Handbook of Gifted Education

Handbook of Gifted Education

Second Edition

Edited by

NICHOLAS COLANGELO *The University of Iowa*

and

GARY A. DAVIS *University of Wisconsin-Madison*

Allyn and Bacon

Boston London Toronto Sydney Tokyo Singapore

Library of Congress Cataloging-in-Publication Data

Handbook of gifted education / edited by Nicholas Colangelo and Gary A. Davis.—2nd ed.
p. cm.
Includes bibliographical references and index.
ISBN 0-205-26085-3
1. Gifted children—Education—United States—Handbooks, manuals, etc. 2. Talented students—Education—United States—Handbooks, manuals, etc. I. Colangelo, Nicholas. II. Davis, Gary A.

LC3993.9.H35 1997
371.95—dc20 96-19246
CIP

Printed in the United States of America
10 9 8 7 6 01 02

We dedicate this book to
Kay and Joseph Colangelo,
Anthony Pullano, and
Marie and Jean Colangelo
and to
Cathy and Kirsten Davis,
Ingrid Frost, and Sonja Thorley
and
In Memoriam
to A. Harry Passow, a pioneering
scholar in gifted education and friend,
who died March 28, 1996.

Contents

Preface

Our vision of this second edition of *Handbook of Gifted Education* was twofold. First, we wanted updates of the dynamic thinking of most of our eminent authors from the first edition. All have built upon or extended their work described in our earlier edition; in many cases, the future directions and goals were predicted in their earlier chapters. Second, we wanted the book to be more comprehensive, to cover more exciting and important bases in gifted education. Even before the first edition was off the press, we regretted some omissions—for example, the impressive talent development research of Benjamin Bloom and Lauren Sosniak, cited in six chapters, as well as program evaluation and programs for secondary students. Further, about the time our first edition was in its final stages the full and destructive impact of detracking and cooperative learning was just being recognized. Essentials indeed. Further, we wished to include other important topics by knowledgeable leaders—for example, teacher preparation and certification, curriculum content guides, legal and ethical issues, international perspectives, and motivation. We also felt we needed more on the important topics of intelligence, eminence, the U.S. government position on gifted children and youth, and that perennial can of worms—identification.

We are both devout students of the Jell-O theory—when you jiggle here, something also jiggles over there. When we increased the number of chapters from 31 to 44, the number of pages threatened to grow to an unacceptable figure. Therefore, most chapters are shorter than in the first edition.

The book remains a scholarly handbook that is at once a text for college senior and graduate courses and a sound resource for university educators and scholar-practitioners in the field.

The history of gifted education has shown an ebb-and-flow pattern in its prominence with both educators and the general public. The current "flow" was born in the 1970s, and the 1980s witnessed a rapid expansion of interest in meeting the academic needs of gifted youngsters. The interest has been worldwide, with legislation and programs sprouting not only in the United States and Canada, but in Mexico, England, Scotland, Ireland, Australia, Indonesia, Micronesia, the Dominican Republic, Costa Rica, Brazil, Colombia, Israel, Egypt, Saudi Arabia, India, China, Taiwan, Japan, Hong Kong, the Philippines, Guam, South Africa, and (at least before the dissolution of the Communist bloc countries) Russia, Poland, and Bulgaria.

In the late 1990s the gifted movement remains strong, but "ebbing" is taking place in some school districts because of budget difficulties and the detracking movement. In addition, the 1994 publication of *The Bell Curve* by Herrnstein and Murray, which argued for a genetic basis of social class differences in intelligence, also is reducing interest in promoting intellectual giftedness.

On the other hand, the 1980s and 1990s have brought a finer focus on social and psychological issues pertaining to the gifted—for example, minority, female, handicapped, and very young gifted children; extraordinarily precocious children and youth; families of the gifted; and subtle dynamics such as extreme sensitivity, excitability, and empathy, as well as near-neurotic levels of perfectionism. The 1993 publication of the national report *National Excellence: A Case for Developing America's Talent* will help set the agenda for the remainder of the 1990s. The report's emphasis on the "quiet crisis" facing the education of America's top students may stem the ebbing forces.

Support for programs and services for the gifted and talented remains enthusiastic and progressive, with occasional exceptions. There has always been conflict—with critics in the general public, who see gifted education as an undemocratic and elitist movement that "gives to the rich"; with some teachers and principals, who install programs only in begrudging response to state mandates or the demands of community parents; and with the academic educational establishment, which has responded too slowly in providing coursework and professional training, sometimes because it does not value "nonrigorous" topics in its research tradition.

Most of the strong interest in—indeed, demand for—college work in gifted education has come from teachers, counselors, and administrators who, after experiencing the realities of schools and classrooms, realize that gifted children present a unique and unmet challenge to the entire educational system. It is these educators who want a better understanding and a repertoire of strategies for teaching gifted students.

This book was conceived with this rapidly growing population of educators in mind. The book is divided into six main sections: (1) an overview and presentation of issues; (2) conceptions and identification; (3) program models and teaching practices; (4) creativity and thinking skills; (5) psychological and counseling services; and (6) special topics, which includes special populations of gifted students as well as teacher training and international and government perspectives. It is a comprehensive text, covering issues, problems, and practical strategies in all central components of gifted education.

In view of the list of unusually authoritative authors, the book provides form and substance, in depth, for scholars who need an up-to-date resource. Those who study these chapters will become familiar with today's issues in the field and with the seasoned ideas and unique insights expected of a resource volume. To help build the next decade of progress in gifted education is part of the vision that created the first and now this second edition.

We wish to thank Pam Bullers, administrative secretary at the Connie Belin and Jacqueline N. Blank International Center for Gifted Education and Talent Development, for her secretarial assistance. We also thank the staff at the Belin-Blank Center for their proofreading and editorial assistance: Frances Blum, Lynette Johnson, Matt Harmston, Paul Hott, Christine Remmert, Melanie Roberts, and Sharron Walker. We also wish to thank Allyn and Bacon editors Ray Short and Mylan Jaixen for their continued support of this second edition. We are most grateful to the contributing authors who collaborated with us in realizing our vision for an expanded second edition.

This text and resource book has been developed with the goal of helping teachers, counselors, and administrators in their day-to-day work with gifted youngsters in schools. We hope this second edition will further enrich the professional development of educators so that they can nurture the talents of students.

Contributors

Susan G. Assouline is associate director of the Connie Belin and Jacqueline N. Blank International Center for Gifted Education and Talent Development at The University of Iowa, where, among other responsibilities, she coordinates the Belin Elementary Student Talent Search. During a postdoctoral fellowship at the Study of Mathematically Precocious Youth program at Johns Hopkins University, she co-authored *Jane and Johnny Love Math: Recognizing and Encouraging Mathematical Talent in Elementary Students* with Ann Lupkowski-Shoplik. She is a column editor for the Research and Evaluation Division of NAGC's newsletter, *Quest.* She co-edited the two volumes of *Talent Development: Proceedings of the H.B. and Jocelyn Wallace National Research Symposium on Talent Development.* She is a former science teacher and school psychologist, holds an adjunct appointment in School Psychology at The University of Iowa, and consults with educators and parents.

Camilla Persson Benbow is a Distinguished Professor and Chair of Psychology at Iowa State University, where she co-directs the Study of Mathematically Precocious Youth (SMPY) and the Office of Precollegiate Programs for Talent and Gifted (OPPTAG). Her research efforts focus on conducting a 50-year longitudinal study of intellectually talented students, which began in 1972 and now involves over 5,000 individuals. She directs research-based summer programs involving over 400 students annually. Dr. Benbow was the first recipient of NAGC's Early Scholar Award in 1985, was the recipient of NAGC's Distinguished Scholar award in 1992, and was inducted into Johns Hopkins University's Society of Scholars in May 1991.

James H. Borland is Associate Professor of Education at Teachers College, Columbia University, where he directs the graduate programs in the education of the gifted. He is author of the books *Planning and Implementing Programs for the Gifted* and *Identifying and Educating Young Economically Disadvantaged Gifted Students* (with Lisa Wright), as well as numerous journal articles. He recently completed a term as co-editor of the Section on Teaching, Learning, and Human Development of the *American Educational Research Journal,* and he is editor of the Education and Psychology of the Gifted series of Teachers College Press. With Lisa Wright he was co-director of Project Synergy and is now the co-director of Project Synergy: Outreach and Project Synergy: Preschool. He has lectured and consulted on the education of gifted students across the United States and abroad.

Victoria W. Carr is an experienced teacher of children who are gifted and children with both gifts and disabilities. She teaches courses in gifted education, classroom management, and interdisciplinary early childhood education at Northern Kentucky University. She is completing her doctoral studies in early childhood special education at the University of Cincinnati. Her speaking, writing, and research interests include assessment, collaboration, and preschool play interactions.

Donna Rae Clasen is a Professor of Educational Psychology at the University of Wisconsin, Whitewater. She also is director of Project STREAM, a Javits Grant program designed to help school districts identify high-ability minority students and increase their educational options. She has published in numerous journals, including the *Gifted Child Quarterly, Roeper Review,* and the *Journal of Youth and Adolescence.* She was named Teacher Educator of the Year by state educators and the Wisconsin Department of Public Instruction.

Robert E. Clasen is Extension Professor of Educational Psychology and Director of University Outreach to the Gifted and Talented at the University of Wisconsin, Madison. He has developed several summer and Saturday programs for gifted children and youth, including College for Kids. He was executive producer, writer, and host of three telecourses dealing with education of the gifted: "Simple Gifts: The Education of the Gifted, Talented, and Creative"; "Programming for the Gifted"; and "Educating Able Learners." He teaches courses and supervises a practicum in gifted education. Among his publications are several books of readings, a telecourse study guide, and articles in the *Gifted Child Quarterly* and *Roeper Review.*

Nicholas Colangelo is the Myron and Jacqueline Blank Professor of Gifted Education and the Director of the Connie Belin and Jacqueline N. Blank International Center for Gifted Education and Talent Development at The University of Iowa. He currently serves on the editorial boards of *Gifted Child Quarterly, Journal of Creative Behavior,* and *Journal for Counseling and Development.* He has authored research and theoretical articles on the affective development and counseling needs of gifted students. He has co-edited two books on gifted: *New Voices in Counseling the Gifted* and the earlier edition of *Handbook of Gifted Education.* In 1991 he received a Distinguished Scholar Award from the National Association for Gifted Children. In 1995 he received an Alumni Achievement Award from the University of Wisconsin–Madison. Also in 1995, he was named Executive Administrator for the World Council for Gifted and Talented Children.

Susan Daniels is an instructor in the Department of Educational Psychology at the University of Wisconsin, Madison, where she teaches graduate and undergraduate courses in creativity and gifted education. She also is Coordinator of Gifted and Talented Programs for the McFarland (Wisconsin) Community Schools. She is a contributing editor to *Roeper Review* and has published articles in the *Journal of Creative Behavior* and other resources. Her research investigates mental imagery in both everyday cognition and creativity. She has received several awards for teaching and scholarship, including a 1992 Graduate Student Award from the National Association for Gifted Children. She also serves as consultant to school districts and agencies, specializing in strategies and techniques for fostering creative behavior.

Gary A. Davis is Professor Emeritus of Educational Psychology at the University of Wisconsin, Madison, where he taught courses in creativity, gifted education, and other areas. He is author of many articles in the areas of creativity, problem solving, moral education, and effective schooling, and of many books, including *Education of the Gifted and Talented* (with Sylvia Rimm), *Creativity Is Forever, Psychology of Problem Solving, Training Creative Thinking, Creative Teaching of Values and Moral Thinking,* and *Effective Schools and Effective Teachers.* He is a reviewer, consulting editor, or editorial board member for *Journal of Creative Behavior, Creativity Research Journal, Roeper Review,* and (formerly) Gifted Child Quarterly.

James R. Delisle is Professor of Education at Kent State University, specializing in education of gifted children. He is author of eight books and more than 200 articles on education, specializing in social and emotional needs of gifted students, developing leadership through curriculum, and adolescent suicide prevention. He is a past president of the Association for the Gifted (CEC-TAG) and serves on the board of directors of the National Association for Gifted Children and the board of trustees for the Roeper School for the Gifted. He teaches one day each week at a middle school in Ohio.

John F. Feldhusen is Robert B. Kane Distinguished Professor of Education at Purdue University and director of the Purdue Gifted Education Resource Institute. He has authored books and articles on gifted education and talent development, is a former editor of *Gifted Child Quarterly,* and currently is editor of *Gifted and Talented International,* the journal of the World Council for Gifted and Talented Children. He is a Fellow of the American Psychological Association and, among many other awards, received a Distinguished Scholar award from the National Association for Gifted Children.

David H. Feldman is Professor and Acting Chair of the Eliot-Pearson Department of Child Development at Tufts University. He also directs the Developmental Science Group at Tufts. His research focuses on extreme precocity, transition processes, emotions and developmental change, and nonuniversal theory. He has authored or co-authored more than 100 publications, including several recent books. Among them are *Beyond Universals in Cognitive Development* (in second edition), *Changing the World: A Framework for the Study of Creativity* (with Mihalyi Csikszentmihalyi and Howard Gardner), and *Nature's Gambit: Child Prodigies and the Development of Human Potential.* He has received numerous grants and awards for his work in developmental and educational psychology, including NAGC's Distinguished Scholar Award in 1981.

Mary M. Frasier is Professor of Educational Psychology and director of the Torrance Center for Creative Studies at the University of Georgia. She is author of numerous articles on identification and program development for gifted students, with a special emphasis on gifted economically disadvantaged and minority students. She currently serves on the editorial board for *Exceptional Children.* She was associate director of the National Research Center on the Gifted and conducted investigations into the effective identification of gifted students from economically disadvantaged and limited-English-proficiency backgrounds. She served as president of the National Association for the Gifted and received a Distinguished Service Award from that organization.

James J. Gallagher is William Rand Kenan, Jr., Professor of Education at the University of North Carolina at Chapel Hill and a senior investigator in the Frank Porter Graham Child Development Center at that University. He has held numerous leadership positions, including the presidencies of the Association for the Gifted, the World Council for the Gifted and Talented, and the National Association for Gifted Children. In addition to numerous articles and monographs, he recently co-authored, with his daughter, Shelagh, the fourth edition of *Teaching the Gifted Child.*

Howard Gardner is Professor of Education and Adjunct Professor of Psychology at Harvard University, Adjunct Professor of Neurology at the Boston University School of Medicine, and co-director of Harvard Project Zero. The recipient of many honors, including a MacArthur Prize Fellowship, Gardner is the author of fourteen books and several hundred articles. In 1990 he was the first American to receive the University of Louisville's Grawemeyer Award in education. He is best known in educational circles for his theory of multiple intelligences, a critique of the notion that there exists but a single human intelligence that can be assessed by standard psychometric instruments. More recently, he and colleagues at Project Zero have been working on the design of performance-based assessments, education for understanding, and the use of multiple intelligences to achieve more personalized curriculum, instruction, and assessment. His newest book is *Leading Minds: Stories of Leaders in Our Time.*

Beth A. Hennessey is Associate Professor of Psychology at Wellesley College, Wellesley, Massachusetts, where she teaches courses in the psychology of creativity, educational psychology, and research methodology. She is a former elementary school teacher, was a recipient of a Spencer Post Doctoral Fellowship/National Academy of Education Grant, and has published research and theoretical articles in the area of the social psychology of motivation and creativity. She is author (with Teresa Amabile) of *Creativity and Learning: What Research Says to the Teacher.*

Nancy Ewald Jackson is Professor of Educational Psychology in the Division of Psychological and Quantitative Foundations, College of Education, The University of Iowa. She has published many empirical, theoretical, and methodological articles on precocious reading and the development of intellectual giftedness, including the chapter "Genius, Eminence, and Giftedness" in the 1994 *Encyclopedia of Human Behavior*. Her empirical work includes several longitudinal studies of the development of precocious readers, and she has been especially concerned with integrating the study of giftedness with broader theoretical accounts of cognition and development. She currently serves on the editorial board of the *Gifted Child Quarterly.*

Lawrence J. Johnson is Associate Dean for Research and Development and director of the Arlitt Child and Family Research and Development Center at the University of Cincinnati. His research expertise relates to the use of interviews and content analysis procedures as research and evaluation tools and conducts research on collaboration and the provision of services to young children and their families. He is co-author of four books and also co-authored a curriculum and assessment instrument. He was editor of *Focus on Research* and associate editor of the *Journal of Early Intervention.* He is a reviewer for many journals in the areas of remedial and special education and gifted education.

Frances A. Karnes is Professor of Special Education at the University of Southern Mississippi, director of the Center for Gifted Studies, and co-director of the Institute for Law and Gifted Education. She is widely known for her research, writing, innovative program developments, and service activities in gifted education and leadership training. She is author or co-author of over 130 articles and co-author of 10 books on gifted education and related areas, including *Gifted Children and the Law* and *Gifted Children and Legal Issues in Education.* She is a former president of the Association for the Gifted and is the founder and first president of the Mississippi Association for Gifted Children. Honors include a Faculty Research Award, granted by the University of Southern Mississippi Alumni Association; an Honorary Doctor of Education degree from her alma mater Quincy University; and an award presented by the Mississippi Legislature for outstanding contributions to academic excellence in higher education.

Merle B. Karnes is Professor Emeritus of Special Education at the University of Illinois. She has published over 200 books, articles, and curricular packages for young disabled children and for gifted children as young as infancy. She is best known for curricular development for young children, for her work with young disabled children who also are gifted, and for her research on the effectiveness of various approaches to educating young children. She has received many awards for research and other contributions, the most recent of which was a

1994 Merit Award from the Division of Early Childhood for her work in the field of exceptional children and her contributions to the professional organization.

Barbara Kerr is Professor of Psychology in Education at Arizona State University. She also has taught at the University of Nebraska and the University of Iowa, where she established guidance and counseling laboratories for gifted and talented students. Her special interests in gifted education include development of talent in women and girls, career development of gifted and talented, and creativity. With colleague Nicholas Colangelo she has published numerous articles ranging from case studies of inventors to large-scale studies of high scorers on the ACT college admissions test. Her books include *Smart Girls, Gifted Women, Handbook for Counseling Gifted and Talented,* and her newest *Smart Girls Two: A New Psychology of Girls, Women, and Giftedness.*

Elizabeth J. Klein is a graduate student in Educational Psychology at The University of Iowa. Her current research interests lie in the study of gifted children and the use of the Internet in education. She is author of the article "Computers and Learning Disabled College Students," published in the computer magazine *Pico*.

Penny Britton Kolloff is Faculty Lecturer at Illinois State University in Normal. Prior to her move to Illinois, she was Director of Curriculum at Cranbrook Schools in Michigan. Before this, in Indiana, she was assistant director of the Gifted Education Resource Institute at Purdue University and later director of the Center for Gifted and Talented Programs at Ball State University. While in Indiana she worked toward the establishment of the Indiana Academy of Science, Mathematics and Humanities. She received an Early Leader award and an Outstanding Research Paper award from the National Association for Gifted Children and has served on the boards of NAGC, the Center for Talent Development at Northwestern University, and the Michigan Alliance for Gifted Education.

Chen-Lin C. Kulik is an educational consultant in Ann Arbor, Michigan, recently retired from the research faculty at the University of Michigan. Her research specialties include psychological measurement and the application of statistical methods in education and the health sciences. She is co-author of the monograph *Meta-Analysis in Educational Research,* published by the *International Journal of Educational Research.*

James A. Kulik is Research Scientist at the University of Michigan's Center for Research on Learning and Teaching. At Michigan he has taught psychology courses, directed university-wide programs of teacher evaluation and student testing and placement, and carried out evaluation studies on educational issues. His major recent research interest has been quantitative integration of research findings in education. He is author of the book *Undergraduate Education in Psychology* and of recent monographs on meta-analysis in education research, ability grouping, and vocational education.

David Lubinski is an Associate Professor of Psychology at Iowa State University and director of its Psychometrics and Applied Individual Differences Division. He also co-directs the Study of Mathematically Precocious Youth program at ISU, and is involved in its 50-year longitudinal study of intellectually gifted participants. Now in its third decade, the study includes over 5,000 mathematically and/or verbally gifted subjects, initially identified before age 13. With expertise in assessing individual differences, his research interests aim at identifying different types of intellectually gifted adolescents (e.g., mathematically, spatially, and/or verbally gifted), and finding optimal ways to facilitate their educational and vocational development.

Ann E. Lupkowski-Shoplik is Director of the Investigation of Talented Elementary Students at Carnegie Mellon University. She conducts the annual Elementary Student Talent Search in the Pittsburgh area and oversees the C-MITES summer program and Weekend Workshops for academically talented third- through sixth-grade children. Her research interests include identifying mathematically talented students younger than age 12 and studying their characteristics and academic needs. She and Susan G. Assouline co-authored *Jane and Johnny Love Math: Recognizing and Encouraging Mathematical Talent in Elementary Students.*

C. June Maker is Associate Professor of Special Education at the University of Arizona, Tucson, where she coordinates graduate degree concentrations in gifted education. She has been active in several organizations, including serving for 19 years on the board of directors of the NAGC. Her publications relate to many topics, including gifted handicapped, teacher training, curriculum development, teaching models, gifted minority students, teaching the gifted in regular classrooms, and alternative assessment of gifted students. She serves on editorial boards for journals in gifted education and special education, and is editor of the book series *Critical Issues in*

Gifted Education. Her current research is on assessment and enhancement of multiple forms of giftedness, in diverse groups, from a problem-solving perspective. She has developed and is conducting research on a unique assessment process (DISCOVER), which is based on observation of students by teachers and other professionals.

Ronald G. Marquardt is chair and Professor of Political Science at the University of Southern Mississippi. He co-authored *Gifted Children and the Law: Mediation, Due Process, and Court Cases* and co-edited *Gifted Children and Legal Issues in Education: Parents' Stores of Hope* (both with Frances Karnes). He has given presentations at national and international gifted association meetings and, writing with Frances Karnes, has published numerous articles related to the law and gifted students.

Patricia Alexander Maurer coordinates programs for gifted and talented students in the Midland (Texas) Independent School District. Her career in Texas public schools spans 25 years of service and includes 17 years of experience in the field of education for the gifted. She is a trainer for both Project IMPACT and the New Jersey Writing Project in Texas. In 1993 and 1994 she was awarded the George Washington Honor Medal by the Freedom Foundation, Valley Forge, for her work on secondary curriculum projects in economics and United States history.

Terry McNabb is an Assistant Professor of Teacher Education at Coe College in Cedar Rapids, Iowa, where she teaches classes in Child and Adolescent Development and Multicultural Education. She worked previously at the Connie Belin and Jacqueline N. Blank International Center for Gifted Education and Talent Development, The University of Iowa, and the American College Testing Program. Her research interests are in academic motivation, gender differences, and academic self-concept.

Martha J. Morelock is Senior Lecturer in Learning, Assessment, and Special Education at the University of Melbourne, Australia. She was a Jessie Smith Fellow at Tufts University and received the Hollingworth Award for her Ph.D. thesis there. Her interests include case studies of extreme giftedness, family influences on the development of talent, emotional aspects of giftedness, and the interplay of general intellectual ability with IQ-independent skills in the shaping of various manifestations of talent. With David Henry Feldman she has co-authored several major articles in the field of gifted education, including chapters in the *International Handbook of Research and Development of Gifted and Talented* and *Assessing and Screening Preschoolers*.

Paula Olszewski-Kubilius is associate director of the Center for Talent Development at Northwestern University. She serves on the editorial boards of *Roeper Review* and the *Journal of Secondary Gifted Education*. Her writing and research interests include the psychological and educational impact of special programs on gifted children, and characteristics and development of economically disadvantaged gifted. She has headed several grant-supported intervention programs for developing the abilities of academically talented low-income minority children. She is coeditor of several books, including *Current Research Methods for Studying Creativity in Youth* and *Patterns of Influence on Gifted Learners: The Home, The Self and the School,* and co-authored the handbook *Helping Gifted Children and Their Families Prepare for College: A Handbook Designed to Assist Economically Disadvantaged and First Generation College Attendees*. In 1987 she received an Early Scholar Award from the National Association for Gifted Children.

A. Harry Passow was Jacob H. Schiff Professor Emeritus of Education at Teachers College, Columbia University, where he served on the faculty for over 40 years. He initiated Teachers College's Talented Youth Project in 1954, directed the project during its 12 years of operation, and co-authored research reports dealing with planning for talented youth, ability grouping, bright underachievers, and other topics. Two books edited by Passow are the 1979 NSSE Yearbook *The Gifted and the Talented* and the *International Handbook of Research and Development of Giftedness and Talent* (with Heller and Monks). He wrote more than 150 journal articles and book chapters. He served as president of the World Council of Gifted Children and was a long-term member of the board of directors for NAGC. He served as senior consultant to the Israel Arts and Science Academy, Israel's residential high school for the gifted and talented. Harry died in March 1996, and this text is dedicated to him.

Philip A. Perrone is Professor of Counseling Psychology at the University of Wisconsin, Madison, where he teaches courses in counseling the gifted, career counseling, and individual assessment. He is author of many articles in the areas of social and emotional development of gifted individuals, developmental guidance programs for school age children, and assisting individuals in the school-to-work transition. He is co-author of the books *Dynamic Counseling, Conflict Management, Guiding the Emerging Adolescent,* and *The Developmental Education and Guidance of Talented Learners.* He has served on the editorial boards of several gifted journals and counseling journals. He twice received the Wisconsin Association for Counseling and Development's Research Award and received the University of Wisconsin Amoco Award for Excellence in Teaching.

Michael M. Piechowski holds Ph.D. degrees in Molecular Biology and Counseling and Guidance, both from the University of Wisconsin. He is Professor of Education at Northland College in Ashland, Wisconsin, where, among other courses, he teaches Transpersonal Psychology. With K. Dabrowski he co-authored a two-volume series entitled *Theory of Levels of Emotional Development.* He has written extensively on the developmental potential of the gifted and on advanced development. He also has studied and written about historically eminent self-actualizing people, such as Saint-Exupery, Eleanor Roosevelt, and Leta Hollingworth, as well as contemporary persons. A favorite (though, he says, largely unappreciated) paper is entitled "The Logical and the Empirical Form of Feeling."

Robert Plomin is MRC Research Professor of Behavioural Genetics and Deputy Director of the Research Centre for Social, Genetic and Developmental Psychiatry at the Institute of Psychiatry in London. The Research Centre aims to bring together research strategies on nature and nurture in the investigation of behavioral dimensions and disorders, a theme that has been the focus of his research. He is first author of the major textbook *Behavioral Genetics: A Primer* (in second edition). He has written eight other books and edited several others. His most recent book is *Genetics and Experience: The Developmental Interplay between Nature and Nurture.*

Valerie Ramos-Ford is an independent educational consultant who writes, lectures, and offers training to educators and parents nationwide in the areas of multiple intelligences and the effects of violence in the lives of children. Prior to her current endeavors, she was a researcher and project manager with Howard Gardner at Project Zero at the Harvard Graduate School of Education. She began her career in education as a preschool teacher.

Sally M. Reis is Associate Professor of Educational Psychology at the University of Connecticut, where she also serves as Principal Investigator for the National Research Center on the Gifted and Talented. She was a teacher for 15 years, 11 of which were spent working with gifted students at the elementary, junior high, and high school levels. She has authored numerous articles, five books, eleven book chapters, and various monographs and technical reports. She is co-author of *The Revolving Door Identification Model, The Schoolwide Enrichment Model, The Secondary Triad Model,* and *The Triad Reader*. She serves on the editorial boards of the *Journal for the Education of the Gifted* and *Gifted Child Quarterly,* and is on the board of the National Association for Gifted Children.

Joseph S. Renzulli is Professor of Educational Psychology at the University of Connecticut, where he also serves as director of the National Research Center on the Gifted and Talented. Throughout his career he has engaged in a variety of research and development activities dealing with identification systems, program development models, a curriculum development model, and a model for evaluating programs for the gifted and talented.

E. Susanne Richert is president of the Global Institute for Maximizing Potential in Brigantine, New Jersey. She has been consultant to state and national departments of education; to school districts in over 30 states, three Canadian provinces, and several nations; and to the United States Supreme Court. She has trained hundreds of teachers worldwide in her research-based staff development model for maximizing student and teacher cognitive, affective, and ethical potential. Additional specialties include equitable identification of disadvantaged and underachieving gifted, shared decision making and team building, and meeting students' emotional needs. She is author of *Maximizing Student Potential,* more than 30 articles and chapters, and the U.S. Department of Education *National Report on Identification.* She has served on the editorial boards of *Gifted Child Quarterly, Roeper Review,* and *Journal for the Education of the Gifted.* Her research and innovative projects include a U.S. Department of Education national leadership training institute; the National Clearinghouse of Gifted Educational Materials; several multidistrict consortia; and APOGEE, a federally funded Javits Grant project.

Sylvia B. Rimm is Clinical Professor at Case Western Reserve University, School of Medicine, in the Departments of Psychiatry and Pediatrics. She directs the Family Achievement Clinic at MetroHealth Medical Center in Cleveland. She is co-author (with Gary Davis) of *Education of the Gifted* *and Talented* and has authored eight other books, creativity tests, and many articles. Her topics include parenting, gifted children, and underachievement. She hosts a regular monthly parenting series on NBC's *Today Show* and a weekly radio program on parenting broadcast nationally on public radio. Her column, "Sylvia Rimm on Raising Kids," is syndicated nationally by Creators Syndicate. Her recent book, *Why Bright Kids Get Poor Grades,* is published by Crowne. She is a member of the board of directors for the National Association for Gifted Children.

Ann Robinson is Professor of Teacher Education at the University of Arkansas at Little Rock. She serves on the Board of Directors for the National Association for Gifted Children and is editor of the *Gifted Child Quarterly*. She is author of the monograph *Cooperative Learning and the Academically Talented Student* and co-author of the book *Recommended Practices in Gifted Education.* Her research addresses the social context of giftedness, curriculum and assessment, and program evaluation. She recently directed a federally funded program for low-income talented middle school students. Dr. Robinson received the Early Scholar Award and the Early Leader Award from the National Association for Gifted Children. She also is director of Project Promise, a federally funded research and service program for gifted middle school students. Her research addresses the social context of giftedness, curriculum, program evaluation, and student–teacher interaction. She has reviewed for several education and gifted education journals.

Patricia O'Connell Ross is director of the Javits Gifted and Talented Education Program in the U.S. Department of Education. She served for three years as Director of Academic Programs at the Center for Talented Youth at Johns Hopkins University and for ten years as the State Director for Gifted Programs in Maine. She was president of the Council of State Directors of Programs for the Gifted and secretary of the Association for the Gifted. She holds undergraduate and advanced degrees in anthropology and museum studies, as well as a master's degree in Education Policy Studies from Harvard University.

Shirley W. Schiever is the Curriculum Specialist at Madge Utterback Middle School, a fine arts magnet school in the Tucson (Arizona) Unified School District. She oversees the program for gifted students as well as other student programs and staff development. She is author of *A Comprehensive Approach to Teaching Thinking* and co-editor of *Critical Issues in Gifted Education: Volume II, Defensible Programs for Cultural Ethnic Minorities.* She has contributed chapters to several books and has written a regular column for the national newsletter *Understanding our Gifted.* Her interests focus on developing higher thinking in students and on recognizing and capitalizing on strengths within Gardner's seven intelligences, especially in ethnic and cultural minority populations.

Carol Schlichter was the original director of Talents Unlimited. She has been a classroom teacher and has served gifted students both as an itinerant teacher and as a resource room teacher. At present, she is Professor of Special Education and Chair of the Program of Gifted and Talented at the University of Alabama. She has authored many articles about the development of creative and critical thinking skills. In 1994 she received the E. Paul Torrance Creativity Award from the Creativity Division of the National Association for Gifted Children.

Linda Kreger Silverman is a licensed psychologist who has counseled gifted children and their families for 30 years. She directs the Gifted Development Center and the Institute for the Study of Advanced Development in Denver, Colorado. She is editor of *Advanced Development: A Journal of Adult Giftedness,* and edited the textbook *Counseling the Gifted and Talented.* For nine years she served on the faculty of the University of Denver in gifted education and counseling psychology. She publishes extensively on all facets of giftedness and lectures throughout the United States and abroad.

Dean Keith Simonton is Professor of Psychology at the University of California, Davis. He has written over 100 articles and five books, including *Genius, Creativity, and Leadership, Scientific Genius,* and *Greatness.* He currently serves on the editorial boards of *Empirical Studies of the Arts,* the *Creativity Research Journal,* and the *Leadership Quarterly,* and is editor of the *Journal of Creative Behavior.* One major research preoccupation concerns the connection between achievement in adulthood and giftedness exhibited in childhood and adolescence.

Lauren A. Sosniak is a Visiting Associate Research Educator at the University of California at Berkeley, School of Education, and project director for Reinventing Communities of Learners. She is the author of many articles on the development of talent, as well as publications in the areas of curriculum theory and curriculum enactment. She currently serves as book review editor for *Educational Researcher* and is a member of the editorial boards for *Journal of Curriculum Studies* and *Review of Educational Research.*

Julian C. Stanley is Professor of Psychology and director of the Study of Mathematically Precocious Youth (SMPY), founded by him in 1971, at Johns Hopkins University. His research, development, and service have involved chiefly finding boys and girls who reason exceptionally well mathematically and helping them get the special, supplemental, accelerative educational opportunities they need and deserve. SMPY has sparked the creation of large annual regional talent searches and residential summer academic programs across the nation, especially at Johns Hopkins University, Duke University, Northwestern University, Iowa State University, and the University of Denver. He edited, co-edited, or sponsored *Mathematical Talent, Intellectual Talent, The Gifted and the Talented, Educating the Gifted, Women and Mathematical Mystique,* and *Academic Precocity.* He is a former president of the American Educational Research Association, the National Council on Measurement in Education, and the Divisions of Educational Psychology and Evaluation and Measurement of the American Psychological Association.

Robert J. Sternberg is IBM Professor of Psychology and Education in the Department of Psychology at Yale University. He is author of *Beyond IQ* and *Metaphors of Mind,* and also co-edited with Janet Davidson *Conceptions of Giftedness.* He is associate director of the National Center for Research on the Gifted and Talented, funded by the U.S. Office of Educational Research and Improvement, and is currently involved in a number of research projects on gifted education. His particular interests are in abilities, creativity, and learning styles. Sternberg is a winner of a number of awards, including the Distinguished Scholar Award of the National Association of Gifted Children.

Abraham J. Tannenbaum, Professor Emeritus of Education and Psychology, Teachers College, Columbia University, is busier than ever as a lecturer, writer, editor, consultant, and researcher, mostly regarding the psychology and education of gifted children. Recently, he has accepted various professional assignments in Israel, Australia, and Greece, as well as the United States.

Joyce VanTassel-Baska is Jody and Layton Smith Professor of Education at the College of William and Mary in Virginia, where she also directs the Center for Gifted Education. She has enjoyed a long career in gifted education at the local, regional, state, and university levels. She is the author or editor of several books and over 200 other publications. Recent books include *Planning Effective Curriculum for Gifted Learners, Comprehensive Curriculum for Gifted Learners,* and *Developing Verbal Talent.* She is a reviewer for several journals in gifted education and contributing editor to *Roeper Review.* In 1993 she received an Outstanding Faculty Award from the State of Virginia.

Herbert J. Walberg is Research Professor of Education at the University of Illinois at Chicago. He has written or edited more than 50 books and contributed more than 380 articles to educational and psychological journals on such topics as educational effectiveness and exceptional human accomplishments. He serves as advisor to the Scholarship Foundation of America, and is currently studying winners of the International Olympiad of Mathematics from Japan, the People's Republic of China, and the United States. Walberg serves as advisor on educational research and improvement to public and private agencies in the United States and other countries, and has testified before state and federal courts and U.S. congressional committees. A fellow of four academic organizations, Walberg has won a number of awards for scholarship and is one of three U.S. members of the International Academy of Education.

S. Lee Winocur is president and executive director of the Center for the Teaching of Thinking in Huntington Beach, California, and national director of the IMPACT project. IMPACT (Increase Maximum Performance by Activating Critical Thinking) is a nationally recognized program for the direct teaching of critical thinking skills, validated by the U.S. Department of Education and disseminated under the auspices of the National Diffusion Network and Phi Delta Kappa. In addition to authoring IMPACT, she designed eight major educational projects and has authored articles on cognitive development, curriculum development, and effective schooling and educational reform. She has lectured at the University of Massachusetts, the University of Southern California, the University of California at Irvine, and the University of San Diego.

Susie Zeiser is a doctoral student in Educational Psychology at the University of Illinois at Chicago and is a former teacher of gifted children. She participates with a group of a dozen scholars who are studying the early childhood traits and conditions of eminent American women and is concentrating on those renowned for their anthropological and feminist contributions.

Guest Foreword: The Second Edition Is Longer and Better Than the First

JULIAN C. STANLEY
Johns Hopkins University

This expertly updated version of the excellent first edition of *Handbook of Gifted Education* incorporates many new features and discards certain topics by means of skillful additions and pruning. There are now 44 chapters, versus the 31 of the initial edition. Not all of the former authors and chapters reappear. Two new additions that seem to me especially desirable are famed behavioral geneticist Robert Plomin's "Genetics and Intelligence" and leading genius researcher Dean Keith Simonton's "When Giftedness Becomes Genius: How Does Talent Achieve Eminence?"

In a brief foreword it is not appropriate to list all the changes, including much rewriting of the earlier chapters that are retained. Suffice it to say that this edition is likely to meet many needs considerably better than its predecessor. By studying it, gifted-child specialists will substantially improve the breadth and depth of their knowledge. Teachers of future teachers of the gifted will find it a comprehensive textbook. Graduate students involved with giftedness, talent, creativity, problem solving, and high achievement should consult it often. School administrators and educational policymakers need its information and wisdom. Parents of the gifted and gifted persons themselves should scan its pages for stimulating ideas. Even the intelligent general reader can find much enlightenment here.

All in all, this second edition is a marvel of speed and quality. It should last out the rest of the century before a third edition becomes needed.

Handbook of Gifted Education

PART I

Introduction

We begin this book with two chapters that survey topics and issues in gifted education, as well as recent and historical background.

Chapter 1 by Colangelo and Davis highlights the need for special services and programs for gifted students—"our most precious natural resource"—and some traditional and contemporary topics and issues, for example, the equity–excellence dilemma, elitism, anti-intellectualism, the National Excellence report, and the detracking and cooperative learning movements. Brief historical overviews of gifted education worldwide and in the United States, along with momentous developments in intelligence testing, put today's investment in gifted education into its larger context. The chapter ends with a summary description of the six sections of the book.

Borrowing a phrase from the 1993 National Excellence report, James J. Gallagher in Chapter 2 aptly labels the state of gifted education "a quiet crisis." He elaborates on issues and trends at the forefront of gifted education. For example, Gallagher reviews new conceptualizations of intelligence and ways to teach thinking and decision making; interactions of genetic and environmental forces; and challenges of serving special populations of gifted students—underachievers, minorities, and females. Stemming from his leadership in formulating public policy in gifted education, Gallagher ends his chapter by naming three national priorities: (1) attending to underserved gifted students, including minorities, those with handicaps, and very young children; (2) forming a support network to improve program quality; and (3) creating collaborative efforts with professionals from other disciplines.

1

Introduction and Overview

NICHOLAS COLANGELO, *The University of Iowa*
GARY A. DAVIS, *University of Wisconsin, Madison*

Nurturing the talents of our most gifted and talented children is one of the most exciting yet controversial issues in education today. The base of the controversy is society's love–hate relationship with giftedness and talent (e.g., Gallagher & Weiss, 1979). On one hand, we admire the talent and drive of individuals who rise from humble backgrounds. On the other, our nation has a longstanding commitment to egalitarianism, reflected in that mighty phrase "All men are created equal." Both educators and people-on-the-street are caught in the confusing tension between encouraging yet restraining individual accomplishment (Gardner, 1982).

Society swings back and forth between the goals of equity versus excellence. When excellence is of concern—as in 1957 when the Soviet Union's Sputnik beat the United States into space and 1983 when the report *A Nation at Risk* jolted American educators—programs for the brightest quickly receive priority. When equity is the primary concern, as in the 1960s, the early 1970s, and resurfacing in the 1990s, planning suitable educational programs for gifted students is put on a back burner or in the closet. *Equity* typically is translated as helping slow-learning, disadvantaged, and other at-risk students become more equal. Unfortunately, treating issues of equity and excellence as antagonistic and mutually exclusive is destructive to the development of sound educational practices that meet the educational needs of every individual student.

It seems that educators, politicians, and others either defend or attack gifted education with enthusiasm, yet typically with little or no factual information. The following are some themes that help account for the ambivalent, even hostile reactions to gifted education, or otherwise lead educators and others to ignore the needs of the gifted.

Giving to the "Haves"

Some resent giving special educational privileges to those who are already basking in talent and who appear to succeed with little or no effort. In fact, it is damaging to talented children and youth to require them to cope with a system that ignores their capabilities, ignores their true educational needs, and requires them to proceed at the pace of below-average students. It also is an unfortunate misperception to equate giftedness with effortlessness. Regardless of native ability, achieving excellence in school or any career field takes hard work—students in gifted-talented (G/T) programs are not "getting something for nothing." The excellent research by Bloom and Sosniak (1981) and studies of eminent individuals emphasize the effort and commitment required to develop high talent.[1]

The Detracking Movement

Jeannie Oakes (1985) and others have argued that tracking plans are racist and discriminatory, deprive slow-track students of educational opportunities, and damage their self-concepts. Such arguments certainly touch the heartstrings of democratic-minded persons. Unfortunately, this "national hysteria" (Reis et al., 1992) has led some districts to abolish not only their accelerated classes, but special

[1] See Chapter 17 by Sosniak, Chapter 27 by Walberg and Zeiser, and Chapter 28 by Simonton.

classes for the gifted and gifted programs themselves. Says Renzulli (1991), with heterogeneous grouping, "bright kids learn nothing new until January."[2]

Cooperative Learning

Detracking is one recent damaging reform movement, cooperative learning is the other. A prototype cooperative learning group consists of four students—two average students, a slower learner, and a fast learner—who work together to complete a worksheet, solve a problem, or otherwise master material. Proponents, who believe cooperative learning should be the primary teaching strategy, cite gains in achievement, motivation, cognitive growth, social skills, and self-confidence, as well as reduced classroom management problems (e.g., Slavin, Madden, & Stevens, 1990). The teaching strategy probably is highly effective—except for gifted students, who (1) prefer not to work in groups because they can learn faster alone; (2) typically get stuck doing most of the work; (3) mainly teach the others; and, most importantly, (4) miss opportunities for accelerated or enriched work that matches their abilities, particularly with other gifted students. In short, cooperative learning diverts attention from more valid educational needs of gifted students.

Elitism and Anti-Intellectualism

Elitism includes the idea that one person or group is inherently superior or more valuable than others. Fear of elitism, however, sometimes leads to a false equation of recognizing differences with holding an elitist point of view. For example, recognizing the skill of a piano virtuoso does not indicate a belief that this skill makes the person "better" than others as a human being.

Youngsters sometimes are perceived as "elite" for a variety of reasons, such as outstanding athletic ability, good looks, or family wealth. The children themselves may act elitist—egotistical and self-important. However, elitism in these areas somehow is considered more acceptable than in children who are intellectually gifted. As a group, gifted youngsters tend to be more understanding and modest than others (e.g., Goldberg, 1965), although snobbishness of gifted students has been reported (Starko, 1990).

Anti-intellectualism is expressed by some who are hostile to the intellectually gifted and to intellectual pursuits generally. Note that if a youngster excels in sports, dance, art, music, or school politics, anti-intellectualism does not arise. However, if a student is labeled *intellectually gifted* and achieves at high levels, then it is another matter. Society allows and applauds certain areas of talent, but high intellectual ability spurs ambivalence. Intellectual giftedness appears to threaten the self-esteem of others, both youngsters and adults, in a way that other talents do not.

"They Will Make It on Their Own"

One common argument against special educational programs for the gifted is the belief that these students "will make it on their own." A corollary is "Give the help to students who really need it." However, many students labeled gifted do *not* make it on their own. Inadequate curriculum, unsupportive educators, social and emotional difficulties, peer pressure, and inadequate parenting all can extinguish the potential high accomplishment of gifted children and adolescents.

The Excitement of Educating Gifted Students

The foregoing are some problems confronting gifted education and gifted students. More difficulties will be noted in later chapters. Nonetheless, there exists tremendous excitement about giftedness. As Sternberg and Davidson (1986) state, "Giftedness is arguably the most precious natural resource a civilization can have" (p. ix). Children who produce and create well beyond our expectations invigorate us and show us the possibilities of

[2] See Chapter 19 by Kulik and Kulik for a discussion of tracking, ability grouping, and the gifted.

human potential. Adults of eminence have left their mark in helping societies develop technologically, aesthetically, and morally. Your authors have never met teachers more excited about teaching than when they work with groups of gifted children.

Historical Overview of Giftedness and Gifted Education

Giftedness Around the World

Identifying and educating gifted youth has intrigued virtually all societies in recorded history. In ancient Sparta, military skills were valued so exclusively that "giftedness" was defined by outstanding combat, warfare, and leadership skills. In Athens, upper-class young boys went to private schools for academics and physical fitness training. Older boys were taught math, logic, rhetoric, politics, culture, and "disputation" by sophists. Plato's academy selected both young men and women on the basis of intelligence and physical stamina, rather than social position. In Rome, although higher education was reserved for males, some gifted women emerged who greatly affected Roman society—for example, the Roman matron Cornelia, mother of statesmen Gaius and Tiberius Gracchus (Good, 1960).

Renaissance Europe sought out and rewarded its gifted artists, architects, and writers with wealth and honor—for example, Michelangelo, Leonardo da Vinci, Boccacio, Bernini, and Dante.

Beginning with the Tang Dynasty (618 B.C.), early China brought its child prodigies to the imperial court, where their gifts were nurtured. China at this time anticipated four principles of contemporary gifted education (Tsuin-Chen, 1961). First, they accepted a multiple-talent conception of giftedness, valuing literary ability, leadership, imagination, reading speed, reasoning, and other talents. Second, they recognized that some precocious youth would grow up to be average; some average youth would later show gifts; and true child prodigies would show gifts and talents throughout their lives. Third, they realized that the abilities of even the most gifted would not develop fully without special training. Fourth, they believed that education should be available to children of all social classes, but that children should be educated according to their abilities.

During the Tokugawa Society period in Japan (1604–1868), Samurai children received training in history, Confucian classics, composition, calligraphy, moral values, etiquette, and martial arts, whereas poor children learned loyalty, obedience, and diligence.

Gifted Education in America

In early America, some gifted youth were accommodated only in the sense that attending secondary school and college was based on both academic achievement and the ability to pay the fees (Newland, 1976). With compulsory attendance laws, schooling became available to all children, but few special services were available for the gifted. Some noteworthy exceptions are these:

- In 1870, St. Louis initiated tracking, allowing some students to complete the first eight grades in less than eight years.
- In 1884, Woburn, Massachusetts, created the "Double Tillage Plan": After the first semester of first grade, bright children were accelerated directly into the second semester of second grade.
- In 1886, Elizabeth, New Jersey, began a tracking system that permitted bright students to progress more rapidly than others.
- In 1891, schools in Cambridge, Massachusetts, developed a similar double-track plan. Students capable of even more accelerated work were taught by special tutors.
- About 1900, some "rapid progress" classes telescoped three years of school work into two.
- In 1901, Worcester, Massachusetts, opened the first special school for gifted children.
- In 1916, special classes for gifted children were created in Los Angeles and Cincinnati; Urbana, Illinois, followed in 1919, and Manhattan and Cleveland in 1922.

By about 1920, approximately two-thirds of all large cities had created some type of program for gifted students. In the 1920s and 1930s, however, interest in gifted education took a nose dive, for two reasons. First, equity and democracy took center stage. Dean Worcester referred to the 1920s as "the age of the common man" and "the age of mediocrity, when the idea was to have everybody just as near alike as they could be . . . administrators had as their ideal to bring everyone to the standard, but they had no interest in carrying anybody beyond the standard" (Getzels, 1977, p. 264). Second, the Great Depression reduced most people's concern to survival. Providing special opportunities for gifted youngsters was not a priority.

Significant Events Preceding Gifted Education Today

Historical events underlying today's strong interest in gifted education center on a half dozen people and one Soviet satellite.

Sir Francis Galton (1822–1911), younger cousin to Charles Darwin, is credited with the earliest significant research and writing on intelligence and intelligence testing. Impressed by his cousin Charles's *Origin of Species,* Galton reasoned that intelligence was related to the keenness of one's senses, which would have survival value. His efforts to measure intelligence therefore involved tests of visual and auditory acuity, tactile sensitivity, and reaction time. A hereditary basis of intelligence appeared to be confirmed by his observation that distinguished persons seemed to come from distinguished families, a conclusion reported in his most famous book, *Hereditary Genius,* published in 1869.

At the turn of the century, Alfred Binet, with his colleague T. Simon, was hired by government officials in Paris to devise a test to identify those dull children who would not benefit from regular classes and who therefore required special training. At the time, some children were placed in schools for the retarded because they were too quiet; too aggressive; or had problems with speech, hearing, or vision. A direct test of intelligence was needed.

A number of Binet's tests failed—hand-squeezing strength, hand speed in moving 50 cm, the amount of forehead pressure that causes pain, detecting differences in hand-held weights, and reaction time to sounds or in naming colors. However, scores on tests of memory, judgment, reasoning, comprehension, and the ability to pay attention tended to agree with the criterion, teachers' judgments of intelligence.

Binet gave us the concept of *mental age,* the notion that children grow in intelligence and that any given child may be measurably ahead or behind the typical intellectual level for his or her actual age. A related notion is that at any given chronological age, children who learn the most do so partly because of greater intelligence.

In 1910, Henry Goddard successfully identified the intelligence of 400 "feebleminded" children with the Binet-Simon tests, and in 1911 he summarized his evaluation of 2,000 normal children (Stanley, 1976). The tests successfully measured intelligence not only at below-average levels, but at average levels and above-average levels as well.

Stanford psychologist Lewis Terman made two historically significant contributions to gifted education that earned him the title of father of the gifted education movement. First, he supervised the modification of the Binet-Simon tests, producing in 1916 the grandfather of all American intelligence tests, the Stanford-Binet Intelligence Scale. The test was revised in 1937, 1960, and 1986.

Terman's second contribution was his identification and longitudinal study of 1,528 gifted children, 856 boys and 672 girls, published in four volumes of *Genetic Studies of Genius* (Terman, 1925; Terman, Burks, & Jensen, 1930; Terman & Oden, 1947, 1959). They have been the most studied group of gifted individuals in the world. In 1921, Terman and his colleagues began administering the Stanford-Binet test to students initially identified by teachers as highly intelligent. The final sample consisted of students from Los Angeles, San Francisco, Oakland, Berkeley, and Alameda, with an average age of 12, who scored above IQ 135, although most were above 140. Jewish children tended to be overrepresented; minority children were underrepresented (e.g., there were two Armenians and one Native American). Chinese children were excluded because they attended special Asian schools at the time. Nearly one-third were from professional families. Thus far, nine major contacts—field studies or mailings—across more than a half century have traced their educational, professional, psychological, social, and even physical development. As a group, they were above average in all of these areas, although no geniuses of the stature of Einstein or Picasso emerged (see, e.g., Golman, 1980; Sears, 1979; Sears & Barbee, 1977).

According to Stanley (1976), Galton was the grandfather of the gifted-child movement, Binet the midwife, Terman the father, and Columbia University's Leta Hollingworth the nurturant mother. Her pioneering contributions consisted of personal efforts supporting gifted education and gifted students in the New York City area, from about 1916 until her death in 1939, and the publication of two major books, *Gifted Children: Their Nature and Nurture* (Hollingworth, 1926) and *Children above 180 IQ Stanford-Binet: Origin and Development* (Hollingworth, 1942). In contrast with Terman's accurate conclusion that gifted children, as a group, are more emotionally stable, Hollingworth drew attention to the strong emotional problems and counseling needs of many gifted students, arguing that the greater the gift, the greater the need for "emotional education."

The last significant historical event to predate the mid-1970s' resurgence of interest in gifted education was the launching in 1957 of the Soviet satellite Sputnik. To many, this represented a clear technological defeat—Soviet scientific minds had hands-down beat ours. Reports that criticized American education, compared it with Russian education, or emphasized that the United States ignored gifted children became popular. For example, a 1959 report entitled *Soviet Commitment to Education* (First Official U.S. Education Mission to the USSR, 1959) claimed that the typical Soviet high school graduate had completed 10 years of math, 5 years of physics, 5 years of biology, 5 years of a foreign language, 4 years of chemistry, and 1 year of astronomy. Tannenbaum (1979) described the aftermath of Sputnik as a "total talent mobilization." Academic coursework was telescoped (condensed) for bright students; college courses were offered in high school; and foreign languages were taught in elementary classes.  Acceleration and ability grouping were used, efforts were made to identify gifted and talented minority children, and new math and science curricula were developed. High schools glowed with new concern for high scholastic standards and career-mindedness. Bright students were expected to take tough courses—to fulfill their potential and submit their developed abilities for service to the nation (Tannenbaum, 1979).

The Sputnik scare and the interest in educating gifted and talented students wore off in about five years.

Today's interest in giftedness began in the early 1970s and grew rapidly until, currently, every state has passed legislation on behalf of gifted children. Schools and districts across the U.S. and Canada and in dozens of foreign countries have created programs and services (e.g., Sisk, 1990). Enthusiasm for creating a suitable education for the gifted—tomorrow's leaders and professionals—remains high among most educators and, particularly, among parents of gifted children.

Handbook of Gifted Education

This book is divided into six main sections. We believe they cover the major topic areas and issues in gifted education.

1. An "Introduction" focuses on the need for gifted education, a brief history, issues and trends, and needs of special groups of gifted students.

2. "Conceptions and Identification" summarizes intellectual and affective components of giftedness, neglected social influences, several conceptions and interpretations of intelligence and their implications for the gifted, and issues and methods in the critical topic of identification.

3. "Instructional Models and Practices" is an extensive section that covers acceleration and enrichment programs, procedures, and activities that foster academic and creative growth; curriculum models that structure and guide acceleration and enrichment practices; examinations of ability grouping and cooperative learning as they relate to gifted programs; mentorships for the gifted; and an often neglected but vital component, evaluating gifted programs.

4. "Creativity, Thinking Skills, and Eminence," as the title suggests, includes discussions of the challenge of identifying the creatively gifted, ways to foster creative growth in all children, goals and a solid program for teaching other thinking skills, and two chapters on the nature and cultivation of eminence.

5. "Psychological and Counseling Services" focuses on the personal, educational, and career counseling needs of the gifted and on how to plan suitable counseling for gifted students and their families. The section includes a close look at the four interrelated topics of motivation, underachievement, perfectionism, and "emotional giftedness"—an intriguing phenomenon of overexcitability and sensitivity of some highly gifted students.

6. Finally, our "Special Topics" section presents a potpourri of pertinent subjects. For example, it includes characteristics, needs, and programs related to special populations of gifted students—the very young, adolescent, handicapped, female, minority, and extremely precocious; teacher training; an international focus in teaching the gifted; legal/ethical issues; and the U.S. government's view of giftedness and its implications for the future.

REFERENCES

Bloom, B. S., & Sosniak, L. A. (1981). Talent development vs. schooling. *Educational Leadership, 39,* 86–94.

First Official U.S. Education Mission to the USSR. (1959). *Soviet commitment to education.* Bulletin 1959, No. 16. Washington, DC: Office of Education, U.S. Department of Health, Education and Welfare.

Gallagher, J. J., & Weiss, P. (1979). *The education of gifted and talented children and youth.* Washington, DC: Council for Basic Education.

Galton, F. (1869). *Hereditary genius.* London: Macmillan.

Gardner, J. W. (1982). *Excellence: Can we be equal and excellent too?* (2nd ed.). New York: Norton.

Getzels, J. W. (1977). General discussion immediately after the Terman Memorial Symposium. In J. C. Stanley, W. C. George, & C. H. Solano (Eds.), *The gifted and the creative: A fifty-year perspective* (pp. 225–269). Baltimore, MD: Johns Hopkins University Press.

Goldberg, M. L. (1965). *Research on the talented.* New York: Bureau of Publications, Columbia University.

Golman, D. (1980). 1,528 little geniuses and how they grew. *Psychology Today, 13*(9), 28–43.

Good, H. G. (1960). *A history of Western education* (2nd ed.). New York: Macmillan.

Hollingworth, L. S. (1926). *Gifted children: Their nature and nurture.* New York: Macmillan.

Hollingworth, L. S. (1942). *Children above 180 IQ Stanford-Binet: Origin and development.* New York: World Book.

Newland, T. E. (1976). *The gifted in historical perspective.* Englewood Cliffs, NJ: Prentice-Hall.

Oakes, J. (1985). *Keeping track.* New Haven, CT: Yale University Press.

Reis, S. M., Westberg, K., Kulikowich, J., Caillard, F., Hebert, T., Purcell, J., Rogers, J., & Smist, J. (1992, April). Modifying regular classroom instruction with curriculum compacting. In J. S. Renzulli (Chair), *Regular classroom practices with gifted students: Findings from the National Research Center on the Gifted and Talented.* Symposium conducted at the annual meeting of the American Educational Research Association, San Francisco.

Renzulli, J. S. (1991). The National Research Center on the Gifted and Talented: The dream, the design, and the destination. *Gifted Child Quarterly, 35,* 73–80.

Sears, P. S. (1979). The Terman genetic studies of genius, 1922–1972. In A. H. Passow (Ed.), *The gifted and the talented* (pp. 75–96). Chicago: National Society for the Study of Education.

Sears, P. S., & Barbee, A. H. (1977). Career and life satisfactions among Terman's gifted women. In J. C. Stanley, W. C. George, & C. H. Solano (Eds.), *The gifted and the creative: A fifty-year perspective* (pp. 28–65). Baltimore, MD: Johns Hopkins University Press.

Sisk, D. A. (1990). Expanding worldwide awareness

of gifted and talented children and youth. *Gifted Child Today, 13*(5), 19–25.

Slavin, R. E., Madden, N. A., & Stevens, R. J. (1990). Cooperative learning models for the 3 R's. *Educational Leadership, 47*(4), 22–29.

Stanley, J. C. (1976). Concern for intellectually talented youths: How it originated and fluctuated. *Journal of Clinical Child Psychology, 5,* 38–42.

Starko, A. J. (1990). Life and death of a gifted program: Lessons not yet learned. *Roeper Review, 13,* 33–38.

Sternberg, R. J., & Davidson, J. E. (Eds.). (1986). *Conceptions of giftedness.* New York: Cambridge University Press.

Tannenbaum, A. J. (1979). Pre-Sputnik to post-Watergate concern about the gifted. In A. H. Passow (Ed.), *The gifted and the talented* (pp. 5–27). Chicago: National Society for the Study of Education.

Terman, L. M. (1925). *Genetic studies of genius: Vol. 1. Mental and physical traits of a thousand gifted children.* Stanford, CA: Stanford University Press.

Terman, L. M., Burks, B. S., & Jensen, D. W. (1930). *Genetic studies of genius: Vol. 3. The promise of youth: Follow-up studies of a thousand gifted children.* Stanford, CA: Stanford University Press.

Terman. L. M., & Oden, M. H. (1947). *Genetic studies of genius: Vol. 4. The gifted child grows up.* Stanford, CA: Stanford University Press.

Terman. L. M., & Oden, M. H. (1959). *Genetic studies of genius: Vol. 5. The gifted group at midlife: Thirty-five years' follow-up of a superior group.* Stanford, CA: Stanford University Press.

Tsuin-Chen, O. (1961). Some facts and ideas about talent and genius in Chinese history. In G. Z. F. Bereday & J. A. Lauwerys (Eds.), *Concepts of excellence in education: The yearbook of education.* New York: Harcourt, Brace and World.

2

Issues in the Education of Gifted Students

JAMES J. GALLAGHER, *University of North Carolina at Chapel Hill*

As the twenty-first century rapidly approaches, it is appropriate to revisit some of the major issues related to education of gifted students that have occupied us during the last few decades, and to speculate on what changes lie ahead. What are the major issues that educators of gifted students face? We are now aware that many of our most difficult problems come from outside our own small domain. For example, the collapse of the Soviet Union as the mortal enemy of the United States removed one of the most persuasive arguments for emphasizing education of gifted students.

For a number of years it had been clear that the allocation of resources for the education of gifted students depended, in a significant measure, upon how worried we were about external threats to our society. Sidney Marland, former U.S. Commissioner of Education, in despair about the lack of support for programs for gifted students, once pleaded for the Russians to "send up more Sputniks" so that we would be scared enough, once again, to divert some resources to this educational issue.

The current U.S. Secretary of Education, Richard Riley, in the significant National Excellence report (Ross, 1993), identifies the education of bright students as a "quiet crisis," meaning that it is similar to problems such as soil erosion and water pollution that must reach a catastrophic level before receiving major national attention, even though the national interest would be better served with some additional attention now.[1] Some of the summary comments of that analysis of our current status were as follows:

- Only a small percentage of students are prepared for challenging college-level work, as measured by tests that are not very exacting or difficult.
- The highest achieving U.S. students fare poorly when compared with similar students in other nations.
- Students going on to a university education in other countries are expected to know more than U.S. students and to be able to think and write analytically about that knowledge on challenging exams.

Major Issues

The following are my candidates for significant issues, and there are many subissues within these broad areas of concern.

- How do we now understand intelligence and from whence it springs, and how does that view affect educational programs for gifted students?
- How do cultural differences affect our identification processes and special programs for gifted students?
- How do we differentiate educational programs and goals for gifted students?
- How do we plan for special subgroups of gifted students—gifted students with learning disabilities, gifted girls, gifted underachievers, and so on?
- How has the educational reform movement affected educational programs for gifted students?

The Nature of Intelligence

As our knowledge of intelligence increases and expands, a portrait of intelligence as a huge storehouse of information has been replaced

[1] See Chapter 44 by Ross.

by a construct of intelligence as a series of interconnected knowledge structures, a network of interrelationships. The gifted student is one who has richer and more complex knowledge structures and, more important, the metathinking skills necessary to continue building that knowledge structure. The more complex the knowledge structure, the more likely it is that new information can be usefully inserted into that structure or across structures. Some have referred to this as the Matthew Principle of intellectual development, in reference to the biblical phrase from the Book of Matthew, "the rich get richer."

The newer conceptualizations of intelligence include, in addition to traditional memory, association, reasoning, and evaluation (e.g., Guilford, 1977), an executive function (decision making), metacognition (thinking about one's thinking processes), and multiple dimensions (Gardner, 1985). The introduction of information-processing models in discussions of intellectual abilities has helped spur interest in the decision-making functions of the intellect (Perkins & Simmons, 1988; Sternberg & Davidson, 1986). Because good judgment (making the appropriate choice between competing options) is one of the hallmarks of gifted individuals, the questions for educators are how this intellectual process functions and what instruction can do to enhance it.

Perkins and Simmons (1988) believe that intellectual competence on a given task depends on three major factors: the power of one's neurological computer, the tactical repertoire one can bring to bear, and a stock of context-specific content and know-how.

These authors conclude that there is great importance in teaching tactics. Tactics must be instructed explicitly because they will not automatically be picked up or "soaked up" by the student, and extensive practice in the use of tactics must be provided so that the skill becomes automatic. Deliberate planning also has to be made for conceptual transfer, because transfer occurs far less often or readily than one might think. The translation of new findings on intellectual functioning into educational curricula and strategies has begun, but a great amount of transformation of thinking by educators will have to take place before the translation is fully completed.

There has been an increase in interest in the relationship between metacognition and giftedness. Cheng (1993) summarized the existing literature on this topic and proposed that metacognition is a key component of giftedness. He reported that gifted children tend to use strategies more efficiently, learn new strategies with greater ease, transfer them to novel tasks more readily, and are able to verbalize their thinking processes more effectively than their age peers. Yet there remain a number of unresolved issues regarding the relative power of metacognitive awareness versus executive control. Is giftedness more related to one's metacognitive knowledge or to one's self-regulatory activities? Also, little is known about the developmental processes in young children by which metacognition emerges. Cheng urges more emphasis on case studies and naturalistic studies to pursue the developmental dynamics of the thinking processes of gifted students.

Kanevsky (1990) indicated that as early as age four or five, youngsters identified as gifted showed superior problem-solving strategies on puzzles such as the Tower of Hanoi, and were superior to average students two or three years older even though their mental levels were roughly equal. Furthermore, the gifted students seemed to be able to transfer their understanding from one problem to related problems more effectively, used information about their own errors to lead to a more correct solution, and had more confidence in their own solutions to the problems.

Early enthusiasm about the development of artificial intelligence appears to have been tempered by an abandonment of a general problem-solving stategy in favor of performance within more restricted domains (Nesher, 1989). In some respects, gifted students appear to be the general problem solvers that artificial intelligence investigators have been unable to create (Perkins & Salomon, 1989).

Regarding creativity, some questions have been raised regarding whether there is such a thing as a general factor of divergent thinking or creativity, or whether creativity or creative performance always has to be considered within a specific domain so that one can think about a creative mathematician or a creative writer, but not a creative person per se (Baer, 1993).

A new challenge appears to be how to measure knowledge structures in these various domains. How does one determine the relationships between concepts? A number of methods being tried include word association, ordered recall, and sorting and ratings of degrees of relatedness. Such devices can produce a matrix of proximity values (Goldsmith, Johnson, & Acton, 1991).

Another way of judging contrasting knowledge structures is the series of comparisons of the behaviors of "experts" versus "novices" in areas from physics to medical diagnosis to chess. Chi, Glaser, and Farr (1988) summarize that literature as follows:

1. Experts excel mainly in their own domains.
2. Experts perceive large meaningful patterns in their domains.
3. Experts are faster than novices at performing the skills of their domains, and they quickly solve problems with little error.
4. Experts have superior short-term and long-term memory.
5. Experts see and represent problems in their domains at a deeper level than do novices; novices tend to represent problems at a superficial level.
6. Experts spend a great deal of time analyzing problems qualitatively.
7. Experts have strong self-monitoring skills.

In other words, experts have knowledge structures that allow them to respond to new experiences in a more thoughtful and analytic fashion, freed from the immediacy of the particular experience.

Personality and Self-Image

It has become increasingly accepted that there are personality patterns that link to creative performance. Sternberg and Lubart (1993) reviewed the literature on this topic and found that tolerance of ambiguity, moderate risk taking, the willingness to surmount obstacles and persevere, the willingness to grow (to admit that old ideas were incomplete or even wrong), and a substantial amount of self-esteem all seem to predispose a person of high mental ability to be creative.[2] It concerns many educators that these characteristics are not often stimulated or supported in the typical public school program, whether for gifted students or for others.

For years there has been a continuing dialogue between psychologists and educators as to whether a positive self-image builds a more effective learner, or whether effective learning builds a more positive self-image. Research evidence suggests that these two constructs are highly interactive. Schunk (1991) pointed out that self-efficacy is a predictor of such diverse outcomes as academic achievement, social skills, smoking cessation, pain tolerance, athletic performance, career choices, assertiveness, coping with feared events, recovery from heart attack, and sales performance. Even more important, it is evident that self-image can be modified by success or failure, by attributions, and by the timing of rewards and feedback from others, particularly teachers. Hoge, Smit, and Hanson (1990) found that the self-esteem of over 300 students in public schools was linked to feedback from teachers and the school climate, whereas their self-esteem in a particular discipline was linked to the grades they received in that discipline. It is clear that self-image is one of the variables that can be influenced through modification of the school environment and teacher–student interaction.

Genetics and Environmental Influences

One major attitudinal shift has been in the increasing realization of the role played by the environment in the development, or *crystallization,* of intellectual abilities. Although evidence gathered from twin studies and from sibling and adoptive studies has clearly established the role of genetics in intellectual development (Plomin & McClearn, 1993), it has become increasingly clear that the early envi-

[2] See Chapter 22 by Davis.

ronment of the child has an important influence on the unfolding of intellectual abilities.

This strong interactive relationship between environment and genetics (Sameroff & Chandler, 1975) helps to explain some otherwise puzzling bits of information about the development of gifted youngsters. For example, it can explain the disproportionate number of males who are achieving well in mathematics, and the disproportionately heavy incidence of giftedness in some ethnic groups in which learning and language development are especially stressed, such as in Jewish and Asian populations. These findings clearly indicate that we are far short of reaching the full potential of our population, because the environmental setting for the full development of intellectual abilities is not positive in the case of many children.

The work of Howard Gardner (1985; see Chapter 5 by Ramos-Ford and Gardner) in describing multiple dimensions of intelligence is of significance to the field, not because of the uniqueness of the idea (after all, Thurstone's Primary Mental Abilities was presented some four decades ago), but because Gardner's ideas have found immediate application in devising alternative identification strategies and differentiated curriculum. Gardner himself has initiated special application programs for his ideas, such as Project Zero, which have demonstrated the utility of his theory.

Subgroups of Gifted Students

Cultural and Ethnic Miinorities

One increasing concern during the last decade has been the particular needs of racial, ethnic, and cultural subgroups of gifted children (see Maker & Schiever, 1989). Black, Hispanic, and Native American children appear in gifted programs at only about one-half or less their prevalence in the larger society, whereas Asian Americans appear at twice their percentage in the U.S. population.

Considerable attention is being paid to possible bias of measuring instruments, which are often held responsible for these differential prevalence rates. However, an alternative explanation is available. Instead of clinging to the discredited idea that intelligence is totally genetically based and impervious to environmental effects, which would be the only reason we might expect equal prevalence of giftedness across ethnic and racial groups, we should consider whether such differential prevalence rates might be explainable through the differential environmental advantages or disadvantages that such subpopulations have had in our society (see Gallagher & Gallagher, 1994; Perkins & Simmons, 1988). Of course, it is easier to change the identifying tests than to change the uneven societal playing field on which these children must compete. The development of the federal Javits program, designed to aid culturally different gifted students, has substantially expanded the search for alternative instruments or strategies (Ross, 1994).

A number of alternative methods and procedures have been suggested by which students from minority populations could be more accurately assessed for their learning potential than by traditional IQ or achievement tests. One procedure that has received considerable attention is the System of Multicultural Pluralistic Assessment (SOMPA) devised by a sociologist, Jane Mercer (1979). Essentially, this procedure adjusts attained IQ scores and achievement scores for unfavorable environmental factors.

One question raised by such alternative assessments of potential is how well such students actually perform in advanced programs. Matthew, Golin, Moore, and Baker (1992) used the SOMPA to identify a sample of gifted African American children. They then compared the performance of the students identified by SOMPA on the Ross Test of Higher Cognitive Processes with students from similar backgrounds who had achieved IQ scores in the gifted range. The results indicated that the SOMPA group was equivalent in its performance on the Ross and in its achievement scores to the non-SOMPA group, suggesting that the SOMPA may, in fact, be a legitimate tool for use in alternative assessments.

R. Gallagher (1989) and Wong and Wong (1989) point out that Asian American gifted students, despite their often high test performances, have many adaptation problems in U.S. society and need special attention.

Problems resulting from, for example, bilingualism, cultural identity, and career choice of lower level occupations call for increases in counseling and support, and there remains the special issue of gifted Asian American girls in a subculture in which males appear to be highly favored.

Maker and Schiever (1989) summed up changes in identification practices designed to maximize the discovery of minority children with special talents. Use objective and subjective multiple assessment procedures; include culturally and linguistically appropriate instruments; and use a case study approach in which decisions are made by a team of qualified individuals.

Special programming. A further question now being explored is what kind of special program would be desired for minority gifted students, once identified. A number of observers have pointed out that the special needs of these subgroups call for differential educational approaches (Baldwin, 1987; Sisk, 1989; Udall, 1989).

Although there is general agreement that the student should be well educated in his or her own cultural heritage and background, the end result of such instruction is not agreed on (Frasier, 1992; Kitano, 1992). Whether the goal for the education of such gifted students is *cultural assimilation,* fitting into the mainstream U.S. culture, or *cultural pluralism,* in which the values of the minority group are considered to be primary, is the center of the controversy. Kitano (1992) believes that the pluralistic approach, allowing gifted students to maintain their own cultural diversity and values, is more desirable than leading the students to assimilation to a mainstream culture which may have a different and dubious set of goals and values. Frasier (1992) also believes in the need to maintain cultural identity, but insists that minority children need to learn what it takes to be successful in mainstream U.S. society.

Maker and Schiever (1989, p. 301) summarized program suggestions from a wide variety of specialists concerned with Hispanic, black, Native American, and Asian American gifted children, as follows:

1. Identify students' strengths and plan a curriculum to develop these abilities.
2. Provide for the development of basic skills and other abilities students may lack.
3. Regard differences as positive rather than negative attributes.
4. Provide for involvement of parents, the community, and mentors or role models.
5. Create and maintain classrooms with a multicultural emphasis.

Although these precepts would seem to be good advice for any student and teacher, increased attention and emphasis should be considered for these factors when planning for multicultural gifted students. We are sure to see an increase in such differential planning in the future as our sensitivity to the special needs of these subgroups intensifies.

Cross-cultural studies. Considerable attention has been given to cross-cultural comparisons of academic performance because of concern that U.S. students are not competing successfully with students in other countries. Stevenson, Lee, and Chen (1994) report on the treatment of gifted students in Japan, China, and Taiwan. While China and Taiwan have developed special programs for gifted students with the specific purpose of fulfilling the need for well-educated citizens for economic growth, Japan, aware of its past elitist military background, has been careful to maintain equity as an educational philosophy. Although Japan has high schools for only high-achieving students, such schools are justified on the grounds that some students have earned this special treatment through their hard work, not their native abilities.

Japanese parents, well aware of the importance of attending the right school, have invested heavily in *jukus,* supplementary schools to improve students' mastery and prepare them for higher education entrance examinations. The *jukus* are a $6 billion industry in Japan. The emphasis in all of these cultures has been on *student effort* as a key element of performance, although innate differences in intelligence are accepted as fact.

These cultures believe an emphasis on hard work and attainment helps all students, both average and gifted, and hence they downplay the importance of innate ability.

Gifted Underachievers

One subgroup that has received little attention over the past decade is that of *gifted underachievers,* students who appear to possess considerable intellectual potential but who are performing in a mediocre fashion or worse in the educational setting. In part, this lack of attention would seem to be due to the tendency of many communities and states to accept the definition of a *gifted* student as one who is productive and effective. Such a definition removes the underachiever from the gifted category. Still, many educators wish to find some ways of stimulating and encouraging such youngsters to use the vast potential that they seem to have (Rimm, 1987; see Chapter 34 by Rimm).

We are still searching for characteristics that separate underachievers from achievers. In a study using a database of over 30,000 high school juniors and seniors, giftedness was measured as a composite score over the 95th percentile on the American College Testing program, and underachievement was defined as a high school grade-point average of less than 2.25 on a 4-point scale. Gifted underachievers defined in this fashion had significantly fewer out-of-class accomplishments in areas of leadership, music, writing, and athletics, and had a significantly lower opinion of their high school education than the high achievers. Colangelo, Kerr, Christensen, and Maxey (1993) sum up the sample as follows: "They are, for the most part, white, male, middle-class young people with some dissatisfactions about their school and some concerns about their own behavior" (p. 160). For these students, the lack of fulfillment of academic promise continues to be a frustrating experience that has resisted easy solution.

The few educational interventions that are reported to be successful for gifted underachievers have stressed programs of intense and consistent intervention over an extended period of time (Bulter-Por, 1987; Whitmore, 1980). It is clear that gifted underachievers have developed complex behavior patterns, established over a long period of childhood, and that such patterns will not be turned around without substantial effort. We do not have available at present a menu of programmatic possibilities to attack that problem of underachievement. This was an issue ten years ago, and it remains an issue today.

Gifted Girls

One subgroup of gifted students that is attracting more and more attention is that of gifted girls and women. The first major indicator of differences between gifted girls and women, compared with gifted males, was found in the longitudinal study of Lewis Terman and his colleagues (Terman & Oden, 1947). From a career perspective, the women in the sample were much less productive than the men.

Although there are clearly complicating factors that explain such differences, particularly the multiple responsibilities of homemaking and child rearing, there are a number of other factors inhibiting the full intellectual development of gifted girls and women in our society as well (Jacklin, 1989). Reis and Callahan (1989) asked whether women have really come such a long way, given their poor representation in legislative halls, the courts, and major corporations.

There remains considerable question as to whether observed differences are the result of genetic differences or the end product of a series of sociocultural interactions and values. Gagne (1993) obtained peer and teacher ratings in areas of aptitude and talent for over 2,000 students in grades 4 through 8 in a major metropolitan area. When he examined the gender distribution of youngsters in the top 10 percent of the categories, he found significant gender differences, with boys more talented in physical abilities and technical tasks, and girls more talented in the arts and socioaffective attitudes. The presence of gender differences at the upper elementary and junior high school levels is perceived clearly by peers and teachers. The fact of gender differences is clear to see, but their genesis is not.

Although some believe that there may be a constitutional difference between males and females in such specific aptitudes as mathematics (Leroux, 1985; Stanley & Benbow, 1986), the mainstream of thought today focuses on the social environment and how it can be modified to encourage gifted female students. One suggestion for a more encouraging environment has been to design programs that exclude boys (Rand & Gibb, 1989), given that research has confirmed that boys dominate classroom discussion, monopolize computer facilities, and so forth (Sadker & Sadker, 1985). Single-sex courses in subject areas such as mathematics and science, to allow the female students to progress without being discouraged by male assertiveness in these subjects, have been tried with apparent good results (see Chapter 38 by Kerr). A great deal of research and creative program development on how to create a facilitating school and societal environment are needed before we are likely to know how far gifted girls can progress, given a more favorable chance to achieve than in the past.

Twice Exceptional Child

The emergence of gifted students with individual disabilities, such as Helen Keller, Franklin Roosevelt, and Woodrow Wilson, reminds us that there also may be substantial hidden talent in individuals whose disabilities have cloaked their giftedness from their teachers, parents, and friends.

Baum and Owen (1988) compared high-ability students with learning disabilities (LD) with a group of average-ability students with learning disabilities and found major differences between the two groups. The gifted LD group were seen as disruptive in class but showing more creativity than the average LD group. The gifted LD group attributed their poor school performance to shyness.

Coleman (1992) carried out a similar study comparing elementary-aged gifted LD and average LD students on coping skills. The gifted LD students revealed significantly more planful problem solving when responding to problem scenarios presented to them. Coleman proposed that coping strategies be directly taught to all LD students, in addition to having a general counseling program.

Groups versus individuals. Whenever people wish to know about gifted students, or to compare subgroups of gifted students to other samples, they ask questions such as "Are they loners?" or "Do they have emotional difficulties?" or "Are they snobbish?" The answers to these questions can come either through *group statistics,* the average, or *individual cases,* the variance; and the answer can vary depending on which choice is made. Group statistics will reveal that gifted students are generally quite socially adept, popular with their peers, and emotionally stable. However, if you focus on one particular child, you may discover that, for example, Burton is emotionally disturbed to the point of suicide and desperately needs help. There are not contradictions between these two statements. We merely need to recognize and take into account the wide variance in this population around any personal characteristic, from height and weight to social skills.

Educational Adaptations for Gifted Students

The issue facing American education is, how does the institution of the schools adapt to differences? A recent publication listed 101 recommended practices for gifted education in a wide variety of educational topics (Shore, Cornell, Robinson, & Ward, 1991).

Acceleration

One of the motivations to accelerate a gifted student—that is, to send him or her through the various educational levels at a faster than normal pace—involves the length of time required to finish a professional or technical program. It is not unreasonable to conceive of students beginning kindergarten at age 5 and not completing their graduate or professional program until age 30 or beyond—spending a quarter of a century in school! Anything that can be done to shorten that period without affecting program or student should receive consideration. But can acceleration create harmful conditions that would outweigh the savings?

One concern about students who have been accelerated is that such an academic move could result in socioemotional problems. The educational practitioners surveyed by Southern and Jones (1991) believed that there were a wide range of potential problems for students who were accelerated. However, Sayler and Brookshire (1993), drawing from a base of almost 25,000 eighth-grade students from the National Education Longitudinal Study, identified those students within this larger sample who were accelerated or gifted. Comparisons of accelerated students, gifted students, and a randomly selected group of regular students revealed that the accelerated students appeared, on average, to be popular, to have a positive self-concept and locus of control, and to be seen as troublemakers significantly less often than the regular group. The authors indicated that the fear that acceleration usually or inevitably leads to academic, social, or emotional maladjustment was *not* supported. The accelerated students displayed levels of emotional adjustment and feelings of acceptance by others that were higher than those of regular students and about the same as those of older students identified as gifted (p. 153).

What actually happens to students who have been accelerated? One answer to this question came from a study of 65 students who entered college two years younger than the norm. These early entrants graduated earlier and had a greater percentage graduating Phi Beta Kappa than was true of the general college population. All but 4 of the 65 accelerated students completed their program (Brody, Assouline, & Stanley, 1990). There was little evidence of any academic malfunctioning of this special group because of their accelerated status. The authors cautioned, however, that such acceleration seems successful when the students have aptitude scores at least equal to the average for college students.

One special condition of acceleration can involve children with very high IQ scores. They may be accelerated more than the one or two grades that is the usual practice. What happens then? Gross (1992) described several such students who were radically accelerated from their own grade level and reported that they were more stimulated intellectually, enjoyed closer and more productive social relationships, and displayed healthier levels of social self-esteem than did gifted students who had been retained with their own age group.

The Desired Educational Environment

While the statement of national goals in *Goals 2000* contains a desire for both equity and excellence, many of the most active reform efforts appear to focus on equity. It is that value which leads one to heterogeneous grouping, whereby no one gets any special programming or privileges, and thus all are "equal."

It is around this issue of heterogeneous grouping versus ability grouping or performance grouping that most of the problems between the educational reform movement and programs for gifted students arise.[3] Gifted programs often rely on ability or performance grouping to provide the proper setting for advanced learning.

Slavin and Braddock (1993), strong proponents of heterogeneous grouping, make the point that only the academically gifted appear to profit from a grouped and accelerated program, and speculate that all students could profit from the style of instruction used in the gifted program, without the grouping.

Gallagher (1993) pointed out that a regular classroom teacher has a primary responsibility to the average student and then to the students who have fallen behind. Time often runs out before a well-meaning teacher can organize special experiences for gifted students. Teachers also often lack special skills in teaching advanced thinking skills.

Growing evidence supports the value of peer stimulation of gifted students with one another. In a review of mathematically gifted students, Sowell (1993) found that "Precocious students enjoy working alongside others who

[3] See Chapter 19 by Kulik and Kulik.

are precocious; the fast pace appears to be invigorating. . . . Situations in which students spend greater amounts of time together appear to be conducive to greater achievement and more positive attitudes than situations in which time with peers is limited" (p. 128). The problem that educational leaders and administrators have is how to put these pieces of information together with the strong current trend toward inclusion and heterogeneous grouping.

The development of the educational reform movement that stresses *equity* has appeared to result in a reduction in the number of special classes for young gifted students and the number of pull-out or resource room settings. This, in turn, increases the need to study gifted students' performance in regular classrooms. Westberg, Archambault, Dobyns, and Salvin (1993) performed an observational study of 46 third- and fourth-grade classrooms across the country. They looked at the teacher–student interaction of one gifted and one average-ability student for a two-day period in each of the classrooms. They found no instructional or curricular differentiation in 84 percent of the instructional activities. The greatest amount of differentiation appeared in mathematics, in which gifted students were given advanced content materials. The majority of gifted students who were observed were not being provided with instructional or curricular experiences commensurate with their abilities.

On the other hand, there is evidence that attending and participating in special programs does change the perceptions, attitudes, and motivation of many gifted students. Barnett and Durden (1993) studied students who had taken special academic advanced courses from the Center for Talented Youth at Johns Hopkins University, and found that they took more advanced college courses at an earlier age and enrolled in more college courses than a comparable group of students who did not attend such courses. On a sadder note, Purcell (1993) indicated that there was a sharp decline in energy, curiosity, and intrinsic motivation to achieve among students who had been in a gifted program that was eliminated by their school system.

Differentiated Curriculum

More concrete examples are now available of just what "differentiated curriculum for gifted students" means (see VanTassel-Baska, 1993; also Chapter 10). Gallagher and Gallagher (1994) presented four major ways to adapt current curriculum to the special needs of gifted students:

- **Acceleration:** Speeding up curriculum so that, for example, eighth-grade algebra might be presented in sixth grade
- **Enrichment:** Extending normal curriculum with differing examples and associations which build complex ideas on the regular curriculum
- **Sophistication:** Direct instruction in complex networks of ideas, such as theories in the sciences or larger generalizations in the humanities
- **Novelty:** Introducing into the curriculum unique ideas not normally found in standard programs, such as the interdisciplinary impact of technology on the society

The choice of which approach or which combination of approaches would be desirable is based on the particular group of students and the preferences of the teacher.

Differentiated curriculum seems to be pursued less often in the humanities than in the sciences. Brandwein (1987) proposed a curriculum in the humanities for gifted students in elementary schools that focuses on extensive exploration of such concepts as *truth, beauty, justice, love,* and *faith.* This is similar to some of the curricular suggestions of Adler (1984), focusing on important concepts and values as the organizing rubric for the gifted curriculum.

Thinking Skills

One consistent strategy has been to provide opportunities for students to problem-solve, problem-find, and create unique and original products. Such thinking skills can lead students to a more independent approach to problems. There probably has never been a more intensive effort in gifted education than the focus on stimulating creative thinking.[4] Despite the continuing interest, there has grown a new realization that such strategies cannot and should not be considered apart from the knowledge base of the student. There is an increasing realization that you cannot be creative in the abstract; you must be creative in something, in mathematics or art or historical research, and to do that you must have some organization of knowledge in that content field (Gallagher & Gallagher, 1994).

One other mental operation that has received attention recently is that by which controlled mental processes are made automatic. Whether in athletics or in intellectual striving, the ability to make complex processes automatic allows easy access to relevant knowledge and frees up attentional resources that can then be directed toward other aspects of the task. A strong knowledge base allows more effective *automaticity*.

In short, cognitive skills or strategies are most useful when they are combined with an effective associative network of concepts and systems of ideas. Such a network increases the effectiveness of memory, allows a better organization of a hierarchy of ideas, and makes it easier to access the information on demand. Obviously, the educational question of moment is how to develop most effectively such an associative network.

Two decades ago, Getzels and Csikszentmihalyi (1976) pointed out that in both art and science, it is the correct selection of the problem to be addressed that distinguishes between the truly creative scientist or artist and the more traditional and routine members of their professions. Only in quite recent times, however (Gallagher, Stepien, & Rosenthal, 1992), has any sustained attention been paid to the development of a problem-finding curriculum with students. Even the education of gifted students has been largely confined to a series of problem-solving exercises, with the teacher carefully constructing the problem in such a way as to ensure the students' mastery.

Problem-based learning was included in an introductory course on Science, Society and the Future for high-aptitude secondary students (Gallagher, Stepien, & Rosenthal, 1992). The students showed significant gains in *fact finding* and *problem finding* over a group of comparable ability lacking the special training. There seems little doubt that it is possible to train students in metacognitive processes to the point that such skills can become functional in the classroom.

With a substantial interest being shown in how students find and solve problems, why is there not more evidence of such strategies being used within the classroom? Onosko (1991) interviewed teachers and administrators and conducted classroom observations to explore barriers to instruction in higher order thinking in the classroom. He found six major barriers: the tradition of instruction as knowledge transmission, the need to cover broad curriculum, low expectations of student abilities, large numbers of students, lack of planning time, and the culture of teacher isolation. A recent national report, *Prisoners of Time* (Jones, 1994), has highlighted the inefficient use of time within the school setting as a major deterrent to more effective instruction. In particular, teachers in the United States spend more time in front of the students providing instruction and less time in planning, thinking, and coordinating efforts with other teachers.

Technology. The potential for the uses of technology is far greater than is realized in the classroom or school. Barr (1990) pointed out that "intuitive learning" (learning through nonrational or nonlogical means) can be enhanced through the use of high-resolution graphics programs that allow students to explore the structure of complex molecules in three dimensions, or through programs that translate complex calculus equations into visual representations that allow for intuitive understandings not possible in two-dimensional print pages.

[4] See Chapter 23 by Hennessey and Chapter 24 by Daniels.

The Vision of Educational Reform

The passage by the Clinton administration of the legislation known as Goals 2000, a later version of America 2000 supported by the Bush administration, was an indication of the desire to set major goals for education in the United States. These goals carried a mix of two major values in our society, the desire for educational equity and the desire for educational excellence, as seen in an equity goal of a 90 percent graduation rate for secondary schools along with a goal for becoming first in the world in mathematics and science, an excellence goal.

Educational Reform and Gifted Students

One of the major issues of concern is the degree to which public policies at the state and federal levels will provide additional assistance for special education for gifted students. The allocation of public funds to some groups of citizens, but not to others, always requires extensive explanation. In the case of children in poverty or children with handicapping conditions, the argument is straightforward. We believe, as a society, that children who are in trouble or are at risk for not developing in an effective way should receive special help. The situation is different when the issue of special education for gifted children arises. Here, one cannot appeal to the sorry state in which such children find themselves. Often as not, they are doing well in school, relatively speaking, and do not seem to have many academic or personal difficulties.

There has been a modest federal initiative called the Javits program (Ross, 1994; see Chapter 44) that provides funds for research, personnel preparation, demonstration, and a National Research Center for the Gifted and Talented (Reis, 1989). Such federal help is designed to add to the investment already made by the states, because states generally prefer to spend money on direct services rather than on research and personnel preparation.

The argument for special attention to gifted children is that many of these youngsters will become the leaders of the next generation in science, politics, the arts, and humanities. If we are to maintain our superior position, from an economic standpoint, over other rapidly developing countries in the world, we will rely heavily on the capabilities of such students. The evidence available at present is that these gifted students are not performing up to their potential and certainly are not performing competitively with their opposite numbers in many other cultures (Ross, 1993; Jones, 1994).

Unlike the argument that it is our duty, as caring members of Western civilization, to provide help for children with disabilities, the argument for special attention to gifted students centers on a degree of "enlightened selfishness." Such an argument brought forth major resources in the Sputnik era (Bruner, 1960; Goodlad, 1964) and seems to have the potential for doing so again while our concern is high regarding our economic viability versus Japan, Korea, Taiwan, Germany, and so forth.

Ten Years from Now?

What can we expect to see at the start of the twenty-first century as issues in the education of gifted students? Surely some continued advances can be expected in the understanding of intelligence itself, which may further redefine what we refer to as gifted students. Decision-making processes and metathinking in intelligent behavior are sure to come under more extensive scrutiny. Some additional and different measures of intelligence, built on information-processing models, also are likely to emerge. Mapping the sequential and developmental processes by which intelligence interacts with environmental factors to create a superior-thinking individual is a difficult task ahead of us.

How far we may progress in educational methods to teach gifted students may very well be determined by the final results of the reform movement on U.S. education. If it generates better curricula and more insights into the virtues of certain instructional strategies, then gifted students will likely profit more from such innovations than any other group of students. In any event, there is good reason to expect continued research and instructional interest in the fate of gifted students in this decade. The needs of the country are too visible and of too much concern to expect otherwise.

REFERENCES

Adler, M. (1984). *The Paidaia program: An educational syllabus.* New York: Macmillan.

Baer, J. (1993). *Creativity and divergent thinking: A task specific approach.* Hillsdale, NJ: Lawrence Erlbaum Associates.

Baldwin, A. (1987). Undiscovered diamonds. *Journal for the Education of the Gifted, 10,* 271–286.

Barnett, L., & Durden, W. (1993). Education patterns of academically talented youth. *Gifted Child Quarterly, 37,* 161–168.

Barr, D. (1990). A solution in search of a problem: The role of technology in educational reform. *Journal for the Education of the Gifted, 14,* 79–95.

Baum, S., & Owen, S. (1988). High ability/learning disabled students: How are they different? *Gifted Child Quarterly, 32,* 321–326.

Brandwein, P. (1987). *The permanent agenda of man: The humanities.* New York: Harcourt Brace Jovanovich.

Brody, L., Assouline, S., & Stanley, J. (1990). Five years of early entrants: Predicting successful achievement in college. *Gifted Child Quarterly, 34,* 138–142.

Bruner, J. (1960). *The process of education.* Cambridge, MA: Harvard University Press.

Butler-Por, N. (1987). *Underachievers in school: Issues and intervention.* New York: Wiley.

Cheng, P. (1993). Metacognition and giftedness: The state of the relationship. *Gifted Child Quarterly, 37,* 105–112.

Chi, M., Glaser, R., & Farr, M. (Eds.) (1988). *The nature of expertise.* Hillsdale, NJ: Lawrence Erlbaum Associates.

Colangelo, N., Kerr, B., Christensen, P., & Maxey, J. (1993). A comparison of gifted underachievers and gifted high achievers. *Gifted Child Quarterly, 37,* 155–160.

Coleman, M. (1992). A comparison of how gifted/LD and average/LD boys cope with school frustration. *Journal for the Education of the Gifted, 15,* 239–265.

Frasier, M. (1992). Response to Kitano: The sharing of giftedness between culturally diverse and non-diverse gifted students. *Journal for the Education of the Gifted, 15,* 20–30.

Gagne, F. (1993). Sex differences in aptitudes and talents of children as judged by peers and teachers. *Gifted Child Quarterly, 38,* 69–77.

Gallagher, J. (1993). An intersection of public policy and social science: Gifted students and education in mathematics and science. In L. Penner, G. Batsche, H. Knoff, & D. Nelson (Eds.), *The challenge in mathematics and science education* (pp. 15–47). Washington, DC: American Psychological Association.

Gallagher, J., & Gallagher, S. (1994). *Teaching the gifted child* (4th ed.). Boston: Allyn and Bacon.

Gallagher, R. (1989). Are we meeting the needs of gifted Asian-Americans? In C. J. Maker & S. Schiever (Eds.), *Critical issues in gifted education: Defensible programs for cultural and ethnic minorites* (Vol. 2, pp. 169–173). Austin, TX: Pro-Ed.

Gallagher, S., Stepien, W., & Rosenthal, H. (1992). The effects of problem-based learning on problem solving. *Gifted Child Quarterly, 35,* 12–19.

Gardner, H. (1985). *Frames of mind* (2nd ed.). New York: Basic Books.

Getzels, J., & Csikszentmihalyi, M. (1976). *The creative vision: A longitudinal study of problem finding in art.* New York: McGraw-Hill.

Goldsmith, T., Johnson, P., & Acton, W. (1991). Assessing structural knowledge. *Journal of Educational Psychology, 83,* 88–96.

Goodlad, J. (1964). *School curriculum reform in the United States.* London: H. M. Stationery Office.

Gross, M. (1992). The use of radical acceleration in cases of extreme intellectual precocity. *Gifted Child Quarterly, 36,* 91–99.

Guilford, J. P. (1977). *Way beyond the IQ.* Buffalo, NY: Bearly Limited.

Hoge, D., Smit, E., & Hanson, S. (1990). School experiences predicting changes in self-esteem of sixth- and seventh-grade students. *Journal of Educational Psychology, 82,* 117–127.

Jacklin, C. (1989). Female and male: Issues of gender. *American Psychologist, 44,* 127–133.

Jones, J. (Ed.) (1994). *Prisoners of time.* Washington, DC: National Commission on Time and Learning.

Kanevsky, L. (1990). Pursuing qualitative differences in the flexible use of a problem solving strategy by young children. *Journal for the Education of the Gifted, 13,* 115–140.

Kitano, M. (1992). A multicultural educational perspective on serving the culturally diverse gifted. *Journal for the Education of the Gifted, 15,* 4–19.

Leroux, J. (1985). *Gender differences influencing gifted adolescents: An ethnographic study of cul-*

tural expectations. Unpublished doctoral dissertation, University of Connecticut, Storrs.

Maker, C. J., & Schiever, S. (Eds.) (1989). *Critical issues in gifted education: Defensible programs for cultural and ethnic minorities* (Vol. 2). Austin, TX: Pro-Ed.

Matthew, J., Golin, A., Moore, M., & Baker, C. (1992). Use of SOMPA in identification of gifted African American children. *Journal for the Education of the Gifted, 15,*(4), 344–356.

Mercer, J. (1979). *System of multicultural pluralistic assessment technical manual.* New York: Psychological Corporation.

Nesher, P. (1989). Microworlds in mathematics education: A pedagogical realism. In L. Resnich, (Ed.) (1989). *Knowing, learning, and instruction: Essays in honor of Robert Glaser.* Hillside, NJ: Lawrence Erlbaum Associates.

Onosko, J. (1991). Barriers to the promotion of higher order thinking in social studies. *Theory and Research in Social Education, 19*(4), 341–366.

Perkins, D. N., & Salomon, G. (1989). Are cognitive skills context-bound? *Educational Researcher, 18,* 16-25.

Perkins, D. N., & Simmons, R. (1988). *The cognitive roots of scientific and mathematical ability.* Washington, DC: U.S. Department of Education, Educational Information Center. ERIC Document No. 307-779 (pp. 1–45).

Plomin, R., & McClearn, G. (Eds.) (1993). *Nature, nurture and psychology.* Washington, DC: American Psychological Association.

Purcell, J. (1993). The effects of the elimination of gifted and talented programs on participating students and their parents. *Gifted Child Quarterly, 37,* 177–187.

Rand, D., & Gibb, L. (1989). A model program for gifted girls in science. *Journal for the Education of the Gifted, 12,* 142–155.

Reis, S. (1989). Reflections on policy affecting the education of gifted and talented students: Past and future perspectives. *American Psychologist, 44,* 399–408.

Reis, S., & Callahan, C. (1989). Gifted females: They've come a long way—or have they? *Journal for the Education of the Gifted, 12,* 99–117.

Rimm, S. (1987). Creative underachievers: Marching to the beat of a different drummer. *Gifted Child Today, 48,* 2–6.

Ross, P. (1993). *National excellence: The case for developing America's talent.* Washington, DC: U.S. Department of Education.

Ross, P. (1994). Introduction to descriptions of Javits grant projects. *Gifted Child Quarterly, 38,* 64.

Sadker, M., & Sadker, M. (1985). Sexism in the schoolroom of the 80's. *Psychology Today, 19*(3), 54–57.

Sameroff, A., & Chandler, M. (1975) Reproductive risk and the continuum of caretaking causality. In F. Horowitz (Ed.), *Review of child development research* (Vol. 4, pp. 187–244). Chicago: University of Chicago Press.

Sayler, M., & Brookshire, W. (1993). Social, emotional, and behavioral adjustment of accelerated students, students in gifted classes, and regular students in eighth grade. *Gifted Child Quarterly, 37,* 150–154.

Schunk, D. (1991). Self-efficacy and academic motivation. *Educational Psychology, 26,* 337–345.

Shore, B., Cornell, D., Robinson, A., & Ward, V. (1991). *Recommended practices in gifted education.* New York: Teachers College, Columbia University.

Sisk, D. (1989). Identifying and nurturing talent among the American Indians. In C. J. Maker & S. Schiever (Eds.), *Critical issues in gifted education: Defensible programs for cultural and ethnic minorities* (Vol. 2, pp. 128–132). Austin, TX: Pro-Ed.

Slavin, R., & Braddock, J. (1993). Ability grouping: On the wrong track. *College Board Review, 168,* 11–18.

Southern, W., & Jones, E. (1991). *The academic acceleration of gifted children.* New York: Teachers College Press.

Sowell, E. (1993). Programs for mathematically gifted students: A review of empirical research. *Gifted Child Quarterly, 37,* 124–132.

Stanley, J., & Benbow, C. (1986). Youths who reason exceptionally well mathematically. In R. Sternberg & J. Davidson (Eds.), *Conceptions of giftedness* (pp. 361–387). New York: Cambridge University Press.

Sternberg, R., & Davidson, J. (Eds.) (1986). *Conceptions of giftedness.* New York: Cambridge University Press.

Sternberg, R., & Lubart, T. (1993). Creative giftedness: A multivariate investment approach. *Gifted Child Quarterly, 37,* 7–15.

Stevenson, H., Lee, S., & Chen, C. (1994). Education of gifted and talented students in mainland China, Taiwan, and Japan. *Journal for the Education of the Gifted, 17,* 104–130.

Terman, L., & Oden, M. H. (1947). *The gifted child grows up: Twenty-five years follow-up of a superior group* (Vol. 4). Stanford, CA: Stanford University Press.

Udall, A. (1989). Curriculum for gifted Hispanic students. In C. J. Maker & S. Schiever (Eds.), *Critical issues in gifted education: Defensible programs for cultural and ethnic minorities* (Vol. 2, pp. 41–56). Austin, TX: Pro-Ed.

VanTassel-Baska, J. (1993). *Comprehensive curriculum planning for gifted learners.* Boston: Allyn and Bacon.

Westberg, K., Archambault, F., Dobyns, S., & Salvin, T. (1993), The classroom practices observation study. *Journal for the Education of the Gifted, 16,* 120–146.

Whitmore, J. (1980). The etiology of underachievement in highly gifted young children. *Journal for the Education of the Gifted, 3*(1), 38–51.

Wong, S., & Wong, P. (1989). Teaching strategies and practices for the education of gifted Cantonese students. In C. J. Maker & S. Schiever (Eds.), *Critical issues in gifted education: Defensible programs for cultural and ethnic minorities* (Vol. 2, pp. 182–188). Austin, TX: Pro-Ed.

PART II

Conceptions and Identification

Part II focuses on how *giftedness* is defined and conceptualized and ways gifted students are—or should be—identified. Several themes emerge. One is that diverse and competing conceptualizations of giftedness exist—for example, emphasizing multiple categories, types, and components of giftedness or intelligence versus highlighting a basic *g* factor. A second theme is the recognition that identification procedures are not always tied to good research or theory. A third is that assessment procedures and instruments are not always equitable, valid, and fair.

In Chapter 3 Abraham J. Tannenbaum first presents a taxonomic definition of giftedness comprising eight combinations that essentially reflect *who, what,* and *how:* Producers of thoughts or tangibles may work creatively or proficiently; performers of staged artistry or human services also may work creatively or proficiently. Tannenbaum's *sea star* model emphasizes five cognitive and noncognitive factors that link high promise with productive adult giftedness. Each of the five factors—general ability, special aptitudes, nonintellectual (especially personality) factors, environmental supports, and chance—have both static and dynamic dimensions. Tannenbaum adds much clarification to our typically glib uses of the word *gifted*.

Robert J. Sternberg in Chapter 4 reviews his triarchic theory of intelligence and its implications for gifted education. His three types of intellectual giftedness include *analytic* giftedness, exhibited by persons who do well on intelligence tests; *synthetic* giftedness, displayed by unconventional, creative, and intuitive thinkers; and *practical* giftedness, adeptness at coping with everyday problems and job challenges. *Giftedness,* says Sternberg, is a well-managed balance of these three abilities. Sternberg also itemizes metacomponents, performance components, and knowledge-acquisition components—aspects of information processing that underlie analytic, synthetic, and practical intelligence. His Triarchic Abilities Test evaluates strengths in the three types of intelligence. Giftedness is not totally fixed, says Sternberg, but is capable of development—by helping students capitalize on their strengths and improve their weaknesses.

Like Sternberg, Valerie Ramos-Ford and Howard Gardner in Chapter 5 challenge the notion of a Binet/Terman "general intelligence." The theory of *multiple intelligences* (MI) includes seven types: linguistic, logical-mathematical, spatial, musical, bodily-kinesthetic, interpersonal, and intrapersonal intelligence. A given individual may be gifted in any combination of the seven intelligences, which "work in concert with one another." *Intelligence,* say Ramos-Ford and Gardner, is the "ability or set of abilities that permit an individual to solve problems or fashion products." The seven intelligences are best evaluated in informal "intelligence-in-operation" ways, rather than by formal testing—for example, via portfolios, board games, and observation of working styles. The authors describe several programs in which MI theory guides learning activities. MI theory has opened the eyes of many educators regarding the definition and identification of "giftedness."

In Chapter 6 Robert Plomin concedes that environmental factors, such as educational interventions, contribute to intellectual development. Nonetheless, he contends that genetics make a "significant and substantial" contribution. Although a knowledge of genetic influence does not dictate specific gifted programming directions, says Plomin, "better decisions ought to be made with knowledge than without it." Adoption studies and twin research indicate heritability estimates—the proportion of differences in IQ due to genetics—of about .50. Heritability estimates are higher for adults than for children; despite logic and popular belief, the influence of environmental factors *decreases* over the years. The finding that genetic effects on intelligence test scores account completely for genetic effects on achievement, notes Plomin, indicates that underachievement is largely due to environmental factors. An exciting current line of research is the hunt for specific genes that affect intelligence.

E. Susanne Richert in Chapter 7 describes pervasive problems in identifying and teaching gifted students. For example, elitist definitions identify white, middle-class, high-achieving students and reward conformity to school values. Multiple criteria are problematic because data often are combined inappropriately. Data from different sources should be used independently, says Richert, not just to confirm other data. Richert describes her APOGEE project, which uses renorming by cultural group and gender to identify poor and minority gifted students and to maintain gender balance. APOGEE, which includes intensive teacher training, has resulted in measurable improvements in thinking skills, reading ability, self-esteem, and reduced behavior problems.

Susan G. Assouline in Chapter 8 continues the identification topic with a focus on testing in assessing gifted students. She notes that critics pan testing, especially intelligence testing, for being superficial, for being unrepresentative of students' capabilities, and for overemphasizing a single (IQ) score. However, in the context of answering questions and making decisions regarding programs for and placement of gifted children, ability and achievement testing are invaluable. Assouline comments on the limitations of group intelligence tests, and recommends the Stanford-Binet and WISC instruments. She presents a Psychological Interpretive Report that describes how the testing-based assessment of "Fred" led to accelerating this remarkable first grader several grades. A second case used the Iowa Acceleration Scale to evaluate "Megan" for a similarly successful acceleration plan.

3

The Meaning and Making of Giftedness

ABRAHAM J. TANNENBAUM, *Teachers College, Columbia University*

Behavioral scientists never tire of searching for *the* childhood abilities that guarantee superior accomplishment later in life. By now, it should be common knowledge that, besides intellect and artistry, *many* attributes of the human psyche interweave with its surroundings in the intervening years to shape a child's future.

A Definition of Giftedness

Outstanding contributors to the arts, sciences, letters, and the general well-being of fellow humans tend often to show signs of promise in childhood. It is therefore reasonable to identify precocious children as the target group from which the highly gifted are most likely to emerge someday. Because there can never be any assurance that these children will fulfill their potential, defining giftedness among them is necessarily risky. One set of criteria may be *ineffective* because it excludes too many children who may grow up to be gifted; other qualifying characteristics may prove *inefficient* by including too many who turn out to be nongifted. There is inevitably a tradeoff between effectiveness and efficiency (Gagne, 1994), and educators invariably opt for a definition that enables them to cast the widest possible net at the outset to be sure not to neglect children whose high potential may be all but hidden from view.

Keeping in mind that developed talent exists only in adults, I propose a definition of giftedness in children to denote their potential for becoming critically acclaimed performers or exemplary producers of ideas in spheres of activity that enhance the moral, physical, emotional, social, intellectual, or aesthetic life of humanity.

In detailing this proposed definition as it pertains to childhood *promise,* it is useful to answer three basic questions about giftedness in its *maturity,* most often in adulthood:

1. *Who* qualifies to join the pool of *possibly* gifted individuals?
2. *What* broad realms of achievement among pool members are judged for signs of excellence?
3. *How* do pool members demonstrate their giftedness in these domains of human accomplishment?

As illustrated in Figure 3.1, the answer to the *who* question is that there are two types of gifted people: *producers* and *performers. What* do *producers* produce? *Thoughts* and *tangibles. What* do *performers* perform? *Staged artistry* and *human services. How* do *producers* of *thoughts* and *producers* of *tangibles* and *performers* of *staged artistry* and *performers* of *human services* go about proving their excellence? By working *creatively* or *proficiently*.

Obviously, the dyads that constitute the *who, what,* and *how* categories are not mutually exclusive. Producers often perform mental or physical rehearsals before (and even during) the acts of production. Performers sometimes produce preliminary conceptual, visual, or auditory sketches to guide their performances. Tangibles are produced with some kind of forethought, afterthought, and continual thinking in between. Thoughts that incorporate heightened ability and affect are sometimes preceded by tangible mockups and by tinkering with materials, some of which inform the emerging ideas. Also, there is something stagey about successful performance of human services, as any virtuoso teacher or physician with a bedside manner will confirm. And of course, brilliant staged artistry always performs an edifying human service. As for

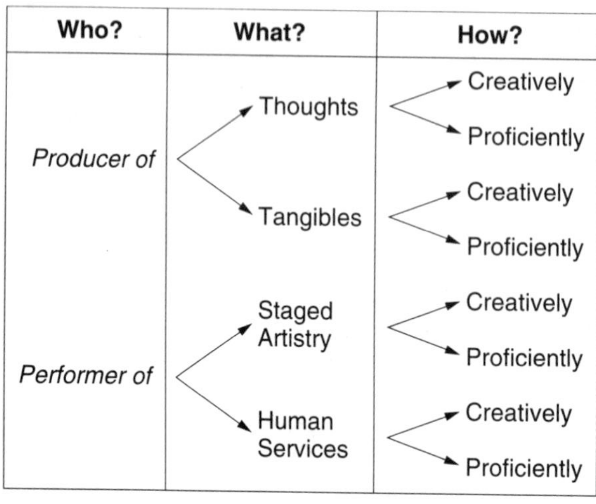

Figure 3.1 Defining *who* may show signs of giftedness, through *what* media it reveals itself, and *how* it can be expressed.

the links between creativity and proficiency, creatives often rely on superior craftsmanship and skill (their own or that of others) to actualize their innovative visions. Conversely, craftspeople and technicians tend to make original adjustments or refinements of their work processes and products.

To further clarify matters, two-dimensional products are classified as *thoughts* rather than *tangibles*. They include all works recorded on surfaces, such as paintings, literature, music notations, choreographic sketches, scientific and mathematical symbols, and the like, all of which can be touched but are really meant to be viewed for the cognitive and aesthetic messages they convey. Sculpture and craftsmanship in stone, metal, or wood, on the other hand, are defined here as *tangibles* because the sense of touch can enhance their appreciation as three-dimensional products.

The reason for making inseparable descriptors in the dyads *appear* separable is to concretize the definition without oversimplifying it. Accordingly, there are eight groups of individuals who are recognized by Western societies for the quality of their work, as follows:

1. The producer of thoughts creatively. This is the philosopher, not the professor of other people's philosophies; the brilliant poet, novelist, essayist, or dramatist, not the voracious reader of literature; the acclaimed painter, composer, or choreographer, not just the lover of the arts; the theoretical or experimental scientist, not the science enthusiast; the historian, not the history buff.

2. The producer of thoughts proficiently. This is the expert who can solve complex problems, as in math or science, even though deep insight, rather than innovation, is needed to work out a solution. Included are the masters of computer programs who are able to use the technology for retrieval and analysis of complex data. Also included are the talented editors who can turn chaotic manuscripts into great literature. Among the most prominent in this category are the efficiency experts, the great troubleshooters with superior critical skills which they use to correct existing schemes or identify those least likely to go away.

3. The producer of tangibles creatively. This is the inventor with enough imagination in science and technology to develop such patentable products as the light bulb, the refrigerator, computer hardware, medical equipment, sophisticated communication devices, and the proverbial better mousetrap. In the arts, there are sculptors, architects, and design engineers whose main talents lie in developing new products that are either aesthetically or functionally appreciated.

4. The producer of tangibles proficiently. This is the precision worker whose strength lies in meticulousness rather than originality. Included are diamond polishers whose perfect facets reflect light brilliantly; stonecutters chiseling intricate figures and ornaments for a cathedral's exterior; the wood craftspersons reproducing traditional furniture faithfully in all its complicated design; toolmakers who work by hand to reproduce precision instruments; and machinists capable of constucting sophisticated, problem-free machines, appliances, and equipment. Some may argue that master forgers of great art should be included in this category.

5. The performer of staged artistry creatively. This is the interpreter or re-creator. Included are the musical recitalists presenting their own understanding of composers' works; dramatic actors breathing life into a character in a play; dancers communicating their idiosyncratic rendition of a choreographed piece; poetry readers; and orchestral conductors whose brilliance lies in their unique renditions of works in these languages. Oratory and debate can also be fitted into this category, although some may count them among the lost arts.

6. The performer of staged artistry proficiently. Included are dancers who translate the choreographer's art into motion faithfully, not interpretively; orchestral musicians whose technique and self-discipline enable the conductor to re-create the wishes of the composer; movie actors carrying out the will of the director and thus turning movie drama into a "director's art"; and chorus members whose musical or dance performance demonstrates the precision needed to blend with that of other members.

7. The performer of human services creatively. Included are innovative teachers, political leaders, social workers, clinical psychologists, and other members of the helping professions. Also deserving mention are action researchers in medicine, the behavioral and social sciences, education, and any other fields that can help the human-to-human condition.

8. The performer of human services proficiently. These are the classroom teachers who follow guidelines faithfully and successfully; physicians with a keen mind for diagnosis and treatment; the psychiatrists who are sensitive to the needs of patients; and administrators of large corporations and service institutions who demonstrate superior managerial skills that require following a predesigned administrative plan competently, rather than designing and executing an original plan.

The Linkages between Promise and Fulfillment

Having defined giftedness in its maturity as comprising eight broad categories, let us now take up the question of what intrapsychic attributes and external circumstances enable a child *over time* to qualify as gifted. As emphasized in the beginning of this chapter, ability alone at an early age is a fair but far from perfect forerunner of eventual success. Much happens in children's life experiences throughout the school years and beyond that helps to account for what these growing individuals may or may not become.

Mental power by itself is not only a limited predictor of *eventual* adult achievement; it is a far from perfect correlate *during* adulthood, for even then there are traces of mediocrity in high places. Some people get ahead on little more than captivating charm or good looks; on aggressive ambition; on nepotism or "nephewism"; or on affiliation with the "right" race, color, or creed. These booster variables propel them through open doors of opportunity, which close immediately behind them. Others enter through merit at a time when career openings happen to be available and they happen to be ready and willing to take advantage of them. Meanwhile, those who qualify after the less able incumbents are comfortably tenured in their positions are not given a chance to break into the fields in which they are superbly talented. Similar discouragements frustrate virtuoso performers who cannot break into their fields because of the glut of talent that arrived ahead of them. These life circumstances can prevent or delay a person's opportunity to enter an advanced-level career, despite outstanding qualifications through ability and training.

Antecedents and Concomitants of Demonstrated Giftedness: The Star Model

There are no simple, foolproof causes of *demonstrated* giftedness. The antecedents and concomitants are complex, elusive, and not entirely known. However, they lie within the filigree of interweaving, interacting factors, five in all, which may be depicted in the form of a sea star (see Figure 3.2).

The five elements that contribute to the critical center mesh that accounts for gifted behavior are: (1) superior general intellect, (2) distinctive special aptitudes, (3) a supportive array of nonintellective traits, (4) a challenging and facilitative environment, and (5) chance—the smile of good fortune at critical periods of life. Each factor consists of static and dynamic subfactors.

Static subfactors denote individual status, usually relating to group norms, group identity, or other external criteria. They tend to portray humans in snapshot-like assessments, single impressions frozen in time and place. What these reveal corresponds to what is seen in an aerial photo of forest land, which is descriptive rather than analytic; it records a panorama of color, density, and variety of trees, without exploring what makes them appear the way they do. Similarly, a static view of children and their life circumstances provides a useful impression of where they stand in comparison to others at a particular moment in time. Such assessment relating to giftedness often comprises survey methods and standardized measures.

Dynamic subfactors, on the other hand, refer to processes of human functioning and of the situational contexts in which individual behavior is shaped. Unlike static impressions, which are basically molar, processes are of a molecular nature and can be discerned only through diagnosis at below-the-surface levels. The objective is to elucidate the individuality of people and the uniqueness of the surroundings with which they interact, thus avoiding classification and labeling through standard methods. Most theories of dynamic processes in gifted children have been validated only through clinical insights and wise armchair speculation.

No combination of four factors can compensate for a serious deficiency in the fifth. The minimal essentials, or threshold levels, for all five vary with every talent domain. For example, giftedness in theoretical physics requires higher general ability and fewer interpersonal skills than does giftedness in the social service professions. Therefore, no single set of criteria can be equally effective and efficient for identifying, for example, both "hard" scientists and politicians. The five factors interact in different ways for separate talent domains, but *all* are represented in some way in every form of giftedness.

Superior General Ability: The Static Dimension

General intellectual ability can be defined roughly as the *g* factor, which is itself defined roughly as some kind of mysterious mental strength denoting abstract thinking ability and shared by a variety of specific competencies. It is usually reflected in measures of general intelligence and in the common variance among tested special aptitudes.

The *g* factor, as revealed in tested general intelligence, figures on a sliding scale on all high-level areas. This means that different threshold IQs are required for various kinds of accomplishment, higher in academic subjects than, for example, in the performing arts. There is no basis for making extreme assertions about the IQ, whether to discount its relevance to giftedness entirely or to accept it without reservation. Instead, positions along this continuum should be adjusted according to the talent area, which means taking a stance closer to one extreme for some kinds of

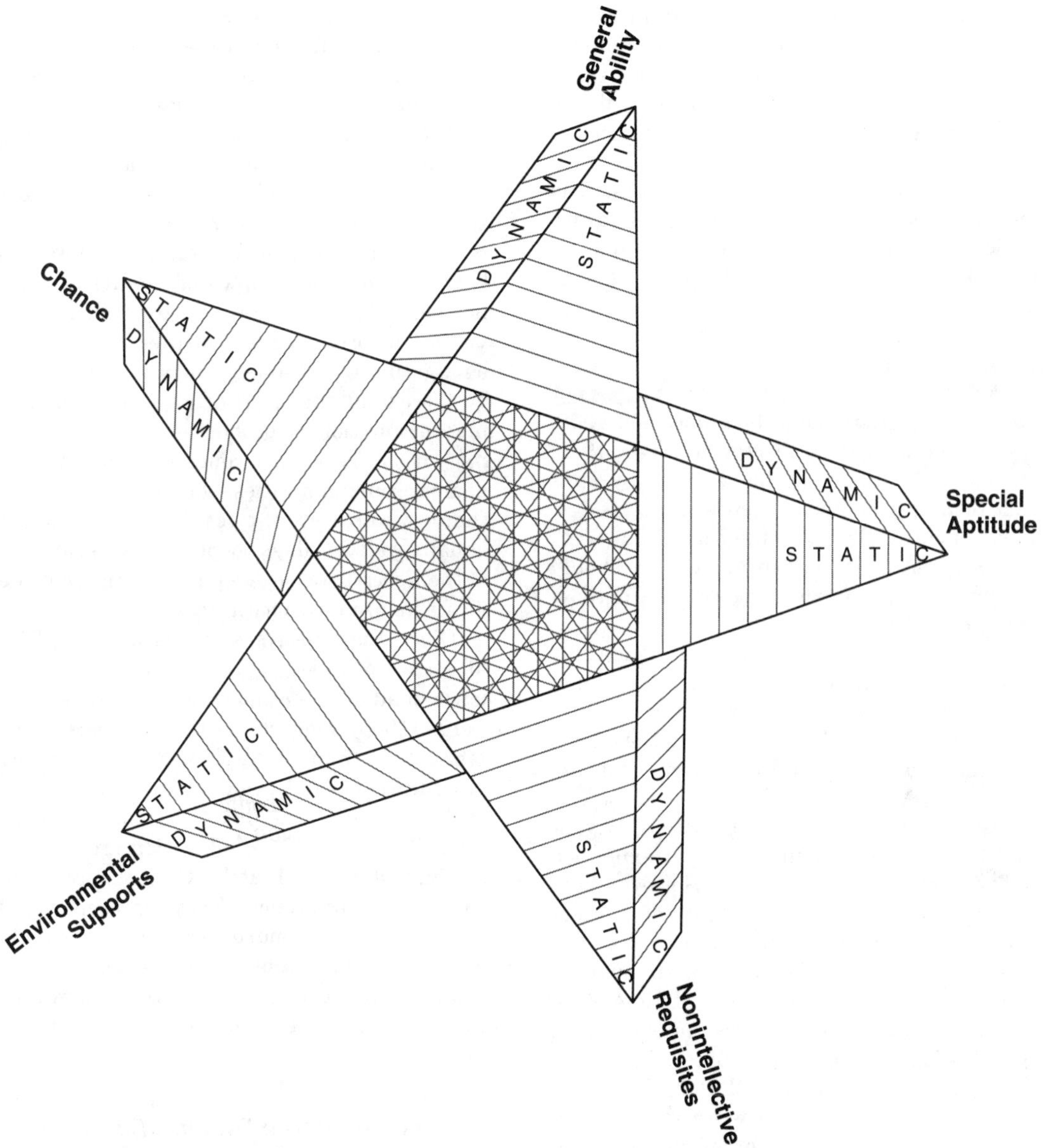

Figure 3.2 A psychosocial filigree of factors accounting for gifted achievements.

giftedness and nearer the opposite extreme for others.

The IQ as a reflector of human ability has been criticized widely in at least two ways. Some (e.g., Lippmann, 1976) argue against its *legitimacy* on grounds that it "acts" as the hand of Fate, dictating what a person as young as age five can and cannot become in later years within not-too-broad limits. The alleged danger is that engaging in such prophesy, and placing strong faith in it, threatens individual freedom to control one's destiny in a democracy where personal ambition and opportunity are cherished. Others (e.g., Gould, 1981) question the IQ's *validity* in realizing its avowed purposes. IQ is seen as a vastly overrated measure of childhood potential, except perhaps in the confines of classrooms emphasizing rigid mastery of simple academic skills and memory of trivial facts, neither of which is important for becoming outstanding producers or performers.

Critics of the IQ's validity argue that it is an inadequate predictor of a child's future achievement in the world of work (McClelland, 1973; Wallach, 1976); it correlates with only a narrow range of human abilities (Sternberg, 1991, 1994); "it is based . . . only marginally, on a theory of how the mind works" (Gardner, 1983, pp. 17, 18); it does not measure creativity (Getzels & Jackson, 1958, 1962); it is socioculturally biased (Davis, 1948; Helms, 1992); it should be replaced by aptitude testing since "the existence of . . . *g* . . . is extremely doubtful" (Guilford, 1973, p. 632); and its emphasis on power testing should give way to process testing (Ramos-Ford & Gardner, 1991).

As a predictor of scholastic achievement, IQ explains somewhere between 25 percent and 40 percent of the variance, which is far from perfect but appreciably higher than the effects of father's education or occupation (Duncan, Featherman, & Duncan, 1973).

As for the prediction of job success, Wigdor and Garner (1982) found that IQ explained only 4 percent of the variance. However, subsequent studies of the trainability of workers seemed to brighten the picture. For example, Ree and Earles (1992) report their own research showing an average correlation of .76 between general ability scores and success in 89 technical job training courses. These researchers also found a correlation of .44 (corrected for attentuation) between general ability and job performance for airmen in eight areas of specialization. Significantly, in neither study did tests of specific aptitudes add much to the prediction. These outcomes are roughly in line with others cited by Ree and Earles (1992).

Probably the most supportive evidence of the high IQ's validity in predicting success in adulthood is Oden's (1968) follow-up study of the Terman population that had scored an average IQ of 150 in childhood. The researcher summarized her results as follows: "Now, after 40 years of careful investigation, there can be no doubt that, for the overwhelming majority of subjects, the promise of youth has been more than fulfilled" (Oden, 1968, p. 51).

The charge that IQ tests are socioculturally biased is intensely emotional; and rightly so, considering that it relates to some of the most sensitive matters involving equity and racial relations. Democracy can tolerate differences between *individuals* in tested intelligence, but not between *subpopulations,* especially if the victims of prejudice are further stigmatized, as a group, by relatively low mean IQ scores. To the extent that IQ, per se, influences people's estimation of each other as *human beings,* it can be rightly condemned for its bias against some minorities. Objectively, however, the test scores predict academic achievement equally well for all subpopulations, regardless of their social status, keeping in mind that the forecasts are far from perfect.

Given that the IQ is comparably valid for all sectors of society, why do some groups score lower than others on average? The answer, as Lorge (1953) suggests, is that the social system rather than the test instrument harbors prejudices, not only against racial and socioeconomic minorities but also against groups classified by sex, age, education, geographic origin, and mental health. IQ scores are sensitive to these differences. They represent one of the *consequences,* not *causes,* of bias in society by showing that some groups are denied a fair chance to achieve excellence. In other words, the test is only a reflector, not a perpetrator, of bigotry.

General Ability: The Dynamic Dimension

In reference to mental powers, dynamic insights focus on the *how* (style and idiosyncrasy) along with the *how well* (quality) of functioning and socialization at molecular levels. This attention to detail seeks to elucidate human individuality in the context of its unique surroundings and experiences. With the help of clinical, componential, factorial, and just plain armchair analysis, cognitive psychologists have generated a huge literature on dynamic functioning in the cognitive domain. Space limitations permit merely a brief sampling of the rich and abundant ideas that relate to gifted productivity and performance.

By far, the greatest interest in dynamic functioning relates to the *how well* rather than the *how* of behavior. However, one of the rare empirical studies in both categories (Kanevsky, 1992) compares young high-IQ children matched in mental age with an older, average-IQ group on the Tower of Hanoi game. The study showed that the high-IQ children not only were more efficient in the task, but also were more apt to engage in "gamesmanship" in which they imposed added challenges on themselves by changing the rules of the exercise. They further demonstrated their unusual playfulness and need for self-betterment by striving repeatedly to improve their speed, accuracy, and independence. As part of their quest for more and more efficiency, they appreciated the opportunity to improve their tactical skills in the course of solving the problem, rather than just to test whether they would succeed or fail at it. These results provide some evidence that bright children possess distinctive styles of behavior in the process of learning.

Other dynamics subsumed under general ability combine both stylistic habits and underlying, particularized skills. For example, in a review of research comparing gifted with nongifted children on cognitive strategies, Rogers (1986) concluded that the more able groups succeeded at (1) recognizing the problem to be solved; (2) quickly devising steps to solution; (3) setting priorities for the direction to take; (4) selecting representation of information more in the way an expert would; (5) deciding which resources to allocate; (6) monitoring solutions systematically; and (7) taking longer preparation time before working on a task.

A subsequent literature review by Shore and Kanevsky (1993) adds more insights. They reported that gifted children, defined on the basis of high IQ and high achievement, know more, know more about what they know, and know how to interconnect their accumulating knowledge better than do less able children. They think faster and are especially proficient in monitoring and guiding their own thoughts when they work on a task. Their representation of a problem extends beyond the information given, which prepares them to include relevant information and exclude the irrelevant. Not only do they have more knowledge, they also have more strategies for applying what they know. The gifted also show more flexibility in shifting from one tactic to another in order to reach the best solution, especially when the problem is filled with complexity, which they prefer.

Special Abilities: Static Dimension

A general factor may predominate, but children also possess special aptitudes, some of which are much more fully developed than others, especially in gifted individuals. Furthermore, there are signs of extraordinary aptitudes even among children who are too young to undergo formal, standardized testing in any domain of specialization. Consider, for example, the case of child prodigies, some of them not yet of school age.[1]

Children who are bright at school, though not at prodigious levels, can be tested formally for special potential only when they reach adolescence. The quality of such measures would seem adequate enough to have persuaded Stanley and Benbow (1986) to use aptitude tests rather than the IQ to identify junior and senior high school students who are exceptionally advanced in mathematics. It would seem that general ability also contributes to the rapid advancement of these young scholars. For in monitoring their progress, Stanley (1991) observed: "To be radically accelerated, I should think that an IQ of at least 140 on the old Stanford-Binet scale (mean 100, standard deviation 16) would be needed to cope comfortably with the academic challenges of a college" (pp. 68, 69). However, IQ reveals little about the child's progress in mathematics specifically; an aptitude test is needed to sharpen the image, especially among gifted adolescents. Special aptitudes take on particu-

[1] See Chapter 35 by Morelock and Feldman.

lar importance at elevated levels of *g* in accounting for the variance in achievement.

Much of the work on identifying special aptitudes has been done through factor analysis. For example, Thurstone's (1958) factor-analytic studies yielded seven special abilities, including verbal reasoning, reasoning, word fluency, number facility, memory, spatial relations, and perceptual speed. Subsequently, Guilford (1967, 1977) proposed a structure-of-intellect model of as many as 150 factors in which five operations (cognition, memory, divergent production, convergent production, and evaluation) convert five types of content (figural [visual and auditory], symbolic, semantic, and behavioral) into six types of products (units, classes, relations, systems, transformations, and implications).

Vernon (1961) proposed a hierarchical model of intelligence, in which verbal ability, numerical facility, logical reasoning, attention, and fluency factors are subsumed under a higher-order verbal-educational factor, whereas drawing, handwork, and technical subjects, along with spatial ability, mechanical information, psychomotor coordination, reaction times, and athletic, ability are clustered under a higher-order spatial-mechanical factor. Nevertheless, as Carroll (1993) pointed out: "There is good evidence . . . for domination of all these factors by some sort of general factor" (p. 60).

Factor analysis is not the only means of recognizing the existence of special aptitudes. Gardner (1983) favors clinical and neurological insights to reveal seven intelligences, including linguistic, logical-mathematical, spatial, bodily-kinesthetic, musical, interpersonal, and intrapersonal.

Not much evidence has been collected thus far on the predictive validity of special aptitude tests. In the most extensive and encouraging work to date, Stanley and Benbow (1986) cite several follow-up investigations of their students. The results indicated that differences among them in initial scores on a mathematical aptitude measure were associated with subsequent differences in mathematical achievement.

However, post hoc studies of adults in a variety of occupations show how difficult it is to forecast success in any particular specialization. One of the best known retrospective research projects was conducted by Roe (1953) on 67 biologists, physical scientists, and social scientists who were creative contributors to their fields. Differences in visual aptitudes, auditory-verbal skills, imageless thought, and kinesthetic abilities were directly relevant to the type of science fields they pursued. For example, geneticists and biochemists obtained higher scores on nonverbal tests than did the physiologists, botanists, and bacteriologists who made up the rest of the biological sciences sample. Anthropologists were relatively low in mathematical ability compared with the psychologists and social scientists. As for the physicists, those dealing more with theory in their respective fields scored higher on verbal tests, in comparison with the experimentalists, who excelled on the spatial measures.

Although Roe's data showed some relationship between specific cognitive strengths and areas of specialization in science, it would be difficult to justify counseling young students about which branches of science they should enter, or even whether they should concentrate on science at all, on the basis of cognitive measures alone, for several reasons:

1. Existing tests seem to be more adequate in retrospective analyses than in making accurate forecasts, except perhaps in mathematics generally, though not in specifying any of its branches.
2. Even though special aptitudes probably do exist in young children, they are more easily measured in adolescents for purposes of making prognoses.
3. Under the best of circumstances, tests of cognition can only reveal whether the person has the intellectual power to qualify for careers in a particular field, but whether such careers *will* be pursued is only partly associated with intellect.

In the last analysis, special aptitudes can help a child excel in a specific discipline, *if* she or he also shows evidence of superior general ability. But to bring giftedness fully to life, these cognitive faculties have to be energized by an encouraging disposition, an enriching environment, and timely elements of chance.

Special Aptitudes: Dynamic Dimension

There seems to be unequal attention paid to process variables associated with the different specializations that are nurtured among the gifted. The area that seems to have attracted the most serious study is fine art.

Getzels and Csikszentmihalyi (1976) focused on the *how* as well as the *how well* of production, and on the relationships between them, by monitoring the work of artists in the course of producing art. They examined 31 college-age artists at work under conditions structured by the researchers. At the disposal of each artist were two tables, one of which was cluttered with approximately thirty still-life objects. The subjects were invited to examine and transfer any number of objects from the first table to the second in order to put together a still-life composition and then to make a drawing of the composition. Each person was observed for signs of distinctive ways of working. It was expected that artistic talent would be associated with the *number* of objects examined, the *uncommonness* of these choices, and the *thoroughness* with which the examination of each was conducted. The results showed that these work styles correlated as highly as .40 with aesthetic value and .54 with originality, based on judgments by a panel of critics who rated the final products.

As for *unique* responses demonstrated by professional artists, Kay (1991) hypothesized what she calls "a personal aesthetic bias" about which little is known, except that it produces a framework and set of organizing principles that guide the highly creative person in setting the stage for extraordinary productivity or performance and in turning the brilliant vision into a reality.

Kay's conception of a personal aesthetic bias seems reminiscent of a process of creativity which, according to Ashby and Walker (1968), is manifested by a sophisticated excursion into *convergent* thinking—a search for the *single solution* that no other person can fathom for a particular problem. The great product or performance is achieved by a process of super-speed selection, from among myriad alternatives, of the appropriate means to reach a goal that is acceptable to the self-critical artist. Successful execution is accomplished through information processing whereby anything leading to less than the envisioned ideal is dismissed so quickly that it appears automatic.

It is interesting to note that scores on power tests of static ability were not associated with the quality of artistic production in both the Getzels and Csikszentmihalyi (1976) and Kay (1991) investigations. There are two possible reasons for these results: First, potential talent in the fine arts can be assessed only through monitoring the processes by which art is produced; second, static differences between the artist and nonartist exist, but instruments for assessing them are inadequate.

Unfortunately, the pioneering research on productive processes in the arts has not received comparable attention in other areas.

Nonintellective Factors: Static Dimension

Relating personality traits to giftedness is a chicken-and-egg problem. Nobody knows for sure whether, and to what extent, these attributes are *causes, concomitants,* or *consequences* of successful achievement.

Of all the personality traits associated with giftedness, none has drawn more attention than motivation to achieve. Renzulli (1978; see Chapter 11) counts high task commitment as one of the only three major factors that characterize giftedness, the other two being creativity and above-average ability.

According to Rosen (1956), the achievement syndrome can be located at the indicated extremes of each of three polarities:

1. *Activistic-passivistic orientation:* This orientation denotes one's perception of control of self. Those who are activistic, or internally controlled, reject the fatalistic view that success is in the cards, but are convinced instead that they can shape their destinies.
2. *Individualistic-collectivistic orientation:* This orientation offers the choice between

self-sufficiency as against dependency on collaboration. The potentially gifted often choose to work at a task they like, even in the company of people they dislike, rather than work with people they like at a task they dislike.

3. *Present-future orientation:* This denotes the choice between immediate gratification versus planning for the future, even if it means sacrificing present gains for eventual compounded gains. The highly motivated take a more optimistic view of their chances of eventual success, whereas the less motivated tend not to make long-range plans.

Some investigators have suggested that an achievement orientation is situational. This means that a child may be motivated to achieve on the ball field but not at school, or on the ball field today but not tomorrow (Katz, 1969; Maehr, 1974). The gifted child, who believes that success or failure at school can make the difference between success and failure in life outside of school, may be faced with a dilemma in choosing between a heavy commitment to academics as against peer pressure to conform to a more conventional adolescent lifestyle.

In their meta-analysis of studies exploring the link between giftedness and self-concept, Hoge and Renzulli (1993) found the evidence inconclusive. They report that the gifted had slightly better self-concepts than average-ability children. However, when the measuring instruments were broken down into separate aspects of personal status, the evidence revealed that the gifted were relatively strongest in academic and behavioral self-concepts, but lower in self-reports of physical and social status.

The question of whether special classes for the gifted tend to raise or lower their self-esteem has not been answered conclusively. Hoge and Renzulli (1993) reported that some studies found a decline in self-esteem when the gifted moved from heterogeneous to homogeneous groupings.[2] However, Kulik and Kulik (1991) reported from their meta-analysis that some studies show improved self-images among the gifted in homogeneous classes, whereas others show no difference due to ability grouping.

As for other personality dimensions, Olszewski-Kubilius, Kulieke, and Krasney (1988) summarized several studies using the California Personality Inventory. The results were consistent for all ages, from elementary school through college. The gifted showed mostly consistent superiority on overall and subtest scores pertaining to such traits as independence, intrinsic motivation, flexibility, self-acceptance, and psychological adjustment.

Nonintellective Factors: Dynamic Dimension

Although motivation is closely associated with gifted accomplishment, a closer look at the dynamics indicates that motivation can stem either from within the individual or from external reward. Hennessey and Amabile (1988) summarize studies involving different age levels and different kinds of rewards and conclude that inner motivation is consistently associated with superior creative output.[3] However, it would be simplistic to conclude that intrinsic motivation is invariably detrimental. As the authors point out, under certain circumstances or with certain individuals, there is an additive relationship between intrinsic and extrinsic forces; they combine to produce a greater impact than could be expected from either one separately.

The importance of autonomously oriented achievement as a dynamic component of motivation is probably what characterizes Piechowski's (1979; see Chapter 30) concept of *overexcitability,* which he defines as an intense personal reaction to an experience. Research suggests that not only are elevated levels of achievement associated with elevated overexcitability profiles, but there is also a relationship between *types* of overexcitability—psychomotor, sensual, intellectual, imaginational, and emotional—and the domains in

[2] See Chapter 29 by Colangelo.

[3] See Chapter 23 by Hennessey.

which superior achievement is demonstrated (Piechowski, Silverman, & Falk, 1985).

It seems also that self-concept has its dynamic underpinnings. Beery (1975) and Covington and Beery (1976) proposed a theory of achievement behavior in which students protect their self-concepts of high ability by exercising little effort to learn. They refuse to submit themselves to a test in which the demands are high, in order to avoid the risk of failure and the implication that their potential is not as high as they think it is.

The Environment: Static Dimension

Giftedness requires social contexts that enable it to mature. These contexts are as broad as society itself and as restricted as the sociology of the classroom. Human potential cannot flourish in an arid cultural climate. It needs nurturance, urgings, encouragement, and even pressures from a world that cares. The most serious societal threat to the cultivation of giftedness occurs when excellence of performance or production is no longer deemed a standard.

Environment plays such an important role in shaping creative activity that Csikszentmihalyi (1988) gives it prominent attention among three forces that initiate creative behavior: (1) the *domain* in which productivity or performance is acceptable and which undergoes substantive and stylistic change from one period in history to another; (2) the *field* of teachers, critics, patrons, and creative peers who judge individual contributions to each domain; and (3) the *person* who creates within the limits of an acceptable domain and sometimes revolutionizes it to the satisfaction of the field. Thus, giftedness does not develop in an environmental vacuum but, rather, interacts with a particular domain and field in a sensitive, meaningful partnership.

Among the more specific environmental influences is social class. Terman (1925) discovered that high-IQ children were overrepresented among the middle and upper socioeconomic classes. The same has been true for National Merit Scholars (Astin, 1964) and highly capable math students in the Study of Mathmatically Precocious Youth (SMPY) program (Benbow & Stanley, 1980).

As for the impact of adolescent peers, Coleman (1960) found that in high schools where students are encouraged by peers to direct most of their energies into athletics and social activities, it is unlikely that intellectual pursuits will be attractive even to the most able among them.

Finally, there is the influence of the classroom. There is no systematic research on charisma among teachers or on the special "chemistry" between some students and some instructors. There is the popular argument, supported by biographies and autobiographies, that this magical encounter between a gifted novice and a special mentor accounts in large measure for the emergence of talent among many potentially gifted. Nobody can ever know how many gifted young minds have languished in obscurity for lack of an education commensurate with their abilities or of an unforgettable relationship with a memorable teacher.

Most of the evidence concerning the effects of schooling centers on experimental administrative plans, including acceleration and ability grouping. A comprehensive meta-analysis of research on grade skipping (Kulik & Kulik, 1984) shows that this form of acceleration is clearly advantageous to the academic growth of its beneficiaries.

There is less consensus on the outcomes of ability grouping as it involves gifted children. Again, through meta-analysis, Kulik and Kulik (1992) found that, except for multilevel classes that provide only minor adjustment of course content for ability groups, all other attempts approximating homogeneity in classrooms, including cross-grade grouping, within-class grouping, enriched classes for the gifted, and accelerated classes for the gifted, prove eminently successful.[4]

Environmental Factors: Dynamic Dimension

The social settings that have been investigated most thoroughly for their dynamic influence are the home and the psychoeducational facilities. Research suggests that the educa-

---

[4] See Chapter 19 by Kulik and Kulik.

tional climate in the home reveals much about motivation at school. In a study of fifth graders stratified according to socioeconomic status, Wolf (1966) hypothesized a positive correlation between what he called "process variables" and performance measures of scholastic ability, and suggested that these coefficients are higher than the ones between socioeconomic standing and scholastic performance. Process variables refer to various means through which parents encourage and provide opportunities for children to engage in learning experiences outside of school. There are three such variables, each having several specific subcomponents:

1. *Press for achievement motivation:*
   - **a.** Nature of the child's intellectual expectations
   - **b.** Nature of the parents' intellectual aspirations for the child
   - **c.** Amount of information parents have regarding the child's intellectual development
   - **d.** Nature of parental rewards for the child's intellectual development
2. *Press for language development:*
   - **a.** Emphasis on use of language in various situations
   - **b.** Opportunities provided for enlarging the child's vocabulary
   - **c.** Emphasis on correct use of language
   - **d.** Quality of language models available in the home
3. *Provisions for general learning:*
   - **a.** Opportunities provided for the child to learn at home
   - **b.** Opportunities for learning outside the home and school
   - **c.** Availability of learning materials at home
   - **d.** Availability of books at home and the public library nearby, and parents' encouragement to use them
   - **e.** Nature and amount of assistance in learning provided by the parents

Wolf measured the process variables through a questionnaire administered to mothers of his sample population. The results showed a startlingly high correlation of .69 between the dynamics of mother–child relationships and the targeted children's IQ scores. An even more impressive coefficient of .80 was obtained in relation to Metropolitan Achievement Test results. These outcomes were subsequently confirmed in a replication by Trotman (1977). Of course, the interaction between parents and children works both ways. Children probably achieve better as a result of parental stimulation, and parental stimulation is further encouraged by how well children respond.

Chance Factors: Static Dimension

The influence of the unexpected and unpredictable on the course of human development is a largely neglected subject in the studies of giftedness. This aversion is understandable, because what is there to say about luck—except that it exists and that it can make a difference between success and failure? Nobody knows what forms it will take, or when or how often it will strike. It is treated almost as if it were a supernatural force, inscrutable and therefore outside the pale of science. Nonetheless, no one can deny its power to facilitate or inhibit, and to direct or redirect, a creative act.

It is hard for educators, parents, and members of the helping professions to realize that their best efforts on behalf of potentially gifted children can be enhanced or nullified by circumstances over which they have no control. Even when a person seems a sure bet for success or failure, the smile or the frown of fortune can turn matters around completely.

Getzels (1979) discovered this in his longitudinal study of talented young art students. After collecting considerable data on backgrounds, abilities, personalities, and processes by which his subjects executed a creative work of art, he conducted a follow-up study five to six years later to see how well earlier signs of talent led to subsequent success in the field. Of the 31 former fine arts students, 7 could not be located and were considered either to have abandoned a career in art or not to have been visibly successful in it. Of the 24 who could be found, 8 had abandoned art as a career, 7 were only marginally involved, and the remaining 9 had achieved various levels of success as fine artists. Consider, in Getzel's own words, the important part chance played in the careers of his subjects: "There were idiosyncratic accidents and exigencies determining each artist's life and achievement that could not be reflected in the group data" (p. 385).

What the study demonstrates to students of gifted behavior is that information gathered about the subjects during their years in art school revealed only a little about their prospects for future success in the field. So much depended on the unpredictable.

According to Atkinson's (1978) view, all human behavior and accomplishment can be ascribed to "two crucial rolls of the dice over which no individual exerts any personal control: the accidents of birth and background. One roll of the dice determines an individual's heredity; the other his formative environment" (p. 221). Chance factors should never be trivialized or neglected in the study of giftedness, especially given that so many eminent people place emphasis on their experiencing unpredictable events that help them reach the top.

Chance Factors: Dynamic Dimension

Is chance simply a stroke of luck, a random event in the life of an individual, totally unrelated to the lawful functioning of the psyche or the environment? Is it a static condition, improbable and fateful, or can the person reach out and develop a dynamic relationship with it? According to Austin (1978), there are four kinds of chance factors. The first is simply luck, good or bad, that befalls a passive person who is in the right (or wrong) place at the right (or wrong) time.

At the second level of chance, a person increases the likelihood of being struck with good fortune by setting the mind and body into constant motion, although the activity is ill defined, restless, and aimlessly driven. Though mostly wasteful, such behavior overcomes inertia by stirring the "pot of random ideas" constantly so that a few will connect in unanticipated combinations.

The third level of chance connects an unforeseen experience with a person who is uniquely equipped to grasp its significance. Social and psychological factors interact to illustrate Louis Pasteur's dictum that "chance favors the prepared mind." Luck strikes rarely, and it is a rare person who can make the most of it; how much less probable it is that the two rarities should come together at all.

Finally, there is a fourth level of chance, which Austin calls *altamirage,* a facility for becoming lucky because of the highly individualized action taken by a person. It is the kind of good fortune "experienced by only *one* quixotic rider cantering in on his own homemade hobby-horse to intercept the problem at an odd angle" (p. 77). Such rare and often eccentric individuals patiently and persistently tinker with ideas and materials until a rare combination clicks brilliantly into place, sometimes without warning.

Of the four levels suggested by Austin, the second and fourth suggest processes of interaction between the individual and "luck." "Stirring the pot" helps persons somehow to insinuate themselves into the right positions when fortune strikes. Altamirage also runs counter to passivity and gives the edge to people who tickle fate with particular off-beat mannerisms that somehow invite the smile of good fortune.

No matter how chance factors are defined, one truism seems irrefutable: Luck interacts with inspiration and perspiration in a mutually dependent way. Without intimations of high potential, no amount of good fortune can help the mediocre person achieve greatness; conversely, without some experience or good fortune, no amount of potential can be truly realized.

Postscript

This chapter defines giftedness operationally and elaborates on the factors that combine to account for gifted behavior. The portrait is of eight types of developed talent, only a few of which are ever demonstrated in childhood. But children can grow up to be gifted in the way adults are if they are made of the right stuff in ability and personality and can make the most of mediated enriching experiences punctuated by timely strokes of luck as they grow older. Until maturation and wise nurturance are allowed to run their courses, all that can be said for precocious children, even the prodigies among them, is that they are *potentially* gifted. Whether, and in what ways, early promise will be fulfilled, only time can tell.

In my treatment of the meaning and making of giftedness, I have revised two long-standing beliefs. First, I no longer subscribe to the notion that only the creative are gifted and that mastery is merely a sign of high-level consumption, of little use to anybody except the consumer. It is true that many of those who ingest and digest huge gobs of trivia, and spew them forth on game shows or at cocktail parties, are only bores with no real qualifications to be counted as gifted. However, there is room for outstanding proficiency in sophisticated domains of production and performance that deserve to be recognized as signs of excellence. Think, for example, of the microsurgeon who operates "by the book" as only few can in order to save life and limb. That kind of proficiency needs to be included in any definition of giftedness.

My second revision pertains to the making of gifted behavior. My old sea-star image of five interacting factors still survives as the model of choice. Each factor, however, is now divided in two: the static and the dynamic. A static dimension of the person comes into focus by standing back and viewing him or her in a somewhat distant perspective, where other people and different surroundings provide illuminating contexts. The dynamic dimension consists of "under-the-skin" images of individuals that reveal how and how well they interact with their surroundings. It is confined to the interiors of human life and thus rounds out the picture provided by static exteriors. Both static and dynamic dimensions of factors effecting and affecting human achievement supply meaning to the making of giftedness.

REFERENCES

Ashby, W. R., & Walker, C. C. (1968). Genius. In P. London & D. Rosenhan (Eds.), *Foundations of abnormal psychology* (pp. 201–225). New York: Holt, Rinehart and Winston.

Astin, A. W. (1964). Socioeconomic factors in the achievements and aspirations of the Merit Scholar. *Personnel and Guidance Journal, 42,* 581–586.

Atkinson, J. W. (1978). Motivational determinants of intellective performance and cumulative achievement. In J. W. Atkinson & J. O. Raynor (Eds.), *Personality, motivation, and achievement* (pp. 221–242). New York: Wiley.

Austin, J. H. (1978). *Chase, chance, and creativity.* New York: Columbia University Press.

Beery, R. (1975). Fear of failure in the student experience. *Personnel and Guidance Journal, 54,* 190–203.

Benbow, C. P., & Stanley, J. C. (1980). Sex differences in mathematical ability: Fact or artifact? *Science, 210,* 1262–1264.

Carroll, J. B. (1993). *Human cognitive abilities.* New York: Cambridge University Press.

Coleman, J. S. (1960). The adolescent subculture and academic achievement. *American Journal of Sociology, 65,* 337–347.

Covington, M. V., & Beery, R. (1976). *Self-worth and school learning.* New York: Holt, Rinehart and Winston.

Csikszentmihalyi, M. (1988). Society, culture, and person: A systems view of creativity. In R. J. Sternberg (Ed.), *The nature of creativity* (pp. 325–339). New York: Cambridge University Press.

Davis, A. (1948). *Social class influences upon learning.* Cambridge, MA: Harvard University Press.

Duncan, O. D., Featherman, D., & Duncan, B. (1973). *Socioeconomic background and achievement.* New York: Seminar Press.

Gagné, F. (1994). Are teachers really poor talent detectors? Comments on Pegnato and Birch's (1959) study of the effectiveness and efficency of various identification techniques. *Gifted Child Quarterly, 38*(3), 124–126.

Gardner, H. (1983). *Frames of mind.* New York: Basic Books.

Getzels, J. W. (1979). From art student to fine artist: Potential, problem finding, and performance. In A. H. Passow (Ed.), *The gifted and talented: Their education and development* (78th Yearbook of the National Society for the Study of Education) (pp. 372–387). Chicago: University of Chicago Press.

Getzels, J. W., & Czikszentmihalyi, M. (1976). *The creative vision: A longitudinal study of problem finding in art.* New York: Wiley.

Getzels, J. W, & Jackson, P. W. (1958) The meaning of "giftedness" —an examination of an expanding concept. *Phi Delta Kappan, 46,* 75–77.

Getzels, J. W., & Jackson, P. W. (1962). *Creativity and intelligence.* New York: Wiley.

Gould, S. J. (1981). *The mismeasure of man.* New York: Norton.

Guilford, J. P. (1967). *The nature of human intelligence.* New York: McGraw-Hill.

Guilford, J. P. (1973). Theories of intelligence. In B. B. Wolman (Ed.), *Handbook of general psychology* (pp. 630–643). Englewood Cliffs, NJ: Prentice-Hall.

Guilford, J. P. (1977). *Way beyond the IQ.* Buffalo, NY: Bearly.

Helms, J. E. (1992). Why is there no study of cultural equivalence in standardized cognitive ability testing? *American Psychologist, 47,* 1083–1101.

Hennessey, B. H., & Amabile, T. M. (1988). The conditions of creativity. In R. J. Sternberg (Ed.), *The nature of creativity* (pp. 11–38). New York: Cambridge University Press.

Hoge, R. D., & Renzulli, J. S. (1993). Giftedness and self-concept. *Review of Educational Research, 63,* 449–465.

Jensen, A. R. (1969). How much can we boost IQ and scholastic achievement? *Harvard Educational Review, 39,* 1–123.

Kanevsky, L. (1992). The learning game. In P. S. Klein & A. J. Tannenbaum (Eds.), *To be young and gifted.* (pp. 204–241). Norwood, NJ: Ablex.

Katz, I. (1969). A critique of personality approaches to Negro performance, with research suggestions. *Journal of Social Issues, 25,* 13–27.

Kay, S. (1991). The figural problem solving and problem finding of professional and semi-professional artists and nonartists. *Creativity Research Journal, 4*(3), 233–252.

Kulik, J. A., & Kulik, C. C. (1984). Effects of accelerated instruction on students. *Review of Educational Research, 54,* 409–425.

Kulik, J. A., & Kulik, C. C. (1991). Ability grouping and gifted students. In N. Colangelo & G. A. Davis (Eds.), *Handbook of gifted education* (pp. 178–196). Boston: Allyn and Bacon.

Kulik, J. A., & Kulik, C. C. (1992). Meta-analytic findings on grouping programs. *Gifted Child Quarterly, 36,* 73–77.

Lippmann, W. (1976). The abuse of the tests. In N. J. Block & G. Dworkin (Eds.), *The IQ controversy* (pp. 18–20). New York: Pantheon.

Lorge, I. (1953). Difference or bias in tests of intelligence. *Proceedings: Invitational conference on testing problems.* Princeton, NJ: Educational Testing Service.

Maehr, M. (1974). *Sociological origins of achievement.* Monterey, CA: Brooks/Cole.

McClelland, D. C. (1973). Testing for competence rather than for intelligence. *American Psychologist, 28,* 1–14.

Oden, M. H. (1968). The fulfillment of promise: Forty-year follow-up of the Terman group. *Genetic Psychology Monographs, 77,* 3–93.

Olszewski-Kubilius, P., Kulieke, M. J., & Krasney, N. (1988). Personality dimensions of gifted adolescents: A review of the empirical literature. *Gifted Child Quarterly, 32,* 347–352.

Piechowski, M. M. (1979). Developmental potential. In N. Colangelo & R. T. Zaffrann (Eds.), *New voices in counseling the gifted* (pp. 25–27). Dubuque, IA: Kendall/Hunt.

Piechowski, M. M., Silverman, L. K., & Falk, R. F. (1985). Comparison of intellectually and artistically gifted on five dimensions of mental functioning. *Perceptual and Motor Skills, 60,* 539–549.

Ramos-Ford, V., & Gardner, H. (1991). Giftedness from a multiple intelligence perspective. In N. Colangelo & G. A. Davis (Eds.), *Handbook of gifted education* (pp. 55–64). Boston: Allyn and Bacon.

Ree, M. J., & Earles, J. A. (1992). Intelligence is the best predictor of job performance. *Current Directions in Psychological Science, 1,* 86–89.

Renzulli, J. S. (1978). What makes giftedness? Reexamining a definition. *Phi Delta Kappan, 60,* 18–24.

Roe, A. (1953). *Making of a scientist.* New York: Dodd, Mead.

Rogers, K. B. (1986). Do the gifted think differently? A review of recent research and its implications for instruction. *Journal for the Education of the Gifted, 10*(1), 17–39.

Rosen, B. C. (1956). The achievement syndrome. *American Sociological Review, 21,* 203–211.

Shore, B. M., & Kanevsky, L. (1993). Thinking processes: Being and becoming. In K. A. Heller, F. J. Monks, and A. H. Passow (Eds.), *International handbook of research and development of giftedness and talent* (pp. 133–147). Oxford, England: Pergamon Press.

Stanley, J. C. (1991). Critique of "Socioemotional adjustment of adolescent girls enrolled in a residential acceleration program." *Gifted Child Quarterly, 35,* 67–70.

Stanley, J. C., & Benbow, C. P. (1986). Youths who reason exceptionally well mathematically. In R. J. Sternberg & J. E. Davidson (Eds.), *Conceptions of giftedness* (pp. 361–387). New York: Cambridge University Press.

Sternberg, R. J. (1991). Giftedness according to the triarchic theory of human intelligence. In N. Colangelo & G. A. Davis (Eds.), *Handbook of gifted education* (pp. 45–54). Boston: Allyn and Bacon.

Sternberg, R. J. (1994). Quoted by Beth Azar in

Psychology weighs in on bell curve debate. *APA Monitor, 25*(2), 1, 22, 23.

Terman, L. M. (1925). *Mental and physical traits of a thousand gifted children.* Stanford, CA: Stanford University Press.

Thurstone, T. G. (1958). *SRA primary mental abilities.* Chicago, IL: Science Research Associates.

Trotman, F. K. (1977). Race, IQ and the middle class. *Journal of Educational Psychology, 69,* 266–273.

Vernon, P. E. (1961). The structure of human abilities (2nd ed.). London: Methuen.

Wallach, M. A. (1976). Tests tell us little about talent. *American Scientist, 64,* 57–63.

Wigdor, A. K., & Garner, W. R. (1982). *Ability testing: Uses, consequences, and controversies.* Washington, DC: National Academy Press.

Wolf, R. (1966). The measurement of environments. In A. Anastasi (Ed.), *Testing problems in perspective* (pp. 491–503). Washington, DC: Council on Education.

4

A Triarchic View of Giftedness: Theory and Practice

ROBERT J. STERNBERG, *Yale University*

Throughout most of this century, intellectual giftedness has been defined as a unidimensional construct. The most frequently used measure of that dimension has been the IQ. Underlying the use of this measure is the belief that intelligence is a single thing and that IQ provides a reasonably good, though not perfect, measure of it. Sometimes achievement test scores as well as IQ test scores are used in the identification of children as gifted. However, achievement test scores tend to be highly correlated with IQ test scores and measure almost the same thing. The basic thesis of this chapter is that we ought to define intellectual giftedness in a broader way that goes beyond what is measured by either the IQ or the achievement tests.

Kinds of Intellectual Giftedness

In my triarchic theory of human intelligence (Sternberg, 1985, 1988b), there are multiple loci of intellectual giftedness. In other words, giftedness cannot possibly be captured by a single number. Unless we examine the multiple sources of giftedness, we risk missing identification of large numbers of gifted individuals. The three main kinds of giftedness are in terms of analytic, synthetic, and practical abilities.

The work reported herein was supported under the Javits Act program (Grant #R206R00001) as administered by the Office of Educational Research and Improvement, U.S. Department of Education. The findings and opinions expressed in this chapter do not reflect the positions or policies of the Office of Educational Research and Improvement or the U.S. Department of Education.

Analytic Giftedness

Giftedness in analytic skills involves being able to dissect a problem and understand its parts. People who are strong in this area of intellectual functioning tend to do well on conventional tests of intelligence, which place a premium on analytical reasoning. For example, analogies require analysis of relations between pairs of terms and pairs of relations; synonyms require analysis of which of several answer options most closely corresponds to a given target word; reading comprehension involves analysis of reading passages; matrix problems involve analysis of interrelations among rows and columns of figures, numbers, or whatever. Analytic giftedness clearly is the kind best measured by existing tests.

I frequently give the example of one of my past students, "Alice," who was a prime example of analytic giftedness. Her test scores were excellent, her undergraduate grades were excellent, her teachers thought that she was extremely smart, and she did well in almost all of the things that are traditionally viewed as part of intellectual giftedness. But Alice proved to have difficulty in her later years of graduate school because, although she was excellent at analyzing ideas, she was not nearly so good at coming up with clever ideas of her own.

Synthetic Giftedness

Synthetic giftedness is seen in people who are insightful, intuitive, creative, or just adept at coping with relatively novel situations. People who are synthetically gifted do not necessarily do well on conventional measures of intelligence. Indeed, if they see more or different things in a problem than did the test-constructor, they may get the problem wrong. They don't see things the way many others do. Thus, people with synthetic giftedness may not be the ones with the highest IQs, but they may be the ones who ultimately make the greatest contributions to such pursuits as science, literature, art, drama, and the like. Synthetic giftedness is important not only in the sciences and the arts. People who make money in the stock market often tend to be contrarians: They can see market phenomena in a way different from that of others who analyze the market. Similarly, people who make money in business tend to be those who see a need for a new product or service, or a new way of delivering a product or service. Synthetic giftedness is important for success in the world but is hardly measured at all by existing tests.

I sometimes give as an example of synthetic giftedness my graduate student "Barbara," who did not do well at all on tests but was recommended to us at Yale as having unusual creative and insight skills. Despite her low test scores, Barbara proved herself to be enormously creative in coming up with ideas for new research. Thus, although she may not have been as strong as Alice in analyzing problems, she was much better at coming up with new problems of her own.

Practical Giftedness

A third kind of intellectual giftedness is practical giftedness, which involves applying whatever analytic or synthetic ability you may have to everyday, pragmatic situations. The practically gifted person is one who can go into an environmental setting, figure out what one needs to do to succeed in that setting, and then go ahead and do it. Many people have strong analytic or synthetic abilities but are unable to apply these abilities to negotiation of successful relations with other people, or to getting ahead in their careers. The practically gifted person specializes in these uses of abilities.

As an example of a practically gifted individual, my graduate student "Celia" had neither Alice's analytic ability nor Barbara's synthetic ability. But Celia was highly successful in figuring out what she needed to do in order to succeed in an academic environment. She knew what kind of research was valued, how to get articles into journals, how to impress people at job interviews, and the like. She did not have the skills of an Alice or a Barbara, but she could turn the skills she had to her advantage in practical settings.

Combining Analytic, Synthetic, and Practical Giftedness

Of course, people do not possess just one of these kinds of skills. Rather, they represent some blend of the three different skills. Moreover, this blend can change over time because intelligence can be developed in various directions. People who are extreme in one of these kinds of giftedness without at least some skill in the others may tend to be less successful in ultimately convincing people of their worth. For example, someone who is very creatively gifted but cannot demonstrate it in practical settings and cannot convince people of the worth of his or her ideas will encounter frustration at every turn. Thus, an important part of giftedness lies in being able to coordinate these three aspects of abilities, and in knowing when to use which one. Giftedness is as much a well-managed balance of these three abilities as it is a high score on any one or more of them. I therefore sometimes refer to a gifted person as a good "mental self-manager."

Loci of Intellectual Giftedness: Components of Intelligence

The kinds of intellectual giftedness described here are general categories of superiority. In order to understand giftedness more fully, one would wish to understand the loci of information processing that contribute to the kinds of giftedness described above.

Metacomponents of Intelligence

In the triarchic theory, executive processes used to plan, monitor, and evaluate problem solving and decision making are referred to as *metacomponents.* Metacomponents are essential to successful problem solving and decision making. I usually refer to eight of them, although I do not claim that this list is exhaustive.

1. Problem recognition. One cannot solve a problem that one does not know exists. Some people excel in problem solving because they are quick to recognize when they have problems or are good at generating important problems to study. Problem recognition, therefore, precedes the normal problem-solving cycle in that it is prerequisite for it.

2. Problem definition. It is not enough to recognize a problem, one also has to understand the nature of the problem being confronted. Problem definition involves figuring out just what a given problem is. Again, some people may be good problem solvers, but frequently will solve the wrong problem. People who excel in problem definition are those who, confronted with a set of environmental contingencies, can figure out exactly what the problem is that needs to be solved. Ironically, schools tend to present children, even gifted children, with problems that they are supposed to solve. In everyday life, however, and in the contributions of great discoverers and inventors, problem recognition and problem definition are key. We should put more emphasis on having students figure out problems, rather than giving the problems to them.

3. Selection of lower-order components for problem solving. This metacomponent involves choosing a set of processes to solve a problem. We have a large array of mental processes at our disposal. No matter how well we may execute any one or more of these processes, they may not be effective for us if we do not know when to use them. Good problem solvers often tend to be people who know which processes to use when.

4. Ordering lower-order processes into a strategy. After choosing a set of processes, it is necessary to sequence them in a way that will lead from the formulation of the problem to its solution. If one chooses the correct processes but misorders their execution, a problem may prove to be insoluble. Individuals who excel in this metacomponent are able to sequence steps correctly.

5. Mental representation of problems. To solve a problem, one needs to represent it mentally in some form. For example, linear syllogisms such as "John is taller than Mary. Mary is taller than Susan. Who is tallest?" are soluble either through a linguistic representation of information, a spatial representation of information, or a combination of the two (Sternberg, 1985). Thus, in this and other problems, options are available for the representation of information. However, not all representations of a given problem are equally useful, and how useful a given representation will be depends not only on the problem but also on the strengths and weaknesses of the individual in exploiting different representations. Someone who excels in mental representation is not necessarily the best utilizer of every representation but, rather, someone who knows what representations to use when, given the constraints of the problem, time to solve the problem, and the individual's own abilities.

6. Allocation of processing resources. In life, we often have too many things to do in a given amount of time. Thus, it is necessary to allocate out time and mental-processing resources to use them as effectively as possible. People who excel in this metacomponent are able to allocate the amounts of time and processing resources that best suit a particular problem. Other people may be good problem solvers but may spend too long on problems that do not deserve a lot of time, or not enough time on problems that may deserve more time. Effective resource allocation is extremely important for successful performance in the complex stream of everyday life.

7. Solution monitoring. Solution monitoring refers to keeping track of how problem solving is going as we are solving a particular problem. In other words, often we start going down a garden path in our problem solving, or we start on a path that may ultimately lead to solution, but only after a long uphill battle. Good solution monitors keep track of where their problem solving is leading them, and, as they see that the path they are on is not taking them where they want to go, consider using an alternative strategy.

8. Solution evaluation. Even after one has finished solving a problem and has produced a solution, the problem-solving cycle is still not complete. We still need to evaluate the quality and appropriateness of the solution we have obtained. Students at various levels of schooling often make errors in their work because their solutions are unacceptable. They never bother to check whether the solutions even make sense, much less whether they are exact. We need to evaluate our solution against the original constraints of the problem. People who excel in this metacomponent are not necessarily the best in the other metacomponents, but they recognize when a solution is not what it should be, and therefore can persevere until they come up with a solution that fits the constraints of the problem.

These metacomponents are interactive with each other. In my experience, it is almost impossible to measure them singly, as almost any task that requires one of them will require at least several more. We have had some success in measuring metacomponents (Sternberg, 1985), but I doubt that any of our measures or anyone else's are pure. An important locus of giftedness is not only in how adept a person is at executing each of the metacomponents, but also in how adept the person is at combining them and utilizing them in a well-integrated way.

Performance Components of Intelligence

Performance components are the processes used to solve a problem. The metacomponents decide what to do, whereas the performance components actually do it. The number of performance components is large, as different performance components are used in the solution of different problems. Nevertheless, there is overlap within classes of tasks. Here I will discuss some of the performance components involved in inductive reasoning. It is important to note, however, that these represent only a small subset of the total number of performance components in human information processing.

1. Encoding. To solve a problem, we first must perceive the terms of the problem and retrieve information in long-term memory relevant to those perceptions. The process involved is called encoding. My own work and that of others (e.g., Siegler, 1978) suggest that encoding is a particularly important process in the solution of problems. If we misencode the terms of a problem, it does not matter how well we operate on the encodings: The answer will be wrong, because the problem is incorrectly perceived. Excellent encoders tend to be people with large knowledge bases, who see more in the terms of a problem than a novice might. Expert encoders do not always encode more quickly than novices. Indeed, some of our research suggests that expert encoders may encode the terms more slowly, in part because they have more knowledge to call on, and in part because strong encoding can facilitate later operations on those encodings (see Sternberg & Rifkin, 1979; S. Sternberg, 1969).

2. Inference. Inference is involved in seeing the relation between two terms or objects. It is used in a large variety of tasks. Excellent inferrers are good at compare-and-contrast tasks in that they easily see relations between different things. Which inferences are made will depend in part on how well the relevant objects are encoded. We may not be able to infer a relation between two objects if we do not know the relevant attributes about which the inference needs to be made.

3. Mapping. Mapping is used to determine relations between relations. For example, it forms the basis for analogical reasoning. We have found that mapping appears somewhat later than other components of performance, perhaps because it involves second-order relations (Sternberg & Rifkin, 1979). It is possible to map relations of successively higher orders, and work with adolescents shows that the acquisition of mapping of successively higher order relations continues throughout adolescence (Case, 1978; Sternberg & Downing, 1982).

4. Application. Application means carrying over a relation from one set of terms to another. For example, in analogies it is used to apply a relation previously inferred (Sternberg, 1977; see Mulholland, Pellegrino, & Glaser, 1980, for an alternative point of view). Good appliers are able to carry over relations they have inferred in one setting to another setting.

Knowledge-Acquisition Components

Knowledge-acquisition components are used to learn new information. Gifted individuals are often particularly effective in the use of these components because they are so often adept at learning new information. Three knowledge-acquisition components are particularly important in learning (Sternberg & Davidson, 1983).

1. Selective encoding. Selective encoding is used to separate information that is relevant for one's purposes from information that is not relevant. For example, when a scientist receives a computer output of data from an experiment, often he or she is confronted by a bewildering array of numbers. The good selective encoder will know which of these numbers are important for the particular scientific purposes. Indeed, selective encoding is important in all walks of life. For example, a business executive needs to know which factors are relevant in making a management decision, and which factors are of less consequence. A writer needs to know what details to include in an article or a book, and what details are of little or no interest. An artist has to decide how detailed to make a particular painting or sculpture. Selective encoding, therefore, is important to giftedness in many different walks of life.

2. Selective combination. Often it is not enough just to decide what details are relevant for a particular purpose. We need to know how to put those relevant pieces of information together. For example, in doing a mathematical proof, the greatest difficulty often is not in figuring out which postulates or theorems are relevant, but in figuring out how to sequence them together so as to reach the desired conclusion. In any aspect of science, we frequently need to put together the pieces of a difficult puzzle, much as a detective would when analyzing clues at the scene of a crime. Similarly, a doctor needs to figure out how a set of symptoms can be used in combination to help diagnose the particular presenting syndrome.

3. Selective comparison. Selective comparison means using old information for new purposes—for example, recognizing how information we have used in one experiment could be carried over to another experiment. Kekule's dream about a snake dancing around and biting its tail was a selective comparison in that it provided the basis for his figuring out the structure of the benzene molecule. Good selective comparers not only see analogies between present problems and past ones, they also see sources of disanalogy between sets of problems. That is, they see the dissimilarities as well as the similarities between the old situation and the new one.

The Role of Experience

The components of intelligence described here are always applied at some particular level or region of experience. In other words, the same components might be applied in a task that is either relatively novel or relatively familiar. In some cases, the components of problem solving will change as we become more familiar with the task and see better ways of doing it. In our research, however, more often the components are executed more rapidly or efficiently, but they do not change as we become more familiar with the problem-solving tasks.

There are two regions of experience for the application of components to tasks that are particularly relevent for understanding intelligence.

1. Relative novelty. Insightful people are often particularly adept at applying components of information processing to problems that are relatively novel. They can take a problem that is quite different from ones they have solved before and can see a new way of solving it that most other people would not see. The student "Barbara," described above, is a case in point. Coping with relative novelty is an important part of synthetic intelligence. I emphasize the word *relative* because problems that are extremely novel do not measure intelligence well at all. For example, it would be pointless to give calculus problems to second graders. The region of interest for measuring synthetic ability is the region in which a problem is new, but not completely so. In assessing these skills, we use insight problems (Davidson & Sternberg, 1984), nonentrenched conceptual projection problems (Sternberg, 1982), and counterfactual analogies (Sternberg & Gastel, 1989). People who are gifted in coping with relative novelty often tend to be our most creative contributors to society.

2. Relative familiarity. The region of relative familiarity is the region in which task performance starts to be automatized. Automatization is a critical part of intelligence in that many of the problem-solving behaviors we need to perform are executed again and again. If they do not consume many resources they can be executed much more efficiently and even can be executed in parallel. For example, reading is initially a difficult and halting process, but it becomes smooth and rapid once the bottom-up processing of words and sentences becomes automatized. Driving, speaking, and writing are all processes that become increasingly automatized with practice.

People who are good automatizers have an edge in problem solving over people who are not, in that their automatization frees processing resources for them to cope with novelty in situations. People who do not automatize need to devote processing resources to the basics of a problem, so that these resources are not free for dealing with the more novel aspects of a given problem.

There is no guarantee that people who are good at coping with relative novelty will be good automatizers. Giftedness does not necessarily apply across the full range of the experiential continuum. A person might be gifted at one level of this continuum or at several levels. I suggested before that superior automatization frees resources for coping with novelty. However, there also can be costs associated with automatization. Sometimes, as experts become more and more routinized in their solution of a problem or a class of problems, they lose flexibility. They begin to have difficulty seeing things in new ways. Our research has even found that this loss of flexibility can impede experts more than novices when a task that is familiar to the experts is changed in its essential aspects (Sternberg & Frensch, 1989).

Contextual Functions

The components of intelligence are applied to various levels of experience in order to serve three different functions in everyday contexts. Understanding practical giftedness of the kind demonstrated by "Celia" requires understanding the three functions that intelligent thinking and behavior can serve.

1. Adaptation. Adaptation refers to the adjustment of ourselves and our behavior to the environment in order to provide a good fit to that environment. When we take on a new job, or a new school, or a new relationship, or any kind of new environment, we usually need to adapt to some degree. Our research suggests that practically intelligent people are often good adapters (Wagner & Sternberg, 1985). People who are practically gifted are not necessarily those who are the most superior in executing the components of intelligence. Rather, their superiority is in exploiting these components in practical settings. Others may be better at executing the components in the abstract, but do not know how to apply them in everyday life.

A critical aspect of environmental adaptation is the acquisition and utilization of tacit knowledge (Sternberg, 1985; Sternberg, Wagner, & Okagaki, 1993). Tacit knowledge is what we need to know in order to adapt to an environment that we are not explicitly taught and that often is not even verbalized. Tacit knowledge comprises the "tricks of the trade" or the "rules of thumb" that lead to successful performance in a given domain. It is possible to identify the tacit knowledge within a given domain (see, e.g., Sternberg, 1988b, for an identification of tacit knowledge relevant to business management). Practically intelligent people are adept at picking up this knowledge. The ability to pick up and to exploit the knowledge does not appear to be closely related to conventional IQ.

2. Selection. It is not always practically intelligent to adapt to an environment. Sometimes, the smart thing is to get out. If you can see that a job, problem, relationship, or whatever is not suitable for you, the best strategy may be to put it behind you. Practically intelligent people know when to get out. It is not useful to think of intellectual giftedness in terms of "levels" of selection; rather, the practically intelligent person achieves a balance between adaptation and selection. He or she knows when to try to conform to an environment, but also when to leave it.

3. Shaping. One does not always leave an environment when it is not just so. For example, we may be in a job that is not ideal, but may see ways to make the job better. Relationships are almost never just what we want, but it is often possible to shape them into something better. If there is a pinnacle of practical intelligence, it is in the ability of an individual to shape an environment. Practically intelligent people balance not only adaptation and selection, but shaping as well. They have a knack for turning environments into what they want them to be. Often, they are able to convince others to work in the environments they set up. Great scientists, artists, writers, politicians, and others are people who succeed in shaping their environments. They set the paradigms that others follow, rather than merely following existing paradigms. Hence, a practically gifted person is able to set standards, not just conform to them.

Capitalization on Strengths and Compensation for and Remediation of Weaknesses

The main point of this chapter has been that there are many different kinds and loci of giftedness. It is naive to assume that intellectual giftedness can be captured through a single number. However, there is one thing that people who are intellectually gifted have in common throughout their lives. That one thing is that they know what they are good at, know what they are not good at, and are able to capitalize on their strengths and compensate for their weaknesses, or to remediate their weaknesses to the point where these weaknesses no longer get in their way. Over short periods of time, it is possible to appear gifted without knowing and exploiting strengths and without knowing and finding ways around weaknesses. But over the long term, in order to exploit our abilities maximally, capitalization and compensation become key.

This view of giftedness is quite different from the standard one. It suggests that people who are intellectually gifted are not necessarily good at lots of things. One cannot add up the scores on a bunch of subtests or items and measure giftedness simply in terms of the number of items answered correctly. A person who is good at one thing may show up as far more gifted than someone who is good at a large number of things. The big question is not how many things we are good at, but how well we can exploit whatever we are good at and find ways around the things that we are not good at.

Measurement of Intellectual Giftedness

The kinds of skills described here are not measured well by conventional tests of intelligence or other cognitive abilities. At best, such tests measure analytical skills, but they do not measure synthetic and practical skills, and often they do not even measure analytical abilities very well (Sternberg, 1984). Conventional tests of creativity attempt to measure divergent thinking abilities but do not measure synthetic intelligence in a way that I consider adequate. Apparently, I am not alone in this perception (see chapters in Sternberg, 1988a).

I am currently using a research version of the Sternberg Triarchic Abilities Test (Sternberg, 1993), which measures the various abilities described in this chapter. It provides separate scores for analytical, synthetic, and practical abilities. One special use of the test is for identifying gifted individuals. The idea is that someone may be gifted with respect to some aspects of the theory but not others. Indeed, few people will be gifted with respect to all aspects of the triarchic theory. There are twelve subtests: nine multiple-choice subtests (equally divided among verbal, quantitative, and figural items) and three essay subtests:

1. *Analytic-Verbal:* Figuring out meanings of neologisms (artificial words) from natural contexts. Students see a novel word embedded in a paragraph and have to infer its meaning.
2. *Analytic-Quantitative:* Number series. Students have to say what number should come next in a series of numbers.
3. *Analytic-Figural:* Matrices. Students see a figural matrix with the lower right entry missing. They have to determine which of the options fits into the missing space.
4. *Practical-Verbal:* Everyday reasoning. Students are presented with a set of everyday problems in the life of an adolescent (who might be themselves or someone else) and have to solve the problems (e.g., what to do about a friend who seems to have a substance-abuse problem).
5. *Practical-Quantitative:* Everyday math. Students are presented with scenarios requiring the use of math in everyday life (e.g., buying tickets for a ball game or making chocolate chip cookies), and have to solve math problems based on the scenarios.
6. *Practical-Figural:* Route planning. Students are presented with a map of an area (e.g., an entertainment park) and have to answer questions about navigating effectively through the area depicted by the map.
7. *Creative-Verbal:* Novel analogies. Students are presented with verbal analogies preceded by counterfactual premises (e.g., money falls off trees). They have to solve the analogies as though the counterfactual premises were true.
8. *Creative-Quantitative:* Numerical matrices with novel symbols. Students are presented with numerical matrices with one entry missing, and they have to fill in the missing entry. However, the matrix contains novel numerical symbols, such as * + 7 = 15, and students have to use these symbols in combination with ordinary numbers.
9. *Creative-Figural:* In each item, subjects are presented first with a figural series that involves one or more transformations; they then have to apply the rule of the first series to a new figure with a different appearance, and complete the new series.

There are three essay items, one each emphasizing analytical, creative, and practical thinking. The high school–level analytical problem requires students to analyze the advantages and disadvantages of having police or security guards in a school building. The creative problem requires students to describe how they would reform their school system to produce an ideal one. The practical problem requires students to specify a problem in their life and to state three practical solutions for solving it.

Thus, the idea of testing is to expand our notion of giftedness and then be able to identifiy as gifted individuals who may be adept in skills that are not measured by conventional tests. There is a need for synthetic and practical thinking as well. These individuals may actually be the ones who make the more important contributions later in life.

Developing Intellectual Giftedness

I do not believe that intellectual giftedness is totally something with which one is born. It is generally accepted that there is some hereditary component to intelligence, but at the same time there is more to intelligence than just the effects of heredity. Although one cannot take a developmentally delayed individual and turn her or him into a budding genius, I believe that it is possible to increase our intellectual skills, and we have now collected evidence that suggests as much (Davidson & Sternberg, 1984; Sternberg, 1987). I have developed a program for teaching intellectual skills at the high school and college levels (Sternberg, 1986) and also have worked with younger children. We combine the idea of development with the idea of testing. We give a first form of an intelligence test, then training, then a second form of the test in order to assess improvement.

Intelligence does not have to be enhanced via a separate course or program. At Yale, for the past two years we have taught a summer psychology course for gifted high school students that infuses instruction via the triarchic theory into the course (Sternberg, 1994). Students have been identified, instructed, and assessed in a way that takes into account all three aspects of their intelligence. The textbook we used (Sternberg, 1995) builds triarchic instruction and assessment into the context of the course.

Triarchic theory can be infused into instruction in *any* area. Table 4.1 shows the kinds of questions that can be used across subject-matter areas to tap triarchic thinking, and Table 4.2 shows the kinds of prompts teachers can use to instruct and assess gifted children triarchically.

What abilities, exactly, should be tapped? My answer to this question is based on my notion of intelligence as ultimately involving capitalization of strengths and compensation for (or remediation of) weaknesses. We need to teach students to make the most of their strengths and to find ways around or ways of improving on their weaknesses. We cannot create enormous changes in everyone. What we can do is help students exploit their intellectual strengths more effectively at the same time that they improve those abilities in need of enhancement.

Teaching intellectual skills does not elimi-

Table 4.1
Triarchic Theory Applied to Student Instruction and Assessment Methods

	Analytic	*Creative*	*Practical*
Psychology	Compare Freud's theory of dreaming to Crick's.	Design an experiment to test a theory of dreaming.	What are the implications of Freud's theory of dreaming for your life?
Biology	Evaluate the validity of the bacterial theory of ulcers.	Design an experiment to test the bacterial theory of ulcers.	How would the bacterial theory of ulcers change conventional treatment regimens?
Literature	In what ways were Catherine Earnshaw and Daisy Miller similar?	Write an alternative ending to *Wuthering Heights* uniting Catherine and Heathcliff in life.	Why are lovers sometimes cruel to each other and what can we do about it?
History	How did events in post–World War I Germany lead to the rise of Nazism?	How might Truman have encouraged the surrender of Japan without A-bombing Hiroshima?	What lessons does Nazism hold for events in Bosnia today?
Mathematics	How is this mathematical proof flawed?	Prove— . . . How might catastrophe theory be applied to psychology?	How is trigonometry applied to construction of bridges?
Art	Compare and contrast how Rembrandt and Van Gogh used light in . . .	Draw a beam of light.	How could we reproduce the lighting in this painting in the same actual room?

Table 4.2
Prompts Utilizing Various Abilities

Memory Abilities	*Analytical Abilities*	*Creative Abilities*	*Practical Abilities*
Who said?	Compare and contrast	Create	Apply
Summarize	Analyze	Invent	Show how you can use . . .
Who did?	Evaluate	Imagine what you would do if you were . . .	Implement
When did?	Critique	Imagine	Utilize
What did?	Say why in your judgment . . .	Design	Demonstrate how in the real world . . .
How did?	Explain why . . .	Show how you would . . .	
Repeat back	Explain what caused . . .	Suppose that . . .	
Describe	Evaluate what is assumed by . . .	Say what would happen if . . .	

nate individual differences. To the contrary, when we have trained both children identified as gifted and children not so identified, almost all of the children have improved, but the amount of difference at the end of training is about the same as at the beginning. The learning curves for the gifted and non-gifted children are roughly parallel. In some cases, there are changes in rank orders of individuals, but we have never found an instance in which we have eliminated differences across individuals in performance.

I do not believe that intelligence is the whole story to giftedness. Creativity is important (see Sternberg & Lubart, 1991), as are personality dispositions and motivational states. Hence, when I have talked about giftedness in this chapter, I have focused only on its intellectual side, not on all sides. We should not believe that the only possible kind of giftedness is with respect to intelligence.

To conclude, it is possible to understand intellectual giftedness in a way that transcends the bounds of our usual conceptions of intelligence. In this chapter I have proposed one model for extending these bounds, the triarchic theory of human intelligence. I believe this theory provides us with a firmer, broader base for understanding intellectual giftedness than we have through existing theories and tests designed to measure intellectual excellence.

REFERENCES

Case, R. (1978). Intellectual development from birth to adulthood: A neo-Piagetian interpretation. In R. Siegler (Ed.), *Children's thinking: What develops?* (pp. 37–71). Hillsdale, NJ: Lawrence Erlbaum Associates.

Davidson, J. E., & Sternberg, R. J. (1984). The role of insight in intellectual giftedness. *Gifted Child Quarterly, 28,* 58–64.

Mulholland, T. M., Pellegrino, J. W., & Glaser, R. (1980). Components of geometric analogy solution. *Cognitive Psychology, 12,* 252–284.

Siegler, R. S. (1978). The origins of scientific reasoning. In R. S. Siegler (Ed.), *Children's thinking: What develops?* (pp. 109–149). Hillsdale, NJ: Lawrence Erlbaum Associates.

Sternberg, R. J. (1977). *Intelligence, information processing, and analogical reasoning: The componential analysis of human abilities.* Hillsdale, NJ: Lawrence Erlbaum Associates.

Sternberg, R. J. (1982). Nonentrenchment in the assessment of intellectual giftedness. *Gifted Child Quarterly, 26,* 63–67.

Sternberg, R. J. (1984). What should intelligence tests test? Implications of a triarchic theory of intelligence for intelligence testing. *Educational Researcher, 13,* 5–15.

Sternberg, R. J. (1985). *Beyond IQ: A triarchic theory of human intelligence.* New York: Cambridge University Press.

Sternberg, R. J. (1986). *Intelligence applied: Understanding and increasing your intellectual skills.* San Diego: Harcourt Brace Jovanovich.

Sternberg, R. J. (1987). Most vocabulary is learned

from context. In M. G. McKeown & M. E. Curtis (Eds.), *The nature of vocabulary acquisition* (pp. 89–105). Hillsdale, NJ: Lawrence Erlbaum Associates.

Sternberg, R. J. (Ed.) (1988a). *The nature of creativity: Contemporary psychological perspectives.* New York: Cambridge University Press.

Sternberg, R. J. (1988b). *The triarchic mind: A new theory of human intelligence.* New York: Viking.

Sternberg, R. J. (1993). *Sternberg Triarchic Abilities Test.* Unpublished test.

Sternberg, R. J. (1994). A triarchic model for teaching and assessing students in general psychology. *The General Psychologist, 30*(2), 42–48.

Sternberg, R. J. (1995). *In search of the human mind.* Fort Worth, TX: Harcourt.

Sternberg, R. J., & Davidson, J. E. (1983). Insight in the gifted. *Educational Psychologist, 18,* 51–57.

Sternberg, R. J., & Downing, C. J. (1982). The development of higher-order reasoning in adolescence. *Child Development, 53,* 209–221.

Sternberg, R. J., & Frensch, P. A. (1989). A balance-level theory of intelligent thinking. *Zeitschrift für Pädagogische Psychologie (German Journal of Educational Psychology), 3,* 79–96.

Sternberg, R. J., & Gastel, J. (1989). If dancers ate their shoes: Inductive reasoning with factual and counterfactual premises. *Memory and Cognition, 17,* 1–10.

Sternberg, R. J., & Lubart, T. I. (1991). An investment theory of creativity and its development. *Human Development, 34,* 1–31.

Sternberg, R. J., & Rifkin, B. (1979). The development of analogical reasoning processes. *Journal of Experimental Child Psychology, 27,* 195–232.

Sternberg, R. J., Wagner, R. K., & Okagaki, L. (1993). Practical intelligence: The nature and role of tacit knowledge in work and at school. In H. Reese & J. Puckett (Eds.), *Advances in lifespan development* (pp. 205–227). Hillsdale, NJ: Lawrence Erlbaum Associates.

Sternberg, S. (1969). Memory scanning. Mental processes revealed by reaction-time experiments. *American Scientist, 4,* 421–457.

Wagner, R. K., & Sternberg, R. J. (1985). Alternative conceptions of intelligence and their implications for education. *Review of Educational Research, 54,* 197–224.

5

Giftedness from a Multiple Intelligences Perspective

VALERIE RAMOS-FORD and HOWARD GARDNER, *Harvard University*

Introduction: The Traditional Approach to the Assessment of Intelligence

There exists an extensive history of approaches to the identification of gifted and talented individuals. One of the most widely implemented methods has been the administration of a standardized test of intelligence, a practice that can be traced principally to the work of Alfred Binet. In light of the expansion of public education in Paris at the turn of the last century, this pioneering psychologist and his colleagues were asked to devise measurements that could assist in identifying students who were likely to fail in elementary school (Binet & Simon, 1905). In response, they created the first successful measure of scholastic intelligence. Binet's concept of *mental age* soon led to its influential by-product, the *intelligence quotient* (IQ).

Binet's ideas made their way swiftly across the Atlantic and were embraced particularly by Lewis Terman and his colleagues at Stanford University, who in 1916 created the Stanford-Binet Intelligence Scale, the most widely used standardized test of intelligence. Although these measures were indisputably of value, they led to a narrow view of intelligence—one inextricably tied to those skills most valued in the schools of the time, linguistic and logical-mathematical skill.

Nearly a century later, many educators, scientists, and lay persons still subscribe to this limited view of intelligence. Consequently, hundreds of tests of this nature have been developed to measure individuals' capabilities and readiness for a range of academic and professional situations. The testing industry has become an increasingly powerful decision maker in society. Results of such tests determine who will be admitted into academic settings from preschool to law school and into professions ranging from police work to teaching. Although many of these tests are useful as a means to specific ends, their proponents often describe the instruments as revealing far more about an individual's capabilities and characteristics than they actually do. Most of these tests rely heavily on a series of rapid-fire, short-answer or multiple-choice questions anchored in the linguistic and logical-mathematical domains. What results is a snapshot of the individual's capabilities at a precise point in time, in a limited range of intellectual spheres, as discerned in the often stressful test-taking situation.

The testing community has had a particularly strong impact on the identification and education of the gifted and talented in our society. Taking a lead from Terman's (1925) widely known longitudinal study of California children with high IQs, the terms *giftedness* and *high IQ* had become virtually synonymous by the 1930s. Despite efforts over the last several decades to broaden the definition and assessment of intelligence (Feldman, 1980; Gardner, 1983; Guilford, 1967; Thurstone, 1938), a majority of children who participate in specialized programs for the gifted and talented today are still admitted on the basis of IQ. A score of 130 might allow one child into such a program, while a score of 129 will keep another out.

We and our colleagues at Harvard Project

The work described in this chapter was supported in part by grants from the Spencer Foundation, the W. T. Grant Foundation, and the Rockefeller Brothers Fund.

Zero set forth a theory-based, pluralistic view of human cognition: the theory of multiple intelligences (MI theory). On the basis of this view, we have developed alternative methods of assessment and instruction for children from preschool to high school. In addition, many educational programs around the country have independently used MI theory as inspiration for developing rich learning environments and holistic, context-sensitive ways to assess and nurture promise and achievement in children of all ages and all levels of cognitive capability. In this chapter, we explore the theory and history of multiple intelligences, and examine one of the approaches to the assessment of intelligence that MI has spawned.

A New Look at Intelligence: The Theory of Multiple Intelligences

The theory of multiple intelligences, first presented by Gardner in *Frames of Mind* (1983; see also Gardner, 1993; Walters & Gardner, 1985, 1986), challenges the notion of *general intelligence* or *g*, on which most current models of intelligence testing are based. From its outset, MI theory questioned the idea that an individual's intellectual capacities can be captured in a single measure of intelligence; instead, it suggests an approach to assessment, and ultimately to instruction, that actively seeks to identify what may be unique about an individual's proclivities and capabilities in a number of domains of knowledge.

One common criticism of MI theory has focused on the use of the word *intelligence* to describe the competences addressed. Some have suggested that some of the intelligences (e.g., musical or bodily-kinesthetic) would more accurately be labeled *talents* or *gifts*. While there is no reason that these competences must be called intelligences, we have deliberately chosen to do so as a challenge to those who consider logical-mathematical and linguistic capability on a different plane than the other capacities considered in MI theory. We have attempted to remove language and logic from the IQ pedestal that they have occupied for generations in Western society. In so doing, we believe we have taken a step toward the democratization of the range of human cognitive capabilities.

We defined *intelligence* as an ability or set of abilities that permit an individual to solve problems or fashion products that are of consequence in a particular cultural setting. Beginning with this definition, we outlined a number of criteria for what constitutes an intelligence. The criteria were drawn from several disparate sources: exploration of trajectories of development in normal and gifted individuals; the breakdown of skills under conditions of brain damage; exceptional populations including prodigies and autistic savants; cross-cultural accounts of cognition; psychometric studies; and studies of the training and generalization of particular skills. From these sources, we arrived at seven candidate intelligences: linguistic, logical-mathematical, spatial, musical, bodily-kinesthetic, and two areas of person-related understanding, interpersonal and intrapersonal.

This list should not suggest that the seven intelligences are the only acceptable candidates; there may be others. Moreover, most if not all of these intelligences can be broken down into subcomponents of skill and understanding. The seven intelligences proposed so far are intended to support the notion of a pluralistic view of intelligence, not to restrict its scope or define it in its entirety. As the term *multiple intelligences* suggests, we believe that human cognitive competence is better described as a set of abilities, talents, or mental skills that we have chosen to call "intelligences." We also suggest that these intelligences are, at most, potentials or proclivities that are either realized or not depending on the cultural context in which individuals are reared and the opportunities presented for the identification, expression, and development of the several intelligences (see Kornhaber, Krechevsky, & Gardner, 1990).

The Seven Intelligences

Linguistic intelligence is one of the most studied human competences. It can be broken down into subcomponents, including syntax, semantics, and pragmatics, as well as more school-oriented skills such as written or oral expression and understanding. It is exemplified in the novelist, lecturer, lawyer, and lyricist, to name a few adult roles that exploit linguistic intelligence. In children, high capability in this domain might manifest itself in the ability to tell rich and coherent stories or to report with accuracy on experiences they have had—not simply in the ability to repeat sentences and define words on a standardized measure of intelligence.

Logical-mathematical intelligence can be divided into an inventory of subcomponents: deductive reasoning, inductive reasoning, computation, and the like. Logical-mathematical intelligence is exemplified in the adult role of mathematician or physicist. In children, an ability in the domain might be demonstrated through facility with counting, calculations, and the ability to create useful notations.

Logical-mathematical and linguistic intelligences represent the skills most addressed and valued in traditional school settings. These forms of intelligence have been considered the archetypes of "raw intelligence," which purportedly cut across all domains. As mentioned earlier, skills in these two domains continue to form the basis of the majority of intelligence tests, even though their usefulness outside of the school setting has been challenged. We list them first not because we consider them to be of greatest importance or value, but because of their prominence in traditional school and testing situations.

Spatial intelligence can be observed in a wide array of vocations and avocations. It entails the capacity to represent and manipulate spatial configurations. The architect, engineer, mechanic, navigator, sculptor, and chess player all rely on spatial intelligence in their work. In the young child, a capability in this domain might be seen as a facility with puzzles or other spatial problem solving, or an attention to elements of design "all the way around" a clay sculpture. Spatial intelligence is not as highly valued or supported in our current educational system as linguistic and logical-mathematical intelligence, but it is clearly a significant constituent of success in a number of valued adult roles.

Bodily-kinesthetic intelligence refers to the ability to use all or part of one's body (like one's hands or one's mouth) to perform a task or fashion a product. Such intelligence is manifest in the dancer, athlete, mime, and surgeon. The child with high bodily-kinesthetic intelligence can be seen moving expressively in response to different musical and verbal stimuli, or demonstrating keen athletic ability in organized sports or on the playground.

Musical intelligence includes pitch discrimination; the ability to hear themes in music; sensitivity to rhythm, texture, and timbre; and, in its most integrated forms, the production of music through performance or composition. The musical child can be seen singing to himself or herself, noticing the different sounds in his environment, and so on.

Finally, MI theory recognizes two domains of intelligence about persons. *Interpersonal* intelligence entails the ability to understand other individuals—their actions and their motivations. In addition, it includes the ability to act productively on the basis of that knowledge. Our interpersonal intelligence is the knowledge that guides us through the social interactions of daily life. In more developed forms, this intelligence can be seen in teachers, therapists, and salespersons, as well as in religious and political leaders. Children skilled in this domain can be perceived as leaders and organizers in the classroom, as cognizant of how and where other children spend their time, and as sensitive to the needs and feelings of others.

The companion to interpersonal intelligence is *intrapersonal* intelligence, a person's understanding of self. It includes knowledge and understanding of one's own cognitive strengths, styles, and intelligences, as well as one's feelings and range of emotions. In addition, it entails the ability to put that knowledge to use in planning and carrying out successful activities. Because this type is the most private of the intelligences, it is usually necessary to gain evidence of it through language, music, visual art, or another form of expression. The young child who demonstrates intrapersonal intelligence might be heard saying to his teacher, "I feel a little sad because my mother didn't bring me to school today. Is it O.K. if I stay with you until I feel better?" or

"Drawing is my favorite activity, even though I don't draw as well as I want to."

The Autonomy of the Intelligences

According to MI theory, each intelligence is a relatively autonomous intellectual potential that is capable of functioning independently of the others. Particularly convincing support for this claim has been found in the neuropsychological literature. For example, research with brain-damaged adults has repeatedly demonstrated that particular faculties can be lost while others remain relatively or even wholly unaffected (Gardner, 1975). To be sure, we are not suggesting that normally functioning individuals will demonstrate intelligences that work completely independently of one another. In fact, it can be assumed that in most cases the intelligences work in concert with one another. What differs among individuals is their profile of intelligences. Theoretically, there could be individuals who perform at the same level or even excel in all of the intelligences. In most cases, however, individuals exhibit a more jagged profile of abilities, exhibiting various strengths and weaknesses across domains. A high level of ability in one domain does not, and should not, fortell a similarly high level in another.

The notion of autonomy of intelligences has significant implications for the gifted and talented community. This notion supports the criticism that the concept of a measurable *g* or *general intelligence* is at best limited, and at worst educationally misleading. For example, it cannot be presupposed that an individual who demonstrates exceptional linguistic and logical-mathematical skills on a standardized measure of intelligence also will display exceptional ability (or even interest) in all other domains. Neither can it be presupposed that a child who performs poorly on such a measure will fail to excel in one or more of the other domains. There are many examples that support the preceding claims: the child with an overall IQ of 130 who has difficulty understanding spatial problems; the ten-year-old violin prodigy who performs poorly on academic subjects; or the poet who has little skill or understanding in the logical-mathematical domain.

Differences among an individual's levels of capability support the notion that each intelligence proceeds along its own developmental trajectory. Individuals thus will differ with regard to the areas in which they are considered to be "at promise" (or "at risk"), and the extent to which they are considered to be so in each domain.

It follows that the use of traditional intelligence tests and similar measures as a means of admitting individuals to gifted and enrichment programs, particularly when these measures are used in lieu of other supporting information, is pedagogically unjustifiable. Further, given the precious and limited resources for gifted programs, it makes no more sense to give arts enrichment to promising scholars than it does to give scholarly enrichment to young artists. Programs should be deployed and children admitted to them in a manner that takes into account each individual's special gift or talent and how it can best be supported and developed.

A Multiple Intelligences Approach to Assessment

There are clearly many areas of human capability that contemporary constructs of intelligence simply fail to explain. Take, for example, the piano virtuoso, the world-class athlete, or the skilled architect. It is likely that the particular "intelligences" involved in each of these individuals' areas of expertise would not be evident in the results of measures of intelligence limited to logical-mathematical or linguistic capabilities. We do not dispute the value of considering IQ as one factor in the identification and placement of a gifted individual; we do suggest that other factors deserve to be taken into account as well. For example, we suggest considering the quality of products that a child has already fashioned, the child's desire for membership in a program and stated goals for participation, the student's performance during a trial week or two with other "gifted" children, and other such unobtrusive measures. Such a combination of approaches would undoubtedly uncover more gifted individuals with more diverse capabilities than would any standardized measure.

An MI approach to assessment makes a conscious move away from traditional testing methods. Toward this goal, we have incorporated the following features into our current approach to assessment.

Assessment versus Testing

What distinguishes *assessment* from *testing* is the former's preference for methods and measures that elicit information in the course of ordinary performances in a comfortable and familiar environment rather than in the decontextualized setting of formal testing. An examination of progress and learning (or lack thereof) should occur every time an individual is involved in a domain and not merely at specified and often artificial points during the year. In our view, educators and the students under their charge should engage in regular and appropriate reflection on their goals, the various means to achieve them, the success (or lack thereof) in achieving these goals, and the implications of this assessment process for rethinking goals and procedures (Gardner, 1991a). One way in which this can be accomplished is through the use of portfolios or, more accurately, "processfolios": meaningful collections of student work that illustrate both exploration of and progress in a particular domain of inquiry as well as examples of best work (see, e.g.,Wolf, Bixby, Glenn, & Gardner, 1991).

Ecological Validity

An essential criterion in our approach is that the assessment be ecologically valid. Assessment of a person's capabilities will be most informed and useful if it takes place in a situation that closely resembles the individual's actual working conditions. This goal can be achieved by supplying classrooms with engaging and enjoyable materials and activities in each of the seven domains of intelligence outlined previously. Doing so maximizes the teacher's opportunities to observe a particular child's strengths and interests, while simultaneously maximizing the child's opportunity to discover and develop his or her capabilities and interests in a variety of domains. Through the direct involvement of teachers and children in the assessment process, the evaluation of various capabilities can become an ongoing, unobtrusive part of the child's natural learning environment.

Intelligence-Fair Assessment

Another criterion in our approach is that the assessment instruments be "intelligence-fair." As already mentioned, most testing instruments rely heavily on the test taker's linguistic and logical-mathematical capabilities as a means of tapping capability in other domains. To the extent possible, our assessment instruments do not confound intelligences. Instead, they look directly at the intelligence-in-operation. For instance, if we are interested in assessing a young child's understanding of numbers, we would not ask the child to express that understanding through a verbal response to a verbally presented problem involving numbers—for example, "If Nick has two apples and Emma has three, how many apples do they have altogether?" Instead, we might ask the child to play a board game in which he or she could demonstrate skill and understanding of numbers and number concepts through the manipulation of various props. Similarly, to learn about a child's social understanding we might observe the child as particular social skills emerge naturally in classroom interactions.

Working Styles

In addition to looking at capabilities in all domains, the MI approach to assessment also considers an individual's approach or working style in each domain. For example, we consider level of engagement, persistence, and distractibility as the person interacts with a variety of materials. Such information helps explain why certain individuals are more likely than others to develop in a given domain or to utilize lessons learned in one domain. Gaining information about an individual's working style also enables the observer to compare a child's mode of attack across tasks. One can determine if the individual has a consistent working style across domains; whether the individual has specific working styles that emerge in some domains but not in others; and whether there is a connection between particular working styles and the individual's success or failure in a given domain. This information, when coupled with the individual's particular profile of intelligences, yields rich information regarding the most effective pedagogical approach for a given individual.

The information from this approach to assessment differs from that yielded by most standardized tests. Whereas the latter usually results in a series of subtest scores and/or an IQ score, the former is communicated in the richer format of a narrative profile. Such profiles present a more balanced and holistic view of an individual's intelligences, one that addresses all domains of knowledge and capability as well as the individual's approach to each domain. In addition, the profile serves as a guide to formal educational opportunities as well as less formal activities that can nurture and support the particular array of capabilities exhibited by an individual. In this way, the assessment process gathers and presents information useful to parents, teachers, and, of course, the children themselves.

In sum, our approach strives toward making assessment and curriculum as engaging and enjoyable for the child as they are informative for the adults who interact with the child. It stresses the importance of assessment as a process that works hand in hand with curriculum, exposure to a wide variety of materials, and the need for a meaningful context in which assessment can take place.

The Education of the Intelligences

Several educational experiments, either wholly or partially influenced by MI theory, have been undertaken over the last decade. Perhaps the foremost effort is the ATLAS Communities Project (Communities for Authentic Teaching, Learning, and Assessment for All Students), a collaboration with the Coalition for Essential Schools at Brown University, the School Development Program at Yale University, and the Educational Development Center in Newton, Massachusetts. As one of nine school reform projects nationwide currently funded by the nonprofit New American Schools Development Corporation (NASDC), this group is attempting to design "break-the-mold schools" for the twenty-first century. At the middle school and high school levels, ARTS PROPEL is a collaboration with Educational Testing Service and the Pittsburgh public schools. PROPEL is a large-scale effort to stimulate artistic learning and to assess its level of competence (Gardner, 1989; Wolf, 1988; Zessoules, Wolf, & Gardner, 1988). In middle school the now completed Practical Intelligence for School (PIFS) Project examined the (practical) intelligences needed for success in school (Gardner, Krechevsky, Sternberg, & Okagaki, 1994). At the elementary level, a number of teachers in Indianapolis founded the Key School. Using MI theory as a point of departure, they developed an approach to education that sought to nurture all intelligences in every child (Olson, 1988).

MI theory is not so much a prescription for educational programs, with a set curriculum or methodology that must be carried out in all settings, but, rather, a provocation for educators and others to think differently about the assessment and education of all individuals. This is evident as we look at the unique ways in which MI-inspired programs around the country have developed (Krechevsky, Hoerr, & Gardner, 1995). Still, many of these extensions of MI theory share common elements. First, each attempts to broaden the notion of intelligence to include a much wider range of human cognitive capabilities. Second, each attempts to personalize education by developing means of discovering and supporting capabilities and interests which are unique in each individual. Finally, MI-inspired programs actively strive to blur the line between assessment and curriculum so that each informs the other in an ongoing process.

In relation to the identification and education of the gifted and talented, MI theory supplies a framework in which we can broaden the notion of intelligence and giftedness to include a much wider range of capabilities, reevaluate what counts as a "gift," and consider how best to assess and nurture promise and achievement in many different cognitive domains.

MI theory has encouraged many educators, parents, and others to abandon the notion that "the cream always rises to the top." This applies to both the gifted and talented children in the population of all children, and to the skills that can be considered the gift of any particular child. The theory suggests that if children are not given many opportunities to experience, explore, and develop an interest or proficiency, we may never discover those domains in which a child holds a special interest or talent. Consider, for example, a potential musical prodigy who never had access to a musical instrument or recorded music, or the potentially gifted athlete who was not encouraged in physical activities. There are, of course, those cases of youth who despite their unpromising milieu reveal their extraordinary talent to the world with little or no provocation, but these extraordinary individuals should be considered the exception rather than the rule.

We do not mean to suggest that every child should be considered "gifted" in the traditional sense. We do suggest that it is critical to have rich environments and holistic, context-sensitive ways to assess and nurture promise and achievement in all children. We have a responsibility as educators to find out what every child is good at and interested in so that we can help children feel good about themselves as learners; and to find ways to make educational capital out of those activities in which children show interest or skill in order to build bridges to areas in which they show less interest or skill.

Project Spectrum is an example of one successful extension of MI theory with preschool children.

Project Spectrum: An Innovative Approach to the Assessment and Education of Intelligences at the Preschool Level

Historically, theories of child development describe what the "normal" child can be expected to do at a given age or stage of development. Jean Piaget (1983) argued that every child must go through a universal sequence of stages when developing skills and understanding in a particular area. In addition, Piaget claimed that individuals should be at essentially the same level of development across all areas, exhibiting a fairly flat profile of cognitive capabilities. We in no way wish to diminish the remarkable contributions of Jean Piaget or other developmentalists of the past. However, research on thinking and learning over the last two decades has found that: The level of a child's understanding or expertise in one area can be largely independent of his or her understanding and expertise in others; and preschool children are far more different from one another than had been previously indicated by educational and psychological literature (Gardner, 1991b).

Project Spectrum, now completed in its phase as a research project, was a collaboration undertaken over the course of several years by many researchers at Harvard Project Zero, David Feldman at Tufts University, and the staff and students of the Eliot-Pearson Children's School at Tufts. Spectrum represented an effort to create a "contextualized" environment in which a wide range of abilities in young children could be observed and assessed. We used Feldman's notion of domain-specific development in nonuniversal domains (Feldman, 1986) and the seven domains of intelligence of MI theory as points of departure. Through a series of close observations of preschoolers in the context of the classroom, we identified what we perceived to be the core abilities of this age group in each domain of intelligence. It was soon apparent that there were subcomponents of each domain that also warranted examination; that the intelligences ought to be described in terms of meaningful cultural activities or domains; and that, as mentioned above, it was equally important to look at the children's working styles or ways of approaching each domain. As a result of Spectrum's initial phase of research, we developed fifteen measures that could be used systematically to tap four-year-olds' cognitive capabilities in seven domains of knowledge, and we identified over a dozen working styles in these children (see Tables 5.1 and 5.2).

The fifteen measures (Table 5.1) were intended as a complement to an enriched classroom environment (described below). They were designed to look specifically at a child's capabilities when there was uncertainty about her level of understanding or skill in a particular domain based on everyday observations in the classroom. The information gained from these measures was always used in concert with other available sources of information. In addition, the information gained was treated as a measure of the child's ability in a domain at a precise point in time, not as a measure of the child's overall potential in a domain. The only way to find out how a child's capability in a domain evolves is to reassess the child on a regular and reliable schedule.

Criteria for Developing Spectrum Assessment Materials

A main criterion in the development of Spectrum assessment materials was that they be stimulating and enjoyable to the preschool-age child. Our materials were sturdy, engaging, and inviting so that children were comfortable working in many content areas regardless of their skill levels. Themes within the activities were geared toward the

Table 5.1
Domains of Knowledge Examined in Project Spectrum

Language	*Mathematics*
Invented narrative measure: Storyboard Activity	Counting/strategy measure: Dinosaur Game
Descriptive narrative measure: Reporter Activities	Calculating/notation measure: Bus Game
Movement	*Visual Arts*
Creative movement measure: Creative Movement Curriculum	Art portfolios Structured Drawing Activities
Athletic movement measure: Obstacle Course	
Music	*Social*
Production measure: Singing Activity	Social analysis measure: Classroom Model Activity
Perception measure: Pitch Discrimination	Social roles measure: Peer Interaction Checklist
Science	
Hypothesis testing measure: Sink and Float Activity	
Logical inference measure: Treasure Hunt Game	
Mechanical measure: Assembly Activity	
Naturalist measure: Discovery Area	

Table 5.2
Measures of Working Style Examined by Project Spectrum

Child is:
- easily engaged/reluctant to engage in activity.
- confident/tentative.
- playful/serious.
- focused/distractible.
- persistent/frustrated by task.
- reflective about own work/impulsive.
- apt to work slowly/apt to work quickly.
- conversational/quiet.

Child:
- responds to visual/auditory/kinesthetic cues.
- demonstrates playful approach.
- brings personal strength/agenda to task.
- finds humor in content area.
- uses materials in unexpected ways.
- shows pride in accomplishment.
- is curious about materials.
- shows concern over "correct" answers.
- focuses on interaction with adult.
- transforms task/materials.

preschooler's world of experiences and interests.

For example, in a Spectrum assessment activity in the area of logical-mathematical intelligence, or number skills, a child plays a board game in which her game piece, a small dinosaur, must escape from the hungry mouth of a large dinosaur. The number and direction of moves is determined by two dice, one of which displays numbers and another that shows plus and minus signs. Through a series of random and deliberate placements of the dice, the child attempts to maneuver the little dinosaur to safety. This activity produces a quantified account of the child's ability to work with the number concepts embedded in the game.

In the Storyboard Activity, a measure of invented narrative (linguistic) skills, a child is presented with an enticing assortment of characters, props, and creatures that can be incorporated into a story. The materials provide a child with a stimulating basis for telling a fanciful story, while offering the teacher an opportunity to look at the child's use of vocabulary and sentence structure, as well as the ability to tell a thematically coherent story. For children who are more comfortable using descriptive language, complementary "reporting" activities tap some of the same components measured by the Storyboard Activity.[1]

Recording Information Gathered through the Spectrum Approach

A strength of the Spectrum approach to assessment is that it provides teachers and others with several means of organizing and recording their observations of individual preschool children. Spectrum's assessment measures employ a variety of different methods for recording and scoring a child's performance in the various domains. Depending on the nature of the activity and the domain on which it focuses, these methods range from the use of fully quantified score sheets to more holistic, observational checklists. An example of the former would be the scoring system used for the Dinosaur Game. An example of the latter would be the checklists we have devised for recording a child's engagement and production in visual arts or creative movement activities. While most teachers will not find it practical, or even possible, to formally administer all fifteen measures to all children in their classes, or to use all of the methods of recording that we provide, our materials and measures can be extremely useful for those times when more structured observation and methods of recording are deemed necessary.

The Spectrum Profile

Through the Spectrum approach, teachers gather a wealth of information about the intellectual strengths and working styles of each child. This information becomes the basis of Spectrum Profiles, relatively brief individualized written reports generated from the child's formal and informal engagement with

[1] For more information, see *Project Spectrum Handbook,* 1994.

Spectrum materials over the course of the school year. In straightforward language, the profile describes the particular pattern of intellectual capabilities and working styles exhibited by each child. It addresses relative strengths and weaknesses within a child's own range of capabilities; and occasionally it records "absolute" strengths when the child's performance stands out in relation to the larger population of preschoolers.

Consistent with our belief that assessment should be in service of individuals, and not simply a means of ranking them, the profile provides concrete yet informal suggestions for follow-up activities for each child. For example, if a child demonstrates a strength or interest in the bodily-kinesthetic domain, his or her report would suggest activities in the home and community that might support the child's capabilities in that domain. Similarly, if a child demonstrates difficulty with number skills, the report might suggest remediation activities such as counting and calculating games.

In summary, the profile presents information to teachers, parents, and others that can be put to use in service of a child's future involvement and success in a range of intellectual undertakings. The Spectrum Profile is intended as a guide to the child's profile of cognitive capabilities and working styles and the specific needs and opportunities which accompany such a profile.

The Spectrum-Inspired Classroom

We realized quickly that unless assessment occurred over time, and after a child had significant opportunity to explore and develop skill in a particular area, the information it produced could be misleading and uninformative. For this reason, the focus of the project shifted from assessment of preschool-aged children to a new approach to early education, one in which curriculum and assessment function hand in hand on an ongoing basis (see, e.g., Adams, & Feldman, 1993; Hatch & Gardner, 1986; Krechevsky, 1991; Krechevsky & Gardner, 1990; Malkus, Feldman, & Gardner, 1988; Ramos-Ford, Feldman, and Gardner, 1988; Wexler-Sherman, Gardner, & Feldman, 1988).

In its phase as a research project, a Spectrum classroom featured a wide variety of materials, games, puzzles, and learning areas that were designed to engage and interest preschoolers. For example, art materials, musical instruments, a dramatic play area, puzzles and games that stimulate numerical and logical thinking, and a natural science corner were continuously available to the children. In addition, there were regularly scheduled activities such as creative movement sessions, and a class newspaper in which children could demonstrate their language skills by reporting on events of their weekends and vacations. In many ways Spectrum was reminiscent of what can be found in many well-implemented preschool classrooms. The difference was that in addition to the usual activities, we interspersed the 15 more formal assessment measures and a series of less formal checklists for each child over the course of the school year. Through careful observations in such a setting, we found that we could gain considerable information about the profile of interests and abilities of individual children while offering them, at the same time, a rich and diverse environment in which to explore and learn.

Rather than suggesting a prescribed method on which all early education programs should be modeled, Spectrum offers a flexible framework within which educators can develop customized, unique programs that more effectively serve all children in their care. The past decade has presented many new applications of the Spectrum approach. These include programs for older children, the gifted, and those in need of special education; programs with children's museums; and apprenticeship programs, to name a few.

A Spectrum-inspired approach to early education also can help to enrich practices already widely used in preschools and other settings. For example, many existing preschool programs use thematic units within which curricular activities are grounded. A teacher familiar with the Spectrum approach might expand and diversify a unit in order to include a variety of materials and activities from many domains, thus maximizing the chances that children of all skill levels and interests can become involved. Or a teacher might choose to incorporate a domain-based approach that allows children to explore a particular area (such as music or natural science) in depth, over time, and from several different perspectives. Having the opportunity to observe each child as an engaged learner in a rich environment, the teacher can make an informed effort to widen each child's experience and build bridges between children's areas of strength and interest and areas they may not as readily explore.

As an example, consider a child who shows interest and skill in the area of music but difficulty with language concepts. Perhaps this child might be offered opportunities to develop vocabulary and skill in forming sentences by creating new words for songs, singing stories, and so on. Or consider a child who demonstrates skill in spatial tasks. Such a child might explore number concepts by keeping track of how many pieces there are in the objects he takes apart and puts together. This "bridging" offers children exposure to new areas of learning and exploration as well as new ways of looking at and entering into already familiar areas.

A Multiple Intelligences Approach to Teacher Training

MI theory can serve as a powerful framework for teacher training and development. The theory itself, as well as the many accounts of how it has been put into practice, can serve as a starting point for a teacher's self-reflection and development. First, it can help a teacher look at his or her own profile of strengths and weaknesses across many areas of human cognition. This self-examination enables a teacher to see where to improve his or her level of understanding in order to teach more effectively. Second, the theory has spawned a number of methods that a teacher can employ to observe individual children more closely and to put the observations to educational use. Finally, MI theory offers a starting point from which teachers can think more concretely about curriculum development.

A common sentiment of teachers who have become familiar with MI theory is that they feel their eyes have been opened to the many subtleties of children's behavior. These educators agree that stimulating materials are not enough if they are not employed in a meaningful way and if a teacher does not have a solid idea about how and why they are used in the classroom. The problem with most prepackaged curricula is that the uniqueness of any given classroom, its teacher, and students cannot be taken into account in their development.

MI theory does not presume to offer one way in which children of any age or level of cognitive capability should be taught. Rather, it serves as a catalyst, and perhaps a challenge, to teachers to find what is best *in* each child and *for* each child (Gardner 1993: Krechevsky, Hoerr, & Gardner, 1995).

Summary: Toward a More Capacious View of Giftedness

MI theory has inspired many successful educational programs over the last decade, each of which incorporate key elements of the new approach to assessment and instruction. We believe that it is an ecologically valid, "intelligence-fair," and unobtrusive approach to assessment, which yields rich information about a child's distinctive profile of capabilities, interests, and styles of learning across the many domains of human cognition. In addition, we believe MI theory presents multiple opportunities to assess and encourage a child's evolving profile of intelligences by bringing the assessment process out of the testing room and into the classroom.

It is particularly important during the preschool and early elementary years that opportunities be maximized for an individual's exploration across a range of domains. While the discovery of particular interests and abilities can happen spontaneously for some gifted children, specifically designed activities, materials, or situations may be needed to instigate such discovery in many children, even those already "at promise." MI-inspired classrooms present all children with opportunities to explore their interests and abilities across domains, while simultaneously providing their teacher with systematic ways of assessing and, more important, responding to each child's needs. Assessment becomes an ongoing process embedded within the learning environment instead of a decontextualized task that occurs without motivation at fixed times during the year.

A multiple intelligences approach to assessment and instruction strives toward identifying and supporting the "gifts" in every individual. We have suggested that the first step toward achieving this goal is to address capabilities in the many domains of human cognition discussed earlier, instead of focusing exclusively on the logical-mathematical and linguistic domains. In addition, we suggest broadening the focus of assessment to include the identification of relative strengths (those an individual exhibits in relation to his or her own profile of cognitive capabilities) as well as absolute strengths (those an individual exhibits in relation to the wider population of peers). In this way one can make informed educational and extracurricular decisions that are based on the learner's complete profile of intellectual capabilities.

A multiple intelligences approach to assessment will likely identify many more children as "at promise" than traditional methods of the past. The identification of a wider array of capabilities in a wider population of individuals presents a challenge not only to the schools but also to families and communities to create opportunities in which these diverse capabilities can be supported and developed. To the extent that children so identified can be included in formal gifted programs, both the children and the programs will be beneficiaries, if they are well matched. But even if it is not possible to include every child, gifted or not, in an ideally designed program, the very exercise of recognizing gifts and laying out options can be expected to have beneficial effects for the child and for the culture.

REFERENCES

Adams, M. L., & Feldman, D. H. (1993). Project Spectrum: A theory-based approach to early education. In R. Pasnak & M. L. Howe (Eds.), *Emerging themes in cognitive development* (Vol. 2, pp. 53–76). New York: Springer-Verlag.

Binet, A., & Simon, T. (1905). Méthodes nouvelles pour le diagnostique du niveau intellectuel des anormaux. *L'année Psychologique, 11,* 245–336.

Feldman, D. H. (1980). *Beyond universals in cognitive development.* New York: Ablex.

Feldman, D. H. (1986). *Nature's gambit.* New York: Basic Books.

Gardner, H. (1975). *The shattered mind.* New York: Knopf.

Gardner, H. (1983). *Frames of mind: The theory of multiple intelligences.* New York: Basic Books.

Gardner, H. (1989). Zero-based arts education: An introduction to Arts Propel. *Studies in Art Education, 30*(2), 71–83.

Gardner, H. (1991a). Assessment in context: The alternative to standardized testing. In B. Gifford & M. C. O'Connor (Eds.), *Future assessments: Changing views of aptitude, achievement, and instruction* (pp. 77–119). Boston: Kluwer.

Gardner, H. (1991b). *The unschooled mind: How children think and how schools should teach.* New York: Basic Books.

Gardner, H. (1993). *Multiple intelligences: The theory into practice.* New York: Basic Books.

Gardner, H., Krechevsky, M., Sternberg, R., & Okagaki, L. (1994). Intelligence in context: Enhancing students' practical intelligences for school. In K. McGilly (Ed.), *Classroom lessons: Integrating cognitive theory and classroom practice.* Cambridge: MIT Press/Bradford Books.

Guilford, J. P. (1967). *The nature of human intelligence.* New York: McGraw-Hill.

Hatch, T., & Gardner, H. (1986). From testing intelligence to assessing competences: A pluralistic view of intelligence. *Roeper Review, 8,* 147–150.

Kornhaber, M., Krechevsky, M., & Gardner, H. (1990). Engaging intelligence. *Educational Psychologist, 25*(3, 4), 177–199.

Krechevsky, M. (1991). Project Spectrum: An innovative assessment alternative. *Educational Leadership, 48*(5), 43–49.

Krechevsky, M., & Gardner, H. (1990). The emergence and nurturance of multiple intelligences. In M. J. A. Howe (Ed.), *Encouraging the development of exceptional abilities and talents.* (pp. 222–245). Leicester, England: British Psychological Society.

Krechevsky, M., Hoerr, T., & Gardner, H. (1995). Complementary energies: Implementing MI theory from the lab and from the field. In J. Oakes & K. H. Quartz (Eds.), *Creating new educational communities: Schools and classrooms where all children can be smart.* Chicago: National Society for the Study of Education.

Malkus, U., Feldman, D. H., & Gardner, H. (1988). Dimensions of mind in early childhood. In A. Pellegrini (Ed.), *The psychological bases of early education* (pp. 25–38). Chichester, England: Wiley.

Olson, L. (1988). Children flourish here: Eight teachers and a theory changed a school world. *Education Week, 7*(1), 18–19.

Piaget, J. (1983). Piaget's theory. In P. Mussen (Ed.), *Handbook of child psychology.* New York: Wiley.

Project Spectrum Handbook (1994). Available from Harvard Project Zero, Longfellow Hall, Cambridge, MA 02138.

Ramos-Ford, V., Feldman, D. H., & Gardner, H. (1988). A new look at intelligence through Project Spectrum. *New Horizons for Learning, 8*(3), 6–7, 15.

Terman, L. M. (1925). *Genetic studies of genius* (Vol. 1). Stanford, CA: Stanford University Press.

Thurstone, L. (1938). *Primary mental abilities.* Chicago: University of Chicago Press.

Walters, J., & Gardner, H. (1985). The development and education of intelligence. In F. Link (Ed.), *Essays on the intellect* (pp. 1–21). Washington, DC: Curriculum Development Associates.

Walters, J., & Gardner, H. (1986). The theory of multiple intelligences: Some issues and answers. In R. Sternberg & R. Wagner (Eds.), *Practical intelligences* (pp. 163–182). New York: Cambridge University Press.

Wexler-Sherman, C., Gardner, H., & Feldman, D. H. (1988). A pluralistic view of early assessment: The Project Spectrum Approach. *Theory into Practice, 28,* 77–83.

Wolf, D. P. (1988). Opening up assessment. *Educational Leadership, 45*(4), 24–29.

Wolf, D. P., Bixby, J., Glenn, J., & Gardner, H. (1991). To use their minds well: Investigating new forms of student assessment. In G. Grant (Ed.), *Review of research in education* (Vol. 17, pp. 31–74). Washington, DC: American Educational Research Association.

Zessoules, R., Wolf, D. P., & Gardner, H. (1988). A better balance: Arts Propel as an alternative to discipline-based arts education. In J. Burton, A. Lederman, & P. London (Eds.), *Beyond DBAE: The case for multiple visions of art education* (pp. 117–130). North Dartmouth, MA: University Council on Art Education, Southeastern Massachusetts University.

6

Genetics and Intelligence

ROBERT PLOMIN, *Institute of Psychiatry, London*

In the field of gifted education, the contribution of genetics has long been neglected. The purpose of this chapter is to suggest that the field has much to gain by taking a more balanced view that recognizes nature (genetics) as well as nurture (environment) in the origins of giftedness. The chapter focuses on the domain about which most is known—genetics and intelligence—and emphasizes the important contribution that genetic research can make toward understanding nurture as well as nature. Properly understood, genetic research does not threaten gifted education but, rather, provides fundamental facts on which the field of gifted education can grow in exciting new directions.

The neglect of genetics in contemporary discussions of giftedness is striking. Part of the reason for this neglect is the legacy of behaviorism in the behavioral sciences, which led to environmentalism and conditioned behavioral scientists to be uncomfortable with biology. The major reason, however, is the concern that finding genetic influence will mean that nothing can be done environmentally. This notion is wrong for three reasons. First, to recognize genetic influence does not imply that a trait is due entirely to genetics. Rarely do genetic factors account for more than half of the variance of behavioral traits. Second, the phrase *genetic influence* in relation to complex traits like intelligence denotes probabilistic propensities, not predetermined programming. For single-gene disorders, such as a type of mental retardation called phenylketonuria (PKU), the gene has its effect regardless of other genes or the environment. Complex traits, however, involve many genes and many environmental influences. For this reason, genetic influences on complex traits are not hard-wired, mechanistic determinants. Rather, genes merely contribute to the odds that development will proceed in a certain direction.

Third, genetic research only describes genetic and environmental influences as they exist on average in a particular population at a particular time. Even if a trait were highly heritable, an intervention could have a dramatic effect on a particular individual. Moreover, a new intervention that did not previously contribute to environmental influences in the population could have a major effect, on average, in the population. In other words, genetic research describes "what is," but it does not predict "what could be."

Genetic research also does not prescribe or proscribe "what should be." Concerns about political implications lie at the core of uneasiness about finding genetic influence. However, finding genetic influence is compatible with a wide range of actions, including no action at all. Values come into play when decisions are made concerning what is to be done with such knowledge.

If genetic research describes "what is" rather than predicting "what could be" or prescribing "what should be," what does it matter whether genetic factors are important? Many educational programs for the gifted would proceed largely unchanged whether or not heredity is important. Moreover, knowledge of genetic influences is unlikely to be of much specific help to the educator confronted with a particular gifted child. Genetic research is likely to contribute in more general ways. Although finding genetic influence bears no necessary implications for social action, better decisions ought to be made with knowledge

Preparation of this chapter was supported in part by Grant HD-27694 from the National Institute of Child Health and Human Development.

than without it. Knowing "what is" should help guide the search for "what could be." Nonetheless, the major reason for wanting to understand the genetic and environmental origins of individual differences in intelligence is the basic science goal of explanation. Basic science, which carries no promise of practical application, often leads to novel and important applications. The driving force behind science is simply curiosity, a curiosity that is shared by educators and parents who wonder why children develop the way they do.

Another preliminary issue concerns *intelligence,* a word that is almost as contentious as the word *genetics* in the field of gifted education. The word *intelligence* has so many different meanings that it may be preferable to use other words in order to avoid confusion. What is meant by *intelligence* in this chapter is general cognitive ability, which represents the well-established fact that nearly all reliable measures of cognitive abilities (such as tests of verbal, spatial, and memory) intercorrelate at least moderately (Carroll, 1993). General cognitive ability is what such tests have in common (Jensen, 1987). More complex cognitive processes, such as abstract reasoning, are better indices of general cognitive ability than less complex processes such as simple sensory discriminations. Because intelligence tests typically assess a broad range of complex cognitive processes, their total scores provide reasonable indices of general cognitive ability, that is, intelligence.

The Contributions of Genetic and Environmental Factors in Intelligence

Family studies show that intelligence does indeed run in families. The average correlation of IQ scores for parents and offspring and for siblings is about .45. The question is whether intelligence runs in families for reasons of nature or nurture. Adoption and twin studies provide a kind of natural experiment to disentangle genetic and environmental influences (Plomin, 1990). If family resemblance is due to heredity, then genetically related individuals adopted apart should be similar even though they do not share the same family environment. If family resemblance is due to shared family environment, then genetically unrelated individuals adopted together should be similar even though they do not share heredity.

The results of dozens of studies indicate that both nature and nurture are important. First-degree relatives include parents and their offspring and siblings, who are related 50 percent genetically. For 1,017 pairs of first-degree relatives who were adopted apart, the average IQ correlation is .22, suggesting that genetic factors account for about half of the IQ correlation of .45 for first-degree relatives who lived together (Bouchard & McGue, 1981). For 2,101 pairs of genetically unrelated adoptive parents and their adopted children and pairs of unrelated children adopted together, the average IQ correlation is about .23, suggesting that shared family environment also makes a contribution.

Thus, in rough summary, "genetic" relatives adopted apart correlate about .22, "environmental" relatives correlate about .23, and "genetic-plus-environmental" relatives correlate about .45. Of the IQ resemblance between first-degree relatives, about half appears to be due to nature and the other half to nurture. *Heritability* is a statistic that describes the proportion of variance in the population that can be attributed to genetic differences among individuals. The heritability estimate from these adoption data is 44 percent, which means that of the differences among individuals in IQ scores, genetic differences can account for approximately 44 percent of this variance. [The correlation of .22 is doubled to estimate heritability because first-degree relatives are only 50 percent similar genetically, as explained elsewhere (e.g., Plomin, 1990).] This means that about half of the IQ differences among individuals in the population can be accounted for by genetic differences among them. Nurture, shared family environment, accounts for an additional 23 percent of the variance. The rest of the variance of IQ scores can be attributed to error of measurement (about 10 percent) and to environmental influences that are not shared by individuals in the same family (about 23 percent).

Twin studies also provide a kind of natural

experiment in which the resemblance of identical twins, who are identical genetically, is compared to the resemblance of fraternal twins, first-degree relatives whose genetic relatedness is .50. If heredity affects a trait, identical twins should be more similar in the trait than fraternal twins. For IQ, the average twin correlations are .86 for identical twins (4,672 pairs) and .60 for fraternal twins (5,546 pairs; Bouchard & McGue, 1981). Because identical twins are twice as similar genetically as fraternal twins, a rough estimate of heritability doubles the difference between the identical and fraternal twin correlations. This estimate of heritability is 52 percent, [(.86 − .60) × 2], not too different from the estimate of 44 percent from adoption studies. It should be noted that the correlation of .60 for fraternal twins exceeds the correlation of .45 for nontwin siblings, which suggests that shared environmental factors contribute more to the resemblance of twins than to nontwin siblings, an issue to which we shall return.

One of the most dramatic adoption designs involves reared-apart identical twins, although the number of such twin pairs is small for obvious reasons. For several small studies involving a total of 65 pairs of identical twins reared apart, the average IQ correlation was .72 (Bouchard & McGue, 1981). Because they are genetically identical and are not reared in the same family, the correlation for identical twins reared apart provides a direct estimate of heritability. This heritability estimate of 72 percent is higher than the estimate of 44 percent from adoption studies and 52 percent from twin studies, and it has been replicated in two recent studies totaling 95 pairs of identical twins reared apart (Bouchard, Lykken, McGue, Segal, & Tellegen, 1990; Pedersen, Plomin, Nesselroade, & McClearn, 1992). A possible explanation for this higher heritability estimate is that, unlike most adoption and twin studies, studies of twins reared apart involved adults rather than children and adolescents. As explained later, heritability appears to be greater later in life.

Model-fitting analyses that simultaneously analyze all of the family, adoption, and twin data yield heritability estimates of about .50 (Chipuer, Rovine, & Plomin, 1990; Loehlin, 1989). Few scientists any longer dispute the conclusion that intelligence shows significant genetic influence (Snyderman & Rothman, 1987). It should be noted that the total variance of IQ test scores includes error of measurement. Corrected for unreliability of measurement, heritability estimates would be higher. Also, the world's research literature includes disproportionate numbers of young children. As will be discussed, new evidence indicates that adults show even greater heritability than children. Regardless of the precise estimate of heritability, genetic influence on IQ test scores is not only statistically significant, it is also very substantial.

What about high intelligence? It cannot be assumed that the etiology of high intelligence is the same as the etiology of the normal range of individual differences (Plomin, 1991). It is surprising that so little is known about the genetic and environmental origins of high intelligence. The issue is whether genetic factors affect high ability, which is different from the usual focus on genetic contributions to intelligence differences among individuals in the population. That is, the reasons that one child has an IQ of 150 and another an IQ of 145 are less important than understanding why both children have such high IQ scores, compared with the rest of the population.

In a follow-up study of Terman's gifted individuals, the average IQ of their offspring was 133, a score in the top few percentile of the distribution of IQ scores (Oden, 1968). This suggests that familial factors contribute importantly to high intelligence. Family studies, however, cannot disentangle genetic and environmental influences. A new genetic approach to this issue has been developed that is essentially an analysis of means. The method, called DF analysis after its developers (DeFries & Fulker, 1985, 1988), compares the mean scores of the partners (co-twins) of high-scoring twin individuals for identical and fraternal twin pairs. If familial (genetic and environmental) factors are not important, co-twins of high-scoring twins should have an average IQ near the population mean of 100. If familial factors are important, co-twins will have an average score that lies between the high-scoring twins and the population average. If genetic factors are important, co-twins of identical twins will have an average score closer to the high-scoring twins than will the co-twins of fraternal twins.

The first attempts to apply this approach to high intelligence suggest that genetic factors are as important at the high end of the distribution of IQ scores as they are are for the rest of the distribution (Plomin & Thompson, 1993). Although more work needs to be done to feel confident about this conclusion, these results suggest an important hypothesis: In terms of genetic influence, high intelligence might merely be the high extreme of the continuous dimension of intelligence. That is, the same genetic deck of cards may be played, but individuals at the high end are dealt a better hand. It should be noted that these results refer only to the top few percentile of IQ scores, not to the rare one-in-a-million genius. Lykken and colleagues (Lykken, McGue, Tellegen, & Bouchard, 1992) have speculated that genetic influences on genius are different from those that affect the normal range of intelligence in that particular rare combinations of many genes may be necessary for genius.

Beyond Heritability

The conclusion that genetic contributions to individual differences in IQ test scores are significant and substantial is one of the most important facts that has been uncovered in research on intelligence. Even when this conclusion is fully accepted, however, we are much closer to the beginning than to the end of the story of heredity and intelligence (Plomin & Neiderhiser, 1991). The rest of the story requires going beyond "anonymous" genetic and environmental components of variance to begin to identify specific genetic and environmental influences and to chart their developmental course.

Identifying Genes

One of the most exciting developments is the emerging possibility that molecular genetic tools can begin to identify specific genes that affect complex behaviors, including intelligence (Plomin, Owen, & McGuffin, 1994). The challenge is to use the thousands of new DNA markers to find genes in complex systems that involve multiple genes as well as multiple nongenetic factors. No genes have as yet been found that contribute to high intelligence, although research on this topic is in progress (Plomin, et al., 1994). Despite the allure of molecular genetic strategies, this chapter forgoes further discussion of this topic because of its promissory nature (see Plomin & Thompson, 1993.)

Three other genetic discoveries deserve mention. First is the remarkable finding that heritability of intelligence increases with age (McCartney, Harris, & Bernieri, 1990; McGue, Bouchard, Iacono, & Lykken, 1993; Plomin, 1986). This finding is especially interesting because it is counterintuitive: People usually assume that environmental factors increasingly account for variance in intelligence as experiences accumulate during the course of life. Another important developmental discovery comes from genetic analyses of age-to-age change and continuity, which find that genetic factors contribute to change as well as continuity, especially during the transition from early to middle childhood (Fulker, Cherny, & Cardon, 1993). What this means is that genetic factors that contribute to individual differences in intelligence in early childhood differ to some extent from genetic factors that affect intelligence in middle childhood. Although this could mean that new genes are turned on in middle childhood, more likely the same genes have different effects in the brains of eight-year-olds as compared to four-year-olds (Plomin, 1986).

The third discovery involves multivariate genetic analysis, which makes it possible to estimate the extent to which genetic effects on one trait overlap with genetic effects on another trait. One example of this approach is the finding that genetic influence on tests of specific cognitive abilities overlap to a surprising extent, suggesting that the generality of intelligence is a genetic phenomenon (Pedersen, Plomin, & McClearn, 1994). Nonetheless, some genetic influence on specific cognitive abilities is independent of general intelligence.

Another example of multivariate genetic analysis involves tests of school achievement, which also show substantial genetic influence. Multivariate genetic analyses have consistently shown that genetic effects on intelligence tests account completely for genetic effects on tests of school achievement (Thompson, Detterman, & Plomin, 1991; Wadsworth, 1994). Conversely, differences between scores on IQ tests and tests of school achievement are exclusively environmental in origin. This finding illustrates the possibility of unanticipated applications of basic research. First, the finding suggests that school achievement scores independent of IQ scores are largely devoid of genetic influence, and would thus provide a better measure of achievement per se. Second, the finding suggests that underachievement, defined as a discrepancy between ability and achievement, is largely due to environmental factors. Research to identify specific environmental factors that lead to underachievement deserves a high priority in order to foster the development of gifted underachievers.[1]

Identifying Environments

Two of the most important discoveries from behavioral genetic research involve nurture rather than nature. The first is the topic of shared and nonshared environments mentioned earlier. The obvious fact that intelligence runs in families has reasonably but wrongly been attributed to shared family environment. To some extent, this is the case prior to adolescence; but in the long run, growing up in the same family does not make children similar in IQ scores. Genetically related children in the same family are indeed similar, but heredity accounts for this familial resemblance. Environmental influences relevant to cognitive development make children in the same family *different,* not similar. This type of environmental influence has been called *nonshared environment,* because environmental influences of this type are not shared by children growing up in the same family (Plomin & Daniels, 1987).

As mentioned earlier, heritability of intelligence appears to increase during the life span. As heritability increases, the effect of shared environment appears to decrease. Also discussed earlier, genetic research involving young children and twins suggests substantial influence of shared environment. However, recent evidence suggests that shared environmental influence is much less after adolescence. Further, as mentioned earlier, twin studies yield inflated estimates of shared environmental influence (Plomin, 1988).

The strongest evidence for the importance of shared environment comes from the correlation for adoptive siblings—that is, pairs of genetically unrelated children adopted into the same families. Their average IQ correlation is about .30 across studies. However, these studies happened to assess adoptive siblings as children. In 1978, the first study of older adoptive siblings yielded a strikingly different result: The IQ correlation was −.03 for 84 pairs of adoptive siblings from 16 to 22 years of age (Scarr & Weinberg, 1978). Other studies of older adoptive siblings have also found similarly low IQ correlations. The most impressive evidence comes from a ten-year longitudinal follow-up study of over 200 pairs of adoptive siblings. At the average age of eight years, the IQ correlation was .26. Ten years later, their IQ correlation was near zero (Loehlin, Horn, & Willerman, 1989). These results suggest that shared environment is important for IQ scores during childhood when children are living at home, then fades in importance after adolescence.

These results also suggest that a priority for research should be the identification of nonshared experiences that account for long-term environmental influences on intelligence. The key is to study more than one child per family in order to ask what environmental experiences make children growing up in the same family so different. Some steps have been taken toward distinguishing intelligence-relevant environmental measures that assess shared environment and those that assess nonshared environment (Chipuer & Plomin, 1992). Measures of shared environment can be expected to correlate with IQ

---

[1] See Chapter 31 by Silverman and Chapter 34 by Rimm.

scores in childhood but not later, at least not for environmental reasons (see below). Measures of nonshared environment, on the other hand, are not expected to correlate with IQ scores during childhood but are the best hope for predicting later IQ scores from earlier experiences.

The second important discovery from genetic research concerning the environment has been called the *nature of nurture* (Plomin & Bergeman, 1991). The phenomenon is this: Measures widely used to assess the environment in fact show genetic influence in twin and adoption studies conducted during the past five years (Plomin, 1994). Although this seems paradoxical, what it means at its simplest level is that ostensible measures of the environment inadvertently assess genetically influenced characteristics (e.g., IQ) of individuals. For example, one of the most widely used observation/interview measures of the home environment (parental behavior) as it relates to cognitive development is a measure called the Home Observation for Measurement of the Environment (HOME; Caldwell & Bradley, 1978).

In an adoption study, mothers' behavior toward each child was assessed using the HOME for nonadoptive and adoptive siblings. Separate HOME scores were obtained for mothers' behavior toward each child when the child was 12 months old and again when each child was 24 months old (Plomin, DeFries, & Fulker, 1988). The question was whether mothers were more similar in their behavior toward genetically related nonadoptive siblings as compared to genetically unrelated adoptive siblings. If so, this pattern of results would suggest genetic influence. Sibling correlations for HOME total scores were .50 and .36, respectively, for nonadoptive and adoptive siblings at 12 months. At 24 months, the pattern of sibling correlations was similar: .50 for nonadoptive siblings and .32 for adoptive siblings. Thus, these data suggest that parental behavior assessed by the HOME substantially reflects genetic differences among children.

If genetic factors contribute to environmental measures such as the HOME, genetic factors might also be involved in the correlation between the HOME and children's cognitive development. This appears to be the case—about half of the HOME's prediction of children's cognitive development can be accounted for by genetic factors (Braungart, Plomin, Fulker, & DeFries, 1992).

These findings on the nature of nurture suggest that research on family environment needs to be embedded in genetic designs that can disentangle nurture from nature (Rowe, 1994). More generally, research on the developmental interface between nature and nurture needs to consider a more active role of children in selecting, modifying, and creating their own environments (Scarr, 1992). This is the more profound meaning of finding genetic influence on measures of the environment: Genes contribute to experience itself (Plomin, 1994).

Conclusions and Future Directions

The convergence of evidence from numerous family, twin, and adoption studies makes it clear that genetics plays a major role in the origins of individual differences in the normal range of intelligence and probably in high intelligence as well. There is still much to be learned about this rudimentary nature–nurture question, especially in relation to specific cognitive abilities (Plomin, 1988). For example, genetic research suggests that broad factors of verbal abilities and spatial abilities are more heritable than other broad factors such as memory and processing speed, but not enough research has been done even to be certain about this simple conclusion.

More research also is needed that focuses on each specific cognitive ability. For example, the broad factor of spatial ability shows moderate heritability, but it seems that this factor includes tests of some of the most highly heritable cognitive abilities and some tests of the least heritable abilities. In contrast, for the broad factor of verbal ability, which also shows moderate heritability, most tests—including tests as diverse as vocabulary and word fluency—show moderate heritability. For memory, tests that involve words seem to be more heritable than other types of memory tests. In addition to questions about the heritability of such traditional specific cognitive abilities, genetic research has just begun to investigate information-processing measures, as well as newer measures of neuroscience such as electroencephalographic evoked potentials, positron emission tomography scans, and functional magnetic resonance imaging (Vernon, 1993).

Although more research of this sort is needed, the theme of this chapter is that genetic research can go far beyond estimating heritability. The emerging ability to identify specific genes involved in intelligence is a particularly exciting possibility that will revolutionize genetic research, for example, by making it possible to identify relevant genotypes directly from a few drops of blood or a few cells scraped from the lining of the cheek. However, most of what is currently known about the genetics of intelligence comes from twin and adoption studies, and such studies will continue to provide valuable information even when molecular genetic research comes on line.

More research is especially needed that takes advantage of new developmental, multivariate, and environmental approaches to genetic analysis. Although such research has just begun, it already has yielded findings of great importance. For example, developmental genetic research indicates that the heritability of intelligence increases with age, and that genetic factors also contribute to age-to-age change, especially during the transition to middle childhood. Multivariate genetic research has concluded that the overlap between intelligence and scholastic achievement is due entirely to genetic factors, whereas the differences between them are environmental in origin. Perhaps most important of all are the environmental findings concerning the importance of nonshared environment and genetic influences on experience.

Incorporating genetic strategies in research on gifted education promises to be stimulating for both fields and synergistic in its contributions to understanding the development of giftedness.

REFERENCES

Bouchard, T. J., Jr., Lykken, D. T., McGue, M., Segal, N. L., & Tellegen, A. (1990). Sources of human psychological differences: The Minnesota Study of Twins Reared Apart. *Science, 250,* 223–228.

Bouchard, T. J., Jr., & McGue, M. (1981). Familial studies of intelligence: A review. *Science, 212,* 1055–1059.

Braungart, J. M., Plomin, R., Fulker, D. W., & DeFries, J. C. (1992). Genetic mediation of the home environment during infancy: A sibling adoption study of the HOME. *Developmental Psychology, 28,* 1048–1055.

Caldwell, B. M., & Bradley, R. H. (1978). *Home Observation for Measurement of the Environment.* Little Rock: University of Arkansas.

Carroll, J. B. (1993). *Human cognitive abilities: A survey of factor-analytic studies.* Cambridge, England: Cambridge University Press.

Chipuer, H. M., & Plomin, R. (1992). Using siblings to identify shared and nonshared HOME items. *British Journal of Developmental Psychology, 10,* 165–178.

Chipuer, H. M., Rovine, M., & Plomin, R. (1990). LISREL modelling: Genetic and environmental influences on IQ revisted. *Intelligence, 14,* 11–29.

DeFries, J. C., & Fulker, D. W. (1985). Multiple regression analysis of twin data. *Behavior Genetics, 15,* 467–473.

DeFries, J. C., & Fulker, D. W. (1988). Multiple regression analysis of twin data: Etiology of deviant scores versus individual differences. *Acta Geneticae Medicae et Gemellologia, 37,* 205–216.

Fulker, D. W., Cherny, S. S., & Cardon, L. R. (1993). Continuity and change in cognitive development. In R. Plomin & G. E. McClearn (Eds.), *Nature, nurture, and psychology* (pp. 77–97). Washington, DC: American Psychological Association.

Jensen, A. R. (1987). Psychometric *g* as a focus of concerted research effort. *Intelligence, 11,* 193–198.

Loehlin, J. C. (1989). Partitioning environmental and genetic contributions to behavioral development. *American Psychologist, 44,* 1285–1292.

Loehlin, J. C., Horn, J. M., & Willerman, L. (1989). Modeling IQ change: Evidence from the Texas Adoption Project. *Child Development, 60,* 993–1004.

Lykken, D. T., McGue, M., Tellegen, A., & Bouchard, T. J. (1992). Emergenesis: Genetic traits that may not run in families. *American Psychologist, 47,* 1565–1577.

McCartney, K., Harris, M. J., & Bernieri, F. (1990).

Growing up and growing apart: A developmental meta-analysis of twin studies. *Psychological Bulletin, 107,* 226–237.

McGue, M., Bouchard, T. J., Jr., Iacono, W. G., & Lykken, D. T. (1993). Behavioral genetics of cognitive ability: A life-span perspective. In R. Plomin & G. E. McClearn (Eds.), *Nature, nurture, and psychology* (pp. 59–76). Washington, DC: American Psychological Association.

Oden, M. H. (1968). The fulfillment of promise: 40 year follow-up of the Terman gifted group. *Genetic Psychology Monographs, 77,* 3–93.

Pedersen, N. L., Plomin, R., & McClearn G. E. (1994). Is there *G* beyond *g*? (Is there genetic influence on specific cognitive abilities independent of genetic influence on general cognitive ability?) *Intelligence, 18,* 133–143.

Pedersen, N. L., Plomin, R., Nesselroade, J. R., & McClearn, G. E. (1992). A quantitative genetic analysis of cognitive abilities during the second half of the life span. *Psychological Science, 3,* 346–353.

Plomin, R. (1986). *Development, genetics, and psychology.* Hillsdale, NJ: Lawrence Erlbaum Associates.

Plomin, R. (1988). The nature and nurture of cognitive abilities. In R. Sternberg (Ed.), *Advances in the psychology of human intelligence* (Vol. 4, pp. 1–33). Hillsdale, NJ: Lawrence Erlbaum Associates.

Plomin, R. (1990). *Nature and nurture: An introduction to human behavioral genetics.* Pacific Grove, CA: Brooks/Cole.

Plomin, R. (1991). Genetic risk and psychosocial disorders: Links between the normal and abnormal. In M. Rutter & P. Casaer (Ed.), *Biological risk factors for psychosocial disorders* (pp. 101–138). Cambridge, England: Cambridge University Press.

Plomin, R. (1994). *Genetics and experience: The interplay between nature and nurture.* Newbury Park, CA: Sage Publications.

Plomin, R., & Bergeman, C. S. (1991). The nature of nurture: Genetic influence on "environmental" measures. *Behavioral and Brain Sciences, 14,* 373–427.

Plomin, R., & Daniels, D. (1987). Why are children in the same family so different from each other? *Behavioral and Brain Sciences, 10,* 1–16.

Plomin, R., DeFries, J. C., & Fulker, D. W. (1988). *Nature and nurture during infancy and early childhood.* New York: Cambridge University Press.

Plomin, R., McClearn, G. E., Smith, D. L., Vignetti, S., Chorney, M. J., Chorney, K. A., Venditti, C., Kasarda, S., Thompson, L. A., Detterman, D. K., Daniels, J. K., Owen, M., & McGuffin, P. (1994). DNA markers associated with high versus low IQ; The IQ QTL Project. *Behavior Genetics, 24,* 107–118.

Plomin, R., & Neiderhiser, J. M. (1991). Quantitative genetics, molecular genetics, and intelligence. *Intelligence, 15,* 369–387.

Plomin, R., Owen, M. J., & McGuffin, P. (1994). The genetic basis of complex human behaviors. *Science, 264,* 1733–1739.

Plomin, R., & Thompson, L. A. (1993). Genetics and high cognitive ability. In R. Bock & K. Ackrill (Eds.), *The origins and development of high ability* (pp. 62–84). Chichester, England: Wiley (Ciba Foundation Symposium 178).

Rowe, D. C. (1994). *The limits of family influence.* New York: Guilford Press.

Scarr, S. (1992). Developmental theories for the 1990s: Development and individual differences. *Child Development, 63,* 1–19.

Scarr, S., & Weinberg, R. A. (1978). The influence of "family background" on intellectual attainment. *American Sociological Review, 43,* 674–692.

Snyderman, M., & Rothman, S. (1987). Survey of expert opinion on intelligence and aptitude testing. *American Psychologist, 42,* 137–144.

Thompson, L. A., Detterman, D. K., & Plomin, R. (1991). Associations between cognitive abilities and scholastic achievement: Genetic overlap but environmental differences. *Psychological Science, 2,* 158–165.

Vernon, P. A. (Ed.) (1993). *Biological approaches to the study of human intelligence.* Norwood, NJ: Ablex.

Wadsworth, S. J. (1994). School achievement. In J. C. DeFries, R. Plomin, & D. W. Fulker (Eds.), *Nature and nurture during middle childhood* (pp. 86–101). Cambridge, MA: Blackwell.

7

Excellence with Equity™ in Identification and Programming

E. SUSANNE RICHERT, *Global Institute for Maximizing Potential, Brigantine, New Jersey*[1]

Gifted education is under severe attack as part of the national restructuring and "detracking" movements in schools. Unless educators can produce models of excellence that do not violate equity, gifted programs will continue to be eliminated nationwide. This chapter addresses the problems of inequity in gifted programs and reports on a research-based solution successfully implemented in the APOGEE Project. APOGEE (**A**cademic **P**rograms for the **G**ifted with **E**xcellence and **E**quity), with assistance from a federally funded Javits grant, offers a practical approach for resolving the apparent conflict between excellence and equity in both identification and programming for students with gifted potential. The model used in APOGEE guarantees equity and has resulted in demographic heterogeneity in the classroom; excellence as well as cost-effectiveness in program design; and statistically significant cognitive, affective, and social benefits to the students served, regardless of culture, economic class, or gender.

Problems with Programs for the Gifted

Elitism in Programs for the Gifted

Beginning with the National Report on Identification (Richert, 1985, 1987; Richert, Alvino, & McDonnel, 1982), I have been criticizing the following elitist practices that continue to jeopardize support for gifted programs: (1) elitist and distorted definitions of giftedness, (2) confusion about the purpose of identification, (3) violation of educational equity, (4) misuse and abuse of tests and test results, (5) cosmetic and improper use of multiple criteria, and (6) elitist program design.

These problems have become evident to many others. The three arguments most frequently made by influential writers Oakes (1985), Goodlad (Goodlad & Oakes, 1988), and Sapon-Shevin (1994), among others, are not easy to refute:

1. Elitist identification practices and definitions of giftedness create school segregation by economic class and cultural groups.
2. The most motivating and challenging curriculum is found in programs for the gifted, while curriculum for other programs is often monotonous and devoid of interest.
3. The best trained and most effective teachers work with the gifted, denying the benefits of these teachers to students of other abilities.

These serious problems have been raised by many educators and parents. Various national education associations have taken formal positions against tracking and various forms of ability grouping. These problems are polarizing champions of heterogeneous grouping versus advocates of differentiated educational provisions for the gifted. Polarization has always been a side effect of programs for the gifted, but the present struggle has eliminated or drastically reduced programs for the gifted in many states and school districts.

In this national wave of school reform, James Madison's fear of "the tyranny of the majority" in a democratic society seems to be realized. Because the gifted and their advo-

[1] 1509 East Shore Drive, Brigantine, NJ 08203

cates are a small minority, their needs often receive a low priority in reform efforts. The responses of educators of the gifted to this seemingly relentless trend toward heterogeneous grouping have fallen into two extremes, neither of which is satisfactory. One position makes uncompromising elitist arguments for serving at least the "most gifted" students, who tend to be defined as exceptionally high IQ students and who coincidentally are typically white and affluent. This elitist stance unfortunately has generated fodder for the "egalitarian" positions of Oakes (1985) and Sapon-Shevin (1994) as well as, ironically, the irresponsible policy recommendations against efforts at equity in education for the poor or culturally diverse made by Herrnstein and Murray (1994) in their widely publicized book, *The Bell Curve*. The other strategy is to ride the bandwagon of egalitarian school reform in a misguided attempt to serve the gifted in full-time heterogeneously grouped classes, or to offer the panacea of "enrichment for all." This approach ignores the research-based needs of the gifted for various kinds of homogeneous grouping so effectively analyzed by Kulik and Kulik (Kulik, 1992; Kulik & Kulik, 1987; see Chapter 19).

Elitist Definitions of Giftedness

Many districts and states still use elitist definitions of giftedness that result in the inclusion of only certain kinds of gifted students, most often those who are white, middle class, and academically achieving. Herrnstein and Murray's controversial book, a major media event heralded by a *Newsweek* magazine cover story (October 24, 1994), explicitly supports this limited concept of ability. The authors claim that educational programs to eliminate bias will not overcome what they misleadingly argue are innate differences in intelligence, as measured by IQ, among various socioeconomic groups in our society. A major purpose of the 1972 federal definition of giftedness (Marland, 1972), as well as the more recent *National Excellence: The Case for Developing America's Talent* (U.S. Department of Education, 1993), was to expand the concept of giftedness beyond IQ. Yet in practice, much more limited definitions still are being applied, especially in states where *gifted* is a special education category and relies on special education funding.

Some state and local definitions distort the intention of these federal definitions by inappropriately distinguishing between *gifted* and *talented* students. This creates an elitist hierarchy. It uses the former for general intellectual ability, as measured primarily by intelligence tests, and the latter for other gifted abilities referred to in the federal definition—that is, specific academic aptitude, creativity, leadership, and ability in the visual and performing arts. Some state departments of education, for example, that of New York, distort Renzulli's (1978) concept of giftedness (the interaction of above-average ability, creativity, and motivation) by designating as *gifted* and thereby eligible for programs, those students who demonstrate all three abilities, and as *talented* those students who exhibit only two abilities (New York State Department of Education, n.d., p. 2).

Such distinctions ignore the differences between the manifestations of giftedness studied in adults, and the potential for giftedness in children that gifted programs are designed to develop. False distinctions between *talented* and *gifted* among children or designating degrees of giftedness ("highly," "severely," "profoundly," or "exotically" gifted) create implicit hierarchies, engenders elitism within programs, and excludes many students with gifted potential. Such hierarchies also ignore the fact that giftedness emerges, as Renzulli (1978), Richert (1985, 1986), Richert et al. (1982), Tannenbaum (1983), and others assert, through the interaction of innate abilities and learning or experience.

The major bias that impels these practices is the prevalent myth that academic achievement is directly related to adult giftedness. Various studies (e.g., Baird, 1982; Hoyt, 1965; Munday & Davis, 1974; Taylor, Albo, Holland, & Brandt, 1985) have repeatedly revealed no correlation, or even a small negative correlation, between academic achievement and adult giftedness in a broad range of fields. This should not be surprising, because many of the evaluation criteria for determining grades, such as propensity for convergent thinking, conformity to expectations of teachers or test makers, and meeting externally determined deadlines, are inversely correlated with adult eminence or original contributions to most fields. These studies demonstrate that test scores predict test scores; grades predict grades. As Nairn (Nairn & Associates, 1980) and others have argued, socioeconomic status predicts both. Giftedness, or original contribution to a field, requires nonacademic abilities unrelated or inversely related to school achievement, such as creativity, passion, and intrinsic motivation.

Confusion about the Purposes of Identification

There are various kinds of confusion about the purposes of identification, often related to the needs and values of the people involved in identification. There are researchers like Terman, and many who followed him, whose interest has been in designating traits that will predict giftedness in adults, rather than in specifying necessary educational provisions. There also are educators who want the identification criteria (e.g., high grades, teacher recommendation) to reaffirm the values of conformity inherent in the school system. Some parents want to have a label for their children to affirm their own self-esteem (Miller, 1981). But these are distortions of the purpose of programs for the gifted, which should be the development of latent and manifest potential in all areas. The identification process should be a *needs assessment* whose primary purpose is the placement of students into educational programs designed to develop their latent potential.

Violation of Educational Equity

Typical identification procedures violate educational equity by consistently excluding large proportions of poor and culturally diverse gifted students. The *National Report on Identification* (Richert, Alvino & McDonnel, 1982) revealed that the measures of academic achievement most frequently used by schools are teacher recommendations, grades, and standardized tests. These often screen out subpopulations that especially need programs, such as underachieving, learning-disabled, handicapped, and culturally different students with gifted potential. A significant finding of the *National Report* is that poor students are most consistently screened out of gifted programs because their disadvantage cuts across every other subpopulation. In addition, as Torrance (1979) argued, the majority of creative and divergent thinkers are excluded by using IQ criteria.

The U.S. Department of Education (1979), Richert et al. (1982), and Zappia (1989) report a 30 to 70 percent underrepresentation of culturally different students in programs for the gifted in the United States. Typical of the national pattern, the eight demographically diverse New Jersey districts that participated in the APOGEE Project originally had 10 to 75 percent underrepresentation of culturally diverse students (Richert & Wilson, 1995). The APOGEE Project also collected significant data on economic bias. The APOGEE districts started with 75 to 600 percent underrepresentation of economically disadvantaged students, defined as receiving free or reduced-priced lunch, in their programs for the gifted. The underrepresentation of poor African-American males, the group most at risk in U.S. schools, was over 800 percent in some districts. This shocking inequity is a problem not only for those excluded from gifted programs but also for those included, in that it makes programs particularly vulnerable to charges of elitism.

Inappropriate, Cosmetic, and Distorting Use of Multiple Identification Criteria

One trend in identification is the use of data from a variety of sources. However, this apparent comprehensiveness is deceptive. Practitioners in many states use test scores (IQ, achievement, or both), teacher observations, and sometimes parent observations in their identification process (Richert et al., 1982). The intent of collecting multiple sources of data is to make the procedure more defensible and inclusive. However, the data are often misused in several ways: The data may be unreliable, used at an inappropriate stage or sequence in the identification process, weighted in indefensible ways, or invalidly placed in a matrix with other data.

The statistically unsound practice of giving equal weighting to data from multiple sources, or even using weighted-scoring procedures, was strongly criticized by a national panel of experts (Richert et al., 1982). Ultimately, such combinations of data continue to screen out poor and culturally diverse students. While the combination of ability, creativity, and task commitment are indisputable requisites for manifestations of adult giftedness, the relative importance and the developmental patterns of each of these have not yet been demonstrated.

Adding the results of various procedures, measures, and test scores and using the sum as the criterion for selection is also questionable, in that it is the statistical equivalent of adding apples and oranges. The range, standard deviations, reliability, and construct and content validity of different measures, whether formal or informal, are not necessarily equivalent.

Combining data inappropriately tends to identify Jacks-of-all-trades, or students who develop ability, creativity, and motivation concurrently. It may eliminate the "masters of some" and the current "masters of none"—those underachieving students who particularly need a gifted program to develop their unmanifested potential.

The national survey of practices reported in the *National Report on Identification* (Richert et al., 1982) revealed that even when multiple measures are used, standardized test scores tend to be given disproportionate weight. The more measures that are used and combined inappropriately, the more likely it becomes that disadvantaged students (poor, minority, creative, and others who tend to be underachievers in schools) will be excluded. The recent move toward procedures that include "authentic" or "alternative" assessment is not necessarily helpful to the poor or culturally different, because, as Asa Hilliard (1993) forcefully argued in a presentation at a National Association for Black School Educators conference, such procedures rely primarily on subjective, white, middle-class expectations. In sum, the use of multiple measures, which may create the appearance of inclusiveness, may reinforce a narrow concept of giftedness and exacerbate the problem of elitism in identification.

Another problem is the sequence in which multiple sources of data are used. If parents or teachers assess the creativity or motivation of students only *after* they have qualified for a talent pool with a high standardized achievement test score, then disadvantaged students already would have been screened out. If individualized IQ tests are given to students only *after* they qualify through a group IQ or achievement test, then underachieving students already will have been excluded. Such procedures are merely cosmetic efforts at equity, which often actually reinforce the exclusion of disadvantaged groups.

There is ample evidence that those without training in characteristics of the gifted are often unreliable sources of identification data (e.g., Baldwin, 1962; Cornish, 1968; Gear, 1976, 1978; Jacobs, 1971; Wilson, 1963). Other sources of information that lead to bias and exclusion include locally designed checklists, and observation forms that are not research based (Richert, 1987; Richert et al., 1982.)

Elitist Program Models

The limited nature of school resources often sets up counterproductive competition among groups vying for funds and services. Many administrators argue that because of limited funds, only small numbers of gifted students can be served. As a result, parents whose children are being served tend to defend the status quo out of fear that their children will be excluded or will receive less if other groups (i.e., culturally different and disadvantaged children) are included. Similarly, parents of children who are not served in these programs argue for using the funding in ways that will benefit their own children. This kind of polarization, as dramatized by Sapon-Shevin (1994), is used to argue that programs for the gifted cause a "disruption of community" and therefore should be eliminated.

One unfortunate outcome of educational reforms attempting to foster excellence has been the reinforcement of elitist programs that serve as few as 1 to 3 percent of students. These programs look for and establish services for the "highly gifted." Program models that delineate a hierarchical pattern (pyramids or ladders) (Cox, Daniel, & Boston, 1985) of degrees of giftedness, rather than an egalitarian and pluralistic model that simply acknowledges various kinds of gifted potential, polarize support for gifted programs and make them vulnerable to attack on grounds of elitism (Sapon-Shevin, 1994).

Academic Programs for the Gifted with Excellence and Equity (APOGEE)

In Project APOGEE, an acronym for Academic Programs for the Gifted with Excellence and Equity, ethical principles and equitable identification procedures that I have been recommending since 1982 (Richert, 1987, 1990, 1994, 1995; Richert et al., 1982) were used in over 30 schools in eight New Jersey school districts of various sizes and demographics. These rural, urban, and suburban districts included student populations that ranged from 185 to 28,464. The proportions of poor and culturally diverse students ranged from 2 to 87 percent. The more than 3,000 students identified for services included over 60 percent poor or culturally diverse students with gifted potential.

Principles of Identification

APOGEE applied identification principles that emerged through the deliberations of the national panel of experts as part of the *National Report on Identification* (Richert et al., 1982) and as further developed in my Maximizing Potential Model (Richert, 1994, 1995; Richert & Wilson, 1995). These six principles are as follows:

1. *Defensibility:* Procedures should be based on the best available research and recommendations.
2. *Advocacy:* Identification should be designed in the best interests of all students. Students should not be harmed by the procedures.
3. *Equity:*
   - Procedures should guarantee that no one is overlooked. Students from all groups should be considered for representation according to their demographic representation in the district.
   - The civil rights of students should be protected.
   - Strategies should be specified for identifying the disadvantaged gifted.
   - Cutoff scores should be avoided because they are the most common way that disadvantaged students are discriminated against. (High scores should be used to include students, but if students meet other criteria—through self or parent nominations, for example—then a lower test score should not be used to exclude them.)
4. *Pluralism:* The broadest defensible definition of giftedness should be used.
5. *Comprehensiveness:* As many learners with gifted potential as possible should be identified and served.
6. *Pragmatism.* Whenever possible, procedures should allow for the cost-effective modification and use of available instruments and personnel.

Defensible Definitions

The *National Report on Identification* (Richert et al., 1982) analyzed a strong trend in the United States over the last half of this century toward broadening definitions to include multiple abilities and factors of giftedness. A few of the contributors to that direction include Guilford's (1967) introduction of his multifactored structure-of-intellect model; Torrance's (1964) research in creativity; Renzulli's (1978) explanation of some of the motivational factors in giftedness; Tannenbaum's emphasis on the nonintellectual and social variables of giftedness (1983; see Chapter 3); Passow's (1988), Roeper's (1982), and Richert's (1986, 1994) suggestions for developing a concept of emotional giftedness; Piechowski and Colangelo's

(1984) elaboration of Dabrowski's conceptualization of a developmental potential intrinsic to giftedness; and my own insistence on the ethical component of giftedness (Richert, 1986, 1994).

In the area of cognitive science, Gardner (1983; see Chapter 5), Sternberg (1985; see Chapter 4), and Gagné (1985), as well as a special issue of the *Roeper Review* (Silverman, 1986), emphasize the recognition of diverse, discrete cognitive abilities in the identification of giftedness. In addition, I have argued for a comprehensive and pluralistic definition, one that not only acknowledges the existence of various exceptional abilities, but also is ethical and will neither harm nor limit the potential of exceptional students from diverse backgrounds (Richert, 1986, 1987, 1994). It is more defensible in terms of the research, and more acceptable in terms of students' self-concepts, to view the identification process as a needs assessment that targets untapped gifted potential. The pragmatic definition for programmatic purposes that we applied in APOGEE from 1990 to 1993 was to identify up to 25 percent of students within each demographic group as requiring a program to develop their diverse exceptional potentials. The new federal definition supports this approach by arguing that "Children and youth of outstanding talent perform or show the potential for performing at remarkably high levels of accomplishment when *compared with others of their age, experience or environment*" (U.S. Department of Education, 1993; emphasis added).

Selection of Tests and Instruments

The misuse of instruments was avoided by using the cautions and recommendations of the panel of experts for the *National Report* about the appropriateness of tests for different abilities, populations, and stages of identification. We followed these precautions in the use of tests:

1. Selection of different measures and procedures to identify each gifted ability.
2. Addressing the following issues before using any test:
    - Is the test appropriate for the ability being sought?
    - Is the test being used at the appropriate stage of identification (i.e., nomination into a broad talent pool; assessment for a specific program option; evaluation within a program)?
    - Is the test appropriate for any disadvantaged groups in the district that are typically discriminated against in measures of academic achievement (e.g., poor, minority, creative, underachieving)?

Three Approaches to Equitable Identification of Disadvantaged Groups

While most states formally subscribe to the comprehensive federal definition of giftedness, in practice many local districts tend to seek—and to find—white, middle-class academic achievers. Measures of academic achievement that are most often used by schools, including teacher recommendations, grades, and most especially standardized tests, have been amply demonstrated to have cultural biases (e.g., Black, 1963; Goolsby, 1975; Hoffman, 1962; Miller, 1974; Nairn & Associates, 1980; Samuda, 1975). The *National Report on Identification* specified the following groups as being severely underrepresented in programs for the gifted:

- Poor students (e.g., students qualifying for free or reduced-price lunch)
- Culturally diverse students
- Students with minimal proficiency in English
- Males (when identifying verbal ability below the fifth grade
- Females (when identifying mathematical ability)
- Intellectually creative, academically underachieving, physically handicapped, and learning-disabled students

The *National Report* recommended that if an identification process results in more than a 5 to 10 percent underrepresentation of any of these subpopulations, one of three procedures (each with inherent advantages and disadvantages) should be used to overcome the bias.

One method to overcome bias is a "culture-free" approach that uses instruments, such as *Raven's Progressive Matrices* (Raven, 1958) or the K-ABC (Kauffman & Kauffman, 1983), that yield results that may be relatively independent of culture (Davidson, 1992). The *National Report* also lists more than twelve additional tests that have been assessed as appropriate for various subpopulations. A disadvantage is that most districts do not have culture-free tests available, so it is expensive to use them for screening all students at the initial stage of identification. Furthermore, few staff are trained in the appropriate use of these instruments.

A second approach uses "culture-specific" measures, instruments, or procedures for each cultural or demographic group. The culture-specific approach is appealing because students of different cultures do not have to meet dominant culture expectations to qualify for a gifted program (Maker, 1992; U.S. Department of Education, 1994).

However, the culture-specific approach is so labor- and resource-intensive that it usually requires university researchers for effective implementation (Maker, 1992). At present, few districts have either the funds or the expertise required to use this method effectively. Another disadvantage is that procedures have not been developed for all cultural groups. What can a district do if, for example, instruments have been developed for its African American students born here, but not for Haitians? How should the very diverse Hispanic groups, such as Cuban, Mexican, Puerto Rican, and Costa Rican, be treated?

Culture-specific approaches also do not address the issues of economic class or gender inequity, which can result in biases in most formal or informal instruments. For example, poor African American males, who are at great educational risk nationally, may be underrepresented by up to 800 percent without some form of gender as well as cultural renorming (Richert & Wilson, 1995). Culture-specific methods also do not directly address the issue of underachieving gifted students (of any demographic group). Too often, instruments measure the quality of instruction or student performance in relation to test makers' expectations, rather than gifted potential.

A third pragmatic approach, used in the APOGEE Project, acknowledges both the bias in typical standardized tests and the differences among the various cultural groups (Richert & Wilson, 1995). The goal is to factor out the bias in tests and only to compare students to their demographic peers or within their social environment. The effect is to create local norms for each subpopulation by disaggregating all data, including tests and various forms of nominations, according to demographic groups. This method is relatively simple and cost-effective in that it relies primarily on existing data and uses the same instruments for all students. Any deficiency is in the tests, not the students!

VanTassel-Baska and Willis (1982) found that test scores of economically disadvantaged students tended to underestimate their potential for success in an academically advanced program. This means that admitting poor students with gifted potential who have lower scores is both justifiable and defensible. The improved performance of the identified students from all demographic groups in APOGEE classes, to be discussed, provides ample support for the effectiveness of this strategy.

Identification Strategies Used in APOGEE

Project APOGEE used a procedure approved by the U.S. Office of Civil Rights (U.S. Department of Education, 1979). The available test scores, teacher nominations (grades K–11), parent nominations (grades K–3), and self-nominations (grades 6–11) were separated according to their various demographics, including categories for economic class, cultural group, and gender. Economic groupings were based on whether students were "disadvantaged," using the federal standard of qualifying for free or reduced-price lunch, or "advantaged—that is, not qualifying for free or reduced-price lunch.

Cultural groups varied by district, but included African American, Hispanic, Indian (from Asia), Asian, Native American, White, Limited English Proficient, and several others. If there was a greater than 15 percent gender inequity, which often occurred among high-risk groups such as poor African

American and Hispanic males, data were renormed for gender. Students were then selected on the basis of their highest score on any one of the rank-ordered lists of various instruments used by the school, which included at least two of the following: standardized achievement tests, teacher recommen-dations, parent recommendations, and self-nominations. This procedure factors out the inherent bias in most standardized tests (Angoff, 1971; Hansen, Hurwitz, & Madow, 1953; Sudman, 1976).

Renorming guarantees the selection of the same percentage of students from *within* each subpopulation present in the school. The purpose of renorming is not merely to achieve equity, but to identify and develop latent gifted potential in all populations. Selecting up to 25 percent of students from each group allowed expanded opportunities for students from all demographic groups, including white middle class. This strategy therefore avoids polarizing demographic groups and generates advocacy among parents of students with diverse backgrounds.

Multiple Sources of Data Should Complement, Not Confirm Each Other

Recent work in the field of cognitive science, as reviewed, presents a very strong case for multiple kinds of intelligence. Each of these "intelligences" must be assessed differently. As the *National Report on Identification* warned, precautions should be taken when using data from various measures. Districts should not combine formal and informal measures as if all were of equal weight. The purpose of using data from different sources is not to validate or confirm one source with another (parent nomination and teacher nomination, or IQ and achievement test scores, for example). The purpose is to have a variety of measures *complement* each other in order to discover gifted potential that a single measure might not indicate.

Data from different sources should be used independently, and any one source should be sufficient to include a student in a program. High scores should be used only to include students. Cutoff scores should not be used because they tend to exclude creative, underachieving, and disadvantaged students. Intellectually creative or disadvantaged students should not be excluded from a program solely on the basis of a test score if there are other indicators of exceptional potential (such as teacher, parent, or self-nominations). In other words, a high score on either a nonstandardized measure *or* a standardized test should be enough to offer entry into a program for at least one year. Students should be able to qualify for a program by scoring high on any of several measures, rather than on most or all. In the APOGEE project, all formal and informal data were renormed, and students qualified by scoring among the top 25 percent of their demographic group on any test score or by teacher, parent, or self-nomination.

Appropriate Use of Data from Students, Parents, Teachers, and Peers

Checklists and other informal data from parents, teachers, and peers are especially important in ensuring identification of students from disadvantaged populations. At the primary (K–3) level, parents are good sources of information about a child's strengths and intrinsic motivations, sometimes demonstrated by extracurricular activities. At all grade levels, teachers trained in identifying characteristics, positive and negative, of the gifted are particularly good sources of observations about creative behaviors (Gear, 1978). A list of some negative characteristics associated with high levels of creativity, critical thinking, or intrinsic motivation is included in the *National Report on Identification* and in a training handbook (Richert, 1994). Without such training, data from teachers may offer information that is even less useful than a standardized test (Gear, 1976, 1978).

Checklists can provide information about students' extracurricular activities that are indicators of intrinsic motivation. Peer nominations are also useful, especially in finding students with leadership potential. It is from peers that leaders emerge and by peers that leaders must first be recognized. Peer nominations also have utility in the area of creativity, because peers have a good basis for judging the exceptionality, imaginativeness, and uniqueness of a fellow student's ideas. The national panel of experts for the *National Report* stressed that the following standards be used for such instruments:

- Characteristics listed should be research-based, not just the product of a well-intentioned local committee.[2]
- The list should include negative or unexpected characteristics indicated by the research.
- Teachers using such instruments must be trained to recognize gifted students on the basis of their negative behaviors.

In addition, nomination forms should produce different scores for diverse abilities. For example, a minimum requirement would be for teacher observation checklists to evaluate both specific academic abilities that the program addresses and intellectual creativity.

Achievement and IQ tests tend to screen out the most creative students, and teachers often have biases against nonconforming students. For this reason, nominations for creativity are especially crucial. With the exception of the Torrance Tests of Creative Thinking (the figural version is especially useful with all populations, including the disadvantaged (Torrance & Ball, 1984) and the Structure of Intellect Learning Abilities Test (Meeker, Meeker, & Roid, 1985), there are very few readily available standardized tests that elicit scores in creativity. The APOGEE Project used easily implemented, research-based, self-, teacher, and parent nomination forms, which then were renormed for the various demographic groups in each district (Richert, 1993).

Self-Nominations

Starting at about grade 4, self-nominations can be very successful identification instruments. Their disadvantage is that students who have high potential but poor self-esteem, or who are underachieving, may not nominate themselves if they have traditional views of giftedness. Therefore, instead of identifying themselves as "gifted," students are asked to express their level of interest in various program options that allow for intrinsic motivation, creativity, and risk-taking. Students first are informed about the curriculum and objectives, and then are invited to visit various program options. They apply for those that they want to pursue. This method taps into the intrinsic motivation and intense interests of the gifted and was, after renorming, a very successful indicator of gifted potential in the APOGEE Project.

Use of Data on Student Progress for Evaluation

The identification process is not concluded upon determination of a list of students to receive services. The last stage of identification is ongoing evaluation and assessment of students' performance and interests. Students should be assessed annually, not to determine whether they are "still gifted," but to see whether they should remain in a particular program option or would be better served in another option or in the regular classroom. The focus is on the best interests of the student, not those of the teacher, parent, or school. The same data gathered to evaluate individual students may be used in aggregate for program evaluation and improvement.

Data on student progress in a program option—related to the program's curriculum objectives to develop higher level cognitive abilities, creative and critical thinking, or higher level emotional and ethical potentials—rather than changes in standardized test scores, should determine whether a student continues in the program each year.[3]

The few standardized tests appropriate at this stage are specified in the *National Report on Identification* (Richert et al., 1982). These tests may provide some assessment of

---

[2] Several instruments are included in Chapter 6 of the *National Report* and are available from the Global Institute.

[3] See Richert (1986, 1990, 1994, 1995) for sources and analyses of the higher levels of cognitive, affective, and ethical taxonomies appropriate for curriculum objectives.

progress in critical thinking ability. However, teacher, self-, and peer product and process evaluations are better indicators of progress. Product evaluations should include assessments of critical thinking and higher-level cognitive skills such as creativity, complexity, and pragmatism (does it work?). Process evaluation by self and teacher should address higher-level affective and social skills, such as independence, intrinsic motivation, risk taking, persistence, decision making, and cooperation. Process and product evaluation may be carried out during the year through the use of various criterion-referenced scales and checklists that address the goals of the program. Many have been collected in a training handbook (Richert, 1994, 1995).

Using Strategies to Develop Potential in the Regular Classroom

The regular classroom is a de facto identification environment whose effectiveness depends on staff development. Ordinarily, the regular classroom develops only those abilities that can be measured by tests or recognized by teachers. As a result, many underachieving or disadvantaged students are overlooked in identification. However, if teachers receive special training, then the regular classroom can indeed develop higher-level cognitive and affective abilities and will offer what may be called a "developmental curriculum" to evoke gifted potential (Richert, 1987, 1994; Richert et al., 1982). The long-range educational goal of schools should be to train all teachers in methods that develop the highest level cognitive, affective, and ethical potential of all students (Richert, 1995). Then, whatever their background, characteristics, or diverse potentials, students could be identified for program options because their abilities would become manifest in the classroom. Another immeasurable benefit of this approach would be the improvement of the quality of education for all students, instead of limiting the best services to a small minority of students. The APOGEE Project was deliberately designed to train teachers to upgrade instruction not only in classes where identified students were homogeneously grouped, but also in regular heterogeneous classes.

Equitable Result of APOGEE's Identification Procedures

The result of renorming the data in the APOGEE Project was an overall increased representation of culturally diverse students by 500 percent, an increase of economically disadvantaged students by 600 percent, and an increase of up to 800 percent of poor, culturally diverse males in program options designed to evoke gifted potential (Richert, 1995). At the same time, representativeness was achieved for all demographic groups in each district.

Low-Cost Program Demonstrates Excellence with Equity

Because of inevitable competition for resources, an inexpensive program design that uses primarily existing resources, rather than hiring many new staff, is necessary to serve the 20 to 25 percent of students with gifted potential. Without a practical and comprehensive program design, broad-based and equitable identification cannot be supported. A crucial advocacy issue is that identifying many fewer than 20 percent of students tends to polarize parents of high-achieving students versus parents of disadvantaged or culturally different students in the competition for places in a program.

In order to develop a high-quality program that can serve the diverse needs of up to 20 or 25 percent of a student population, I have recommended a five-step plan for modifying the diversity of existing district resources (including homogeneous grouping in required subject areas, the regular classroom, cocurricular activities, and electives, among many others; Richert et al., 1982). Two of the most crucial steps in this approach are equitable identification and intensive staff development for those faculty who will be teaching in the various program options.

The APOGEE Program design modified existing resources to serve the top 25 percent within each demographic group. Depending on the number of classes per grade level in each building, the top 20 to 25 percent of students in grades K–11 (for placement in grades 1–12) from *within* each subpopulation was then selected for a class that would meet daily for at least one required subject area. Instruction for teachers in differentiating required subject areas for individual interests, learning styles, and achievement levels in order to evoke maximum cognitive, affective, and ethical potential was provided by offering training in my Maximizing Potential Model™ (Richert, 1994, 1995; Richert & Wilson, 1995). In the elementary grades, which had self-contained classes, identified students were regrouped across classes at each grade level, a minimum of 45 minutes a day, for at least their reading class. Some districts chose to have one- to three-hour reading/language arts blocks. Other districts added math or a math–science block. At the middle or secondary levels, additional advanced or honors sections were taught by trained teachers. The net effect is that at least *twice* the original number of students take advanced courses, and those courses now include representative numbers of students from all demographic groups. Equity is not violated; economic or cultural groups are not "segregated."

As a major caution, equitable identification and placement by themselves are not sufficient to meet the needs of nontraditional students. Fragmented pull-out programs cannot meet the needs of underachieving students who need modification of required subject areas where they are not excelling. Without intensive staff development for teachers who will be serving students with gifted potential who are not usually identified (such as highly creative, culturally diverse, and poor students), these students will be set up for failure.

Intensive training to meet the needs of the gifted in required subject areas was offered through the APOGEE Project to over 150 regular classroom teachers, grades 1 to 12. The process included three kinds of instruction over a two-year period: (1) 45 hours of direct training, (2) from 10 to 30 hours of follow-up sessions, and (3) on-site, in-class coaching sessions for each teacher. Trained teachers then used 36 Strategies for Maximizing Cognitive, Affective and Ethical Potential™ (Richert, 1995) not only with classes of identified students, but also with their heterogeneously grouped classes. The training included many strategies for individualizing instruction for students' interests, learning styles, abilities, and emotional and academic needs over a wide range of achievement levels. The staff development ensured that excellence was not sacrificed for equity. This approach is not only cost-effective, with a one time per pupil cost of less than $20, but it overcomes the objection that only the highest achieving students get the most effective instruction or the best trained teachers (Oakes, 1985; Sapon-Shevin, 1994).

Administrative support for the program model and staff development was most often based on its benefits for all students, not just those with gifted potential. For example, in one southern New Jersey district that applied this approach for several years before the APOGEE project began, teachers keep discovering more students with high potential within the regular classroom. In this district, over 20 percent of the students are economically disadvantaged. The district now has almost 40 percent of its students in advanced or honors classes. Parents of students with gifted potential become strong program advocates because students are being served consistently in academic subject areas where they get credit for their work, rather than in fragmented enrichment or pull-out programs that do not improve their academic performance. This approach also avoids the politically correct, but cosmetic and ineffective, approach of "enrichment for all," which sacrifices excellence for equity.

Pre–postassessment of over 2,000 students in APOGEE, over 50 percent of whom were poor and culturally diverse, demonstrated statistically significant improvements in critical thinking skills (measured by the Cornell Test of Critical Thinking; Ennis, Millman, & Tomko, 1990), reading ability (measured by each district's standardized tests), self-esteem (measured by the Coopersmith Self-Esteem Inventory; Coopersmith, 1967), and reduced behavioral problems (reported by teachers and quantified in at least one building case study) (Richert & Wilson, 1995). These results are extremely important not just for those students who benefited from this program, but for the policy implications as well. Analysis of the data revealed that gains in performance were made both by high achievers and by students previously considered either "not gifted" or "underachievers."

It is intriguing that the greatest gains in critical thinking were made by students who had been previously identified as gifted through typical measures of academic achievement. It seems that the students who had earlier been placed in traditional academically advanced and honors classes were in fact underachievers in self-esteem and critical thinking. Their improvement suggests that the homogeneous classes and accelerated curriculum differentiation that typically is offered to high achievers was actually limiting their critical thinking and self-esteem.

The significant gains made by newly included potentially gifted students who were poor or culturally diverse demonstrates, contrary to Herrnstein and Murray's (1994) irresponsible recommendations, that changes in delivery of instruction can indeed improve the performance of traditionally underserved populations.

Conclusions

My eighteen years of experience with equitable identification, comprehensive and low-cost program design, and intensive staff development used in the APOGEE Project have taught me a great deal. First, there is enormous underachievement among students of all cultures and economic circumstances. We will never know how many students are capable of high-level work unless we first meet their needs in the regular classroom. Second, if programs for the gifted are to survive attacks from many quarters, it is essential that we offer equitable, practical models for both identification and programming, along with intensive staff development for all teachers so that students of all abilities, including the gifted, will achieve their maximum potential.

I therefore urge that we celebrate diversity, which, as Alexis de Tocqueville observed, is the hallmark of American democracy. Rather than developing identification procedures and programs that are elitist and exclusive, programs for the gifted should reflect American pluralism.

Programs for students with gifted potential can be both equitable and defensible if the following practices are followed:

1. Adopt a comprehensive and pluralistic definition that includes diverse abilities and emphasizes potential and need among all populations.
2. Recognize that the purpose of identification and programmatic provisions for the gifted is not to label or to reward achievement or conformity to school expectations, but to find and develop exceptional potential.
3. Use data about cognitive (especially creative) and noncognitive abilities from sources beyond academic achievement to identify diverse and discrete gifted abilities.
4. Appropriately assess data from multiple sources.
5. Renorm academic achievement and other instruments to overcome bias against various disadvantaged groups, particularly the poor and the culturally diverse.
6. Identify up to 25 percent of a school's student population so that if errors are made, they are errors of inclusion rather than exclusion.
7. Develop cost-effective, multiple program options to serve the diverse needs of a heterogeneous population with gifted potential.
8. Fund intensive staff development to upgrade the skills of all teachers.

This pluralistic approach incorporates the expanding conceptualizations of giftedness and provides equitable, comprehensive, defensible, and pragmatic identification procedures and strategies that can serve the needs of both students and our society.

REFERENCES

Angoff, W. H. (1971). Scales, norms and equivalent sources. In R. L. Thorndike (Ed.), *Educational measurement* (pp. 514–515). Washington, DC: American Council on Education.

Baird, L. L. (1982). *The role of academic ability in high level accomplishment and general success* (College Board Report No. 82). New York: College Board Publications.

Baldwin, J. W. (1962). The relationship between teacher judged giftedness, a group intelligence test and an individual test with possible gifted kindergarten pupils. *Gifted Child Quarterly. 6,* 153–156.

Black, H. (1963). *They shall not pass.* New York: Morrow.

Coopersmith, S. (1967). *The antecedents of self-esteem.* San Francisco: Freeman.

Cornish, R. C. (1968). Parents', teachers', and pupils' perception of the gifted child's ability. *Gifted Child Quarterly, 12,* 14–47.

Cox, J., Daniel, N., & Boston., B. 0. (1985). *Educating able learners.* Austin: University of Texas Press.

Davidson, K. L. (1992). A comparison of Native American and white students as measured by the Kaufman Assessment Battery for Children. *Roeper Review, 14,* 111–115.

Ennis, R. H., Millman, J., and Tomro, T. N. (1990). *Carnell critical thinking tests.* Costa Mesa, CA: Critical Thinking Press.

Gagné, F. (1985). Giftedness and talent: Reexamining a reexamination of the definitions. *Gifted Child Quarterly, 29,* 103–112.

Gardner, H. (1983). *Frames of mind.* New York: Basic Books.

Gear, G. H. (1976). Teacher judgment in identification of gifted children. *Gifted Child Quarterly, 10,* 478–489.

Gear, G. H. (1978). Effects of training on teachers' accuracy in identifying gifted children. *Gifted Child Quarterly, 12,* 90–97.

Goodlad, J. I., & Oakes, J. (1988, February). We must offer equal access to knowledge. *Educational Leadership,* pp. 16–22.

Goolsby, T. M. (1975). *Alternative admissions criteria for college: Non traditional approaches to assess the academic potential of black students.* Atlanta, GA: Southern Regional Education Board.

Guilford, J. P. (1967). *The nature of human intelligence.* New York; McGraw-Hill.

Hansen, M., Hurwitz, W., & Madow, W. (1953). *Sample survey methods and theory* (Vol. 1). New York: Wiley.

Herrnstein, R. J., & Murray, C. (1994). *The bell curve.* New York: Simon & Schuster.

Hilliard, A. (1993). Presentation at the National Association for Black School Educators, Houston, Texas.

Hoffman, B. (1962). *The tyranny of testing.* New York: Crowell-Collier.

Hoyt, D. P. (1965). *The relationship between college grades and adult achievement: A review of the literature* (ACT Research Report No. 7). Iowa City: The American College Testing Program.

Jacobs, J. C. (1971). Effectiveness of teacher and parent identification of gifted children as a function of school level. *Psychology in the Schools, 8,* 140–142.

Kauffman, A., & Kauffman, N. (1983). *Kauffman assassmen battery for children.* Circle Pines, MN: American Guidence Service.

Kulik, J. A. (1992). *An analysis of the research on ability grouping: Historical and contemporary perspectives.* Storrs: The National Research Center on the Gifted and Talented, University of Connecticut.

Kulik, J. A., & Kulik, C. (1987). Effects of ability grouping on student achievement. *Equity and Excellence, 23,* 22–30.

Maker, J. (1992). Intelligence and creativity in multiple intelligences: Identification and development. *Educating Able Learners. 17*(4), 12–19.

Marland, S. P., Jr. (1972). *Education of the gifted and talented.* Report to the Congress of the United States by the U.S. Commissioner of Education. Washington, DC: U.S. Department of Health, Education, and Welfare.

Meeker, M. N., Meeker, R., & Roid, G. (1985). *Structure of the intellect learning abilities test* (SOI-LA). Los Angeles: Western Psychological Services.

Miller, A. (1981). *Prisoners of childhood: How narcissistic parents form and deform the emotional lives of their gifted children.* New York: Basic Books.

Miller, L. P. (Ed.) (1974). *The testing of black students.* A symposium. Englewood Cliffs, NJ: Prentice-Hall.

Munday, L. S., & Davis, J. C. (1974). *Varieties of accomplishment after college: Perspective of the meaning of academic talent* (ACT Research Report No. 7). lowa City: The American College Testing Program.

Nairn, A., & Associates (1980). *The reign of ETS: The corporation that makes up minds* (the Ralph Nader report on the Educational Testing Service). Washington, DC: Ralph Nader.

New York State Department of Education. (n.d.). *Guidelines for the identification of the gifted and talented.* Albany: New York State Department of Education.

Oakes, J. (1985). *Keeping track: How schools structure inequality.* New Haven, CT: Yale University Press.

Passow, A. H. (1988). Educating gifted persons who are caring and concerned. *Roeper Review, 11,* 13–15.

Piechowski, M. M., & Colangelo, N. (1984). Developmental potential of the gifted. *Gifted Child Quarterly, 8,* 80–88.

Raven, J. C. (1958). *Standard progressive matrices.* London: H. K. Lewis.

Renzulli, J. S. (1978). What makes giftedness: Reexamining a definition. *Phi Delta Kappan, 60,* 108–184.

Richert, E. S. (1985). The state of the art of identification of gifted students in the United States. *Gifted Education International, 3,* 47–51.

Richert, E. S. (1986). Toward the Tao of giftedness. *Roeper Review, 8,* 197–204.

Richert, E. S. (1987). Rampant problems and promising practices in the identification of disadvantaged gifted students. *Gifted Child Quarterly, 31,* 149–154.

Richert, E. S. (1990). Patterns of underachievement among gifted adolescents. In J. Genshaft & M. Bireley (Eds.), *The gifted adolescent: Personal and educational issues.* New York: Teachers College Press.

Richert, E. S. (1993). *Richert teacher, parent and self nomination forms.* Brigantine, NJ: Global Institute for Maximizing Potential.

Richert, E. S. (1994). *Training handbook for maximizing student potential.* Brigantine, NJ: Global Institute for Maximizing Potential.

Richert, E. S. (1995). *Maximizing student potential.* Brigantine, NJ: Global Institute for Maximizing Potential.

Richert, E. S., Alvino, J., & McDonnel, R. (1982). *The national report on identification: Assessment and recommendation for comprehensive identification of gifted and talented youth.* Sewell, NJ: Educational Information and Resource Center, for U.S. Department of Education.

Richert, E. S., & Wilson, R. B. (1995). APOGEE: Academic Programs for Gifted with Excellence and Equity: Preliminary research results. In G. Ohiwerei (Ed.), *Developing strategies for excellence in urban education.* New York: Nova.

Roeper, A. (1982). How the gifted cope with their emotions. *Roeper Review, 5,* 21–24.

Samuda, R. J. (1975). Alternatives to traditional standardized tests, introduction. In R. J. Samuda (Ed.), *Psychological testing of American minorities* (pp. 131–157). New York: Dodd, Mead.

Sapon-Shevin, M. (1994). *Playing favorites: Gifted education and the disruption of community.* Ithaca: State University of New York Press.

Silverman, L. K. (Ed.) (1986). The IQ controversy (Special Issue). *Roeper Review, 8.*

Sternberg, R. (1985). *Beyond IQ.* Cambridge: Cambridge University Press.

Sudman, S. (1976). *Applied sampling.* New York: Academic.

Tannenbaum, A. J. (1983). *Gifted children: Psychological and educational perspectives.* New York: Macmillan.

Taylor, C. W., Albo, D., Holland, J., & Brandt, G. (1985). Attributes of excellence in various professions: Their relevance to the selection of gifted/talented persons. *Gifted Child Quarterly, 29,* 29–34.

Torrance, E. P. (1964). *Education and the creative potential.* Minneapolis: University of Minnesota Press.

Torrance, E. P. (1979). *The search for satori and creativity.* Buffalo, NY: Creative Education Foundation.

Torrance, E . P., & Ball, O. E. (1984). *Torrance tests of creative thinking: Streamlined* (Revised manual, figural A and B). Bensenville, IL: Scholastic Testing Service.

U.S. Department of Education. (1979). *Office of Civil Rights report.* Washington, DC: Author.

U.S. Department of Education. (1993). *National excellence: A case for developing America's talent.* Washington, DC: Author.

U.S. Department of Education. (1994). *Identifying outstanding talent in American Indian and Alaska Native students.* Washington, DC: Author.

VanTassel-Baska, J., & Willis, G. (1982). A three year study of the effects of low income on SAT scores among the academically able. *Gifted Child Quarterly, 31,* 4.

Wilson, C. (1963). Using test results and teacher evaluation in identifying gifted pupils. *Personnel and Guidance, 41,* 720–721.

Zappia, I. (1989). Identification of gifted Hispanic students. In C. J. Maker & S. Scheiver (Eds.), *Critical issues in gifted education: Defensible programs for cultural and ethnic minorities* (Vol. 2, pp. 19–26). Austin, TX: Pro-Ed.

8

Assessment of Gifted Children

SUSAN G. ASSOULINE, *The University of Iowa*

The purpose of this chapter is to discuss the role of psychological and educational assessments in the lives of gifted children. An assessment is a data-gathering procedure designed to help answer a question and make a decision. An assessment often includes testing because some decisions about gifted children require information obtained from tests, either psychological or educational. Anastasi (1988) described the function of psychological tests as the ". . . measure [of] differences between individuals or between the reactions of the same individual on different occasions" (p. 3). She defined *psychological tests* as "like other tests in science, insofar as observations are made on a small but carefully chosen *sample* of an individual's behavior" (p. 24). In other words, psychological tests measure individual differences in behavior. The behaviors being measured may be sampled from broad domains, such as intelligence or personality. Psychological tests can do no more than measure behavior; they do not actually create the construct of intelligence or personality. *Educational tests* are also measures of behavior, but, as defined by Anastasi, ". . . have been specifically developed for use in educational contexts, predominantly at the elementary and high school levels" (p. 411).

Because the distinction between psychological and educational tests is not clear, the term *psychoeducational* has come to mean that the information used will include results from psychological as well as educational tests. Tests are not the only component of a psychoeducational assessment—behavioral observations as well as background and anecdotal information are also typically included in an assessment—but tests are often the major component. The focus of this chapter is on the role of tests in an assessment.

Traditional Testing: Questions and Answers

Why promote the use of tests as part of an assessment when the present trend is to discount traditional testing and its results?

Even though traditional psychoeducational testing—for example, IQ and achievement testing—is relatively new, misuses of information from traditional testing situations have been associated with the tests since their creation. The present trend toward so-called authentic assessment implies that traditional testing is somehow false or artificial, and the results not useful.

The major complaint about traditional testing, as expressed by Wiggins (1993), is that:

> Students are tested not on the way they use, extend, or criticize "knowledge" but on their ability to generate a superficially correct response on cue. They are allowed one attempt at a test that they know nothing about until they begin taking it. For their efforts, they receive—and are judged by—a single numerical score that tells them little about their current level of progress and gives them no help in improving. (p. 2)

In his attack on testing, and on single scores (e.g., IQs) in particular, Wiggins ignores the fact that these scores are obtained through a carefully structured one-on-one interview that was professionally developed to measure a *sample* of a child's behavior. Wiggins questions whether or not tests are even in a student's best interest. This question gets at the heart of my chapter. The pages that follow will demonstrate why, when, how, and what tests are in the gifted child's best interest, and who should be testing the child.

What types of educational decisions are conducive to testing?

Again, the purpose of an assessment is to gather information relevant to making a decision. In educational settings, decisions about students typically fall into one of two categories: program or placement. A *program,* or curriculum, decision requires information about an individual's achievement within a curriculum domain. The information then guides decisions about which curriculum the learner needs. A *placement* is a classification decision. Placement decisions require information to help predict how successful an individual will be in a certain placement (Thorndike & Hagen, 1986).

Placement is a direct result of an identification process. Until recently, the primary reason for assessing a child was to make a decision regarding placement. For gifted children, this traditionally has been associated with a measure of general intellectual ability (IQ). Feldhusen and Jarwan (1993) asserted that the practice of identifying students as *gifted* on the basis of IQ scores is strongly connected with identification practices of special educators and is a deeply entrenched educational practice.

Although there is general agreement that gifted children exist, there is limited agreement over what characterizes a gifted child and how that child should be educated. Whether or not a test *creates* a gifted child is part of the current controversy in the use of tests. Hanson (1993) declared, "By their very existence, tests modify or even create that which they purport to measure" (p. 47). However, a different perspective was expressed by Stanley (1977): "If people have individual differences, and if we prize and value those differences, then why not measure them? . . . Measurement of individual differences involves the belief that human beings have differential talents and that these can be measured, are valuable to society, and should be cultivated" (p. 8). The question seems to be: Do the tests create the differences, or do the differences exist independently of the test, and are such differences concretely represented by being measured and therefore quantified?

It is my position that well-constructed tests measure differences that exist among individuals. A child's giftedness exists independently of a test, and an extensive, professional assessment that includes information from tests can guide educators and parents in developing an appropriate educational plan for the child.

An appropriate assessment will carefully evaluate *characteristics* of a child. The purpose of an assessment is never to evaluate the person's value or worth. Assessments should present objective and useful information that will form a foundation for sound educational decisions about children. Tests are among the most reliable and valid ways to acquire that information.

What is the historical context in which present-day testing occurs?

Intelligence, intelligence testing, and IQs are hotly debated topics in today's education circles. Publications such as *The Bell Curve* (Herrnstein & Murray, 1994) have exacerbated the controversy that surrounds IQ and the testing of intelligence.

Intelligence and giftedness have been linked since the 1800s, beginning with the publication of Galton's (1869) *Hereditary Genius.* That link was inexorably forged by Lewis Terman, who in 1916 published the U.S. version of Binet and Simon's individual intelligence test, the Stanford-Binet Intelligence Scale, and in 1922 launched a study of 1,528 gifted children. The results of the study are published in a series entitled the *Genetic Studies of Genius,* the first volume of which was published in 1925 (Terman, 1925).

In Terman's work we see the shift in terminology from *genius* to *gifted* (Feldhusen & Jarwan, 1993). Terman's extensive longitudinal studies established the connection between identifying gifted students on the basis of intellectual potential as measured by an individualized intelligence test. However, early in the days of developing the Stanford-Binet, Terman cautioned test users:

> We must guard against defining intelligence solely in terms of ability to pass the tests of a given intelligence scale. It should go without say-

ing that no existing scale is capable of adequately measuring the ability to deal with all possible kinds of material on all intelligence levels. (Terman, 1921, p. 131)

These precautionary statements were prescient to more recent theoretical work that goes beyond the scales as originally conceptualized by Binet (see Chapter 4 by Sternberg and Chapter 5 by Ramos-Ford and Gardner, in this text, and Hanson, 1993).

What are present-day policies and their effect on programming and placement?

Legislative policy regarding the education of gifted children varies from state to state. Most state policies regarding gifted education can trace their beginnings to the 1970s with the publication of the 1972 commissioned report, *Education of the Gifted and Talented* (commonly called the Marland Report), and the enactment of Public Law 94-142, the Education for All Handicapped Children Act, in 1975 (Passow, 1993). The Marland Report provided a definition that became the U.S. Office of Education definition, and served to guide many states in formulating their policies. The definition (see Table 8.1) seems to ensure that tests of intelligence will continue to play a role in the identification of gifted children.

Table 8.1
1972 U.S. Office of Education Definition

Public Law 91-230, Section 806)
Gifted and talented children are those identified by professionally qualified persons, who by virtue of outstanding abilities are capable of high performance. These are children who require differentiated educational programs and/or services beyond those normally provided by the regular school program in order to realize their contribution to self and society.

Children capable of high performance include those with demonstrated achievement and/or potential ability in any of the following areas, singly or in combination:

1. General intellectual ability
2. Specific academic aptitude
3. Creative or productive thinking
4. Leadership ability
5. Visual and performing arts
6. Psychomotor ability[a]

It can be assumed that utilization of these criteria for identification of the gifted and talented will encompass a minimum of 3 to 5 percent of the school population.

[a] The area of psychomotor ability was later removed from the definition.

What tests of intelligence are used?

Group intelligence tests are often used as a way of initially screening for students of high academic ability, but beyond that their uses are limited. Two tests widely used are the Cognitive Abilities Tests (Thorndike & Hagen, 1993) and the Otis-Lennon School Ability Test (Otis & Lennon, 1988). In general, scores obtained from group intelligence tests tend to be lower than those from individually administered intelligence tests (Sattler, 1988). Because they are more economical, group-administered tests of intelligence are used far more extensively than are individually administered intelligence tests.

A standardized, individually administered intelligence test is the best instrument for identifying gifted children on the criteria of *general ability.* The two tests primarily used are the "Binet IV" (Thorndike, Hagen, & Sattler, 1986), and the WISC-III (Wechsler, 1991). The Binet IV is a revision of the Stanford-Binet test, and the WISC-III is the third edition of the Wechsler Intelligence Scales for Children. The history of the development of the Binet IV and the WISC-III are summarized in Table 8.2.

Is an IQ a measure of intelligence?

It would be ridiculous to consider the score obtained from an administration of an intelligence test to be synonymous with intelligence. Nevertheless, a well-designed test can provide relevant and useful information about behaviors that typically are associated with "intelligence."

Intelligence tests measure behavioral *at-*

Table 8.2
Important Dates and Context of the Binet and Wechsler Scales

Binet Scales

1905 In Paris, France, Alfred Binet and Theodore Simon developed a 30-item test intended to measure judgment, comprehension, and reasoning of school-aged children (based on testing that began in the 1890s). The test was called the Binet-Simon Scale.

1908 The Binet-Simon Scale was introduced in the United States and standardized on 2,000 American children under the direction of Goddard. The scale was used primarily for the evaluation of mentally retarded individuals.

1916 Stanford University Professor Lewis Terman published an extended, standardized form of the Binet-Simon Scale under the name of the Stanford Revision and Extension of the Binet-Simon Scale. This version was the result of many years of extensive modification.

The concept of IQ (intelligence quotient), as a ratio of mental age to chronological age, was introduced with this version of the scale.

An age-scale format for the scale was established. This means that test items were standardized on a representative group of children at various ages. The underlying assumption with an age-scale format is that the appearance of certain behaviors is developmental, and so the items on the test are organized for different age groups.

1937 The 1916 version of the Binet-Simon Scales was revised by Lewis Terman and Maude Merrill and renamed the Stanford-Binet Intelligence Scale.

1960 The Stanford-Binet was revised by selecting the best items from two 1937 forms and combining them into one form (Form L-M). The "L" is for Lewis, the "M" is for Maude.

1973 New norms for the Stanford-Binet Intelligence Scale (Form L-M) were published. The Stanford-Binet (Form L-M) is regarded as an extremely reliable and valid instrument for use in predicting academic success. It is designed to be used with individuals as young as 2 years of age through adult.

1986 The Stanford-Binet Intelligence Scale: Fourth Edition (Binet IV) is published. The Binet IV covers approximately the same age range as the Stanford-Binet (Form L-M), and has maintained much continuity with the Stanford-Binet (Form L-M) by keeping many of the items the same. Instead of the age scale format used by the Stanford-Binet (Form L-M), however, the Binet IV is comprised of 15 subscales which yield an over-all score measuring general cognitive functioning.

Silverman and Kearney (1992a, 1992b) make an excellent case for continuing to use the Stanford-Binet (Form L-M) with extraordinarily able students because it does a better job of differentiating exceptionally gifted from moderately gifted children. This is important because children with IQs above 160 tend to have social-emotional needs that differ from those of gifted students with lower IQs.

Wechsler Scales

1914 David Wechsler became involved in intelligence testing as a U.S. Army private during World War I when the Army was conducting large-scale testing.

This introduction to the measurement of intelligence resulted in Wechsler eventually developing an intelligence test that would take into consideration factors contributing to a global concept of intelligence.

1949 The Wechsler Intelligence Scale for Children (WISC), designed for children ages 6 to 16, was published. The Wechsler tests use a point-scale format. The underlying assumption of a point scale format is that items are designed to measure specific functions or aspects of behavior at every age.

Wechsler considered IQ, defined as the ratio of mental age to chronological age, as inappropriate, especially for adults. He developed the notion of a *deviation IQ* in which the examinee's score is compared with scores earned by other individuals of the examinee's age.

Table 8.2 *(Continued)*

1955	The Wechsler Adult Intelligence Scale (WAIS), designed for individuals aged 16 to adult, was published.
1967	The Wechsler Preschool and Primary Scale of Intelligence (WPPSI), designed for children ages 3 to 7, was published.
1974	The WISC was revised and renamed the WISC-R.
1981	The WAIS was revised and renamed the WAIS-R.
1991	The WISC-R was revised again and named the WISC-III.

tributes of intelligent behavior, not intelligence as a separate, fixed *entity.* No intelligence test is perfectly designed to measure all attributes of intelligent behavior, but when used correctly, information from a well-designed, individually administered intelligence test can be one of the best indicators regarding an individual's range of knowledge and cognitive skills at a given point in time (Sattler, 1988).

What does an intelligence test score mean? As a way of summarizing the information gathered from the administration of an intelligence test, a score is calculated on the basis of the examinee's responses to a number of different items. This score is called an *intelligence quotient* or IQ. IQs obtained from administering the Wechsler Scales or Binet Scales have a mean (average) score of 100. The IQ score from an assessment is most meaningful when it is converted to a percentile ranking, as this allows the student, parent, or educator to know how the child's performance compares with that of other children of his or her age. The comparison is actually the primary reason for administering an intelligence test: to see how one child responds to a standard set of questions compared to the other children of his or her age. If a child scores 100 on one of these tests, his or her percentile rank is 50. This means that the child scored higher than 50 percent of the children in the comparison group. As the child's score goes over 100, the percentile ranking increases beyond 50, indicating that the performance surpasses that of a larger percentage of the child's age-mates. Correspondingly, the academic materials that were appropriate for the child at the 50th percentile become less appropriate for the child at the 90th percentile. For example, a child earning a score of 132 on the WISC-III would have a percentile ranking of 92, thus indicating that this child's performance surpasses that of 92 percent of children his or her age.

The percentile ranking can be misleading, however, for scores at the lower and upper end of the range of IQs. For example, at the upper end all scores above 148 on the WISC-III have a percentile ranking of 99. When looking at students who score at the upper end of the test, it becomes important to look at how the child performed on specific *subtests* and the *pattern* of those scores.

Using Testing in an Assessment

In this section, a psychoeducational report is analyzed to demonstrate how testing can be used in a comprehensive assessment. The case is that of a 6-year-7-month boy who was in the first grade. His parents wanted him placed in grade 7, but the school refused. His parents came to The Connie Belin & Jacqueline N. Blank International Center for Gifted Education and Talent Development (Belin-Blank Center) as the last stage before going to court.

Psychological Interpretive Report
The Connie Belin & Jacqueline N. Blank International Center
for Gifted Education and Talent Development

Assessment

STUDENT: Fred D. BIRTHDATE: 4/11/–
AGE: 6 years, 7 months GRADE: 1
REPORT DATE: 12/1/–
EVALUATION DATE: November 12–14
PSYCHOLOGIST: Susan G. Assouline, Ed.S., Ph.D.

Reason for Referral:

The superintendent of schools recommended that Dr. D. refer his son, Fred, to the Belin-Blank Center for an evaluation of Fred's academic achievement and for recommendations based upon that evaluation. At the time of the referral, Fred had been withdrawn from first grade in the local public school of his home town and was being schooled at home.

Background Information and Observations:

Fred had been evaluated previously at the age of 5 years, 1 month, and 6 years, 5 months. Each evaluation included the administration of an individual intelligence test (Stanford Binet, Fourth Edition, and Wechsler Intelligence Scale for Children—Revised) and each evaluation resulted in confirmation of Fred's superior intellectual ability. The academic achievement tests administered dur-ing the previous evaluations were designed to provide a general indication of Fred's achievement in reading, mathematics, and spelling. The tests administered at the age of 6 years, 1 month were the Wide Range Achievement Test—Revised (WRAT-R) and the Basic Achievement Skills Individual Screener. *On these screening instruments, Fred performed at the seventh-grade level for reading, math, and spelling.* The primary recommendation from each of those reports was that consideration be given to Fred's program of study to determine the best way in which to meet his needs for academic stimulation and appropriate socialization with his schoolmates.

Reports from the previous evaluations indicated that Fred had excellent concentration and attention, and my observations of Fred's

Analysis of Assessment

A good assessment begins with a question to be answered. There are two questions concerning this student: (1) What is the correct grade placement? and (2) what is the appropriate academic program?

Two individual administrations of an intelligence test had been administered within a sixteen-month period. There was no need for a third test.

Was the information from the previous administrations of achievement sufficient? No, the tests used were designed for screening; the information from them was inappropriate for a placement or a program decision. This is obvious in the vague recommendations.

This is an example of nontest data that was part of the assessment. This is used in the recommendations.

ability to concentrate and attend to tasks during the present evaluation were similar.

Fred is right-handed and has worn corrective lenses for four months.

Interpretation of Results:
Tests Used:

- Raven's Progressive Matrices (RPM)
- Stanford Diagnostic Reading Test (Green Level, Form A)
- Standard Reading Inventory
- Stanford Diagnostic Mathematics Test (Green Level, Form A)
- Sequential Tests of Educational Progress (STEP) Basic Concepts and Computation

One of the goals of the present evaluation was to determine Fred's academic progress relative to his ability. Fred was asked to complete the Raven's Progressive Matrices (RPM), an untimed nonverbal test of figural reasoning. For this test, the individual is presented with 60 meaningless figures and is asked to discern the nature of the pattern for each figure and complete the relations. Fred correctly completed 41 out of 60 figures in 35 minutes and earned a score surpassing 98% of the *8-year-olds* in the normed sample (the highest raw score earned by the 6½-year olds in the normed sample was 34). Thus, compared to the highest score earned by his *age-mates* in the normed sample, he was able to answer correctly 7 more items than the top-scoring individual(s). This is a significant discrepancy from the highest score earned by his age-mates and confirms that Fred's ability to form comparisons, reason by analogy, and organize spatial perceptions into systematically related wholes, as measured by this well-standardized instrument, is superior—even when compared to children two years older than he.

How do Fred's abstract reasoning skills compare to his age-mates? To older children? This is important because abstract reasoning skills will be part of an advanced curriculum.

From Dr. D's description of Fred's routine at home, it is obvious that he has been presented with considerable factual knowledge; however, all evidence indicates that he is more than ready to receive this knowledge and to process it with reasoning skills that

Some educators believed that Fred was being pushed by his parents and that he was not ready for advanced material.

surpass those of bright students in higher grades.

Superior ability to process information and to attend to presented learning tasks is extremely rare and requires careful tailoring of an individualized educational plan that will provide an optimal match between Fred's ability and achievement.

This part is the crux of the reason for completing the assessment.

The two previous psychoeducational reports included a screening of his spelling, reading, and mathematics achievement. The present assessment of reading and mathematics was more diagnostic in nature.

This is a lead-in to the specific tests used to suggest where to begin programming.

Reading: Form A of the Green Level Stanford Diagnostic Reading Test was administered. The Green Level is designed for students in grades 3, 4, and 5 and provides comparative scores for a sample of students in those grades. Fred worked quickly through the subtests. The final passages were to be read silently, but Fred subvocalized each of those passages. Even though he worked quickly, he was not impulsive in his responses and he rechecked his answers to the questions.

Since reading is one of the most important elementary school activities, a careful assessment of Fred's reading skills were critical. Additionally, this case almost went to court because the initial screening information suggested a "reading level of seventh grade," and the parents used that information to advocate that Fred be placed in grade 7. School personnel reacted strongly against this and wanted to keep Fred in grade 1.

When compared to fourth graders, Fred earned the percentile rankings reported below. Grade equivalent scores represent the typical performance of students in a specified grade. Because Fred is not a typical student, grade equivalents are not generally good comparative indicators; however, for our purpose of determining where to begin instruction, it was appropriate.

Stanford Diagnostic Reading	*Percentile*	*Grade Equivalent*
	(Compared with Fourth Graders)	
(Green Level–Form A)		
Auditory Discrimination	92	7.3
Phonetic Analysis	95	>12
Structural Analysis	83	6.8
Auditory Vocabulary	51	3.9

Literal Comprehension	74	4.7
Inferential Comprehension	43	3.7

The "lowest" grade equivalent score (earned for inferential comprehension) was two grade levels above his present placement. The highest (earned for phonetic analysis) was beyond grade 12. *Relatively* speaking, Fred's auditory vocabulary, literal comprehension, and inferential comprehension, as measured by these subtests of the Stanford Diagnostic Reading Test, are not as well developed as his ability to discriminate auditorily, analyze the relationships between sounds and letters (phonetic analysis), and decode words through the analysis of word parts (structural analysis). In other words, the skills measured by the cognitively less demanding tasks of recognizing words and decoding them are more advanced than his *understanding* of common words and his general reading comprehension, especially his inferential comprehension.

This is an important point because it begins to explain why the parents and educators could not see eye to eye. The parents were focusing on the highly developed decoding skills, and the educators "knew" that Fred would not survive in seventh-grade classes—even though he could "read" the material.

The Standard Reading Inventory was also administered, and the hypothesis that Fred's decoding skills were more developed than his comprehension skills was confirmed by the results of the Standard Reading Inventory. He orally read the fourth- and fifth-grade passages with only a few minor pronunciation errors. It was noted that he read in a monotone. We did not go beyond the fourth- and fifth-grade passages, but he could probably read passages at a much higher grade level. However, it is unlikely that he could comprehend passages at the junior high grade levels. His silent reading speed was at the instructional level for grade 4, but not for grade 5.

Instructionally, Fred reached frustration (correctly answered 4 out of 10 comprehension questions for both silent and oral reading) at the fourth grade level. He correctly answered four of the ten comprehension questions for the fifth-grade oral reading passage, but he answered only two of the ten comprehension questions correctly for the fifth-grade silent reading passage. He subvocalized while he was reading this passage.

Coupled with the information from the Stanford Diagnostic Reading Test, it appears that providing materials at an advanced third- or fourth-grade level would be instructionally appropriate. Fred's ability to decode written words will continue to be far superior to his ability to comprehend for several more years. Fred could probably read a sixth- or seventh-grade social studies text, but his thinking is not yet sophisticated enough to comprehend the material fully and draw inferences. He needs time to allow underlying cognitive functions necessary for comprehending to develop and mature.

All of the above information leads to this recommendation regarding programming.

Fred probably needs only limited instruction in decoding or phonics. It is recommended that an instructional program emphasize the development of his comprehension skills. His overall comprehension is at an advanced third-grade or beginning fourth-grade level, and instruction with materials at these levels would probably provide sufficient challenge. Fred needs two things to continue developing his comprehension skills: (1) time for the underlying cognitive processes to mature and (2) the opportunity to interact with students who are at a similar level of comprehension. These students will most likely be found in higher grades. If Fred is accelerated into third or fourth grade, it would be most appropriate to place him with the most advanced reading group.

This recommendation is based on the information obtained from the assessment.

Although his reading comprehension skills are (relatively) not as superior as his skills at decoding words, they are still superior when compared to those of his age- or grade-mates. The fact that his ability to comprehend ranges from two to four grade levels above his age-mates means he will need special arrangements for reading instruction. A whole-language approach to reading and writing instruction might foster Fred's progress in each of these areas. However, it would be important *not* to use a grade-level basal for whole-language instruction. Rather,

Fred will need exposure to literature such as that provided by the Great Books Series.

Mathematics: Three mathematics tests were administered before finding one that was appropriately difficult. The Green Level (Form A) of the Stanford Diagnostic Mathematics Test was the first test administered. The green level was developed for students in grades 4, 5, or 6. Fred finished the whole test in less than an hour (95 minutes is allowed). When compared to fifth graders, he earned the following percentiles for the three subtests:

Mathematics was the other curriculum area for which programming recommendations were needed.

"Appropriately difficult" is another way of saying that I had to go way above grade level to find a test with sufficient ceiling.

Stanford Diagnostic Mathematics Test percentile rank (compared to fifth graders)	
Number System and Numeration	86
Computation	85
Applications	94

The Stanford Diagnostic Mathematics Test did not appear to be sensitive enough to prescribe specific instruction. Therefore, the Computation and Basic Concepts tests of the Sequential Tests of Educational Progress (STEP) were administered. The level designed for grades 6–9 was too difficult, as evidenced by his performance: Fred required all 40 minutes to answer 24 of the 50 questions; and he answered only 14 questions correctly, which placed him at the 8th percentile when compared to ninth graders. It was decided not to give him the middle school/junior high level of the Computation test.

The information from this diagnostic test was not sufficient to generate programming recommendations.

The preceding level of the STEP Basic Concepts and Computation tests, which were designed for grades 3–5, was administered. On this level of the Basic Concepts test, Fred answered 38 out of 50 items correctly in 35 minutes. When compared to second-semester fifth graders, this score is at the 83rd percentile. Eight of the 12 missed items were items that required manipulation of number concepts. On the Computation subtest, Fred answered 53 out of 60 items correctly in 28 minutes. This is at the 90th percentile when compared to second-semester fifth graders. He did not seem to miss many items that were specific to one area.

The fact that Fred did so well on both of the tests designed for third through fifth graders indicates that he has relatively few, if any, gaps in his mathematics knowledge base. The biggest concern is that he not rush too quickly into prealgebra and algebra because he needs time to allow for the development of the necessary cognitive structures that will foster success in more abstract mathematics such as algebra. Unlike many extremely precocious students, Fred has not developed sloppy habits. He does not do all of his work in his head; rather, he was careful to work out the problems on scratch paper. However, if he remains unchallenged, he will most likely develop poor work habits because performing computations mentally will be one of the only ways that he has to mentally challenge himself.

For a more complete discussion of elementary students who are mathematically talented, see *Jane and Johnny Love Math: Recognizing and Encouraging Mathematical Talent in Elementary Students* (Lupkowski & Assouline, 1992).

Summary and General Recommendations:
Given Fred's superior performance on the two previously administered individual intelligence tests, as well as his superior performance on the RPM, one would predict that his academic achievement would be at least two grade levels above that of his age- or grade-mates. Indeed, Fred has fully utilized his superior academic ability and has achieved at a level commensurate with that ability. Fred has excellent concentration and attending skills and could easily succeed in third- or fourth-grade material. For some tasks, e.g., decoding and basic computation, even fourth-grade material will be too easy for him. With regard to his general reading comprehension, however, placing him in an advanced third-, fourth-, or fifth-grade class seems most appropriate.

This was the major recommendation.

The more routine school tasks (i.e., decoding of words and basic mathematics computation) are about as fully developed as can be expected for a 6½-year-old child, and his ability to concentrate and attend has been well honed. *Fred is at a critical point in his academic development. He will not lose his ability to learn, but if he is not sufficiently challenged he may lose his love for learning and likely develop poor study habits.* Because his reading and math comprehension skills seem to

The parents feared that Fred would not remain as able if he did not receive adequate programming.

be equally developed, it would make sense to consider whole-grade rather than subject-matter acceleration. For subjects such as science and social studies, Fred is probably ready to begin receiving instruction at a third-, and fourth-, or even fifth-grade level. Pretesting in these subject areas would be appropriate.

This is a placement recommendation.

The school system is fortunate that Fred's parents are able and willing to fill in any gaps in Fred's instruction that might occur as a result of accelerating Fred by two or more grades.

When students who have superb ability to learn are tutored at home, it is sometimes believed that the parent's opinion is suspect because parents have invested so much in their child's education. My sense of the situation is that Dr. D has tapped into his son's strengths and has helped his son realize those strengths. Fred took the tests at the Belin-Blank Center by himself and demonstrated extremely mature behavior. His behavior was more similar to that of a mature, extremely intelligent eight- or nine-year-old. His demeanor is like that of a well-behaved upper elementary student.

Fred has achieved through home schooling provided by his parents, but he needs the opportunity to interact with peers. He also needs exposure to extracurricular activities and contests, such as spelling bees, the Mathematical Olympiad for Elementary Students (MOES), and science projects that are typically assigned in the upper elementary grades. In determining an appropriate placement for Fred, attention should be paid to the most academically comfortable setting, i.e., third, fourth, or fifth grade, as well as the most emotionally comfortably setting. The receiving teacher(s), parents, and administrator(s) should discuss the most appropriate setting.

In this case, his peers likely will *not* be his age-mates.

An understanding teacher who can adequately prepare his or her class to welcome a new student (who is younger, yet equally able), and who can communicate effectively with the parents is most important.

This point cannot be overemphasized.

I have recommended that Dr. and Mrs. D continue to provide enriching educational experiences for their son. However, it was suggested that these experiences might be focused on opportunities that are not traditionally offered in the regular, public school. For example, Fred would probably do well in learning one or two foreign languages, as well as a musical instrument. Activities in sports and social groups such as Cub Scouts are also to be encouraged. When he is old enough (probably around age 11 or 12), Fred would probably benefit from summer programs offered by universities such as the University of Iowa and Iowa State.

Follow-up every three or four months with the Belin-Blank Center Staff, to be initiated by Dr. and Mrs. D, is strongly recommended.	Follow-up is a critical component of a successful assessment and intervention.

Susan G. Assouline, Ph.D.

Postscript

Six months after the results from the psychoeducational assessment were used to place Fred and develop a program for him, the unanimous conclusion was that the placement was tremendously successful. Currently, Fred is thriving in school, and the school personnel have a new appreciation of Fred's ability and achievement. The discussions about Fred opened up new opportunities for other gifted students.

In providing an actual report of psychoeducational testing, I demonstrated that testing fit into the assessment of this youngster, and that the information from the tests was necessary in order to make an informed decision about Fred's academic placement. The test results and their interpretation also helped in developing the recommendations for programming.

A critical component of the testing was the professional administration and interpretation of the tests. It is evident that specialized training in the administration and interpretation of the tests is imperative. An appreciation for the special programming needs of academically able students also is crucial. Additionally, the psychologist needed to be able to convey this information to parents and educators in a way that would serve the child.

The tests were administered in a safe setting, and Fred's performance validated what his parents had observed. The test results helped those who were advocating for appropriate placement and programming. The assessment documented in this psychoeducational report needed to happen prior to gathering additional data to document Fred's ongoing progress. Assessment methods that are now being called "authentic" are certainly appropriate and, indeed, are part of the everyday planning that occurs for this child. (Update: As of March, 1996, Fred is doing well as a second-year pharmacy student at Purdue University, at age 12.)

Is testing needed for decisions that aren't so extreme?

In this next section we present the case of a second-grade girl for whom acceleration to third grade is being considered. Acceleration is a highly controversial issue. The Iowa Acceleration Scale (IAS; Assouline, Colangelo, & Lupkowski, 1993) was developed as a guidance tool to facilitate decisions about acceleration. A completed IAS follows (Figure 8.1).

THE IOWA ACCELERATION SCALE

DR. SUSAN ASSOULINE, Associate Director
DR. NICHOLAS COLANGELO, Director
The Connie Belin National Center for Gifted Education
The University of Iowa

DR. ANN E. LUPKOWSKI-SHOPLIK, Director
Investigation of Talented Elementary Students
Carnegie Mellon University

THE IOWA ACCELERATION SCALE (IAS)

PURPOSE OF THE IAS:

While there has been considerable research on the positive effects of acceleration, the decision to accelerate a student remains one of the more difficult and controversial decisions for educators and parents. There is hesitancy because acceleration breaks the "mold" of grade-sequential schooling. Educators and parents are concerned about the effects of acceleration on both the academic and social aspects of the student. There is worry about making a decision that will adversely affect a child.

The Iowa Acceleration Scale (IAS) was developed in response to the important concerns expressed by educators and parents. Its purpose is to provide a comprehensive guide for making decisions regarding:

- Whole-grade acceleration (skipping)
- Early entrance to school
- Early graduation from school

DEVELOPMENT OF THE IAS:

The IAS is the outcome of a thorough review of the literature and research on acceleration, interviews with educational experts, clinical experiences with grade-accelerations, and pilot-testing of the IAS.

SUMMARY OF THE SCALES:

The IAS is comprised of a General Information section and four subscales. The four subscales provide an individualized and comprehensive profile of the student. The subscales cover the four major areas that should be considered when making a decision regarding acceleration. They are:

- Academic Ability and Achievement
- School Information
- Interpersonal Skills
- Attitude and Support

WHAT IS NEEDED TO COMPLETE THE IAS:

- All standardized test scores
- Student's cumulative folder
- Psychoeducational reports (private and/or school generated)

WHO SHOULD COMPLETE THE IAS:

The IAS should be completed by a team of educators and the child's parents. The IAS should be used as a guide in the decision-making process. Team members should include principal, present and receiving teachers, and parents.

HOW TO USE THE IAS:

- Each subscale provides a score and recommendations regarding acceleration are based upon the scores from the subscales and a total score. This total is recorded on the last page of the IAS.
- The IAS manual provides additional information on administration and score interpretation (the manual is still in draft form). Until the manual is complete, the Belin Center staff will serve as consultants to a school requesting the IAS.

Figure 8.1 The Iowa Acceleration Scale.

THE IOWA ACCELERATION SCALE

GENERAL INFORMATION

Student Name: Megan Date: Nov. 10

Date of Birth: October 11 Gender: F

School: Elementary Present Grade: 2

NAMES/POSITIONS OF INDIVIDUALS COMPLETING IAS:

Principal: Ms. K Parent (Guardian): Mrs. S.

Present Teacher(s): Ms. B Receiving Teacher(s): Ms. A

Other: M. D. (Media/TAG Specialist)

FAMILY INFORMATION:

Names and Occupations of Parents or Guardians Living in the Home:

Father—Not in the home

Mother—Medical Technologist

Names of Siblings:	Gender:	Age:	Grade in School:	Public/Private
Michael	M	5	K	Public

PRIOR SCHOOL EXPERIENCE:

	Name of School Attended	(Public/Private)	Approx. Size (less than 300; 300-600; 600-1000; more than 1000)
Pre-school			
Kindergarten	Megan has attended the same school since kindergarten.	Public	300
Grade 1		"	"
Grade 2		"	"
Grade 3			
Grade 4			
Grade 5			
Grade 6			
Grade 7			
Grade 8			
Grade 9			

1

Figure 8.1 (*Continued*)

THE IOWA ACCELERATION SCALE

Has the student done any of the following? (check all that apply):

- ☐ Already skipped one grade
- ☐ Entered kindergarten or first grade early
- ☐ Accelerated in one or more subjects

If yes, explain:

Please comment regarding the success of the acceleration:

Which of the following standardized tests has the student taken? (mark all that apply)

- ☐ ITBS
- ☐ California Achievement Test
- ☐ Stanford
- ☒ Metropolitan
- ☒ Other: (please specify)

Attach copies of all test results available.

Has the student ever been given an evaluation by a psychologist, social worker, learning specialist? (Circle one)

Yes (No)

f yes, attach copies of all reports.

Does the student have a diagnosed learning or physical disability?

Yes (No)

If yes, please explain and give diagnostic information used to determine the disability:

Has the student ever received special educational services or been on medication?

Yes (No)

If yes, please explain.

ACADEMIC ABILITY AND ACHIEVEMENT

Directions: For each item below circle the response that most often or best describes the student's *current* behavior or attitude.

MEASURE OF INTELLIGENCE (IQ SCORE)

Name of Test: ________

Average (100-114) 0

1 standard deviation above the mean (115-129) .... (2)

2 standard deviations above the mean (130-144) 4

3 standard deviations (or more) above the mean (145-above) 7

If a score is unavailable, an individualized IQ test needs to be administered.

Comments: Cognitive Abilities Test-Grade 2

NOTE: These are most likely an underestimate

Verbal	90% ile
Quantitative	92% ile
Nonverbal	88% ile

MEASURE OF ACHIEVEMENT

Name of Test: ________

Less than one full grade equivalent above 0

Grade equivalent of 1 to 1.5 years above 2

Grade equivalent of 1.5 to 2 years above .... (4)

Grade equivalent of 2 years or more above 7

Comments:

Based upon results of the Woodcock Reading Mastery Tests

Note: decoding skills are higher than comprehension

Academic Ability and Achievement Subtotal: 6

If subtotal score < 4, acceleration is not recommended.

SCHOOL INFORMATION

GRADE PLACEMENT UNDER CONSIDERATION

Accelerate one grade within building .... (1)

Early entrance to kindergarten or first grade 2

The acceleration will result in a change in building (e.g., elementary to next level) 2

The acceleration will result in a move to a new district 3

Comments:

Figure 8.1 (*Continued*)

THE IOWA ACCELERATION SCALE

Attendance at School

Has a history of unexcused absences and tardiness 0
Has a history of absences due to illness or for family issues 1
Absences and tardiness not a problem 2
Excellent attendance .... (3)

Comments:

Physical Size

Smaller than students in present grade 1
About the same size as students in present grade 2
Larger than students in present grade .... (3)

Comments:

Motor Coordination

Less coordinated than students in present grade 1
About as coordinated as students in present grade .... (2)
More coordinated than students in present grade 3

Comments:

Age

Student is among the youngest in the present grade 1
Student is among the oldest in the present grade .... (2)

Comments:

Participation in School Extracurricular Activities (e.g., athletics, clubs)

Student does not participate 0
Student has limited participation in activities .... (1)
Student has extensive participation (i.e., two or more activities) 2
Student has a leadership role or has received wide recognition in one or more activities 3

Comments:
Activities not offered at this level

Motivation

Doesn't complete assignments and appears disinterested in schoolwork .. 0
Needs one-on-one encouragement to complete assignments 1
Completes those tasks that are of interest to him or her 2
Completes assignments and shows positive attitude 3
Completes assignments more quickly and more comprehensively than other classmates .... (5)

Comments:

Attitude Towards Learning

Disinterested and/or frustrated when presented with new academic challenges 0
Completes assignments competently, but rarely seeks further challenges .. 1
Is enthusiastic and enjoys new challenges 2
Actively seeks and persists in new and rigorous academic challenges ..... (4)

Comments:

School Information
Subtotal: 21

Interpersonal Skills

Participation in Non-School Extracurricular Activities (e.g., religious groups, 4-H, scouts)

Student does not participate 0
Student has limited participation in activities .... (1)
Student has extensive participation (i.e., two or more activities) 2
Student has a leadership role or has received wide recognition in one or more activities 3

Comments:

Relationships with Peers

Poor interpersonal skills and no friends 0
Prefers to be with younger children rather than same-aged children 0
Interpersonal skills are not as well-developed as age mates 1
Prefers to be with older children and/or adults rather than age-mates .. (2)
Interpersonal skills are appropriate for age 3
Good interpersonal skills with age mates as well as students both older and younger 5

Comments:

Relationships with Teachers

Has poor interpersonal relationships with all teachers 0
Has poor interpersonal relationships with some teachers 1
Has very good relationships with one or two teachers .... (2)
Has excellent relationships with most teachers 3

Comments:

3

Figure 8.1 (*Continued*)

THE IOWA ACCELERATION SCALE

EMOTIONAL DEVELOPMENT
(of these categories, which is most like the student)

Exhibits a fairly strong pattern of emotional disturbances (e.g., depressed, inappropriate affect, aggressive behavior, etc.—see manual) 0
Very sensitive to criticism or remarks 1
Reacts aggressively towards criticism or remarks 1
Self-concept as a student is poor 1
Has an inflated ego about self and ability . . . . (1)
Has a positive and realistic self-concept about personal and academic abilities 3

Comments:
NOTE: No comment from School

BEHAVIOR

Has had behavior problems that have led to contact with law enforcement 0
History of behavior problems in classroom, home, or community 0
Has occasional discipline problems . . . . (1)
Has no history of discipline problems 3

Comments:
NOTE: This was not specified

PARENT INVOLVEMENT

Parents are overly involved in their child's progress and pressure the child 0
Parents are uninterested and uninvolved in their child's school progress . . 1
Parents are supportive and appropriately involved in their child's progress . 2
Parents are strongly committed to working with the school in meeting the child's academic needs . . . . (3)

Comments:

GRADE PLACEMENT OF SIBLINGS

Student would be accelerated into the same grade as an older sibling 0
Student presently has a sibling in the same grade 0
Sibling is one grade above or below the current grade 1
Sibling is two or more grades above or (below) the student's current grade (2)
Student has no siblings 3

Comments:

Interpersonal Skills
Subtotal: 12

ATTITUDE AND SUPPORT

STUDENT'S ATTITUDE REGARDING ACCELERATION

Student does not want to be accelerated 0
Student is unsure about acceleration 1
Student is positive about acceleration . . . . (2)
Student is enthusiastic about acceleration 3

Comments:

SCHOOL SYSTEM SUPPORT (ATTITUDE)

Widespread nonsupport among school personnel 0
Educators most directly involved (e.g., teacher and principal receiving the student are not supportive) 0
Minimal or ambivalent support for acceleration 1
Enthusiastic support for acceleration . . . . (4)

Comments:

PRIOR PLANNING FOR ACCELERATION

No planning or staff meetings have occurred 0
Limited staffing and information sharing regarding the student's placement 1
Extensive staffing and discussion regarding the student's placement . . . . (3)

Comments:

Attitude and Support
Subtotal: 9

SUBSCALE TOTALS

Academic Ability and Achievement Subtotal: 6

School Information Subtotal: 21

Interpersonal Skills Subtotal: 12

Attitude and Support Subtotal: 9

IAS Total: 48

Name & Position of Belin Center Consultant:
Susan Assouline, Associate Director

Signature of Belin Center Consultant:
Dr. Susan G. Assouline

4

Figure 8.1 (*Continued*)

Postscript

Megan is almost the ideal candidate for acceleration. She is already eight years old, like most of the third graders in the class to which she would be accelerated. Additionally, there seems to be enthusiastic support from school personnel as well as parents. Overall, she seems to be more like a third grader than a second grader.

In evaluating the form, note that on page 4 the responders indicated that she "has inflated ego about self and ability." When students are underchallenged, it often appears that their ego is inflated, when in fact, that is a sign of tenacity. This may be connected with the response to the next item, Behavior (see page 4), where it was indicated that she has occasional discipline problems.

Megan's acceleration was successful. She is doing well in her new class, where the gifted teacher monitors her progress.

Conclusion

By presenting two cases in which testing was used to make informed educational decisions and generate relevant recommendations, I hoped to demonstrate that testing is not passé. It was my intention to show the actual uses of the results of tests, and to prove that the tests did not "create" the condition but did help educators understand the learning needs of the student.

REFERENCES

Anastasi, A. (1988). *Psychological testing* (6th ed.). New York: Macmillan.

Assouline, S. G., Colangelo, N., & Lupowski, L. (1993). *Iowa Acceleration Scale.* The Belin-Blank Center, The University of Iowa, Iowa City.

Feldhusen, J. F., & Jarwan, F. A. (1993). Identification of gifted and talented youth for educational programs. In K. A. Heller, F. J. Monks, & A. H. Passow (Eds.), *International handbook of research and development of giftedness and talent* (pp. 233–252). Oxford, England: Pergamon.

Galton, F. (1869). *Hereditary genius.* New York: Macmillan.

Hanson, F. A. (1993). *Testing, testing: Social consequences of the examined life.* Berkeley: University of California Press.

Herrnstein, R. J., & Murray, C. (1994). *The bell curve.* New York: Simon & Schuster.

Lupkowski, A. E., & Assouline, S. G. (1992). *Jane and Johnny love math: Recognizing and encouraging mathematical talent in elementary students.* Unionville, NY: Trillium Press.

Otis, A. S., & Lennon, R. T. (1988). The *Otis-Lennon school ability test* (6th ed.). San Antonio, TX: The Psychological Corporation.

Passow, H. (1993). Nation/state policies regarding education of the gifted. In K. A. Heller, F. J. Monks, & A. H. Passow (Eds.), *International handbook of research and development of giftedness and talent* (pp. 29–46). Oxford, England: Pergamon.

Sattler, J. M. (1988). *Assessment of children* (3rd ed.). San Diego, CA: J. M. Sattler.

Silverman, L. K., & Kearney, K. (1992a). The case for the Stanford-Binet L-M as a supplemental test. *Roeper Review, 15,* 34–37.

Silverman, L. K., & Kearney, K. (1992b). Don't throw away the old Binet. *Understanding Our Gifted, 4*(4), 1, 8–10.

Southern, W. T., & Jones, E. D. (1991). *The academic acceleration of gifted children.* New York: Teachers College Press, Teachers College, Columbia University.

Stanley, J. C. (1977). The gifted child movement. In J. C. Stanley, W. C. George, & C. H. Solano (Eds.), *The gifted and the creative: A fifty year perspective* (pp. 1–27.) Baltimore, MD: Johns Hopkins University Press.

Terman, L. M. (1921). A symposium: Intelligence and its measurement. *Journal of Educational Psychology, 12,* 127–133.

Terman, L. M. (1925). *Genetic studies of genius* (Vol. 1). Stanford, CA: Stanford University Press.

Thorndike, R. L., & Hagen, E. P. (1986). *Measurement and evaluation in psychology and education* (4th ed.). New York: Macmillan.

Thorndike, R. L., & Hagen, E. P. (1993). *The cognitive abilities test* (Form 5). Chicago: Riverside.

Thorndike, R. L., & Hagen, E. P., & Sattler, J. M. (1986). *Stanford-Binet intelligence scale* (4th ed.). Chicago: Riverside.

U.S. Commissioner of Education (1972). *Education of the gifted and talented* (Report to the Congress). Washington, DC: U.S. Government Printing Office.

Wechsler, D. (1991). *Manual for the Wechsler Intelligence Scale for Children—third edition (WISC-III).* San Antonio, TX: The Psychological Corporation.

Wiggins, G. P. (1993). *Assessing student performance.* San Francisco: Jossey-Bass.

PART III

Instructional Models and Practices

Part III considers various ways the educational needs of gifted youngsters may be addressed. There is an array of programs and practices. Enrichment programs allow students to broaden their school experiences by pursuing topics in greater depth or by studying topics not offered at all in the regular curriculum. Acceleration programs permit students to progress through material at faster rates or at younger ages than is conventional. Selection of program options—always—should be based first on the needs of students, second on administrative convenience.

In Chapter 9 Shirley W. Schiever and C. June Maker note that *enrichment* can refer to program delivery services, such as Saturday classes or resource room (pull-out) programs, or to the curriculum, which may stress, for example, thinking processes, academic content, or the creation of products. *Acceleration,* too, can refer to either the form of service, such as grade skipping or early admission to kindergarten or college, or the curriculum content. Most acceleration plans provide only an advanced curriculum, not a differentiated one. A sensible program will include both, according to student characteristics and needs. The authors use catastrophe theory to describe how a new state—qualitatively different curriculum—appears as a product of enrichment and acceleration efforts. Their Spiral Model of Thinking offers a structure for integrating enrichment and acceleration principles into curriculum for the gifted.

Looking at curriculum matters, Joyce VanTassel-Baska in Chapter 10 argues that gifted programs should be less process–product oriented, and more focused on rich content knowledge—organized around "systems of thought and great ideas." She supports an Integrated Curriculum Model (ICM) that draws the best from individual curriculum models, specifically mentioning Joseph Renzulli's Schoolwide Enrichment Model (Chapter 11), Talent Search approaches (Chapters 12 and 13), Talents Unlimited (Chapter 26), and others. Three components of the author's ICM thus include advanced content knowledge, thinking skills, and a focus on "major issues, themes, and ideas." VanTassel-Baska also describes the translation of ICM into her successful National Language Arts Curriculum Project and National Science Curriculum Project for High Ability Learners. The author's ideas and efforts square well with current interest in developing the talents of all children.

In Chapter 11, Joseph S. Renzulli and Sally M. Reis present the *Schoolwide Enrichment Model* (SEM), which incorporates Renzulli's earlier *Enrichment Triad Model.* As two central features, the SEM brings enrichment activities into the regular classroom for all students, and identifies the most able 15 to 20 percent of the students for a talent pool. Talent Pool students, and other students who show motivation and creativity, volunteer for independent research projects. The authors review new elements of SEM, such as enrichment clusters and the continuum of special services (e.g., counseling or assistance with projects), which promote talent development for all students. Renzulli and Reis cap their chapter with summaries of curriculum modification techniques and enrichment learning and teaching.

Camilla P. Benbow and David Lubinski in Chapter 12 present the Study of Mathematically Precocious Youth (SMPY), which includes (1) identifying and providing programs and services to intellectually talented students, typically beginning at grade 7, and (2) conducting a long-term study of the educational and career development of past SMPY participants. The authors argue that gifted students are intellectually precocious; therefore, acceleration is the best curricular practice for them. SMPY is said to be supported by the theory of work adjustment, which stresses accommodating both a person's skills and personal preferences.

The major spinoff from the original math-only SMPY program is the equally successful Talent Search programs. Like SMPY, Talent Search typically emphasizes summer short courses for gifted junior high school students, but in a potpourri of verbal and math/science areas. In Chapter 13 Susan G. Assouline and Ann Lupkowski-Shoplik describe the above-level testing used to identify junior high school participants, as well as the testing used to identify elementary school students for the newest version of Talent Search: Elementary Talent Search. The authors also summarize the many doors of opportunity that open to both junior high and elementary Talent Search participants.

Paula Olszewski-Kubilius in Chapter 14 explains that summer, Saturday, and other types of precollege programs and competitions provide suitable learning experiences for gifted students. Such programs offer high-level accelerated courses, opportunities for in-depth study, or introductions to several subject areas. Benefits include social support from gifted peers, better self-concepts, stronger feelings of involvement, improved study skills and independence, increased academic skills, and sometimes college credit for high school and even middle school students. Research by Olszewski-Kubilius and others indicates that accelerated summer math classes lead gifted girls to continue to take advanced math and science courses. The authors note two problematic issues: overlap with regular school curricula and limited access to the programs due to location or cost.

In Chapter 15 John F. Feldhusen raises our eyebrows by recommending that, at the secondary level, we discard the term *gifted* and the "gifted program" concept along with it. He argues that talent development for secondary students does not require a "program" but, rather, calls for a diversity of well-selected courses and extra-school experiences. Some examples are honors, AP, and accelerated math classes; concurrent enrollment in college; Saturday and summer programs; working with local drama or historical societies; and counseling. Feldhusen describes Growth Plans, which include identification of talent and a statement of one's experiences, strengths, interests, goals, and planned education. Feldhusen's *Purdue Pyramid* illustrates educational experiences that lead to an understanding of one's talents and a commitment to their development.

Penny Britton Kolloff in Chapter 16 describes a growing strategy for meeting the educational needs of high school students with exceptional math and science abilities. Residential high schools, which have located on college campuses, two former hospitals, and one vacated high school, foster excellence in math and science as well as in communications, art, and sometimes humanities areas. Kolloff describes several specific schools, objective and subjective admission criteria, faculty (who need not be certified teachers), curriculum (including AP courses), and extracurricular activities, and explains why the schools are superbly successful. Currently, just a handful of residential high schools exist, but the concept is a sound and growing one.

In Chapter 17 Lauren A. Sosniak outlines the original purpose, surprising results, and provocative conclusions of the landmark Bloom and Sosniak research on talent development. She begins by asking how individuals talented in sports, art, and academic fields were identified and then helped to grow. In fact, these youth were "discovered" only after they became highly talented; there were few early signs of extraordinary capability. Three phases of learning included an early "romance" with the talent area, strongly rewarded by parents and teachers; followed by a period of developing the technical skills, vocabulary, rules, and logic of the discipline; and finally a stage of intense commitment and work. Throughout, Sosniak stresses the essential social context in the form of strong support by parents, teachers, and society—outside experts, competitive awards, news coverage—rather than any obvious display of early advantage.

We typically think of mentorships as a high school plan—placing the interested student on the job with a local engineer or printer for a few hours per week to learn about the profession and the mentor's skills and lifestyle. In Chapter 18 Donna Rae Clasen and Robert E. Clasen describe how mentorships, ancient in origin, are used effectively with gifted students at elementary and secondary levels. They note criteria for mentors, such as eagerness, sensitivity, and communication and creativity skills; readiness characteristics of the protege, for example, high ability, enthusiasm, and commitment; and how the mentor and mentee should be matched. Clasen and Clasen describe several mentorship programs, how to structure mentorships, and report marvelous benefits, for example, for gifted minority, disadvantaged, and female students.

In Chapter 19 James A. Kulik and Chen-Lin C. Kulik note that, historically, reviews of effects of ability grouping have reflected the philosophy of the times: With the 1920s advent of intelligence testing, ability grouping was seen as valuable; the 1930s' democratic focus on children's feelings led to negative perceptions; in the 1950s the Cold War again promoted ability grouping; but the 1960s' civil rights movement turned attitudes sour. The ethnographic studies of anti–ability grouping leader Jeanie Oakes interpret such grouping as damaging, but the authors and other critics disagree. Statistical regression research on tracking is intricate and also open to interpretation. The Kuliks conclude from meta-analyses that ability grouping without changes in curriculum may help little but that grouping with enrichment and acceleration is beneficial.

In Chapter 20 Ann Robinson takes issue with claims (e.g., by Robert Slavin) that cooperative learning helps all students with achievement, social skills, and academic motivation. Robinson notes that effects on gifted students have been ignored; gifted students do not prefer cooperative learning over individualistic learning; they often wind up as tutors; "free riders" produce "sucker effects" in high-ability group leaders; and, importantly, gifted students miss acceleration and enrichment opportunities that better match their abilities. In one study, advocates of gifted education were not enthusiastic about mixed-ability cooperative learning groups but favored the use of such groups within ability levels. Robinson also notes complications in assessing results of cooperative learning; for example, group performances overestimate the accomplishments of individuals.

The final chapter in Part III, Chapter 21 by James H. Borland, addresses a too-often ignored component of gifted education—program evaluation, which can provide answers to questions as elementary as "Do these programs work?" and is essential for program improvement. Evaluation, notes Borland, has been variously conceived as judgmental, descriptive, or improvement-oriented. He points out subtle functions of evaluation, such as sociopolitical ones aimed only at raising the program's stature. The author describes common evaluation problems—for example, ambiguous goals (e.g., "to create leaders"), lack of suitable tests, ceiling effects, and inappropriate comparison norms. Outside evaluators are specialists who bring objectivity, says Borland, but have limited inside knowledge. The author describes a four-step evaluation procedure that requires no psychometric training. He also recommends authentic assessment centered on student products.

9

Enrichment and Acceleration: An Overview and New Directions

SHIRLEY W. SCHIEVER, *Tucson Unified School District, Tucson, Arizona*
C. JUNE MAKER, *University of Arizona*

The question "Is this an enrichment or an acceleration program?" is indicative of two problems associated with these terms. First, an implication is made that no program could be both enriched and accelerated, that one mode must be chosen and adhered to, and that never the twain shall meet. Second, referring to enrichment or acceleration programs creates confusion. Does *enrichment* refer to the curriculum or to the service delivery of the program? Does an acceleration program deliver an accelerated curriculum, or does it provide for the (grade) acceleration of students? The purpose of this chapter is to clarify the existing confusion and to make a case for the complementary nature of enrichment and acceleration and the need to include both in curriculum for gifted students. To this end, we will provide a brief overview of enrichment and acceleration practices, offer an application of catastrophe theory to curriculum for the gifted, and present a model of thinking as a structure for developing and examining curricula.

Enrichment

The term *enrichment* is used to refer to curriculum as well as program delivery services. *Enriched curriculum* refers to richer, more varied educational experiences, a curriculum that has been modified or added to in some way (Davis & Rimm, 1994; Howley, Howley, & Pendarvis, 1986). These modifications or additions may be in content or teaching strategies, and ideally they are based on the characteristics of the learners for whom they are designed.

An enrichment program goal is to offer students curriculum that is greater in depth or breadth than that generally provided. After-school or Saturday classes, resource rooms, additions to regular classroom curriculum, or special interest clubs may be used as ways to implement an enrichment program. The key element for an enrichment program should be a systematic plan for extended student learning.

Howley, Howley, and Pendarvis (1986) describe three approaches to enrichment: process oriented, content oriented, and product oriented. Each of these approaches will be considered briefly as it applies to curriculum.

The *process-oriented* approach to enrichment is designed to develop students' higher mental processes and, in some cases, their creative production as well. Students usually are taught the steps or components of one or more models, such as Bloom's Taxonomy of Cognitive Objectives (Bloom, Englehart, Furst, Hill, & Krathwohl, 1956); Creative Problem Solving (Parnes, 1981); or the Structure of Intellect (Guilford, 1967), and are required or encouraged to apply the focus skills through using learning centers, engaging in discussions, and/or conducting independent studies on topics of interest to them.

One concern regarding this approach is that frequently the thinking processes are taught and/or practiced in isolation from content, or subject matter. The resulting fragmentation is not likely to promote transfer of the higher thinking skills to other content areas or to daily problems or situations. Many times, games that require strategic planning or problem solving are used to "teach thinking." However, thinking processes are best taught and practiced using substantive content. If students are expected to think, they need something to think *about.*

Content-oriented approaches to enrichment stress the presentation of a particular content area. Generally, the curriculum for mathematics, science, language arts, or the social sciences is treated with a greater breadth and depth than is possible in the regular curriculum. Offerings may be in the form of mini-courses, museum and science center programs, college options for precollege students, and mentorships (Howley et al., 1986). For example, at the elementary level students might be offered a mini-course in prealgebra; at the middle school level students could be offered a mentorship with an astronomer; or at the high school level students might enroll in Advanced Placement Biology, Calculus, Chemistry, English, or American History, or in classes held on a college campus. AP classes also are considered to be a content acceleration method.

The disadvantage of mini-courses and special programs is that usually the enrichment is separated from the curriculum of the regular classroom. This violates developmental and curricular principles. From a developmental standpoint, learning experiences should be sequential if skills and the information base are to develop in a logical progression and rest on a solid foundation. Such detached offerings also violate the curriculum principle of *organization for learning value* (Maker, 1982a, 1982b; Maker & Nielson, 1996); that is, all or major portions of instruction and learning experiences should be organized around basic concepts or abstract generalizations that enable students to learn efficiently and to see the interconnectedness among concepts and disciplines.

Product-oriented enrichment programs emphasize primarily the *result* or *product* of instruction rather than the content or processes involved. Products may be tangible, such as a report, painting, novel, or presentation, or intangible, such as improved mental health (Howley et al., 1986) or coping skills. Commonly, enrichment programs purportedly emphasize processes (higher levels of thinking) but in reality process instruction is directed toward demonstrating the processes learned by developing products. This situation may result from the pressure exerted on teacher and student alike to "show" what happens in the program for the gifted—that is, to produce evidence that learning is occurring and that it *is* different from regular class activities.

A criticism of product-oriented enrichment is that frequently it results in a "make it and take it" system, in which students churn out products without establishing a knowledge base or striving for accuracy and excellence in the product. Quantity becomes the yardstick rather than quality. Such situations represent a lack of understanding of the necessity for, and role of, process, content, *and* product in curriculum enrichment for gifted students.

Certain models or approaches to enrichment are comprehensive, integrating content, process, and product orientations. These include the Schoolwide Enrichment Model (Renzulli & Reis, 1985; see Chapter 11 in this volume) and the Autonomous Learner Model (Betts, 1985). Other models include Group Investigations (Sharan & Sharan, 1992) and Problem-Based Learning (Stepien, Gallagher, & Workman, 1993). Although an approach such as Problem-Based Learning may at first seem to be a content model, much more is involved. Students are presented with complex, real-life problems and are expected to solve them using the methods and thinking processes of professionals who grapple with these types of "ill-structured" problems on a daily basis. Processes and products different from the regular curriculum are natural outcomes of the focus on realistic interdisciplinary situations. Adopting approaches in which the three dimensions of content, process, and product are integrated or making a conscious effort to combine methods from the three orientations will minimize criticism and increase the likelihood that comprehensive enrichments will occur.

Research on Enrichment

Because so many varied approaches are labeled "enrichment," research on this general practice is difficult to summarize. However, one available body of research provides strong support for the practice. Because the debate on ability grouping has continued for many years and has become somewhat heated, several meta-analyses of research and best-evidence syntheses have been conducted in an attempt to bring a scientific perspective to these arguments. The research indicates clearly that programs in which all ability groups follow the same curriculum have little or no effect on student achievement, whereas grouping programs that involve a more substantial adjustment of curriculum to ability have clear positive effects on children (Kulik, 1992; see Chapter 19 by Kulik and Kulik in this volume). Rogers (1991) concluded that ability grouping for curriculum extension in a pullout program produces an academic effect size of .65 (.30 is considered substantial), which is reflected in general achievement, critical thinking, and creativity; and Kulik (1992) reported that talented students from enriched classes "outperform initially equivalent students from conventional classes by 4 to 5 months on grade equivalent scales" (p. v).

Evidence for the success of enrichment practices also can be found in research on individual models and approaches advocated for use with gifted students. Reviews of several of these models can be found in Maker and Nielson (1995).

Acceleration

The term *acceleration* commonly is used to denote models of both service delivery and curriculum delivery. Acceleration as a service delivery model includes early entrance to kindergarten or to college; grade skipping; or part-time grade acceleration, in which a student enters a higher grade level for part of the school day to receive advanced instruction in one or more content areas. Service delivery acceleration offers standard curricular experiences to students at a younger-than-usual age or a lower-than-usual grade level. Acceleration as a curriculum model involves speeding up the pace at which material is presented and/or expected to be mastered. Such acceleration may occur in a regular classroom, in a resource room, or in special classes. It may take the form of telescoping, whereby students complete two or more years' work in one year, or self-paced studies. Each type of acceleration has its advantages and its disadvantages.

Early entrance to kindergarten or first grade allows children who are ready for the academic rigors and structure of school to encounter learning that may be challenging. Early entrance also allows students to complete schooling at a relatively young age, leaving more time for career and professional development. However, early entrance may tax the physical maturity of some children. They may tire before older students or may experience frustration with the level of their psychomotor development. That is, their fine motor coordination may be underdeveloped by kindergarten standards, and they may have difficulty manipulating crayons or pencils. Additionally, this placement does not provide intellectual peers for the gifted child; average five-year-old children do not think in the same ways or about the same topics as gifted four-year-old children. Early entrance to college usually holds fewer perils than early entrance to kindergarten, unless the gifted students hope to socialize with college students of normal college age. Even then, the intellectual stimulation and challenges of good college courses may override this disappointment.

Full-time grade acceleration (grade skipping) is an economical way to provide for gifted students. For some students, usually those in the primary grades, parents and students may find grade skipping to offer sufficient challenges and therefore to be a viable placement. However, grade skipping may put gifted students at a maturational disadvantage similar to that of the young kindergartner. This disadvantage becomes more pronounced during the middle and high school years, when physical maturation determines athletic prowess and influences heavily an individual's self-confidence.

Acceleration as a service delivery model also fails to provide a differentiated curriculum for gifted learners. Students receive instruction and have learning experiences that are designed for average students who are older than the gifted students, but the curriculum is not changed to match the needs of the gifted. The pace and content remain unchanged; the learner merely experiences them at an earlier age than usual.

Telescoping curriculum content so that gifted students may cover more material in less time and self-paced learning are types of curriculum acceleration. Bright students may master material rapidly and feel good about their accomplishments in this type of acceleration, and it is an economical plan. Telescoping and content acceleration generally present more problems to teachers and administrators than to students. Teachers need the requisite skills and time to telescope curriculum, and self-paced content acceleration for individual students also requires planning time and special management techniques.

Like acceleration as a service delivery model, acceleration as a curriculum model offers "the same but sooner and/or faster" to gifted students. The content, learning processes, and expected products remain the same for students, whether they are gifted or not; only the onset and pace change.

Research on Acceleration

Researchers have studied acceleration of the various types and at different grade levels, and generally report academic achievement and social adjustment equal to or better than that of nonaccelerated, similar-ability peers, with no discernible negative effects from the acceleration. Kulik (1992), for instance, concluded from his meta-analyses of research that "talented students from accelerated classes outperform non-accelerates of the same age and IQ by almost one full year on achievement tests" (p. v). Other reported advantages of acceleration include (1) improved motivation, confidence, and scholarship; (2) prevention of lazy mental habits; (3) early completion of professional training; and (4) reduction of the cost of education (VanTassel-Baska, 1986).

In spite of evidence supporting the efficacy of acceleration for gifted students, widespread resistance to the concept and practice exists. The current organizational structure of most schools is geared to average students, with few provisions for the gifted; teachers and administrators are reluctant to allow or create variances for individual students. Service delivery acceleration and individually paced learning also challenge the purpose of school in terms of the democratic ideal and the concept of socialization with age peers. Additionally, acceleration as it has been practiced frequently has meant only covering more material faster, and the belief exists that acceleration is responsible for social maladjustment or that it creates skill gaps in core areas (VanTassel-Baska, 1986).

Enrichment and Acceleration as Complementary Program Components

Combining or integrating enrichment and acceleration for gifted students is not a radical or a revolutionary idea. In practice, meeting the needs of gifted students as determined by their learning characteristics requires that abstract and complex concepts be taught (enrichment) and that students proceed at a pace more rapid than that of the average learner (acceleration). Additionally, support for such integration may be found in the literature. Fox (1979) believes that acceleration means the adjustment of learning time to meet student capabilities and this adjustment will lead to higher levels of abstraction, more creative thinking, and mastery of more difficult content. VanTassel-Baska (1981) has stated that the term *enrichment* has no meaning for the gifted unless it is inextricably bound to good acceleration practices. Davis and Rimm (1994), in asking whether a special math, computer, or foreign language class in the elementary school is considered enrichment or acceleration, implied that in many cases the dichotomy is a false one.

As evidenced by practice and the literature, enrichment and acceleration are complementary components of comprehensive curriculum for gifted learners. In the remainder of this chapter, using the concept of catastrophe theory as rationale and organizer, we will make a case for the necessity of including both enrichment and acceleration components in curriculum for gifted students.

Catastrophe Theory and Curriculum for Gifted Students

As explained by Berliner (1986), catastrophe theory is a mathematical system to account for abrupt changes in the nature of objects. It was developed by René Thom, a topological mathematician, and first published in 1968 in France. The theory may be applied to phenomena that are discontinuous, sudden, and unpredictable, wherein change occurs imperceptibly or gradually to a point and then suddenly a new state occurs. The simplest example from the physical world is the change of water into steam. As water heats, at some point (depending on the interaction of temperature, volume, pressure, and chemical particles), the water changes from liquid to gas. More heat has become the agent of a qualitative change; an interaction among factors has occurred. In Berliner's (1986) words, "more leads to different" (p. 34).

When applying catastrophe theory to curriculum, the critical factors are curriculum content, process, and product, along with acceleration and enrichment. Curriculum content, processes, and products must be accelerated and enriched to that point at which *more* becomes *different.* This is the point when an interaction occurs; the curriculum becomes *qualitatively differentiated.*

One recommended modification to the *content* of curriculum for gifted students is an increase in the level of abstractness (Maker, 1982a; Maker & Nielson, 1996). The concepts selected to be taught should be abstract rather than concrete; thus, they should be concepts such as culture, values, and mathematical patterns. Choosing abstract concepts *enriches* the curriculum, but the presentation and exploration of the concepts also must be *accelerated* if the dynamic of catastrophe theory is to be activated, if the curriculum is to become qualitatively different. For example, a regular sixth-grade curriculum might include study of the Eastern Hemisphere. Gifted students need to establish a factual information base, just as others do. However, gifted students should spend the majority of their time dealing with abstract concepts such as culture, cause–effect relationships, or political and economic systems. The abstractness of the content provides a type of enrichment, as this is "beyond" the regular curriculum, but the pace of presentation also must be accelerated.

The *processes* of instruction and learning included in curriculum for gifted students should be modified in a variety of ways, including an emphasis on higher levels of thinking (Maker, 1982a; Maker & Nielson, 1996). For example, gifted students should spend the majority of their time critically examining, synthesizing, and evaluating ideas, rather than memorizing and applying information and procedures. Focusing on higher thought processes enriches the curriculum. These skills should be taught and practiced at an accelerated rate—at younger-than-usual ages, and with instruction paced more rapidly than normal.

Student products reflect content learned and processes engaged in before and during the creation of the product. Products of gifted students should demonstrate the results of enrichment and acceleration of content and process instruction by the sophistication of the concepts included and the presentation, form, or format of the finished product. For example, average fourth-grade students, on completion of a unit of study on their state of residence, might submit reports of factual information about the state, and include a map and drawings of the state flag, flower, and bird. A more abstract approach suitable for gifted fourth-grade students might focus on the effects of political forces on their state's government and economic climate. After examining and evaluating these forces, these students might develop and give presentations to state legislators regarding the effect of, for example, underfunding educational programs on the attraction of new industry to the state.

Applying catastrophe theory to the acceleration and enrichment of the content, processes, and products of curriculum for gifted students provides a conceptual framework for differentiating such curriculum. The critical point is that all three factors, content, process, and product, must be both enriched *and* accelerated. Without both enrichment and acceleration, more is simply more; the point of the interaction that produces a qualitative difference is not reached. Acceleration and enrichment are necessary but not sufficient factors in developing and presenting curriculum to gifted learners. The catastrophic change that produces differentiated curriculum occurs only when all factors are present to a sufficient degree.

The Spiral Model of Thinking

Schiever (1990) developed a model of thinking that provides a framework within which to examine the role of acceleration and enrichment in curriculum development. A brief explanation of the Spiral Model of Thinking follows.

Schiever envisions thinking skills and the development of thinking as a spiraling continuum of skills, maturation, and experiences. The continuum of thought originates with *enabling skills* and includes *developmental processes, complex thinking strategies,* and *solving undefined or real-life problems.*

In the Spiral Model, the most basic building blocks of cognition are the enabling skills. These skills drive and make possible all thinking; they feed directly into the developmental processes but are present in complex thinking strategies and in solving undefined or real-life problems. Although all of the enabling skills are basic and relatively simple, some are more complex than others. For example, encoding and remembering are relatively simple cognitive operations; determining relevance and comparing and contrasting are more complex skills. The enabling skills vary depending on the task at hand or the problem to be solved, as well as the maturity and cognitive sophistication of the thinker. For example, comparing and contrasting concrete objects, such as buttons, is a lower level operation than comparing and contrasting thought systems.

The developmental processes vary from simple to complex—*classification, concept development, deriving principles, drawing conclusions,* and *making generalizations* (see Figure 9.1). Any of the developmental processes may be transformed and applied to complex thinking tasks *at the level of the thinker's maturity and experience.* For example, young children may classify blocks according to shape and/or color to make a pattern (solve a defined problem). As thinkers mature and incorporate more experiences into their cognitive bank, they are able to, for example, classify increasingly abstract and complex ideas. They move from concrete (objects and experiences) to high levels of abstraction and complexity (concepts such as *love, altruism,* or *infinity*).

The developmental processes spiral through developmental stages and life experiences, gradually spiraling upward toward transformation and application. The developmental processes are transformed—that is, adapted selectively to the situation at hand and then applied to the complex thinking strategies of (1) *defined problem solving,* (2) *decision making,* (3) *critical thinking,* (4) *creative/productive thinking,* and (5) *evaluation.* The complex thinking strategies are interrelated and make possible the solving of undefined or real-life problems (see Figure 9.1), which Schiever sees as the ultimate goal of all formal and informal cognitive instruction and development.

Curriculum for the Gifted

Experts in the field (e.g., Clark, 1988; Kaplan, 1979; Maker, 1982a) agree that curriculum for gifted students should be differentiated from that offered other students, according to the characteristics and needs of the gifted. A number of models and checklists have been developed as ways to approach developing such differentiated curricula (Feldhusen & Wyman, 1980; Kaplan, 1974; Maker, 1982a; Sato & Johnson, 1978). On the basis of current research, preferred practices, a reconceptualization of the thinking process, and catastrophe theory, we offer a new approach. This approach illustrates the interdependent and interactive nature and roles of enrichment and acceleration in developing curricula for gifted students.

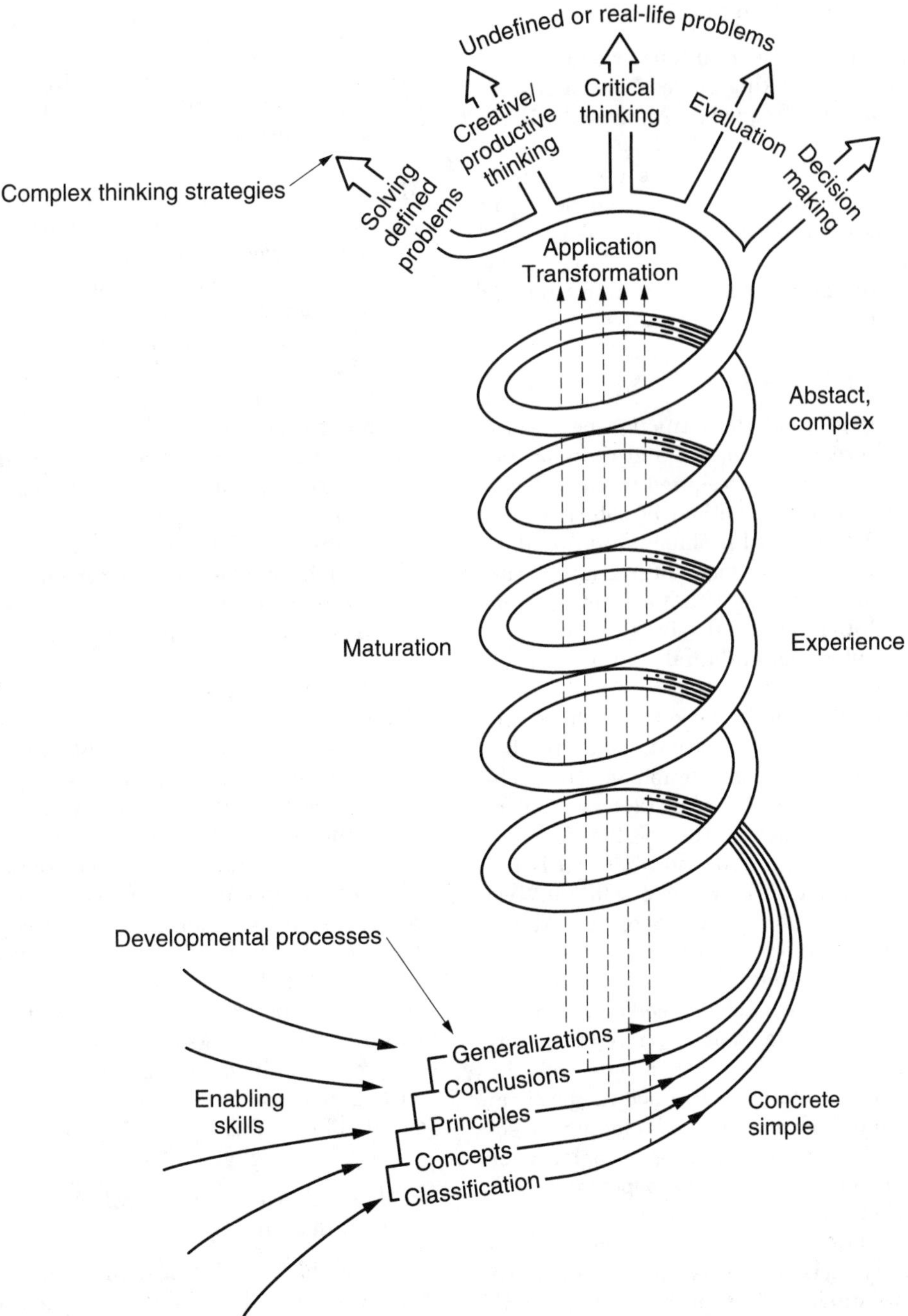

Figure 9.1 Spiral model of thinking.

Problem Solving and the Curriculum

As educators focus more intensely on thinking skills and the thinking process, problem solving is mentioned frequently. Anderson's (1980) definition of problem solving as any goal-directed sequence of cognitive operations is very broad, but he is not alone in believing that thinking *is* problem solving. This belief leads to a natural progression of examining and/or planning curriculum for gifted students from a problem-solving perspective.

Types of Problems

Getzels (1964) made a distinction between a *presented problem situation* and a *discovered problem situation*. A presented problem has a known formulation, method of solution, and solution. A discovered problem situation does not yet have a known formulation, and therefore has no known method of solution and no known solution. On the basis of this concept, Getzels and Csikszentmihalyi (1967) developed a conceptual distinction between types of problems. According to these researchers, one can distinguish problem situations on the basis of (1) how clearly and completely the problem is stated at the beginning, (2) how much of the method for reaching the solution is available to the solver, and (3) how general is the agreement about an acceptable solution. Two ends of a continuum can be identified. At one end is a situation in which the problem, method, and solution are known to the presenter. The problem solver needs only to employ the appropriate steps to arrive at the correct solution. At the other end of the continuum is a situation in which the problem is not formulated, and no known method of solution or solution exists. Most problems, or tasks and projects in people's personal and professional lives, are of the latter type.

Maker (1986) expanded the model produced by Getzels and Csikszentmihalyi (1967, p. 81) to produce four problem types, and Schiever (1990) identified a fifth type. These problem types differ in what is known both to the problem presenter and the problem solver:

I. The problem and the method of solution are known to the problem presenter and the problem solver, but the solution is known only to the problem presenter.

II. The problem is known by the presenter and the solver, but the method of solution and solution are known only to the presenter.

III. The problem is known to the presenter and the solver, more than one method may be used to solve the problem, and the solution or range of solutions is known only to the presenter.

IV. The problem is known to the presenter and the solver, but the method and the solution are unknown to both the presenter and the solver.

V. The problem is unknown or undefined, and the method and the solution are unknown to both the presenter and the solver (see Table 9.1). In the classroom setting, problems of this type may be presented so that students use skills necessary to solve real-life problems.

School learning experiences typically consist of primarily Type I problems, wherein students are presented a clearly defined problem (such as in math) and taught the steps necessary to reach a solution. However, if one believes that the goal of curricula is to prepare students to be adults who cope successfully with both personal and career problems, curricula also must include solving problems of Types II, III, IV, and V if the necessary skills are to be taught and practiced. If gifted students are to become leaders and professionals with the capabilities society wants and needs, and/or self-fulfilled adults, their school experiences must prepare them to be effective solvers of undefined, real-life problems.

Problem Solving, The Spiral Model, and Curriculum

Viewing the Spiral Model in terms of problem types provides a useful approach to curriculum development. The developmental processes each can be considered in light of problem types; that is, in what ways can, for example, classification be taught as a Type I, II, III, IV, or V problem? Curriculum content provides the context for teaching the develop-

Table 9.1
Types of Problem Situations

	Problem		*Method*		*Solution*	
Type	*Presenter*	*Solver*	*Presenter*	*Solver*	*Presenter*	*Solver*
I	K	K	K	K	K	U
II	K	K	K	U	K	U
III	K	K	R	U	R	U
IV	K	K	U	U	U	U
V	U	U	U	U	U	U

Source: Adapted with permission from *The Creative Vision* by J. W. Getzels and M. Csikszentmihalyi, 1976, page 80, Table 6.1. Copyright © 1976 by John Wiley & Sons, New York.

Note: K = Known, U = Unknown, R = Range.

mental processes within the problem-solving perspective. The following examples are based on the belief that requiring students to memorize the results of other people's thinking is not a preferred teaching practice. Rather, students should be allowed and enabled to develop their own classification categories, concept delineations, principles, conclusions, and generalizations.

A social studies curriculum designed to teach the three key concepts of *difference, interdependence,* and *societal control* (Taba, Durkin, Fraenkel, and McNaughton, 1971) will be used to illustrate how content and process (thinking skills) can be taught within a problem solving framework. Content objectives for the concept *differences* in Grade 1 encompass differences in (1) family composition and size, (2) family responsibility, and (3) family lifestyle. The teaching of these dimensions of *difference* can be organized according to the developmental processes and the problem types. For example, to teach the skill of classification as a Type I problem in the context of *differences,* the teacher might ask students to find out how many children are in each family represented in the classroom. The families then could be classified according to teacher-provided categories related to size. This classification experience is within the parameters provided by the teacher and serves primarily as a foundation for the development of the concept of *differences.* The students would be solving a defined problem (a complex thinking strategy), but the Type I structure dictates the low level of the classification behaviors and the limitations on the use of other developmental processes or complex thinking strategies. Increasing the pace (acceleration) of experiences will not result in differentiated curriculum, since neither content nor processes are enriched.

A Type II activity might require students to classify families according to whether they are the same or different from the (individual) student's family, according to teacher-provided criteria. The problem again is defined by the teacher and known to him or her and the students, but only the teacher would know how the students should structure and accomplish classification if they were to reach the preferred (or "right") solution. For example, categories such as type of pet(s), language(s) spoken, or length of time living in the current house might be established. The teacher could collect and record the necessary data on the chalkboard, then ask students individually or in small groups to put their families in the appropriate categories. Type II structure keeps the classification behaviors at a relatively low level, because the criteria and categories are provided by the teacher. However, some low-level evaluation and decision making may be required, such as whether to count a parent's knowledge of a language or a student's after-school Hebrew lessons as a second (or third) language. Again, students have solved a defined problem and may have used developmental processes and complex thinking strategies infrequently and at a low level. Neither content nor processes have been enriched, so acceleration will not result in differentiated curriculum.

The Type III problem might be presented in this way: Group the families represented in our class into three groups that are equal or nearly equal in size. The problem is stated, but a range of possible methods and solutions exists. Students would evaluate and make decisions regarding categories and classification, develop concepts, and reach conclusions. Content and processes are enriched in this example, so acceleration of pacing would result in differentiation.

The Type IV problem might be defined through a question such as, "How can we find and group the differences between our families?" The problem would be known to teacher and students, but the method and solution would be unknown and probably would evolve as the process unfolded. Students must generalize about observed differences between families; decide on which differences they will focus; and determine categories and levels of differentiation (e.g., by number in family, such as 2, 3, or 4, or small [2–3], medium [4–6], and large [7 or more]). Because information must be processed prior to classification, the classification behaviors will be at a higher level of abstraction than for Types I and II, and more complex categories are likely to be developed. In this example, content and processes are enriched. If accelerated pacing is included, as well as enriched and accelerated student products, the interaction that produces a differentiated curriculum may be expected to occur.

The key question for a Type V classification activity could be, "In what ways might families be grouped, compared, or contrasted?" Students therefore would need to define the problem in some way that gives them a direction in which to move toward solution. Conceivably, students could engage in most or all of the developmental processes and complex thinking strategies as they solved the problem. For example, students would have to (1) make decisions and arrive at conclusions before they gathered data, (2) examine the data critically and evaluate the data, (3) derive the principles of *familyness,* and (4) generalize from their sample to families in general. Drawing on their individual concepts of *family* and *different,* students might attempt to derive the principles that would enable them to select (draw conclusions, make decisions) and convey the essence of what they had generalized about familial differences. The developmental processes would be transformed as needed to fit the content and the task to be performed. As in the Type IV task, when families are classified within this activity, the levels of thinking will reflect the prior processing of information. The structure of this Type V problem may lead to the discovery and processing of information related to differences between family responsibilities and lifestyles (other learning objectives for this unit). As with the Type IV problem, curriculum content and processes have been enriched. Accelerated pacing and enriched and accelerated products may be expected to result in qualitatively different learning experiences.

At the middle school or junior high level, the context for expanding the concept of differences is the United States—its people and development (Taba et al., 1971). Content objectives include *differences* in (1) regional economics and points of view and (2) goals, such differences resulting in conflicts.

Using a Type I problem and the classification process, students might be required to learn about and classify geographic regions of the United States according to economic characteristics or the industry base, as defined by the teacher. The problem and its solution are well defined, and enabling skills and a low level of classification behavior are the primary cognitive requirements. In this example, neither the processes nor the content of the curriculum have been enriched.

A Type II problem might require students to group geographic regions of the United States according to their predominant political allegiance. The students would have to ascertain how to determine predominant political allegiance and classify the regions on the basis of existing political parties, all of which would be known to the teacher. Some low-level decisions (complex thinking strategy) might be required for regions without a clear or decisive political leaning, but most of the cognition would consist of enabling skills and low-level classification behaviors. Neither content nor processes would be enriched.

A Type III problem might consist of asking students to identify characteristics of subregions of their county. On the basis of these characteristics, small groups could make defensible predictions of conflict or harmony during the next 25 years. This task would require drawing conclusions, making generalizations, evaluating, thinking critically, and making decisions. Curriculum content and process would be enriched and accelerated in terms of grade level.

In a Type IV problem, students could be asked to determine differences among teacher-identified regions and project future areas of possible conflict based on the differences. In this approach, the problem is defined (by the teacher), but a variety of methods and solutions are open to students. Additionally, more content objectives are likely to be met as students look for regional characteristics that may aid them in finding similarities. Their approach will be more open, and more content necessarily will be included. During the solution of this problem, students will develop concepts related to regional differences (which may be either concrete or abstract), derive principles about causes of conflict (an abstract concept), draw conclusions about the effects of differences (abstract concept), and generalize (higher level thinking) about differences, regions, and conflict. In solving this problem, students also will be required to transform and apply information and skills to evaluate, make decisions, engage in critical and creative thinking, and solve defined subproblems. The structure of this activity not only teaches the content objective (the concept), but also incorporates meaningful experience with higher levels of thinking. Content and processes are enriched and accelerated in terms of level of abstractness for grade level.

Using a Type V situation, in which the problem definition is unknown to both the teacher and the students, a teacher might direct students to explore regional points of view related to economics (two abstract concepts). Students first would need to define the problem (i.e., what is a region, which regions to focus on). This definition would require classification of regional characteristics and elements, derivation of the principles underlying regional delineations, generalizing about many regions from one or a few, drawing conclusions about specific regions, and making decisions about the focal points for the investigation. The problem solutions require intricate interplay of the developmental processes and complex thinking strategies. The concept will have been taught at a high level of abstractness, and the cognition therefore will be at a correspondingly complex and abstract level. Curriculum content and process have been enriched and accelerated in terms of abstractness for grade level.

Curriculum Development

Each developmental process (classification, concept development, deriving principles, drawing conclusions, and making generalizations) may be examined and taught through superimposing the concept of problem type on the skill in the context of content to be learned, and then structuring learning experiences accordingly. The purpose of the five problem types is to suggest a way to approach curriculum design. The reader should note that Type V problems necessarily move the thinker to the top of the spiral model, where undefined and real-life problems are found. When Classification and Type V problems intersect, other developmental processes and complex thinking strategies are transformed and applied to the problem. In other words, by definition, Type V problems entail all of the developmental processes, and thus require complex thinking strategies. Classification or any other developmental process may be used or taught in a Type V format, but the skill will not be used in isolation. The interrelatedness of complex cognitive operations is apparent in the above analysis of Type V situations.

Enrichment. Using the Spiral Model/problem-solving approach to plan curriculum enables teachers to examine the thinking processes being taught, practiced, and learned, and facilitates the enrichment of curriculum content. As increasing numbers of Types III, IV, and V problems are planned, thematic organization and more abstract and complex content may be included. By moving away from clearly defined, rote memory, and comprehension-based activities and concept attainment, the progression is naturally toward bigger ideas that are more inclusive and more abstract. For example, if students were to learn about the values of people in different periods of time (Taba et al., 1971) through a variety of independent methods (Type IV), a natural progression would lead toward the causes and effects of those values in the various societies. This progression toward the abstract and complex is natural when the structure for curriculum design incorporates higher levels of thinking and problem solving within the context of the content to be taught and learned.

Acceleration. Acceleration of learning experiences for gifted students must occur in two ways. First, gifted students are developmentally advanced, and the intellectually gifted can process more abstract ideas at an earlier age than other students. This means that a concept of *difference* designed to be taught to eighth-grade students, such as differences in goals that result in conflict (Taba et al., 1971), probably is appropriate for sixth-grade gifted students.

Second, gifted students can move through, or process, information and ideas more quickly than other students. For example, intellectually gifted students not only begin processing abstract concepts such as *conflict* at an earlier age than their age peers, but they also move more quickly through developmental process activities and are able to apply the concept to undefined or real-life problems far sooner than their age-mates (Gallagher & Gallagher, 1994). An instructional unit that might require six weeks for most students not only should be taught earlier and at a higher or more abstract level, but also may be completed by gifted students within three or four weeks.

Level of material and pace of instruction are dimensions of acceleration that mesh with the inclusion of enriched learning within a problem-solving approach to curriculum development. The spiral model of thinking may be used as an infrastructure for acceleration and enrichment of content, process, and product. When these factors are in place, the stage is set for the catastrophic event, the desired change, and the emergence of a qualitatively different curriculum.

Summary

Acceleration and *enrichment* are terms used to describe both curriculum and service delivery models. The primary focus of this chapter is on the curricular aspects of both, and their necessarily complementary nature. Components of curriculum, the content, instructional and learning processes, and expected student products, all must be enriched *and* accelerated. The resulting curriculum is not just enriched, nor is it just accelerated. Through a dynamic interaction of factors, it becomes differentiated for gifted learners.

REFERENCES

Anderson, J. R. (1980). *Cognitive psychology and its implications.* San Francisco: Freeman.

Berliner, D. C. (1986). Catastrophes and interactions: Comments on "the mistaken metaphor." In C. J. Maker (Ed.), *Critical issues in gifted education: Defensible programs for the gifted* (pp. 31–38). Rockville, MD: Aspen.

Betts, G. (1985). *Autonomous learner model for the gifted and talented.* Greeley, CO: Autonomous Learning Publications and Specialists.

Bloom, B. S., Englehart, M. D., Furst, E., Hill, W. H., & Krathwohl, D. R. (1956). *Taxonomy of educational objectives, Handbook I: Cognitive domain.* New York: McKay.

Clark, B. (1988). *Growing up gifted* (3rd ed.). Columbus, OH: Merrill.

Davis, G. A. and Rimm, S. B. (1994). *Education of the gifted and talented* (3rd ed.). Boston: Allyn and Bacon.

Feldhusen, J. F., & Wyman, A. R. (1980). Super Saturday: Design and implementation of Purdue's special program for gifted children. *Gifted Child Quarterly, 24,* 15–21.

Fox, L. H. (1979). Programs for the gifted and talented: An overview. In A. H. Passow (Ed.) *The gifted and the talented* (pp. 104–126). Chicago: National Society for the Study of Education.

Gallagher, J. J. & Gallagher, S. A. (1994). *Teaching the gifted child* (4th ed.). Boston: Allyn and Bacon.

Getzels, J. W. (1964). Creative thinking, problem solving, and instruction. In E. R. Hilgard (Ed.), *Theories of learning and instruction.* NSSE 66th Yearbook (pp. 240–267). Chicago: University of Chicago Press.

Getzels, J. W., & Csikszentmihalyi, M. (1967). Scientific creativity. *Science Journal, 3*(9), 80–84.

Guilford, J. P. (1967). *The nature of human intelligence.* New York: McGraw-Hill.

Howley, A., Howley, C. B., & Pendarvis, E. D. (1986). *Teaching gifted children.* Boston: Little, Brown.

Kaplan, S. N. (1974). *Providing programs for the gifted and talented.* Ventura, CA: Office of the Ventura County Superintendent of Schools.

Kaplan, S. N. (1979). *Inservice training manual: Activities for developing curriculum for the gifted and talented.* Ventura, CA: Office of the Ventura County Superintendent of Schools.

Kulik, J. A. (1992). *An analysis of the research on ability grouping: Historical and contemporary perspectives.* Research-Based Decision Making Series. Storrs, CT: National Research Center on the Gifted and Talented, University of Connecticut.

Maker, C. J. (1982a). *Curriculum development for the gifted.* Austin, TX: Pro-Ed.

Maker, C. J. (1982b). *Teaching models in education of the gifted.* Austin, TX: Pro-Ed.

Maker, C. J. (1986). *Frames of discovery: A process approach to identifying talent in special populations.* Unpublished paper available from author, Department of Special Education and Rehabilitation, University of Arizona, Tucson, AZ 85721.

Maker, C. J., & Nielson, A. B. (1995) *Teaching models in education of the gifted.* Austin, TX: Pro-Ed.

Maker, C. J., & Nielson, A. B. (1996). *Curriculum development in the education of the gifted.* Austin, TX: Pro-Ed.

Parnes, S. J. (1981). CPSI: The general system. In W. B. Barbe & J. S. Renzulli (Eds.). *Psychology and education of the gifted.* New York: Irvington.

Renzuli, J. S., & Reis, S. A. (1985). *The school-wide enrichment model: A comprehensive plan for educational excellence.* Mansfield Center, CT: Creative Learning.

Rogers, K. B. (1991). *The relationship of grouping practices to the education of the gifted and talented learner.* Research-Based Decision Making Series. Storrs, CT: National Research Center on the Gifted and Talented, University of Connecticut.

Sato, I. S., & Johnson, B. (1978). Multifaceted training meets multidimensionally gifted. *Journal of Creative Behavior, 12,* 63–71.

Schiever, S. W. (1990). *A comprehensive approach to teaching thinking.* Boston: Allyn and Bacon.

Sharan, Y., & Sharan, S. (1992). *Expanding cooperative learning through group investigations.* New York: Teachers College Press.

Stepien, W. J., Gallagher, S. A., & Workman, D. (1993). Problem based learning for traditional and interdisciplinary classrooms. *Journal for the Education of the Gifted, 16*(4), 338–357.

Taba, H., Durkin, M.C., Fraenkel, J. R., & McNaughton, A. H. (1971). *A teacher's handbook to elementary social studies: An inductive approach.* Reading, MA: Addison-Wesley.

VanTassel-Baska, J. (1981, December). *The great debates: For acceleration.* Speech presented at the CEC/TAG National Topical Conference on the Gifted and Talented Child, Orlando, Florida.

VanTassel-Baska, J. (1986). Acceleration. In C. J. Maker (Ed.), *Critical issues in gifted education. Defensible programs for the gifted* (pp. 179–196). Austin, TX: Pro-Ed.

10

What Matters in Curriculum for Gifted Learners: Reflections on Theory, Research, and Practice

JOYCE VANTASSEL-BASKA, *College of William and Mary, Williamsburg, Virginia*

How can educators help a gifted student to excel? The answer to this question is a complicated one; much of our research on what has an impact on the lives of gifted individuals relates, for example, to the role of parents (Feldman, 1985; Bloom, 1985), the role of internal factors and significant others (VanTassel-Baska & Olszewski-Kubilius, 1989), the role of crystallizing experiences (Gardner, 1985), and even the role of chance (Tannenbaum, 1983). Yet the quality and character of a school's curriculum are vital ingredients to the eventual realization of a child's capacity. Gifted and talented students, like all students, have the right to a continuity of educational experience that meets their present and future academic needs. When an organized, thoughtful curriculum plan is in place and when that curriculum is supported by articulate, informed educational leadership, the probability of capturing the interest and energy of our ablest young thinkers is markedly enhanced. Certainly an organized curriculum is a key ingredient in the complex blending of circumstance so central to the transformation of a gifted learner's initial capacity for intellectual activity into a mature competence for academic and professional accomplishment.

Several key beliefs and assumptions have guided the thinking of most recent curriculum theory in gifted education (Gallagher, 1985; Maker, 1982; Passow, 1982; VanTassel-Baska, 1993). These beliefs may be stated succinctly as follows:

1. All learners should be provided curriculum opportunities that allow them to attain optimum levels of learning.
2. Gifted learners have different learning needs compared with typical learners. Therefore, curriculum must be adapted or designed to accommodate these needs.
3. The needs of gifted learners cut across cognitive, affective, social, and aesthetic areas of curriculum experiences.
4. Gifted learners are best served by a confluent approach that allows for both accelerated and enriched learning.
5. Curriculum experiences for gifted learners need to be carefully planned, written down, implemented, and evaluated in order to maximize potential effect.

The purpose of this chapter is to present a view of curriculum for the gifted that is consonant with these assumptions and also recognizes key characteristics of the learner, the research and development evidence for curricular approaches in the education of the gifted, and the application of coherent curriculum theory to practice. The Integrated Curriculum Model (ICM) described within the chapter represents a synthesis of several approaches, forged to create greater complementarity in translating appropriate curriculum for the gifted learner into meaningful practice.

Historical Development of Curriculum in Gifted Education

For close to 20 years the field of gifted education has favored a process–product orientation to curriculum. Fueled by the practical application of the Enrichment Triad Model (Renzulli, 1977) in pullout resource classrooms primarily at the elementary level, this approach gained further support as the cognitive science movement developed, calling for higher order thinking skills, relevant real-world products, and emphasis on different modes of thinking (Gardner, 1983; Sternberg, 1985).[1] Maker (1982) viewed curriculum as the use of various instructional models that could be organized to provide for gifted students in any classroom setting. By modifying an instructional model and its components along content, process, and product dimensions, gifted curriculum would result as long as certain differentiating factors were taken into account. Any model of curriculum that followed these early examples of the process–product paradigm tended to gain easy acceptance in the field. The Autonomous Learner Model (Betts, 1991), the Purdue Three-Stage Model (Feldhusen & Kolloff, 1978), and the IPPM (Individualized Programming Planning Model; Treffinger, 1986) all made the underlying assumption that good curriculum for gifted learners was developed on the basis of individual learner interest and emphasized higher order skills used in the service of creating meaningful products.

This dominance in thinking about curriculum for the gifted has limited the development and use of models of curriculum derived from the disciplines of knowledge themselves rather than from educational psychology. Thus, many gifted programs have lacked the rich substance that only the world of content knowledge might bring when linked to important ideas and issues. Ward (1981) pressed for a curriculum framework that would honor the traditional disciplines of study at the same time that it extended ideas about differential education of the gifted. Ward actually sought to provide a meaningful structure to curriculum for the gifted, one that would emphasize systems of thought and great ideas as organizers, rather than emphasize individual skills or topics. Yet Ward's model was conceptually too abstract for easy translation and use by teachers, although several curriculum efforts were spawned using his approach (VanTassel-Baska & Feldhusen, 1981; Ward, 1979).

[1] See Chapter 4 by Sternberg and Chapter 5 by Ramos-Ford and Gardner.

Another approach to curriculum began to find favor in the late 1970s as a reaction against the trivialization of curriculum spawned by the misapplication of process–product models. Like Ward, Stanley's diagnostic-prescriptive content-based approach to curriculum (Stanley, Keating, & Fox, 1974; see also Keating, 1976) was concerned about students' learning important subject matter, but did not advocate radical reorganization of existing school curriculum, merely its speeding up or acceleration for gifted learners. Based on Scholastic Aptitude Test scores derived from national talent searches that identify over 120,000 talented middle school–age students each year, the application of this curriculum approach has been widely implemented in university-based summer and academic year offerings.[2] Begun initially as a fast-paced, credit-producing series of course options primarily in mathematics, the application of this model has now spread to all content areas, with speed of course completion and mastery of course content the major defining emphases, whether credit is subsequently awarded or not. Yet this approach as an option in schools had limited appeal for many school practitioners because it offered nothing new in curriculum substance, only a prescription for flexible pacing of what already existed. The current practice of *curriculum compacting* offers a more limited variation of the central ideas of diagnostic-prescriptive intervention at more discrete levels of classroom work (Reis & Purcell, 1993).

Rationale for an Integrated Curriculum Model

While these approaches have all been used by schools in their programs for the gifted, the emphasis of curriculum intervention has been at the level of program model, not day-to-day classroom practice. It is also fair to say that these approaches to curriculum for the gifted have not sustained an ongoing development of

[2] See Chapter 12 by Benbow and Lubinski and Chapter 13 by Assouline and Lupkowski-Shoplik.

planned curriculum experiences. Rather, they have been interpreted and reinterpreted by a host of practitioners, all with a special interest or passion to incorporate. What the field has lacked is a comprehensive and cohesive curriculum framework sensitive to what good curriculum design contains, that honors the disciplines under study, and sufficiently differentiates for gifted students. Thus it is time to support an integrated model of curriculum for gifted learners, one that draws the best from each curriculum approach already advocated.

There are other important reasons for advocating an integrated model for curriculum for the gifted. One stems from the need to address all salient characteristics of the gifted learner simultaneously, attending to precocity, intensity, and complexity as integrated characteristics representing cognitive and affective dimensions of the learner. Integrating curriculum approaches allows for this broad-based response to student needs. A second reason relates to current delivery models for curriculum. As pullout programs have decreased in number, more gifted students are served in heterogeneous or self-contained settings, contexts where integrated curriculum approaches can work well if applied diligently and systematically. Thus, an integrated curriculum may be thought of as a total curriculum package in an area of learning rather than an "add-on" curriculum.

A third reason for an integrated approach rests with the current research on learning. Studies have documented that better transfer of learning occurs when higher order thinking skills are embedded in subject matter (Perkins & Saloman, 1989), and that teaching concepts of a discipline is a better way to produce long-term learning than teaching facts and rules (Marzano, 1992). Our understanding of creativity also has shifted toward the need for strong subject matter knowledge as a prerequisite (Amabile, 1983).

A fourth reason for using an integrated model for curriculum is related to a clear shift of emphasis in the field from the focus on the individual gifted learner to the process of collective talent development for all learners. As this shift has occurred, the wedding of curriculum principles important for the gifted have been seen as the province of all learners developing talents in both traditional and nontraditional domains, accomplished through employing interdisciplinary, concept-based curriculum, and higher order thinking. This development calls for a close alignment of meaningful subject matter with its higher order manipulation by skills and ideas.

For all of these reasons the integrated curriculum model offers a cogent exemplum for curriculum design and development for gifted learners.

The Integrated Curriculum Model

The theoretical model advocated for use is the Integrated Curriculum Model (ICM) first proposed by this author in 1986 (VanTassel-Baska, 1986) and further explicated in subsequent publications (VanTassel-Baska, 1992, 1993). This model comprises three interrelated curriculum dimensions, each responsive to a very different aspect of the gifted learner. These curriculum dimensions may be thought of as (1) emphasizing advanced content knowledge that frames disciplines of study, (2) providing higher order thinking and processing, and (3) focusing learning experiences around major issues, themes, and ideas that define both real-world applications and theoretical modeling within and across areas of study (see Figure 10.1).

This model synthesizes what I believe are the three best approaches to curriculum development and implementation documented in the literature (Benbow & Stanley, 1983; Maker, 1982; Ward, 1981). The fusion of these approaches is central to the development of coherent curriculum that is responsive to diverse needs of gifted students and yet provides rich challenges for optimal learning.

The Talent Development Approach in Action

The recent interest in talent development for all learners in schools has spawned new curriculum work in the field. Of particular interest has been the adaptation of Gardner's multiple intelligences model to school curriculum (Gardner, 1983). This approach assumes that the majority of children have some talent area

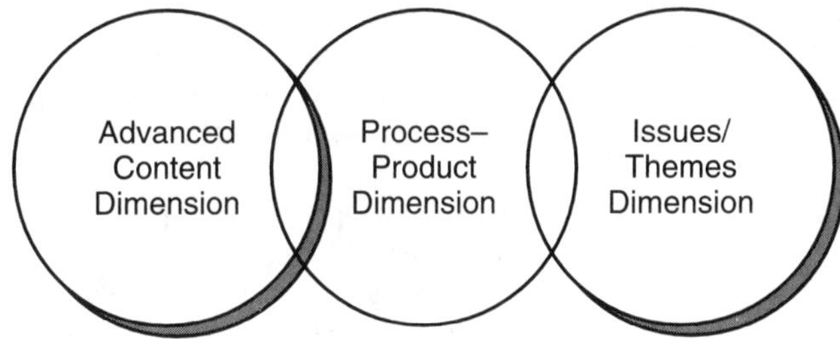

Figure 10.1 The Integrated Curriculum Model for gifted learners.

or intelligence that can be developed through focused curriculum attention. Similar in practice to the Talents Unlimited model developed in the 1970s by Calvin Taylor and continued by Schlichter (see Chapter 26), the talent development model also eschews identification of children as "gifted," but rather favors the use of diagnostic information to determine strengths that can be used to develop an appropriate set of curriculum options. Highly individualized, this approach has been implemented in several school-based settings (e.g., Bolanos, 1991) and has been viewed as a way to focus all schools on the talent development concept. Implications for use of the model in developing validated curriculum units of study or demonstrating student growth, however, have not been detailed.

A second approach to the talent development concept of curriculum has been explored through two recent national curriculum projects in science and language arts, developed to respond to the needs of gifted learners for a challenging curriculum and to demonstrate alignment with the new curriculum reform paradigm (VanTassel-Baska, 1993). Funded through the U.S. Department of Education Javits Act, these curriculum development projects at the College of William and Mary provide field-validated models for direct use in classrooms or as models for further development. Each set of units was developed by a team of curriculum specialists that included a classroom teacher, a content expert, and others with both curriculum and gifted and talented expertise.

The translation of the ICM to the National Language Arts Curriculum Project was accomplished by developing a curriculum framework addressing each of the dimensions. To satisfy the need for *advanced content,* the language arts curriculum used advanced literature selections, works that were at a reading level two years beyond grade level and sophisticated with respect to meaning. The writing emphasis was placed on persuasive essays, developing argument in written form, a more advanced form of writing than is typically taught at elementary levels. Use of advanced vocabulary and the mastery of English syntax at the elementary level also were stressed. The *process–product* dimension of the curriculum was addressed by use of the embedded model of reasoning developed by Paul (1992) and the use of a research model developed to aid students in generating original work. Products were encouraged through both written and oral work. The *issue/theme* dimension of the curriculum was explicated by focusing on the theme of *change* as it applied to works of literature selected for the unit, the writing process, language study, and learners reflecting on their own learning throughout the unit. Additionally, selecting an issue of significance to study was emphasized as a part of the research project for each unit. To date, six units have been developed, validated, piloted, and revised using this framework.

The translation of the ICM to the National Science Curriculum Project for High Ability Learners was driven by the overarching theme of *systems,* which became the conceptual organizing influence in each of seven units of study. Students learned the elements, boundaries, inputs, and outputs as well as interactions of selected systems. Through a problem-based learning approach, they also learned how science systems interact with real-world social, political, and economic systems. The *process–product* dimension of the curriculum model was addressed through engaging students in a scientific research process that led them to create their own experiments and to design their own solutions to the unit's central problem. The *content* dimension was addressed by selecting advanced science content for inclusion in each unit and encouraging in-depth study of selected content relevant to understanding the central problem of the unit. These units are being used in classrooms across the country to incorporate the new science emphasis, and have been found successful in heterogeneous as well as more restricted settings.

Curriculum Reform Design Elements

These national curriculum projects for high-ability learners were developed with an understanding of appropriate curriculum dimensions for gifted students, but they also demonstrate the use of key design features of curriculum reform strongly advocated by the national standards projects (O'Day & Smith, 1993) and the middle school movement (Erb, 1994). Thus the projects employ the following emphases:

- The curriculum is *meaning-based* in that it emphasizes depth over breadth and concepts over facts, and is grounded in real-world issues and problems that students care about or need to know. In science, students study the implications of daily occurrences like acid spills on interstate highway systems. In language arts, they relate to the impact of the treatment of minorities in this country as it has changed over a sixty-year period.
- The curriculum incorporates *higher order thinking* as integral to all content areas. The units provide students opportunities to demonstrate their understanding of advanced content and interdisciplinary ideas through strategies such as concept mapping, persuasive writing, and designing experiments.
- The curriculum emphasizes *intra- and interdisciplinary connections* through using overarching concepts, issues, and themes as major organizers. Thus, students study systems of cities, of government, of economies, and of language as well as chemistry and biology. The concept of *change* in language arts is relevant to literature, writing, and language as well as to mathematics, art, and music.
- The curriculum provides opportunities for *metacognition,* student reflection on learning processes. Students are involved in consciously planning, monitoring, and assessing their own learning for efficient and effective use of time and resources.
- The curriculum develops *habits of mind* through cultivating modes of thinking that resemble those of professionals in various fields with respect to skills, predispositions, and attitudes. In science, curiosity, objectivity, and skepticism are openly nurtured; in language arts, the mode of reflection and revision is consistently encouraged.
- The curriculum promotes *active learning* and *problem solving* through putting students in charge of their own learning. In the problem-based science units, students find out what they know, what they need to know, and how to pursue important knowledge in working on a real-world problem in small investigatory teams. In language arts, students team to discover how language functions and is structured.
- The curriculum is *technology-relevant* in that it uses various new technologies as tools for the learning process, from doing library research via CD-ROM, to composing at the word processor, to communicating with students across the world by e-mail. The units of study in both science and language arts incorporate activities that require these applications.
- The curriculum sets *learner outcomes of significance.* Expectations for learning are identified at targeted grade levels that reflect the priorities of the new curriculum for being broad-based, conceptual, and relevant to real-world application. In each set of units, learner outcomes reflect content, process, and concept emphases.
- The curriculum employs *authentic assessment* by tapping into what students

know as a result of meaningful instruction. Using approaches like portfolios and performance-based activities, the units engage learners in assessment as an active part of the learning process.

All of these reform elements formed the basis for initial curriculum development work. Tailoring of the curriculum for gifted learners occurred through ensuring the following kinds of emphasis:

- Provisions for acceleration and compression of content
- Use of higher order thinking skills (e. g., analysis, synthesis, evaluation)
- Integration of content by key ideas, issues, and themes
- Advanced reading level
- Opportunities for students to develop advanced products
- Opportunities for independent learning based on student capacity and interest
- Use of inquiry-based instructional techniques

Thus, the systematic fusion of integrated curriculum considerations was effected.

Implementation Considerations

The implementation of the Integrated Curriculum Model (ICM) is based on several considerations in the school setting. Most important among them is the nature of the gifted learner. For such students, regardless of the richness of the core curriculum base, there will be a need to address certain powerful characteristics through flexible implementation of such a model.

The Learner: Characteristics, Aptitudes, and Predispositions

There are many characteristics of gifted learners on which one might focus for a discussion of creating an optimal match between learner and curriculum. Several lists have been discussed as a basis for curriculum work (e.g., Maker, 1982; VanTassel-Baska, 1993). However, in our studies with curriculum it has become apparent that three such characteristics remain pivotal for purposes of curriculum planning and development.

The *precocity* of the learner is a key characteristic to consider in curriculum development. Gifted learners almost by definition evidence advanced development in some school-related curriculum area. The most common tested areas for such development are in the verbal and mathematical subject domains. Most students identified for gifted programs are at least two years advanced in one or both areas. Such evidence of advanced development provides a basis for curriculum planning at a more advanced level and for the expectation that such students can master new material in one-third to one-half the time of typical learners. For very gifted learners, there is a powerful motivation to "learn fast and move ahead."

In addition to precocity, another key characteristic that deserves attention for curriculum development is the *intensity* of gifted learners. This intensity may be manifested affectively in the realm of emotional responsiveness, as when students react strongly to the death of a pet or a classroom injustice committed by a teacher. But this characteristic also has saliency in the cognitive realm. Students exhibit intensity through the capacity to focus and concentrate for long periods of time on a subject that fascinates them or an idea they find intriguing. Such a characteristic can just as quickly become dissipated in uninteresting busywork or lack of depth in the exploration even of a subject of interest. This characteristic, like precocity, needs curricular attention.

The third learner characteristic of curricular interest is *complexity,* the capacity of gifted learners to engage in higher level and abstract thinking even at young ages. It also refers to their preference for hard and challenging work, often at levels beyond their current functioning. They also enjoy working on multiple levels simultaneously, as when solving complex real-world problems that have many parts and perspectives to study. Just as with precocity and intensity, the characteristic of complexity in the gifted demands a curriculum responsiveness because it is openly desired by the learner as well as indicated by student behavior.

These three characteristics each dictate an approach to curriculum that honors the various facets of the gifted mind and personality; and curriculum models for the gifted have responded variously to these characteristics. The Integrated Curriculum Model represents a fusion of these approaches such that the most powerful characteristics of the gifted are directly reflected in the curriculum intervention. Although this model has salience for all learners, based on a talent development paradigm, the variable of time becomes crucial in implementation. Not all learners will be ready at the same stage of development in each area for advanced, intensive, and complex study. The judicious application of this curricular model for all learners is thus advised.

Context Variables

What are the context variables that need consideration in order for the ICM to work in schools? While the need for a match between the learner and the intervention already has been described, it also is important to highlight contextual considerations that could have an impact on the successful use of this curriculum model in school settings. At least four variables must be considered.

Flexibility in Student Placement and Progress

Even an enriched and accelerated curriculum developed for high-ability learners and addressing all of the educational reform principles cannot be used with such learners without careful consideration of entry skills, rate of learning, and special interests and needs. Thus, ungraded multiage contexts where high-ability learners may access appropriate work groups and curriculum stations is a crucial component of the implementation context. Pretesting of students on relevant skills is a central part of the new curriculum projects, and diagnosing unusual readiness or developmental spurts that may occur in a curriculum sequence is also important. Schools may notice and use such data as a basis for more in-depth work in an area of a particular teaching unit.

Grouping

As curriculum for high-ability learners is implemented, attention must be paid to the beneficial impact of grouping for instruction. As Kulik's latest reanalysis of the grouping data points out, when curriculum is modified for gifted students, the effects of grouping become more prominent (Kulik, 1993; see Chapter 19 by Kulik and Kulik). Moreover, recent classroom studies have verified that little differentiation is occurring in heterogeneous classrooms for gifted students (Archambault et al., 1993), and the majority of teachers in our schools are not trained to teach gifted learners (Westberg, Archambault, Dobyns, & Salvin, 1993). Thus, forming instructional groups of gifted students for implementation of differentiated curriculum is clearly the most effective and efficient way to deliver it. Whether such grouping occurs in separate designated classes or in regular classrooms is a local consideration.

Trained Teachers

On the basis of recent data confirming the significant role of teacher training in providing differentiated instruction for the gifted (Hansen & Feldhusen, 1994; see also Chapter 43 by Feldhusen) and the availability of coursework in the education of the gifted (Parker & Karnes, 1991), there is little reason not to place gifted students with teachers who have received at least twelve hours of professional training. The benefits to the gifted learners become greater when differentiated curriculum is handled by those sensitive to the nature and needs of such students.

A Climate of Excellence

For gifted learners to perform at optimal levels, the educational context must offer challenging opportunities that provide generative situations (Feldhusen, VanTassel-Baska, & Seeley, 1989), yet also demand high standards of excellence. More than ever, a climate of excellence matters if curriculum standards are to be raised successfully for any student. For gifted students in particular, such a climate must be in place to ensure optimal development, positive attitudes toward learning, and high engagement. Such a climate also is essential for disadvantaged gifted youth, who are put more at risk by lowered expectations for performance (House & Lapan, 1994).

Preliminary Results and Implications

Current studies are underway to assess the cognitive and affective impacts of the Integrated Curriculum Model in the two content domains with high-ability and other learners (VanTassel-Baska, 1994). Data are being collected in the educational contexts in which the curriculum is being implemented, and the implications of the context variables described above are being examined. On the basis of pilot efforts to date, however, there are several important results and implications that may be discussed.

One finding is the responsiveness of gifted learners to such a curriculum. Preliminary pilot data have shown significant cognitive growth gains for students in both science and language arts on meaningful content tasks (Hughes, VanTassel-Baska, Boyce, & Quek, 1994). Moreover, students have developed sophisticated products and participated in intellectual discussions about key concepts and ideas taught in the curriculum (Sher, VanTassel-Baska, Gallagher, & Bailey, 1993). Motivational aspects of the curriculum also appear to be high, with many students unwilling to leave their classrooms at the appointed time (Darby, 1994). Thus, such an approach can be argued to be appropriate based on both student learning and interest grounds.

One implication thus far is the need to find teachers who are comfortable and flexible with the content area to be taught, as well as teachers trained in gifted education. For both science and language arts, growth gains were greater and student motivation better in those pilot classrooms where teachers grasped the structure of the discipline being taught and could reinforce it in powerful ways throughout the units. Although much of the instructional methodology advocated in the projects is open-ended, inquiry-based, and facilitative, subject matter knowledge that can informally be brought in to back up the use of such strategies is clearly beneficial, even at the early elementary levels.

Also, language arts classrooms that provided some form of instructional grouping showed greater gains for gifted learners on several dimensions than did classrooms that were totally heterogeneous. This finding was due in part to the extensive use of advanced reading materials in the units and in part to teacher frustration in trying to cope with all learners engaged in complex activities different from the basals. Another implementation suggestion from the language arts pilot research was to use the pilot curriculum in lieu of the core curriculum in the district on a daily basis rather than as a pull-out option. Reasons for this approach included the broad scope of the units developed, the importance of ongoing practice with the concepts and higher order skills being taught, and the need for more time in implementing a curriculum that incorporates all of the language arts strands.

Conclusion

The Integrated Curriculum Model offers the best combinational approach to date for restructuring curriculum for gifted learners at the same time that it responds to the curriculum reform agenda. It offers practitioners concrete units of study to implement in classrooms nationally. By meeting the criteria for exemplary curriculum design, exemplary content considerations, and differentiation for gifted learners, the units developed at the College of William and Mary provide the translation from theoretical principles to practice. Only multiple replications and long-term use will yield the more complete answers we seek to questions of long-term effectiveness with gifted learners.

REFERENCES

Amabile, T. (1983). *The social psychology of creativity.* New York: Springer-Verlag.

Archambault, F. X., Westberg, K. L., Brown, S., Hallmark, B. W., Zhang, W., & Emmons, C. (1993). Regular classroom practices with gifted students: Findings from the classroom practices survey. *Journal for the Education of the Gifted, 16,* 103–119.

Benbow, C. P., & Stanley, J. C. (Eds.) (1983). *Academic precocity: Aspects of its development.* Baltimore, MD: Johns Hopkins University Press.

Betts, G. (1991). The autonomous learner model for the gifted and talented. In N. Colangelo & G. A. Davis (Eds.), *Handbook of gifted education* (pp. 142–153). Boston: Allyn and Bacon.

Bloom, B. (1985). *Developing talent in young people.* New York: Ballantine.

Bolanos, P. (1991). *Curriculum for the key school.* Presentation at National Javits Project Director meeting, Washington, DC.

Darby, D. (1994). *Presentation at National Summer Institute on Teaching Science to High-Ability Learners.* Williamsburg, VA: Center for Gifted Education.

Erb, T. (1994). The middle school: Mimicking the success routes of the information age. *Journal for the Education of the Gifted, 17*(4), 385–408.

Feldhusen, J., & Kolloff, P. (1978, January–February). A three stage model for gifted education. *G/C/T,* 3–5, 53–57.

Feldhusen, J., VanTassel-Baska, J., & Seeley, K. (1989). *Excellence in educating the gifted.* Denver, CO: Love.

Feldman, D. (1985). *Nature's gambit.* New York: Basic Books.

Gallagher, J. (1985). *Teaching the gifted child.* Boston: Allyn and Bacon.

Gardner, H. (1983). *Frames of mind.* New York: Basic Books.

Gardner, H. (1985). The role of crystallizing experience. In F. Horowitz & M. O'Brien (Eds.), *Developmental perspectives on the education of the gifted.* Washington, DC: American Psychological Association.

Hansen, J., & Feldhusen, J. (1994). Comparison of trained and untrained teachers of gifted students. *Gifted Child Quarterly, 38*(3), 115–123.

House, E., & Lapan, S. (1994). Evaluation of programs for disadvantaged gifted students. *Journal for the Education of the Gifted, 17*(4), 441–466.

Hughes, C. E., VanTassel-Baska, J., Boyce, L. N., & Quek, C. G. (1994). *The William and Mary pilot of Change and the Search for Meaning: A national language arts unit for high ability students in grades 4–6.* Williamsburg, VA: Center for Gifted Education, College of William and Mary.

Keating, D. (1976). *Intellectual talent.* Baltimore, MD: Johns Hopkins University Press.

Kulik, J. (1993). *An analysis of the research on ability grouping: Historical and contemporary perspectives.* Storrs, CT: National Research Center on the Gifted and Talented.

Maker, C. J. (1982). *Curriculum development for the gifted.* Rockville, MD: Aspen Systems.

Marzano, R. (1992). *Cultivating thinking in English.* Urbana, IL: National Council of Teachers of English.

O'Day, J. A., & Smith, M. S. (1993). Systemic reform and educational opportunity. In S. H. Fuhrman (Ed.), *Designing coherent education policy* (pp. 250–311). San Francisco: Jossey-Bass.

Parker, J., & Karnes, F. (1991). Graduate degree programs and resource centers in gifted education: An update and analysis. *Gifted Child Quarterly, 35,* 43–48.

Passow, A. H. (1982). *Differentiated curriculum for the gifted/talented.* Ventura County, CA: Office of the Superintendent of Schools.

Paul, R. (1992). *Critical thinking: What every person needs to survive in a rapidly changing world.* Rohnert Park, CA: Critical Thinking Foundation.

Perkins, D., & Saloman, G. (1989). Are cognitive skills context bound? *Educational Research, 18*(1), 16–25.

Reis, S. M., & Purcell, J. H. (1993). An analysis of content elimination and strategies used by elementary classroom teachers and the curriculum compacting process. *Journal for the Education of the Gifted, 16,* 147–170.

Renzulli, J. (1977). *The enrichment triad.* Mansfield Center, CT: Creative Learning Press.

Sher, B. T., VanTassel-Baska, J., Gallagher, S. A., & Bailey, J. M. (1993). *Developing a curriculum framework in science for high ability learners K–8.* Williamsburg, VA: Center for Gifted Education, College of William and Mary.

Stanley, J., Keating, D., & Fox, L. (1974). *Mathematical talent.* Baltimore, MD: Johns Hopkins University Press.

Sternberg, R. J. (1985). *Beyond IQ.* New York: Basic Books.

Tannenbaum, A. (1983). *Gifted children.* New York: Macmillan.

Treffinger, D. (1986). Fostering effective, independent learning through individualized programming. In J. S. Renzulli (Ed.), *Systems and models for developing programs for the gifted and talented* (pp. 429–468). Mansfield Center, CT: Creative Learning Press.

VanTassel-Baska, J. (1986). Effective curriculum and instructional models for the gifted. *Gifted Child Quarterly, 30,* 164–169.

VanTassel-Baska, J. (1992) *Effective curriculum planning for gifted learners.* Denver, CO: Love.

VanTassel-Baska, J. (1993). *Comprehensive curricu-*

lum for gifted learners (2nd ed.). Boston: Allyn & Bacon.

VanTassel-Baska, J. (1993). Theory and research on curriculum development for the gifted. In K. Heller, F. Monk, & A. H. Passow (Eds.), *International handbook of research and development of giftedness and talent* (pp. 365–386). London: Pergamon Press.

VanTassel-Baska, J. (1994). Development and assessment of integrated curriculum: A worthy challenge. *Quest, 5*(2), 1–5.

VanTassel-Baska, J., & Feldhusen, J. (Eds.). (1981). *Concept curriculum for the gifted K–8.* Matteson, IL: Matteson School District #162.

VanTassel-Baska, J., & Olszewski-Kubilius, P. (1989). *Patterns of influence: The home, the self, and the school.* New York: Teachers College Press.

Ward, V. (1979). The governor's school of North Carolina. In A. H. Passow (Ed.), *The gifted and the talented, their education and development: NSSE yearbook committee and associated contributors* (pp. 209–217). Chicago: University of Chicago Press.

Ward, V. (1981). *Differential education for the gifted.* Ventura County, CA: Office of the Superintendent of Schools.

Westberg, K. L., Archambault, F. X., Dobyns, S. M., & Salvin, T. J. (1993). An observational study of classroom practices used with third- and fourth-grade students. *Journal for the Education of the Gifted, 16,* 120–146.

11

The Schoolwide Enrichment Model: New Directions for Developing High-End Learning

JOSEPH S. RENZULLI and SALLY M. REIS, *University of Connecticut*

Two afternoons a week, twelve-year-old Kelvin goes to an enrichment cluster at the Noah Webster School in Hartford, Connecticut. When he was selected for the program, Kelvin said, "It feels good, but I was amazed. I was about to faint! I was super, super surprised." The reason for Kelvin's amazement is that he had never considered himself to be a good student, at least not in the way we usually view students. And the program was not exactly the place where you usually found kids like Kelvin, who lives in subsidized housing and whose family manages to survive on a monthly welfare check and food stamps.

The program Kelvin is enrolled in looks at talent development in a different way, as it is based on a plan called the Schoolwide Enrichment Model (SEM). In this model a broad range of talents and potential talents are identified in all students through the use of a strength assessment guide called the Total Talent Portfolio. This guide helps to focus attention on student interests and learning style preferences as well as strengths in traditional subjects. These strengths serve as building blocks for advanced achievement. Kelvin's strongest academic area is mathematics, and through a process called Curriculum Compacting he is now being provided with mathematics material that is two grade levels above the level of math being covered in his classroom.

Kelvin, a bright underachiever who once described himself as a "mental dropout," now finds school a much more inviting place. He hopes to enter the research he is doing on airplane wing design in his enrichment cluster into a state science fair competition. He is also thinking about a career in engineering, and the enrichment specialist at his school has helped him apply for a special summer program at the University of Connecticut that is designed to recruit and assist minorities into mathematical and engineering-related professions. "School," says Kelvin, "is a place where you have must-dos and can-dos. I work harder on my must-dos so I can spend more time working on my can-dos."

In this chapter, the new developments that enabled Kelvin to be involved in the SEM despite poor grades and chronic underachievement are described, along with a brief chronology of how the SEM evolved and an overview of research conducted on the model.

History and Chronology of the SEM

The original Enrichment Triad Model (Renzulli, 1976) was developed in the mid-1970s and implemented by school districts primarily in Connecticut. The model, which was initially field-tested in several districts, proved to be quite popular, and requests from all over the country for visitations to schools using the model and for information about how to implement the model increased. A book about the Enrichment Triad Model (Renzulli, 1977) was published, and more and more districts began asking for help in implementing this approach. It was at this point that a clear need was established for research about the effectiveness of the model and for other vehicles that could provide technical assistance for interested educators to help develop programs in their schools. Thus began almost twenty years of field testing, research, and dissemination.

The Triad Model (see Figure 11.1) was designed to encourage the creative productivity of young people by exposing them to various topics, areas of interest, and fields of study;

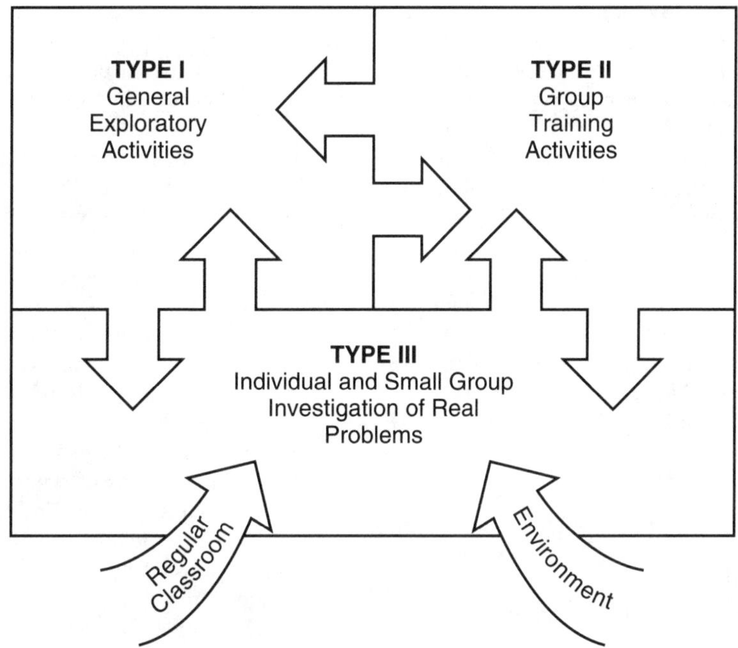

Figure 11.1 The Enrichment Triad Model.

and to further train them to *apply* advanced content, process-training skills, and methodology training to self-selected areas of interest. Accordingly, three types of enrichment are included in the Enrichment Triad Model.

Type I enrichment is designed to expose students to a wide variety of disciplines, topics, occupations, hobbies, persons, places, and events that ordinarily would not be covered in the regular curriculum. In schools that use this model, an enrichment team consisting of parents, teachers, and students often organizes and plans Type I experiences by contacting speakers; arranging minicourses, demonstrations, or performances; or by ordering and distributing films, slides, videotapes, or other print or non-print media. The following Type I invitation from a Triad Program provides an example of Type I enrichment:

> On Tuesday, December 8, Mr. Martin Nagel will be here to give a presentation on coins and stamps to interested primary students. Martin is an attendance counselor with the Richland County Office of Education and also a very avid coin and stamp collector. He has given numerous talks to students in our county system and has just recently completed teaching a course on "Coin and Stamp Collecting" at our Saturday Enrichment School. In addition to giving students some facts and history on coins and stamps, he will also share part of his valuable collection with the students.
>
> It is our hope that some students who attend this Type I will be interested in pursuing a Type III project in this area and perhaps starting collections of their own.

Type II enrichment consists of materials and methods designed to promote the development of thinking and feeling processes. Some Type II enrichment is general, consisting of training in areas such as creative thinking and problem solving, learning-how-to-learn skills such as classifying and analyzing data, and advanced reference and communication skills. Type II training, usually carried out both in classrooms and in enrichment programs, includes the development of (1) creative thinking and problem solving, critical thinking, and affective processes; (2) a wide variety of specific learning-how-to-learn skills; (3) skills in the appropriate use of advanced-level reference materials; and (4) written, oral, and visual communication skills. Other Type II enrichment is specific, cannot be planned in advance, and usually involves advanced instruction in an interest area selected by the student. For example, students who became interested in botany after a Type I on plant tropisms pursued follow-up training in this area by doing advanced reading in botany; compiling, planning and carrying out plant experiments; and learning more about advanced research methods in this field.

Type III enrichment occurs when students become interested in pursuing a self-selected area and are willing to commit the time necessary for advanced content acquisition and process training in which they assume the role of a first-hand inquirer. The goals of Type III enrichment include:

- Providing opportunities for applying interests, knowledge, creative ideas, and task commitment to a self-selected problem or area of study
- Acquiring advanced-level understanding of the knowledge (content) and methodology (process) that are used within particular disciplines, artistic areas of expression, and interdisciplinary studies
- Developing authentic products that are primarily directed toward bringing about a desired impact on a specified audience
- Developing self-directed learning skills in the areas of planning, organization, resource utilization, time management, decision making, and self-evaluation
- Developing task commitment, self-confidence, and feelings of creative accomplishment

An example of a Type III enrichment experience is provided in Figure 11.2.

As our experience with Triad Programs grew, our concern about who was being identified to participate in these programs also grew. We became increasingly concerned about students who were not able to participate in enrichment programs because they did not score in the top 1 to 3 percent of the population on achievement or intelligence tests. Research conducted by Torrance (1962, 1974) had demonstrated that students who were rated high on creativity measures do well in school and on achievement tests, but often are not selected for gifted programs because their scores are below the cutoff for admission. Research (Reis, 1981) indicated that when a broader population of students (15 to 20 percent of the general population, called the *talent pool*) were able to participate in Types I and II enrichment experiences, they produced Type III products as good as those of the traditional "gifted" students (the top 3 to 5 percent). This research produced the rationale for the Revolving Door Identification Model (RDIM) (Renzulli, Reis, & Smith, 1981), in which a talent pool of students receives regular enrichment experiences and the opportunity to "revolve into" Type III creative productive experiences. In RDIM, we recommend that students be selected for participation in the talent pool on the basis of multiple criteria that include indices of creativity, because we believe that one of the major purposes of gifted education is to develop creative thinking and creative productivity in all students. Once identified and placed in the talent pool—through the use of test scores; teacher, parent, or self-nomination; or creative potential or productivity—students are observed in classrooms and enrichment experiences for signs of advanced interests, creativity, or task commitment. We have called this part of the process "action information" and have found it to be an instrumental part of the identification process in assessing students' interest and motivation to become involved in Type III creative productivity. Further support for this approach has been offered by Kirschenbaum (1983) and Kirschenbaum and Siegle (1993), who demonstrated that students who are rated or test high on measures of creativity tend to do well in school and on measures of achievement. The development of the RDIM led to the need for a guide for how all of the components of the previous Triad and the new RDIM could be implemented. The resulting work was entitled the *Schoolwide Enrichment Model* (Renzulli & Reis, 1985).

In the SEM, a talent pool of 15 to 20 percent of above-average-ability or high-potential students is identified through a variety of measures, including achievement tests, teacher nominations, assessment of potential for creativity, and task commitment, as well as alternative pathways of entrance (self-nomination, parent nomination, etc.). High achievement test and IQ scores automatically include a

"Bobby Bones"

by Jerry Beach
Allison Roxby
Donny Capnano
Merri Petrovits
Eric Chadwick
Rebecca Christian
Stephanie Durstin

East School
Torrington, Connecticut

Grade 4

Brief Description

Bobby Bones is a life-size model of the human skeletal structure with a taped mini-course designed to be presented to other youngsters. Thomas Hébert, the resource teacher who provided managerial assistance to the students, indicated that he was delighted with the "ownership" involved in the completion of this Type III. The physical education teacher in East School, Janet Beck, supervised the building of the skeleton and helped Tom to coordinate the entire project. The students' classroom teacher, Steve Ksenych, compacted the curriculum for the entire school year, enabling the project to be completed. The art teacher, Elaine Towne, provided advice and helped the students build Bobby Bones. Another classroom teacher who had outstanding talent in music, helped the students to write a song that accompanied the mini-course in anatomy that was developed after the skeleton was built. This Type III required two years to complete and was subsequently presented to every third-grade classroom in Torrington as a Type II mini-course in conjunction with the third-grade health curriculum.

Bobby Bones

THE REGISTER
LITCHFIELD COUNTY'S NEWSPAPER
Torrington, Connecticut

Tuesday, May 10, 1983 **Second Section** **Page 13**

Usually students of anatomy take a skeleton apart to learn about its structure but students at East School are putting one together. 'Bobby Bones' is the name of the bigger-than-life-size papier mâché skeleton that eight fourth-grade students from teacher Steve Ksenych's language arts class at East School have been constructing since October. The students, participants in the Talented and Gifted Program, are constructing the skeleton under the direction of art teacher Elaine Towne. Physical education teacher Janet Beck, TAG teacher Tom Hébert, and Ksenych are assisting in the project which is part of an enrichment activity and helps the students learn more about anatomy, science and art. With the addition of ribs, fingers and a coat of shellac the skeleton should be finished in about three weeks. It will be put on display at the TAG project fair to be held at the end of the year.

Figure 11.2 Example of Type III enrichment.

student in the talent pool, enabling those students who are underachieving in their academic work to be included.

Once students are identified for the talent pool, they are eligible for several kinds of services. First, interest and learning-styles assessments are used with talent pool students. Informal and formal methods are used to create or identify students' interests and to encourage students to further develop and pursue these interests in various ways. Learning-style preferences that are assessed include projects, independent study, teaching games, simulations, peer teaching, programmed instruction, lecture, drill and recitation, and discussion. Second, curriculum compacting is provided to all eligible students; the regular curriculum is modified by eliminating portions of previously mastered content. This elimination or streamlining of curriculum enables above-average students to avoid repetition of previously mastered work and guarantees mastery while simultaneously finding time for more appropriately challenging activities (Reis, Burns, & Renzulli, 1992; Renzulli, Smith, & Reis, 1982). A form entitled the Compactor (Renzulli & Smith, 1978) is used to document which content areas have been compacted and what alternative work has been substituted. Third, the Enrichment Triad Model offers three types of enrichment experiences. Types I and II enrichment are offered to all students; however, Type III enrichment is usually more appropriate for students with higher levels of ability, interest, and task commitment.

Separate studies of the SEM demonstrated its effectiveness in schools with widely differing socioeconomic levels and program organization patterns (Olenchak, 1988; Olenchak & Renzulli, 1989). The SEM has been implemented in several hundred school districts across the country (Burns, 1992) and interest in this approach continues to grow.

New Challenges for Gifted Education

Through field tests with numerous districts, we began to explore how many of the components of SEM could be provided to a broader range of students. These opportunities enabled us to develop instructional procedures and programming alternatives that emphasize the need (1) to provide a broad range of advanced level enrichment experiences for *all* students, and (2) to use the many and varied ways that students respond to these experiences as stepping stones for relevant follow-up on the parts of individuals or small groups. This approach is not viewed as a new way to identify who is or is not "gifted"! Rather, the process simply identifies how subsequent *opportunities, resources,* and *encouragement* can be provided to support continuous escalations of student involvement in both required and self-selected activities. This approach to the development of high levels of multiple potentials in young people is purposefully designed to sidestep the traditional practice of labeling some students "gifted" (and by implication, relegating all others to the category of "not-gifted"). The term *gifted* is used in our lexicon only as an adjective, and even then it is used in a developmental perspective. Thus, for example, we speak and write about *the development of gifted behaviors* in specific areas of learning and human expression, rather than about giftedness as a state of being. This orientation has allowed many students opportunities to develop high levels of creative and productive accomplishment that otherwise would have been denied through traditional special program models.

Practices that have been a mainstay of many special programs for "the gifted" are being absorbed into general education by reform models designed to upgrade the performance of all students. This integration of gifted program knowhow is viewed as a favorable development for two reasons. First, the adoption of many special program practices is indicative of the viability and usefulness of both the knowhow of special programs and the role enrichment specialists can and should play in total school improvement. Second, *all* students should have opportunities to develop higher order thinking skills and to pursue more rigorous content and first-hand investigative activities than those typically found in today's "dumbed-down" textbooks. The enthusiastic ways in which students respond to enriched learning experiences should be used as a rationale for providing all students with advanced-level opportunities. This approach reflects a democratic ideal that accommodates the full range of individual differences in the entire student population, and it opens the door to programming models that develop the talent potentials of many at-risk students who traditionally have been excluded from anything but the most basic types of curricular experiences. To operationalize this ideal, we need to get serious about the things we have learned during the past several years about both programming models and human potential.

The application of gifted program knowhow to general education is supported by a wide variety of research on human abilities (Bloom, 1985; Gardner, 1983; Renzulli, 1986; Sternberg, 1984). This research clearly and unequivocally provides a justification for much broader conceptions of talent development. These conceptions argue against the restrictive student selection practices that guided identification procedures in the past. Lay persons and professionals at all levels have begun to question the efficacy of programs that rely on narrow definitions, IQ scores, and other cognitive ability measures as the primary methods for identifying which students can benefit from differentiated services. Traditional identification procedures have restricted services to small numbers of high scoring students and excluded large numbers of at-risk students whose potentials are manifested in other ways that will be described later in a new SEM component called the Total Talent Portfolio. Special services should be viewed as opportunities to develop "gifted behaviors," rather than merely finding and certifying them. In this regard, we should judiciously avoid saying that a young person is either "gifted" or "not gifted." It is difficult to gain support for talent development when we use as a rationale statements such as "Elaine is a gifted third grader." These kinds of statements offend many people and raise the accusations of elitism that have plagued special programs. But note the difference in orientation when we focus on the *behavioral characteristics* that brought this student to our attention in the first place: "Elaine is a third grader who reads at the adult level and is fascinated by biographies about women of scientific accomplishment." And note the logical and justifiable services provided for Elaine:

1. Under the guidance of her classroom teacher, Elaine was allowed to substitute more challenging books in her interest area for the third-grade reader. The schoolwide enrichment teaching specialist helped the classroom teacher locate these books, which were purchased with funds from the enrichment program budget.
2. Elaine was allowed to leave the school two afternoons a month (usually on early dismissal days) to meet with a mentor who is a local journalist specializing in gender issues. The schoolwide enrichment teaching specialist arranged transportation with the help of the school's parent volunteer group.
3. During time made available through curriculum compacting in her strength areas (reading, language arts, and spelling), the schoolwide enrichment teaching specialist helped Elaine prepare a questionnaire and interview schedule to be used with local women scientists and women science faculty members at a nearby university.

Could anyone argue against the logic or the appropriateness of these services? When programs focus on developing the behavioral potential of individuals or of small groups who share a common interest, it is no longer necessary to organize groups merely because they all happen to be "gifted third graders."

New Components in the Schoolwide Enrichment Model

The programming model that we have advocated since the early 1970s has always argued for a behavioral definition of giftedness and a greater emphasis on applying gifted program knowhow to larger segments of the school population. The model currently is being used in hundreds of school districts across the country, including major urban areas such as New York City, Detroit, St. Paul, San Antonio, and Fort Worth. The present reform initiatives in general education have created a more receptive atmosphere for flexible approaches that challenge all students. Accordingly, we have organized the Schoolwide Enrichment Model so that it blends into school improvement activities that currently are taking place throughout the country. Space does not permit a detailed description of the full model, which is described in a book called *Schools for Talent Development* (Renzulli, 1994); however, the following sections will describe the school structures on which the model is targeted and the three service delivery components. A graphic representation of the model is presented in Figure 11.3.

School Structures

1. The regular curriculum. The regular curriculum consists of everything that is a part of the predetermined goals, schedules, learning outcomes, and delivery systems of the school. The regular curriculum might be traditional, innovative, or in the process of transition, but its predominant feature is that authoritative forces (policymakers, school councils, textbook adoption committees, state regulators) have determined that the regular curriculum should be the centerpiece of student learning. Application of the SEM influences the regular curriculum in three

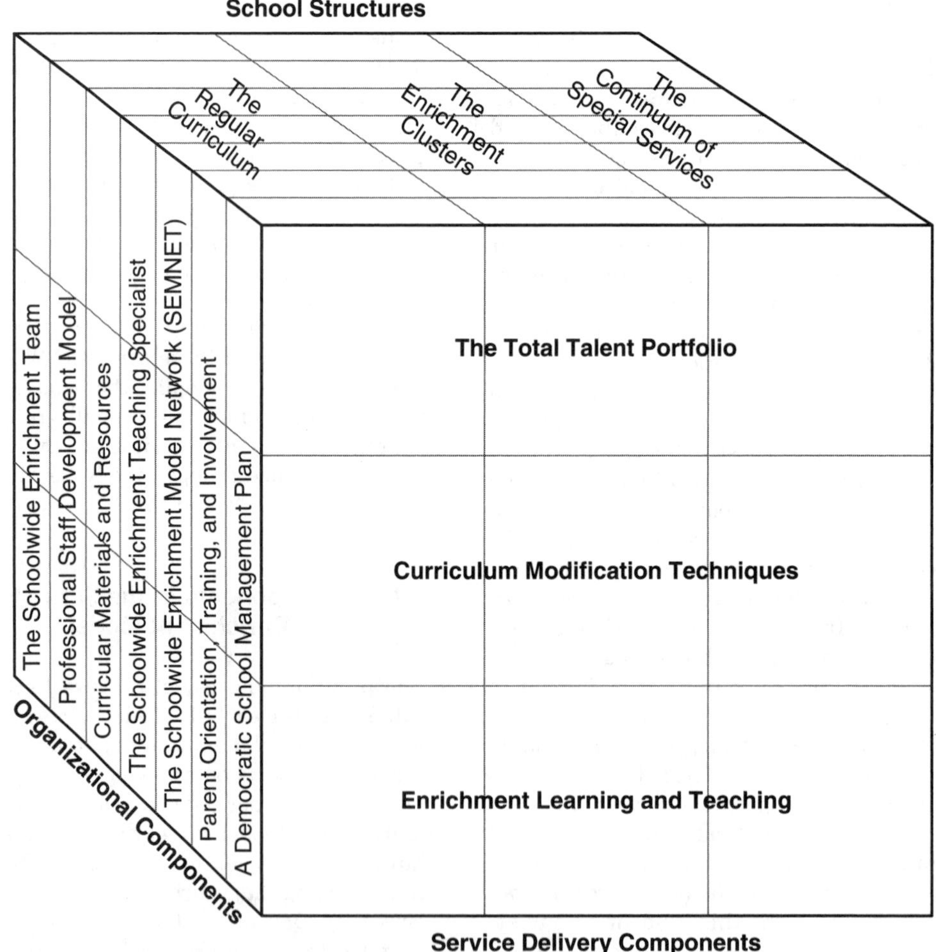

Figure 11.3 The Schoolwide Enrichment Model: Relationship between two types of components of the model and school structures.

ways. First, the challenge level of required material is differentiated through processes such as curriculum compacting, textbook content modification procedures, and group jumping strategies. Second, the systematic content intensification procedures, which replace eliminated content with selected in-depth learning experiences, increase the challenge level by introducing the broad underlying principles of a discipline. Third, types of enrichment recommended in the Enrichment Triad Model (to be described) are integrated selectively into regular curriculum activities. Although our goal in the SEM is to influence rather than replace the regular curriculum, application of certain SEM components and related staff development activities have resulted in substantial changes in both the content and instructional processes of the entire regular curriculum.

2. Enrichment clusters. *Enrichment clusters* are nongraded groups of students who share common interests and who come together during specially designated time blocks to pursue these interests. As with extracurricular activities and programs such as 4-H and Junior Achievement, the main rationale for participation in one or more clusters is that *students and teachers want to be there.* All teachers (including music, art, physical education, etc.) are involved in teaching the clusters; teacher involvement in any particular cluster is based on the same type of interest assessment used for students. Community resource persons should also be invited to organize enrichment clusters.

The model for learning used with enrichment clusters is based on an inductive approach to the pursuit of real-world problems rather than on traditional, didactic modes of teaching. This approach, entitled *enrichment learning and teaching,* is purposefully designed to create a learning environment that places a premium on the development of higher order thinking skills and the authentic application of these skills in creative and productive situations. The theory underlying this approach is based on the work of constructivist theorists such as Jean Piaget, Jerome Bruner, and John Dewey, and on applications of constructivist theory to classroom practice. Enrichment clusters are excellent vehicles for promoting cooperativeness within the context of real-world problem solving, and they also provide superlative opportunities for promoting positive self-concepts. A major assumption underlying the use of enrichment clusters is that *every child is special if we create conditions in which that child can be a specialist within a specialty group.*

Enrichment clusters are organized around major disciplines, interdisciplinary themes, or cross-disciplinary topics (e.g., an electronic music group or a theatrical/television production group that includes actors, writers, technical specialists, costume designers, etc.). The clusters are modeled after the ways in which knowledge utilization, thinking skills, and interpersonal relations take place in the real world. Thus, all work is directed toward the production of a product or service. There are no lesson plans or unit plans. Rather, direction is provided by the following key questions:

1. What do people with an interest in this area do?
2. What products or services do they provide?
   - a. What are the different roles that are necessary to produce the product or service?
   - b. What are the methods and resources used by professionals to produce high-quality products?
3. How, and with whom, do they communicate the results of their work?
4. Who are the people in our community interested in the product or service we will produce or provide?
5. What steps need to be taken to ensure that our product or service will have an impact on our audience?

The enrichment clusters are not intended to be the total program for talent development in a school, but they are a major vehicle for stimulating interests and developing talent potentials across the entire school population. They are also vehicles for staff development in that they provide teachers an opportunity to participate in enrichment teaching, and subsequently to analyze and compare this type of teaching with traditional methods of instruction. In this regard the model promotes a spillover effect by encouraging teachers to become better talent scouts and talent developers and to apply enrichment techniques to regular classroom situations. Enrichment clusters are used by some schools on a half-day-per-week basis; in other schools they meet daily. At the Webster Elementary Magnet School in St. Paul, Minnesota, which is based on SEM, for example, a broad array of interdisciplinary clusters is offered daily. At the Southeast School in Mansfield, Connecticut, enrichment clusters are offered two afternoons a month and are taught jointly by teachers, administrators, and parent volunteers. One of the most popular clusters, called "Flight School," was organized by the superintendent of schools, who is a licensed pilot.

3. The continuum of special services. A broad range of special services is the third school structure that is targeted by the model. A diagram representing these services is presented in Figure 11.4. Although the enrichment clusters and the SEM-based modifications of the regular curriculum provide a broad range of services to meet individual needs, a program for total talent development still requires supplementary services that challenge young people who are capable of working at the highest levels of their special interest areas. These services, which cannot ordinarily be provided in enrichment clusters or the regular curriculum, typically include individual or small group counseling, direct assistance in facilitating advanced level work, arranging for mentorships with faculty members or community persons, and making other types of connections between students, their families, and out-of-school persons, resources, and agencies. For example, the schoolwide enrichment coordinator in the LaPorte, Indiana, School Corporation developed a Parent–Teacher Enrichment Guide of the city and surrounding area that includes information about a wide

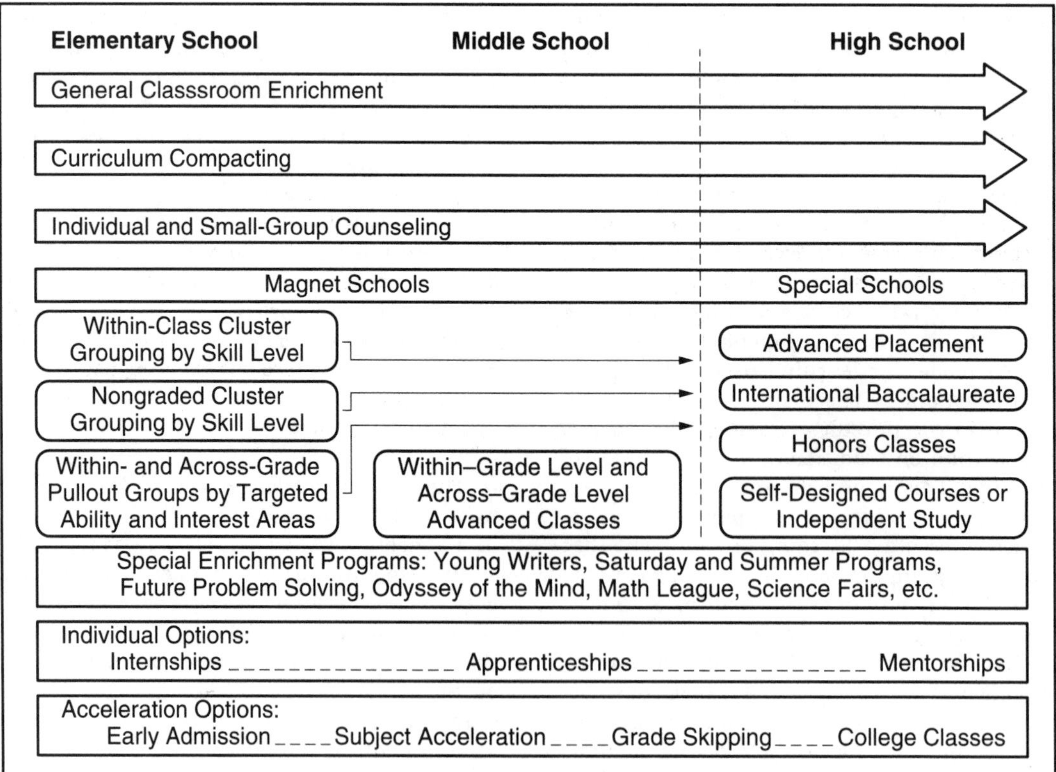

Figure 11.4 The continuum of services for total talent development.

variety of enrichment opportunities for parents and teachers.

Direct assistance also involves setting up and promoting student, faculty, and parental involvement in special programs such as Future Problem Solving, Odyssey of the Mind, the Model United Nations program, and state and national essay, mathematics, and history contests. Another type of direct assistance consists of arranging out-of-school involvement for individual students in summer programs, on-campus courses, special schools, theatrical groups, scientific expeditions, and apprenticeships at places where advanced-level learning opportunities are available. Provision of these services is one of the responsibilities of the schoolwide enrichment teaching specialist or an enrichment team of teachers and parents who work together to provide options for advanced learning. A schoolwide enrichment teaching specialist in Barrington, Rhode Island, estimates that she spends two days a week in a resource capacity to the faculties of two schools, and three days providing direct services to students.

Service Delivery Components

The Total Talent Portfolio

The case study of Elaine presented earlier is an example of the ways in which the Schoolwide Enrichment Model targets specific learning characteristics that can serve as a basis for talent development. Our approach to targeting learning characteristics uses both traditional and performance-based assessment to compile information about three dimensions of the learner—abilities, interests, and learning styles. This information, which focuses on strengths rather than deficits, is compiled in a folder called the Total Talent Portfolio (see Figure 11.5). It is used to make decisions about talent development opportunities in regular classes, in enrichment clusters, and in the continuum of special services. Two questions summarize the intent of the Total Talent Portfolio: What are the very best things we know and can record about a student's best work, and what are the best ways we can utilize the information to nurture the student's talent? This expanded approach to identifying talent potentials is essential if we are to make genuine efforts to include more underrepresented students in a plan for *total* talent development. This approach is also consistent with the more flexible conception of *developing* gifts and talents that has been a cornerstone of our work and our concerns for promoting equity in special programs.

Curriculum Modification Techniques

The second service delivery component of the SEM is a series of *curriculum modification techniques* that are designed to: (1) adjust levels of required learning so that all students are challenged, (2) increase the number of in-depth learning experiences, and (3) introduce various types of enrichment into regular curricular experiences. The procedures used to carry out curriculum modification are curriculum compacting, textbook analysis, and surgical removal of repetitious material from textbooks, and a planned approach for introducing greater depth into regular curricular material.

Curriculum compacting (Reis & Renzulli, 1992) is a systematic procedure for modifying or streamlining the regular curriculum to eliminate repetition of previously mastered material, upgrading the challenge level of the regular curriculum, and providing time for appropriate enrichment and/or acceleration activities. This process includes (1) defining the goals and outcomes of a particular unit or segment of instruction, (2) determining and documenting which students have already mastered most or all of a specified set of learning outcomes or are capable of mastering them in less time than their peers, and (3) providing replacement activities for material already mastered through the use of instructional options that enable a more challenging and productive use of the student's time. These options include content acceleration, individual or group research projects, peer teaching, and involvement in nonclassroom activities discussed in the section on the continuum of services. A key feature of these options is that students have some freedom to make decisions about the topic and the methods through which the topic will be pursued. Curriculum compacting might best be thought of as *organized common sense,* because it simply recom-

Abilities	Interests	Style Preferences			
Maximum Performance Indicators[a]	*Interest Areas*[b]	*Instructional Styles Preferences*[c]	*Learning Environment Preferences*[d]	*Thinking Styles Preferences*[e]	*Expression Style Preferences*[f]
Tests • Standardized • Teacher-made Course gades Teacher ratings Product evaluation • Written • Oral • Visual • Musical • Constructed (Note differences between assigned and self-selected products) Level of participation in learning activities Degree of interaction with others	Fine Arts Crafts Literary Historical Mathematical/Logical Physical Sciences Life Sciences Political/Judicial Athletic/Recreation Marketing/Business Drama/Dance Musical Performance Musical Composition Managerial/Business Photography Film/Video Computers Other (specify)	Recitation and drill Peer tutoring Lecture Lecture/discussion Discussion Guided independent study[g] Learning/interest center Simulation, role playing, dramatization, guided fantasy Learning games Replicative reports or projects[g] Investigative reports or projects[g] Unguided independent study[g] Internship[g] Apprenticeship[g]	*Inter/Intra Personal* • Self-oriented • Peer-oriented • Adult-oriented • Combined *Physical* • Sound • Heat • Light • Design • Mobility • Time of Day • Food Intake • Seating	Analytic (School Smart) Synthetic/ Creative (Creative, Inventive) Practical/ Contextual (Street Smart) Legislative Executive Judicial	Written Oral Manipulative Discussion Display Dramatization Artistic Graphic Commercial Service
[a]*Sources:* General tests and measurements literature.	[b]*Sources:* Renzulli (1977).	[c]*Sources:* Renzulli & Smith (1978). [g]With or without a mentor.	[d]*Sources:* Amabile (1989); Dunn, Dunn, & Price (1981); Gardner (1983).	[e]*Sources:* Sternberg (1984).	[f]*Sources:* Renzulli & Reis (1985).

Figure 11.5 Dimensions of the Total Talent Portfolio.

mends the natural pattern that teachers ordinarily follow when individualizing instruction, or teaching in the days before textbooks were invented. Compacting might also be thought of as the mirror image of remedial procedures that have always been used in diagnostic/prescriptive models of teaching.

The second procedure for making adjustments in regular curricular material is the examination of textbooks to determine which parts can be economized on through textbook analysis and "surgical removal" of repetitious drill and practice. The textbook *is* the curriculum in the overwhelming majority of today's classrooms. Despite rhetoric about school and curriculum reform, this situation is not likely to change in the near future. Until high-quality textbooks are universally available, it is essential to deal with the curriculum situation as it currently exists. Although curriculum compacting is one procedure that can be used to get an unchallenging curriculum off the backs of students who need curriculum modifications, it is merely a form of damage control. We need to take a more proactive stance to overcome the well-documented low levels of American textbooks.

The procedures for carrying out the textbook analysis and surgical removal process are based on the argument that less is better when it comes to content selection, and it is necessary to make wise decisions when determining which material will be covered in greater depth. The first step in the process might best be described as textbook triage. Each unit of instruction is examined by grade-level teams to determine which material is needless repetition of previously covered skills and concepts. When repetition is eliminated, teachers then decide which material is necessary for review, and which material is important enough to cover in either a survey or an in-depth manner. What teachers teach is at the very heart of professional competency. The textbook analysis and surgical removal process offers teachers an opportunity to come together as a group of professionals around specific tasks within and across grade levels and subject areas to perform these important operations.

Adding more in-depth learning experiences is the third curriculum modification procedure. This approach is based on the work of Phenix (1964), who recommended that a focus on representative concepts and ideas is the best way to capture the essence of a topic or area of study. Representative ideas or concepts consist of themes, patterns, main features, sequences, organizing principles and structures, and the logic that defines an area of study. Representative ideas and concepts can also be used as the bases for interdisciplinary or multidisciplinary studies.

While the use of representative concepts allows teachers to capture the essence of an area of study, it also allows them to introduce economy into content selection. The vast amount of material within any given discipline prevents unlimited coverage of content; therefore, material must be selected so that it is both representative and maximally transferable. Excellent resources are available to assist in this process. Books such as the *Dictionary of the History of Ideas* (Weiner, 1973) contain essays that cover every major discipline, and the emphasis of the essays is on interdisciplinary and cross-cultural relationships. The essays are cross-referenced to direct the reader to other articles which contain similar ideas in other domains. Additional resources can be found in books such as the *Syntopicon: An Index to the Great Ideas* (Adler, 1990), which lists concepts, ideas, and themes around which curriculum can be developed.

In-depth teaching also concerns the level of advancement or complexity of the material. First and foremost, the material must take into consideration the age, maturity, previous study, and background experiences of students. Beyond these considerations, three principles of content selection are recommended. First, curricular material should be selected so that it escalates along the hierarchy of knowledge dimensions: facts, conventions, trends and sequences, classifications and categories, criteria, principles and generalizations, and theories and structures. Second, movement toward the highest level, theories and structures, should involve continuous recycling to lower levels so that facts, trends and sequences, and the like can be understood in relation to a more integrated whole rather than as isolated bits of irrelevant information. Third, the cluster of diverse procedures surrounding the acquisition of knowledge, that dimension of learning commonly referred to as process or thinking skills, should themselves be viewed as a form of content. These more enduring skills form the cognitive structures and problem solving strategies that have the greatest transfer value.

A final characteristic of in-depth learning is a focus on methodology. This focus is designed to promote an understanding of, and appreciation for, the *application* of methods to the kinds of problems that are the essence of fields of knowledge. The goal of this emphasis on methodology is to cast the young person in the role of a first-hand inquirer rather than a mere learner-of-lessons, even if this role is carried out at a more junior level than that of the adult professional. This role encourages young learners to engage in the kinds of thinking, feeling, and doing that characterize the work of the practicing professional because it automatically creates confrontations with knowledge necessary for active rather than passive learning!

Enrichment Learning and Teaching

The third service delivery component of the SEM is enrichment learning and teaching. Enrichment learning and teaching is based on the ideas of a small but influential number of philosophers, theorists, and researchers.[1] The work of these theorists, coupled with our own research and program development activities, has given rise to the concept we call *enrichment learning and teaching.* The best way to define this concept is in terms of the following four principles:

1. Each learner is unique, and therefore all learning experiences must be examined in ways that take into account the abilities, interests, and learning styles of the individual.
2. Learning is more effective when students enjoy what they are doing, and therefore learning experiences should be constructed and assessed with as much concern for enjoyment as for other goals.
3. Learning is more meaningful and enjoyable when content (knowledge) and process (thinking skills, methods of inquiry) are learned within the context of a real and present problem; and therefore attention should be given to opportunities to personalize student choice in problem selection, the relevance of the problem for individual students at the time the problem is being addressed, and authentic strategies for addressing the problem.
4. Some formal instruction may be used in enrichment learning and teaching, but a major goal of this approach to learning is to enhance knowledge and thinking skills through *applications* of knowledge and skills, which result in students' own construction of meaning.

The ultimate goal of learning that is guided by these principles is to replace dependent and passive learning with independence and engaged learning. Although all but the most conservative educators will agree with these principles, much controversy exists about how these (or similar) principles might be applied in everyday school situations. Also, a danger exists that these principles might be viewed as yet another idealized list of glittering generalities that cannot be manifested easily in schools that are entrenched in the deductive model of learning. Developing a school program based on these principles is not an easy task. Over the years, however, we have achieved a fair amount of success by gaining faculty, administrative, and parental consensus on a small number of easy-to-understand concepts and related services, and by providing resources and training related to each concept and service delivery procedure. Numerous research studies (summarized in Renzulli & Reis, 1994) and field tests in schools with widely varying demographics have been conducted. These studies and field tests have provided opportunities for the development of

[1] Although it is beyond the scope of this chapter to review the work of these eminent thinkers, the group includes William James, Alfred North Whitehead, John Dewey, Maria Montessori, Jean Piaget, Paul Torrance, Jerome Bruner, Philip Phenix, Howard Gardner, Robert Sternberg, and Albert Bandura.

large amounts of practical knowhow that are readily available for schools that would like to implement the SEM.

Summary

For the past eighteen years, we have been developing, field-testing, and carrying out research on the Schoolwide Enrichment Model in numerous schools throughout the United States, Canada, and several nations overseas. For at least the following four reasons, the model caught on, and user satisfaction can be documented through evaluation and research studies, commendations by educators using the model, and site visits to places where the model is being used.

Practicality and Existing Know-how

The first reason for the success of SEM is its clarity, practicality, and flexibility. The roles and responsibilities of participating teachers, students, and administrators are easy to learn and are described in ways that avoid complex language or ponderous rhetoric. Although the model is directed toward a small number of common goals, each school is encouraged to develop its own unique program within the framework of general goals, guides, and "how-to" information. This flexibility has produced numerous examples of local pride and ownership, and it also has generated many practitioner-developed contributions to the model that have been shared locally and nationally.

In order for a model to work, it must be based on sound ideas and research, but every idea must be backed up with practical information, strategies, and materials. The following list represents categories of the broad array of service delivery components that we have developed and field-tested over the years:

- Print and video staff development materials
- Planning guides and worksheets for each major component of the model
- Instruments for assessing students' strengths, interests, and learning styles
- Procedures for developing schoolwide enrichment teams
- A slide presentation and script for parent orientation
- A taxonomy of specific thinking skills
- Guidelines for preparing interest development centers
- Procedures for developing a scope and sequence for thinking skills
- A directory of within- and across-discipline enrichment materials
- A directory of how-to books for first-hand investigative activities
- Sample letters, memos, and pamphlets for parents, students, and faculty
- Guidelines for developing a faculty/community mentor system
- Procedures for establishing a student "research foundation"
- A set of slides and script to train students in the investigative process
- Planning worksheets and documentation forms
- A community resources survey and classification system
- Easy-to-understand charts, diagrams, and summary sheets that facilitate staff development and student and parent orientation
- Evaluation forms and instruments for each major component of the model
- A residential summer staff development institute for advanced training and the training of trainers
- A national network and directory of school districts using the model
- A directory of practitioner consultants who have extensive experience in using the model
- Technical reports verifying the research base underlying the model.

Underlying Theory and Research

A second reason for the success of SEM has been the practicality of the theory underlying the model and the research that has been carried out over the years to support various aspects of the model. The underlying theory is divided into two dimensions. The first dimension focuses on a broadened conception of human potential and creative productivity (Gardner, 1983; Renzulli, 1978, 1986); the second dimension concentrates on pedagogical issues that are directly related to improving high-level acts of learning.

Most proposed changes in educational systems are implemented because of good intentions and desperate needs for improvement in the status quo. We have taken the time over the years to examine the effectiveness of the model in a broad range of school settings (Renzulli & Reis, 1994), and this research is summarized in Table 11.1. We also have compiled numerous examples of program materials and documents that point out a broad variety of implementation activities in districts with widely differing demographic characteristics.

Attractiveness to All Types of Schools

The third reason for the success of SEM has been the quality and commitment of persons who have implemented the model at the local level. For a variety of reasons, the model has attracted energetic teachers and administrators who believe that schools can be more effective and caring places. Many of these persons first became involved with the SEM because of their work in special programs for high-ability students. They initially were attracted to our written material and summer training programs at the University of Connecticut because of our concerns for equity as well as excellence in learning and teaching, and because of the flexible and common sense features of the model. And as the model evolved toward more specific recommendations and procedures for total school enrichment, most of these people "stuck with us" and became emissaries for change in their local districts.

Concern for At-Risk Populations

A final reason for the growing popularity of the Schoolwide Enrichment Model is our concern for providing special enrichment opportunities for students from low socioeconomic backgrounds and for students who show potentials for superior performance in areas that are not easily assessed by traditional ability measures. Low achievement among economically disadvantaged students represents the single most glaring failure of our educational system. The lack of results from years of compensatory programs and expenditures of billions of dollars have caused a small but growing number of educators at all levels to realize that we must explore creative alternatives to traditional models.

Conclusion

The general attitude that many educators and educational reform leaders have toward special programs for the gifted has resulted in barriers toward the broader implementation of any set of ideas with "gifted roots." Overt charges of elitism have been directed toward a field that historically has found its greatest support in school districts that serve the white middle class. Some of these criticisms are not unfounded. Quota requirements for the funding of special programs and identification guidelines that are based predominantly on ability test scores are still in effect in most states, and the conservative branch of the field's leadership continues to argue for some students to be identified as the "truly gifted." Conservatives also look with suspicion on identification procedures that are alternatives to IQ scores, and models such as SEM have been viewed with particular scorn by some in our field who believe the concept of giftedness has been "watered down." Some also have criticized our more flexible approach to identification because *our* advocacy for developing thinking skills in all students is viewed as a usurping of their early "discovery" of the process models. These process models were their stock-in-trade; therefore, our recommendation for a broader based use is viewed as giving away the family jewels!

All of these forces act against the provision of special enrichment opportunities for students from low socioeconomic backgrounds or students who may have potentials for superior performance in areas that are not as easily assessed as those measured by traditional ability tests. Compounding the problem is the slow but certain movement toward a test-driven, basic skills curriculum that has gained a strong foothold in many states. This movement, directed primarily toward "getting the scores up" on state and national wall charts, is

Table 11.1
Effectiveness of SEM over a Broad Range of School Settings

Author & Date (School Setting[a])	Major Finding
	Effectiveness of SEM as Perceived by Teachers, Administrators, and Parents
Reis, 1981 (E,P)	Teachers preferred RDIM over more traditional methods of identification; teachers reported that a high level of involvement with the program influenced their teaching practices.
Olenchak, 1988 (E)	The SEM contributed to improved teachers', parents', and administrators' attitudes toward education for high-ability students.
Cooper, 1983 (8 Districts)	Administrators attitudes to SEM included: greater staff participation in the education of high-ability students, more positive staff attitudes toward the program, fewer concerns about identification, positive changes in how the guidance department worked with the students, and more incentives for students to work toward higher goals.
	Creativity and SEM: Quality of Student Products
Reis, 1981 (P,E)	Products of above-average students were as good as the products completed by students who were identified for the program using traditional methods.
Gubbins, 1982 (E)	Students who did not generate Type IIIs attributed the lack of product development to time management and idea-generating difficulties.
	Creativity and SEM: Effects of Skill Training
Burns, 1987 (E)	Students receiving process skill training were 64% more likely to initiate Type IIIs than students who did not receive the training.
Newman, 1991 (E)	Students with training in the Talents Unlimited model were more likely to complete Type IIIs than students who did not receive the training.
	Creativity and SEM: Creative-Productive Behavior
Delcourt, 1988 (S)	Students completing Type IIIs displayed changes in skills required for project completion (e.g., writing), personal characteristics (e.g., increased patience), and decisions related to career choices.
Starko, 1986 (E)	Students who became involved with Type IIIs more often initiated their own creative products both inside and outside school than did qualified students who did not receive services.
	SEM and Personal and Social Development
Delisle, 1981 (E)	Students with high academic self-concepts tended to revolve into the program, initiate Type IIIs, and internalize their academic successes.
Olenchak, 1991 (E)	SEM, when used as an intervention, was associated with improved attitudes toward learning and improved self-concept in high-ability students with learning disabilities.
	SEM and Social Acceptability
Skaught, 1987 (E)	Studies identified for a SEM program were positively accepted by their peers.

(continued)

Table 11.1 *(Continued)*

Author & Date	*Major Finding*
Heal, 1987 (E)	SEM was associated with a reduction in the negative effects of labeling.
	SEM and Underachievement
Emerick, 1988	Reasons attributed to the reversal of academic underachievement included: the use of curriculum compacting, exposure to Type I activities, opportunities to be involved in Type IIIs, and a close match between the learning modes of students and a teacher who understands the modes.
Baum, Renzulli, & Hébert, in preparation (E,M)	A positive gain in classroom performance was made by underachieving students who undertook a Type III.
Taylor, 1992 (S)	Secondary vocational-technical students who undertook Type IIIs changed college plans from attending 2.6 years to attending 4.0 years.
	SEM and High-Ability/Learning Disabled Students
Baum, 1988 (E)	The Type III, when used as an intervention with high-ability, learning-disabled students, was associated with improvement in student behavior, time management, self-esteem, and the development of specific instructional strategies.
	SEM and Self-Efficacy
Schack, 1986 (E,M)	Self-efficacy was a significant predictor of initiation of Type IIIs. A mini-course on research methodology increased student self-efficacy.
Starko, 1986 (E)	The number of completed Type IIIs was a highly significant predictor of self-efficacy.
	SEM and Learning Styles
Stewart, 1979 (E)	High-ability students tend to prefer instructional methods that emphasize independence, while students in the general population prefer instructional methods with more structure.
	SEM and Curriculum Compacting
Reis et al., 1992 (P,E)	Ninety-five percent of teachers were able to identify high-ability students in their classes and document students' strength areas. Teachers were able to eliminate an average of 45%–50% of curriculum for high-ability students.
	SEM and Logitudinal Research
Delcourt, 1993	Students who participated in Type IIIs maintained interests in college and career aspirations that were similar to those manifested during their public school years.
Hébert, 1993	Type III interests of students affected postsecondary plans. Type IIIs serve as important training for later productivity.

[a]Settings: P—Primary (K–2), E—Elementary (grades 3–5), M—Middle (grades 6–8), S—Secondary (grades 9–12).

SEM = Schoolwide Enrichment Model.

Type I = General exploratory experiences.

RDIM = Revolving Door Identification Model.

Type III = Self-selected creative project.

already resulting in cutbacks in library and media programs, arts programs, extracurricular activities, and just about anything else that makes school an enriching and inviting place. Improving test scores is indeed an important national priority, and a goal of the SEM. But thirty years of federal and state support for compensatory education have produced negligible results; yet, the present focus on "outcomes" is predicated on the same didactic model of learning. At-risk students have been the major victims of this "drill-and-kill" approach to learning, an approach that has almost become public policy in the nation's schools. It is the children of the poor who suffer most from declining enrichment opportunities. It is the families of these young people who cannot afford the computer camps, the dance lessons, the well-stocked home bookshelves, the summer on-campus science programs, and the SAT prep courses that the middle class uses to compensate for unchallenging schools.

The SEM is an enrichment model that cuts across all activities that take place in a school by creating *an enriched learning environment in which young people want to participate.* The Schoolwide Enrichment Model is purposefully designed to create such an environment by blending the kinds of activities that promote challenge, effort, and enjoyment into the entire curriculum. These types of activities have been used for years in special programs, and we believe they can improve general education while simultaneously challenging high-achieving students.

REFERENCES

Adler, M. J. (Ed.). (1990). *The syntopicon: An index to the great ideas.* Chicago: Encyclopedia Britannica.

Baum, S. (1988). An enrichment program for the gifted learning disabled students. *Gifted Child Quarterly, 32*(1), 226–230.

Baum, S., Renzulli, J. S., & Hébert, T. P. (1995). *The prism metaphor: A new paradigm for reversing underachievement.* Storrs, CT: National Research Center on the Gifted and Talented.

Bloom, B. S. (Ed.). (1985). *Developing talent in young people.* New York: Ballantine Books.

Burns, D. E. (1987). *The effects of group training activities on students' creative productivity.* Unpublished Ph.D. dissertation, The University of Connecticut, Storrs.

Burns, D. E. (1992). *SEM network directory.* The Talent Development Program, The University of Connecticut, Storrs.

Cooper, C. (1983). *Administrators' attitudes toward gifted programs based on the enrichment triad / revolving door identification model: Case studies in decision-making.* Unpublished Ph.D. dissertation, The University of Connecticut, Storrs.

Delcourt, M. A. B. (1988). *Characteristics related to high levels of creative/product behavior in secondary school students: A multi-case study.* Unpublished Ph.D. dissertation, The University of Connecticut, Storrs.

Delcourt, M. A. B. (1993). Creative productivity among secondary school students: Combining energy, interest and imagination. *Gifted Child Quarterly, 37*(1), 23–31.

Delisle, J. R. (1981). *The revolving door identification and programming model: Correlates of creative production of behavioral change.* Unpublished Ph.D. dissertation, The University of Connecticut, Storrs.

Dunn, R., Dunn, K., & Price, G. E. (1981). *Learning style inventory.* Lawrence, KS: Price Systems.

Emerick, L. J. (1988). *Academic underachievement among the gifted: Students' perceptions of factors relating to the reversal of the academic underachievement pattern.* Unpublished Ph.D. dissertation, The University of Connecticut, Storrs.

Gardner, H. (1983). *Frames of mind.* New York: Basic Books.

Gubbins, E. J. (1982). *Revolving door identification model: Characteristics of talent pool students.* Unpublished Ph.D. dissertation, The University of Connecticut, Storrs.

Heal, M. M. (1989). *Student perceptions of labeling the gifted: A comparative case study analysis.* Unpublished Ph.D. dissertation, The University of Connecticut, Storrs.

Hébert, T. P. (1993). Reflections at graduation: The long term impact of elementary school experiences in creative productivity. *Roeper Review, 16(*1), 22–28.

Kirschenbaum, R. J. (1983). Let's cut out the cut-off score in the identification of the gifted. *Roeper Review, 5,* 6–10.

Kirschenbaum, R. J., & Siegle, D. (1993, April). *Predicting creative performance in an enrichment program.* Paper presented at the Association for the Education of Gifted Underachieving Students 6th Annual Conference, Portland, OR.

Newman, J. L. (1991). *The effects of the Talents Un-*

limited model on students' creative productivity. Unpublished Ph.D. dissertation, The University of Alabama, Tuscaloosa.

Olenchak, F. R. (1988). The schoolwide enrichment model in the elementary schools: A study of implementation stages and effects on educational excellence. In J. S. Renzulli (Ed.), *Technical report on research studies relating to the Revolving Door Identification Model* (2nd ed.). Storrs, CT: Bureau of Educational Research, The University of Connecticut.

Olenchak, F. R. (1991). Assessing program effects for gifted/learning disabled students. In R. Swassing & A. Robinson (Eds.), *NAGC 1991 research briefs.* Washington, DC: National Association for Gifted Students.

Olenchak, F. R., & Renzulli, J. S. (1989). The effectiveness of the schoolwide enrichment model on selected aspects of elementary school change. *Gifted Child Quarterly, 33,* 36–46.

Phenix, P. (1964). *Realms of meaning.* New York: McGraw-Hill.

Reis, S. M. (1981). *An analysis of the productivity of gifted students participating in programs using the revolving door identification model.* Unpublished doctoral dissertation, The University of Connecticut, Storrs.

Reis, S. M., Burns, D. E., & Renzulli, J. S. (1992). *Curriculum compacting: The complete guide to modifying the regular curriculum for high ability students.* Mansfield Center, CT: Creative Learning Press.

Reis, S. M., & Renzulli, J. S. (1992). Using curriculum compacting to challenge the above-average. *Educational Leadership, 50* (2), 51–57.

Reis, S. M., Westberg, K. L,. Kulikovich, J., Caillard, F., Hébert, T., Plucker, J., Purcell, J. H., Rogers, J. B., & Smist, J. M. (1993). *Why not let high ability students start school in January?* Storrs, CT: National Research Center on the Gifted and Talented.

Renzulli, J. S. (1976). The enrichment triad model: A guide for developing defensible programs for the gifted and talented. *Gifted Child Quarterly, 20,* 303–326.

Renzulli, J. S. (1977). *The enrichment triad model: A guide for developing defensible programs for the gifted and talented.* Mansfield Center, CT: Creative Learning Press.

Renzulli, J. S. (1978). What makes giftedness? Reexamining a definition. *Phi Delta Kappan, 60*(3), 180–184, 261.

Renzulli, J. S. (1986). The three-ring conception of giftedness: A developmental model for creative productivity. In R . J. Sternberg & J. E. Davidson (Eds.), *Conceptions of giftedness* (pp. 332–357). New York: Cambridge University Press.

Renzulli, J. S. (1994). *Schools for talent development: A practical plan for total school improvement.* Mansfield Center, CT: Creative Learning Press.

Renzulli, J. S., & Reis, S. M. (1985). *The schoolwide enrichment model: A comprehensive plan for educational excellence.* Mansfield Center, CT: Creative Learning Press.

Renzulli, J. S., & Reis, S. M. (1994). Research related to the Schoolwide Enrichment Model. *Gifted Child Quarterly, 38,* 2–14.

Renzulli, J. S., Reis, S. M., & Smith, L. H. (1981). *The revolving door identification model.* Mansfield Center, CT: Creative Learning Press.

Renzulli, J. S., & Smith, L. H. (1978). *The compactor.* Mansfield Center, CT: Creative Learning Press.

Renzulli, J. S., Smith, L. H., & Reis, S. M. (1982). Curriculum compacting: An essential strategy for working with gifted students. *Elementary School Journal, 82,* 185–194.

Schack, G. D. (1986). *Creative productivity and self-efficacy in children.* Unpublished Ph.D. dissertation, The University of Connecticut, Storrs.

Skaught, B. J. (1987). *The social acceptability of talent pool students in an elementary school using the schoolwide enrichment model.* Unpublished Ph.D. dissertation, The University of Connecticut, Storrs.

Starko, A. J. (1986). *The effects of the revolving door identification model on creative productivity and self-efficacy.* Unpublished Ph.D. dissertation, The University of Connecticut, Storrs.

Sternberg, R. J. (1984). Toward a triarchic theory of human intelligence. *Behavioral and Brain Sciences, 7*(2), 269–316.

Stewart, E. D. (1979). *Learning styles among gifted / talented students: Preferences for instructional techniques.* Unpublished Ph.D. dissertation, The University of Connecticut, Storrs.

Taylor, L. A. (1992). *The effects of the secondary enrichment triad model and a career counseling component on the career development of vocational-technical school students.* Unpublished Ph.D. dissertation, The University of Connecticut, Storrs.

Torrance, E. P. (1962). *Guiding creative talent.* Englewood Cliffs, NJ: Prentice-Hall.

Torrance, E. P. (1974). *Norms–Technical manual: Torrance tests of creative thinking.* Bensenville, IL: Scholastic Testing Service.

Weiner, P. P. (Ed.). (1973). *Dictionary of the history of ideas.* New York: Scribner's Sons.

12

Intellectually Talented Children: How Can We Best Meet Their Needs?

CAMILLA P. BENBOW and DAVID LUBINSKI, *Iowa State University*

The Study of Mathematically Precocious Youth (SMPY) was founded by Julian C. Stanley in September 1971 at Johns Hopkins University. Its work has spanned more than two decades and is now located at two sites—Johns Hopkins University and Iowa State University. Regional centers, based on SMPY's philosophy and procedures, have been established at four universities as well. They are the Center for Talented Youth (CTY) at Johns Hopkins, the Talent Identification program at Duke University, the Center for Talent Development at Northwestern University, and the Rocky Mountain Talent Search at the University of Denver. Within CTY is the Study of Exceptional Talent (SET), providing counseling and services in the SMPY tradition to our nation's most intellectually talented adolescents (top 1 percent and beyond). In addition, there are numerous other local programs across the nation and world based on SMPY's work. Together, these programs serve approximately 150,000 students on an annual basis, making them a dominant feature of our educational landscape.

SMPY always has been concerned with the optimal development of intellectually precocious youth, particularly mathematically talented youth. Its empirical investigations are predicated on conducting research *through service* to intellectually gifted adolescents. By developing and providing innovative educational programs and educational counseling, SMPY attempts to discover those mechanisms that promote both intellectual and social well-being (they are not unrelated) among the gifted.

By simultaneously conducting research on and providing services to gifted youth, SMPY developed a dual focus. First, it created a set of programs and services constituting what has become known as the *SMPY model* for serving intellectually talented sudents (Benbow, 1986; Stanley, 1977; Stanley & Benbow, 1982, 1986). The SMPY model was field-tested extensively (e.g., Benbow & Stanley, 1983a) and then widely disseminated. Second, SMPY launched a longitudinal study to investigate the development of intellectually talented students and to assess the impact of educational interventions on their educational and career development (Lubinski & Benbow, 1994). About five thousand talented individuals currently are being tracked throughout their adult lives. The SMPY longitudinal study, which we are conducting at Iowa State University, is similar to the classic Terman (1925–1959) study. SMPY's study, however, contains over three times as many subjects, and these participants are identified using a specific aptitude test, not a general intelligence test. They were comprehensively assessed at age 13 in terms of both their intellectual and nonintellectual personal attributes.

Both the programmatic and research strands of SMPY will be described in this chapter. First, however, the theoretical model guiding SMPY's educational programming and its empirical research on the dispositional determinants of scientific educational/career paths of the gifted is provided. It serves as the foundation for our work.

The Theoretical Model Guiding SMPY's Work

The conceptual framework guiding SMPY's scholarly work and its educational programs/interventions draws on three theoretical perspectives (Dawis & Lofquist, 1984;

Tannenbaum, 1983; Zuckerman, 1977), while incorporating information about the development of talent and personal preferences for contrasting educational/vocational paths (Benbow & Lubinski, 1994; Lubinski & Benbow, 1994). Since its beginning, SMPY's work has been consistent with a well-established model of vocational adjustment (see Figure 12.1), the Theory of Work Adjustment (TWA), a model developed over the past thirty years by René V. Dawis and Lloyd H. Lofquist at the University of Minnesota (Lofquist & Dawis, 1969, 1991). Although formulated to allow a better understanding of adjustment in the world of work, an especially attractive feature of this model is that it can be readily extended to critical *antecedents* to vocational adjustment, such as choice of educational program. Currently SMPY is, in fact, explicitly extending the model to explain just that—educational adjustment.

According to the TWA, to ascertain the optimal learning and work environment for an individual, one must first parse the individual's work (or academic) personality *and* environment into two broad yet complementary subdomains. An individual's work personality primarily comprises his or her (1) repertoire of specific skills or abilities and (2) personal preferences for content found in contrasting educational/vocational environments. In contrast, different environmental contexts (educational curricula and occupations) are classified in terms of (1) their ability requirements and (2) their capability to reinforce personal preferences. Optimal educational and work environments for an individual are those for which two levels of correspondence can be established, *satisfactoriness* and *satisfaction.* Satisfactoriness refers to the correspondence between an individual's abilities and the ability requirements of a particular environment (e.g., occupation or educational curriculum), whereas satisfaction denotes correspondence between an individual's preferences and the types of reinforcers provided by the environment. Good educational and career choices maximize satisfactoriness and satisfaction and, consequently, the degree of commitment to one's choice.

An important implication of this model is that *both* abilities and preferences must be assessed, concurrently, to ascertain the readiness of a given individual for a particular educational or career track (see, e.g., Lubinski & Thompson, 1986). Similarly, components of the educational/vocational environment (response requirements *and* reward systems) need to be evaluated simultaneously to estimate whether both dimensions of correspondence are likely to be achieved. It is important to keep in mind that correspondence, and thus personal fulfillment for any one individual, whether gifted or not, is not likely to be found but in a few educational or career tracks. Multipotentiality is not prevalent among the gifted (Achter, Lubinski, & Benbow, 1996).

To provide a practical illustration of TWA and its implications, we will focus on the physical sciences, given their special place in SMPY's research. For these disciplines, we know that the ability requirements involve especially high mathematical reasoning ability (e.g., Benbow & Arjmand, 1990; Green, 1989; Walberg, Strykowski, Rovai, & Hung, 1984). Yet high spatial/mechanical reasoning abilities are also important, probably the second most critical personal attribute for satisfactoriness all along the math/science pipeline (Humphreys, Lubinski, & Yao, 1993). Verbal ability is *relatively* less critical, but still valuable. In terms of preferences, investigative interests (scientific) and theoretical values (intellectual, philosophical) are among the most salient personal preferences for gravitating toward scientific environments, finding their content reinforcing for developing one's intellectual talent, and maintaining a commitment toward these kinds of disciplines (e.g., Dawis, 1991; Holland, 1985; Lubinski & Benbow, 1992, 1994; Roe, 1953). The physical sciences also require intense abilities and preferences for manipulating and working with sophisticated things and gadgets. Individuals with pronounced or relatively higher social values (or stronger need for people contact), in contrast, are not as readily reinforced in such environments. These are the abilities and preferences that are important for adjustment in scientific environments and, thus, must be assessed and in place for an individual considering entrance into them (Lubinski, Benbow, & Sanders, 1993). Moreover, these personal attributes, coupled with an intense commitment

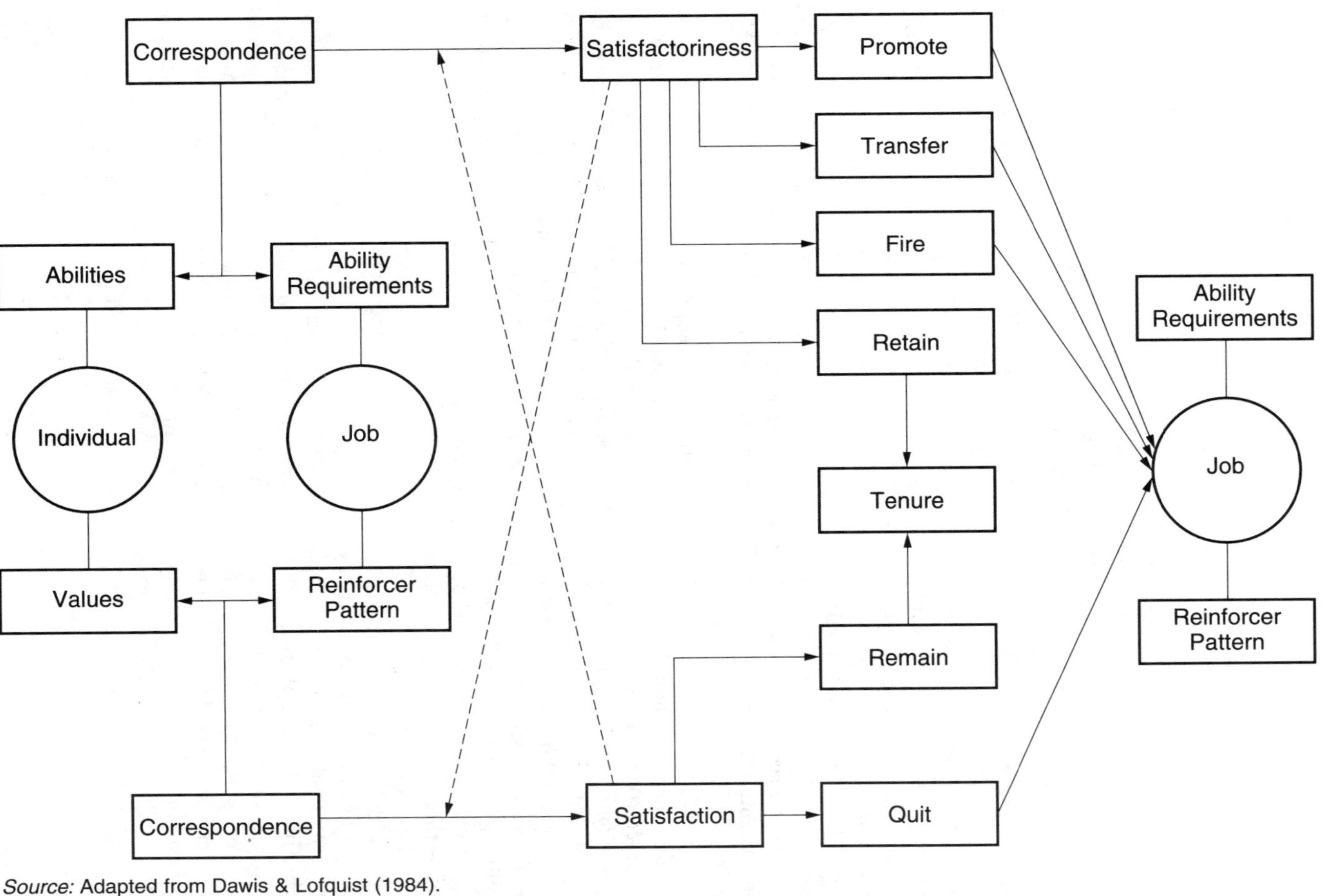

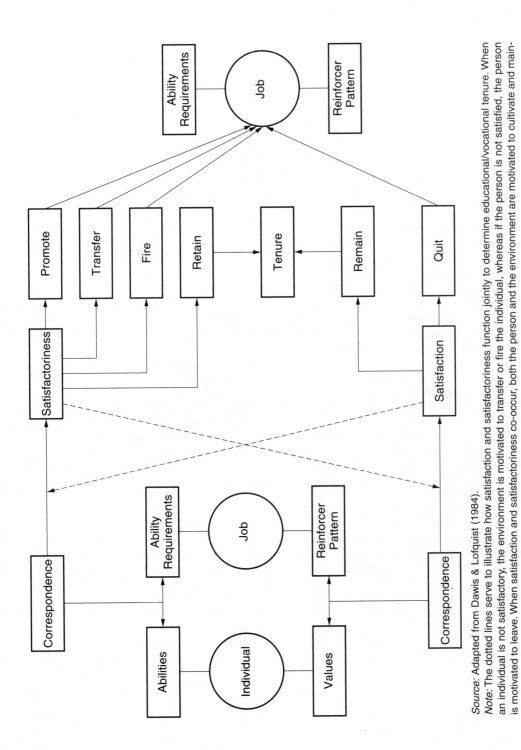

Source: Adapted from Dawis & Lofquist (1984).
Note: The dotted lines serve to illustrate how satisfaction and satisfactoriness function jointly to determine educational/vocational tenure. When an individual is not satisfactory, the environment is motivated to transfer or fire the individual, whereas if the person is not satisfied, the person is motivated to leave. When satisfaction and satisfactoriness co-occur, both the person and the environment are motivated to cultivate and maintain interactions with one another.

Figure 12.1 A depiction of the theory of work adjustment.

to mastery of one's chosen discipline and substantial energy for work (to be discussed), are the sine qua non for high scientific achievement.

It should be noted, however, that possession of this constellation of personal attributes (though rare) is still not sufficient for the manifestation of exceptional scientific achievement. That is even rarer. Those who have the personal potentialities also require special encounters with the appropriate environment to facilitate the emergence of world-class scientific achievement. This is the second aspect of SMPY's theoretical model, to which we now turn.

Bloom (1985) noted from his interviews of talented performers in a variety of disciplines that special experiences, sometimes interventions, are important in their development.[1] Moreover, Zuckerman (1977), in her analysis of Nobel Laureates' careers, saw that their development or emergence fit well with the model of "the accumulation of advantage." That is, individuals who produce exceptional scientific advances almost universally show promise extremely early in their lives, and this evidenced precocity not only responds to but also creates greater opportunities for intellectual development.[2] For example, most Laureates receive an advantage in graduate work by attending the most distinguished universities (10 universities produced 55% of the Laureates) and by studying with the best minds of the day—thereby begetting a pattern of eminence creating eminence.

Tannenbaum (1983), furthermore, postulated that great performances or productivity results from a rare blend of superior general intellect, distinctive special aptitudes, the right combination of nonintellective traits, a challenging environment, *and* the smile of good fortune at crucial periods of life (see Chapter 3 in this volume). The first three components seem to parallel the abilities and preferences discussed in the Theory of Work Adjustment, and the latter two the work of Zuckerman. According to Tannenbaum, success depends on this *complete* configuration of personal propensities and experiential facilitators, whereas failure results from even a single deficit. By virtue of its synergetic significance, then, every one of Tannenbaum's five qualifiers is a necessary requisite for high achievement, and none alone is sufficient to overcome inadequacies in the others. We have adopted that view as well. Thus, for the optimal development or actualization of talent to occur, not only must the individual possess the necessary personal attributes critical for success and satisfaction in his or her chosen vocational track, but he or she also must be given (or create, or seek out) the opportunity to develop in an appropriate educational-learning environment. All components are vital.

The practical implications for SMPY were that we must first identify the appropriate educational and vocational environments for the individual under consideration, and then attempt to arrange educational interventions congruent with the individual's abilities and needs. Until recently SMPY focused most of its efforts on optimizing satisfactoriness by using acceleration to provide a better fit between the individual's abilities and the learning environment. We now turn to how this was accomplished by describing the SMPY educational model.

The SMPY Model

SMPY's educational intervention activities over the past two decades can be captured succinctly by a pseudochemical formula devised by Stanley: MT:D_4P_3. This stands for Mathematical Talent: Discovery, Description, Development, and Dissemination of its Principles, Practices, and Procedures (Stanley, Keating, & Fox, 1974). SMPY's focus is on the individual student, and its first step is to understand that student, who initially was the mathematically talented student. This is accomplished through the identification (i.e., participation in a talent search, to be described) and characterization phases of its model (i.e., the first

---

[1] See Chapter 17 by Sosniak.

[2] Sandra Scarr (1992; Scarr & McCartney, 1983) has written insightfully on how people actually seek out and create environments for themselves that correspond to their personal attributes.

two D's), where students become aware of their distinct profile of abilities and preferences. Once the students' ability and preference profiles are known, students are encouraged to adapt their educational program to create an appropriate learning environment, one that is commensurate with and responsive to their abilities (the third D, Development). This is accomplished through use of acceleration or following the principle of placement according to competence. Students are prompted, through personal correspondence, newsletters, and the like, to look at the entire curriculum available to them, including postsecondary curriculum as well, in order to locate where in each subject they might be appropriately placed according to their demonstrated competence (not age). Then they are encouraged and supported in their attempts to gain access to appropriate curricula or educational experiences that may or may not be within their home schools (e.g., MathCounts). In essence, SMPY promotes primarily competence rather than age as the criterion to be used in determining who obtains access to what curricula and experiences, and at what time. The goal is to develop a combination of accelerative options, enrichment, and out-of-school opportunities (already available resources) that reflect the best possible alternative for educating a specific child and, thereby, enhancing satisfactoriness. This approach has been labeled *curricular flexibility.*

Much of SMPY's programmatic research has been aimed at refining this model for identifying and serving mathematically and verbally gifted youth. We now explore its components in greater depth.

Talent Search

To identify large numbers of mathematically talented students, SMPY developed the concept of an annual *talent search* and conducted six separate searches in March 1972, January 1973, January 1974, December 1976, January 1978, and January 1979. During those years, 9,927 intellectually gifted junior high school students in the Mid-Atlantic region between 12 and 14 years of age were tested. Students were eligible to participate in a SMPY talent search if they had scored in the upper 5 percent (1972), 2 percent (1973 and 1974), or 3 percent (1976, 1978, and 1979) in mathematical ability on the national norms of a standardized achievement test battery administered as part of their schools' regular testing program (e.g., the Iowa Test of Basic Skills).

All of these students then took the College Board Scholastic Aptitude Test (SAT), both the mathematics (SAT-M) and verbal (SAT-V) sections. (In 1972 and 1974 the SAT-V was not administered.) Their resulting SAT score distributions consistently were indistinguishable from those typically observed for above-average high school students, the students for whom the test was designed (Benbow, 1988). This form of assessment, using tests designed for older students with younger gifted students, is known as *out-of-level testing* and is especially powerful in measuring analytical reasoning ability when the test is the SAT (Benbow & Wolins, in press; Minor & Benbow, in press).

For the adolescents participating in talent searches, the SAT is ideal for revealing systematic sources of intellectual differences among the gifted that are hidden by the ceiling effects observed with conventional instruments. These individual differences are psychologically meaningful and important to assess for purposes of structuring accelerative educational opportunities. The differences in academic accomplishments among individuals in the top 1 percent are remarkable. Benbow (1992) showed that over a ten-year time frame, between ages 13 and 23, the academic achievements of those individuals in the *top quarter of the top 1 percent* in mathematical ability were much more impressive than the achievements of those in the *bottom quarter of the top 1 percent,* who were, nonetheless, themselves high achievers. Hence differential expectations for individuals in this range, which spans the range of IQ scores from approximately 135 to over 200, are justified and should be established.

Through out-of-level testing in talent searches, which began by serving and studying mathematically talented students only but then spread to students high in verbal and/or overall general intellectual ability, students are able to learn about their relative strengths and weaknesses with respect to the two most critical intellectual attributes for academic excellence, mathematical and verbal reasoning. Overlooked by this process, however, is the assessment of spatial ability, the remaining major marker of general intelligence (Lubinski & Dawis, 1992). Because of SMPY's interest in the sciences and the importance of spatial ability for success in that domain (Humphreys et al., 1993), this ability (along with preferences) is assessed in the supplemental testing sessions offered to those who score highly on the SAT (Cohn, 1977; Lubinski & Benbow, 1992, 1994). Through talent searches and supplemental testing sessions, the first two D's, Discovery and Description, of the SMPY model are handled.

SMPY's Smorgasbord

The primary purpose of identification, in SMPY's view, is to help assess what educational interventions and services are not only appropriate but necessary for the student's optimal intellectual development. In 1971, when SMPY began, it was not clear what was appropriate for facilitating the education of intellectually precocious youth. It did appear, however, that acceleration, though rarely utilized, was the method with the most empirical support. Thus, SMPY began experimenting with various educational innovations based on the principle of acceleration to determine some of the optimal means of providing academic challenges to gifted students.

Some of the educational alternatives that SMPY began experimenting with and then included in its smorgasbord of accelerative options (Southern, Jones, & Stanley, 1993) are: early admittance to school, grade skipping, entering college early with or without the high school diploma (most high schools will award a high school diploma after completion of one year of college) (Brody & Stanley, 1991; Eisenberg & George, 1979; Stanley & Benbow, 1983), entering a college early-entrance program such as Simon's Rock or the Texas Academy for Math and Science (Stanley, 1991), International Baccalaureate (see description in Cox, Daniel, & Boston, 1985), taking a course (e.g., Algebra 1) one or two years earlier than typical, taking college courses on a part-time basis while in secondary school (Solano & George, 1976), taking special fast-paced classes during the summer or academic year (Durden, 1980; Stanley & Stanley, 1986; Swiatek & Benbow, 1991b, VanTassel-Baska, 1983), completing two years of a subject in one year, compressing curricula, taking Advanced Placement (AP) courses and examinations (AP courses are college-level courses taught in high school, which may garner college credit for the student if final AP exam scores are sufficiently high) (Zak, Benbow, & Stanley, 1983), individual tutoring in advanced subject matter (Stanley, 1979), earning a master's degree simultaneously with the bachelor's degree, and joint B.A./M.D. or B.A./Ph.D. programs. Essentially, SMPY uses already available resources, curricula, or programs designed for older students, but with younger gifted students (Benbow & Stanley, 1983a). This is consistent with basic research findings revealing that gifted students are simply precocious or developmentally advanced (Dark & Benbow, 1990, 1991; Elkind, 1988). It also makes recommended interventions highly cost-effective (Benbow, 1991).

In conjunction with the aforementioned work involving experimentation with various forms of acceleration, SMPY developed fast-paced classes where, for example, students master one full year of high school subject matter in just three intensive weeks during the summer. This effort began in 1972 with a mathematics class of some 30 students (Fox, 1974). Today, about 10,000 students are served annually through such classes, which are offered during the summer and academic year in verbal, mathematical, and scientific areas.

The fast-paced mathematics classes, an innovation for which SMPY is especially noted, cover precalculus mathematics. In three intensive summer weeks or on alternate Saturdays throughout the academic year, the typical student completes one to two high school mathematics courses. Some students are prepared by the end of the program to take calculus as eighth graders (Bartkovich &

Mezynski, 1981). We summarize next how they achieve this remarkable feat.[3]

Diagnostic Testing—Prescriptive Instruction

SMPY's initial experiences in working with mathematically talented students, through its Wolfson I and II precalculus mathematics classes, involved covering the entire precalculus sequence in 14 months of classes conducted on Saturdays or else in the summer. All units were taught to all students, but at a rate dictated by the ablest members of the class. Much success was experienced (Benbow, Perkins, & Stanley, 1983; Swiatek & Benbow, 1992). These classes revealed not only that these students could learn mathematics extremely rapidly but also that many of them already knew mathematical concepts not yet explicitly taught to them (Bartkovich & George, 1980; Bartkovich & Mezynski, 1981; Stanley, Keating, & Fox, 1974). Moreover, the rate at which unknown mathematical concepts and principles were acquired also varied. These findings illuminated a need for developing a teaching approach that could accommodate both the individual's idiosyncrasies in knowledge of mathematics and his or her rate of learning. The results of experimenting led to the diagnostic testing followed by prescriptive instruction (DT-PI) model (Stanley, 1978, 1979), which was first piloted in the summer of 1978 with remarkable success (Bartkovich & Mezynnski, 1981).

This individualized instructional approach, which can be used in both individual and group settings, is a strategy for teaching gifted students at a rate dictated by their abilities, and only those concepts or units in a subject they have not mastered. It is a sequential method of (1) determining the student's current level of knowledge using appropriate tests, (2) pinpointing areas of weakness by analyzing items missed on a given test, (3) devising an instructional program that targets those areas of weakness and allows the student to achieve mastery on a second form of the test, and (4) proceeding to the next higher level and repeating steps 1 to 3.

The DT-PI model has been used successfully with students as young as 6 years of age and has been used to help students master arithmetic or basic mathematics, precalculus, calculus, the sciences, and other courses such as the mechanics of standard written English. Not only teachers but also paraprofessionals, mentors, and qualified volunteers from the community can use this approach. It is an extremely flexible instructional model.

The SMPY Longitudinal Study

We now turn our attention to the other facet of SMPY—its longitudinal study, planned to extend fifty years. Through this study we are working toward developing a comprehensive and refined understanding of the processes whereby precocious forms of intellectual talent develop into noteworthy forms of adult achievement and creative accomplishment. How various educational interventions or opportunities, such as acceleration, facilitate the development of potential into actual achievement and creativity is a question of special importance to SMPY's research program.

Design

A description of the longitudinal study is provided in Table 12.1. There are five cohorts in all (extensive detailing is provided in Lubinski & Benbow, 1994): Four were assembled through talent searches, while a fifth cohort is composed of 750 graduate students in top U.S. mathematics and physical science departments. Each of the first four cohorts is separated in age by a few years, while cohort 5 overlaps with cohort 4. Combined, the cohorts span more than twenty years; therefore, findings from each cohort can serve in part as replications for similar analyses conducted in other time frames. In addition, because the students in the first four cohorts were identified over a twenty-year period using the same criteria and are studied at the same junctures, the study allows for a reasonable assessment

[3] A more detailed description can be found in Benbow (1986).

Table 12.1
The Five Cohorts of SMPY's Longitudinal Study

Cohort	*N*	*When Identified*	*Age at Identification*	*SAT Criteria*	*Ability Level*
1	2,188	1972–1974	12–13	Verb. ≧ 370 or Math ≧ 390	1%
2	778	1976–1979	12	Top 1/3 of Talent Search Participants	0.5%
3	423	1980–1983		Math ≧ 700 or Verb. ≧ 630	0.01%
Comparison Groups	150	1983	12	SAT-M + SAT-V ≦540	5%
		1982	12	500–590 Math 600–690 Math	0.5%
4>	1,000	1987–	12	Math ≧ 500 or Verb. ≧ 430	0.5%
5>	750	1992	23	Graduate students in top-ranked engineering, math, and science departments in the United States	

of historical effects and also for some degree of quasi-control of historical influences.

Another unique aspect of this study is the ability to modify and add new assessment materials. Cohort 4 grows by approximately 400 participants each year, allowing us to ask questions not possible in the early 1970s. Finally, a retrospective but also longitudinal study of graduate students in this nation's top engineering, mathematics, and physical science departments was initiated (Cohort 5) to ascertain whether such students differ in experiential or psychological ways from students identified via conventional talent searches. Data from Cohort 5 will help determine how well SMPY's findings, based on students identified by the SAT at age 13, generalize to other groups of gifted individuals.

The Cohorts

The first four SMPY cohorts were formed using different ability cutoffs on the SAT. The first three cohorts are successively more able; the fourth, consisting of primarily Midwestern residents who are being identified through the Office of Precollegiate Programs for Talented and Gifted (OPPTAG) at Iowa State University, represents the same ability level as Cohort 2. A detailing of each cohort is outlined in Table 12.1.

Cohort 1 comes from SMPY's March 1972, January 1973, and January 1974 Talent Searches. As seventh- or eighth-graders, they scored SAT-M ≥ 390 or SAT-V ≥ 370 (Benbow, 1983, 1992; Benbow & Arjmand, 1990). Those cutoff scores were selected because they represented the average performance of a random sample of high school females on the SAT at that time. The 2,118 students were drawn primarily from the state of Maryland, with a heavy concentration from the greater Baltimore area. Cohort 2 comprises at least the top one-third of seventh-grade students from SMPY's December 1976, January 1978, and January 1979 Talent Searches, using cutoff scores at or above the top 0.5 percent in general intellectual ability. These 778 students were drawn from the Mid-Atlantic states. These first two cohorts are separated by at least three years. About 60 percent of the participants are male.

Cohort 3 comprises three groups and is national in its representation. It consists of nearly 300 students who scored at least 700 on SAT-M before age 13 between November 1980 and November 1983, plus more than 150 students scoring at or above 630 on SAT-V before age 13. These scores represent the top 1 in

10,000 for mathematical and verbal reasoning abilities, respectively. Finally, for comparison purposes, Cohort 3 includes two additional groups. The first group consists of 150 seventh-grade students scoring slightly above chance on the SAT (i.e., SAT-M + SAT-V ≤ 540) in the 1983 Talent Search conducted by the Center for Talented Youth (CTY) at Johns Hopkins University. Because chance performance tends to imply low ability, it is important to keep in mind that this last group's ability level is still in the top 3 to 5 percent on national norms (only students in the top 3 to 5 percent in ability can enter a Talent Search); thus, by most definitions they too would be considered at least modestly gifted. The second comparison group consists of 50 seventh graders, in the early 1980s, whose SAT-M scores were either in the 500–590 range or in the 600–690 range.

Cohort 4 currently consists of 1,000 students, primarily Midwesterners, scoring before age 13 at least 500 on SAT-M, 430 on SAT-V, *or* 930 or more on SAT-M + SAT-V. Like Cohort 2, they represent the top 0.5 percent in ability. Students in Cohort 4 had enrolled in Iowa State's summer program for intellectually talented youth,[4] a program based purely on the SMPY model. Several comparison groups also are being formed from the Iowa Talent Search, which screens students with abilities in the top 3 percent in the nation, as well as from students in the normative ability range.

Finally, Cohort 5 contains over 750 individuals from various engineering, mathematics, and physical science disciplines who were enrolled in this nation's top graduate programs in 1992. Approximately 50 percent of the sample consists of females. This sample was surveyed in the spring of 1992, with a response rate of 93 percent.[5]

Collectively, the five cohorts of SMPY comprise approximately 5,000 highly able students. This number will soon increase to about 6,000, the target number for the study. All of the students in the five cohorts are being surveyed at critical junctures throughout their youth and adult lives. Each cohort, moreover, will be surveyed at the same ages to ensure comparability of findings across cohorts.

To date, we have surveyed Cohort 1 at age 13, 18, 23, and 33 (in progress). Cohort 2 also has been surveyed at ages 13, 18, and 23, with the last survey just being completed. Cohort 3 has been surveyed at ages 13, 18, and 23 (in progress). Cohort 4 has been surveyed at age 13 and 18 (in progress). Cohort 5 has been surveyed at age 23 only, but that survey included much retrospective information. Response rates to our several follow-up surveys range from 75 percent to well over 90 percent. Respondents do not differ significantly from nonrespondents on key variables, including ability, family background, and college attendance (Benbow & Arjmand, 1990).

Preliminary Findings

What are some of the major findings that have emerged so far from the longitudinal study? Perhaps the most important one is that we can identify at age 13 most of those students who have the potential to become our nation's great scientific achievers (Benbow, 1992; Lubinski & Benbow, 1992, 1994; Lubinski, Benbow, Eftekhari-Sanjani, & Jensen, in preparation). Students labeled as mathematically talented on the basis of high SAT-M scores at age 13 do disproportionally enter careers in the math/science pipeline. Indeed, graduate students in Cohort 5 who happened to take the SAT-M at age 13 earned scores comparable to those of participants in Cohort 2. More specifically, we know that among the gifted, those choosing to enter the math/science areas as adults have especially strong mathematical reasoning and spatial abilities and investigative/realistic or theoretical preferences (Lubinski, Benbow, & Sanders, 1993). This holds for both genders and is consistent with the Theory of Work Adjustment.

We also have learned from longitudinal analyses that most mathematically talented students seem to be successful in translating their potential into academic achievement. At

[4] See Lubinski and Benbow (1992, 1994) for a profile of their abilities, interests, and values.

[5] Some of the findings from this survey are reported in Lubinski, Benbow, Eftekhari-Sanjani, and Jensen (in preparation).

the end of high school and college, these students were high academic achievers (Benbow, 1983, 1992; Benbow & Arjmand, 1990). For example, by age 23 at least 85 percent of Cohort 1 had graduated from college with excellent academic records; almost half of them were pursuing graduate training. The achievements of Cohorts 2 and 3, however, are even more impressive, as expected given their initially greater ability level (Lubinski & Benbow, 1994). Moreover, there appears to be no threshold effect for ability in its relationship to subsequent academic achievement; those with the most ability tend to show the strongest record of academic achievement (Benbow, 1992).

Results of studies evaluating SMPY's programmatic innovations have been uniformly positive (e.g., Benbow, Lubinski, & Suchy, in press; Benbow & Stanley, 1983a; Brody & Benbow, 1987; Kolitch & Brody, 1992; Richardson & Benbow, 1990; Stanley & Benbow, 1983; Swiatek & Benbow, 1991a, 1991b, 1992). Even though intellectually gifted students as a group do achieve academically at a high level (Benbow, 1992; Benbow & Arjmand, 1990), it does appear that they do not achieve as highly if deprived of an education that corresponds to their level of competence. Moreover, students themselves view SMPY's services and programs as satisfying and personally beneficial several years later (Benbow, Lubinski, & Suchy, in press). Especially valued, beyond the sheer intellectual stimulation, was the acknowledgment of their abilities and the contact with intellec-tual peers. This was especially true for females.

Although multiple studies have been conducted on the variety of acceleration options that SMPY has promoted with its participants (see Benbow, 1992, for a review), we can summarize the results quite succinctly: When differences are found, they favor the accelerates over the nonaccelerates irrespective of the mode of acceleration (e.g., Swiatek & Benbow, 1991a, 1991b). In addition, students are satisfied with their acceleration in both the short and the long term (Richardson & Benbow, 1990; Swiatek & Benbow, 1992).

To date SMPY has been concerned primarily with enhancing *satisfactoriness* as defined by TWA through the provision of educational interventions that are accelerative in nature.[6] Although preferences were assessed and considered throughout SMPY's history, work directly experimenting with ways to optimize *satisfaction,* the other dimension of correspondence within TWA, has not been systematic. We now know that we are able to forecast salient features of gifted students' adult vocational interest profile by assessing their interests at age 13 with instruments designed for adults (Lubinski, Benbow, & Ryan, 1995). Therefore, interventions directly aimed at also enhancing satisfaction now seem timely and appropriate for SMPY to develop. Optimizing satisfaction as well as satisfactoriness should lead to even greater educational and vocational adjustment and well-being among the gifted.

Gender differences have been striking among the participants in SMPY's longitudinal study and very much publicized by the popular media (e.g., Pool, 1994). What are the facts? There are more males than females who are markedly talented in mathematics at age 13 (Benbow, 1988; Benbow & Stanley, 1980, 1983b). Moreover, highly able males and females, when considered as a group, have differing ability and preference profiles (Lubinski & Benbow, 1992, 1994; Lubinski, Benbow, & Ryan, 1995; Lubinski & Humphreys, 1990a, 1990b; Lubinski, Schmidt, & Benbow, in press). When evaluating these differences in the light of the Theory of Work Adjustment, the data inevitably lead to the prediction that highly able males and females will find personal fulfillment in differing educational and career tracks. That is, the psychological profiles of mathematically talented males are often more congruent with studying in the physical sciences than are those of mathematically gifted females, and these predictions have been borne out by the longitudinal data collected by SMPY (Lubinski & Benbow, 1992;

[6] It should be noted, however, that this work appears to enhance satisfaction indirectly (Lubinski et al., 1993, footnote 3). Providing an appropriate educational environment tends also to provide an appropriate social environment.

Lubinski, Benbow, & Sanders, 1993). As adults, mathematically talented males are more heavily represented in the physical sciences and at the highest educational levels than their female counterparts.

In the social and emotional arena, we find that intellectually gifted students have positive self-concepts, especially in academics, and self-esteem (Swiatek, 1993). They possess an internal locus of control; and, on average, their psychological health does not differ much from that of normative or socioeconomically privileged samples (Jensen, 1994). There are indications, however, that modestly gifted students appear to be somewhat better adjusted than the highly gifted and that verbally gifted females are at a somewhat greater risk for emotional distress. As for moral reasoning, the highly gifted score at a level comparable to college students four to five years their senior. Yet moral reasoning, as currently measured, seems to be just another measure of verbal ability (Sanders, Lubinski, & Benbow, 1995). Hence, the underlying meaning of "advanced moral reasoning ability" among the gifted is equivocal.

Finally, what are some of SMPY's basic findings from research on the biological nature of giftedness. Extremely talented youth show a higher proportion of left-handers, suffer more frequently from allergies, and tend to be myopic (Benbow, 1986); overall, however, mathematically gifted individuals possess better physical health than both their average-ability and socioeconomically privileged peers (Lubinski & Humphreys, 1992). Intellectually gifted males, in particular, evince enhanced right-hemisphere functioning. This has been determined using standard tasks, such as dichotic listening, and the EEG (O'Boyle, Alexander, & Benbow, 1991; O'Boyle & Benbow, 1990). Moreover, studies from both cognitive and psychometric approaches to intelligence converge on the notion that intellectually gifted students are simply precocious. They do not solve problems in qualitatively the same manner as average-ability individuals of their age, but in a manner similar to individuals four to five years older. Mathematically gifted students are especially strong at manipulating information in working memory and in handling numeric/spatial stimuli within working memory. The verbally gifted, in contrast, are better at representing word stimuli in working memory.

Summary and Conclusion

SMPY's work has focused on the optimal development of intellectual talent since its founding in 1971 by Julian C. Stanley. This has been accomplished through both intervention research and a planned fifty-year longitudinal study. Through this programmatic research agenda, it systematically developed an identification procedure based on out-of-level testing (i.e., the Talent Search; see Chapter 13 by Assouline and Lupkowski-Shoplik), which has diagnostic value for gifted individuals and has demonstrated predictive validity over 10-year intervals (Benbow, 1992). We learned, through SMPY's longitudinal research, that the future pool of truly exceptional scientists and engineers will consist mostly of talent-search-identifiable individuals (Benbow, 1992; Benbow & Arjmand, 1990). Within this group of gifted individuals we now have identified, by utilizing the Theory of Work Adjustment as a guide, the psychological profiles at age 13 of those who eventually do enter the math/science pipeline (Lubinski, Benbow, & Sanders, 1993).

Moreover, through its programmatic work SMPY experimented with ways to best provide an education that is commensurate with a gifted student's advanced abilities. Acceleration in its many variants seemed to be the procedure of choice; and indeed it was. Those who accelerate perform better academically than those who do not accelerate their education, irrespective of mode of acceleration (e.g., Swiatek & Benbow, 1991a, 1991b). Put simply, our results point to the generalization that gifted individuals will not achieve as highly if not provided with a challenging education that is structured at a pace commensurate with their ability level. Acceleration appears to be the best method for achieving this goal.

Current reform efforts seem bent on making no provisions for the gifted. This can only result in loss of a precious resource within our society. On the basis of the current empirical evidence, not allowing gifted children to accelerate is simply educational malpractice (Benbow & Stanley, in press).

Finally, sound empirical investigations have shown that SMPY's procedures are educationally efficacious. No other model for educating gifted children has gathered so much empirical support for its practices and procedures. It is no wonder, then, that the SMPY model has had such a significant effect on education, particularly gifted education, as documented by VanTassel-Baska (in press).

REFERENCES

Achter, J., Lubinski, D, & Benbow, C. P. (1996). Multipotentiality among the intellectually gifted: It was never there in the first place, and already it's vanishing. *Journal of Consulting Psychology,* 43, 65–76.

Bartkovich, K. G., & George, W. C. (1980). *Teaching the gifted and talented in the mathematics classroom.* Washington, DC: National Education Association.

Bartkovich, K. G., & Mezynski, K. (1981). Fast-paced precalculus mathematics for talented junior-high students: Two recent SMPY programs. *Gifted Child Quarterly, 25,* 73–80.

Benbow, C. P. (1983). Adolescence of the mathematically precocious: A five year longitudinal study. In C. P. Benbow & J. C. Stanley (Eds.), *Academic precocity: Aspects of its development* (pp. 9–37). Baltimore, MD: Johns Hopkins University Press.

Benbow, C. P. (1986). SMPY's model for teaching mathematically precocious students. In J. S. Renzulli (Ed.), *Systems and models in programs for the gifted and talented* (pp. 1–25). Mansfield Center, CT: Creative Learning Press.

Benbow, C. P. (1988). Sex differences in mathematical reasoning ability among the intellectually talented: Their characterization, consequences, and possible explanation. *Behavioral and Brain Sciences, 11,* 169–183, 225–232.

Benbow, C. P. (1991). Meeting the needs of gifted students through acceleration: A neglected resource. In M. C. Wang, M. C. Reynolds, & H. J. Walberg (Eds.), *Handbook of special education* (Vol. 4, pp. 23–36). New York: Pergamon Press.

Benbow, C. P. (1992). Academic achievement in mathematics and science of students between ages 13 and 23: Are there differences among students in the top one percent of mathematical ability? *Journal of Educational Psychology, 84,* 51–61.

Benbow, C. P., & Arjmand, O. (1990). Predictors of high academic achievement in mathematics and science by mathematically talented students: A longitudinal study. *Journal of Educational Psychology, 82,* 430–441.

Benbow, C. P., Arjmand, O., & Walberg, H. J. (1991). Productivity predictors among the intellectually talented. *Journal of Educational Research, 84*(4), 215–223.

Benbow, C. P., & Lubinski, D. (1994). Individual differences among the gifted: How can we best meet their educational needs? In N. Colangelo, S. G. Assouline, & D. L. Ambroson (Eds.), *Talent development* (pp. 83–100). Dayton: Ohio Psychology Press.

Benbow, C. P., Lubinski, D., & Suchy, B. (in press). The impact of the SMPY model and programs from the perspective of the participant. In C. P. Benbow & D. Lubinski (Eds.), *Psychometric and social issues concerning intellectual talent.* Baltimore, MD: Johns Hopkins University Press.

Benbow, C. P., & Minor, L. L. (1990). Cognitive profiles of verbally and mathematically precocious students: Implications for identification of the gifted. *Gifted Child Quarterly, 34,* 21–26.

Benbow, C. P., Perkins, S., & Stanley, J. C. (1983). Mathematics taught at a fast pace: A longitudinal evaluation of SMPY's first class. In C. P. Benbow & J. C. Stanley (Eds.), *Academic precocity: Aspects of its development* (pp. 51–78). Baltimore, MD: Johns Hopkins University Press.

Benbow, C. P., & Stanley, J. C. (1980). Sex differences in mathematical ability: Fact or artifact? *Science, 210,* 1262–1264.

Benbow, C. P., & Stanley, J. C. (1981). Mathematical ability: Is sex a factor? *Science, 212,* 118–121.

Benbow, C. P., & Stanley, J. C. (1982). Consequences in high school and college of sex differences in mathematical reasoning ability: A longitudinal perspective. *American Educational Research Journal, 19,* 598–622.

Benbow, C. P., & Stanley, J. C. (1983a). An eight-year evaluation of SMPY: What was learned? In C. P. Benbow & J. C. Stanley (Eds.), *Academic precocity: Aspects of its development* (pp. 205–214). Baltimore, MD: Johns Hopkins University Press.

Benbow, C. P., & Stanley, J. C. (1983b). Sex differences in mathematical reasoning ability: More facts. *Science, 222,* 1029–1031.

Benbow, C. P., & Stanley, J. C. (in press). Current educational equity policies: Are they equitable? *Psychology, Public Policy, and the Law.*

Benbow, C. P., & Wolins, L. (in press). Utility of out-of-level testing for gifted seventh graders using SAT-M: An examination of item bias. In C. P. Benbow & D. Lubinski (Eds.), *Psychometric and social issues concerning intellectual talent.* Baltimore, MD: Johns Hopkins University Press.

Bloom, B. (1985). *Developing talent in young people.* New York: Ballantine.

Brody, L. E., & Benbow, C. P. (1987). Accelerative strategies: How effective are they for the gifted? *Gifted Child Quarterly, 31,* 105–110.

Brody, L. E., & Stanley, J. C. (1991). Young college students: Assessing factors that contribute to success. In W. T. Southern & E. D. Jones (Eds.), *The academic acceleration of gifted children* (pp. 102–132). New York: Teachers College Press.

Chronicle of Higher Education, Inc. (1992). *Almanac of higher education.* Chicago: University of Chicago Press.

Cohen, J. (1988). *Statistical power analysis for the behavioral sciences* (2nd ed.). Hillsdale, NJ: Lawrence Erlbaum Associates.

Cohn, S. J. (1977). Cognitive characteristics of the top-scoring participants in SMPY's 1976 talent search. *Gifted Child Quarterly, 22,* 416–421.

Cohn, S. J. (1991). Talent searches. In N. Colangelo & G. A. Davis (Eds.), *Handbook of gifted education* (pp. 166–177). Boston: Allyn and Bacon.

Cox, J., Daniel, N., & Boston, B. O. (1985). *Educating able learners: Programs and promising practices.* Austin: University of Texas Press.

Dark, V. J., & Benbow, C. P. (1990). Mathematically talented students show enhanced problem translation and enhanced short term memory for digit and spatial information. *Journal of Educational Psychology, 82,* 420–429.

Dark, V. J. & Benbow, C. P. (1991). Differential enhancement of working memory with mathematical and verbal precocity. *Journal of Educational Psychology, 83,* 48–60.

Dawis, R. V. (1991). Vocational interests, values, and preferences. In M. Dunnette & L. Hough (Eds.), *Handbook of industrial and organizational psychology* (2nd ed.) (Vol. 2, pp. 833–871). Palo Alto: Consulting Psychologist Press.

Dawis, R. V. (1992). The individual differences tradition in counseling psychology. *Journal of Counseling Psychology, 39,* 7–19.

Dawis, R. V., & Lofquist, L. H. (1984). *A psychological theory of work adjustment.* Minneapolis: University of Minnesota Press.

Dunber, S. L., & Benbow, C. P. (1990). Aspects of personality and peer relations of extremely talented adolescents. *Gifted Child Quarterly, 34,* 10–15.

Durden, W. J. (1980). The Johns Hopkins program for verbally gifted youth. *Roeper Review, 2,* 34–37.

Eisenberg, A. R., & George, W. C. (1979). Early entrance to college: The Johns Hopkins experience. *College and University, 54,* 109–118.

Elkind, D. (1988). Acceleration. *Young Children, 43,* 2.

Fox, L. H. (1974). A mathematics program for fostering precocious achievement. In J. C. Stanley, D. P. Keating, & L. H. Fox (Eds.), *Mathematical talent: Discovery, description, and development* (pp. 101–125). Baltimore, MD: Johns Hopkins University Press.

Green, K. C. (1989). A profile of undergraduates in the sciences. *American Scientist, 77,* 475–480.

Holland, J. L. (1985). *The making of vocational choices: A theory of vocational personalities and work environments* (2nd ed.). Englewood Cliffs, NJ: Prentice-Hall.

Humphreys, L. G., Lubinski, D., & Yao, G. (1993). Utility of predicting group membership: Exemplified by the role of spatial visualization in becoming an engineer, physical scientist, or artist. *Journal of Applied Psychology, 78,* 250–261.

Jensen, M. B. (1994). *Psychological well-being of intellectually precocious youth and peers at commensurate levels of socioeconomic status.* Unpublished master's thesis, Iowa State University, Ames, IA 50011.

Kolitch, E. R., & Brody, L. E. (1992). Mathematics acceleration of highly talented students: An evaluation. *Gifted Child Quarterly, 36,* 78–86.

Lofquist, L. H., & Dawis, R. V. (1969). *Adjustment to work.* New York: Appleton-Century-Crofts.

Lofquist, L. H., & Dawis, R. V. (1991). *Essentials of person–environment–correspondence counseling.* Minneapolis: University of Minnesota Press.

Lubinski, D., & Benbow, C. P. (1992). Gender differences in abilities and preferences among the gifted: Implication for the math–science pipeline. *Current Directions in Psychological Science, 1,* 61–66.

Lubinski, D., & Benbow, C. P. (1994). The Study of Mathematically Precocious Youth (SMPY): The first three decades of a planned fifty-year longitudinal study of intellectual talent. In R. Subotnik & K. Arnold (Eds.), *Beyond Terman: Longitudinal studies in contemporary gifted education* (pp. 255–281). Norwood, NJ: Ablex.

Lubinski, D., Benbow, C. P., Eftekhari-Sanjani, H., & Jensen, M. B. (in preparation). *The psychological profile of our future scientific leaders.*

Lubinski, D., Benbow, C. P., & Ryan, J. (1995). Stability of vocational interests among the intellectually gifted: A fifteen-year longitudinal study. *Journal of Applied Psychology, 80,* 196–200.

Lubinski, D., Benbow, C. P., & Sanders, C. E. (1993). Reconceptualizing gender differences in achievement among the gifted. In K. A. Heller, F. J. Monks, & A. H. Passow (Eds.), *International handbook for research on giftedness and talent* (pp. 693–707). Oxford, England: Pergamon Press.

Lubinski, D., & Dawis, R. V. (1992). Aptitudes, skills, and proficiency. In M. D. Dunnette & L. M. Hough (Eds.), *Handbook of industrial and organizational psychology* (2nd ed.) (Vol. 3, pp. 3–59). Palo Alto, CA: Consulting Psychologists Press.

Lubinski, D., & Humphreys, L. G. (1990a). A broadly based analysis of mathematical giftedness. *Intelligence, 14,* 327–355.

Lubinski, D., & Humphreys, L. G. (1990b). Assessing spurious "moderator effects": Illustrated substantively with the hypothesized ("synergistic") relation between spatial and mathematical ability. *Psychological Bulletin, 107,* 385–393.

Lubinski, D., & Humphreys, L. G. (1992). Some bodily and medical correlates of mathematical giftedness and commensurate levels of socioeconomic status. *Intelligence, 16,* 99–115.

Lubinski, D., & Thompson, T. (1986). Functional units of human behavior and their integration: A dispositional analysis. In T. Thompson & M. Zeiler (Eds.), *Analysis and integration of behavioral units* (pp. 275–314). Hillsdale, NJ: Lawrence Erlbaum Associates.

Lubinski, D., Schmidt, D. B., & Benbow, C. P. (in press). Educational-vocational preferences among intellectually gifted adults are forecastable from age-13 assessments: A 20-year stability analysis of the study of values. *Journal of Applied Psychology.*

Minor, L. L., & Benbow, C. P. (in press). Construct validity of the SAT-M: A comparative study of high school students and gifted seventh graders. In C. P. Benbow & D. Lubinski (Eds.), *Psychometric and social issues concerning intellectual talent.* Baltimore, MD: Johns Hopkins University Press.

O'Boyle, M. W., Alexander, J. E., & Benbow, C. P. (1991). Enhanced right hemisphere activation in the mathematically precocious: A preliminary EEG investigation. *Brain and Cognition, 17,* 138–153.

O'Boyle, M. W., & Benbow, C. P. (1990). Enhanced right hemisphere involvement during cognitive processing may relate to intellectual precocity. *Neuropsychologia, 28,* 211–126.

Pool, R. (1994). *Eve's rib: Searching for the biological roots of sex differences.* New York: Crown Publishers.

Richardson, T. M., & Benbow, C. P. (1990). Long-term effects of acceleration on the social and emotional adjustment of mathematically precocious youth. *Journal of Educational Psychology, 82,* 464–470.

Roe, A. (1953). *The making of a scientist.* New York: Dodd, Mead.

Sanders, C. E., Lubinski, D., & Benbow, C. P. (1995). Does the Defining Issues Test measure psychological phenomena distinct from verbal ability?: An examination of Lykken's query. *Journal of Personality and Social Psychology, 69,* 498–504.

Scarr, S. (1992). Developmental theories for the 1990s: Development and individual differences. *Child Development, 63,* 1–19.

Scarr, S., & McCartney, K. (1983). How people make their own environments: A theory of genotype → environment effects. *Child Development, 54,* 424–435.

Solano, C. H., & George, W. C. (1976). College courses and educational facilitation for the gifted. *Gifted Child Quarterly, 20,* 274–285.

Southern, W. T., Jones, E. D., & Stanley, J. C. (1993). Acceleration and enrichment: The context and development of program options. In K. A. Heller, F. J. Monks, & A. H. Passow (Eds.), *International handbook for research on giftedness and talent* (pp. 387–409). Oxford, England: Pergamon Press.

Stanley, J. C. (1977). Rationale of the Study of Mathematically Precocious Youth (SMPY) during its first five years of promoting educational acceleration. In J. C. Stanley, W. C. George, & C. H. Solano (Eds.), *The gifted and the creative: A fifty-year perspective* (pp. 73–112). Baltimore, MD: Johns Hopkins University Press.

Stanley, J. C. (1978). SMPY's DT-PI model: Diagnostic testing followed by prescriptive instruction. *Intellectually Talented Youth Bulletin, 4,* 7–8.

Stanley, J. C. (1979). How to use a fast-pacing math mentor. *Intellectually Talented Youth Bulletin, 6,* 1–2.

Stanley, J. C. (1991). A better model for residential high schools for talented youths. *Phi Delta Kappan, 72,* 471–473.

Stanley, J. C., & Benbow, C. P. (1982). Educating mathematically precocious youths: Twelve policy recommendations. *Educational Researcher, 11,* 4–9.

Stanley, J. C., & Benbow, C. P. (1983). Extremely young college graduates: Evidence of their success. *College and University, 58,* 361–371.

Stanley, J. C., & Benbow, C. P. (1986). Youths who reason exceptionally well mathematically. In R. J. Sternberg & J. E. Davidson (Eds.), *Conceptions of giftedness* (pp. 361–387). New York: Cambridge University Press.

Stanley, J. C., Keating, D. P., & Fox, L. H. (1974). *Mathematical talent: Discovery, description and development.* Baltimore, MD: Johns Hopkins University Press.

Stanley, J. C., & Stanley, B. S. K. (1986). High-school biology, chemistry, or physics learned well in three weeks. *Journal of Research in Science Teaching, 23,* 237–250.

Swiatek, M. A. (1993). *Academic and psychosocial perspectives on giftedness during adolescence.* Unpublished Ph.D. dissertation, Iowa State University, Ames.

Swiatek, M. A., & Benbow, C. P. (1991a). Ten-year longitudinal follow-up of ability-matched accelerated and unaccelerated gifted students. *Journal of Educational Psychology, 83,* 528–538.

Swiatek, M. A., & Benbow, C. P. (1991b). A ten-year longitudinal follow-up of participants in a fast-paced mathematics course. *Journal for Research in Mathematics Education, 22,* 138–150.

Swiatek, M. A., & Benbow, C. P. (1992). Nonintellectual correlates of satisfaction with acceleration: A longitudinal study. *Journal of Youth and Adolescence, 21,* 699–723.

Tannenbaum, A. (1983). *Gifted children: Psychological and educational perspectives.* New York: Macmillan.

Tannenbaum, A. (1986). The enrichment matrix model. In J. S. Renzulli (Ed.), *Systems and models for developing programs for the gifted and talented* (pp. 391–428). Mansfield Center, CT: Creative Learning Press.

Terman, L. M. (1925–1959). *Genetic studies of genius* (Vols. I–V). Stanford, CA: Stanford University Press.

VanTassel-Baska, J. (1983). Illinois statewide replication of the Johns Hopkins Study of Mathematically Precocious Youth. In C. P. Benbow & J. C. Stanley (Eds.), *Academic precocity: Aspects of its development* (pp. 179–191). Baltimore, MD: Johns Hopkins University Press.

VanTassel-Baska, J. (in press). Contributions to gifted education of the talent search concept. In C. P. Benbow & D. Lubinski (Eds.), *Psychometric and social issues concerning intellectual talent.* Baltimore, MD: Johns Hopkins University Press.

Walberg, H. J., Strykowski, B. F., Rovai, E., & Hung, S. S. (1984). Exceptional performance. *Review of Educational Research, 54,* 84–112.

Zak, P. M., Benbow, C. P., & Stanley, J. C. (1983). AP exams: The way to go! *Roeper Review, 6,* 100–101.

Zak, P. M., Benbow, C. P., & Stanley, J. C. (1983). Several factors associated with success as an undergraduate chemistry major in college. *College and University, 58,* 303–312.

Zuckerman, H. (1977). *Scientific elite: Nobel laureates in the United States.* New York: Free Press.

13

Talent Searches: A Model for the Discovery and Development of Academic Talent

SUSAN G. ASSOULINE, *The University of Iowa*
ANN LUPKOWSKI-SHOPLIK, *Carnegie Mellon University*

A [person's] reach should exceed his [or her] grasp, or what's a heaven for?
—Robert Browning

In Browning's quote, we see the foundation for the Talent Search model. The founder of the Talent Search model is Julian C. Stanley, and Browning's quote is one of Professor Stanley's favorites. Talent Search is a two-step process that involves, first, the identification of students who have demonstrated, or "grasped," a high level of academic achievement, as documented by high performance on grade-level tests. Second, these identified students are invited to take a test above their grade level to determine their "reach," or potential for academic challenge. The primary goal is *discovery* of students who are exceptionally able academically.

The goals of Talent Search, however, extend beyond the discovery of academically talented youth. They include three other goals, which complement each other and make the Talent Search model comprehensive. Together, the four goals are *discovery, development, description,* and *dissemination* (J. C. Stanley, personal communication, March 15, 1994). In this chapter, we focus primarily on the discovery of academic talent, although we will discuss briefly the goal of talent development. The previous chapter by Benbow and Lubinski and Chapter 14 by Olszewski-Kubilius offer more complete information regarding the development of academic talent.

The history of Talent Search is detailed elsewhere (see Benbow, 1991; Cohn, 1991; Keating & Stanley, 1972; Stanley, 1991; Stanley, George, & Solano, 1977; Stanley, Keating, & Fox, 1974; VanTassel-Baska, in press). There are new aspects of the Talent Search model that merit discussion, specifically the work that has been done with elementary students (Assouline & Lupkowski, 1992; Colangelo, Assouline, & Lu, 1994; Lupkowski-Shoplik & Assouline, 1993; Mills & Barnett, 1992). The purpose of this chapter is to provide an overview of how the Talent Search model has been used with junior high school students and then to describe its recent application with elementary students.

The Talent Search model is based on the notion that students differ in academic ability, and that these differences can be identified through standardized testing. A well-designed standardized test will produce results that, when plotted in graph form, yield a bell curve (see Figure 13.1, Section A). Standardized tests have enough items to provide reliable and valid information for a representative sample of test takers. However, it would not be efficient for test developers, students, or their educators to have enough items on each test that are *easy* enough and *difficult* enough for all test takers, especially those at the extremes of the bell curve. An efficient way to acquire more information about students at the extremes of the curve is to use tests that are out-of-level. In this chapter, we focus on the use of above-level tests for students at the upper end of the bell curve, and as the primary mechanism of Talent Search. As can be seen in Section B of Figure 13.1, the above-level test spreads out the scores of students who were clustered at the upper percentiles on the grade-level tests (Section A), and actually creates a new distribution of scores. The above-

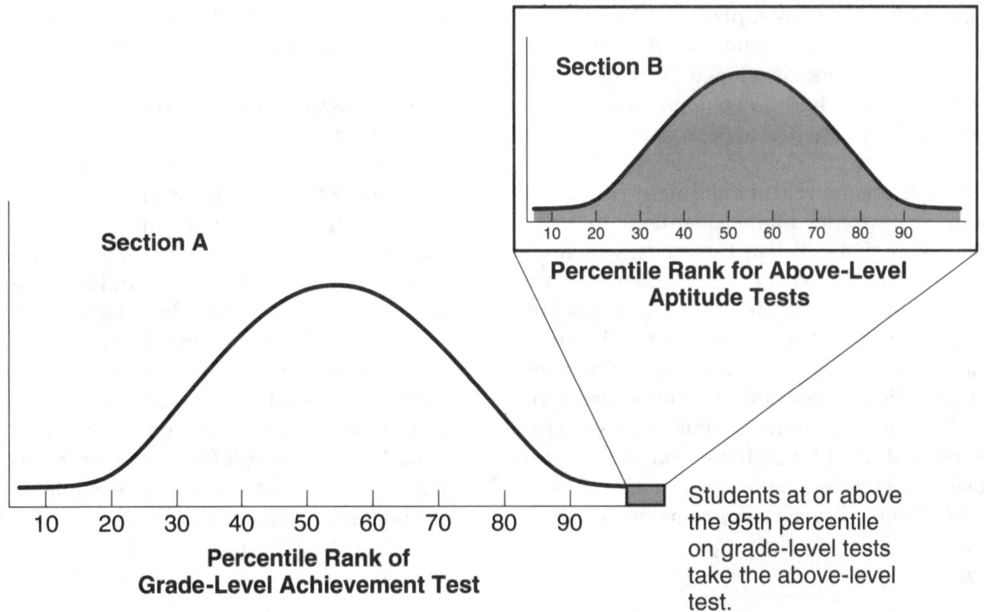

Figure 13.1. Above-level test score distribution for students scoring high on grade-level test.

level test provides a more precise assessment of ability and readiness for additional challenge.

How Does the Talent Search Work?

As mentioned, the Talent Search is a two-step process. The first step is to identify students who have scored well on a grade-level standardized test such as the Iowa Tests of Basic Skills, California Achievement Test, Stanford Achievement Test, or the Texas Assessment of Academic Skills, and invite these students to take an above-level test. How well do students need to score on the grade-level tests before being invited to take an above-level test? This is an important question, because educators need to be responsible in identifying those students who would benefit from above-level testing, but not be overly frustrated by the experience. For junior high students, the grade-level criterion of the 97th percentile has been found to be an appropriate cutoff for participation in the Talent Search (Ebmeier & Schmulback, 1989). For elementary students, the grade-level criteria for participation in the Talent Search range from the 95th to the 97th percentile. The major factor to consider in establishing the initial criteria for invitation to the Talent Search is the degree to which the Talent Search test will be above-level (Assouline, Colangelo, McNabb, Lupkowski-Shoplik, & Sayler 1993).

The second step in the Talent Search process is for the student to take the above-level test. A test is "above-level" if it is at least two years above the student's present grade placement. By taking an above-level test, the student is presented with more challenging items. The student's performance on the above-level test is an indication of the degree to which he or she needs additional challenge in a particular subject area.

How Successful Is the Talent Search Model?

In the spring of 1972, Julian C. Stanley initiated the junior high Talent Search at Johns Hopkins University. Since then, several hundred thousand students, primarily in grades 7 and 8, have taken the Scholastic Aptitude Test (SAT), which was developed as college entrance tests for high school juniors and seniors. In the 1980s, the college entrance exam of the American College Testing Program (ACT) became an additional Talent Search instrument for junior high students.

Today, regional Talent Searches, which are university-based, cover each state in the United States as well as a few countries outside the United States (e.g., China, Ireland). In addition to the regional Talent Searches, each of which serves several states, there are additional local searches. Some local searches are housed in universities and others are housed in state educational organizations. A list of Talent Search programs is found in Table 13.1.

Which Above-Level Tests Are Used with Junior High Students?

Scholastic Aptitude Test. Initially, Stanley was interested in finding adolescents who were exceptionally talented in mathematics, so he sought a test that would measure high-level mathematical reasoning abilities. He wanted a test that was professionally prepared, standardized, secure, and reliable, and that had several forms. In addition, Stanley needed a test difficult enough so there would be virtually no perfect scores and the average examinee would score halfway between a perfect score and a chance score. This test should also have well-known, meaningful, normative interpretations of scores available. The mathematics section of the Scholastic Aptitude Test (SAT-M) proved suitable in content,

Table 13.1
Talent Search Centers

University-based Regional Talent Searches

Elementary (Third, Fourth, Fifth, and Sixth Grades)
The Belin-Blank Center, The University of Iowa, 210 Lindquist Center, Iowa City, IA 52242
Center for Talent Development, Northwestern University, 617 Dartmouth Place, Evanston, IL 60208
Center for Talented Youth, Johns Hopkins University, 3400 N. Charles Street, Baltimore, MD 21218
Talent Identification Program, Duke University, Durham, NC 27708

Middle School/Junior High (Sixth, Seventh, and Eighth Grades)
Center for Talent Development, Northwestern University, 617 Dartmouth Place, Evanston, IL 60208
Center for Talented Youth, Johns Hopkins University, 3400 N. Charles Street, Baltimore, MD 21218
Rocky Mountain Talent Search, University of Denver, Denver, CO 80208
Talent Identification Program, Duke University, Durham, NC 27708

University-based Local Talent Searches

Elementary (Third, Fourth, Fifth, and/or Sixth Grades)
California State University at Sacramento, 600 J Street, Sacramento, CA 95819–6098
Elementary Student Talent Search, Carnegie Mellon University, 227 C Student Center, Pittsburgh, PA 15213

Middle School/Junior High (Sixth, Seventh, and Eighth Grades)
California State University at Sacramento, 600 J Street, Sacramento, CA 95819–6098
Iowa Talent Search, Iowa State University, Office of Precollege Programs for Talented and Gifted, W172 Lagomarcino Hall, Ames, IA 50011–3180.
Joseph-Baldwin Academy, Northeast Missouri State University, McClain Hall (203), Kirksville, MO 63501

State-based Talent Searches
Illinois Talent Search, Illinois State Board of Education, 100 North First Street, Springfield, IL 62777–0001

difficulty, and meaningfulness (Stanley, 1977a, 1977b; Stanley & Benbow, 1986). After using the SAT-M with several large groups of talented seventh graders, Stanley and his colleagues "concluded that the SAT-M must function far more at an analytic reasoning level for Talent Search participants than it does for high-school juniors and seniors" (Stanley & Benbow, 1986, p. 362). They also realized that the Verbal section of the SAT (SAT-V) was useful for identifying verbally talented youth.

The original SAT was composed of three sections: Mathematics, Verbal, and Test of Standard Written English (TSWE). In 1994 the SAT was revised and renamed the Scholastic Assessment Test (SAT I); it now consists of only the Verbal and Mathematics-sections. The SAT I, like its predecessor, was designed to measure mathematical and verbal reasoning abilities of college-bound high school students. Scores are reported on a scale of 200 to 800 on the SAT-Verbal and SAT-Mathematics. In 1994 the average high school senior (representing the 50th percentile) earned a score of 423 on the Verbal section and 479 on Mathematics.[1] The average score for Talent Search participants was 362 on the Verbal section and 414 on Mathematics (CTY, 1995). Approximately 20 percent of the seventh-grade students who participate in Talent Searches score as well as or better than the average college-bound twelfth grader (CTY, 1995).

When seventh graders take the SAT, it is presumed to be a measure of reasoning ability, which is similar but not identical to the test's purpose for college-bound eleventh and twelfth graders. Benbow (1991) described the thinking of Stanley and his colleagues when selecting the SAT-M as a measure of mathematical reasoning ability:

> Our rationale is that most of these students were demonstrably unfamiliar with mathematics from algebra onward, yet many of them were able to score high on a difficult test of mathematical reasoning. Presumably, this could occur only through extraordinary analytic ability. We concluded that the SAT-M must function far more at an analytic reasoning level for the SMPY[2] students than it does for high-school juniors and seniors, most of whom have studied abstract mathematics for several years. (Benbow, 1991, p. 156)

The same reasoning process is used to justify the use of the SAT-Verbal for identifying verbally talented youth.

American College Testing Program. The other major college entrance exam is the American College Testing Program (ACT). The ACT was pilot-tested as a potential Talent Search instrument in 1987 (Sawyer & Brounstein, 1988) and was found to be valid as an above-level instrument in the search for academic talent (Dreyden & Stanley, 1988; Maxey & Dreyden, 1988; Stanley & York, 1988). The ACT comprises four tests of educational development: English, mathematics, reading, and science reasoning. The questions on these tests are designed to tap students' knowledge and skills in major curriculum areas and therefore measure educational progress in curriculum-related areas. The ACT assessment is available to students in all 50 states, as well as several foreign countries. Scale scores on each of the tests of the ACT range from 1 to 36. The

[1] The score scale for the Scholastic Assessment Test has been adjusted as of April 1, 1995, so the scores are recentered at 500 for both sections of the test. Data reported in this chapter were collected before the recentering occurred.

[2] SMPY is the Study of Mathematically Precocious Youth. It was started in 1971 by Professor Julian C. Stanley at Johns Hopkins University. The first Talent Search took place in the spring of 1972, and the Talent Search process was part of SMPY until 1979. In 1979, a separate, independent unit was created on the Johns Hopkins Campus to conduct Talent Searches and summer programs. That unit, known as the Center for the Advancement of Academically Talented Youth (CTY), is a thriving organization that has contributed to the academic development of thousands of students.

average score for college-bound seniors is 21 for each test of the ACT. The average ACT scores for Talent Search participants were 18 for English, 17 for Mathematics, 18 for Reading, and 19 for Science. Approximately 35 percent of Talent Search participants earned scaled scores that were equal to or surpassed those of average college-bound twelfth graders (R. Sawyer, personal communication, April 25, 1995).

The SAT and the ACT are both college entrance exams, and are extremely effective as above-level tests for junior high students. Students may take either test independently of the organized, university-based Talent Searches at any one of the established testing sites publicized by the Educational Testing Service (SAT) or the American College Testing Program (ACT). However, by participating in one of the regional Talent Searches, students benefit from the organized planning and dissemination of information that are available through Talent Searches.

Although the SAT and ACT both measure mathematical and verbal skills, the tests are different. For example, the ACT provides a Science Reasoning score and separates its verbal assessments into two tests: Reading and English. Conceptually, the ACT was designed as a measure of achievement in each of the areas tested. The SAT was designed to measure reasoning skills in the math and verbal areas without being heavily tied to specific curriculum. However, both tests have undergone major revisions in recent years, and the differences between the philosophies of the two testing organizations seem to have narrowed.

When seventh and eighth graders do well on a test that has relatively unfamiliar content and was developed for older students, the underlying assumption is that these students have excellent reasoning abilities. Both the ACT and the SAT have proved to be effective instruments for that purpose. In most of the regional Talent Searches, both tests are an option for junior high students; only the search at Johns Hopkins University relies exclusively on the SAT. Parents and educators often wonder which test their junior high students should take. It is recommended that students in junior high take the SAT one year and the ACT the following year.

Which Above-Level Tests Are Used with Elementary Students?

Because the Talent Search model, now in its third decade, worked so well at the junior high level, it seemed a natural extension to implement the model at the elementary level. Simultaneously, researchers at Johns Hopkins University, Carnegie Mellon University, the University of Iowa, and the University of North Texas began investigating the feasibility of various above-level tests to be used with elementary students.

Secondary School Admission Test. The first test to be researched carefully was the Secondary School Admission Test (SSAT), which was developed by Educational Testing Service and is now administered by the SSAT Board. The SSAT is a multiple-choice, secure test that is suitable for administration to large groups and is given numerous times per year in many locations. Many of the over 40,000 students who take the test each year are applying for admission to independent elementary, junior high, or high schools. The Lower Level of the SSAT was developed for fifth through seventh graders and the Upper Level for eighth through eleventh graders. The test contains quantitative, verbal, and reading comprehension sections.

We have used the Lower Level of the SSAT as an identification instrument for students younger than age 12 (Assouline & Lupkowski, 1992; Lupkowski-Shoplik & Assouline, 1993). Third- through fifth-grade students scoring at the 95th percentile on a grade-level standardized test took the SSAT as part of several regional Talent Searches for elementary school students. The Center for Talented Youth (CTY) at Johns Hopkins University also has used the SSAT as an above-level instrument for their Young Students Talent Search, which serves fifth- and sixth-grade students.

Although both levels of the SSAT were effective for finding academic talent in students younger than seventh grade, there were two major drawbacks to continuing the use of the SSAT: (1) While the test is administered in a number of private schools, it remains primarily inaccessible to most elementary students in the United States, and (2) the cost of the SSAT is considerably higher than that of some other tests.

PLUS Academic Abilities Assessment. At present, Johns Hopkins University's Center for Talented Youth uses a test developed by the Educational Testing Service. The PLUS Academic Abilities Assessment is used in the CTY search for exceptional mathematical and/or verbal reasoning abilities among fifth and sixth graders. The PLUS reports verbal and quantitative scores. CTY's talented fifth graders are compared to the national sample of eighth graders, while CTY sixth graders' scores are compared to those of a national sample of ninth graders.

EXPLORE. In 1992 American College Testing completed its development of an assessment for eighth graders, EXPLORE (American College Testing, 1992). The EXPLORE assessment consists of four multiple-choice tests: English, Mathematics, Reading, and Science Reasoning. In addition to a score for each area, a composite score, which is the average of the four scores, is provided. EXPLORE was developed by ACT to measure students' curriculum-related knowledge as well as complex cognitive skills. It first was used as an above-level test for elementary students in 1993 (Colangelo, Assouline, & Lu, 1994), and has been adopted by university-based elementary Talent Searches at the University of Iowa, as well as Carnegie Mellon, Northwestern, and Duke Universities.

The scale scores on EXPLORE range from 1 to 25. The average scale score earned by eighth graders is 14.2 for each test (i.e., English, Mathematics, Reading, and Science Reasoning) and 14.4 for the Composite score. The results of the nearly 10,000 first-time test takers of the University of Iowa's Belin Elementary Student Talent Search (BESTS) are found in Table 13.2A and 13.2B.

What Do the Scores Earned by Talent Search Participants Mean?

Goal 2 of the Talent Search model is *development* of academic talent. This development usually takes place with course work offered during summers or on weekends. The above-level test scores earned by Talent Search participants are useful indicators of readiness for fast-paced coursework. Cutoff scores for the fast-paced, accelerated programs typically correspond to the 50th percentile of the distribution of scores for the group for whom the test was developed, that is, college-bound seniors for the ACT and SAT, and eighth graders for the EXPLORE. Although these criteria seem rather narrow, and there is a risk that some students may be overlooked by setting these cutoff scores, "We identified more youths who reason exceptionally well mathematically [and verbally] than we could handle" (Benbow, 1986, p. 3). Goldstein, Stocking, and Sawyer (1992) reported that approximately 6 percent of the total seventh-grade Talent Search participants actually qualify for the *fast-paced* precollege programs offered during the summer. Students who do not earn scores that indicate a need for fast-paced, accelerative course work also may participate in summer and weekend programs, but the content of those programs tends to be oriented more toward enrichment and exploration of topics not typically covered in schools.

In addition, the above-level scores can be used to determine the appropriateness of a variety of educational options, depending upon the availability of local resources. A range of educational options, compiled from Boatman, Davis, and Benbow (1995), Cohn (1991), and VanTassel-Baska (in press), is shown in Figure 13.2. We have divided the performance of students on the above-level test into two general categories: *talented* and *extremely talented.* All students who participate in a Talent Search are talented and should be proud that they were chosen to be part of such a challenging experience. Students who earn scores above the 50th percentile (e.g., 14 or above on any of the EXPLORE tests) in the above-level distribution are extremely talented and would most likely benefit from the more accelerative

Table 13.2A
Eighth Graders in the National Sample

English	Mathematics	Reading	Science Reasoning	Composite
14.2	*14.2*	*14.2*	*14.2*	*14.4*

Table 13.2B
The Average EXPLORE Test Scale Scores Earned by BESTS Participants

	English			*Math*			*Reading*			*Science Reasoning*			*Composite*		
Grade	*M*	*F*	*Total*	*M*	*F*	*Total*	*M*	*F*	*Total*	*M*	*F*	*Total*	*M*	*F*	*Total*
3	9.5	9.8	9.7	9.0	8.5	8.8	9.2	9.4	9.3	10.0	9.8	9.9	9.5	9.5	9.5
4	12.9	13.5	13.2	11.2	10.6	10.9	12.7	13.5	13.1	12.9	12.6	12.8	12.5	12.7	12.6
5	**15.2**	**16.2**	**15.7**	13.3	12.8	13.0	**15.7**	**16.5**	**16.1**	**15.4**	**15.3**	**15.3**	**15.0**	**15.3**	**15.2**
6	**16.9**	**18.1**	**17.4**	**15.5**	**15.1**	**15.3**	**18.0**	**18.9**	**18.4**	**17.6**	**17.7**	**17.6**	**17.1**	**17.6**	**17.3**

[a] Boldface scores are higher than the mean of the national sample of eighth graders.
[b] The average scores for sixth graders are well above the eighth-grade average of 14.
[c] With the exception of mathematics, the average scores for fifth graders are above the eighth-grade average of 14.
[d] With the exception of mathematics, the average scores for fourth graders are very close to the average scores of eighth graders.
[e] Whereas the third graders scored considerably lower than fourth, fifth, or sixth graders, they still did very well, especially considering that they took a test that was designed for students with five more years of school experience.

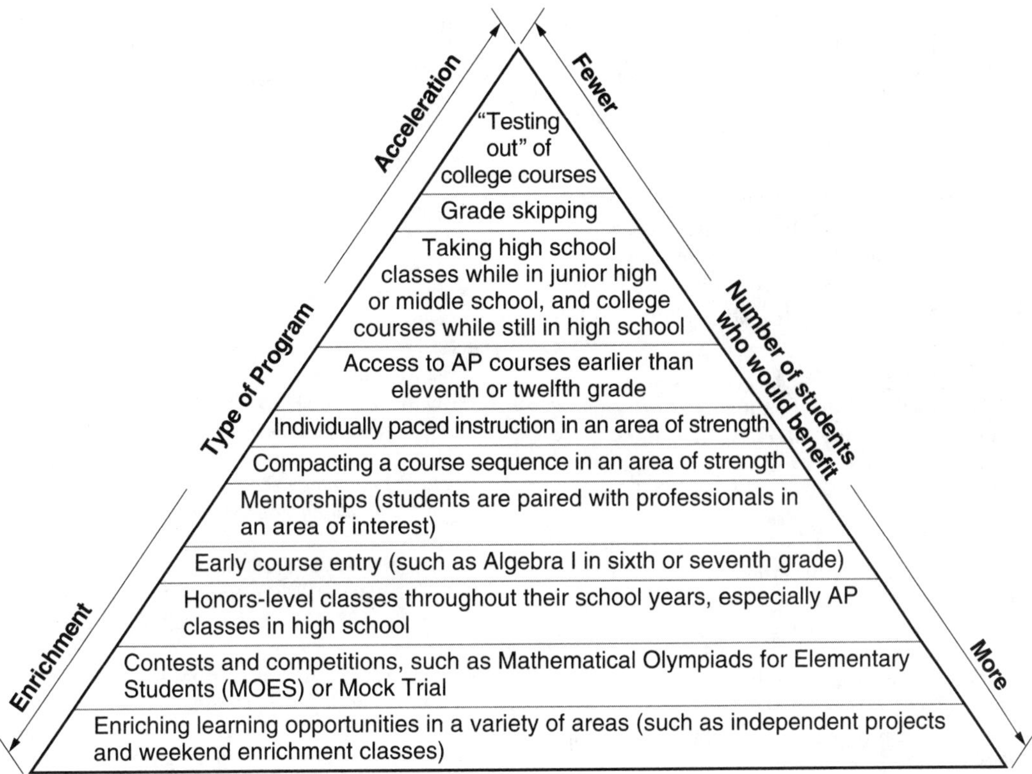

Figure 13.2. Pyramid of curricular options for talent search participants. The options are in ascending order from least accelerative (enrichment) to most accelerative. Talented students, defined as participants in a Talent Search, but scoring below the 50th percentile, should consider the options at the base of the pyramid. Extremely talented students, scoring above the 50th percentile on the Talent Search test, should consider the options at the top of the pyramid as well as those close to the base.

opportunities found at the top of Figure 13.2. Motivation, past achievement, maturity, interest, and availability of resources also play a role in making programming decisions.

What Are the Benefits of Participating in Talent Searches?

We know from our many phone conversations and letters from the parents of the talented students who participate in these searches that the opportunities offered are both necessary and successful. The primary benefit to participation is the opportunity to learn more about the specific academic talents of the student, both individually and compared to his or her academic peers. Additionally, participating in a Talent Search often opens the door to educational opportunities in the student's academic strength. Finally, students who participate in university-based Talent Searches become part of an educational information network. Through newsletters, mini-conferences, symposia, letters, and telephone calls, experts at the university level inform students of a vast array of educational opportunities. They encourage students to participate in academic programs and competitions offered by many different institutions, suggest books to read during summer vacation, offer "food for thought" for students selecting courses to take in school and making long-term educational plans, and provide research-based recommendations concerning acceleration and ability grouping. Participation in a university-based Talent Search provides educational counseling tailored to the interests and needs of academically talented students.

We obviously are advocates of the Talent Search model. The model has generated hundreds of programs and other opportunities for thousands of talented students. VanTassel-Baska (in press) highlights the benefits as follows:

> [T]he direct benefits to students as a result of these programs are enormous. For many it becomes a way: (1) to earn advanced high-school and even college credit in an economical manner, (2) to associate for the first time with an equally able peer group, (3) to develop the "habits of mind" associated with serious study on a college campus, and (4) to gain a sense of academic competence through receiving a worthy challenge to learn more difficult material. This list does not mention the enormous personal gains in the area of social and emotional development that these students seem to experience as judged by anecdotal reports.

Elementary and junior high students with superior academic talent clearly need educational opportunities commensurate with their capabilities. The Talent Search model is a proven process for meeting this need.

REFERENCES

American College Testing. (1992). *EXPLORE school program guide.* Iowa City, IA: ACT Publications.

Assouline, S. G., Colangelo, N., McNabb, T., Lupkowski-Shoplik, A. E., & Sayler, M. (1993, October). *An investigation to determine guidelines for recommending above-level testing of talented elementary students.* Presentation at the National Association for Gifted Children, Atlanta, Georgia.

Assouline, S. G., & Lupkowski, A. E. (1992). Extending the Talent Search model: The potential of the SSAT-Q for identifying mathematically talented elementary students. In N. Colangelo, S. G. Assouline, & D. L. Ambroson (Eds.), *Talent development: Proceedings from the 1991 Henry B. and Jocelyn Wallace National Research Symposium on Talent Development* (pp. 223–232). Unionville, NY: Trillium.

Benbow, C. P. (1986). SMPY's model for teaching mathematically precocious students. In J. S. Renzulli (Ed.), *Systems and models for developing programs for the gifted and talented* (pp. 3–66). Mansfield Center, CT: Creative Learning Press.

Benbow, C. P. (1991). Mathematically talented children: Can acceleration meet their educational needs? In N. Colangelo & G. A. Davis (Eds.), *Handbook of gifted education* (pp. 154–165). Boston: Allyn and Bacon.

Boatman, T. A., Davis, K. G., & Benbow, C. P. (1995). Best practices in gifted education. In A. Thomas & J. Grimes (Eds.), *Best practices in school psychology III* (pp. 1083–1095). Washington DC: National Association of School Psychologists.

Cohn, S. J. (1991). Talent Searches. In N. Colangelo & G. A. Davis (Eds.), *Handbook of gifted education* (pp. 166–177). Boston: Allyn and Bacon.

Colangelo, N., Assouline, S. G., & Lu, W-H. (1994). Using EXPLORE as an above-level instrument in the search for elementary student talent In N. Colangelo, S. G. Assouline, & D. L. Ambroson (Eds.), *Talent development: Proceedings from the 1993 Henry B. and Jocelyn Wallace National Research Symposium on Talent Development* (pp. 281–297). Dayton: Ohio Psychology Press.

CTY. (1995). *1995 Talent Search report.* Baltimore, MD: Johns Hopkins University Press.

Dreyden, J. I., & Stanley, G. E. (1988, April). *College entrance test score and demographic profile information for talented seventh grade youth.* Paper presented at the Annual Meeting of the National Council on Measurement in Education, New Orleans, Louisiana.

Ebmeier, H., & Schmulbach, S. (1989). An examination of the selection practices used in the Talent Search Program. *Gifted Child Quarterly, 33,* 134–141.

Goldstein, D., Stocking, V. B., & Sawyer, R. N. (1992). The talented adolescent: Data from TIP's first decade. In N. Colangelo, S. G. Assouline, & D. L. Ambroson (Eds.), *Talent development: Proceedings from the 1991 Henry B. and Jocelyn Wallace National Research Symposium on Talent Development* (pp. 298–318). Unionville, NY: Trillium.

Keating, D. P., & Stanley, J. C. (1972). Extreme measures for the exceptionally gifted in mathematics and science. *Educational Researcher, 1*(9), 3–7.

Lupkowski-Shoplik, A. E., & Assouline, S. G. (1993). Identifying mathematically talented elementary students: Using the Lower Level of the SSAT. *Gifted Child Quarterly, 37*, 118–124.

Maxey, E. J., & Dreyden, J. I. (1988, April). *Measures of validity between the ACT assessment and other achievement variables for talented seventh-grade youth.* Paper presented at the Annual Meeting of The National Council on Measurement in Education, New Orleans, Louisiana.

Mills, C. J., & Barnett, L. B. (1992). The use of the Secondary School Admission Test (SSAT) to identify academically talented elementary school students. *Gifted Child Quarterly, 36*, 155–159.

Sawyer, R., & Brounstein, P. (1988, April). *The relationship between ACT and SAT score among academically talented seventh grade students.* Paper presented at the Annual Meeting of the National Council on Measurement in Education, New Orleans, Louisiana.

Stanley, G. E., & York, A. V. (1988, April). *The ACT Assessment as a Measure for Identifying Talented Seventh Grade Youth.* Paper presented at the Annual Meeting of the National Council on Measurement in Education, New Orleans, Louisiana.

Stanley, J. C. (1977a). The predictive value of the SAT for brilliant seventh and eighth graders. *College Board Review*, No. 106, pp. 2–7. (Reprinted in *International Schools Journal* [1981], No. 2, pp. 39–48.)

Stanley, J. C. (1977b). Rationale of the Study of Mathematically Precocious Youth (SMPY) during its first five years of promoting educational acceleration. In J. C. Stanley, W. C. George, & C. H. Solano (Eds.), *The gifted and the creative* (pp. 75–112). Baltimore, MD: Johns Hopkins University Press.

Stanley, J. C. (1991). An academic model for educating the mathematically talented. *Gifted Child Quarterly, 35*, 36–42.

Stanley, J. C., & Benbow, C. P. (1986). Youths who reason exceptionally well mathematically. In R. J. Sternberg & J. E. Davidson (Eds.), *Conceptions of giftedness* (pp. 361–387). New York: Cambridge University Press.

Stanley, J. C., George, W. C, & Solano, C. H. (Eds.). (1977). *The gifted and the creative: A fifty-year perspective.* Baltimore; MD: Johns Hopkins University Press.

Stanley, J. C., Keating, D. P., & Fox, L. H. (Eds.). (1974). *Mathematical talent: Discovery, description, and development.* Baltimore; MD: Johns Hopkins University Press.

VanTassel-Baska, J. (in press). Contributions to gifted education of the Talent Search concept. In C. P. Benbow & D. Lubinski (Eds.). *Psychometric and social issues concerning intellect and talent.* Baltimore; MD: Johns Hopkins University Press.

14

Special Summer and Saturday Programs for Gifted Students

PAULA OLSZEWSKI-KUBILIUS, *Center for Talent Development, Northwestern University*

Increasingly, special programs that occur outside typical school hours are being developed for academically gifted students. There is more funding for such programs and greater demand for them on the part of students and parents. This chapter will explore some of the issues involved with extracurricular programming and their role in talent development. Results of research on the long- and short-term effects of summer and Saturday programs will also be presented.

Why Special Programs?

One important question is why special programs should exist for gifted learners. Are they needed? If so, why? Many individuals believe that summer and Saturday programs are absolutely necessary for gifted children because of their special learning needs (Olszewski-Kubilius, 1989). Typically, these programs provide a level of challenge and a pace of learning that is more suitable to the intellectual capabilities of gifted students and very different from what they encounter in school. There are more opportunities for independent inquiry, in-depth study, and accelerated learning. For many gifted children, this is the first time they are placed in a learning situation that requires study and concentrated work.

In addition, the talent development process requires intensive instruction that goes beyond what schools can or are willing to provide (Bloom, 1985). It is well known and widely accepted that developing musical or athletic talent to a high level requires lessons, special teachers, and long hours of devoted study over a period of years. In these areas, school programs typically provide only initial exposure to the talent field and an arena for identification of talent by coaches or teachers. Parents expect to supplement their child's learning and development through outside programs. Similarly, research has indicated that gifted scientists, writers, and others spent considerable time learning in their talent area from parents and mentors, or in tinkering and studying on their own (Bloom, 1985). As with musical and athletic talent, however, parents may not be knowledgeable enough to instruct their child in the talent area beyond a certain point or to provide appropriate educational materials. Even in the best schools, the amount of instruction in an area for a gifted child may not be sufficient to develop the talent or to satisfy the child's hunger for learning.

Even if a parent or mentor is capable of providing additional instruction, academically gifted children need to have friendships and interaction with intellectual peers. Most academically gifted children spend little of their time in school in homogeneous classes with other gifted children (Cox, Daniel, & Boston, 1985). The emphasis in most schools is on grouping children according to age, not ability. However, classes with other gifted children are more likely to foster friendships based on common interests and priorities and social support for educational pursuits and talent development (Olszewski-Kubilius, Grant, & Seibert, 1993). In addition, these settings can provide more intellectual stimulation and challenge.

Another reason extracurricular programs for gifted children are needed is that schools simply fail to provide for these children, especially for special subgroups such as underrepresented minorities and the economically disadvantaged (Alamprese, Erlanger, & Brigham, 1988; VanTassel-Baska, Patton, & Prillaman, 1990). Reasons include lack of funds and other resources, lack of qualified teachers, too few students to justify setting up classes in rural settings, and lack of commitment to gifted learners. Parental demand for special opportunities often have fueled the development of special summer and Saturday programs.

Finally, special programs for some academically gifted children may be necessary to save them from a pattern of underachievement or poor study habits that can result from spending time in "easy" or "boring" classes (Rimm, 1991) and lack of peer support for academic achievement. Thus, special outside-of-school programs are becoming vital to the education of gifted youths.

General Issues with Special Programs

Regardless of who sponsors special programs or their content, some general issues exist.

Relationship to In-School Programs

A frequent concern of educators is the articulation between in-school programs and outside-of-school programs. Often, gifted students take courses they would normally take in school (e.g., algebra) in special summer and Saturday programs. When students accelerate themselves in a content area at the seventh or eighth grade through a special program, there can be both immediate and long-term consequences. Immediate consequences include how to respond to the course just completed and what kind of course the student should now be placed in. Long-term consequences include how to accommodate a high school junior who has completed all of the mathematics the high school has to offer. Schools may actively discourage students from participating in special programs because of these articulation issues, or they may discourage them indirectly by not responding appropriately after the experience. Research has shown that students who complete high school course work in summer programs often do not receive credit for such work, and many are not even subsequently appropriately placed in the content area. Some students even end up repeating the course in their home school (Olszewski-Kubilius, 1989). Nothing is more demoralizing to a good student, especially one who seeks challenging courses in special programs, than being required to retake a course.

Access to Special Programs

Special summer and Saturday programs most often are sponsored by institutions of higher education. Most charge tuition. As a result, many are simply out of reach of academically gifted children who are economically disadvantaged. Minority children are less likely to be identified as gifted and less likely to be placed in special programs within their schools (Alamprese, Erlanger, & Brigham, 1988; VanTassel-Baska, Patton, & Prillaman, 1990). They also are underrepresented in talent search and other outside-of-school educational programs. But gifted minority students, especially those who are economically disadvantaged, are in dire need of the services provided by special programs. The costs of residential summer programs often are too high for even moderate-income families. And commuter programs may be too distant, especially in more rural areas. Thus, although special summer and Saturday programs are increasingly seen as vital to talent development, access to them is too often limited to economically advantaged gifted students and those in resource-rich geographic locations.

Instructional Models and Program Types

Summer and Saturday programs vary on many dimensions, such as content, duration, intensity, sponsorship, and overall purpose. There also are many different program and instructional models. Program attributes are important because they determine the type of student for whom the experience is most appropriate. Summer programs that offer intensive accelerated courses are a better match for very able students with good study skills and an ability to learn independently (Bartkovich & Mezynski, 1981; Benbow & Stanley, 1983; Lynch, 1992; Olszewski-Kubilius, Kulieke, Willis, & Krasney, 1989). Programs that offer students an opportunity to study a single subject in great depth are more suited to students with intense, focused interests (VanTassel-Baska, 1988). Some programs give students a chance to sample several different courses (e.g., students take one class in the morning and one in the afternoon). Some Saturday programs are single-shot events that have career awareness as the primary focus, while some summer programs include these as a small component of their academic classes. Some programs offer typical elementary, high school, or college classes with the goal of accelerating students in the content area, while others offer enrichment types of classes that generally pose fewer articulation problems for local schools (Feldhusen & Sokol, 1982). Some programs consist of mentorships, internships, or shadowing an adult professional on the job.

Other types of precollege programs include dual enrollment, in which high school students typically take high school and college classes simultaneously; by-mail or correspondence programs for both high school (offered by regional talent searches; see Sawyer, DeLong, & von Brock, 1987) and college-level courses; early entrance programs to college (e.g., the Early Entrance Program at the University of Washington, Simon's Rock College, or the Program for the Exceptionally Gifted at Mary Baldwin College); and memberships in organizations or clubs that offer informational newsletters and other opportunities (the Study of Exceptional Talent at Johns Hopkins University).

Some programs attempt to serve gifted students with a wider range of abilities; others focus on a more homogeneous group, for example, extremely precocious students. These latter types of programs typically use off-level testing as a way of discerning high levels of talent within an area. Some programs target students typically underrepresented in gifted programs, such as minority or economically disadvantaged students or females (Brody & Fox, 1980; Fox, Brody, & Tobin, 1985). Characteristics of special programs are important to educators who often must respond to gifted students' experiences at the local school level, to parents who are seeking programs that will further their child's talent development, and to gifted students who desire suitable, supportive, enjoyable learning environments.

Benefits of Special Programs

Organizers of special programs believe that gifted students benefit greatly from them. Research evidence actually exists on very few of these proposed benefits, and this body of research will be reviewed in the next section. However, the purported benefits of special programs include the following (Olszewski-Kubilius, 1989):

- Perceptions of increased social support for learning and achievement due to homogeneous grouping with other gifted students and support from teachers and counselors
- Positive feelings due to involvement in a learning situation that presents a more appropriate match between the students' intellectual abilities and the challenge or rigor of a course
- Development of study skills as a result of immersion in an intellectually challenging course
- Development of independence and enhancement of general living skills because of living away from home on one's own
- Increased knowledge about university programs and college life
- Raising of expectations and aspirations for educational achievement due to success in a challenging learning environment
- Reinforcement for risk taking as a result of extending oneself both intellectually and socially
- Growth in acceptance of others, knowledge of different cultures, and an enhanced world

view as a result of living and socializing with a more diverse group of students

- Self-testing of abilities due to placement in an intellectually challenging situation and subsequent reevaluations and goal setting that can further a student's progress in attaining excellence

Research on the Effects of Special Programs

Self-Esteem, Self-Concept, Self-Perceptions

Parents, educators, and researchers are interested in the effects of special programs on gifted students' self-concept, self-esteem, and self-perceptions. Students and parents seek out these programs because they believe they will provide a better and more appropriate environment, both socially and academically. In general, the research suggests that they provide positive experiences for most students.

Previous research has shown that gifted children tend to have higher scores on global self-concept measures, compared with nongifted children (see Olszewski, Kulieke, & Willis, 1987; Hoge & Renzulli, 1993, for reviews of this literature). Thus, while giftedness per se normally is not associated with reduced levels of self-esteem, the question is whether placement in a special program for gifted students results in any changes in self-esteem or self-perceptions. As Olszewski et al. (1987) noted, a change in environment, which involves a change in friends, social climate, or academic rigor or challenge, can have an impact on self-perceptions. Such changes result from a reevaluation of one's competence in a particular area based on a new reference group.

Previous research on in-school programs has shown varied results. Maddux, Scheiber, and Bass (1982) found no statistically significant differences on a self-concept measure for children enrolled in a totally segregated or partially segregated gifted program versus those not enrolled in any special program, although segregated children did have higher scores. These authors also found that segregated children in the first year of the program were rated less positively by peers, but this was transitory and disappeared by year 2.

In contrast, research by Coleman and Fults (1982, 1985) showed that gifted fourth-, fifth-, and sixth-grade children who were enrolled in a segregated, one-day-a-week pullout program had lower self-concept scores than gifted children in the regular classroom. Scores fluctuated over time and were more positive upon return to the regular classroom for sixth graders and prior to placement in the segregated program for fourth graders. These results substantiate the social comparison basis for changes in self-concept for in-school programs.

Studies specifically conducted on children enrolled in special summer or Saturday programs also show varied results. Kolloff and Moore (1989) measured the self-concepts of fifth through tenth graders attending three different two-week summer residential programs. Their results indicated that students' self-concepts were more positive at the end of the program than at the beginning, as measured by two separate instruments. Changes, however, were small to moderate on the average. The authors noted that an enhanced self-concept is the result of a more appropriate academic setting and greater peer acceptance.

VanTassel-Baska and Kulieke (1987) found an increase in self-esteem for seventh- through ninth-grade students enrolled in a summer program conducted at a national research laboratory and designed to foster scientific talent development. However, these findings were not replicated in a second summer, when results showed no pre- to postprogram changes on an instrument that measured global self-worth. Olszewski et al. (1987) used an instrument that assessed various domains of self-concept with seventh- through ninth-grade students participating in two summer residential programs. Students were measured before the programs and on the first and last days of the programs. Results showed declines in academic self-concept over time, an initial decline followed by an increase in social acceptance, and positive changes for physical and athletic competence over the course of the three-week programs.

Cooley, Cornell, and Lee (1991) reported that African American students who attended a predominantly white university summer enrichment program were accepted by other students and were comparable in self-concept and academic self-esteem as assessed by teachers. These authors concluded that summer programs for gifted students that are white-dominated can provide a supportive environment for gifted black students.

In summary, although research results are mixed, it appears that negative effects of placement in special programs on self-esteem, self-concept, and self-perceptions, due to a higher level comparison group, are slight to moderate and probably transitory.

Effects of Fast-Paced Summer Programs

One instructional model used extensively in summer programs across the United States involves fast-paced courses. These programs developed subsequent to the creation of the regional talent searches for seventh and eighth graders.[1] Fast-paced summer courses typically are open to students scoring at the mean for high school seniors who plan to attend college (roughly 500 SAT-Mathematics and 430 SAT-Verbal). They offer an array of honors-level high school courses that students seek to complete in a reduced time frame—150 hours of in-school instruction is reduced to 75 hours of instruction during the summer—and they encourage excellence, hard work, and a positive attitude toward academic accomplishment.

Research has shown that the SAT scores used as cutoffs for entrance into these types of programs are valid and select students who will succeed academically (Olszewski-Kubilius, Kulieke, Willis, & Krasney, 1989). Research also has shown that student achievement is high. On average, students complete two courses in precalculus mathematics within 50 hours of instruction (Bartkovich & Mezynski, 1981) and perform higher on standard tests than students who spend an entire year in similar mathematics classes (Stanley, 1976). Similar achievement levels have been found for fast-paced science classes (Lynch, 1992). Better performance, especially in mathematics, is associated with well-developed, independent study skills (Olszewski-Kubilius et al., 1989).

Students who take fast-paced courses differ in their motivations for participating in them (Brounstein, Holahan, & Sawyer, 1988). Some students are motivated primarily by academic interests and concerns while others have modest academic expectations and are interested mainly in the social value of the experience (i.e., relationships with other students and staff). A relatively small group of students are motivated equally by academic and social outcomes (Brounstein et al., 1988).

The evidence regarding how schools respond to fast-paced summer classes is equivocal. Lynch (1990) reported that 80 percent of students who asked for credit for high school courses completed in a summer program received it, although many schools required students to take a school exam. Appropriate placement in the content area subsequent to a summer course was a more frequent response by schools (Lynch, 1990).

However, Olszewski-Kubilius (1989) reported that only 50 percent of students who achieved proficiency (i.e., scored at or above the mean for high school seniors on a standardized test) in fast-paced summer classes received credit or appropriate placement in their home schools. Additionally, these rates varied by subject area: They were higher for cumulatively organized subjects such as algebra or Latin, and lower for verbal classes such as writing or literature.

Research has shown that fast-paced, accelerative summer programs can significantly influence many aspects of students' academic careers, occupational choices, and aspirations. A five-year study by the Center for Talented Youth of Johns Hopkins University compared talent search participants who took an accelerated summer class to a similar group, matched on gender and SAT scores, who participated in the talent search selection process but did not take courses (Barnett & Durden, 1993). The summer program participants took

---

[1] See Chapter 12 by Benbow and Lubinski and Chapter 13 by Assouline and Lupkowski-Shoplik.

advanced placement (AP) calculus and the calculus AB and BC exams earlier than search-only participants, were more likely to take college courses while still in high school, and entered more academically competitive colleges.[2] Although the summer program students had taken a variety of summer courses, in general they pursued a more rigorous course of study in mathematics than did the students who had not had a summer experience. Males who participated in programs were more accelerated in math than males who had participated only in the search, but there were no differences between groups of females.

Olszewski-Kubilius and Grant (1994) found that students who had participated in an accelerated summer program continued a pattern of high academic achievement throughout high school and college. Students, especially females, who took a mathematics class benefited more than students who took other subjects in the summer. Specifically, math females accelerated themselves more in mathematics, earned more honors in math, took more AP classes of any type in high school and more math classes in college, participated more in math clubs, more often majored in math or science in college, and had higher educational aspirations. Females who took nonmath courses consistently reported the least acceleration and relatively lower levels of achievement and lower aspirations (Olszewski-Kubilius & Grant, 1994).

Because of the underrepresentation of females in advanced math courses and math and science careers, some studies have specifically examined gender differences in the effects of summer programs on academically talented students' educational and vocational decisions and achievements. For example, Fox, Brody, and Tobin (1985) and Brody and Fox (1980) reported on the effects of a fast-paced, noncompetitive summer algebra class designed for seventh-grade females talented in mathematics. The experimental girls were compared to control groups of males and females who had participated in a talent search, females who had participated in a career awareness program, and students who had participated in school-based math programs. Two to three years after the intervention, the experimental girls were more accelerated in mathematics than the control boys or girls. By grade 11, however, the number of accelerated experimental girls remained stable, the number of accelerated control girls declined, and the number of accelerated control boys increased dramatically. The authors suggest that the intervention helped mathematically talented girls to keep even with boys who accelerated themselves without any intervention. Additional effects of the summer program for girls included a greater commitment to full-time work in the future and higher educational aspirations (Fox, Brody, & Tobin, 1985).

Several studies have shown that intensive outside-of-school academic programs, other than summer programs, can have powerful, positive effects. As described in Benbow, Perkins, and Stanley (1983) and Swiatek and Benbow (1991), students in an accelerative math program that compressed four and a half years of high school mathematics into two years were compared to three other groups of students: those who qualified for the program but did not participate, those who entered the program but dropped out, and those who were initially in the program but later were placed in a slower paced mathematics class. Students who completed the program had higher SAT-M scores at the end of high school and were more likely to have completed calculus and taken AP calculus and the BC calculus exam. They took high school math classes earlier; took more college-level classes in high school; scored higher on the College Board Achievement tests; were more likely to earn at least a National Merit Letter of Commendation and to participate in math competitions; attended more intellectually challenging colleges; were more likely to enter college early; and were more likely to study applied math in graduate school. The only gender difference obtained was that girls who completed the class were

---

[2] The AB exam is less comprehensive and less rigorous than the BC exam. A score of 3 to 5 on the AB exam generally will earn one semester of college credit, while those scores on the BC exam earn two semesters of credit.

more likely to attend graduate school; there was no similar effect of participation on boys. However, the number of subjects in the study was small, making results of gender comparisons tenuous.

In summary, special intensive programs in mathematics, particularly summer programs, can positively affect students' educational and career decisions.

Effects of Other Programs

Research on the effects of other kinds of special programs for gifted children and youth is generally sparse. Sawyer, DeLong, and von Brock (1987) studied middle school students who completed advanced course work in a correspondence program. They reported that 98 percent of students who studied AP courses by correspondence scored at 3 or above on the AP exam (a score of 3 generally earns college credit). This is especially impressive given that these students were younger than typical high school students who take AP exams. By-mail or correspondence courses are a good alternative for gifted secondary students whose schools offer no AP classes or only a limited number of them.

A few outside-of-school programs have career education or counseling as their main focus. Colson (1980) investigated the effects of a community-based career guidance program on gifted high school students. The program included educational awareness, career awareness, self-awareness, planning and decision making, shadowing of a university professor, and an active hands-on internship. Participants queried one year after program completion felt that the career education program was the single most significant event of their senior year and that it was the best preparation for later decision making.

Several outside-of-school programs reported in the literature focus on particular groups of gifted students considered in need of special services because they are underrepresented in school gifted programs. For example, Lynch and Mills (1990) provided Saturday and summer classes to sixth-grade minority students who were economically disadvantaged. The classes provided instruction in mathematics and language arts. The results showed that students made greater gains on standardized tests in mathematics, although not in reading, compared with a group of similar students who did not receive special instruction. The author reported that as a result of the gains students made, some qualified for their in-school gifted program without affirmative action measures.

Confessore (1991) reported a longitudinal follow-up of students who participated in a university-based summer arts program ten years prior. The students were adolescents at the time of participation and took college-level classes in art, music, dance, theater, or creative writing. Survey results showed that, in general, students remained active in the arts subsequent to the program, and 83 percent stated that the program helped them confirm their identity as artists. Participants also reported that contact with other artistically talented adolescents was a major benefit of the program. Like academically oriented programs, special outside-of-school programs in the arts can have positive long-term effects for gifted students.

Contests and Competitions

Other programs in which gifted students can participate are contests, competitions, and olympiads. Many such programs exist within the United States and across Europe (see Goldstein & Wagner, 1993, for a description). The preparation for these programs gives students advanced training and skills. Some, like the Westinghouse Science Talent Search, involve years of preparation, significant cash prizes, and several levels of competitions (i.e., state, regional, and national).

Little research exists on the effects of contests and competitions. Longitudinal follow-ups on participants in the Westinghouse Science Talent Search found that most had continued to pursue mathematics and science related fields (Subotnik & Steiner, 1994). However, more females had left these fields than males, although their reasons for doing so did not differ. It appears that some students who received a great deal of support from mentors in preparation for talent competitions did not receive the same level of support after high school (Subotnik & Steiner, 1994).

The Future of Special Programs

It is likely that the demand for outside-of-school programs for gifted students will increase. The form that these programs take may change, however. Computer technology offers exciting possibilities for delivery of special courses and programs, including "telelearning" and "telementoring" (Lewis, 1989; McBride & Lewis, 1993). These technologies can increase access for gifted students, especially those who are geographically isolated or in schools with limited instructional resources. Research must continue to assess the long-term effects and benefits of special programs for students and the validity of entrance and selection criteria against student performance. Especially lacking are large scale, well-designed studies that empirically demonstrate the purported positive effects of summer programs and the high levels of achievement of participants. These are needed to convince educators and policymakers that gifted children can indeed learn at faster rates than other children and need and profit in specific ways from special educational services. Summer and Saturday programs have become vital to the talent development of academically gifted students, but the educational models they embody need to become an essential part of the local school curriculum.

REFERENCES

Alamprese, J. A., Erlanger, W. J., & Brigham, N. (1988). *No gift wasted: Effective strategies for educating highly able disadvantaged students in math and science* (Vols. 1–2). USOE Contract #300-87-0152.

Barnett, L. B., & Durden, W. G. (1993). Education patterns of academically talented youth. *Gifted Child Quarterly, 37*, 161–168.

Bartkovich, K. G., & Mezynski, K. (1981). Fast-paced precalculus mathematics for talented junior-high students: Two recent SMPY programs. *Gifted Child Quarterly, 25*, 73–80.

Benbow, C. P., Perkins, S., & Stanley, J. C. (1983). Mathematics taught at a fast pace: A longitudinal evaluation of SMPY's first class. In C. P. Benbow & J. C. Stanley (Eds.), *Academic precocity: Aspects of its development* (pp. 51–78). Baltimore, MD: Johns Hopkins University Press.

Benbow, C. P., & Stanley, J. C. (Eds.). (1983). *Academic precocity: Aspects of its development.* Baltimore, MD: Johns Hopkins University Press.

Bloom, B. S. (Ed.). (1985). *Developing talent in young people.* New York: Ballantine.

Brody, L., & Fox, L. H. (1980). An accelerative intervention program for mathematically gifted girls. In L. H. Fox, L. Brody, & D. Tobin (Eds.), *Women and the mathematical mystique* (pp. 164–178). Hillsdale, NJ: Lawrence Erlbaum Associates.

Brounstein, P. J., Holahan, W., & Sawyer, R. (1988). The expectations and motivations of gifted students in a residential academic program: A study of individual differences. *Journal for the Education of the Gifted, 11*(3), 36–52.

Coleman, J., & Fults, B. (1982). Self-concept and the gifted classroom: The role of social comparisons. *Gifted Child Quarterly, 26,* 116–120.

Coleman, J., & Fults, B. (1985). Special-class placement, level of intelligence, and the self-concepts of gifted children: A social comparison perspective. *Remedial and Special Education, 6*(1), 7–12.

Colson, S. (1980). The evaluation of a community-based career education program for gifted and talented students as an administrative model for an alternative program. *Gifted Child Quarterly, 24,* 101–106.

Confessore, G. J. (1991). What became of the kids who participated in the 1981 Johnson Early College Summer Arts Program? *Journal for the Education of the Gifted, 15*(1), 64–82.

Cooley, M. R., Cornell, D. G., and Lee, C. C. (1991). Peer acceptance and self-concept of Black students in a summer gifted program. *Journal for the Education of the Gifted, 14,* 166–170.

Cox, J., Daniel, N., & Boston, B. O. (1985). *Educating able learners: Programs and promising practices.* Austin: University of Texas Press.

Feldhusen, J., & Sokol, L. (1982). Extra-school programming to meet the needs of gifted youth: Super Saturday. *Gifted Child Quarterly, 26,* 51–56.

Fox, L. H., Brody, L., & Tobin, D. (1985). The impact of early intervention programs upon course-taking and attitudes in high school. In S. F. Chipman, L. R. Brush, & D. M. Wilson (Eds.), *Women and mathematics: Balancing the equation* (pp. 249–274). Hillsdale, NJ: Lawrence Erlbaum Associates.

Goldstein, D., & Wagner, H. (1993). After school programs, competitions, school olympics, and summer programs. In K. A. Heller, F. J. Monks, & A. H. Passow (Eds.), *International handbook of research and development of giftedness and talent* (pp. 593–604). New York: Pergamon Press.

Hoge, R. D., & Renzulli, J. S. (1993). Giftedness and self-concept. *Review of Educational Research, 63,* 449–465.

Kolloff, P. B., & Moore, A. D. (1989). Effects of summer programs on the self-concepts of gifted children. *Journal for the Education of the Gifted, 12*(4), 268–276.

Lewis, G. (1989). Serving the gifted in rural areas. Telelearning: Making maximum use of the medium. *Roeper Review, 11,* 195–202.

Lynch, S. J. (1990). Credit and placement issues for the academically talented following summer studies in science and mathematics. *Gifted Child Quarterly, 34*(1), 27–30.

Lynch, S. J. (1992). Fast-paced high school science for the academically talented: A six-year perspective. *Gifted Child Quarterly, 36,* 147–154.

Lynch, S., & Mills, C. J. (1990). The Skills Reinforcement Project (SRP): An academic program for high potential minority youth. *Journal for the Education of the Gifted, 13*(4), 364–379.

Maddux, C. D., Scheiber, L. M., & Bass, J. E. (1982). Self-concept and social distance in gifted children. *Gifted Child Quarterly, 26,* 77–81.

McBride, R. O., & Lewis, G. (1993). Sharing the resources: Electronic outreach programs. *Journal for the Education of the Gifted, 16*(4), 372–386.

Olszewski-Kubilius P. (1989). Development of academic talent: The role of summer programs. In J. VanTassel-Baska & P. Olszewski-Kubilius (Eds.), *Patterns of influence on gifted learners: The home, the self and the school* (pp. 214–230). New York: Teachers College Press.

Olszewski-Kubilius, P., & Grant, B. (1994). Academically talented females in mathematics: The role of special programs and support from others in acceleration, achievement and aspiration. In K. D. Noble & R. F. Subotnik (Eds.), *Remarkable women: Perspectives on female talent development.* Creskill, NJ: Hampton Press.

Olszewski-Kubilius, P., Grant, B., & Seibert, C. (1993). Social support systems and the disadvantaged gifted: A framework for developing programs and services. *Roeper Review, 17,* 20–25.

Olszewski, P., Kulieke, M., & Willis, G. B. (1987, Summer). Changes in the self-perceptions of gifted students who participate in rigorous academic programs. *Journal for the Education of the Gifted, 10*(4), 287–303.

Olszewski-Kubilius, P., Kulieke, M. J., Willis, G. B., & Krasney, N. (1989). An analysis of the validity of SAT entrance scores for accelerated classes. *Journal for the Education of the Gifted, 13*(1), 37–54.

Rimm, S. (1991). Underachievement and superachievement: Flip sides of the same psychological coin. In N. Colangelo & G. A. Davis (Eds.), *Handbook of gifted education* (pp. 328–343). Boston: Allyn and Bacon.

Sawyer, R. N., DeLong, M. R., & von Brock, A. B. (1987). By-mail learning options for academically talented middle-school youth. *Gifted Child Quarterly, 3,* 118–120.

Stanley, J. C. (1976). Special fast-mathematics classes taught by college professors to fourth through twelfth grades. In D. P. Keating (Ed.), *Intellectual talent: Research and development.* Baltimore, MD: Johns Hopkins University.

Subotnik, R. F., & Steiner, C. L. (1994). Adult manifestations of adolescent talent in science: A longitudinal study of 1983 Westinghouse Science Talent Search winners. In R. F. Subotnik & K. D. Arnold (Eds.), *Beyond Terman: Contemporary longitudinal studies of giftedness and talent* (pp. 52–76). Norwood, NJ: Ablex.

Swiatek, M. A., & Benbow, C. P. (1991). Ten-year longitudinal follow-up of ability matched accelerated and unaccelerated gifted students. *Journal of Educational Psychology, 3,* 528–538.

VanTassel-Baska, J. (1988). Curriculun design issues in developing a curriculum for the gifted. In J. VanTassel-Baska (Ed.), *Comprehensive curriculum for gifted learners.* Boston: Allyn and Bacon.

VanTassel-Baska, J., & Kulieke, M. J. (1987). The role of community-based scientific resources in developing scientific talent: A case study. *Gifted Child Quarterly, 31,* 111–115.

VanTassel-Baska, J., Patton, J., Prillaman, D. (1990). The nature and extent of programs for the disadvantaged gifted in the United States and territories. *Gifted Child Quarterly, 34,* 94–96.

15

Secondary Services, Opportunities, and Activities for Talented Youth

JOHN F. FELDHUSEN, *Purdue University*

Two major shifts in orientation are needed if we hope to enhance or facilitate the development of talent among adolescents during the middle school and high school years. One is to abandon the *program* concept and the other is to abandon the *gifted* concept. "Program" often connotes a specific and restricted set of activities exclusively for an explicitly identified group of students labeled "gifted." The extent of activities is often limited to an hour or two of pull-out time from a math, English, or science class for some bland and often worthless enrichment activities (Cox, Daniel, & Boston, 1985). Little good is accomplished with such "programs."

The full development of youth's talent calls for a wide diversity of experiences in well-selected courses of instruction, extracurricular activities, and extra-school experiences in the wider community. The latter, extra-school activities, might include participation in special Saturday or summer programs (Feldhusen, 1991), concurrent enrollment in college or university courses, or work with a local drama or historical society. Our major emphasis is that talent development calls for a rich variety of experiences through which highly able youth carry out a self-identification process to understand better their special aptitudes and talents, grow in knowledge in the fields related to their talents, and increasingly commit themselves to the full development of their talents.

The second shift is away from the concept and label *gifted* to a *talent* orientation. A recent report from the United States Office of Education (U.S. Department of Education, 1993) concluded that "The term 'gifted' connotes a mature power rather than a developing ability and, therefore, is antithetic to recent research findings about children" (p. 26). The report generally uses the term *talent* or *talented* rather than *gift* or *gifted* and offers the following definition:

> Children and youth with outstanding talent perform or show the potential for performing at remarkably high levels. . . . (p. 26)

It is clear, then, that our task is to find youth who are precocious in their talent development and to identify their specific talent strength or strengths. Some will possess multiple talents calling for several accelerated learning experiences; others will have only one or two talent strengths and a more limited need for special educational opportunities. In any event, these are youth who *need* accelerated, enriched, fast-paced, challenging instruction to sustain their talent development (Feldhusen & Sokol, 1982).

Efforts to search for and identify talented youth have become excessively formal, statistical, and dependent on tests. The process of identification also has resulted in excessive labeling behavior on the part of school personnel, especially in so-called gifted programs. A process of searching for and selecting youth for special educational opportunities to meet their particular needs surely can be carried out without the intermediate step of labeling them as gifted. Rather than labeling and categorizing them, it is preferable to use the language of special education and denote them as children with special talents, aptitudes, abilities, or needs (Feldhusen, 1993).

Search and Selection

A variety of methods can be used to search for talented youth. Regional talent searches using the Scholastic Aptitude Test (SAT) (VanTassel-Baska, 1984) serve well to identify youth with high-level aptitude in mathematics or verbal talent. An elementary version of the SAT, EXPLORE (from ACT), is also now available.[1] A variety of other competitions also serve to identify talented, precocious youth. Standardized achievement test results can be used to identify special talents, but we recognize that low ceilings on such tests often impose severe restrictions on the highest score levels attainable by talented youth.

Teachers can be trained to structure educational activities and opportunities in their classrooms to enable youth to reveal their talents. Teachers typically need training to enable them to recognize the behavioral signs that reveal special talent strengths.

Preliminary screening in the talent search can be facilitated with rating scales such as the Scales for Rating the Behavioral Characteristics of Superior Students (SRBCSS; Renzulli, Smith, Callahan, White, & Hartman, 1976), the Purdue Academic Rating Scales (Feldhusen, Hoover, & Sayler, 1990), and the Purdue Vocational Talent Scales (Feldhusen, Hoover, & Sayler, 1990). Interest inventories such as the Interest-A-Lyzer (Renzulli, Hebert, & Sorenson, 1994) also can be useful in the search for talent strengths.

The ten scales of the SRBCSS include several of particular interest for talent assessment, namely Leadership, Art, Music, Creativity, Expressiveness, Drama, and Planning. The Purdue Academic Rating Scales focus on five talent domains: Science, Mathematics, English, Social Studies, and Foreign Languages. The Purdue Vocational Talent Scales assess special aptitude in Home Economics, Trade and Industrial Areas, Vocational Agriculture, and Business. All of these instruments are useful as preliminary indicators of talent.

Ultimately, youth talents are best revealed in challenging, rich learning situations and best assessed by teachers who create learning experiences in which talent can be shown and who recognize the superior talents manifested by their students. The process is then cyclical in that preliminary identification by a teacher leads to increasingly well tailored instruction to sustain the challenge and to keep the talent growing and developing.

Secondary Services, Opportunities, and Activities

The locus of educational provision for talented adolescents is in classes, extracurricular activities, counseling, and extra-school opportunities (Feldhusen, Hoover, & Sayler, 1990). A wide variety of services should be available to meet the special needs of talented youth for enriched, advanced, and challenging learning experiences. Table 15.1 presents a smorgasbord of educational services that are appropriate at the middle and high school levels for talented youth. The lists are suggestive and not limiting. Talented students should have many opportunities to study and learn with other talented, precocious youth, and to accelerate their learning program to fit their own precocity (Feldhusen & Moon, 1992; Feldhusen, Moon, & Rifner, 1989).

Although there has been much debate in recent years about special high-track classes, as well as some shifting to heterogeneous grouping, we agree wholeheartedly with Kulik and Kulik (1991; see Chapter 19), who concluded:

> Programs of separate instruction for high aptitude and gifted students are usually effective; . . . and they are necessary if we wish to cultivate our nation's resources of intellectual talent. (p. 191)

Talented youth *need* the stimulation and challenge that can only come with advanced and enriched instruction, highly knowledgeable teachers, and equally talented/precocious peers. It is of no academic value to bide one's

[1] See Chapter 13 by Assouline and Lupkowski-Shoplik.

Table 15.1
Talent Development Services, Resources, and Activities

Junior High or Middle School Services	*High School Services*
1. Counseling A. Group B. Individual	1. Counseling A. Group B. Individual
2. Honors classes	2. Honors classes
3. Future problem solving	3. Advanced Placement classes
4. Junior Great Books	4. Foreign languages
5. Odyssey of the Mind	5. Seminars
6. Career education	6. Mentorships
7. Seminars	7. Internships
8. Mentors	8. Concurrent college enrollment
9. AP or college classes	9. College classes in high school
10. Acceleration A. Math B. Science C. English	10. Special opportunities A. Art B. Music C. Drama D. Dance
11. Special opportunities A. Art B. Music C. Drama D. Dance	11. Special projects for vocationally talented
12. Special projects for vocationally talented	12. Debate
14. Correspondence study	13. Correspondence study
15. Independent study	14. Independent study

time in low-level, slow-paced instruction or cooperative learning activities. Grouping for special classes should be on a subject-by-subject basis and based on youth talents and precocity, not on a general tracking plan. However, it is clear that some youth are talented in so many areas—multitalented—that their entire program should be advanced in all subjects and in the company of other talented students.

Talented youth should be allowed, encouraged, and counseled to take Advanced Placement (AP) courses whenever and wherever they are available (College Board, 1989). The AP exams also offer excellent tests of talent strengths as well as college credit for those students who score well.

Concurrent college or university enrollment affords another way for talented youth to experience higher level academic challenges (Feldhusen & Cobb, 1989). Several state education departments now require high schools to award academic credit toward high school graduation for college courses that parallel high school courses. The student also earns college credit for courses completed successfully.

Extracurricular activities afford many opportunities for talent development. For verbally talented youth, debate and other forensic activities afford excellent opportunities to develop talents in public speaking, group leadership, library research, writing, planning, and organizing. Language clubs make it possible to develop speech capabilities in a foreign language. Youth organizations in vocational subjects provide many opportunities for talent development in project work, leadership, and artistic design. Most high schools offer an abundance of extracurricular opportunities.

Counselors should be able to identify youth with special talents and provide educational and career guidance for their optimum development (Silverman, 1993). Academic records in junior and senior high schools should serve to identify the specific talent strengths of students and should be used in writing short- and long-range talent development plans for individual students. The Growth Plan concept will be presented in the next section.

Talented youth need to select courses wisely in junior and senior high school to ready themselves for college programs. Some should plan to attend one of the residential high schools of mathematics and science now operating in ten states.[2] Early admission to college, preferably a major university, affords many talented youth the only route to challenging learning experiences that sustain talent development. Counselors can and should provide guidance to the right courses in middle school and the freshman and sophomore years of high school to assure readiness of tal-

[2] See Chapter 16 by Kolloff.

ented youth for concurrent college enrollment, early admission to college, or admission to one of the academies.

Extra-school opportunities also can contribute significantly to the process of talent development. These are the educational opportunities, resources, and activities in the community, state, and region that are accessible after school, evenings, weekends, and summers (Feldhusen, 1991; Goldstein & Wagner, 1993). Some schools and chambers of commerce have published catalogs of such opportunities for their areas. The offerings also are reported in newspapers or brochures distributed in the community. The activities often center at colleges, universities, museums, libraries, historical sites, or institutes and may consist of public lectures, classes, courses, exhibits, and the like.

Talented youth should especially be led to opportunities on college or university campuses (Trost, 1993). Concurrent enrollment in college classes, as noted earlier, can provide challenging learning experiences. Mentorships with college professors, special classes on Saturdays and in summers, research internships, use of library and computer facilities, and association with the college theater are some of the resources that are often open to talented youth who live near colleges and universities.

We conclude that effective talent development depends on a wide variety of resources in school and community and on the motivation of talented youth and their parents, with guidance from school teachers and counselors, to make optimum use of the available resources. Too often, programs for the gifted have conveyed the message that only the special services offered in the program qualify as educational provision for the gifted. In contrast, our view is an eclectic one: Use all available resources even though they are not officially designated "gifted program," and add services as needed such as Advanced Placement classes, seminars, honors classes, and special clubs. Absence of a formal gifted program often leads to hand wringing and desperation on the part of parents of talented youth. Ideally, their responses should be (1) to seek out the best current options for their talented child and (2) to press the school to offer more advanced, challenging learning opportunities.

Growth Plans

Talents grow into full-blown, mature expertise or competence when there is explicit planning during childhood and adolescence for their development. The process begins with recognition by parents, teachers, counselors, or others of the young person's special talents, aptitudes, and abilities as well as the intense interest that often accompanies special talent in a domain. Ultimately, it is the child and then the adolescent who must come to see and understand his or her own talent strength and commit to the development of the talent(s). Parents and school personnel can help a great deal, but they cannot force children to become motivated to develop their own talents. Challenging and exciting teachers in the early years and increasingly competent, expert teachers in the middle years (Bloom, 1985), along with supportive and knowledgeable parents, can provide the initial impetus for the eventual takeover of the task by talented youth themselves.

The concept of a Growth Plan is a formal mechanism or procedure for inducing more specific thought about talent development. A Growth Plan for an eighth-grade adolescent is presented in Figure 15.1. The planning process is best carried out in school, led by a counselor or talent development coordinator, in a series of four to eight meetings of 40 to 60 minutes each with students in small groups of 12 to 20. The development of the Growth Plan is done by the students with assistance from the counselor or coordinator.

The first section of the Growth Plan is an inventory or review of self, abilities, interests, and accomplishments to date. The planning process often is carried out in the late spring as a preparation for the next school year and beyond. Test scores are made available to students as much as possible for their age and are interpreted with the assistance of the counselor or coordinator to help students achieve as much self-understanding as possible.

Name K.M. Phone (715) XXX-9214

Grade level entering 8th grade

Current courses STAR I: A Voyage Through the Digestive System of Mammals and The Chemistry of Aquatics Environments At Home School: Most Abled Math and Most Abled Language Arts.

Clubs, organizations Science Olympiad and Sports Teams

Awards, honors Science Olympiad State Finalist; Highest Math Student in the Seventh Grade; Scholastic Awards in Math, Science, Social Studies and Language

Test scores SAT V= 540, Q= 490; ACH: Science: 97%; Math: 92%; IQ: 147

Prior experience in gifted program Has been enrolled in Most Abled (Accelerated) classes at his home school

Interest Analysis K.M. has a wide variety of interests including writing, sciences, and reading. He enjoys going to movies and investigating science topics.

Learning styles K.M. likes to learn in a hands-on, highly active environment. He prefers tasks and projects which are highly structured and which allow him to examine the components carefully. He likes to work in groups and by himself.

Student's own goals	Recommended classes for next year
Short-term— *Raise SAT scores. *Progress faster in science studies *Become more responsible (i.e., getting homework completed). Long-term— *Pursue career interests in radiology, ecology, or chemistry.	*Continue in Most Abled (Accelerated) Classes.
Recommended activities in school	**Recommended extra-school activities**
*Continue participation in Science Olympiad. *Pursue athletic activities as determined by K.M. and his parents. *Pursue interests in mathematics, science, and ecology through school clubs.	*Visit more aquariums to continue studies in ecology. *Contact and/or secure mentor to assist with further ecological studies.

Final plan ________________

Figure 15.1 Growth Plan.

The next phase of Growth Plan activity is goal setting. Students are led in the process of developing and/or clarifying their short- and long-term personal, social, academic, and career goals. This may require class and out-of-class time for students to reflect on the directions of their lives and their aspirations for the future. The goals are recorded on the Growth Plan.

The next phase is selecting classes, courses, and academic experiences for the year ahead and possibly several years ahead if they contemplate early college admission. Counselors should be ready to guide students in linking their goals to necessary academic steps. Extracurricular activities also are planned and incorporated into the Growth Plan. Finally, thought is given to extra-school opportunities. Throughout this planning process the counselor's role includes making students aware of appropriate resources and activities in relation to their goals.

When a tentative draft of the Growth Plan has been written, it should be taken home for discussion with parents and revised according to the realities that flow from students' perceptions of parent feedback and suggestions. In most cases talented students will be dependent on parent support, especially for extra-school activities such as Saturday and summer programs or concurrent college enrollment that involve additional costs.

The Growth Plan process should increasingly be guided by students themselves. Hopefully they will come to see themselves as capable of planning for and guiding their own talent development.

Purdue Pyramid Model of Talent Development

Figure 15.2 presents a summary pyramid model of the talent development process. The base suggests that talented youth, like all youth, need acceptance as legitimate, valid human beings. Peer pressure to be normal or average is a major problem for talented teenagers (Brown, Clasen, & Eicher, 1986). Typically, they can best achieve peer acceptance in the company of other talented youth. The model then suggests, in the vertical segments, a variety of educational experiences that facilitate talent development. Again, the suggestions represent a sampling, not a definitive list.

Out of the educational opportunities, as a result of challenging educational experiences, talented youth come to better understand their talents, aptitudes, abilities, interests, motivation, potentials, and limitations. Self understanding is a necessary prelude to the final pyramidal stage—commitment to the full development of one's talents and abilities. Such a commitment is linked to an awareness of career goals as well as knowledge of the educational routes to those goals.

Through the teenage years, parent support is a vital ingredient of talent development. Parents provide the financial resources for the extra-school opportunities, they are the sounding board for discussion of opportunities, they provide guidance and motivation, and they afford emotional support throughout the process.

Summary and Comment

Three major research projects have yielded insights about the talent development process. The first was conducted by Benjamin Bloom and reported in 1985 in *Developing Talent in Young People.*[3] Studying athletes, artists, and scientists who had achieved world class recognition, Bloom tried to find the conditions in youth that facilitated their talent development. He found that early identification of talent strengths, highly supportive and encouraging parents, and stimulating and knowledgeable teachers were key elements in their early development. The youth themselves showed early capacity to learn rapidly and well. Long-term commitment of the youth themselves to the development of their talent emerged in later adolescence and characterized those who went on to high-level achievement.

---

[3] See Chapter 17 by Sosniak.

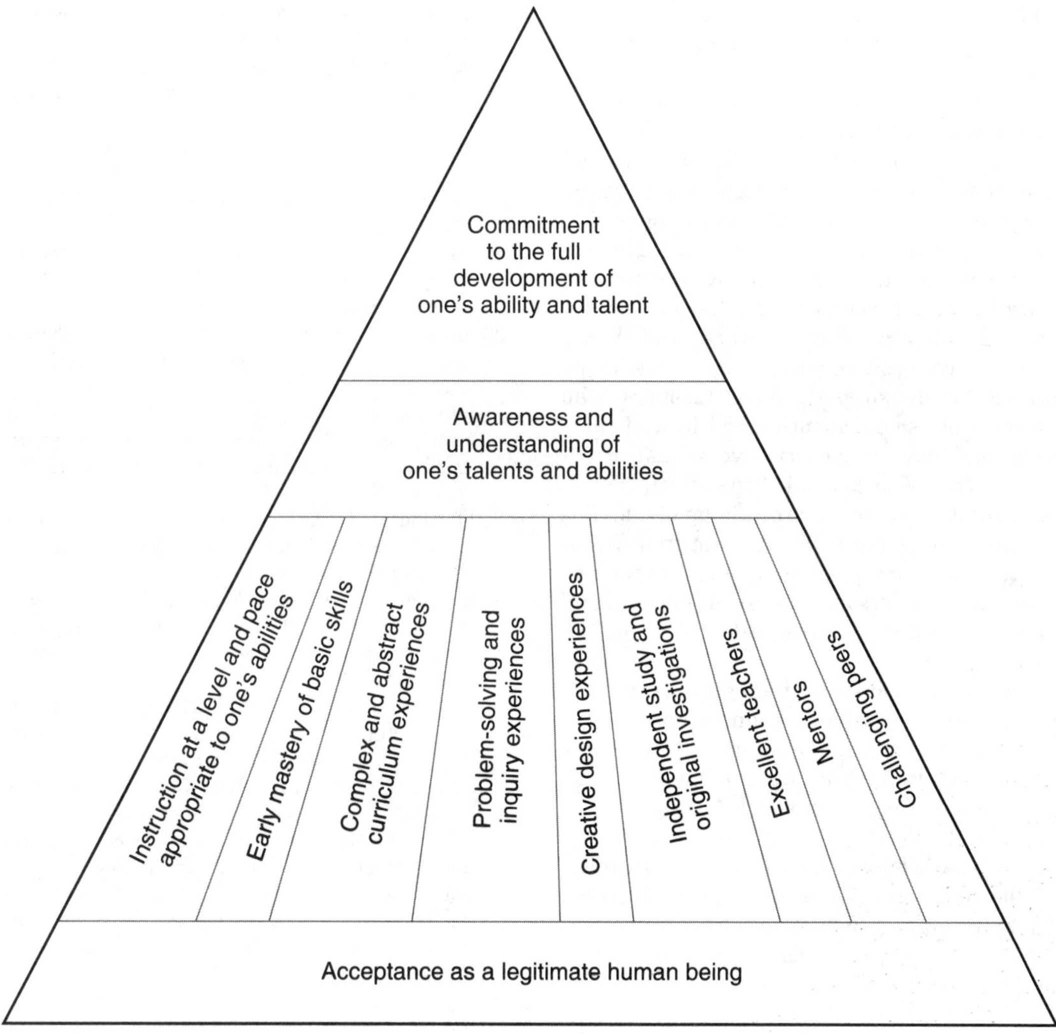

Figure 15.2 The Purdue Pyramid Model of Talent Development

In *Multiple Intelligences: The Theory in Practice,* Howard Gardner (1993) reminds us of the emerging role of the multiple talents conception, first presented by him in 1983 and now having a powerful impact on school reform in the United States.[4] As opposed to the old conception of a single general intelligence, or *g,* Gardner's new theory proposes seven basic talents or intelligences: logical-mathematical, linguistic, musical, spatial, bodily-kinesthetic, interpersonal, and intrapersonal. Implementation of the theory in schools is being carried out and evaluated. Gardner, Walters, and Hatch (1992) concluded that "Within the area of education, the applications of the theory are . . . tentative and speculative" (p. 35). Nevertheless, observers are almost uniformly optimistic that the mul-

[4] See Chapter 5 by Ramos-Ford and Gardner.

tiple intelligences approach in education bodes well for talent development in U.S. schools.

A recent book by Csikszentmihalyi, Rathmude, and Whalen (1993), *Talented Teenagers,* described research that followed 208 youth through their high school years. They showed talent precocity in mathematics, science, music, art, and athletics. The researchers concluded that talents continue to grow in youth through the adolescent years if they develop productive work and study habits, have positive personality traits, enjoy strong family support, have teachers who model professional identity and love of their field, and have a conservative sexual orientation. They also concluded that talent development is a complex process involving differentiation of one's talents, aptitudes, and abilities and integration of one's capacities into a unified persona that experiences "flow" or total absorption in the talent field activities.

The junior and senior high school years are critical times for talent recognition and development. The recent publication *National Excellence: A Case for Developing America's Talent* (U.S. Department of Education, 1993) stresses the need for a new view and conception of youth talents and urges abandonment of the term and conception *gifted.* It seems likely that this transition will lead to more effective ways of discovering and nurturing youth talents.

REFERENCES

Bloom, B. S. (1985). Generalizations about talent development. In B. S. Bloom (Ed.), *Developing talent in young people* (pp. 507–549). New York: Ballantine Books.

Brown, B. B., Clasen, D. R., & Eicher, S. A. (1986). Perceptions of peer pressure, peer conformity dispositions, and self-reported behavior among adolescents. *Developmental Psychology, 22,* 521–530.

College Board (1989). *A guide to the Advanced Placement program.* Princeton, NJ: College Entrance Examination Board.

Cox, J., Daniel, N., & Boston, B. O. (1985). *Educating able learners: Programs and promising practices.* Austin: University of Texas Press.

Csikszentmihalyi, M., Rathunde, K., & Whalen, S. (1993). *Talented teenagers.* New York: Cambridge University Press.

Feldhusen, J. F. (1991). Saturday and summer programs. In N. Colangelo & G. A. Davis (Eds.), *Handbook of gifted education* (pp. 197–208). Boston: Allyn and Bacon.

Feldhusen, J. F. (1993). Talent identification and development in education (TIDE). *Gifted Education International, 10,* 10–15.

Feldhusen, J. F., & Cobb, S. J. (1989). College courses for high school credit. *G/T Indiana, 1*(6), 2.

Feldhusen, J. F., Hoover, S. M., & Sayler, M. F. (1990). *Identification and education of the gifted and talented at the secondary level.* Monroe, NY: Trillium Press.

Feldhusen, J. F., & Moon, S. M. (1992). Grouping gifted students: Issues and concerns. *Gifted Child Quarterly, 36,* 63–67

Feldhusen, J. F., Moon, S. M., & Rifner, P. J. (1989). Educating the gifted and talented: Strengths, weaknesses, and prospects. *Educational Perspectives, 26*(122), 48–55.

Feldhusen, J. F., & Sokol, L. (1982). Extra-school programming to meet the needs of gifted youth. *Gifted Child Quarterly, 26,* 51–56.

Gardner, H. (1983). *Frames of mind: The theory of multiple intelligences.* New York: Basic Books.

Gardner, H. (1993). *Multiple intelligences: The theory in practice.* New York: Basic Books.

Gardner, H., Walters, J., & Hatch, T. (1992). If teaching had looked beyond the classroom: The development and education of intelligences. *Innotech Journal, 16*(1), 18–36.

Goldstein, D., & Wagner, H. (1993). After school programs, competitions, school olympics, and summer programs. In K. A. Heller, F. J. Monks, & A. H. Passow (Eds.), *International handbook of research and development of giftedness and talent* (pp. 593–604). New York: Pergamon Press.

Kulik, J. A., & Kulik, C. C. (1991). Ability grouping and gifted students. In N. Colangelo & G. A. Davis (Eds.), *Handbook of gifted education,* (pp. 178–196). Boston: Allyn and Bacon.

Renzulli, J. S., Hebert, T. P., & Sorenson, M. F. (1994). *Secondary interest-a-lyzer.* Mansfield Center, CT: Creative Learning Press.

Renzulli, J. S., Smith, L. H., Callahan, C. M., White, A. J., & Hartman, R. K. (1976). *Scales for rating the behavioral characteristics of superior students.* Mansfield Center, CT: Creative Learning Press.

Silverman, L. K. (Ed.) (1993). *Counseling the gifted and talented.* Denver, CO: Love.

Trost, G. (1993). Prediction of excellence in school, university, and work. In K. A. Heller, F. J. Monks, & A. H. Passow (Eds.), *International handbook of research and development of giftedness and talent* (pp. 325–336). New York: Pergamon Press.

U.S. Department of Education (1993). *National excellence: A case for developing America's talent.* Washington, DC: U.S. Government Printing Office.

VanTassel-Baska, J. (1984). The talent search as an identification model. *Gifted Child Quarterly, 28,* 172–176.

16

Special Residential High Schools

PENNY BRITTON KOLLOFF, *Illinois State University, Normal*

This chapter describes a growing national trend in the education of gifted students, the development of special residential high schools for young people of exceptional intellectual and academic ability. Since 1980, at least ten states have established these schools, and others are in various stages of planning similar schools. Stanley (1987) recommended that any state that has at least 300 National Merit semifinalists each year should explore the possibility of a residential high school.

Rationale

Since the early 1970s, programs for gifted students have proliferated across the United States as local schools have created various accommodations for their high-ability learners. Approaches for high school students have generally taken the form of advanced or honors courses, opportunities for acceleration to higher level classes, or, in some cases, enrollment in college classes while still in high school (Cox, Daniel, & Boston, 1985). Depending on the local or state definition of *gifted*, programs of these types usually are directed at meeting the needs of up to 10 percent of the students in a school. If these students are considered a homogeneous group, however, then the most academically and intellectually advanced among them will still have unmet needs.

The typical high school is unable to offer the number of advanced courses or a sufficiently diverse curriculum to provide for the gifted learner who, for example, is capable of mastering all the mathematics courses the school has to offer within a year or two of entrance. At a time when many of the nation's secondary schools do not offer a physics course, some do not include a course in chemistry, and the majority of students do not have an opportunity to go beyond the second year of a foreign language, concerns must focus on making advanced courses accessible to the most intellectually capable students. Also, if small, perhaps rural, schools do not have large enough enrollments to offer the most advanced classes or are not able to provide teachers for those courses, then educators, parents, and students themselves must seek alternatives for students who need such experiences. It is this advanced group of students for whom special schools are being developed.

Certain characteristics define students for whom a special residential school may be the most appropriate educational approach. They are individuals who are capable of mastering content in much less time than is required by other students and who are at the same time able to engage in complex processes at high levels of abstraction. Because of these capabilities, such gifted students often exhaust the curricular offerings of their local high school well before they are able to graduate. In short, these are students who need a different educational experience from that offered by most schools.

Instruction for these students requires faculty who are specialists in areas of advanced content and who are capable of delivering appropriately fast-paced, high-level instruction. Again, most schools, necessarily addressing the needs of the majority of their students, do not have such faculty available.

There is yet another recognized need of gifted students, that of interaction with others of similar ability in a supportive climate. At best, schools provide these opportunities on a limited basis (several hours a week, perhaps in one or two classes in which students are grouped by ability). However, fears of elitism, strong feelings against tracking, and parent or teacher resistance prevent schools from going further to group students for large portions of their time. Current backlash against grouping students by ability has resulted in a movement among local school districts to eliminate special programs and classes for gifted students (Purcell, 1993; Renzulli & Reis, 1991).[1]

These conditions, combined with the relatively recent goals of (1) achieving academic excellence in our country's educational systems; (2) developing the talented as a source of future economic and social leadership; and (3) establishing highly visible efforts linking political, economic, and educational institutions have led to the realization that special residential schools are an appropriate way of meeting the needs of many of the nation's most talented young people. Recognition of the importance of meeting these needs, and an acknowledgment that long-term benefits may accrue from an investment in the education of the exceptionally gifted, have resulted in proposals to state legislatures to create and sustain residential high schools for highly gifted students selected from within the state.

National Excellence: A Case for Developing America's Talent (U.S. Department of Education, 1993) cites six broad recommendations for ensuring that education in this country will meet the needs of our students as they fulfill their potential and as they compare to students in other countries. Five of these recommendations relate directly to the goals and activities of state residential schools for gifted students. The recommendations call for an appropriately challenging curriculum, high-level learning opportunities, opportunities for disadvantaged and minority students, appropriate teacher training and technical assistance, and the attainment of world-class performance.

States that create residential high schools for high-ability students will position themselves well to respond to these recommendations. Each state that establishes a school has the opportunity to create a program that (1) directly benefits its own students and (2) provides leadership in the state educational community. This leadership emerges as curricula are developed and tested with the residential students, as programs bring teachers from local schools to the campus to work with the students and faculty, and through activities that take the resources of the residential school to other schools in the state. A sense of commitment to the larger community, stemming from the need to return some of the investment by the state, keeps the residential school from becoming insular. Initiatives for educational reform and innovation can begin in such a school and spread throughout the state.

An Early Example

In 1978, then Governor James B. Hunt, Jr., and the General Assembly of North Carolina proposed the first residential high school for gifted students of that state. In the fall of 1980, the North Carolina School of Science and Mathematics, in Durham, accepted its first class of junior-year students and began a program designed to meet the academic, social, and emotional needs of a cross-section of the brightest students in the state. In addition to the direct benefits to the students who have attended and graduated from the school, the North Carolina school has pioneered ways for developing and disseminating new curricula and teaching methods to other schools throughout the state.

The North Carolina school, which has been a model for similar schools throughout the country, serves a student body of juniors and seniors drawn from all geographic areas of the state. These classes represent a balance among race, socioeconomic level, and sex. The faculty is composed of individuals with content expertise, many of whom hold doctoral degrees, and for whom there is no requirement that they be certified teachers. The curriculum itself offers opportunities for students to accelerate and enrich their academic programs. The overall program incorporates independent study, community service, and other extracurricular elements, and seeks to provide a balanced experience for students.

[1] See Chapter 19 by Kulik and Kulik.

This most successful school, which has received a great deal of national attention, also can point to benefits to the state that invested in the plan. A large number of graduates elect to attend colleges and universities in North Carolina, and many of them will choose to remain in the state to enter professional careers and raise their families. Many businesses and industries have chosen to locate in North Carolina in part because of the state's demonstrated commitment to excellence in education. These are persuasive arguments as other state legislatures consider similar plans.

Characteristics of Special Residential Schools

The Students

Most residential high schools admit students at grade 11 for the beginning of a two-year experience. Illinois, an exception, admits students who are beginning grade 10. Because they are established through legislative action supported by state funds, the schools are committed to enrolling a student body that profiles the population of the state. Consideration is given to balancing the various groups that make up the state. Sizes of the schools range from about 150 to over 600.

Identification and selection of students for participation in a special residential school is a complex process that starts well before the beginning of the academic year in which a student is admitted. Applicants take standardized tests such as the SAT-I: Reasoning Tests (formerly the Scholastic Aptitude Test or SAT), the PSAT, or similar off-level tests. Most of the existing schools use test scores, high school grades, recommendations, writing samples, portfolios of artwork or auditions in other talent areas, and interviews to assemble a profile of each applicant. Subjective and objective assessments are combined to arrive at admissions decisions.

In addition to evidence of academic achievement and ability, residential schools look for students who show potential to succeed in a program that requires independent work and who also demonstrate the maturity to live away from home while attending a rigorous academic school.

Recent research by Jarwan and Feldhusen (1993) affirms the importance of linking the identification and selection process to the particular curriculum and program of the school. A good match between student and program will help ensure that both the students and the school will be successful. Systematic training for those involved in the identification and selection process is also critical, so that subjective assessments of prospective students made by a group of professionals will achieve maximum reliability.

The Faculty

Instructors for these exceptionally talented students come from high schools, colleges and universities, and the private sector. Most residential schools report that their faculties comprise individuals with advanced degrees, with about half having earned doctorates. There is great flexibility concerning the requirements for "certification" of teachers in these schools. Efforts are made to recruit teachers with outstanding academic credentials and the ability to work well with gifted students. Schools want individuals who can inspire gifted students both inside and outside of the classroom, offer support for creative ideas, and become role models as productive adults.

Residential schools often have special visiting teacher/scholar programs that bring teachers from around the state to the residential site to work with the students. These individuals work with students, develop curricula, observe and implement teaching methods, and return home to adapt the techniques and materials for their high-ability students and share them with other teachers.

Facilities

Special residential schools require special facilities. Because of the nature of the schools, there must be a complex of buildings designed to accommodate both the instructional and the living components of the programs. Existing residential schools have addressed this need in several ways. The first of these special schools for gifted students, the North Carolina School of Science and Mathematics, is located in a former hospital complex that has been converted into dormitories, classrooms, laboratories, a library, and recreational areas. The Arkansas residential high school also is housed in a former hospital in Hot Springs. The Illinois Math and Science Academy moved into a vacant high school building. Initially, some classrooms were turned into dormitory rooms; others remained classrooms or became laboratories or other needed spaces. Dormitories have since been constructed on the academy campus.

Several residential high schools are located on college or university campuses where the needed facilities already exist with little need for modification. The Louisiana School for Math, Science, and the Arts is located on the campus of Northwestern State University in Nachitoches. The Texas Academy of Mathematics and Science is part of the University of North Texas, Denton. The Indiana Academy for Science, Mathematics and Humanities is on the campus of Ball State University in Muncie. The Mississippi School for Math and Science is on the campus of the Mississippi University for Women in Columbus. The South Carolina Governors' School for Science and Mathematics is located at Coker College in Hartsville. In most of these situations, although the residential high school and the college or university exist on the same campus, there are separate facilities for the two student bodies. Dormitories house only high school students, and restrictions are placed on interaction between high school and older students. A unique situation exists at the Indiana Academy, where the residential high school, Ball State University, and the Burris Laboratory School (a K–12 school affiliated with the university) share some facilities and provide students with flexibility in course taking and extracurricular choices, while still preserving certain limitations.

The Curriculum

At the heart of residential schools for gifted students are curricula especially designed to meet their needs. With an emphasis on mathematics and science in most programs, students usually advance rapidly through high-level course work in these and other areas. Curricular offerings in these schools may fit one of several different models. For some, the College Board Advanced Placement (AP) program is the foundation of the curriculum. Students who spend two years in a residential high school may take many AP classes and/or exams, thus enabling them to begin college or university with a year or more of credit in several areas. Stanley (1987), in fact, urges that the curriculum for a school of this kind include courses that prepare students to take AP exams in calculus, physics, chemistry, computer science, and biology. At the Illinois Mathematics and Science Academy, the completion of the three-year curriculum takes students through a beginning university curriculum and prepares them to take a variety of AP exams in mathematics, sciences, English, and foreign languages.

Residential schools located on college or university campuses incorporate university courses into the curriculum of the high school. Students may take courses (e.g., languages) not offered in the residential school curriculum or other specialized courses that balance and supplement the curriculum of the high school. The curriculum of the Texas Academy of Mathematics and Science consists of university honors courses, for which students earn college credit in addition to completing the requirements for high school graduation. In their two years at Texas Academy, students simultaneously complete the last two years of high school and the first two years of college. Students attending the Indiana Academy for Science, Mathematics and Humanities may take courses in areas such as Latin or fine arts at Ball State University or music at Burris Laboratory School (Dixon, 1993).

Although the major emphasis of special residential high schools is typically science and mathematics, these schools incorporate strong communications and arts programs into the curriculum. The Louisiana School for Math, Science, and the Arts goes a step further in offering students the opportunity to focus on math/science, humanities, or the creative and performing arts. A student may select one or more of these areas in which to concentrate. The Indiana Academy incorporated humanities into the name of the school, and the curriculum reflects this emphasis.

Most of these special high schools also develop unique curricular offerings in addition to the AP courses and college courses. Humanities, English, and social studies courses may be organized in ways different from the traditional secondary curriculum. The nature of the learners and the faculty lends itself to the development of courses that explore broad, interdisciplinary themes, epistemology, and the historical and philosophical foundations of disciplines. The Illinois Mathematics and Science Academy developed an approach known as Problem-Based Learning in which students are given realistic problems to investigate using their problem-solving abilities. The "fuzzy situations" require students to exercise their question-asking, information-gathering, hypothesis-formulation, and testing skills while their teachers assume the roles of facilitators and coaches. These experiences engage students in studying the content of various disciplines in nontraditional but real-world ways (Stepien & Gallagher, 1993; Stepien, Gallagher & Workman, 1993). The curriculum at the Indiana Academy for Science, Mathematics and Humanities includes a number of thematic interdisciplinary courses that focus on history and English. Examples of these include Dickens and the Industrial Revolution (a literature and history course), Russian Literature (a history, literature, and culture course) and Sylvia Beach and the Lost Generation (a study of the culture and literature of the American ex-patriates in Paris in the 1920s). In addition to these courses, all students enroll in a course called Colloquium that meets once a week to discuss selected great issues (Dixon, 1993).

Overall, the curriculum of special residential high schools is characterized by its gifted students. These schools offer a program of advanced courses in a curriculum with considerable breadth and depth. Students can pursue a sequence of advanced courses in mathematics and sciences rarely available in high schools. Both advanced and nontraditional offerings in other areas also may be available in residential schools.

Several additional curricular components also are a part of residential high schools. Mentorships, internships, and research and independent study opportunities are incorporated into the program to allow various degrees of individualization for the students. In many of the schools, students are encouraged to pursue original research projects. Residential schools located on university campuses may arrange for students to work on projects with faculty mentors. Schools located near high-tech centers, research and medical facilities, or other industries in the scientific field are able to place students in mentorships and internships where they experience involvement in the actual workings of these organizations. In 1992–1993, for example, a total of 121 students at the Illinois Mathematics and Science Academy worked in 38 laboratories in the Chicago area (Marshall, 1993).

Extracurricular Program

Beyond the academic day, residential students may be involved in community service projects, recreational activities, faculty–student projects, clubs, and competitions and contests. Residential schools offer many of the same activities students would find in their local schools, including musical and theatrical performance groups; individual and team sports; foreign language, science, and math organizations; and service clubs. The campuses develop diverse extracurricular programs based on the students' interests and talents. Students often have opportunities to attend seminars, lectures, symposia, and other events that take place at the schools themselves and on nearby college campuses.

Following the example set by the North Carolina school, most other institutions have established a requirement that students become involved in campus and community service. Projects may involve activities such as tutoring, volunteering in hospitals or similar institutions, or assisting local agencies and organizations.

Benefits of Special Residential Schools

A number of groups benefit from special residential schools for gifted students. Most important, of course, are the students themselves who attend and are challenged at their levels by an appropriately rigorous curriculum. These students experience an education designed for them, taught by faculty who are experts in their fields and who are committed to providing appropriate education for the gifted, and in an environment where they are energized and sparked by other students with similar abilities and interests.

Recognizing that there is potential for wider benefits to education in the state, the majority of residential schools have outreach programs. Among the variety of outreach efforts, a particularly effective approach involves bringing teachers from schools around the state to the residential site as visiting scholars and instructors. Some teachers spend a full academic year, others a semester. These teachers then return to their home schools with teaching methods and curriculum that may be adopted or adapted for local students.

In some cases, residential schools are using satellite capabilities to transmit courses from their site to schools throughout the state where other students may take advantage of the curriculum. The Indiana Academy uses the Indiana Higher Education Telecommunications System (IHETS) to provide courses in areas such as physics, Russian, Chinese, AP calculus, and human genetics to rural schools where there is student interest but no teacher is available or enrollment is too low to offer the class. The Director of the Indiana Academy reports that in the 1994–1995 academic year, these classes are in 949 classrooms throughout the state (V. Roberts, personal communication, September 23, 1994).

Still other outreach efforts include workshops and institutes at the residential schools or other sites which bring teachers together to learn about techniques and materials for educating the gifted. The Illinois Mathematics and Science Academy awards grants to Illinois teachers to prepare innovative teaching activities, which are then shared throughout the state. The Illinois academy also hosts conferences on special topics such as problem-based learning and produces materials such as the *IMSA Math Journal* for dissemination to schools throughout the state. Students may benefit directly from such activities as Summer "AD" Ventures, a summer math, science, and technology program for Illinois students in grades 7 through 10 (Marshall, 1993).

Special Issues

The establishment of special residential high schools raises a number of issues that must be resolved before such a school can open. One of the first is a concern of communities that the residential schools will take their top students away from the local high schools in a kind of "brain drain." This fear has proved to be unfounded, generally, because residential schools enroll students from throughout the state, and no one community or local area sends a disproportionate number of students.

An important issue raised by legislators, parents, and local schools is that of young people leaving home two or three years before they ordinarily would leave to attend college. For residential high schools located at colleges and universities, there are additional concerns to be addressed related to placing high school–age students on campuses with older students. Existing residential high schools have limited the interactions among high school and college students by housing them separately and segregating the two groups for social and, in most cases, academic activities.

Another often repeated concern is that placing the most talented students together in a school of this type will lead to feelings of superiority and special favor among the selected students, and a perception that they are entitled to receive special opportunities and benefits with nothing expected in return. Schools address this concern by structuring involvement in outside community and volunteer activities, and by requiring that they share responsibility for maintaining their school. Most schools communicate to the students the expectation that the students will repay in these ways the investment in their education made by the state.

When considering state-supported residential high schools, questions always are raised about the composition of the student body, Schools are asked by legislators and funding groups to ensure that the classes will be balanced in terms of geographic, racial, ethnic, gender, and socioeconomic representation.

This brings up the question—often unspoken—of quotas. How does a school balance the student body while homogeneously grouping the students in terms of academic and intellectual ability? Most of the schools specify in their written materials that they are committed to achieving a student body that is diversified and that geographic and other variables are considered by the admissions committee. Stanley (1987), however, in discussing residential high schools for mathematically talented youth, urges that minimum ability levels be established for selection and that these levels not be modified to accommodate outside pressures. According to Stanley, these minimum levels should be developed by each state and should use as a reference point the average SAT scores achieved by male college-bound seniors in that state. In accord with Stanley's view, the Texas Academy of Mathematics and Science has set a minimum acceptable score of 550 on the mathematics portion of the SAT with an overall minimum of 1000 on the combined verbal and mathematics parts of the test. The North Carolina School of Science and Mathematics, in contrast, has set no minimum scores in the belief that admissions criteria must be flexible to allow for special situations—for example, to accommodate a student who has recently emigrated to this country and is not yet fluent enough in English to achieve the minimum scores on the SAT (Eilber, 1987).

Despite the intention of state residential high schools for gifted students to reflect the demographics of the population, Jarwan and Feldhusen (1993) found that representation of ethnic groups in the composition of these schools does not mirror the representation of these groups in the general population: African Americans, Hispanics, and Native Americans are underrepresented in these schools, and Asian students are overrepresented.

Another major consideration affecting the establishment of special residential schools is the provision of a total, rounded experience for the students who attend. This involves support services, such as academic and personal counseling, and a program of extracurricular opportunities including athletics, recreation, arts clubs and performing groups, and social activities. Because students are on campus 24 hours a day, seven days a week, planning must be comprehensive and must address the needs of the total student. Residential staff must be prepared to assist students as they adjust to living away from home for the first time, encountering an extremely demanding curriculum, and balancing their academic and social interests and commitments in a new community.

Existing residential high schools for the gifted carefully and thoughtfully plan their calendars to include long weekends at home, as well as opportunities for students to become involved in outside interests at the school. Staff members are alert to signs of stress, depression, and homesickness, and they are attuned to student behaviors that reveal problems in adjusting to the new environment, such as missing classes, failing to complete assignments, socializing excessively, or withdrawing from interactions with others. Although there may be relatively few instances of these types of difficulties, they are the kinds of issues that set residential schools apart from other schools and must be addressed in planning for and staffing such a school.

Judging Success of Residential Schools

The impact of special residential schools is assessed in several ways. The North Carolina School of Science and Mathematics evaluated aspects of the program that originally were stated as potential benefits. For example, surveys taken after ten years revealed that 67 percent of the graduates had enrolled at in-state colleges and universities for their freshman year; by their junior year, 73 percent were registered at in-state colleges and universities (Johnston, 1988); and 82 percent were studying science or mathematics in college. The Indiana Academy for Science, Mathematics and Humanities reports that 43 percent of the 1994 graduating class chose to remain in Indiana to attend college or university, thus fulfilling one of the proposed benefits to the state, that of retaining a group of its most talented young people.

Additional benefits to the state's educational system are evidenced in the number and scope of the outreach programs. Academically talented students from throughout the state attend the North Carolina school in the summer for advanced instruction in math and science. Teachers from the state spend summer months on campus working with the school's faculty to learn techniques that can be used in their home schools. There is anecdotal evidence that the school has encouraged local schools throughout the state to provide more math and science to students (Johnston, 1988).

Graduating classes of residential schools typically have produced very large numbers of National Merit Scholar semifinalists and finalists. For example, in the 1993 Illinois Mathematics and Science Academy graduating class, a full 33 percent were National Merit semifinalists (Marshall, 1993).

A final indicator of success is that students graduating from residential high schools have attracted millions of dollars in scholarship offers as well as recognition for their outstanding performance in academic competitions. The Louisiana School for Math, Science, and the Arts reported that the first four graduating classes received scholarship offers amounting to over $12 million. Individual awards and recognition have included student-designed experiments for the NASA space shuttle program and membership on the International Physics Olympiad. Illinois Mathematics and Science Academy students have placed first in the Westinghouse Science Talent Search (1993) and first in the American High School Math Exam, and, as individuals and teams, have placed in numerous national and international mathematics, computer science, and science competitions.

Conclusions

The establishment of state-supported residential schools for gifted students is a movement whose time has come. States are seeking ways to meet the educational needs of high-ability students, and they recognize that for the most gifted of their students, an appropriate and effective method for meeting those needs is to group them together in one location and offer them an educational program more advanced and more challenging than those in the local schools.

Beginning slowly, with the North Carolina School of Science and Mathematics and the Louisiana School for Math, Science and the Arts, the movement has gained momentum. At present, one-fifth of the states have established academic-year residential high schools for gifted students, and the issue is being studied by other states. As perceptions of the success and "return on investment" increase, more states are certain to follow the examples of those that have assumed leadership in the development of special residential high schools. Particularly meaningful and convincing will be evidence that these schools benefit not only those who attend, but also education statewide and nationwide. Further support will come from evidence that they provide incentives for the long-term economic growth of the states in which they exist.

As a final comment, there is a growing recognition among educators and legislators of the need for different kinds of services and programs to correspond to different types and levels of giftedness. While many local schools will continue to address these needs through cluster groups, pullout programs, self-contained classrooms, and honors courses, state leaders will heed the recommendations of experts and the examples of states pioneering in the development of residential high schools and establish such schools for their most talented and, perhaps, most underserved population of gifted students.

REFERENCES

Cox, J., Daniel, N., & Boston, B. (1985). *Educating able learners.* Austin: University of Texas Press.

Dixon, F. A. (1993). *History of the Indiana Academy for Science, Mathematics and the Humanities.* Unpublished manuscript.

Eilber, C. R. (1987). The North Carolina School of Science and Mathematics. *Phi Delta Kappan, 68,* 773–777.

Jarwan, F. A., & Feldhusen, J. F. (1993). *Residential schools of mathematics and science for academically talented youth: An analysis of admission programs.* (CRS93304). Storrs, CT: National Research Center for Gifted and Talented.

Johnston, F. (1988, March 14). School of science and math—10 years old and growing. *The Durham Morning Herald.*

Marshall, S. P. (1993). *Illinois' investment.* Annual report. Aurora: Illinois Mathematics and Science Academy.

Purcell, J. H. (1993). The effects of elimination of gifted and talented programs on participating students and their parents. *Gifted Child Quarterly, 37,* 177–187.

Renzulli, J. S., & Reis, S. M. (1991). The reform movement and the quiet crisis in gifted education. *Gifted Child Quarterly, 35,* 26–35.

Stanley, J. C. (1987). State residential high schools for mathematically talented youth. *Phi Delta Kappan, 68,* 770–772.

Stepien, W. J., & Gallagher, S. A. (1993). Problem-based learning: As authentic as it gets. *Educational Leadership, 50,* 25–28.

Stepien, W. J., Gallagher, S. A., & Workman, D. (1993). Problem-based learning for traditional and interdisciplinary classrooms. *Journal for the Education of the Gifted, 16,* 338–357.

U. S. Department of Education. (1993). *National excellence: A case for developing America's talent.* Washington, DC: U.S. Government Printing Office.

17

The Tortoise, the Hare, and the Development of Talent

LAUREN A. SOSNIAK, *University of California, Berkeley*

The hare was once boasting of his speed before the other animals . . . "I shall challenge any one here to race with me."

"The tortoise will not have a chance!" cried the fox.

"Wait and see," said the owl.

—The Hare and the Tortoise
An Aesop Fable

The moral to *The Hare and the Tortoise* concerns the power of perseverance and determination over more obvious (and frequently physical) attributes. The fable has been constructed carefully to favor purposefulness over natural ability and early advantage: The race was sufficiently long and the hare sufficiently distracted (and distractible) for the "unexpected" result to occur. If the course had been a short one, or the hare had been single-minded, there is no doubt that the outcome would have been different.

It is my contention that the development of talent needs to be understood as a variant of this well-known Aesop fable. I will argue in this chapter that the development of talent is a long-term process, and the time it takes for such development has important consequences for the ways we need to think about supportive educational theory and practice. I will also argue that because the development of talent is a lived experience, it needs to be considered in light of the attractions and distractions associated with motivation to pursue a particular course of study over an extended period of time.

Reprinted from M. J. A. Howe (Ed.), *Encouraging the Development of Exceptional Skills and Talents* (pp. 149–164). Leicester, UK: BPA Books. Reprinted by permission of the British Psychological Society

Author's note: This chapter in *The Handbook of Gifted Education* and the research on which it is based challenge traditional conceptions of the development of exceptional talent. The long period of time necessary for such development calls into question traditional interest in early identification. It also invites rethinking of instructional practices and educational support systems necessary for promoting exceptional accomplishment among even larger numbers of youth.

An Empirical Foundation

The data that provide the foundation for description and argument in this chapter are drawn from the Development of Talent Research Project, a five-year study conducted by a team of researchers, under the direction of Benjamin Bloom, at the University of Chicago (Bloom, 1985). The subjects for that study were groups of individuals who, though relatively young, had realized exceptional levels of accomplishment in one of six fields: concert piano, sculpture, swimming, tennis, mathematics, and research neurology (two artistic disciplines, two psychomotor activities, and two academic/intellectual fields). The focus of the investigation was on the roles of the home, teachers, schools, and other educational and experiential factors in discovering, developing, and encouraging unusually high levels of competence.

More specifically, the study was concerned with questions like: How did an individual's involvement with the chosen field begin? How did he or she work at the activity—how were time, materials and other resources used?

What roles did family and teachers play in the learning process? How were interest and involvement maintained? The plan was to search for regularities and recurrent patterns in the educational histories of groups of clearly accomplished individuals, hoping that such consistencies might shed light on how the development of talent is achieved.

The project explored the lives of 120 talented individuals in all, approximately 20 in each field. Retrospective, semistructured, face-to-face interviews were conducted with the individuals who met criteria of exceptional achievement set by experts in their respective fields. Parents were interviewed as well, by telephone, for corroborative and supplementary information. All interviews were tape-recorded. Data analysis was a process analogous to superimposing the unique histories one on the other, and identifying the patterns that were common across most cases—first within each field and later across the fields (see, for example, Glaser, 1965).

The Long-Term Nature of the Development of Talent

The educational histories of the individuals we studied indicate, without exception, that the development of talent takes a considerable amount of time. None of the individuals in our sample demonstrated remarkable talent in short order. All spent many years developing the understanding, the skills, and the attitudes that would eventually allow them to be recognized as experts in their respective fields.

How long does it take to develop talent? The question is not easy to answer with any precision. In fields such as playing concert piano or swimming, there are markers one can use to estimate the length of the process. In our study we found that pianists worked for an average of 17 years from their first formal lessons to their first international recognition. The fastest "made it" in 12 years; the slowest took 25. For the swimmers, 15 years elapsed, on average, between the time individuals began swimming just for fun and the time they earned a place on an Olympic team.

The scientists, mathematicians, and sculptors were unlikely to be recognized for truly outstanding achievement much before their 30th birthday. Unfortunately, we have no clear markers in these fields to use as indications of initial involvement. We do have reason to believe, however, that the process of developing talent even in these areas began very early. For our sample as a whole, parents' values and interests, which were translated into family activity involving even the youngest children, typically helped us understand the direction, although certainly not the degree, of the talented individuals' subsequent development (Sloane, 1985).

Of course, the fact that it takes a long time to develop talent is hardly surprising. Others have noted the same phenomenon (Gruber, 1986; Glaser & Chi, 1988). In fact, our interview schedule was constructed to reflect this possibility. We were quite surprised, however, by two findings related to the long-term development of talent. First, as far as we could tell, for much of the time the individuals spent learning to be as good as they are today, it would have been impossible to predict their eventual accomplishments. Second, the process of developing talent over the long term apparently divided itself into three distinct phases with qualitatively different concerns and consequences. Each of these findings will be discussed in turn.

The Unpredictability of the Development of Talent

Unlike the hare in Aesop's fable, the individuals in our study typically did *not* show unusual promise at the start of the long-term experience. They were not "prodigies" in the way that the stereotype of talent development would have us expect—regardless of whether we define prodigiousness by demonstrated ability or by subjective recollections from parents or the individuals themselves. Early in their experiences with their fields they did not demonstrate abilities significantly beyond those appropriate for their age; they may well have had such abilities, of course, but these either were not noticed or not noticeable.

The pianists, for example, had begun taking lessons by the age of six, on average, and were playing in small recitals organized by their neighborhood teachers within a year or so. Seven years later, by the time they were 13 or 14, most were playing in local competitions, or at annual adjudicated contests. Even after seven years of study and practice, the youngsters reportedly were as likely to fall short in these competitions as they were to outshine their peers. Similarly, the swimmers spent an average of eight years swimming in national competitions before they began to place (to come first, second, or third) in those events.

Parents were somewhat more generous in their subjective recollections of early unusual promise than could be verified by objective evidence. ("He was always the hit of the [recital] because he was so far advanced than the other children who had been taking lessons.") Still, for every parent who had seen a talent just waiting to be developed, there was a counterpart who was taken quite by surprise, many years later, when his or her child began demonstrating considerable talent in a particular area. One pianist's father who was more knowledgeable about music than most recalled: "I would have started [the child] with a better teacher—at a conservatory—if I had known he was going to become a concert pianist . . . At that time, I didn't think it was important." A number of mothers told us they perceived another child in the family to have more "talent," but were subsequently impressed by the tenacity of the sibling who was eventually to become part of our sample.

The individuals themselves were similarly divided in their assertions regarding early unusual promise. Some remembered being told at an early age "I was going to be great and famous, and how unusual I was." More were quite explicit that their "talent" was not noticeable for a considerable number of years. "I was not a wunderkind," they told us in various ways. "They didn't say I had talent until age 16. . . . By then I had worked my ass off!"

Although in large measure our sample did not show unusual promise at the start of the long-term process of developing talent, a small number of individuals could be identified objectively as unusually accomplished at an early age. We believe that these exceptions are as notable for what they reveal about the larger group, and about the nature of traditional means for marking unusual promise, as for the unusual potential they signal in a small portion of our sample. The most prodigious individuals in our study include: two of the 21 concert pianists who won children's competitions which gave them the opportunity to play with a symphony orchestra by the age of 10; one of the swimmers who was a national champion in his age group by the age of 11; and one of the mathematicians who was enrolled in college mathematics courses by the age of 13.

These achievements are considerable indeed. Still, they must be compared side by side with the early demonstrated ability of the much larger number of individuals in our study, which was either inconsistent ("one of the top ten year olds in the country; at eleven years, she was at the bottom of the heap"), strong but certainly not outstanding, or even mediocre. Furthermore, at least in the case of the musicians and the swimmer referred to above, we must keep in mind that the extraordinary achievements reflect norm-referenced rather than criterion-referenced standards. That is, the individuals had demonstrated they were better than their peers at activities that their age-mates were also undertaking.

We began our study with the question of how individuals were discovered and then, once identified, how they were helped to develop their talents; we found much the reverse. The youngsters spent several years acquiring knowledge and developing skills and dispositions appropriate for their fields before they were "discovered" as the most talented in their family or in their neighborhood and accorded the status of biggest fish in their small ponds. In turn, a discovery of this sort, by a parent or teacher, typically led to increased opportunities for development. Then, after several more years of work at increasingly more sophisticated levels, the youngsters were *re*discovered, and so on (Sosniak, 1985a). Gradually, the individuals we studied moved into increasingly more exclusive groups of potentially talented individuals. So slowly did the identification of extraordinary talent take place that the individuals were almost unaware of it happening. This pattern, unpredicted at the start, became more understandable in light of the systematic changes in the nature of teaching and learning over the long term which we found.

Phases of Learning and Teaching

The individuals we studied not only spent many years acquiring the knowledge and developing the skills and dispositions associated with exceptional talent, they did so for a considerable amount of time without any clear idea of where they were heading. There was no intention, at the start, to work toward a standard of excellence in a particular field of study; neither the individuals nor their parents had plans for a long-term commitment or dreams of eventual accomplishment. Exactly what was to be learned, and where it would lead, were decisions made and remade many times in the process of unusually successful learning. Without having to think about the enormity of all that was before them, the individuals and their parents did what seemed good or necessary for the moment.

The very long series of moments appear to have divided themselves into three distinct phases, periods reminiscent of Whitehead's (1929) writings on the rhythms of romance, precision, and generalization in education (Sosniak, 1985b; Sosniak, 1988). Each phase emphasized a particular view of what was being learned, and a particular attitude toward the processes of learning and teaching. Each phase presented different demands on the learner and those with whom he or she worked, and had qualitatively different consequences. The phases were not discrete, but they were dramatic in their particular emphases.

The earliest years of developing talent were filled with opportunities to explore field-specific content without the need for behaving systematically or with demonstrated skill. Initiation to the field of talent most typically came early, and as a natural consequence of membership in a family that valued the activity. Although the parents of the individuals in our study seldom were professionally involved in the areas in which their child would later excel, more often than not they held an avocational interest in the field or closely related activity. As a consequence, the young children were exposed to activities associated with their subsequent talent fields, they were supported and rewarded for behaviors associated with the fields, and they learned a good deal in informal ways about knowledge and skills associated with the activity in which they would eventually excel.

The pianists, for example, listened to music almost from the time they were born, and learned to identify the names of well-known composers, musicians, or musical pieces without anyone being conscious of the process of education. Mathematicians played with numbers and scientific ideas in similar ways. "This is half, this is a quarter, this is an eighth," a mathematician's father reportedly would say to his child as he fed him a breakfast omelette. Parents bought their children field-specific toys and showed genuine interest in the child's various field-specific activities. The talent field provided amusement for children and their parents, and an interest for them to share.

Early formal instruction in the fields for which special instruction was sought was similarly notable for the playfulness of the experiences. First teachers were remembered as having made lessons "fun." These teachers were said to be warm and enthusiastic and quick to provide a variety of rewards for any signs of interest or involvement. They threw coins to the bottom of a swimming pool to encourage children to learn to hold their breath and keep their eyes open under water. They put stars on the top of each page in a music book when the child had finished working on that page.

For the most part, during the early years of learning there was little attention to or concern about the "correctness" of the work. The encouragement of interest and involvement took precedence over the assessment of progress in any formal way. Students, teachers, and parents seemed unconcerned with objective measures of achievement. Virtually any effort was applauded by parents or teachers or both. The emphasis during this period was on engaging in lots of field-specific playful activity, and exploring the possibilities inherent in the activity. In the short run, this emphasis may have obscured or even inhibited early signs of unusual talent; in the long run, however, the extended period of early playful activity may have paid dividends of considerable consequence.

For relatively little effort, the learner got more than might be expected. The effect of the early years of playful, almost romantic involvement with a field seemed to be to get the learner involved, captivated, "hooked"—motivated to pursue the matter further. Of course as would be true about playful situations of many sorts, the more time and attention the individuals paid to the matter, the more skilled they became. In the process of exploring, the students inevitably acquired knowledge and skill that would contribute to subsequent studies. Most importantly, perhaps, this knowledge and skill was gained in a manner that would encourage subsequent development. The individuals apparently had prepared themselves for the second phase of the development of talent.

During the second phase of the development of talent, teaching and learning became much more focused on the systematic acquisition of knowledge and development of skill. Playfulness gave way largely, but seldom entirely, to precision. The nature of the transition from the playful period to the period of precision is not clear, but the fact of the transition is obvious.

The second period of learning was marked by considerable attention to detail. The technical skills and vocabulary of the discipline, as well as its rules and logic, were addressed systematically by teacher and student alike. Youngsters who had toyed with the field earlier invested in the acquisition of specific pieces of knowledge and mastery of narrowly defined objectives. They were willing to engage in the same activity over and over, now consciously making slight variations each time, in the service of achieving some mark of excellence modeled by acknowledged experts in the field.

Instruction became more rational and less informal and personal than it had been earlier. Objective measures of achievement—the results of competitions and the like—provided both a personal sense of accomplishment and a means of planning subsequent instruction. Knowledgeable criticism from teachers and other experts in the field became as rewarding as applause had been earlier. The personal bond between teachers and students shifted from one of love to one of respect.

The student–teacher relationship was carried well beyond the regular lessons. Teachers encouraged, enticed, and prodded students to take part in public activities—recitals, competitions, science fairs, mathematics clubs, and so forth. Teachers arranged for the students to participate in activities with like-minded youngsters after school and during the summers, and they arranged meetings with professionals or expert teachers in the area. They introduced the student to important historical dimensions of the field through literature, recordings, collected works of art, and the like. In various ways teachers provided a rich context for the more focused work that ruled this period.

In response to the students' involvement, parents began making significant sacrifices of time and money to arrange for better teachers, purchase necessary equipment, and travel to important events. Parents also began rearranging life in their homes to accommmodate the demands of the children's developing talents. Someone was always available to chauffeur the children to classes or special events. Meals and weekend activities were planned around talent-related concerns. Parents became more knowledgeable about the talent area along with their children.

The individuals themselves devoted increasing amounts of time to the talent area. This frequently required sacrificing other activities that previously had been a part of the youngsters' lives. They became strongly identified with the area by their age-mates and, often, by adults in their community. Over time, they began to identify themselves in terms of their area of interest and growing expertise.

During this second phase of learning the individuals developed skills, feelings of competence, and a modicum of awareness of the long-term possibilities of work in their respective talent fields. In the end, they were extraordinarily able, but still not sufficiently accomplished to be included among the best in their respective fields. Technical mastery still had to be integrated with a personal desire to pursue the field to its limits, and with a personal vision or style which could redefine the field in terms of the work of the individual rather than defining the individual in terms of the existing field.

The transition to the third phase of talent development was the most difficult, perhaps, and the most uncertain. It required a commitment of unprecedented proportion; virtually all of one's time, emotional energy, and other resources had to be invested in field-specific activity. In fact, it was typically toward the end of the second phase of learning, or the beginning of this third phase, that the individuals made their first conscious and visible commitments to the pursuit of excellence in their respective fields.[1] At last there was a clear end in sight for the work the individuals had been engaged in almost as matter of fact to this point.

During the third phase of learning the individuals typically studied with master teachers—teachers who were known either for their personal expertise in the field or for their work with students who had become acknowledged masters in the field. The opportunity to work with such individuals—a result of previous experiences which made the teachers known to the students and prepared the students to meet the teachers' prerequisite requirements—was viewed at first with considerable awe. The individuals reported being "overwhelmed" by the idea of spending time with these role models, and feeling "electricity in the air" when they were in the company of these teachers.

The nature of the teaching/learning relationship changed dramatically. A close personal bond between student and teacher was no longer an especially important part of instruction. Instead, the student had to share with the teacher a dedication to the field itself, and a devotion to advancing the work of the field in a personal way. An emphasis on specific details also fell by the wayside, in favor of a broader and more inclusive exploration of the activity of the field.

Instruction almost always took place in the context of the real-world activity as it is engaged in by the most talented individuals in the field. Pianists "performed" for their teachers, and analyzed both their performance and the piece of music with their teachers as professional musicians might do in the course of their working lives. Mathematicians watched their teachers "doing mathematics," and in turn were watched by their teachers while they tried their hand.

With the help of expert teachers, and like-minded peers who were similarly engaged in pursuit of excellence in the field, the individuals began to identify and develop personal concerns and ways of working. They began finding and solving their own problems, and working to satisfy themselves rather than their teachers. They immersed themselves completely and wholeheartedly in the worlds of their respective talent fields, and ultimately they became models of excellence in those fields.

In sum, the long-term process of developing talent was not simply a matter of becoming quantitatively more knowledgeable and skilled over time, or of working more intensely for longer hours. It was, predominantly, a matter of qualitative and evolutionary transformations (Sosniak, 1987). These were transformations of the individual, of the substance of what was being learned, and of the manner in which individuals engaged with teachers and field-specific content. Students progressively adopted different views of who they were, of what their fields of expertise was about, and of how the field fitted into their lives.

Movement through the three phases was

[1] The lack of early and conscious commitment to the field is obvious in multiple ways. The mathematicians provide one example: Typically, they made decisions about which colleges to attend as undergraduates without any attention to the quality of the education they might receive in mathematics. Fewer than half were entertaining the idea of mathematics as a career at the end of high school (Gustin, 1985). By the time these individuals applied to graduate school, however, the primary and often sole criterion for the selection of a university was the quality of the mathematical experience they believed would be possible.

not always smooth, but it became quite predictable as we analysed the talented individuals' educational histories.[2] The individuals proceeded at different rates and in different ways. They did so with an enormous amount of prompting, guidance, structure, encouragement, and support from parents and teachers. The talented individuals demonstrated in compelling fashion that the process of unusually successful learning is not all of one kind; rather, it must be understood in relation to the amount of experience the learner has with some subject matter, the meaning of the subject matter for the learner, and the purposes the learning might serve.

The three phases of learning identifiable in educational histories of extremely talented individuals make sense pedagogically. Together they seem to reflect the entirety of a learning experience—from getting involved; through mastery of skills and understanding; to finding the larger meaning and making the learning personal and worthwhile, and becoming educated about something. Furthermore, that which can be gained from each phase seems to be prerequisite for being able to make the most of the subsequent phases. If these phases of talent development are supported by further investigation, they will pose serious challenges to our historical concern for identifying talent early. They will also suggest new ways of thinking about teaching and the assessment of learning with the potential for developing talent more broadly than we can currently imagine. Given the long-term nature of developing talent, and qualitative shifts in teaching and learning over time, obvious early advantage may matter very little in our future efforts to promote success in various endeavors.

[2] This brief outline of phases in the development of talent necessarily ignores negative evidence. Our data do include examples of instances where learning did *not* proceed smoothly in the manner identified. In fact, these made the pattern all the more obvious because of the "corrections" that inevitably took place in the individuals' experiences. Some youngsters, for example, were asked to do the work of the phase of precision before they had developed an intense interest in their talent field. They and their parents remember a point at which they were ready to abandon their work in the field entirely, an option never taken apparently because of the sensitivity of a parent who arranged for a change of teacher who found a more engaging way of working with the student. Other youngsters moved too slowly or too quickly to the third phase, and found themselves floundering until changes were made in teachers or teaching strategies.

The Social Context of the Lived Experience

The development of talent did not take place in a vacuum. It was not the experience of a single individual working alone to release the muse within. The development of talent was, quite clearly, a tribute to the support of many people and communities that valued the activities at which the individuals would eventually excel and valued the individuals' efforts in pursuit of excellence. Without considerable interpersonal support (from family, teachers, peers, and others), and without the less personal but no less social support of organized segments of society engaged in work in the different fields, it is unlikely that the individuals we studied would ever have been identified for their exceptional accomplishments.

As discussed earlier, initial interest in and value of the talent field was typically a consequence of membership in a family with adults who held those interests and values. Initial motivation to work at the activity, toward unspecified ends, was derived in no small measure from the very immediate and interpersonal rewards such work provided. There was no intention or indication that initial efforts might lead to a long-term investment in the pursuit of excellence in the field. Early interest and effort were sustained and nurtured by teachers and other adults who orchestrated activities which added to the amusement the youngsters could find in the talent field and gave them the opportunity to be rewarded by applause.

Later, teachers and other adults would help to maintain the students' interests and efforts by introducing the students to challenges which appealed to their developing competence and by making special opportunities available for summer study and for public demonstration of the students' skill. Parents supplied the resources and the encouragement that allowed the students to take advantage of the opportunities their teachers made available.

For much of the time that it took to develop talent, the individuals we studied were too young to find or create for themselves the host of activities and opportunities that teachers and parents made available. One of the more remarkable aspects of the educational histories of the individuals we studied surely must be the interdependent and self-sustaining system of mutual encouragement and support that was created with and for the individuals by parents, teachers, and other adults with whom the individuals had sustained personal contact. Parents and teachers were willing and able to respond to a learner's development, and to change and grow with the learner in response to that development. Parents, teachers, and the individuals appear to have alternately prodded one another, their changes being mutually dependent and enhancing. No one person was responsible for the long-term investment in the development of talent; together, however, a group of supportive adults was able to find multiple ways of maximizing the possibility that the individuals would be able to sustain their involvement in the process of learning.

The group of people supporting the development of a single new talent did considerably more than merely applaud and reward. In fact, perhaps the most difficult task they faced over the years was to support the individual's efforts when interest flagged or skills stalled. There were many examples of such moments in the educational histories of the individuals we studied. There were moments of frustration and disappointment, and attempts at flight from the field. In these moments of failure and discouragement the commitment of parents and teachers was as strong as or stronger than when things were going well. The ability of parents and teachers to provide support after failure as well as after success, and to see less than exceptional performance as a challenge rather than a sign of failure, seem important in the development of talent, although we don't yet understand this well.

The development of talent depended greatly on the efforts of a wide variety of people on behalf of the accomplishment of one. It depended also on the less personal but no less social support provided by larger communities organized around the various fields. The talented individuals in our study were introduced to these communities initially by parents and teachers; over time these communities assumed an increasingly central role in helping to maintain the student's interest and support his or her development.

The larger communities included agemates and slightly older youngsters from other parts of town and the country. They included adults who came to watch the youngsters in public performances and, sometimes, to report on these activities for local newspapers. They included adults who engaged in activity that on the surface was very similar, and who garnered fame (and sometimes fortune) for their work. Exposure to these communities thus placed the child's activity in the context of a valued activity in society, and this context provided substantial support for the student's interest and involvement.

Introduction to the larger communities organized around the different fields seemed to serve various functions. Most obviously, young students were provided with role models of various ages. The oldest and most expert of these models were typically admired from a distance and treated as heroes. They legitimized the activities that the younger students were engaged in, generally without providing much direction for the students' work.

Role models who were closer in age and expertise tended to have more influence on the specific activities our students were engaged with. The slightly older students of the field were used to set an agenda of skills to be mastered and goals to be achieved. They provided a challenge and offered support and guidance. They served as a regular reminder that the individual was not really alone, despite the hours spent in solo pursuit of one sort of mastery or another.

The communities organized around the different fields provided not only role models but also specific and varied opportunities to acquire the knowledge and skills associated with the development of talent. Typically, each community had its own publications which broadened students' opportunities for instruction and inspiration. These talent-specific publications provided information about people, events, and ways of thinking and working; they helped the individuals identify additional resources for learning, and connect to work they were engaged in with teachers. In many cases, each community organized public events of various sorts which provided the individuals in our study both with an audience and with opportunities to see others engaged in similar activity.

Perhaps the most important function of the communities that supported the learning of the individuals we studied was the fact that they provided repeated demonstrations that the students were engaged in learning which was relevant to their lives, rather than merely school learning or learning appropriate only for children. Learning in the process of the development of talent resembled more closely learning out of school, as Resnick (1987) describes it, than learning in school. It often involved a shared experience, and almost always involved direct engagement with the objects and situations that define the field, contextualized reasoning, and the development of situation-specific competencies. Learning connected so directly with our experiences in the world, Dewey (1944) reminds us, has the potential for staying with us longer and making a deeper impression. "The more human the purpose, or the more it approximates the ends which appeal in daily experience, the more real the knowledge" (p. 198).

Learning, for the talented individuals we interviewed, was much more than a matter of acquiring knowledge and skill in the abstract. Most importantly, it was a vital and valued part of their lives, growing from and into their worlds of experience. In this context, distractions were minimized. Even as the individuals grew older, and their lives became more complex, few other activities could compete with the attraction of the field they knew richly and within which they had already developed some skill.

If the hare in *The Hare and the Tortoise* had had the support of its community for the length of the race, if it had been encouraged to defer the immediate satisfaction of food or rest for the sake of an activity all agreed was worthwhile, if the hare had been in the company of others who were leading by a length or nipping at its heels, surely the tortoise never would have turned out to be so outstanding in the long run. But the race was long and the hare was expected to sustain the activity alone. The talented individuals we interviewed ran a long race too; in this instance, however, they ran with the help of parents, teachers, and the larger community which apparently prevented them from getting so distracted that they lost the chance to excel.

Challenging Traditional Ideas About Talent Development

Gruber (1986) raised serious questions about the necessity and sufficiency of "the stereotyped idea of a 'normal' sequence for a creative life: precocity in childhood, early commitment and achievement, single-minded pursuit of creative goals, a lifetime of elaboration of these beginnings, eventual decline" (p. 255). The findings from our study of the development of talent strongly support his argument. The educational histories we collected from clearly talented young adults were remarkably lacking in evidence not only of precocity in early childhood and early achievement, but also of early commitment and single-minded pursuit of field-specific goals.

The individuals we studied did not spring to life demonstrating the skills, understandings, and dispositions which mark extraordinary talent in the various fields. Instead, they grew into their aptitudes and attitudes in the context of supportive adults, peers, and societies of persons who valued and engaged in activity of a similar sort. Experiences and expectations related to the development of talent were integrated gradually into the individuals' lives and the lives of their families. Thanks to the absence of large goals at the start, there was never so much still to be learned that the task would seem overwhelming.

Aptitudes and attitudes developed in concert, or almost so. The individuals were willing to invest human and material resources in increasingly difficult tasks as the field became an ever more vital and valued part of their lives. They learned to work toward more distant goals as they learned to care about achieving those goals. The students built a reservoir of good feeling about their talent fields, and their abilities, which helped them learn the patience and persistence that apparently are prerequisites of unusually successful achievement.

The process of growing into a person of extraordinary talent involved considerable exposure to and experience with field-specific content. As Duckworth (1987) reminds us:

> Intelligence cannot develop without matter to think about. Making new connections depends on knowing enough about something in the first place to provide a basis for thinking of other things to do—of other questions to ask—that demand more complex connections in order to make sense. The more ideas about something people already have at their disposal, the more new ideas occur and the more they can coordinate to build up still more complicated schemes. (p. 14)

The development of talent involved a clear focus on particular subject matter, with multiple opportunities of various sorts over a long period of time to come to know and appreciate that subject matter.

Cognitive scientists recently have begun making the case that considerable exposure to domain-specific content is an essential early component of the development of human competence. "The obvious reason for the excellence of experts is that they have a good deal of domain knowledge" (Glaser & Chi, 1988, p. xvii). Rich exposure to domain-specific knowledge is said to have important consequences for the development of automaticity, which in turn is believed to help explain the impressive coding and chunking abilities of experts. The study of expertise is leading increasingly to the assertion that "the problem of producing an expert may be, to a large extent, that of creating and maintaining the motivation for the long training that is necessary" (Glaser & Chi, p. xxii).

Findings from the study of the development of talent suggest that their conclusion is at least partially correct. Creating and maintaining the conditions which would support the potential for the development of high levels of competence, over the long term, does seem to be our greatest challenge. To meet this challenge we must become sensitive to the variety of motivations that contribute in different ways at different times to a long-term investment of effort. Our study suggests further that we must recognize the variety of dimensions of teaching and learning which contribute in different ways at different times to the development of people with considerable expertise. Motivating individuals to work at inappropriate tasks in inappropriate ways will hardly do.

To meet the challenge of creating conditions which support long-term involvement with a field of activity, we will have to confront quickly the role of society in the work of educational institutions. The development of talent apparently requires that students come to know their subject matter in socially meaningful ways. The work of educators apparently cannot be seen in isolation from the values of parents and the influences of larger communities. Educational institutions must learn to make learning a vital and valued part of our students' lives, growing from and into their worlds of experience. In many contexts, this may also require that we work to promote particular values and interests in the larger community.

The development of talent apparently is possible for far greater numbers of people than we ever imagined. Our challenge is to learn to provide appropriate opportunities for its development and to create conditions which support the long-term commitment to learning that is required.

Author's Note

Much work on the development of talent focuses on the responsibilities of schools for such development (e.g., U.S. Department of Education, 1993). However, the research just reported reminds us that the development of exceptional abilities probably cannot and certainly should not depend solely on work done in K–12 classrooms. Attention to the out-of-school lives of youth, and the roles of extra-school organizations in the development of talent, would seem to have special import for researchers in the areas of gifted and talented education. Promising avenues for researchers lie in the theoretical work of McLaughlin and Irby (1994; McLaughlin, Irby, & Langman, 1994) and in the changing practices of gifted education programs like the Academic Talent Development program at the University of California at Berkeley (Sosniak, 1995).

REFERENCES

Bloom, B. S. (Ed.) (1985). *Developing talent in young people*. New York: Ballantine Books.

Dewey, J. (1944). *Democracy and education*. New York: Free Press.

Duckworth, E. (1987). *The having of wonderful ideas*. New York: Teachers College Press.

Glaser, B. (1965). The constant comparative method of qualitative analysis. *Social Problems, 12,* 436–445.

Glaser, R., & Chi, M. T. H. (1988). Overview. In M. T. H. Chi, R. Glaser, & M. J. Farr (Eds.), *The nature of expertise*. Hillsdale, NJ: Lawrence Erlbaum Associates.

Gruber, H. E. (1986). The self-construction of the extraordinary. In R. J. Sternberg & J. E. Davidson (Eds.), *Conceptions of giftedness* (pp. 247–263). New York: Cambridge University Press.

Gustin, W. C. (1985). The development of exceptional research mathematicians. In B. S. Bloom (Ed.), *Developing talent in young people* (pp. 270–331). New York: Ballantine Books.

McLaughlin, M. W., & Irby, M. A. (1994). Urban sanctuaries: Neighborhoods that keep hope alive. *Phi Delta Kappan, 76*(4), 300–306.

McLaughlin, M. W., Irby, M. A., & Langman, J. (1994). *Urban sanctuaries: Neighborhoods in the lives and futures of inner city youth*. San Francisco: Jossey-Bass.

Resnick, L. B. (1987). Learning in school and out. *Educational Researcher, 16*(9), 13–20.

Sloane, K. D. (1985). Home influences on talent development. In B. S. Bloom (Ed.), *Developing talent in young people* (pp. 439–476). New York: Ballantine Books.

Sosniak, L. A. (1985a). A long-term commitment to learning. In B. S. Bloom (Ed.), *Developing talent in young people* (pp. 477–506). New York: Ballantine Books.

Sosniak, L. A. (1985b). Phases of learning. In B. S. Bloom (Ed.), *Developing talent in young people* (pp. 409–438). New York: Ballantine Books.

Sosniak, L. A. (1987). The nature of change in successful learning. *Teachers College Record, 88*(1), 519–535.

Sosniak, L. A. (1988). Changing relationships between student and teacher in the development of talent. *Education and Society, 6*(1,2) 79–86.

Sosniak, L. (1995). Inviting adolescents into academic communities: ATDP as an alternative perspective on systemic reform. *Theory into Practice, 34*(1), 35–42.

U.S. Department of Education (1993). *A case for developing America's talent*. Washington, DC: U.S. Government Printing Office.

Whitehead, A. N. (1929). *The aims of education*. New York: Macmillan.

18

Mentoring: A Time-Honored Option for Education of the Gifted and Talented

DONNA RAE CLASEN, *University of Wisconsin, Whitewater*
ROBERT E. CLASEN, *University of Wisconsin, Madison*

The mentor has another function, and this is developmentally the most crucial one: to support and facilitate the realization of the Dream.

—*Levinson et al. (1978)*

Mentoring is a time-honored means of educating the gifted and talented. It comes to us across centuries and from almost all cultures. Since ancient times, great leaders have counseled and instructed young protégés showing promise of maintaining their legacy; master artisans have worked with talented novices to develop their skills; philosophers and spiritual leaders have attended to like-minded young intellectuals. In all these mentoring relationships, the master transfers the knowledge, expertise, and experiences of a science, art, skill, or philosophy to a protégé who may eventually establish new frontiers in the field, break existing records, and create new traditions.

For gifted and talented young people whose skills and ability levels are beyond the scope of usual school resources, a mentorship is often a successful means of meeting their specific needs. The matching of a promising novice with an established expert provides the novice with appropriate challenge and continued encouragement in the development of his or her talent. It can be a productive and meaningful experience for both mentor and mentee, offering the potential of a long-term relationship. Mentorships, however, have their pitfalls and particular challenges. Without structure, allowances for systematic feedback, and a good match between mentor and mentee, the mentorship may flounder, disappointing all concerned. Although mentorships vary greatly in description and application, the probability of their success can be increased by the application of several general principles. These principles will be explored in this chapter.

What Is Mentoring?

A mentorship typically involves an older expert, usually but not always an adult, working with a younger but talented individual in an area of mutual interest. The term *mentor* comes to us from classical Greek, where Homer tells us that Mentor (believed to be Athena in disguise) became teacher and counselor to Odysseus' son Telemachus during the father's odyssey and long absence from his family. Mentor guided the boy Telemachus in becoming a man. While definitions and practices of mentorships vary substantially in the current gifted and talented field, characteristics of classical mentoring are informative. The classical mentorship was a one-to-one relationship; a wise, experienced person guided a neophyte; a long-term commitment was made by both individuals; and both found satisfaction in the mentorship.

In current practice, vestiges of traditional mentorships remain, with varying degrees of differences. Duration of the relationship is an example. Although a minimum of a year is recommended (Zorman, 1993), the time span depends on the purpose of the mentorship and the age and maturity of the mentee. Mentorships for elementary students frequently range in time from several weeks to a semester (Reisner, Petry, & Armitage, 1990).

High school students are often engaged for at least a year, particularly in mentorships with a strong academic focus (Clasen & Hanson, 1987; Lupkowski, Assouline, & Stanley, 1990). However, partnerships ranging from 10 to 18 weeks are not uncommon with high school students (Beck, 1989; Gray, 1983). Regardless of the time involvement, commitment is presumed for a successful experience (Boston, 1976; Cox & Daniel, 1983). Both mentor and mentee must be committed to the undertaking and to the effort and involvement necessary in a flourishing partnership.

The classical expectation was that the mentor would help a neophyte grow and develop beyond intellectual and skill areas. While this goal may be less practical in some current, short-term mentorships, the concept still is embraced. Cox and Daniel (1983) regarded the goal of mentoring as "the shaping of the student's life outlook." Gourley and Richert (1978) offered a similar premise in their description of a mentor as "someone who assists a gifted student in his or her intellectual, affective, social and career development in a specific area" (p. 25).

Need for Mentorships

Mentorships regularly have been regarded as a valuable option for meeting the special needs of high ability students (Cox, Daniel, & Boston, 1985; Stanley, 1979; Torrance, 1984); and as growing demands are placed on education and multiple requests are made for limited resources, mentoring is increasingly being encouraged. Mentorships are especially recommended for extremely precocious students (Lupkowski et al., 1990), for gifted students who have exhausted the resources of the school (Reilly, 1992), and for children of disadvantaged circumstances whose potential may never be realized without special opportunities (Hamilton & Hamilton, 1992; Wright & Borland, 1992).

The need to offer mentoring as an educational option for some high-ability students is reinforced by national reports criticizing the performance of the United States' most able students. In a monograph from the National Association for Gifted Children, Callahan (1993) noted that "findings from international studies provide devastating evidence that the achievements of the most able students in the United States are far behind those of other industrialized nations" (p. 1). Callahan's concern was echoed by Ross (1993) in the most recent national review of gifted education in the United States, *National Excellence: A Case for Developing America's Talent.*[1]

> The United States is squandering one of its most precious resources—the gifts, talents, and high interests of many of its students. In a broad range of intellectual and artistic endeavors, these youngsters are not challenged to do their best work. This problem is especially severe among economically disadvantaged and minority students, who have access to fewer advanced educational opportunities and whose talents often go unnoticed. (p. 1)

One recommendation from the national report clearly calls for mentoring or mentoring-like activities: the establishment of high-level learning opportunities that are as "diverse as the talents of the children" and that permit more in-depth work, appropriate pacing, and work in community settings. The report urges a strong school–community link and use of valuable resources within the community. Mentorships respond to these recommendations.

The Mentor and the Mentee

Characteristics and Roles of a Mentor

Much of the success of a mentorship will be determined by the mentor. Not everyone who is an expert can be a mentor; expertise and skill in a field are necessary but not sufficient. The mentor must be willing—even eager—to share expertise with a novice whose energy and questions may be taxing and with whom patience and understanding likely will be required. Sensitivity to the mentee's developmental needs in areas such as socialization and peer affiliations is essential. Other desir-

---

[1] See Chapter 44 by Ross.

able qualities include good communication and problem-solving skills, creativity, and flexibility. An inventory of good mentor characteristics by Mattson (1983) also included strong personal integrity, optimism, and a sense of humor.

During a mentorship, the mentor will assume several interlocking roles:

1. *Teacher:* As teacher, the mentor helps the mentee push the boundaries of knowledge and skills. The mentor provides systematic feedback on work and helps the novice analyze and evaluate progress and products.
2. *Expert:* The mentor has the ability and experience to create opportunities, to introduce the novice to an expert's view of a field, and to share traditional accumulated wisdom.
3. *Guide:* The mentor knows the path to success and the obstacles to reaching goals and shows the way while allowing for individual exploration.
4. *Advisor:* The mentor advises the mentee regarding expectations and possibilities, introduces the mores and standards of the field, and helps in problem solving and decision making. As advisor, the mentor confronts the novice if behavior is inappropriate.
5. *Friend:* The mentor is a source of emotional support, someone the mentee can trust and with whom feelings can be shared.
6. *Role Model:* As a role model, the mentor becomes an exemplar of certain values, attitudes, and behavioral patterns that the mentee will often strive to emulate.

Some argue that the mentor's most important role is to support the young person's dream and to facilitate its realization (Levinson, Darrow, Klein, Levinson, & McKee, 1978). Boston (1976) ascribes similar responsibility to the mentor, whose task he believes is "the transformation of potential into actuality" (p. 39). While many short-term mentorships in gifted education may not be expected to have such impact on an individual's life, the influence of a mentor should never be underestimated. Even a short-term partnership can have an impact on self-esteem, feelings of competence, and sense of worth (Reisner, Petry, & Armitage, 1990).

Characteristics of the Mentee

While mentor characteristics must be given careful consideration in establishing a mentorship, it is equally important to attend to characteristics of the protégé or mentee, as the student frequently is called. Not all gifted and talented students are either ready or able to enter into a mentorship. Readiness should be assessed carefully before the mentorship begins. Readiness involves possessing exceptional ability and potential to excel in a field, abiding interest and enthusiasm for an area of study, perseverance, and a willingness to commit time and energy to study and exploration. Commitment, in particular, is a prominent factor in evaluations of readiness (Atkinson, Hansen, & Passman, 1992; Boston, 1976; Clasen & Hanson, 1987).

Age also is an issue. Boston (1979) maintained that most elementary students lack the developmental maturity for a one-to-one relationship with an adult and for the required autonomous study. However, a variety of successful mentorships for younger students have been reported, especially in areas of career exploration and skill building. Lengel (1989) argued that early attention is essential for underachieving high-ability students and described a successful mentorship program involving underachieving students in grades 3 through 6 who worked with teacher mentors throughout the school year. Other successful programs involving students as early as fourth and fifth grade have been reported by Ellingson, Haeger, and Feldhusen (1986), Gray (1983), and Reisner et al. (1990). Stanley (1979) and Lupkowski, Assouline, and Stanley (1990) reported successful mentorships for precocious math students as young as 6 and 10 years old.

Reilly (1992) suggested another readiness consideration. She argued that a protégé should take advantage of current school opportunities before turning to a professional mentor. While admitting that determining readiness for a mentor "is a judgment call at best," Reilly outlined a sequence of steps for reaching the decision to arrange for a professional mentor. The process permits assessment of the potential protégé's need for a one-on-one relationship, as well as the student's readiness in terms of the commitment and time-intensiveness of a mentorship. As a very brief summary, the steps included the following:

1. Asking who perceives the need for enrichment (the student, the parent, or the teacher)
2. Finding out the student's needs (e.g., with a student profile)
3. Asking parents about their past help to the student and their willingness to provide future help (e.g., transportation, equipment, supplies)
4. Compiling a list of the student's existing accomplishments (courses, clubs, independent work)
5. Brainstorming activities and resources for the student
6. Asking someone within the school to work with the student
7. Asking a district specialist to help the student
8. Arranging for the student to meet with experts at their workplace
9. Arranging the mentorship or internship

Note that several of these steps focused on accessing existing school resources. Reilly cautioned that a student's desire to "study on my own" may be interpreted incorrectly as indicating a need for a mentor when, in fact, there may be another valid interpretation, such as a desire to explore a subject in more depth and breadth.

Matching Mentor and Mentee

The success of a mentorship will often depend on the match between mentor and mentee, and the time spent in finding a compatible partnership will be rewarded. Frequently, a gifted and talented coordinator, teacher, or counselor will make the match in consultation with mentor and mentee. Background information, interest surveys, and interviews often are used in determining the match. In some instances, however, students and mentors have an opportunity to select each other. The City University of New York Student Mentor Program is a good example. In this program, before mentoring began high school students and university mentors met after school for several weeks and engaged in informal conversation, games, and interviews. By the fifth week, when mentoring started, a mutual selection usually had occurred (Reisner et al., 1990). Because matching in such a case is more spontaneous and natural, the partnership is likely to be strong and enduring.

Depending on the purpose of the mentorship, pairing according to gender and cultural and ethnic backgrounds may also be important. For example, when role models are a priority, it is desirable to match girls with successful women, or young minority students with minority leaders (Beck, 1989; Reisner et al., 1990). However, while pairing on the principle of similarity may be preferable in some instances, the number of available mentors will not always allow this choice. Furthermore, many successful mentorships have been cross-gender and cross-cultural.

Types of Mentorships

In an annotated bibliography of mentor programs, Noller and Frey (1994) dichotomized mentoring into *spontaneous* and *instrumental* arrangements. Spontaneous arrangements occur when two individuals see a mutually desirable relationship with common benefits and decide to undertake it. Spontaneous mentorships have the potential advantage of natural commitment and free-flow planning. Their success may be at risk, though, without a common understanding of roles and responsibilities and a structure to ensure execution of tasks and completion of projects.

Instrumental mentorships are purposeful arrangements, usually done by a teacher, gifted and talented coordinator, or counselor. They are planned with assigned responsibilities and take into account characteristics of the mentor and the mentee. They have the advantage of a third party who attempts to match the mentor and student in personality and learning style and who can help clarify roles and expectations. The vast majority of gifted and talented mentorships in education are of the instrumental variety because young people have limited opportunities for spontaneous mentorships and many would lack the confidence to pursue such an opportunity even if available.

Within arranged mentorships there is great diversity in mentorship profiles. What is considered a "mentorship" in one school district might not be identified as such in another. Broadened definitions have resulted in community service projects, apprenticeships, internships, and "shadowing" being identified as forms of mentorship (Cox, Daniel, & Boston, 1985). Each of these has the potential of being a true mentorship, but none qualifies as such without certain critical components, basic among them a one-on-one relationship with an expert in the field serving as guide, advisor, teacher, and friend.

Following a review of the mentorship literature, Zorman (1993) concluded that five characteristics distinguish mentoring from other relationships:

1. Mutual passion for a specific area of interest
2. A match of teaching and learning styles
3. Lifelong trust
4. Mutual perceptions of symmetry—that is, a movement toward equality in the relationship as the protgégé advances in knowledge and skill
5. A sharing of lifestyle as the novice gradually adopts patterns of the engineer, teacher, artist, or other professional

One characteristic, lifelong trust, is problematic. Although trust is necessary for building a mentorship, *lifetime* trust cannot be assured. Levinson et al. (1978), for example, reported that a rupture in the relationship was not unusual later in life when the mentee's need for complete autonomy reached its zenith. Many mentors will be surpassed in fame and fortune by the protgégé and must be comfortable with this possibility if trust is to be maintained.

Although mentorships frequently are recommended as a component of gifted programming, those who work with school districts recognize that mentorships involving gifted students actually are not common. Of the 913 articles on mentoring annotated by Noller and Frey (1994), only 68 were categorized for gifted students, and these included descriptions of mentorships for gifted students in other countries. A spring 1994 ERIC search using the conjoint of *gifted* and *mentor* showed 79 entries. The articles are instructive regarding the form and function of mentorships in gifted education.

Most mentorships involved junior and senior high school students (Beck, 1989; Comer, 1989; Lupkowski, Assouline, & Vestal, 1992), but increasingly mentoring programs for elementary students have been reported (Emerson-Stonnell & Carter, 1994; Lupkowski et al., 1992; Reisner, Petry, & Armitage, 1990; Wright & Borland, 1992). Most mentorships focused on career exploration or a specific discipline but the focus might also include leadership, critical thinking, underachievement, and research skills. Tan-Willman's (1992) Canadian program for elementary students focused on highly creative students. The Gifted Handicapped Mentor Program in New York was built around specific abilities of gifted students who had special learning or physical challenges (Levey & Dolan, 1988).

Mentors included community volunteers, teachers within the school district, and university faculty and students. Many programs relied on community volunteers (Atkinson et al., 1992; Comer, 1989; Milam & Schwartz, 1992). Others found mentors within the school district to work with a student outside their usual grade level (Lengel, 1989) or drew upon both school and community volunteers (Cellerino, 1983). University students served as mentors to younger students in a number of successful programs (Duln, Lammers, Mason, & Graves, 1994; Gray, 1983; Prillaman & Richardson, 1989), with university students usually receiving training and college credit for their involvement. Wright and Borland (1992) reported positive results when gifted adolescents served as mentors for young, disadvantaged elementary students. In one instance, a brilliant 10-year-old served as a mentor for a precocious 6-year-old student (Stanley, 1979).

Most mentorships focus in general on three goals:

1. The development of cognitive capabilities
2. The development of affective characteristics
3. The development of physical or psychosocial skills

By taking permutations of 1, 2, and 3 and listing the numbers in order of emphasis, it is possible to illustrate kinds of mentorships. This can be a helpful device when structuring a mentorship in terms of identifying purpose, planning activities, and determining evaluation criteria.

In general, goals are interlocking; each will be of importance in most mentoring relationships. Further, while one goal will likely dominate when the mentorship is established, as time progresses and needs shift, the goal emphasis also may shift.

Most Emphasis		Least Emphasis	Mentorship Exemplar
1	2	3	Studying higher level mathematical applications
1	3	2	Exploring a science concept in the laboratory
2	1	3	A mentee working with emotionally disabled children
2	3	1	Guiding an art student to a higher developmental level
3	1	2	A gymnast developing increasingly more difficult moves
3	2	1	A veterinary mentee working in animal surgery

Mentorships for Disadvantaged Students

Increasingly, mentorships are recommended as a means of helping students who may face extraordinary obstacles in realizing their potential (Hamilton & Hamilton, 1992; Olszewski-Kubilius & Scott, 1992). For many students the support, encouragement, and opportunity necessary for talent development are missing or minimal in their lives. Mentorships can help provide these factors. Perhaps most important, a mentoring relationship may have a positive impact on attitudinal and self-concept factors before a student's orientation toward education, achievement, and success become limited.

A report prepared for the U.S. Department of Education (Reisner et al., 1990) described several programs for disadvantaged youth in which college students served as mentors. The CUNY Student Mentor Program was one of the more extensive. CUNY'S program involved 226 college mentors matched with an equal number of high school students from disadvantaged backgrounds. Partners met once a week for two hours over a semester's time. The curriculum base was career-oriented but also stressed personal goal development and decision-making skills. Program evaluations reported the mentorships were especially helpful in empowering students to establish educational and career goals.

Although research on the effectiveness of mentoring for disadvantaged youth is limited, several preliminary findings support their value. Reisner et al. (1990) reported that their survey of local project evaluations of mentorships presented evidence of improvement in three areas: (1) academic performance, (2) motivation and attitudes toward school, and (3) self-esteem and confidence. Flaxman, Ascher, and Herrington (1988), in their review of research on mentoring, concluded that carefully planned, intensive mentoring could "solve some of the contradictions" disadvantaged youth experience in realizing their potential.

Mentorships for Females

Several reviews of mentorships have stressed the importance of mentors for girls and women (Collins, 1983; Halcomb, 1980; Kaufmann, Harrel, Milam, Woolverton, & Miller, 1986). Women who are leaders in their field can provide much needed role modeling for young women as well as insight and advice regarding career experiences and expectations. Despite the obvious benefits of same-sex mentoring, most gifted and talented girls are paired with male mentors, in part because fewer female mentors are available (Beck, 1989).

Although research is needed to explore possible differences in the effectiveness of same-gender and cross-gender mentorships, several studies offer evidence of the general importance of mentors for girls and women (Beck, 1989; Collins, 1983). For example, Kaufmann et al. (1986) concluded that having a mentor helped equalize earning power between career men and women. In Beck's (1989) study, young women in high school paired with female college mentors reported that the mentorship promoted risk-taking and their ability to work independently. It also helped them consider ways to integrate a career and family. Beck pointed out that female mentors can be particularly helpful in aiding young women in overcoming psychological barriers to achievement because they have confronted those barriers successfully themselves.

Mentorships of the Future

In the future, technology will play an important role in mentorships as computers, interactive video, and distance learning become part of mentor relationships. Such advancements may help alleviate some problems currently faced in mentorships, such as finding sufficient time for communication, scheduling meeting times, and containing travel time and costs. E-mail and faxing allow for quick communication and eliminate the need for some travel. In addition, technology may be one means of expanding the mentor pool for more students, increasing both the number and diversity of mentors.

One mentorship program at the University of Minnesota involving university students and ninth graders explored a mentorship using telecommunications (Duln et al., 1994). University students became mentors to young writers, communicating with them electronically via delayed file sharing. Mentors responded to student writing by offering suggestions and raising questions intended to advance the mentee's writing capability. Emphasizing a nurturing process, mentors committed substantial time to developing and maintaining relationships and in fact devoted most responses to interpersonal comments. The role of technology in mentorships calls for careful study, but holds great promise for helping to meet the needs of more gifted students.

Structuring a Mentorship

Mentorships, like all partner relationships, are more likely to succeed when they are entered into purposefully, with commitment on both sides, and with a reasonably clear understanding of the roles and responsibilities of each partner. To increase the likelihood of success, several mentor programs have established guidelines for structuring a partnership. Although suggested procedures for setting up a mentorship vary, a number of characteristics are common (Clasen & Hanson, 1987; Cox & Daniel, 1983; Prillaman & Richardson, 1989; Reilly, 1992; Zorman, 1993). The following ten-step process involving three phases incorporates the most frequently suggested components.

Phase 1: The Preparation

1. *Establish need.* The first step is to determine whether or not a mentorship is the best educational option for a student or group of students at the present time. The answer must consider the students, available mentors, and other educational possibilities. Student desire and ability to commit to a mentorship are considered in the initial assessment.

2. *Recruit mentors.* Mentors are recruited from universities, businesses, community groups, and organizations. Usually, this includes a personal contact by someone who describes the program and explains needs. Once a program becomes established, it is likely that a pool of potential mentors will always be available.

3. *Select potential mentors.* Screening of mentors varies in intensity but often includes an interview, recommendations by their peers, and reviews of their previous experiences working with young people. Final selection is determined by the best match between mentor and mentee.

4. *Match mentee and mentor.* Because the compatibility of the mentor and mentee will be a major factor in the success of the mentorship, time and effort must be expended on this step. This is especially crucial when the mentorship is expected to be long term. Interest surveys, biographical data, and teaching and learning-style inventories can be helpful in finding partners. Mentor and mentee need to meet and chat informally before the final decision is made. A visit to the mentor's place of work also can be helpful.

5. *Provide orientations.* An introduction to the mentorship concept is valuable for all participants. For university students mentoring younger students, classes or workshops are usually part of the process (Prillaman & Richardson, 1989; Reisner et al., 1990). Reisner et al. noted that orientation may be especially important "when there are racial, cultural and socioeconomic differences between tutors and mentors and the students they serve" (p. 39). Equally important are orientation sessions for mentees (Atkinson et al., 1992; Milam & Schwartz, 1992) and for their parents (Prillaman & Richardson, 1989).

Phase 2: The Mentorship

6. *Determine the conceptual contract and work plan.* Together, the mentor and mentee identify their roles and responsibilities, often with a third party, such as a teacher or program director, facilitating. In an early meeting a work plan or schedule is agreed on by the mentor and mentee and, when appropriate, a specific area of study is outlined. Academic needs of the student are considered and work may be assigned. Asking the mentee to keep a journal of activities, thoughts, and learning experiences is common in many mentorships.

7. *Arrange for systematic feedback.* Systematic feedback allows for mentor and mentee to regulate the mentorship, maintain an open relationship, and make changes as needed. Feedback also may come from the mentee's teachers, parents, and program coordinator.

8. *Allow the mentorship to take its course.* The mentorship will include some planned activities; but it also is shaped by emerging needs, interests, and issues as mentor and mentee explore a domain. Ideally it will allow time to move forward, to back up, to retrench, to reflect—even to dream.

Phase 3: The Culmination

9. *Realize a final product.* Whether it is a written report, a science project, or an art show or exhibition, a final product brings closure to a mentorship and creates a sense of satisfaction for all involved. A culminating activity also offers the mentee an opportunity to share his or her work and the mentoring experience with an audience.

10. *Evaluate the mentorship.* Systematic feedback provides formative evaluation of the mentorship, but a summative or final evaluation should be done by all interested parties: mentor and mentee, school personnel, parents, and other significant individuals. Evaluations might include case studies, questionnaires, surveys, and self-reports from mentor and mentee regarding the process and effectiveness of the mentorship.

Evaluations must reflect the goals of the program. For example, mentorships for underachievers or disadvantaged students might assess changes in attitude, achievement, or self-concept (Reisner et al., 1990). Academic mentorships might assess skill development, academic acceleration, or the quality of a final product (Lupkowski et al., 1990; Atkinson et al., 1992).

One important point regarding assessment was noted by Wright and Borland (1992). In many mentorships, the long-term goals cannot be immediately evaluated. The impact of a mentorship on future success of the mentees will not be known for some time, especially in mentorships with young children. Nonetheless, informal evaluations relying on participants' perceptions of the immediate experience constitute a reasonable approach to assessment.

Caveats: Things to Keep in Mind When Setting Up Mentorships

Whether setting up a mentoring program or a single mentorship, attention to several critical factors can mitigate or eliminate later difficulties.

1. Setting the numbers. Individuals responsible for establishing mentorships must determine how many relationships can effectively be managed over a given period of time. Additional resources should be required before expanding beyond the magic number.

2. The tender years. The developmental level of the student is a major consideration. Some elementary students are ready for a mentorship; some high school students are not. Instrumental mentorships arranged for younger students must stand the test of reasonableness and prudence. Obviously, parental permission is required for any deviation from the normal school routine; and this should be gathered in face-to-face contact, not the return of a signed form. Someone must be responsible for closely monitoring the arranged partnership.

3. Developmental needs. Some mentors, though skilled experts in their fields, may be unable or unwilling to handle some of the critical developmental needs of the mentee. This is as important for adolescents as for elementary-age children. Clasen and Hanson (1987) argued that success of a mentorship often depended upon attention to developmental needs. They recommended *double mentoring,* where a second mentor, often a teacher, helped the student in areas important to both his or her personal growth and to the success of the mentorship. They identified several areas in which the second mentor could be particularly effective, including the development of skills for communicating with adults, especially those in power positions; time management; personal reflection on the mentorship; and provision of opportunities for mentees to interact with peers engaged in mentorships.

4. Support systems. In addition to support for the mentee, four additional kinds of continuing support must be considered.

- *Support for the mentor.* Mentors must be valued and supported; their contributions should receive formal recognition from the school. Further, the mentor may need support in learning how to cope with the mentee in terms of age, cultural background, or attitude and value differences. As the relationship advances, changes in equity within the relationship will affect the mentor, who may need support in effectively empowering the mentee.
- *Support for the coordinator.* Beyond being matchmaker, the coordinator often becomes communicator, negotiator, a second mentor, and counselor. Much of the scaffolding of the mentorship is done by the coordinator, and as a result she or he may be held accountable by the school for the success or failure of the mentorship. This is an awesome responsibility, and the individual assigned the task should be given the necessary time, space, and resources to handle the job.
- *Support for the family.* Parents or significant family members may feel threatened by the role of the mentor in the life of their child. As much as possible, they should share in the process in terms of being kept informed, attending occasional meetings, and visiting the mentor and student at mutually agreed-on times.
- *Support for the mentorship.* Most mentorships are not part of the school budget. Mentors usually contribute their services and their institutions or agencies provide access to resources such as libraries or laboratories. Some money should be budgeted, however, for possible transportation costs, incidental expenses, fees for special events or special resources, and of course the coordinator's role.

5. What to do if the mentorship fails. Sometimes a mentorship will not work. This may be due to unexpected events or life changes, or because one or both of the partners find the relationship incompatible. This possibility should be dealt with before the mentorship begins. Mentor and mentee need to know that they are expected to work at the relationship and do all they can to make it succeed, but they also need assurance that they are free to dissolve the mentorship if absolutely necessary. In such a case, both should be able to leave the mentorship without assessing blame, but should be able to evaluate what happened.

Benefits of Mentorships

The endurance of mentoring across the ages suggests that the practice not only is highly regarded by mentorship partners, but that communities have long valued it as a reasonable means for educating promising young people. Much of the staying power of mentorships is due to a broad range of mentoring benefits (Edlind & Haensly, 1985; Moore, 1992; Runions & Smyth, 1985). Among them, seven are especially compelling.

1. Meeting exceptional ability needs. Mentorships provide high-level learning experiences for students with the need and the readiness to move beyond the regular school provisions and into a relationship that will motivate, stimulate, and challenge ability and interest levels. For students with a passion for an area of development, it is an opportunity to meet others who share the passion and who can nurture the interest in a broader context.

2. Career exploration and development. The proliferation of mentorships with a career emphasis indicates the value placed on mentoring for career development across many disciplines. Researchers have documented the influence of mentorships on individuals' careers (Kaufmann et al., 1986; Levinson et al., 1978; Torrance, 1984). Merriam's (1983) review indicated that the mentor often is the principal force in a successful person's career. The mentorship is especially valuable when young people are still questioning their abilities and interests, for the mentorship can "affirm their specialness without limiting it too early" (Albert, 1981, p. 4).

3. Development of potential. The abilities of many talented young people will be realized *only* through special opportunities such as a mentorship. In many cases talent development depends entirely upon opportunity; capabilities and interest alone do not suffice (Clasen, 1993). A mentoring relationship may provide the necessary environment for a change in attitude and achievement for students often screened out of gifted and talented programs or accelerated classes. These include underachieving, learning-disabled, handicapped, economically disadvantaged, and minority students (Richert, 1991).

4. Psychosocial advancement. During the mentorship, self-reliance, personal responsibility, and self-directed learning are encouraged and enhanced. From the mentor, the mentee can learn interpersonal skills, self-monitoring of feelings, and ways of interacting with others (Moore, 1992). The total experience can increase self-esteem, feelings of competence, and a sense of identity.

5. Connections with the larger world. Mentorships can help students see that they and their interests are part of a larger world and that their work contributes to a number of domains that interlock with their particular field of study.

6. Shared rewards. As in any partnership, the mentorship should be mutually beneficial to the partners. While mentees garner advanced knowledge and skills, insights into careers, and emotional support, the mentor has the satisfaction of passing tradition to a new generation. And through the views of the novice, the mentor may find renewed energy and enthusiasm for the field. In reviewing literature on mentorships in gifted education, Edlind and Haensly (1985) found four areas in which mentors were rewarded:

(1) completion of a project, (2) stimulation of new ideas and perspectives, (3) long-term friendships, and (4) personal satisfaction in terms of preparing the next generation, the process that social psychologist Erik Erikson (1968) termed "generativity."

7. Community and school collaborations. Collaborations involving schools and the public and private sectors provide access to many resources that can supplement the needs of gifted and talented students (Atkinson et al., 1992) The partnerships also can develop positive public relations. As school personnel, community leaders, university faculty, and area experts work together on behalf of students, a bond is forged between school and community.

Conclusion

Mentoring can be a powerful experience and frequently has a long-lasting impact on both partners in the relationship. It requires commitment, hard work, and negotiation. In return it offers opportunities for sharing mutual interests, confronting appropriate challenges, and developing a keener understanding of life possibilities.

Under certain circumstances a mentorship will be the most effective educational strategy for meeting the needs of a gifted and talented student and should be an available option (Beck, 1989; Boston, 1976; Gray, 1983; Prillaman & Richardson, 1989). The one-on-one relationship between a young person and a talented, caring adult can encourage, promote, and validate a talent at a critical period. Whether the mentorship focuses on advancing a super talent or nurturing promising potential, the relationship may mean the difference between a dream withered and a dream realized.

REFERENCES

Albert, R. (1981). Special programs require special people. *Roeper Review, 4*(2), 2–4.

Atkinson, C., Hansen, D., & Passman, B. (1992, May–June). A school–community partnership for developing talent. *Gifted Child Today, 15*(3), 18–22.

Beck, L. (1989). Mentorships: Benefits and effects on career development. *Gifted Child Quarterly, 33*, 22–28.

Boston, B. O. (1976). *The sorcerer's apprentice: A case study in the role of the mentor.* Reston, VA: Council for Exceptional Children.

Boston, B. O. (1979). *Developing a community based mentorship program for the gifted and talented.* (Contract No. 300-78-0530). Washington, DC: U.S. Office of Education.

Callahan, C. M. (1993). The performance of high ability students in the United States on national and international tests. *Monograph of the National Association for Gifted Children*. Washington, DC: National Association for Gifted Children.

Cellerino, M. B. (1983). A mentor-volunteer program for the gifted and talented. *Roeper Review, 6*(1), 45–46.

Clasen, D. R. (1993). Resolving inequities: Discovery and development of talents in student populations traditionally underrepresented in gifted and talented programming. *Journal of the California Association for the Gifted, 23*(4), 25–29.

Clasen, D., & Hanson, M. (1987). Double mentoring: A process for facilitating mentorships for gifted students. *Roeper Review, 10,* 107–110.

Collins, N. (1983). *Professional women and their mentors.* Englewood Cliffs, NJ: Prentice-Hall.

Comer, R. (1989). A mentorship program for gifted students. *The School Counselor, 36*(3), 224–228.

Cox, J., & Daniel, N. (1983, September–October). The role of the mentor. *G/C/T, 29,* 54–61.

Cox, J., Daniel, N., & Boston, B. O. (1985). *Educating able learners: Programs and promising practices.* Austin: University of Texas Press.

Duln, A., Lammers, E., Mason, L., & Graves, M. (1994). Responding to ninth-grade students via telecommunications: College mentor strategies and development over time. *Research in the Teaching of English, 28*(2), 117–153.

Edlind, E. P., & Haensly, P. A. (1985). Gifts of mentorships. *Gifted Child Quarterly, 29*, 55–60.

Ellingson, M., Haeger, W., & Feldhusen, J. (1986, March–April). The Purdue mentor program. G/C/T, 2–5.

Emerson-Stonnell, S., & Carter, C. (1994). Math mentor programs. *Gifted Child Today, 17*(1), 34–36, 41.

Erikson, E. (1968). *Identity: Youth and crisis.* New York: Norton.

Flaxman, E., Ascher, C., & Harrington, C. (1988, September). *Mentoring programs and practices:*

An analysis of the literature. New York: Institute for Urban and Minority Education, Columbia University.

Gourley, T., & Richert, S. (1978). Beyond the classroom: Programs for the gifted and talented. *NJEA Review,* 24–26.

Gray, W. (1983). *Challenging the gifted and talented through mentor-assisted enrichment projects.* Bloomington, IN: Phi Delta Kappa Educational Foundation.

Halcomb, R. (1980). Mentors and the successful woman. *Across the Board, 8*(2), 13–18.

Hamilton, S. F., & Hamilton, M. A. (1992). Mentoring programs: promise and paradox. *Phi Delta Kappan, 73*(7), 546–550.

Kaufmann, F., Harrel, G., Milam, C., Woolverton, N., & Miller, J. (1986). The nature, role, and influence of mentors in the lives of gifted adults. *Journal of Counseling and Development, 64,* 576–578.

Lengel, A. (1989, January–February). Mentee/mentor: Someone in my corner. *Gifted Child Today, 12,* 27–29.

Levey, S., & Dolan, J. (1988, May–June). Addressing specific learning abilities in gifted students. *Gifted Child Today, 11,* 10–11.

Levinson, D., Darrow, C., Klein, E., Levinson, M., & McKee, B. (1978). *The seasons of a man's life.* New York: Ballantine Books.

Lupkowski, A. E., Assouline, S. G., & Stanley, J. C. (1990, March–April). Applying a mentor model for young mathematically talented students. *Gifted Child Today, 13,* 15–19.

Lupkowski, A. E., Assouline, S. G., & Vestal, J. (1992, May–June). Mentors in math. *Gifted Child Today, 15,* 26–31.

Mattson, B. (1983, March–April). Mentors for the gifted and talented: Whom to seek and where to look. *G/C/T, 27,* 10–11.

Merriam, S. (1983). Mentors and protégés: A critical review of the literature. *Adult Education Quarterly, 33*(3), 161–173.

Milam, C., & Schwartz, B. (1992, May–June). Mentorship connection. *Gifted Child Today, 15,* 9–13.

Moore, K. M. (1992). The role of mentors in developing leaders in academe. *Educational Record, 63*(1), 23–28.

Noller, R. B., & Frey, R. (1994). *Mentoring: Annotated bibliography (1982–1992).* Sarasota, FL: Center for Creative Learning.

Olszewski-Kubilius, P. M., & Scott, J. M. (1992). An investigation of the college and career counseling needs of economically disadvantaged, minority gifted students. *Roeper Review, 14,* 141–148.

Prillaman, D., & Richardson, R. (1989). The William and Mary mentorship model: College students as a resource for the gifted. *Roeper Review, 12,* 114–118.

Reilly, J. (1992, May–June). When does a student really need a professional mentor? *Gifted Child Today, 15,* 2–8.

Reisner, E. R., Petry, C. A., & Armitage, M. (1990, April). *A review of programs involving college students as tutors or mentors in grades K–12.* (Vol. 1) (Contract No. LC 89089001). Washington, DC: Policy Studies Associates.

Richert, E. S. (1991). Rampant problems and promising practices in identification. In N. Colangelo & G. A. Davis (Eds.), *Handbook of gifted education* (pp. 81–96). Boston: Allyn and Bacon.

Ross, P. O. (Ed.). (1993). *National excellence: A case for developing America's talent.* Washington, DC: U.S. Department of Education.

Runions, T., & Smyth, E. (1985). Gifted adolescents as co-learners in mentorships. *Journal for the Education of the Gifted, 8*(2), 127–132.

Stanley, J. C. (1979). How to use a fast-pacing math mentor. *Intellectually Talented Youth Bulletin, 5*(6), 1–2.

Tan-William, C. (1992). The prime mentors of Canada: A junior–senior partnership for the development of creative potential. In W. Wu, C. Kuo, & J. Steeves (Eds.), *Second Asian conference on giftedness proceedings* (pp. 351–357). Taipei: National Taiwan Normal University.

Torrance, E. P. (1984). *Mentor relationships: How they aid creative achievement, endure, change and die.* New York: Bearly Limited.

Wright, L., & Borland, J. H. (1992). A special friend: Adolescent mentors for young, economically disadvantaged, potentially gifted students. *Roeper Review, 14,* 124–129.

Zorman, R. (1993). The life-stage mentoring model for the gifted. *Gifted International, 8*(1), 4–8.

19

Ability Grouping

JAMES A. KULIK and CHEN-LIN C. KULIK, *University of Michigan*

Ability grouping was controversial when it was first used in U.S. schools at the turn of the twentieth century, and it stirs up debate today. Parents and teachers still discuss it at school meetings. Reporters still write about it in newspapers and magazines. Experts still analyze its pros and cons in professional journals.

Ability grouping is not only a controversial topic, but also a confusing one. People define the term in different ways, and they characterize the effects of grouping differently. Some say grouping helps children, while others say it hurts them. People sometimes support their positions by citing research, but the literature on grouping is so extensive that people use it—like the Bible—to support almost any view.

Those in gifted education are concerned about the controversy and confusion. Although gifted education is not the same thing as ability grouping, the two topics are clearly related. Gifted programs usually attract a select group of high-aptitude students, and the programs usually provide separate instruction for these students. Thus, most programs for the gifted involve ability grouping. Teachers of the gifted are therefore eager to see the confusion about ability grouping cleared up and the controversy resolved.

Fortunately, researchers have been energetically studying ability grouping during the past decade. Although their work has not yet produced complete agreement on all issues, it has at least cleared up some of the confusion, and it may provide the groundwork for a future consensus. In this chapter we describe this recent work, but we begin with simple questions of terminology and a review of older findings.

Definition of Terms

Ability grouping occurs when school personnel use test scores and school records to assign same-grade children to classes or instructional groups that differ markedly in characteristics affecting school learning. Ability grouping is therefore a broad concept that fits a number of different school programs. Schools use it when they assign children to high, middle, and low classes in the elementary grades; when they assign middle and high school students to different classes in core subjects such as English and mathematics; when they assign children to reading groups according to reading level rather than school grade or age; when they provide special classes for the gifted and talented; and when they use within-class grouping in arithmetic or reading classes.

Most writers distinguish between ability grouping and tracking. Educational researchers usually reserve the term *tracking,* or *curricular tracking,* for high school programs in which students choose either college-preparatory, general, or vocational classes on the basis of their educational and career goals. The *Dictionary of Education* (Good, 1973) defines a *track* system as follows:

> a plan to guide students, in accordance with both their abilities and their probable future destinations, into one of several series of high school courses; the various series include alternate courses in the same subject field, such as mathematics, or courses in different fields; the track for academically talented pupils, for example, includes no vocational courses and that for vocational pupils no foreign language. (p. 612)

It is important to note that students themselves select their curricular tracks, whereas preferences of pupils and their parents seldom play a role in placement into ability groups. In addition, curricular tracking occurs only in high schools, whereas ability grouping can and does occur at all levels of education.

Popular writers sometimes use the term *tracking* in a different sense. Singal (1991), for example, defines tracking as "a practice in which students are sorted out at an early age according to their scores on intelligence tests and placed in separate 'tracks' for fast, medium, and slow learners, where they remain through high school" (p. 73). For Singal and other writers, tracking is a rigid and onerous form of ability grouping. Researchers are aware that the term *tracking* is used in this sense:

> The term "tracking" has been used to refer to two phenomena. It sometimes describes rigid ability grouping where students take all their classes in a high- or a low-ability group. Here, however, it will be used in the second, more narrow sense to refer to differentiated curricula for secondary students. College preparatory, vocational, and general tracks are typical. (Eyler, Cook, & Ward, 1983)

Like Eyler and her colleagues, most researchers use the term tracking in the narrower sense to refer to high school curricular programs.

Ability grouping is also different from *curricular differentiation.* A differentiated curriculum provides different courses of study for same-age children with different learning needs and preferences. Programs of bilingual education and special education, for example, involve curricular differentiation. It is important to note that a school may have curricular differentiation without ability grouping. For example, the general and vocational programs in a high school are different curricular programs, but the students who follow them usually score at about the same level on tests of school aptitude. It is also important to note that ability grouping often occurs without curricular differentiation. That is, schools sometimes prescribe the same course of study for high, middle, and low groups.

Extent of Grouping in Schools

Ability grouping is a pervasive feature in elementary and secondary schools in the United States today. McPartland, Coldiron, and Braddock (1987) have provided conclusive evidence on this point. Their data came from the National Assessment of Educational Progress and from a comprehensive survey of schools in the state of Pennsylvania. They found that ability grouping increases with grade level. About 50 percent of schools they surveyed had mixed-ability classes in grade 1, but only 10 percent of schools had mixed-ability classes in all subjects by grade 7. That is, more than 90 percent of the schools used between-class ability grouping for all or some school subjects by the junior high grades.

When within-class ability grouping is added to the total picture, ability grouping starts to seem like a universal feature of U.S. education. McPartland and his colleagues found, for example, that within-class ability grouping is used in well over 90 percent of schools in the primary grades and between 85 percent and 90 percent of schools in the upper elementary grades. The analysis by McPartland and his associates suggests, therefore, that almost all schools group children homogeneously for some or all of their work, either within classes or in separate classrooms, and that schools use this homogeneous ability grouping at every grade level.

Early Research Reviews

Research on ability grouping has a long history. Worlton (1928) conducted one of the first studies of its effects in Salt Lake City, Utah. At the beginning of the school year, he identified two equivalent groups of elementary school children. He arranged for assignment of pupils in one group by ability into homogeneous classes and pupils in the other group to mixed-ability classes. At the end of the school year, Worlton found that children from the homogeneous classes outperformed those from the mixed classes by about two months on a grade-equivalent scale. Hundreds of other researchers carried out similar experiments in the years that followed.

Dozens of reviewers tried to draw conclusions from the accumulated studies, but they did not all reach the same conclusions. During the four decades from the 1930s through the 1960s, in fact, they painted at least four pictures of research results on grouping. The pictures differed as much as the decades that produced them.

The first picture of the research comes from the late 1920s, when the mental testing movement was at its height in U.S. education. Mental tests had just proved their value in the evaluation of recruits during World War I, and many mental testers expected even greater benefits from the use of tests for selection and placement of children in schools. Reviewers of the time shared the optimism about testing and, not surprisingly, had positive things to say about ability grouping. Their most important conclusions, repeated in review after review in the early 1930s, was that grouping led to better school outcomes when ability groups worked with methods and materials that suited their aptitude levels (e.g., Miller & Otto, 1930; Turney, 1931). The reviewers also noted that grouping programs had little or no effect when groups at all levels used the same methods and materials.

As a second picture, in the 1930s John Dewey's philosophy of progressive education became an important influence on U.S. schools, and with its rise enthusiasm about grouping began to fade. Progressive educators held that the social spirit of the classroom did as much for children as formal instruction did, and they criticized grouping programs both for fostering undemocratic feelings in children and for promoting traditional content teaching. Their reviews (e.g., Keliher, 1931) focused on negative effects of grouping. They reported that students learned less and also declined in self-concept and leadership skills in grouped classes.

Our third picture occurred during the 1950s, when the pendulum of opinion about grouping began to swing back. The United States and the Soviet Union were fighting a Cold War for scientific and technological supremacy, and U.S. schools were expected to contribute to the struggle by emphasizing academic and scientific excellence. Reviewers did their part by reexamining research results on grouping. The new reviews (e.g., Goldberg, 1958; Ekstrom, 1961; Passow, 1958) reported that higher aptitude youngsters made notable gains when taught in special enriched and accelerated classes. The reviewers reported that accelerated and enriched classes helped talented children academically and seemed to have no detrimental effects on their social and emotional adjustment.

Finally, the civil rights movement of the 1960s inspired researchers to think more deeply about questions of educational equity and led ultimately to still another reevaluation of grouping research. A number of reviewers reported seeing a different pattern in newer research results on grouping (e.g., Eash, 1961; Findley & Bryan, 1971; Heathers, 1969). According to these reviewers, newer studies suggested that no one benefits from ability grouping and that children in the middle and lower groups clearly suffer a loss in achievement, academic motivation, and self-esteem.

Four educational eras thus produced four pictures of grouping effects. Although the pictures fit their times, they do not fit together. Reviewers saw one thing in one era and something entirely different in the next era. Instead of bringing four decades of research into focus, therefore, the reviews provide only a kaleidoscope of views of grouping.

New Research Approaches

Frustrated by these inconclusive reviews, researchers set out in three new directions. One group borrowed ethnographic tools from anthropology and carried out observational studies. Another group armed itself with the tools of survey research and carried out regression studies on data from national educational surveys. Still another group used the newly developed technique of meta-analysis to carry out quantitative analyses of the accumulated literature on ability grouping.

Ethnographic Studies of Tracking

Researchers using ethnographic methods observed teacher and student behaviors in upper and lower tracks and drew conclusions from their comparisons. The earliest ethnographic studies examined British streamed schools (Ball, 1981; Hargreaves, 1967; Lacey, 1970), but later influential studies focused on U.S. schools and classes (Oakes, 1985; Page, 1991; Rosenbaum, 1976). Although some ethnographic studies include quantitative data, most provide only qualitative descriptions of grouped classes based on observations and interviews. As Gamoran and Berends (1987) pointed out, these ethnographic studies were designed to uncover the subjective meaning of the events and patterns of life in schools.

Perhaps the best known example of ethnographic research on tracking is that reported by Oakes (1985) in her book *Keeping Track.* Oakes and her co-workers made their observations for a project that John Goodlad described in his 1984 book *A Place Called School.* They observed in 299 English and math classes (75 high-track, 85 average-track, 64 low-track, and 75 heterogeneous classes) in a national sample of 25 junior and senior high schools. The observations covered course content, quality of instruction, classroom climate, and student attitudes in each of the classes.

Oakes saw a pattern in the results. Instruction seemed to be better in the higher tracks. For example, in English classes, the percentage of time spent on instruction was 81 for the high track and 75 for the low track; in math classes, percentage of time spent on instruction was 81 for the high track and 78 for the low track. In English classes, percentage of time off task was 2 for the high track and 4 for the low; in math classes, it was 1 for the high track and 4 for the low. In all, more time was spent on instruction and less time was spent off task in the high tracks.

Oakes also reported that there were curricular differences in high- and low-track classes. For example, low-track classes seemed to cover less demanding topics, whereas high-track classes covered more complex material. High-track teachers also seemed to encourage competent and autonomous thinking, whereas low-track teachers stressed low-level skills and conformity to rules and expectations. Oakes did not provide quantitative data to support these observations, however.

Gamoran and Berends (1987) summarized the main results from the ethnographic studies of Oakes and others. They reported that the ethnographers reached four main conclusions: (1) Instruction is conceptually simplified and proceeds more slowly in lower tracks; (2) more experienced teachers and those regarded as more successful seem to be disproportionately assigned to the higher tracks; (3) teachers view high-track students more positively and low-track students more negatively; (4) most of a student's friends are found in the same track.

Other researchers have argued, however, that the evidence does not support these conclusions. First of all, they point out that when quantified, the differences found by ethnographers are tiny (Gamoran & Berends, 1987). The difference of 2 or 3 percent in time on instruction or time off task, for example, is not large. It amounts to a difference of less than 10 minutes per day in time on instruction or off task for low- and high-track classes. Tracks thus appear to be much more alike than they are different.

Critics have also noted that ethnographic analyses do not disentangle the effects due to grouping and those due to student characteristics. Slavin (1990a) suggested that high- and low-aptitude students might differ as much or more in ungrouped situations as they do in grouped ones. Noting that time on task is often found to be lower in low-track classes, for example, he asks: "Might it be that low-achieving students are more likely to be off-task no matter where they are?" (p. 505). Ethnographers usually do not provide data from untracked control classes, and without such control data it is impossible to disentangle effects of the educational treatment from students characteristics.

Finally, critics have suggested that ethnographers may be misinterpreting some of their observations. Slavin makes the following point:

> On the quality of instruction issue, the variables typically found to differentiate high- and low-track classes are ones that cannot be separated from the nature of the students themselves. For example, many studies find that there is less content covered in low-track classes. But is this by its nature an indication of low quality? Might it be that low-track classes need a slower pace of instruction? The whole idea of ability grouping is to provide students with a level and pace of instruction appropriate to their different needs. (Slavin, 1990a, p. 505)

That is, the teacher and curricular differences described by Oakes may represent appropriate responses to the different educational and emotional needs of different schoolchildren.

Although these ethnographic studies raise provocative questions about ability grouping, they do not provide real answers. The studies are simply too casual. Ethnographers deal too much with surface differences and too little with underlying causality. They observe differences between upper and lower groups, but without quantification and control conditions they cannot tell what causes the observed differences nor can they tell how the differences can be reduced. For definitive results, studies must include controls and quantification.

Regression Studies of Tracking

Regression studies have used quantification and statistical control to throw more light on underlying causes. Coleman's massive Equality of Educational Opportunity Survey (EEOS) was the initial stimulus for these studies (Coleman et al., 1966). One key finding of the survey was that achievement varies far more within schools than between schools. This finding led sociologically oriented researchers to wonder whether within-school tracking might be the major cause of this within-school variation. To find out, the researchers carried out regression analyses of survey data modeled on Coleman's analysis.

A study by Jencks and his colleagues illustrates the survey approach (Jencks, 1972). To investigate the effects of high school tracking, the researchers looked at 91 predominantly white comprehensive high schools throughout the United States that had tested their students for Project Talent in the ninth grade and had retested them in the twelfth grade. They found that students who reported that they were in the college preparatory curriculum averaged slightly higher on grade 12 tests than did students of comparable aptitude in other tracks.

Regression studies of survey data on tracking address two main questions. First, what factors influence students to enroll in different curricular tracks? Survey researchers have been especially interested in determining whether academic ability or socioeconomic status plays a more important role in track placement. Second, how much do curricular tracks influence students? Researchers explored the influence of tracks on such educational outcomes as high school achievement, postsecondary attainment, and self-esteem.

Jencks (1972) wrote one of the best summaries of results on the first question. He drew four main conclusions about determinants of track placement:

- Personal preference is the most important determinant. The Equality of Educational Opportunity Survey, for example, found that 85 percent of all high school seniors are in the curriculum they want to be in (Coleman et al., 1966).
- After personal preference, the next most important determinant of curriculum placement seems to be academic ability. Jencks reported that the correlation between test scores and curriculum assignment is around .50.
- Social class does not seem to play an important role in high school curriculum placement, except insofar as it influences test scores.
- Race plays an even smaller role in track placement. Blacks have a *higher* probability of ending up in the college preparatory track than do whites of equivalent aptitude and socioeconomic status.

The picture has not changed in the years since Jencks wrote his review. Garet and DeLany

(1988) drew similar conclusions from their review of the four most influential studies of student placement into curricular tracks (Alexander, Cook, & McDill, 1978; Hauser, Sewell, & Alwin, 1976; Heyns, 1974; Rosenbaum, 1980). Gamoran and Mare (1989) also drew similar conclusions from these studies and from their own analysis of High School and Beyond data.

The effects of track placement on student achievement are less clear. Gamoran and Berends (1987) reviewed 16 national or statewide studies with relevant data. Some of the studies found that track membership accounted for a significant amount of variation in test scores; others found that it accounted for a nonsignificant amount. The effects of tracking on educational attainment after high school are clearer. Gamoran and Berends reported that all studies find that students who are in college preparatory programs are more likely to enroll in college than are equally able students from the general and nonacademic tracks. Gamoran and Berends did not report any other consistent findings from national surveys of high school students.

It is possible to be more precise about the size of these tracking effects (J. Kulik, 1994). It should be noted, first of all, that test scores of high school students completing academic and nonacademic programs are clearly different. Academic students on the average score at the 71st percentile on standardized achievement tests given at the end of high school (or about 0.56 standard deviations above the mean); nonacademic students score on the average at the 33rd percentile (or about 0.44 standard deviations below the mean). The achievement gap at high school graduation is therefore equivalent to about 1.0 standard deviation.

Not all of this gap is an effect of tracking. Regression analyses show that the most important cause of the achievement gap is self-selection (J. Kulik, 1994). The results suggest that if similar students selected academic and nonacademic programs, the gap would be about 0.2 standard deviation. Thus, 80 percent of the difference in test scores of academic and nonacademic students at the end of high school is due to the difference in aptitude of the students who enter the programs. If nonacademic students were similar to academic students in aptitude and took the same number of advanced courses in core subjects, the achievement gap between academic and vocational students would be no more than 0.1 standard deviations. Thus, an additional 10 percent of the achievement gap is due to the different number of advanced courses taken by academic and vocational students. The remaining 10 percent of the gap is due to other curricular and program factors.

The educational attainments of academic and nonacademic students are also clearly different (J. Kulik, 1994). About 75 percent of students from academic programs and about 25 percent of students from nonacademic programs enter college. The average student from a high school academic program completes about two years of college; the average student from a nonacademic program completes only a few months. The difference between academic and nonacademic students is therefore substantial, and regression results suggest that even if similar students enrolled in academic and nonacademic programs, they would still differ in how much schooling they complete.

Slavin (1990a) discussed the problems with drawing conclusions from regression analyses, and concluded that these problems are severe. He believes, first of all, that the statistical controls in the regression analyses are inadequate:

> One problem is statistical; when groups are very different on a covariate, the covariate does not adequately "control" for group differences. To the degree that the covariate has a reliability less than 1.0, it tends to undercontrol for group differences, but even small differences in within-group slopes of the covariate on the dependent measure can cause major errors when there are large group differences (see Reichardt, 1979). When comparing high- to low-ability groups, pretest or covariate differences of one to two standard deviations are typical. No statistician on earth would expect that analysis of covariance or regression could adequately control for such large differences. (p. 506)

Another problem with regression analyses of data from tracked schools is the failure to measure and control for all differences between high tracks and low tracks. Slavin (1990a) again describes the problem clearly:

> In addition, the logic of such comparisons is simply difficult to accept. Do students at Harvard learn more than those at East Overshoe State, controlling for SAT scores and high school grades? Are the San Francisco Forty-Niners better than the Palo Alto High School football team, controlling for height, weight, speed, and age? Such questions fall into the realm of the unknowable. Comparing the achievement gains of students in existing high versus low tracks is not so different. Many factors go into track placement—achievement, behavior, attitudes, motivation, prior course selection, and so on—and each of these is likely to affect posttest achievement regardless of track placement. No study will ever adequately control for all these factors, and as a result studies comparing high to low track will always tend to show higher achievement for the high track students. (p. 506)

Beyond these methodological problems lies a more fundamental conceptual difficulty. Writers who cite regression results in arguments against tracking miss the point. Regression analyses at best show what would happen to certain students in a track system if they were moved to another track. The analyses do not show what would happen if a track system were eliminated and replaced by something different. Effectiveness might be *greater or less* in an untracked system than in any of the tracks in a multitrack system. The most serious problem with these regression analyses, therefore, is their omission of data from schools and classes that are untracked. Leaving control data out of the tracking equations is a serious error. Without such data, the equations cannot be solved, and the important questions about tracking effects cannot be answered.

Meta-analytic Studies of Ability Grouping

The meta-analytic evidence on grouping comes from studies with both experimental and control groups. Meta-analysts have used quantitative methods to analyze the results of such studies in order to determine the nature and size of grouping effects. Meta-analytic methodology itself was first described in 1976 by Gene V. Glass in his presidential address to the American Educational Research Association. Glass used the term *meta-analysis* to refer to the analysis of analyses or, more formally, the application of quantitative statistics to the collected results of a large number of independent studies for the purpose of integrating the findings. To carry out a *meta-analysis,* a reviewer usually (1) finds as many studies as possible of an issue through an objective search of the literature; (2) codes the characteristics of these studies; (3) expresses the results of each study on a common metric; and (4) uses statistical methods to describe relationships between study characteristics and outcomes.

Meta-analysts express treatment effects in studies as *effect sizes,* which are in standard deviation units. In principle, the computation of effect sizes is simple. A reviewer simply finds the difference between an experimental group's gain on an outcome measure and a control group's gain or loss. The reviewer then divides this difference by an estimate of the population standard deviation on the measure. The effect size is thus simply a standardized measure of the treatment effect. An effect size is positive when there is a gain from the treatment and negative when there is a loss. An effect size is large when its absolute value is around 0.8, medium when around 0.5, and small when around 0.2.

Among the most comprehensive meta-analytic investigations of grouping are those carried out by our research group at the University of Michigan (e.g., C.-L. Kulik & J. Kulik, 1982, 1984; J. Kulik & C.-L. Kulik, 1984, 1987, 1991, 1992) and by Robert Slavin at Johns Hopkins University (e.g., Slavin, 1987, 1990b). These meta-analyses have shown that different kinds of programs produce different effects. Some grouping programs have little or no effect on students, other programs have large effects, and still other programs have moderate effects. The key distinction is among (1) programs in which all ability groups follow the same curriculum; (2) programs that make curricular adjustments for the special needs of highly talented learners; and (3) programs in which all groups follow curricula adjusted to background and ability.

Grouping without curricular adjustment. In 1919 Detroit became the first large U.S. city to introduce into its schools a formal plan of ability grouping (Courtis, 1925). The Detroit plan called for intelligence testing of all schoolchildren at the start of Grade 1 and then placement of children into X, Y, and Z groups on the basis of test results. The top 20 percent went to the X classes, the middle 60 percent to Y classes, and the bottom 20 pecent to Z classes. Standard materials and methods were used in all classes, and all classes covered material at the same grade level.

Many school systems followed the Detroit model and instituted their own plans of multilevel grouping. Some developed comprehensive XYZ plans, in which the groups remained separate for the whole day. Other schools used single-subject grouping. Few of the plans relied as much as the Detroit plan on intelligence tests for initial placements, and few separated students at such an early age. Most plans, however, were like the Detroit plan in their basic goal. They were designed to make the teacher's job easier by reducing pupil variation in their classes, but they were not used as a way of providing a highly differentiated curriculum to different ability groups.

The Michigan meta-analyses covered 22 studies of comprehensive XYZ programs and 29 studies of single-subject XYZ grouping (J. Kulik, 1992). The Johns Hopkins analyses covered 30 studies of comprehensive XYZ grouping and 19 studies of single-subject XYZ grouping (Slavin, 1987, 1990b). Slavin used the term *ability-based class assignment* for XYZ grouping and the term *single-subject grouping* for single-subject XYZ grouping.

The Michigan meta-analyses found that lower and middle aptitude students learn about the same amount in grouped and mixed classes. Middle and lower aptitude students who gain about 1.0 years on a grade-equivalent scale after a year in a mixed class would also gain about 1.0 years when taught in homogeneous classes. The Michigan meta-analysis also showed that XYZ grouping has a slight positive effect on the achievement of higher aptitude students. A higher aptitude student who gains 1.0 years on a grade-equivalent scale after a year in a mixed class would gain 1.1 years in a homogeneous class.

The Johns Hopkins results are similar. Like us, Slavin found no effects of grouping on middle and lower aptitude students, but unlike us, he was unable to find a significant effect of XYZ grouping on higher aptitude students. He found that a student who gains 1.0 years on a grade-equivalent scale after a year in a mixed-ability class would also gain 1.0 years if taught in a homogeneous class, and this result is equally true for higher, middle, and lower aptitude students.

Why are the effects of XYZ grouping on student achievement so small? Perhaps curriculum is a key determinant of learning outcomes, and XYZ programs do not prescribe different curricular materials for the stratified classes. For example, children in the high group in a grade 5 program may be ready for work at the sixth-grade level; children in the middle group are usually ready for work at the fifth-grade level; and children in the low group may need remedial help to cover fifth-grade material. Yet all groups work with the same materials and follow the same course of study in most XYZ programs; they are programs of differential placement but not differential treatment.

Some of the studies of comprehensive XYZ classes also examined effect of grouping on student self-esteem. The Michigan meta-analyses covered results from 13 such studies (J. Kulik, 1992). XYZ classes appeared to have a small effect on student self-esteem. On average, self-esteem scores went up slightly for low-aptitude learners in XYZ programs and went down slightly for high-aptitude learners. Thus, brighter children appear to lose a little of their self-assurance when they are put into classes with equally talented children, whereas slower children gain a little in self-confidence when they are taught in classes with other slower learners.

How can we explain these effects on self-esteem? Social factors probably have a direct influence on a child's self-image. Children judge themselves as inferior when they fail on tasks on which peers succeed, and they judge themselves as superior when they excel on tasks on which others fail. Social comparison theory thus predicts a drop in self-esteem for high-achieving students when placed in a homogeneous group of high achievers, and it predicts a rise in self-esteem of low achievers when placed in a group of slow learners. The evidence supports these predictions.

It should also be noted that the evidence does not support the predictions of labeling, or stigma, theory. Labeling theory says that self-esteem will rise for children who are put into a group identified as high-ability, and self-esteem will fall for children in a group identified as low-ability. In fact, just the opposite happens. Labels are apparently a less powerful influence on self-conceptions than the conclusions that people draw from their own comparisons with those around them.

Curricular adjustment for high-aptitude learners. U.S. education has a long tradition of providing special classes for children whose educational needs differ from those of the majority. Special classes have been formed of children who are physically handicapped, emotionally or socially maladjusted, lacking in proficiency in English, and so on. One of the longest traditions is providing special classes for gifted and talented children.

The first classes devised especially for gifted and talented children were accelerated ones (Tannenbaum, 1958). The Cambridge Double Track Plan of 1891 put bright children into special classes that covered the work of six years in four, and the special-progress classes of New York City, originally established in 1900, allowed pupils to complete the work of three years in two. The basic idea of educational acceleration is to modify a school program so that students complete it at an earlier age or in less time than is usual.

In the early years of this century, accelerated programs were the major method by which schools met the special needs of their high-aptitude students. But by the 1920s some educators were concerned that accelerated programs did not meet the emotional and social needs of gifted youngsters. To many of them, enriched classes of the sort that Leta Hollingworth had set up in the city schools of New York City in 1916 seemed an attractive alternative to acceleration. In these classes, children did not simply follow a telescoped regular curriculum. Instead, they spent about half of their school hours working on the prescribed curriculum, and about half pursuing enriching activities. In classes that Hollingworth set up for 7- to 9-year-olds, for example, enrichment activities included conversational French; the study of biography; study of the history of civilization; and a good deal of extra work in science, mathematics, English composition, and music (Gray & Hollingworth, 1931).

The Michigan meta-analyses covered 23 studies of accelerated classes for high-aptitude learners (J. Kulik, 1992). The studies compared the achievement of equivalent students in accelerated classes and nonaccelerated control classes. All of the studies examined moderate acceleration of a whole class of students rather than acceleration of individual children. In each of the comparisons involving students who were initially equivalent in age and intelligence, the students in accelerated classes outperformed the students in nonaccelerated classes. In the typical study, the average superiority for the students in accelerated classes was nearly one year on a grade-equivalent scale of a standardized achievement test.

The Michigan meta-analyses also covered 25 studies of enriched classes for talented students. Twenty-two of the 25 studies found that talented students achieved more when they were taught in enriched rather than regular mixed-ability classes. In the average study, students in the enriched classes outperformed equivalent students in mixed classes by about 4 to 5 months. Children receiving enriched instruction gained 1.4 to 1.5 years on a grade-equivalent scale in the same period during which equivalent control children gained only 1.0 year.

The strong effects of accelerated and enriched classes are probably due to curricular differentiation. In XYZ classes, curricular adjustment is minimal; in accelerated and enriched classes, it is maximal. In these classes, teachers introduce a good deal of above-grade-level material for students who are willing and able to meet the challenge. The test scores show the results. High-aptitude students benefit from taking these advanced classes, and they suffer when they are held back in regular classes.

Curricular adjustment for all students. Unlike XYZ plans, programs of *cross-grade* grouping provide different curricula for children at different ability levels. The best known approach to cross-grade grouping is the Joplin plan, which was first used during the 1950s for reading instruction in the Joplin, Missouri, elementary schools. During the hour reserved for reading in the Joplin schools, children in grades 4, 5, and 6 broke into nine different groups that were reading at anything from the grade 2 to grade 9 level. The children went to their reading classes without regard to their regular grade placement, and returned to their regular age-graded classrooms at the end of the hour. Almost all formal evaluations of cross-grade grouping involve the Joplin plan for reading instruction in elementary schools.

Within-class grouping programs also provide different curricula for children at different ability levels. The most popular model for within-class grouping was developed in the 1950s for teaching arithmetic in elementary schools. A teacher following the model would use test scores and school records to divide the class into three groups for arithmetic lessons, and would use textbook material from several grade levels to instruct the groups. The high group in Grade 6, for example, would use texts from Grades 6, 7, and 8; the middle group would use texts from grades 5, 6, and 7; and the low group would use texts from grades 4, 5, and 6. The teacher would present material to one group for approximately 15 minutes before moving on to another group. Other approaches to within-class grouping are possible, but almost all controlled evaluations examine within-class programs that follow this model.

Both the Michigan and Johns Hopkins meta-analyses found that cross-grade and within-class programs in elementary and middle schools usually produce positive results (J. Kulik, 1992; Slavin, 1987). The Michigan analysis, for example, covered 14 studies of cross-grade grouping and 11 studies of within-class grouping. More than 80 percent of the studies of each type reported positive results. The average gain attributable to cross-grade or within-class grouping was between 2 and 3 months on a grade equivalent scale. The typical pupil in a mixed-ability class might gain 1.0 years on a grade-equivalent scale in one year, whereas the typical pupil in a cross-grade or within-class program would gain 1.2 to 1.3 years. Effects were similar for high-, middle-, and low-aptitude pupils.

Cross-grade and within-class programs appear to work because they provide different curricula for pupils with different aptitude. In cross-grade programs, students move up or down grades to ensure a match between their reading ability and their reading instruction. In within-class programs, teachers divide students into ability groups so that all children can work on arithmetic materials for which they are properly prepared. Curriculum varies with student aptitude in both cross-grade and within-class programs. The programs thus differ in an important respect from most programs of XYZ grouping.

Discussion and Conclusions

The older reviews of the research literature may serve as a source of hypotheses about grouping effects, but the reviews are not very helpful as guides to theory or practice. The reviews are not only nonquantitative and imprecise, but more important, they are subjective and unreliable. Conclusions vary from one review to another, and the reviews seem to reflect the educational philosophies of their times as much as they reflect the research findings.

Ethnographic studies of grouping are no more enlightening. Ethnographers have reported that in lower track classes the curriculum is debased, teachers are inexperienced, and instruction is poor; but careful scrutiny of the ethnographic evidence provides little support for such interpretations. When ethnographers have quantified their observations, for example, differences between instruction in upper and lower track classes appear to be small. The interpretation of the differences also is unclear. The reported differences between upper and lower track classes may simply indicate that teachers try to adjust the pace of their instruction to the preparation of their students.

Regression analyses show that the achievement gap between students in upper and lower tracks is due mostly to student self-selection. If the same types of students enrolled in collegiate and noncollegiate tracks at the beginning of high school, graduates of the two programs would differ very little in test scores at the end of high school. A second, less important factor that may contribute to the achievement gap is the different number of advanced courses in core subjects taken by students in collegiate and noncollegiate tracks. A third factor may be a difference in the way that the same courses are taught for collegiate and noncollegiate students. Regression analyses do not provide conclusive evidence on the second and third factors, however. The controls for self-selection in these analyses are not adequate, and so conclusions from regression analyses are tentative at best.

Meta-analytic studies are currently the only dependable guide to the effects of grouping on children. These meta-analyses show that effects depend on both the type of student and the type of grouping that is involved. Different types of programs have different effects on different students.

The meta-analyses show, first of all, that higher aptitude students benefit academically from ability grouping. The academic benefits are positive but usually small when the grouping is done as a part of a broader program for students of all abilities. For example, XYZ classes, in which little or no effort is made to adjust curriculum to group ability level, raise the test scores of higher ability students by about 0.1 standard deviations. Within-class and cross-grade programs, which entail curricular adjustment, boost test scores of higher aptitude students by about 0.2 to 0.3 standard deviations.

Benefits for higher aptitude students are usually largest in special accelerated and enriched classes. Classes in which talented children cover four grades in three years, for example, boost achievement levels a good deal. Test scores of children accelerated in this fashion are about one year higher on a grade-equivalent scale than if the children were not accelerated. Enriched classes, in which students have a varied educational experience, boost student achievement by more moderate amounts. The average gain on a grade-equivalent scale is 4 months in a typical program. A gain of this size is still impressive, given that some enriched classes spend as much as half their time on cultural material (e.g., foreign languages and music) not covered on standard achievement tests.

Grouping programs usually have smaller effects on middle and lower aptitude learners. XYZ classes, for example, have virtually no effect on the achievement of such students. Test scores of middle and lower aptitude students learning in XYZ classes are indistinguishable from those of similar students in mixed-ability classes. Cross-grade and within-class programs, however, usually raise test scores of middle and lower aptitude pupils by between 0.2 and 0.3 standard deviations. The adjustment of curriculum to pupil ability in within-class and cross-grade programs may be the key to their effectiveness.

Evidence on noncognitive outcomes of grouping is less clear. Despite their importance, noncognitive instructional outcomes are not often studied by educational researchers, and only tentative conclusions can be drawn. One of these conclusions is that grouping programs usually have only small effects on student self-esteem. The programs certainly do not lead talented students to become self-satisfied and smug, nor do they cause a precipitous drop in the self-esteem of lower aptitude students. If anything, grouping programs push children slightly in the opposite direction; quick learners lose a little of their self-assurance, and slower learners gain some badly needed self-confidence.

These conclusions are obviously quite different from the well-known conclusions about grouping reached by Oakes (1985) in her book *Keeping Track*. According to Oakes, students in the top tracks gain nothing from grouping, and other students suffer clear and consistent disadvantages, including loss of academic ground, self-esteem, and ambition. Oakes also believed that tracking is unfair to students because it denies them their right to a common curriculum. She therefore called for the detracking of American schools. Detracked schools would provide the same curriculum to all and would not provide special educational opportunities to any on the basis of ability, achievement, or interests.

Oakes's conclusions, however, were based on her own selective and idiosyncratic review of older summaries of the literature and on her uncontrolled classroom observations. Objective analysis of findings from controlled studies provides no support for her speculations. Whereas Oakes believed that grouping programs are unnecessary, ineffective, and unfair, we conclude that the opposite is true. U.S. education would be harmed by the elimination of programs that provide instruction that is adapted to children's different instructional needs.

The effects of detracking would vary according to the type of grouping program that was eliminated. If typical XYZ classes were eliminated from all schools, the achievement level of the country's brightest students would fall slightly, but the effects would not be noticeable on most other students. If the grouping programs that were eliminated were ones that actually adjusted methods and materials to student aptitude, the damage to student achievement would be greater, and the effects would be felt more broadly. Both higher and lower aptitude students would suffer academically from such detracking. But the damage would be truly profound if, in the name of detracking, schools eliminated enriched and accelerated classes for their brightest learners. The achievement level of such students would fall dramatically if they were required to move at the common pace. No one can be certain that there would be a way to repair the harm that would be done.

REFERENCES

Alexander, K. L., Cook, M. A., & McDill, E. L. (1978). Curriculum tracking and educational stratification. *American Sociological Review, 43,* 47–66.

Ball, S. J. (1981). *Beachside comprehensive: A case-study of secondary school.* New York: Cambridge University Press.

Coleman, J., Campbell, E., Hobson, C., McPartland, J., Mood, A., Wienfield, F., & York, R. (1966). *Equality of educational opportunity.* Washington, DC: U.S. Government Printing Office.

Courtis. S. A. (1925). Ability-grouping in Detroit schools. In G. M. Whipple (Ed.), *The ability grouping of pupils,* 35th Yearbook of the National Society for the Study of Education (Part I, pp. 44–47). Bloomington, IL: Public School Publishing.

Eash, M. J. (1961). Grouping: What have we learned? *Educational Leadership, 18,* 429–434.

Ekstrom, R. B. (1961). Experimental studies of homogeneous grouping: A critical review. *School Review, 69,* 216–226.

Eyler, J., Cook, V. J., & Ward, L. E. (1983) Resegregation: Segregation within desegregated schools. In C. Rossell & W. D. Hawley (Eds.), *The consequences of school desegregation.* Philadelphia: Temple University Press.

Findley, W. G., & Bryan, M. (1971). *Ability grouping: 1970 status, impact, and alternatives.* Athens: Center for Educational Improvement, University of Georgia. (ERIC Document Reproduction Service No. Ed 060-595)

Gamoran, A., & Mare, R. D. (1989). Secondary school tracking and educational inequality: Compensation, reinforcement, or neutrality. *American Journal of Sociology, 94,* 146–183.

Gamoran, G., & Berends, M. (1987). The effects of stratification in secondary schools: Synthesis of survey and ethnographic research. *Review of Educational Research, 57,* 415–435.

Garet, M. S., & DeLany, B. (1988). Student, courses, and stratification. *Sociology of Education, 61,* 61–77.

Glass, G. V. (1976). Primary, secondary, and meta-analysis of research. *Educational Researcher, 5,* 3–8.

Goldberg, M. L. (1958). Recent research on the talented. *Teachers College Record, 60,* 150–163.

Good, C. V. (1973). *Dictionary of education* (3rd ed.). New York: McGraw-Hill.

Goodlad, J. I. (1984). *A place called school.* New York: McGraw-Hill.

Gray, H. A., & Hollingworth, L. S. (1931). The

achievement of gifted children enrolled and not enrolled in special opportunity classes. *Journal of Educational Research, 24,* 255–261.

Hargreaves, D. H. (1967). *Social relations in a secondary school.* London: Tinling.

Hauser, R. M., Sewell, W. H., & Alwin, D. F. (1976). High school effect on achievement. In W. H. Sewell, R. M. Hauser, & D. Featherman (Eds.), *Schooling and achievement in American society.* New York: Academic Press.

Heathers, G. (1969). Grouping. In R. Ebel (Ed.), *Encyclopedia of educational research* (4th ed., pp. 559–570). New York: Macmillan.

Heyns, B. (1974). Social selection and stratification within schools. *American Journal of Sociology,* 79, 1434–1451.

Jencks, C. (1972). *Inequality.* New York: Basic Books.

Keliher, A. C. (1931). *A critical study of homogeneous grouping.* New York: Bureau of Publications, Teachers College, Columbia University.

Kulik, C.-L. C., & Kulik, J. A. (1982). Effects of ability grouping on secondary school students: A meta-analysis of evaluation findings. *American Educational Research Journal, 19,* 415–428.

Kulik, C.-L. C., & Kulik, J. A. (1984, August). *Effects of ability grouping on elementary school pupils: A meta-analysis.* Paper presented at the annual meeting of the American Psychological Association, Toronto. (ERIC Document Reproduction Service No. ED 255 329)

Kulik, J. A. (1992). *An analysis of the research on ability grouping: Historical and contemporary perspectives.* Monograph of the National Research Center on the Gifted and Talented, No. 9204. Storrs: University of Connecticut.

Kulik, J. A. (1994). *High school vocational education and curricular tracking.* Monograph prepared for the National Assessment of Vocational Education. Ann Arbor: Center for Research on Learning and Teaching, University of Michigan.

Kulik, J. A., & Kulik, C.-L. C. (1984). Effects of accelerated instruction on students. *Review of Educational Research, 54,* 409–426.

Kulik, J. A., & Kulik, C.-L. C. (1987). Effects of ability grouping on student achievement. *Equity and Excellence, 23,* 22–30.

Kulik, J. A., & Kulik, C.-L. C. (1991). Ability grouping and gifted students. In N. Colangelo & G. A. Davis (Eds.), *Handbook of gifted education* (pp. 178–196). Boston: MA: Allyn and Bacon.

Kulik, J. A., & Kulik, C.-L. C. (1992). Meta-analytic findings on grouping programs. *Gifted Child Quarterly, 36,* 73–77.

Lacey, C. (1970). *Hightown grammar.* Manchester, England: Manchester University Press.

McPartland, J. M., Coldiron, J. R., & Braddock, J. H. (1987). *School structures and classroom practices in elementary, middle, and secondary schools.* Baltimore, MD: Center for Research on Elementary and Middle Schools, Johns Hopkins University. (ERIC Document Reproduction Service No. ED 291 703)

Miller, W. S., & Otto, H. J. (1930). Analysis of experimental studies in homogeneous grouping. *Journal of Educational Research, 21,* 95–102.

Oakes, J. (1985). *Keeping track: How schools structure inequality.* New Haven: Yale University.

Page, R. N. (1991). *Lower-track classrooms: A curricular and cultural perspective.* New York: Teachers College Press.

Passow, A. H. (1958). Enrichment of education for the gifted. In N. Henry (Ed.), *Education for the gifted,* 57th Yearbook of the National Society for the Study of Education (Part II, pp. 193–221). Chicago: University of Chicago Press.

Rosenbaum, J. E. (1976). *Making inequality.* New York: Wiley.

Rosenbaum, J. E. (1980). Track misperceptions and frustrated college plans: An analysis of the effects of tracks and track perceptions in the National Longitudinal Survey. *Sociology of Education, 53,* 74–88.

Singal, D. J. (1991, November). The other crisis in American education. *The Atlantic Monthly, 268,* 59–74.

Slavin, R. E. (1987). Ability grouping and student achievement in elementary schools: A best evidence synthesis. *Review of Educational Research, 57,* 293–336.

Slavin, R. E. (1990a). Ability grouping in secondary schools: A response to Hallinan. *Review of Educational Research, 60,* 505–507.

Slavin, R. E. (1990b). Achievement effects of ability grouping in secondary schools: A best evidence synthesis. *Review of Educational Research, 60,* 471–499.

Tannenbaum, A. J. (1958). History of interest in the gifted. In N. Henry (Ed.), *Education for the gifted,* 57th Yearbook of the National Society for the Study of Education (Part II, pp. 21–38). Chicago: University of Chicago Press.

Turney, A. H. (1931). The status of ability grouping. *Educational Administration and Supervision, 17,* 110–127.

Worlton, J. T. (1928). The effect of homogeneous classification on the scholastic achievement of bright pupils. *Elementary School Journal, 28,* 336–345.

20

Cooperative Learning for Talented Students: Emergent Issues and Implications

ANN ROBINSON, *University of Arkansas at Little Rock*

In 1990, a debate between Robinson and Slavin appeared in the *Journal for the Education of the Gifted* on the use of cooperative learning with talented students. Prior to their debate, little attention was focused on talented learners in cooperative learning groups, other than to give advice to cooperative learning advocates for managing concerned parents of gifted children (Johnson & Johnson, 1991). The purposes of this chapter are to review the initial debate briefly, to examine recent additions to the research base on cooperative learning and talented students, and to identify emerging issues in the discussion.

A brief review of the Robinson and Slavin debate on cooperative learning and talented students sets the context for an update of the issues. As an advocate for cooperative learning, Slavin (1990a) linked ability grouping, specialized programs for gifted students, and cooperative learning. He questioned the effectiveness of gifted programs and stated a preference for accelerative rather than enrichment models. He criticized schools for engaging in whole-class ability grouping and suggested cooperative learning as an alternative and as an effective means of organizing heterogeneously grouped classes. According to Slavin (1990a), the benefits of cooperative learning for talented students included:

1. Opportunities to explain material to groupmates, which leads to increased retention of the material.
2. Gains in social outcomes such as self-esteem, friendships across ethnicities and with students with disabilities, liking of the subject, and working cooperatively with others. These positive outcomes were advanced for all learners rather than focused on talented students.

In addition to the benefits listed above, Slavin responded to two criticisms of cooperative learning for talented students. The criticisms were the use of high achievers as junior teachers and the concern that the pace of instruction would be slowed to the level of the lowest achieving members of the group. According to Slavin (1990a),

> Neither of these perceptions is accurate. In the forms of cooperative learning we have developed at Johns Hopkins University (Slavin, 1986), all students are learners and teachers; all have an equal responsibility to explain to others and discuss with others. The pace of instruction is similar to what it would be in a traditional class, so high achievers are exposed to the same material they would have otherwise been taught. (pp. 6–7)

Elsewhere, he stated that he believed the situation "in which gifted students who already know the material are used to teach others is atypical" (Slavin, 1990b, p. 28). Finally, he suggested that cooperative learning among relatively homogeneous groups of gifted children could be used in advanced and accelerated classes.

Robinson (1990a, 1990b; also 1991) approached the debate by examining the research base on cooperative learning for its applicability to talented students and by exploring the potential for abuse of cooperative learning in the education of talented students. The research base on cooperative learning was found to have several weaknesses with respect to talented students. These included the following:

1. *Lack of attention to talented students in the research literature on cooperative learning*: Studies rarely included identified gifted students overtly in the analyses.
2. *Poorly defined samples of high-achieving students:* Studies tended to define *high-achieving* as the top one-half or top one-third of the class.
3 *Weak treatment comparisons, which included traditional classrooms with a basic skills orientation or "individualistic" comparisons which prevented normal classroom interaction among students:* Cooperative learning was not compared with other types of small-group learning or with accelerative models recommended for talented students.
4. *Emphasis on low-level achievement outcome:* The majority of cooperative learning studies, particularly those of the Slavin-inspired models, relied on basic skills outcomes.
5. *Contradictory results for higher level outcomes:* In the 1990 review, few studies examined academic outcomes with high-level tasks.

In addition to weaknesses in the research base on cooperative learning, Robinson (1990a) raised two issues related to classroom practice. First, the use of high-achieving students as tutors or "explainers" prevented their being exposed to material new to them. Because time is a fixed resource in the classroom, if students are explaining material they already know or can learn in a fraction of the time a group takes to learn it, high-achieving students are restricted in their opportunities to learn. The second issue concerned expectations educators hold for academically talented students. If educators believe talented students are especially in need of socialization to group norms, they may justify cooperative learning on the basis of such misconceptions about bright children and youth. In addition, the expectation most confusing to high-achieving students was to make them feel responsible for group success, yet to blame them when they dominated groups to move toward task completion effectively and efficiently.

In summary, the initial debate centered primarily on the issues of benefits of cooperative learning for talented students, with Slavin (1990a) suggesting both academic and social benefits as likely outcomes and with Robinson (1990a) questioning the research support for such claims and commenting on cooperative learning practices likely to be deleterious for talented learners.

New Additions to the Knowledge Base on Talented Students

One of the criticisms leveled at cooperative learning advocates in the initial debate was that the research literature did not investigate the effects on talented students. The initial computer searches of the PSYCHINFO and ERIC databases resulted in fewer than five entries on the topic, only one of which presented data (Smith, Johnson, & Johnson, 1982). To investigate new additions to the knowledge base, these two data sources were searched again for the years beginning in 1989 and extending through July 1994. The combined searches resulted in 41 entries. The greatest proportion of these entries were position statements, debates, or reviews. Only six presented either quantitative or qualitative data on the use of cooperative learning with academically talented students. Thus, although interest in the topic of cooperative learning and talented students has been stimulated, that interest has yet to be translated into a healthy number of studies published in journals.

This review concentrates on two types of studies relevant to the knowledge base on cooperative learning and talented students: (1) studies that include identified gifted students in the sample and specifically investigate the effects of cooperative learning on talented students, and (2) general cooperative learning studies, which raise new issues that have implications for academically talented students.

Studies with Identified Gifted Students as the Population of Interest

Studies that include identified gifted students in the sample are exploratory and varied. At present, none represents a programmatic commitment to the investigation of cooperative learning as it relates to talented students. Thus, identifying trends or even organizing research into aggregates is premature. However, new studies do exist.

In terms of student outcomes, the studies tend to focus on attitudinal and social outcomes, although achievement also is monitored. For example, Elmore and Zenus (1994) examined the effects of cooperative learning on the self-esteem and achievement of gifted middle school students in an accelerated mathematics class. In a pretest–posttest one-shot design, the students exhibited statistically significant gains in both math achievement and self-esteem. The average math gains were quite small for the highest and middle achieving students, and just slightly larger for the lowest achievers. Unfortunately, as the authors state, it is not possible to attribute these gains to cooperative learning. The study did not make comparisons with other goal structures (competitive or individualistic), with other small group strategies, or with students who had not received cooperative learning. Anecdotally, the authors noted that both high and low achievers tended to withdraw from the groups. Although the participants were all high-achieving students in an accelerated class, the lowest (relative) achievers in the group tended toward passivity; the highest (relative) achievers were frustrated by the nonresponsive pace.

Since 1990, three classroom-based studies of cooperative learning with affective outcomes and talented students as the population of interest have appeared. In an ethnographic study, Stout (1993) examined "the 'hunch' that cooperative learning is a viable practice for use with gifted students in heterogeneous or homogeneous situations" (p. 2). She observed fourth through sixth graders working in homogeneous cooperative groups on science tasks in a districtwide pullout program for talented students, interviewed 23 of the observed students, and interviewed 12 home school teachers who reported that they used cooperative learning in their heterogeneous classrooms. Student behaviors were categorized by the author as inappropriate behavior, appropriate behavior, inappropriate conversation, and appropriate conversation. However, no systematic sampling plan appeared to be included, and the frequencies of behavior and conversation were not charted for analysis. Information from the teacher interviews is difficult to characterize. Overall, the author noted that classroom teachers reported a range of student reactions to participation in cooperative groups. In terms of limitations, Stout (1993) stated that her role in the district as the cooperative learning trainer may have affected both students' behaviors and the interview responses of the teachers. Thus, beyond the simple conclusions that talented students will engage in cooperative learning in a pull-out program and that classroom teachers perceive differences in the ways students participate in cooperative learning groups, it is difficult to extract much from this study.

Two studies compared the reactions of talented students to various goal structures. Ramsay and Richards (1993) investigated the effects of cooperative learning environments on the academic attitudes of gifted sixth-through eighth-grade students. There were three treatment conditions: classrooms in which cooperative learning was the predominant method, classrooms in which cooperative learning was used occasionally, and classrooms in which no cooperative learning was used. The outcome measure, the Estes Attitude Scales, indicated that for all students the treatment condition in which cooperative learning is used only occasionally, rather than predominantly, is related to better attitudes toward academic subjects. The researchers did not find evidence that gifted students, compared with their nonidentified peers, were either more or less positive about cooperative learning.

In contrast, preferences were more distinct in a study by Li and Adamson (1992), who examined 169 secondary students' learning-style preferences across the content areas of mathematics, science, and English. In comparison to individualistic and competitive styles, high-ability students did not prefer a cooperative learning style, nor was the cooperative style positively correlated with students' academic achievement in the three content areas. Mathematics presented the clearest pattern, with boys preferring individualistic and, to a lesser degree, competitive styles, while girls preferred individualistic to other styles. Other content areas were more mixed, but cooperative learning styles were least preferred overall.

Two studies that investigated directly through face-to-face interviews how students feel about cooperative learning documents some of the negative responses feared by critics. Matthews (1992) interviewed 15 students and reported that gifted students felt frustrated when explaining material to groupmates who were uninterested. They were especially concerned about the quality of group products. Similar frustrations were uncovered by Clinkenbeard (1991) in a study of middle schoolers. Gifted students reported feelings of frustration with the perceived injustice of carrying the instructional workload for groupmates who exerted low effort. Clinkenbeard's findings are especially revealing as she was not specifically investigating cooperative learning and asked no questions that would have led students to express opinions concerning group work. The theme of frustration with group work in heterogeneous settings emerged from a broader, qualitative investigation of classroom experiences of talented students.

Finally, one study investigated the beliefs and attitudes of cooperative learning advocates and educators of the gifted concerning the use of cooperative learning with talented students (Nelson, Gallagher, & Coleman, 1993). The authors surveyed educators to identify and compare the perspectives of cooperative learning advocates and advocates of gifted education to identify and compare their perspectives. There were differences between the two groups of educators in terms of the curriculum. Advocates of cooperative learning believed that the curriculum was challenging enough for gifted students, that all students in a heterogeneous cooperative group learned, and that cooperative learning effectively developed social and leadership skills. Advocates of gifted education were less likely than cooperative learning advocates to adopt these beliefs. Both groups did agree, however, that administrators might use cooperative learning as a means to eliminate specialized programs for talented students and that teachers needed more training in the appropriate use of cooperative learning with talented students. In a further analysis of respondents' open-ended comments, the authors concluded that the issue of heterogeneous and homogeneous grouping within cooperative groups elicited the most comment from both groups of educators. Both groups commented favorably on the use of cooperative groups *within* ability groups, but only the cooperative learning advocates commented favorably on the use of heterogeneous groups with gifted students. Some comments indicated that cooperative learning advocates recognized the danger of overburdening gifted students.

Old Insights and New Practices: Implications for Talented Learners

The recent research on cooperative learning with the most pressing implications for talented students focuses on two general areas: (1) the nature of interaction and behavior among members of cooperative learning groups, and (2) the use of cooperative groups for the purpose of student assessment.

Research on Group Member Interactions and Behavior

Research on student interactions in cooperative groups is not new, but the most recent studies are examining the *nature* of student interactions and group members' behaviors rather than just tallying the numbers of them (Hertz-Lazarowitz, Kirkus, & Miller, 1992). The newer studies indicate that there are differences in the ways various students interact in cooperative groups; some students are active and some are more passive than others.

An early study by Webb (1985) indicated that students who gave explanations to groupmates benefited by increased achievement. Webb's finding and other similar findings led to the interpretation (not by Webb, but by others) that cooperative learning is beneficial to gifted students because they are the explainers (Johnson & Johnson, 1991; Slavin, 1990a). However, it has also led to statements that high-achieving students in cooperative groups dominate the group and advantage themselves at the expense of school strugglers. For example, Johnson and Johnson (1992) comment,

> High-ability group members may be deferred to and may take over the important leadership roles in ways that benefit them at the expense of the other group members (the rich-get-richer effect). In the learning group, for example, a more able group member may give all the explanations of what is being learned. Because the amount of time spent explaining correlates highly with the amount learned, the more able member learns a great deal while the less able members flounder as a captive audience. (pp. 178–179)

Athough Johnson and Johnson's statements about high-ability students do not appear to be based on empirical research, some studies have investigated the differences between high and low achievers in the cooperative context. In a study of two cooperative learning groups in an elementary classroom, King (1993) reported that students who were passive in the learning groups tended to be low achievers. Because passivity can indicate general disengagement from learning, it is cause for concern. In comparing high and low achievers, King noted, and other studies have confirmed, that high achievers tend to be active, even dominant, in the group (Good, Reys, Grouws, & Mulryan, 1989–1990; Mulryan, 1992). These data indicate that statements by cooperative-learning advocates that all students contribute equally to the cooperative group and that no one student is cast in the role of "junior teacher" are not borne out by data on student interactions. The evidence that students respond differentially to cooperative learning and that patterns of passivity develop in cooperative learning as well as in whole-class instruction has implications for all students, including the population of interest in this review—academically talented students.

Lessons from Social Psychology

An important consideration is what underlies disengagement and passivity in groups. The body of literature that examines motivation losses in groups has relevance for the ways in which cooperative learning operates in practice. Early researchers in group process noted that under certain conditions, persons working in groups tended to exert less effort. Reduced effort or motivation in turn resulted in lowered productivity.

Social loafing. One branch of the research on group behavior and motivation losses in groups was based on the concept of *social loafing* (Karau & Williams, 1993). In a series of experiments involving persons pulling on ropes in a tug-of-war task, Ringelmann noted that as the size of the group increased, individual members of the team reduced their efforts (Latane, Williams, & Harkins, 1979). Other researchers noted that in matters of altruism, bystanders in large groups were less likely to assist someone in distress if the bystanding group were large rather than small. It was assumed that the diffusion of individual responsibility encouraged people to let others step forward or at least inhibited them from doing so themselves.

Ringlemann's work was further developed by social psychologists who posited two related effects to explain the loss of motivation in groups. These are the *free-rider effect* and the less frequently cited *sucker effect*. Both of these effects are relevant to the experiences of talented students in cooperative learning groups.

Free-rider effect. The free-rider effect occurs when the possibility arises that some other member of the group can and will provide what is needed, thus making one's own contribution to the group unnecessary. In other words, an individual member in a cooperative learning group may not contribute because he or she does not perceive a need to do so. Both the Johnsons (1992) and Slavin (1992) have noted the possibility of free-rider effects, particularly in cooperative-learning models where there is little individual accountability. Slavin (1992) comments that filling out one copy of a worksheet or turning in one group product are examples of cooperative learning practices which invite free riding. Slavin's concern is that the most likely free rider is the low-performing child in the group. By free-riding, the child gives up the opportunity to learn the material and thereby is unlikely to achieve. Slavin's concern receives indirect support from the King (1993) and Mulryan (1992) studies which document the disengagement of low-attaining students from group work. Although neither researcher explicitly links free-rider effects with the disengagement of school strugglers, the data are suggestive.

While the free rider is usually assumed to be the lowest performing or least motivated member of the group, a series of experiments by Kerr and Bruun (1983) demonstrated that different group members exerted effort or free-rode under different task conditions. When the group's evaluation depended on the highest score, high-ability members worked harder; when the worst score defined the group's evaluation, the low-ability members worked harder. Thus, both high- and low-ability members would free-ride under certain conditions, even when their contributions to the group were identifiable.

Sucker effect. The sucker effect was suggested by Orbell and Dawes (1981) to explain a second source of motivation loss in groups. If there is a possibility that a member can free-ride, there is also a danger that other group members will feel forced to carry the free rider. Orbell and Dawes labeled this the *sucker effect* and hypothesized that people find it so aversive to be played for a sucker that they will reduce their own contributions to the group in order to avoid exploitation. Kerr (1983) designed a series of experiments to determine the existence of such an effect. Although he studied college students working with a motor task rather than an academic one, the sucker effect clearly operated. In fact, it was so potent that capable partners "sometimes preferred to fail at the task rather than be a sucker and carry a free rider" (p. 823). Further, while the free-rider effect was most likely to operate at the beginning of a set of learning tasks, the sucker effect was more powerful at the end of them. It should be noted that most group members were tolerant of low-performing individuals when they perceived the low performance to be due to low ability rather than low effort. In short-term tasks, they willingly carried a low-performing, low-ability member. However, high-performing members did not carry low-performing, low-effort members and would fail themselves rather than exert effort.

Robinson and Clinkenbeard (1993) suggested that the sucker effect has implications for the motivation of high-attaining students in several cooperative-learning models. A plausible, though untested, hypothesis is that the cumulative effects over time of a free-riding member in a cooperative learning group might depress the performance or encourage the disengagement of previously high-achieving, highly motivated members. This effect might be especially potent if a high-achieving member felt powerless to affect the unmotivated members of the group or to change group affiliation.

What is the state of the evidence concerning the operation of free-rider and sucker effects in cooperative learning groups? There are no tightly controlled laboratory studies of such effects. However, in some field studies of cooperative learning, evidence is mounting that student passivity occurs in groups (King, 1993) and that it may occur for a variety of reasons. For example, Mulryan (1992) reported that fifth- and sixth-grade students responded differentially to cooperative learning. She noted that the major finding of her study was that "some students, mainly low achievers, mainfested a high level of passive behavior in cooperative small groups" (p. 261). However, she identified some high-achieving students who were passive as well. According to Mulryan (1992), these students could be characterized as despondent, bored, or "intellectual snobs." Interview transcripts indicate that one despondent student was passive because another group member "says mean things." A bored student indicated that the task was too easy. A student that Mulryan characterized as an intellectual snob expressed frustration because the task was easy for him but difficult for others in the group, thus slowing him down.

To date, research on student passivity in cooperative learning groups has focused largely on low-achieving students and the deleterious effects of free riding on low-attaining free riders. No studies have directly investigated the nature and potency of the sucker effect on high-attaining students in the popular forms of cooperative learning. It would be fruitful to know, for example, whether the drive for excellence in terms of a group product results in compensatory effort by a talented student in an unproductive group. In other words, does the student "work overtime" to compensate for missing information or poor quality products which were the initial responsibility of low-effort members? If so, what are the motivational and emotional outcomes for the high-attaining, highly motivated student? How aversive must being "played for a sucker" become before it affects a talented student's individual achievement, academic productivity, and continuing motivation for school tasks?

Research on Assessment in Cooperative Learning Groups

Enthusiasm for cooperative learning as an instructional technique has extended to the use of cooperative learning in classroom and state assessments for accountability. According to Webb (1993), however, little is known about the extent to which such cooperative assessments allow us to infer what individual students know and are able to do.

To understand the implications of group assessment for talented students, it is useful to examine Slavin's discussion of group productivity and individual achievement. In a review of the research base on cooperative learning, Slavin (1992) commented that some cooperative-learning studies confuse group productivity with individual learning. To argue that cooperative learning affects individual student learning, the outcome measure must be of individual achievement. His example has much resonance for educators concerned with talented students. He explained,

> Leonard Bernstein and I could write a brilliant concerto together, about twice as good as the average of the concerto he could write and the one I could write working separately (I can barely read music). But how much would we *learn* from working cooperatively? I doubt that Leonard Bernstein would learn much about writing concertos from me, and I might do better to take a course on music than to start by watching a composer write a concerto. The point of this example is to illustrate that *learning is completely different from "group" productivity*. It may well be that working in a group under certain circumstances does increase the learning of the individuals in that group more than would working under other arrangements, but a measure of group productivity provides no evidence one way or the other on this; only an individual learning measure that cannot be influenced by group member help can indicate which incentive or task structure is best. Learning takes place only between the ears of the learner. If a group produces a beautiful lab report, but only a few students really contributed to it, it is unlikely that the group as a whole learned more than they might have learned had they each had to write their own (perhaps less beautiful) lab reports under an individualistic or competitive incentive structure. In fact, what often happens in cooperative groups that produce a single report, worksheet, or other group product is that the most able group members simply do the work or give the answers to their teammates, which may be the most efficient strategy for group productivity but is a poor strategy for individual learning. (pp. 150–151)

The implications of Slavin's cautions about the use of single products to assess individual achievement or understanding are straightforward for talented students. Leaving aside the previous concerns related to free-rider and sucker effects, assessment in cooperative groups presents problems of ambiguity. If we assess students in the group context, we simply may not know what each student in the cooperative group knows and can do. If we cannot assess student needs and accomplishments accurately, we cannot present instruction to meet those needs. Without certain safety checks, group assessment can confound individual achievement with group productivity.

The use of cooperative assessments is beginning to occur both in classroom assessment for instructional purposes and in state-level accountability programs. Each of the uses of cooperative assessments has implications for academically talented students and is one of the important emergent issues in the examination of cooperative learning as it relates to talented students.

Cooperative Assessment for Accountability

We consider state accountability issues first as they have great consequences for students. Connecticut, California, Maryland, and New York state assessments, for example, all include cooperative learning tasks. With such increases in high-stakes state assessments, an important question is how well student performance in groups reflects individual competence. To investigate this question, Webb (1993) compared the performance of students working collaboratively on a mathematics task with their performance on a similar task accomplished individually two weeks later. She coded student behavior into the following categories: (1) solved problems correctly aloud without assistance, (2) showed difficulty and received assistance, (3) copied other students' work, and (4) did not contribute to group discussion. Webb examined students who needed help to solve the problem in the group context separately and found that the presence of more than one noncontributing member in a group was related to lowered performance for these students.

Webb concluded that group performances overestimate the individual performances of students. Her chief concern was that overestimation has serious consequences for low-achieving students. If failure to acquire important skills and concepts is masked by group contexts or by the confounding effects of a single product submitted by a group, then students who need additional assistance to succeed may not receive the instruction they require.

The difficulties presented by group assessments for high-achieving students differ from those suggested by Webb but are also of concern. In Webb's study, the group performance resulted in ceiling effects for a majority of the students who were tested in the cooperative-learning context. Thus, we do not know what the students might have been able to do if they had been presented with a group task that tested the limits of performance. It is as possible to encounter ceiling effects in group assessments as it is in the individual basic skills tests or minimum performance tests they are to replace. Advocates for talented students have been effective in speaking out about the artificial depression of student achievement by low-level individual assessments; they will find that group assessments generate some of the same concerns. Presenting a task in a group context does not make it inherently more challenging or less vulnerable to ceiling effects.

Cooperative Assessments in the Classroom

Cooperative group assessment in the classroom will be as vulnerable to free-rider and sucker effects as cooperative group instruction. To address these deleterious effects, teachers who implement such group assessments will need to establish "safety nets" of individual performance opportunities.

For example, the Educational Testing Service developed assessment materials, called PACKETS, for the middle school that require students to work in cooperative learning groups (Katims, 1994). As a sample task, in "Million Dollar Getaway" students are given information about a bank robbery, then placed in groups to work on a group report to be presented to an imaginary news editor (actually to other members of the class). Again, the same cautions about free riding and sucker effects apply to a single product for assessment purposes as they do to cooperative tasks for instruction. Also, many school districts have policies that dictate that grades can be given for individual work only. Accordingly, the developers of PACKETS built in some safety checks for individual learning. For example, teachers observe students individually before the group activity occurs. The cooperative product also can be modified so that each student turns in his or her own product after learning in the group context (Katims, Nash, & Tocci, 1993).

These safety checks are crucial if the concerns associated with cooperative learning and talented students are to be addressed in the assessment context. Although there have been few investigations into cooperative group assessments, the early indications are that group performance can overestimate individual learning (Webb, 1993) and that cooperative learning *and* cooperative assessment used together result in lowered scores for students who are subsequently tested individually (Lambiotte et al., 1987). In other words, the cooperative learning and assessment did not transfer when students later were presented with an individual task. Further studies are needed to determine if this effect is robust.

Summary

In conclusion, a review of the emerging literature on cooperative learning and talented students leads to four general observations. First, the empirical research has begun. In 1990 only one study that included gifted students in the sample was located (Smith, Johnson, & Johnson, 1982). Its usefulness was limited by the small number of gifted students (14) and by the authors' focus on other populations rather than the talented students. In contrast, as of late 1994 more cooperative-learning studies that focus on talented students were beginning to appear.

Second, programmatic research has yet to emerge. Each of the studies reviewed in this chapter is by a different author or authors, and no clear lines of sustained inquiry have been established.

Third, the new research on cooperative learning and talented students validates some of the reservations expressed in the earlier debate; it is less clear on others. For example, talented students often do not prefer cooperative contexts. However, what factors influence those preferences and what effects these preferences have on student motivation and achievement are not fully described.

Finally, new issues have emerged. In the next few years, investigations incorporating the concepts historically of interest to social psychologists—social loafing, free riding, and sucker effects—may prove to enlighten us about subtle interactions in cooperative learning groups. These insights should be especially fruitful to our understanding of cooperative group dynamics for students who are consistently low and high attainers. As pressures to implement cooperative assessments increase to keep pace with exhortations for cooperative learning and for high-stakes accountability, educators concerned with talented students will find much fertile ground for needed investigation.

REFERENCES

Clinkenbeard, P. R. (1991). Unfair expectations: A pilot study of middle school students' comparisons of gifted and regular classes. *Journal for the Education of the Gifted, 15,* 56–63.

Elmore, R. E., & Zenus, V. (1994). Enhancing social-emotional development of middle school gifted students. *Roeper Review, 16,* 182–185.

Good, T. L., Reys, B., Grouws, D. A., & Mulryan, C. M. (1989–1990). Using work groups in mathematics in an attempt to improve students' understanding and social skills. *Educational Leadership, 47*(4), 56–62.

Hertz-Lazarowitz, R., Kirkus, V. B., & Miller, N. (1992). Implications of current research on cooperative interaction for classroom application. In R. Hertz-Lazarowitz & N. Miller (Eds.), *Interaction in cooperative groups: The theoretical anatomy of group learning* (pp. 253–280). New York: Cambridge University Press.

Johnson, D. W., & Johnson, R. T. (1991, January). *What to say to people concerned with the education of high ability and gifted students.* Unpublished manuscript.

Johnson, D. W., & Johnson, R. T. (1992). Positive interdependence: Key to effective cooperation. In R. Hertz-Lazarowitz & N. Miller (Eds.), *Interaction in cooperative groups: The theoretical anatomy of group learning* (pp. 174–199). New York: Cambridge University Press.

Karau, S. J., & Williams, K. D. (1993). Social loafing: A meta-analytic review and theoretical integration. *Journal of Personality and Social Psychology, 65*, 681–706.

Katims, N. (1994). *The PACKETS program: An illustration of classroom-based alternative assessment.* Paper presented at the annual meeting of the American Educational Research Association, New Orleans, Louisiana.

Katims, N., Nash, P., & Tocci, C. M. (1993). Linking instruction and assessment in a middle school mathematics classroom. *Middle School Journal, 25*(2), 28–35.

Kerr, N. L. (1983). Motivation losses in small groups: A social dilemma analysis. *Journal of Personality and Social Psychology, 45,* 819–828.

Kerr, N. L., & Bruun, S. E. (1983). The dispensability of member effort and group motivation loses: Free-rider effects. *Journal of Personality and Social Psychology, 44,* 78–94.

King, L. H. (1993). High and low achievers' perceptions and cooperative learning in two small groups. *Elementary School Journal, 93,* 399–416.

Lambiotte, J. G., Dansereau, D. F., Rocklin, T. R., Fletcher, B., Hythecker, V. I., Larson, C. O., & O'Donnell, A. M. (1987). Cooperative learning and test taking: Transfer of skills. *Contemporary Educational Psychology, 12,* 52–61.

Latane, B., Williams, K., & Harkins, S. (1979). Many hands make light the work: The causes and consequences of social loafing. *Journal of Personality and Social Psychology, 37,* 822–832.

Li, A. K. F., & Adamson, G. (1992). Gifted secondary students' preferred learning style: Cooperative, competitive, or individualistic? *Journal for the Education of the Gifted, 16*(1), 46–54.

Matthews, M. (1992). Gifted students talk about coooperative learning. *Educational Leadership, 50*(2), 48–50.

Mulryan, C. M. (1992). Student passivity during cooperative small groups in mathematics. *Journal of Educational Research, 85,* 261–273.

Nelson, S., Gallagher, J., & Coleman, M. R. (1993). Cooperative learning from two different perspectives. *Roeper Review, 16,* 117–121.

Orbell, J., & Dawes, R. (1981). Social dilemmas. In G. Stephenson & J. H. Davis (Eds.)., *Progress in applied social psychology,* (*Vol. 1,* pp. 37–65). Chichester, England: Wiley.

Ramsay, S. G., & Richards, H. C. (1993). *Cooperative learning environments: Effect on academic attitudes of school-identified gifted students.* Paper presented at the annual meeting of the American Educational Research Association, Atlanta, Georgia.

Robinson, A. (1990a). Cooperation or exploitation? The argument against cooperative learning for talented students. *Journal for the Education of the Gifted, 14*(1), 9–27.

Robinson, A. (1990b). Response to Slavin: Cooperation, consistency, and challenge for academically talented youth. *Journal for the Education of the Gifted, 14*(1), 31–36.

Robinson, A. (1991). *Cooperative learning and the academically talented student.* Monograph of the National Research Center on the Gifted and Talented. Storrs: University of Connecticut Press.

Robinson, A., & Clinkenbeard, P. R. (1993). *Cooperative learning and theories of motivation.* Paper presented at the Henry B. and Jocelyn Wallace National Research Symposium on Talent Development, Iowa City, Iowa.

Slavin, R. E. (1990a). Ability grouping, cooperative learning and the gifted. *Journal for the Education of the Gifted, 14*(1), 3–8.

Slavin, R. E. (1990b). Response to Robinson: Cooperative learning and the gifted: Who benefits? *Journal for the Education of the Gifted, 14*(1), 28–30.

Slavin, R. E. (1992). When and why does cooperative learning increase achievement? Theoretical and empirical perspectives. In R. Hertz-Lazarowitz & N. Miller (Eds.), *Interaction in cooperative groups: The theoretical anatomy of group learning* (pp. 145–173). New York: Cambridge University Press.

Smith, K., Johnson, D. W., & Johnson, R. (1982). The effects of cooperative and individualistic instruction on the achievement of handicapped, regular, and gifted students. *Journal of Social Psychology, 116,* 277–283.

Stout, J. (1993). *The use of cooperative learning with elementary gifted students: Practical and theoretical implications.* Paper presented at the annual meeting of the American Educational Research Association, Atlanta, GA.

Webb, N. M. (1985). Student interaction and learning in small groups: A research summary. In R. E. Slavin, S. Sharan, S. Kagan, R. Hertz-Lazarowitz, C. Webb, & R. Schmuck (Eds.), *Learning to cooperate, cooperating to learn* (pp. 147–172). New York: Plenum Press.

Webb, N. M. (1993). Collaborative group versus individual assessment in mathematics: Processes and outcomes. *Educational Assessment, 1*(2), 131–152.

21

Evaluating Gifted Programs

JAMES H. BORLAND, *Teachers College, Columbia University*

The evaluation of programs for gifted students poses some unique and daunting problems for both practitioners and scholars, problems that are conceptual (what exactly *is* program evaluation?), psychological (who really *wants* to be evaluated?), and practical (for example, how do you measure growth in students who start out at the ceiling level of a test?). Too often, confronted by the welter of difficulties posed by evaluating programs for gifted students, educators throw in the towel and decide either that a systematic evaluation is not necessary, feasible, or affordable or that distributing questionnaires to students and parents to gauge how happy they are with the program will suffice.

This is unfortunate for several reasons, two of which are particularly salient. First, the infrequency with which programs for gifted students are subjected to careful, systematic evaluations impoverishes us as a field. If program evaluation were to be done on a routine and widespread basis, we would have a broader database on which to draw to answer some important questions concerning our practice. Most basic among these is the simple question, "Do these programs work?" I find this question to be very embarrassing because, although I think the answer is a qualified *yes,* I cannot adduce much in the way of good empirical evidence to substantiate my belief. The absence of data on outcomes leaves programs for gifted students open to serious questions regarding their efficacy. This, in turn, can make such programs vulnerable, especially when school authorities must contend with the pressures of economic exigency and questions about the fairness of special programs for gifted students (e.g., Sapon-Shevin, 1994).

The second problem is perhaps even more critical: It is difficult to maintain and increase the quality of a program that does not undergo frequent systematic assessment. As Fetterman (1993) writes, "Gifted and talented education programs, perhaps more acutely than most educational programs, require a clear-sighted and self-critical awareness of program strengths and goals" (p. 1). Improving the programs we offer our students is a professional and moral obligation, one we cannot discharge effectively unless we assess the programs in the first place. Thus, on both the national and the local level, we suffer when we neglect the important task of evaluating programs for gifted students.

The foregoing assumes two important goals of program evaluation: (1) assessing efficacy and (2) fostering program improvement. These, however, are not the only reasons we evaluate programs. Rather than assume that the nature and functions of evaluation and other important concepts are familiar to every reader, let me discuss some of these.

What Is Program Evaluation?

It is often asserted that there is confusion regarding what program evaluation is and how it should be defined. The real issue, however, is not so much a matter of confusion as of different conceptions of evaluation, many of them valid, each with its own implications with respect to purposes and practices. Depending on which conception of evaluation one adopts, if only for a particular task, different procedures and outcomes will be appropriate. A brief overview of some of the leading conceptions, which overlap to some extent, might be useful here.

Evaluation as Judgment

People typically think of program evaluation as a judgmental process, and there are, indeed, definitions of evaluation that emphasize this dimension. For example, the definition put forth by the Joint Committee on Standards for Educational Evaluation (1981) defines evaluation simply as "the systematic investigation of the merit or worth of some object" (p. 12). The Joint Committee's definition implies a distinction between a program's *merit* (its intrinsic quality or degree of excellence) and its *worth* (its value or importance to some person or some group), qualities that can be independent of each other.

For example, some programs for gifted students, although high in merit, have been regarded by school authorities as having little worth. Such programs, when budgets become tight or educational trends unfavorable, face elimination if they are not mandated, marginalization if they are. Unfortunately, too, programs of questionable merit may have undeniable worth to school districts for their public relations value or their ability to mollify assertive parents. Whether the emphasis is on merit, worth, or both, evaluation can be conceived of as largely judgmental, especially in its summative function (see p. 256).

Evaluation as Description

Evaluation can be descriptive instead of, or as well as, being judgmental, as Stake (1967) acknowledges when he writes that evaluation is "an activity comprised of both description and evaluation" (p. 525). Guba and Lincoln (1989), recounting the history of educational evaluation, describe the "second generation of evaluation" as "an approach characterized by *description* of patterns of strengths and weaknesses with respect to certain stated objectives" (p. 28). The central figure of this generation—which followed the first-generation measurement approach of Wundt, Galton, Binet, Goddard, Terman, and others and preceded the third-generation judgmental approach—was Ralph Tyler, the so-called Father of Evaluation.

Objective- or goal-oriented evaluation. Tyler (1950) defined *evaluation* as "the process of determining to what extent . . . educational objectives are actually being realized" (p. 69). This is a classic conception of the evaluation process, one with considerable utility since it is straightforward both in conception (a program is successful to the extent that it satisfies its objectives) and execution (one devotes one's efforts to gathering information on whether or not established objectives have been met). Public and private funding agencies implicitly adopt this approach when they ask grant applicants to propose an evaluation plan that is keyed to the objectives of the proposed project and when they ask grant recipients to provide evidence that they have made progress toward meeting program objectives.

Objective- or goal-free evaluation. In contrast, Michael Scriven proposed a form of evaluation in which the evaluator ignores program goals and objectives altogether, one that involves "gathering data directly on program effects and effectiveness without risking contamination by goals" (Patton, 1986, p. 111). According to Scriven (1972), knowledge of program goals is not only "an unnecessary but also a possibly contaminating step" (p. 2) in the evaluation process. Knowledge of goals and objectives can introduce "perceptual biases" that may make the evaluator oblivious to important unanticipated program outcomes, whereas being unaware of the goals and objectives can "maintain evaluator objectivity and independence through goal-free conditions" (Patton, 1986, p. 112).

Whether one focuses on program goals and objectives or chooses to remain completely ignorant of them, the broader conception of evaluation implied here is a descriptive one. The evaluator either describes what was intended, what was accomplished, and the gap between the two or, ignoring program goals, describes what happened as a result of program implementation.

Evaluation as Program Improvement

The Stanford Evaluation Consortium (Cronbach et al., 1980) defined evaluation as a "systematic examination of events occurring in and consequent of a contemporary program . . . conducted to assist in improving this program and other programs having the same general purpose" (p. 14). In addition to suggesting that evaluation ought to embrace some of the functions of evaluation research in the phrase "and other programs having the same general purpose," the definition is notable here for its emphasis on program improvement. No mention is made of judging or describing, although these activities are not necessarily antithetical to program improvement as a final goal.

Program improvement is one of the most important outcomes of program evaluation and maybe the most compelling reason to undertake the process. As I suggest above, improving programs for gifted students is one of our imperatives, and this goal ought to be part of our general conception of the purposes of program evaluation. This is especially germane to the *formative* function of evaluation, which I discuss later.

Utilization-Focused Evaluation

Patton (1986) argued that "much of what passes for program evaluation is not very useful" and, sensibly, that "evaluation ought to be useful" (p. 7). He called attention to a "utilization crisis" caused by the practice of conducting or commissioning program evaluations and then ignoring their findings in future decision making, which led him to the concept of "utilization-focused evaluation." Patton defined this as "the systematic collection of information about the activities, characteristics, and outcomes of programs for use by specific people to reduce uncertainties, improve effectiveness, and make decisions with regard to what those programs are doing and affecting" (p. 14).

Patton emphasizes the importance of identifying the stakeholders, those who have a vested interest in the outcome of the evaluation; determining what they want or need to know; and providing information that they are likely to use in making decisions about the program under review. In Patton's approach, the overriding concern is whether "there is an immediate, concrete, and observable effect on specific decisions and program activities resulting directly from evaluation findings" (p. 30)—in other words, whether evaluation data are used.

Postpositivist Evaluation

One result of the so-called "paradigm wars" (e.g., Gage, 1989) has been increased application of the methods of qualitative, naturalistic, constructivist, hermeneutic, or postpositivist (to cite only a few of the terms in current use) inquiry to the problems of educational evaluation (see, e.g., Guba & Lincoln, 1989; Patton, 1986). Although awareness and use of postpositivist methods have lagged in the field of education of gifted students, this appears to be changing (Cross, 1994). This is to the good, because the axioms and methods of postpositivism are quite compatible with inquiry into and assessment of giftedness.

It is not possible to describe postpositivism in a few sentences (see, instead, Borland, 1990; Lincoln & Guba, 1985), but at its core is a rejection of the positivist notion that the methods thought to characterize inquiry in the physical sciences are applicable to the study of human beings, their behavior, and their institutions. Among its axioms are the belief that realities are multiple and constructed; that the act of observation affects that which is being observed; that generalization is undesirable and perhaps impossible; and that inquiry cannot be, and should not pretend to be, objective and value-free. Methodologically, postpositivists stress qualitative methods; purposive, instead of random, sampling; human beings as data-gathering instruments; letting one's research or evaluation design emerge as one progresses instead of following a prespecified design; allowing theory to emerge from one's engagement with one's respondents instead of starting with or testing a theory; close description of specific settings (idiographic interpretation) instead of generalizable findings (nomothetic laws); negotiating outcomes with respondents; and case-study reporting.

In the realm of evaluation, this means that the relevant data, are not, in Guba and Lincoln's words, "discovered" as if they had always been 'out there'. . . . [Instead,] the results are *literally*—we stress *literally*—*created* . . . as a product of an interaction between humans" (1989, p. 67; emphasis in the original). As a result, "different stakeholders will have different constructions, which, while perhaps differing in the scope of already constructed knowledge accounted for and in their level of sophistication, are nonetheless legitimate to hold and worthy to honor" (p. 67). Therefore, evaluation should in part involve forcing various stakeholders in a program to confront their own and others' constructed knowledge about the program, resulting in "more informed and sophisticated personal constructions" (p. 67).

As should be clear, there are many ways to conceive of program evaluation, each of which has important considerations for practice. This may seem more confusing than helpful, but it reflects the true state of the art. Some clarification may come from considering the various functions that program evaluation can serve.

What Are the Functions of Evaluation?

Scriven (1967) has drawn a well-known and useful distinction between two major functions of program evaluation, the *summative* and the *formative,* a distinction that is useful in understanding how evaluation can be used.

The Summative Function

Summative evaluation is, I suspect, what most people think of when they think of program evaluation. The focus in summative evaluation is on program outcomes at or near the end of a program's life span or after some significant period of time (such as an academic year), and the major concern is with issues of program efficacy and accountability. Summative evaluation has both a retrospective and a prospective aspect. It is retrospective in that there is an attempt to determine whether a program has been effective. It is prospective in that it is frequently used to make major decisions about a program's future, such as whether to continue or terminate a program, increase or decrease its funding, and so forth. Because summative evaluations are often the basis for administrative decisions, the audience for these data is usually higher level administrators who have the responsibility for such decisions.

The Formative Function

Formative evaluation differs from summative evaluation chiefly in that it serves a diagnostic function. This form of evaluation involves the collection of data at various points during the life of a program—during an academic year, for example—so that problems can be detected and responded to while the program is still operating. Thus, the goal is to improve the program now, not to answer questions of accountability or the program's long-term fate. For this reason, formative data are probably of more interest to those involved in the program's day-to-day management and decision making than they are to higher level administrators.

The distinction is, however, not an absolute one. For one thing, formative data can be incorporated into summative evaluation. Moreover, the effectiveness of formative evaluation in helping educators identify and alleviate problems will affect overall program effectiveness and, thus, the results of summative evaluation. In this sense, formative evaluation is a program component that, like other program components, should be one focus of a summative evaluation.

Other Functions of Evaluation

Nevo (1983) mentioned two other functions that deserve brief attention. The *psychological,* or *sociopolitical,* functions are just that: evaluation whose intended ends are either psychological or sociopolitical. The goal is either to affect the thinking or behavior of one or more people, or to achieve some objective with respect to the status of an individual, group, or program within a particular social structure such as a school, school district, academic department, or state bureaucracy. I have, on occasion, been hired as an evaluator for a program for gifted students only to learn that the intent (though not, I hope, the result) of the evaluation is psychological (e.g., to remind program staff that they are accountable to administrators or to the school board) or sociopolitical (e.g., to enhance the program's stature within a school district).

There is also an *administrative* evaluation function, whereby X evaluates Y for no reason other that as a statement or reminder that X *can* evaluate Y by virtue of a higher position in the administrative hierarchy. It is difficult to regard this as a legitimate function of evaluation, but it does occur and should be noted.

Thus, not only can program evaluation be defined in different ways; it also can serve a variety of functions. These are obviously related; evaluation as judgment is more likely to be summative, whereas evaluation as program improvement is more likely to be formative. All this is important because a clear conception of the forms and functions of program evaluation enhances one's ability to plan and carry out an effective evaluation. This is especially crucial in the case of programs for gifted students because evaluating these programs is particularly problematic. Let me now turn to a discussion of these special difficulties.

Problems in Evaluating Programs for Gifted Students

Problems with Goals and Objectives

Clear, unambiguous program goals and objectives are important in evaluation. This is especially true if the evaluation effort focuses on whether the program has met, or is meeting, its stated goals. But even if the evaluator or evaluators choose to conduct a goal-free evaluation (which is usually not the case), the stakeholders will have difficulty interpreting the evaluation results if they do not have a clear idea of what their program originally set out to accomplish.

Problems with goals and objectives come in a variety of forms. One of these is, to be a bit facetious, the analog of goal-free evaluation: the goal-free program. It has, unfortunately, not been uncommon in my experience to receive nothing but blank stares in response to the question, "What are the goals of your program?" In a surprising number of cases, the implicit but overriding goal seems to be, "To have a gifted program." Although that goal has the undeniable virtue of being easily met, it is a less-than-compelling basis for the creation of a special educational program. The problem here should be obvious: If nobody knows why the program exists, in terms of valid educational outcomes, not only is evaluation problematic, so is nearly every aspect of program operation.

Even when program goals exist, there can be problems. For example, some goals are so grand and lofty as to make it extremely unlikely that a mere educational program could reach them. Wanting to have a positive effect on "the future of our country" and aspiring to "create a cadre of leaders for the world of tomorrow" are well and good, but perhaps ambitious for a single program in a single school district. In any case, such goals certainly do not bode well for a positive summative evaluation. Other goals are just the opposite; they are so trivial as to prompt a response of "So what?" whether they are met or not. Establishing as a program goal the identification of a certain percentage of the student body as gifted or the delivery of inservice education to a certain number of teachers is to substitute administrative responsibilities for program objectives. These goals are easily met, a fact that has little bearing on the merit, worth, or effectiveness of the program. The point I am attempting to make here is a straightforward one. Goals that do not specify what benefits will accrue to students as a result of the program's existence are of little use in program evaluation.

Problems with Measurement

Evaluation nearly always involves some form of measurement or assessment, although this does not necessarily have to involve tests. This presents a host of potential problems.

Lack of adequate tests. One problem, or apparent problem, is the paucity of valid tests for measuring a number of the things we would like to measure in programs for gifted students. One example of this is creativity, valid measures of which have been the Holy Grail for some test constructors for a number of years. This is understandable, for creativity looms large in the goals and activities of a number of programs. However, I believe that attempts to capture this elusive construct with standardized paper-and-pencil measures have been largely unsuccessful (see, e.g., Crockenberg, 1972; Perkins, 1981; Wallach, 1985; see Torrance, 1975, 1988, for a different view).

Now, for a number of people, often including stakeholders in program evaluations, the only valid way to measure something is through the use of an objective test. As House (1993) wrote, although "standardized test scores are not entirely suitable for this purpose [program evaluation]" (p. 2), "there is a demand for test results from policy makers and legislatures that cannot be denied" (p. 11). This, I suspect, is because for many people the terms *objective* and *valid* have become fused, which is unfortunate: Whether a test is objective or not has nothing to do with its validity. Furthermore, frankly subjective methods can outperform objective ones, as is shown by the success Amabile (e.g., 1983) has had with *consensual assessment* relative to the poor record achieved by objective tests of creativity.

However, the absence of valid tests does not imply the absence of tests altogether. Moreover, many of us are so awed by tests that, however skeptical we may be as consumers of other products, we become credulous test consumers, ignoring or not reading what is written in the research journals or the *Mental Measurements Yearbooks*. Thus, the existence of legitimate program goals that refer to psychometrically elusive constructs can have two unhappy outcomes. One, resulting from the belief that valid assessment requires a test, and reinforced by a tendency to believe that if a test is published it must be valid, is to use objective, but invalid, measures. The second is to conclude that no assessment is possible. There is an alternative, as I implied earlier in referring to Amabile's work, and I will return to this later when I discuss *authentic assessment*.

Lack of sufficient ceiling on tests. Another measurement problem is caused by *ceiling* effects on tests. On some tests, especially achievement measures, the test ceiling may be too low for advanced students. All this means is that the test is not difficult enough for the ablest students and/or that there is not enough range at the top end of the score distribution to reveal differences among the highest scorers. This problem would crop up were one to attempt to assess my leaping ability relative to that of a professional basketball player by asking both of us to jump over a bar placed one foot off the ground, then raising the bar in one-inch increments, stopping at a height of two feet. Because the highly gifted athlete and I would both clear the two-foot-high bar, this "test" would suggest that we have equal leaping ability, which is obviously not the case. The test would not be difficult enough; the upper range would be restricted; the ceiling would be too low. Were the bar to be raised a few more times in six-inch increments, the true differences between us would soon become apparent.

This problem can affect evaluations when there is an attempt to assess growth due to program intervention by computing gain scores, differences between posttest scores and pretest scores (often done, but not a good idea because it can compound measurement error). If a test with a low ceiling is used as a pretest to assess students' status prior to exposure to the program, many students may start out with the highest score possible, making it impossible for them to show gains, should there be any. This ceiling problem also can affect better evaluation designs, such as posttest-only designs, by restricting the variance on the measure in question.

Because of ceiling effects, some educators have recommended out-of-level testing for gifted students. This simply means switching to a test designed for chronologically older students. If many gifted third graders are scoring at the ceiling level on a given test, one could administer, say, the fifth-grade test instead.

Probably the best example of this approach is found in the work of the Study of Mathematically Precocious Youth (e.g., Stanley, 1981), in which the mathematics section of the Scholastic Aptitude Test, as it was called then, was used to assess mathematical precocity among middle school students.[1] One thing to keep in mind, as the SMPY researchers themselves point out (e.g., Benbow, 1986), is that a test may be qualitatively different when used with an age group other than the one for which it was designed or on which it was normed. The SAT-M, for example, may be an achievement test for high school seniors who have been exposed to the mathematics curriculum it covers, but for younger students who have had no such exposure it may function as a test of mathematical reasoning, problem solving, creativity, persistence, or whatever.

Regression effects. Regression toward the mean—a phenomenon whereby groups whose mean score on one administration of a test is extreme in one direction or the other, tend, upon retesting, to shift their group mean score in the direction of the population mean for no reason other than the retesting itself—can pose problems for those interested in the assessment of gifted learners. Regression would be likely to happen, for example, if one were to administer an aptitude test to a large group of students, select those who scored in the top 5 percent, and then retest the group after a short interval. The mean score for the group would more often than not be lower on the second testing, although there would be no reason other than the psychometric phenomenon of regression.

It should be clear how regression effects can work against the measurement of real gains, attenuating them if not canceling them out. For this reason, it is important not to use the same instrument for identifying gifted students and later for assessing their progress. By the same token, if a test used as a posttest measure of student growth or status correlates strongly with the test (or battery of indicators) used for identifying students, regression effects can also occur.

[1] See Chapter 12 by Benbow and Lubinski.

Inappropriate norms. In this field, we are more often than not concerned with test scores at the upper extreme of the score distribution. Because this is where we often want to make distinctions between students, we need to be confident that, when raw scores are translated into percentiles, normal curve equivalents, or some other normative score, these latter scores are reliable. Unfortunately, this is not always the case.

Instead, it is frequently the case that norms at the upper end of the score distribution are derived from a subsample of the norming sample that is too small for the task. Put simply, a number of tests used to assess gifted students have had too few gifted students in their norming samples. Scores in the upper range may, therefore, be less reliable, or a range of raw scores may be pegged to a single ceiling percentile so that true differences between students are obscured. The reliability of high scores on a test should be treated with skepticism until one consults the test manual to learn about the norming sample and the standard error of scores over the range of the score distribution.

Problems with Evaluation Designs

For good reasons, it is difficult to design program evaluations in the way one would like to design a good experiment. To build in appropriate controls, it is useful to have a treatment group and a control group, one that does not receive the treatment whose effectiveness is being investigated, and to assign individuals to these groups randomly. One can quickly see why there might be objections were there to be a control group consisting of students who qualified for the gifted program in question, but who were randomly assigned to the group that was not given the program. Even when comparisons are made between students in a program for gifted students and other students "matched for ability," there are problems. As Slavin (1991) convincingly argues, the groups are probably *not* comparable; the comparison group is not in the program for a reason. Thus, to the extent that program evaluations are intended to be experimental designs, they are typically one-group designs, which are problematic (Campbell & Stanley, 1963).

There are some ways around this without encountering the ethical and political problems attendant upon asking some parents to place their gifted students in the "no-program" control group. One is to use some variation of a counterbalanced design (Campbell & Stanley, 1963) in which parts of the program, such as exposure to different curricular components, are presented to different groups of students at different times. For example, students in a program might be divided into two groups, ideally through a random process, with one group receiving exposure to one curricular component, with distinct objectives and methods, while the other group receives exposure to another component altogether. When this phase of the program concludes, the two groups can be assessed, with each group serving as the control for the other in a quasi-experimental two-group design.

We faced a similar problem at Teachers College in planning the second three years of Project Synergy, our Javits Grant project designed to develop ways to identify and educate young economically disadvantaged gifted students, although our solution was different. A goal of the project is to compare the effectiveness of the full intervention process, developed in our first three-year project, with the effectiveness of a program consisting of teacher inservice and parent workshops. For research purposes, we also wanted to have a third group, a control group that would receive no treatment. However, we were concerned about the ethics of identifying but not serving poor potentially gifted students. We decided, therefore, to provide inservice education to teachers only in grades 3 and above in the school attended by students in the control group. During the three years of the project, the control students identified as potentially gifted in kindergarten would have completed kindergarten, first grade, and second grade. The following year, after the project has ended, we hope these students will derive benefits from being in classrooms with teachers who had received inservice education.

Design problems can be daunting, but they can be overcome. Evaluating programs for gifted students is, I believe, more difficult than evaluating most other programs. Nonetheless, it should be done, and I would like to turn now to a discussion of some ways this can be accomplished.

Using an Outside Evaluator

One approach is to bring in an outsider, or group of outsiders, to conduct an evaluation. This could be someone from academia, perhaps with a specialization in evaluation or the education of gifted students; a professional evaluator; an educational consultant; or, if one is near a college with a graduate program in education, students conducting a supervised practicum. An outside evaluation has some things to recommend it.

One advantage an outsider brings is a greater degree of objectivity than is possible for someone inside the system. One can, at times, be too close to a program to see what someone with a fresher perspective can see. Of course, complete objectivity is impossible, but at least someone from outside brings a different subjectivity to the task. In addition, because he or she does not owe his or her livelihood to the powers that be, an outside evaluator possesses a degree of independence of thought and expression not enjoyed by those on the inside. Finally, an experienced evaluator can bring a breadth of experience, derived from work with many types of programs, to bear on the task. Knowing what has and has not worked in other settings can be of great value, especially when significant program changes are being considered. In short, an outside evaluator can provide a valuable service if his or her talents can be afforded.

However, total reliance on outsiders for program evaluation is a mistake. For one thing, some of the very virtues of an outside evaluator—an outside perspective, freedom from negative repercussions from evaluation findings—have their negative sides. An outside perspective, though affording greater breadth, affords limited depth and precludes the sort of local knowledge (Goldenberg & Gallimore, 1991) and tacit knowledge (Lincoln & Guba, 1985) that accrue to one by virtue of long experience in a given setting. In addition, freedom from the consequences of evaluation findings is counterbalanced by lower commitment, less of a stake in how the evaluation results in program improvement. This is not to argue that outside evaluations are not useful, only that, like most things, they have both positive and negative aspects.

Another problem is that outside evaluations tend to be summative only, neglecting the formative function that is so important for program improvement. This does not have to be the case, but it is not unusual for an evaluator to be approached in the spring of the school year when all that can be done is some form of summative evaluation. The best time to begin to discuss an evaluation with a consultant is well before the school year begins, so that a careful evaluation plan, with provisions for formative evaluation, can be developed.

Finally, few schools and school districts have the resources to commission evaluations by outsiders on an annual basis. Frequent evaluation is important for program improvement, and this requires that program evaluation, conducted internally, be built into the program as an essential component. As I argue in my book on program planning (Borland, 1989), evaluation ought to be an integral component of every program for gifted students, one that is no less necessary than, say, identification procedures. How, then, can local evaluations be carried out by school personnel who, in most cases, have little knowledge or experience of program evaluation?

A Framework for Program Evaluation

The following approach to program evaluation is but one of a number of possible approaches to the task. It revolves around program goals, and is straightforward, practicable, and requires no psychometric expertise.

Step 1: Defining or Clarifying Program Goals

Clear, sensible program goals greatly facilitate the evaluation process. The first step, therefore, is to review and to clarify the goals of the program, making certain they refer to benefits that will accrue to students as a result of program intervention.

Step 2: Selecting Goals for the Current Evaluation

Typically, programs come with quite a few goals. To try to make them all the focus of any single evaluation effort could make the process too unwieldy. Therefore, it makes sense to focus on a few goals, perhaps three or four—maybe fewer, maybe more—in any annual evaluation. Which goals are chosen depends on various factors, perhaps special emphases for the upcoming year or perceived program deficiencies that need work. In any case, because program evaluation will take place on an annual basis, there is no need, nor is it advisable, to try to cover every goal every year. At this point, forms can be made, perhaps something like the one shown in Figure 21.1, on which the goals can be written and additional information noted. This should be done prior to the beginning of the academic year so that formative as well as summative data can be planned for.

Step 3: Identifying Program Activities, Outcomes, and Criteria Related to the Selected Goals

Over the course of the coming year, various program activities will take place that are designed to achieve goals or that involve students in behaviors that reflect on goal attainment. The next step, therefore, is to list on each form those activities in which student behavior can be observed that will shed light on progress toward the goal. For example, if a targeted goal is for students to develop research skills, student work on independent projects is one obvious activity in which to observe students for behavior that indicates how they are progressing toward the goal. For each

Program Goal:

Activity	*Behavior or Outcome*	*Observation Points*	*Criterion*	*Performance*	*Analysis*

Synthesis:

Figure 21.1 Form for planning goal-based program evaluation.

goal, then, one lists as many activities as can be anticipated, and one can add activities as they are planned during the year.

Each of these activities will have a behavior or outcome that is to some extent observable, and these should also be listed, as should the observation points, when the behaviors or outcomes will be observed. Finally, the criteria, or desired level of performance, should be specified. Using the above example, depending on past experience, one might stipulate a certain percentage of students completing projects as one criterion for the goal.

Step 4: Recording and Analyzing Student Performance

As each activity related to the program goal takes place, one can record the students' actual level of performance. Then, comparing this with the previously established criterion, one can record a few analytical comments relating to the degree to which the criterion was met and what this implies. Once this is done for all activities listed in the first column, one or two synthesizing paragraphs can be written commenting on the degree to which the goal was met, what should be done in the future, and so forth. Once these have been done for all targeted goals, they can be integrated into an evaluation report containing short-term and long-term recommendations for the program.

The overall goal is to gather as much evidence as possible from direct observation of student work and behavior to shed light on the degree of progress made toward selected program goals. It is likely that most of the data collected will not be test data, and much of the data will be subjective. This should not be a concern. The important thing is to gather as many data as possible and to make the evaluation practicable within the constraints posed by available resources and the evaluation expertise of the educators conducting the evaluation. It should be clear that no particular expertise in program evaluation is required to carry out an evaluation of this sort, and that is by design. To the extent that evaluation is viewed as arcane, highly technical, and imposed from outside or above, it is less likely to be done or used.

Some Other Thoughts on Program Evaluation

Authentic Assessment and Program Evaluation

Much has been written lately on the topic of *authentic assessment,* assessment that more closely resembles the actual curriculum and instruction whose effects are being measured (see, e.g., "Using Performance Assessment," 1992; Wiggins, 1989; Wright & Borland, 1993). An obvious example, provided by House (1993), is the use of essays instead of multiple-choice examinations to assess writing ability or the success of a writing program, because the activity required in the assessment, writing, is more closely matched to what has been taught.

This is a promising area that already has borne fruit in Amabile's (1983) work on *consensual assessment,* the judgment by consensus of creative products within a specific domain by individuals who have expertise in that domain. There is an obvious advantage to this method: It mirrors the way we do things in the real world, in which the products of individuals working in, say, various artistic domains are assessed by individuals and groups within those domains: critics, gallery owners, curators, editors, conductors, and so forth. It is, in that respect, authentic assessment.

These ideas can be brought into the realm of program evaluation quite readily. To the extent that programs exist to assist students in acquiring certain skills, assessing those skills as part of program evaluation can, and arguably should, be done in as authentic a manner as possible. For example, if enhancing students' creativity is a major goal of the program, one could place students in situations that require them to respond creatively to problems in relevant domains.

Evaluation of Programs Designed to Serve Traditionally Underrepresented Gifted Students

Unfortunately, there is ample evidence (e.g., Passow, 1989; Richert, 1987; VanTassel-Baska, Patton, & Prillaman, 1989) that, despite good intentions, we have failed to do enough to identify and serve gifted students who are outside society's mainstream, including students who are economically disadvantaged, especially students from racial and ethnic minority groups. There has been progress in this area, however, as evidenced by the programs for underrepresented students funded though the provisions of the Jacob Javits Gifted and Talented Students Program. But with progress in this area will come new concerns related to program evaluation.

Some of these are obvious, such as the need to accommodate the needs of students with limited English proficiency. Others, however, stem from a complex web of social and cultural factors that derive from significant differences between subcultures within our society. Cultural values and assumptions are implicit in the educational goals, methods, and assessments that prevail in this country, and these are not always consistent with the values of all subcultures. The anthropologist John Ogbu (e.g., 1978, 1985, 1992; see also Fordham, 1988, 1991; Fordham & Ogbu, 1986; and, in this field, Ford, 1992, 1993) states that those minorities he refers to as *involuntary minorities* differ from the white middle class by virtue of what he calls *secondary cultural differences,* which arise under conditions of prolonged inequality and denial of full assimilation into the mainstream. These can take the form of *cultural inversion,* in which mainstream values—such as striving for academic success—are anathematized and seen as emblematic of an oppressive majority. Fordham discusses "the burden of acting white," with which academically successful minority students frequently must contend, and how this can create considerable distress because, although it facilitates academic success and upward mobility, it can alienate minority students from their peers and family members.

Successful evaluation of programs specifically for underrepresented gifted students or of mainstream programs that are more inclusive will require an understanding that giftedness manifests itself in different ways in different cultures and settings, and that in order to understand these manifestations, one must understand the culture and the setting. As Armour-Thomas (1992) argues, cognitive potential and cultural experience cannot be understood apart from each other. Fuller recognition of this fact will facilitate our success in evaluating the increasing range of programs for gifted students that the future is likely to present us.

Conclusion

I hope I have not emphasized the difficulties of program evaluation too much, for it is a practicable and necessary part of operating a program for gifted students. If planning and conducting a program evaluation appears to be a daunting prospect, keep in mind that maintaining and improving a program that is not evaluated is even more daunting. Evaluation is a form of inquiry, which is a search after knowledge. If we do not even attempt to evaluate our programs, we are stating implicitly that we are content to remain ignorant, something that we would find difficult to justify both to our students and to ourselves.

REFERENCES

Amabile, T. M. (1983). *The social psychology of creativity.* New York: Springer-Verlag.

Armour-Thomas, E. (1992). Intellectual assessment of children from culturally diverse backgrounds. *School Psychology Review, 21,* 552–565.

Benbow, C. P. (1986). SMPY's model for teaching mathematically precocious students. In J. S. Renzulli (Ed.), *Systems and models for developing programs for the gifted and talented* (pp. 1–26). Mansfield Center, CT: Creative Learning Press.

Borland, J. H. (1989). *Planning and implementing programs for the gifted.* New York: Teachers College Press.

Borland, J. H. (1990). Postpositivist inquiry: Implications of the "new philosophy of science" for the field of the education of the gifted. *Gifted Child Quarterly, 34,* 161–167.

Campbell, D. T., & Stanley, J. C. (1963). *Experimental and quasi-experimental designs for research.* Chicago: Rand McNally.

Crockenberg, S. (1972). Creativity tests: Boon or boondoggle for education? *Review of Educational Research, 42,* 27–45.

Cronbach, L. J., Ambron, S. R., Dornbusch, S. M., Hess, R. D., Hornik, R. C., Phillips, D. C., Walker, D. E., & Weiner, S. S. (1980). *Toward re-*

form of program evaluation. San Francisco: Jossey-Bass.

Cross, T. (1994). A commentary: Alternative inquiry and its potential contribution to gifted education. *Roeper Review, 16*, 284–285.

Fetterman, D. M. (1993). *Evaluate yourself.* Storrs, CT: National Research Center on the Gifted and Talented.

Ford, D. Y. (1992). Determinants of underachievement as perceived by gifted, above-average and average black students. *Roeper Review, 14,* 130–136.

Ford, D. Y. (1993). An investigation of the paradox of underachievement among gifted black students. *Roeper Review, 16*, 78–84.

Fordham, S. (1988). Racelessness as a strategy in black students' school success: Pragmatic strategy or pyrrhic victory? *Harvard Educational Review, 58*(1), 54–84.

Fordham, S. (1991). Peer proofing academic competition among black adolescents: "Acting white: Black American style." In C. E. Sleeter (Ed.), *Empowerment through multicultural education* (pp. 69–93). Albany: State University of New York Press.

Fordham, S., & Ogbu, J. U. (1986). Black students' school success: Coping with the burden of "acting white." *The Urban Review, 18*, 176–206.

Gage, N. L. (1989). The paradigm wars and their aftermath: A "historical" sketch of research on teaching since 1989. *Educational Researcher, 18,* 4–10.

Goldenberg, C., & Gallimore, R. (1991). Local knowledge, research knowledge, and educational change: A case study of early Spanish reading improvement. *Educational Researcher, 20*(8), 2–14.

Guba, E. G., & Lincoln, Y. S. (1989). *Fourth generation evaluation.* Beverly Hills, CA: Sage.

House, E. R. (1993). *Evaluation of programs for disadvantaged gifted students.* Unpublished manuscript, University of Colorado, Boulder.

Joint Committee on Standards for Educational Evaluation. (1981). *Standards for evaluations of educational programs, projects, and materials.* New York: McGraw-Hill.

Lincoln, Y. S., & Guba, E. G. (1985). *Naturalistic inquiry*. Beverly Hills, CA: Sage.

Nevo, D. (1983). The conceptualization of educational evaluation: An analytical review of the literature. *Review of Educational Research, 53*, 117–128.

Ogbu, J. U. (1978). *Minority education and caste: The American system in cross-cultural perspective.* New York: Academic Press.

Ogbu, J. U. (1985). Minority education and caste. In N. Yetman (Ed.), *Majority and minority* (4th ed., pp. 370–383). Boston: Allyn and Bacon.

Ogbu, J. U. (1992). Understanding cultural diversity and learning. *Educational Researcher, 21*(8), 5–14.

Passow, A. H. (1989). Needed research and development in educating high ability children. *Roeper Review, 11*, 223–229.

Patton, M. Q. (1986). *Utilization-focused evaluation* (2nd ed.). Beverly Hills, CA: Sage.

Perkins, D. N. (1981). *The mind's best work.* Cambridge, MA: Harvard University Press.

Richert, E. S. (1987). Rampant problems and promising practices in the identification of disadvantaged gifted students. *Gifted Child Quarterly, 31,* 149–154.

Sapon–Shevin, M. (1994). *Playing favorites: Gifted education and the disruption of community.* Ithaca: State University of New York Press.

Scriven, M. (1967). The methodology of evaluation. In R. E. Stake (Ed.), *AERA monograph series on curriculum evaluation,* No. 1. Chicago: Rand McNally.

Scriven, M. (1972). Pros and cons about goal-free evaluation. *Journal of Educational Evaluation, 3*(4), 1–7.

Slavin, R. E (1991). Are cooperative learning and "untracking" harmful to the gifted? *Educational Leadership, 48*(6), 68–71.

Stake, R. E. (1967). The countenance of educational evaluation. *Teachers College Record, 68,* 523–540.

Stanley, J. C. (1981). Rationale of the study of mathematically precocious youth (SMPY) during its first five years of promoting educational acceleration. In W. B. Barbe & J. S. Renzulli (Eds.), *Psychology and education of the gifted,* (pp. 248–283). New York: Irvington.

Torrance, E. P. (1975). Creativity research in education: Still alive. In I. A. Taylor & J. W. Getzels (Eds.), *Perspectives in creativity* (pp. 278–296). Chicago: Aldine

Torrance, E. P. (1988). The nature of creativity as manifest in testing. In R. J. Sternberg (Ed.), *The nature of creativity* (pp. 43–75). New York: Cambridge University Press.

Tyler, R. W. (1950). *Basic principles of curriculum and instruction.* Chicago: University of Chicago Press.

Using performance assessment [Special issue]. (1992). *Educational Leadership, 49* (8).

VanTassel-Baska, J., Patton, J., & Prillaman, D. (1989). Disadvantaged gifted learners: At risk for educational attention. *Focus on Exceptional Children, 22*(3), 1–15.

Wallach, M. A. (1985). Creativity testing and giftedness. In F. D. Horowitz & M. O'Brien (Eds.), *The gifted and talented: Developmental perspec-*

tives (pp. 99–123). Washington, DC: American Psychological Association.

Wiggins, G. (1989). A true test: Toward more authentic and equitable assessment. *Phi Delta Kappan, 70*(9), 703–713.

Wright, L., & Borland, J. H. (1993). Using early childhood developmental portfolios in the identification and education of young, economically disadvantaged, potentially gifted students. *Roeper Review, 15*, 205–210.

PART IV

Creativity, Thinking Skills, and Eminence

Every statement of goals for gifted programs names growth in creative thinking and other thinking skills as prime objectives. Part IV helps clarify these complex topics, how they may be strengthened in gifted children, and how they and other factors pertain to adult eminence.

In Chapter 22 Gary A. Davis emphasizes that tests are just one way to identify creative students. Observation of personality and motivational characteristics; biographical information, especially evaluations of past creative activities; and informal estimations of creative abilities (including intelligence) are valid ways to distinguish students with creative tendencies and capability. He notes that creative traits and motivations are built into Renzulli's concept of "action information." Davis itemizes complexities of "creativity" and emphasizes that current creativity tests therefore cannot demonstrate high validity. Further, each type of test—divergent thinking tests and personality inventories—evaluates only part of the creative person. Creativity tests can be useful, says Davis, particularly if combined with other information.

Beth A. Hennessey in Chapter 23 outlines social and environmental conditions that have an impact on children's creative development by affecting their motivation to create. A three-component creativity model includes domain-relevant skills (knowledge and technical skills), creativity-relevant skills (e.g., independence, an interest in novel ideas), and task motivation. Hennessey stresses the core role of intrinsic motivation—interest, enjoyment, and satisfaction—that brings domain and creativity skills to bear on creative performance. The author reviews the effects of intrinsic motivation and extrinsic constraints—such as expecting to be evaluated—on creative performance. Hennessey's own research included successful efforts to "immunize" children against damaging factors by helping them focus on interesting, fun, and playful aspects of assignments.

In Chapter 24 Susan Daniels notes that creativity should be nourished throughout the school day, not just in well-defined creativity programs. She elaborates on ways to strengthen twelve central traits that underlie creative capability. A preliminary requirement, notes the author, is a receptive "psychologically safe" classroom environment. Curriculum can include helping students understand creativity, giving choices in ways to study and prepare projects, infusing brainstorming into discussions, allowing affective and kinesthetic expression, employing creative drama, and using questioning to encourage and respond to curiosity. The authors's sensorial/perceptual diagram helps students organize sensory and imaginational aspects of experience. Daniels also explains how exercises in visual thinking and visual synthesis, some of which are humorous and playful, can stretch imaginations.

In Chapter 25 S. Lee Winocur and Patricia A. Maurer describe Project IMPACT, a remarkably imaginative, engaging, and successful program for teaching thinking skills. Three components of the IMPACT approach include the Universe of Critical Thinking (22 thinking skills such as logical reasoning, evaluating, and analyzing), 10 teaching behaviors (e.g., sequencing cognitive skills, modeling, questioning, and teaching for transfer), and a lesson design that permits improving and developing lessons. The authors present their *Zooley* exercise to illustrate both the dynamics and the enjoyability of the program. Project IMPACT is for all children; in a demonstration project, IMPACT dramatically reduced the number of students defined as "at risk."

Carol Schlichter in Chapter 26 outlines how she transformed Calvin Taylor's Multiple-Talent Totem Pole concept into an effective teacher training strategy, the Talents Unlimited (TU) model. The focus is on methods and activities to teach the talents, or thinking skills, of productive thinking (creativity), decision making, planning, forecasting, and communication, as well as academic content and skills. TU is the elementary training model; TU^2 is the model for secondary teachers. The inservice training includes introductory sessions on multiple talent theory, modeling and demonstrations, classroom practice with feedback, and individual and small-group planning. Talents Unlimited is a schoolwide enrichment plan for all students. However, it is especially valuable in helping gifted students focus and manage independent projects and deal with such development issues as peer problems, parents' expectations, or perfectionism.

Herbert J. Walberg and Susie Zeiser in Chapter 27 outline educational productivity factors that increase efficiency in academic learning and contribute to exceptional talent and even eminence. Nine interacting productivity factors, identified mainly from two decades of studying talented adolescents and eminent people, include, for example, ability, time engaged in learning, quality of instruction, a home life that supports intellectual development, peers outside school, and the negatively related factor of exposure to mass media and popular culture—particularly television. Walberg and Zeiser stress the key role of motivation, which leads to sustained effort, feelings of satisfaction, and motivation for further learning. Recent studies of eminent women essentially replicate factors leading to eminence in men—for example, intelligence, perseverance, inquisitiveness, creativity, and stimulating social environments.

In Chapter 28 Dean Keith Simonton elaborates on the complicated relationship of giftedness and genius. He notes that many of Terman's high-IQ children did not achieve eminence and that many eminent adults in Cox's biographical study would not have met Terman's IQ criterion. Simonton proposes a multiplicative relationship—among, for example, intellect, motivation, personality, childhood experience, and education—which predicts the disproportionate number of lifetime achievements by just a handful of persons. High drive and dedication are essential, notes Simonton, but mental disturbance and childhood emotional trauma also are common among eminent persons. Further, first-borns are more likely to be successful in traditional areas, later-borns in artistic and nontraditional areas; and extensive education apparently provides no great advantage.

22

Identifying Creative Students and Measuring Creativity

GARY A. DAVIS, *University of Wisconsin, Madison*

There are many ways to *identify* students with above-average to high creative potential. Using tests, inventories, or rating scales to *measure* creative abilities, affective characteristics, or the creativeness of past innovative products is just one way.

Attitudes toward identifying versus measuring creativity can differ dramatically. On one hand, the majority of educators committed to fostering giftedness agree that students with creative potential can and should be *identified* for special programs. On the other hand, some critics hold the opinion that "creativity" cannot be *measured* by currently available creativity tests; the search for a convincing CQ (Creativity Quotient) is futile (e.g., Perkins, 1981). This apparent difference of opinion is partly semantic, centered on whether we focus on students who possess abilities and personality dispositions that dispose them toward creative thinking and behavior, versus adults who have demonstrated outstanding creative achievement. We can, within limits, identify students with creative capability; we cannot predict which of them eventually will show adult creative genius.

Identifying some creative children and adolescents is easy. They stick out like the proverbial sore thumb: They are bright, active, energetic, and inquisitive; have quick and lively imaginations and a terrific sense of humor; and they probably relish their creative enterprises, for example, in art, writing, theater, science, social action, entrepreneurship, or at the microcomputer.

Complexity of "Creativity"

Looking beyond the obviously creative kids, identifying creative potential admittedly can be difficult and prone to error because of the inherent complexity of creativity and creative people. A few dimensions of this complexity, which can plague identification of creative persons, are these (Davis, 1989, 1992):

- Individuals can be creative in any part—or all parts—of their personal, educational, and adult professional lives. Said Torrance (1966b, 1979), we can be creative in an infinite number of ways.
- Cognitive and noncognitive traits—intellectual and information-processing capabilities, attitudes, personality traits, motivations, and family and school opportunities and experiences—must combine to orient students toward creativity thinking.
- Some persons are high in Maslow's (1954) *self-actualized* creativity, the mentally healthy tendency to be creative in all aspects of one's life. Others will show *special-talent* creativity, which refers to persons with a great talent who may not be mentally healthy. Still others will possess both self-actualized and special-talent creativity. A long-standing literature couples creativity with psychopathology (e.g., Andreason, 1978; Barron, 1969; Flach, 1990; Richards, 1981), even among regular college students (Schuldberg, 1990; Schuldberg, French, Stone, & Heberle, 1988).
- We have small-scale creative insights and projects, as when a child creates a poem or solves a problem in a novel way; we also have larger scale creative productivity, as when a student writes and produces a high school play.
- Creativity can be "forced," as when we set a time and place for classroom brainstorming; it also happens suddenly and unpredictably,

as when problem solutions pop into consciousness, composers hear symphonies in their heads, or, as Hemingway once said, "The stuff comes alive and turns crazy on ya'" (Bass, 1968).

- Creative innovation may stem from lengthy hard work and planning; it also happens in sudden inspirations and insights. Analogical connections, for example, may appear in an instant, as when cartoonist Gary Larson substitutes house flies for adoring mothers: "Oh my, what a cute little maggot."
- Creativity involves logical thinking and analysis as well as irrational and unrestrained fantasy.
- Creative talent will remain repressed and hidden without a psychologically safe (Rogers, 1962) social and cultural environment that supplies opportunities and reinforcement for creativity.
- Wakefield (1991) noted that *problem finding* is a hallmark of creative accomplishment. His creativity model described four combinations of problem finding (open or closed) and problem solving (open or closed): (1) convergent logical problem solving (closed problems/closed solutions); (2) divergent thinking (closed problems, open solutions); (3) problem invention or discovery (as in insight puzzles; open problem finding, closed solutions); and (4) true creativity (open problem finding/open solutions).

As we will see briefly in the next section, if we examine characteristics and conditions for creative eminence, the complexity of "creativity" multiplies.

Pessimism about Creativity Testing

There are many reasons for pessimism regarding our present ability to "measure creativity." First, the accurate perception that creativity is multiplex and mysterious implies to some that creativity tests are totally without merit, which is inaccurate.

A second reason for pessimism lies with built-in statistical difficulties. Efforts to build an omnibus, sweeping "CQ test" of creative abilities and tendencies—regardless of topic area; stability of the criterion measure; or student personality, motivation, intelligence, education, opportunities, experience, family and school support, interest in taking the test, and so on—simply cannot produce validity coefficients that are large, yet meaningful.

A third reason for pessimism is that, as noted earlier, some critics define creativity in a post hoc way, as a capability possessed only by persons who achieve recognition for their accomplishments. Current creativity tests admittedly cannot predict greatness. By way of comparison, our esteemed intelligence tests do not predict professional eminence one whit better. Among Terman's 1,528 gifted children, nearly all of whom had scored above IQ 140 (some above 180) on his new *Stanford-Binet Intelligence Scale,* not one reached the eminence of an Einstein, Picasso, or Howard Hughes (Golman, 1980).

The reason, perhaps obvious, for the failure of creativity or intelligence tests to predict creative eminence is that too many factors are part of the elusive formula. In addition to the complexity factors listed earlier, Simonton adds chance, birth order, social skills and leadership ability (often depressed by a too-high IQ), and even an unhappy childhood as pieces in the creative eminence puzzle (see Chapter 28). Similarly, Feldman's (1991) *Co-Incidence* theory describes extraordinary achievement at an early age as the joint occurrence of intraindividual, environmental, and historical factors—for example, high ability, passionate commitment, a family that values and fosters ability, exposure to master instruction, and available cultural knowledge (see Morelock and Feldman, Chapter 35). *Coincidence* is the right word, perhaps modified by *lucky.*

On the upside, as we will see later, and speaking from experience in developing creativity tests (Davis, 1975; Davis & Rimm, 1982), many creativity tests in fact are on target, moderately valid, and helpful—when we bear in mind certain limitations. A common difficulty is false negatives—the failure of a test to identify a truly creative person, due to a Grand Canyon of difference between test content and the person's particular form of creativeness. False positives are not likely.[1] A high score almost invariably means the student has creative potential and/or creative experience. That capability may have been invisible or underestimated because, for example, of the student's reticence or a classroom that does not ask for or reward creative ideas.

Measurement limitations mean that creativity test results must be used cautiously, and should be combined with other information regarding students' creativeness in order to identify students with above-average creative potential. If creativity tests or nominations are used, I recommend using at least two such criteria—for example, scores on a divergent thinking test along with scores on a personality/biographical inventory, or else either a creativity test or inventory score plus a teacher's (or parent's) rating of creativeness. If a student scores high on two criteria, you may feel comfortable about identifying him or her as having creative potential. On the other hand, if a student scores average or below on a single creativity test, it easily could be a mistake to accept that score as a true measure of creative capability.

Creativity and Intelligence

Early research by Barron (1969), MacKinnon (1961, 1978), Getzels and Jackson (1962), and Wallach and Kogan (1965) confirmed our commonsense suspicion that creativity and intelligence are different, yet related cognitive capabilities.

One major difference lies in the role of personality and motivation. No one claims that high intelligence depends on one's personality and motivational characteristics. On the other hand, creative thinking and behavior requires not only creative abilities, but logically relevant affective characteristics—attitudes, awarenesses, and personality and motivational traits—that have been confirmed repeatedly by research (e.g., Barron, 1969, 1988; Davis, 1975; MacKinnon, 1961, 1978; Torrance, 1962, 1965, 1977, 1988). In Sternberg's (1988) three-facet model of creativity, two factors included a mix of thinking styles, personality traits, and motivation (e.g., a preference for creating one's own rules; tendencies to simplify; an enjoyment of writing, designing, and creating; flexibility; drive and persistence; and moderate risk taking). His third factor was intelligence.

Getzels and Jackson (1962) made the important observation that their high-intelligence students were not incapable of thinking creatively; they simply were not disposed to do so. Their conclusion underscores the key role of attitudinal, personality, and motivational characteristics, with "creativity consciousness" at the forefront.

A related matter is the Barron and MacKinnon *threshold* concept (e.g., MacKinnon, 1978): Over the wide range of intelligence, they found creativity and intelligence to be moderately related; but, above a threshold IQ, which they pegged at 120, the relationship essentially disappeared. The threshold concept implies that high intelligence is not enough, nor is it the same as creativity. Walberg and Herbig (1991), in reviewing characteristics of eminent persons, concluded that "the very brightest, by estimated IQ, are not necessarily 'the best'" (p. 251; see Chapter 27).

There is little doubt that intelligence and creativity are different animals, but, important to the present argument, they also are related. We know from research by Catharine Cox (1926), the Goertzels (Goertzel, Goertzel, & Goertzel, 1978), Walberg and Herbig (1991; see Chapter 27), and Simonton (1988)—again, along with our intuitions—that high intelligence is a requisite trait for high-level creativity. Consider the following kinds of abilities that are part of high intelligence, and ask yourself if they are relevant to creative capability.

---

[1] Some types of creativity tests are fakable, if a (creativity) test-wise person is so inclined. For example, when so instructed, college students can deliberately score high on an inventory assessing creative personality characteristics (Ironson & Davis, 1979); students also can inflate originality scores on divergent thinking tests by deliberately listing "wild" ideas.

The abilities to . . .

think logically	analyze situations
make inferences	see relationships
separate relevant from irrelevant	ask good questions
define and redefine problems	evaluate
anticipate consequences	make good decisions
think analogically	visualize and transform
	understand complex issues
	impose structure on disorganization or chaos

You probably answered "yes" to each trait.

Consider also for a moment Gardner's *musical* intelligence (see Chapter 5). A person strong in this type of intelligence probably would be judged "creative" because of his or her interpretational, compositional, and/or improvisational skills. But would not a person high in Gardner's other types of intelligence—especially linguistic, logical-mathematical, spatial, interpersonal, and bodily-kinesthetic—also be better equipped and likely to improvise and "compose" in his or her area of high intelligence?

Simonton (1988) tells us that intelligence fills the brain with images, sounds, phrases, and abstract concepts, and the highly intelligent person has a greater chance of forming the novel combinations of ideas, images, and symbols that constitute a masterpiece than does someone with just a "starter set." In a *Newsweek* article about genius, Begley (1993, p. 50) wrote: "Ph.D.s have a vast, complicated neural web, but high-school dropouts only a sparse, inefficient one. (This could explain why geniuses are more adept at bringing together disparate images, thoughts and phrases: Their brains look like Ma Bell's network.)"

The point is that young people with high intelligence have a unique potential for creative productivity, perhaps creative eminence. Therefore, high intelligence is a strong clue for identifying high creative potential.

Informal Identification of Creative Students

Like other means for identifying giftedness, creativity identification methods may be classed as *formal* or *informal,* depending on whether the identification strategy is based on objective test scores or on subjective opinions of teachers, parents, peers, or students themselves. Between formal and informal methods lies a gray area in which formal-looking questionnaires and rating scales are used to record informal impressions of students' creative abilities, characteristics, or past creative achievements.

Biographical Information: Creative Activities

A sure way to locate creative students at any grade level is to look for a background of creative activities. Does the elementary child constantly make or build things? Does he or she have wide interests, unusual hobbies, unique collections? Perhaps dinosaurs, magic, Egyptology, Charlie Chaplin impressions, or a collection of animal bones? Does the child have unusual experience or talent in art, poetry, creative writing, handicrafts, music, dance, computer programming, or a science area? Perhaps you have a "photography kid" or a child who knows more about Picasso, Napoleon, Maya Angelou, Shirley Chisolm, or Russian cosmonauts than do the teachers.

If a child or adolescent happens to be a "theater kid," you need look no further. In my experience, a background in theater is one of two indicators of high creativity that is 100 percent accurate. The other is having had an imaginary playmate. Creative secondary students and adults may laughingly say, "I still do." Typically, the young child will talk to and play with the imaginary companion, have tea parties, blame things on the playmate ("I didn't break it, Bopsy did!"), and make Mom—or the restaurant waitress—set an extra place at the table. Sometimes there are many imaginary friends; sometimes they are animals. Some creative children do a continuous ventriloquist act, talking back and forth with a stuffed animal or doll. The imaginary friend usually disappears after children enter kindergarten (Somers & Yawkey, 1984). Like theater kids, students who report having had an imaginary playmate inevitably show other personality or background traits of creativity.

Creative activities inventories. Research verifies that self-reported involvement in creative activities is a solid indicator of present and probably future creativeness (e.g., Bull & Davis, 1980; Davis, 1989; Holland, 1961; Richards et al., 1988). The face validity of such information is high. Holland, for example, found that high school students who currently were creatively talented in art or science could be identified by assessing their history of creative activities. He concluded that past creative achievement is the single best predictor of future creative achievement. Bull and Davis (1980) asked college students to "List any creative activities (artistic, literary, technical, or scientific) in which you are or have been engaged in the past 2–3 years." The derived creativity scores showed good correlations (validity coefficients) with other criteria of creativity—for example, .41 with scores on How Do You Think? (Davis, 1975) and .40 with an original measure of internal sensation seeking (which evaluated, e.g., desire for fantasy/daydreaming and vividness of imagery), created by Bull.

It is not difficult to create a self-report inventory or one to be completed by parents that simply asks about student's past or present strong interests or hobbies. For example:

> Describe any hobbies, collections, or strong interests that you [your child may] have had. For example, have you [has your child] been really interested in reptiles, writing poetry or stories, magic tricks, theater, computers, Egypt, dinosaurs, collections, science, art, handicrafts, or music? Other hobbies or collections? If so, list them.

A few statements indicating outstanding past creative involvement no doubt would float to the top.

Action information. Renzulli and his colleagues developed the concept of *Action Information* (Renzulli, 1994; Renzulli & Reis, 1985; see Chapter 11). Action Information is either (1) students' ideas for independent research projects—Renzulli's Type III Enrichment—or (2) teachers' observations of students' strong interests, accompanied by high motivation to explore and create within their topic. In short, Action Information is a realistic means of identifying motivated, creative students.

The following are a few of Renzulli's examples of Action Information.[2] A young person shows high creativity and motivation when he or she:

> Goes "above and beyond the call of duty" in completing, for example, an art, writing, or science project that shows superlative quality.
>
> Is labeled by others (not always in complimentary ways) as the "math marvel," "computer whiz kid," "poet in residence," or "mad scientist."
>
> Is sought out by others because he or she is an expert in a particular area.
>
> Is obsessed with a particular topic or area of study.
>
> Has extracurricular activities that are more important than regular school work.
>
> Wants to "get something going," for example, a club, interest group, money raising, or other project (e.g., film making or a class newspaper), field trip, or action on a social problem ("Let's write to the governor about our polluted lake!").
>
> Voluntarily visits museums, laboratories, power plants, etc., on his or her own.
>
> Forgets to come back to class or is always late when returning from a particular course or special interest area, for example, the computer, art, or industrial arts room.
>
> Is a clever humorist—sees whimsical or zany implications of otherwise serious situations.
>
> Has set up a laboratory, photography darkroom, or other special interest area at home on his or her own.
>
> Feels compulsion to begin work on a topic ("I have to write it down before I go nuts").
>
> Is eager to share what he or she has learned or worked on.

---

[2] Adapted from J. S. Renzulli and S. M. Reis, *Schoolwide Enrichment Model* (1985), by permission of the authors and Creative Learning Press, Mansfield Center, CT.

> Goes out of his or her way to make a point or prove someone else wrong; may disagree strongly with the teacher, a noted authority, or a particular law or regulation.
>
> Continues to work on a project even though he or she is discouraged by lack of progress.

While the tight relationship between past and present creativity is not surprising, it can be highly useful in identifying creative giftedness.

Consensual assessment. Amabile's (1982, 1983) *consensual assessment* technique assumes that people familiar with a particular domain recognize creativity when they see it. Teachers elicit samples of creative work with assignments that leave room for flexibility and novelty—for example, creative art and writing—as well as tasks for which the range of responses is limited. Groups of teachers then evaluate the creativeness of the products. As Borland notes (Chapter 21), evaluating actual products reflects the way talent and capability are recognized in the real world.

Like biographical reports of creativity and Renzulli's Action Information, consensual assessment is a valid, nontest way to identify students with creative capability.

Personality and Motivational Information

Creative people must possess a particular collection of personality and motivational dispositions that enable them to think differently and independently, become absorbed in their projects, behave in unconventional and original ways, and risk failure and making fools of themselves in the process. Creative people are unique individuals, but they have a lot in common.

A few years ago (Davis, 1992), I reviewed over a hundred adjectives and short phrases that describe personality characteristics of creative persons, drawn from many sources. I informally sorted the traits into seemingly interrelated subgroups, and was surprised to find only twelve categories. Some categories included large numbers of approximate synonyms; especially recurrent were words that generally meant *original, energetic,* or *independent.* I confess to being a global thinker, and a more analytic person probably could make finer distinctions and produce more categories. My twelve categories, with a few representative synonyms in each category, are these:

1. *Aware of creativeness* (creativity conscious, values originality and creativity, values own creativity)
2. *Original* (imaginative, flexible in ideas and thought, is a "what if?" person, resourceful, unconventional, challenges assumptions, irritated and bored by routine and obvious)
3. *Independent* (self-confident, internally controlled, individualistic, sets own rules, self-accepting, unconcerned with impressing others, may resist societal demands)
4. *Risk-taking* (does not mind consequences of being different, not afraid to try something new, willing to cope with hostility, willing to cope with failure, optimistic)
5. *Energetic* (adventurous, sensation seeking, enthusiastic, excitable, spontaneous, impulsive, driving absorption, goes beyond assigned tasks)
6. *Curious* (questioning, experimenting, inquisitive, wide interests)
7. *Sense of humor* (playful, plays with ideas, childlike freshness in thinking)
8. *Attracted to complexity* (attracted to novelty, asymmetry, the mysterious; is a complex person; tolerant of ambiguity, disorder, incongruity; tends to believe in psychical phenomena, flying saucers)
9. *Artistic* (artistic interests, aesthetic interests)
10. *Open-minded* (receptive to new ideas, receptive to other viewpoints, open to new experiences and growth, liberal, altruistic)
11. *Needs alone time* (needs privacy, reflective, introspective, internally preoccupied, sensitive, may be withdrawn, likes to work by himself or herself)
12. *Intuitive* (perceptive, sees relationships, uses all senses in observing)

There also are *negative* traits—ones that teachers, parents, or peers may not like, but that also can be used to help identify creative children and adolescents. These may in part have their roots in creative students' inclinations toward independence, originality, high energy, and risk taking. Some examples from Torrance (1981b), Smith (1966), and other sources are the following:

- Indifferent to conventions and courtesies
- Challenges rules and authority
- Rebellious, uncooperative
- Capricious, careless, disorderly
- Absentminded, forgetful
- Argumentative, cynical, sarcastic
- Sloppy with details and unimportant matters
- Egocentric, intolerant, tactless
- Temperamental, emotional
- Overactive physically and mentally

Despite recurring commonalities in personality traits, creative students will differ dramatically from one another. Some will be high achievers whose creativity will take artistic, scientific, or other socially valued forms. Other creative students will be more unconventional in appearance and behavior, perhaps visibly rebellious and "antiestablishment"—unwilling to tolerate a bureaucracy perceived as inflexible and irrelevant to world problems or their own concerns. Many creative students will be energetic, outgoing, confident, and comical; some artistic, poetic, or scientific-minded students will be anxious and introverted.

In rating or nominating "creative" students, teachers may not recognize characteristics of creativity, and many will favor "teacher pleasers" over sometimes unconventional, near-hyperactive students who think oddly, dress oddly, ignore rules and conventions, ask too many questions, do poor work when not interested, and/or are generally radical and rebellious. Some energetic and unconventional students will be perceived by their teachers as having attention deficit hyperactivity disorder (ADHD; Cramond, 1994). Such teachers are more likely to recommend consulting a physician about medication than to recommend the child for a gifted/talented program.

In secondary school, very bright students may display the "emotional giftedness" or "overexcitabilities" described by Piechowski (Chapter 30) and Delisle (Chapter 37)—high energy marked by rapid speech and impulsive actions; keen sensual awareness; questioning; reading; theoretical and moral thinking; animistic imagery and magical thinking; and intense emotionality, with high highs and self-critical, even suicidal lows. However, secondary teachers also must watch for the pretentious pseudocreatives, who dress and act the way they believe eccentric creative people should.

A teacher, psychologist, counselor, or parent who is aware of personality indicators of creativeness, both positive and negative, can capitalize on this information to informally identify creative potential in children and adolescents.

Formal Identification Procedures: Inventories and Tests

There are two main categories of creativity tests, *personality inventories* and *divergent thinking tests*. The personality inventories evaluate the kinds of attitudes, personality dispositions, motivational characteristics, interests, and activities described in the previous section—but they ignore cognitive abilities. Divergent-thinking tests evaluate a sample of cognitive abilities but ignore personality traits and background information, except as these may affect test performance.[3]

Creative Personality and Motivational Inventories

Creativity inventories may be administered and scored relatively easily; some can be machine scored. To begin with a shining example of on-target efficiency, Renzulli's ten-item creativity rating scale, part of his Scales for Rating the Behavioral Characteristics of

[3] Space does not permit an evaluation of reliability and validity data for each instrument.

Superior Students (Renzulli, 1983), is used by teachers to rate the creativeness of students of any age (Table 22.1). Its carefully assembled contents compare well with other descriptions of the creative personality.

My How Do You Think (HDYT) test (Davis, 1975; Davis & Bull, 1978; Davis & Subkoviak, 1978) evaluates traits mentioned earlier—independence, confidence, risk-taking, energy, adventurousness, curiosity, reflectiveness, humor and playfulness, liking for complexity, artistic interests, creative interests and activities, as well as belief in ESP and flying saucers.[4] HDYT was validated against actual creative products—creative writing, art, and invention projects required for a college creativity class. It also works well with high school students. Internal consistency reliabilities have ranged from .90 to .96. Research by others has supported construct and criterion-

[4] HDYT is available from the author.

Table 22.1
Creativity Characteristics

	1[a]	*2*	*3*	*4*
1. Displays a great deal of curiosity about many things; is constantly asking questions about anything and everything.	_____	_____	_____	_____
2. Generates a large number of ideas or solutions to problems and questions; often offers unusual ("way out"), unique, clever responses.	_____	_____	_____	_____
3. Is uninhibited in expressing opinion; is sometimes radical and spirited in disagreement; is tenacious.	_____	_____	_____	_____
4. Is a high risk taker; is adventurous and speculative.	_____	_____	_____	_____
5. Displays a good deal of intellectual playfulness; fantasizes; imagines ("I wonder what would happen if . . ."); manipulates ideas (i.e., changes, elaborates on them); is often concerned with adapting, improving, and modifying institutions, objects, and systems.	_____	_____	_____	_____
6. Displays a keen sense of humor and sees humor in situations that may not appear to be humorous to others.	_____	_____	_____	_____
7. Is unusually aware of his or her impulses and more open to the irrational in himself or herself (freer expression of feminine interest for boys, greater than usual amount of independence for girls); shows emotional sensitivity.	_____	_____	_____	_____
8. Is sensitive to beauty; attends to aesthetic characteristics of things.	_____	_____	_____	_____
9. Is nonconforming; accepts disorder; is not interested in details; is individualistic; does not fear being different.	_____	_____	_____	_____
10. Criticizes constructively; is unwilling to accept authoritarian pronouncements without critical examination.	_____	_____	_____	_____
			Total Score	_____

Source: From Renzulli's (1983) *Scales for Rating Behavioral Characteristics of Superior Students.*
[a] Scoring weights: 1 = Seldom or never; 2 = Occasionally; 3 = Considerably; 4 = Almost always.

related validity (e.g., Moss, 1991; Runco, Okuda, & Thurston, 1988; Schuldberg, 1993; Schuldberg et al., 1988).

There have been several spinoffs from HDYT. The Group Inventory for Finding Interests II (GIFFI II; Davis & Rimm, 1982), for high school students, is simply a shortened, published version of HDYT; the Group Inventory for Finding Interests I (GIFFI I), for middle school students, is a combination of items from HDYT and from Rimm's elementary school Group Inventory for Finding (Creative) Talent (GIFT; Rimm & Davis, 1976). Rimm (1983) also developed the Preschool and Kindergarten Interest Descriptor (PRIDE), which parents fill out to describe their 4- or 5-year-old child.

Two published creativity inventories for elementary children are Schaefer's (1971) Creativity Attitude Survey, normed on fourth- and fifth-grade children; and Williams's (1980) Exercise in Divergent Feeling, for ages 8 through 18. Feldhusen, Denny, and Condon (1965) created an unpublished inventory, the Creativity Self-Report Scale, that consists of 67 descriptive phrases compiled by Torrance (1965). Junior or senior high school students simply indicate which of the phrases "is true of you."

Domino (1970) devised a scoring key for the Adjective Check List (ACL; Gough & Heilbrun, 1965), which includes 59 of the 300 ACL adjectives.[5] Gough (1979) himself validated a 30-item creativity scale for the ACL that he believes is better. Gough's scale also is more easily scored because there is no correction for total number of adjectives checked. The creativity score is simply the number of positive items checked minus the number of negative items checked. The positive items are *capable, clever, confident, egotistical, humorous, individualistic, informal, insightful, intelligent, interests wide, inventive, original, reflective, resourceful, self-confident, sexy, snobbish,* and *unconventional.* The negative items are *affected, cautious, commonplace, conservative, conventional, dissatisfied, honest, interests narrow, mannerly, sincere, submissive,* and *suspicious.*[6]

For adolescents and adults there also are the Khatena and Torrance (1976) Something About Myself and What Kind of Person Are You? inventories.

Divergent-Thinking Tests

By far the most popular creativity test battery is the Torrance Tests of Creative Thinking (TTCT; Torrance, 1966a). Torrance inadvertently may have led others to believe that his tests measure creativity, all creativity, and nothing but creativity, but he did not delude himself. Here is an excerpt from his norms-technical manual (Torrance, 1974):

> Since a person can behave creatively in an almost infinite number of ways, . . . it would be ridiculous even to try to develop a comprehensive battery of tests of creative thinking that would sample any kind of universe of creative thinking abilities. The author does not believe that anyone can now specify the number and range of test tasks necessary to give a complete or even an adequate assessment of a person's potentialities for creative behavior. He does believe that the sets of test tasks assembled in the [TTCT] sample a rather wide range of the abilities in such a universe. (p. 21)

The TTCT have a twenty-five-year developmental history, the most complete administration and scoring guides and norms, laudable longitudinal validation (e.g., Torrance, 1974, 1981a, 1990b; Torrance & Wu, 1981), and have been translated into thirty-four languages.

The verbal battery (seven subtests or "activities" in each of forms A and B) requires students, for example, to ask questions about an odd picture, list unusual uses for a cardboard box or tin can, list improvements for a stuffed elephant or monkey, or list consequences of an unlikely event (e.g., clouds are so low you can see only people's feet). The sixth subtest, Unusual Questions, is no longer scored—nor is it even mentioned—in the 1990 scoring

[5] Domino's scoring key is available in Davis (1992).

[6] Reprinted by permission of Harrison G. Gough and the American Psychological Association.

guide, worksheet, or norms (Torrance, 1990a). The nonverbal/figural battery (three subtests, forms A and B) includes three subtests, all of which require the test taker to create a meaningful drawing from an incomplete or abstract form. According to Torrance (1977), the figural tests are more culture-fair. The verbal tests may be group administered from the fourth grade through graduate school, and individually administered from kindergarten through the third grade; the figural tests may be group administered from kindergarten through graduate school.

The four basic scores of the original Torrance battery evaluate four abilities: *fluency* (number of ideas), *flexibility* (number of different categories of ideas), *originality* (statistical uniqueness), and *elaboration* (in the figural tests, number of pertinent details or ideas added to the original stimulus figure, its boundaries, or the surrounding space). Currently, Torrance recommends the streamlined scoring system for the figural tests (Torrance, 1990b; Torrance & Ball, 1984), intended to both expedite scoring and evaluate a total of 18 creative abilities. The streamlined scoring evaluates 5 norm-referenced measures: fluency, originality, elaboration, abstractness of titles, and resistance to premature closure; and 13 criterion-reference measures (creativity strengths): emotional expressiveness, story-telling articulateness, movement or action, expressiveness of titles, synthesis of incomplete figures, synthesis of lines (or circles), unusual visualization, internal visualization, extending or breaking boundaries, humor, richness of imagery, colorfulness of imagery, and fantasy. The new verbal scoring guide and figural norms-technical manual (Torrance, 1990a, 1990b) present normative data by grade and test form for the five norm-referenced measures, an average standard score, and a "creativity index" (average standard score plus number of creativity strengths).

Given the complexity problems described earlier and Torrance's own caution, validity data seem reasonable, despite criticisms. For summaries of pros and cons, see Callahan (1991), Chase (1985), Treffinger (1985), and Torrance (1979, 1988, 1990b).

The Getzels and Jackson (1962) tests and the Wallach and Kogan (1965) tests are published only in their books and apparently may be used without charge. Other published divergent thinking tests include the Guilford (1970) Creativity Tests for Children; the Monitor Test of Creative Potential for age 7 and older (Hoepfner & Hemenway, 1973); and Exercise in Divergent Thinking for ages 8 through 18 (Williams, 1980).

Torrance's (1981c) Thinking Creatively in Action and Movement is unique in that it was designed for very young children. Subtests, for example, ask children to show as many ways as they can to walk or run from one spot to another, or to put a paper cup in a wastebasket.

Thinking Creatively with Sounds and Words (Torrance, Khatena, & Cunnington, 1973) includes two different tests that are scored only for originality. With Onomatopoeia and Images, the test taker writes one idea stimulated by each of the 10 word stimuli (e.g., *zoom, moan, fizzy, jingle*); with Sounds and Images the person describes one idea stimulated by each of four abstract sounds. Sounds and Images could use updated scoring norms to accommodate contemporary associations to the sounds; for example, "racquetball" is a common response to one sound, yet earns maximum originality points according to the 1973 scoring guide.

Many unpublished creativity tests can be found, some of which try to evaluate creativity in specific subject areas. For example, the Detroit Public Schools Creativity Scales (Parke & Byrnes, 1984) are based on factors that experts use to evaluate creativity in music composition, music performance, dance, art, short story and novel writing, drama, poetry, and speech. The Judging Criteria Instrument (Eichenberger, 1978) is used by peers or oneself to evaluate creativity in a physics class, using rating scales that evaluate fluency, flexibility, originality, elaboration, usefulness, social acceptance, and worth to science.

If a G/T program planner wished to scour the literature for old and/or obscure tests for a particular purpose, some lists that include an astonishing variety of instruments appear in

Davis (1971, 1973), Kaltsoonis (1971, 1972), and Kaltsoonis and Honeywell (1980). As a sample, one scale measures the capacity to empathize with story characters; there also is a creative writing evaluation form, a preference for polygons task, a motor creativity test, several math creativity tests, a chemistry creativity test, a creative background inventory, an "experiential curiosity measure," a pun test, and an ingenuity test.

Summary and Conclusions

Identifying students with creative capability extends well beyond objective testing; in fact, several subjective procedures may have higher validity. Especially, information regarding a student's past and present creative activities is a disarmingly excellent indicator. In the same category are Renzulli's Action Information and Amabile's consensual assessment approaches. Observations of creative personality dispositions (positive and negative), high motivation, creative abilities, and even high intelligence are appropriate clues.

Creativity tests are of two main types, divergent-thinking tests and creative personality inventories; measures of creativity in subject areas also can be located. Creativity tests and inventories are useful when scores are combined with other information—perhaps scores on a second test or teachers' ratings—in order to make reliable judgments. False negatives pose a common hazard; truly creative students may not produce a high score when asked to decorate a picture of a cake, solve matchstick puzzles, or list unusual uses for a bucket.

The complexity of creativity and the effects of innumerable personal, familial, and environmental factors do not permit the development of a comprehensive, highly valid CQ test that can make long-range predictions of outstanding creative achievement.

REFERENCES

Amabile, T. (1982). Social psychology of creativity: A consensual assessment technique. *Journal of Personality and Social Psychology, 43,* 997–1013.

Amabile, T. (1983). *The social psychology of creativity.* New York: Springer-Verlag.

Andreason, N. C. (1978). Creativity and psychiatric illness. *Psychiatric Annals, 8,* 113–119.

Barron, F. (1969). *Creative person and creative process.* New York: Holt.

Barron, F. (1988). Putting creativity to work. In R. J. Sternberg (Ed.), *The nature of creativity* (pp. 76–98). New York: Cambridge University Press.

Bass, S. (1968). *Why man creates* (film). Oakland, CA: Kaiser Aluminum.

Begley, S. (1993, June 28). The puzzle of genius. *Newsweek,* pp. 46–51.

Bull, K. S., & Davis, G. A. (1980). Evaluating creative potential using the statement of past creative activities. *Journal of Creative Behavior, 14,* 249–257.

Callahan, C. M. (1991). The assessment of creativity. In N. Colangelo & G. A. Davis (Eds.), *Handbook of gifted education* (pp. 219–235). Boston: Allyn and Bacon.

Chase, W. I. (1985). Review of the Torrance Tests of Creative Thinking. In J. Mitchell (Ed.), *Ninth mental measurements yearbook* (Vol. 2, pp. 1630–1634). Lincoln, NE: Buros Institute of Mental Measurement.

Cox, C. M. (1926). *Genetic studies of genius. Vol. II: The early mental traits of three hundred geniuses.* Stanford, CA: Stanford University Press.

Cramond, B. (1994). Attention-deficit hyperactivity disorder and creativity—What is the connection? *Journal of Creative Behavior, 28,* 193–210.

Davis, G. A. (1971). Instruments useful in studying creative behavior and creative talents: Part II. *Journal of Creative Behavior, 5,* 162–165.

Davis, G. A. (1973). *Psychology of problem solving.* New York: Basic Books.

Davis, G. A. (1975). In frumious pursuit of the creative person. *Journal of Creative Behavior, 9,* 75–87.

Davis, G. A. (1989). Testing for creative potential. *Contemporary Educational Psychology, 14,* 257–274.

Davis, G. A. (1992). *Creativity is forever* (3rd ed.). Dubuque, IA: Kendall/Hunt.

Davis, G. A., & Bull, K. S. (1978). Strengthening affective components of creativity in a college course. *Journal of Educational Psychology, 70,* 833–836.

Davis, G. A., & Rimm, S. (1982). Group inventory for finding interests (GIFFI) I and II: Instruments for identifying creative potential in the junior and senior high school. *Journal of Creative Behavior, 16,* 50–57.

Davis, G. A., & Subkoviak, M. J. (1978). Multidimensional analysis of a personality-based test of creative potential. *Journal of Educational Measurement, 12,* 37–43.

Domino, G. (1970). Identification of potentially creative persons from the Adjective Check List. *Journal of Consulting and Clinical Psychology, 35,* 48–51.

Eichenberger, R. J. (1978). Creativity measurement through use of judgment criteria in physics. *Educational and Psychological Measurement, 38,* 221–227.

Feldhusen, J. F., Denny, T., & Condon, C. F. (1965) *Manual for the creativity self-report scale.* Unpublished manuscript, Purdue University, West Lafayette, IN.

Feldman, D. H. (with Goldsmith, L. T.). (1991). *Nature's gambit: Child prodigies and the development of human potential.* New York: Teachers College Press.

Flach, F. (1990). Disorders of the pathways involved in the creative process. *Creativity Research Journal, 3,* 158–165.

Getzels, J. W., & Jackson, P. W. (1962). *Creativity and intelligence.* New York: Wiley.

Goertzel, M. G., Goertzel, V., & Goertzel, T. G. (1978). *300 eminent personalities.* San Francisco: Jossey-Bass.

Golman, D. (1980, February). 1528 little geniuses and how they grew. *Psychology Today,* pp. 28–53.

Gough, H. G. (1979). A creative personality scale for the Adjective Check List. *Journal of Personality and Social Psychology, 37,* 1398–1405.

Gough, H. G., & Heilbrun, A. B., Jr. (1965). *The Adjective Check List manual.* Palo Alto, CA: Consulting Psychologists Press.

Guilford, J. P. (1970). *Creativity tests for children: A manual of interpretation.* Orange, CA: Sheridan Psychological Services.

Hoepfner, R., & Hemenway, J. (1973). *Test of creative potential.* Hollywood, CA: Monitor.

Holland, J. L. (1961). Creative and academic performance among talented adolescents. *Journal of Educational Psychology, 52,* 136–147.

Ironson, G., & Davis, G. A. (1979). Faking high or low creativity scores on the Adjective Check List. *Journal of Creative Behavior, 13,* 139–145.

Kaltsoonis, B. (1971). Instruments useful in studying creative behavior and creative talents: Part I. Commercially available instruments. *Journal of Creative Behavior, 5,* 117–126.

Kaltsoonis, B. (1972). Additional instruments useful in studying creative behavior and creative talents: Part III. Noncommercially available instruments. *Journal of Creative Behavior, 6,* 268–274.

Kaltsoonis, B., & Honeywell, L. (1980). Additional instruments useful in studying creative behavior and creative talent: Part IV. Noncommercially available instruments. *Journal of Creative Behavior, 14,* 56–67.

Khatena, J., & Torrance, E. P. (1976). *Manual for Khatena-Torrance Creative Perceptions Inventory.* Chicago: Stoelting.

MacKinnon, D. W. (1961). Creativity in architects. In D. W. MacKinnon (Ed.), *The creative person* (pp. 291–320). Berkeley: Institute of Personality Assessment and Research, University of California.

MacKinnon, D. W. (1978). Educating for creativity: A modern myth? In G. A. Davis & J. A. Scott (Eds.), *Training creative thinking* (pp. 194–207). Melbourne, FL: Krieger.

Maslow, A. H. (1954). *Motivation and personality.* New York: Harper & Row.

Moss, M. A. (1991). *The meaning and measurement of Jung's construct of intuition: Intuition and creativity.* Unpublished Ph.D. dissertation, University of Wisconsin, Madison.

Parke, B. N., & Byrnes, P. (1984). Toward objectifying the measurement of creativity. *Roeper Review, 6,* 216–218.

Perkins, D. N. (1981). *The mind's best work.* Cambridge, MA: Harvard University Press.

Renzulli, J. S. (1983, September/October). Rating the behavioral characteristics of superior students. *G/C/T,* 30–35.

Renzulli, J. S. (1994). *Schools for talent development: A practical plan for total school improvement.* Mansfield Center, CT: Creative Learning Press.

Renzulli, J. S., & Reis, S. M. (1985). *Schoolwide enrichment model.* Mansfield Center, CT: Creative Learning Press.

Richards, R. L. (1981). Relationships between creativity and psychopathology: An evaluation and interpretation of the evidence. *Genetic Psychology Monographs, 103,* 261–324.

Richards, R. L., Kinney, D. K., Lunde, I., Benet, M., & Merzel, A. P. C. (1988). Creativity in manic-depressives, cyclothymes, their normal relatives, and control subjects. *Journal of Abnormal Psychology, 97,* 281–288.

Rimm, S. B. (1983). *Preschool and kindergarten interest descriptor.* Watertown, WI: Educational Assessment Service.

Rimm, S. B., & Davis, G. A. (1976). GIFT: An instrument for the identification of creativity. *Journal of Creative Behavior, 10,* 178–182.

Rogers, C. R. (1962). Toward a theory of creativity. In S. J. Parnes & H. F. Harding (Eds.), *A source book for creative thinking* (pp. 63–72). New York: Scribner's.

Runco, M. A., Okuda, S. M., & Thurston, B. J. (1988). Psychometric properties of four systems for scoring divergent thinking tests. *Journal of Psychoeducational Assessment, 5,* 149–156.

Schaefer, C. E. (1971). *Creativity attitude survey.* Jacksonville, IL: Psychologists and Educators, Inc.

Schuldberg, D. (1990). Schizotypal and hypomanic traits, creativity, and psychological health. *Creativity Research Journal, 13,* 219–232.

Schuldberg, D. (1993). Personal resourcefulness: Positive aspects of functioning in high-risk research. *Psychiatry, 56,* 137–152.

Schuldberg, D., French, C., Stone, B. L., & Heberle, J. (1988). Creativity and schizotypal traits: Creativity test scores and perceptual aberration, magical ideation, and impulsive nonconformity. *Journal of Nervous and Mental Disease, 176,* 648–657.

Simonton, D. K. (1988). *Scientific genius: A psychology of science.* Cambridge, England: Cambridge University Press.

Smith, J. M. (1966). *Setting conditions for creative teaching in the elementary school.* Boston: Allyn and Bacon.

Somers, J. V., & Yawkey, T. D. (1984). Imaginary play companions: Contributions of creativity and intellectual abilities of young children. *Journal of Creative Behavior, 18,* 77–89.

Sternberg, R. S. (1988). A three-facet model of creativity. In R. J. Sternberg (Ed.), *The nature of creativity* (pp. 125–147). New York: Cambridge University Press.

Torrance, E. P. (1962). *Guiding creative talent.* Englewood Cliffs, NJ: Prentice-Hall.

Torrance, E. P. (1965). *Rewarding creative behavior.* Englewood Cliffs, NJ: Prentice-Hall.

Torrance, E. P. (1966a). *Torrance tests of creative thinking.* Bensenville, IL: Scholastic Testing Service.

Torrance, E. P. (1966b). *Torrance tests of creative thinking: Norms-technical manual.* Princeton, NJ: Personnel Press.

Torrance, E. P. (1974). *Torrance tests of creative thinking: Norms-technical manual* (revised). Bensenville, IL: Scholastic Testing Service.

Torrance, E. P. (1977). *Creativity in the classroom.* Washington, DC: National Education Association.

Torrance, E. P. (1979). *The search for satori and creativity.* Buffalo, NY: Creative Education Foundation.

Torrance, E. P. (1981a). Empirical validation of criterion-referenced indicators of creative ability through a longitudinal study. *Creative Child and Adult Quarterly, 6,* 146–140.

Torrance, E. P. (1981b). Non-test ways of identifying the creatively gifted. In J. C. Gowan, J. Khatena, & E. P. Torrance (Eds.), *Creativity: Its educational implications* (2nd ed.) (pp. 165–170). Dubuque, IA: Kendall/Hunt.

Torrance, E. P. (1981c). *Thinking creatively in action and movement.* Bensenville, IL: Scholastic Testing Service.

Torrance, E. P. (1988). The nature of creativity as manifest in its testing. In R. W. Sternberg (Ed.), *The nature of creativity* (pp. 43-75). New York: Cambridge University Press.

Torrance, E. P. (1990a). *Torrance tests of creative thinking: Manual for scoring and interpreting results. Verbal, forms A and B.* Bensenville, IL: Scholastic Testing Service.

Torrance, E. P. (1990b). *Torrance tests of creative thinking: Norms-technical manual. Figural (streamlined) forms A and B.* Bensenville, IL: Scholastic Testing Service.

Torrance, E. P., & Ball, O. E. (1984). *Torrance tests of creative thinking: Streamlined (revised) manual, figural A and B.* Bensenville, IL: Scholastic Testing Service.

Torrance, E. P., Khatena, J., & Cunnington, B. F. (1973). *Thinking creatively with sounds and words.* Bensenville, IL: Scholastic Testing Service.

Torrance, E. P., & Wu, T. H. (1981). A comparative longitudinal study of the adult creative achievements of elementary school children identified as highly intelligent and as highly creative. *Creative Child and Adult Quarterly, 6,* 71–76.

Treffinger, D. J. (1985). Review of the *Torrance Tests of Creative Thinking.* In J. Mitchell (Ed.), *Ninth mental measurements yearbook* (Vol. 2, pp. 1632–1634). Lincoln, NE: Buros Institute of Mental Measurement.

Wakefield, J. F. (1991). The outlook for creativity tests. *Journal of Creative Behavior, 25,* 184–193.

Walberg, H. J., & Herbig, M. P. (1991). Developing talent, creativity, and eminence. In N. Colangelo & G. A. Davis (Eds.), *Handbook of gifted education* (pp. 245-255). Boston: Allyn and Bacon.

Wallach, M. A., & Kogan, N. (1965). *Modes of thinking in young children.* New York: Holt.

Williams, F. (1980). *Creativity assessment packet.* Buffalo, NY: DOK.

Teaching for Creative Development: A Social-Psychological Approach

BETH A. HENNESSEY, *Wellesley College*

What is the relationship between giftedness and creativity? Should creative performance be expected to flow naturally from children who have been identified as gifted, or can such students be directly helped to develop their creative abilities? Although the answers to such questions are highly complex, an examination of the social-psychological literature can do much to inform educators interested in these issues.

Social psychologists focus on "creative situations," the particular social and environmental conditions that can have a positive or negative impact on the creativity of most individuals. Investigations into the social psychology of creativity reveal a direct relation between the motivational orientation an individual brings to a task and the creativity of that person's performance on the task (Amabile, 1983a). It is the environment, or at least certain aspects of the environment, that in large part determines that motivational orientation. In essence, people have been found to be most creative when they feel motivated primarily by the interest, enjoyment, satisfaction, and challenge of the work itself—not by external pressures. This relationship between creativity and motivation was first stated formally as the *intrinsic motivation principle of creativity:* The intrinsically motivated state is conducive to creativity, whereas the extrinsically motivated state is detrimental (Amabile, 1983a, 1983b; Hennessey & Amabile, 1988a).

Experimental and nonexperimental evidence gathered in the last few years has recently led to a revision of this formulation. Amabile (1993) proposed a theory of motivational synergy which suggests that although intrinsic motivation is necessary for high levels of creativity, extrinsic motivation need not always be detrimental. Extrinsic motivation may sometimes combine positively with intrinsic motivation to boost overall levels of creativity, particularly when there is a high initial level of intrinsic motivation and when the motivators are perceived as supporting, rather than limiting, autonomy and competence.

Importantly, however, many theorists and practitioners contend that in the classroom intrinsic motivation is always preferable to extrinsic incentives. There is a great deal of research evidence to suggest that intrinsic motivation leads to better problem solving and deeper levels of conceptual understanding (e.g., McGraw, 1978). In the classroom, extrinsic motivation typically will lead to better performance only on tasks requiring rote recitation, precise performance under strong time pressure, and the completion of familiar repetitive procedures. On the basis of such findings, many educational experts agree that classrooms fraught with rewards, competition, and frequent evaluation do not offer the best situations for learning. There is no question that they are not the best situations for fostering students' creativity.

A Three-Component Model

A few social-psychological theorists working in the area of creativity have proposed process models designed to explain how it is that the motivational orientation brought to a task can be especially influential in determining creativity of performance. Amabile's (1983a,

The author wishes to thank Malcolm W. Watson and Teresa Amabile for their helpful comments on this chapter.

1983b, 1988) componential conceptualization of creativity was one of the first and most influential of these attempts; and it is this model that has most influenced my own work and the work of many of my colleagues.[1] In addition to intrinsic task motivation, this formulation also includes aspects of knowledge, talent, personality, and cognitive style.

Domain-Relevant Skills

The first of the three components in the Amabile scheme, *domain-relevant skills,* lays the foundation on which any creative performance must be built. This component includes factual knowledge, technical skills, and special talents in the domain in question. Domain-relevant skills are the set of cognitive pathways for solving a particular problem or doing a particular task. Some of these paths are more well traveled and are practiced more than others, and the entire set of pathways can be either quite extensive or quite limited. The larger the set, the greater the chance of developing a novel combination of steps and producing something new.

Creativity-Relevant Skills

The second component, *creativity-relevant skills,* constitutes what Amabile terms the "something extra" of creative performance. Assuming that an individual has some incentive for task engagement, performance will be adequate providing that the necessary domain skills are available. Even in instances where these domain skills are exceptionally well developed, however, creative performance will not result if creativity-relevant skills are lacking. Creativity-relevant skills include a cognitive approach conducive to looking at problems from new perspectives, a willingness to explore new cognitive pathways and a knack for exploring them, and a working style conducive to persistence and the energetic pursuit of a novel idea or solution. Personality characteristics that have been found to co-occur often with a high level of skills in this component include independence, self-discipline, a willingness to take risks, tolerance for ambiguity, and little or no concern for social approval (Feldman, 1980; Golan, 1963; Hogarth, 1980; Stein, 1974, 1975).

Task Motivation

The final building block in this conceptual model involves *task motivation.* A person can have either no motivation for doing a task, a primarily intrinsic motivation, or a primarily extrinsic motivation. *Intrinsic motivation* is defined as the motivation to do an activity for its own sake, because it is intrinsically interesting, enjoyable, or satisfying (Amabile, 1983a; Lepper, Greene, & Nisbett, 1973). In contrast, *extrinsic motivation* is defined as the motivation to do an activity primarily in order to achieve an extrinsic reward (Amabile, 1983a; Lepper et al., 1973). As explained earlier, intrinsic motivation is crucial to creativity of performance. Within Amabile's componential model, task motivation comprises two elements: the individual's baseline attitude brought to a task and that individual's perceptions of the reasons that she or he is engaging in that task. In any given situation, extrinsic constraints that may be present in the environment and the individual's strategies for dealing with those constraints combine to influence a person's level of intrinsic task motivation.

Giftedness and the Componential Model

There is no one "recipe" for giftedness. As Gardner's (1983) and Sternberg's (1985) theories of multiple intelligences remind us, individuals can have a variety of different strengths.[2] How might the gifted child be characterized according to Amabile's model? Whatever definition of giftedness one subscribes to, it would seem that, where creativity is concerned, gifted children can be expected to fare especially well. In fact, Renzulli's (1982) conceptualization of gifted-

[1] A similar componential model was also subsequently proposed by Sternberg and Lubart (1993).

[2] See Chapter 4 by Sternberg and Chapter 5 by Ramos-Ford and Gardner.

ness includes each of Amabile's three basic components: above-average general ability and knowledge (domain-relevant skills), a high level of task commitment or motivation to achieve in certain areas, and a high level of creativity-related skills.

The Importance of Intrinsic Motivation

Intrinsic task motivation is considered by Amabile, myself, and others to be the most important of the three creativity components. It is the easiest to influence in a systematic way because intrinsic/extrinsic motivational orientation is highly subject to social influence. In addition, no amount of domain-relevant or creativity-relevant skills can compensate for a lack of intrinsic motivation to perform an activity, whereas, to some extent, a high level of intrinsic motivation has been shown to make up for a deficiency in the other two component areas. Task motivation makes the difference between what an individual *can* do and what she or he *will* do (Amabile, 1983b). It is task motivation that determines whether domain skills and creativity skills will be adequately and efficiently tapped in the service of creative performance.

While Gallagher (1992) and others report that intellectually gifted children typically have strong levels of intrinsic motivation, one should not take this tendency for granted. As many contemporary theorists are quick to point out, it is important to consider motivational orientation both as a relatively enduring trait *and* as a temporary, situation-specific state. Laboratory and field-based research tells us that intrinsic motivation is a most delicate and often fleeting entity. Even those persons who are generally more highly intrinsically motivated quickly fall prey to outside influences. Intrinsic motivation cannot be taught. It cannot be coerced. Rather, intrinsic interest must come from *within* the individual. This motivational state springs in large part from a passion and excitement about the task itself and is particularly susceptible to undermining effects of extrinsic constraints (see Hennessey & Amabile, 1988a).

Empirical Evidence: The Undermining Effects of Expected Reward

In order to test hypotheses about the impact of environmental constraints on creativity in an appropriate fashion, the experimental task not only must be intrinsically interesting but also must meet a number of criteria:

1. The task must be open-ended and allow for a variety of responses;
2. it must not depend heavily on specialized skills; and
3. it must be a task in which subjects produce an observable product or response that can be recorded and later presented to experts to be judged on creativity and related dimensions (Hennessey & Amabile, 1988b).

Among the first to recognize these research requirements were Lepper, Greene, and Nisbett, who in 1973 investigated the effect of expected reward on children's motivation and artistic performance. These investigators found that, for preschoolers who initially displayed a high level of intrinsic interest in drawing with felt-tip markers, working for an expected "Good Player Award" decreased their interest in the task. When compared with an unexpected reward group and a control (no reward) group, the subjects motivated to receive Good Player Awards spent significantly less time using the markers during subsequent free-play periods. This decrement in interest persisted for at least a week beyond the initial experimental session. Furthermore, the rated "quality" of the drawings produced under expected reward conditions was lower than that of the unexpected reward or control groups. Taking a similar approach, Greene and Lepper (1974) and Kernoodle-Loveland and Olley (1979) later replicated these results.

A number of studies focused specifically on the effect of reward on creative aspects of subjects' performance. One of the earliest, by Kruglanski, Friedman, and Zeevi (1971), involved Israeli high school students who either had or had not been promised a reward if they would complete two open-ended creativity tasks. Product originality was assessed by two judges, and a clear and statistically significant superiority for nonrewarded subjects emerged. In addition, intrinsic motivation differences were found between the two groups in terms of subjects' expressed enjoyment of the activities and their willingness to volunteer for further participation.

Amabile (1982) also examined the effect of expected reward on the creativity of subjects' performance. The experimental task involved artistic creativity, and the reward was introduced in a competitive setting. Girls ranging in age from 7 to 11 years made paper collages during one of two parties. Subjects in the experimental group competed for prizes, whereas those in the control group expected that the prizes would be raffled off. Artist-judges later rated each collage, and the control group was judged significantly higher than the experimental group on collage creativity.

Each of these investigations points to the same conclusion. For subjects who initially display a high level of interest in a task, working for an expected reward decreases their motivation and undermines the creativity and globally assessed quality of their performance.

Several intrinsic motivation theorists have proposed that in order to undermine intrinsic interest, a reward must be salient (Ross, 1975) and must be perceived as a means to an extrinsic end (Calder & Staw, 1975; Deci, 1975; Kruglanski et al., 1971; Lepper et al., 1973). One method of demonstrating this crucial role of perceiving a task as a means to an end is to offer subjects a choice concerning task engagement. If subjects perceive themselves as freely choosing to perform an activity for which a reward is offered, they may well adopt an extrinsic motivational orientation toward that activity—viewing the task as a means to an end, and their own engagement as motivated by external pressures. On the other hand, if subjects are simply presented with a task and told that they will be paid, with no choice in the matter, this same detrimental effect of extrinsic constraints may not emerge. This phenomenon has in fact been demonstrated in a study conducted by Folger, Rosenfield, and Hays (1978). These researchers found that under conditions of choice, rewarded subjects showed significantly less interest than did nonrewarded subjects. Under conditions of no choice, however, rewarded subjects showed more task interest.

In an investigation of the interactive effects of reward and choice on children's creativity, Amabile, Hennessey, and Grossman (1986, Study 2) directly manipulated the meaning of "reward" by varying its method of presentation. We employed a design in which the presence or absence of choice was completely crossed with the presence or absence of reward. We predicted that creativity would be undermined only in those children who explicitly contracted with the experimenter to perform a task later in order to obtain a reward first. Either reward or no choice alone was not expected to have a significant undermining effect.

Analyses of the creativity scores for both stories and collages produced by participants revealed the predicted interaction between reward and choice. Subjects in the choice-reward condition produced products lower in creativity than did subjects in the other three groups. This study demonstrated that it is not reward per se but, rather, the functional significance of reward as controlling of performance that undermines creativity.

In an effort to replicate these findings conceptually, we carried out a second investigation (Amabile et al., 1986, Study 3) in which reward and choice were again crossed. In this instance, however, the subjects were adult women and the reward was delivered only after the task had been completed. Analyses again revealed a significant reward × choice interaction, resulting largely from the very low creativity exhibited by subjects in the contracted-for reward group (choice-reward). As predicted, and as in the earlier study, the lowest level of creativity was observed in this condition.

Imposing restrictions on how subjects may choose to complete a task has also proved detrimental to creativity. In an investigation conducted with nursery school children, Amabile and Gitomer (1982) asked their young subjects to make paper collages under one of two conditions. Children assigned to the choice condition were allowed to choose 5 out of 10 boxes of materials to use in this task. For children in the no-choice condition, however, the experimenter made the box selections—yoking the two conditions in a matched-pairs design. All subjects then completed their collages, which were later rated for creativity by artists. Two weeks after this initial session, a behavioral measure of subsequent intrinsic interest in the collage activity was obtained. As predicted, subjects in the choice condition made collages that were significantly more creative than those made by subjects in the no-choice condition. In addition, children in the choice condition later spent somewhat more time with collage materials during free play than did children in the no-choice condition.

Other Extrinsic Constraints

Having established the deleterious effects of reward and conditions of restricted choice, what other extrinsic constraints might also have a negative impact on subjects' creativity? One body of research has consistently demonstrated that expecting to be evaluated produces similar decrements in interest and task performance. The initial study of evaluation expectation (Amabile, 1979) was designed to test the hypothesis that such constraint will undermine creative performance on open-ended tasks. The task was a collage-making activity, and it was predicted that subjects placed under constraint (evaluation expectation) would show lower levels of both creativity and intrinsic interest in the task than would nonconstraint controls. The subjects in this study were 95 undergraduate women. As a cover story, the experimenter explained that this investigation was actually a pretest for another experiment to be done the following quarter. The alleged purpose of the pretest was to identify activities that would affect subjects' moods. Subjects assigned to the control condition were told that their designs would not be used as a source of data—that the only measure of interest was the mood they reported on a questionnaire. In contrast, subjects assigned to the evaluation condition were told their finished designs would be rated by graduate artists from the university's art department and would serve as important sources of information.

After working on her collage for fifteen minutes, each subject was asked to complete a Mood Questionnaire (in keeping with the cover story) and an Art Activity Questionnaire that included a number of questions designed to assess subjects' interest in and attitude toward the collage task. Results supported the hypothesis that evaluation expectation is detrimental to creativity, with control (nonevaluation) subjects producing significantly more creative products than experimental (evaluation) subjects. In addition, control subjects scored higher in self-rated interest than did experimental subjects.

In order to establish firmly that an expected evaluation has negative effects on adults' creativity, two further investigations were undertaken. In both studies, a replication with an artistic activity (Amabile, Goldfarb, & Brackfield, 1982, Study 1) and a verbal activity (Amabile et al., 1982, Study 1), there was a significant main effect of evaluation expectation on the creativity ratings. Nonevaluation subjects made collages and wrote poems that were judged significantly more creative than those produced by evaluation subjects.

In a related study (Berglas, Amabile, & Handel, 1981), the effects of prior evaluation on children's subsequent artistic creativity were examined. As predicted, there was an overall negative impact of prior evaluation on creativity of performance—even though that evaluation had been positive.

Finally, Koestner, Ryan, Bernieri, and Holt (1984) set out to determine the impact of another extrinsic constraint—behavioral limits—on children's motivation and creativity. In this study, 5- and 7-year-old children were asked to engage in an intrinsically interesting painting activity under three conditions of limit setting that varied along an information/control dimension. In the controlling-limits group, restrictions pertaining to task neatness were stated in terms of "should" and "must." The "milder" informational group was given a verbal communication conveying the same constraints, but with reduced external pressure and an acknowledgment of possible conflicting feelings about the imposed limits. For the control (no-limits) group, no mention was made of neatness.

Following the period during which the children made their paintings, they were left alone for a free-play session. The amount of time spent during this period was used as a measure of intrinsic motivation. Finally, the children were asked to rate how much they had enjoyed the painting activity. The results showed that subjects in the no-limits and informational-limits groups spent more free-choice time painting than did controlling-limits subjects. Thus, intrinsic motivation was significantly greater for children in the nonlimitational and informational conditions than for children in the controlling condition. In addition, a marginal difference between the three groups emerged on the self-report measure of enjoyment. Effects of limit-setting were also found for creativity, with the no-limits group showing significantly more creativity than the controlling-limits group. The informational-limits group was intermediate.

Applying the Research to the Classroom

Clearly, there exists considerable research evidence to support the fact that environmental features such as expected reward, expected evaluation, and other extrinsic constraints can have a negative impact on both students' motivation and their creativity. Further, these deleterious effects seem to occur across the life span: People from preschoolers to college students (and beyond) can be expected to suffer the same kind of negative impact.

When presenting this research to my college classes, I often ask that they perform what I call the "Martian experiment." I ask my students to imagine that they have just landed their spaceship on the playground of a prototypical American public elementary school. They know nothing at all about the U.S. educational system, but they are familiar with the work of Hennessey and colleagues, as these researchers' reputation is galaxy-wide. Wishing to learn as much as possible about our planet, the space aliens enter a third-grade classroom. They are shocked by what they find: an environment fraught with restrictions, evaluation, competition, and reward systems too numerous to mention. Have this nation's educators launched some sort of a campaign purposefully constructed to destroy their students' intrinsic motivation? Have they decided that creativity is something to be squelched rather than nurtured? From the Martian viewpoint, this would certainly seem to be the case.

Of course, in reality, nothing could be further from the truth. Programs designed to enhance creativity in the classroom abound, and recent surveys of teachers have revealed that many educators both in the United States and abroad believe that the enhancement of student creativity should be a primary professional goal (Dialdin, 1993; Fryer & Collings, 1991a, 1991b). The difficulty rests in the fact that parents and educators have failed to understand that the motivation so necessary for creative performance cannot be engendered from without. Extrinsic incentives such as promised rewards, expected evaluations, and in-class competitions only undermine student motivation and performance. The intrinsic interest so necessary for creativity must come from *within* the individual (see Hennessey, in press).

Keeping Intrinsic Motivation Alive in the Classroom

What can be done to keep intrinsic motivation and creativity alive in our schools? There are many formal programs designed to foster creativity in the classroom. These interventions have been constructed to *teach* children to think creatively, and the majority focus not on intrinsic motivation per se but on creativity-relevant skills. Programs are available in a wide variety of forms, including The Purdue Creative Thinking Program (Feldhusen, Treffinger, & Bahlke, 1970); *Synectics, Making It Strange* (Gordon, 1961, 1974), and other workbooks by Gordon and Poze (1971, 1972a, 1972b); and several workbooks by Stanish (1977, 1979, 1981, 1988; Eberle & Stanish 1985).

While these programs and others like them have met with some real success, the focus of this chapter has been primarily on the pervasive everyday factors that can influence children's motivation and creativity. The message is clear: No creativity-enhancement techniques can be truly successful until teachers have removed from the classroom routine as many of the killers of motivation as possible. Yet old habits die hard, and it will take a good deal of time to wean teachers, students, administrators, and parents from the reward-, evaluation- and competition-based approaches they have been taught. In the interim, determined teachers will find that even small changes in curricular content and teaching practices may yield marked results.

Teachers should carefully examine their instructional biases and ask themselves if any restrictions, rewards, evaluations, or competitive elements might reasonably be eliminated from the school day. In situations in which reward or evaluation components seem necessary, a substitution of self-evaluation or self-reward systems for the more usual teacher-centered paradigms is suggested. Teachers also can pay careful attention to the subtle and not-so-subtle messages they are conveying to students. As Deci and Ryan (1985) explain, the interpersonal context within the classroom is experienced by students along an autonomy-supportive/controlling continuum. Students of teachers who favor controlling over autonomous techniques are more likely to adopt an extrinsic motivational set (Boggiano, Barrett, Main, & Katz, 1985; Deci, Nezlek, & Sheinman, 1981). As mentioned earlier, even constraints (such as the promise of reward) that have been shown to undermine motivation can have less negative impact if they are introduced within a supportive interpersonal environment that promotes children's feelings of self-determination and the perception that they are agents rather than pawns within the classroom setting (DeCharms, 1968; Koestner et al., 1984).

Finally, three recent investigations conducted by my colleagues and myself suggest one other recommendation for those wishing to promote intrinsic motivation and creativity in the classroom. Teachers are strongly advised to engage in directed discussions designed to "train" children to maintain an intrinsic focus even when extrinsic factors are present (see Hennessey & Zbikowski, 1993).

The Immunization Studies

In the first effort (Hennessey, Amabile, & Martinage, 1989, Study 1), we set out to determine whether special training sessions designed to directly address motivational orientation could "immunize" children against the usually damaging effects of reward on intrinsic motivation and creative aspects of performance. Elementary students (ages 7 to 11) were randomly assigned to an intrinsic motivation focus or a control group and met with an experimenter over two consecutive days to view videos and engage in directed discussion. The tapes shown to subjects in the intrinsic motivation focus condition depicted two attractive 11-year-olds talking with an adult about various aspects of their schoolwork. Scripts for this condition helped subjects focus on the intrinsically interesting, fun, and playful aspects of a task. Ways to make even the most routine assignment exciting were suggested, and subjects were helped to distance themselves from socially imposed extrinsic constraints such as rewards. Tapes shown to subjects in the control condition featured the same two 11-year-old actors talking about, for example, food, music groups, movies, and seasons.

Following the training, all subjects met individually with a second adult for testing. Half the children in each of the two conditions were told that, as a reward, they could take two pictures with an instant camera only if they promised to tell a story later for the experimenter. For children in the no-reward conditions, this picture taking was presented simply as the first in a series of "things to do."

In this 2×2 design, presentation of reward was completely crossed with type of training received. It was expected that children who had gone through intrinsic motivation training, unlike untrained children, would suffer no decline in their creativity under expected reward. The data from this first investigation not only confirmed these expectations but also gave us reason to believe that our intervention had much more of an impact than we had expected. We found that the offer of reward actually *augmented* the creativity of the trained group. The creativity of the children who had received intrinsic motivation training and were expecting a reward for their performance was significantly higher than that of any of the other three groups.

Two follow-up investigations of our intrinsic motivation focus techniques (Hennessey, Amabile, & Martinage, 1989, Study 2; Hennessey & Zbikowski, 1993) were subsequently carried out, each designed as a conceptual replication of Study 1. In Study 2, it was again the children who had received immunization training and were expecting a reward who produced the most creative products (paper collage), although in this instance the effect was far less dramatic. Statistical comparisons revealed that the creativity of those children receiving training and expecting a reward for their performance was significantly different from that of only one of the other three design groups. Was the outstanding performance of the reward/intrinsic motivation group in Study 1 a fluke?

In the third investigation in this series, subjects assigned to the intrinsic motivation focus/reward condition again produced the most creative products, but their performance was only significantly different from that of the no-training/reward group.

Taken together, the combined results of the three studies indicate that we cannot expect that subjects exposed to our intrinsic motivation training and offered a reward for their performance will demonstrate unusually high levels of creativity. We can expect, however, that children who have been specifically instructed in ways to overcome the usually negative effects of extrinsic constraints at the very least will maintain baseline levels of intrinsic motivation and creativity under reward conditions.

Clearly, our intrinsic motivation tapes and discussion sessions met their intended goal: In each of three separate studies, two brief fifteen-minute meetings were sufficient to overcome the negative impact of reward on creative performance. The results of the most recent investigation offer the clearest demonstration yet of this basic immunization effect. In the face of expected reward, control group subjects showed significant decrements in creativity of performance; whereas subjects receiving training experienced no such deleterious effects.

An important question remains: What is it about our tapes and conversations that allows children to maintain their creativity in the face of reward? The training sessions seem to engender certain attitudes or self-perceptions that give our subjects a "natural immunity" to the negative effects usually associated with extrinsic constraints. Children exposed to our training techniques learn to deemphasize the importance of reward and approach our experimental tasks with playfulness and a willingness to take risks, which many researchers believe are crucial to creativity (Amabile, 1983a; Barron, 1968; Dansky & Silverman, 1975; Davis, 1992; Lieberman, 1965; Stein, 1974).

If experimenters, virtual strangers, were able to affect this much attitudinal and behavioral change in only two fifteen-minute sessions, think how much more could be done by classroom teachers who build naturalistic discussions about motivation, interest, and playfulness into the school day.

Conclusions

What practical applications can be derived from these research endeavors? The lessons are many, and teachers of the gifted should keep in mind that their students' advanced intellectual capacities and problem-solving skills often will not be enough to ensure that creativity will flourish within the classroom. An intrinsic task orientation is essential for creative production. Such intrinsic interest cannot be taught; it must come from within. Yet teachers wishing to facilitate the creative process can do much to ensure that their students' intrinsic motivation will not be undermined. The following are suggestions:

1. Remember that students will be most creative when they enjoy what they are doing.
2. Use tangible rewards as little as possible; instead, encourage students to take pride in what they have accomplished.
3. Avoid competitive situations within the classroom.
4. Downplay your evaluation of students' creative work; instead, help them become more proficient at recognizing their own strengths and weaknesses.
5. Whenever possible, give students choices about what they will do and how they will accomplish their goals.
6. Make intrinsic motivation a regular focus of class discussions; encourage students to become aware of their own special interests and help them to distance themselves from extrinsic constraints.
7. Encourage students to become active, independent learners, and allow them to take confident control of their own learning process.
8. In any ways that you can, show students that you value creativity—that you not only allow it but also actively engage in it.
9. Show students that you are an intrinsically motivated individual who enjoys thinking creatively.

REFERENCES

Amabile, T. (1979). Effects of external evaluation on artistic creativity. *Journal of Personality and Social Psychology, 37,* 221–233.

Amabile, T. (1982). Children's artistic creativity: Detrimental effects of competition in a field setting. *Personality and Social Psychology Bulletin, 8,* 573–578.

Amabile, T. (1983a). *The social psychology of creativity*. New York: Springer-Verlag.

Amabile, T. (1983b). Social psychology of creativity: A componential conceptualization. *Journal of Personality and Social Psychology, 45,* 357–377.

Amabile, T. (1988). A model of creativity and innovation in organizations. In B. M. Staw & L. L. Cummings (Eds.), *Research in organizational behavior* (Vol. 10). Greenwich, CT: JAI Press.

Amabile, T. (1993). Motivational synergy: Toward new conceptualizations of intrinsic and extrinsic motivation in the workplace. *Human Resource Management Review, 3,* 185–201.

Amabile, T., & Gitomer, J. (1982). *Children's artistic creativity: Effects of choice in task materials.* Unpublished manuscript, Brandeis University.

Amabile, T., Goldfarb, P., & Brackfield, S. C. (1982). *Effects of social facilitation and evaluation on creativity.* Unpublished manuscript, Brandeis University.

Amabile, T., Hennessey, B., & Grossman, B. (1986). Social influences on creativity: The effects of contracted-for reward. *Journal of Personality and Social Psychology, 50,* 14–23.

Barron, F. (1968). *Creativity and personal freedom.* New York: Van Nostrand.

Berglas, S., Amabile, T., & Handel, M. (1981). *Effects of evaluation on children's artistic creativity.* Unpublished manuscript, Brandeis University.

Boggiano, A., Barrett, M., Main, D., & Katz, P. (1985). *Mastery–motivation in children: The role of an extrinsic vs. intrinsic orientation.* Paper presented at the American Educational Research Association, Chicago.

Calder, B., & Staw, B. (1975). Self-perceptions of intrinsic and extrinsic motivation. *Journal of Personality and Social Psychology, 31,* 599–605.

Dansky, J., & Silverman, I. (1975). Play: A general facilitator of fluency. *Developmental Psychology, 11,* 104.

Davis, G. A. (1992). *Creativity is forever* (3rd ed.). Dubuque, IA: Kendall/Hunt.

DeCharms, R. (1968). *Personal causation: The internal affective determinants of behavior.* New York: Academic Press.

Deci, E. (1975). *Intrinsic motivation.* New York: Plenum Press.

Deci, E., Nezlek, J., & Sheinman, L. (1981). Characteristics of rewarder and intrinsic motivation of rewardee. *Journal of Personality and Social Psychology, 40,* 1–10.

Deci, E., & Ryan, R. (1985). *Intrinsic motivation and self-determination in human behavior.* New York: Plenum Press.

Dialdin, D. (1993). *A cross-national examination of the consensual assessment technique.* Unpublished manuscript, Wellesley College.

Eberle, B., & Stanish, B. (1985). *CPS for kids.* Carthage, IL: Good Apple.

Feldhusen, J., Treffinger, D., & Bahlke, S. (1970). Developing creative thinking: The Purdue Creativity Program. *Journal of Creative Behavior, 4,* 85–90.

Feldman, D. (1980) *Beyond universals in cognitive development.* Norwood, NJ: Ablex.

Folger, R., Rosenfield, D., & Hays, R. (1978). Equity and intrinsic motivation: The role of choice. *Journal of Personality and Social Psychology, 36,* 557–564.

Fryer, M., & Collings, J. (1991a). British teachers' views about creativity. *Journal of Creative Behavior, 25,* 75.

Fryer, M., & Collings, J. (1991b). Teachers' views about creativity. *British Journal of Educational Psychology, 61,* 207.

Gallagher, J. J. (1992). Gifted persons. In M. C. Alkin (Ed.), *Encyclopedia of educational research* (6th ed.) (pp. 544–549). New York: Macmillan.

Gardner, H. (1983). *Frames of mind: The theory of multiple intelligences.* New York: Basic Books.

Golan, S. (1963). Psychological study of creativity. *Psychological Bulletin, 60,* 548–565.

Gordon, W. (1961). *Synectics.* New York: Harper & Row.

Gordon, W. (1974). *Making it strange.* Books 1–4. New York: Harper & Row.

Gordon, W. J. J., & Poze, T. (1971). *Metaphorical way of learning and knowing.* Cambridge, MA: SES Associates.

Gordon, W. J. J., & Poze, T. (1972a). *Strange and familiar.* Cambridge, MA: SES Associates.

Gordon, W. J. J., & Poze, T. (1972b). *Teaching is listening.* Cambridge, MA: SES Associates.

Greene, D., & Lepper, M. (1974). Effects of extrinsic rewards on children's subsequent interest. *Child Development, 45,* 1141–1145.

Hennessey, B. (in press). Social, environmental and developmental issues and creativity. *Educational Psychology Review.*

Hennessey, B. A., & Amabile, T. M. (1988a). The conditions of creativity. In R. J. Sternberg (Ed.), *The nature of creativity.* New York: Cambridge University Press.

Hennessey, B., & Amabile, T. (1988b). Story-telling: A method for assessing children's creativity. *Journal of Creative Behavior, 22,* 235–246.

Hennessey, B., Amabile, T., & Martinage, M. (1989). Immunizing children against the negative effects of reward. *Contemporary Educational Psychology, 14,* 212–227.

Hennessey, B., & Zbikowski, S. (1993). Immunizing children against the negative effects of reward: A further examination of intrinsic motivation training techniques. *Creativity Research Journal, 6,* 297–307.

Hogarth, R. (1980). *Judgment and choice.* Chichester, England: Wiley.

Kernoodle-Loveland, K., & Olley, J. (1979). The effect of external reward on interest and quality of task performance in children of high and low intrinsic motivation. *Child Development, 50,* 1207–1210.

Koestner, R., Ryan, R., Bernieri, F., & Holt, K. (1984). Setting limits on children's behavior: The differential effects of controlling vs. informational styles on intrinsic motivation and creativity. *Journal of Personality, 52,* 233–248.

Kruglanski, A., Friedman, I., & Zeevi, G. (1971). The effects of extrinsic incentive on some qualitative aspects of task performance. *Journal of Personality, 39,* 606–617.

Lepper, M., Greene, D., & Nisbett, R. (1973). Undermining children's intrinsic interest with extrinsic rewards: A test of the "overjustification" hypothesis. *Journal of Personality and Social Psychology, 28,* 129–137.

Lieberman, J. (1965). Playfulness and divergent thinking: An investigation of their relationship at the kindergarten level. *Journal of Genetic Psychology, 107,* 219–224.

McGraw, K. (1978). The detrimental effects of reward on performance: A literature review and a predication model. In M. Lepper & D. Greene (Eds.), *The hidden costs of reward.* Hillsdale, NJ: Lawrence Erlbaum.

Renzulli, J. S. (1982). Dear Mr. and Mrs. Copernicus: We regret to inform you . . . *Gifted Child Quarterly, 26,* 11–14.

Ross, M. (1975). Salience of reward and intrinsic motivation. *Journal of Personality and Social Psychology, 32,* 245–254.

Stanish, B. (1977). *Sunflowing.* Carthage, IL: Good Apple.

Stanish, B. (1979). *I believe in unicorns.* Carthage, IL: Good Apple.

Stanish, B. (1981). *Hippogriff feathers.* Carthage, IL: Good Apple.

Stanish, B. (1988). *Hearthstone traveler.* Carthage, IL: Good Apple.

Stein, M. (1974, 1975). *Stimulating creativity* (Vols. 1, 2). New York: Academic Press.

Sternberg, R. (1985). *Beyond IQ: A triarchic theory of human intelligence.* New York: Cambridge University Press.

Sternberg, R., & Lubart, T. (1993). Creative giftedness: A multivariate approach. *Gifted Child Quarterly, 37,* 7–15.

24

Creativity in the Classroom: Characteristics, Climate, and Curriculum

SUSAN DANIELS, *University of Wisconsin, Madison*

"All right class, I need you to be sitting quietly in your seats with your workbooks open to page . . ."

"Since Kristin got the best score in the class, her paper has a star on it and will go up on our bulletin board for the rest of this week . . ."

"So, while we'll all be studying the Renaissance this month, you will have a choice as to the particular topic and presentation format for your projects. Some will want to look at the art of the time, others may be interested in a comparative study of the political structure of different countries. While you'll all be required to write a brief research paper, you can select the format for your project presentation: An architectural model, a dramatic reenactment, a debate, or a musical performance are just a few of the possibilities."

"What an interesting response, Tony! Please tell me more about what you mean and how you came upon this idea."

Creativity is an ability or—more accurately—a constellation of traits and abilities which most programs for the gifted wish to enhance (Davis, 1991; Parke, 1989), yet a "program" per se in training creative thinking is not enough. Rather, creativity must be acknowledged and nurtured throughout the school day, both within and across areas of the curriculum. Defining creativity is an ongoing challenge for practitioners in many fields (Feldman, Csikszentmilhalyi, & Gardner, 1994) and something that has been likened to nailing Jello to the wall—just when you think you've "got it," something changes, something shifts. Creativity is *generally* characterized by uniqueness, originality, and the ability to make something new, novel, and useful (Tardif & Sternberg, 1988).

The author is indebted to Tim Connell, Ellen Fiedler, and Karen Kaether for their assistance during the development of this chapter.

Uniqueness, originality, and novelty are relative concepts—things are more or less unique or original relative to what has come before. Quantum shifts in the way the world is perceived are extraordinarily rare and usually are built upon hundreds of previous efforts (Clasen & Clasen, 1986; Csikszentmihalyi, 1994). Certain individuals will persist in creative pursuits; others will become discouraged, distracted, or uninterested (Gardner, 1993). Determinants of persistence in creative activity emerge from an interaction of personal and environmental variables (Feldman, 1988).

Some environments, Zeitgeists, or social milieus support and further creative enterprise; others stifle creativity. Similarly, in schools, some classrooms, teachers, and curricular approaches address, foster, and support creative traits, abilities, and endeavors (see Chapter 23 by Hennessey); others seemingly ignore and, in the extreme, actively suppress creative enterprise (Sternberg & Lubart, 1993). The purpose of this chapter is to present the twelve most common traits and abilities associated with creativity (Davis, 1992; see Chapter 22) and to address classroom climate, instructional strategies, activities, and curricular approaches that serve to support and enhance creativity.

Creative Characteristics

Creative people in varying degrees and combinations tend to be (or have):

1. Self-aware regarding their own creativity
2. Independent
3. Risk taking
4. Energetic
5. Curious
6. Sense of humor
7. Attracted to complexity and novelty
8. Artistic
9. Open-minded
10. Need for privacy/alone time
11. Perceptive
12. Original/imaginative

Of course, not all traits will be evident in all creative people. Other cognitive, affective, social, and environmental factors may interact with and serve to mediate these characteristics. In addition, and to a large extent dependent on environment, these characteristics may serve a productive purpose or present difficulties (challenges) for teacher and student alike. Table 24.1 provides an overview of these twelve characteristics and their related educational implications. A detailed examination of each follows.

Awareness of Creativity

Creative individuals tend to be aware of their own creative abilities. This self-awareness in turn may lead to a heightened awareness of the creativity of others. In addition, such metacognitive understanding of creativity serves to be self-reinforcing. A certain "creativity consciousness"—receptivity to and valuing of creative ideas and innovations—seems to underlie and support an individual's creative potential.

Independence

Independence is central to creativity. The creative individual must be ready and willing to make waves, to go against the crowd, and at times to stand alone. Independence can manifest in a variety of ways: by standing apart from one's peers in viewpoint, appearance, activity, and a host of other personal choices. At times, independence will emerge in the form of a direct challenge toward a teacher. A certain self-confidence on the part of the teacher is necessary to allow, respond to, and appropriately direct such challenges.

Risk Taking

Creative individuals often take intellectual, social, psychological, and emotional risks. Whenever a unique approach or opinion is ventured, the creative individual risks rejection and isolation. Some creative individuals, often those talented and creative in the bodily-kinesthetic areas, will be inclined to take physical risks as well (Farley, 1976; Gardner, 1983). Thus, careful guidance, support, and a balance of limits and choices are essential to the well-being and development of the creative individual.

High Energy

It is not surprising that *driving absorption, passionate interest, intense dedication,* and *unwilling to give up* are all phrases used to describe the energy, perseverance, commitment, and motivation of highly creative individuals (Amabile, 1989; see Chapter 23 by Hennessey). Such energy and drive are often evidenced in early childhood and maintained into adulthood. Most creative accomplishments are not the result of a spontaneous event or of an overnight discovery but of a lifetime of work and commitment to a particular field or endeavor (Csikszentmihalyi & Getzels, 1973; Wallace & Gruber, 1989).

Curiosity

Along with creativity come curiosity and questioning. The creative impulse inclines one toward exploration and investigation. "How

Table 24.1
Characteristics of Creativity

Characteristics	*Attributes*	*Classroom Challenges*	*Educational Strategies*
Aware of their own creativeness	Values originality and creativity; values own creativity; actively tries to be creative	Rejects societal norms and standards; may be indifferent to common conventions and courtesies; prone to non-conforming, unconventional behavior.	Provide a psychologically safe, nonthreatening environment, which allows for disagreement and a degree of controversy.
Independent	Inner directed; self-aware; self-sufficient; intrinsically motivated	Uncooperative; resists domination/ authority; may resist societal demands	Shift focus of learning to the student; allow choice; engage student as a partner in curricular design.
Risk taking	Not afraid to try something new; willing to cope with failure; optimistic	Rejects limits imposed by others; may engage in "inappropriate" or dangerous behaviors	Set clear, simple, and reasonable limits, which afford physical and psychological safety; allow choice and flexibility within these limits.
Energetic	Spontaneous; persistent; driven; unwilling to give up	Impulsive; unable to "switch gears" when highly focused; excitable	Allow for movement and reasonable noise in classroom.
Sense of humor/playfulness	Playful; childlike	May seem silly; class clown; may find humor in situations others don't; likely to enjoy puns; may overdo	Acknowledge humor; provide time and outlet for humor; include humor in teaching; include creative dramatics.
Curious	Questioning; experimenting; displays wide interests	Always into things; sometimes destroys things to find out about them; always asks "why . . ."	Encourage sampling, browsing, and exploring varied topics; allow for questioning and probing; provide hands-on activities.

Attracted to complexity and dialectical thinking	Enjoys new topics and activities; tolerant of ambiguity; tolerant of disorder; engages in "combinatorial play," often with seemingly disparate concepts	Bored with routine and rote learning	Employ integrated and broad thematic approaches to curriculum development; approach problems as opportunities for novel solutions; incorporate metaphor and analogies in instructional practices.
Open-minded	Receptive to new ideas; receptive to others' viewpoints; adaptable	Challenges "facts"; always asks "What if . . ."	Provide situations/activities that are open-ended, provocative, and multidisciplinary.
Artistic	Aesthetic interests; often prefers personal metric to expert judgment	Lack of attention to mundane details or may fixate on the quixotic or unusual	Allow multimedia approaches to assignments; provide materials for artistic expression in all content areas.
Needs privacy/alone time	Reflective; introspective	May be withdrawn; may not participate in class activities; may be affected by insights no one else shares	Allow individual work time and provide a space and time for quiet thinking and reflection.
Perceptive	Sees relationships; uses all senses in observing; sensitive	May be overstimulated; may have difficulty focusing on narrowly defined tasks, multiple choice tests, etc.	Discuss multiple perspectives and encourage sensorial exploration of materials; accept emotions and explore affective responses.
Original/imaginative	Resourceful; flexible; enjoys pretending and fantasizing; imagery is common in everyday thought	Prone to radical and fanciful thinking; may be a daydreamer and forgetful	Provide for individualization and differentiation in curriculum and materials; include opportunities for the use of imagery in educational activities.

does this work?" "How can we make it better or different?" "Why is it like that?" "Can it be like this instead?" "Why couldn't we do it this way also?" are considerations that often compel the curious and creative to understand, to interact with, and to effect change on aspects of their environment.

Sense of Humor/Playfulness

Humor is associated with an ability to approach problems, and life in general, in a fresh, childlike, and playful manner. Humor in the form of puns, satire, and farce engages the imagination in approaching a topic with an unusual "twist." A unique juxtaposition of entities, ideas, words, and images often lends a humorous note to a creative product. Numerous inventions and creations have resulted from fooling around with ideas and playing with possibilities, in contrast to more rule-bound approaches and traditions (Davis & Rimm, 1989).

Attracted to Complexity

Creativity is not a simple concept or process. Often creative enterprises bridge disciplines, styles, materials, techniques, cultures, geography, and periods. Creative people tend to be drawn to complexity. Thus, an environment rich and varied in resources, materials, and modes of interaction may contribute to an increase in creative activity.

Several investigations of creativity suggest that the creative process involves a struggle with the perceived world and that out of this struggle a new synthesis is created (Forisha, 1978). Old forms are disrupted as the creative process transcends the traditional cultural world with which one is familiar (Schachtel, 1959). Creative thinking often is presented as a dialectic between two modes of thought: the organized structure of form and the free play of imagination (May, 1975), the alternating experience of diffusion and integration (Barron, 1963), the tension between realistic and primitive modes of functioning (Bowers & Bowers, 1972), and the interplay of convergent and divergent thought processes (Isaksen & Treffinger, 1985).

Artistic

The studies of Csikszentmihalyi and Getzels (1973, 1988; Getzels & Csikszentmihalyi, 1968a, 1968b, 1976) indicate that personality and value differences characterize young people engaged in a creative career and further differentiate those who are successful in creative pursuits. More specifically, art students were found to hold social and economic values in lower esteem, and they ascribed to aesthetic values much more than average college students. The more original the art student, the more extreme were his or her values. Many creative scientists also value a personal sense of aesthetics and elegance over commercial reward or public recognition.

Open-Minded

Creative people are open-minded, willing to consider multiple possibilities, and able to tolerate ambiguity while exploring an idea. Open-mindedness, though not necessitating a complete rejection of convergence or convention, approaches what *is* as a starting point for what *might* be—a starting place for more original explorations of what might be possible in a future context (Samples, 1987).

Need for Privacy and Alone Time

Graham Wallas's (1926) analysis of the creative process included four stages: preparation, incubation, illumination, and verification. *Preparation* is foundational in this view, as it is the stage that involves exploring, clarifying, gathering, and reviewing data; collecting resources and materials; and so on. The next stage, *incubation*, is perhaps the hallmark of the Wallas model. Incubation is a period during which the creative activity or problem is, deliberately or incidentally, put out of one's mind. Incubation is a period of preconscious, fringe-conscious, or unconscious processing during which one is not giving the creative project or idea deliberate attention; instead, one is involved in another activity, such as jogging, resting, reading, walking in the woods, or possibly even sleeping. It is after such periods of relaxation and reflection that the "Aha!" or "Eureka!" associated with *illumination* in the creative process occurs. Such processes generally do not evolve in periods or environments of high levels of interpersonal interaction (Storr, 1988). On the contrary, creative individuals place considerable value on the inner life of their mind, their imagination, and the relationship of reflection and contemplation to creative pursuits. Numerous creators in wide and varied fields have reported a need for extended periods of solitude for nurturing and exploring creative ideas (Gardner, 1993; Storr, 1988).

Perceptiveness

A high degree of perceptiveness often is associated with giftedness (Ehrlich, 1982; Lovecky, 1986, 1993). Creatively gifted individuals are particularly sensitive to stimuli from the environment, especially with regard to the following: identifying patterns; discerning details; and noticing both similarities and distinctions among seemingly disparate entities, items, or ideas (Daniels-McGhee & Davis, 1994; Torrance, 1962). Heightened sensory awareness coupled with both a well-developed intuitive capacity and the ability to apprehend multiple layers of meaning simultaneously allows the perceptively gifted to assess people and situations rapidly (see Chapter 30 by Piechowski). Such heightened awareness is also what enables the creative individual to see past the obvious and, in noting fine points, to see possibilities where others may not.

Originality and Imagination

A creative individual tends to fantasize, daydream, and imagine to a greater extent than less creative peers. Imagery plays a key role in the thinking and conceptualizing of the creative individual (Daniels, 1995). Creative individuals employ more purposeful forms of mental imagery in their everyday thinking and problem solving and generally have greater control of their mental representations (Flowers & Garbin, 1989) as well as the external form in which they find expression.

Classroom Climate

Environments shape behaviors, and classroom environments shape—foster or inhibit—creative behaviors. Carl Rogers (1962) asserted that a *psychologically safe* environment was necessary to foster creativity. Rogers identified flexibility and receptivity as two key components of a creativity-conducive environment. In his view, awareness of and encouragement for novel and unusual ideas is essential to ultimate creative development. Students' curiosity and independence must be acknowledged as aspects of both the creative person and the creative process.

Teachers are central in establishing environments that support student creativity. Teachers who acknowledge and applaud students' creative pursuits, model risk taking, teach with a sense of humor, and approach matters of curriculum and instruction with open-mindedness inevitably teach creatively and build creative learning environments. Generally, classrooms that can be described in the same terms that describe creative individuals will enhance and support creative potential. In contrast, classrooms with controlling, rigid, and inflexible structures will inhibit creative expression and growth.

Curriculum and Instruction

Various aspects of curriculum and instruction may be adapted to accommodate and foster creativity. Curriculum can be designed specifically to address and heighten awareness of creativity, and instructional strategies can be employed that both model and allow for independence, risk taking, high energy levels, curiosity, playfulness, preference for complexity, aesthetic inclinations, open-mindedness, reflection, and heightened perception.

Metacognitive Understanding of Creativity

Curriculum that includes the deliberate study of creative individuals and their work will heighten awareness of creativity in general and domain-specific creativity as well. Biographical and anecdotal material dealing with the study of creative lives can be included in the study of all disciplines, and specific discussion questions may highlight the individuals and processes associated with notable examples of discovery and invention.

Examples:

What influenced the design of the first geodesic dome? How so?

Was Einstein's childhood happy? What prompted his interest in science? Was he imaginative?

What environmental aspects had the greatest impact on the early art of Georgia O'Keefe? What role did her life as a child play in her later artistic development?

Instructional strategies that enhance awareness of creativity must include taking time to respond positively to creative ideas as they occur. Again, questioning can be useful.

What made you think of that?

What ideas did you put together to come up with such a unique approach?

I'm not sure I know what you mean, yet my curiosity is certainly piqued. Can you tell me more?

Such responses honor the originality inherent in creative expression.

Student Choice

Independence is fostered by shifting the focus of learning to the student, allowing choice, and engaging the student as a partner in curricular design. Whole-group instruction and identical culminating assignments for all students are anathema to independence and creativity, foster conformity, and squelch individual pursuits. Creativity requires options and choice. Choice can be readily incorporated in the curriculum through a variety of means and without much extra effort in the design process.

Although the broad themes selected for study in any given subject area might be determined by an appropriate authority, students can be allowed choices of specific topics and areas of interest. For instance, as suggested in the example at the very beginning of the chapter, while a whole class may be studying the Renaissance, individual students can research different countries or different issues, for example:

The art of the time
Clothing and costumes
Architecture
Social organization
Political structure
Chivalry
Inventions
Women's roles
Mortality
Medicine

Potential projects and products might include:

A slide show
An illustrated children's book
A model
A script for a play or mock trial
A replica of an invention appropriate to the time
A work of art in the style of the time
A piece of music
An illustrated time-line
A diorama
A social diary of an eminent individual of the time
Hand-made examples of illuminated text
A video
A monologue on a pertinent topic
An interview with a museum curator

In determining products, the teacher can make a specific recommendation and, of course, accept suggestions and ideas from students, thereby both providing a forum for creative expression and allowing individual students' intrinsic motivation and personal learning goals to emerge (Amabile, 1989).

Boundaries

Although rules and boundaries are necessary for safety and a positive social climate, freedom of expression should be encouraged. Some creative ideas that are expressed in the classroom are perceived as odd or weird by others. Unless an idea is directly confrontational or intended to be injurious—psychologically or physically—to the teacher or another classmate, unusual ideas should be given time and a forum for expression.

Instances of ideas that initially seemed odd or unusual but which ultimately led to productive discoveries can be pointedly discussed. Both whole-group and small-group brainstorming sessions can be employed as a means of learning both to defer judgment and to take creative intellectual risks with unusual ideas.

Brainstorming can be readily infused into all curricular areas and incorporated into class discussions: "What are all the adjectives we might use to describe Dill in *To Kill a Mockingbird?"* In a primary math class, the students might be asked to: "List all the ways you can to depict the number 100 and then choose 5 to present to the class."

Divergence and respect for individual and out-of-the-ordinary responses are prerequisite to the intellectual playfulness and risk taking associated with creativity in the classroom. Too often, curricula and instructional strategies are designed around a convergent "find-the-one-right-answer" approach. Open-ended assignments and multiple possibilities are absolutely necessary for productive risk taking. Nothing will squelch a student's willingness to take an intellectual risk and venture forth with an unusual response more rapidly than a fear of not meeting expectations—a fear of failing to determine the "one right answer" (Haberman, 1991).

Sometimes, answers that initially seem bizarre or irrelevant ultimately prove to be novel, creative, and fruitful. If an idea seems too wacky or disconcerting to a teacher, a period of *incubation* can be suggested as a means to acknowledge and encourage the student while not discrediting the idea. Simply put, a teacher can respond by saying, "I'm not sure quite what you mean or how that would work, but why don't you think about it for a while longer and see if some other pieces come to you?"

Time, Space, Movement, and Laughter

Creative students are frequently described as *energetic*—intense, driven, passionate, active, absorbed, excitable. These personality characteristics often bring with them prolonged and focused concentration, emotional involvement in the subject matter, kinesthetic activity, or some combination thereof. To accommodate this intensity within the learning environment, extended time-blocks must be provided for immersion in an area of study, and students must be allowed the space and environment for both affective and kinesthetic expression.

Creative Dramatics

Incorporating creative drama activities across curricular areas is an excellent approach for accommodating the emotional and physical energy often associated with creativity. The creative dramatics process is dynamic. The leader guides the group to explore, develop, express, and communicate ideas, concepts, and feelings through dramatic enactment. In creative drama the group improvises action and/or dialogue appropriate to the content being explored; elements of drama give form and meaning to the experience.

Creative drama activities run the gamut from the simple and spontaneous—a game of "statues"—to the planned and complex—a full staging of an original play. One creative drama text (Heinig, 1988) presents the following as a continuum of drama activity variables:

	Easier	***More Advanced***
1.	Use of desk area	Use of large space/theater
2.	Teacher direction	Creative/independent play making

3. Pantomime warm-ups	Pantomime stories—verbal pieces
4. Individual playing	Pair or group work
5. Unison playing for self-satisfaction	Playing to share or communicate with others
6. Reader's theater	Full-scale productions
7. Humorous or "light" material	Highly dramatic or "serious" material
8. Minimal information content	High data content

Pantomime warm-ups. Pantomime warm-ups and pantomime stories can be readily incorporated into a lesson with little or no additional preparation and no special training in theater technique (Davis, 1992), as long as the classroom facilitator (teacher) is willing to "play" also.

Pantomime warm-ups include the following:

- *Circles*: Students stand in large circle. Each person, in turn, thinks of a way to make a circle by using his or her body. All others make the same circle. The circle can be made with part of the body, or all of the body; it can be a fixed circle (e.g., a halo) or a moving circle (e.g., a circular motion of the foot or rolling on the floor). Names add to the fun (e.g., "This is a halo circle," "This is an eyeball circle," This is a chicken circle," "This is a Groucho Marx circle").
- *Mirrors*: This activity requires students to work with a partner. One student becomes a "mirror" that mimics the movements of the partner who might be combing hair, making faces, or putting on makeup. Roles are then reversed.
- *Obstacles:* With chalk, draw "start" and "finish" lines about eight feet apart on the floor. One at a time, students make up an imaginary obstacle which must be climbed over, dodged past, waded through, or overcome in some other way to get from start to finish.
- *Nature's Shapes:* Children shape their bodies to become a tree, stone, leaf, growing flower, rain, sun, etc.

Pantomime stories. Pantomime stories are readily adapted to a variety of subjects, topics, and themes. Pantomime stories can be initiated in a variety of ways, including the following:

- *Who Am I (Are We)?* Students act out community helpers and characters, historical or literary characters, or individuals from current events.
- *What Am I (Are We)?* Students mime animals, inanimate objects, machinery, toys, plants, or mythical creatures.
- *What Am I (Are We) Seeing, Hearing, Tasting, Smelling, Touching?* Students mime reactions to loud sounds, tasting a bitter fruit, smelling strong fumes, or touching a hot stove.
- *Where Am I (Are We)* Students mime being in various locations, such as a museum, boat, foreign land, or on a spaceship.
- *Occupations.* Students can mime activities associated with various jobs, occupations from other times, or occupations in other locations or countries.
- *Inventions.* Students can mime using or *being* an invention.
- *Musical Instruments.* Students mime an instrument of personal choice or one from a category, such as orchestral, marching band, percussion, woodwind, and brass. Instruments from a particular region or country might be the focus.
- *Countries and Customs.* Students enact a custom or celebration associated with a particular country of study: British afternoon tea, Spanish or Mexican bullfight, Japanese kite-flying contest.

Pantomime stories may be extended by adding a verbal one-liner at the end in summary or conclusion of the mimetic act, or to emphasize a moral, add a humorous note, or as a means to continue into more elaborate play-making activities.

Curiosity = Questioning

Curiosity is one of the traits most frequently mentioned by parents of creative students

(Louis & Lewis, 1992). Eighty-eight percent of parents in one study (Parkinson, 1990) stated that their children were curious and inclined toward actively exploring the environment and asking penetrating questions.

Questioning in the classroom is key to both encouraging and responding to curiosity. Burning questions can drive creativity. Questions often underlie the *investigation, contemplation,* and *imagination* that contribute to creative activity.

How might life be different if we couldn't read?
How might life be different if there was no gravity?
How might life be different if we only "kept" memories for a year?
How might life be different if sleep was not necessary?

"What if" and "how might" questions can serve as springboards for creative projects in all subject areas—literature, science, art, social studies—and as starting points for cross-disciplinary investigations.

A sizeable body of literature has accumulated over recent decades pertaining to classroom discourse (Good & Brophy, 1973). Many findings indicate that questions occupy much of classroom "talk-time," but the questions generally originate with the teacher (as many as 400 questions per school day), and the majority of questions posed by the teacher are geared for straight recall responses. Rarely are students asked questions that require analytical, evaluative, or imaginative thinking, and even more rarely are students asked to generate *their own questions.*

A multipurpose, two-part activity that can be adapted for all curricular areas to stimulate thinking and curiosity at the introduction of a new concept relies heavily on student-generated questions. First, students can be asked to generate a representative list of all they currently know about a given topic. Next, students individually, in small groups, or as a class can generate, in brainstorming fashion, a list of questions about what more they would like to know. Question journals can be kept to record ideas for further exploration, and students can be encouraged to build on each other's questions in order to probe issues in greater depth and in more divergent ways.

Student A: Why are airplane wings the size they are?
Student B: What might happen if we made them smaller?

Question prompts such as those included in Table 24.2 (adapted from Wiederhold, 1991) can be used as starting points for encouraging investigation, contemplation, and imaginative explorations.

The journalistic questions—Who? What? When? Where? Why? How?—are excellent starting points for engaging student curiosity. However, the most provocative question teachers can pose to a group of students is "What are *your* questions?" (Anders, 1991).

Table 24.2
Creativity/Curiosity Question Matrix

	WHO	*WHAT*	*WHERE/WHEN*	*WHY*	*HOW*
Investigation	Who is . . . ?	What is . . . ?	Where/when is . . . ?	Why is . . . ?	How is . . . ?
Contemplation	Who can . . . ?	What can . . . ?	Where/when can . . . ?	Why can . . . ?	How can . . . ?
Imagination	Who might . . . ?	What might . . . ?	Where/when might . . . ?	Why might . . . ?	How might . . . ?

Linking Perception and Imagination: A Bridge to Possible Worlds

Creative ideas often result from a shift in perception (Davis & Rimm, 1989). The directed interplay and deliberate manipulation of perception and transformational imagery (imagination) has led both creative scientists and artists to original hypotheses, inventions, and creations (Daniels-McGhee & Davis, 1994).

Perceptual abilities may be purposefully accessed and enhanced in the classroom through activities that direct students' attention to their perceptions of the environment. Activities that explore student perceptions and imaginal experiences afford opportunities to heighten affective and aesthetic awareness, enhance flexible thinking, and increase original and creative production.

Purposeful perceptions: Awareness and observation. A sensorial/perceptual diagram may be used in classroom activities to record perceptions of actual events as they are experienced. Or the diagram may be used as a means of organizing reflections and images associated with past experiences. For example, a weekend recreational experience might be recorded as shown in Figure 24.1. Such reflections often bring emotion-laden memories and associations (Hess, 1987). Thus, the "feeling" slice of the diagram is divided into two parts: One section is for recording tactile content and the other section is for recording affective content.

This sensorial/perceptual diagram may be applied in various curricular areas and learning contexts. It may be used as a perceptual diary, maintained by teacher and students, to log responses to field trips and outings. Vivid, detailed pictures can be used as a starting point for imagining what else might be experienced if one were able to "walk into" the given scene. This format also can be used for organizing thoughts about the experiences of:

- A family traveling west by covered wagon
- Anne Frank's experience
- A Victorian girl at afternoon tea
- Sitting at a medieval feast

These responses and writings may be maintained simply for extending student awareness, or they may be used as starting points for creative writing, for example, poetry, short

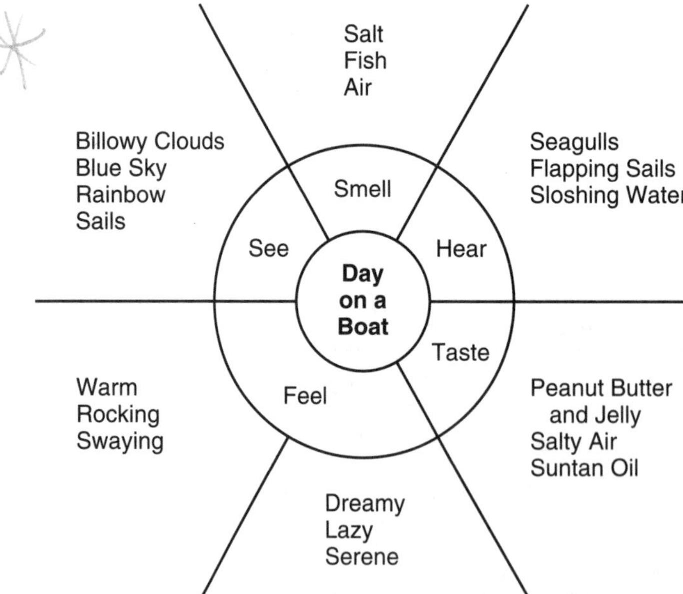

Figure 24.1 A sensorial/perceptual diagram documenting perceptions of past experiences.

stories, or fictionalized diaries, or as impetus and inspiration for works of art, such as painting, sculpture, montage, or other media. The possibilities are as boundless as the imagination.

Playful perceptions. Once students have participated in experiences constructed to heighten awareness of one's perceptual abilities, additional activities can build on and extend initial perceptions in playful and imaginative ways (Leff, 1984). Assumptions are altered and new perspectives taken with activities such as:

- Try to notice aspects of the environment you normally wouldn't.
- Imagine environments and events as the *reverse* of what you normally think they are. (Reverse visual orientation: Imagine far as near, top as bottom, etc.)
- Search for *mundane* aspects of the environment and then look for something interesting about them.
- Analyze what aspects of the environment around you *communicate* to you.
- Look for repetitive patterns in your life and surroundings.
- Make and check predictions about what is going to happen around you in a matter of minutes, hours, or days.
- Randomly choose two items or events from your surroundings and then imagine ways in which they might be compatibly combined.
- Look at the world through *different value systems;* for instance, as an environmentalist, an architect, or an urban planner might.
- Imagine improvements in *problem spots* around you.
- Imagine improvements in already *pleasant* things around you.

Given that much of this type of exploration involves visual perception and visual thinking, students may want to document their ideas with visual representations as well as with words (Arnheim, 1969; Daniels-McGhee, 1994; Gardner, 1982; McKim, 1972).

Visual Thinking, Discovery, and Invention

Visual thinking is conducted in three primary modes:

- *Perception*: The images we *see*
- *Imagination:* The images we *imagine*, recall, invent, combine, and/or transform internally in our "mind's eye" independent of immediate perception
- *Depiction:* The images we represent externally—those that we *draw*, sketch, paint, or model

Visual thinking also involves various cognitive processes and operations that take place both within and across these modes of thought. These include, but are not limited to:

- *Pattern-seeking*: Finding patterns, matching, filling in gaps, categorizing, and completing patterns.
- *Rotation*: Inverse drawing, mental manipulations, and orthographic imagination (imagining how a solid object looks from several directions).
- *Visual reasoning*: Spatial analogy and visual induction.
- *Comprehension of dynamic structures:* Mental representation of three-dimensional *motion* (paper folding, visualizing a knot being tied, the movements of a pulley, moving a piano through a hallway).
- *Visual synthesis*: Combining multiple images. In creative synthesis, new entities emerge that are both different from and greater than the sum of their parts.

While all of these processes may be applied in solving problems, *visual synthesis* is perhaps the most intimately connected with novel, creative, and generative responses to problem situations. Visual synthesis (and its near relative *metaphorical thinking*) have resulted in creativity, invention, and discovery in many different fields and contexts.

Numerous discoveries and inventions have resulted from perceptual "play" and the deliberate transformation of visual images. Albert Einstein is purported to have thought almost purely in images (Wallace & Gruber, 1989) and to have taken delight in the mental manipulation of the images and models he generated. As he said,

> The words or the language, as they are written or spoken, do not seem to play any role in my mechanism of thought. The psychical entities which seem to serve as elements in thought are certain signs and more or less clear images which can be "voluntarily" reproduced and combined. (Einstein, 1952)

Nikola Tesla, who designed the fluorescent light and the alternating current electrical generator, projected images of machines and potential inventions "in his mind's eye." Tesla described these projections as complete and even more detailed than most blueprints or renderings (McKim, 1980).

Modeling, drawing, and thought. In contrast to Tesla's detailed mental imaging, James D. Watson (1968), discoverer of the DNA molecule, described working with a model as a tangible, graphic aid. For Watson, drawing and thinking were nearly inseparably linked. He wrote:

> Only a little encouragement was needed to get the final soldering accomplished in the next couple of hours. The brightly shining metal plates were then immediately used to make a model in which for the first time all the DNA components were present. In about an hour I had arranged the atoms in positions which satisfied both the X-ray data and the laws of stereochemistry. The resulting helix was right-handed with the two chains running in opposite directions . . . Another fifteen minutes' fiddling by Francis [Crick] failed to find anything wrong, though for *brief* intervals my stomach felt uneasy when I saw him frowning. (McKim, 1980)

Drawings serve as a physical representation of constructions of the visual mind. Drawings assist in analyzing, testing, and modifying particular visions. Drawing clarifies visual images and provides a visual record of the design throughout the problem-solving process. Drawing also aids invention in that only the most visually able mind can maintain multiple mental images at once (e.g., Tesla), whereas multiple drawings may be simultaneously viewed more easily for purposes of comparison, contrast, and evaluation of possibilities.

Facilitating visual thinking in the classroom requires an environment that provides students with materials and opportunities for interacting visually with ideas. While visual ideas can be captured with whatever is at hand (e.g., an eyebrow pencil on a candy bar wrapper), visual thinking benefits from exposure to appropriate and varied materials.

Young students' thinking and experimentation might benefit from contact with and the availability of:

- Multicolored chalk
- Chalkboards
- Crayons
- Paints
- Paintbrushes of varying sizes
- Plastic-coated wire
- Paper scraps of different colors and textures
- Cardboard
- Styrofoam shapes
- Clay
- Scissors
- Rulers
- Swatches of material
- Needles
- Thread
- Scraps of wood (checked for splinters)
- Glue

Older students might prefer:

- Carbon, charcoal, pastels, and standard colored pencils
- Soft drawing pencils
- Large pads of newsprint
- Tracing paper
- Erasing gum
- A plastic triangle
- Drafting templates
- Rapidograph or Koh-i-noor pens
- Foamcore
- Artist-quality blank books for permanent records, journals, and logs of ideas

Students will benefit from exposure to many different types of materials, and will find that some ideas are best expressed with certain materials rather than others. However, they initially should be encouraged to work in a free-hand fashion; the constrained or restrictive use of precision tools may slow down and consequently impede the idea-generating process. A slower, more reflective approach can be applied to modifying and improving original ideas on a second or third pass. Also, students should be encouraged to experiment with materials in unconventional ways and in multimedia combinations, as these are the circumstances in which novel ideas, uses, and applications might emerge.

Integrated Thematic Instruction: Combinations, Complexity and Creativity

Bridging disciplines, methods, and modes of expression produces possibilities for complex associations and creative interactions (Kovalik, 1993). Activities that bridge perceptual systems and subject areas often yield products of "effective surprise" (Bruner, 1986) and responses of "Why, of course. How creative! Why didn't I think of that?"

This phenomena is evidenced in numerous cross-modality poetic metaphors, such as in the following literary examples (Marks, 1982):

- The murmur of gray twilight (Poe)
- The sound of coming darkness (Poe)
- Sunset hovers like the sound of golden horns (Robinson)
- The world lay luminous; every petal and cobweb trembled music (Aiken)
- A soft yet glowing light, like lulled music (Shelley)
- Music suddenly opened like a luminous book (Aiken)
- The notes entered my breast like luminous arrows (Gautier)
- Music bright as the soul of light (Swinburne)
- The silver needle-note of a fife (Auslander)
- The dawn comes up like thunder (Kipling)

Inspired apprehensions and articulations such as these may emerge spontaneously in thought, but as educators and curriculum planners we have the opportunity to orchestrate experiences for our students that might enhance creative interactions with the learning environment.

One such curricular approach (Ruef, 1994) utilizes student observation along with methods from the arts and the sciences to foster creativity in the form of analogical, metaphorical, and theoretical thought. The student is invited to become a poet, a scientist, and an artist by approaching the world with an interdisciplinary mind, a jeweler's loupe (magnifying glass), and one good question: "What does it remind me of?" A second question, "Why is it like that?," provides a starting point for further creative and academic explorations.

The jeweler's loupe intensifies seeing, wonder, and concentration. With heightened visual sensitivity, students approach their environment—the natural and man-made world—with a fresh perspective. Fingerprints, popcorn, pebbles, feathers, and pinecones become new "worlds" unto themselves. After careful observation, posing the question "What does it remind me of?" opens the door to creative activity by incorporating analogy, simile, and metaphor. "My fingerprint is like a slice of onion" becomes my fingerprint is a whirlpool, a yo-yo, a plate of spaghetti, a planet, a piece of antique lace, or a butterfly wing—and the metaphorical foundation for generating even more creative and inventive literary, scientific, and artistic possibilities (Fowler, 1990; Lakoff & Johnson, 1980). Such explorations might serve to spark the beginnings of a poem, drawing, sculpture, invention, or model. Further investigations of other "fingerprints" in the world, such as fish skin, pollen grains, or tree bark, coupled with the second question, "Why is it (are they) like that?", sets the stage for hypothesizing and theorizing in many and varied domains. Again, the possibilities are limitless, bounded only by the collective imagination and creative capacities of the teacher and class. Vast potential indeed!

Comments

Opportunities for creative development will most readily be infused in various contexts of learning by adapting curriculum both within and across content areas. Existing curriculum and classroom structures need to be considered as possible avenues for enhancing creative endeavor.

In view of the 4 P's of creativity, *person, process, press* (environment), and *product,* one must consider the role of the teacher, the curriculum, and the classroom climate as well as the student and his or her creative characteristics, behaviors, and potential if that creative potential is to be acknowledged, appreciated, and developed.

REFERENCES

Amabile, T. (1989). *Growing up creative: Nurturing a lifetime of creativity*. New York: Crown.

Anders, P. (1991). Personal communication, annual meeting of American Educational Research Association, Chicago, Illinois.

Arnheim, R. (1969). *Visual thinking*. Berkeley: University of California Press.

Barron, F. (1963). *Creative person and creative process*. New York: Holt.

Bowers, K. S., & Bowers, P. G. (1972). Hypnosis and creativity: A theoretical and empirical rapproachment. In E. Fromm & P. Shor (Eds.), *Hypnosis* (pp. 255–292). Chicago: Aldene-Atherton.

Bruner, J. (1986). *Actual minds, possible worlds*. Cambridge, MA: Harvard University Press.

Clasen, R. E., & Clasen, D. R. (1986). *Programming for high creatives*. Madison, WI: University of Wisconsin-UTAG.

Csikszentmihalyi, M. (1994). The domain of creativity. In D. G. Feldman, M. Csikszentmihalyi, & H. Gardner (Eds.), *Changing the world: A framework for the study of creativity* (pp. 135–158). Westport, CT: Praeger.

Csikszentmihalyi, M., & Getzels, J. W. (1973). The personality of young artists: An empirical and theoretical explanation. *British Journal of Psychology, 64*(1), 91–104.

Csikszentmihalyi, M., & Getzels, J. W. (1988). Creativity and problem finding. In F. H. Farley & R. W. Neperud (Eds.), *The foundations of aesthetics, art, and art education* (pp. 91–106). New York: Praeger.

Daniels, S. (1995). *Images of creativity: The relationship of imagery, everyday cognition, and the creative potential of high school students with exceptional abilities in the arts and sciences*. Unpublished Ph.D. thesis, University of Wisconsin, Madison.

Daniels-McGhee, S. (1994). Visual thinking, imagination, and problem solving. In P. J. Hillmann, D. R. Clasen, & R. E. Clasen (Eds.), *Teachers tackle thinking*. Madison: University of Wisconsin–Madison Education Extension Programs.

Daniels-McGhee, S. & Davis, G. A. (1994). The imagery–creativity connection. *Journal of Creative Behavior, 28,* 151–177.

Davis, G. A. (1991). Teaching creative thinking. In N. Colangelo & G. A. Davis (Eds.), *Handbook of gifted education* (pp. 236–244). Boston: Allyn and Bacon.

Davis, G. A. (1992). *Creativity is forever* (3rd ed.). Dubuque, IA: Kendall/Hunt.

Davis, G., & Rimm, S. (1989). *Education of the gifted and talented* (2nd ed.). Englewood Cliffs, NJ: Prentice-Hall.

Ehrlich, V. (1982). *Gifted children: A guide for parents and teachers*. Englewood Cliffs, NJ: Prentice-Hall.

Einstein, A. (1952). Letter to Jacque Hadamard. In B. Ghiselin (Ed.), *The creative process* (pp. 43–44). Berkeley: University of California Press.

Farley, F. H. (1976). Arousal and cognition: Creative performance, arousal, and the sensation-seeking motive. *Journal of Perceptual and Motor Skills, 43,* 703–708.

Feldman, D. H. (1988). Creativity: Dreams, insights, and transformations. In R. J. Sternberg (Ed.), *The nature of creativity*. New York: Cambridge University Press.

Feldman, D. H., Csikszentmilhalyi, M., & Gardner, H. (Eds.). (1994). *Changing the world: A framework for the study of creativity.* Westport, CT: Praeger.

Flowers, J. H., & Garbin, C. P. (1989). Creativity and perception. In J. A. Glover, R. R. Ronning, & C. R. Reynolds (Eds.), *Handbook of creativity*. New York: Plenum Press.

Forisha, B. L. (1978). Mental imagery and creativity: Review and speculations. *Journal of Mental Imagery, 2,* 209–238.

Fowler, C. (1990). One nation, undercultured and underqualified. In W. J. Moody (Ed.), *Artistic intelligences: Implications for education*. New York: Teacher's College Press.

Gardner, H. (1982). *Art, mind, and brain: A cognitive approach to creativity*. New York: Basic Books.

Gardner, H. (1983). *Frames of mind.* New York: Basic Books.

Gardner, H. (1993). *Creating minds: An anatomy of creativity seen through the lives of Freud, Einstein, Picasso, Stravinsky, Eliot, Graham, and Gandhi.* New York: Basic Books.

Getzels, J. W., & Csikszentmihalyi, M. (1968a). On

the roles, values, and performance of future artists: A conceptual and empirical exploration. *Sociological Quarterly, 9,* 516–530.

Getzels, J. W., & Csikszentmihalyi, M. (1968b). The value orientation of art students as determinants of artistic specialization and creative performance. *Studies in Art Education, 10,* 5–16.

Getzels, J. W., & Csikszentmihalyi, M. (1976). *The creative vision.* New York: Wiley.

Good, T. L., & Brophy, J. E. (1973). *Looking in classrooms.* New York: Harper & Row.

Haberman, M. (1991). The pedagogy of poverty vs. good teaching. *Phi Delta Kappan, 73*(4), 290–294.

Heinig, R. B. (1988). *Creative drama for the classroom teacher.* Englewood Cliffs, NJ: Prentice-Hall.

Hess, K. H. (1987). *Enhancing writing through imagery: Using mental imagery to encourage confidence in creative expression.* Monroe, NY: Trillium Press.

Isaksen, S. G., & Treffinger, D. J. (1985). *Creative problem solving: The basic course.* Buffalo, NY: Bearly Limited.

Kosslyn, S. (1983). *Ghosts in the mind's machine.* New York: Norton.

Kovalik, S. (1993). *Integrated thematic instruction: The model.* Oak Creek, AZ: Books for Educators.

Lakoff, G., & Johnson, M. (1980). *Metaphors we live by.* Chicago: University of Chicago Press.

Leff, H. L. (1984). *Playful perception.* Burlington, VT: Waterfront Books.

Louis, B., & Lewis, M. (1992). Parental beliefs about giftedness in young children and their relation to actual ability level. *Gifted Child Quarterly, 36,* 27–31.

Lovecky, D. (1986). Can you hear the flowers singing? Issues for gifted adults. *Journal of Counseling and Development, 64,* 590–592.

Lovecky, D. (1993). The quest for meaning: Counseling issues with gifted children and adults. In L. K. Silverman (Ed.), *Counseling the gifted and talented.* Denver: Love.

Marks, L. E. (1982). Synesthetic perception and poetic metaphor. *Journal of Experimental Psychology: Human Perception and Performance, 8,* 15–23.

May, R. (1975). *The courage to create.* New York: Norton.

McKim, R. H. (1972). *Experiences in visual thinking.* Monterey, CA: Brooks/Cole.

McKim, R. H. (1980). *Thinking visually.* Palo Alto, CA: Dale Seymour.

Parke, B. N. (1989). *Gifted students in regular classrooms.* Boston: Allyn and Bacon.

Parkinson, M. L. (1990). Finding and serving gifted preschoolers. *Understanding Our Gifted, 4*(5), 5–6.

Reuf, K. (1994). *The private eye: (5X) Looking/thinking by analogy.* Seattle, WA: Private Eye Project.

Rogers, C. R. (1962). Toward a theory of creativity. In S. J. Parnes & H. F. Harding (Eds.), *A sourcebook for creative thinking* (pp. 63–72). New York: Scribner's.

Samples, B. (1987). *Openmind/wholemind: Parenting and teaching tomorrow's children today.* Rolling Hills Estates, CA: Jalmar Press.

Schachtel, E. G. (1959). *Metamorphosis: On the development of affect, perception, attention, and memory.* New York: Basic Books.

Sternberg, R. J., & Lubart, T. I. (1993). Creative giftedness: A multivariate investment approach. *Gifted Child Quarterly, 37,* 7–15.

Storr, A. (1988). *Solitude: A return to the self.* New York: Macmillan.

Tardif, T. Z., & Sternberg, R. J. (1988). What do we know about creativity? In R. J. Sternberg (Ed.), *The nature of creativity: Contemporary psychological perspectives* (pp. 429–440). New York: Cambridge University Press.

Torrance, E. P. (1962). *Guiding creative talent.* Englewood Cliffs, NJ: Prentice-Hall.

Wallace, D. B., & Gruber, H. E. (1989). *Creative people at work.* New York: Oxford University Press.

Wallas, G. (1926). *The art of thought.* London: Cape.

Watson, J. (1968). *The double helix.* New York: Atheneum.

Wiederhold, C. (1991). *Cooperative learning and critical thinking: The question matrix.* San Juan Capistrano, CA: Resources for Teachers.

25

Critical Thinking and Gifted Students: Using IMPACT to Improve Teaching and Learning

S. LEE WINOCUR, *Center for Teaching of Thinking, Huntington Beach, California*
PATRICIA A. MAURER, *Midland Independent School District, Midland, Texas*

Systematic Instruction in Thinking Skills Benefits Gifted Students

One all-too-common phenomenon illustrates the importance of systematic thinking skills instruction for gifted students. Young gifted children have an uncanny ability for intuitive responses—they just seem to know things. Unfortunately, this mesmerizing effect sometimes masks gaps in their learning.

On Monday, presented with a new and unique problem, the gifted child may demonstrate a flash of brilliance. On Tuesday, faced with a similar problem in a different context, the child may be unable to perform. The "Aha!" just won't come. This phenomenon happens because the child does not know how he or she arrived at the first answer. Unable consciously to describe and replicate the thinking that occurred, the child reaches an impasse. Without the ability to transfer learning from one context to another, children cannot develop competence.

Over time, a lack of "response-ability," the ability to respond successfully, erodes children's confidence in their own intellect. The spontaneous behaviors that distinguish young gifted children—a wide range of interests, high motivation, problem-solving ability, commitment to inquiry, intuitive insight, and logical reasoning—become less apparent. Children's thinking becomes tentative and reluctant.

We learn thinking in a social context. A child's ability to activate good thinking at the appropriate time results from the supported dialogue which occurs in thoughtful classrooms.

Teaching for thinking means teaching for intelligent behavior, an activity too important to be left to chance, even for gifted children.

Three Components of Impact

IMPACT (Increase Maximal Performance by Activating Critical Thinking) organizes three important components of a sound thinking skills program. First, IMPACT provides teachers with a curriculum framework of 22 skills, the Universe of Critical Thinking, which integrate thinking both within and across disciplines.

The Universe of Critical Thinking includes skills that accelerate performance in academic subjects. By focusing student attention on transfer of a common set of skills to varied learning tasks, IMPACT increases efficient and effective use of student time. Students develop competence with thinking tools which help them to access, process, and apply new information.

Second, IMPACT introduces 10 teaching behaviors that engage and sustain critical thinking on the part of individual students and classroom groups. These behaviors include:

- Promotion of interaction through cooperative learning
- Sequencing of cognitive skills from simple to complex
- Sequencing of modalities from concrete to abstract
- Modeling and demonstrating

- High-level questioning to promote thoughtful dialogue
- Cueing with the language of thinking
- Probing with a well-planned series of questions
- Symbolizing ideas using graphic organizers
- Reflecting with wait-time
- Teaching for transfer

By supporting development of effective teaching practices, IMPACT provides a structure for total school improvement. Teaching with IMPACT requires thoughtful planning and implementation. Because IMPACT also asks teachers to think, they model intelligent behavior for students.

Third, IMPACT includes a *lesson design* that can be used to develop and remodel lessons which elicit quality thinking. The lesson design helps teachers analyze the prerequisites needed for success with each new thinking skill. The lesson design targets specific objectives, outlines teaching strategies, and provides for applications and variations. Teachers learn to structure lessons that capitalize on a student's previous knowledge and provide relevant entry points for new learning.

In IMPACT classrooms, the three components work together to provide a scaffold which supports thinking and learning.

In the preface to the September 1984 issue of *Educational Leadership,* Ron Brandt discussed a balanced approach to teaching thinking. His suggestions included teaching of thinking, teaching for thinking, and teaching about thinking. IMPACT contributes to the development of each dimension.

- The Universe of Critical Thinking and the lesson design assist teachers in their efforts to provide direct instruction in how to think consciously and solve problems—*teaching of thinking.*
- The 10 teaching behaviors and the lesson design assist teachers in their efforts to foster classroom conditions that encourage thinking—*teaching for thinking.*
- The interaction of the 10 teaching behaviors, lesson design, and Universe of Critical Thinking creates a climate in which both teachers and students are talking about and working to improve the quality of their thinking—*teaching about thinking.*

Why Use IMPACT?

When selecting a thinking skills program, three basic approaches are available:

- Programs that emphasize the attitudes or dispositions associated with critical thinking, such as a spirit of inquiry, curiosity, and openness to questions.
- Programs that target the critical thinking processes, such as the scientific method or creative problem solving.
- The IMPACT approach, which focuses on the skills of critical thinking.

The original authors of IMPACT identified skills necessary for improved performance in the classroom and improved performance on standardized measures of ability and achievement. They selected skills through an analysis of curriculum guides, textbooks, and tests. They asked themselves two simple questions: What do we expect students to do in school? How do we measure student learning?

In an academic setting, students' abilities to gather, organize, analyze, evaluate, and apply information improve performance in reading, language arts, mathematics, science, and social studies. When internalized, these skills transfer to any learning task. They assist students in constructing and shaping an understanding of the world in which they live.

In describing the constructivist approach to teaching and learning, Jacqueline and Martin Brooks (1993) suggested:

> Schools can be student-centered and successfully prepare students for their adult years by understanding and honoring the dynamics of learning; by recognizing that, for students, schooling must be a time of curiosity, exploration, and inquiry, and memorizing information must be subordinate to learning how to find information to solve real problems.

The IMPACT approach values student questions. Lessons begin with concrete, active experiences which undergird concept formation. Teachers facilitate learning through interaction with students. Students work independently as well as in groups. Teachers affirm, cue, and probe to extend thinking.

One can define critical thinking as the ability to correctly assess statements. Such a definition is based on a commitment to orderly and detailed habits. The skills of critical thinking help students to acquire, select, and apply information with greater precision.

Specific assumptions undergird the IMPACT program:

- All students are capable of higher level thinking.
- Thinking skills can be taught and learned.
- Teachers' behavior can enhance student thinking.
- Thinking skills should be taught in context.
- Thinking skills are basic to learning and interdisciplinary in nature.
- The transfer of thinking skills can be taught.

The components of IMPACT interact to make students better at thinking and better at the business of school.

Special programs for gifted students sometimes attract negative attention because they are organized around activities labeled *enrichment.* Although IMPACT lessons and strategies serve to enrich the cognitive development of students, they are essential, not supplementary. IMPACT positively affects the level of intellectual engagement of all students in a classroom.

IMPACT lessons allow for open-ended response. They support the concept, suggested by experts in the field of identification of gifted students, that "giftedness" can be found by observing students' behavior—in their responses.

Using IMPACT to Differentiate Curriculum

The Universe of Critical Thinking includes three major categories, each containing subskills arranged in hierarchical order (see Figure 25.1). When students integrate and apply the skills from each level, they move toward the goal of improved critical thinking.

The Universe of Critical Thinking guides planning for instruction in an IMPACT classroom. The framework focuses teacher and student attention on the types of thinking required by any learning experience.

In IMPACT, lesson guides for language arts and mathematics are available. Although lessons originally were designed for at-risk high school students, they are easily adapted for use with students at all age and ability levels. In addition, they serve as models for developing new lessons.

Lessons provide memory cues to help students activate and transfer the skills. Once the thinking skills are introduced, teachers can embed and reinforce them in every lesson, in every subject.

IMPACT training includes the lesson, "Can You Zooley" (see Figure 25.2). Take a few minutes and try it. The answers are at the end of the chapter.

Two questions provide insight into the purposes and outcomes of the Zooley activity. First, how did you feel when you first looked at the activity page. "Overwhelmed" is a fairly standard response. Thinking critically is hard work. Without specific strategies at hand to guide the process, difficult problems initially appear impossible.

Second, how many different thinking skills were required to complete the activity successfully? You may have discovered that each skill in the Universe of Critical Thinking, beginning with observation and including deductive reasoning, must be applied in order to complete Zooley.

The complexity of critical thinking reveals itself through a game. No student ever forgets the experience of Zooley. Additionally, students remember that the lesson illustrates the process of working from general to specific.

Teachers often ask students to "think harder." However, the term *think* represents an abstraction that students cannot capture. The specific language of the Universe of Critical Thinking signals or cues specific needed action. Students use the taxonomy of

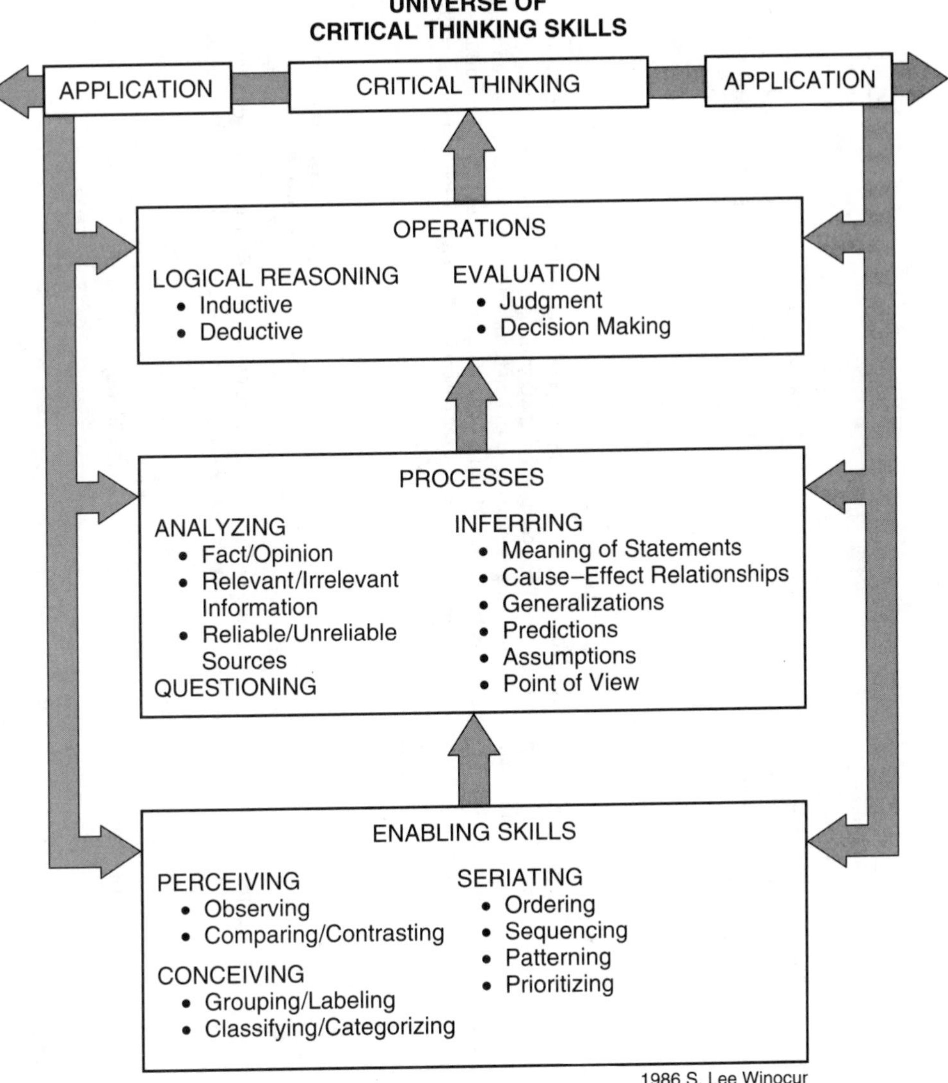

Figure 25.1 Universe of Critical Thinking Skills.

skills as a tool for opening an internal dialogue about their own thinking. When students purposefully select specific thought processes, they become overt thinkers.

Overt thinkers act with independence and autonomy. They metacognitively process new ideas, new challenges, and new problems. They are able to think about the quality of their thinking and to make choices which improve it.

The term *differentiate* refers to a process of building and/or modifying curriculum to match the needs of learners. Differentiated curriculum for gifted students must include planned experiences to develop productive, complex, and higher level thinking skills.

Gifted students often are asked to deal with broad-based issues, problems, or themes that integrate concepts across subject areas. If a child's thinking skills have not been cultivated and polished, the level of abstraction required

CRITICAL THINKING LEVEL
OPERATIONS

SKILL
LOGICAL REASONING
Deductive

OBJECTIVE(S)
Given the game "Zooley," the student will answer 18 or more questions correctly and will justify the answers

PREREQUISITE SKILL(S)
Comparing/contrasting
Patterning, testing hypotheses
Observing

TAXONOMY LEVEL(S)
Application
Analysis
Evaluation

MATERIALS/EQUIPMENT
Study Sheet 1

INTRODUCTION

Thinking logically helps you to analyze information and reach a conclusion that makes sense. In this lesson we will play a game called "Zooley." Logical thinking skills are needed in order to play this game. Deductive thinking skills are used by a doctor to figure out which disease a patient has, by a mechanic to decide what might be wrong with a car, or by a detective in solving a crime. You will use deductive logic to play this game.

TEACHING STRATEGY
The teacher will:

A. Introduce the activity.
   1. Distribute copies of the "Zooley Game." Explain that the object of the game is to figure out which animals inhabit the zoo. The accompanying diagram is a map of the zoo. Instruct the students to observe that the cages are arranged in two rows, which are separated by an aisle or corridor. The animals live in the cages. At the bottom of the map is a key to the inhabitants' names and the designs that represent them. After observing the map closely, students are to answer the questions on Study Sheet 1.
   2. Arrange students in pairs.

B. Model the thinking skills and provide guided practice.
   1. Model the thinking involved in answering the first question. The question is, "Which family is visiting the polar bears?" *(the Zuffs)* How do you know? *(The design for that family is in the aisle between cages; the design matches the one for Zuff in the "Key to Family Names"; they appear to be visiting; or, they are on the outside.)* If students have difficulty in understanding this analysis, continue to discuss the responses together, trying not to answer the questions for the students.
   2. Ask open-ended questions that encourage students to think for themselves. For example: What do you notice is different about the location of certain families? What might this tell you? What is the key word in the first question? *(visiting)* Who might be visiting animals in a zoo? *(people)*

Figure 25.2 Zooley.

TEACHING STRATEGY, CONTINUED

3. Review the reasoning associated with selected responses. For example:
   Question 4: Which is the family of spiders?
   Answer: Lesger.
   Reasoning: What is different about spiders? *(Spiders have eight legs.)*

   ① ②
   If the Lesger design shows eight legs, then the Lesger family is made up of spiders.

   ①
   The Lesger design shows eight legs.

   ②
   Therefore, the Lesger family is made up of spiders.

   Continue this analysis for 2 or 3 other questions.
4. Say, "Often when we think through the answer to a question, our thinking follows a pattern. The pattern we have identified in this lesson is one form of deductive logic."

CONCLUSIONS AND APPLICATION

When the game is completed, ask, "What skills were you using while you were playing this game? *(observation, drawing conclusions, inferring, thinking logically, etc.)* What other situations do you think would require you to use these skills?" *(When I'm lost and need directions; when I'm doing research for a paper; when I'm planning a trip, etc.)*

Learning to be a critical thinker can be hard work. You have to process information, recognize patterns, and use these to find the answer. But learning to be a critical thinker can be satisfying too!

VARIATIONS

Assign Home Enrichment Learning Packet (H.E.L.P.), "Deductive Logic."

3.2.1 *ZOOLEY*
Study Sheet 1

Can You Zooley?

Key to Family Names

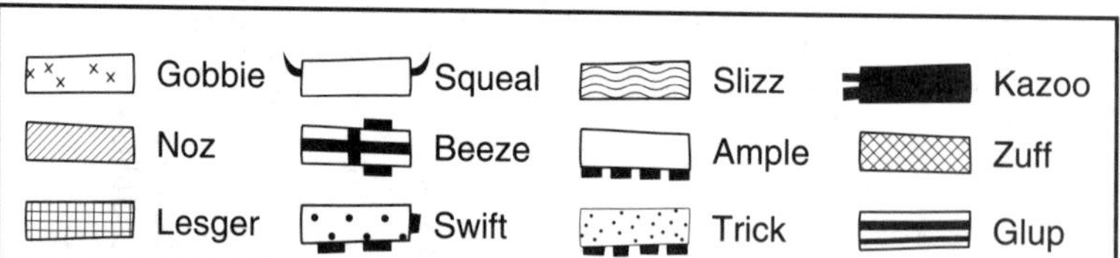

3.2.1 ZOOLEY
Study Sheet 1 (continued)

HOW DO YOU ZOOLEY?

1. What family is visiting the polar bears?
2. What kind of family are they?
3. Whose family is the largest?
4. Which is the family of spiders?
5. Whose son has Mr. Crocodile just swallowed?
6. Which swimming family has only 3 sons?
7. Which family has just 3 daughters?
8. Is the polar bear's cub male or female?
9. Which family has no offspring?
10. Which is a family of snakes?
11. Which is a kangaroo?
12. What will be the surname of the elephant's baby, which is soon to be born?
13. How many sons has Mr. Giraffe?
14. Which family has no father?
15. Which mother is away at the hospital?
16. Who are the neighbors of the monkeys?
17. A wee pelican has wandered into whose cage?
18. Which is a family of pelicans?
19. Give the names of each kind of animal.
20. What is the zookeeper's name?
21. What are the three other objects in the zoo?

Figure 25.2 (*continued*)

may result in disappointing performance. IMPACT bridges the gap between intuitive knowing and conscious competence.

Using IMPACT for Total Program Improvement

Greathouse Elementary School, Midland Independent School District, Midland, Texas, opened its doors for the first time in September 1993. Prior to opening, all teachers received IMPACT training and the staff agreed to serve as a national demonstration site for the IMPACT project.

In response to a desegregation plan, Greathouse Elementary School draws a fifth-grade population from three different Midland neighborhoods. During the 1993–1994 school year, 241 students attended fifth-grade classes. The following demographic data describes the diversity within the group:

Ethnicity		
African American	27	11%
Hispanic	60	25%

White	154	64%
Free/reduced meals	77	33%
Special programs		
Learning-disabled	19	8%
Gifted/talented	19	8%

In the fall of 1993, 87 students—33 percent of the fifth-grade population—were identified as "at-risk" for failure to master one or more sections of the state-mandated TAAS (Texas Assessment of Academic Skills) Test. By the spring of 1994, the number of "at-risk" students had been reduced to 49.

Passing rates for individual sections of the TAAS reflect the growth that occurred for subpopulations within this group (see Table 25.1). The TAAS test specifically targets higher level thinking skills in reading and math. The staff attributes the positive growth in test performance to the direct teaching of thinking skills within each content area. Also, teachers feel they are beginning to close the gap between subpopulations.

Dr. Bill Maurer, principal of Greathouse Elementary School, indicated "Increased test performance provides only one piece of the picture. Because all students participate in a continuous dialogue about thinking, the level of cognitive engagement in classrooms has been elevated."

This observation has important implications for gifted students. At Greathouse Elementary, gifted students attend special "gifted" classes as part of their regular schedule. However, in a sense these students are not gifted part of the time. When direct instruction in thinking skills raises the level of cognitive engagement in classrooms, the new degree of challenge mitigates differences among students.

This does not mean that gifted students do not need regularly scheduled opportunities to work with other gifted students. However, thinking skills training provides one way to increase the level of challenge within heterogeneously grouped classrooms.

Conclusion

Direct instruction in thinking skills is an essential component of a program for gifted students. Gifted students need to become consciously competent in applying thinking skills. They cannot be allowed to depend solely on intuitive insight. They must have a repertoire of strategies available to improve the quantity and quality of their thinking. IMPACT provides a reasonable solution to meeting this need.

REFERENCE

Brooks, J. G., & Brooks, M. G. (1993). *In search of understanding: The case for constructivist classrooms.* Alexandria, VA: Association for Supervision and Curriculum Development.

Table 25.1
Passing Rates by Ethnicity and Subject Area

		African American	*Hispanic*	*White*
Reading	Passing, 1993	27%	54%	85%
	Passing, 1994	52%	64%	96%
Math	Passing, 1993	13%	51%	87%
	Passing, 1994	44%	65%	85%
Passing ALL tests, 1993		5%	36%	78%
Passing ALL tests, 1994		40%	54%	82%

3.2.1 ZOOLEY
Answer Key

1. Zuff
2. Humans. They are outside the cages observing other animals.
3. Kazoo.
4. Lesger. Spiders have eight legs.
5. Beeze's son was swallowed. Thus, Gobbie are crocodiles and gender of each animal is designated by shape.
6. Squeal. Note flipper and name similarity (i.e., Seal-Squeal).
7. Lesger. Spiders.
8. Male.
9. Slizz. There are only adults in the cage.
10. Slizz. See lines similar to shape of snake.
11. Swift. See pocket on side of female.
12. Ample. See baby inside female; not a Gobbie because a male is inside a male.
13. Mr. Noz has none.
14. Squeal.
15. Noz. No female is in the cage.
16. Trick. This is a family of polar bears.
17. Gobbies. This wee animal proves to be a pelican.
18. Beeze.
19. Gobbie: crocodiles — Beeze: pelicans — Trick: polar bears
    Noz: giraffes — Swift: kangaroo — Kazoo: monkeys
    Lesger: spiders — Slizz: snakes — Zuff: humans
    Squeal: seals — Ample: elephants — Glup: ?
20. Mr. Glup.
21. These symbols have no specific meaning. This question allows the student to use divergent thinking skills. Accept any answer.

26

Talents Unlimited Model in Programs for Gifted Students

CAROL SCHLICHTER, *University of Alabama*

Talents Unlimited (TU) is a staff development model for training both regular classroom teachers and specialists in gifted education to identify and nurture students' multiple thinking talents. Classroom-based research, beginning in 1971 and continuing today, links Calvin Taylor's multiple talent theory (1968) with practice in thinking skills instruction. In this model, traditional *academic* talent helps students to gain knowledge in a variety of disciplines, while five other talents—*productive thinking, decision making, planning, forecasting,* and *communication*—assist students in processing or using the knowledge to create new solutions to problems. The five thinking talents plus the academic talent represent some, but not all, of the ways in which people express intelligence. Indeed, Taylor (1986) identified three additional talents which, when detailed and elaborated by future classroom research, may account for additional student talent potential.

The teacher is perceived to be the key person in student talent development. Therefore, from its inception, the TU model was intended to focus on teacher training. Training for teachers and other instructional personnel in the TU model is provided by two distinct, but coordinated, programs:

1. Talents Unlimited, Inc., in Mobile, Alabama, is a developer-demonstrator model of the National Diffusion Network (USDE), which provides training for elementary teachers, grades 1–6.
2. Talents Unlimited to the Secondary Power (TU^2) in Tuscaloosa, Alabama, comprises the training model for secondary teachers, grades 7–12.

Four major categories of activities and strategies are employed in the staff development model: (1) input sessions on multiple talent theory and talent skills definitions, (2) modeling and demonstration, (3) classroom practice and feedback sessions, and (4) one-to-one and small-group planning.

The results of over twenty years of implementation with teachers and their students (Chisson & McLean, 1993; Schlichter, 1986) have made TU one of the most widely used thinking skills models in the world. "In the project reporting period from October 1, 1990, to September 30, 1991, TU was introduced by 8,691 trained educators in 2,146 school sites to approximately 416,923 students, more than any of the other 500 National Diffusion Network programs" (Haskew, 1993, p. 74). It was identified by *Learning* magazine (Baum, 1990) as one of the top ten thinking skills models in the United States. A cadre of more than 270 state and national certified trainers, guided by Talents Unlimited, Inc., and TU^2, makes possible this broad diffusion of TU and ensures the integrity of the model's implementation.

Classroom Applications of Talents Unlimited

A major strength of the TU model is its effectiveness with groups of students representing diversity in intellectual ability and achievement, socioeconomic level, and interests. Gifted students, as well as "slow learners," were included in the population of the original research. Rural and other minority groups also were represented in this and subsequent studies. Numerous successful adoptions of the

TU model in sites representing all areas of the United States and several foreign countries attest to the validity of this program in enhancing the multiple thinking talent development of students of diverse backgrounds and abilities (Schlichter, 1983).

The effectiveness of TU in enriching the learning of all youngsters is directly related to its integration into the instructional program. Table 26.1 describes the talent areas included in the model, as well as illustrative instructional activities at varying grade levels.

Table 26.1
Description of the Talents Unlimited Model

Talent Areas	*Definition*	*Sample Activity*
Productive Thinking	To generate many, varied, and unusual ideas or solutions and to add detail to the ideas to improve or make them more interesting	During a science unit on sea life, students generate many, varied, unusual strategies for grouping an array of sea animal specimens to help others understand how the animals are alike and different.
Decision Making	To outline, weigh, make final judgments, and defend a decision on the many alternatives to a problem	Students decide which of several graphing methods they have studied is the best way to present information about a given topic of interest, weighing the alternative with criteria such as clarity in presentation of main ideas, provision for greatest detail in information, visual attractiveness, etc.
Planning	To design a means for implementing an idea by describing what is to be done, identifying the resources needed, outlining a sequence of steps to take, pinpointing possible problems, and showing improvements in the plan	Students plan a school activity to celebrate Martin Luther King Day, detailing their objective, materials and equipment needed, a sequence of steps required, possible problems, and improvements for their plan.
Forecasting	To make a variety of predictions about the possible causes and/or effects of various phenomena	In a class on astronomy, students predict the possible effects on life on earth if our planet suddenly stopped spinning on its axis but continued to revolve around the sun.
Communication	To use and interpret both verbal and nonverbal forms of communication to express ideas, feelings, and needs to others	Students generate many, different single words to describe their feelings if they had to live in hiding for two years to help them analyze character development in *The Diary of Anne Frank.*
Academic	To develop a base of knowledge and/or skill about a topic or issue through acquisition of information and concepts	Students read from a variety of resources to gain information about the Impressionist period and then share the information in a discussion of a painting by Monet.

Thinking Skills Instruction as Enrichment for All Students

Educators and researchers in the field of gifted education have made concerted efforts to bridge the gap between regular classroom programs and special education services to bright students and to develop a sense of ownership among school personnel for the enrichment of *all* students. Models for schoolwide enrichment have helped to clarify program objectives that are appropriate for all students and those that primarily address the needs and interests of more able students (e.g., Feldhusen & Kolloff, 1978; Renzulli & Reis, 1985; Treffinger, 1980). One of the staple components of schoolwide enrichment models is training for thinking and feeling processes; this component is viewed as appropriate for all students, regardless of ability level.

Thinking skills instruction certainly is not new to educators of gifted students. What is newer, perhaps, is the increasing emphasis given by both regular educators and educators of gifted students to the use of thinking skills models with all students, not just with students identified as gifted. The idea that the teaching of thinking skills is an important but underdeveloped component of the basics of school instructional programs leads many school districts to implement models like TU.

TU is an infusion model for the teaching of thinking, integrating thinking skills instruction across the curriculum. When faculty and students share a common language and goals for thinking, the likelihood that students will see relationships among disciplines and among the diversity of thinking strategies is increased, and the possibility for transfer of learning is enhanced.

One of the concepts that emerged quickly during the early development of the TU model was that students vary in their use of certain talent skills across subject areas. Apparently, students' preferences and aptitudes for certain subject areas interact to some extent with their skill in using the talent clusters. Thus, implementation of the model across all aspects of the school curriculum is desirable.

Examples of Classroom Applications of the TU Model

The *Productive Thinking* talent employs four divergent thinking skills analogous to Torrance's (1962) fluency, flexibility, originality, and elaboration factors. Expressed in user-friendly language, these skills encourage "possibility thinking" intended to stretch thinking beyond what the student already knows or has been taught. In an Illinois high school, a math teacher who had taught students ways to determine the areas of regular geometric figures challenged them to generate many, different, and unusual strategies for finding the area of *nonregular* geometric figures. Using their existing base of knowledge, students were encouraged to discover pathways new to them through manipulation of known ideas and methods. Similarly, in a nearby class on architectural drafting, students who already had house designs were given an example of a topographical plot plan and asked to make sketches to show a variety of unique settings/locations for their houses on the plot. At a later time, they evaluated their ideas with real-world criteria.

An elementary teacher used productive thinking in sharing with her class *Dr. De Soto* by William Steig (1982), a story about a mouse dentist who uses wit instead of might in handling a tricky fox with a bad toothache. Stopping the story at the point where Dr. DeSoto is trying to think of a humane solution to the fox problem, the teacher encouraged her students to use what they knew about Dr. DeSoto and his work *and* their productive thinking to think of their own clever solutions. Their solutions were later used in an extension activity in which they rewrote the ending to the book.

While deferment of judgment is a basic principle of productive thinking, examination and evaluation of ideas does eventually occur. Often, it is the *Decision Making* talent that guides student thinking. For example, first graders listed a variety of alternative topics for their Earth Day posters and then submitted them to various criteria: Can I draw this? Is this a good message to send? Is this idea something I want to do to help save the earth?

Their discussion of answers to the questions about each alternative helped them weigh choices and make final decisions that they could defend orally with varied reasons. Such careful evaluation gave students confidence as they took their chosen poster topics to the planning stage.

In a middle school social studies class, students engaged in a study of early American history were presented this challenge for a group decision-making activity: *Some historians argue that the colonial years were not a "Golden Age" for women, while others believe that women in colonial America had the best possible lives. Take a stand on this issue.* After a lively class effort in generating criteria questions (Did women contribute to life in colonial America in a variety of ways? Were their contributions valued? Were women allowed to achieve goals they had for themselves? Did women's roles give them power?), group members used their academic talent skills to read and research material for answers to these questions. Then in group discussion they used a decision-making matrix to rate the relative merits of the alternatives in the issue and arrive at a final decision, which they would then defend in a class debate.

Advanced Placement and honors classes often draw students talented in specific subject areas. If little attention is given to training students in how to wrestle with ideas, these classes can result only in a "more and harder" pursuit of academic mastery. Not so in an AP biology class in Michigan, where students were challenged to determine the best method for slowing or even reversing eutrophication (plant growth) in local lakes. Over several weeks, students used their knowledge of nitrogen and phosphorous cycles, along with site visits and additional research by local environmentalists, as guides in generating alternatives and establishing criteria (Is the strategy technically possible? Is it cost-effective? Will the strategy provide a long-term solution? Will it be least likely to place other aspects of the ecosystem at risk?). Alternatives were weighed and decisions were defended with full documentation to a panel of local experts who provided friendly feedback to these young people.

Planning is the talent of nitty-gritties, a cluster of skills designed to help thinkers move from a more general idea to specific detailing of a scheme for putting the idea into action. For example, the first graders described earlier (who made decisions on topics for posters) later used the planning talent to focus their topics with a specific sketch of the poster design, a list of materials and equipment needed, a sequence of steps for carrying out the poster making project, a list of possible problems, and improvements or revisions written directly on the plan.

Planning also was an important tool for eighth graders in a physical science class in San Antonio, Texas. As a culminating project for a unit on Newton's laws of motion/gravity, this assignment was given: *Develop a plan for making a model of a carnival ride that demonstrates a law of motion or a law of gravity. Make a sketch of your model and complete the other parts of the planning guide: materials and equipment needed, a sequence of steps, and possible problems. Indicate any improvements directly on your plan in a different color.* Students received feedback on their plans from their peers, as well as the teacher, and had opportunities to make further revisions before beginning implementation. The high rate of student success in presenting interesting and credible demonstrations using their academic knowledge was likely due to the careful blend of product and process: a stimulating hands-on activity with the organizing and management tools of the planning talent. Too often, teachers provide what could be exciting, challenging projects but fail to provide training in the how-to's of thinking required to bring the project to fruition.

The thinking talent that deals with predicting causes or effects of events and situations is *Forecasting.* Frequent practice in predicting possible explanations for an event and in predicting potential outcomes or consequences of a set of circumstances can inhibit a condition that J. P. Guilford (1956) termed *hardening of the categories,* the inability to shift one's point of view.

An elementary science teacher asked students to predict many and varied causes for the extinction of dinosaurs, encouraging them to explore widely for possibilities. Some of the causes involved changes to which dinosaurs might not have been able to adapt, such as changes in temperature or humidity, disappearing food sources, increase in the numbers of predators, or a combination of factors. Some student predictions could be discussed in light of present knowledge; but even highly speculative predictions were accepted and discussed in terms of newly developing scientific knowledge and techniques for uncovering new ideas. Often, it is the speculativeness and open-endedness of this kind of thinking that stimulates some students to do further research, engage in creative writing, or create projects based on their predictions.

In a Tech-Prep program in an Illinois high school, students in a beginning food services course were reading a newspaper listing of numerical ratings given to local restaurants by health inspectors. Spurred by the curiosity of students concerning explanations for the widely varying restaurant ratings, including some of their favorite hangouts, the teacher easily engaged them in predicting different events or circumstances that might cause a restaurant to fail to meet hygiene standards. The transition from these student-generated speculations to follow-up activities, including text reading and interviewing local health inspectors, was not only painless but also exciting to students as they verified some predictions and generated additional ones regarding this real-world problem.

Predicting effects comes closer, perhaps, to the type of activity teachers think of when the term *forecasting* is used. "What if" questions are the signals for predicting outcomes and consequences of varied circumstances. "What might happen if all animals were predators?" was a question that helped young scientists take a different look at the animal kingdom. In an elementary math class, students were asked to predict the effects *if stores allowed you to purchase only in whole units and omitted fractional parts of units.* A high school business education class was asked to predict the consequences *if a company did not prepare departmental margin statements.* Students in a social studies class were challenged to predict the effects on U.S. business and politics *if the muckrakers of the late 1800s had been censored.* All of these questions are strategies for helping students avoid simplistic, pigeonholed thinking and begin examining the connections among events that result from inferential thinking.

The *Communication* talent represents just a starter set of skills related to facility in using verbal and nonverbal language to share thoughts, ideas, and feelings. Fluency and flexibility in the use of language are major aims of the communication skills, but form, clarity, richness of expression, and completeness of ideas are supporting goals.

Two skills of this talent—using single words to describe feelings and networks of ideas to convey complete thoughts—were evoked during an ecology unit when a powerful video on predators and prey was shown. To help students articulate their strong emotional responses to the video, they were asked to think of single words to describe their feelings about the predator–prey relationship. Later, these word lists served as the basis for developing cohesive paragraphs describing the viewpoint of either the predator or the prey.

Some uses of communication talent skills call for imaginative uses of knowledge in composition activities. In a biology class, students were challenged to demonstrate their knowledge of the circulatory system in a more inventive and personal manner with this assignment: *Imagine that you have been shrunk and injected into a vein of a frog. Trace your flow through the frog's circulatory system, and compare it to your own circulatory system by writing an on-the-scene report. Use a variety of complete thoughts as you compose your network of ideas.*

The application of a model such as TU in the basic instructional program provides all students multiple opportunities to process information in their preferred styles and, at the same time, creates a stimulating environment for active learning. This latter outcome is particularly important for gifted students who spend the majority of their school hours in the basic instructional program which, too often, emphasizes basic mastery.

Identifying Student Talents Requiring Additional Enrichment

The staff development involved in the Talents Unlimited model plays an important role in sensitizing teachers to specific behaviors of students which indicate talent potential and in enhancing teaching strategies for the encouragement of these specific talents. Missy, a case in point, is described next.

A primary-grade social studies class was introduced to the culture of ancient Egypt with a guided tour, via slides, led by their enthusiastic teacher. In a follow-up discussion, the youngsters were encouraged to identify topics about Egypt they would like to pursue further. One third grader, Missy, was fascinated by the fashions of ancient Egypt. Needless to say, the number of holdings on this topic in the elementary school library was limited. Missy's teacher enlisted the assistance of the theater department of a local university, and additional resources were made available to Missy. Her interest in fashions persisted and, when encouraged to think of what she could do with her increasing knowledge of Egyptian fashions, Missy decided to make Egyptian paper dolls with accompanying paper fashions that she could manipulate during an oral presentation/demonstration to other students in her school.

To help Missy think through the many details of this project, the teacher employed the skills of the Planning talent, using the "drawing board" format for primary students. This illustrations-with-labels approach to planning relieves young students, even bright ones, of the often burdensome task of writing all of their ideas. Additionally, it can assist in the mental imaging of all the bits and pieces needed in the management of a long-term plan. On one sheet, Missy was asked to *draw a sketch of the Egyptian paper dolls you want to make.* On second and third sheets she was encouraged to *draw and label a list of materials/equipment you will need for the paper doll project and a list of steps to follow, in order, to complete the paper doll project.* A final sheet was used to *identify any problems you might have with your project.* Then, through discussion, Missy was encouraged to *note, in a different color, any changes you need to make to improve your plan.*

Planning skills are tools of task analysis, an important aid in projects that last for several weeks. When young thinkers have their own pictures/words as a guide to all the parts of a project of interest, they are more likely to work independently on the project because the plan provides step-by-step directions of the student's own making.

Classroom teachers, even those trained in Talents Unlimited, do not always have the time or skill needed to provide in-depth assistance to students they identify as having special talent potential. Such students may be prime targets for participation in enrichment or gifted programs. Indeed, Reis and Jordan (1993) noted that staff development in Talents Unlimited appears both to increase the incidence of teacher nomination of students for enrichment programs and to enhance dialogue about the goals of an enrichment program and the types of gifts and talents developed in the program. The following sections discuss strategies for using the skills of the TU model in special programs.

Thinking Skills Instruction in Special Programs for Gifted Students

The Talents Unlimited model is useful as one component in programs for gifted students, but it is not a substitute for the provision of services representing other important dimensions of gifted education, such as assessing interest, streamlining the regular academic curriculum, or developing research skills. As a model for nurturing students' multiple thinking talents, TU can be implemented as a support system for gifted students in several ways: (1) to help students focus and manage independent projects, (2) to provide methodological assistance as students conduct investigations of problems of interest to them, and (3) to help students deal with developmental issues.

Focusing and Managing Independent Projects

Earlier sections presented illustrations of the use of Talents clusters in discrete activities within the curriculum. It is important to recognize that the six talents of this model interact dynamically; that is, they form natural linkages for a comprehensive problem-solving model not unlike well-documented models used by adult problem solvers in the world of work. Helping students apply the talent processes in a linking manner to projects/problems of special interest to them can nurture creative productivity, a major goal of gifted education. Newman (1991, 1993), for example, reported the positive effects of Talents training on the completion rate and quality of student products in enrichment programs.

An enrichment teacher in Fort Benton, Montana, used Talents in a linking format to guide an elementary resource group in focusing and developing an idea for a special project: an *endangered species trunk* to teach other classes about the endangered species of Montana. *Productive Thinking* was used to generate and elaborate many, varied, and unusual examples of hands-on learning activities students would make to include in the trunk. Because Productive Thinking focuses on *possibility thinking,* the students' list of activity ideas included more ideas than could be used, as well as ideas representing a wide variation in quality and interest for individual students. Evaluation skills were needed, and the *Decision Making* talent was invoked. Using a decision-making matrix, each student listed four or five alternatives of some initial interest; the entire group generated possible criteria questions to be used in the matrix (Will this activity teach something important about endangered species in Montana? Do I have the knowledge/skills to make this activity? Can I get the materials needed for this activity? Would others enjoy doing this activity?). Students then weighed each alternative against the criteria to help them arrive at defensible choices for the activity that would be the focus of their work over the next several weeks.

Of course, a decision is just an intermediate step to the final product. The *Planning* talent, with accompanying guide, helped students detail the exact nature of the activity they would complete, along with identification of resources needed, a sequence of actions to bring the project to fruition, possible problems, and improvements in the plan. This detailed plan served as the day-to-day implementation guide, making several weeks of demanding activity more manageable and palatable for young students. Many communication skills were employed as students prepared written materials, recorded tapes, and otherwise articulated their activities for use by others.

The networking of talents also served as a support system for students in a ninth-grade English talent pool class, who were well into studying the works of Shakespeare. Their teacher told them about a local community college instructor who was an expert on Shakespeare and challenged them to figure out how they might make use of this resource person. These Talents-trained young people linked the thinking clusters in the following manner:

1. *Productive Thinking* to generate a list of many, different, unusual strategies the speaker might use to share ideas about Shakespeare (e.g., dramatic interpretations, question/answer session, videotapes of Shakespeare productions by community college students)
2. *Decision Making* to evaluate which of the strategies generated would be best (actual decision was a *Meet the Press* format, with the speaker assuming the role of Shakespeare for an interview)
3. *Planning* to develop in detail the resources needed, actions to be taken (including who was responsible and the estimated dates of completion), possible problems, and changes/improvements in the plan
4. *Communication* to carry out one of the steps in the plan: developing the set of interview questions to ask Shakespeare
5. *Communication,* again, following implementation of the plan, to write an article about the interview with Shakespeare for the school newspaper

Providing Methodological Assistance

Once students focus on a project or problem, their implementation efforts often provide opportunities to use the Talents as troubleshooting skills. Such a situation occurred with a group of bright middle school students who were involved in survey research.

Following a work session with a resource person on selecting questions and developing procedures for implementing an opinion poll, students discussed the management of data. The issue of confidentiality in handling data developed during the discussion. To help students explore important implications of this issue, the teacher asked students to "forecast what might occur if confidentiality of information were not honored in the survey process." The resulting predictions pointed to possible problems and led students to ask what could be done to protect confidentiality. The obvious next steps were Productive Thinking for the development of possible safeguards, and then Decision Making for the selection of the best ideas to implement to ensure confidentiality.

A similar strategy provided methodological assistance to a bright student who was preparing to field test an original game he had designed. When asked how he planned to conduct the field test, the student initially gave a vague response about "asking other kids what they think of the game." The teacher responded by asking the student to use one of the Communication skills to generate questions that would give him both general reactions and more specific feedback that could be used to revise and improve the game. The teacher also reminded the student of the Planning talent skills. With a little guidance and encouragement, the student was able to develop a thoughtful, orderly scheme for discovering what he wanted to determine about his product.

Assisting with Developmental Needs

An important ingredient of programs for gifted students focuses on their affective development. Many gifted students suffer from the challenges of growing up in a world geared to the average. Too often they are ridiculed by peers for independent thinking and overburdened by parental expectations. Sometimes, they are their own worst enemy, imposing on themselves unattainable goals of perfection.

Bibliotherapy is a technique that can assist young people with the challenges of developmental tasks through a responsive interaction with literature. Given the appropriate content and encouragement, students often are able to articulate their own feelings about issues a story character is facing. Sometimes this discussion, facilitated by the teacher, leads students to an exploration and possibly a resolution of a problem or concern, or it may provide primarily an emotional catharsis. In implementing bibliotherapy, the largest amount of time is spent on responding to the literature. These discussions provide opportunities for students to connect their feelings about events and characters in a book to their own experiences, to achieve personal insights.

Although the kinds of questions used to facilitate students' reflections and responses vary for each literature selection depending on the needs and interests of students, more *why* questions than *what* questions are asked. The development of a menu of questions for a bibliotherapy session is facilitated by a teacher's skill in using the Talents clusters. Two examples will be provided. Other illustrations are documented by Schlichter and Burke (1994) and Hebert (1991).

Many gifted students must face issues associated with some aspect of discrimination. In *Words by Heart* (Sebestyen, 1979), a book especially suited to the junior high school age, Lena feels the sting of repeated racial discrimination and is confused by her father's insistence on nonviolence. She must make her own decision of how to respond to the discrimination she faces. Some of the facilitator's questions make use of the TU model:

1. What are some different and unique ways people your age might feel discriminated against (*Productive Thinking*)?
2. Have you ever had an experience similar to Lena's in which you had to try to decide how to treat someone who had discriminated against you? Share your story (*Communication*).
3. Decide what you would have done in Lena's situation (*Decision Making*), and write her a letter, supporting your advice by relating it to similar incidents or feelings in your own life (*Communication*).

For gifted females (and gifted males), *The Practical Princess* (Williams, 1969) provides a forum for discussing the issue of gender role conflicts. Princess Bedelia, unlike traditionally depicted fairytale princesses, is a confident, take-charge, creative problem-solving figure; but she is not particularly appreciated by the males in her community, who view her virtues as unfeminine. The following are a few of the Talents-framed tasks/questions that helped stimulate discussion of nonstereotyped sex roles for both boys and girls:

1. Tell about any experiences you have had when someone thought you shouldn't do something just because you were a girl/boy (*Communication*).
2. What other clever strategies might someone use in responding to that same experience (*Productive Thinking*)? In what new and special ways might you help others view you as capable of many, different kinds of activities (*Productive Thinking*)? What varied effects might occur if you are successful (*Forecasting*)?
3. Suppose that Bedelia kept a diary about her life. Develop a network of complete thoughts in the form of a diary entry that she might have written about the dragon episode or a dream she had of her future (*Communication*).

Teachers can assist students in developing greater awareness of their use of the Talents skills as problem-solving strategies with guided discussions, whether the focus is on cognitive or affective program objectives. The linking of talents and applying them to problems and issues of personal interest may reap more benefits for students than merely using the processes as discrete skills in unrelated exercises.

Summary

Talents Unlimited is a staff development model for training teachers to recognize and nurture diversity in students' intellectual potential, grades K–12. It is effectively used to differentiate instruction in the regular classroom and to provide a support system of problem-solving skills as bright students conduct independent investigations. While TU does not represent a complete program for gifted students, it can be an important component of any enrichment program, focusing on the empowerment of students by teaching them thinking strategies for processing and accessing knowledge. Further, these strategies can be used as gifted students resolve affective challenges associated with their special talents and gifts.

REFERENCES

Baum, R. (1990). Ten top programs. *Learning, 18*(6), 51–55.

Chissom, B. S., & McLean, J. E. (1993). Research and evaluation related to the Talents Unlimited model: Review and recommendations. In C. L. Schlichter & W. R. Palmer (Eds.), *Thinking smart: A primer of the Talents Unlimited model* (pp. 171–197). Mansfield Center, CT: Creative Learning Press.

Feldhusen, J. F., & Kolloff, M. B. (1978). A three-stage model for gifted education. *G/C/T, 1*(4), 3–5, 53–58.

Guilford, J. P. (1956). Structure of intellect. *Psychological Bulletin, 53,* 267–293.

Haskew, B. (1993). Talents Unlimited: Reflections, directions, projections. In C. L. Schlichter & W. R. Palmer (Eds.), *Thinking smart: A primer of the Talents Unlimited model* (pp. 63–81). Mansfield Center, CT: Creative Learning Press.

Hebert, T. P. (1991). Meeting the affective needs of bright boys through bibliotherapy. *Roeper Review, 13,* 207–212.

Newman, J. L. (1991). *The effects of the Talents Unlimited model on students' creative productivity.* Unpublished Ph.D. dissertation, University of Alabama, Tuscaloosa.

Newman, J. L. (1993). The effects of the Talents Unlimited model on students' creative productivity. In C. L. Schlichter & W. R. Palmer (Eds.), *Thinking smart: A primer of the Talents Unlimited model* (pp. 141–158). Mansfield Center, CT: Creative Learning Press.

Reis, S. M., & Jordan, T. (1993). Using the Talents Unlimited model in enrichment programs. In C. L. Schlichter & W. R. Palmer (Eds.), *Thinking smart: A primer of the Talents Unlimited model* (pp. 119–140). Mansfield Center, CT: Creative Learning Press.

Renzulli, J. S., & Reis, S. M. (1985). *The schoolwide enrichment model.* Mansfield Center, CT: Creative Learning Press.

Schlichter, C. L. (1983). The multiple talent approach: Stretching limits for all children. *Eastern Kentucky University Educational Review, 6*(2), 15–29.

Schlichter, C. L. (1986). Talents Unlimited: An in-service education model for teaching thinking skills. *Gifted Child Quarterly, 30,* 119–123.

Schlichter, C. L., & Burke, M. (1994). Using books to nurture the social and emotional development of gifted students. *Roeper Review, 16,* 280–283.

Sebestyen, O. (1979). *Words by heart.* New York: Little, Brown.

Steig, W. (1982). *Dr. De Soto.* New York: Farrar, Straus and Giroux.

Taylor, C. W. (1968, December). Be talent developers as well as knowledge dispensers. *Today's Education,* 67–69.

Taylor, C. W. (1986). The growing importance of creativity and leadership in spreading gifted and talented programs world-wide. *Roeper Review, 8,* 256–263.

Torrance, E. P. (1962). *Guiding creative talent.* Englewood Cliffs, NJ: Prentice-Hall.

Treffinger, D. J. (1980). *Encouraging creative learning for the gifted and talented.* Ventura, CA: Ventura County Superintendent of Schools, LTI Publications.

Williams, J. (1969). *The practical princess.* New York: Parents' Magazine Press.

27

Productivity, Accomplishment, and Eminence

HERBERT J. WALBERG and SUSIE ZEISER, *University of Illinois at Chicago*

During the last quarter century, educational psychologists have completed and compiled the findings of more than 8,000 studies on how educational productivity factors during the first two or three decades of life influence academic learning. More efficient educational productivity of academic and related learning may allow more time to develop childhood and adolescent giftedness and adult eminence. The productivity factors that enhance academic learning, moreover, also appear to develop exceptional talent, since learning is a fundamental ingredient of notable human accomplishment. The theory of educational productivity based on meta-analysis of the outcomes of many studies (Walberg, 1984a), coupled with the theory of human capital (Walberg & Stariha, 1992), emphasizes the importance of broad learning through the primary agencies of families, teachers, peer groups, mass media, and the efficient use of human time.

This chapter reviews corroborative findings as well as current primary research. It suggests that alterations in the productivity factors have proved beneficial for ordinary and extraordinary human achievement. It makes clear that the amount of time invested by parents, educators, coaches, and learners themselves multiplies the effects of educational and environmental factors to increase academic learning, talent development, and adult eminence.

Accordingly, for better realization of human potential, efficient procedures are required. Efficiency streamlines the acquisition of basic skills and cultural literacy so that general education can be accomplished in less time and thus earlier in the life span. The time savings can result in greater supplies of time for the pursuit of general all-roundedness or specialized exceptionality. Such time use allows for greater accomplishments, including transformation and novel application of existing knowledge (Walberg & Herbig, 1991; Walberg & Stariha, 1992; Walberg & Tsai, 1984).

Educational Productivity

Research synthesis suggests that nine factors, when controlled for each other and for other factors, consistently and strongly influence academic learning (Walberg, 1984a):

1. Ability or prior achievement as measured by the usual standardized tests
2. Chronological age or stage of development
3. Motivation or self-concept as indicated by perseverance on tasks
4. Instructional time engaged in learning
5. Quality of instruction, including both curricular and psychological aspects
6. The curriculum of home life
7. Classroom group environment
8. Peer group selected outside school
9. Exposure to mass media and popular culture, notably television (which is the only factor inversely related to learning outcomes)

These factors are the main direct influences on cognitive, affective, and behavioral learning in childhood and adolescence. No single factor, however, accounts for high accomplishment. It is the combination and interaction of these factors, taken together, that appear to do so. High ability and large quantities of instructional time, for example, may have little effect on unmotivated students, on students whose home environment may discount the importance of school, or on those receiving poor-quality instruction.

School, Home, and Peer Group

Constructive relations among parents and teachers are required for optimum performance. The goals for intellectual development of the child, then, must be shared among these chief agents of education if it is to be maximally productive. World-class test scores in culture-free subjects such as mathematics and science in Japan can be explained in part by this communality of interest. It has been observed, for example, that Asian families sometimes purchase not one, but two textbooks for their children. The second textbook is for the mother to use to help her child be successful in school. Such dedication has huge effects on children's learning.

The first five of the above nine factors were included in the educational models of Bloom, Bruner, Carroll, and Glaser (see Walberg, 1984b). Syntheses of research, however, suggest that social/psychological factors, both inside and outside the school, also significantly influence valued outcomes.

Factor 6, the curriculum of the home, refers to such activity as informal parent–child conversation and communication about everyday observations and events. These may include discussions and/or critical analysis of school-related discoveries, leisure reading, television programs, and friends. Among such serious efforts, as Walberg and Herbig (1991) pointed out, are the no less important expressions of affect and relatedness: happiness, laughter, caprice, and serenity.

With respect to television, estimates suggest that American adolescents watch television around 28 hours per week. After 10 hours per week, however, television has deleterious influences on learning. The 18 "excessive" hours per week might better be reallocated to other pursuits such as homework, leisure reading, projects, hobbies, and talent development.

Noncognitive Outcomes

Much of the research on the productivity factors focused on cognitive outcomes. Still, these are hardly all of what educators and parents want from schooling. Raven's (1981) summary of surveys in Western countries, including England and the United States, suggests that attitudinal, social, and emotional goals are more important to educators, parents, and students than academic ones. Given a choice, Raven reports, all three groups rank cooperation, self-reliance, constructive attitudes, lifelong learning incentives, and critical thinking as more important than specific academic achievement reflected in school grades or standardized test scores. At the same time, no one has shown that cognitive mastery interferes with the less measurable outcomes of schooling; presumably, the mastery of school subjects enhances self-concept, learning-to-learn skills, and the basic knowledge required for beginner's status in most academic and nonacademic fields

Raven's findings, however, may underscore the value of active participation, interaction, and human relationships for learning in the home, the classroom, and friendship circles. These not only influence learning directly but also indirectly influence ability and motivation, which, in turn, influence responsiveness to instruction (Walberg & Stariha, 1992). The dynamic and interactive qualities of the model of educational productivity suggest that if we provide a great deal of exceptional instruction—with the support of the home and with the active participation and cooperation of a peer culture and popular culture that do not actively promote anti-intellectual values—motivation and ability to learn will increase.

"Matthew Effects"

In general, research on the productivity model suggests that early educational advantages multiply (as in the Matthew's Gospel story of the rich getting richer or what sociologists call "cumulative advantage"). In modern times, Merton (1968), in portraying distinguished scientific careers, depicted how the initial advantages of university study, work with eminent scientists, early publication, job placement, and citation combine multiplicatively to confer tastes, skills, habits, rewards, and further opportunities that cumulate to produce highly skewed productivity in scientific work. That is, relatively few scientists account for much of publications, citations, and discoveries. Similar processes and advantages appear to explain the precocity and accomplishments of talented children and adolescents who accumulate multiplicative advantages through the educational productivity factors. Still, unless they can maintain optimal conditions with respect to most of the factors, they may not reach and maintain world-class status (see Walberg & Tsai, 1984).

Motivation and Productivity

Although Herbert Simon's (1954) motivational theory pertains to foreign language learning, it appears to generalize and parsimoniously explain much of human learning and exceptional performance. Simon notes that in choosing frequent practice (that is, high amounts of self-instruction time), we eventually experience the learning activity as easier; with ease comes an increase in the pleasantness of the activity; with an increase in pleasantness come greater desire and motivation to engage in further learning. Knowledge of results, whether self-recognized or pointed out by others, enhances such motivation.

Sustained, concentrated effort over time appears to be one of the necessary factors of distinguished accomplishment. Catharine Cox (1926), who analyzed over 300 biographical accounts, found that eminent adults were characterized, in part, by persistence, intellectual energy, and unusual ambition—all constructs indicative of motivation. Block (1971) also found impressive endurance of aspiration levels in his analysis of the Berkeley Growth Studies, a fifty-year longitudinal project. Kagan and Moss (1962) found that gifted children placed a high value on intellectual and cognitive activities, which also endured over time. Thus, an accomplished adolescence and adult life may be attributable in part to sustained motivation and habits of perseverance acquired early in life.

Motivation, Activity, and Accomplishment

During the 1960s, creativity came to be misconstrued as an instant phenomenon. True enough, an apparently sudden insight may be a part of artistic and scientific discoveries. But insight alone is hardly sufficient. Its coming to consciousness requires intense preparation, and most insights require vast testing and planning if they are to come to fruition. For example, an entry in the journal of the great mathematician Karl Gauss reveals the progress of his discovery: "Finally, two days ago, I succeeded. . . . Like a sudden flash of lightning, the riddle happened to be solved. I myself cannot say what was the conducting thread which connected what I previously knew with what made my success possible" (p. 84, cited in Getzels & Jackson, 1962). But for years Gauss had been working on a proof for this theorem, which converged at a moment in time. Similarly, the great English scientist Isaac Newton believed that his record of discoveries was achieved "by always thinking about them."

A Knowledge Base

More recently, of 16 programs of research on creativity (Tardif & Sternberg, 1988), 11 cited the individual's use of existing knowledge for novel ideas as the most frequently observed cognitive characteristic of creativity. The necessity of the familiar component in creative discovery is supported by a large-scale review of psychological studies of eminent painters, writers, musicians, philosophers, religious leaders, and scientists of the current and past centuries, as well as by the study of prize-winning adolescents of today (Walberg, 1982, 1969). All reveal early, intense concentration and interest in previous work in their fields (Bloom, 1985).

Simon (1981) estimated that 70 hours of concentrated, prodigious work per week for 10 years is required for expert mastery of a special field today. Recent evidence, even in the study of so-called idiot savants, suggests that social withdrawal contributes enormous amounts of time in thought toward the propensities in which persons show brilliance (Howe, 1989; Howe & Smith, 1988). Showing, for example, that perfect pitch is a learned ability, Howe's work suggests that no person has ever managed to create outstanding accomplishments without undergoing a long period of intense and careful preparation.

Although eminent creators sometimes produce some inferior work, the quality of work generally varies directly with the amount of work produced (Albert, 1978; Barron, 1961; Simonton, 1984). It is interesting to note how extremely productive some highly creative people are. For example, Bach composed an average of 20 pages of finished music per day; Picasso produced over 20,000 paintings, sculptures, and drawings; Poincaré published 500 papers and 30 books; Edison held 1,093 patents; Freud had 300 publications and Einstein 248 (Simonton, 1984). Only enduring motivation and persevering activity can account for such prodigious production of outstanding works (Ochse, 1990; Simonton, 1987).

Knowledge, Experience, and Novelty

Acquisition of knowledge alone cannot account sufficiently for eminent accomplishment. Creativity is something more than mere mastery (Walberg & Herbig, 1991). The growth of human capital and cultural progress is accounted for by more than the mere transmission of knowledge and its embodiment in people; creativity refers ultimately to the new knowledge, techniques, and applications that promote human welfare (Walberg, 1988). Still, novelty or creativity has been accorded more mystery and inspiration than it probably deserves, and a parsimonious account deriving from the natural sciences may well serve as a working explanation

In the theory of biological evolution, Darwin showed that new species evolve by trial and error; Skinner similarly showed that differential rewards or "positive reinforcements" determine what randomly emitted behavior is increased; and subsequent research on humans showed that given powerful enough needs and reinforcers, human behavior also can be strongly influenced, if not determined (Lea, 1978). Similarly, Campbell (1960) cogently argued that trial and error suffices to explain creative thought as well as other mental processes.

Campbell held that blind-variation-and-selective-retention processes are "fundamental to all inductive achievements, to all genuine increases in knowledge, to all increases in fit of system to environment" (p. 380). For this reason, three conditions for creativity are necessary: "a mechanism for introducing variation, a consistent selection process, and a mechanism for preserving and reproducing the selected variations" (p. 381). Campbell cites many illustrative examples of such creative trial-and-error thought in autobiographical works by such mathematicians and scientists as Mach, Poincaré, and Hadamard, as well as works by psychologists such as Thurstone, Tolman, Hull, Miller and Dollard, and Mowrer.

The significance of the models of both Campbell and Simon lies in their parsimony and applicability to real-world problems and solutions. Notable in their work are the limitations and trade-offs in time, memory, and retrieval that constrain learning and thought.

Having a large fund of knowledge and experience confers advantages in discovering novel solutions, but such funds are hardly preconditions. Even novices can think of novel and workable ideas, particularly if they are encouraged to do so. Teachers and parents who understand and point out the possibilities of discovering and applying ideas may show novel applications of familiar ideas and experience—a good service, especially for exceptional students. In a national sample of high school students, those winning competitive awards in the arts and in science chose creativity over wealth and power as the most valued development in life (Walberg, 1969).

Eminent Men

Many of the ideas expressed here derived from our studies of eminent people (see Walberg & Stariha, 1992). Even though concerned about tomorrow's achievement results, educators, psychologists, and others also should think about what they are doing today that may affect students' adult accomplishments. For more than two decades, we have been researching the early lives of people who achieved eminence in such fields as the visual arts, music, politics, and science. In our initial research, we studied the biographies of

Leonardo da Vinci, Abraham Lincoln, Isaac Newton, and others (nearly all men). We and their biographers rated each person on the educative conditions of their families and schools that promoted their accomplishments.

As children, the eminent men showed intellectual competence and motivation, social and communication skills, general psychological wholesomeness, and both versatility and persevering concentration during childhood. Most were stimulated by the availability of cultural stimuli and materials related to their field and by teachers, parents, and other adults.

Large percentages of the sample were exposed to stimulating family, educational, and cultural conditions during childhood. Only slightly more than half were encouraged by parents, but a solid majority were encouraged by teachers and other adults and were exposed to many adults at an early age. Significantly more than half, 60 percent, were exposed to eminent persons during childhood.

About 80 percent were successful in school, the majority liked it, and less than a quarter had school problems. Seventy percent had clear parental expectations for their conduct; but nearly 9 out of 10 were allowed to explore their environments on their own, obviously a delicate, important balance in child rearing and teaching.

Other sources corroborate these findings. Psychologists who have employed case studies and other methods to discover the conditions of creativity suggest similar traits and conditions. In addition, national surveys of accomplished adolescents who won competitive awards for achievements in the arts and sciences suggested similar trends. Still, prior psychological studies concentrated largely on males, and the survey research employed the criterion of promising adolescent accomplishment rather than actual adult eminence.

Eminent Women

For these reasons, we made content analyses of biographies of 256 eminent women of this century. They included, for example, skater Sonja Henie, actress Ethel Barrymore, singer Mahalia Jackson, athlete Babe Didrikson Zaharias, business woman Helena Rubinstein, blind and deaf leader Helen Keller, poet Marianne Moore, painter Grandma Moses, reformer Margaret Sanger, educator and civil rights leader Mary McLeod Bethune, scientist Rachel Carson, suffragist Jeannette Rankin, and political leader Eleanor Roosevelt.

We wanted to depict childhood character and conditions of eminent women. One goal was to help to identify and encourage distinguished accomplishments in others. We recognize, nonetheless, at least three problems: the shortcomings of biography, biases in our own ratings, and the possibility that the present may require different patterns of traits and conditions than did the past. Thus, our findings can be taken only as hints for the present and should be compared with other research findings and personal experience.

Childhood Traits

What was the most common psychological trait of eminent women shown during childhood? It was the same as that shown by eminent American and European men of previous centuries—intelligence. More than 50 percent of the women showed high intelligence in their early years. Equally unsurprising, the other top-ranking traits for women, as for men, were the propensities to persevere and work hard, especially women eminent in music and the visual arts.

Shared by more than 3 in 10 girls, especially political activists and college administrators, was success in school. Seven in 10 women, nonetheless, were not particularly successful in school. Many contemporary studies show little relation of academic grades to adult success for people with a given amount of education.

Parental and Other Social Influence

Because they can be altered, environmental influences are of practical interest. About one-third to one-half of the sample were directly taught or strongly encouraged by their fathers, mothers, or other adults. Seven in 10 had clear parental expectations for their conduct, yet nearly one-fourth were allowed to explore on their own, and 32 percent learned much outside school.

Forty-six percent came from financially advantaged families, although more than half came from culturally advantaged families. More than one-third were extensively exposed to cultural materials and stimulation (not necessarily in their later fields of accomplishment). Part of the sample were exposed to one or more of the following advantages:

The presence of many adults other than their parents
The presence of eminent adults other than their parents
Social milieux that were open and receptive to varied cultures
A revolutionary period in their future fields
Special tutoring
External incentives for accomplishment

The rarest environmental condition was cultural emphasis on immediate gratification. Just one percent of the women grew up under this condition.

Conclusion

The results of our analyses of talented adolescents and the biographies of eminent men and women confirm findings from prior research. As a whole, the research suggests that accomplished adults and boys and girls in many fields resemble one another more than less accomplished peers. They are intelligent, hard working, and follow through on activities despite difficulties. Many are inquisitive and original enough to question conventions.

Despite such free thinking, they benefited from encouragement, stimulation, and direct teaching provided by their parents, teachers, and other adults. Many lived in social environments receptive to varied ideas and cultures; many were tutored and given special recognition for their early accomplishments.

The most frequent traits of accomplished people—intelligence, perseverance, and stimulating social environments—are hardly guarantees of adult success. Combinations of other traits and conditions undoubtedly play influential roles in combination at various stages of childhood, adolescence, and adulthood. Luck and the vicissitudes of opportunity also play their parts. Still, the findings that regularly turn up suggest that parents, educators, and others should think carefully about how to encourage constructive psychological traits and to design stimulating conditions that seem likely to enable boys and girls to fulfill their potential.

REFERENCES

Albert, R. S. (1978). Observations and suggestions regarding giftedness, familial influence and the achievement of eminence. *Gifted Child Quarterly, 22,* 201–211.

Barron, F. (1961). Creative vision and expression in writing and painting. In D. W. McKinnon (Ed.), *The creative person* (pp. 231–247). Berkeley: Institute of Personality Assessment Research, University of California.

Block, J. (1971). *Lives through time.* Berkeley, CA: Bancroft Books.

Bloom, B. S. (1985). Generalizations about talent development. In B. S. Bloom (Ed.), *Developing talent in young people.* New York: Ballantine.

Campbell, D. T. (1960). Blind variation and selective retention in creative thought as in other knowledge processes. *Psychological Review, 67,* 380–400.

Cox, C. M. (1926). *The early mental traits of three hundred geniuses.* Stanford, CA: Stanford University Press.

Getzels, J. W., & Jackson, P. W. (1962). *Creativity and intelligence: Explorations with gifted students.* New York: Wiley.

Howe, M. J., (1989). Separate skills or general intelligence: The autonomy of human abilities. *British Journal of Educational Psychology, 59,* 351–360.

Howe, M. J., & Smith, J. (1988). Calendar calculating in "idiots savants": How do they do it? *British Journal of Psychology, 79,* 371–386.

Kagan, J., & Moss, H. A. (1962). *Birth to maturity.* New York: Wiley.

Lea, S. E. G. (1978). The psychology and economics of demand. *Psychological Bulletin, 85,* 441–466.

Merton, R. K. (1968). The Matthew effect in science. *Science, 159,* 56–63.

Ochse, R. (1990). *Before the gates of excellence: The determinants of creative genius.* New York: Cambridge University Press.

Raven, J. (1981). The most important problem in education is to come to terms with values. *Oxford Review of Education, 7,* 253–272.

Simon, H. A. (1954). Some strategic considerations in the construction of social science models. In P. Lazarsfeld (Ed.), *Mathematical thinking in the social sciences.* Glencoe, IL: Free Press.

Simon, H. A. (1981). *Sciences of the artificial.* Cambridge, MA: MIT Press.

Simonton, D. K. (1984). *Genius, creativity and leadership: Historiometric inquiries.* Cambridge, MA: Harvard University Press.

Simonton, D. K. (1987). Developmental antecedents of achieved eminence. *Annals of Child Development, 5,* 131–169.

Tardif, T. Z., & Sternberg, R. J. (1988). What do we know about creativity? In R. J. Sternberg (Ed.), *The nature of creativity.* New York: Cambridge University Press.

Walberg, H. J. (1969). A portrait of the artist and scientist as young men. *Exceptional Children, 36,* 5–11.

Walberg, H. J. (1982). Childhood traits and environmental conditions of highly eminent adults. *Gifted Child Quarterly, 25,* 103–107.

Walberg, H. J. (1984a). Improving the productivity of America's schools. *Educational Leadership, 41,* 19–27.

Walberg, H. J. (1984b). *National abilities and economic growth.* Chicago: University of Illinois Office of Evaluation Research.

Walberg, H. J. (1988). Creativity and talent as learning. In R. J. Sternberg (Ed.), *The nature of creativity: Contemporary psychological perspectives* (pp. 340–361). New York: Cambridge University Press.

Walberg, H. J., & Herbig, M. P. (1991). Developing talent, creativity, and eminence. In N. Colangelo & G. A. Davis (Eds.), *Handbook of gifted education* (pp. 245–255). Boston: Allyn and Bacon.

Walberg, H. J., & Stariha, W. E. (1992). Productive human capital: Learning, creativity and eminence. *Creativity Research Journal, 5,* 323–340.

Walberg, H. J., & Tsai, S.-L. (1984). Matthew effects in education. *American Educational Research Journal, 20,* 359–374.

28

When Giftedness Becomes Genius: How Does Talent Achieve Eminence?

DEAN KEITH SIMONTON, *University of California, Davis*

Lewis M. Terman's multivolume *Genetic Studies of Genius* has long been recognized as one of the secure classics in the literature on giftedness. Each volume of this monumental work contains important insights about the nature and development of intellectual giftedness across the life span. Yet we must recognize the reason why the set of five volumes must be referred to as *studies* rather than as a *study.* The plural is mandated because Terman's magnum opus actually contains two rather different types of investigations.

In the first place, the bulk of *Genetic Studies* is devoted to Terman's ambitious longitudinal study of gifted children. Volume 1 describes how the large sample of children was selected and then details their characteristics, such as family background, physical health, scholastic performance, interests and hobbies, and personality traits (Terman, 1925). Volume 3 examines the same children some years later to discern continuities and changes in their early development (Burks, Jensen, & Terman, 1930). Volume 4 looks at these "Termites" when they have become young adults at the thresholds of their careers (Terman & Oden, 1947). And, lastly, Volume 5, published posthumously (Terman & Oden, 1959), scrutinized this same intellectually gifted sample as it entered middle age, enabling the researchers to determine directly their adulthood achievements (see also Oden, 1968). In many respects this last volume is the most crucial, for Terman was by then obligated to show that those whom he identified as talented children did in fact become highly accomplished adults. Childhood gifts may even produce adulthood genius.

But we skipped Volume 2, which was published in 1926, and is the only volume of the five that does not list Terman as a co-author. This 842-page tome was instead written by one of his doctoral students, Catharine Cox, who chose a rather contrary approach to the study of giftedness across the life span. Rather than identify a group of gifted children and then follow them through adulthood to see if they attained distinction in some significant domain, Cox decided to reverse the procedure: She would identify a group of obviously eminent adults and then peer into the biographies of their early childhood to find out whether they had displayed any signs of giftedness. Thus, Terman's longitudinal study of children was supplemented by Cox's retrospective study of adults. The explicit hope was that these two studies would obtain complementary results. The gifted children would become geniuses, and the geniuses would prove themselves to have been gifted children. Certainly Terman had no regrets about including this aberrant study among the set. In his last years, when he was doing what he could to finish Volume 5, he firmly believed that giftedness and genius were intimately related. The two concepts simply represented the two end points of an underlying process of talent development that stretched from birth until death.

But how valid is this belief? Does giftedness necessarily develop into genius? If not, why not? Conversely, does all genius exhibit giftedness in childhood? If not, again, why not? Note that this is a problem about which Terman himself expressed some concern. Not all of his gifted children made good, and he took great pains to explain these misfits and failures. Cox, too, showed awareness of this issue. Many of the 301 geniuses in her sample would not have qualified for inclusion in

Terman's longitudinal study, a discrepancy that she tried to handle in various ways. Hence, the connection between childhood and adulthood talent may be more complex than the main argument of *Genetic Studies of Genius* would like us to think.

I wish to devote this chapter to discussing some of the intricacies involved. I will examine the consistencies and the incongruities that have arisen in longitudinal and retrospective studies of talent development. I will, quite frankly, pose more puzzles than provide firm solutions. My goal is simply to outline what we know so far and to indicate how far we must go before we know what we need to know.

Parallels and Paradoxes

Space is insufficient to discuss all the questions about the conversion of talent into eminence (see Simonton, 1994). Next, I focus on three key research sites: intelligence, personality, and development. These three issues were first introduced, implicitly or explicitly, in *Genetic Studies of Genius.*

Intelligence

Terman's sample was specifically selected according to performance on the Stanford-Binet intelligence test, which Terman had developed only a few years earlier. If a child earned an IQ score of 140 or better, he or she was identified as sufficiently gifted that the label *genius* might not be inappropriate. Indeed, the average IQ across the entire sample of over 1,500 children was about 150, a truly admirable figure. For Cox's 301 geniuses, IQ scores were also calculated, only this time in an entirely different manner. Obviously the Stanford-Binet cannot be administered to deceased subjects, and so Cox substituted a historiometric assessment for the psychometric one. Because the intelligence quotient is conceived as the ratio of mental age to chronological age (multiplied by 100), she and her fellow raters—including Terman—applied this definition to biographical information about the ages at which members of her sample acquired certain skills and demonstrated certain accomplishments. Actually, Cox was following a procedure first introduced by Terman (1917) in a paper on the IQ of Francis Galton. Without going into the details, it suffices to say that her 301 geniuses also tended to be very bright, with IQ scores also averaging around 150 (before introducing her "correction" for data reliability).

Both Terman and Cox thought of *genius* as a quantitative rather than a qualitative attribute. The higher a person's IQ, the greater the intellectual talent, and hence the higher the level of genius. Accordingly, the IQ score should correlate highly with an individual's ultimate achievement. It did not turn out that way. In the Terman sample, not every gifted child became an eminent adult. Worse still, any differentials in IQ could not distinguish those who where successful from those who failed (Terman & Oden, 1959). The outcome was not much better for the Cox sample. Although she reported a small positive correlation between IQ and eminence, this correlation has been shown to be largely artifactual (Simonton, 1976). Subsequent research has obtained comparable results for both psychometric and historiometric samples (e.g., McClelland, 1973; Simonton, 1984c; see also Barrett & Depinet, 1991). Only on rare occasions does variation in intellectual ability prove to be a conspicuous predictor of attained distinction (e.g., Simonton, 1986, 1991b). Why is it that a high IQ, however measured, does not always translate into adulthood genius?

Thresholds and triangular distributions. Often, intelligence functions as a necessary but not sufficient agent of achievement. Below a certain IQ—the figure is often put at around IQ 120—the probability of adult eminence is minimal, but beyond that threshold level further increases in IQ will not necessarily translate into proportional amounts of distinction (Barron & Harrington, 1981; Guilford, 1967; Simonton, 1985a). To be sure, an exceptionally high intellect *may* permit more attainments than an intellect somewhat less stratospheric (Benbow, 1992), but there are no guarantees. The outcome is a peculiar triangular distribution, as depicted in Figure 28.1.

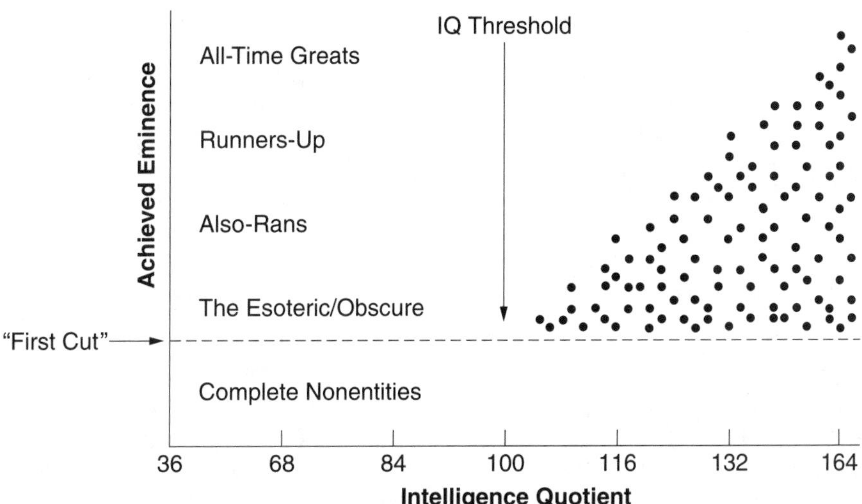

Figure 28.1 Hypothetical scatterplot between IQ and fame showing a triangular distribution and a threshold function.
Source: D. K. Simonton, *Greatness: Who Makes History and Why* (New York: Guilford Press, 1994), Figure 8.3, p. 233.

Curvilinear relationships. It can get worse. Under certain conditions an individual might actually be penalized for possessing an IQ excessively high. For example, unusual precocity may interfere with the development of the social skills absolutely essential to the emergence of an adult capable of adapting to the world. The stories of intellectual prodigies who failed to realize their potential as adults for this very reason are sadly all too numerous. The case of William James Sidis provides the classic illustration (Montour, 1977). Moreover, social maturity aside, extremely brilliant individuals often experience difficulty trying to communicate the value of their ideas. Too often they will talk over the heads of their audience and find themselves dismissed by possible appreciators as prohibitively "highbrow," "cerebral," "theoretical," "eccentric," "radical," or "avant garde." This liability is particularly urgent in domains where success depends on the cultivation of a broad constituency. A theoretical physicist can afford to be understood by only a handful of colleagues; a politician, entrepreneur, commander, or religious figure cannot.

One mathematical model predicts that for those areas of achievement where it is necessary to appeal to the masses, the relationship between IQ and effectiveness should be curvilinear, with a peak at around 119. The predicted curve (Figure 28.2) has been shown to be consistent with a considerable body of psychometric and historiometric research (Simonton, 1985a). Evidence also appears in the Terman and Cox samples. Very few of the "Termites" attained distinction in areas of leadership that required the individual to reach large masses of people. And of the Cox 301, those who did achieve a reputation of broad appeal—such as the U.S. presidents in her sample—exhibited much lower IQs than did the rest of her geniuses. It is possible to have too much of a good thing.

Multiple intelligences. In the first few decades of the twentieth century, psychologists tended to view intelligence as a single, homogeneous construct. This unity has even been titled "Spearman's *g*" to reflect Spearman's (1927) advocacy of a single, *general* factor underlying performance on all tests of intellectual ability. Terman and Cox were no exception. They both implicitly subscribed to Samuel Johnson's (1781, p. 5) claim that "the true Genius is a mind of large general powers,

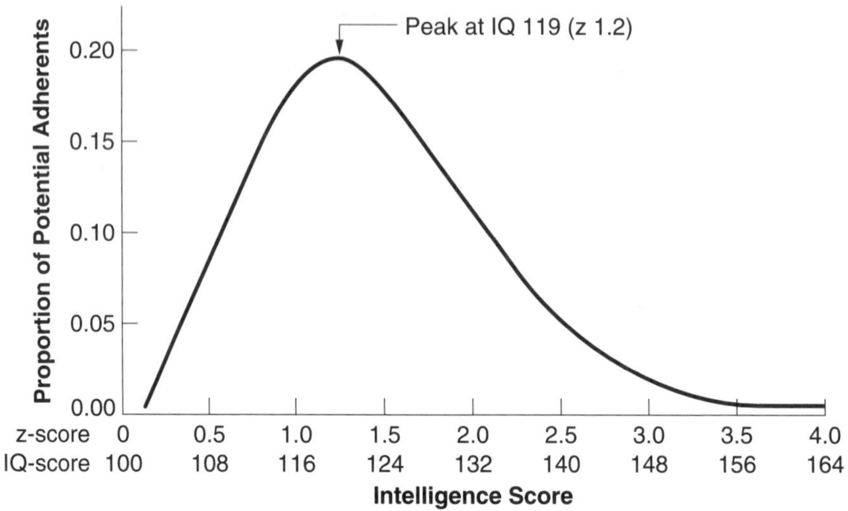

Figure 28.2 The expected proportion of potential followers as a function of intelligence, according to a theoretical model that specifies the trade-offs for various levels of IQ.
Source: D. K. Simonton, "Intelligence and Personal Influences in Groups: For Nonlinear Models," *Psychological Review,* Vol. 92, Figure 8.3, p. 540.

accidentally determined to some particular direction."

However, research since Terman, Cox, and Spearman suggests that intelligence is a far more complicated concept that any single-factor theory would lead us to suspect (Guilford, 1967; Sternberg, 1985). In Gardner's (1983) frequently discussed theory, for example, there are seven distinct intelligences: verbal, logical-mathematical, spatial-visual, bodily-kinesthetic, musical, intrapersonal, and interpersonal.[1] Accordingly, there should be at least seven kinds of intellectual giftedness, as well as seven varieties of genius. In fact, Gardner (1993) recently examined T. S. Eliot, Albert Einstein, Pablo Picasso, Martha Graham, Igor Stravinsky, Sigmund Freud, and Mahatma Gandhi as twentieth-century exemplars of these alternative intellects. Yet it is clear that the Stanford-Binet test on which Terman based his IQ scores is slanted heavily toward the first two or three of these intelligences. No wonder, then, that most of his children became professors, lawyers, doctors, and scientists rather than artists, choreographers, composers, psychoanalysts, or world leaders.

This is, of course, a problem that yet plagues some modern definitions of giftedness and genius. Children can still be selected for gifted programs on the basis of performance on narrowly defined psychometric instruments. And we still have people calling themselves "geniuses" because they score so many standard deviations above the mean on some equally limited test. Thus, an IQ of 132 admits you into Mensa, IQ 164 allows you to join Four Sigma, and IQ 228 makes you the "brightest person in the world" (Marilyn Vos Savant). These conceptions of talent exalt one specific type of intellect and unfairly exclude many other equally valuable forms of intelligence.

Is this critique contradicted by the results of Cox's retrospective study? Not at all! Cox's operational definition of IQ was actually quite different from Terman's. In compiling evidence of childhood and adolescent precocity, she did not impose a one-size-fits-all conception of intelligence. Instead, she let her 301 geniuses

[1] See Chapter 5 by Ramos-Ford and Gardner.

individually decide the specific intelligence on which they were going to be evaluated. Pascal's IQ was based largely on his early mathematical prowess, Mozart's on his being a musical prodigy, J. S. Mill's on his phenomenal analytical precocity, and so forth. None were penalized for being mediocre or even retarded in some cognitive domain captured by the Stanford-Binet. Cox's IQs were implicitly predicated on the doctrine that there exist multiple forms of intelligence.

Skewed distributions. Terman and Cox, following Galton (1869), believed that intellectual capacity, like so many psychological characteristics, is normally distributed in the population. That assumption is valid, at least approximately (Burt, 1963). The frequency distribution of IQ scores indeed looks like the bell-shaped curve, with about two-thirds of the population having IQs within one standard deviation of the mean. Not only is the distribution roughly symmetrical, but virtually the entire human population will have an IQ score within four deviations from the mean. For instance, only one person out of a million can be admitted into the Mega Society, which requires an IQ of 176.

If intelligence enjoys an intimate relationship with achievement, then the distribution of achievements also should be approximately described by a normal distribution. But that is far from true. The discrepancy is best observed when we look at an objective index of accomplishment such as income, influence, or productivity (Burt, 1943; Price, 1963; Simonton, 1988a). Take creative output, for example. No matter what domain of creative activity we examine, the distribution of lifetime productivity is highly skewed, with a small proportion of the contributors creating the overwhelming proportion of the total contributions (Albert, 1975; Dennis, 1954a, 1954b, 1955). This skewed distribution is so well established that it has actually inspired the announcement of corresponding scientific laws (Lotka, 1926; Price, 1963). According to the Price Law, for instance, if k is the number of individuals active in a creative domain, then $\sqrt{k}$ gives the number in that elite that is responsible for *half* of everything accomplished in the field (Price, 1963). To illustrate, of the 250 composers who have added something durable to the classical repertoire, the number of composers who are credited with half of that repertoire is $16 \approx 15.8 = \sqrt{250}$ (Simonton, 1984b, Chapter 5). To show what this means more dramatically, suppose we translated this elitist distribution into the same terms as IQ scores, calling them "productivity quotients" or PQs (Simonton, 1988c, Chapter 4). Then the highest PQs would be almost 200 points higher than the highest IQs! We often speak of geniuses as giants in their fields: Imagine meeting a true giant whose height is 21 standard deviations above the population mean! That's the magnitude of distortion we are talking about here.

How can we explain this conspicuous discrepancy? There are several possible explanations (Simonton, 1988c, Chapter 4), but I would like to consider just one provocative account (Burt, 1943; Eysenck, 1993; Shockley, 1957). When trying to identify the predictors of some phenomena, behavioral scientists are accustomed to think in terms of additive models, where each cause makes an independent contribution to the effect; the total effect is simply the sum of the separate effects. Moreover, if the various components are normally distributed, any summation of those components also will be normally distributed. Yet outstanding talent may be a phenomenon that demands *multiplicative* interaction effects. All the diverse components of exceptional achievement—intellect, motivation, personality, developmental experiences, education, and so on—are multiplied together rather than merely added. Significantly, the multiplicative product of normally distributed variables yields a highly skewed *lognormal* distribution, in accord with what we see in distributions of lifetime achievements.

Such a multiplicative model is also compatible with the threshold and triangular distribution seen in Figure 28.1. Individuals who are very low on just one of the contributing factors will not manifest any gifts as adults. Zero times any number is zero. Therefore, below the minimum intellectual requirement, we cannot expect genius to emerge. Yet additional increases in intelligence beyond that threshold value will not automatically increase the chances for success. The contribution of exalted intelligence to the overall product can be negated by deficiencies in other components of the product. In fact, this is precisely what happened to those in Terman's sample who ended up as adulthood underachievers. However high their IQs, some key factor was missing from their constitution.

In contrast, others with appreciably lower IQs may feature compensating factors that enable them to accomplish much more than Terman's unrealized talents. An instance may be found in William Shockley (Eysenck, 1993). As a child, Shockley was among the many children whom Terman originally tested for possible inclusion in the longitudinal sample, but his IQ was not high enough to certify him as a psychometrically proven genius. Rather than become a gifted child, Shockley became a famous scientist instead, co-inventing the transistor and receiving a Nobel Prize in Physics! No member of Terman's sample achieved so high a level of acclaim. Clearly, Shockley had other things going for him that could easily compensate for a subgenius IQ score.

Personality

Cox was aware of the possibility of such tradeoffs. After gauging the personality characteristics of a subsample of 100 geniuses, she observed that drive and determination could more than compensate for a less than stratospheric IQ. In particular, she admitted that "high but not the highest intelligence, combined with the greatest degree of persistence, will achieve greater eminence than the highest degree of intelligence with somewhat less persistence" (Cox, 1926, p. 187). This motivational aspect of talent development is sine qua non of success. Attainment requires an adult capable of overcoming the numerous frustrations and obstacles that always block the path to greatness. Even after notable achievers establish their reputations, their position is never secure, and failures will accompany successes throughout their lives (Simonton, 1977, 1985b). Moreover, to attain distinction in any domain typically requires a childhood and adolescence packed with arduous training and practice. Research shows that potential talents have to grapple with their chosen domain several hours per day for a full decade before that latent capacity becomes actualized (Bloom, 1985; Ericsson, Krampe, & Tesch-Römer, 1993; Hayes, 1989; Simonton, 1991a). Such a commitment of time and energy is not for the weak of heart. Those of the Cox sample who became famous despite mediocre intellects obviously had this essential quality. Those of Terman's sample who failed to live up to expectations often missed this requirement (Terman & Oden, 1959).

Lack of zeal is not the only character flaw that may prevent a gifted child from becoming an adult genius. The personality profile needed to attain success in maturity is very complex, demanding that a developing talent be high on some traits and low on others (Cattell, 1963; Cox, 1926; Simonton, 1991b). Yet this profile for achievement is not necessarily selected for when intelligence tests are used to identify talent. The classic studies by Getzels and Jackson (1962) and Wallach and Kogan (1965) illustrate this point rather well. Children picked on the basis of high IQs tend to have rather different personality profiles than those who are chosen according to their unusual performance on tests that purport to measure creativity. For instance, the latter tend to be more playful and humorous, to be less conventional in their ambitions, and to conform less in their attitudes about school and life.

But the most remarkable discrepancy has to do with psychopathology. Terman (1925) was almost preoccupied with the personality profiles of his precocious subjects. He wanted to counter the then-prevalent view that genius was close to madness. Accordingly, he took great pains to show that his gifted children were not only not abnormal, but actually *super*normal. Both psychologically and physically, the "Termites" were healthier than average, not less healthy. I believe that this demonstration was misguided: There is some truth to Dryden's (1681, p. 6) famous lines, "Great Wits are sure to Madness near ally'd, / And thin Partitions do their Bounds divide."

I lack space to review all the relevant literature on behalf of this proposition, which already has been done by others anyway (e.g., Eysenck, 1993; Prentky, 1989; Richards, 1981). It may suffice here merely to make the following four points:

1. Historiometric studies show that notable achievers exhibited incidence rates for various mental disorders that exceed the rates in the general population (Ellis, 1926; Ludwig, 1992; Martindale, 1972).
2. Psychiatric studies found similarly high proportions of mental or emotional pathologies among famous contemporaries (Andreasen, 1987; Jamison, 1989; Juda, 1949).
3. Psychometric studies of eminent individuals have found them to obtain high scores on the clinical subscales of various personality measures, such as the Minnesota Multiphasic Personality Inventory or the Eysenck Personality Questionnaire (Barron, 1969; Götz & Götz, 1979a, 1979b; MacKinnon, 1978; Rushton, 1990).
4. Genetic studies of family pedigrees indicate that distinguished achievers are most likely to appear in lineages that display conspicuously high percentages of mental illness (Andreasen, 1987; Juda, 1949; Karlson, 1970).

All of this evidence corroborates the basic conclusion that genius-level talents probably reside at the delicate boundary between a healthy and an unhealthy personality. Furthermore, we have reason to believe that this precarious location is not incidental. There actually are certain advantages that accrue to individuals who lie at the edge. Such personalities are less conforming, more unconventional, even iconoclastic (Eysenck, 1993). They may experience manic periods full of optimistic activity that motivate a large corpus of outstanding works (Jamison, 1993; Slater & Meyer, 1959). And they may entertain bizarre thoughts, crazy associations, or offbeat metaphors or analogies that enable them to arrive at path-breaking insights (Eysenck, 1993; Woody & Claridge, 1977). Of course, all of these tendencies can go too far; you can have too much of a bad thing. Those who inherit or acquire a disposition to go beyond the frontier into never-never land may never develop their gifts (Rothenberg, 1990). Or, like Schumann and Van Gogh, they may not allow their talents to advance as far as they would have otherwise. Nonetheless, it's disastrous to talent development for a gifted individual never to break out of the shell of a conventional and courteous complacency.

I suspect that Terman's procedures for obtaining his original sample of gifted children militated against his identifying talents that had this essential component of potential greatness. He did not test the entire student population but, rather, relied on teacher nominations to provide a first screening. One can only guess how many kids were not named because their teachers thought them weird rather than bright. Moreover, even if a few oddballs managed to get through this first filter, I wonder how many of them would have taken the tasks in the Stanford-Binet seriously enough to provide meaningful answers to the interviewer's probes. How many future geniuses would have had a good time offering unconventional and humorous answers that would necessarily earn them low scores on the test? Of course, we will never know. Yet maybe William Schockley was one of them!

Development

In the previous section I observed that the borderline pathology that contributes to the realization of intellectual talent may be inherited, for exceptional individuals often come from pathological family pedigrees. Hence, the family lines of "natural ability" documented by Galton (1869) seem to have been supplemented by family lines of "unnatural abilities." However, it would be incorrect to conclude that where two such genetic lineages happen to intersect in precisely the proper proportions, giftedness always becomes genius. Genius is not just born; it is also made—by the environment in which talented youth emerge. Genetic endowment merely offers the raw materials on which must operate the events and circumstances of childhood and adolescence. Here, too, we can witness some intriguing discrepancies between potential and actual talents. I will focus on three sets of environmental influences that probably have received the most attention: (1) birth order, (2) traumatic events, and (3) education and training (Simonton, 1987).

Birth order. Terman (1925) made the observation that first-borns seemed to be overrepresented in his sample of gifted children. A similar pattern seems to hold for child prodigies as well (Feldman & Goldsmith, 1986). Furthermore, some early studies of adult notables appear to suggest the same advantage of primogeniture, beginning with Galton's (1874) study of eminent British scientists (see, e.g., Albert, 1980; Ellis, 1926). However, subsequent work indicates that the picture is not so simple. First-borns are more likely to attain distinction in some domains of achievement, whereas those in other ordinal positions are more prone to achieve success in rather different domains. Thus, while first-borns become famous scientific creators (Clark & Rice, 1982; Eiduson, 1962; Roe, 1952; Terry, 1989), later-borns become the notable artistic creators (Bliss, 1970; Clark & Rice, 1982), with the exception that classical composers are more aligned with the scientists on this developmental event (Schubert, Wagner, & Schubert, 1977). An analogous distribution holds in leadership, where the first-borns provide the politicians (Wagner & Schubert, 1977; Zweigenhaft, 1975), while the last-borns populate the revolutionaries (Stewart, 1977, 1991). Of course, as with all generalizations in the behavioral sciences, there are many exceptions to these statements. However, some of these departures end up supporting the more general proposition. For instance, later-borns who do go into science have a higher likelihood of becoming scientific revolutionaries who work to overthrow the established paradigms (Sulloway, in preparation). Hence, the overall tendency is for first-borns to achieve eminence in prestigious positions that are well integrated with the Establishment, whereas the later-borns are more likely to succeed as rebellious agents of a new order or even as advocates of disorder.

We need not discuss the reasons for these divergent outcomes, except to say that this pattern fits nicely with Adler's (1938) classic theory of the first-born as the "dethroned king." The more important point to make here is that this tendency helps us appreciate why Terman's gifted children turned out the way they did. When first-borns predominate in a sample, we should expect a high percentage of doctors, lawyers, professors, and other professionals (Schachter, 1963) but a low percentage of artists, writers, and others who are less willing to conform to societal definitions of success. And that is how the story came out in the end. Moreover, this developmental pattern may also explain the prominence of first-borns among the Termites in the first place. First-borns may have been more likely to seek the scholastic attention that would have earned them a teacher nomination, and more eager to earn additional academic kudos by performing well during the IQ screening. In fact, I wonder if the trend for IQ to decline with ordinal position tells us more about attitudes than aptitudes (cf. Zajonc, 1976, 1983). Later-borns may have less respect for the authorities who decide that these measures assess anything important, and may be too iconoclastic to accept the presumption that the questions have a single right answer.

Whatever the status of the last conjecture, one conclusion must be stressed. Birth order may not really decide the magnitude of adulthood distinction (cf. Helmreich, Spence, Beane, Lucker, & Matthews, 1980). Rather, ordinal position primarily determines the domain of achievement in which that distinction is attained. To call first-borns more successful because they are more likely to be identified as gifted children or because they become well-respected professionals serves only to perpetuate a first-born view of the world. Such a prejudice may invite a later-born revolt!

Traumatic events. Empirical studies of eminent personalities repeatedly record that a large proportion experienced less than idyllic childhoods (Goertzel & Goertzel, 1962; Goertzel, Goertzel, & Goertzel, 1978). The family may have experienced tremendous fluctuations in economic and emotional well-being, and the home was often the locus of tragedy. Of the diverse ways that misfortunes can visit a talent's early development, the one that has received the most empirical attention has been orphanhood or parental loss (e.g., Albert, 1971; Eisenstadt, Haynal, Rentchnick, & De Senarclens, 1989). For both creators and leaders, the percentage of geniuses who lost one or both parents before reaching early adulthood is appreciably larger than what appears to hold in the general population or any other comparable group (e.g., Berrington, 1974; Martindale, 1972; Silverman, 1974; Walberg, Rasher, & Parkerson, 1980).

What makes statistics like these especially remarkable is the contrast with the far more benign home environments that Terman's group enjoyed as children and adolescents (Terman, 1925). His children were more likely to grow up in comfortable, intact families where everything transpired as in storybooks. Child prodigies, too, are more prone to emerge from such nurturant environments (Feldman & Goldsmith, 1986). What's the problem here? Why the discrepancy?

It may very well be that some form of "trials and tribulations" in early childhood and adolescence is an integral part of talent development. The beneficial impact may arise from three sources (cf. Simonton, 1987, 1994). First, such events may disrupt ordinary socialization practices to such an extent that the individual will find it less easy to conform to societal expectations. After all, parents play a big role in inculcating societal norms and values, both as instructors and as models. Second, the child may undergo a bereavement reaction that puts the developing talent into a permanent emotional disequilibrium that can be alleviated only by attaining fame and fortune (Eisenstadt, 1978). Third, the experience of traumatic events may facilitate the development of an emotional robustness that enables the individual to handle disappointments and frustrations far better than those who emerged from more tranquil family backgrounds (Simonton, 1994, Chapter 6). These three sources are not mutually exclusive.

Before any parents try to do their kids a favor by making their childhoods more rough-and-tumble, some caveats are in order. The advantage gained from an unhappy childhood or adolescence varies according to the domain of achievement. For example, although the rates of parental loss are higher among scientists than among the general population, the rates among literary creators are higher still (Berry, 1981). Evidently, artistic creativity requires more turmoil than does scientific creativity. In addition, the influence of traumatic events must be weighed against the youth's personal resources that are used to overcome the sometimes severe emotional disabilities that also can ensue from a painful childhood or adolescence. Juvenile delinquents and suicidal depressives also exhibit high incidence of parental loss (Eisenstadt, 1978). Hence, there probably exists an optimal level of developmental stress for each youth. What might not be enough challenge for one developing talent might be just right for a second, and far too much for a third. Thus, the many famous personalities who attained distinction *without* having to suffer orphanhood may be those for whom their development was optimized by less dramatic tests of character.

Whatever the complexities, I cannot help but think that most of Terman's children were not sufficiently challenged. They often seem to fit Dylan Thomas's remark that "There's only one thing that's worse than having an unhappy childhood, and that's having a too-happy childhood" (Ferris, 1977, p. 49).

Education and training. Terman loved to boast about the academic success of his intellectually gifted children. They tended to get excellent grades and to obtain advanced degrees. Child prodigies, too, often make their first big splash in the newspapers by phenomenal displays of scholastic prowess. One occasionally reads about "brains" who entered high school at 10 and graduated at 11 with straight As and full scholarships to Ivy League colleges.

Yet when we turn to those who actually made a name for themselves, the role of education becomes more ambiguous. First of all, those who get excellent grades and high honors are not necessarily more prone to achieve distinction in their chosen fields; the correlations are either zero or very weakly positive (Cohen, 1984; Hudson, 1958; McClelland, 1973). As a consequence, there are many examples of unquestioned geniuses who were mediocre or even miserable scholars. Moreover, the relationship between level of formal education and realization of talent is not always straightforward. This became evident when the 301 members of the Cox (1926) sample were subjected to a more detailed analysis (Simonton, 1976, 1983a). If you plot the eminence scores that she derived from Cattell's (1903) rankings against their level of formal education, and fit curves to the creators and leaders separately, you obtain the results shown in Figure 28.3. Notice that for creative geniuses, achieved eminence peaks somewhere in the last half of undergraduate training. For leaders, in contrast, the connection is strictly negative. In neither case can we conclude that adult accomplishment is a positive linear function of the level of education obtained. Other studies based on more contemporary samples lead to the same general conclusion: Higher levels of education are not always an advantage, and sometimes may be a disadvantage (Simonton, 1984b, Chapter 4).

Of course, it is one matter to uncover a provocative empirical association, quite another to interpret its theoretical implications. In the present case, several explanations can be offered for curves like those seen in Figure 28.3 (Simonton, 1994, Chapter 6). Here, I would just like to mention one obvious possibility: Formal education may not always make a positive contribution to talent development, and in some instances may detract from the growth of certain kinds of talent.

Thus, on the one hand, those who plan to become lawyers, doctors, professors, and other professionals—the kinds of attainments that predominated in Terman's sample—have much more to benefit from advancing to higher academic degrees. Indeed, the career demands in these domains give them no choice! These days it is virtually impossible to get anywhere in these fields without a J.D., M.D., or Ph.D.

On the other hand, most artistic creators, revolutionary scientists, and other more unconventional achievers may have much to lose and little to gain from continuing with more than a smattering of higher education. They may need enough formal training to acquire certain basic knowledge and skills, such as the ability to write well and to carry on an informed conversation. Beyond that, the increased inculcation of more specialized disciplinary preoccupations may only interfere

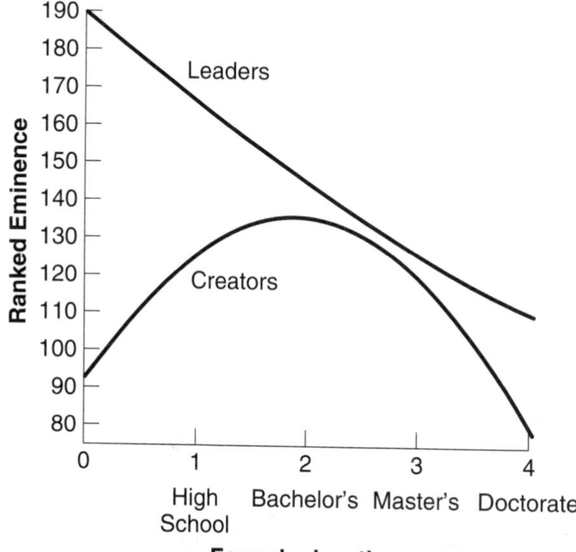

Source: D. K. Simonton, "Formal Education, Eminence, and Dogmatism: The Curvilinear Relationship," *Journal of Creative Behavior,* Vol. 17, Figure 1, p. 152.

Figure 28.3 Ranked eminence as a function of formal education for the 301 historic geniuses of the Cox (1926) sample.

with more important pursuits. For instance, success in many fields is strongly correlated with voracious and omnivorous reading, an undisciplined activity that may suffer under academic demands (McCurdy, 1960; Simonton, 1984b, p. 74). In addition, many domains of achievement require the slow acquisition of highly specialized techniques that are not always taught—or taught well—in formal academic settings. Whatever the details, we must recall that it usually takes about ten years of intense study to master the materials of a domain. The implication is clear: When formal schooling is not directly contributing to that mastery, it is necessarily delaying that mastery. Distaste for that interference leads many talented young adults to become college dropouts—to their benefit.

When a developing talent must seek an education outside the educational system proper, one form of extracurricular training is especially important: mentoring. This was not a topic that attracted much attention from either Terman or Cox. Yet studies of talented youths show that this is a crucial factor in their development (Bloom, 1985; Feldman & Goldsmith, 1986).[2] The young talent must find a suitable teacher who is well matched to the youth's current capacity, and must frequently change teachers as that capacity continues to grow. Furthermore, retrospective studies of eminent personalities reveal the impact of the same developmental influence, but with some critical differences that are often overlooked in the longitudinal literature (Simonton, 1983b, 1992a).

To begin with, mentors can have a detrimental effect on talent growth if they are driven to clone themselves through their students. It is partly for this reason that it is usually more advantageous to have multiple mentors rather than rely on just one (Simonton, 1984a, 1992b).

In addition, the connection between mentor characteristics and successful talent development is often complex, with interaction effects, curvilinear relationships, and other niceties (Simonton, 1977, 1984a, 1992b). For example, the most effective mentors tend to be those at the peak of their own careers rather than those who are past their prime and thus are less receptive to new ideas.

Finally, we must also recognize that a developing talent may receive considerable benefits from nonpersonal relationships with predecessors in their domain of creative activity. Role models of eminent achievement can be admired and emulated at a distance, even when those paragons of excellence are deceased. This indirect mentoring can be as powerful as one-on-one training (Simonton, 1975, 1984a, 1988b, 1992b). Albert Einstein had the portraits of three deceased predecessors hanging in his study—Newton, Faraday, and Maxwell. These three probably had far more influence on the development of Einstein's special talents than did any of his teachers. To borrow Newton's metaphor, they were the giants on whose shoulders Einstein stood.

Conceivably, many of Terman's children did not grow up to become highly distinctive adults because they failed to form the right links with those greats who represented the best in their particular area of talent. Without the deep desire to surpass admired predecessors, even the greatest gifts will seldom become genius.

Conclusion

In this short chapter I could do no more than offer a preliminary probe of a very profound enigma. Many critical questions have necessarily been ignored. We have not discussed, for example, the difficult question of gender differences on the realization of latent talents, nor have we treated the matter of how the "spirit of the times" (or *Zeitgeist*) moderates the emergence and expression of genius. And we have omitted any discussion of the possible role of crystallizing experiences, marginality, socioeconomic class, religious affiliation, and many other possibly critical developmental events (for further discussion, see Simonton, 1994). Nevertheless, those topics that I have managed to cover should convey the develop-

[2] See Chapter 17 by Sosniak.

mental complexities behind the conversion of inherent into actual gifts. We are still a long way from understanding all forces that impinge upon talent development. We are even farther from comprehending how all these forces converge and interact in the creation of an exceptional achiever. Future research must try to bring these complexities together into a single life span developmental framework. Besides incorporating the large inventory of pertinent developmental influences, it must articulate all the interaction effects, curvilinear relationships, and other causal functions that greatly entangle the impact of these influences. Furthermore, this account must provide answers to what I consider to be two absolutely fundamental issues.

First, why is it that so many gifted children fail to realize their fullest potential as adults? In concrete terms, why did so many of Terman's children end up falling short of the highest expectations? Where did the developmental process go astray? What are the most common blind alleys? Which of these dead ends are one-way streets and which are culs de sac from which a fortunate talent can reverse direction and reenter the main highway to success?

Second, how can it be that many eminent adults displayed no obvious signs of giftedness in either childhood or adolescence? Why is it, for instance, that more than half of Cox's 301 geniuses had IQ scores below the minimum threshold required for entrance into the Terman sample? Is the developmental trajectory for these apparently unpromising children qualitatively different from that which guides the precocious who eventually make good?

The first issue is the enigma of the "nipped bud," the second that of the "late bloomer." These exceptional individuals are in many respects far more central to the emergence of a sound theoretical interpretation than the minority in the Cox sample who easily would have qualified for entrance into the Terman sample. The nipped buds and the late bloomers are anomalies that should help us isolate the idiosyncrasies in the thin garden path between the promise of youth and the triumph of maturity. After all, nipped buds and late bloomers are far more common than those lucky few—like Pascal, Mozart, and J. S. Mill—whose transitions from giftedness to genius were comparatively smooth and untroubled. With a better understanding of these developmental discontinuities, we may someday learn how to ensure that the more auspicious path becomes the norm rather than the exception. Maybe the subjects of a future longitudinal study of gifted children will all later qualify for inclusion in a subsequent retrospective study of genius adults.

REFERENCES

Adler, A. (1938). *Social interest: A challenge to mankind* (J. Linton & R. Vaughan, Trans.). London: Faber & Faber

Albert, R. S. (1971). Cognitive development and parental loss among the gifted, the exceptionally gifted and the creative. *Psychological Reports, 29,* 19–26.

Albert, R. S. (1975). Toward a behavioral definition of genius. *American Psychologist, 30,* 140–151.

Albert, R. S. (1980). Family positions and the attainment of eminence: A study of special family positions and special family experiences. *Gifted Child Quarterly, 24,* 87–95.

Andreasen, N. C. (1987). Creativity and mental illness: Prevalence rates in writers and their first-degree relatives. *American Journal of Psychiatry, 144,* 1288–1292.

Barrett, G. V., & Depinet, R. L. (1991). A reconsideration of testing for competence rather than for intelligence. *American Psychologist, 46,* 1012–1024.

Barron, F. (1969). *Creative person and creative process.* New York: Holt, Rinehart & Winston.

Barron, F., & Harrington, D. M. (1981). Creativity, intelligence, and personality. *Annual Review of Psychology, 32,* 439–476.

Benbow, C. P. (1992). Academic achievement in mathematics and science of students between ages 13 and 23: Are there differences among students in the top one percent of mathematical ability? *Journal of Educational Psychology, 84,* 51–61.

Berrington, H. (1974). Review article: *The Fiery Chariot:* Prime ministers and the search for love.

British Journal of Political Science, 4, 345–369.

Berry, C. (1981). The Nobel scientists and the origins of scientific achievement. *British Journal of Sociology, 32,* 381–391.

Bliss, W. D. (1970). Birth order of creative writers. *Journal of Individual Psychology, 26,* 200–202.

Bloom, B. S. (Ed.). (1985). *Developing talent in young people.* New York: Ballantine.

Burks, B. S., Jensen, D. W., & Terman, L. M. (1930). *The promise of youth: Follow-up studies of a thousand gifted children.* Stanford, CA: Stanford University Press.

Burt, C. (1943). Ability and income. *British Journal of Educational Psychology, 12,* 83–98.

Burt, C. (1963). Is intelligence distributed normally? *British Journal of Statistical Psychology, 16,* 175–190.

Cattell, J. M. (1903). A statistical study of eminent men. *Popular Science Monthly, 62,* 359–377.

Cattell, R. B. (1963). The personality and motivation of the researcher from measurements of contemporaries and from biography. In C. W. Taylor & F. Barron (Eds.), *Scientific creativity: Its recognition and development* (pp. 119-131). New York: Wiley.

Clark, R. D., & Rice, G. A. (1982). Family constellations and eminence: The birth orders of Nobel Prize winners. *Journal of Psychology, 110,* 281–287.

Cohen, P. A. (1984). College grades and adult achievement: A research synthesis. *Research in Higher Education, 20,* 281–293.

Cox, C. (1926). *The early mental traits of three hundred geniuses.* Stanford, CA: Stanford University Press.

Dennis, W. (1954a). Bibliographies of eminent scientists. *Scientific Monthly, 79,* 180–183.

Dennis, W. (1954b). Productivity among American psychologists. *American Psychologist, 9,* 191–194.

Dennis, W. (1955). Variations in productivity among creative workers. *Scientific Monthly, 80,* 277–278.

Dryden, J. (1681). *Absalom and Achitophel: A poem.* London: Davis.

Eiduson, B. T. (1962). *Scientists: Their psychological world.* New York: Basic Books.

Eisenstadt, J. M. (1978). Parental loss and genius. *American Psychologist, 33,* 211–223.

Eisenstadt, J. M., Haynal, A., Rentchnick, P., & De Senarclens, P. (1989). *Parental loss and achievement.* Madison, CT: International Universities Press.

Ellis, H. (1926). *A study of British genius* (rev. ed.). Boston: Houghton Mifflin.

Ericsson, K. A., Krampe, R. T., & Tesch-Römer, C. (1993). The role of deliberate practice in the acquisition of expert performance. *Psychological Review, 100,* 363–406.

Eysenck, H. J. (1993). Creativity and personality: Suggestions for a theory. *Psychological Inquiry, 4,* 147–148.

Feldman, D. H., & Goldsmith, L. T. (1986). *Nature's gambit: Child prodigies and the development of human potential.* New York: Basic Books.

Ferris, P. (1977). *Dylan Thomas.* London: Hodder & Stoughton.

Galton, F. (1869). *Hereditary genius: An inquiry into its laws and consequences.* London: Macmillan.

Galton, F. (1874). *English men of science: Their nature and nurture.* London: Macmillan.

Gardner, H. (1983). *Frames of mind: A theory of multiple intelligences.* New York: Basic Books.

Gardner, H. (1993). *Creating minds: An anatomy of creativity seen through the lives of Freud, Einstein, Picasso, Stravinsky, Eliot, Graham, and Gandhi.* New York: Basic Books.

Getzels, J., & Jackson, P. W. (1962). *Creativity and intelligence: Explorations with gifted students.* New York: Wiley.

Goertzel, M. G., Goertzel, V., & Goertzel, T. G. (1978). *300 eminent personalities: A psychosocial analysis of the famous.* San Francisco: Jossey-Bass.

Goertzel, V., & Goertzel, M. G. (1962). *Cradles of eminence.* Boston: Little, Brown.

Götz, K. O., & Götz, K. (1979a). Personality characteristics of professional artists. *Perceptual and Motor Skills, 49,* 327–334.

Götz, K. O., & Götz, K. (1979b). Personality characteristics of successful artists. *Perceptual and Motor Skills, 49,* 919–924.

Guilford, J. P. (1967). *The nature of human intelligence.* New York: McGraw-Hill.

Hayes, J. R. (1989). *The complete problem solver* (2nd ed.). Hillsdale, NJ: Lawrence Erlbaum Associates.

Helmreich, R. L., Spence, J. T., Beane, W. E., Lucker, G. W., & Matthews, K. A. (1980). Making it in academic psychology: Demographic and personality correlates of attainment. *Journal of Personality and Social Psychology, 39,* 896–908.

Hudson, L. (1958). Undergraduate academic record of Fellows of the Royal Society. *Nature, 182,* 1326.

Jamison, K. R. (1989). Mood disorders and patterns of creativity in British writers and artists. *Psychiatry, 52,* 125–134.

Jamison, K. R. (1993). *Touched with fire: Manic-*

depressive illness and the artistic temperment. New York: Free Press.

Johnson, S. (1781). *The lives of the most eminent English poets* (Vol 1). London: Bathurst et al.

Juda, A. (1949). The relationship between highest mental capacity and psychic abnormalities. *American Journal of Psychiatry, 106,* 296–307.

Karlson, J. I. (1970). Genetic association of giftedness and creativity with schizophrenia. *Hereditas, 66,* 177–182.

Lotka, A. J. (1926). The frequency distribution of scientific productivity. *Journal of the Washington Academy of Sciences, 16,* 317–323.

Ludwig, A. M. (1992). Creative achievement and psychopathology: Comparison among professions. *American Journal of Psychotherapy, 46,* 330–356.

MacKinnon, D. W. (1978). *In search of human effectiveness.* Buffalo, NY: Creative Education Foundation.

Martindale, C. (1972). Father absence, psychopathology, and poetic eminence. *Psychological Reports, 31,* 843–847.

McClelland, D. C. (1973). Testing for competence rather than for "intelligence." *American Psychologist, 28,* 1–14.

McCurdy, H. G. (1960). The childhood pattern of genius. *Horizon, 2,* 33–38.

Montour, K. (1977). William James Sidis, the broken twig. *American Psychologist, 32,* 265–279.

Oden, M. H. (1968). The fulfillment of promise: Forty-year follow-up of the Terman gifted group. *Genetic Psychology Monographs, 77,* 3–93.

Prentky, R. A. (1989). Creativity and psychopathology: Gamboling at the seat of madness. In J. A. Glover, R. R. Ronning, & C. R. Reynolds (Eds.), *Handbook of creativity* (pp. 243–269). New York: Plenum Press.

Price, D. (1963). *Little science, big science.* New York: Columbia University Press.

Richards, R. (1981). Relationships between creativity and psychopathology: An evaluation and interpretation of the evidence. *Genetic Psychology Monographs, 103,* 261–324.

Roe, A. (1952). *The making of a scientist.* New York: Dodd, Mead.

Rothenberg, A. (1990). *Creativity and madness: New findings and old stereotypes.* Baltimore, MD: Johns Hopkins University Press.

Rushton, J. P. (1990). Creativity, intelligence, and psychoticism. *Personality and Individual Differences, 11,* 1291–1298.

Schachter, S. (1963). Birth order, eminence, and higher education. *American Sociological Review, 28,* 757–768.

Schubert, D. S. P., Wagner, M. E., & Schubert, H. J. P. (1977). Family constellation and creativity: Firstborn predominance among classical music composers. *Journal of Psychology, 95,* 147–149.

Shockley, W. (1957). On the statistics of individual variations of productivity in research laboratories. *Proceedings of the Institute of Radio Engineers, 45,* 279–290.

Silverman, S. M. (1974). Parental loss and scientists. *Science Studies, 4,* 259–264.

Simonton, D. K. (1975). Sociocultural context of individual creativity: A transhistorical time-series analysis. *Journal of Personality and Social Psychology, 32,* 1119–1133.

Simonton, D. K. (1976). Biographical determinants of achieved eminence: A multivariate approach to the Cox data. *Journal of Personality and Social Psychology, 33,* 218–226.

Simonton, D. K. (1977). Eminence, creativity, and geographic marginality: A recursive structural equation model. *Journal of Personality and Social Psychology, 35,* 805–816.

Simonton, D. K. (1983a). Formal education, eminence, and dogmatism: The curvilinear relationship. *Journal of Creative Behavior, 17,* 149–162.

Simonton, D. K. (1983b). Intergenerational transfer of individual differences in hereditary monarchs: Genes, role-modeling, cohort, or sociocultural effects? *Journal of Personality and Social Psychology, 44,* 354–364.

Simonton, D. K. (1984a). Artistic creativity and interpersonal relationships across and within generations. *Journal of Personality and Social Psychology, 46,* 1273–1286.

Simonton, D. K. (1984b). *Genius, creativity, and leadership: Historiometric inquiries.* Cambridge, MA.: Harvard University Press.

Simonton, D. K. (1984c). Leaders as eponyms: Individual and situational determinants of monarchal eminence. *Journal of Personality, 52,* 1–21.

Simonton, D. K. (1985a). Intelligence and personal influence in groups: Four nonlinear models. *Psychological Review, 92,* 532–547.

Simonton, D. K. (1985b). Quality, quantity, and age: The careers of 10 distinguished psychologists. *International Journal of Aging and Human Development, 21,* 241–254.

Simonton, D. K. (1986). Presidential personality: Biographical use of the Gough Adjective Check List. *Journal of Personality and Social Psychology, 51,* 149–160.

Simonton, D. K. (1987). Developmental antecedents of achieved eminence. *Annals of Child Development, 5,* 131–169.

Simonton, D. K. (1988a). Creativity, leadership, and

chance. In R. J. Sternberg (Ed.), *The nature of creativity: Contemporary psychological perspectives* (pp. 386–426). New York: Cambridge University Press.

Simonton, D. K. (1988b). Galtonian genius, Kroeberian configurations, and emulation: A generational time-series analysis of Chinese civilization. *Journal of Personality and Social Psychology, 55,* 230–238.

Simonton, D. K. (1988c). *Scientific genius: A psychology of science.* New York: Cambridge University Press.

Simonton, D. K. (1991a). Emergence and realization of genius: The lives and works of 120 classical composers. *Journal of Personality and Social Psychology, 61,* 829–840.

Simonton, D. K. (1991b). Personality correlates of exceptional personal influence: A note on Thorndike's (1950) creators and leaders. *Creativity Research Journal, 4,* 67–78.

Simonton, D. K. (1992a). Leaders of American psychology, 1879–1967: Career development, creative output, and professional achievement. *Journal of Personality and Social Psychology, 62,* 5–17.

Simonton, D. K. (1992b). The social context of career success and course for 2,026 scientists and inventors. *Personality and Social Psychology Bulletin, 18,* 452–463.

Simonton, D. K. (1994). *Greatness: Who makes history and why.* New York: Guilford Press.

Slater, E., & Meyer, A. (1959). Contributions to a pathography of the musician: 1. Robert Schumann. *Confinia Psychiatrica, 2,* 65–94.

Spearman, C. (1927). *The abilities of man: Their nature and measurement.* New York: Macmillan.

Sternberg, R. J. (1985). *Beyond IQ: A triarchic theory of human intelligence.* New York: Cambridge University Press.

Stewart, L. H. (1977). Birth order and political leadership. In M. G. Hermann (Ed.), *The psychological examination of political leaders* (pp. 205–236). New York: Free Press.

Stewart, L. H. (1991). The world cycle of leadership. *Journal of Analytical Psychology, 36,* 449–459.

Sulloway, F. J. (in preparation). *Born to rebel: Radical thinking in science and social thought.* Cambridge, MA: MIT Press.

Terman, L. M. (1917). The intelligence quotient of Francis Galton in childhood. *American Journal of Psychology, 28,* 209–215.

Terman, L. M. (1925). *Mental and physical traits of a thousand gifted children.* Stanford, CA: Stanford University Press.

Terman, L. M., & Oden, M. H. (1947). *The gifted child grows up.* Stanford, CA: Stanford University Press.

Terman, L. M., & Oden, M. H. (1959). *The gifted group at mid-life.* Stanford, CA: Stanford University Press.

Terry, W. S. (1989). Birth order and prominence in the history of psychology. *Psychological Record, 39,* 333–337.

Wagner, M. E., & Schubert, H. J. P. (1977). Sibship variables and United States presidents. *Journal of Individual Psychology, 33,* 78–85.

Walberg, H. J., Rasher, S. P., & Parkerson, J. (1980). Childhood and eminence. *Journal of Creative Behavior, 13,* 225–231.

Wallach, M. A., & Kogan, N. (1965). *Modes of thinking in young children: A study of the creativity-intelligence distinction.* New York: Holt.

Woody, E., & Claridge, G. (1977). Psychoticism and thinking. *British Journal of Social and Clinical Psychology, 16,* 241–248.

Zajonc, R. B. (1976). Family configuration and intelligence. *Science, 192,* 227–235.

Zajonc, R. B. (1983). Validating the confluence model. *Psychological Bulletin, 93,* 457–480.

Zweigenhaft, R. L. (1975). Birth order, approval-seeking, and membership in Congress. *Journal of Individual Psychology, 31,* 205–210.

PART V 

Psychological and Counseling Services

A critical and growing feature of programs for the gifted is a strong emphasis on psychological needs. Gifted students no longer are viewed simply as extraordinary and efficient learners, but as complex personalities with exceptional sensitivities and recurrent vulnerabilities.

Despite Terman's opposite conclusion, many bright children do have emotional and adjustment problems. Nicholas Colangelo in Chapter 29 traces the real need for counseling programs from Leta Hollingworth to current counseling centers featuring personal, career, and family counseling. Colangelo elaborates on the nature and significance of gifted students' self-concept, especially pertaining to one's own giftedness. Group counseling is particularly recommended, and the author describes concrete goals, techniques, and topics. Interest in family counseling is growing, focusing, for example, on sibling stresses. Colangelo's parent–school interaction model includes the four combinations of parents or schools being either concerned with or uninterested in special programming. A good counseling program, says Colangelo, is developmental—well planned, ongoing, and grounded in cognitive and affective needs—rather than dealing with problems as they arise in a remedial way.

Michael M. Piechowski in Chapter 30 elaborates on the extraordinary sensitivity, intensity, and "overexcitability" of many highly gifted students. Characteristics in the five areas of psychomotor, sensual, intellectual, imaginational, and emotional help us make sense of bright and creative students who show rapid speech, self-criticism, powerful empathy and morality, active mental imagery, extraordinary sensitivity, and extreme emotional highs and lows. They may wonder "What's wrong with me?" Others may be surprised when such a student selects morally correct action over socially expected behavior ("positive maladjustment"). Piechowski relates giftedness to self-actualization and traces emotional growth in gifted students, contrasting a rational-altruistic pattern with an introspective-emotional one.

In Chapter 31 Linda Silverman reviews unique problems in families of gifted students. She notes, for example, issues pertaining to early assessment, suitable home stimulation, school placement, working with school personnel, locating resources, as well as common personality characteristics of gifted children, such as independence, questioning, introversion, high sensitivity, and perfectionism. Peer relations are problematic partly because of the higher maturity of gifted children; getting gifted peers together is a good solution. Silverman also notes family tensions caused, for example, by the existence of an equally gifted—but ignored—sibling. The author reminds us that giftedness runs in families—gifted children typically means gifted parents. Despite rumors of overprotective, incompetent, bragging parents who antagonize school districts, most families of the gifted have healthy interaction patterns and good psychological adjustment.

Philip A. Perrone in Chapter 32 elaborates on career counseling needs of gifted students. He points out that many gifted females underestimate their abilities and still gravitate toward sex-role stereotypic choices. Perrone recommended helping gifted females learn about career possibilities and exposing them to professional women models. Mentorships provide valuable career experiences for boys and girls. Perrone ties Gottfredson's stage theory of conceptual development to evolving career interests—from childish orientations to size and power, through sex-appropriate and socially valued choices, to selections that fit unique needs and, finally, to choices based on an "integrated world view." Holland's model describes qualitatively different areas of career interest—investigative, artistic, social, enterprising, and conventional. Perrone ends with a list of psychological, psychocreative, and social factors that influence career choices of gifted students.

Terry McNabb in Chapter 33 addresses the topic of intrinsic motivation and asks why some high-ability students "lose, suppress, or sidestep" motivation and become underachievers. Family problems, failures of teachers to encourage achievment, and classroom boredom reduce motivation, notes McNabb. According to attribution theory and locus-of-control theory, students' perceptions of their ability and control will influence school performance. One dilemma is that, to some students, high effort means low ability. McNabb also reviews implications of goal theories: Students who view intelligence as fixed will see high performance as a measure of their ability; students who view intelligence as malleable will see learning as the route to high ability. The author recommends that teachers emphasize the effort–outcome connection, use rewards sparingly, and model the incremental (malleable) view of intelligence.

Ten to 20 percent of high school dropouts test in the gifted range; 40 percent of the top high school graduates do not complete college. In Chapter 34 Sylvia B. Rimm identifies subtle pressures that contribute to underachievement, such as anti-intellectual and antigifted attitudes, rigid and unchallenging classes, an absence of education-oriented parent models, or perhaps a sibling who receives the title of "special." Some warning signs are procrastination, disorganization, and careless work. Virtually all underachievers have low self-esteem, notes Rimm, followed by avoidance of academic tasks and, consequently, deficient skill development. Underachievers may be dependent or dominant, conforming or nonconforming, creating four behavior patterns. Rimm describes her six-step TRIFOCAL model that has reversed underachievement. With some underachieving students, Rimm used acceleration (!) to motivate them.

29

Counseling Gifted Students: Issues and Practices

NICHOLAS COLANGELO, *The University of Iowa*

Educating gifted students has focused mostly on meeting their learning needs. Counseling needs, though long recognized, are a relatively recent emphasis. The focus of this chapter is on the counseling needs of gifted students: defining what these needs are and how they can be addressed. Although I fully recognize that teachers are also "counselors" to students, this chapter focuses on the role of school counselors.

Historical Overview

A brief historical overview of counseling with gifted students will help set the present-day context. The gifted-child movement in the United States can be traced back to Lewis M. Terman, whose pioneering longitudinal study of 1,528 gifted children formed the project titled Genetic Studies of Genius (Burks, Jensen, & Terman, 1930; Terman, 1925; Terman & Oden, 1947, 1959). The Terman studies grounded the study of giftedness in an empirical and psychometric tradition. Also, the work dispelled negative myths and traditions regarding the gifted. For example, Terman and his colleagues showed that gifted children were physically superior and psychologically and socially more stable than their intellectually average peers. The studies indicated that giftedness was a "positive" and derailed any initial concerns of a psychological nature. I say *derailed* because the findings seemed to provide evidence that concern for social/psychological needs was not well founded. I also say *derailed* because the Terman sample has been shown to be nonrepresentative of giftedness and of the wider population of gifted youngsters.

Terman's sample was identified by use of the Stanford-Binet intelligence test, and his sample was nearly exclusively white and middle-class youngsters. The original group recommended for the Stanford-Binet testing was picked by teachers, and so some teacher biases probably entered even before the standardized testing. Further, although Terman erased a number of myths, he created others, most notably the myth that gifted children are uniformly well adjusted and therefore do not need counseling services. Thus, counselors and those in related professions were not an integral part of gifted education during its early development (Kerr, 1986; Webb, Meckstroth, & Tolan, 1982).

Leta Hollingworth (1926, 1942) was the first to contribute evidence indicating that gifted children do have social and emotional needs meriting attention. Hollingworth also emphasized strongly that the regular school environment did not meet the educational needs of the gifted. Rather, she wrote that the school environment was more likely to lead to apathy with these youngsters. She anticipated some of the emotional difficulties and peer problems that receive attention today. Especially, noting that there is often a gap between a gifted student's intellectual and emotional development, she stated, "To have the intellect of an adult and the emotions of a child combined in a childish body is to encounter certain difficulties" (Hollingworth, 1942, p. 282).

The 1950s witnessed some major attention to counseling gifted students and the establishment of research and guidance programs. John Rothney, a counselor educator, founded the Wisconsin Guidance Laboratory for Superior Students (University of Wisconsin–Madison), which was headed by Rothney and later by Marshall Sanborn. The Guidance Laboratory, later renamed the Guidance Institute for Talented Students (GIFTS), was headed by Charles Pulvino, followed by Nicholas Colangelo and then by Philip Perrone (Colangelo & Zaffrann, 1979).

John Curtis Gowan was a major force from the 1950s to 1970s in promoting counseling services for the gifted. The 1960s and 1970s also witnessed increased sensitivity to issues dealing with gifted women, minorities, and disadvantaged students, including counseling needs.

The 1980s saw the establishment of the Supporting the Emotional Needs of Gifted (SENG) program by James T. Webb at Wright State University after the suicide of Dallas Egbert, a highly gifted 17-year-old. SENG has continued its focus on addressing the counseling and psychological needs of gifted students. James Delisle at Kent State University expanded on the concepts of depression and suicide among the gifted (e.g., Delisle, 1992).

In 1982 Barbara Kerr established the Guidance Laboratory for Gifted and Talented at the University of Nebraska–Lincoln, to extend the work of both GIFTS and SENG (Myers & Pace, 1986). Linda Silverman, a psychologist, established the Gifted Child Development Center at Denver, Colorado. In 1988, The University of Iowa established the comprehensive Connie Belin National Center for Gifted Education (renamed the Connie Belin & Jacqueline N. Blank International Center for Gifted Education and Talent Development in 1995) with Nicholas Colangelo as director. The Belin-Blank Center has a strong focus on personal counseling, career guidance, family counseling, and psychological assessment. The clinical programs at the Belin-Blank Center are headed by Susan Assouline, associate director and school psychologist.

Since the publication of the first edition of this *Handbook* (Colangelo & Davis, 1991), a growing aspect of counseling has been family counseling and family therapy. One example is the development of a family counseling program at the Belin-Blank Center. This counseling program is based on brief, solution-focused therapy. Typically, families are seen for a maximum of five sessions, with a strong emphasis on providing the family with problem-solving skills. At the Belin-Blank Center, we have found that families of gifted students have a number of strengths that can be channeled to correcting difficulties. The counseling staff helps families use their own strengths in new and effective ways.

In my chapter on counseling in the first edition, I anticipated that counseling and psychological issues would become one of the distinguishing features in the education of gifted children. Several events have taken place since the first edition that highlight the growing importance of counseling gifted students. These include:

1. The publication of several texts focusing on counseling and related issues—for example, *The Handbook for Counseling the Gifted and Talented* (Kerr, 1991), *Guiding the Social and Emotional Development of Gifted Youth* (Delisle, 1992), and *Counseling the Gifted and Talented* (Silverman, 1993).
2. The increasing attention to qualitative research and its application to research with gifted children (see review by Asher & Moon, 1993). Qualitative research methodology consists of observation analysis, case studies, conversational analysis, and naturalistic inquiry. These methods are particularly well suited for research on social and emotional issues. Thus, there will likely be increased research in the affective domain of gifted youngsters.
3. The 1994 Clinton administration added two goals to the original six of Goals 2000, which is the federal government's main agenda for the nation's education for the remainder of the 1990s. Of relevance is Goal 8: "By the year 2000, every school will promote partnerships that will increase parental involvement and participation in the social, emotional and academic growth of children" (McKernan, 1994, p. 11). This goal lies explicitly in the realm of counseling and psychological issues, and I anticipate that this general thrust in education will have specific crossover to the counseling and psychological development of gifted students.

In the remaining six sections of this chapter I will discuss counseling issues and strategies under these six headings: self-concept, group counseling, counseling with families, parent–school interactions, underachievement, and school counseling programs for gifted students.

Self-Concept

The self-concept construct has deep historical roots in psychology and education. The self-concept can be viewed as a "powerful system of cognitive structures that is quite likely to mediate interpretation of and response to events and behaviors directed at or involving the individual" (Nurius, 1986, p. 435). The definition of self-concept has evolved from a "collection of self-views" (e.g., Rogers, 1951; Snygg & Combs, 1949) to general good and bad feelings about oneself (McGuire, 1984; Shavelson, Hubner, & Stanton, 1976) to recent theory and research on operationally defining the structures and contents of the self-concept (Colangelo & Assouline, 1995; Marsh, 1990; Nurius, 1986).

Self-concept of gifted youngsters has received considerable attention this past decade. These studies typically have investigated (1) how gifted and average children's self-concepts compare (Hoge & Renzulli, 1993; Karnes & Wherry, 1981; Kelly & Colangelo, 1984; Loeb & Jay, 1987); (2) whether self-concept is a developmental construct (Harter, 1982; Hoge & McSheffrey, 1991; Hoge & Renzulli, 1993; Karnes & Wherry, 1981; Marsh, 1992, 1993); and (3) how programming affects a child's self-concept (Kelly & Colangelo, 1984; Loeb & Jay, 1987; Maddux, Scheiber, & Bass, 1982).

Self-concept and giftedness represent complex constructs, and the study of each is made more difficult by theoretical controversies within each field. For example, the developmental nature and processes of self-concept have been debated (Harter, 1982; Karnes & Wherry, 1981; Ketcham & Snyder, 1977). Additionally, there are concerns about the reliability and validity of measures of self-concept (Marsh, 1990, 1994; Wylie, 1989). In the area of gifted education, the question of unidimensionality versus multidimensionality has also permeated almost every aspect of the field.

Closely related to self-concept is the attitude that gifted students have toward their own giftedness. Three books—*On Being Gifted* (American Association for Gifted Children, 1978), *Gifted Children Speak Out* (Delisle, 1984), and *Gifted Kids Speak Out* (Delisle, 1987)—present testimonials from gifted children describing the impact of giftedness on their lives. One conclusion that can be drawn from these testimonials is that these children have mixed feelings about their giftedness. Research has provided some confirmation of this ambivalence. Colangelo and Kelly (1983) found that while gifted youngsters were positive about being labeled gifted, they perceived nongifted peers and teachers as having negative views of them. A study by Kerr, Colangelo, and Gaeth (1988) indicated that the attitude of gifted adolescents toward their own giftedness was multifaceted. Adolescents reported that being gifted was a positive in terms of their own personal growth and in terms of academics. In terms of social peer relations, however, they reported it to be a negative. In a partial replication of Kerr and colleagues' study, Monaster, Chan, Walt, and Wiehe (1994) supported the finding that attitudes toward giftedness are multifaceted. In addition, Monaster and colleagues found that those who knew the gifted child well had positive attitudes toward the child, and that attitudes became more negative toward "giftedness" as respondents were removed from personal knowledge of a gifted youngster.

The Kerr et al. and Monaster et al. findings are very relevant for school counselors because the issues focus on human interaction. In individual counseling sessions, counselors can discuss issues such as: What does it mean to be gifted? What do I like about being gifted? What do I not like about being gifted? If I were not gifted, what would be better for me? If I were not gifted, what would be worse for me?

Group Counseling

It is my observation that gifted students are considerably smarter about course work than about themselves. They have the ability to be insightful about themselves, but seldom the opportunity to articulate and share their insights.

I can offer no more powerful tool for the social and emotional growth of gifted students than group counseling. Group counseling is a rich arena that affords students a rare opportunity to share with one another their struggles and questions about growing up and what it means to be "gifted."

But, simply sitting around talking about feelings and values is not enough. Group counseling is a structured situation with a trained leader (e.g., a school counselor) who has knowledge of both gifted youngsters and group dynamics.

Why Group Counseling for Gifted Students?

All students grow by having opportunities to discuss feelings and perceptions in an atmosphere of trust and understanding. Also, students need to share with peers. To think of *peers* as one's age-mates trivializes the concept. A peer is more a soul-mate than an age-mate—someone who understands what you mean, has experienced what you are talking about, and can respond to you. Gifted students seldom have the opportunity to talk to one another about what it means to be gifted or how it feels to understand things that many age-mates cannot seem to grasp. These are subjects that educators do not encourage for discussion, and gifted students are bright enough to know it's best to keep such things to oneself.

Grouping gifted students for the sole purpose of helping them discuss, in a safe and open atmosphere, issues of a more personal and social nature gives them an opportunity to enjoy and grow from their peers. Most of the time gifted students "hide" who they are (Colangelo, 1991). Group counseling is a situation in which they are encouraged to share themselves—with others who understand and accept. I would guess that if gifted students were given a chance to meet as a small group for the purpose of self-discovery, for most of them this would be the first opportunity they ever had to share with true "peers." If a rationale is needed for group counseling with gifted students, it is that in the course of school life, such a situation will not arise naturally.

Topics for Group Counseling

A counselor may wonder what topics are useful or of interest to a group of gifted students meeting for group counseling sessions. These students will not find it difficult to generate discussion. In my own experience with groups, the challenge is in ending the discussions rather than in starting them.

A counselor needs to set the atmosphere for a group. He or she must be clear on the purpose, rules, and norms. The overall purpose is for gifted students to be able to talk about themselves and learn about one another in an atmosphere of safety and respect.

The following are some stems that a counselor may use in generating discussions:

1. What does it mean to be gifted?

I have found exciting and varied discussions generated by such a question. Students will see it in different ways. Questions that help elaborate this topic are:

1a. What do your parents think it means to be gifted?

1b. What do your teachers think it means to be gifted?

1c. What do other kids in school think it means?

2. How is being gifted an advantage for you? How is it a disadvantage?

3. Have you ever deliberately hidden your giftedness? If so, how?

Colangelo (1991) reported on group discussions with gifted students in which they talked about "deliberate underachievement"—purposely getting lower grades so that their friends would be more accepting of them. Many gifted students will be able to articulate how they make decisions to avoid demonstrating their giftedness.

4. How is your participation in this group different from your regular school day?

Colangelo (1991) also reported that students in groups talked about how "Finally, I can be myself" or "I can say what's on my mind without someone making fun of me or saying I'm a snob."

5. What is different about being gifted and being a girl? Boy? Black, Hispanic, white, etc.?

In studies reported by Colangelo and Kerr (1990) and Kerr and Colangelo (1988), it is obvious that gender and ethnicity are important variables related to giftedness. A variation of questions I have found useful are: Would you rather be a gifted boy or a gifted girl? How would it be better or worse? You can ask this same question in terms of ethnicity. Students will find it stimulating to discuss such issues. Also, they will achieve much better insight into gender and ethnic issues.

6. Is there a time in school (elementary, middle, high school) when it is easiest to be gifted? Most difficult? Why?

The foregoing questions are by no means exhaustive and they will lead to other related questions and directions.

Dynamics and Techniques

One of my primary teaching responsibilities over the past several years has been training and supervising counselors in group counseling. I have found that many counselors have been trained to use their individual counseling skills in a group setting and call this group counseling. Group counseling is quite distinct from individual counseling, although they are not mutually exclusive. And although many of the skills one learns in doing one-on-one counseling are useful and applicable to group counseling, such skills are not the essence of group counseling. To rely only on individual skills in a group setting is to make inadequate use of group dynamics.

The essence of group counseling is to transform students from *spectators* to *participants.* Although there is evidence of the positive effects of being a spectator in a group, its value pales compared to the value of being a participant (Yalom, 1985). To be a spectator means to observe and listen, but to be only tangentially associated with the topic of discussion. A group is not effective when the primary role of its members is that of spectator.

A counselor can transform spectators into participants by taking opportunities to make any topic of discussion a connector to each group member. Following is a specific example using the concepts of *vertical* and *horizontal* self-disclosures.

Let's say a student is talking about her feelings about having been labeled *gifted.* The counselor could ask her questions to help her elaborate on these feelings: "How long have you felt this way?" "Is it changing at all for you?" "Who knows that you feel this way?" All of these are good questions that help the student talk more about her feelings. These questions lead to what can be called *vertical* self-disclosure (Yalom, 1985) because they help "build" more information on how the student feels about labeling. As we build this mound of information, the rest of the students in the group are listening (perhaps nodding in agreement), being empathic, and so on. Their role is primarily that of spectators (albeit sympathetic and interested ones) in that they are observing this interaction between the one student and the counselor.

Using the same incident, the counselor could transform the group members from spectators to participants by moving from vertical to *horizontal* self-disclosure. Instead of asking for more information on the feelings about labeling, the counselor asks the student, "Who in this group do you think feels the same way you do?" or "Who in this group do you think feels most different from you about labeling?" These types of questions are *horizontal* in that they connect students to one another (Yalom, 1985). The students in the group are no longer simply spectators, listening to one girl talk about labeling. Instead, they are actively involved in their own feelings and perceptions about labeling participants.

In every group there will be countless opportunities to take what a student says and make *horizontal* connections. Every *horizontal* connection makes better use of group dynamics and generates more energy and participation.

The second technique I want to share is not so much focused on transforming spectators to participants as it is on helping students to pay better attention to the processes in their group. At the end of every group session, the counselor can ask one student to "process for the group." What this means is to take the last three to five minutes of the session to articulate to everyone what he or she thought happened in the group. This group process time is an opportunity to share how the group went about its task for the session. This simple technique accomplishes several important tasks. First, over time, it gives each student a chance to share what he or she "saw" happening in group. It also offers other students a chance to hear the perspective of one member on what happened during a session. To paraphrase T. S. Eliot, you can have the experience but miss the meaning. This technique minimizes the possibility of missing the meaning. Second, ending every session with group process time is a good way to summarize and tie up the session. Third, the group process time can often be an excellent stem for the start of the next group session. For instance, it is not uncommon in groups I have led to have a student start a session with, "When Bob did group process last week, he said some things that I saw very differently. I want to talk about how I saw them . . ." The group session is off and running.

Group counseling is an effective means of helping gifted students in their social and emotional growth. It is rare that gifted students ever have the opportunities for grouping when the primary purpose is personal growth rather than academics. Group counseling is most vibrant when members are *transformed* from spectators to participants. For a more extensive treatment of group counseling with the gifted, see Colangelo and Peterson (1993).

Counseling with Families

The family has been recognized as a primary and critical component in the development of talent and the success of children in school. Bloom's (1985; Bloom & Sosniak, 1981) seminal work on talent development made a compelling case for the demands on, as well as the influences of, the family on the development of talent (see Chapter 17 by Sosniak). Although research and writings on families of gifted students have increased in the last two decades (see review by Colangelo & Assouline, 1993), counseling with families is still an area of exceptional need and challenge.

In the special anniversary issue of *Roeper Review,* I emphasized that one of the most significant trends in gifted education over the next ten years would be a focus on families (Colangelo, 1988). Although there has been an increase in counseling families, counselors and therapists who work with families of gifted children rarely have expertise in the area of gifted (Wendorf & Frey, 1985). Their expertise is in family counseling.

Sibling Relationships and the Label "Gifted"

School counselors should anticipate difficulties in families when a child is first labeled *gifted.* It is at this time that the family needs assistance. First, school counselors need to be certain that parents clearly understand why their child has been identified as gifted. Many counselors hold parent discussion groups to clarify this issue. Second, counselors should help families anticipate changes as they attempt to adjust to the label. For siblings, the *gifted* label throws into question their role and their importance in the family.

Cornell and Grossberg (1986) found that in families with labeled gifted children, the nonlabeled children are more prone to personality adjustment problems. Grenier (1985) reported increased competition and diminished cooperation by nonlabeled siblings (see review by Jenkins-Friedman, 1992).

The good news is that the family will become accustomed to the label and positive adjustments are likely over time. Colangelo and Brower (1987) reported that, after a while, the negative effects of labeling disappear. Counselors can effectively ease the initial strain and disruption by helping the family communicate openly about the gifted label.

Also, families simply alerted to likely changes seem better able to take some strain and disruption in stride and thus appear to adjust even more quickly.

Giftedness as a Family Organizer

In working with families of gifted children, it is fair to ask, "To what extent is any issue simply what all families must confront, and to what extent is this issue unique because of the presence of a gifted child?" Giftedness in many families becomes an "organizer"—that is, a rationale for understanding behavior and actions (see Jenkins-Friedman, 1992). In some families, behaviors are tolerated because the parents perceive that "this is how it is with a gifted child" or not tolerated because "such behavior should not come from a gifted child." The giftedness of a child can structure how parents relate to him or her as well as to siblings. Many families feel they must put greater energy and resources into the development of a gifted child's talents. Negatives from such organizers can occur when a family loses "balance" with regard to the needs of other children. As in any case of exceptionality (e.g., a handicapped child), the "specialness" can organize the energy and resources of a family, at times to the detriment of other aspects of the family.

A Family Counseling Program

At the Connie Belin & Jacqueline N. Blank International Center for Gifted Education and Talent Development, we have established a family counseling program to respond to the needs of families with a gifted child. The counseling lasts a maximum of five to six sessions per family. The focus is on helping the family develop its own strengths in the resolution of issues. Families receive services at no cost, and in return for these services they participate in research related to family counseling.

We have found that although a child's "giftedness" may be the stated reason for seeking counseling, there often are other issues within these families that have been subsumed under giftedness (e.g., marital discord, alcoholism, delinquency).

Parent–School Interactions

One of the most important issues confronting counselors is the parent–school relationship (Colangelo & Dettmann, 1983, 1985; Dettmann & Colangelo, 1980). The underlying issue regarding this relationship is the role the school should take in providing special educational opportunities for gifted students. Colangelo and Dettmann (1982) developed a counseling model conceptualizing four types of parent-school interactions involving gifted students (Figure 29.1).

Type I (cooperation) is an interaction based on the attitude by both parents and schools that the school should be active in gifted education. The tendency here is for open sharing of information about the child and cooperation between parents and schools. Typically, the gifted are identified and given special educational opportunities commensurate with their needs. The underlying assumption by both parents and schools is that the most effective way to develop exceptional ability is through overt special educational considerations (e.g., honors classes, advanced classes, resource rooms, independent projects, ability groupings, and grade skipping).

Type II (conflict) is an interaction based on conflicting attitudes by (active) parents and a (passive) school regarding the role of the school. Parents believe that their gifted child needs special programming by the school in order to develop his or her abilities. However, the school believes that the typical school curriculum is adequate to meet the needs of all youngsters, including the gifted. Also, it is typical for the school to believe that special programs should be a priority for students with disabilities. The school in this situation feels that parents are pushy and demand unnecessary attention for gifted youngsters. The parents feel they must be aggressive, or the school will ignore the needs of their child.

Type II interactions often are the most difficult for parents and school. These schools

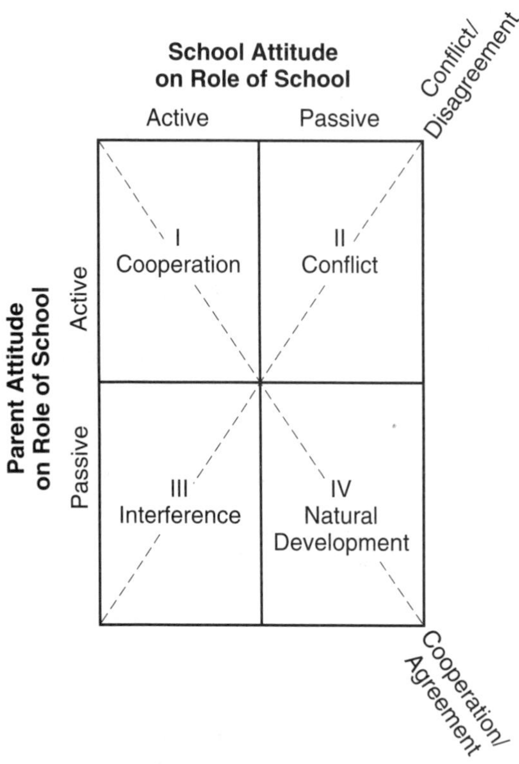

Source: Reprinted by permission of the authors and publisher from N. Colagnelo and D. F. Dettmann (1982), "A Conceptual Model of Four Types of Parent–School Interactions," *Journal for the Education of the Gifted,* Vol. 5, pp. 120–126, Figure 1.

Figure 29.1 Interaction model depicting attitudes of parents and schools regarding the role of the school in gifted education.

tend to view gifted education as an albatross. Parents tend not to support the school and often blame the school for problems their child may have with boredom or lack of motivation and achievement. Parents sometimes encourage the child not to accept the school's evaluations and requirements (e.g., report card grades, classwork) as accurate assessments of his or her abilities.

I have found that parents usually take one of three approaches in this Type II conflict. One is that they continually fight the school. They may either demand meetings for further discussion or join forces with other parents to assert their position. In the second approach, parents take it upon themselves to provide the special programs needed by a child. These may include summer enrichment activities, museum trips, college courses, tutors, mentors, and sometimes even private schools. Obviously, this approach is limited by the educational background and financial resources of the parents. The third approach occurs when parents feel hopeless. They believe that they can have no real effect and that all they can do is complain. For many parents, the end result is a withdrawal from direct communication with the school.

Type III (interference) interactions are also based on conflict, but with a reversal of the dynamics found in Type II. In Type III the school actively wants to provide for the gifted child, but the parents do not agree. Parents are unsure if special programs for the gifted are helpful or necessary. They are concerned about what effect identification and labeling may have on their (gifted) child as well as on siblings who may not be identified. Parents may be concerned that special recognition will damage their child's peer relationships. Parents also may view identification and special programs as an interference in the normal educational development of their child. Meanwhile, the school believes that the child *does* need special consideration and is willing to provide it. Of course, the school is often frustrated by the parents' refusal to let their child participate in the school's special program.

Type IV (natural development) interactions are based on agreement by both parents and schools that the role of the school should be passive. This belief is founded on the premise that high ability will take care of itself ("cream rises to the top") and that very little can be done meaningfully to nourish extraordinary ability. Essentially, both parents and schools view the typical school curriculum and extracurricular activities as providing enough challenge and variety to stimulate the development of high potential and ability. In Type IV interactions, parents and schools recognize and support the youngster's efforts but believe that the natural development of talent will take its course, if the talent is truly there.

Implications of Parent–School Interactions

The model in Figure 29.1 accounts for both *process* and *outcome.* The process relates to the nature of the interactions—that is, cooperative or conflictual. The outcome relates to the four possible types of content and results of the interactions when parents and school communicate about the school's role in gifted education.

The model can be used as a diagnostic instrument for helping both parents and school staff understand their interactions. The model also provides counselors with a framework for understanding their interactions with parents and other school staff—thus gaining insight into *how* they will deal with issues regarding programming for gifted children. Counselors can use this mode not only to determine the type of interaction that *exists* between the school and parents, but also to assess what type of interaction would be *preferred.*

Underachievement

Perhaps the most intense counseling focus has been on the underachieving gifted student. In the Family Counseling Program at the Connie Belin & Jacqueline N. Blank International Center for Gifted Education and Talent Development, underachievement has been the number one presenting problem. The issue of underachievment is confusing because of disagreement about its definition and the inconsistency of results from interventions (Dowdall & Colangelo, 1982; Whitmore, 1980).[1]

Underachievement is seen as a discrepancy between assessed potential and actual performance. The discrepancy may be between two standardized measures (e.g., IQ and achievement tests), between a standardized measure and performance (e.g., IQ and grades), or two nonstandardized measures (e.g., teacher expectation and performance on daily assignments). To a school counselor, the discrepancy between scores is not as critical as the interpersonal dynamics involved in underachievement. Rather than looking at it as a psychometric event, I see it as a relationship between the gifted student and teachers, parent(s), and sometimes peers.

I have found that for some gifted students underachievement is a way to express either a need for attention or a need for control over a situation. Underachieving brings considerable attention from both teachers and parents, in extreme cases almost doting behavior. Adults are so concerned that the gifted youngster will not make good use of his or her gifts that they give a great deal of energy and time to him or her.

Counselors often can break the attention-getting cycle by having parents and teachers avoid responding too strongly to the underachieving behavior, or even ignore it. They can give attention when the child achieves well

[1] For a more comprehensive treatment of underachievement, see Chapter 34 by Rimm.

and minimize attention when the child is not achieving. The equation is simple. If the child wants attention, he or she will soon learn that the attention is forthcoming only when certain achieving behaviors (and attitudes) are present. The child will want to do more of these kinds of behaviors because the reward is the attention.

A gifted youngster who uses underachievement as a means to gain control of a situation offers a more difficult challenge. For such youngsters, poor achievement is a way to show teachers and parents that they (the students) can do what they want. A typical reaction by teachers and parents to this kind of defiance is to attempt to force the student to do the task and do it at levels comparable to expectations. This situation can lead to a vicious and nonproductive cycle.

The counselor can work with teachers and parents to help them quit the fight. It is likely the student will diminish the fight relationship if there is no one to fight with. Minimizing the power struggle will allow more opportunity for the student to perform because he or she is more free to do so.

Again, I am a strong proponent of group counseling to help gifted students better understand their behaviors and motives and learn new patterns of interactions. It is in the rich atmosphere of a group of peers with a trained leader (school counselor) that a gifted youngster can explore motives and consequences of underachieving behavior.

Finally, it is important for the school counselor to use school records as a source of information in understanding gifted underachievers, especially at the secondary level. In a comprehensive study of 153 gifted underachievers, grades 7–12, Peterson and Colangelo (1996) found data on attendance, tardiness, course selection, and course grades, by gender and by age, that provided differential patterns that distinguished gifted students who achieved from those who underachieved. Peterson and Colangelo reported that patterns of underachievement established in junior high school, though not impossible to alter in high school, do tend to persist through high school. The school records are ubiquitous in schools and are a good resource for counselors.

School Counseling Programs for Gifted Students

There are two ways to envision a school counseling program for gifted students: as *remedial* or as *developmental*. In the remedial approach, the emphasis is on problem solving and crisis intervention. In this approach, the counselor is primarily a "therapy expert" who intervenes in problem situations either to help solve the problem or to minimize the difficulty. The counselor is involved in staffing, referrals, and one-on-one counseling. Where there is group counseling, the students are selected because they share a common problem (e.g., underachievement, behavior problems), and the purpose is to correct the problem.

In the developmental approach, the counselor does use his or her expertise to serve a therapy function and is available for problem solving, but these functions are not primary. The real work of the developmentally oriented counselor is to establish an environment in school that is conducive to the educational growth of gifted students. Such an approach is predicated on knowledge of both affective and cognitive needs of gifted youngsters.

The focus of individual counseling is to get to know students and help them better understand their own strengths and weaknesses as decision makers and formulators of their lives. Group counseling focuses on sharing perceptions and learning more effective interpersonal skills. Group members do not necessarily have a common problem to resolve. Work with families is based not on a problem with their child, but on the recognition that gifted children pose unique challenges to parents. Family work is based more on discussion groups with parents in which the parents share information and connect with other families.

I strongly advocate a developmental approach to counseling with gifted students. Giftedness is not a problem to be solved but a unique challenge to be nourished. Also, a developmental approach does not depend on research evidence that gifted youngsters are "at risk." In a therapy model, such evidence would be necessary to justify having a counselor with expertise in working with the gifted.

A developmental counseling program requires the following components:

1. An articulated and coherent rationale
2. A program of activities based on the affective and cognitive needs of youngsters
3. Trained counselors who are well grounded not only in counseling but also in giftedness
4. A minimum of attention to rehabilitative (therapy) services, but a strong component of individual, family, and teacher consultations
5. Input and participation from teachers, administrators, parents, and the youngsters who are served
6. A component for the continued professional development of the counselor so that he or she may keep pace with the latest research and practices on the counseling needs of gifted youngsters

Summary

Although concern for the counseling needs of gifted students can be traced back to Leta Hollingworth's work of nearly seventy years ago, the emergence of counseling as a major force in the education of the gifted and talented is a phenomenon of the last fifteen years. Since the first edition of the *Handbook* (Colangelo & Davis, 1991) several factors have strengthened the focus on counseling for the gifted:

1. Publications focusing on counseling the gifted
2. A continuing appreciation for qualitative research approaches that lend themselves to studies focusing on affective issues
3. The inclusion of social and emotional issues in *Goals 2000*

Individual, group, and family counseling are predicated on the assumptions and evidence that youngsters with exceptional ability and talents also have unique social and emotional needs. These unique needs exist and interact in the successful or unsuccessful development of talent. Counseling is a necessary component in the successful development of talent. For counselors to be successful, they need knowledge and expertise both in counseling and in giftedness. A developmental counseling program in a school will foster both the cognitive and the affective growth of gifted youngsters.

REFERENCES

American Association for Gifted Children. (1978). *On being gifted.* New York: Walker & Company.

Asher, J. W., & Moon, S. M. (1993). Quantitative and qualitative guidelines for research in gifted education. *Quest, 4,* 7–10.

Bloom, B. S. (Ed.). (1985). *Developing talent in young people.* New York: Ballantine Books.

Bloom, B. S., & Sosniak, L. A. (1981). Talent development vs. schooling. *Educational Leadership, 39,* 86–94.

Burks, B. S., Jensen, D. W., & Terman, L. M. (1930). *Genetic studies of genius: Vol. 3. The promise of youth.* Stanford, CA: Stanford University Press.

Colangelo, N. (1988). Families of gifted children: The next ten years. *Roeper Review, 11,* 16–18.

Colangelo, N. (1991). Counseling gifted students. In N. Colangelo & G. A. Davis (Eds.), *Handbook of gifted education* (pp. 273–284). Boston: Allyn and Bacon.

Colangelo, N., & Assouline, S. G. (1993). Families of gifted children: A research agenda. *Quest, 4,* 1–4.

Colangelo, N., & Assouline, S. G. (1995). Self-concept of gifted students: Patterns by self-concept, domain, grade level, and gender. In F. Monks (Ed.), *Proceedings from the 1994 European council on high ability conference* (pp. 66–74). New York: Wiley.

Colangelo, N., & Brower, P. (1987). Labeling gifted youngsters: Long-term impact on families. *Gifted Child Quarterly, 31,* 75–78.

Colangelo, N., & Davis, G. A. (Eds.). (1991). *Handbook of gifted education.* Boston: Allyn and Bacon.

Colangelo, N., & Dettmann, D. F. (1982). A conceptual model of four types of parent-school interactions. *Journal for the Education of the Gifted, 5,* 120–126.

Colangelo, N., & Dettmann, D. F. (1983). A review of research on parents and families of gifted children. *Exceptional Children, 50,* 20–27.

Colangelo, N., & Dettmann, D. F. (1985). Families of gifted children. In S. Ehly, J. Conoly, & D. M. Rosenthal (Eds.), *Working with parents of exceptional children* (pp. 233–255). St. Louis: C. V. Mosby.

Colangelo, N., & Kelly, K. R. (1983). A study of student, parent, and teacher attitude towards gifted programs and gifted students. *Gifted Child Quarterly, 27,* 107–110.

Colangelo, N., & Kerr, B. (1990). Extreme academic talent: Profiles of perfect scorers. *Journal of Educational Psychology, 82,* 404–409.

Colangelo, N., & Peterson, J. S. (1993). Group counseling with gifted students. In L. S. Silverman (Ed.), *Counseling the gifted and talented* (pp. 111–129). Denver: Love.

Colangelo, N., & Zaffrann, R. T. (Eds.). (1979). *New voices in counseling the gifted.* Dubuque, IA: Kendall Hunt.

Cornell, D. G., & Grossberg, I. W. (1986). Siblings of children in gifted programs. *Journal for the Education of the Gifted, 9,* 252–264.

Delisle, J. R. (1984). *Gifted children speak out.* New York: Walker.

Delisle, J. R. (1987). *Gifted kids speak out.* Minneapolis: Free Spirit.

Delisle, J. R. (1992). *Guiding the social and emotional development of gifted youth.* New York: Longman.

Dettmann, D. F., & Colangelo, N. (1980). A functional model for counseling parents of gifted students. *Gifted Child Quarterly, 24,* 139–147.

Dowdall, C. B., & Colangelo, N. (1982). Underachieving gifted students: Review and implications. *Gifted Child Quarterly, 26,* 179–184.

Grenier, M. E. (1985). Gifted children and other siblings. *Gifted Child Quarterly, 29,* 164–167.

Harter, S. (1982). The perceived competence scale for children. *Child Development, 53,* 87–97.

Hoge, R. D., & McSheffrey, R. (1991, December–January). An investigation of self-concept in gifted children. *Exceptional Children,* pp. 238–245.

Hoge, R. D., & Renzulli, J. S. (1993). Exploring the link between giftedness and self-concept. *Review of Educational Research, 63,* 449–465.

Hollingworth, L. S. (1926). *Gifted children: Their nature and nurture.* New York: Macmillan.

Hollingworth, L. S. (1942). *Children above 180 IQ.* New York: World Book.

Jenkins-Friedman, R. (1992). Families of gifted children and youth. In M. J. Fine & C. Carlson (Eds.), *The handbook of family school interventions: A systems perspective* (pp. 175–187). Boston: Allyn and Bacon.

Karnes, F. A., & Wherry, J. N. (1981). Self-concepts of gifted students as measured by the Piers-Harris children's self-concept scale. *Psychological Reports, 49,* 903–906.

Kelly, K. R., & Colangelo, N. (1984). Academic and social self-concepts of gifted, general, and special students. *Exceptional Children, 50,* 551–554.

Kerr, B. A. (1986). Career counseling for the gifted: Assessments and interventions. *Journal of Counseling and Development, 64,* 602–604.

Kerr, B. (1991). *Handbook for counseling the gifted and talented.* Alexandria, VA: AACD Press.

Kerr, B., & Colangelo, N. (1988). The college plans of academically talented students. *Journal of Counseling and Development, 67,* 42–48.

Kerr, B., Colangelo, N., & Gaeth, J. (1988). Gifted adolescents' attitudes toward their giftedness. *Gifted Child Quarterly, 32,* 245–247.

Ketcham, B., & Snyder, R. T. (1977). Self-attitudes of the intellectually and socially advantaged student: Normative study of the Piers-Harris children's self-concept scale. *Psychological Reports, 40,* 111–116.

Loeb, R. C., & Jay, G. (1987). Self-concept in gifted children: Differential impact in boys and girls. *Gifted Child Quarterly, 1,* 9–14.

Maddux, C. D., Scheiber, L. M., & Bass, J. E. (1982). Self-concept and social distance in gifted children. *Gifted Child Quarterly, 26,* 77–81.

Marsh, H. W. (1990). A multidimensional, hierarchical model of self-concept: Theoretical and empirical justification. *Educational Psychology Review, 2,* 77–172.

Marsh, H. W. (1992). Content specificity of relations between academic achievement and academic self-concept. *Journal of Educational Psychology, 84,* 35–42.

Marsh, H. W. (1993). The multidimensional structure of academic self-concept: Invariance over gender and age. *American Educational Research Journal, 30,* 841–860.

Marsh, H. W. (1994). Using the national longitudinal study of 1988 to evaluate theoretical models of self-concept: The self-description questionnaire. *Journal of Educational Psychology, 86,* 439–456.

McGuire, W. J. (1984). Search for self: Going beyond self-esteem and reactive self. In R. A. Zucher, J. Arnoff, & A. I. Rubin (Eds.), *Personality and the prediction of behavior* (pp. 73–120). New York: Academic Press.

McKernan, J. R. (Chair). (1994). *The national education GOALS report.* Washington, DC: U.S. Government Printing Office.

Monaster, G. J., Chan, J. C., Walt, C., & Wiehe, J. (1994). Gifted adolescents' attitudes toward their giftedness: A partial replication. *Gifted Child Quarterly, 38,* 176–178.

Myers, R. S., & Pace, T. M. (1986). Counseling gifted and talented students: Historical perspectives and contemporary issues. *Journal of Counseling and Development, 64,* 548–551.

Nurius, P. S. (1986). Reappraisal of the self-concept

and implications for counseling. *Journal of Counseling Psychology, 33,* 429–438.

Peterson, J. S., & Colangelo, N. (1996). Gifted achievers and underachievers: A comparison of patterns found in school files. *Journal of Counseling and Development, 74,* 399–407.

Rogers, C. (1951). *Client-centered therapy: Its current practice, implications, and theory.* Boston: Houghton Mifflin.

Shavelson, R. J., Hubner, J. J., & Stanton, G. C. (1976). Validation of construct interpretations. *Review of Educational Research, 46,* 407–441.

Silverman, L. K. (Ed.). (1993). *Counseling the gifted & talented.* Denver: Love.

Snygg, D., & Combs, A. W. (1949). *Individual behaviors: A perceptual approach to behavior* (rev. ed.). New York: Harper.

Terman, L. M. (1925). *Genetic studies of genius* (Vol. 1). *Mental and physical traits of a thousand gifted children.* Stanford, CA: Stanford University Press.

Terman, L. M., & Oden, M. H. (1947). *Genetic studies of genius* (Vol. 4). *The gifted child grows up.* Stanford, CA: Stanford University Press.

Terman, L. M., & Oden, M. H. (1959). *Genetic studies of genius* (Vol. 5). *The gifted group at mid-life.* Stanford, CA: Stanford University Press.

Webb, J. T., Meckstroth, E. A., & Tolan, S. S. (1982). *Guiding the gifted child.* Columbus: Ohio Psychology Press.

Wendorf, D. J., & Frey, J. (1985). Family therapy with intellectually gifted. *American Journal of Family Therapy, 13,* 31–37.

Whitmore, J. (1980). *Giftedness, conflict, and underachievement.* Boston: Allyn and Bacon.

Wylie, R. C. (1989) *Measures of self-concept.* Lincoln: University of Nebraska Press.

Yalom, I. D. (1985). *The theory and practice of group psychotherapy* (3rd ed.). New York: Basic Books.

30

Emotional Giftedness: The Measure of Intrapersonal Intelligence

MICHAEL M. PIECHOWSKI, *Northland College, Ashland, Wisconsin*

In my chapter "Emotional Development and Emotional Giftedness" in the first edition of this handbook, I assumed that emotional development and emotional giftedness were expressions of intrapersonal intelligence. A closer look at Gardner's description of intrapersonal intelligence showed white areas in need of being chartered. The present chapter brings together emotional giftedness, emotional growth, and moral sensitivity with the concepts of developmental potential (overexcitabilities), self-evaluative processes, and inner transformation. A fuller and more comprehensive understanding of intrapersonal intelligence is thus served.

The Concept of Developmental Potential

Emotional sensitivity and emotional intensity are often cited as distinguishing most gifted children, and especially the highly gifted (e.g., Piirto, 1992; Silverman, 1983; Tolan, 1994). These traits account for their vulnerabilities in childhood and their troubles in school (Kurcinka, 1991; Richert, Alvino, & McDonnel, 1982; Roedell, 1984; Vail, 1987). Seeing themselves so different from "normal," they doubt themselves and ask, "What is wrong with me?"; they realize the discrepancy between their feelings and those of others, and to account for the lack of fit they judge themselves to be wanting. In fact, some intellectually precocious youngsters actually look in the catalog of mental disorders to find a label that could apply to them (Tolan, 1987). They are too young, of course, to see that the lack of fit is not evidence of mental disturbance. Alas, even gifted adults are often not free from this fallacy, for such is the power of the pressure to be normal. But not all this pressure comes from the outside.

One of the basic human faculties is the capacity for making comparisons and evaluations. In the personal domain this means self-evaluation—comparing ourselves with others—and responsiveness to how others evaluate us (Bandura, 1986). But this process may be taken a step further, and a very significant step it is—namely, comparing ourselves in the present with what we can become—our potentials, possibilities, and above all, our ideal self.

It is likely that to be emotionally sensitive entails a range and speed of evaluative processes that is greater than average. Combined with great imagination and intellectual power this may lead to brooding and devastating self-criticism. It may turn morbid or neurotic. Or it may mobilize one's whole psyche toward the goal of self-realization in creativity; in service to others; or in a higher, transpersonal consciousness in which the illusion of separateness gradually lifts.

Dabrowski (1967, 1972) studied the mental health of intellectually and artistically gifted youths. Recognizing that creative individuals tend to live more intensely, Dabrowski took the intensity of their emotions, their sensitivity and emotional extremes, as part and parcel of their psychophysical makeup. In their intensified manner of experiencing, feeling, thinking, and imagining, he perceived a potential for further growth. Inner forces were at work that often generated overstimulation, conflict, pain, but also—and this is significant—a search for a way out of it. An escape route may lead to addiction, or to inner growth and transformation.

To Dabrowski the seemingly typical signs of morbidity and neurosis spelled genuine potential for advanced development. Dabrowski's (1937) early study of self-mutilation led him to examine this phenomenon among writers, artists, and other highly creative people and to conclude that self-aggression represents a psychologically higher level than aggression against others. Individuals who experience great inner turmoil, the result of the tension created by the combined forces of several overexcitabilities, may be pushed toward self-mutilation. This happens—Van Gogh cutting off his ear comes to mind—because these individuals find themselves in a climate of misunderstanding and alienation, without emotional support.

Dabrowski's concept of *developmental potential* includes talents, specific abilities, and intelligence, plus five primary components of psychic life: psychomotor, sensual, intellectual, imaginational, and emotional overexcitabilities (see Table 30.1).

To varying degrees, these five dimensions give talent its power (Piechowski, 1979, 1986). They may be thought of as modes of experiencing or as channels through which flow the colors, textures, insights, visions, currents, and energies of experience. These channels can be wide open, narrow, or barely present. Dabrowski called them "forms of psychic overexcitability" to emphasize the intensification of felt experience much beyond the ordinary. Overexcitabilities contribute to the individual's psychological development, and their strength can be taken as a measure of developmental potential. They are easily observed in children, and they stand out loud and clear in gifted children. Kurcinka (1991) had the felicity of calling them *spirited*—"children who are more intense, sensitive, perceptive, persistent, energetic."

It is unfortunate that the stronger these overexcitabilities are, the less peers and teachers welcome them unless they, too, are gifted. Children exhibiting strong overexcitabilities are often made to feel embarrassed and guilty for being "different." Criticized and teased for what they cannot help, they begin to believe there is something wrong with them. Sometimes they learn to disguise their intensity, sometimes they seek refuge in fantastic worlds of their own creation, sometimes they try to "normalize" it and, as a result, suffer depression or ill-defined anxiety. These reactions are the consequences of being forced into denying their own potential.

Intensity and Emotional Sensitivity

The intensity of emotional reactions, especially in children, may sometimes be difficult to understand, especially when they strike seemingly out of the blue, when the child seems terribly upset over "nothing." Parents and teachers must show considerable patience and knowledge of the child to see that this apparent overreaction comes from the child's sensitivity and need for his or her own order of things to be preserved. That children need order and predictable routines is well known. To a sensitive and intense child who may be disequilibrated, often by his own emotions, a departure from routine (for instance, in the way a story is told), may be extremely upsetting because the need for reliable markers of consistency and support is all the greater. Without doubt, the strongest support is the parent's loving patience and acceptance.

To illustrate how emotional intensity and sensitivity are experienced, a few examples taken from written responses of subjects who answered an overexcitability questionnaire are given next. This questionnaire was designed to tap the five dimensions of developmental potential (Lysy & Piechowski, 1983; Piechowski, 1979; Piechowski & Cunningham, 1985; Piechowski, Silverman, & Falk, 1985).

Positive feelings take the form of being "flooded by unexpected waves of joy," feeling "incredibly alive—every cell, muscle, etc., feels stimulated. I have incredible energy then and hardly need any rest," or "Sometimes I can be so happy that I want to laugh and cry or be silent and shout, all at the same time." The beauty in music or nature can move a person to tears. Pain can have a different aspect: "Even the greatest pain that I have felt has been ecstatic and full of life." Just as they are capable of communion with nature, of merging with a painting or a piece of music, a religious or spiritual experience can overtake such people completely.

Intense individuals feel their emotions very strongly; they soar high and plunge into black glooms with sometimes rapid and bewildering

Table 30.1
Forms and Expressions of Psychic Overexcitability

Psychomotor

Surplus of energy:
Rapid speech, marked excitation, intense physical activity (e.g., fast games and sports), pressure for action (e.g., organizing), marked competitiveness
Psychomotor expression of emotional tension:
Compulsive talking and chattering, impulsive actions, nervous habits (tics, nail biting), workaholism, acting out

Sensual

Enhanced sensory and aesthetic pleasure:
Seeing, smelling, tasting, touching, hearing, and sex; delight in beautiful objects, sounds of words, music, form, color, balance
Sensual expression of emotional tension:
Overeating, sexual overindulgence, buying sprees, wanting to be in the limelight

Intellectual

Intensified activity of the mind:
Curiosity, concentration, capacity for sustained intellectual effort, avid reading; keen observation, detailed visual recall, detailed planning
Penchant for probing questions and problem solving:
Search for truth and understanding; forming new concepts; tenacity in problem solving
Reflective thought:
Thinking about thinking, love of theory and analysis, preoccupation with logic, moral thinking, introspection (but without self-judgment), conceptual and intuitive integration; independence of thought (sometimes very critical)

Imaginational

Free play of the imagination:
Frequent use of image and metaphor, facility for invention and fantasy, facility for detailed visualization, poetic and dramatic perception, animistic and magical thinking
Capacity for living in a world of fantasy:
Predilection for magic and fairy tales, creation of private worlds, imaginary companions; dramatization
Spontaneous imagery as an expression of emotional tension:
Animistic imagery, mixing truth and fiction, elaborate dreams, illusions
Low tolerance of boredom

Emotional

Feelings and emotions intensified:
Positive feelings, negative feelings, extremes of emotion, complex emotions and feelings, identification with others' feelings, awareness of a whole range of feelings
Strong somatic expressions:
Tense stomach, sinking heart, blushing, flushing, pounding heart, sweaty palms
Strong affective expressions:
Inhibition (timidity, shyness); enthusiasm, ecstasy, euphoria, pride; strong affective memory; shame; feelings of unreality, fears and anxieties, feelings of guilt, concern with death, depressive and suicidal moods

Table 30.1 *(Continued)*

Capacity for strong attachments, deep relationships
Strong emotional ties and attachments to persons, living things, places; attachments to animals; difficulty adjusting to new environments; compassion, responsiveness to others, sensitivity in relationships; loneliness
Well-differentiated feelings toward the self
Inner dialogue and self-judgment

Source: From R. F. Falk, M. M. Piechowski, & S. Lind, "Criteria for Rating Intensity of Overexcitabilities (Manual)," Unpublished manuscript, Northland College, Ashland, Wisconsin, 1994.

succession. By contrast, individuals lacking in intensity feel their emotions mildly and only with minor fluctuations; their lives lack the complexity and spice of those living at a higher pitch (Sommers, 1981). The degree of emotional intensity is a stable individual characteristic and quite independent of what actually evoked the emotion. Emotional intensity, or its lack in unemotional people, is a characteristic of temperament observable early in life (Larsen & Diener, 1987).

Emotional sensitivity is another matter. Emotionally intense individuals can also be very sensitive to the feelings of others, to others being hurt, to injustice, but also to criticism and pain. If an emotional child grows up with too much criticism and ridicule, the child will begin to seek self-protection in emotional withdrawal and may create an inner shield. The price for such withdrawal and denied feelings is high: loss of emotional vitality, lack of enjoyment of one's successes and achievements, and lack of the sense of who one is, in short, a process of emotional deadening (Miller, 1981, 1983).

The Case for Emotional Giftedness

Annemarie Roeper (1982, p. 24) suggested that the emotionally gifted are persons who have "the capacity to integrate emotions, intellect, and creativity against enormous odds":

> Some gifted children show enormous empathy with others, surpassing at times the compassion of adults who are more limited by society's expectations. As a result, adults may not understand a child's reaction. For example, during a chess tournament, John, the obvious winner, began to make careless mistakes and lost the game. When asked what happened, he replied, *I noticed my opponent had tears in his eyes, I could not concentrate and lost my desire to win.* John's empathy was greater than his ambition. Many adults, especially those who supported John, were disappointed. Yet, one could argue that his reaction was a more mature one than theirs for his self esteem did not depend on winning the competition. (emphasis in the original)

In the film *Searching for Bobby Fisher,* the supercharged competitive drive of the parents, some of whom want a victory at any cost, contrasts sharply with the distinctly more sane behavior of the young competitors. It takes a great deal of fortitude and moral courage to resist the pressure to win and the prospect of a barrage of accusations: "Why did you do that?!" "How *could* you?" In a competitive climate, young John's action made no sense. Yet it is a clear-cut example of what Dabrowski called *positive maladjustment.* Winning the tournament would have been the socially expected and approved act; it would have made John a well-adjusted champion. But this conflicted with his empathy for the opponent. A win at the price of the other boy's tears was—to John—unacceptable. One could say that to John, in face of this, a victory was morally wrong. Doing what is morally right is a positive action. When morally right action conflicts with social expectations and pressures, it is positive maladjustment.

Instances of empathy, unselfishness, and consideration for others are readily found among gifted children. Seymour (1987) described two such boys. The older was accelerated from second to fourth grade. The boy's exceptional intelligence and verbal facility impressed everyone. His brother, a year younger and also highly gifted, was, by contrast, considered "average." His great imagination and sensitivity attracted less attention than his brother's obvious scholastic brilliance. The older boy had a temper and often hit his younger brother who, although in fact he was the larger of the two, did not strike back but would walk away instead; despite his anger and obvious pain, he controlled himself—and he was only seven years old. On a school trip to the zoo this very young boy, unlike his classmates, showed a concentrated interest in every animal. There was a goat he wanted to feed. But when he was given a bag of corn by some visitors, instead of running with it to the goat, he first offered the corn to each of his classmates so that they could have the pleasure of feeding the goat, too. Seymour found attention to others to be a consistent trait in this boy. From responses to her parent questionnaire, Silverman (1983, 1994) collected numerous observations of emotional sensitivity, compassion, and moral sensitivity in gifted children (above 130 IQ) as young as age $2^1/_2$ or 3.

Considerateness, understanding of others, of their feelings, motives, and aspirations characterize what Gardner (1983) called *inter*personal intelligence. Empathic acts—a response to another's distress and a desire to soothe—have been observed in infants (Borke, 1971; Hoffman, 1983). The capacity for empathy and unselfish acts is readily observed in preschoolers (Radke-Yarrow, Zahn-Waxler, & Chapman, 1983). Empathy is the foundation out of which grow the moral emotions (Damon, 1988).

Intrapersonal Intelligence *in Extenso*

Introspective individuals who are keenly and accurately aware of their own emotional life are characterized by *intra*personal intelligence or self-knowledge. Gardner (1983, 1993a, 1993b; see Chapter 5) defined intrapersonal intelligence as introspective capacity. Gardner further noted that through continued development this capacity may culminate in a mature sense of self and inner wisdom. However, there is a gap in this picture. By what developmental process is the mature self realized? What has to take place in a person's development to make gaining advanced self-knowledge and wisdom possible? To fill this gap, we must turn to Dabrowski's theory of emotional development, and particularly to his concept of *multilevel development.* By multilevel, Dabrowski meant the type of inner growth in which a split between the higher and lower in oneself is strongly felt. The split is healed by concerted emotional labors of aligning one's life with the ideal of becoming a better human being.

Originally Gardner (1983, p. 252) included in his formulation of intrapersonal intelligence a "continued development, where an individual has an option of becoming increasingly autonomous, integrated, or self-actualized. . . . The end goal of these developing processes is a self that is highly developed and fully differentiated from others," but subsequently he did not include or develop it further. In multilevel development, the goal is to confront the whole truth about oneself as a prelude to a far-reaching inner transformation. As Eleanor Roosevelt astutely observed, such truth can make you wince. To make Gardner's definition of intrapersonal intelligence full, and in keeping with his original conception, we must include the process of inner growth that leads to profound self-knowledge of the kind that is characteristic of a highly developed sense of self.

Moral Exemplars

Individuals who are guided by compassion, emotional sensitivity, and moral certainty are given the appellation of moral exemplars. Gandhi's life is a classic instance of spiritual growth powered by deep emotions. Gandhi's emotional giftedness lay in his ardent concern to have no blemish on his character (punishment for an infraction caused him the greatest pain by the very fact that he deserved it), his ability to befriend people, his joy in serving others (he tells how he developed a passion for nursing the sick), and his dedication to abolishing any kind of discrimination based on color, caste, religion, nationality, social position, or wealth (Gandhi, 1948/1983). He taught himself to follow the inner voice: "I delighted in submitting to it. To act against it would have been difficult and painful to me" (p. 118). Following it, this very shy and sensitive man was transformed into a radical reformer who championed the rights of those who were denied human rights, who were exploited and in bondage. Although Gardner (1993a) chose him as the epitome of *inter*personal intelligence, it must be recognized that without persevering with utmost honesty and rigor in his self-knowledge and the task of inner transformation, Gandhi could not have become a Mahatma—a Great Soul.

Gandhi's goal was to live a life of truth so that he could find God. When he started his law practice, his goal was to resolve the conflict rather than to win the case for one side only:

> I felt that my duty was to befriend both parties and bring them together. I strained every nerve to bring a compromise. . . . [In the end] both were happy over the result, and both rose in public estimation. My joy was boundless. I had learnt the true practice of law. I had learnt to find out the better side of human nature and to enter men's hearts. I realized that the true function of a lawyer was to unite parties riven asunder. (Gandhi, 1948/1983, p. 117)

As a child and as a man Gandhi was intensely emotional, sensual, exquisitely sensitive (he was extremely shy), endowed with rich imagination, and engaged in relentless intellectual and spiritual inquiry. In other words, his experiential channels—overexcitabilities—were wide open.

In the life of Eleanor Roosevelt we get a close look at the inner workings of emotional giftedness par excellence (Piechowski, 1990; Piechowski & Tyksta, 1982). The driving forces of her life were a sense of duty, a desire for love and to belong, a willingness to be of service, and a determination to develop her individual identity on an equal basis with her powerful husband. She was propelled by compassion toward those in need, whether material, emotional, or to fulfill a personal goal. Because she made sense of the sorrows of her own childhood, she had a thorough understanding of the emotional needs of children and adolescents (Vander Ven, 1984). At the same time her behavior, though outwardly ladylike, was radical and revolutionary.

Guided by humility, compassion, and understanding of human nature, the conscience of such individuals is a reliable guide for acting in accordance with the highest principles of fairness and compassion. From the point of view of giftedness, one is prone to ask: In what way can such a conscience be considered a talent? How did it develop? How was it trained?

Briefly, we find that some do achieve their inner knowledge as a result of guidance and training, exemplified in the spiritual traditions of the East and West. Spiritual directors and masters guide their disciples' inner growth (Nixon, 1994). But there are certain individuals who arrive at self-knowledge by guidance from within. For instance, Brennan and Piechowski (1991) and Grant (1988) described persons who were taught, as it were, by an "inner voice"; their inner growth was guided almost entirely from within.

Inner growth and transformation, as we are beginning to discover, can follow different paths. The moral exemplars described by Colby and Damon (1992) appear to tread the path of increasing moral certainty; those studied by others show growth through inner struggle and self-chosen work at inner transformation (Dabrowski, 1967; Nixon, 1994; Piechowski, 1990, 1992, 1993). Nevertheless, moral exemplars are not entirely free from inner conflict generated by a clash between the unquestioned beliefs they grew up with and the face-to-face encounter with oppression, poverty, social injustice, and denial of basic human rights.

To sum up, the young chess player who chose to lose the championship for the sake of another player, the 7-year-old who refrained from fighting despite his advantage in size and strength, Gandhi's submission to his inner voice, Eleanor Roosevelt's self-knowledge and life of service, are outstanding examples of emotional giftedness or intrapersonal intelligence in its full sense. They are strongly empathic, introspective, self-analytical, and self-corrective; they possess emotional intensity, depth, and devotion. And they are "positively maladjusted" as well!

Dabrowski's Theory and Bandura's Self-System: Self-Knowledge and Self-Evaluation Conjoined

The examination of the nature of this process of inner transformation is the core of Dabrowski's theory of emotional development which he called "positive disintegration" (Dabrowski, 1964, 1967; Dabrowski & Piechowski, 1977). By this paradoxical name he emphasized the dismantling and tearing down that takes place in one's inner being once the process of emotional growth is launched in earnest. What is experienced as "lower" gradually is removed and replaced by what is "higher." Self-evaluation and self-judgment play a strong part. Since the process is usually experienced as a movement from a lower to a higher level, it has been called "multilevel." The split between higher and lower in oneself takes many forms but is distinctly and spontaneously experienced by emotionally gifted people. [The theory is too elaborate and too broad to attempt a sketch here, but serviceable outlines exist (Nelson, 1989; Piechowski, 1975, 1992).]

Emotional giftedness grows out of emotional overexcitability when there is a will to change oneself and to help others, whether materially, emotionally, or in the realization of their potential. Naturally, intellectual and imaginational overexcitabilities play a strong role. The examples of Mohandas Gandhi and Eleanor Roosevelt underscore the link between robust emotionality and finding one's mission in life by serving others. Dabrowski's theory is very much about this quest that comes from a deep longing for an ideal of love, an ideal of brotherhood, an ideal of beauty, an ideal of caring, an ideal of humility, an ideal of truth, or all such ideals. It is a call to a higher, more deeply meaningful life.

Children who advance in development more rapidly than their peers, especially emotionally and intellectually, feel this call early but often find themselves misunderstood. Clark (1983, p. 126) noted that an intense sense of justice and unwavering idealism appear early in the emotional growth of gifted children and that it is hard for them to understand why adults are not doing anything to correct what is so blatantly wrong and unfair in the world. Such children have trouble adjusting to a world where everything appears to stand on its head; it makes them "positively maladjusted."

This presents the practical problem of how to coach gifted children when they show signs of positive maladjustment. Delisle and Galbraith (1987) offer survival strategies. Specialists in conflict resolution teach win–win strategies (Fisher & Ury, 1981).

Silverman (1994) reports that in the extensive files of the Gifted Development Center there are

> dozens of cases on record of gifted children fighting injustice, befriending and protecting handicapped children, conserving resources, responding to others' emotional needs, becoming terribly upset if a classmate is humiliated, becoming vegeterian in meat-eating families, crying at the violence in cartoons, being perplexed at why their classmates push in line, refusing to fight back when attacked because they considered all forms of violence—including self-defense—morally wrong, writing letters to the President to try to end the Gulf War, and writing poems of anguish at the cruelty in the world. I have found that the higher the child's IQ, the earlier moral concerns develop and the more profound effect they have on the child. But it usually takes maturity before the child can translate moral sensitivity into consistent moral action. (p.111)

The association of high IQ with moral sensitivity, moral character, and early ethical concerns was already noted by both Terman and Hollingworth. Although it is easy to recall cases of extremely bright people who appear to lack the emotions that make for moral responsibility—"whiz kids" who become devious presidential advisors, Wall Street manipulators, athletic saboteurs, scientists who forge data—one cannot ignore such individuals' life histories, how they were raised and what they were taught, the choices they made, and the developmental context that led to their conscience ending up muffled. Life has many pressures and decision points arising from the dominant value system, which prizes achievement and status at nearly any price. Lives can go wrong in countless ways and, when in the service of established authority, often without catching on that "something is rotten in the state of Denmark."

Bandura (1986) identified eight mechanisms by which we can get around our conscience, our self-evaluative process. Activation of these mechanisms can be gradual, or limited to certain situations. For instance, it is easier to do something unethical when one tells oneself that what other people are doing is much worse, or when the responsibility is diffused or relegated to a higher authority, or when one finds moral justification in carrying out heinous acts as did Hitler's SS *(Stutzstaffel),* his special force for ethnic cleansing and racial purity. The SS was trained to believe in *their* moral superiority which then justified extermination of people deemed morally inferior, degenerate, or subhuman (Moczarski, 1981). However, there have always been cases of those whose emotional system rebels, whether through psychosomatic illness or doubt, leading to positive maladjustment. Conscientious objectors are cases in point, such as Lieutenant Louis Font (Piechowski, 1992), the airman Daniel Cobos, and others who broke ranks with established but dishonest and secretive power structures (Everett, 1989). At least half of those described by Everett were people in jobs requiring exceptional intelligence.

It is significant that the emotional and moral sensitivity of high-IQ children is frequently and consistently observed. It is imperative that it be recognized, understood, supported, and perhaps emulated as well. In order to be able to understand this association we will have to study the way in which high levels of abstract reasoning, in combination with emotional sensitivity, accelerate development of evaluative and, particularly, self-evaluative processes. In Bandura's (1986) terms, we will have to study more closely the *self-system* in emotionally precocious children.

What emerges from the examples given earlier is a natural progression from emotional overexcitability to emotional giftedness with a strong component of moral sensitivity, from which moral responsibility and moral action arise. The strong potential for inner transformation begins with a reaction to how things are in the world in which one lives, then shifts to evaluating one's moral responsibility and preparing to act on it.

Dabrowski outlined a typology of personality development (Table 30.2) with special attention to inner growth in which the split between "what is," the current state of one's being, and "what ought to be," the call to an ideal higher state, is so acutely felt that it spurs further growth. The process of self-correction becomes inner transformation in multilevel growth. Inner transformation is also the process of creating a new self or realization of the higher, transpersonal, or transcendental self (Assagioli, 1965; Csikszentmihalyi, 1993; Piechowski, 1974, 1993).

As an example, Etty Hillesum, a young Jewish woman who lived in Holland at the time of the Holocaust, felt at the age of 27 a spiritual restlessness, inner chaos, depression, and despair. She took up the inner struggle to overcome it by deep reflection, acts of will, and prayer. Under the horrifying conditions of arrests and deportation of Jews, she attained serenity and inner peace entirely free of hatred toward the Germans. She realized that to give in to hate, as she was initially moved to do, would mean to become just like them. Instead, as a way of preparation for the inevitable, she volunteered for the transit camp in Westerbork from which she was eventually shipped to the gas chambers of Auschwitz. She left behind a diary, an absorbing document of her inner transformation (Hillesum, 1981/1985; Piechowski, 1992; Spaltro, 1991). Surprisingly, the horrors of war are placed as if on the periphery. Her diary is "in the first place a journey through her inner world, and that inner world of hers is not governed by the threat of war" (Gaarlandt, 1985).

Strong developmental potential, in its combination of talents, abilities, and strong overexcitabilities, is the necessary condition for self-actualization. In all cases of self-actualization studied so far, there is evidence of a very

Table 30.2
Levels of Emotional Development According to Dabrowski's Theory of Positive Disintegration

Level V: Secondary Integration
The struggle for self-mastery has been won. Inner conflicts regarding the self have been resolved through actualization of the personality ideal. Disintegration has been transcended by the integration of one's values into one's living and being. The life is lived in service to humanity. It is lived according to the highest, most universal principles of loving—compassionate regard for the worth of every individual.
A magnetic field in the soul—Dag Hammarskjφld

Level IV: Organized Multilevel Disintegration
Individuals are well on the road to self-actualization. They have found a way to reach their own ideas, and they are effective leaders in society. They show high levels of responsibility, authenticity, reflective judgment, empathy for others, autonomy of thought and action, self-awareness, and other attributes associated with self-actualization.
Behind tranquility lies conquered unhappiness—Eleanor Roosevelt

Level III: Spontaneous Multilevel Disintegration
Multilevelness arises. The person develops a hierarchical sense of values. Inner conflict is vertical, a struggle to bring up one's behavior to higher standards. There is a dissatisfaction with what one is, because of a competing sense of what one could and ought to be (personality ideal). This internal struggle between higher and lower can be accompanied by existential despair: anxiety, depression, and feelings of dissatisfaction with the self (inferiority, disquietude, astonishment).
Video meliora proboque deteriora sequor[a]—Marcus Tullius Cicero

Level II: Unilevel Disintegration
Individuals are influenced primarily by their social group and by mainstream values, or they are moral relativists for whom "anything goes," morally speaking. They often exhibit ambivalent feelings and indecisive flip-flop behavior because they have no clear-cut set of self-determined internal values. Inner conflicts are horizontal, a contest between equal, competing values.
A reed shaken in the wind—Matthew, XI, 7

Level I: Primary Integration
Egocentrism prevails. A person at this level lacks the capacity for empathy and self-examination. When things go wrong, someone else is always to blame; self-responsibility is not encountered here. With nothing within to inhibit personal ambition, individuals at Level I often attain power in society by ruthless means.
Dog-eat-dog mentality

Source: Adapted from Nelson (1989), Maxwell (1992), and Piechowski (1992).
[a] "I regard the better but follow the worse."

strong developmental potential—that is, besides special talents and high intelligence there are necessarily very strong overexcitabilities (Brennan & Piechowski, 1991; Piechowski, 1978). Although self-actualization and emotional giftedness are not the same, in the cases cited here they go together (Piechowski, 1992).

By what signs can we recognize the potential for self-actualization and for emotional giftedness in young people? Some signs have been mentioned: emotional overexcitability expressed in the intensity and sensitivity to others' feelings and one's own; empathy and understanding of others; early emergence of moral concerns about being fair to others; self-judgment; and worrying about subtle issues in how others are affected by one's actions. In other words, the signs of emotional giftedness can be read in anything that we can recognize as proper to the dual domain of *inter-* and *intra*personal intelligences, but only if combined with compassion, caring, and corrective self-judgment. In other words, as conceived here, it is called *emotional growth*.

Emotional Growth of Gifted Children and Adolescents

In a two-year follow-up study conducted in collaboration with Nicholas Colangelo, self-reports were obtained from gifted youngsters. At the beginning of the project the children were 12 to 17 years old. The purpose of the study was to find individual patterns of emotional growth. The youngsters were given an open-ended questionnaire asking what evokes in them strong positive feelings, what stimulates their mind, what is their conception of self, and so on. The items were designed to tap the five overexcitabilities enumerated in Table 30.1.

Two contrasting types of emotional growth were found (Piechowski, 1989). In one type the orientation is pragmatic, with well-defined and not-too-distant goals and not much inner exploration. This type of growth was called *rational-altruistic* because it closely fits with the type of character development described by Peck and Havighurst (1960). For example, a female high school student gave this response to the question, "If you ask yourself, 'Who am I?' what is the answer?":

> *I am a 17-year-old girl who is smart, dependable, responsible, tall, hardworking, but lazy at times, kind, active in clubs, has high ideals, who functions best in an organized environment, somewhat slow, involved, and tired.*

At 19 she gave the following reply to the same question:

> *I am an intelligent young woman who enjoys being with others and who likes to do things for them. I like to learn and I like to do things well. I am a person who likes things to be clearly defined—I want to know what is expected of me in a given situation. Right now, I am someone who is making difficult decisions about the future and what I really want to do with my life.*

In these and other of her responses we see a strong goal orientation. The framework is rational and altruistic. Satisfaction comes from involvement in many activities, service to others, and seeing clearly what ends it all serves. In another place she said, "I dislike activity that has no purpose." Such response could come from a self-actualizing "doer" (Maslow, 1971), and, although we do not see here a high degree of emotional intensity, rich imagination, or intellectual thirst for knowledge, it is worth remembering that Eleanor Roosevelt, who had all these traits, also disliked activities that had no purpose.

The other type is characterized by an awareness of inner life quite unlike the typical self-conscious adolescent. This type was called *introspective-emotional*. It is in this type of emotional growth that we see the potential for advanced development as described by Dabrowski's theory. Several characteristics emerged (see Table 30.3). By a striking coincidence, Averill and Nunley's (1992) steps toward an emotionally creative life resemble the characteristics of emotional growth found in gifted adolescents.

Unlike many adolescents who live for the moment, are very peer-conscious, or are much worried about their future, we find in a number of gifted children an early awareness of their personal growth and its numerous possibilities—an eager anticipation and making ready for what is to come. At age 12 one girl wrote, "I dream of being an adult," and similarly at age 14, "I dream about how my life will be when I grow up. I dream lots and lots of ways I could be."

In response to the question about what attracts his attention in books, a boy of 17 expressed an intense inner push for emotional growth: "I want to be moved, changed somehow. I seek change, metamorphosis. I want to grow (not just in relation to books, either)."

Awareness of feelings and emotions gains importance. In reply to the question about who they are, several youngsters described themselves in distinctly emotional terms:

> *[I am] A person who needs attention and a person that needs to be accepted. He can't be turned away because he gets hurt easily. (Male, age 16)*

> *I am a very misunderstood person. . . . People think that my life is easy because I am talented, but I have a lot of problems of my own just be-*

Table 30.3
Parallels in Emotional Growth and Emotional Creative Life

Characteristics of Emotional Growth of Introspective Gifted Adolescents (Piechowski, 1989)	*Steps Toward a Creative Emotional Life (Averill & Nunley, 1992)*
1. Awareness of growing and changing; awareness of many possible developmental paths	1. Making a commitment to one's possible self
2. Awareness of feelings and conscious attention to them, interest in others and empathy toward others	2. Acquiring knowledge of emotions and how they can be developed
3. Feelings of unreality occasionally present, marking periods of particularly intense emotional growth	
4. Inner dialogue and self-judgment, at times quite severe	4. Setting goals
5. Searching and questioning—problem finding; asking basic, philosophical, existential questions	5. Achieving results
6. Awareness of one's real self	3. Gaining self-awareness

> *cause of these talents. I often even get cut down for something good that I do. This is very hard to cope with. I am a very sensitive and emotional person. I get angered or saddened very easily. I can also get happy easily. I think I like this part of me. All these emotions somehow make me feel good about myself. . . . I am not a very confident person, though people think I am. (Male, age 16)*

> *I am a person who has feelings. . . . I have friends. I love life. . . . NOTE: I HAVE FEELINGS. (Female, age 12)*

The note of insistence on feelings shows at once the frustration when they are ignored by others and also how important they are to these gifted children's self-definition.

Empathy and understanding of others can be quite conscious as for the girl just quoted, who two years later at age 14 said: "I can see myself in other people, I can see things I've done in what other people do. I *really* understand people's thoughts and actions because I think of times I was in their place." Expressions of understanding and caring for others are frequent in the responses of these youngsters.

Although developmentally adolescence is a time when interest in one's own and others' feelings comes to focus, the articulateness and insight of these gifted youngsters are rather exceptional. The emotional maturity and sensitivity that some youngsters achieve in late adolescence appear in the gifted—those engaged in emotional growth—in early adolescence.

Periods of intense emotional growth can bring on such sudden inner shifts as to produce moments of disequilibrium and estrangement. One feels at odds with the sourroundings, as if suddenly alien to what was familiar before. Such feelings of unreality are not necessarily a cause for concern. What calls for concern is the fact that great emotional intensity and sensitivity combined with high intelligence make a youngster acutely aware of the precariousness of human existence and of the precarious condition of our world. Because of this, and because others understand it so little, gifted children can be extremely vulnerable and at risk (Leroux, 1986; Roedell, 1984; Silverman, 1993, 1994).

Feelings of unreality are the natural product of great emotional intensity and of feeling "different." For example, "Sometimes I think I am going insane and I wish I had someone intelligent to talk to" (female, age 16). In the next excerpt the feeling of unreality is combined with emotional experimentation and a shift in a perspective—thinking of parents as strangers: "When I ask myself who I am, sometimes I wonder if I'm really here. Or, I'll look at mom and dad and ask myself, who are these people, and I try to picture them as total strangers" (female, age 15).

To be self-critical is common among the

gifted. To some it spells the danger of developing a negative self-image. However, in each case one must try to distinguish if the self-criticism is a spur toward growth or an obstacle in the person's inner growth.

Here are some examples of how these youngsters monitor themselves. Their sensitive conscience is fitted with a spur to self-correction—the opposite of most adolescents who, paradoxically, can be very critical of everything and everyone and yet be lacking in self-judgment (Elkind, 1984). The following inner dialog was a response to the question, "Do you ever think about your own thinking? Describe."

> *When I take a stand on something, I later wonder why I did that. I think about how I came to that conclusion. I think about if I was right, according to the norms of society. I think about my friends and other people I know and wonder if I really feel the way I let on, and if I am fooling myself by thinking things I really feel. (Male, age 17)*

Issues of right and wrong figure prominently here, in itself not unusual, but the process of sorting them out is already strongly autonomous. He examines the origin of his convictions and asks himself whether they are genuine or perhaps just self-deceptions.

Here is a response to the question "In what manner do you observe and analyze others?" from another 17-year-old youngster.

> *Critically. I have an unusual ability for finding people's faults and discovering their vulnerabilities. I use this knowledge, too—sometimes even unconsciously. . . .*
>
> *I am a manipulator, and it sometimes bothers me. I know how to handle friends, family, teachers, etc., which makes things comfortable for me but does sometimes bother my conscience. (Fleetingly, though.)*

One might be inclined to wonder whether future development of this boy will lead him to continue to muffle his conscience and become an even more skillful puppeteer pulling the strings in others to his own advantage, or if this awareness will help him to transcend it. In answer to the question about what attracts his attention in a book, he wrote that the characters were important and that he wanted "to be able to understand them and relate to them—to sympathize with them." A person to whom such feelings are important is not likely to ignore them in others nor the impact of his actions on others.

Searching, inquiring, and problem finding are those special abilities that enable one to discover things that need discovering, questions that need to be asked, and problems that have yet to be conceived (Getzels & Csikszentmihalyi, 1975). Questioning, self-scrutiny, and the search for truth go together. Gifted youngsters often ask philosophical and existential questions and ask them early (Hollingworth, 1942). Somehow they develop not only a sense of objective truth but of inner truth as well:

> *Lots of times I wish I wouldn't think so much. It makes me very confused about a lot of stuff in the world. And I always wish I could think up answers instead of just questions. . . . My parents and all my adult friends don't understand. I wish I could talk to somebody who would have the same questions I do, and the answers to them. Maybe instead of somebody intelligent, I need somebody insane. (Female, age 16) (Piechowski, 1989)*

In Delisle's (1984) extensive collection of responses from younger children, one can find similar responses about arguing with teachers or persistence in asking questions. But moral evaluations and issues of personal responsibility are more typical of adolescents. Colangelo (1982) found this to be prevalent in moral dilemmas voiced by gifted adolescents.

> *I think about my morals and what I really think is right and wrong. I often find that how I feel is a contradiction of what society thinks. This makes me wonder if there is something wrong with me. I concentrate on why and how I became this way and if I will always be this way. (Male, age 17)*

> *I live day to day like everyone else but I am continually frustrated with the shallowness of how we live and relate to one another.*
>
> *Sometimes I hate myself because I am lazy and I feel unable to change. (Female, age 16) (Piechowski, 1989)*

We see in these excerpts keen questioning and self-scrutiny. We can recognize the expression of Dabrowskian dynamisms of astonishment (first excerpt), dissatisfaction with oneself (second excerpt), and "positive maladjustment" (in both). These youngsters are gifted not only in terms of their talents and abilities but also in terms of character growth—they sincerely want to become better persons. Their self-knowledge is impressive for this age.

Awareness of one's real self appears early in those engaged in intense emotional growth. Gifted youngsters quickly realize that their self-knowledge, the way they know and understand themselves, differs from the way others see and know them. They thus realize that their real self is hidden from others, and they can even be aware of keeping it hidden.

> *I'm somebody no one else knows. Some people see one part of me, others see other parts, it's like I'm acting. The real me is the one inside me. My real feelings, that I understand but can't explain. (Female, age 14)*

The development of self-awareness and self-understanding of these gifted youngsters traces the general direction of most adolescents. What is distinctive in the gifted is an acceleration of development and a greater intensity of existential questioning. Importantly, they value their emotional side. These young people not only are aware of their moods, feelings, and emotions, but they also realize that the emotional sphere is an essential part of their selves.

Finale: Off to a Good Start—the Budding Cartography of Intrapersonal Intelligence

We are just beginning to pull together insights and observations from different sources into a coherent picture relating emotional development, emotional giftedness, and intrapersonal intelligence. Three theories are the principal sources for this synthesis: Dabrowski's theory of emotional development, Bandura's social cognitive theory of thought and action, and Gardner's theory of multiple intelligences. These three theories have very different origins.

Dabrowski's theory grew out of his desire to map out the types of personality development from the most emotionally limited and deficient to those most advanced and altruistic, motivated by a powerful pull toward the ideal of becoming a better human being, perhaps even a Mother Teresa or an Albert Schweitzer. Dabrowski's theory encompasses both the emotional and moral aspects of personality development.

Bandura's theory grew out of his interest to delineate the social foundations of how we think and act. Bandura's theory describes a self-system and its main moving gears—that is, self-evaluation processes.

Gardner developed his theory out of curiosity about how children develop their abilities to draw, sing, think metaphorically, and use symbols, and out of his urge to find an alternative to the psychometric definition of human abilities. This he found in the functions and specializations of the brain that define the core skills of distinct talent domains, or intelligences, and which are particularly valued in one culture or another.

I have attempted to present an expanded view of the development of intrapersonal intelligence. In doing so a number of observations, concepts, and developmental processes have been brought head to head:

1. The concept of developmental potential—the overexcitabilities that impart characteristic intensity, sensitivity, and richness of inner life but also create problems of experiential overload and disequilibration
2. Moral sensitivity and moral emotions in children and adults
3. Positive maladjustment that creates an inner imperative to correct social wrongs
4. Self-evaluative processes that move from self-judgment to self-correction in the emotional and moral sphere
5. Introspective emotional growth that encompasses all of the above
6. Inner transformation, which is the essence

of emotional growth on the path toward a transcendent self

7. Inter- and intrapersonal intelligences

It is good and right that flowerings so diverse can be brought together into one luxuriant landscape. The blank areas stretching in the initial outline of intrapersonal intelligence become filled with specific emotional, evaluative, corrective, and creative processes.

Intrapersonal development, the true knowledge of self, is thus not a domain apart, the way musical or spatial intelligence can be, but in the deepest and ineffable sense the development of a person as a whole being. Although Gardner (1983, p. 274) realized that perhaps a knowledge of self is a "higher level, more integrated form of intelligence, . . . one that ultimately comes to control and to regulate more 'primary orders' of intelligence" he did not develop the idea further. The elaboration presented here complements Gardner's original thought by putting advanced development and emotional giftedness on the map of intrapersonal intelligence.

REFERENCES

Assagioli, R. (1965). *Psychosynthesis.* New York: Viking.

Averill, J. R., & Nunley, E. P. (1992). *Voyages of the heart: Living an emotionally creative life.* New York: Free Press.

Bandura, A. (1986). *Social foundations of thought and action.* Englewood Cliffs, NJ: Prentice-Hall.

Borke, H. (1971). Interpersonal perception of young children: Egocentrism or empathy? *Developmental Psychology, 5,* 263–269.

Brennan, T. P., & Piechowski, M. M. (1991). A developmental framework for self-actualization: Evidence from case studies. *Journal of Humanistic Psychology, 31,* 43–64.

Clark, B. (1983). *Growing up gifted* (2nd ed.). Columbus, OH: Merrill.

Colangelo, N. (1982). Characteristics of moral problems as formulated by gifted adolescents. *Journal of Moral Education, 11,* 219–232.

Colby, A., & Damon, W. (1992). *Some do care: Contemporary lives of moral commitment.* New York: Free Press.

Csikszentmihalyi, M. (1993). *The evolving self.* New York: HarperCollins.

Dabrowski, K. (1937). Psychological bases of self-mutilation. *Genetic Psychology Monographs, 19,* 1–4.

Dabrowski, K. (1964). O dezyntegracji pozytywnej. *(Positive disintegration).* Warsaw: Panstwowy Zaklad Wydawnictw Lekarskich.

Dabrowski, K. (1967). *Personality-shaping through positive disintegration.* Boston: Little, Brown.

Dabrowski, K. (1972). *Psychoneurosis is not an illness.* London: Gryf.

Dabrowski, K., & Piechowski, M. M. (1977). *Theory of levels of emotional development* (2 vols.). Oceanside, NY: Dabor.

Damon, W. (1988). *The moral child: Nurturing children's natural moral growth.* New York: Free Press.

Delisle, J. (1984). *Gifted children speak out.* New York: Walker.

Delisle, J., & Galbraith, J. (1987). *The gifted kids' survival guide II.* Minneapolis, MN: Free Spirit.

Elkind, D. (1984). *All grown up and no place to go.* Reading, MA: Addison-Wesley.

Everett, M. (1989). *Breaking ranks.* Philadelphia: New Society.

Fisher, R., & Ury, W. (1981). *Getting to yes.* New York: Penguin.

Gaarlandt, J. G. (1985). Introduction. In E. Hillesum: *An interrupted life: The diaries of Etty Hillesum, 1941–43.* New York: Washington Square Press, 1985.

Gandhi, M. K. (1948/1983). *Autobiography.* New York: Dover.

Gardner, H. (1983). *Frames of mind: The theory of multiple intelligences.* New York: Basic Books.

Gardner, H. (1993a). *Creating minds.* New York: Basic Books.

Gardner, H. (1993b). *Multiple intelligences: The theory in practice.* New York: Basic Books.

Getzels, J. W., & Csikszentmihalyi, M. (1975). *The creative vision.* New York: Wiley.

Grant, B. A. (1988). *Four voices: Life history studies of moral development.* Unpublished doctoral dissertation, Northwestern University, Evanston, Ilinois.

Hillesum, E. (1981/1985). *An interrupted life: The diaries of Etty Hillesum, 1941–43.* New York: Washington Square Press.

Hoffman, M. (1983). Empathy, guilt, and social cognition. In W. F. Overton (Ed.) *The relationship between social and cognitive development* (pp. 1–51). Hillsdale, NJ: Erlbaum.

Hollingworth, L. S. (1942). *Children above 180 IQ.* New York: World Book.

Kurcinka, M. S. (1991). *Raising your spirited child. A guide for parents whose child is more intense, sensitive, perceptive, persistent, energetic.* New York: HarperCollins.

Larsen, R. J., & Diener, E. (1987). Affective intensity as an individual difference characteristic: A review. *Journal of Research in Personality, 21,* 1–39.

Leroux, J. A. (1986). Suicidal behavior in gifted adolescents. *Roeper Review, 9,* 77–79.

Lysy, K. Z., & Piechowski, M. M. (1983). Personal growth: An empirical study using Jungian and Dabrowskian measures. *Genetic Psychology Monographs, 108,* 267–320.

Maslow, A. H. (1971). *The farther reaches of human nature.* New York: Viking.

Maxwell, E. (1992). Self as a phoenix: A comparison of Assagioli's and Dabrowski's developmental theories. *Advanced Development, 4,* 31–48.

Miller, A. (1981). *Prisoners of childhood.* New York: Basic Books.

Miller, A. (1983). *For your own good.* New York: Farrar, Straus & Giroux.

Moczarski, K. (1981). *Conversations with an executioner.* Englewood Cliffs, NJ: Prentice-Hall.

Nelson, K. C. (1989). Dabrowski's theory of positive disintegration. *Advanced Development, 1,* 1–14.

Nixon, L. (1994). Multilevel disintegration in the lives of religious mystics. *Advanced Development, 6,* 57–74

Peck, R. F., & Havighurst, R. J. (1960). *The psychology of character development.* New York: Wiley.

Piechowski, M. M. (1974). Two developmental concepts: Multilevelness and developmental potential. *Counseling and Values, 18*(2), 86–93.

Piechowski, M. M. (1975). A theoretical and empirical approach to the study of development. *Genetic Psychology Monographs, 92,* 231–297.

Piechowski, M. M. (1978). Self-actualization as a developmental structure: A profile of Antoine de Saint-Exupéry. *Genetic Psychology Monographs, 97,* 181–242.

Piechowski, M. M. (1979). Developmental potential. In N. Colangelo & R. T. Zaffrann (Eds.), *New voices in counseling the gifted* (pp. 25–57). Dubuque, IA: Kendall/Hunt.

Piechowski, M. M. (1986). The concept of developmental potential. *Roeper Review, 8,* 190–197.

Piechowski, M. M. (1989). Developmental potential and the growth of the self. In J. VanTassel-Baska & P. Olszewski-Kubilius (Eds.), *Patterns of influence: The home, the self, and the school* (pp. 87–101). New York: Teachers' College Press.

Piechowski, M. M. (1990). Inner growth and transformation in the life of Eleanor Roosevelt. *Advanced Development, 2,* 35–53.

Piechowski, M. M. (1991). Emotional development and emotional giftedness. In N. Colangelo & G. A. Davis (Eds.), *Handbook of gifted education.* (pp. 285–306). Boston: Allyn and Bacon.

Piechowski, M. M. (1992). Giftedness for all seasons: Inner peace in time of war. In N. Colangelo, S. G. Assouline, & D. L. Ambroson (Eds.), *Talent Development.* Proceedings of the Henry B. and Jocelyn Wallace National Research Symposium on Talent Development (pp. 180–203). Unionville, NY: Trillium.

Piechowski, M. M. (1993). Is inner transformation a creative process? *Creativity Research Journal, 6,* 89–98.

Piechowski, M. M., & Cunningham, K. (1985). Patterns of overexcitability in a group of artists. *Journal of Creative Behavior, 19,* 153–174.

Piechowski, M. M., & Tyska, C. A. (1982). Self-actualization profile of Eleanor Roosevelt, a presumed nontranscender. *Genetic Psychology Monographs, 105,* 95–103.

Piechowski, M. M., Silverman, L. K., & Falk, R. F. (1985). Comparison of intellectually and artistically gifted on five dimensions of mental functioning. *Perceptual and Motor Skills, 60,* 539–549.

Piirto, J. (1992). *Understanding those who create.* Dayton: Ohio Psychology Press.

Radke-Yarrow, M., Zahn-Waxler, C, & Chapman, M. (1983). Children's prosocial dispositions and behavior. In P. Mussen (Ed.), *Carmichael's manual of child psychology* (4th ed., Vol. 4, pp. 469–545). New York: Wiley.

Richert, S. E., Alvino, J. J., & McDonnel, R. C. (1982). *National report on identification.* Sewell, NJ: Educational Improvement Center–South.

Roedell, W. C. (1984). Vulnerabilities of highly gifted children. *Roeper Review, 6,* 127–130.

Roeper, A. (1982). How the gifted cope with their emotions. *Roeper Review, 5,* 21–24.

Seymour, D. (1987). *A case study of two young gifted brothers.* Unpublished manuscript.

Silverman, L. K. (1983). Personality development: The pursuit of excellence. *Journal for the Education of the Gifted, 6*(1), 5–19.

Silverman, L. K. (1993). The gifted individual. In L. K. Silverman (Ed.), *Counseling the gifted and talented.* Denver: Love.

Silverman, L. K. (1994). The moral sensitivity of gifted children and the evolution of society. *Roeper Review, 17,* 110–116.

Sommers, S. (1981). Emotionality reconsidered: The role of cognition in emotional responsiveness. *Journal of Personality and Social Psychology, 41,* 553–561.

Spaltro, K. (1991). "A symbol perfected in death": Etty Hillesum as moral exemplar. *Advanced Development, 3,* 61–73.

Tolan, S. S. (1987). Parents and "professionals," a question of priorities. *Roeper Review, 9,* 184–187.

Tolan, S. S. (1994). Psychomotor overexcitability in the gifted: An expanded perspective. *Advanced Development, 6,* 77-86.

Vail, P. L. (1987). *Smart kids with school problems.* New York: New American Library.

Vander Ven, K. (1984). *The development of Eleanor Roosevelt and her relationships with children and youth.* Paper presented at the Eleanor Roosevelt Centennial Conference, Vassar College, Poughkeepsie.

31

Family Counseling with the Gifted

LINDA KREGER SILVERMAN, *Gifted Development Center and the Institute for the Study of Advanced Development, Denver, Colorado*

A gifted child in the family is a mixed blessing. From birth on, these children present an unusual set of challenges. They tend to begin life as active babies, sleeping less than other infants, responding intensely to their environment, often colicky. When they appear, parents are often puzzled as to how to meet their needs, with very little in the way of understanding or support in the community.

Gifted children have *asynchronous development,* which means that whereas their intellectual skills are advanced, their social and motor skills are usually age-appropriate (Tannenbaum, 1992; Wright, 1990). The unevenness of their development leads to frustration—for themselves and for their parents. Decisions that are quite simple for other families (such as "Where should we send our child to school?") often are agonizingly difficult for parents of advanced children. Grade placement is another problem, and peer relations also can be a source of strain. Gifted children often enjoy playing with children older than themselves, mothering children younger than themselves, and talking to adults; however, their relations with children their own age usually leave something to be desired.

Any exceptionality places a heavy burden of responsibility on the parent, but parents of gifted children have the added stress of being continuously discounted. There are great emotional risks in going to the principal and saying, "I believe my child is gifted and has special needs." Too often, they hear the patronizing reply, "Yes, Mrs. Maxwell, *all* our parents think their children are gifted." Zealots of egalitarian school reform movements label parents of gifted children "elitist" and accuse them of seeking "to twist the structure of the schools to the benefit of their children" (George, 1988, p. 27). Parents of handicapped children are treated with more respect.

Concerns of Families of the Gifted

Most parents experience some degree of anxiety upon learning that they have a gifted child. When I share test results with parents of exceptionally gifted children, the tissue box is always close by. For some, it is as big a shock as being told that their child is developmentally handicapped. They mourn the loss of having a "normal" child whose needs will be taken care of easily within the regular classroom. Parents often feel inadequately prepared to meet the needs of a gifted child. These problems are compounded by many factors: myths and misinformation about the gifted, blatant or covert hostility toward the intellectually advanced, lack of information about available resources, and limited financial resources of parents. Gifted children can be very expensive to raise, and there is no financial assistance available.

In counseling parents of the gifted for the last thirty years, I have found a dozen unique concerns that provoke them to seek psychological services:

- Observing that their child is developing differently from other children
- Obtaining assessment of the child's strengths and weaknesses
- Determining appropriate methods of home stimulation
- Deciding appropriate school placement
- Needing assistance with school personnel
- Ascertaining information about available resources (such as enrichment programs)

- Coping with underachievement and lack of motivation
- Dealing with the child's intensity, perfectionism, heightened sensitivity, introversion, or depression
- Assisting the child in developing better peer relations
- Experiencing increased tension in the family as a result of the special needs of their gifted child(ren)
- Helping the child move from dependence to the self-discipline of independence
- Understanding their own giftedness

They also engage in counseling for reasons similar to those of other parents: poor family dynamics, stress-related disorders, conflicting perceptions of parents, divorce, sibling rivalry, depression or suicidal ideation in an adolescent, and so on. Counselors with special training in the psychology of giftedness are needed to reassure parents and help them meet the needs of their exceptional children.

Recognizing Giftedness

Parents of identified gifted children often begin to notice signs of giftedness in their children in the first five years. In Kaufmann and Sexton's (1983) study, 83 percent of the 98 parents were aware of their children's abilities prior to school age. Gogel, McCumsey, and Hewett (1985) surveyed 1,039 parents of gifted children: 87 percent recognized their children's abilities by the age of 5. Nearly half suspected that their children were gifted before their toddlers were 2 years old.

When parents believe their children are advanced, they are usually right. Reported accuracy levels of parental judgment range from 47 to 90 percent (Hanson, 1984; Louis & Lewis, 1992; Robinson, 1987; Silverman, Chitwood, & Waters, 1986). Accuracy increases dramatically after the children are 4 years old—not because parents become more astute, but because children become infinitely easier to assess. The greatest source of error is *underestimating* their children's abilities. Parents often fail to recognize their children's giftedness, especially if other family members and friends' children show similar advancement (Munger, 1990; Rogers, 1986).

The first signs usually reported by parents are alertness and responsiveness of their infants (Gogel et al., 1985). Next they notice that their toddlers progress through the developmental milestones at a faster pace than the baby books indicate—particularly in the development of vocabulary, verbal abilities, memory, and abstract reasoning ability (Lewis & Louis, 1991; Roedell, 1989). When they realize that their children are quite advanced compared to neighbors' children, parents begin to worry that their child will be out of step with playmates or with the school curriculum. This is often the beginning of a barrage of bad advice from well-meaning friends, relatives, and educators. The methods of good childrearing that serve as the basis for this advice are appropriate for average children (Ross, 1964; Sebring, 1983) and are frequently no more applicable for children who are developmentally advanced than for children who are developmentally delayed. Because gifted children "look normal," it is more difficult for the adults in their lives to be aware of their unique needs. Parents of young children are more likely to seek the help of professionals when they match their child's traits to a list of characteristics of giftedness (see Table 31.1) (Munger, 1990; Silverman et al., 1986).

Obtaining Assessment

Early identification of handicapped children is essential for their well-being because it enables *early intervention.* The same is true for the gifted. The earlier gifted children are identified, the more favorable their development. Individual intelligence testing is the best means available for determining the discrepancy between the child's mental age and chronological age. From the time Binet and Simon (1908) invented *mental age,* gifted children have been defined as those who reason more like older children than like age-mates. Chronological age correlates with physical development, handwriting speed, emotional

TABLE 31.1
Early Signs of Giftedness

Unusual alertness in infancy
Less need for sleep in infancy
Long attention span
High activity level
Smiling or recognizing caretakers early
Preference for novelty
Intense reactions to noise, pain, frustration
Advanced progression through the developmental milestones
Extraordinary memory
Enjoyment and speed of learning
Early and extensive language development
Fascination with books
Curiosity; asks many questions
Excellent sense of humor
Keen powers of observation
Abstract reasoning, problem-solving skills, ability to generalize
Early interest in time

needs, and social skills, whereas mental age correlates with interests, peer relations, learning rate, amount of information mastered, and awareness of the world. Diagnostic assessment provides valuable information about a child's relative strengths, weaknesses, learning style, and learning needs, and is the surest way to detect learning disabilities in bright children. The ideal age for evaluation is during the preschool and primary years—before gifted girls go into hiding (Silverman, 1986b).

Although many parents recognize advanced development in preschoolers, the majority rely on the schools for official determination of their children's giftedness (Dembinski & Mauser, 1978). However, "giftedness" usually is defined as being selected for a gifted program, and since numerous schools have abandoned their gifted programs (e.g., Benbow, 1992), many children are not identified. Typically, gifted programs begin in third grade, and participants are selected on the basis of gross screening devices: combinations of group achievement test scores, grades, and teacher recommendations. When giftedness is equated with *achievement*, children who do not excel in their regular schoolwork will not be recognized. This group includes gifted children with learning disabilities; the exceptionally gifted who are bored; culturally diverse students for whom the curriculum may be irrelevant; creative children who need different teaching styles; gifted girls, second-born children, and children with anti-intellectual peer groups, who are hiding their abilities; introverts who don't speak up in class; and children for whom English is a second language. Only the scholastically gifted will be seen.

The unpopular IQ test has a much better track record than portfolios and other achievement measures for locating hidden gifted learners (Silverman, 1994). In most schools, however, individual intelligence testing is available only for children with problems. Group IQ tests, used as part of the selection process in some districts, are not as reliable. Whitmore (1980), for example, described an underachiever who attained 89 on a group IQ test and 163 on an individual test—a difference of 74 points.

Parents who decide to obtain assessment of their children's abilities outside of school face another set of roadblocks. It is often difficult to find a psychologist or agency sufficiently experienced with gifted children. Introverted, perfectionistic children will only answer questions they are certain they can answer accurately. An examiner who has no experience with the gifted may take their "I don't knows" at face value, whereas a seasoned professional will overcome their reticence to perform. Interpreting test scores for gifted children is complex because discrepancies in scores obtained on various instruments are much greater for the gifted than for any other population (Silverman & Kearney, 1992a, 1992b) because of *ceiling effects.* A recent comparison of scores of 20 highly gifted children on the Wechsler Intelligence Scale for Children, Third Edition (WISC-III) and the Stanford-Binet (Form L-M) revealed an average difference of 37 IQ points (more than two standard deviations), with discrepancies as high as 60 points (Silverman, 1995). One child achieved a score of 124 on the Kaufman-ABC, 137 on the WISC-R, and 229+ on the Binet L-M—a difference of 105 points (Silverman & Kearney, 1992b).

Because most tests have insufficient room at the top for very bright children to demonstrate the full strength of their abilities, it is recommended that students who score in the ceiling range on two or three subtests be administered the Stanford-Binet (Form L-M) as a supplemental test (Rimm & Lovance, 1992; Silverman & Kearney, 1989, 1992a, 1992b). This old Binet has a higher range of items because it was designed to assess adults as well as children. Stanley (1990) considers it "the original examination suitable for extensive out-of-level testing" (p. 167). Also, as the newer tests place undue emphasis on response speed (Kaufman, 1992), it is suggested that untimed tests like the Binet be used to assess children with motor or processing-speed problems.

Another means of locating gifted students is through the national talent searches originated by Julian Stanley (1990), in which junior high or middle school students take college entrance exams (SAT and ACT) designed for high school seniors.[1] Some drawbacks are that gifted girls are less likely to be identified than gifted boys (Silverman, 1986b), the exams may be biased against lower income children (VanTassel-Baska, 1989), and seventh grade is late in the developmental sequence to identify giftedness.

After the child is identified, the counselor's job begins in earnest. Parents need guidance in understanding strengths and weaknesses, dealing with the implications of various ranges of ability, locating appropriate resources, sorting through the options, and coming to terms with the meaning of the child's giftedness for everyone in the family system. Although children seem to react favorably to the testing, it may take months or even years for parents and siblings to adjust to the results of the assessment (Colangelo & Brower, 1987; see Chapter 29 by Colangelo).

Home Stimulation

Researchers consistently have found parenting to be the most potent factor in the development of giftedness, creativity, and eminence (e. g., Bloom, 1985; Kulieke & Olszewski-Kubilius, 1989; Tannenbaum, 1992). Yet, many parents are confused as to how much and what type of home stimulation is appropriate. Some parents even apologize for their children's advancement (Roedell, 1989). Parents have exclaimed anxiously, "Honestly, I didn't teach her to read. She picked it up on her own." The fear that they will be seen as "pushy" prevents many parents from exercising their rightful role as educators.

A major study of individuals who achieved world class recognition by the age of 30 (Bloom, 1985; see Chapter 17 by Sosniak) highlights the important role parents play and provides information about the most effective familial support for the development of talent:

> . . . the parents' participation in the child's learning contributed significantly to his or her achievement in the field. . . . these children could [not] have gotten good teachers, learned to practice regularly and thoroughly, and developed a value of and commitment to achievement in the talent field without a great deal of parental guidance and support. (p. 476)

Further insights about the role of the family in nurturing giftedness comes from a study of MacArthur fellows, all of whom received substantial awards for their outstanding creativity (Cox, Daniel, & Boston, 1985).

> *Almost without exception the MacArthur Fellows pay tribute to their parents.* While the educational level of the parents varied, and the level of financial backing as well, virtually all the parents let their children know the value of learning by personal example. The parents supported without pushing. Their homes had books, journals, newspapers. They took the children to the library. The parents themselves read, and they read to their children. Most important, they respected their children's ideas. (p. 24; emphasis in original)

Feldman (1986; see Chapter 35 by Morelock and Feldman) describes parents of prodigies quite similarly. He did not find them controlling; instead, "the parents' role seems to be to respond, support and encourage" (p. 156). Families of early achievers usually are stable

[1] See Chapter 12 by Benbow and Lubinski and Chapter 13 by Assouline and Lupkowski-Shoplik.

and cohesive; they establish patterns of achievement, independence, and perseverance in early childhood, and focus attention and resources on their gifted children (Robinson & Noble, 1991). Perhaps the most striking impression from various studies is the high degree of parental involvement with their children (Kulieke & Olszewski-Kubilius, 1989; Robinson & Noble, 1991; Silverman & Kearney, 1989). When parents of gifted children are asked to describe their interests, the first response of many mothers is "my children."

Gogel, McCumsey, and Hewett (1985) asked over 1,000 families to list the most successful ways they work with their gifted children at home. The most cited activity was reading together. Second was consistent encouragement and praise for their children's achievements. Other methods listed included frequent conversations, participation in community activities, field trips to museums, vacations, discussions, listening, and asking and answering questions. Other studies indicate that parents assist the development of their gifted young by providing strong family values, clear standards of conduct, and good role models (MacKinnon, 1962); by mutual trust and approval (Piechowski, 1987); through emotional support from extended family members (VanTassel-Baska, 1989); by supporting their children's interests (Bloom & Sosniak, 1981); by encouraging curiosity and active exploration (Kulieke & Olszewski-Kubilius, 1989); by holding high expectations for their children (Albert, 1978; Bloom & Sosniak, 1981); by encouraging autonomy; by valuing creative and intellectual endeavors; through emotional and verbal expressiveness (Robinson & Noble, 1991); by avid reading and reading frequently to children (Cox et al., 1985); by quality time and communication (Delisle, 1992); and by helping their children to believe in their dreams (M. Darnell, personal communication, November 15, 1988).

Parents should be encouraged to provide a stimulating home environment—including instruction—if the child is eager, interested, and enjoying the activities. On the other hand, parents should be discouraged from pushing unwanted enrichment on their child. Ironically, the more skillful parents are at home stimulation, "the greater dissonance there will be when the child enters school" (Munger, 1990, p. 58).

Determining Appropriate School Placement

Part of the guidance parents desire is information about school options: public and private. The counselor needs to be aware of the availability of various special programs for the gifted and the supportiveness of administrators of different schools. Parents need to determine which of several alternatives is best for their child. A recurring question is the impact on social development of transporting children to a magnet or private school away from the neighborhood school. Parents are reassured to learn that gifted children often have different sets of peers for different types of activities (Roedell, 1985) and usually develop two sets of companions: school friends and neighborhood friends.

If public school offerings are limited, private schools should be explored. Parents should visit several potential schools and determine which ones are responsive to giftedness, are located within a reasonable distance, appear congruent with their own philosophy, and are affordable. After they have narrowed the choice to two or three alternatives, they should take their child to spend a morning or afternoon in each environment and request input from the child. Even 4-year-old gifted children are capable of selecting an appropriate school for themselves. They often notice factors that parents miss, for example, how the children treat each other on the playground.

When no gifted programs are available or affordable, or a highly gifted child is bored in the gifted program, acceleration should be considered. Unfortunately, although many children have benefited from acceleration, it remains unpopular with educators. "Indeed, school personnel frequently assume that cognitive maturity is altogether unrelated to psychosocial maturity and for that reason they take a strong stand against accelerative options" (Robinson & Noble, 1991, p. 60). Excellent criteria for determining whether early entrance or grade advancement is appropriate are provided by Feldhusen (1992).

Unfortunately, many parents are pressured to move in the opposite direction: to hold back instead of accelerate. Holding gifted boys back at the kindergarten level has become an accepted practice, on the erroneous assumption that it will enhance their social relationships. Intellectually advanced boys are sometimes branded "immature" because they refuse to play the "baby" games of their age-mates. A more appropriate solution to social adjustment difficulties is to find the boy true peers—age-mates of similar ability with whom he can be socially comfortable.

An additional option is home schooling. Families of highly gifted children frequently select this option for some period of time when it is difficult for them to find suitable placements for their children. Robinson and Noble (1991) reported that a high percentage of eminent persons were home tutored. The most frequently voiced drawback to home schooling is the lack of socialization opportunities. To meet social needs, home schooling families may get together for group instruction, participate in church groups, or enroll their children in extracurricular activities.

Assistance with School Personnel

At times, the school counselor is called upon to act as an advocate for a gifted student. The counselor can help select the most effective teachers for the child and can help teachers adapt their methods to meet the student's needs. If a student is unhappy and the teacher is unresponsive to the parents' attempts to ameliorate the situation, the counselor may need to intervene. For example, if parents feel their daughter would be better served in first grade, but her teacher feels that she is not ready to leave kindergarten, the counselor can observe her in both kindergarten and first grade and can mediate between the teacher and the parent.

Private therapists also can advocate for the child with school personnel. A junior high student whose grades were D's and F's came to our center at midterm for counseling. The boy couldn't see the point of trying to improve, because even if he turned in all his assignments for the rest of the semester his final grades would reflect the months of noncompliance. The counselor intervened on the student's behalf, explained to each of his teachers that the youth was now in counseling, and asked that he be allowed a fresh start. Most of his teachers were willing to give the student a second chance.

According to the study conducted by Gogel et al. (1985), parental persistence is the key factor in success in working with schools. Techniques parents used included initiating contact with school personnel at all levels, volunteering parent services, and assuming leadership roles. If they encountered resistance, they usually asked a staff member to intercede on their behalf, sought outside testing, or changed schools. A cooperative partnership between the home and the school is essential.

Locating Available Resources

Counselors should be acquainted with various resources in the community. Parents need to know about after-school enrichment programs, early college entrance, simultaneous enrollment in high school and college, internships, mentorships, and scholarships. In addition, parents request information about support groups and conferences, periodicals, and books on parenting the gifted. If a student needs assistance in certain skill areas, it is helpful to have on hand the names of competent tutors. Referral sources of other professionals in the community (e.g., audiologists, optometrists, occupational therapists, speech therapists, play therapists, specialists and support groups, for Attention Deficit/Hyperactivity Disorder [ADHD], and allergists) should be provided for various difficulties revealed in the assessment.

Extended family members cannot be overlooked as important sources of support for gifted students, particularly those from disadvantaged backgrounds (VanTassel-Baska, 1989). Grandparents and other relatives should be included in family counseling efforts so that all who have a direct impact on the child are familiar with his or her strengths, weaknesses, and needs. If extended family is not available, mentors and role models can be sought from groups of retired persons or professional groups in the child's areas of interest. Local businesses can be contacted to provide computers and scholarship assistance to economically disadvantaged children with intellectual promise.

Reversing Underachievement

One of the main reasons parents of gifted children seek counseling is their children's underachievement. Children who are underachieving should receive comprehensive diagnosis as early as possible (Whitmore, 1980). It is important to ascertain whether the difficulty is short-term or long-term, school-based or home-based. In my clinical practice I begin by asking the parents when they first noticed the problem. If they say that the child was an easy baby, was wonderful for the first five years, but everything fell apart when he or she started school, it is likely that the problem is in part educational. On the other hand, if they say that their child has been difficult from birth, that he or she fights incessantly with siblings, and that life on the home front resembles a war zone, then it is apparent that family counseling is needed. A student who has been underachieving for less than a year can be turned around much more quickly than one who has developed a pattern of chronic underachievement for several years.

The next step is assessment. Diagnostic assessment is indispensable in working with underachievers. Too many times a child is called "lazy" or parents are blamed when the problem may be physiological. Hidden learning disabilities have proved to be the primary cause of underachievement in the population served by the Gifted Development Center (Silverman, 1989). We administer an individual intelligence test, an achievement battery, a self-concept measure, a projective assessment, an introversion scale, and an inventory of causes of underachievement to the child, and the Myers-Briggs Type Inventory (MBTI; Myers, 1962) to all family members. In addition, we obtain a detailed developmental questionnaire from the parents, records of previous testing, and information from the teachers, parents, and student via phone and personal interviews.

We have found remarkable consistencies in the test profiles of underachieving gifted students: They tend to achieve high scores in vocabulary, abstract reasoning, spatial relations, and mathematical analysis, coupled with low scores in sequential tasks (e.g., repeating digits, coding, computation, spelling). If the discrepancies are mild, the problem may be simply a mismatch between the student's spatial learning style and the teachers' teaching style. This can be ameliorated by providing the teacher with some different strategies for reaching the student (see Silverman, 1989), and by helping the student understand his or her own learning style.

However, if the discrepancies are severe (e.g., a WISC Verbal/Performance split of 20 points or more, at least a 7-point spread between high and low subtest scores, or differences of 30 points between IQ and achievement scores), then the student may be learning disabled. It is extremely difficult to recognize learning disabilities in gifted students because the strengths and weaknesses tend to mask each other, making the children appear average. In addition, the newer tests (i.e., WISC-III, WPPSI-R) put so much emphasis on processing speed (Kaufman, 1992) that a gifted/learning-disabled child's IQ score is likely to be seriously depressed. The diagnostic checklist in Table 31.2 provides additional observational data to help determine if a sensorimotor disability is present. If many of these signs appear, the student needs a complete evaluation, followed by therapy.

Different types of therapy are recommended depending on the profile that emerges from the assessment. Low Performance scores in comparison with Verbal scores may indicate the need for a vision evaluation. Low scores on Digit Span, coupled with a history of chronic ear infections, may signify the need for further assessment of auditory processing. Children

Table 31.2
Diagnostic Checklist of Writing Disability

1. Is his writing posture awkward?
2. Does he hold his pencil strangely?
3. Can you see the tension run through his hand, arm, face?
4. Does it take him much longer to write than anyone else his age?
5. Does he fatigue easily and want to quit?
6. Does he space his letters on the paper in an unusual way?
7. Does he form his letters oddly (e.g., starting letters at the top that others would start at the bottom)?
8. Does he mix upper and lower case letters?
9. Does he mix cursive and manuscript?
10. Are his cursive letters disconnected?
11. Does he prefer manuscript to cursive?
12. Does his lettering lack fluidity?
13. Does he still reverse letters after age 7?
14. Is his handwriting illegible?
15. Is his spelling poor?
16. Does he avoid writing words he can't spell?
17. Does he leave off the endings of words?
18. Does he confuse singulars and plurals?
19. Does he mix up small words, like *the* and *they*?
20. Does he leave out soft sounds, like the *d* in *gardener*?
21. Is his grasp of phonics weak? (Is it difficult to decipher what he was trying to spell?)

with poor eye–hand coordination and speed often profit from sensorimotor integration therapy, using a computer for written assignments, and the elimination of timed tests. Children with cyclic mood swings or enuresis are referred to an allergist to rule out food allergies. If high levels of distractibility are evident during the testing, the parents are given a checklist of the symptoms of ADHD, and further evaluation is recommended to see if medication is needed. If emotional difficulties surface, counseling or play therapy is recommended. Counseling is usually the last recommendation, after all of the physiological factors have been examined.

Educational options must also be evaluated. If the problem began when the child started school, then placement with another teacher or in another school may be the solution. Roeper (1992) warns parents not to assume that the problem always resides within their child; inappropriate education diminishes a gifted student's motivation (Gross, 1992).

The MBTI (Myers, 1962) is helpful in assessing family dynamics. Clashes between parents and children often can be traced to differences in personality style. The parent who was most like the child in learning style and behavior usually "gets on the child's case" the most. Very often these are father/son dyads, wherein the father was an underachiever in school and the son mirrors those qualities that the father most disliked in himself. Discussions of learning style, personality style, and the combination of giftedness and learning disabilities can help the father understand himself better as well as understanding his son. With the assistance of the counselor, the father begins to realize that he can become his son's greatest ally. He can teach his son how he compensated for his weaknesses or became more organized. A deeper bonding ensues between the father and son through these discussions. Teachers who were among the "organizationally impaired" at some point in their lives also are effective in teaching underachievers organizational skills.

Additional strategies employed with underachievers include tutoring (Freed, 1990); counseling groups for underachievers (Mendaglio, 1993); discussion groups that include underachievers (Colangelo & Peterson, 1993); group counseling for families in which parents are matched with someone else's children (Shaw & McCuen, 1960); family counseling (Colangelo; see Chapter 29); role playing (Olenchak, 1991); grade advancement (Rimm & Lovance, 1992); creating a more caring environment in school with better communication (Seeley, 1993); alternative schools; special class placement and interventions (Whitmore, 1980); individual plans with parent, teacher and student (Fine & Pitts, 1980); adapting the curriculum to the student's learning style; teaching to the student's strengths; teaching the student compensation techniques; bibliotherapy; and using the student's interests to make school relevant (Emerick, 1992). The bottom line is that underachievement can be reversed.

Personality Characteristics

A number of personality traits are correlated with giftedness (see Table 31.3). Children's argumentativeness and questioning of authority are mentioned frequently in the literature as a chief source of parents' concern (Meckstroth, 1991; Munger, 1990). Parents seem to find children's persistent questions particularly annoying (Strom, Johnson, Strom, & Strom, 1992). Strom et al. contend that questioning is natural for the gifted child; it reflects the child's growing independence and need to understand. Sebring (1983) suggested that conflicts can be avoided if parents understand that gifted children are independent thinkers and are really analyzing what is expected of them when they argue.

Another characteristic that causes concern to parents is introversion. Although only 25 or 30 percent of the U.S. population are introverted, introverts comprise at least half of the gifted population (Gallagher, 1990; Hoehn & Bireley, 1988; Myers, 1962). Gallagher studied 1,725 adolescents enrolled in three programs for talented students and found that 50 percent were introverted. In our studies of the highly gifted at the Gifted Development Center, it appears that introversion increases with IQ (Silverman, 1986a; see also Dauber & Benbow, 1990); more than 75 percent of the 234 children we have found above 160 IQ are introverted—three times the national average. It is important for those who counsel gifted children and their families to understand this personality type. Differences between introverts and extraverts can be found in Table 31.4.

Intensity, perfectionism, and heightened sensitivity are the three emotional tributaries that most often flow through the gifted personality. "There is among gifted individuals a greater intensity of feeling, greater awareness of feeling, and greater capacity to be concerned" (Piechowski, 1987, p. 22; see Chapter 30). Intensity is the hallmark of passion, an important variable in the achievement of excellence (Feldman, 1979); perfectionism is the driving force behind the pursuit of excellence; and heightened sensitivity is the basis of compassion. These three qualities combine to create a unique personality structure governed by the vision of the ideal. In adult life, they may create a powerful force for changing the world, but in childhood these are very difficult traits to live with.

Gifted adolescents frequently feel that they should not have conflicts or negative feelings. They have been labeled "*too* sensitive," "*too* intense," and "*too* perfectionistic" by so many people in their lives that they internalize the message that there is something really wrong with them. The counselor's first task is clearing up the misconception that intense feelings are inappropriate.

It is confusing to raise a child who is at

Table 31.3
Intellectual and Personality Characteristics

Intellectual Characteristics	*Personality Characteristics*
Exceptional reasoning ability	Insightfulness
Intellectual curiosity	Need to understand
Rapid learning rate	Need for mental stimulation
Facility with abstraction	Perfectionism
Complex thought processes	Need for precision/logic
Keen sense of justice	Questioning of rules/authority
Early moral concern	Sensitivity/empathy
Passion for learning	Intensity
Analytical thinking	Acute self-awareness
Vivid imagination	Excellent sense of humor
Divergent thinking/creativity	Nonconformity
Powers of concentration	Perserverance
Capacity for reflection	Tendency toward introversion

Table 31.4
Extraversion and Introversion

Extraverts	*Introverts*
Get energy from interaction	Get energy from inside themselves
Feel energized by people	Feel drained by people
Have a single-layered personality (same in public and private)	Have a persona and an inner self (show best self in public)
Are open and trusting	Need privacy
Think out loud	Mentally rehearse before speaking
Like being the center of attention	Hate being the center of attention
Learn by doing	Learn by observing
Are comfortable in new situations	Are uncomfortable with changes
Make lots of friends easily	Are loyal to a few close friends
Are distractible	Are capable of intense concentration
Are impulsive	Are reflective
Are risk takers in groups	Fear humiliation; quiet in large groups

many developmental ages at once. Parents need help in differentiating dysfunctional behavior from behavior that is normal for gifted children or for children their child's age. For example, a 5-year-old was being reprimanded by her mother for acting childish. "Act your age!" scolded her mother. "But, Mom, I'm acting like all the other kids in my class," the kindergartner retorted. When a child talks and reasons like a much older person, it is easy to forget what is age appropriate. Whitmore (1979) pointed out that the child may not perceive a behavior (e.g., argumentativeness) as a problem, and that it may be more of a problem for the parents. In this case, the parents may need the counseling more than the child. Everyone in the family can profit from stress reduction techniques, as well as communication and negotiation skills.

Peer Relations

Parents often are more concerned about their children's social adjustment than their scholastic accomplishments. For gifted children also, the number one priority is usually finding a friend. The most important factor in determining their friendship choices appears to be mental age (Gross, 1989); true peers are intellectual equals.

Many assume that gifted children experience greater social adjustment difficulties than their classmates. However, a comprehensive review of the literature disclosed that the majority of gifted students enjoy positive relations with peers (Robinson & Noble, 1991). Gifted children appear to be more mature than their age-mates in play interests, social understanding, choice of friends, fears, and world view. The picture is not as not as uniformly positive for the highly gifted, gifted adolescent girls, and gifted minority group members.

Observation of the friendship patterns of the gifted reveals that they seek children with similar interests and abilities, and that age and gender are of lesser importance. Grouping gifted children together for instruction is one obvious way to enhance their social development. Programs for the gifted have a highly beneficial effect on social relationships (Feldhusen, Sayler, Nielsen, & Kolloff, 1990; Olszewski-Kubilius, 1989).

Contrary to superstitions that associations with other gifted students prevent these children from adjusting to the "real world," in fact their ability to relate to heterogeneous groups *increases* when they find others like themselves. Higham and Buescher (1987) reported a carryover effect from the positive social experiences of adolescents in summer enrichment programs to their regular school experiences: They felt more comfortable and socially adept. Once they have found friends who truly appreciate them, laugh at their jokes, and enjoy their company, their self-confidence increases in other situations. They demand less from average peers because they know that someone, somewhere, likes them just the way they are. When peer problems exist, the solution is usually to locate gifted peers. Programs for the gifted, enrichment courses, computer bulletin boards, pen pals, and support groups for families of the gifted are all methods of finding children of similar abilities.

Children only learn to love others when they have achieved self-love. The process usually involves the following stages: (1) self-awareness; (2) finding kindred spirits; (3) feeling understood and accepted by others; (4) self-acceptance; (5) recognition of the differences in others; and, eventually, (6) the development of understanding, acceptance and appreciation of others. Counselors can help gifted children find true peers, help them gain self-acceptance, and guide them toward accepting others.

Increased Tension

There are reports of increased conflict in families when a child has been labeled *gifted* (Cornell, 1984; Dirks, 1979). Two frequent concerns are confusion about the child's role in the family and conflicting expectations of the child by the parents (Colangelo & Dettmann, 1983). There may be jealousy and competitiveness in families in which there are both gifted and "nongifted" siblings (Cornell, 1984; Grenier, 1985). However, Kaufmann and Sexton (1983) found that only 20 percent of the siblings of gifted children in their study had negative reactions, and Colangelo and Brower (1987) reported that problems disappeared within five years. In cases where there is increased friction, the gifted label usually catches the lion's share of the blame. Yet, one variable that has not been systematically investigated is the effect on children of being perceived as nongifted when they are equally as bright as an identified sibling.

When one child in the family is gifted, the rest usually are not far behind. Reviewing the IQ scores of 148 sets of siblings, we found that almost 36 percent were within 5 points, 61.5 percent were within 10 points, and 73 percent were within 13 points of each other (Silverman, 1988). Discrepancies greater than 13 points occurred when one of the siblings had a learning disability or a history of chronic ear infections, or there was a substantial age difference between the siblings at the time of testing. The "nongifted" child, then, is most probably a gifted child who did not test as high as the identified sibling because of learning disabilities or other factors, or who does not achieve sufficiently to gain acceptance in the gifted program. The factors that depressed the child's performance, coupled with the perception that the child is not as bright as his or her sibling, could account for a considerable amount of jealousy and competitiveness. Much of the jealousy is alleviated when the so-called nongifted child is properly identified.

Increased stress also occurs when the family focuses on the achievements of one child over those of other children or when children's achievements are compared (Delisle, 1992). Sloane (1985) reported that parents who devoted their lives to the tennis champion, concert pianist, or Olympic swimmer in their families experienced occasional twinges at the neglect of other siblings. Tension also is created when parents hold differing views of giftedness. In one study, mothers believed the school's "gifted" designation while fathers were skeptical (Cornell, 1983). Fathers tend to perceive giftedness as achievement, whereas mothers perceive giftedness in terms of developmental differences (Silverman, 1986b). These discrepant points of view can be discussed in counseling, which usually resolves the conflict.

The counselor can dispel myths and misunderstandings about giftedness and can provide parents who need them with some basic parenting skills (such as remembering who's in charge, presenting a united front, and not comparing their children), but tensions are still likely to be present in the gifted family. Characteristics of gifted children—intensity, perfectionism, sensitivity, and argumentativeness—are not limited to one family member. Everyone shares in them to some degree—a perfect setting for high drama! Meckstroth (1989) called it "crisis cubed": "The effects of life situations, feelings, and ideas become magnified in the gifted family. It is as if there is a geometric progression of intensity with each family member involved" (p. 11). The counselor can help the family understand that strong feelings are healthy. Compassion and problem solving grow out of this enhanced awareness.

Fostering Self-Discipline

Gifted youngsters have a keen sense of justice; they respond well to democratic approaches in which they have a voice in decision making, and poorly to authoritarian parenting styles. "Do it because I said so!" is both ineffective and self-defeating. Fortunately, most parents of gifted children reason with their children rather than resort to punishment and other forms of external power (Abelman, 1991). Nevertheless, many people in our culture take "ageism" for granted—the conviction that since adults have more power they are entitled to more rights and privileges than children. Gifted children do not share that assumption. "Respect your elders" is a hierarchical concept that leaves the young without respect. To bring this point home, I engage parents in the following exercise:

> Close your eyes and imagine that you are asking your mother-in-law to get off the phone. Observe everything you can about yourself. Now imagine that you are asking your child to get off the phone. What differences do you notice in your choice of words? . . . tone of voice? . . . facial expression? . . . body posture? . . . amount of wait time?

Parents usually laugh, but they do gain an awareness of the difference in respect that they award individuals older and younger than themselves. The key to family harmony is respect for all members: a simple concept, but one that is difficult to implement.

Gifted children tend to behave manipulatively or disrespectfully in situations in which they feel powerless or not respected. The antidote is to help parents create a family system with a balance of power in which all members feel supported.

One method of balancing power in a family is by establishing a family council—usually a regularly scheduled meeting of the entire family. A family council provides direct experience in democratic decision making. Everyone is given an opportunity to air grievances, request changes in rules, learn negotiation skills and conflict resolution techniques, and practice effective communication skills on a routine basis. Family council meetings can also be a vehicle for building self-esteem and family solidarity. A time for compliments can be included as well as a time for complaints, and the meetings can conclude with shared activities such as reading aloud. Gifted children can participate competently in family council meetings at about 7 years old, although even preschoolers respond well to this approach. Family council meetings initially can be set up in the counselor's office, with the counselor acting as facilitator until the family feels comfortable facilitating meetings by themselves.

Gifted Children, Gifted Parents

When a child is identified as gifted, the parents are probably gifted too. It is painful for parents to acknowledge their own giftedness. However, "it is hard to help one's child resolve issues one has not yet resolved for oneself" (Tolan, 1992, p. 8).

It is not fashionable to speak of the hereditary component of giftedness, but the assumption that gifted children are randomly assigned to nongifted parents does a disservice to their parents, exacerbating their feelings of inadequacy. Too many writers mistakenly assume that mismatches in intellectual power between parents and children occur on a regular basis, as in the stereotypic portrayal of the mother in the movie *Little Man Tate*. Most parents of the gifted are intellectually equipped to raise their children effectively. The children will probably outdistance their parents in knowledge of a specific field, but parents and children tend to be well matched in terms of intellectual abilities.

It often comes as a surprise to parents to learn that they are as bright as their children. After having their children tested, some parents have had radically altered self-perceptions, resulting in taking on new career aspirations, going back to school, and applying for scholarships. Many mothers flatly deny any possibility of their own giftedness: "She gets it from her father." They may have gifted parents, spouses, siblings, and children, and still see themselves as not gifted—as if the phenomenon just skipped over them. They suffer from the conception that giftedness equals achievement, so they have no basis for recognizing themselves as gifted. When they identify with the characteristics of giftedness in children, this perception slowly begins to change. It is imperative that mothers, as their daughters' major role models, acknowledge their own abilities. Otherwise, their daughters come to believe, "If mommies can't be gifted, how can I be?" Tolan (1992) reminds parents that "one of the best things about raising gifted children may be the selves we discover along the way" (p. 10).

Conclusions

Giftedness is a family affair, with far-reaching implications for every member of the family. Whether gifted children are recognized or not, labeled or not, encouraged or not, there is no escape from the impact of giftedness on the family system: The characteristics and needs will still be there. Many of the normal attributes of giftedness are misjudged and misinformation about the gifted continues to be propagated. Few counselors are aware of the unique concerns of gifted families or prepared to give them appropriate guidance. Without this knowledge base, counselors may prove more harmful than helpful to these families. Counselors need to be willing to explore their own biases and recognize and deal with their own feelings before they can be of help.

The literature about families of the gifted can also be counterproductive. Much of it paints an unattractive picture of parents who label one child as the "star" for their own narcissistic ego needs (Cornell, 1984), teach their children they are superior, make invidious comparisons between their children, brag, have unrealistic expectations, are competitive and jealous, parentify their children, have weak role definitions, are overprotective, are incompetent in their parenting skills, and antagonize school districts with their unreasonable demands. The healthy, functional parents, who make up the vast majority of the 2,000 families with whom I've worked, cannot even turn to the literature for guidance with their complex family and school problems. Contrary to these negative depictions, families of the gifted tend to have healthy interaction patterns and a higher level of psychological adjustment than the norm (Mathews, West, & Hosie, 1986). But parents of gifted children feel abandoned within the field as well as outside of it.

A developmental counseling program recognizes that gifted children pose unique challenges to parents and includes ongoing work with families (see Chapter 29 by Colangelo). Meckstroth (1991) offers a comprehensive guide for conducting parent workshops and seminars. Counselors can help parents understand the meaning of IQ scores, help family members become adjusted to labeling, and give parents instruction on how to interact effectively with schools. Parents also can be helped to come to terms with the meaning of *giftedness* in their own lives. With appropriate counseling, myths can be dispelled, options presented, and support services obtained. Counselors are desperately needed who have special training in the area of giftedness, who understand the powerful emotional lives of their gifted clients, and who have a deep appreciation and respect for the difficult task involved in raising gifted children.

REFERENCES

Abelman, R. (1991). Parental communication style and its influence on exceptional children's television viewing. *Roeper Review, 14,* 23–27.

Albert, R. S. (1978). Observations and suggestions regarding giftedness, familial influence, and the achievement of eminence. *Gifted Child Quarterly, 22,* 201–211.

Benbow, C. P. (1992). Everywhere but here! *Gifted Child Today, 15*(2), 2–8.

Binet, A., & Simon, T. (1908). Le développement de l'intelligence chez les enfants. *L'Année Psychologique, 14,* 1–94.

Bloom, B. S. (Ed.). (1985). *Developing talent in young people*. New York: Ballantine.

Bloom, B. S., & Sosniak, L. A. (1981). Talent development vs. schooling. *Educational Leadership, 39*(2), 86–94.

Colangelo, N., & Brower, P. (1987). Labeling gifted youngsters: Long-term impact on families. *Gifted Child Quarterly, 31*, 75–78.

Colangelo, N., & Dettmann, D. F. (1983). A review of research on parents and families of gifted children. *Exceptional Children,* 50(1), 20–27.

Colangelo, N., & Peterson, J. S. (1993). Group counseling with gifted students. In L. K. Silverman (Ed.), *Counseling the gifted and talented* (pp. 111–-129). Denver: Love.

Cornell, D. G. (1983). Gifted children: The impact of positive labeling on the family system. *American Journal of Orthopsychiatry, 53,* 322–336.

Cornell, D. G. (1984). *Families of gifted children*. Ann Arbor, MI: UMI Research Press.

Cox, J., Daniel, N., & Boston, B. O. (1985). *Educating able learners: Programs and promising practices*. Austin: University of Texas Press.

Dauber, S. L., & Benbow, C. P. (1990). Aspects of personality and peer relations of extremely talented adolescents. *Gifted Child Quarterly, 34,* 10–15.

Delisle, J. R. (1992). *Guiding the social and emotional development of gifted youth: A practical guide for educators and counselors*. New York: Longman.

Dembinski, R. J., & Mauser, A. J. (1978). Parents of the gifted: Perceptions of psychologists and teachers. *Journal for the Education of the Gifted, 1,* 5–14.

Dirks, J. (1979). Parent's reactions to identification of the gifted. *Roeper Review, 2*(2), 9–10.

Emerick, L. J. (1992). Academic underachievement among the gifted: Students' perceptions of factors that reverse the pattern. *Gifted Child Quarterly, 36,* 140–146.

Feldhusen, J. F. (1992). Early admission and grade advancement for young gifted learners. *Gifted Child Today, 15*(2), 45–49.

Feldhusen, J. F., Sayler, M. F., Nielsen, M. E., & Kolloff, P. B. (1990). Self-concepts of gifted children in enrichment programs. *Journal for the Education of the Gifted, 13*, 380–387.

Feldman, D. (1979). The mysterious case of extreme giftedness. In A. H. Passow (Ed.), *The gifted and talented: Their education and development* (pp. 335–351). The seventy-eighth yearbook of the National Society for the Study of Education, Part I. Chicago: University of Chicago Press.

Feldman, D. H., with L. T. Goldsmith. (1986). *Nature's gambit: Child prodigies and the development of human potential*. New York: Basic Books.

Fine, M. J., & Pitts, R. (1980). Intervention with underachieving gifted children: Rationale and strategies. *Gifted Child Quarterly, 24*, 51–55.

Freed, J. N. (1990). Tutoring techniques for the gifted. *Understanding Our Gifted, 2*(6), 1, 11–13.

Gallagher, S. A. (1990). Personality patterns of the gifted. *Understanding Our Gifted, 3*(1), 1, 11–13.

George, P. (1988). Tracking and ability grouping. *Middle School Journal, 20*(1), 21–28.

Gogel, E. M., McCumsey, J., & Hewett, G. (1985, November–December). What parents are saying. *G/C/T,* 7–9.

Grenier, M. E. (1985). Gifted children and other siblings. *Gifted Child Quarterly, 29*, 164–167.

Gross, M. U. M. (1989). The pursuit of excellence or the search for intimacy? The forced-choice dilemma of gifted youth. *Roeper Review, 11,* 189–193.

Gross, M. U. M. (1992). The use of radical acceleration in cases of extreme intellectual precocity. *Gifted Child Quarterly, 36*, 91–99.

Hanson, I. (1984). A comparison between parent identification of young bright children and subsequent testing. *Roeper Review, 7,* 44–45.

Higham, S. J., & Buescher, T. M. (1987). What young gifted adolescents understand about feeling "different." In T. M. Buescher (Ed.), *Understanding gifted and talented adolescents: A resource guide for counselors, educators, and parents* (pp. 77–91). Evanston, IL: Center for Talent Development, Northwestern University.

Hoehn, L., & Bireley, M. K. (1988). Mental processing preferences of gifted children. *Illinois Council for the Gifted Journal, 7,* 28–31.

Kaufman, A. S. (1992). Evaluation of the WISC-III and WPPSI-R for gifted children. *Roeper Review, 14,* 154–158.

Kaufmann, F. A., & Sexton, D. (1983). Some implications for home-school linkages. *Roeper Review, 6*, 49–51.

Kulieke, M. J., & Olszewski-Kubilius, P. (1989). The influence of family values and climate on the development of talent. In J. VanTassel-Baska & P. Olszewski-Kubilius (Eds.), *Patterns of influence on gifted learners: The home, the self, and the school* (pp. 40–59). New York: Teachers College Press.

Lewis, M., & Louis, B. (1991). Young gifted children. In N. Colangelo & G. A. Davis (Eds.), *Handbook of gifted education* (pp. 365–381). Boston: Allyn and Bacon.

Louis, B., & Lewis, M. (1992). Parental beliefs about giftedness in young children and their relation to actual ability level. *Gifted Child Quarterly, 36,* 27–31.

MacKinnon, D. W. (1962). The nature and nurture of creative talent. *American Psychologist, 17,* 484–495.

Mathews, F. N., West, J. D., & Hosie, T. W. (1986). Understanding families of academically gifted children. *Roeper Review, 9,* 40–42.

Meckstroth, E. (1989). Guarding the gifted child. *Understanding Our Gifted, 1*(5), 1, 10–12.

Meckstroth, E. (1991). Guiding the parents of gifted children: The role of counselors and teachers. In R. M. Milgram (Ed.), *Counseling gifted and talented children: A guide for teachers, counselors, and parents.* Norwood, NJ: Ablex.

Mendaglio, S. (1993). Counseling gifted learning disabled: Individual and group counseling techniques. In L. K. Silverman (Ed.), *Counseling the gifted and talented* (pp. 131–149). Denver: Love.

Munger, A. (1990). The parent's role in counseling the gifted: The balance between home and school. In J. VanTassel-Baska (Ed.), *A practical guide to counseling the gifted in a school setting* (2nd ed., pp. 57–65). Reston, VA: Council for Exceptional Children.

Myers, I. B. (1962). Manual for the *Myers-Briggs type indicator.* Palo Alto, CA: Consulting Psychologists Press.

Olenchak, F. R. (1991). Wearing their shoes: Role playing to reverse underachievement. *Understanding Our Gifted, 3*(4), 1, 8–11.

Olszewski-Kubilius, P. (1989). Development of academic talent: The role of summer programs. In J. VanTassel-Baska & P. Olszewski-Kubilius (Eds.), *Patterns of influence on gifted learners: The home, the self, and the school* (pp. 214–230). New York: Teachers College Press.

Piechowski, M. M. (1987). Family qualities and the emotional development of older gifted students. In T. M. Buescher (Ed.), *Understanding gifted and talented adolescents* (pp. 17–23). Evanston, IL: Center for Talent Development, Northwestern University.

Rimm, S. B., & Lovance, K. J. (1992). The use of subject and grade skipping for the prevention and reversal of underachievement. *Gifted Child Quarterly, 36,* 100–105.

Robinson, N. M. (1987). The early development of precocity. *Gifted Child Quarterly, 31,* 161–164.

Robinson, N. M., & Noble, K. D. (1991). Social-emotional development and adjustment of gifted children. In M. C. Wang, M. C. Reynolds, & H. J. Walberg (Eds.), *Handbook of special education: Research and practice, Volume 4: Emerging programs* (pp. 57–76). New York: Pergamon Press.

Roedell, W. C. (1985). Developing social competence in gifted preschool children. *Remedial and Special Education, 6*(4), 6–11.

Roedell, W. C. (1989). Early development of gifted children. In J. VanTassel-Baska & P. Olszewski-Kubilius (Eds.), *Patterns of influence on gifted learners: The home, the self, and the school* (pp. 13–28). New York: Teachers College Press.

Roeper, A. (1992). Whose problem is it? *Understanding Our Gifted, 4*(4), 5.

Rogers, M. T. (1986). *A comparative study of developmental traits of gifted and average youngsters.* Unpublished doctoral dissertation, University of Denver.

Ross, A. O. (1964). *The exceptional child in the family.* New York: Grune & Stratton.

Sebring, A. D. (1983). Parental factors in the social and emotional adjustment of the gifted. *Roeper Review, 6*(2), 97–99.

Seeley, K. R. (1993). Gifted students at risk. In L. K. Silverman (Ed.), *Counseling the gifted and talented* (pp. 263–275). Denver: Love.

Shaw, M. C., & McCuen, J. T. (1960). The onset of academic underachievement in bright children. *Journal of Educational Psychology, 51,* 103–108.

Silverman, L. K. (1986a). Parenting young gifted children. *Journal of Children in Contemporary Society, 18,* 73–87.

Silverman, L. K. (1986b). What happens to the gifted girl? In C. J. Maker (Ed.), *Critical issues in gifted education, Vol. 1: Defensible programs for the gifted* (pp. 43–89). Austin, TX: Pro-Ed.

Silverman, L. K. (1988, October). The second child syndrome. *Mensa Bulletin,* No. 320, pp. 18–20.

Silverman, L. K. (1989). Invisible gifts, invisible handicaps. *Roeper Review, 12,* 37–42.

Silverman, L. K. (1995). Highly gifted children. In J. Genshaft, M. Bireley, & C L. Hollinger (Eds.), *Serving gifted and talented students: A resource for school personnel* (pp. 217–240). Austin, TX: Pro-Ed

Silverman, L. K. (1994). The moral sensitivity of gifted children and the evolution of society. *Roeper Review, 17,* 110–116.

Silverman, L. K., Chitwood, D. G., & Waters, J. L. (1986). Young gifted children: Can parents identify giftedness? *Topics in Early Childhood Special Education, 6*(1), 23–38.

Silverman, L. K., & Kearney, K. (1989). Parents of the extraordinarily gifted. *Advanced Development, 1,* 41–56

Silverman, L. K., & Kearney, K. (1992a). The case for the Stanford-Binet L-M as a supplemental test. *Roeper Review, 15,* 34–37.

Silverman, L. K., & Kearney, K. (1992b). Don't throw away the old Binet. *Understanding Our Gifted, 4*(4), 1, 8–10.

Sloane, K. D. (1985). Home influences on talent development. In B. S. Bloom (Ed.), *Developing tal-*

ent in young people (pp. 439–476). New York: Ballantine.

Stanley, J. C. (1990). Leta Hollingworth's contributions to above-level testing of the gifted. *Roeper Review, 13,* 166–171.

Strom, R., Johnson, A., Strom, S., & Strom, P. (1992). Designing curriculum for parents of gifted children. *Journal for the Education of the Gifted, 15*, 182–200.

Tannenbaum, A. J. (1992). Early signs of giftedness: Research and commentary. *Journal for the Education of the Gifted, 15*, 104–133.

Tolan, S. S. (1992). Only a parent: Three true stories. *Understanding Our Gifted, 4*(3), 1, 8–10.

VanTassel-Baska, J. (1989). The role of the family in the success of disadvantaged gifted learners. *Journal for the Education of the Gifted, 13*, 22–36.

Whitmore, J. R. (1979). Discipline and the gifted child. *Roeper Review, 2*(2), 42–46.

Whitmore, J. R. (1980). *Giftedness, conflict, and underachievement.* Boston: Allyn and Bacon.

Wright, L. (1990). The social and nonsocial behavior of precocious preschoolers during free play. *Roeper Review, 12*, 268–274.

32

Gifted Individuals' Career Development

PHILIP A. PERRONE, *University of Wisconsin, Madison*

Assisting gifted students with career planning and decision making is more possible today because a number of psychologists have identified what is unique in gifted students' career development and decision making and have tested specific interventions that show promise. I believe that Gottfredson's (1981) structure best explains the career processes and decision making of gifted students and that Holland's (1962, 1973) model best explains the direction of many gifted students' career choices. Recent literature also notes that gifted females' career development and career decisions are confounded by social and cultural expectations regarding parenting responsibilities.

Significance of Career Development

Herr and Cramer (1988) define *career development* as "understanding the factors underlying free and informed choice, the evolution of personal identity in regard to work, and the transition, induction, and adjustment to work" (p. 98). Their definition suggests that successful career development is consistent with the promises of a democracy, namely, making free and informed choices. Their definition also suggests that free and informed career choices relate to good adult mental health.

Unique Facets of Gifted Students' Career Development and Decision Making

Specific Female Considerations

The effect of social stereotypes and social pressure on females' career plans is readily apparent. In 1989 only 1 percent of females taking the ACT exam indicated they planned to major in physical sciences, 2 percent in biological sciences and engineering, and none in mathematics (American College Testing Program, 1989). Not only are the career options of gifted females restricted, but society loses when nearly half of its members fail to consider science- and math-related careers.

The expressive trait described by Hollinger (1988) is particularly significant in understanding the career decisions of gifted adolescent females. Hollinger notes that in making decisions, gifted females consider both *instrumental* traits, which contribute to a sense of personal agency, and *expressive* traits, which contribute to social acceptance. These two traits work against one another in gifted females' decisions and thus eliminate many occupational options.

In her study of 284 gifted adolescent females, Hollinger found that females possessing instrumental qualities prefer Realistic and Investigative ("thing-idea" oriented) occupations. Regardless of self-perceptions, gifted females preferred occupations that were predominantly sex-role stereotypic, indicative of the strong influence of social stereotypes on females.

Further support for a restricted career vision by gifted females, which is a product of family, friends', and teachers' expectations, is shown in the work of Houser and Garvey (1985). They studied the relationships among college women's career choices, personality, and social support. They found that women who enrolled in nontraditional college programs received more support and encouragement from family, friends, teachers, and counselors, with teachers and counselors exerting the largest influence. Phillips (1987) and Dickens (1990) confirmed Houser and Garvey's findings in their studies of high-ability students. These findings contradict those of

Parsons, Adler, and Kaczala (1982), who concluded that parents' beliefs about their child's math ability had a greater impact on children's mathematical self-esteem than grades given by math teachers. The overriding influence of social factors and self-concepts also is found in Rosser's (1989) conclusion that females underestimate their abilities and plan to attend less prestigious colleges than boys with similar grade-point averages.

Female career stereotypes and self-concept of math ability clearly are critical limiting factors in females' career planning and decision making. Liking and doing well in mathematics is fundamental to choosing math-science and business careers. *Mathematics is the most critical academic area to focus on in order to maximize gifted females' career options.*

The significance of mathematics in females' career planning also is evident in Eccles's (1987) study of gender differences in math-science interests. She suggested that it is more helpful to learn how females' interest in math-science compares with their interest in other subject areas than to be concerned with how their interests compare with male interests.

Eccles's earlier (1984) study illustrates the relevance of involving females' parents in career planning as early as possible in order to keep their math-science options open. In that study, females who excelled in both math-science and language arts were considered better in language arts by their parents, and parents communicated to their daughters that doing well in language arts was more important. Parents of males who excelled both in language arts and mathematics communicated the opposite to their sons

Read (1991) found relatively low participation of gifted girls in special math programs offered in 142 high schools. Participation by females was negatively influenced by perceived peer pressure, administrator attitudes, program content, counselor attitudes, and how the gifted girls were identified. Program content and the identification process can be changed to make special math programs more attractive to females. Today, administrator and counselor attitudes certainly should be supportive.

Arnold's (1993) ten-year follow up of 46 female and 35 male high school valedictorians and salutatorians shows gender differences regarding the pursuit of scientific careers. She found that, beginning in the sophomore year of college, women reported a decrease in their intellectual self-esteem. By their senior year they were concerned about how to resolve the expected conflict between family and career. Women also reported that faculty expectations regarding their future careers were vague. Attrition of women from science-related career paths occurred throughout the ten-year period while males maintained their interest.

Arnold compared 22 women with high career aspirations and 24 women with low career aspirations. He reported that women in the high group were greatly influenced by their mothers' education and by their professional work experience while in college (e.g., teaching and research assistantships), and that they placed less importance on working with people. The high career aspiration group expected to marry and have children later.

Given these findings, how should education frame a comprehensive approach to help gifted females achieve their potential. Silverman (1991) identified several key career interventions for both females and males, for example, learning about women's career potentialities and exposing students to professional women engaged in different career-family patterns. Specific suggestions for females are arranging for shadowing of career women, helping females set long-term career goals, analyzing dual (marriage and family) career paths, encouraging females to remain in advanced math and science classes, and actively seeking advanced educational opportunities and scholarships for females.

General Career Development Considerations for Gifted Students

Katchadourian and Boli (1985) identified two primary learning motives among college undergraduates: "careerism" and "intellectualism." Students who score high on careerism seek marketable skills, financial security, and establishing professional contacts as reasons for attending college. Students high in intellectualism are motivated to think critically and develop artistic and aesthetic taste and judgment. Some students scored high on both scales, and others scored low on both. On the basis of this finding, the writers outlined a four-part topology: *careerists,* who are high on career and low on intellectual; *intellectuals,* high on intellectual and low on career; *strivers,* high on both; and *unconnected,* low on both. Interestingly, careerists do not expect to enjoy their studies.

Reviewing the above and other research, Howley (1989) concluded that whatever route gifted students choose, they eventually will have misgivings. He suggested that beginning in grade school, gifted children should learn economics and what a quality adult life means and requires. He felt this could best be achieved through on-the-job mentorship programs.

Kelly (1992) found that among 21 gifted seventh- and eighth-grade females and 20 males there were fewer perceived career barriers than among 152 pupils in regular classes. In contrast to an earlier study by Kelly and Colangelo (1990), gifted students were not found to be higher in career maturity than students in regular classrooms. Gifted boys expressed a greater need for occupational information than gifted girls, and girls in regular classrooms expressed interest in a wider array of occupations than gifted girls. Kelly suggested that gifted girls acquire career information informally and by happenstance, while gifted boys seek career information both informally and formally.

The importance of females gaining a better understanding of the economics of work appears again in a study by Kelly and Cobb (1991). Thirty-eight gifted females and 69 gifted males between the ages of 11 and 14 were as knowledgeable regarding career decision-making factors as high school juniors and seniors, and were slightly more advanced in career planning than others in their age group. No cultural differences were found. While females were more knowledgeable about career options than males, their career aspirations were lower.

Milgram and Hong's (1992) 18-year follow-up of 67 high school seniors underscores the important contribution of nonacademic experiences to adult accomplishments. Seventeen of 48 subjects whose adolescent leisure activities matched their adult occupations were found to have more on-the-job responsibility and to have accomplished more at work. Also, the measure of creativity administered in high school, an adaptation of the Wallach and Kogan tests (1965), was a better predictor of adult accomplishment than aptitude test scores or school grades.

Emmett and Minor (1993) conducted in-depth interviews with 16 male and 14 female graduates from a gifted high school program, 10 each from the classes of 1985, 1987, and 1989. These students identified 180 career-related decisions made between the ages of 14 and 22. The researchers analyzed the decisions using cluster analysis. Cluster I included expectation-related items such as *others' expectations, a sense of responsibility,* and *not being ordinary*. Cluster II was labeled *perfectionism* and included *making a difference* and *achieving a sense of accomplishment*. Cluster III was labeled *self-centeredness* and included *maintaining autonomy* and *being true to oneself*. Cluster IV focused more on issues of superior intelligence, including *wanting a challenge, variety,* and *continuing to learn*. Cluster V involved difficulties making decisions due to one's *multipotentiality*. Emmett and Minor concluded that sensitivity to others' expectations and perfectionistic tendencies are dominant considerations in gifted students' career planning.

Emmett and Minor summarized the major career decision problems facing gifted adolescents: wanting to delay a decision as long as possible, frequently changing their mind and their major, feeling "stuck" in a field because of the early investment made in the choice and the expectations of parents and teachers, having made a premature choice from among a limited number of career options, and selecting an occupation beneath one's ability. They recommended helping gifted students view career decision making as an ongoing process rather than a one-time choice.

Multipotentiality, greater ego involvement in work, acquiring more career information than is typical of one's age group, high career expectations, and perfectionistic tendencies set gifted students apart from others. It is important that gifted students learn the economic consequences of their career decisions and understand that they may be "blinded" by their altruism or self-actualizing tendencies in making decisions.

Gottfredson's Theory of Occupational Aspirations

Gottfredson (1981) presented a theory of how occupational aspirations develop from early childhood through the college years. She based her theory on the writings of Van den Daele's (1968) description of cognitive development and the formation of children's ego-ideals (see Table 32.1). She took some liberty in compacting his 10 levels into 5 stages. Also, Gottfredson did not develop her theory in regard to Van den Daele's ninth and tenth levels of conceptual development. That is, she failed to elaborate on a fifth stage because only a tiny fraction of adolescents were seen as exhibiting behavior at this high level of career development. Because, according to Van den Daele, intelligence largely determines the rate at which children and adolescents move through these stages, gifted adolescents are more likely to make career plans and decisions from the referent point that characterizes this stage.

Gottfredson's theory rests on the assumption that individuals seek jobs compatible with images of themselves. Gottfredson concurred with Van den Daele that social class, intelligence, and gender are the important determinants of self-concept and of career aspirations. The compromises made in career planning and career decisions revolve around *expectations,* which are products of social class; job *accessibility,* which is largely dependent on having the aptitude and opportunity to meet entry requirements; and one's self-definition relative to sex roles.

Overview of Gottfredson's Theory

Gottfredson described four stages of conceptual development and hypothesized that conceptual development and career development build on one another. The four stages are

Table 32.1
A Comparison of Van den Daele's and Gottfredson's Stages

Van den Daele's Stages of Cognitive Development	*Gottfredson's Stages of Occupational Aspiration*
1. "I" distinct from others 2. Dichotomous organization of thought (pleasing others)	1. Orientation to size and power (3 to 5 years)
3. Distinction of *before* and *after* (conflict avoidant) 4. Generalization of common characteristics (little man or woman)	2. Orientation to sex roles (6 to 8 years)
5. Orientation to general sex-role expectations (one of the group) 6. Cues in on others' feelings, intentions (social conformist)	3. Orientation to social valuation (9 to 13 years)
7. Orientation to internalized principles (values) (social agent) 8. Self-style valued more highly (personal goal orientation) (independent agent)	4. Orientation to the internal, unique self (beginning about 14 years)
9. Integration from among apparent diversity (creative) (striving for personal social good) 10. Striving for transcendent good (self-actualization)	[a]5. Integrated world view (late adolescence, young adulthood)

[a]Elaborated by the present author.

(1) orientation to size and power (ages 3 to 5), (2) orientation to sex roles (ages 6 to 8), (3) orientation to social valuation (ages 9 to 13), and (4) orientation to the internal, unique self (beginning around age 14). There is a fifth career development stage paralleling Van den Daele's ninth and tenth levels of conceptual development, which Gottfredson described as an integrated world view evidenced through reflective consideration of the human situation.

Children and adolescents, and probably even most adults, do not focus on job activities in career decision making but, rather, on the lifestyle that corresponds to the occupation and the personalities of individuals they know in the occupation. Prior to preparing for a career, little usually is known about what people really do on the job.

The Five Stages

1. *An orientation to size and power (ages 3 to 5):* This is when the child first has an inkling of what it means to be an adult. Career aspirations at this stage involve fantasy and immediate gratification, with little consideration of the future. The adult is perceived as controlling all the resources relative to both activity and gratification, and thus adulthood is valued because of controlling desired resources.

2. *An orientation to sex roles (ages 6 to 8):* Gender self-concept is thought to be consolidated in this stage of development, and children's occupational preferences reflect a concern with doing what is sex-appropriate. Gottfredson suggests that the developmental pattern regarding sex roles is tied to level of cognitive development.

3. *An orientation to social valuation (ages 9 to 13):* During this period social class and ability become determinants of behavior and expectations. Differences in the prestige associated with various jobs are recognized, and social class and intellectual differences in behavior and attitude become more apparent. Peer influence on behavior and aspirations is considerable. The emerging adolescent is able to cue into social class and intellectual differences, for example, in speech and dress. In effect, the development of social class stereotypes and occupational stereotypes parallel one another, with preferences for higher occupational levels corresponding with higher levels of intelligence. Gottfredson (1981) noted: "More able students aspire to higher level jobs, and within all ability groups the higher social class youngsters have the higher aspirations" (p. 563). The combination of higher intelligence and higher social class frees the individual to aspire to a wide range of high-level occupations because most occupations are seen as accessible. For the most gifted, going to college is a foregone conclusion.

4. *An orientation to the internal, unique self (beginning around age 14):* As Gottfredson noted, this age frequently marks the beginning of the adolescent identity crisis. During this stage additional criteria are used to assess compatibility with various occupations. Gottfredson noted that, typically, occupations that are perceived as inappropriate for one's sex are discarded first, followed by occupations that are outside one's social class "comfort range," either too low or to high. The amount of effort required to attain different occupational levels within different fields of occupational endeavor is assessed, with individuals discarding any that appear to demand excessive effort—a thought that may not enter the minds of many gifted students. Holland's (1962) schema for differentiating between occupational fields will be introduced later in this chapter because it helps to explain the direction that gifted students' career aspirations may take.

5. *An integrated world view evidenced through reflective consideration of the human situation (beginning in late adolescence or young adulthood):* Van den Daele noted that the transition into his highest two levels of conceptual development (Gottfredson's fifth stage) are not explained in terms of changes in cognitive processes. He implied that rich and diverse life experiences are necessary precursors to attaining the conceptual level that constitutes this fifth stage. Van den Daele further discussed finding a striking difference in the career motivation of males and females, with *achievement* being more congruent with a masculine identity and *morality* more congruent with a feminine identity. One can only speculate whether child-rearing practices and adult role models of both sexes have changed sufficiently to bring this 1960s' view into question.

What characterizes fifth-stage thought processes and behaviors? Van den Daele's descriptors include the following: Self–society relationships are attended to from both an immediate and a historical perspective; intuition is trusted and valued; conflicts with society are recognized, accepted, and even welcomed; a world view is superordinate to self-interest; the emphasis is on becoming; means are construed as coequal with ends; and the individual engages in poetic, dialectical thinking (Van den Daele, 1968).

A linear, rational, self-occupation congruence model of career planning and decision making is not applicable to a person's functioning at this value-based stage of conceptual wisdom. Probably, this fifth stage also is best reflected in the second series of career decisions that follow the completion of a college degree and possibly working for a few years.

In Gottfredson's view, the typical pattern of compromise is to sacrifice one's primary vocational interests first, job level second, and sex type last. The individual first compromises those attributes that are least central to his or her self-concept and social identity. She also noted that as new criteria for judging self-occupation compatibility are applied, preferences become more complex and narrower.

Holland's Theory

While Gottfredson provided an explanation of how career aspirations evolve, Holland (1962, 1973, 1977) proposed a model that explains particular directions that gifted individuals' career aspirations take. Holland (1962) developed his model by analyzing responses from National Merit finalists, which suggests the model should be relevant to understanding the career paths that gifted persons pursue.

Holland's theory is based on the assumption that most people can be categorized into one of six personality types and that there are six corresponding kinds of career environments. People are assumed to search for compatible environments that will let them exercise their skills and abilities and express their attitudes and values (Holland, 1973). Briefly, Holland's six personality types are:

1. *Investigative (I):* This type prefers activities in which he or she can observe, communicate using symbols, and be creative. The phenomena under investigation may be physical, biological, or social-cultural.
2. *Artistic (A):* The artistic person prefers freedom to manipulate one or more of the different modes of human expression to create art forms.
3. *Social (S):* This personality type prefers training, supporting, and teaching others while avoiding explicit, systematic activities.
4. *Enterprising (E):* The enterprising person prefers manipulating others to achieve his or her own goals or the goals of the organization while avoiding explicit, systematic procedures.
5. *Conventional (C):* The conventional type prefers explicit, ordered manipulation of data and has a low tolerance for ambiguous, unsystematic activities.
6. *Realistic (R):* This type prefers explicit, ordered manipulation of tools, machines, or animals and has a low tolerance for ambiguity.

Individuals seldom fall exclusively into one of these types, and so a system was devised to indicate primary and secondary types. Individuals are encouraged to explore various occupations listed under both the primary and the secondary personality types. In essence, Holland hypothesized a *goodness-of-fit* model of career development wherein individuals match their self-stereotypes with their stereotypes of primary work personalities.

Post-Kammer and I (Post-Kammer & Perrone, 1983) used Holland's model as part of a follow-up study in 1982 of 300 gifted males and 348 gifted females who graduated from 44 different Wisconsin high schools between 1962 and 1975. Respondents ranged in age from 24 to 35. We inquired about perceptions of their career development since graduating from high school and asked several questions regarding their current work activities and future plans. Interestingly, the age of the respondents was not a differentiating factor when analyzing responses, but there were gender differences.

Both females (73 percent) and males (57 percent) indicated that marriage or a close relationship with a significant other was their most important source of satisfaction. Work was listed as the most important satisfier by 37 percent of the males and 35 percent of the females. This finding would suggest that theories of career development should pay attention to the "coupling" tendency of most individuals and the importance of a close interpersonal relationship in overall life satisfaction.

When asked whether they had lived up to their full educational and vocational capabilities, few said yes, but most said they had done reasonably well vocationally (males 66 percent, females 61 percent) and educationally (males 56 percent, females 55 percent). In terms of work itself, males placed more importance on their income while females emphasized the importance of good relationships with co-workers and supervisors. This finding is consistent with Van den Daele's findings (noted earlier) that males are more achievement oriented and females more morality oriented.

Further analysis of these data (not reported in the original article) showed none of the respondents were engaging in *realistic* occupations. No males and only a few females were engaged in *conventional* occupations. Very few females or males were in *artistic* occupations, and those who were had been fully involved in some art form since high school. The majority of females were engaged in *investigative* and *social* occupations such as teaching and social work. There were females who reported entering social occupations largely because of parents' and teachers' expectations.

Within the investigative occupations, there were differences among those pursuing physical science, biological science, and social science careers. Those in physical science careers wanted to unravel the mysteries of the universe. Those in biological careers wanted to find cures and ways to prevent the physical destruction of humanity. Those in social science careers wanted to solve mysteries of the mind and learn how social organizations can function more effectively.

Providing the Necessary Environment for Talent Development

Bloom and Sosniak (1981) detailed the learning conditions experienced by persons achieving excellence in three areas: *artistic* (concert pianists and sculptors), *psychomotor* (Olympic swimmers and tennis players), and *cognitive* (research mathematicians and research neurologists).[1] A retrospective interview was used to obtain data from the most capable Americans they could locate in these three areas who had achieved an internationally recognized level of accomplishment. Their main findings related to career development were as follows

1. The majority had become highly involved in their particular field before age 12, and their parent(s) or a relative had a strong interest in the talent area. This significant person supported and encouraged development in the specific talent field.
2. The curriculum of the home consisted of language, resources needed to develop the special talent area, and high expectations for the child.
3. Most instruction was one to one.
4. Parents made adjustments in their lives in order for the child to develop her or his talent.
5. Emphasis was more on mastery than on competition.
6. By adolescence, the parents' instructor role was transferred to an outside teacher.
7. Recitals, contests, or concerts served to heighten the level of learning and emotions prior to as well as during the performance.

---

[1] See Chapter 17 by Sosniak.

Effective teachers used the opportunity afforded by these performances to relate current skills to long-term goals.

8. Once the child embarked on developing his or her talent, from age 10 or so, other activities became subordinate.
9. During adolescence 15 to 25 hours a week were spent practicing. During this period their aspirations (career goals) ruled much of their lives.

The factors considered essential in the development of their talent provide convincing evidence that talent does not develop on its own and that high-level career aspirations are a major factor in the career attainment of exceptionally gifted and productive individuals.

Career Interventions That Hold Promise

Programmatic Intervention

Beck (1989) investigated how participants benefited from a specific eighteen-week mentorship program. An orientation phase focused on formulating a plan for investigating an interest area, selecting an appropriate mentor, and discussing possible projects. The orientation was followed by three weeks of in-school instruction preparing students to work with their mentors. About 14 weeks, eight hours weekly, involved implementing the plan with the mentor. During this time, weekly two-hour group discussions were held. Major benefits of the program included having the opportunity to examine lifestyles and personal attributes of mentors, seeing first-hand how mentors interact with others, and even making future job contacts. Overall, students gained a realistic idea of what a career totally involves. Females found the mentorship particularly valuable when they had the opportunity to discover ways to integrate career and family. Beck emphasized the need for professional female mentors for female students. It would seem beneficial, though for different reasons, for gifted males to have female mentors as well.

Another programmatic approach focused on motivating gifted students to seek out and use career information. Willings (1986) cited several reasons that gifted students are "turned off" by conventional career searches and then provided an outline for an "enriched" career search. A few of the problems mentioned regarding conventional searches are that the process is boring, the information is trivial, and information systems seem to operate on the assumption students should find one best career option.

Among the more interesting aspects of Willings's enriched program is introducing students to Paterson's (1955) theory of two complementary drives—the drive to "be somebody" and the drive to do something worthwhile. He recommends encouraging students to fantasize careers and consider what is possible, and discussing with them the economic consequences of different career choices. He also teaches a mini-course on how to study jobs, including how to locate hidden factors.

Individual-Programmatic Intervention

Kerr and Erb (1991) describe a focused, value-based career intervention at the Connie Belin and Jacqueline N. Blank International Center for Gifted Education and Talent Development which proved effective with academically talented college students and would seem to have promise for talented high school students. The intervention is designed to address possible identity diffusion experienced by multitalented high school students. Their intervention is predicated upon Strong's (1968) social influencing model. In phase 1, the counselor strives to enhance clients' perception of their competence. In phase 2, the attempt is made to encourage clients to change an attitude or viewpoint.

Kerr and Erb tested their model first on 26 female and 15 male college honor students; 14 females and 5 males served as a control group. The control group later became a second study group. Participants were engaged in three sessions: a group (5 to 8 participants) life-planning workshop; an assessment session; and an individual (exit) counseling session. One surprising finding was that multipotential students were found to have both a sense of purpose and identity; they did not experience identity diffusion. Another finding was that participants significantly increased their self-confidence in the process.

Factors Contributing to Career Development in Gifted Students

Thirty years of studying gifted persons' career development has led me to believe that three sets of factors contribute to their unique career development: *psychological, psychocreative,* and *social.* By describing what I believe is unique in gifted individuals' career development, I am defining *giftedness* from a career developmental perspective.

Psychological Factors

1. Traditional sex-role stereotypes are slightly less of a factor in the self-identity of gifted persons compared with others.
2. There is a greater likelihood of gifted persons working at one job for life.
3. Work is central to the identity of gifted persons (high ego involvement).
4. They have a strong need to achieve mastery in their chosen field.
5. They have a strong desire, seemingly an innate need, to make an impact on society.
6. The gifted individual frequently feels exhilarated, rather than exhausted, when pursuing a valued goal; both means and ends are highly satisfying.

Psychocreative

7. There is constant testing of personal and environmental limits, a challenge of the status quo, continual questioning of self and others, and less need for closure.
8. Gifted individuals are highly capable of creating their own futures.
9. They are risk takers.
10. They actually create, and even seek to maintain, dissonance in their lives as proof to themselves that they are fully engaged in life.

Social Factors

11. They have a more worldly view.
12. They have a greater sense of social responsibility.

Conclusions

Conceptual development and career development seem interdependent for gifted persons. The two do leap-frog one another: Fostering career development is essential to furthering conceptual development, and vice versa. Gifted persons are more likely to make decisions based on the values characteristics of the fifth, value stage of development. Therefore, traditional, deductive, career decision-making strategies are inappropriate for these individuals. Rather, creative and intuitive approaches to decision making are required.

Because aptitudes are high in several areas, they usually have unlimited academic areas they can pursue successfully. The status level of acceptable occupations is high and the ceiling unlimited ("You can be whatever you want to be"). Freedom to choose can be frightening and even destructive without some guidance and support from others and a sense of what they want to give and receive from their work life. Gifted women receive conflicting and confusing signals from society relative to the level of career that is deemed appropriate and the specific fields that are considered gender-appropriate. Gifted children from economically disadvantaged backgrounds require early intervention to reduce the limiting effects of a lower social class background and to raise career expectations.

Gifted individuals seem oriented primarily toward Holland's *investigative* and *enterprising* occupations, suggesting the need to provide more precise information regarding the activities and lifestyles of individuals engaged in these occupational areas. Conflicting feelings may arise from having to engage in a lengthy preparation period prior to entering one's chosen career. Long-term training periods prolong dependency, which is in conflict with gifted students' strong need for independence.

REFERENCES

Arnold, K. D. (1993). Undergraduate aspirations and career outcomes of academically talented women: A discriminant analysis. *Roeper Review, 15*, 169–175.

American College Testing Program. (1989). *State and national trend data for students who take the ACT Assessment.* Iowa City, IA: American College Testing.

Beck, L. (1989). Mentorships: Benefits and effects of career development. *Gifted Child Quarterly, 33,* 22–28.

Bloom, B. S., & Sosniak, L. A. (1981). Talent development vs. schooling. *Educational Leadership, 39*(2), 86–94.

Dickens, M. (1990). *Parental influences on the mathematics self-concept of high achieving adolescent girls.* Unpublished Ph.D. dissertation, University of Virginia, Charlottesville.

Eccles, J. (1984). Sex differences in mathematics participation. In M. Steinkamp & M. Maehr (Eds.), *Women in science* (pp. 93–137). Greenwich, CT: JAI Press.

Eccles, J. (1987). *Understanding motivation: Achievement beliefs, gender roles and changing educational environments.* Paper presented at the annual meeting of the American Psychological Association, New York.

Emmett, J. D., & Minor, C. W. (1993). Career decision-making factors in gifted young adults. *Career Development Quarterly, 41,* 350–366.

Gottfredson, L. S. (1981). Circumspection and compromise: A developmental theory of occupational aspirations. *Journal of Counseling Psychology Monograph, 28,* 545–579.

Herr, E. L., & Cramer, S. H. (1988). *Career guidance and counseling through the life span.* Glenview, IL: Scott, Foresman.

Holland, J. L. (1962). Some explorations of a theory of vocational choice: One- and two-year longitudinal studies. *Psychological Monographs,* 76(26 Whole No. 545).

Holland, J. L. (1973). *Making vocational choices: A theory of careers*. Englewood Cliffs, NJ: Prentice-Hall.

Holland, J. L. (1977). *The self directed search.* Palo Alto, CA: Consulting Psychologists Press.

Hollinger, C. L. (1988). Toward an understanding of career development among G/T female adolescents. *Journal for the Education of the Gifted. 12*(1), 62–79.

Houser, B. B., & Garvey, C. (1985). Factors that affect nontraditional vocational enrollment among women. *Psychology of Women Quarterly, 9,* 105–117.

Howley, C. B. (1989). Career education for able students. *Journal for the Education of the Gifted, 12*(3), 205–217.

Katchadourian, H., & Boli, J. (1985). *Careerism and intellectualism among college students.* San Francisco: Jossey-Bass.

Kelly, K. (1992). Career maturity of young gifted adolescents: A replication study. *Journal for the Education of the Gifted, 16*(10), 36–45.

Kelly, K., & Cobb, S. J. (1991). A profile of the career development characteristics of young gifted adolescents: Examining gender and multicultural differences. *Roeper Review, 13,* 202–206.

Kelly, K., & Colangelo, N. (1990). Effects of academic ability and gender on career development. *Journal for the Education of the Gifted, 13,* 168–175.

Kerr, B., & Erb, C. (1991). Career counseling with academically talented students: Effects of a value-based intervention. *Journal of Counseling Psychology, 38,* 309–314.

Milgram, R. M., & Hong, E. (1992). Creative thinking and creative performance in adolescents as predictors of creative attainments in adults: A follow-up after 18 years. *Roeper Review, 15,* 135–139.

Parsons, J., Adler, T., & Kaczala, C. (1982). Socialization of achievement attitudes and beliefs: Parental influences. *Child Development, 53,* 310–321.

Paterson, T. T. (1955). *Morale in war and work.* London: Parrish.

Phillips, D. (1987). Socialization of perceived academic competence among highly competent children. *Child Development, 58,* 1308–1320.

Post-Kammer, P., & Perrone, P. A. (1983). Career perceptions of talented individuals: A follow-up study. *Vocational Guidance Quarterly, 31,* 203–211.

Read, C. R. (1991). Achievement and career choices: comparisons of males and females. *Roeper Review, 13*, 188–193.

Rosser, P. (1989). *Sex bias in college admissions tests: Why women lose out.* Cambridge, MA: National Center for Fair and Open Testing.

Silverman, L. K. (1991). Helping gifted girls reach their potential. *Roeper Review, 13,* 122–123.

Strong, S. R. (1968). Counseling: An interpersonal influence process. *Journal of Counseling Psychology, 15,* 215–224.

Van den Daele, L. (1968). A developmental study of the ego-ideal. *Genetic Psychology Monographs, 78,* 191–256.

Wallach, M. A., & Kogan, N. (1965). *Modes of thinking in young children.* New York: Holt.

Willings, D. (1986). Enriched career search. *Roeper Review, 9*, 95–100.

33

From Potential to Performance: Motivational Issues for Gifted Students

TERRY McNABB, *Coe College, Cedar Rapids, Iowa*

The role of motivation in academic achievement has been a subject of scientific inquiry for over forty years. Variously described as task commitment, persistence, intrinsic interest, challenge seeking, desire, and effort expenditure, the concept of motivation is understood by researchers, educators, and lay people to represent the difference between *potential* and *performance*. The role of motivation is especially salient with highly able students, where this difference can be substantial and extremely frustrating for parents, teachers, and the students themselves.

In his three-ring conception of giftedness, Renzulli (1978; see Chapter 11) identifies task commitment, one way of operationalizing motivation, as one of the three components (along with above-average ability and creativity) of gifted behavior. In this conceptualization, the three components are necessary and sufficient to demonstrate giftedness. While Renzulli's model broadens the definition of giftedness beyond the psychometrically driven one used by Terman, it causes some confusion in the understanding of underachievement (Gagne, 1991). If motivation is a necessary condition for gifted behavior, then how do we deal with students who are deemed capable of, but do not demonstrate, gifted behavior? At the crux of the underachievement issue is the realization that high ability does not guarantee high achievement—that is, giftedness does not guarantee gifted behavior.

The pertinent question for educators and parents is: Assuming that children possess an "intrinsic" desire to learn, why do some high-ability children lose, suppress, or sidestep this "intrinsic motivation"? Further, what is meant, specifically, by *motivation* and how can we better understand the psychological mechanisms that underlie low motivation? While little of the motivation research over the past forty years has directly addressed motivational issues that relate to high-ability students, many well-developed and well-researched theories can shed light on the critical question of why some students with high academic ability do not meet, or even attempt to meet, their potential. The purpose of this chapter is to explore several psychological explanations for the underachievement of some gifted students.

Underachievement as a Motivation Problem

Academic underachievement can be the product of many causes; indeed, in most situations it is likely to be the student's reaction to a constellation of variables. Some cases of underachievement have psychometric explanations: Individual or group tests have been incorrectly administered or scored, test results have been misinterpreted, or measurement error has been excessive. These explanations, however, probably account for very few instances of underachievement. In many cases the source of the underachievement is environmental. Family problems can inhibit a child's ability to give schoolwork the attention it requires, or the school environment might be such that it does not allow the full expression of giftedness. Sometimes exceptional performance is not encouraged or is even discouraged by beleaguered school personnel, through limited course offerings, on the one hand, and negative classroom interactions on the other. Many children express their boredom in school through misbehavior, which, in turn, elicits negative reactions from teachers and reinforces the child's perception that his or her achievement needs are unreasonable.

Even when a challenging curriculum is offered, an encouraging academic environment is present, and no serious family problems exist, there remain a large number of high-ability students who, for psychological reasons, exhibit one or more of the following academic behaviors: low effort, challenge avoidance, unreasonably low or unreasonably high self-expectations, low persistence at difficult tasks, or lack of joy in learning. It is these students whose self-defeating behaviors can be better perceived through the lens of motivational research.

The constellation of behaviors described here has generally been considered to typify the student who lacks "intrinsic motivation"—that is, a tendency to engage in a behavior in the absence of external reward. As motivation research has become more precise, its focus has been on identifying specific academic behaviors that are associated with desirable academic outcomes. Research has generally focused on three factors—challenge seeking, persistence, and task enjoyment—as indicating the presence of intrinsic motivation. These factors are considered "adaptive" academic behaviors, and their opposites—challenge avoidance, giving up, and lack of enjoyment—are considered "maladaptive" academic behaviors. This more precise conceptualization avoids the tendency to think of motivation as a trait and focuses instead on situation-specific behaviors. Similarly, it encourages the realization that students are not either "motivated" or "unmotivated"; although they might not be motivated to meet the teacher's or the school's academic goals, they *are* motivated to meet their own psychological needs.

Theories of Motivation

All of the theories to be discussed are cognitive theories of motivation. That is, they rest on the assumption that behavior stems from the way that people interpret and internalize information. Many cognitive theories of achievement behavior are guided by the assumption that a child's perception of his or her ability is a better predictor of achievement-related behaviors than are objective measures of that ability (e.g., standardized test scores, grades). Research from many theoretical perspectives has borne this out (Bandura, 1977; Covington, 1984; Harter, 1978; Nicholls, 1982; Parsons, 1982; Phillips, 1984; Weiner, 1979). This assumption leads us to pay special attention to constructs related to self-concept of ability, perceived competence, self-efficacy, and the like as they help us to understand children whose academic behaviors are not consistent with their capabilities. Put another way, why do children who are academically exceptional behave as if they were not? The focus will be on how each of these theories can be applied to the underachievement question: What is preventing this child from exhibiting adaptive academic behaviors?

Locus-of-Control Theory

In 1966, in the context of his development of social learning theory, Julian Rotter identified the tendency of people to perceive that outcomes in a particular arena were either within or outside their control, and found that this tendency was related to the expectations they held for future success in that area. He called this construct *locus of control,* which has since been applied to issues in numerous realms, including health, interpersonal relationships, and academics. People with an internal locus of control have been found to take more responsibility for their behavior and to demonstrate typical *expectancy shifts,* or changes in their expectations for their performance after a particular event. A typical expectancy shift would be to raise one's expectations after experiencing success, and to lower one's expectations following failure (James & Rotter, 1958). People who have an external locus of control feel that forces outside themselves control their fortunes and act as if there were little relationship between what they do and what happens to them. As a consequence, they exhibit "atypical" expectancy shifts (i.e., low expectancy after success, high expectancy after failure) which are often manifested as low confidence in their own ability, even following success.

This pattern of atypical expectancy shifts would seem to describe the behaviors of some underachievers, in that they appear to have either low or unrealistically high academic goals. The student who avoids enrolling in a high-level mathematics course despite high achievement test scores and high grades in previous math classes is demonstrating an atypical expectancy shift.

Rotter's theory has generated voluminous research into the antecedents, correlates, and consequences of a student's locus of control for academic subjects. Generally, it has been found that there is a tendency for locus of control to be a generalized trait, but that there is variation within and between domains or areas. For example, a student who exhibits an internal locus of control in athletic activities could also hold an external locus for schoolwork, or hold an internal locus for math but an external locus for English.

Locus of control is thought to derive from a person's reinforcement history, and therefore is sensitive to environmental variations. One of the most pertinent areas of research, conducted in the early 1970s, proposed that intrinsic motivation can be undermined by external reward, and that the mechanism through which this happens is locus of control. Lepper, Green, and Nisbitt (1973) conducted a program of research on the "overjustification hypothesis," in which children were given rewards for performing activities that they already enjoyed. Many experiments using varying types of rewards (e.g., verbal praise, candy, symbolic rewards) showed that children showed less interest and enjoyment in an activity that they had initially engaged in for its intrinsic interest after being promised and given a reward for engaging in that same activity (Deci, 1971; Dollinger & Thelen, 1978; Greene & Lepper, 1974; Lepper & Greene, 1975). The authors proposed that when a reward was imposed on an already rewarding activity, the children's locus of control for that activity was shifted from internal to external. Later research by Amabile and others (Amabile, 1985; Amabile, Goldfarb, & Brackfield, 1990; Ambile, Hennessey, & Grossman, 1986) has shown that a similar phenomenon occurs when artists and authors are rewarded for their creative products; stories or artwork produced under contract were judged to be less creative than work produced without a promised "reward."[1]

The implications for some gifted students seem clear. For those who are vulnerable to the undermining effect of reward, and we know little about why some are and some are not, their loss of control over school work would seem to begin as soon as grades are assigned. Constantly praised and rewarded for doing what comes naturally to them (i.e., excellent work), students come to depend on external evaluation and, worse, come to view their own behavior as driven by the external agent.

While the controversy over the appropriate use of reward continues (see Cameron & Pierce, 1994), it seems clear that for some students, a loss of a sense of control over their own learning could be at the root of their underachievement problems.

Attribution Theory

Research on locus of control was absorbed to a great degree by a newer theoretical formulation that emerged in the 1970s. Weiner's (1974, 1979) introduction of *attribution theory* proposed that locus of control was one of two dimensions that characterized the explanations (or attributions) that students give for their successes and failures in the classroom. According to Weiner, the four chief explanations that students give for academic outcomes focus on ability, effort, task difficulty, or luck. These four attributions vary not only in terms of their *locus* (internal or external), but also in terms of their *stability* or permanence (stable or unstable). Using these two dimensions, locus and stability, Weiner constructed a four-celled taxonomy (see Figure 33.1). Ability was perceived to be an internal, stable explanation; effort was an internal, unstable

[1] See Chapter 23 by Hennessey.

		LOCUS OF CONTROL	
		Internal	External
STABILITY	Stable	Ability	Task Difficulty
	Unstable	Effort	Luck

Figure 33.1 Four attributions that explain academic outcomes.

explanation; task difficulty was external and stable; and luck was external and unstable.

Twenty years of subsequent research on attribution theory has led to the consideration of a third dimension, *controllability,* as well as other refinements of the theory, but the original conceptualization is still the best known and will be the subject of this discussion (see Weiner, 1994, for an example of how attribution theory has evolved).

Attribution theory has linked specific academic behaviors to particular attributions: Attributing success to ability is associated with high expectations for future success, challenge seeking, and persistence, while attributing failure to ability is associated with low expectations for future success, challenge avoidance, and low persistence. Students who believe that their failures are due to a lack of ability believe that their low ability will make future failures more likely. Diener and Dweck (1978) claimed that such students exhibit "learned helplessness" in academic settings; they see poor academic outcomes as outside of their control because the outcomes are due to low ability, and so they give up easily, avoid challenges, and dislike school. Adaptive academic behaviors, then, are clearly associated with ability attributions for success, but not for failure.

Effort attributions, on the other hand, are associated with adaptive behaviors when used to explain failure. Because effort is generally perceived to be under one's control, therefore unstable, it is changeable. Students who believe that their school work can be improved through their own effort are likely to maintain high expectations for success and to "try harder" next time. The picture becomes much more complicated with success outcomes.

The Ability–Effort Relationship. The way that students think about *ability* and *effort,* especially as these concepts relate to each other, has enormous implications for understanding high-ability students' motivation problems. Nicholls (1976, 1982) reported developmental trends in this area. Preschool and kindergarten children generally do not distinguish between effort and ability, and seem to have an "all good things go together" attitude (i.e., smart kids work hard and are good in class). In the early elementary grades, the two concepts become discrete, and effort is seen as more important. By early adolescence, individual differences in conceptions of ability become more apparent, and many children come to have a compensatory view of effort and ability; that is, smart kids don't have to try hard, and if you do have to try hard, you're not smart. Also, ability is seen as more important, and as placing limits on achievement.

Consider the implications of these beliefs for students who have been labeled and treated as "gifted" from a young age. Suppose that a student, on his first algebra test (a new task), receives a grade that he considers to be low (this could be a "B") after working very hard. Having made ability attributions for his good performance in math for his entire life (since he has been told that he is "good in math" since early childhood), he is now confronted with a situation where he must explain to himself how this could be. The fact that he had to work so hard on the test already has shaken his confidence in his ability. Many students in such circumstances begin to avoid situations where they have to work hard, not out of laziness, but out of fear, to protect a self-concept of high ability.

Within the attribution theory framework, several researchers have addressed the effort–ability conundrum. Covington and Omelich (1979) called effort the "double-edged sword" because of the problems mentioned here and because of the way that teachers view effort. Whereas some students typically avoid high-effort situations because of their implications for ability, teachers value and reward high effort on the part of students. One solution to this situation might be to expand the four-celled attribution conceptualization in Figure 33.1 to include other explanations that students might already use, or might be encouraged to use, for their academic outcomes (e.g., strategy).

Attribution retraining, which involves teaching students to give unstable rather than stable attributions for failure, has been found to be successful with many groups of students. Most of these retraining studies (e.g., Schunk, 1983) have given students effort feedback (e.g., "You are working hard on that") to encourage the use of effort attributions. Other studies have trained students to focus on the methods they used rather than simply the effort they exerted (Clifford, 1986a, 1986b; McNabb, 1987). For example, students can be encouraged to focus on their study techniques rather than the amount of time they spend studying, or they can think about the particular techniques they used to solve a math problem. Perhaps a more broad-based understanding of what *effort* means, particularly one that recognizes both the direction and intensity aspects of "trying," would give underachieving students a way out of the effort–ability box. That is, because strategy seems to incorporate aspects of both effort and ability, it could give gifted students a way to keep trying (by trying something else) without threatening their sense of competence.

Goal Theories

Carol Dweck and her colleagues (Dweck, 1986, 1991; Dweck & Leggett, 1988; Elliot & Dweck, 1988) proposed that adaptive achievement behaviors (challenge seeking, persistence in the face of obstacles, positive affect) and maladaptive achievement behaviors (challenge avoidance, low persistence, negative affect) have more to do with differences in students' classroom goals than with differences in their academic abilities. Further, students' goals in academic situations are related to the way they think about their intelligence (see Figure 33.2).

According to Dweck, there are two basic views of intelligence, the *entity* view and the *incremental* view. Students who have an entity view believe that intelligence is a fixed trait. It is something they "have," and they are motivated to engage in activities that will give them favorable judgments of their ability. Entity theorists adopt *performance* goals; they see achievement situations (performance) as a test of their competence. When they approach

Theory of Intelligence	*Goal Orientation*	*Confidence in Present Ability*	*Behavior Pattern*
Entity theory (Intelligence is fixed)	**Performance goal** (Goal is to gain positive judgments/avoid negative judgments of competence)	**If high**→	**Mastery-oriented** Seek challenge High persistence
		but	
		If low →	**Helpless** Avoid challenge Low persistence
Incremental theory (Intelligence is malleable)	**Learning goal** (Goal is to increase competence)	**If high**→ or **low**	**Mastery-oriented** Seek challenge (that fosters learning) High persistence

Figure 33.2 Dweck's model of achievement motivation.
Source: From "Motivational Processes Affecting Learning," by C. S. Dweck, 1986, *American Psychologist,* 41, p. 1041.

a learning situation about which they are confident, they will demonstrate adaptive learning behaviors. When, however, they approach a situation about which they have low confidence (a new situation or one that has been challenging in the past), they exhibit maladaptive behaviors. Entity theorists tend to see ability and effort as inversely related, so they doubt their ability after high-effort successes.

Incremental theorists view their intelligence as malleable and a product of effort. They see achievement situations as opportunities to increase their competence, and orient toward activities that help them develop their intellect and skills. Incremental theorists thus have *learning* rather than performance goals. They see effort and ability as positively related, so they focus on trying harder when they are challenged. Incremental theorists demonstrate adaptive academic behaviors regardless of their level of confidence in a particular task. According to Dweck and Leggett (1988, p. 260):

> Adaptive individuals effectively coordinate performance and learning goals. It is when an overconcern with proving their adequacy to themselves or to others leads individuals to ignore, avoid, or to abandon potentially valuable learning opportunities that problems arise.

Change *adequacy* to *giftedness* in the above quote, and the plight of the gifted underachiever becomes clear. It would seem difficult for a child who has been referred to as "gifted" for all of his or her childhood to have an incremental view of intelligence. In fact, the child has likely heard enough low effort–high ability messages (e.g., "That was so easy for you, you must be really smart"; "You got that answer so quickly, you are really good at math") by early adolescence to have a firmly entrenched entity view. Also, by this time, being gifted is likely to be central to the child's identity, providing further incentive to protect the self-concept of high ability. Unfortunately, as early adolescents enter middle school, they face greater academic challenges than previously encountered, many of them in novel situations where their confidence is questionable. Entity theorists, for whom the goal is a favorable evaluation of their ability, must be confident of their ability before displaying it for judgment. But confidence is fragile, because exertion of effort calls ability into question. In this framework, self-defeating, self-handicapping behaviors like avoiding difficult courses, not studying for tests, and causing problems in class become easier to understand.

Implications for Teachers

Research that directly ties children's perceptions of their giftedness with their achievement behaviors remains to be conducted. It seems likely that a better understanding of how high-ability children view effort will contribute greatly to understanding the underachievement phenomenon. In the meantime, teachers can do the following:

1. *Emphasize the role of effort in learning by focusing on the process and progress rather than on the outcome and external evaluation.* For example, point out to students the concepts they have mastered since the last test, rather than the grades they received. Ideally, grades should serve an informational function by telling students what they know or have mastered.
2. *Sacrifice accuracy, occasionally, for risk taking.* For example, reward students for assuming challenging tasks by weighting the credit received by the level of difficulty. Give pass/fail credit for especially difficult assignments.
3. *Help students to see the relationship between their effort and outcomes.* Praise students for exceptional effort, especially those who hesitate to demonstrate it. Comment on how good grades on tests or assignments are related to hard work or good study methods (e.g., "It looks like you put a lot of time into this paper. I can really tell by the quality of the work.")
4. *Use rewards sparingly, and only to reinforce behaviors that are not already rewarding.* Help students to recognize the rewards intrinsic in a challenging task with comments like "Doesn't it make you feel

great to be able to do a tough problem like that?"

5. *Model an incremental view of intelligence by emphasizing the importance of skill acquisition and downplaying normative performance.* Recognize students who make good progress relative to their own achievement. Many gifted students can come out on top without much effort, and do not work to the best of their own ability. Show respect for people who have achieved a lot through effort, as well as those whose accomplishments seem to be related to their innate abilities (even Larry Bird spent many hours practicing free throws).

REFERENCES

Amabile, T. M. (1985). Motivation and creativity: Effects of motivational orientation on creative writers. *Journal of Personality and Social Psychology, 48,* 393–399.

Amabile, T. M., Goldfarb, P., & Brackfield, S. (1990). Social influences on creativity: Evaluation, coaction, and surveillance, *Creativity Research Journal, 3,* 6–21.

Amabile, T. M., Hennessey, B. A., & Grossman, B. S. (1986). Social influences on creativity: The effects of contracted-for reward. *Journal of Personality and Social Psychology, 50,* 14–23.

Bandura, A. (1977). Self-efficacy: Toward a unifying theory of behavioral change. *Psychological Review, 84,* 191–215.

Cameron, J., & Pierce, W. D. (1994). Reinforcement, reward, and intrinsic motivation: A meta-analysis. *Review of Educational Research, 64,* 363–403.

Clifford, M. M. (1986a). The comparative effects of strategy and effort attributions. *British Journal of Educational Psychology, 56,* 75–83.

Clifford, M. M. (1986b). The effects of ability, strategy, and effort attributions for educational, business, and athletic failure. *British Journal of Educational Psychology, 56,* 169–179.

Covington, M. V. (1984). The self-worth theory of achievement motivation: Findings and educational implications. *Elementary School Journal, 85,* 5–20.

Covington, M. V., & Omelich, C. L. (1979). Effort: The double-edged sword in school achievement. *Journal of Educational Psychology, 71,* 169–182.

Deci, E. L. (1971). Effects of externally mediated rewards on intrinsic motivation. *Journal of Personality and Social Psychology, 18,* 105–115.

Diener, C. I., & Dweck, C. S. (1978). An analysis of learned helplessness: Continuous changes in performance, strategy and achievement cognitions following failure. *Journal of Personality and Social Psychology, 36,* 451–462.

Dollinger, S. J., & Thelen, M. H. (1978). Overjustification and children's intrinsic motivation: Comparative effects of four rewards. *Journal of Personality and Social Psychology, 36,* 1259–1269.

Dweck, C. S. (1986). Motivational processes affecting learning. *American Psychologist, 41,* 1040–1048.

Dweck, C. S. (1991). Self-theories and goals: Their role in motivation, personality, and development. In R. A. Dienstbier (Ed.), *Nebraska symposium on motivation: Vol. 38. Perspectives on motivation* (pp. 199–235). Lincoln: University of Nebraska Press.

Dweck, C. S., & Leggett, E. L. (1988). A social-cognitive approach to motivation and personality. *Psychological Review, 95,* 256–273

Elliot, E. S., & Dweck, C. S. (1988). Goals: An approach to motivation and achievement. *Journal of Personality and Social Psychology, 54,* 5–12.

Gagne, F. (1991). Toward a differentiated model of giftedness and talent. In N. Colangelo & G. A. Davis, (Eds.), *Handbook of gifted education* (pp. 65–80). Boston: Allyn and Bacon.

Greene, D., & Lepper, M. R. (1974). Effects of extrinsic rewards on children's subsequent intrinsic interest. *Child Development, 45,* 1141–1145.

Harter, S. (1978). Effectance motivation reconsidered: Toward a developmental model. *Human Development, 21,* 34–64.

James, W., & Rotter, J. B. (1958). Partial and 100% reinforcement under chance and skill conditions. *Journal of Experimental Psychology, 55,* 397–403.

Lepper, M. R., & Greene, D. (1975). Turning play into work: Effects of adult surveillance and extrinsic rewards on children's intrinsic motivation. *Journal of Personality and Social Psychology, 31,* 479–486.

Lepper, M. R., Greene, D., & Nisbett, R. E. (1973). Undermining children's intrinsic interest with extrinsic reward: A test of the overjustification hypothesis. *Journal of Personality and Social Psychology, 28,* 129–137.

McNabb, T. F. (1987). *The motivational effects of strategy and effort attribution training.* Unpublished manuscript, University of Iowa.

Nicholls, J. G. (1976). Effort is virtuous but it's better to have ability: Evaluative responses to perceptions of effort and ability. *Journal of Research in Personality, 10,* 306–315.

Nicholls, J. G. (1982). Conceptions of ability and achievement motivation. In R. Ames & C. Ames (Eds.), *Research in motivation in education: Student motivation* (pp. 39–73). New York: Academic Press.

Parsons, J. E. (1982). Expectancies, values and academic behaviors. In J. T. Spence (Ed.), *Assessing achievement.* San Francisco: Freeman.

Phillips, D. (1984). The illusion of incompetence among high-achieving children. *Child Development, 55,* 2000–2016.

Renzulli, J. S. (1978). What makes giftedness? Reexamining a definition. *Phi Delta Kappan, 60,* 180–184, 261.

Rotter, J. B. (1966). Generalized expectancies for internal versus external control of reinforcement. *Psychological Monographs, 80,* (1, Whole No. 609).

Schunk, D. H. (1983). Ability versus effort attributional feedback: Differential effects on self-efficacy and achievement. *Journal of Educational Psychology, 74,* 548-556.

Weiner, B. (Ed.). (1974). *Achievement motivation and attribution theory.* Morristown, NJ: General Learning Press.

Weiner, B. (1979). A theory of motivation for some classroom experiences. *Journal of Educational Psychology, 71,* 3–25.

Weiner, B. (1994). Integrating social and personal theories of achievement striving. *Review of Educational Research, 64,* 557–573.

34

Underachievement Syndrome: A National Epidemic

SYLVIA B. RIMM, *Case Western Reserve School of Medicine and the MetroHealth Center, Cleveland, Ohio*

A five-minute interview with this author on NBC's *Today* show covering the topic of gifted underachieving children and an offer of free information about underachievement attracted over 20,000 phone calls and thousands of letters from distressed parents. Letters about elementary school age children, middle and high school adolescents, and floundering young adults in and out of college emphasized the extent of the underachievement problem. Parents described peer pressures, behavior problems, and their children's lack of understanding of the effort needed for school. Young adults commented on the effects of competition that caused them anxiety, depression, and feelings of alienation and inadequacy. Excerpts from a few letters from around the United States are included in Figure 34.1.

It is impossible to determine accurate percentages of gifted underachievers. The National Commission on Excellence in Education (1983) reported that half of gifted students do not perform to their tested abilities. High school dropout studies found that between 10 and 20 percent of those who do not complete high school are in the tested gifted range (Lajoie & Shore, 1981; Nyquist, 1973; Whitmore, 1980). Underachievement of gifted students emerges dramatically again in college. Of the top 5 percent of this country's high school graduates, 40 percent do not complete college (DeLeon, 1989).

Being intellectually or creatively gifted does not assure educational or creative success or productivity. There are risks and pressures that accompany high intelligence which detour potentially high-achieving children toward defensive and avoidance patterns (Rimm, 1987b). The determinants of whether gifted children move toward high achievement or fall into underachieving patterns appear to be related to their home, school, and/or peer environments (Rimm, 1986b, 1995).

The Pressures

The main pressures that gifted children seem to feel include: (1) the need to be extraordinarily intelligent and/or "smartest"; (2) the wish to be extremely creative and unique, which they may translate as nonconformity; and (3) the concern with being admired by peers for appearance and popularity.

Although parents are often accused of pressuring their gifted children, these pressures typically arise because of the children's giftedness. Gifted children often internalize a sense of stress because many adults in their environments have admired them for their academic accomplishments, their unusual ideas, and/or their appearance. The profuse praise they receive not only reinforces their motivation but, when too extreme or frequent, may cause them to feel as if they are expected to accomplish the goals that are so admired or valued by others. They not only may feel pressure to achieve, but they also may acquire a dependence on attention and find it difficult to function without continuous praise and reinforcement (Deci, 1986; Hom, Gaskill, & Hutchins, 1988).

If school and home environments foster successful relationships between effort and outcomes, it is more likely that children will manage the internalized pressures and will incorporate them as motivations toward achievement (Rimm, 1987b). School environments that foster underachievement would be those that either do not value high achievement or, conversely, set achievement outcomes too high. In either case, children may make

North Carolina:
My son, an 11th grader, is a gifted student and having a lot of problems this year. I'm afraid he is throwing away all his chances for the future.

Florida:
Zachary is 5 years old and in kindergarten. He's been reading since he was two years of age. However, I am concerned with his behavior. He gives up very easily. Sometimes he'll throw a pencil. Zachary also demands attention and excessive praise, which is not easy to deliver to one child in a class of 27 children.

Tennessee:
My son, Kevin, was told he would be in the school's Academic Olympics. Since he isn't doing his work, his teacher is considering sending someone else in his place. He cried about it because he wants very much to be a part of this. He claims he tries, but he just cannot seem to get assignments turned in.

Iowa:
Our son is definitely experiencing all the problems you mentioned. Jerod is 16 and had a 90th percentile in all his basic skills tests. He's getting D's and F's in every academic subject. He had to repeat sophomore English because he just would not turn in assignments. He just does not do homework at all.

In grade school he got perfect papers almost consistently and was in a TAG program and loved the extra challenges the teachers provided him. In junior high there was no TAG money and hence no program. He became extremely bored with humdrum classes and this started his downward spiral.

Texas:
I have a college student who was a National Merit Scholar who is on scholastic probation because she hasn't a clue about what studying entails. The process is foreign to her since she floated through high school. She is quite devastated, and we really don't know how to teach her to study.

Pennsylvania:
My daughter is 18, has 1340 on her SATs and is getting C and D minuses in her postgraduate year.

Idaho:
I am interested in where I can read more about the topic of gifted kids who don't hand in papers, stop going to classes in college, etc. Sounds like you have met my son, recently readmitted to Middlebury College (VT) for his "last chance."

Figure 34.1 Excerpts from *Today* Show viewers' letters.

appropriate efforts but do not gain satisfaction from their successful efforts. Some school environments that do not value excellent school achievement include the following:

- An anti-intellectual school atmosphere that sets high priorities for athletics or social status but not for intellectual attainment or preparation for higher level education (Brown & Steinberg, 1990; U.S. Department of Education, 1993)
- An anti-gifted atmosphere that considers gifted programming elitist and emphasizes the importance of all students adjusting and fitting into the same mold
- A rigid classroom environment that encourages all children to study identical materials at similar speeds or in similar styles. Gifted children may teach others, but their actual learning is not valued.
- Teachers who rigidly fail to see the quality of children's work because of different values, personal power struggles, or cultural or racial prejudice. These cause children to feel unable to accomplish outcomes despite their efforts (Rimm, 1980; Davis & Rimm, 1994).

School environments that value children's accomplishments but only provide tasks that are too easy and do not encourage challenge or sustained efforts also foster underachievement. The schools value good grades and performance, and initially grades reflect excellent performance. Children tend to feel positively about school, but they are not sufficiently challenged because the work is too easy. Reis and Purcell (1993) found that gifted children in elementary school already have accomplished 35 to 50 percent of the skills they will be taught in a specific grade before they have entered it. Children learn that achievement is easy, that success is readily attainable, and that learning and study are effortless. Occasionally, they may comment about boredom or lack of challenge, but as long as grades continue to be high, they exhibit no behavior problems.

When the curriculum becomes more complex or when students enter higher grades where peer populations are more intellectually competitive, gifted children feel as though they are not as intelligent as they believed they were earlier. Some learn more appropriate study habits. Others hide from their threatening feelings. They worry that they are not as smart as they would like to be, and they invent or discover a whole group of rituals and excuses that prevent them from making further effort.

One college student thought her "brain cells might be dissolving." Another explained that something was missing, and he no longer felt special and, therefore, just gave up. Many bright high school students have reminded me that "if you're smart, schoolwork should be easy." Peer messages about being "casual" or "cool" also reinforce a model of not making "too much" school effort. A fifth-grade boy's conclusion that he would like to "get all A's without carrying a book" emphasizes that point well.

Procrastination, incomplete assignments, disorganization, and careless work become typical symptoms that initiate underachievement syndrome for these students. These symptoms will disappear only when the students are gradually persuaded to take the risk of making school effort. Only then will they find out that they are, indeed, highly capable. Perhaps even with appropriate effort they will be required to set more realistic goals. Their past school environments simply have not taught them the challenging *process* of achievement. Bias among teachers against accelerated curriculum and grade skipping often prevents schools from challenging these students (Rimm & Lovance, 1992).

Underachievement occurs when children's habits, efforts, and skills cause them to lose their sense of control over school outcomes. Teachers are less likely to identify these children as gifted because their intelligence or creativity may no longer be evident in the classroom. Even parents begin to doubt their children's abilities. They may recall that their children were "smart" at some point in the past, but now they may be willing to settle for very average and sometimes far below average achievement. Passing grades become acceptable.

High-Risk Home Environments

Family characteristics of underachievers have been described in several studies (Frasier, Passow, & Goldberg, 1958; French, 1959; Whitmore, 1980; Zilli, 1971). Rimm and Lowe (1988) targeted some critical differences between the families of 22 gifted underachievers and the findings from family studies of achievement and eminence. The findings are summarized and the main differences are highlighted in Tables 34.1, 34.2, and 34.3.

Although parents of both groups showed concern about achievement for their children, the modeling of intrinsic and independent learning, positive commitment to career, and respect for school were remarkably, though unintentionally, absent from families of underachieving gifted children. The enrichment and fun of early childhood were often replaced by a plethora of activities and lessons which were so time consuming that they left little energy for intrinsically interesting home learning, independent projects, or family game playing. Management of students' homework by parents resulted in dependent patterns and parent–child arguments.

Many parents of underachieving gifted children openly opposed teachers and school policies. Parents were involved in opposition to schools in 90 percent of the families. In some cases, parents' battles were—appropriately—based on lack of challenge. They rarely shared their own career interests with their children. Most fathers spoke quite negatively about their own work even when they had invested many years in preparation for their high-level careers. Well-educated mothers who centered their lives on their children and volunteer activities often voiced frustration at their "nonprofessional" role. Green, Fine, and Tollefson (1988) also found that parents' attitudes toward their careers were related to their children's underachievement.

Unlike the families in the studies of giftedness and eminence (Bloom, 1985; MacKinnon, 1965; Walberg et al., 1981), the theme of family organization and consistent and predictable expectations for conduct was noticeably absent in the homes of the under-

Table 34.1
Family Structural Characteristics

Characteristics	*Eminence and Giftedness*	*Underachieving Gifted*	*Comparison*
Size of family	Small	2.59 children	Similar
Birth order	More than half oldest	59% oldest	Similar
Only children	Percentage varied	27%	Similar to some, different from some
Adopted children in family	Not reported	23%	Not reported, probably different
Male/female	More males	More males	Similar
Specialness	Earned specialness	Specialness displaced for 81%; 18% never earned specialness	Different
Age of parents at marriage	Older parents fairly typical	Mother—30 Father—32	Similar
Education of parents	Higher education fairly typical	Mother—15.7 Father—17.9	Similar
Parent loss	Low parent divorce, some parent loss	Low parent divorce, some parent loss	Similar

Source: "Family Environments of Underachieving Gifted Students" by S. B. Rimm and B. Lowe, 1988, *Gifted Child Quarterly, 32*(4), Fall, pp. 353–359.

Table 34.2
Family Climate

Characteristics	*Eminence and Giftedness*	*Underachieving Gifted*	*Comparison*
Child centeredness	Child centered High adult personal interests	Child centered early; low adult personal interests	Similarities and differences
Discord and trauma vs. secure supportive families	Mixed findings: artists, authors more traumatic; scientists, mathematicians more secure	Considerable discord	Different
Parenting style	Mixed, but nonauthoritarian and consistent	Early liberal, then changed to 95% inconsistent "ogre" rituals	Different
Family relationships:			
Father/mother	Usually very good	68% good, 32% bad	Some differences
Child/mother	Usually good	59% poor	Different
Child/father	Usually good	63% poor	Different
Child/siblings	Usually good	45% poor	Different
Structure and organization	Consistent and predictable	Inconsistent: 95% indicated manipulating one or both parents	Different

Source: "Family Environments of Underachieving Gifted Students" by S. B. Rimm and B. Lowe, 1988, *Gifted Child Quarterly, 32*(4), Fall, pp. 353–359.

achieving children studied by Rimm and Lowe (1988). Differences between parents in the standards, limits, and expectations provided unclear guidelines. Ninety-five percent of the students (all but one) indicated that they could manipulate one or both parents much of the time, and the parents of these children confirmed their children's observations. The absence of consistent leadership among these parents was remarkable.

Although most children spent their early childhoods with parents who considered their parenting techniques to be quite liberal and flexible, only one couple maintained a consistent parenting philosophy. By the time their children were of school age, extreme differences in parenting styles emerged. In 95 percent of the families, one parent played the role of the parent who challenged and disciplined, while the other took the role of protector. There was increasing opposition between parents as the challenger became more authoritarian and the rescuer became increasingly protective. In 54 percent of the families the father took the role of disciplinarian; in 41 percent the mother played the authoritarian role. These authoritarian/rescuer rituals are described by Rimm (1986b; 1995) as "ogre" games.

When children were asked which of their parents was easier, only five children (23 percent) indicated that their parents had similar expectations. Twenty-five percent of the boys thought their father was easier, and 50 percent chose their mother as the easier parent. Three of the girls (60 percent) considered their father to be easier. Only one girl said her mother was easier.

According to their parents, 81 percent of the gifted underachievers were considered by their families to be "special." This sense of specialness was either attached to the parents' early discovery of their child's gifted abilities or based on a long-awaited birth or unusual circumstance. Later, that specialness was withdrawn, and the "special" attribution was

Table 34.3
Values Espoused and Modeled by Parents

Characteristics	*Eminence and Giftedness*	*Underachieving Gifted*	*Comparison*
Achievement orientation expressed	Valued work and achievement	Valued work and achievement	Similar
Grade expectations	Reasonable and unpressured	Reasonable and unpressured: Mothers—3.2 GPA Fathers—3.2 GPA	Similar
Early enrichment and activities	Provided	Provided	Similar
Social adjustment of children	Mixed	73% not well accepted by peers	Some differences
High energy of parents	Dramatically consistent	Mainly true	Some differences
Father's career	Mainly committed, positive and sharing interests	Considerable frustration with career or, if positive, not sharing interests	Different
Mother's career	Mainly homemakers, volunteers, busy and happy	Mainly homemakers, volunteers, busy but not satisfied	Different
Identification with same-sexed parent	Mixed research on identification, mainly positive for achievement with boys and girls with fathers	25% of males identified with father, 20% identified with mother	Different
School–home relationship	Mainly good and supportive Reasonable school adjustments	90% were oppositional, problem in school environments	Different
Homework independence	Independence plus additional independent learning projects; some parent monitoring	59% were homework dependent, absence of independent learning projects; oppositional monitoring	Different
Intrinsic learning	Frequently modeled by parents	Rarely modeled by parents	Different

Source: "Family Environments of Underachieving Gifted Students" by S. B. Rimm and B. Lowe, 1988, *Gifted Child Quarterly, 32*(4), Fall, pp. 353–359.

given to another family member. Sometimes the sense of specialness was lost as part of school adjustment (Rimm, 1990a, 1990b). Clinical interviews indicated that all of the samples were given a great deal of early attention. More than half (54 percent) had that attention withdrawn dramatically by a second sibling, who then received the "special" designation, or by a parent's remarriage to a stepparent. In 27 percent (6) of the cases, only children adjusted poorly to sharing attention at school. In 18 percent (4) of the cases, children never established a sense of specialness because another sibling was already designated as having that role.

The following examples provide insights into the trauma felt by children whose specialness is displaced:

Maureen, a gifted ninth grader, had been adopted. She was showered with extreme amounts of adult attention for the first six years of her life. Her younger sister was an unexpected birth child to her parents. Maureen was an underachiever throughout school and shared with the therapist that she could remember always resenting her younger sister, although she could not explain any reasons for her feelings.

Sandy was born to a single mother who felt guilty about her out-of-wedlock pregnancy. Sandy's mother spent almost every waking moment with her child. When her mother married, Sandy felt disempowered and angry at her stepfather with whom she was determined not to share her mother's attention.

When the "special" designation was withdrawn, the early dependence on extreme amounts of attention had the effect of causing the children to feel "attention neglected." The search for a way to retrieve the special attention involved behaviors that parents and teachers often labeled as "spoiled" or "arrogant." These children often behave as if they had an attention deficit disorder (Rimm, 1994). Efforts by teachers and parents to "put these children back in their places" only increased the children's feelings of neglect and their defiant or nonproductive behaviors.

Characteristics and Directions of Underachievement

The characteristic found most frequently and consistently among underachieving children is low self-esteem (Davis & Rimm, 1994; Fine & Pitts, 1980; Whitmore, 1980). Although the children acknowledge that they are intelligent, they do not believe themselves capable of accomplishing what their families or teachers expect of them. They may mask their low self-esteem with displays of bravado, rebellion, or highly protective defense mechanisms (Covington & Beery, 1976; Fine & Pitts, 1980; Rimm, 1986b). For example, they may openly criticize the quality of the school or the talents of individual teachers, or claim that they "don't care" or "didn't really try" in regard to a mediocre test score or class grade.

Related to their low self-esteem is their sense of low personal control over their own lives (Rimm, 1986b, 1995). If they fail at a task, they blame their lack of ability; if they succeed, they may attribute their success to luck. Thus, they may accept responsibility for failure, but not for success (Felton & Biggs, 1977). This attribution process in educational achievement has been related to the original theory of *learned helplessness* advanced by Seligman (1975). If a child does not see a relationship between his efforts and the outcomes, he is likely to exhibit characteristics of learned helplessness and will no longer make an effort to achieve. Weiner (1974, 1980) also emphasized that children's subsequent performance will be strongly influenced by whether they attribute successes and failures to ability, effort, task difficulty, or luck. Attributing success to *effort* leads to further effort, while attributing success to *task ease* or *luck* does not (see Chapter 33 by McNabb).

Low self-esteem leads the underachiever to nonproductive avoidance behaviors both at school and at home. For example, underachievers may avoid making a productive effort by asserting that school is irrelevant and that they see no reason to study material only to receive a diploma. Students may further assert that when they are really interested in learning, they can do very well. They complain that teachers should make the work more interesting. These avoidance behaviors protect underachievers from admitting their feared lack of productive ability. If they study, they risk *confirming* their possible shortcomings to themselves and to important others. If they do not study, they can use the nonstudying as a rationale for the failure, thus protecting their precarious feelings of self-worth (Covington & Beery, 1976).

Extreme rebellion against authority, particularly school authority, provides another route to protect the underachiever. The student may be eager to tell teachers, the principal, the superintendent, even the board of education exactly how they ought to run the school. Faulting the school helps the underachiever avoid the responsibility of achieving by blaming the system.

Expectations of low grades and perfectionism, though apparent opposites, also serve as defense mechanisms for the underachieving child with low self-esteem. If the underachiever expects low grades, he or she lowers the risk of failure. Setting goals that are impossibly high also provides safety for underachievers. They can use the "too high" goals as an excuse for not making efforts. By contrast, achieving children set realistic goals that are reachable, and failures are constructively used to indicate weaknesses needing attention.

Two main directions of responses have been described by Rimm (1986b, 1995). She has found that underachievers exhibit their defenses by either dependent or dominant behaviors. Figure 34.2 shows these two directions. Conforming underachievers differ from those in the nonconforming category by their visibility. That is, conforming dependent and dominant students have characteristics that may lead to underachievement problems, but their underachievement is not as serious or apparent. Nonconforming dependent and dominant underachievers are already exhibiting serious problems. The prototypical names used in Figure 34.2—"Passive Paul," "Rebellious Rebecca," and so forth—are used to emphasize the main characteristics of these underachievers, but any one child typically exhibits a group of these symptoms. Rimm also points out that some underachievers exhibit both dependent and dominant qualities. Cornale (1988) found that by adolescence, most underachievers exhibit both dependent and dominant symptoms.

Reversal of Underachievement

The underachieving gifted child continues to underachieve because the home, school, and/or peer group unintentionally reinforce that underachievement. The student is no longer motivated to achieve, and there may be deficiencies in skills necessary for achievement. Working below one's abilities affects both immediate educational success and eventual career achievement.

Although it is certainly difficult to reverse long-standing patterns of underachievement, Rimm's TRIFOCAL Model has been proven successful in approximately 80 percent of her cases (Rimm, 1986b, 1995). She has found that the treatment of underachievement involves the collaboration of school and family in the implementation of six steps (see Figure 34.3).

1. Assessment
2. Communication
3. Changing expectations
4. Role model identification
5. Correction of deficiencies
6. Modifications of reinforcements

In addition to the use of the TRIFOCAL model, parents and teachers should prepare to be equipped with "patience, dedication, and support" (Hoffman, Wasson, & Christianson, 1985).

Step 1: Assessment of Skills, Abilities, and Types of Underachievement

The first step in the underachievement reversal process is an assessment that involves the cooperation of the school psychologist, teacher of the gifted, and parents. It's critical that these people are aware of characteristics of gifted and creative children.

An *individual* intelligence test continues to be a highly recommended first assessment instrument. The venerable IQ number has the potential to communicate important expectations related to a child's abilities. Since gifted underachieving children have not been motivated, it is likely that *group* intelligence test scores have underestimated their intellectual potential. The underachievement also may have had a depressing effect on scores obtained by individual testing. The WISC-R, WISC III, or the Stanford-Binet L-M must be individually administered by a psychologist. There are other individual intelligence tests that can be administered by a psychologist to evaluate learning potential for culturally diverse, nonverbal, non-English-speaking, blind, or deaf gifted children who also need to be individually assessed. Some of these instruments are questionable in terms of their equivalence to the most conventionally accepted tests, namely the Wechsler and Binet scales, but all provide a reasonably acceptable predictor of a child's school-related capability.

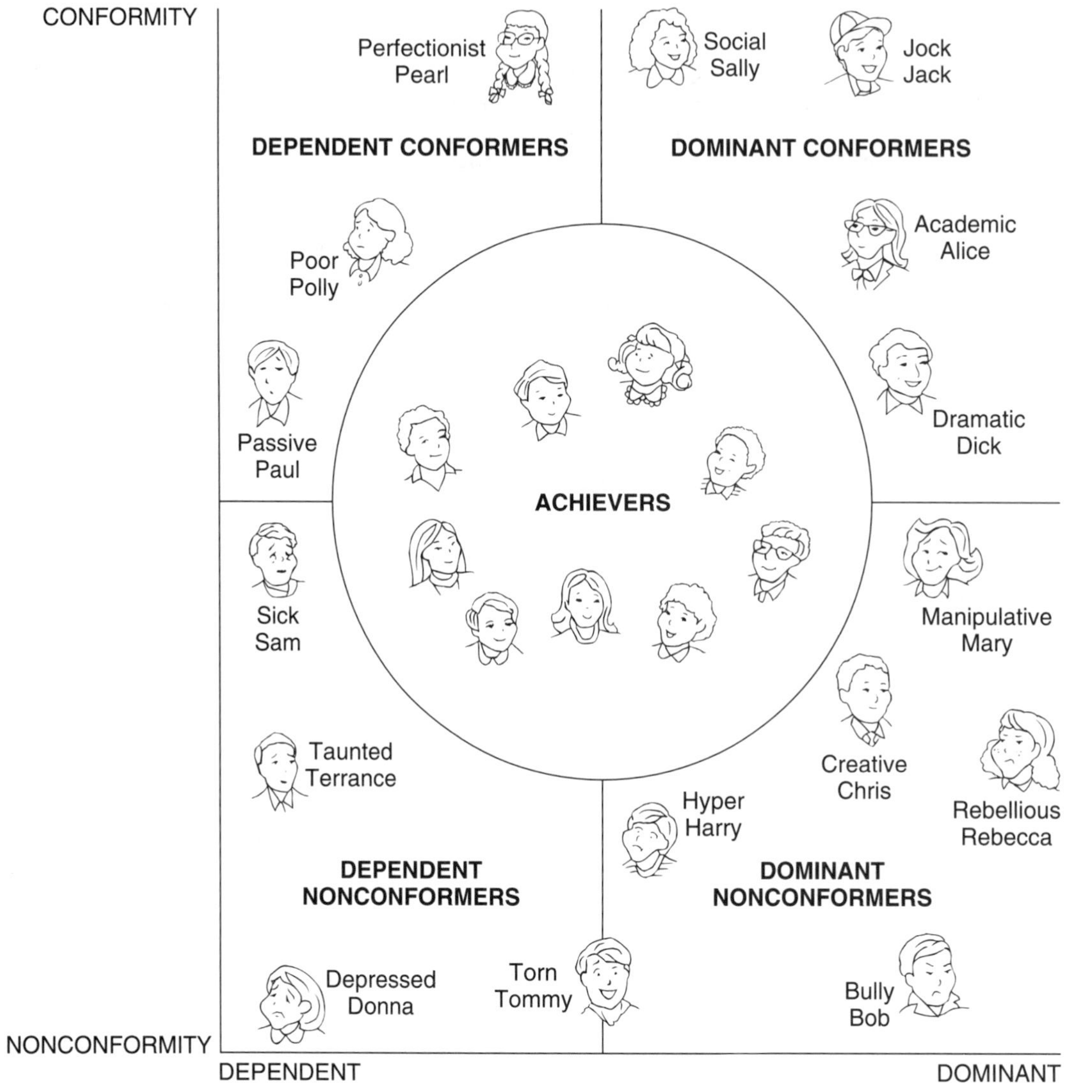

Source: Underachievement Syndrome: Causes and Cures by Sylvia B. Rimm, 1986, Watertown, WI: Apple Publishing Company. Reprinted with permission.

Figure 34.2 The inner circle of achievers.

For culturally diverse children, scores may be lower than actual abilities.

During testing the psychometrist should be especially aware of particular task-relevant characteristics of the child: symptoms of tension, attention to the task, perseverance at the task, responses to frustration, problem-solving approaches, defensiveness, and dependence on personal encouragement by the examiner. These reflect, in miniature, approaches to educational tasks that the child very likely uses in the classroom and home environments. Intelligence testing should be followed by individual achievement tests to as-

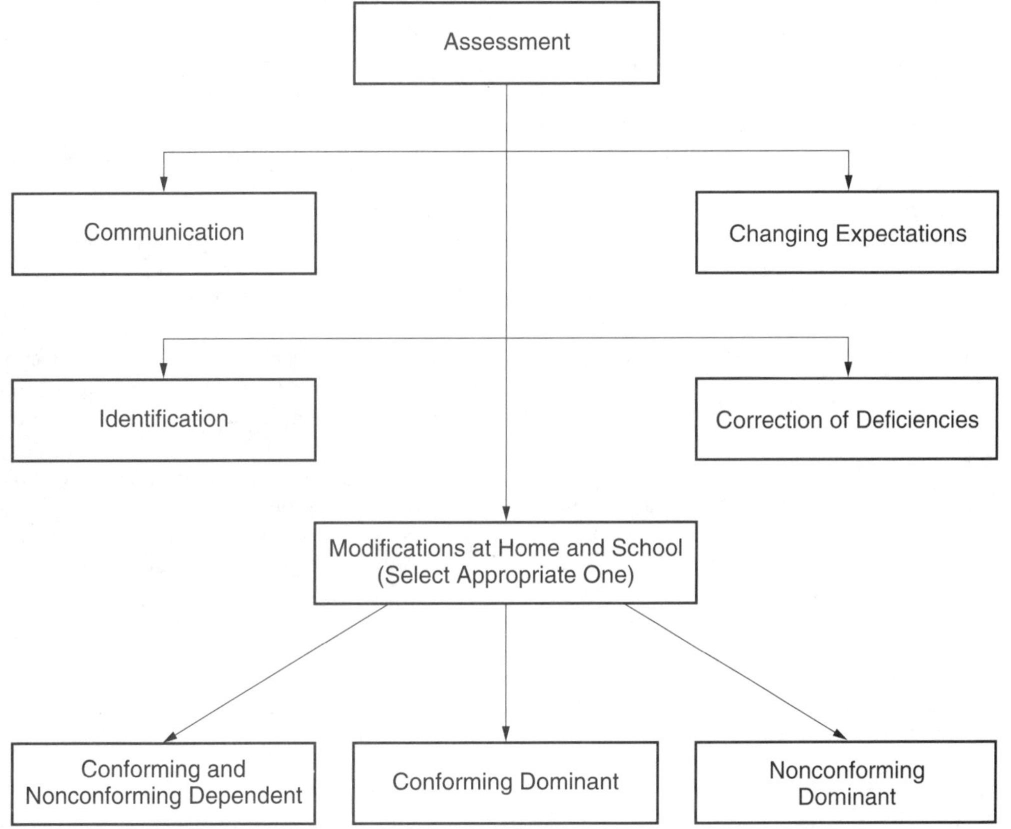

Source: Underachievement Syndrome: Causes and Cures by Sylvia B. Rimm, 1986, Watertown, WI: Apple Publishing Company. Reprinted with permission.

Figure 34.3 TRIFOCAL model for curing underachievement syndrome.

sess clearly the child's strengths and deficits in basic skills, particularly reading and math. Achievement tests that do not require writing are a better measure for the many underachievers who have handwriting problems.

A creativity test or inventory, which can be administered by the teacher or by a psychologist, should also be part of the assessment. These produce not only a norm-referenced creativity score but also descriptions of abilities, characteristics, and interests that are relevant to understanding the child's personality, creative potential, and learning style. The GIFT and GIFFI tests include dimension scores such as Independence, Self-confidence, Imagination, Interests, and Challenge-Inventiveness that provide important insights into understanding the student.

AIM (Achievement Identification Measure; Rimm, 1986a), GAIM (Group Achievement Identification Measure; Rimm, 1987a), and AIM-TO (Achievement Identification Measure—Teacher Observation; Rimm, 1988) are inventories developed for the identification of children's characteristics related to achievement or underachievement. GAIM can be used with students from grades 5 through 12. AIM is completed by parents, and AIM-TO is a teacher observation instrument. The latter two instruments also can be completed for any school-age student. The scores will provide a description of the extent and type of the person's underachievement. Dimension scores will reveal whether the student is mainly dependent or dominant or combines a mixture of both. Scores will also permit insights into parent consistency in messages about achievement. A description of the dimension scores is provided in Figure 34.4.

Finally, a parent interview also can be very helpful in identifying underachieving patterns unintentionally maintained at home or in school. Ideally, both parents should be at the interview. If only one appears, it would be important to ask about the other parent's relationship to the child.

Step 2: Communication

Communication between parents and teachers is an important component of the cure for underachievers. Either a parent or the teacher may initiate the first conference. The initiator should assure the other person of support rather than placing blame. If it appears to a teacher that the parents are not interested in or capable of consistent follow-through, the teacher should select another child advocate in the school with whom to work around the child's underachievement. Schools have facetiously labeled this adaption of the TRIFOCAL model the "bifocal" model. Reversing the pattern without parent assistance is not as efficient but is nevertheless effective for many children. A counselor, gifted coordinator, resource teacher, or even another classroom teacher will often be an excellent child advocate.

The content of the communication between parents and teachers should include a discussion of assessed abilities and achievements and the child's expressions of dependence or

Competition
High scorers enjoy competition whether they win or lose. They are good sports and handle victories graciously. They do not give up easily.

Responsibility
High scorers are responsible in their home and schoolwork. They tend to be well organized and bring activities to closure. They have good study habits and understand that their efforts are related to their grades.

Achievement Communication
Children who score high are receiving clear and consistent messages from parents about the importance of learning and good grades. Their parents have communicated positive feelings about their own school experiences, and there is consistency between mother and father messages of achievement.

Independence/Dependence
High scorers are independent and understand the relationship between effort and outcomes. They are able to share attention at home and in the classroom.

Respect-Dominance
High scorers are respectful toward their parents and teachers. They are reasonably well-behaved at home and school. They value education. They are not deliberately manipulative.

Source: Guidebook—Underachievement Syndrome: Causes and Cures, by S. Rimm, M. Cornale, R. Manos, and J. Behrend, 1989, Watertown, WI: Apple Publishing Company. Reprinted with permission.

Figure 34.4 Dimension scores for AIM, GAIM, and AIM-TO.

dominance. Teachers should communicate in clear English. There is a tendency for educators to employ jargon that mystifies intelligent adults who are not educators. Communication is especially important so that adults at home and at school do not fall into the trap of continually reinforcing these problem patterns (Rimm, 1986b, 1995).

Step 3: Changing the Expectations of Important Others

Self, parent, teacher, peer, and sibling expectations are difficult to change. As noted above, IQ scores, if higher than anticipated, are very effective in modifying expectations. Anecdotal information also can provide convincing evidence of the child's abilities. For example, a teacher who is trying to convince an adolescent or his or her parents of the adolescent's mathematical talent can explain that he or she solves problems in an unusually clever way or seems to learn math concepts more quickly than anyone else in the class. A psychologist who is trying to convince a teacher that a child has unusual talent can describe the unusual vocabulary or problem-solving skills that the child reveals during testing. Specific descriptions of special strengths are good evidence of giftedness.

It is important to underachieving children that parents and teachers are able to honestly say to them that they believe in their ability to achieve (Perkins & Wicas, 1971). The expectations of these important others are basic to the personal change in self-expectations that is necessary to reverse underachievement to high achievement.

Rimm and Lovance (1992) reported the effectiveness of grade skipping or subject acceleration in changing students' self-expectations. Although these were only components of the reversal of underachievement, they were very effective for building a gifted student's confidence and internal locus of control. Table 34.4 describes how both grades and subject skips were used in the prevention and reversal of underachievement. Following is a letter from an eighth grader who completely reversed his underachievement. Although many parenting and some school changes were made for this young man, he attributed his success mainly to his subject skip to high school algebra.

> *My life has changed through working with you because I realized that I was an underachiever. I started working to my ability and got to go to school at my high school a year early.*
>
> *Now every day I get to go to North and take Algebra 1. I have learned very much in terms of my education, self-confidence, and respect. I have become very good friends with my Algebra teacher and am getting very good grades in his class, something I didn't think I would do.*
>
> *I treat my parents with more respect because I have more respect for myself. I rarely get into trouble anymore, and at my middle school I haven't received any more referrals and am getting straight A's. I have more, better quality friends who are very trustworthy and nice.*

Rimm and Olenchak (1991) found that involvement in Future Problem Solving proved helpful in the reversal of underachievement. It undoubtedly changed both self and peer expectations for the underachiever. Rimm (1995) finds group sessions effective for helping children change expectations. Figure 34.5 includes typical topics discussed or played out.

Jackson, Cleveland, and Mirenda (1975) showed in their longitudinal research with bright fourth-, fifth-, and sixth-grade underachievers that positive expectations by parents and teachers had a significant long-range effect on achievement in high school. Bloom's (1985) studies of talent development found that parents of research neurologists and mathematicians always expected their children to be very good students. An interesting true story which emphasizes the role of teacher expectation for achievement follows:

> *It was the first teacher conference of the new year, a time when teachers may not yet know all the parents of their students. Ms. Dunn, a fourth-grade teacher, had two Janets in her class. One was an excellent student, positive, and well-adjusted; the other had multiple problems and was very negative. When the second Janet's parents came for conference, Ms. Dunn mistook them for the first Janet's parents. She welcomed them*

Table 34.4
Results of Subject and Grade Skipping

Summary of Case Events

Gender of Child	*Presenting Problems*	*Wechsler FS IQ and Binet[a] Score (If Available)*	*Grades / Subjects Skipped to Date*	*Time for Adjustment (Teacher Perceptions)*	*Additional Therapy Required*	*Grade[e]*	*Projected Future Accelerations*
F	Parent concern about boredom; behavior problems at home	147+[b] 151	Early placed kindergarten	One semester	Yes—brief[c]	1	NYD[f]
F	Parent concern about boredom	141	Early placed kindergarten Subject skipping	None	Yes—brief	6	NYD[f]
F	Behavior problems in preschool	139	Early placed kindergarten	One semester	Yes—brief	K	NYD[f]
M	Behavior problems at home and school	144 172	Skipped 1st grade	One quarter	Yes—brief	2	Math and reading skips or computer curriculum
M	Parent concern about boredom; peer adjustment problems; dependency	151+ 185+	Skipped 1st grade; math acceleration in 4th	One semester	Yes—brief	4	Further extreme math acceleration
F	Refusal to do school work	152+ 160+	Skipped 1st grade reading; 2nd grade math; other English, math, science, foreign language	One semester	Yes—occasional[d]	8	Subject skips and early graduation
M	Parent concern about boredom	141+ 173	Skipped 1st and 2nd grade reading, 2nd grade math; skipped last half of 1st grade; skipped 4th grade math	None	None	4	Subject and grade skips

F	Teacher concern about boredom	133+	Skipped last half of 2nd and first half of 3rd grade	None	None	7	None likely—AP courses available in high school
F	Unfinished work; disorganization; complaints of boredom; poor peer relations	127	Skipped 2nd grade; math accelerated later	One semester	Yes—1 semester	8	AP classes; NYD[f]
M	Behavior problems at home and school; disorganization, unfinished work	149+	Skipped 3rd grade	One year	Yes—occasional	6	AP classes available in high school; NYD[f]
F	Parent and child concern about boredom	126+	Skipped 4th grade reading and math	None for reading One quarter for math	Yes—brief	8	Possible grade skip in high school
F	Parent concern about boredom	139+	Skipped 2nd grade math, 4th grade reading; skipped 6th grade science	None	Yes—brief	6	Likely subject skips; NYD[f]
F	Teacher concern about boredom, perfectionism	135	Skipped 2nd grade math, 3rd grade reading; skipped 6th grade entirely	None	None	9	None likely—AP courses available in high school
M	Behavior problems, disorganization; incomplete work	149+	Skipped subjects in math, science, French, history, and Latin	One quarter	Yes—brief	10	Early graduation

Source: "The Use of Subject and Grade Skipping for the Prevention and Reversal of Underachievement," by S. B. Rimm, and K. J. Lovance, 1992, *Gifted Child Quarterly, 36*(2), pp. 100–105.

[a] Stanford-Binet, Form L-M

[b] Indicates ceiling scores

[c] Brief therapy refers to no more than 4 sessions.

[d] Several initial sessions followed by therapy sessions 2 or 3 times during the school year

[e] Grade at time of interview

[f] Not yet determined.

Competition—Game Playing
Discussion of Feelings

Competition—Comparison to Sports

Peer Relations—Popularity vs. Friendship
Reading and Discussion—*It's Dumb to Be Smart*

Competition and Siblings
Reading and Discussion—*Brothers and Sisters*

Pressure—How to Cope and How Much Is Too Much

Leadership vs. "Bossyship"

Understanding Parents

Responsibility

Perfectionism

Creative Problem Solving

Source: Adapted from *Gifted Kids Have Feelings Too* by S. B. Rimm and *Exploring Feelings* by S. B. Rimm and C. Priest, 1990, Watertown, WI: Apple Publishing Company.

Figure 34.5 Topics for small-group sessions for students.

with an enthusiastic description of their daughter's positive attitude, only to be greeted by their shocked expression. She immediately realized her mistake, but rather than embarrass herself and the parents, she continued her discussion about a "few areas" where Janet needed improvement.

The parents left the conference feeling more positive about their daughter than ever before and conveyed this excitement to their child. The next day, to Ms. Dunn's surprise, Janet entered school with a big smile and a positive attitude. Her self-confidence and her school efforts were completely transformed. She ended the school year with B's instead of the usual D's that had been typical of earlier report cards. A chance faux pas had led to a dramatic change for Janet. Yes, it really is a true story!

Because sibling competition is frequently a causal component of underachievement syndrome, changing the expectations of siblings may help. In the sibling rivalry that often exists, an achieving child may have assigned the role of "loser" to a brother or sister, and the anticipated change of that role may feel threatening to the "winner." An individual and personal communication to the "winner" about the expected change is helpful. Parents should provide the assurance that the sibling's changed status will not displace the achiever's role. Genetically and environmentally, a "whole smart family" is not only possible but likely.

Rachel, an eleventh-grade gifted high achiever, seemed to take a real pleasure in helping her ninth-grade underachieving brother get into trouble at home and in school. Although she mainly believed she was doing this because she loved her brother, it was also clear that she viewed the reversal of his long-standing underachievement problems as threatening to her own highest performance. (Rimm, 1995)

Step 4: Model Identification

A critical turning point for the underachieving child is the discovery of one or more role models for identification. All other treatments for underachievement dim in importance compared with strong identification with achieving models. As noted, Bloom's (1985; Bloom & Sosniak, 1981) biographical research with highly talented students showed that parents modeled the values and the lifestyles of successful achievers in the child's talent area.[1] Research indicates that the best family environment for a gifted boy includes a father who is competent and strong, is pleased with his job, and permits his son to master tasks independently. Because this ideal situation is

[1] See Chapter 17 by Sosniak.

rarely provided for the gifted underachiever, parents and teachers need to manipulate the environment to encourage students to identify with appropriate role models. A long-term longitudinal study of culturally disadvantaged children who grew up on the island of Kauai indicated that role models are very important for successful young people (Werner, 1989).

Research on parent identification (Mussen & Rutherford, 1963) indicates that the selected parent identification figure is nurturant, powerful, and shares common characteristics with the child. As a warning, however, an underachieving adolescent sometimes selects a powerful, nurturant model who shares the *underachieving* characteristics of the adolescent. This person may then become a strong model for underachievement.

Underachieving children should be matched with achieving persons to serve as models for them. Such persons can serve in model capacities for more than one child. The model's actual role may be as tutor, mentor, companion, teacher, parent, sibling, counselor, psychologist, minister, scout leader, doctor, and so on. One teacher may serve as a role model for many students. Although that may sound relatively simple, one teacher who was the only male on the faculty in his elementary school commented that he "was tired of being the only available role model for so many boys." Persons who may serve as appropriate role models may be invited to schools to talk to students about their careers. Videotaping these talks may provide a continuing role model for others.

Step 5: Correcting Skill Deficiencies

The underachieving gifted child almost always has skill deficiencies as a result of inattention in class and poor work and study habits. However, because he or she is gifted the skill deficiencies may be easily overcome. This is less of a problem for very young children because the deficiencies are less likely to be extensive. Tutoring should be goal-directed, with movement to a higher reading or math group or acceptance into an accelerated class as the anticipated outcome. It should be of specified duration—for example, weekly for two months until the child takes a proficiency test—rather than ongoing. Ideally, the tutoring should be done by an experienced and objective adult who recognizes the child's underachievement and giftedness. Parents or siblings are seldom appropriate because the personal relationships are likely to cause the child additional pressure and dependency. Children have often described the assistance given by an older sibling as helpful but having a secondary effect of "making them feel dumb." The correction of skill deficiencies must be conducted carefully so that (1) the independent work of the underachieving child is reinforced by the tutor, (2) manipulation of the tutor by the child is avoided, and (3) the child senses the relationship between effort and the achievement outcomes. Charting progress during tutoring helps to confirm visually the rapid progress to both child and tutor.

Sometimes underachieving gifted students actually have learning disabilities. Other times their dependent patterns look like learning disabilities. Table 34.5 compares dependencies to disabilities and can provide teachers with a diagnostic guide for detecting actual disabilities.

Step 6: Modification of Reinforcements at Home and School

Parent and teacher discussions will certainly identify some manipulative rituals that were discussed in the home and school etiology sections. These behaviors need to be modified by setting important long-term goals and some short-term objectives that can ensure immediate small successes for the child both at home and at school. These successful experiences may be temporarily reinforced by a variety of rewards.

There are many effective rewards within the value system of parents and within the capabilities of teachers to administer, for example, free time on the computer. Any rewards used should be based on activities completed or the quality of the activity. Rewards should never be given for incomplete work or when work is not attempted.

Modifying reinforcements for homework and study are an important component of

Table 34.5
Ways to Discriminate between Dependence and Disability

Dependence	*Disability*
1. Child asks for explanations regularly despite differences in subject matter.	Child asks for explanations in particular subjects which are difficult.
2. Child asks for explanation of instructions regardless of style used, either auditory or visual.	Child asks for explanations of instructions only when given in one instruction style, either auditory or visual but not both.
3. Child's questions are not specific to material but appear to be mainly to gain adult attention.	Child's questions are specific to material, and once process is explained, child works efficiently.
4. Child is disorganized or slow in assignments but becomes much more efficient when a meaningful reward is presented as motivation.	Child's disorganization or slow pace continues despite motivating rewards.
5. Child works only when an adult is nearby at school and/or at home.	Child works independently once process is clearly explained.
6. Individually administered measures of ability indicate that the child is capable of learning the material. Individual tests improve with tester encouragement and support. Group measures may not indicate good abilities or skills.	Both individual and group measures indicate lack of specific abilities or skills. Tester encouragement has no significant effect on scores.
7. Child exhibits "poor me" body language (tears, helplessness, pouting, copying) regularly when new work is presented. Teacher or adult attention serves to ease the symptoms.	Child exhibits "poor me" body language only with instructions or assignments in specific disability areas and accepts challenges in areas of strength.
8. Parents report whining, complaining, attention getting, temper tantrums, and poor sportsmanship at home.	Although parents may find similar symptoms at home, they tend to be more sporadic than regular, particularly the whining and complaining.
9. Child's "poor me" behavior appears only with one parent and not with the other; only with some teachers and not with others. With some teachers or with the other parent, the child functions fairly well independently.	Although the child's "poor me" behaviors may only appear with one parent or with solicitous teachers, performance is not adequate even when behavior is acceptable.
10. Child learns only when given one-to-one instruction but will not learn in groups even when instructional mode is varied.	Although child may learn more quickly in a one-to-one setting, he/she will also learn efficiently in a group setting provided the child's disability is taken into consideration when instructions are given.

It is critical to realize that some children who are truly disabled have also become dependent. The key to distinguishing between disability and dependence is the child's response to adult support. If the child performs only with adult support when new material is presented, he/she is too dependent whether or not there is also a disability.

Source: Underachievement Syndrome: Causes and Cures by Sylvia B. Rimm, 1986, Watertown, WI: Apple Publishing Company. Reprinted with permission.

reversing underachievement syndrome. However, this modification by itself will not be sufficient. Dozens of other recommendations for home and school changes are given by Rimm (1986b, 1995) in her books specifically written about underachievement syndrome.

Ramifications for Parenting

General recommendations for parenting gifted children emerge from the comparisons of gifted underachievers with high achievers.

The preschool years. Child-centered environments are typical for gifted children. However, conferring adult status on children carries the risk of later "disempowerment." Although some praise is certainly healthy and encouraging, too much praise and admiration and the use of frequent superlatives confer a "specialness" that can rarely be adjusted to in school. Dependence on too much positive reinforcement may reduce intrinsically motivated behaviors (Rimm, 1990b).

Parenting styles. Styles of parenting seem to be much less important than consistency in parenting. Dissimilarities between parents, with one expecting too much and the other overprotecting, are a main source of problems for children (Rimm, 1990a).

Homework and learning. Gifted children do not need regular help with homework. Positive monitoring of homework and study habits is effective. Encouraging intrinsically interesting learning experiences and independence is important.

Modeling. Valuing of personal careers and work by parents provides an important model for children's achievement; they internalize what they see and hear.

Organization. Reasonable standards of organization provide a model for organization and leave more time for development of family interests and independence. The writer and filmmaker John Sayles describes the kind of education that worked best for him (U.S. Department of Education, 1993):

> In general, I feel like what was most helpful about school when it worked was the existence of a structure, but with the leeway to go beyond it if you had the inclination. I think both the structure and the freedom were equally important; the structure giving something to react to or from, and the freedom being that there was some encouragement for original thinking as long as you didn't make too much trouble. (p. 21)

Clinical experiences with underachievers indicate that school, home, and peer environments can and should be modified to cure underachievement syndrome in gifted children. Although the reversal is difficult, the satisfaction felt by the child and family and the achievement of potential contributions to society make the extraordinary efforts worthwhile.

REFERENCES

Bloom, B. S. (Ed.). (1985). *Developing talent in young people.* New York: Ballantine.

Bloom, B. S., & Sosniak, L. A. (1981). Talent development vs. schooling. *Educational Leadership, 39,* 86–94.

Brown, B. B., & Steinberg, L. (1990). Academic achievement and social acceptance: Skirting the "brain–nerd" connection. *Education Digest, 55*(7), 55–60.

Cornale, M. (1988). *Dependence and dominance in preadolescent academic underachievers.* Unpublished research paper, University of Wisconsin–Madison.

Covington, M. V., & Beery, R. G. (1976). *Self-worth and school learning.* New York: Holt.

Davis, G. A., & Rimm, S. B. (1994). *Education of the gifted and talented.* Boston: Allyn and Bacon.

Deci, E. L. (1986). Motivating children to learn: What can you do? *Learning 86, 14*(7), 42–44.

DeLeon, P. H. (1989, February). *Why we must attend to minority gifted: A national perspective.* Presented at the Johnson Foundation Wingspread Conference, Racine, Wisconsin.

Felton, G. S., & Biggs, B. E. (1977). *Up from underachievement.* Springfield, IL: Charles C Thomas.

Fine, M. J., & Pitts, R. (1980). Intervention with underachieving gifted children: Rationale and strategies. *Gifted Child Quarterly, 24,* 51–55.

Frasier, A., Passow, A. H., & Goldberg, M. L. (1958). Curriculum research: Study of underachieving gifted. *Educational Leadership, 16,* 121–125.

French, J. L. (1959). *Educating the gifted: A book of readings.* New York: Holt.

Green, K., Fine, M. J., & Tollefson, N. (1988). Family systems characteristics and underachieving gifted adolescent males. *Gifted Child Quarterly, 32,* 267–272.

Hoffman, J. L., Wasson, F. R., & Christianson, B. P. (1985, May–June). Personal development for the gifted underachiever. *G/C/T,* 12–14.

Hom, H. L., Jr., Gaskill, B., & Hutchins, M. (1988). *Motivational orientation of the gifted student, thread of evaluation and its impact on performance.* Paper presented at the meeting of the American Educational Research Association, New Orleans, Louisiana.

Jackson, R. M., Cleveland, J. C., & Mirenda, P. F. (1975). The longitudinal effects of early identification and counseling of underachievers. *Journal of School Psychology, 13,* 119–128.

Lajoie, S. P., & Shore, B. M. (1981). Three myths? The over-representation of the gifted among dropouts, delinquents, and suicides. *Gifted Child Quarterly, 25,* 138–141.

MacKinnon, D. W. (1965). Personality and the realization of creative potential. *American Psychologist, 20,* 273–281.

Mussen, P. H., & Rutherford, E. (1963). Parent-child relations and parental personality in relation to young children's sex-role preferences. *Child Development, 34,* 589–607.

National Commission on Excellence in Education. (1983). *A nation at risk: The imperative for educational reform.* Washington, DC: U.S. Government Printing Office.

Nyquist, E. (1973). *The gifted: The invisibly handicapped, or there is no heavier burden than a great potential.* Paper presented at the National Conference on the Gifted, Albany, New York.

Perkins, J. A., & Wicas, E. A. (1971). Group counseling bright underachievers and their mothers. *Journal of Counseling Psychology, 18,* 273–278.

Reis, S. M., & Purcell, J. H. (1993). An analysis of content elimination and strategies used by elementary classroom teachers in the curriculum compacting process. *Journal for the Education of the Gifted,16*(2), 147–170.

Rimm, S. B. (1980, September–October). Congratulations Miss Smithersteen, you have proved that Amy isn't gifted. *G/C/T,* 23–24.

Rimm, S. B. (1986a). *AIM: Achievement identification measure.* Watertown, WI: Educationa Assessment Service.

Rimm, S. B. (1986b). *Underachievement syndrome: Causes and cures.* Watertown, WI: Apple.

Rimm, S. B. (1987a). *GAIM: Group achievement identification measure.* Watertown, WI: Educational Assessment Service.

Rimm, S. B. (1987b). Why do bright children underachieve? The pressures they feel. *Gifted Child Today,10*(6), 30–36.

Rimm, S. B. (1988). *AIM-TO: Achievement identification measure—teacher observation.* Watertown, WI: Educational Assessment Service.

Rimm, S. B. (1990a). *How to parent so children will learn.* Watertown, WI: Apple.

Rimm, S. B. (1990b). A theory of relativity. *Gifted Child Today,13*(3), 32–36.

Rimm, S. B. (1994). *Keys to parenting the gifted child.* New York: Barrons Educational Series.

Rimm, S. B. (1995). *Why bright kids get poor grades and what you can do about it.* New York: Crown.

Rimm, S. B., & Lovance, K. J. (1992). The use of subject and grade skipping for the prevention and reversal of underachievement. *Gifted Child Quarterly, 36,* 100–105.

Rimm, S. B., & Lowe, B. (1988). Family environments of underachieving gifted students. *Gifted Child Quarterly, 32,* 353–359.

Rimm, S. B., & Olenchak, F. R. (1991). How FPS helps underachieving gifted students. *Gifted Child Today, 14,* 19–22.

Seligman, M. E. (1975). *Helplessness: On depression, development and death.* San Francisco: Freeman.

U.S. Department of Education. (1993). *National excellence: A case for developing America's talent.* Washington, DC: Office of Educational Research and Improvement.

Walberg, H., Tsai, S., Weinstein, T., Gabriel, C. L., Rasher, S. P., Rosencrans, T., Rovai, E., Ide, J., Truijillo, M., & Vukosavich, P. (1981). Childhood traits and environmental conditions of highly eminent adults. *Gifted Child Quarterly, 25,* 103–107.

Weiner, B. (1974). Achievement motivation and attribution theory. Morristown, NJ: General Learning Press.

Weiner, B. (1980). *Human motivation.* New York: Holt.

Werner, E. (1989). Children of the garden island. *Scientific American, 234*(1), 106–111.

Whitmore, J. R. (1980). *Giftedness, conflict, and underachievement.* Boston: Allyn and Bacon.

Zilli, M. G. (1971). Reasons why the gifted adolescent underachieves and some of the implications of guidance and counseling of this problem. *Gifted Child Quarterly, 15,* 279–292.

PART VI

Special Topics

Part VI includes special areas that are important foci in our concern for educating gifted children and youth. For example, we will look at identifying and meeting the educational needs of culturally diverse, handicapped, and female gifted students, as well as unique issues concerning preschool and adolescent gifted learners. Some thought-provoking topics in this section include adult eminence, child prodigies and prodigious savants, international perspectives, legal and ethical issues, teacher training and certification, and U.S. government perspectives on the future of gifted education.

In Chapter 35 Martha J. Morelock and David H. Feldman describe three types of extremely precocious children: children with extraordinarily high IQs, child prodigies, and so-called idiot savants—persons with mental retardation who also have spectacular islands of brilliance. High-IQ children and prodigies are a curious mixture of child and adult; prodigies and savants intuitively understand the regularities of a domain. High-IQ children may dislike school, have poor peer relationships, and possess intelligence that outstrips their emotional development. Like Simonton, the authors puzzle over why high IQ does not necessarily become genius. Feldman's coincidence theory describes the melding of favorable intraindividual, environmental, and historical forces and time frames.

Nancy Ewald Jackson and Elizabeth J. Klein in Chapter 36 define *gifted behavior* in young children and infants as precocious, excellent, productive, and measurable. The authors comment on precocity in speaking, comprehension, and especially reading, all of which reflect high verbal intelligence. Children precocious in language "pattern analysis" often, but not always, later show advanced abilities in other analytic areas, such as math, music, chess, or computers. Regarding origins, intelligent parents create a favorable environment for learning and thinking—which tangles the effects of genetics and environment. The authors note issues and problems in the long-term prediction of adult gifted behavior from childhood precocity. They present a flowchart model that traces how genotypic influences, learning opportunities, motivational influences, and precocious achievements may evolve over the years into talent in music, math, or language productivity. Parent reports and ability tests are useful in identifying young gifted children, note Jackson and Klein.

In Chapter 37 James R. Delisle notes that gifted adolescents are "first and foremost" teenagers, much like all other teenagers. Their intensity or overexcitability can lead to remarkable achievement, but also sometimes to suicide. Delisle's programming recommendations focus on both intellectual challenge and personal validation. He recommends involving them in social action and service; using internships for career guidance; and involving them in literature by thinkers who have grappled with the adolescents' problems. In a thought-provoking statement, Delisle describes underachievement as a myth—a mismatch of others' expectations and the adolescent's own passions. For gifted adolescents, notes Delisle, "peer problems" do not exist simply because they prefer the company of like-minded older students to that of agemates.

Barbara Kerr in Chapter 38 discusses the "gradual disengagement" of many bright female students from high aspirations, and the value conflicts that dog achieving women. Kerr notes that gifted girls tend not to enroll in advanced math class or to participate in gifted programs; sex-role stereotypes continue to be taught; and even feminist teachers treat boys and girls differently. Kerr observes that selection tests loaded with math and science will favor boys, an effect that can be offset with lower cutoff scores for girls. Kerr's chapter includes many other positive suggestions and recommendations for educating gifted girls, such as multidimensional selection criteria to tap into girls' creativity and leadership; perhaps single-sex schooling; encouraging girls to take challenging courses and to take risks; helping them develop high expectations; and encouraging them to "fall in love with an idea."

Minority students are vastly underrepresented in gifted programs. Mary M. Frasier in Chapter 39 argues for a reframing of issues regarding African-American and other minority students. She notes that most problems fall into four categories: access to gifted programs, assessment procedures that overemphasize test scores, accommodating cultural and linguistic differences, and negative attitudes regarding giftedness in minority students. Frasier's reconceptualization takes a multigroup perspective. Instead of trying to fit minority students into the existing (majority) approach to assessment and teaching, we should recognize cultural differences in beliefs, values, and varying styles of communication, thought, and learning. A multidimensional, culturally relevant approach to identification is thus at the top of her list of recommendations. In her final section, Frasier summarizes her F-TAP model for identification and for planning educational services.

Like minority students, gifted children with disabilities also are vastly underserved, note Lawrence J. Johnson, Merle B. Karnes, and Victoria W. Carr in Chapter 40. That is unfair to them and to society. The authors review the history of concern for gifted disabled, then itemize barriers that hinder identification and programming-for example, inappropriate identification; stereotyped attitudes of how "gifted kids" should look and act; lack of information about their developmental delays; inadequate training of professionals; and a shortage of programming models, supportive technology, counseling, and funding. Most of the authors' recommendations revolve around correcting these common problems—for example, by using multidimensional identification procedures, improving training for educators, providing career counseling services, and focusing on strengths instead of deficits. Karnes's Retrieval and Acceleration of Promising Young Handicapped Talented (RAPYHT) model has proved successful in identifying and providing effective services for these children.

A. Harry Passow in Chapter 41 tells us that the challenge of educating gifted students has been a worldwide concern since Biblical times. However, talent priorities vary from culture to culture, with selection rooted in customs, laws, caste systems, institutions, or the school system. The focus may be on developing talent for social needs, developing each individual for self-fulfillment, or both. The birth of the World Council for Gifted and Talented Children, as well as regional organizations, emphasizes the transnational concern for gifted students. Passow notes that programs worldwide deal with issues of elitism, egalitarianism, and whether G/T programs are even necessary. Sternberg's and Gardner's expanded definitions of giftedness are making an international impact, as is Renzulli's Enrichment Triad Model and Stanley's radical acceleration approach. Ability grouping, tracking (streaming), and special classes, says Passow, are more accepted in other countries.

In Chapter 42 Frances A. Karnes and Ronald G. Marquardt review legal issues and procedures, a topic that until recently existed only at the fringes of gifted education. The authors emphasize that disputes are best and most cheaply resolved at the lowest levels. One works up the ladder from direct negotiation with responsible persons to, in turn, the principal, the superintendent, and the school board. A mediator helps decide issues at the state board of education level; this is followed by more costly and adversarial due process procedures and then by state or federal courts. The authors present cases and thoughtful ideas related to these recurring issues: early admission, program provision, racial balance, transferring students, appropriateness of instruction, teacher certification, transportation, liability for injury, fraud and misrepresentation, and home schooling.

In Chapter 43 John F. Feldhusen addresses the training of teachers of the gifted. Good teachers of the gifted, says Feldhusen, tend to be intelligent, experienced, enthusiastic about the gifted, achievement-oriented, organized, able to relate to the gifted, and imaginative, with cultural and intellectual interests and a sense of humor. They need to understand gifted students and their cognitive and affective needs, identification procedures, and methods and materials for teaching them. They also must be competent in directing independent research, teaching creativity and thinking skills, individualizing instruction, counseling, and working with culturally different gifted students. Feldhusen also describes his own research, which confirmed the benefits of graduate course work that covers these competencies as well as program development and program evaluation.

Finally, Patricia O'Connell Ross in Chapter 44 traces the attitudes and legislation of the U.S. government relating to the education of gifted and talented students, from the launching of Sputnik in 1957 to the 1993 *National Excellence: A Case for Developing America's Talent* report—which she helped write—and President Clinton's 1994 *Goals 2000: Educate America Act.* Quoting legislation, she describes how the focus has evolved from cultivating math and science talent during the Cold War to the current position of improving expectations for and education of all students, including those with gifts and talents.

35

High-IQ Children, Extreme Precocity, and Savant Syndrome

MARTHA J. MORELOCK, *University of Helbourne, Australia*
DAVID H. FELDMAN, *Tufts University*

People have long been fascinated by extreme precocity in childhood. In this chapter, types of extremely precocious children are described, compared, and contrasted, incorporating discussion of educational programming. A taxonomy of manifestations of extreme precocity is presented, and implications for research are explored.

The Extremely Precocious Child

The Biblical story of the child Jesus, who, at the age of 12, astonished the rabbis with his understanding, is perhaps the first recorded allusion to an extremely precocious child.[1] It was not until the 1700s, however, that more detailed narrative accounts of childhood precociousness began to appear in what was to become a developing literature of child psychology (Hollingworth, 1942). The earliest of these, written in 1726, described the child Christian Friedrich Heinecken. Barlow (1952) provides a synopsis of the life of Heinecken:

> Christian Friedrich Heinecken, a German, who was known as the "Infant of Lubeck," from the place where he was born in 1721, is said to have talked within a few hours after his birth. Besides his remarkable faculty for numbers, he is said to have known, at the age of one year, all the principal events related in the Pentateuch; at two was well acquainted with the historical events of the Bible, and at three had a knowledge of universal history and geography, Latin and French. People came from all parts to see him, and the King of Denmark had him brought to Copenhagen in 1724, in order to assure himself of the truth of what he had heard regarding him. But shortly after this, little Heinecken was taken ill and predicted his own death, which took place in 1725, at the tender age of four. (Barlow, 1952, pp. 135–136)

Admittedly, the facts of this account may be exaggerated a bit as a result of extensive word-of-mouth dissemination prior to being recorded in writing in 1726. Nevertheless, Christian Heinecken's life synopsis suggests that the child was extraordinarily precocious when it came to the ability to absorb and verbalize abstract knowledge. Childhood precocity, however, comes in numerous guises and raises a multitude of questions. There are, for example, child prodigies whose extraordinary performance in particular fields rivals that of adult professionals. Such a prodigy was the child musician and composer Wolfgang Amadeus Mozart (1756–1791), who, at the age of 6, toured Europe with his father, Leopold, and sister, Maria Anna, exhibiting the children's musicianship—particularly young Wolfgang's mastery of the violin, piano, and organ (Barlow, 1952).

Then, of course, there are astonishing cases like George and Charles—identical twin calendar calculators (Hamblin, 1966). George at the age of 6 and Charles at the age of 9 could answer spontaneously questions such as, "On what day of the week was your third birthday?" "The year is 31275; on what day of the week will June 6th fall?" Given a date, these twins could give the day of the week over a span of 80,000 years—40,000 backward or 40,000 forward. Such feats are the more astounding because the twins' tested IQs were

[1] This story may be found in the Bible, King James Version, Luke 2:46–47.

between 40 and 50. Incredibly, although they could not count to 30, they swapped 20-digit prime numbers for amusement. They could easily factor the number 111 and remember 30 digits, but could not add.

Heinecken, Mozart, and George and Charles reflect the three major types of extremely precocious children found in the literature. Although young Heinecken lived prior to the development of IQ tests, his academic precocity was characteristic of the gifted child of extraordinarily high IQ. Mozart was a supreme example of the child prodigy, while George and Charles are classified as *idiot savants.* We will examine each of these variations of extreme precocity, noting the similarities and differences between them.

The Child of Extraordinarily High IQ

To understand the child of extraordinary IQ, it is necessary to understand something about the instrument that first defined and selected such children. Lewis M. Terman's Stanford-Binet Intelligence Scale, which first appeared in 1916, was an extension and revision of the 1908 Binet-Simon Scale, which had been devised by the French psychologist Alfred Binet and T. Simon, his physician collaborator. The Binet-Simon scale was a practical screening device for identifying children who, unable to succeed in the public schools of Paris, were in need of special programs. Terman's scale, however, incorporated a new theoretical premise—a definition of human intelligence. Terman defined *intelligence* as the ability to acquire and manipulate concepts—the shorthand symbols necessary for abstract thinking (Terman, 1975).

In extending the standardized instrument so that it reached higher levels of ability in late childhood, Terman and his associates paved the way for studies of the gifted (Segoe, 1975). Terman himself began the first broad-scale study of gifted children (Terman, 1925–1959). A mammoth longitudinal project, it followed over 1,500 children with IQs of at least 140 into adulthood, middle age, and beyond.

It remained for Terman's contemporary Leta S. Hollingworth (1942) to conduct the first systematic in-depth study devoted solely to children of extraordinarily high IQ. Hollingworth's observations concerning the special psychological, social, and educational needs of children above 180 IQ remain valuable today.

Leta Hollingworth and Children above 180 IQ

Hollingworth (1942) conducted case studies of 12 children (8 boys and 4 girls) testing above 180 IQ on the Stanford-Binet Intelligence Scale. She found that, although no one characteristic could be singled out as identifying accelerated development, early talking and reading most clearly differentiated these children from the average. Although this is an interesting finding, it is not a surprising one. The capacity for abstract, symbolic thought that Terman aimed at identifying through the Stanford-Binet was chiefly language-based conceptual facility. Consequently, children most adept at encoding and communicating logical thought through language were destined to be designated "the highly gifted." Early talking and reading are likely manifestations of such verbal-conceptual ability.

Hollingworth observed that early recognition and provision of opportunities for their abilities consistently proved to foster the optimal development of such children. Although all her subjects showed superior learning ability, their actual accomplishments and the quality of their personal and social adjustment depended heavily on the way they were treated by those responsible for them.

Hollingworth discerned three major adjustment problems risked by children of above-180 IQ (Witty, 1951). First, they frequently failed to develop desirable work habits in a school setting geared to the capacities of average children. In such a setting, they generally spent considerable time in idleness and daydreaming. Consequently, they learned to dislike school.

To remedy this, Hollingworth (1942) proposed a combination of acceleration through the normal elementary curriculum plus enrichment experiences aimed at providing knowledge about cultural evolution as manifested through the development of common things such as clothing, lighting, trains, etiquette, and so forth. She believed that by understanding how things had developed in the past, these children would be encouraged to become innovative thinkers themselves.

A second problem noted by Hollingworth was difficulty in finding satisfying companionship. Consequently, these children risk becoming socially isolated. Children of extraordinarily high IQ, she observed, typically strive to play with others. Their efforts commonly fail, however, since age-mates do not share their interests, vocabulary, or desire for more complex activities. While older children may satisfy the extraordinarily gifted child's need for intellectual rapport, physically the younger child is at a disadvantage.

Because of this problem, Hollingworth believed that children of extraordinarily high IQ need to be educated for leisure. She especially espoused games like chess or checkers, which could be enjoyed by people of all ages and potentially could assist these children in bridging social gaps.

Hollingworth's research suggested that children of extraordinarily high IQ are unlikely to be accepted as leaders by age-mates. Leaders, Hollingworth (1926) concluded, are likely to be "more intelligent, but not too much more intelligent, than the average of the group led" (p. 131). Consequently, she believed that beyond IQ 160, children have little chance of being popular leaders in a regular school setting. To develop leadership skills, asserted Hollingworth, such children need to be placed in special classes with others like themselves.

A third problem cited by Hollingworth was a certain vulnerability because of these children's intellectual capacity to understand and grapple with major philosophical and ethical issues before they are emotionally ready to deal with them. Hollingworth wrote, for example, of a 6-year-old boy of IQ 187 who "wept bitterly after reading how the North taxed the South after the Civil War" (Hollingworth, 1942, p. 281).

Hollingworth cautioned that such vulnerabilities must be understood and dealt with patiently by adults so as to avoid engendering lifelong emotional problems. She concluded, "To have the intelligence of an adult and the emotions of a child combined in a childish body is to encounter certain difficulties" (Hollingworth, 1942, p. 282).

Children of Extraordinarily High IQ in Australia

It was 50 years after Hollingworth's research before another systematized in-depth study devoted to extraordinarily high IQ children appeared in the literature. In 1993, Australian researcher Miraca U. M. Gross (1993) published her research documenting the academic, social, and emotional development of 15 children scoring at IQ 160+ in the eastern states of Australia. The group consisted of 10 males and 5 females ranging in age from 5 years, 3 months, to 13 years, 5 months. Only four of the children—all males—scored 175+ on the Stanford-Binet L-M, suggesting they were on a par with Hollingworth's children. Three of the children attained IQ scores of 200 or higher, prompting Gross to publish detailed individualized case studies of them (Gross, 1992) prior to the publication of her larger study. Only one of Hollingworth's children had attained an IQ score of 200.

Gross used structured child and parent interviews as well as questionnaires to collect data about family history and facts about physical and psychosocial development, school history, and family characteristics. In addition, she collected results of academic achievement tests in reading, mathematics, and spelling. Because Gross's study, like Hollingworth's, emphasized the children's school experience, many of the issues reported by Gross—for example, the trials of negotiating appropriate educational experiences in a school system geared toward the norm and the emotional and social difficulties stemming from inappropriate placements—echoed those first documented by Hollingworth.

One of the most interesting aspects of Gross's study is her use of psychosocial assessment instruments not available in Hollingworth's day. Her use of the Coopersmith Self-Esteem Inventory (Coopersmith, 1981) documented scores on the social self–peers subscale significantly below the mean of their age-peers. This tendency revealed that the children's awareness that they were rejected and disliked by age-mates caused problems in self-concept. Furthermore, to eight of her children, Gross administered Rest's (1986) Defining Issues Test (DIT), a test of moral judgment based on Kohlberg's stages of moral development. The results showed that the children exhibited accelerated levels of moral development. On questions of moral or ethical significance, the children (ranging in age from 10 to 13) resembled junior high, high school, or college students. Thus, Gross's findings provided additional support for clinical observations that had been made about children of extraordinarily high IQ since the days of Hollingworth.

The Child of Extraordinarily High IQ in the Family Context: Families with Children above 200 IQ

Morelock's (1994) ongoing and in-depth study of extraordinarily high IQ children views these children from a developmental perspective. This research looks not only at child characteristics of mentality and personality, but also at the families giving rise to such extraordinary children. The investigation includes some of the most profoundly gifted children, in IQ terms, ever studied. All of the children have IQ's of 180+; six have IQ scores well above 200. The children ranged from 5 through 11 years of age at the time of the interviews, and included seven boys and one girl. In terms of acceleration and achievement, these children are indeed extraordinary. For example, one child boasts the distinction of being, at age 10, the youngest person ever to have graduated from college. Another, at the age of 8 years, 4 months, achieved a score of 760 out of a possible 800 on the math portion of the SAT, winning the distinction of attaining the highest score for that test ever recorded at such an early age. One of Gross's (1993) subjects had set the former record, achieving the same score at the age of 8 years, 10 months. Only 1% of college-bound 17- and 18-year-olds in the United States attain a score of 750 or more. A third child and the only female in Morelock's group—an 11-year-old writing prodigy—writes poetry rivaling that of professionals, not only in mastery and creative use of language, but also in her extraordinary spiritual, mystical, and psychological insights.

The study examines family environment as well as "transgenerational influences" —themes, values, and behavior patterns transmitted across family generations that serve to shape and channel the children's giftedness and talent (Feldman & Goldsmith, 1986; Morelock, 1988, 1994). The research centers more strongly on the family than have former studies of children of extraordinarily high IQ. Additionally, the study seeks to enter into the phenomenological realities of the children and families through interviews with family members as well as input from individuals outside the family who have had close interactions with the focus child (teachers, members of the extended families, psychologists, etc.). Aspects of family environment are assessed through the Moos Family Environment Scale (FES) (Moos & Moos, 1994). While the analysis of research data is still taking place, some intriguing trends have emerged:

1. A striking finding is that family values and themes traced over the generations reveal themselves not only in patterns of child rearing by parents, but even in the language and mode of thought of the children. It appears that the facility with language that is characteristic of extraordinarily high IQ children enables them to absorb and express the values and modes of thought encoded in that language more readily than can average children. Consequently, they become sensitive distillers and reflectors of family values and themes at a very early age. This is manifested remarkably clearly in their behavior, talk, and thought processes.

2. These children develop extraordinary uniqueness and individuality at a very early age. It is as if the mastery of concepts and facility with language encourage a precocious and curious mixture of adult and child. In the group studied by Morelock, however, some children "lead" with the adult, while others "lead" with the child. That is, in first meeting the majority of these children, one is immediately struck with the sophistication of thought and language—so much so that one must remind oneself that this person *is,* chronologically at least, a *child.* With others, one must be persistent in order to penetrate through the child persona to the underlying adult brilliance. The father of 10-year-old college graduate Michael Kearney, for example, talks of the ability of his child to "normalize"—to blend like a chameleon into the expectations of those around him by modifying his language and behavior so that he can appear to be a normal child rather than a brilliant college-educated person (Kearney & Kearney, 1994). This case is unusual. It is more common that these children display their capabilities whether or not they want to—often to their own puzzlement and distress. Michael Kearney's ability to normalize heightens some difficulties that he shares with other extraordinarily brilliant children. When he was in college, he was constantly challenged to prove himself by unbelieving adults who insisted in seeing him as nothing more than a "normal" child. Michael's father commented that it was as if Michael were invisible. The underlying reasons for these individual differences in mode of child/adult manifestation of personality remain to be explored.

3. Assessment of families with the Moos Family Environment Scale (Moos & Moos, 1994) suggests that these families are more *cohesive* (the degree to which family members are committed to one another and help and support each other) and more *expressive* (acting openly and expressing feelings directly) than are average families. The expressiveness pertains not only to feelings but also to the free exchange and exploration of ideas. This is captured through the Intellectual-Cultural Orientation subscale of the FES, which measures the degree of interest in political, social, intellectual, and cultural activities manifested in families. These families scored higher than average families on this subscale. In addition, the mean score on this subscale for Morelock's eight families was higher than for families of gifted children in former studies (who also scored above the norm) (Cornell, 1984; Tabackman, 1976). Although an intriguing trend, it is questionable how much significance can be attached to it at this point because of the small number of families in Morelock's study.

Interestingly, the families tended to score *lower* than average on scales measuring orientation toward achievement or competition, participation in active social and recreational activities, degree of importance of clear organization and structure in family activities and responsibilities, and the extent to which set rules and procedures are used to run family life. The FES assessed conflict as occurring less in these families than in average families; while the extent to which family members are assertive, self-sufficient, and make their own decisions (the Independence subscale) is higher than average.

Generally, these results are consistent with FES assessments in former studies of families with gifted children (Cornell, 1984; Kulieke & Olszewski-Kubilius, 1989; Tabackman, 1976). Only minor differences were revealed, especially in the more extreme scores reflected in the Expressiveness and Intellectual-Cultural Orientation subscales. It is interesting to speculate about the extent to which the differences in these subscales result from and feed into the extraordinariness of verbal-conceptual abstract reasoning abilities manifested in the IQ scores of the Morelock group.

4. A fascinating birth order trend emerged in these families with regard to self-definition among siblings. Consistent with earlier studies of giftedness and talent (e.g., Feldman, 1991), the children identified as profoundly gifted in Morelock's study were first-borns. The second-born children in these families tended to describe themselves and their talents in terms of what they could *do* rather than how they could *think.* Their talents were centered around *products*—construction and mechanical or architectural design (with construction or mechanical toys), dancing, or artistic abilities. The 7-year-old younger brother of the writing prodigy declared, "I'm a doer, not a talker," and proceeded to show his numerous mechanical designs and building constructions to the researcher. Michael Kearney's 8-year-old younger sister, Maeghan, announced to her family that she was the "creative" one in the family and took up drawing and the construction of doll clothes. The younger brother of the SAT-Math whiz also took up construction as a hobby, and delighted in showing the researcher a small building he had designed and his efforts at constructing a hot-air balloon. A younger sister of an 11-year-old highly talented in mathematics, logical thought, and chess became an extraordinary dancer. Her brother reported that he was a "thinker" whereas she was an "applier." Generally, the second-borns were much more at ease when demonstrating their active talent areas than when talking in an interview. This was distinctly unlike their older siblings, who delighted in exploring concepts and inner feelings through the interviews. Interestingly, the only family in which this general pattern failed to hold true was one that valued sports, athletics, and "doing things in the real world" to such an extent that it may have overridden the usual pattern. In this particular family, the focus child reported that he wanted to be a professional athlete. His younger sister, who was only 4 at the time of the interview, was talented in drama, singing, and dance. Thus, *both* children were, at the time of the interviews, oriented toward more traditionally "second-born talents."

It may be that the second-borns differentiate themselves from their intellectual older siblings by gravitating toward a talent area involving a product, thereby providing concrete undeniable proof that they, too, are talented. This can serve to offset the fact that they arrived on the scene considerably handicapped in the time they have had to develop thinking skills. Generally, for the second-born the product seems more the central *reason* for thinking. In contrast, for the first-born the focus is an intense exploration of thought and concepts for its own enjoyment. Any resultant product appears to be a secondary spinoff from that. Second-borns also apparently gravitate toward areas in which they do not have to compete with their older siblings.

Extraordinarily High IQ and Achievement

Since the advent of the IQ scale, extraordinarily high IQ aroused expectations of extraordinary achievement. On the basis of her longitudinal observations, Hollingworth concluded that children testing above 180 IQ constituted the "top" among graduates—the ones who predictably would win honors and prizes for intellectual work. Furthermore, she considered them "potential geniuses" (Witty, 1951); that is, she saw in them the possibility of original contributions of outstanding and lasting merit. A study conducted in 1984, however, raised questions about the prediction of genius-level contributions solely on the basis of extraordinary IQ.

Feldman's (1984) study using Terman's (Terman, 1925–1959) original research files compared the lives of the 26 subjects scoring 180 or above on the Stanford-Binet with 26 of their counterparts of lesser IQ randomly selected from the original sample of over 1,500. A difference of 35 IQ points differentiated the average IQs of the groups in question (150 vs. 185). Although there was some evidence that the above-180-IQ subjects were more successful in their careers than the 150-IQ group, the difference was slight. A small number of distinguished *men* emerged from the above-180-IQ group (e.g., an academic psychologist of international repute, a celebrated landscape architect, a judge, and a promising pollster who committed suicide at age 28), while a comparable group failed to emerge from either the 150-IQ women, the 150-IQ men, or the 180-IQ women. Even so, the degree of distinction of these 180-IQ men could not be considered to be on a par with genius. What factors may have caused these highly capable individuals to fail to fulfill their promise?

Explaining the Reluctance of Genius to Emerge

Research suggests several possible answers to the questions posed above. A first explanation is suggested by research pointing out the social and psychological risks plaguing those of extraordinarily high IQ (Hollingworth, 1926, 1942; Morelock, in press). Intellectual ability of this type may well lay the groundwork for future eminence, especially in fields requiring academic excellence or exceptional general intellectual ability combined with specific talents. It may be, however, that the higher the IQ, the more the benefits are counterbalanced by psychosocial adjustment problems imposed by such capacity. In addition, the females targeted by Feldman's study had to surmount the barriers traditionally imposed by societal stereotypes of acceptable female roles and behavior (Terman, 1975) and the psychological spinoff effects of such stereotypes (Clance & Imes, 1978; Horner, 1972).

All of the above notwithstanding, it may be that in predicting genius-level achievement, one needs to consider more than individual capabilities or even motivation. Simonton (1984, 1994; see Chapter 28 by Simonton) proposes that works of genius and great contributions to society are the results of a fortuitous melding of historical, social, and individual ingredients, where the Zeitgeist, or spirit of the times, generates an economic, political, and philosophical backdrop that determines the sociocultural receptiveness to an individual with a particular set of abilities. Genius, according to Simonton, is a matter of being the right person at the right place at the right time. This is a sentiment strikingly in accord with Feldman's (1980) observation that genius-level achievement is as much a matter of the developmental readiness of a domain to respond to and assimilate particular contributions as it is a matter of an individual's capacity to make those contributions.

In searching for explanations for the nonemergence of genius, we have gone briefly from the individual to the sociocultural and historical. There is one area, however, that remains to be examined—the IQ test itself. As originally conceived by Alfred Binet, the IQ test was a means for gauging an individual's capability to succeed in school as it exists in Western culture. To assume that such a test can select the potential for works of creative genius in any of a multiplicity of fields is requiring more than it was ever equipped to do.

A related question is the relevance of the concept of genius and achievement in the first place. In recent years, some writers have begun to see the IQ score as an index of *asynchronous development* (Morelock, 1992). As such, it gauges the degree to which the rate of a child's cognitive development is in sync with his or her rates of physical, social, and emotional development. According to the proponents of the asynchronous development view, the IQ score should be regarded as a diagnostic tool to assist in providing educational programming, counseling, and parenting addressing the child's varying developmental levels and needs—not as a predictive device for ferreting out potential achievers.

The questions of whether an IQ score can be used in any sense to select potential high achievers, whether it is instead an index of asynchrony to assist in educational programming, parenting, and counseling, or whether it is simply a cultural construct of limited significance may shortly become issues of mere academic interest. Indeed, today some are questioning whether we may soon lose altogether the capability of psychometrically identifying the extraordinarily high IQ child.

The Extraordinarily High IQ Child—An Endangered Species[2]

The identification of highly academically able children so that their needs can be met is not always easy in the classroom. Such children may fail to exhibit the interest and enthusiasm others expect of gifted children. Psychometric data may prove especially helpful in identifying quick minds not obvious to the eye.

From the Stanford-Binet's first appearance in 1916 through its 1973 Terman-Merrill revision (Stanford-Binet, Form L-M), Terman's instrument remained the instrument of choice for identifying academically able children. However, the Stanford-Binet: Fourth Edition, issued in 1986, is an instrument based on a construct of intelligence fundamentally different from that formulated by Terman. Consequently, some (Silverman & Kearney, 1989) argue that if older versions of the scale focusing more strongly on verbal-conceptual facility cease to be available, we may lose the ability to psychometrically identify the types of children studied by Hollingworth.

[2] The suggestive term *endangered species* is taken from Linda Silverman's May 1988 presentation at the Second National Conference on the Exceptionally Gifted, The Hollingworth Center for Highly Gifted Children, Auburn, Maine. Dr. Silverman's presentation was entitled "The Extraordinarily Gifted: An Endangered Species?"

While psychometric data should always be used in conjunction with other sources of information (e.g., parent and teacher observations) (Morelock & Feldman, 1992), to be left without an instrument of proven value for identifying extraordinarily academically able children would be unfortunate. We still know comparatively little about these rapid assimilators of abstract knowledge—and the congenitive processes lying beneath the identification achievable through the IQ index.

Educating the Extraordinarily High IQ Child

Literature on educating "highly gifted children" generally incorporates a range extending from IQ 145 through IQ 180 and over (Silverman, 1989). Some writers choose to subdivide this span into the "exceptionally gifted" (IQ 150 and over) and the "profoundly gifted" (IQ 180 and over) (Webb, Meckstroth, & Tolan, 1982). From the time of Hollingworth (1942), however, it has generally been implicitly assumed that the differences in educational needs among these subgroups is more a matter of degree than kind. Consequently, literature aimed at the "highly gifted" includes these more extreme categories.

Generally, an individualized program is essential in educating the highly gifted (Silverman, 1989). Two children with comparable measured IQs are likely to have quite different profiles of specific academic and nonacademic strengths and weaknesses. Additionally, it is common for these children's profiles of abilities, on the Wechsler Intelligence Scale for Children—Revised, for example, to show peaks and valleys very similar to those seen with learning-disabled children (D. Wertlieb, personal communication, March 8, 1989).[3] A 7-year-old child with some abilities equal to those of a 14-year-old and others that are at the normal level for his or her chronological age cannot be regarded as learning disabled because none of the measured abilities fall below the norm. Functionally, however, the child is dealing with the same kinds of wide discrepancies of ability that plague a learning-disabled child. Like learning-disabled children, highly gifted children need support in dealing with the frustration inherent in such a situation. Also like learning-disabled children, highly gifted children need individualized educational programs addressing their various levels of ability.

Silverman notes that with these children's increased ability to deal with complexity, abstraction, and advanced concepts, "the need for repetition dramatically decreases, and the pace of instruction increases accordingly" (Silverman, 1989, p. 78). For optimal learning, Silverman recommends full-day programs conducted by specially trained teachers using a specially tailored curriculum. The menu of possible provisions includes the following (Silverman, 1989, p. 78).

Individualized education programs (IEPs)
Fast-paced, challenging courses
Self-contained classes
Acceleration
University-based programs
Mentors or tutors
Special schools or programs
Community enrichment opportunities
Home teaching
Counseling

Although peaks and valleys are commonly reflected in the ability profiles of extraordinarily high IQ children, they are most dramatic in the two other major categories of extreme precocity we will discuss—the prodigy and the idiot savant.

The Prodigy

A *prodigy* is a child who, before the age of 10, performs at the level of an adult professional in some cognitively demanding field (Feldman, 1991). As a uniquely defined category of extreme precocity, the prodigy came

[3] Dr. Donald Wertlieb is associate professor and chairman of the Eliot-Pearson Department of Child Study, Tufts University. He also maintains a private practice as a clinical-developmental psychologist.

into being less than two decades ago (Feldman, 1979). This is in spite of the fact that *prodigy* has been used loosely to refer to extraordinary youngsters for many years. The term historically meant any unnatural occurrence portending impending change (Feldman, 1991). Thus, it referred to an entire range of phenomena extending across the advent of happenings notable as uncanny or extraordinary and the existence of humans or animals regarded as "freak."

Eventually, as the term began to be used to refer more narrowly to extreme human precocity, the "sign" or "portent" aspect of its meaning was dropped, while the essential connotation of "unnatural" or "inexplicable" remained. Within this narrowed context, *prodigy* continued to be used indefinitely to refer to a broad range of manifestations of precocity (for example, see Barlow, 1952).

With the advent of IQ and its general acceptance as the measure of giftedness, the child prodigy became subsumed under the IQ umbrella (Feldman, 1979). Children who could compose sonatas at the age of 6 were assumed—implicitly, at least—to be high IQ children with penchants for given fields.

While the notion of IQ was beginning to dominate American concepts of giftedness, there appeared in the European literature two systematic research studies of child prodigies failing to support the congruence of prodigiousness and extraordinarily high IQ (Baumgarten, 1930; Revesz, 1925). Indeed, these were, until 1980 (Feldman, 1980), the only scientific studies of child prodigies in the world literature.[4] We turn now to examine the only three prodigy studies existing in the research literature.

[4] Although these are the only systematic scientific studies of child prodigies on record, a number of biographical or psychohistorical accounts have been published providing interesting insights into the life of the prodigy. See, for example, Kathleen Montour's (1977) "William James Sidis: The Broken Twig"; Norbert Wiener's 1953 autobiography, *Ex-Prodigy: My Childhood and Youth;* Amy Wallace's 1986 book (also about William James Sidis), *The Prodigy;* and Fred Waitzkin's 1984 book, *Searching for Bobby Fischer: The World of Chess, Observed by the Father of a Child Prodigy.*

The Prodigy as Reflected in Research Literature

Revesz and Erwin Nyiregyhazi. Revesz (1925) conducted an in-depth case study of the 7-year-old Hungarian musical prodigy Erwin Nyiregyhazi, using a combination of interviews; observations of Erwin in and out of performing situations; anecdotes from family, teachers, and acquaintances; and formal assessments employing the available techniques of the day (e.g., the 1908 Binet-Simon Scale).

By parental accounts, Erwin was remarkable from a very early age. By the age of 2 he could reproduce correctly tunes sung to him, and by the end of his third year he demonstrated perfect pitch by reproducing on the mouth organ any melody sung to him. At 4 he began to play the piano and compose melodies. In his fifth year the family began providing Erwin with formal music lessons. From age 6 to 12 Erwin became a celebrated performer, playing before the British royal family and other audiences in Budapest and Vienna.

Revesz provided a detailed analysis of Erwin's musical abilities, favorably comparing them with those of other legendary prodigies and great musicians of the day.

Additionally, Revesz used the Binet-Simon scale to assess Erwin's general mental capacity. Erwin scored a mental age 3 years beyond his chronological age of 7, or by modern reckoning slightly above 140 IQ.

Revesz, however, asserted that the test inadequately revealed Erwin's brilliant intellect, noting that the child "analyzed his own inner life in the manner of a trained psychologist" and "expressed himself with great caution and in remarkably pregnant phraseology" (Revesz, 1925, p. 42).

In spite of Erwin's remarkable musical talents and exhibited brilliance, Revesz asserted that the prodigy was indeed, in every aspect other than his music, a child: "Erwin was a child in the full sense of the word; a clever, gay, friendly, charming boy. . . . He played as children play, was fond of boyish exploits, and enjoyed them very much" (Revesz, 1925, pp. 57–58). The mixture of child and adult found by Revesz was noted again by Baumgarten, to whose work we next turn.

Baumgarten's nine prodigies. Baumgarten (1930) studied nine child prodigies including two pianists, two violinists, one orchestra conductor, one artist, one geographer, and one chess prodigy. Focusing specifically on the children as whole personalities rather than on their extraordinary achievements alone, she also examined patterns of different abilities manifested by them. Like Revesz, she wrote of the intriguing mixture of adult and child and the frequently noticeable display of childlike naïveté demonstrated by her subjects. Additionally, they appeared ambitious, pragmatic, wary of those who might harm their careers, passionately devoted to their fields, unafraid of public performance, and desirous of using their gifts to benefit their families.

On a battery of standardized intelligence tests, the children performed well as a whole—but not with the degree of extraordinariness conveyed by their special talents. Translated into contemporary IQ terms, the scores ranged from 120 to at least 160. Baumgarten concluded that her subjects' overall intellectual competence, as reflected in the test results, could not explain their outstanding performances in particular fields.

Baumgarten found surprising contrasts between various abilities within subjects. For example, violinists and pianists demonstrated poor hand coordination in bending wire, drawing, and folding and cutting—though one girl violinist had a talent for drawing. Additionally, a 6-year-old boy showing difficulty in making a circle out of two or three sections or a pentagon from two sections was, at the same time, extraordinarily good at map drawing.

Baumgarten concluded that it was necessary to go beyond the testing of intellectual abilities to explain the remarkable achievements of child prodigies. She felt that factors of inheritance, temperament, family, education, environment, and culture must be examined.

Child Prodigies and Human Potential

A study of six prodigies begun in 1975 (Feldman, 1991, 1994) included two chess players, a young mathematician, a musician-composer, a writer, and an "omnibus prodigy" who showed prodigious achievement in a number of areas, but who eventually began to focus on music composition and performance.[5] What eventually developed into an open-ended effort to observe, understand, and explain the prodigy phenomenon began as a straightforward psychological experiment designed to refute an esoteric point in cognitive-developmental psychology. The point in question was the Piagetian assertion that, universally, children's cognitive development proceeds in major predictable sequential stages grossly encompassing all of a child's thinking capacities at any given point in time. Accordingly, to account for a prodigy's adult level performance in a specific field, one would have to assume that the child's overall cognitive development was generally advanced beyond his or her years.

To test this assertion, four cognitive-developmental measures were administered to the two 8-year-old chess players and the 10-year-old musician-composer (Bensusan, 1976).[6] The results of the testing showed that these child prodigies in chess and music com-

---

[5] At the age of 3½, when Adam, the omnibus prodigy, first entered the study, he was reported to read, write, speak several languages, study mathematics, and compose for the guitar (Feldman, 1980).

[6] The four measures given were: (1) Inhelder and Piaget's (1958) five chemicals task, a test of the level of acquisition of various concrete and formal logical operations; (2) a role-taking task devised by John Flavell (1968) and his associates at the University of Minnesota, the aim of which is to test social-cognitive development by assessing the level of ability to take another's point of view; (3) a map-drawing exercise, an adapation of Piaget and Inhelder's (1948) layout diagram task (Snyder, Feldman, & La Rossa, 1976), which gives a general estimate of the level of the coordination of spatial-logical reasoning; and (4) a psychometric measure of level of moral judgment and reasoning prepared by James Rest (1986), based on Kohlberg's stages of moral development (Feldman, 1991).

position performed age-appropriately in logic, role-taking, spatial reasoning, and moral judgment. The traditional Piagetian conceptualization of cognitive development was thus seriously challenged.

These findings, like those of Revesz and Baumgarten, suggest that prodigious abilities, rather than being the manifestation of a generalized endowment, are domain-specific.

Association with these six prodigies and their families has extended beyond a decade and has resulted in a theoretical framework, the *co-incidence theory,* seeking to explain not only prodigious development, but also all human achievement.

Co-Incidence Theory

Co-incidence is defined as the melding of the many sets of forces interacting in the development and expression of human potential (Feldman, 1994). These include intraindividual (e.g., biological and psychological), environmental (e.g., familial, societal, or cultural), and historical forces. We can think of them as comprising at least four different time frames bearing on the prodigy's appearance and development: the individual's life span, the developmental history of the field or domain, historical and cultural trends bearing on individuals and fields, and evolutionary time. Each of these will be discussed briefly.

Life span of the individual. Aspects of this time frame include, first of all, biological propensities predisposing an individual toward giftedness in certain fields. An example might be Gardner's (1993) concept of multiple brain-based intelligences (i.e., linguistic, musical, logical-mathematical, spatial, bodily-kinesthetic, interpersonal, and intrapersonal intelligences), each of which holds more or less potential for development within a particular individual (see Chapter 5 by Ramos-Ford and Gardner). Conceivably, a child "at promise" for prodigious achievement in music is equipped at birth with the intellectual, physical, and acoustic facilities necessary for extraordinary musical sensibility and performance.

Another factor included in this time frame is the point in the child's physical, social, and emotional developmental history when he or she is introduced to a domain. Playing the violin, for example, requires a certain degree of dexterity. Some children may develop the required dexterity earlier than others. The time of introduction to the instrument may thus be an important factor in whether violin playing becomes a source of pleasure or a source of frustration. Additionally, Csikszentmihalyi and Robinson (1986) noted that children's levels of social and emotional development may play important roles in determining their receptivity to domains. An adolescent grappling with age-appropriate issues of peer acceptance and popularity may opt out of long hours of piano practice and choose, instead, to spend the time socializing with peers. In the case of one chess prodigy, for example, the attractions of the peer group proved powerful enough to jeopardize an intense commitment to the study of chess (Feldman, 1991; Goldsmith, in press).

Another factor encompassed by the individual time frame is how likely the child's family is to nurture talent in a particular field. Mozart's musician-father, for example, fortuitously possessed the musical ability enabling him to instruct his son. He also must have valued the domain and been interested in it enough to spend many hours tutoring his children and accompanying them on their concert rounds—aside from any opportunistic motives he also may have had.

Degree of forthcoming parental support may also be affected by the child's gender. Goldsmith (1987) noted that, historically, general cultural undervaluing of feminine achievement has resulted in (1) less likelihood that parents would provide necessary support for a female would-be prodigy to realize her potential and (2) a scarcity of documentation about existing girl prodigies.

Whether or not parents encourage domain-specific talents may be influenced by values or child-rearing patterns passed down from prior generations. Such transgenerational influences were apparently at work, for example, in the family of child-prodigy violinist Yehudi Menuhin. Menuhin's family had for centuries prior to his birth been shaped by a Hasidic

Jewish tradition emphasizing not only the transcendent and communicative power of music, but also the development of boy prodigies groomed to assume religious leadership as rabbis. The fervor with which the Menuhin family encouraged Yehudi's musical talent may have had its roots in this centuries-old tradition.

Developmental history of the field. Bodies of knowledge, like human beings, develop and change over time.[7] Consequently, the performance requirements and opportunities in various fields change as well. The life span of a would-be prodigy coincides with some portion of a domain's developmental history, the joint existence of the two allowing for a particular expression of the child's potential.

Prodigious achievement can only occur within domains accessible to children. This means that the domains must require little prerequisite knowledge and be both meaningful and attractive to children. Equally important is the adaptability of the domain's media and techniques to children (e.g., child-size violins are necessary for child prodigy violinists). Given these prerequisites, music performance and chess seem especially amenable to budding prodigies—as is substantiated by the fact that the largest proportion of child prodigies in recent decades emerges from these fields. Other fields produce comparatively few prodigies. There have been occasional writing prodigies, child prodigy visual artists (Goldsmith & Feldman, 1989), and on rare occasion a child prodigy in mathematics.

Historical and cultural time frame. This time frame reflects historical and cultural trends affecting opportunities for learning. Prodigious achievement is necessarily influenced by the cultural importance attached to various domains. The revived interest in science and math during the 1950s because of the Soviet satellite initiatives is one example. Another is that a potential chess prodigy in the former Soviet Union was more likely to find institutionalized support and interest than would the same child in the United States.

Evolutionary time frame. Cultural and biological evolution provide the context within which all the other factors in prodigy development interact. Through biological variation and natural selection, human capabilities come into being and either flourish or cease to exist. Parallel evolutionary forces operate on cultures and their artifacts. This qualitative flux in the essence of humanity and the products of humankind necessarily influences options for the expression of potential.

Co-incidence and Prodigious Achievement

The child prodigy is the manifestation of a fortuitous concordance of the various forces of coincidence in such a way as to maximize the expression of human potential. In each of the cases of prodigiousness contained in the research literature, there was, first of all, a child of unquestionably extraordinary native ability. This child was born into a family that recognized, valued, and fostered that ability when the child's introduction to the culturally available domain revealed its presence. The child was invariably exposed to the instruction of master teachers possessing superior knowledge of the domain and its history and imparting that knowledge in a way most likely to engage the interest and sustain the commitment of the child. For the child's part, there was generally exhibited a combination of inner-directedness and a remarkably passionate commitment to the field of extraordinary achievement. Such commitment holds social and emotional repercussions for the life of the prodigy, as we will see in the following sections.

---

[7] We choose to define *genius* in terms of developmental changes in bodies of knowledge. That is, a creative contribution meriting the designation of genius is one that transforms an entire domain of human knowledge. One of such caliber, for example, was Albert Einstein's theory of relativity, which did, indeed, transform the domain of physics (Feldman, 1982).

Social and Emotional Concomitants of Prodigiousness

The prodigy shares with the extraordinarily high IQ child difficulties in establishing satisfactory peer relationships. The inner drive to master the domain of interest typically demands long hours of exacting effort. It is effort gladly devoted by the child pushed by the passion for mastery. Nevertheless, this extensive commitment leaves little time for more childlike pursuits and the forging of bonds with age-mates. In addition, because of the inability of other children to keep up with the prodigy in his or her area of interest, the burden of finding some common ground for a friendship often falls to the prodigy. Consequently, friendships may become restricted to a very small group of others sharing interest in the area of prodigious specialization.

Family Relationships

The family is the catalyst for the co-incidence process (Feldman, 1991). It is the prodigy's parents who must locate necessary teachers and resources and facilitate the child's access to them. At times, this entails commuting to other cities or even uprooting the family unit permanently to resettle closer to a desired mentor. Because a prodigy progresses so rapidly, frequent changes may be required as the child outgrows a succession of mentors.

Such close parental involvement results in a longer and more intense period of dependence for prodigies than is the case in families with more typical children. As with families of handicapped children, especially close family ties may be engendered through common efforts to protect a "special" child from a potentially insensitive outside world.

The strong commitment to talent development shared by prodigies and their families generally means some sacrifice by other family members. While many prodigies are only children, some do have siblings. Limited family resources may dictate that sibling talent goes unsupported. On the other hand, the prodigy's presence may influence the channeling of sibling potential. When Hepzibah Menuhin, the younger sister of child prodigy violinist Yehudi, asked to learn to play the violin like her older brother, her parents encouraged her to play the piano instead—since Yehudi needed an accompanist. When Yalta, the youngest sibling, later showed interest in the piano, she was often told to make herself useful around the house instead because the family didn't need another musician. Yet many believed Hepzibah and Yalta to be equally as talented as Yehudi (Rolfe, 1978).

Having caught a glimpse of the dramatic showcasing of domain-specific talent characterizing the prodigy, we now turn to our last form of extreme precocity—the idiot savant.

The Idiot Savant

The phenomenon of the "idiot savant," like that of the high-IQ child and the child prodigy, has its own unique history. The term was coined in 1887 by Dr. J. Langdon Down of London (Down, 1887) to refer to severely mentally handicapped persons displaying advanced levels of learning in narrowly circumscribed areas.

Although intriguing in its own right, the term *idiot savant* fails to describe the individuals it labels, since they are generally neither "idiots" nor "savants." In Down's time, *idiot* referred to individuals operating at the lowest level of retarded intellectual functioning, as classified by practitioners on the basis of evaluation of speech and language capabilities. With the advent of IQ tests, idiocy was translated as encompassing the lowest portion of the IQ scale, spanning an IQ range of 0 to 20.[8] In reality, however, the IQs of all known tested idiot savants have been above 20—usually in the range of 40 to 70 (Treffert, 1989).

The *savant* part of the term is a straightforward adaptation from the French word "to know" or "man of learning," which, although

[8] The term *idiot* was used from 1910 to 1968 to refer to this portion of the IQ scale. In 1968, the World Health Organization adopted the term *profoundly retarded* to refer to this same range (Craft, 1979).

perhaps slightly more appropriate, is nevertheless a misnomer as well.[9]

Given the inappropriateness of the term as a whole and the pejorative connotation of the first part of it, Treffert (1989) proposed *savant syndrome*—or just *savant*—as a more desirable name for the phenomenon. Treffert described the phenomenon and proposed more precise classification terminology as well as a theoretical explanatory framework. His thoughts provide a valuable base as we continue to explore the savant.

Savant Syndrome—Definition and Description

Treffert defined *savant syndrome* as follows:

> Savant Syndrome is an exceedingly rare condition in which persons with serious mental handicaps, either from developmental disability (mental retardation) or major mental illness (early infantile autism or schizophrenia), have spectacular islands of ability or brilliance which stand in stark, markedly incongruous contrast to the handicap. In some, savant skills are remarkable simply in contrast to the handicap (talented savants or savant I). In others, with a much rarer form of the condition, the ability or brilliance is not only spectacular in contrast to the handicap, but would be spectacular even if viewed in a normal person (prodigious savants or savant II). (Treffert, 1989, p. xxv)

Treffert noted that the condition can be either congenital or acquired by a normal person after injury or disease of the central nervous system. It occurs six times as often in males as in females. Intriguingly, the skills can appear—and disappear—in an unexplained and sudden manner. Savant brilliance occurs only within very few areas: calendar calculating; music, chiefly limited to the piano; lightning calculating (the ability to do extraordinarily rapid mathematical calculations); art (painting, drawing, or sculpting); mechanical ability; prodigious memory (mnemonism); or, on rare occasion, unusual sensory discrimination (smell or touch) or extrasensory perception. Prodigious savants, however, occur primarily within the areas of music, mathematics (lightning and calendar calculating), and memory.

Research reveals a number of characteristics generally true of all savants.

Characteristics of Savant Functioning

Generally, savants display minimal abstract reasoning ability combined with almost exclusive reliance on concrete patterns of expression and thought. One savant (Scheerer, Rothman, & Goldstein, 1945), for example, could memorize and sing operas in several languages, yet he had no comprehension of the abstract conceptual and symbolic meaning of words. In addition, there is a general incapacity for metacognition, or reflection upon one's internal thinking processes (LaFontaine, 1974; Scheerer, Rothman, & Goldstein, 1945; Treffert, 1989). Calendar calculators, for example, commonly respond correctly to queries (e.g., "On what day of the week did September 1, 1744, fall?) without being able to explain how they arrived at the correct response. Those able to articulate rule-based strategies tend to have higher IQs than do their counterparts (Hermelin & O'Connor, 1986).

Another characteristic of savants is an immediate—seemingly intuitive—access to the underlying structural rules and regularities of their particular domain, be it music (Treffert, 1989), mathematical calculation (Hermelin & O'Connor, 1986; O'Connor & Hermelin, 1984), or art (O'Connor & Hermelin, 1987). Furthermore, the domain-specific rules intuitively "known" by savants are the same rules applied by those of normal or high reasoning ability who are skilled in the same area. Savants, however, bound by the structural rules of their domain, are incapable of being creative in the sense of producing totally original work. Thus, while a musical savant may imitate, improvise, or embellish based on preestablished constraining musical rules, he

[9] Bernard Rimland (1978) claims that the *idiot* in *idiot savant* is from the French *idiot,* meaning "ill-informed or untutored." This interpretation captures the paradoxical nature of the phenomenon (i.e., "untutored man of learning") without confusing the issue with IQ-associated connotations.

or she is generally incapable of composing (Treffert, 1989).

A further frequently noted aspect of the savant is a restricted range of emotion that precludes the experience of heightened passion, excitement, or sentiment. This takes the form of generally flattened affect and—in the case of the performance of musical savants—shallow, imitative expressiveness lacking subtlety or innuendo.

While the talent of the mnemonist savant lies solely in his or her impressive memory for miscellaneous or mundane happenings, all savants claim incredibly powerful memories narrowly limited to their domains of achievement.

Treffert (1989), the first researcher to differentiate between *talented* and *prodigious* savants, reported that there have been only about 100 known prodigious savants in the world literature—2 to 15 of whom are currently living. Leslie Lemke is one who was portrayed in depth by Treffert.

Leslie Lemke

Leslie Lemke was born prematurely and given up for adoption at birth. Within the first few months of life, he developed retrolental fibroplasia—a condition common to premature babies in which the retina proliferates uncontrollably and that sometimes, as in Leslie's case, results in glaucoma with associated blindness. Consequently, Leslie had to have both eyes surgically removed.

At 6 months of age, Leslie, who was then blind, palsied, and mentally handicapped, was placed in a foster home under the care of 52-year-old May Lemke. May was an experienced nurse and governess who was well known for her skill as well as the love and devotion she showed in caring for children. When Leslie first arrived at the Lemke household, he was hardly able to cry, move, or swallow. May, however, refused to lose hope for Leslie, and, with her constant attention, Leslie was indeed able to develop.

By age 5½ Leslie was able to walk in spite of his spasticity. He also could repeat verbatim a whole day's conversation while impersonating each speaker's voice. Leslie's speech, however, was mainly repetitious, rather than social; he responded to questions by repeating them. About this age also, Leslie was discovered under a bed rhythmically strumming the bedsprings as if playing an instrument.

When Leslie was between the ages of 7 and 8, a piano was added to the Lemke household, and May, who played by ear, introduced Leslie to it by playing and singing for him and running his fingers up and down the keyboard. Leslie, too, began to play be ear. By age 8, under May's loving tutelage, Leslie also played the bongo drums, the ukelele, the concertina, the xylophone, and the accordian. By age 9, although he still required help in dressing and feeding himself, he could play the chord organ.

One incident marked in May's mind the fruition of the "miracle" of Leslie. One evening, when Leslie was 14 years old, the family watched a movie on television, after which May and her husband, Joe, retired for the evening. They were awakened at about 3:00 A.M. by strains of Tchaikovsky's Piano Concerto No. 1, the theme song to the movie they had seen earlier. Thinking that the television had been left on, May went into the living room to check and discovered Leslie at the piano playing the piece vigorously and flawlessly after having heard it only once.

Leslie has performed for concert audiences around the world. They are amazed by his prodigious memory. After once hearing a 45-minute opera tape, Leslie can transpose the music to the piano and sing the score back in its original foreign language. In addition, his songs are stored indefinitely, with Leslie recalling them and performing them without error after several years of intervening time. His repertoire includes thousands of pieces.

Leslie's IQ measures 58.

Explaining the Prodigious Savant

Treffert (1989) proposed an intriguing explanation for the phenomenon of the prodigious savant. Drawing upon the research of Geschwind and Galaburda (1987), he suggested that pre- or postnatal injury to the left hemisphere of the brain results in compensatory growth in the right hemisphere. This is manifested by the impairment of language and analytic thought (functions dominated by the left hemisphere) and a heightened capacity for right-brain-dominated functions (e.g., musical and spatial abilities).

Savant memory, proposes Treffert, is the manifestation of altered (compensatory) brain circuitry. Injury to the cerebral cortex, which normally manages conscious, cognitive-associative memory, causes memory functions to be shifted to a more primitive area of the brain (the *corticostriatal system*). Memory becomes nonassociative, habitual, emotionless, and nonvolitional. It becomes, in essence, a conditioned response.

Treffert affirmed, however, that even such extreme alterations in brain function and circuitry fail to explain the prodigious savant's extensive access to the structural rules of domains. Such access, suggested Treffert, may be based on some inherited ancestral memory transmitted across generations.[10] This domain-specific memory, he continued, is inherited separately from general intelligence. Treffert concluded that once the groundwork is laid for savant skills, intense concentration, obsessive repetition, reinforcement from others for display of the special ability, and an unstoppable drive to exercise the ability produce the prodigious savant.

Juxtaposing the Extremes—What We Learn from the Child of Extraordinary IQ, the Prodigy, and the Savant

We have examined a broad range of manifestations of human precocity. Each type, however, can be characterized in terms of (1) degree of generalized abstract reasoning ability and (2) extent and nature of domain-specific capability. Table 35.1 presents a breakdown of the various gradations and combinations of these, reflected by the cases mentioned in this chapter. A number of interesting contrasts and similarities emerge from the research on these various forms of precocity.

Speculations on Abstract Reasoning, Emotion, and Precocity

All the types of precocious children mentioned in the research literature are described as highly attracted to and motivated by their respective areas of achievement. We suspect that this attraction derives at least partly from brain functioning particularly compatible with the cognitive demands of the area of activity. Descriptive terminology characterizing this attraction, however, ranges from *drive* to *passion,* depending on the type of precocity under discussion.

Passion has been used to describe prodigies—those with sufficient generalized abstract reasoning abilities and concomitant conscious associative memory to come to love their domain of expertise. *Drive,* on the other hand, denotes the bare-bones motivation of the idiot savant. It is the motivation, according to Treffert, of those whose "habit" memory and lack of cognitive associations prevent a more interpretive and emotional type of mastery. We speculate that the intensity with which the savant and the prodigy conduct their pursuits is equally strong. Only the capacity for interpretation of that intensity differs.

An example of this interpretive difference is found in the way savant mental calculators and nonsavant mental calculators are reported as referring to their calculating ability. Nonsavant calculators are, first of all, generally conscious of the mental process by which they, over time, have explored the relationships among various numbers (Smith, 1983).

Furthermore, nonsavant calculators speak of numbers having become their "friends" in childhood. The Dutch mental calculator Wim Klein states, "Numbers are friends for me, more or less. It doesn't mean the same for you, does it, 3,844? For you it's just a three and an eight and a four and a four. But I say 'Hi, 62 squared.'" Similarly, Hans Eberstark, in recalling his lifetime experience with mental

[10] Treffert is not the first to suggest the possibility of genetically transmitted qualities of intellect. The idea has had a fair amount of support since, at least, Francis Galton's (1892) book *Hereditary Genius.* Also, Brill (1940) proposed inherited transmission of domain-specific gifts as a factor in lightning calculator abilities.

Table 35.1
A Taxonomy of Extreme Precocity

Type of Child	*Characteristics*
Extraordinarily high IQ—omnibus prodigy	Extraordinarily high abstract reasoning capability[a] plus extraordinarily advanced domain-specific skills in multiplicity of domains. Performs at adult professional level in multiple domains. Displays passionate involvement with numerous domains of prodigious achievement. Voracious appetite for academic knowledge.
Prodigy	Displays anywhere from above-average to extraordinarily high generalized abstract reasoning capability plus extraordinarily advanced domain-specific skill in a single domain. Performs at adult professional level in a single domain. Displays passionate involvement with domain of prodigious achievement. May demonstrate voracious appetite for academic knowledge.
Extraordinarily high IQ child	Extraordinarily high generalized abstract reasoning capability and possibly notable domain-specific skills in one or more areas. May be intensely drawn to a number of different areas. May have a problem committing to a single area of interest. Voracious appetite for academic knowledge.
Prodigious savant	Minimal generalized abstract reasoning capability and islands of extraordinarily advanced domain-specific skill in one or more areas. Appears driven to exercise domain-specific capabilities. Concrete thinker.

Note: These classifications reflect the types of extreme precocity found in the research literature to date. Certain groups, such as mental calculators and mnemonists, are anomalous in that they display anywhere from minimal to extraordinarily high generalized abstract reasoning ability along with their islands of advanced skill. When minimal generalized abstract reasoning capability exists, such persons are classified as prodigious savants. According to the definition here, however, they cannot be classified as prodigies—even at higher levels of abstract reasoning ability—because standards for adult professional-level performance do not exist in their areas of achievement.

[a] The generalized abstract reasoning capability referred to in this table is logical, verbal-conceptual facility.

calculation, said he had different emotional reactions to various numbers, calling 36 arrogant, smug, and self-satisfied, whereas he harbored a personal affection for "the ingenious, adventurous 26, the magic, versatile 7, the helpful 37, the fatherly, reliable (if somewhat stodgy) 76" (Smith, 1983, p. xiii).

In contrast, the savant calculating twins, George and Charles, apparently never had any awareness of their methods. When asked how they did what they did, the twins simply replied "It's in my head and I do it" (Hamblin, 1966, p. 107). Their straightforward, concrete response—unembellished with associated nuances—is typical of the savant.

The concrete thought and flattened affect of the savant is in striking opposition to the thought and affect of the extraordinarily high IQ child. Silverman (1989) notes that extraordinarily high IQ children "manipulate abstract symbol systems with ease and become animated when dealing with complex relations involving many variables"—yet they may have difficulty with more concrete material, such as the rote memorization of facts (Silverman, 1989, p. 75). Equally intriguing is the fact that a tendency toward emotional intensity is cited as one of the hallmarks of this form of giftedness (Piechowski, 1979; see Chapter 30).

Structure of the Talent Domain and Requirements for Achievement

Something about the extraordinary domain-specific abilities of prodigies and savants may be revealed through studying the characteristics and structuring of the relevant domains (Goldsmith & Feldman, 1988, 1989; Miller, 1989; Morelock & Feldman, 1993; Treffert,

1989). For example, comparative studies of prodigy and savant talent in music and art (Morelock & Feldman, 1993) reveal similarities in the way both prodigies and savants intuit the rules and regularities underlying the organization of the domains. At the core of these two domains, there appear to be syntactical structures functionally equivalent to the one found in language—an "image lexicon" in the case of art (O'Connor & Hermelin, 1987) and absolute pitch in the case of music (Miller, 1989)—which allow for the development of higher order structures and provide a basis for higher order pattern extraction from visual or auditory experience. Prodigies and savants seem to assimilate these syntactical rules and regularities intuitively. The process seems akin to the way normal children intuitively grasp the syntactical rules of language and then manifest that implicit understanding through language comprehension and expression. Yet, the general intellectual abilities surrounding the domain-specific talent of the prodigy lend a depth of quality and a connectedness to the outside world which is not found in savant talent. Thus:

> Possibly, the savant provides us with an opportunity to observe domain-specificity in its purest form. Perhaps the purest essence of domain-specific talent is the ability to holistically intuit the syntactic core of rules and regularities lying at the heart of a domain of knowledge: the pattern of relationships between numbers, the pattern of tones in a musical scale, the pattern of images in the visual world, the pattern of words in a language. . . . In the prodigy, we see this same domain-specific talent. But through the facilitation of general intellectual capacities, it becomes enlarged, embellished, imbued with meaning, intimately connected with both the phenomenological reality of the child . . . and the materialistic reality of the external world. (Morelock & Feldman, 1993, p. 179)

Intriguing questions remain. Extraordinary musical talent among both savants and prodigies is relatively common, while phenomenal artistic ability is rare. What explains this difference in incidence? What makes the underlying structures of domains differentially assimilable into the human psyche? What are the relative roles played by general IQ-type abilities and IQ-dependent domain-specific skills in the creation of varieties of achievement in talent domains? Is there interplay between them? And if so, what is the nature of it? Research into the structural cores of various domains may spur important insights about the human capacities that create and respond to those structures.

The Catalytic Family

Research concerning high-IQ children (Fowler, 1981; Gross, 1993; Morelock, 1994), prodigies (Feldman, 1991; Feldman & Goldsmith, 1986), and prodigious savants (Treffert, 1989) confirms the critical importance of the family in coordinating and encouraging the development of extraordinary giftedness. Frequently, this is not a conscious effort, but merely the unconscious establishment of a family milieu favoring particular activities or ways of looking at the world (Feldman & Goldsmith, 1986; Fowler, 1981, Morelock, 1994). The fit of child to family may be a key issue here. Had Leslie Lemke or Wolfgang Amadeus Mozart grown up in a nonmusical family, it is questionable whether either would have developed the astonishing talent each eventually displayed.

Conclusion

It appears that there is much to be gained from additional comparative research in this area. Through it, perhaps we can begin to assemble the mysterious jigsaw puzzle before us. It is, after all, remarkable that the manifestations of extreme precocity fit together as they do, each highlighting the uniqueness of the others. Placed in careful juxtaposition, they begin to reveal the marvelous complexity and beauty residing in the spectrum of human potential.

REFERENCES

Barlow, F. (1952). *Mental prodigies.* New York: Philosophical Library.

Baumgarten, F. (1930). *Wunderkinder psychologische Untersuchungen.* Leipzig: Johann Ambrosius Barth.

Bensusan, R. (1976). *Early prodigious achievement: A study of cognitive development.* Unpublished master's thesis, Tufts University, Medford, Massachusetts.

Brill, A. A. (1940). Some peculiar manifestations of memory with special reference to lightning calculators. *Journal of Nervous and Mental Disease, 90,* 709–726.

Clance, P. R., & Imes, S. A. (1978). The imposter phenomenon in high achieving women: Dynamics and therapeutic intervention. *Psychotherapy: Theory, Research, and Practice, 15,* 241–245.

Coopersmith, S. (1981). *The antecedents of self-esteem.* Palo Alto, CA: Consulting Psychologists Press.

Cornell, D. G. (1984). *Families of gifted children.* Ann Arbor, MI: UMI Research Press.

Craft, M. (Ed.) (1979). *Tredgold's mental retardation* (12th ed.). London: Bailliere Tindall.

Csikszentmihalyi, M., & Robinson, R. (1986). Culture, item, and the development of talent. In R. J. Sternberg & J. E. Davidson (Eds.), *Conceptions of giftedness* (pp. 264–284). New York: Cambridge University Press

Down, J. L. (1887). *On some of the mental affections of childhood and youth.* London: Churchill.

Feldman, D. H. (1979). The mysterious case of extreme giftedness. In A. H. Passow (Ed.), *The gifted and the talented* (Seventy-eighth yearbook of the National Society for the Study of Education, pp. 335–351). Chicago: University of Chicago Press.

Feldman, D. H. (1980). *Beyond universals in cognitive development.* Norwood, NJ: Ablex.

Feldman, D. H. (1982). A developmental framework for research with gifted children. In D. H. Feldman (Ed.), *Developmental approaches to giftedness and creativity: New directions for child development* (pp. 31–45). San Francisco: Jossey-Bass.

Feldman, D. H. (1984). A follow-up of subjects scoring above 180 IQ in Terman's "Genetic studies of genius." *Exceptional Children, 50,* 518–523.

Feldman, D. H. (with Goldsmith, L. T.). (1991). *Nature's gambit: Child prodigies and the development of human potential.* New York: Teachers College Press.

Feldman, D. H. (1994). *Beyond universals in cognitive development* (2nd ed.). Norwood, NJ: Ablex.

Feldman, D. H., & Goldsmith, L. T. (1986). Transgenerational influences on the development of early prodigious behavior: A case study approach. In W. Fowler (Ed.), *Early experience and the development of competence: New directions for child development* (pp. 67–85). San Francisco: Jossey-Bass.

Flavell, J. H. (1968). *The development of role-taking and communication skills in children.* New York: Wiley.

Fowler, W. (1981). Case studies of cognitive precocity: The role of exogenous and endogenous stimulation in early mental development. *Journal of Applied Developmental Psychology, 2,* 319–367.

Galton, F. (1892). *Heredity genius: An inquiry into its laws and consequences* (2nd ed.). New York: D. Appleton.

Gardner, H. (1993). *Frames of mind: The theory of multiple intelligences.* (Tenth anniversary edition). New York: Basic Books.

Geschwind, N., & Galaburda, A. M. (1987). *Cerebral lateralization: Biological mechanisms, associations, and pathology.* Cambridge, MA: MIT Press.

Goldsmith, L. T. (1987). Girl prodigies: Some evidence and some speculations. *Roeper Review, 10,* 74–82.

Goldsmith, L. T. (in press). Tracking trajectories of talent: Child prodigies growing up. In C. Friedman & B. Shore (Eds.), *Talents within: Cognitive and developmental aspects.* Washington, DC: American Psychological Association.

Goldsmith, L. T., & Feldman, D. H. (1988). Idiots savants—thinking about remembering: A response to White. *New Ideas in Psychology, 6*(1), 15–23.

Goldsmith, L. T., & Feldman, D. H. (1989). Wang Yani: Gifts well given. In W.-C. Ho (Ed.), *Yani: The brush of innocence* (pp. 50–62). New York: Hudson-Hills.

Gross, M. U. M. (1992). The early development of three profoundly gifted children of IQ 200. In P. S. Klein & A. J. Tannenbaum (Eds.), *To be young and gifted* (pp. 94–138). Norwood, NJ: Ablex.

Gross, M. U. M. (1993). *Exceptionally gifted children.* New York: Routledge.

Hamblin, D. J. (1966, March 18). They are idiot savants—Wizards of the calendar. *Life,* pp. 106–108.

Hermelin, B., & O'Connor, N. (1986). Idiot savant calendrical calculators: Rules and regularities. *Psychological Medicine, 16,* 1–9.

Hollingworth, L. (1926). *Gifted children: Their nature and nurture.* New York: Macmillan.

Hollingworth, L. (1942). *Children above 180 IQ Stanford-Binet—Origin and development.* Yonkers-on-Hudson, NY: World Book.

Horner, M. S. (1972). Toward an understanding of achievement related conflicts in women. *Journal of Social Issues, 28,* 157–175.

Inhelder, B., & Piaget, J. (1958). *The growth of logical thinking from childhood to adolescence.* New York: Basic Books.

Kearney, K. J., & Kearney, C. Y. (1994). *The accidental genius.* Manuscript submitted for publication.

Kulieke, M. J., & Olszewski-Kubilius, P. (1989). The influence of family values and climate on the development of talent. In J. L. VanTassel-Baska & P. Olszewski-Kubilius (Eds.), *Patterns of influence on gifted learners: The home, the self, and the school* (pp. 40–59). New York: Teachers College Press.

LaFontaine, L. (1974). *Divergent thinking abilities in the idiot savant.* Unpublished Ed.D. dissertation, School of Education, Boston University.

Miller, L. K. (1989). *Musical savants: Exceptional skill in the mentally retarded.* Hillsdale, NJ: Lawrence Erlbaum Associates.

Montour, K. (1977). William James Sidis: The broken twig. *American Psychologist, 32,* 267–279.

Moos, R. H., & Moos, B. S. (1994). *Family environment scale manual: Development, application, research* (3rd ed.). Palo Alto, CA: Consulting Psychologists Press.

Morelock, M. J. (1988). *Transgenerational influences on the development of children's talents, gifts, and interests.* Unpublished master's thesis, Tufts University, Medford, Massachusetts.

Morelock, M. J. (1992). Giftedness: The view from within. *Understanding Our Gifted, 4*(3), 11–14.

Morelock, M. J. (1994). *The profoundly gifted child in family context: Families with children above 200 IQ.* Manuscript in preparation.

Morelock, M. J. (in press). The child of extraordinarily high IQ from a Vygotskian perspective. In R. C. Friedman & B. Shore (Eds.), *Talents within: Cognitive and developmental aspects.* Washington, DC: American Psychological Association.

Morelock, M. J., & Feldman, D. H. (1992). The assessment of giftedness in preschool children. In E. Vazquez Nuttal, I. Romero, & J. Kalesnik (Eds.), *Assessing and screening preschoolers: Psychological, social, and educational dimensions.* Boston: Allyn and Bacon.

Morelock, M. J., & Feldman, D. H. (1993). Prodigies and savants: What they have to tell us about giftedness and human cognition. In K. A. Heller, F. J. Monks, & A. H. Passow (Eds.), *International handbook of research and development of giftedness and talent* (pp. 161–181). New York: Pergamon Press.

O'Connor, N., & Hermelin, B. (1984). Idiot savant calendrical calculators: Math or memory? *Psychological Medicine, 14,* 801–806.

O'Connor, N., & Hermelin, B. (1987). Visual and graphic abilities of the idiot savant artist. *Psychological Medicine, 17,* 79–80.

Piaget, J., & Inhelder, B. (1948). *The child's conception of space.* London: Routledge.

Piechowski, M. M. (1979). Developmental potential. In N. Colangelo & R. T. Zaffrann (Eds.), *New voices in counseling the gifted* (pp. 25–57). Dubuque, IA: Kendall/Hunt.

Rest, J. R. (1986). *Defining issues test: Manual.* Minneapolis, MN: Center for Ethical Development, University of Minnesota.

Revesz, G. (1925). *The psychology of a music prodigy.* New York: Harcourt.

Rimland, B. (1978, August). Inside the mind of the autistic savant. *Psychology Today,* pp. 68–80.

Rolfe, L. (1978). *The Menuhins: A family odyssey.* San Francisco: Panjandrum/Aris.

Scheerer, M., Rothman, E., & Goldstein, K. (1945). A case of "idiot savant": An experimental study of personality organization. *Psychology Monograph, 58,* 1–63.

Segoe, M. B. (1975). *Terman and the gifted.* Los Altos, CA: Kaufmann.

Silverman, L. K. (1989). The highly gifted. In J. F. Feldhusen, J. VanTassel-Baska, & K. R. Seeley (Eds.), *Excellence in educating the gifted* (pp. 71–82). Denver, CO: Love.

Silverman, L. K., & Kearney, K. (1989). Parents of the extraordinarily gifted. *Advanced Development, 1,* 41–56.

Simonton, D. K. (1984). *Genius, creativity, and leadership.* Cambridge, MA: Harvard University Press.

Simonton, D. K. (1994). *Greatness: Who makes history and why.* New York: Guilford Press.

Smith, S. B. (1983). *The great mental calculators: The psychology, methods, and lives of calculating prodigies, past and present.* New York: Columbia University Press.

Snyder, S., Feldman, D. H., & La Rossa, C. (1976). *A manual for the administration and scoring of a Piaget-based map drawing task,* Tufts University, Medford, Massachusetts. Summarized in O. Johnson (Ed.), (1976), *Tests and measurements in child development: A handbook II.* San Francisco: Jossey-Bass.

Tabackman, M. J. (1976). *A study of family psycho-social environment and its relationship to academic achievement in gifted adolescents.* Unpublished doctoral dissertation, University of Illinois, Urbana-Champaign.

Terman, L. M. (Ed.). (1925–1959). *Genetic studies of genius* (Vols. 1–5). Stanford, CA: Stanford University Press.

Terman, L. M. (1975). Human intelligence and achievement. In M. V. Seagoe (Ed.), *Terman and the gifted* (pp. 216–228). Los Altos, CA: Kaufmann.

Treffert, D. A. (1989). *Extraordinary people: Understanding "idiot savants."* New York: Harper.

Waitzkin, F. (1984). *Searching for Bobby Fischer: The world of chess, observed by the father of a child prodigy.* New York: Random House.

Wallace, A. (1986). *The prodigy.* New York: Dutton.

Webb, J. T., Meckstroth, E. A., & Tolan, S. S. (1982). *Guiding the gifted child.* Columbus, OH: Child Psychology.

Weiner, N. (1953). *Ex-prodigy: My childhood and youth.* Cambridge, MA: MIT Press.

Witty, P. (1951). *The gifted child.* Boston: Heath.

36

Gifted Performance in Young Children

NANCY EWALD JACKSON and ELIZABETH J. KLEIN, *The University of Iowa*

In this chapter we first describe behaviors that might be called manifestations of intellectual giftedness in young children. Second, we look at origins of gifted performance. Third, we summarize what is known about the long-term predictive significance of these behaviors. Fourth, we consider the practical issue of how young children with intellectual gifts can be identified. We define as *young children* those in the approximate age range from 2 through 6 years and *infants* as below 2 years of age. Although we touch occasionally on questions about gifted performance in infancy, our primary focus is on young children and on connections between their behavior and giftedness later in childhood.

We refer whenever possible to gifted behaviors rather than gifted children. We think it would be salutary for scholars in the field of giftedness to adopt the practice, now common among those who study individuals with disabilities, of "putting the person first" (Jackson, 1993). The literature provides little support for the assumption that giftedness in childhood is an enduring and unchanging property of the individual. Rather, different forms of giftedness emerge at different ages, sometimes in different children (Gross, 1992; Horowitz, 1992).

Manifestations of Giftedness in Young Children

What Is Gifted Performance in Young Children?

Sternberg (1993) suggested that gifted performance must have all of five qualities: (1) It must be excellent, relative to the performance of peers who are the same age or who have had the same degree of instruction; (2) it must be rare among the same peers; (3) it must be demonstrable on some reliable and valid assessment instrument; (4) it must be productive, or suggest potential for productivity; and (5) it must have some societal value.

Many behaviors that might be displayed by young children and infants meet Sternberg's first three criteria, including talking at 7 months, using elaborate language or drawing recognizable pictures at 30 months, or reading fluently at 4 years. These performances are excellent relative to age norms, are rare, and reliably demonstrable on validated standard instruments. Satisfying Sternberg's last two criteria is more difficult.

"Productivity" implies work, and young children are not expected to be workers. Therefore, in a tradition that goes back to Terman (1925), we often think of giftedness in children in terms of potential for adult productivity. From this perspective, a judgment that precocious talking, drawing, or reading indicates "potential for productivity" must be based on evidence from longitudinal studies (Jackson, in press). However, we prefer not to define a child's current behavior by reference to its long-term predictive significance. That significance is important to determine, but it can be assessed separately from any categorization of a young child's current behavior as *gifted.*

A more manageable way to evaluate the productivity of a young child's behaviors is to consider the extent to which an exceptional behavior pattern produces important immediate changes in the lives of the child and his or her family, teachers, and other companions. From this perspective, behaviors such as precocious talking and precocious reading easily qualify as productive, because they are important in everyday life in our society.

An 18-month-old who comprehends and produces sophisticated language lives in a social world dramatically different from the world of peers who cannot speak at length or comply with complex directions. Similarly, 5-year-olds who read fluently and independently are able to learn in ways that are not yet open to other children their age. We also propose that a preschooler's precocious talent in the graphic arts, music, or arithmetic has an immediate impact on the child's daily life, and therefore qualifies as productive.

Sternberg's final criterion, value, also can be applied to the behaviors of young children. In mainstream American culture, we value verbal sophistication, literacy, and numeracy in our children. These values are reflected in the content of educational television programs, preschool curricula, and popular children's toys and books. Other intellectual, artistic, social, and physical skills also are valued, but the definition of *excellence* and opportunities for children to develop a skill vary considerably across groups. Perhaps for this reason, research on the development of intellectual giftedness in young children has focused primarily on precocious oral language development and the early development of reading, writing, and arithmetic skill, with some case study literature (e.g., Feldman, 1986; Gross, 1992; Morelock & Feldman, 1993; Tannenbaum, 1992) documenting the early emergence of talent in music or the graphic arts.[1] We shall touch on the latter literature only briefly.

Tests of intelligence are not administered routinely to children of preschool age and play a less central role in our conceptualization of gifted performance than they do in considering giftedness during the school years. Practical issues related to the assessment of intelligence in children who have displayed gifted behaviors are discussed later in this chapter.

Giftedness in Oral Language Production and Comprehension

Precocity in the production and comprehension of oral language has been noted consistently as an indicator of high verbal intelligence in children of preschool age and as a predictor of continued giftedness in linguistic performance (Crain-Thoreson & Dale, 1992; Tannenbaum, 1992). Identifying a child's language development as precocious is facilitated by the fact that language acquisition follows a set sequence in which skills emerge in a predictable order, though at widely varying individual rates.

Linguistic precocity can be defined by performance on professionally administered standard tests of language comprehension and production, by analysis of tape-recorded language samples, and from parents' reports (Crain-Thoreson & Dale, 1992; Fenson et al., 1994). In one study, measures taken at 24 months that indicated continuing advanced development included vocabulary size and the length and grammatical complexity of a child's sentences (Crain-Thoreson & Dale, 1992). The various aspects of language often develop in synchrony with one another, but individual children may be especially advanced in some oral language skills, but not others (Fenson et al., 1994). For example, Henderson, Jackson, and Mukamal (1993) studied a 2-year-old whose sentences were exceptionally long and grammatically complex, even though the words he used and topics discussed were not unusually sophisticated. Sentences produced by this child at age 2 years, 7 months, included, "I'm going to show you the cranberry bread that mother baked in the oven," and, "I want to leave the garlic there because haveta don't get paint on it."

In one recent study (Crain-Thoreson & Dale, 1992), parents of children whose language development was found to be advanced at ages 20 and 24 months reported that their children began talking at an average age of 7.2 months, which is consistent with other reports of precocious oral language development in children who have earned high intelligence test scores (e.g., Terman, 1925). However, the case study literature also includes reports of highly intelligent children, and adults of great intellectual achievement, who did not begin talking especially early. One exceptionally intelligent boy studied by Gross (1992) did not utter his first word until 21 months, echoing

[1] See Chapter 35 by Morelock and Feldman.

the developmental history reported for Albert Einstein.

The mother of another high-IQ boy reported a recurring pattern in the case study literature—language production that did not begin early but progressed rapidly thereafter:

> . . . . Once he decided he was going to talk he went from single words to complete sentences with incredible speed and with virtually no transition stage. And there were very few pronunciation errors. . . As for correctness of grammar; most children carry on for some time saying "he comed" or "I falled," but Ian only had these stages momentarily and then it was straight on into absolute accuracy." (Gross, 1992, p. 115)

Giftedness in Reading and Writing

Children are expected to become skilled producers and comprehenders of oral language during their preschool years, but a minority demonstrate unusually gifted performance by becoming literate as well. Some of the most extremely precocious readers we have known have been able to recognize a large number of words, and even sound out unfamiliar ones, before passing their third birthday (Henderson et al., 1993; Jackson, 1988a). Precocious readers may be able to read simple (or not-so-simple) texts on their own at the age of 3 or 4 years, comprehending what they have read (Jackson, 1988b, 1992a).

High verbal intelligence is neither necessary nor sufficient to make a child become a precocious reader, although highly intelligent children are more likely to begin reading early. Across a series of studies, children who learned to read before beginning first grade have had an average IQ of about 130 (Jackson, 1992a). This is well above the average IQ of 100 for the population as a whole; in fact, an IQ of 130 is often the threshold for identifying a child as gifted. However, remember that if the *average* precocious reader has an IQ of about 130, one-half of precocious readers would be expected to earn IQs *below* 130. Precocious readers often have IQs in the moderately above-average range, and the earliest readers are not always the children who are the most extremely advanced in verbal knowledge and reasoning ability (Jackson, 1992a; Jackson, Donaldson, & Cleland, 1988).

Cognitive profiles of precocious readers. What other cognitive characteristics are associated with a child's becoming a precocious reader? There are no clear-cut answers to this question. Even when one knows something about the children's intellectual characteristics, it is difficult to determine exactly which toddlers will be precocious readers (Jackson, 1992a). For example, most children whose oral language development is extremely advanced at age 2 years do not become precocious readers by the time they are 4, even when they come from homes in which their parents have supported their literacy development in appropriate ways (Crain-Thoreson & Dale, 1992). However, early talkers are likely to be superior readers by age 6½ years (Dale, Crain-Thoreson, & Robinson, 1995).

Research on the intellectual characteristics of precocious readers suggests that they may have minds that do some kinds of basic information processing with superior efficiency (Jackson & Myers, 1982; Jackson, 1992a). Perhaps individual differences in mental processing efficiency influence the pace with which children learn from the literacy-supporting experiences in their daily lives. In working with precocious readers and their parents, one gets the impression that the children's interests and rapidly developing abilities shape parents' behavior at least as much as parents lead their children (Henderson et al., 1993).

Interests. The interests of precocious readers are much like those of other children their age, except for interests in reading and writing. These latter interests may be the result, rather than the cause, of exceptionally rapid development (Thomas, 1984). The reading-related interests of precocious readers tend to fall into two categories, which can be described as *literary* and *technical* interests. Literary interests include reading fiction and writing poems and stories. Technical interests include reading for information and drawing maps and diagrams. Boys tend to have more technical interests, girls more literary interests. This gender difference remains stable from the summer after kindergarten until late in elementary school (Jackson et al., 1988; Mills & Jackson, 1990). However, we do not know whether boys and girls *begin* learning to read for different reasons.

Reading skill patterns. Extensive studies of precocious readers' skill patterns have revealed that, at least by the time they have finished kindergarten and can comprehend text at or beyond the second-grade level, these children typically have a solid repertoire of skills. One need not worry that they have not learned to read "the right way." After a few years of reading, 5- or 6-year-old precocious readers typically have well-developed word identification skills that draw on both knowledge of letter–sound correspondences and an ability to recognize words directly by sight (Jackson & Donaldson, 1989; Jackson, Donaldson, & Mills, 1993). The kinds of errors that precocious readers make in reading stories aloud are similar to the kinds of errors made by typical readers (Jackson, Donaldson, & Cleland, 1988). Precocious readers use information from context to help identify words, but they do not depend entirely on context for word identification (Jackson & Donaldson, 1989).

Precocious readers read both isolated words and text passages accurately, but the most striking feature of their skill repertoire is a tendency to read text very rapidly (Jackson & Donaldson, 1989; Jackson, in press). Being a faster-than-average beginning reader is useful. Children who read through a passage quickly are likely to find it easier to comprehend. They still have the beginning of a sentence in mind by the time they reach the end, which makes it easier to link up and make sense of the whole (Breznitz & Share, 1992).

We can conclude that precocious readers typically have developed their ability in ways that give them a firm foundation for future learning. However, this picture of precocious readers as well rounded needs to be qualified in three ways. First, like many typical readers in a very early stage of reading acquisition, precocious readers in their preschool years, or those who are just a bit ahead of their kindergarten classmates, do not always have strong phonological decoding skills (Henderson et al., 1993; Jackson, 1992a). Some precocious readers make an unusual degree of progress on the basis of sight-word reading skills alone before they eventually figure out and start using the phonological system (Jackson, 1988b). Second, individual children who are all exceptionally advanced readers differ markedly from one another in the relative strengths of their various skills (Jackson et al., 1988; Jackson et al., 1993). Third, the school language arts curriculum for most kindergarten and primary classes encompasses a range of activities related to reading, spelling, and composition that is much broader than the set of skills measured in studies of precocious readers.

Precocious writing and spelling. The relation between precocity in reading and precocity in writing has not been studied extensively, and it seems to vary across children. Durkin (1966) described precocious readers as "pencil and paper kids" whose interest in reading, according to their parents' retrospective reports, seemed to flow from an even earlier interest in writing. We have known precocious readers like this (e.g., Jackson, 1988a). Some children create and use systematically nonstandard spelling systems (e.g., spelling *giraffe* as *GRF*) before they become aware that what they write can be read (Read, 1971). However, we have also known precocious readers whose spelling and writing skills did not emerge until several years after they began to read words (e.g., Henderson et al., 1993; Jackson, 1988a).

Other Manifestations of Gifted Performance in Young Children

Children of preschool age who master reading, and sometimes writing, at an unusually early age might be expected to demonstrate other intellectual gifts as well. Learning to read an alphabetic language such as English requires analytic code-breaking skill of a sort that also should be useful in breaking the codes of other representational systems, such as those of mathematics and music.

Although Gardner (1983) has argued that linguistic, logical-mathematical, and musical "intelligences" are distinct, case studies of child prodigies and eminent adults are consistent with the hypothesis that there are strong links between the skills used to learn alphabetic writing systems, mathematics, music, and computer languages (e.g., Csikszentmihalyi & Robinson, 1986; Gross, 1992; Feldman, 1986; Jackson, 1992a, 1992b; Tannenbaum, 1992). Similar analytic abilities may be involved in learning to sound out or spell words; play, read, and write music; or do elementary mathematics. Published case studies and our own experience suggest that skill in reading and music can emerge as early as age 2 or 3 years, but mathematical talent is more likely to be clearly evident at age 4 or 5 years.

Gross (1992) reported case histories of three Australian boys with extremely high Stanford-Binet IQs that illustrate how gifted performance may occur in different domains as children grow up. All three boys were reading before their third birthday, and all also showed precocious talent in mathematics. In their elementary school years, the boys' interests and precocious achievements spanned music, computer programming, Latin, physics, chess, and structural analysis of transportation systems. The analytic quality that linked one boy's interests across various domains is evident in the following observation:

> Ian always seemed to look for different things in reading . . . he's never been interested in fantasy or imaginative stories. The sort of things that excited him were factual books, books on computing or logic, or compendiums of math puzzles. He had a craze, at one stage, for "Choose Your Own Adventure" stories, because he liked working out the different permutations of changes and endings. But even in writing, he doesn't go in for imaginative stories. When he was 7 his teacher said to me that she would throw a party on the day he wrote an imaginative story because anything she asked him to do he would convert into a diagram, a maze, a flowchart, a timetable, calendar—everything had to be set out and analyzed. (Gross, 1992, pp. 123–124)

We have known a number of "pattern analyzers" like Ian, not all of them boys. However, we also have known highly intelligent children who were extremely precocious readers but whose interests and abilities were more specifically linguistic and literary (e.g., Jackson 1988a, 1992b). No child's gifted performance should be dismissed because he or she does not show other characteristics sometimes associated with that kind of performance.

Precocious talent in the graphic arts is mentioned less frequently in the case study literature than precocious reading, mathematics achievement, or musical talent. However, unusual degrees of representational skill have been reported in children of preschool age (Winner & Martino, 1993). Precocious talent in drawing may be a child's most striking demonstration of giftedness, but such talent also can co-occur with advanced performance on tests of visual-spatial reasoning and with reading precocity (Jackson, 1992a).

Although young children may demonstrate giftedness in various aspects of their art work, the representation of space is especially interesting because children typically progress slowly through regular steps toward complete and integrated representations of three dimensions. Case (1992) and Porath and Arlin (1992) argued that even the most precocious child artists are not extremely advanced in the way they represent space. However, Winner and Martino describe several cases of precocity in spatial representation, including an Israeli boy who invented ways to represent depth in his drawings beginning at age 2½. Western children typically do not begin dealing with this problem until about age 8, and developmental theorists who emphasize the importance of maturational limits (e.g., Case, 1992) would be hard pressed to explain such precocity.

Early Giftedness and Savant Syndrome

Gifted performances in areas such as reading and mathematics and, to a lesser extent, in music and drawing, occur most often in children who also would earn high scores on tests of general or verbal intelligence. However, each of these talents also can occur in a peculiarly encapsulated form in what is known as *savant syndrome.*

Savants, sometimes also called by the French term *idiots savants,* are individuals whose general intelligence is well below average, but who can perform brilliantly in particular areas. Many, but not all, savants are autistic. Savant readers are called *hyperlexics,* and they are likely to become able to sound out words, even unfamiliar nonsense words, before reaching school age, despite limited ability to use language for communication (e.g., Healy, 1982). Savant musicians, such as Eddie, studied by Miller (1989), typically become expert pianists at an early age despite low intelligence and the visual impairment particularly characteristic of this form of savant syndrome. Savant abilities are also evident in forms of mathematical calculation or in memory for tightly organized bodies of knowledge.

The skill and enthusiasm with which some highly intelligent young children master closed symbol systems by capitalizing on a sensitivity to rules and patterns is echoed in reports of savants' performances (Gross, 1992; Miller, 1989; Morelock & Feldman, 1993). The key difference between the two types of precocious achievers is in the lack of flexibility and generalizability of savants' talents. However, some savants have developed skills that would meet all of Sternberg's criteria for gifted performance.

Origins of Gifted Performances in Young Children

When a child demonstrates remarkably gifted performance, we wonder why that particular child has become exceptional in that particular way. One way of looking at this question is to try to identify the extent to which the behavior is an expression of a genetic predisposition or an exceptionally supportive environment.

Imagine a child like the 2-year-old reader Max (Henderson et al., 1993). On his second birthday, Max surprised his parents by reading a restaurant sign that said "Pizza." From that time on, his mother systematically encouraged his rapidly developing literacy. Perhaps Max's precocity reflected experiences provided by his parents. After all, his mother had been trained as a reading teacher. Although she had not consciously taught him to read before age 2, she had supported his learning in many informal ways from infancy onward. On the other hand, Max's highly intelligent parents also had passed on genes that may have given him the potential to learn rapidly.

Genes and environment work together within families in ways that are impossible to disentangle unless one compares birth and adoptive families. For example, Max's parents' high intelligence, education, and literary interests probably influenced their choice to create a home environment in which the value of reading was clearly evident. Parents' genes can affect their children indirectly, through the environments they create, as well as by transmission through egg and sperm (Scarr & McCartney, 1983).

This mixing of heredity and environment is important when we try to plan interventions based on what has seemed to work well for parents and children who were doing what came naturally to them. Parenting practices that have been associated with the development of gifted behavior will not necessarily produce gifted behavior if applied out of context.

Research on the development of precocious reading (Jackson, 1992a) illustrates the distinction between patterns of parental behavior naturally associated with gifted performance and the consequences of systematic attempts to create such performances. Children identified as precocious readers at age 5 or 6 years are likely to continue to be good, though not always exceptional, readers (Mills & Jackson, 1990). However, intensive early instruction in reading and other academic skills typically has not had lasting effects (Coltheart, 1979; Rescorla, Hyson, & Hirsh-Pasek, 1991).

In observing how young gifted children interact with their parents, one often is struck simultaneously by the precocity of a child's current achievement and the skill with which the parent exploits opportunities to help the child reflect on and extend his or her learning. For example, the parent of a 5-year-old who had been reading for several years told a story about her son's emerging skill in mathematics.

The boy surprised his mother by asking, "Do you know how much 3 times 8 is?" She answered, "I think I do. Do you?" He then replied, "Yes. It's 24. Do you know how I know? It's because 3 times 4 is 12."

Although this boy's independently developed understanding of mathematics is impressive, his mother's response is also noteworthy. She answered her son's question in a way that led him to express his knowledge and reasoning, rather than terminating the interchange by saying, "Yes, it's 24" (Jackson, in press).

The dynamic interplay between a child's developing abilities and interests and a parent's sensitive nurturing is evident in Moss's (1992) comparison of the teaching strategies of mothers of 3- and 4-year-olds with high and average Binet IQs. Moss asked each mother to choose challenging tasks for their children and videotaped the mother helping her child complete a puzzle and a peg game and engaging in free play with blocks. The children with high IQs were more verbally fluent and able to engage their partners in longer and more sophisticated conversations. They also demonstrated more self-regulation of their problem solving, perhaps as a response to their mothers' greater use of helping strategies such as predicting consequences of future actions and monitoring the activity by commenting on the appropriateness of moves. In contrast, mothers of children with average IQs were more likely to focus the child's attention on behavior related to getting back on task, rather than on ways of actually doing the task.

Moss interpreted her observations from a Vygotskyan perspective, suggesting that the mothers of children with high IQs were more likely to converse in ways that stretch a child's existing competence by structuring "a context in which the child is sensitively manipulated into finding his or her own solution." (p. 297). The kinds of behaviors demonstrated by the high-IQ children and their mothers are consistent with other findings suggesting that highly intelligent children have more metacognitive, or thinking-about-thinking, skills than children of average intelligence (Jackson & Butterfield, 1986; Kanevsky, 1992). Unfortunately, this study does not allow us to separate the extent to which parents have developed a focus on teaching metacognitive skills over time, because it always has worked for their child, from the extent to which the approach works now because the parent has been using it consistently for years.

Although an interaction style designed to encourage the child's ability to manage problem solving independently may characterize many interactions between children with intellectual gifts and their parents, the case study literature also suggests that parents of individuals who have become eminent adults may incorporate specific agendas in their teaching. For example, Nobel-laureate physicist Richard Feynman (1988) reported that while he was still in his high chair, his father taught him to create patterns with colored tiles as an introduction to mathematics.

In recent years, middle-class Americans have become more and more concerned with fostering the development of academic skills in their preschool-age children (Zigler & Lang, 1985). This phenomenon may have contributed to the precocious emergence of reading in more children who were ready to learn, but early academic pressure does not seem to confer any lasting benefit on most middle-class children, whether the pressure comes from home or a structured preschool program (Coltheart, 1979; Jackson, 1992a; Rescorla et al., 1991). Our impression is that the most sophisticated and enthusiastic precocious readers are children who have driven their parents and teachers to keep up with them.

Although gifted children sometimes are assumed to be the product of affluent homes, effective parent–child interactions can take place in any setting. For example, precocious readers come from a wide range of family backgrounds. Some have come from families rich in literacy but little else (Durkin, 1982; Torrey, 1979). Durkin found that most of the good readers from low-income African-American families in one urban school district had learned to read at home before beginning elementary school. In working with hundreds of parents of precocious readers, the first author has formed the impression that they tend to be exceptionally thoughtful, well-organized people who are strongly committed to supporting their children's development. Parents of precocious readers typically supported their young children's developing literacy in activities such as reading with them and teaching letter names, but many parents provide the same kinds of support without having their child make exceptionally rapid progress (Durkin, 1966; Jackson et al., 1988).

Predictive Significance of Young Children's Gifted Performances

Methodological Issues

Giftedness, by definition, is rare. This fact alone makes it difficult to determine the long-term predictive significance of young children's demonstrations of giftedness. Longitudinal studies are expensive and difficult to manage, even when they include samples of only a few hundred children. To do a complete study of relations between gifted performances in young children and gifted performances later on *in a sample representative of the population in general,* one would need to study thousands of children. Furthermore, the experience of participation in such a study could turn parents' and children's attention to issues studied by the investigators in ways that would make the sample unrepresentative. Therefore, efforts to understand the long-term predictive significance of gifted performances in early childhood probably will remain dependent on incomplete evidence gleaned from an assortment of imperfect approaches.

One such incomplete approach is a simplification of the comprehensive longitudinal design described earlier. Records of major longitudinal studies, which were designed for other purposes, are scanned to identify children whose very early behavior was remarkable in some way or who later demonstrated some form of giftedness, typically high intelligence. Such studies (e.g., Willerman & Fiedler, 1974) have been useful. However, their records rarely contain the kind of information that would be optimal for a study of the development of giftedness. For example, the researchers in such studies are not likely to have looked for or measured behaviors such as precocious reading.

A second approach is the retrospective case study. Children who earned high intelligence test scores (e.g., Hollingworth, 1942; Terman & Oden, 1947) or demonstrated some other talent or prodigious achievement (e.g., VanTassel-Baska, 1989; Feldman, 1986) are identified, usually in elementary school. The children, their parents, and others are asked for retrospective accounts of the child's earliest years. However, memory for past events may be incomplete and distorted. Also, retrospective reports of the early childhoods of children who performed well at later ages tell us nothing about children who may have displayed similar behaviors in early childhood, but who were *not* later identified as gifted performers. Retrospective case studies of eminent adults have the same limitations, but to an even greater degree.

A third approach is to identify and follow the subsequent development of infants or, more likely, very young children who already have demonstrated some form of giftedness such as precocious language use (Crain-Thoreson & Dale, 1992), precocious reading (Jackson & Myers, 1982; Mills & Jackson, 1990), or a variety of precocious achievements (Roedell, Jackson, & Robinson, 1980; Robinson, 1993). This focused approach is less costly than longitudinal studies of unselected groups of children. It complements retrospective studies by identifying children who behave in remarkable ways in their early years but may not qualify as gifted performers later on. Such studies could include comparison groups of children who did not display the remarkable early behavior of interest. However, even when such comparison groups are available, they cannot be assumed to be the same as the focal group in all but the gifted performance for which the focal group was selected. Such groups also may be too small to include cases of late-developing giftedness. Therefore, focused prospective longitudinal studies provide either potentially biased or no information about children who become gifted performers without showing early signs of their talent.

Continuities and Changes in the Development of Gifted Performance

Limits of the research notwithstanding, the literature does suggest that infants who later will earn high IQ scores are somewhat more likely than others to become rapidly bored with repeated presentations of the same picture or sound and to turn to novel stimuli more rapidly than other children their age (Borkowski & Peck, 1986; McCall & Carriger, 1993; Tannenbaum, 1992). As preschoolers, children who eventually will earn high IQs or high scores on out-of-level tests of mathematics and verbal reasoning are more likely than other children to have excellent memories, be advanced in language development (Terman & Oden, 1947), and read early (Terman & Oden, 1947; VanTassel-Baska, 1989). Furthermore, children who display these characteristics during their preschool years are likely to continue to perform well intellectually (Crain-Thoreson & Dale, 1992; Dale, Crain-Thoreson, & Robinson, 1995; Mills & Jackson, 1990; Robinson, 1993).

Demonstrations of gifted performance during the preschool years may be linked to later achievements that seem, at least superficially, to be quite different. As noted before, a child whose first remarkable accomplishment is early reading is not necessarily destined for a literary career. Instead, early reading ability sometimes may presage later interest and remarkable achievement in another symbol system such as music, mathematics, or computer science. This kind of nonobvious continuity in development is called *heterotypic continuity* (Kagan, 1971). Although the term has been used in describing many different aspects of development, it may be especially useful in thinking about the development of gifted performances across age.

Gifted performances are most likely to be evident in domains in which new forms of competence emerge as a result of a universal or culturally imposed timetable. For example, toddlers face the universal developmental task of mastering their native language. They also may encounter culture-specific symbol systems such as pictures and written language. At the age of 2 or 3 years, the children most likely to be identified as gifted perfomers in a literate society are those who talk, read, write, or draw unusually early or exceptionally well for their age. However, neither talking nor reading is a noteworthy accomplishment among 8-year-olds. Even though a child may continue to do these things exceptionally well, gifted performance may be more salient in domains such as mathematics or science to which the child has been introduced just recently.

Later Development of Precocious and Nonprecocious Readers

Reading precocity is reported often in case histories of eminent adults and children who have been selected for remarkable accomplishments (Cox, 1926; Feldman, 1986). Reading precocity is especially common among children whose IQs are extraordinarily high (Hollingworth, 1942; Terman & Oden, 1947). However, estimates of the prevalence of reading precocity among moderately high IQ children have ranged widely from study to study (Terman & Oden, 1947; Ehrlich, 1978; Jackson, 1992a), perhaps because of differences in the degree of encouragement and instruction the children received in different communities and different eras.

Some very bright children do not learn to read early, even if they have had some encouragement (Jackson, 1992a; Jackson & Myers, 1982). High-IQ children and eminent adults occasionally have had great difficulty learning to read (Jackson, 1992a), but a more common pattern for bright children is to make rapid progress in reading after beginning at a typical age (Dale et al., 1995). At the same time, children who received an exceptionally early start may slow down a bit in their elementary school years (Mills & Jackson, 1990).

The skills involved in beginning to identify words differ from those required of a mature reader of sophisticated texts (Curtis, 1980). As children grow older and their reading skills develop, those who had a head start because they learned very early to break the code of print may be overtaken by later bloomers who, once they also figure out the code, have the general world knowledge and language and reasoning skills required to comprehend increasingly advanced texts. In one study of children who had begun reading somewhat early, the best predictor of individual differences in reading comprehension in fifth or sixth grade was the child's verbal intelligence, although how well the child was reading just after kindergarten also predicted later comprehension (Mills & Jackson, 1990).

Precocious readers almost always remain at least average in their reading ability, and most stay well above average, even though their reading performance in fifth or sixth grade is much more likely to be within the range of their classmates' performance than it was in kindergarten (Mills & Jackson, 1990). Some investigators claim that precocious readers remain superior in reading achievement throughout their elementary school years, relative to other children of comparable intelligence who were not early readers (Durkin, 1966; Pikulski & Tobin, 1989; Tobin & Pikulski, 1988). However, the meaning of these findings is hard to evaluate. Does an early start in reading in itself give a child a lasting advantage, or do other factors, such as persistence, interest in learning, or parental support, contribute both to the early emergence of reading and to continued good achievement? The general absence of long-term gains from experimental programs designed to create precocious readers suggests that getting an early start in reading may not, in itself, be important for most middle-class children. A head start in reading may be more important for children who have a special need to begin school with skills that will help them, and their teachers, recognize their ability (Durkin, 1982; Jackson & Roller, 1993).

A Conceptual Model of the Development of Gifted Performance

Figure 36.1 (Jackson, in press) is a conceptual model suggesting ways in which precocious readers, the young gifted performers we know best, may demonstrate precocious achievements in different ways at different ages. The kinds of achievement included in the model all have been observed in children. Except for literary production and verbal intelligence, all rest heavily in the mastery of closed symbol systems. Forms of precocious achievement are placed in the model according to their most likely age of emergence, and most of the specified developmental paths have been documented in the individual-differences literature.

This model is designed to encourage further speculation and the formulation of alternative hypotheses; it is not a proven account of how giftedness develops. Some omissions or placements are judgment calls. Environmental influences and motivational and other mediators of achievement (e.g., gender) that are likely to be important at different stages of development are indicated only very generally by large boxes meant to suggest potentially complex and important effects. The term *metacognitive input* refers to the kinds of parental scaffolding of learning observed by Moss (1992) and described earlier. Further specification and testing of models such as this one depend on longitudinal studies that may start with focused identification of young children with remarkable characteristics but that are designed to test for heterotypic as well as homotypic continuity in development.

Identification of Young Children with Intellectual Gifts

Describing versus Identifying Gifted Performance

In previous sections we described aspects of gifted performance in young children. However, presenting a picture of what gifted performers are like is different from the task of identifying those children. When descriptions of the "typical" gifted young child become transformed into checklists of characteristics for parents or teachers to use in deciding whether or not a child qualifies as gifted (e.g., Parkinson, 1990), a number of factors influence whether a characteristic works to discriminate between gifted and less exceptional performers.

For example, most young gifted performers

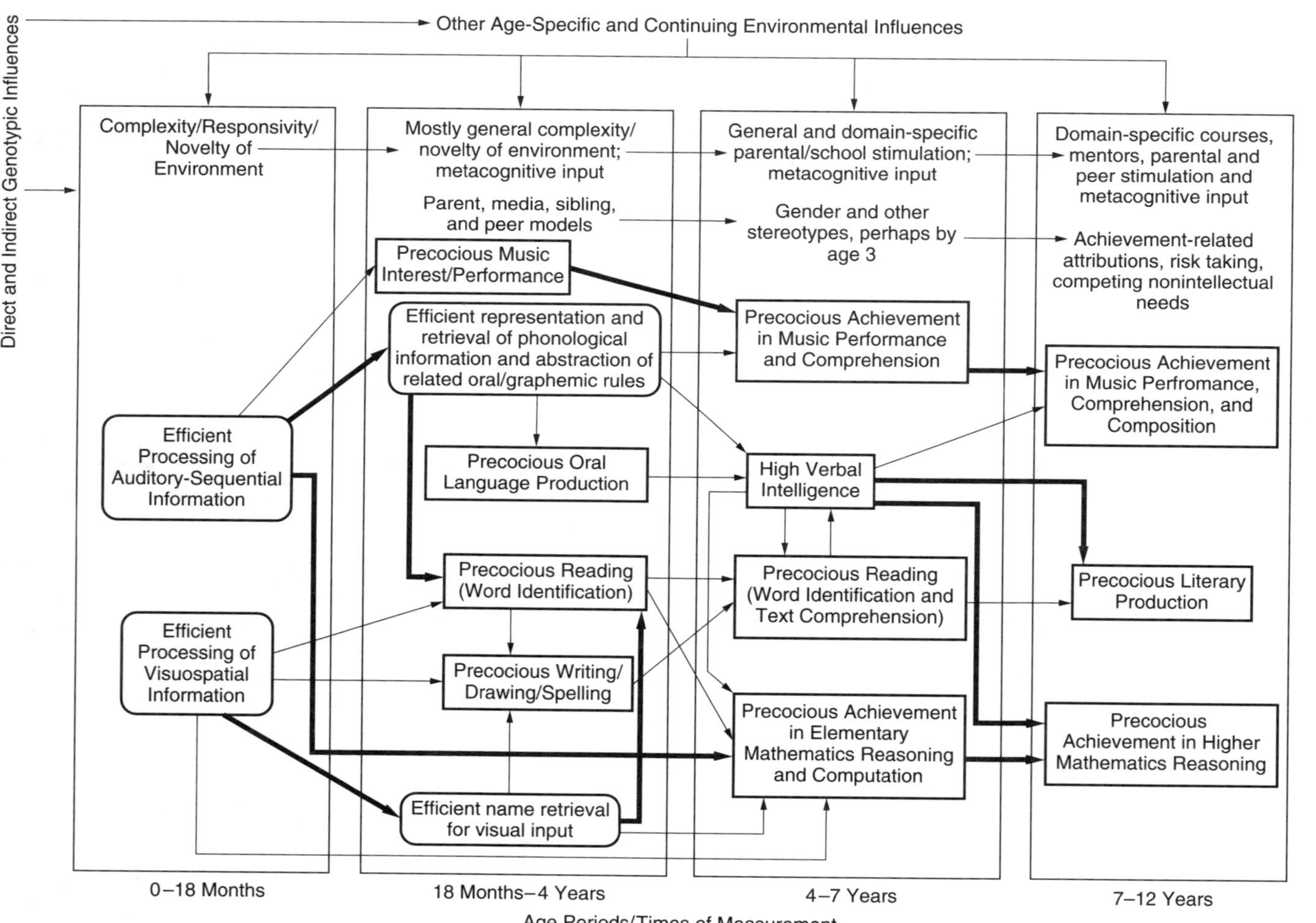

Source: Adapted from Figure 1 in Jackson (in press).

Figure 36.1 A conceptual model of continuities in the development of gifted performances in reading, mathematics, language, and music. The hypothesized strength of each path is indicated by the thickness of the arrow depicting it.

could be described as "intensely curious," "investigative," and "asks penetrating questions," but so could many young children whose performance would not fit the Sternberg criteria we summarized earlier. Furthermore, a parent's judgment about what degree or kind of curiosity is unusual for a young child may differ from the judgment of a teacher or psychologist who has observed many children of that age. Perhaps this is why parents' perceptions of gifted performance are most likely to have diagnostic utility for skills such as reading, in which the difference between age-expected and exceptionally advanced behavior is widely known and easy to observe (Robinson, 1993).

On the other hand, concrete accomplishments are not necessarily the basis for parents' most accurate perceptions of a young child's giftedness. Louis and Lewis (1992) asked parents of children with a mean age of 33 months about the reasons why they had brought their child to a specialized clinic for gifted children. Parents of children with higher tested IQs (mean = 149) were more likely to refer to their child's exceptional memory, imagination, and abstract thinking, whereas parents of the children with lower IQs (mean = 118) were more likely to mention their child's specialized knowledge of body parts, the alphabet, and or numbers. Unfortunately, interpretation of this and other similar findings is complicated by the fact that parents' perceptions may be influenced as much or more by their own intellectual sophistication and educational histories as by their children's behaviors.

Using Standard Tests to Identify Young Gifted Performers

Standard tests designed to measure individual differences in infant development generally have not been successful in identifying children who would demonstrate intellectual precocity in their later preschool or elementary school years, although high-scoring children are more likely to maintain their precocity if the initial assessment was motivated or supported by parents' perceptions of the child's everyday behavior (Shapiro et al., 1989; Willerman & Fiedler, 1974). Recently developed measures of infant attention and memory ultimately may do better (McCall & Carriger, 1993), which would be useful to theorists trying to understand the development of giftedness. However, there rarely is any practical reason to use standard tests to evaluate the extent to which an infant or young child is displaying gifted behaviors.

The purpose of standard tests is to compare a particular child's abilities against those of others the same age. Unless correctable developmental problems are suspected, the only reason to compare young children's abilities with those of their peers is to provide a common language in which parents and institutions can communicate easily about a child's educational needs, relative to others in a group. Children's scores on standard tests, like their abilities, change from year to year. If the practical question at hand is the appropriate kindergarten program for a 5-year-old, the child's IQ or other characteristics demonstrated a year or two earlier are not very helpful. However, a comprehensive assessment of a child's general intelligence, specific academic skills, and social maturity can be critical in matching a child with the right program at the time of school entry (Jackson & Roller, 1993; Roedell et al., 1980).

Psychologists disagree about the most appropriate way to assess the general or verbal intelligence of preschool-aged children suspected of being intellectually precocious. The Stanford-Binet was long favored for this purpose because its flexible format and broad range of norms was conducive to eliciting extremely advanced performances from young children whose attentiveness and willingness to respond verbally might be limited. However, the most recent version of this test has been restructured and renormed in ways that have reduced the frequency with which children earn extremely high IQs. Some psychologists therefore have resorted to using the earlier form of the test and its outdated norms. We agree with those who have argued that this practice destroys much of the value of a standard assessment (Robinson & Robinson, 1992).

In assessing young children's advanced academic skills, as well as general intelligence, the examiner faces a tradeoff between choosing an instrument that is well standardized and widely respected by school personnel and using one that is likely to be sensitive to a young child's sometimes spotty advanced knowledge. Children with advanced skills in areas such as reading may fail simple preliminary test items designed to tap supposedly prerequisite skills (Henderson et al., 1993). Two relatively unfamiliar tests that may be useful in assessing 3- and 4-year-olds' reading and mathematics skills are the Test of Early Mathematics Ability (Ginsburg & Baroody, 1990) and the Test of Early Reading Ability—2 (Reid, Hresko, & Hammill, 1989). However, the more widely used and better standardized Woodcock-Johnson Psychoeducational Battery (Woodcock & Johnson, 1989) provides similar information. In any standard assessment, a child's test performance should be interpreted in the context of other information, including reports from parents, about the child's everyday behavior.

Summary

Young children's gifted performances are most evident in those areas of development in which new skills which have social and practical importance are emerging, such as oral language and reading. Giftedness demonstrated during the preschool years may change form or disappear as a child matures, but threads of developmental continuity may be detectable in the underlying abilities being expressed. It may never be possible to disentangle heredity from environment in accounting for the emergence of gifted performances, and the study of how giftedness develops has been restricted by practical and methodological factors. Identifying gifted performances in young children involves dealing with issues different from those involved in the scientific study of the development of giftedness.

REFERENCES

Borkowski, J. G., & Peck, V. A. (1986). Causes and consequences of metamemory in gifted children. In R. J. Sternberg & J. E. Davidson (Eds.), *Conceptions of giftedness* (pp. 182–200). New York: Cambridge University Press.

Breznitz, Z., & Share, D. L. (1992). Effects of accelerated reading rate on memory for text. *Journal of Educational Psychology, 84,* 193–199.

Case, R. (1992). *The mind's staircase: Exploring the conceptual underpinnings of children's thought and knowledge.* Hillsdale, NJ: Lawrence Erlbaum Associates.

Coltheart, M. (1979). When can children learn to read—and when should they be taught? *Reading research: Advances in theory and practice* (Vol. 1, pp. 1–30). New York: Academic Press.

Cox, C. M. (1926). *Genetic studies of genius:* Vol. 2. *The early mental traits of three hundred geniuses.* Palo Alto, CA: Stanford University Press.

Crain-Thoreson, C., & Dale, P. S. (1992). Linguistic precocity, preschool language, and emergent literacy. *Developmental Psychology, 28,* 421–429.

Csikszentmihalyi, M., & Robinson, R. E. (1986). Culture, time, and the development of talent. In R. J. Sternberg & J. E. Davidson (Eds.), *Conceptions of giftedness* (pp. 264–284). New York: Cambridge University Press.

Curtis, M. E. (1980). Development of components of reading skill. *Journal of Educational Psychology, 72,* 656–669.

Dale, P. S., Crain-Thoreson, C., & Robinson, N. M. (1995). Linguistic precocity and the development of reading: The role of extralinguistic factors. *Applied Psycholinguistics, 16,* 173–187.

Durkin, D. (1966). *Children who read early.* New York: Teachers College Press.

Durkin, D. (1982, April). *A study of poor black children who are successful readers.* Reading Education Report No. 33, Center for the Study of Reading, University of Illinois at Urbana-Champaign.

Ehrlich, V. Z. (1978). *The Astor program for gifted children.* New York: Columbia University.

Feldman, D. H. (1986). *Nature's gambit: Child prodigies and the development of human potential.* New York: Basic Books.

Fenson, L., Dale, P. S., Reznick. J. S., Bates, E., Thal, D. J., & Pethick. S. J. (1994). Variability in early communicative development. *Monographs of the Society for Research in Child Development,* Serial No. 242, Vol. 59, No. 5.

Feynman, R. P. (1988). *"What do you care what other people think?" Further adventures of a curious character.* New York: Norton.

Gardner, H. (1983). *Frames of mind.* New York: Basic Books.

Ginsburg, H. P., & Baroody, A. J. (1990). *Test of early mathematics ability.* Austin, TX: Pro-Ed.

Gross, M. U. M. (1992). The early development of three profoundly gifted children of IQ 200. In P. Klein & A. J. Tannenbaum (Eds.), *To be young and gifted* (pp. 94–140). Norwood, NJ: Ablex.

Healy, J. M. (1982). The enigma of hyperlexia. *Reading Research Quarterly, 17,* 319–338.

Henderson, S. J., Jackson, N. E., & Mukamal, R. A. (1993). Early development of language and literacy skills of an extremely precocious reader. *Gifted Child Quarterly, 37,* 46–50.

Hollingworth, L. S. (1942). *Children above 180 IQ.* New York: World Book.

Horowitz, F. D. (1992). A developmental view on the early identification of the gifted. In P. Klein & A. J. Tannenbaum (Eds.), *To be young and gifted* (pp. 73–93). Norwood, NJ: Ablex.

Jackson, N. E. (1988a). Case study of Bruce: A child with advanced intellectual abilities. In J. M. Sattler (Ed.), *Assessment of children* (3rd ed., pp. 676–678). San Diego: Sattler.

Jackson, N. E. (1988b). Precocious reading ability: What does it mean? *Gifted Child Quarterly, 32,* 200–204.

Jackson, N. E. (1992a). Precocious reading of English: Sources, structure, and predictive significance. In P. Klein & A. J. Tannenbaum (Eds.), *To be young and gifted* (pp. 171–203). Norwood, NJ: Ablex.

Jackson, N. E. (1992b). Understanding giftedness in young children: Lessons from the study of precocious readers. In N. Colangelo, S. G. Assouline, & D. L. Ambroson (Eds.), *Talent Development: Proceedings from the 1991 Henry B. and Jocelyn Wallace National Research Symposium on Talent Development* (pp. 163–179). Unionville, NY: Trillium Press.

Jackson, N. E. (1993). Moving into the mainstream? Reflections on the study of giftedness. *Gifted Child Quarterly, 37,* 46–50.

Jackson, N. E. (in press). Strategies for modeling the development of giftedness in children: Reconciling theory and method. In R. C. Friedman & B. Shore (Eds.), *Talents within: Developmental and cognitive aspects.* Washington, DC: American Psychological Association.

Jackson, N. E., & Butterfield, E. C. (1986). A conception of giftedness designed to promote research. In R. J. Sternberg & J. E. Davidson (Eds.), *Conceptions of giftedness* (pp. 151–181). New York: Cambridge University Press.

Jackson, N. E., & Donaldson, G. (1989). Precocious and second-grade readers' use of context in word identification. *Learning and Individual Differences, 1,* 255–281.

Jackson, N. E., Donaldson, G., & Cleland, L. N. (1988). The structure of precocious reading ability. *Journal of Educational Psychology, 80,* 234–243.

Jackson, N. E., Donaldson, G., & Mills, J. R. (1993). Components of reading skill in postkindergarten precocious readers and level-matched second graders. *Journal of Reading Behavior, 25,* 181–208.

Jackson, N. E., & Myers, M. G. (1982). Letter naming time, digit span, and precocious reading achievement. *Intelligence, 6,* 311–329.

Jackson, N. E., & Roller, C. M. (1993). *Reading with young children.* Research-based Decision Making Series, No. 9302. Storrs, CT: National Research Center on the Gifted and Talented.

Kagan, J. (1971). *Change and continuity in infancy.* New York: Wiley.

Kanevsky, L. (1992). The learning game. In P. Klein & A. J. Tannenbaum (Eds.), *To be young and gifted* (pp. 204–241). Norwood, NJ: Ablex.

Louis, B., & Lewis, M. (1992). Parental beliefs about giftedness in young children and their relationship to actual ability level. *Gifted Child Quarterly, 36,* 27–31.

McCall, R. B., & Carriger, M.S. (1993). A meta-analysis of infant habituation and recognition memory performance as predictors of later IQ. *Child Development, 64,* 57–79.

Miller, L. K. (1989). *Musical savants: Exceptional skills in the mentally retarded.* Hillsdale, NJ: Lawrence Erlbaum Associates.

Mills, J. R., & Jackson, N. E. (1990). Predictive significance of early giftedness: The case of precocious reading. *Journal of Educational Psychology, 82,* 410–419.

Morelock, M., & Feldman, D. (1993). Prodigies and savants: What they have to tell us about giftedness and human cognition. In K. A. Heller, F. J. Monks, & A. H. Passow (Eds.), *International handbook of research and development of giftedness and talent* (pp. 161–181) New York: Pergamon.

Moss, E. (1992). Early interactions and metacognitive development of gifted preschoolers. In P. Klein & A. J. Tannenbaum (Eds.), *To be young and gifted* (pp. 278–320). Norwood, NJ: Ablex.

Parkinson, M. L. (1990). Finding and serving gifted preschoolers. *Understanding Our Gifted, 2* (5), 1, 13.

Pikulski, J. J., & Tobin, A. W. (1989). Factors associated with long-term reading achievement of early readers. In S. McCormick & J. Zutell (Eds.), *Cognitive and social perspectives for liter-*

acy research and instruction. Thirty-eighth yearbook of the National Reading Conference (pp. 123–124). Chicago: National Reading Conference.

Porath, M., & Arlin, P. (1992, February). *Developmental approaches to artistic giftedness.* Paper presented at the second annual Esther Katz Rosen Symposium on the Psychological Development of Gifted Children. University of Kansas, Lawrence.

Read, C. (1971). Preschool children's knowledge of English phonology. *Harvard Educational Review, 41,* 1–34.

Reid, D. K., Hresko, W. P., & Hammill, D. D. (1989). *Test of early reading ability—2.* Austin, TX: Pro-Ed.

Rescorla, L., Hyson, M. C., & Hirsh-Pasek, K. (1991). *Academic instruction in early childhood: Challenge or pressure?* San Francisco: Jossey-Bass.

Robinson, N. M., (1993). Identifying and nurturing gifted, very young children. In K. A. Heller, F. J. Monks, & A. H. Passow (Eds.), *International handbook of research and development of giftedness and talent* (pp. 507–524). New York: Pergamom.

Robinson, N. M., & Robinson, H. B. (1992). The use of standardized tests with young gifted children. In P. Klein & A. J. Tannenbaum (Eds.), *To be young and gifted* (pp. 141–170). Norwood, NJ: Ablex.

Roedell, W. C., Jackson, N. E., & Robinson, H. B. (1980). *Gifted young children.* New York: Teachers College Press.

Scarr, S., & McCartney, K. (1983). How people make their own environments: A theory of genotype—> environment effects. *Child Development, 54,* 424–435.

Shapiro, B.K., Palmer, F. B., Antell, S. E. , Bilker, S., Ross, A., & Capute, A. J. (1989). Giftedness: Can it be predicted in infancy? *Clinical Pediatrics, 28,* 205–209.

Sternberg, R. J. (1993). Procedures for identifying intellectual potential in the gifted: A perspective on alternative "metaphors of mind." In K. A. Heller, F. J. Monks, & A. H. Passow (Eds.), *International handbook of research and development of giftedness and talent* (pp. 185–208). New York: Pergamon.

Tannenbaum, A. J. (1992). Early signs of giftedness: Research and commentary. In P. Klein & A. J. Tannenbaum (Eds.), *To be young and gifted* (pp. 3–32). Norwood, NJ: Ablex.

Terman, L. M. (1925). *Genetic studies of genius:* Vol. 1. *Mental and psychological traits of a thousand gifted children.* Palo Alto, CA: Stanford University Press.

Terman, L. M., & Oden, M. H. (1947). *Genetic studies of genius*: Vol. 4. *The gifted child grows up.* Palo Alto, CA: Stanford University Press.

Thomas, B. (1984). Early toy preferences of four-year-old readers and nonreaders. *Child Development, 55,* 424–430.

Tobin, A. W., & Pikulski, J. J. (1988). A longitudinal study of the reading achievement of early and non-early readers through sixth grade. In J. Readance & R. S. Baldwin (Eds.), *Dialogues in literacy research. Thirty-seventh yearbook of the National Reading Conference* (pp. 49–55). Chicago: National Reading Conference.

Torrey, J. W. (1979). Reading that comes naturally: The early reader. In T. G. Waller & G. E. MacKinnon (Eds.), *Reading research: Advances in theory and practice* (Vol. 1, pp. 117–144). New York: Academic Press.

VanTassel-Baska, J. (1989). Profiles of precocity: A three-year study of talented adolescents. In J. VanTassel-Baska & P. Olszewski-Kubilius (Eds.), *Patterns of influence on gifted learners: The home, the self, and the school* (pp. 29–39). New York: Teachers College Press.

Willerman, L., & Fiedler, M.F. (1974). Infant performance and intellectual precocity. *Child Development, 45,* 483–486.

Winner, E., & Martino, G. (1993). Giftedness in the visual arts and music. In K. A. Heller, F. J. Monks, & A. H. Passow (Eds.), *International handbook of research and development of giftedness and talent* (pp. 253–282). New York: Pergamon.

Woodcock, R. W., & Johnson, M. B. (1989). Woodcock-Johnson Psycho-educational Battery-Revised. Allen, TX: DLM Teaching Resources.

Zigler, E., & Lang, M. E. (1985). The emergence of "superbaby": A good thing? *Pediatric Nursing, 11,* 337–341.

37

Gifted Adolescents: Five Steps toward Understanding and Acceptance

JAMES R. DELISLE, *Kent State University*

A Preamble

Most persons reading this chapter were probably gifted adolescents themselves not all that long ago. Here's why I make this assumption: If you're reading this book, you are most likely enrolled in a college course focusing on gifted students and their education. Generally, most people who support gifted education are pretty bright themselves (although they are often loath to admit this in the company of others—"too embarrassing and egocentric!"), putting to rest the common myth that "opposites attract." Indeed, it is the challenge of teaching students whose talents outshine the average that provides teachers of the gifted, perhaps you, both the personal pleasure and the professional satisfaction that gets them out of bed each morning and headed to the schoolhouse. They share a wavelength—able students, able teacher—and this similarity makes their job worthwhile.

Given this commonality, take a minute or two to reflect on your own wishes and desires as a gifted 15-year-old. What were your dreams and hopes? What were your fears? Go ahead . . . think. I'll wait.

Welcome back!

If I'm not mistaken, your hopes and fears as a gifted adolescent had little to do with your talents and lots to do with the fact that you were 15. College, grades, careers, class rank—they all got your due attention, I'm sure. Still, your overriding concerns were probably more like these:

- Will anyone find me attractive enough to want to date me?
- Will I pass my driver's license test on the first try?
- What will my new teachers be like next year?

Gifted adolescents, since time began, have been more *like* their high school and junior high classmates than *unlike* them. They might be bright, aware, and globally conscious, but to the majority, it still matters if they're liked and it's still important that they have access to Nike's newest Air Jordan or Pearl Jam's latest CD.

First and foremost, gifted adolescents are teenagers (give or take two years), and the teacher or counselor or parent who forgets the prominence of this age factor in understanding what makes these able young people tick does so at the risk of alienating this very astute, yet very teenage, population.

Then How Do They Differ, These Gifted Adolescents? What Makes Them Unique?

What distinguishes gifted adolescents from other adolescents is as individualistic and unique as is each of the students who wears this label. Often, the same characteristics and behaviors that were present when these adolescents were young—advanced vocabulary and thought patterns, emotional intensity, an awareness of the needs and fears of others—are still there in overabundance. Now, though, there may be an unsettling air of sophistication in these gifted young people. Piechowski (1991; see Chapter 30), citing the work of Dabrowski (1964), calls these "overexcitabilities," which involve virtually every realm of an adolescent's life: intellectual, psychomotor, emotional, sensual, and imaginational. Each overexcitability, unique yet overlapping, pinpoints areas of arousal that cause the gifted adolescent to be noticed by others as "just a little different" or "a cut above the rest." Such overexcitability can be seen in adolescents like Catherine Murray who, at age 17, began the Global Teen Club, an international network of culturally diverse and socially aware teens; or Sarah Plunkett, an 18-year-old girl from Texas who has raised more than $600,000 for breast cancer awareness since the age of 14; or Matthew Sterling, a 17-year-old high school senior who took his own life 5 days before graduation, after discovering that someone else, not he, would be named valedictorian.

. . . That's right, suicide. No one ever said that emotional intensities and overexcitabilities all ended in rosy pictures or glowing reports of life successes. Like any other of life's important qualities—love, loyalty, compassion—there is a mixture of positive and negative to be found in each. Perhaps this admixture can best be expressed through the words of a gifted adolescent:

> I'd never heard the phrase "transcend the human condition." But I knew that was what I longed to do. But once I did that, where would I go from there? . . . If I do transcend, are there other degrees or is there just one more? If there is just one more, maybe in its experience there is serenity at the end? (American Association for Gifted Children, 1978, pp. 18–19)

Gifted adolescents seldom need to be "identified" in the lockstep, test score–based format so unfortunately common in elementary schools. Rather, parents and other educators can use much more sophisticated and unbiased "equipment" to locate the latent or expressed talents in adolescents: their own eyes and ears. By listening carefully and by observing those situations that bring out a teenager's passions in life—music, politics, rock climbing, writing—the first important step in talent fruition will have been satisfied: acknowledgment.

The Role of Education in the Life of Gifted Adolescents

Because the majority of gifted identification at the secondary level is through self-selection, a bigger concern is the development of talents possessed by these able young people. As expressed by Betts (1991):

> When working directly with gifted and talented students in a school setting, it becomes apparent that a broad range of experiences is necessary. Besides emphasizing the cognitive, it also is essential to include emotional and social development. (p. 143)

At this point, I could offer a whole set of prescriptions about how junior high and high schools should change to accommodate the intellectual and emotional needs of their most able students. However, as a realist, I sense that such prescriptions would be seen the way most prescriptions usually are: as overpriced solutions that leave a bad taste in one's mouth.

Instead, I prefer to offer suggestions that could be accomplished with or without school support, in settings as different as Dime Box, Texas, and Scarsdale, New York. The common themes that will pervade these suggestions are two:

1. Each requires initiative beyond the classroom from its student participants.
2. Each meshes two areas of importance to gifted adolescents: personal validation and intellectual challenge.

1. Service, Service, Service

It has long been noted by counselors of gifted students (Hollingworth, 1926; Mendaglio, 1993; Roeper, 1982) that they possess a more mature grasp of community and world concerns than would be expected for their chronological ages. Whether it is the nuclear potential of far-off nations or the house fire across town that left a family of six homeless, situations that demand attention and action capture the minds of many gifted adolescents.

A not-uncommon adult response to this desire for involvement is to rely on someone else for the solutions. "But it's not our problem" or "that's why people buy insurance" offers scant solace to the kid who wants action. As adults, it is up to us to guide students who wish to act upon their caring. If *not* us, then who?

By raising money for a neighborhood family shelter, or sending good wishes to strangers who were victims of violent crime, or purchasing rain forest acreage, or refurnishing an entire household of goods lost to a flash flood (all activities completed in one school year by the same group of 12- and 13-year-olds), adolescents can turn misery into magic. In the process, they also learn that, wherever they live, they are able to make a difference in the lives of others and, as a rewarding by-product, in their own lives as well.

Three resources that provide guidance for teachers or students seeking such involvement are: *The Kid's Guide to Social Action* (Lewis, 1991); *Kidstories: Biographies of Twenty Young People You'd Like to Know* (Delisle, 1991); and *The Kids Can Help Book* (Logan, 1992). Each book provides specific evidence that leadership ability is alive and well in today's adolescents.

2. Internships toward the Future

One common characteristic of gifted adolescents is the *multipotential* many of them possess. An interest in many career directions, coupled with a proficiency to excel in multiple areas of endeavor, often complicates the process of focusing on a college major or a career direction. As stated by one student,

> When I look for a career in my future, the clouds really thicken. There are so many things I'd like to do and be, and I'd like to try them all; where to start is the problem . . . I'd like to be a physical therapist, a foreign correspondent, a psychiatrist, an anthropologist, a linguist, a folk singer, an espionage agent, and a social worker. (Sanborn, 1979, p. 285)

This lack of a singular career focus may appear, at first glance, as a frivolous problem. After all, if one is blessed with an embarrassment of riches allowing for any number of vocational directions, what exactly is the problem?

As noted time and again by gifted adolescents (Delisle, 1987; Post-Kammer & Perrone, 1983), the dilemma comes when one realizes that the career direction selected is more than just making a "job choice." Involving years of advanced preparation with a singular focus, choosing a career path is a commitment that might include a decade or more of time beyond high school graduation before one is allowed to practice the chosen profession. This is as true in the arts as it is in medicine or law or engineering, and this preparation phase often leaves even the brightest young person financially and emotionally dependent on others. In essence, this prolongs one's adolescence into the mid- or late twenties, by which time many of their contemporaries would already be earning decent salaries and living a more independent lifestyle.

Further, in choosing a career direction that involves an extended preparation phase, the gifted adolescent may question frequently whether he or she *really* wants to be a podiatrist or a civil engineer for the next thirty years. Despite evidence that points to the fact that most individuals will experience six or more *job* changes in the course of a career, highly skilled professionals seldom make a 180° shift in occupational focus. Once a podiatrist, *always* a podiatrist, even if you shift locations of employment from a general hospital to a specialized practice. Feet are feet, bridges are bridges, and talented adolescents fear that by selecting one area over others, they are dismissing the multiplicity of talents and interests that are part and parcel of being bright. A practicing trial lawyer who does tonsillectomies on the side? Doubtful. A concert pianist who moonlights as a social worker? Unlikely.

Career guidance in high schools that focuses on multipotential students is rare (Berger, 1989). As an alternative, a useful strategy employed by more and more capable students is the internship, an intensive hands-on exploration of possible careers conducted from the inside. Thus, for students interested in telecommunications or media, working at a local television or radio station (or, in fact, the local utility company) will give students face-front exposure to the joys, benefits, tedium, and pressures of a world of work they might wish to pursue. Best arranged through local contacts or "friends of friends," these internships can help convince a student whether a particular career direction is as fulfilling in practice as it is on paper. Businesses, hospitals, hotels, law firms—most are eager to help ambitious students explore their career interests; they just need to be asked.

High schools can help with the mechanics of internships in several ways:

- They can offer graduation credit for internships done by students during the school year or in the summer.
- They can arrange flexible scheduling for juniors and seniors so that internships can be completed during a part of each school day or week.
- They can compile a list of local agencies and businesses willing to accept student interns.
- They can hold "career seminar days," during which time local professionals discuss the high points and hassles of their own careers and their preparation for their careers.

Today's college-bound students who eventually attend graduate or professional schools for advanced degrees or certificates may end up with $50,000 or more in educational bills before even embarking on their careers. This financial investment, coupled with the equally expensive commitments of time, energy, and deferred independence, make it essential that gifted adolescents explore as fully as possible their future life's work. An internship is an inexpensive, valuable way to do just this.

3. The Myth of Underachievement

The luckless Charlie Brown, in a telling sobriquet of his innermost worries, confided to Linus that "There is no heavier burden than a great potential."

So true, because when one is identified as "gifted," a whole array of extraordinary expectations cojoins that label. In fact, in the eyes of many, gifted students are often considered "underachievers" because they did not live up to the high, high standards that seem preordained when one is anointed as a "gifted child."

I call this issue the "Aunt Peggy syndrome" in honor of one of my most annoying relatives. Here's the story: When I received my Ph.D. in educational psychology in 1981, I was the first person in our far, far extended family to have achieved that level of academic attainment. In celebration of my achievements (and to brag a little to their friends), my parents threw a congratulatory party for me. Friends and relatives I'd neither seen nor thought about in years attended, including Aunt Peggy. As she was chugging her cheap wine and recalling her images of me as an overweight 10-year-old ("Thanks, Aunt Peggy"), she uttered a one-liner that will remain forever a family legend.

"Jim," she said, "we're all so proud of you—your achievements and your degree. But ya know?" she added, "I always thought you'd become a *real* doctor—you know, the kind of doctor who really helps people."

Zap.

In one tactless moment, Aunt Peggy had dismantled my pride, replacing it with self-doubts as to whether this Ph.D. was worth the years of toil it took to complete. In Aunt Peggy's mind then, and still today, I am an underachiever. ("Thanks, Aunt Peggy.")

Unfortunately, Aunt Peggy is not just *my* relative. And just as surely as her words had their impact on me, the Aunt Peggys in life with whom gifted adolescents must contend will leave a mark on them. It may be a shallow mark, its deepness toned down by the fact that Aunt Peggy's opinion means very little to me, but what it lacks in depth it makes up for in length—14 years later, I can still hear her voice, her disappointment in me.

This retelling of family folklore has a purpose: Sooner or later, in the lives of all of the gifted adolescents you meet, they will be thought of as "underachievers" by someone or other who thought their lives should have taken a different direction. If this opinion gets internalized, several scenarios could occur:

1. The so-called underachiever begins to seek ways to make *everyone* happy, by running at breakneck speed in too many new directions.
2. The "underachiever" shuts down, figuring that by not performing *at all,* she or he can

stave off the criticism that results when a goal attempted is not completely attained.

3. The "underachiever" "blows off" the criticism, disregarding either the words, their source, or both as just uninformed opinions about something that is no one else's business: my life's choices.

This last option, the healthiest of the three, is not readily believed despite some superficial bravado that would make it seem that it is. For gifted adolescents who sincerely question, deep down, whether their decisions were right or their performance acceptable, the threat of being perceived as an underachiever is enough to make them believe that Charlie Brown, if anything, understated the problems with "potential."

As caregiving educators, there are several steps we must take to ensure the "survival of the fittest," intellectually speaking. First, we must begin to convince ourselves and our students that, for the most part, *underachievement is a myth,* a convenient invention of twentieth-century pop psychology devised to make adolescents feel guilty and all others feel blameless for a student's lack of effort or progress in school. Adolescents are already ripe victims for self-doubt without adults adding on the pressure that giftedness requires peak performance on a daily basis.

Next, we must recognize that every gifted adolescent will have a passion—a beautiful term to describe falling in love with anything, coined by George Betts—about one or more things, be it roller blading, beachcombing, fly fishing, or embryology. By using these passions as vehicles to enhance learning in other, related areas (rather than as "rewards" for good behavior or high grades), gifted adolescents will receive the positive notoriety and self-confidence that accompanies unconditional acceptance of one's selected loves in life. Unless they are physically or emotionally harmful to self or others, or blatantly illegal or immoral, passions and the people who have them must be treated with the respect they deserve. John Gardner (1961) once said that "the world needs both gifted plumbers and gifted philosophers, or neither our pipes nor our theories will hold water." A more reverential sentiment in tribute to passions has never been uttered.

The bottom line when it comes to underachievement among gifted adolescents is that most of the books and articles written on this topic should be disregarded. Too often, you will find prescriptions on how to write student contracts, how to reserve rewards for special moments of success, and how to convince a 15-year-old that answering questions out of a social studies text that is older than he is really does make a difference in his learning. Almost nowhere will you find what this gifted adolescent, typical among thousands, expresses so eloquently:

> I would have loved one of [my] teachers to recognize me and ask, " What are you thinking?" How I would have loved for my teacher to ask, "What's on your mind?" Instead I was called on to answer a question that I could not have cared less about, because it was hers, not mine. (American Association for Gifted Children, 1978, p. 58)

Underachievement? See it as the paper tiger that it truly is.

4. Appreciating Whoever You Are: The Impact of Philosophical Discourse on Gifted Students

The most capable student I ever met was a 10-year-old named Nathan who would get physically ill on Wednesday afternoons, just prior to leaving for his Hebrew class. It wasn't merely a dislike of this after-school school that bothered Nathan; his illness was prompted by something much more profound and personal. As he expressed it tearfully to me on the occasion of my discovering him vomiting in the boy's bathroom:

> My rabbi doesn't take me seriously. When I disagree with him or question something he says, he tells me I'm "too young and stupid to have my own opinions about religion."

On the contrary, Nathan was asking the types of questions that bother the analytical minds of gifted children: "How do we know there's a God?" "How do we know that Judaism is the 'right' religion?" "If my mom remarries a non-Jew, what does that make me?" "Shouldn't I be able to choose a religion when I'm older instead of being forced to have one while I'm a kid?"

Unappreciated by an elder who was angered and perplexed by his maturity, Nathan turned inward, against himself, believing there was something wrong with him. None of his Hebrew school classmates seemed concerned about the issues that bothered Nathan, and that made him feel even more isolated and weird. Worst of all, he began to see himself as "stupid," obviously incapable of understanding something that both his classmates and his rabbi accepted at face value.

Little did Nathan know that his questions and concerns were shared (and asked) by people he'd never heard of: Plato, Aristotle, Sartre, and Nietszche. And only when I introduced him to a picture-book version of Thoreau's *Walden* did Nathan begin to believe that there was a bigger picture of the world than was afforded him through the concave lens of experiences he had had thus far. Nathan was—and is—a philosopher, and the only legitimate way to address and resolve his inner conflicts was to introduce him to the giants of philosophical thought: If it worked for Nathan, at 10, it can work for older gifted adolescents as well.

Methods of incorporating the great works from centuries past into rigorous and legitimate self-study are available in Ward (1980), White and Schlagger (1993), and Mehorter (1964), all of whom provide concrete outlines for introducing able students to universal questions and themes. Through this self-study (which is enhanced when students are able to discuss their questions with similarly disposed adults or agemates), students not only learn about the foundations of world culture and knowledge, they also begin to see themselves within the personal reflections of others. The result is a deeper awareness of and bond with the intellectual rumblings that make one tick.

An additional resource, *The Courage of Conviction* (Berman, 1986), highlights the personal philosophies of prominent contemporaries such as the Dali Lama, Steve Allen, Billy Graham, Mario Cuomo, Petra Kelly, and Jane Goodall, who cites the importance of individual worth in this stunning quote:

> The way in which my own life touches those of so many others, those I know and thousands of those I don't, has strengthened my belief that each human has his or her own unique place in the ocean of existence. . . . At all different levels the ripples and currents pass or mingle, and some merge inextricably. With each merging a new force is created, itself as unique as the two beings that forged it. What joys the world would have lost if some of these forces had never been created, and what pain in other cases would it have been spared. (Berman, 1986, p. 76)

A related area of study is bibliotherapy, defined by Schlichter and Burke (1994) as "a process of dynamic interaction between an individual and literature through facilitated dialogue . . . its focus is *not* on checking the reader's comprehension of the story but on helping individuals recognize, sort out, and evaluate their feeling responses to the literature" (p. 280). In bibliotherapy, the big questions are asked by characters as diverse as J. D. Salinger's Holden Caulfield and Judy Blume's Ramona Robinson, and the issues range from existential crises to slumber party arguments. Frasier and McCannon (1981) and Piirto (1994) suggest books whose central characters are gifted adolescents, and *The Bookfinder* (Spreddman-Dreyer, 1989) is a four-volume compilation of synopses of young adult literature dealing with virtually every aspect of growing up.

Back to Nathan: After meeting with Nathan's rabbi and talking with her son, Nathan's mother decided to seek a new source for spiritual education. The new rabbi, more open to Nathan's questions and concerns, allowed Nathan to mature into a young man capable of dealing with life's inconsistencies. By the time you are reading this, Nathan will have already celebrated his Bar Mitzvah.

5. First among Equals: Finding and Fitting into a Peer Group

None of you reading this chapter has a peer group; neither do I. But before bemoaning our lot as rugged individualists, understand this:

The reason none of us has a peer group is that there's *no such thing* as "a" peer group.

For some unknown reason, and at some now-forgotten moment in time, the term *peer* became synonymous with *age-mate.* When this occurred, the era of "peer problems" for gifted children began. Now, if a gifted 9-year-old didn't participate in school or free-time activities with other 9-year-olds, a problem with "peer identification" was said to exist. Never mind the reality that this very able 9-year-old fully enjoyed talking and working alongside 12-year-olds; and disregard the fact that this same child was adored by first graders and adults alike as an affable, knowledgeable young person. If this highly intelligent 9-year-old got along with just about everyone except his or her age-mates, "peer problems" were said to exist.

Talk about seeing a glass half-empty instead of half-full!

T. Ernest Newland (1976) saw the absurdity behind this error of logic and coined the term *peerness* to explain the situation that exists when the mental age and reasoning abilities of a gifted child cause him or her to seek out the company of people who think and talk as he or she does—which, mostly, means people chronologically older than he or she is. Peerness affects both young children who seek soulmates, not just playmates, and gifted adolescents whose behaviors and social needs deal less with "Who's wearing what?" and "Who's dating who?" and more with the bigger issues of justice and fairness and responsibility. It's not that these adolescents don't enjoy an occasional burger and fries with age-mates, and they don't always wear their existential hearts on their sleeves, but gifted adolescents do benefit by associating with people of like minds who aren't afraid to let either their true emotions or their advanced vocabulary show.

Yet the myth persists that if sophomores don't hang out with other sophomores, something is wrong; something needs to be fixed. Before rushing headlong to remedy a problem that doesn't need a solution, make sure to ask these questions:

- Whose problem *is* this? If a gifted adolescent is content to have a peer group of older (and often, smaller in number) friends, does a problem really exist? And if so, who owns it?
- Is the gifted adolescent *unable* to make friends of his or her own age, or does she or he simply *choose* not to associate with classmates on a frequent basis?
- Does the gifted adolescent find fulfillment in solitary or small-group activities rather than in large, boisterous, and frequent social gatherings?

These questions should be asked *to* gifted adolescents by the persons concerned that a peer problem exists. With a little coaxing and some honest discussion, adults may find that they have one less worry about the care and feeding of that highly able adolescent whose interests and social preferences align more with our own than those of classmates.

Of course, problems in social relations *can* exist among gifted adolescents. For example, if they are unable to locate intellectual peers of *any* age, then loneliness and isolation may occur. If the gifted adolescent has the social skills of Hannibal Lecter and the low-key attitude of Murphy Brown, social relationships might be difficult to establish or maintain. Or if the gifted adolescent is simply obnoxious, wanting everything done in a certain way or at a certain time, then friendships may be few and far between. For these adolescents, a crash course in social skills instruction or a thorough reading of *The Gifted Kid's Survival Guide II* (Delisle & Galbraith, 1987) is in order.

However, for the vast majority of gifted adolescents, whose social problems are more in the eye of the beholder than anywhere else, it will be enough to introduce them to the concept of *peerness* and to acknowledge that, after high school, no one pegs social relationships to a specific chronological age. Those realities of growing up gifted, coupled with the exposure of gifted adolescents to others with similar styles and attributes (e.g., in honors classes, summer enrichment programs, or gifted programs) may be all the social skills instruction they need.

Isolation is the refuge of genius, not its goal, reminds Leta Hollingworth (1942). By allowing gifted adolescents to seek their own level of social contacts, we validate two very important attributes: their uniqueness and their commonality with others.

In Conclusion

This chapter on gifted adolescents was written in a style that reflects the minds of its subject—a bit irreverent, not altogether serious, and providing as many questions as answers. I hope that you, the reader, are able to glean the main points about this unique, yet remarkably similar population: that they deserve to express their opinions and lifestyle choices; that they want to succeed as surely as we want them to (albeit, in some different areas of focus); and that despite their advanced intellects and stunning powers of mind, they are still teenagers concerned about zits and dates and cars and clothes and college. In many ways, gifted adolescents are the "us" we were several decades ago, seeking similar challenges, dreaming magical thoughts of omnipotence. If we treat them with the same degree of personal respect that we wanted from others when we were 12 or 17 or 21, we will be on the right path in providing them with appropriate guidance.

REFERENCES

American Association for Gifted Children. (1978). *On being gifted.* New York: Walker.

Berger, S. (1989). *College planning for gifted students.* Reston, VA: Council for Exceptional Children.

Berman, S. (1986). *The courage of conviction.* New York: Dodd, Mead.

Betts, G. T. (1991). The autonomous learner model for the gifted and talented. In N. Colangelo & G. A. Davis (Eds.), *Handbook of gifted education* (pp. 142–153). Boston: Allyn and Bacon.

Dabrowski, K. (1964). *Positive disintegration.* Boston: Little, Brown.

Delisle, J. (1991). *Kidstories: Biographies of twenty young people you'd like to know.* Minneapolis: Free Spirit.

Delisle, J. (1987). *Gifted kids speak out.* Minneapolis: Free Spirit.

Delisle, J., & Galbraith, J. (1987). *The gifted kid's survival guide II.* Minneapolis: Free Spirit.

Frasier, M., & McCannon, C. (1981). Using bibliotherapy with gifted children. *Gifted Child Quarterly, 25,* 81–85.

Gardner, J. W. (1961). *Excellence: Can we be equal and excellent too?* New York: Harper.

Hollingworth, L. S. (1926). *Gifted children: Their nature and nurture.* New York: Macmillan.

Hollingworth, L. S. (1942). *Gifted children above 180 IQ Stanford Binet: Origin and development.* New York: World Book.

Lewis, B. A. (1991). *The kid's guide to social action.* Minneapolis: Free Spirit Publishing.

Logan, S. (1992). *The kids can help book.* New York: Perigee.

Mendaglio, S. (1993). Sensitivity: Bridging affective characteristics and emotions. *Journal of Secondary Gifted Education, 5(1),* 10–13.

Mehorter, J. T. (1964). *Self and society: An independent study course for gifted high school students.* Ph.D. dissertation, University of Virginia. *Dissertation Abstracts International, 25,* 3879-A. (University Microfilms #64-10909)

Newland, T. E. (1976). *The gifted in socio-educational perspective.* Englewood Cliffs, NJ: Prentice-Hall.

Piechowski, M. M. (1991). Emotional development and emotional giftedness. In N. Colangelo & G. A. Davis (Eds.), *Handbook of gifted education* (pp. 285–306). Boston: Allyn and Bacon.

Piirto, J. (1994). *Talented children and adults: Their development and education.* New York: Macmillan.

Post-Kammer, P., & Perrone, P. A. (1983). Career perceptions of talented individuals: A follow-up study. *Vocational Guidance Quarterly, 31,* 203–211.

Roeper, A. (1982). How the gifted cope with their emotions. *Roeper Review, 5,* (21–24).

Sanborn, M. (1979). Career development: Problems of gifted and talented students. In N. Colangelo & R. Zaffrann (Eds.), *New voices in counseling the gifted* (pp. 294–300). Dubuque, IA: Kendall/Hunt.

Schlichter, C. L., & Burke, M. (1994). Using books to nurture the social and emotional development of gifted students. *Roeper Review, 16,* 280–283.

Spreddman-Dreyer, S. (1989). *The bookfinder.* Circle Pines, MN: American Guidance Services.

Ward, V. S. (1980). *Differential education for the gifted.* Ventura, CA: National/State Leadership Training Institute, Ventura County Superintendent of Schools.

White, D. A., & Schlaggar, S. (1993, July–August). Gifted sixth graders and primary source philosophy. *Gifted Child Today,* 25–29.

38

Developing Talents in Girls and Young Women

BARBARA KERR, *Arizona State University*

Teachers who work closely with gifted students have long observed and lamented the failure of gifted girls to fulfill their early intellectual promise. They watch in frustration as little girls who were once so eager to demonstrate their intelligence and creativity grow into teenagers who carefully obscure their achievements or blithely pass up opportunities for special programming designed to nurture their talents. Counselors who work with gifted young women may notice a gradual disengagement with goal setting but are unable to pinpoint exactly what seems to be holding bright females back. Those of us who study characteristics of gifted females have what seems to be a straightforward task: Discover the barriers to gifted females' achievement and investigate means of overcoming them. This was indeed the focus of Lynn Fox's work in the mid-1970s with mathematically gifted junior high school girls (Fox, 1976; Fox, Benbow, & Perkins, 1983), Elyse Fleming and Constance Hollinger's Project Choice (1979) with gifted girls identified according to U.S. Commissioner of Education guidelines (1972), and my own research related to academically talented and high-IQ girls and women (Kerr, 1983, 1985, 1994). The results of this earlier work and the findings of the many studies now being published show that the problem of gifted females' failure to realize their potential is complex and the task of guiding gifted girls anything but straightforward. In addition, recent trends in intelligence research, in gifted females' behavior, and in the values of society as a whole have brought about rapid changes in how we perceive, teach, and guide gifted girls.

Females and Giftedness: Recent Changes

First, the concept of giftedness itself is undergoing transformation. New concepts of intelligence such as Sternberg's (1986) triarchic theory and Gardner's (1983) theory of multiple intelligences challenge the notion of the unitary IQ score as a predictor of extraordinary intellectual performance. However, the new theories of intelligence have little or nothing to say about gender, and it will probably be decades before a body of research exists on such topics as "gender differences in information processing" or "effects of gender on personal intelligences."

A second problem that occurs when we try to summarize the state of the art in educating gifted girls and women is that our subjects are changing before our very eyes. In the last ten years there have been extraordinary changes in bright young women's career choices and aspirations. Studies in the early 1980s showed gifted adolescent girls and young women to have lower aspirations than their gifted male age-mates (Kerr, 1983). Currently, however, young gifted women are choosing professional careers in almost equal proportions to gifted young men. For example, business has replaced education as the most popular career choice of bright high school–age young women (Kerr & Colangelo, 1988). Among middle school gifted children, however, differences still exist in career goals, with bright girls having somewhat lower aspirations than gifted boys (Kelly & Hall, 1994).

Changes are occurring in phenomena once thought to be fixed aspects of the psychology of women, such as fear of success and math anxiety. Research studies indicate that "fear of success" was short-lived as a phenomenon (Tressemer, 1977). It is now clear that women's attitudes toward competition are complex and based on context (Meara & Day, 1993). By the mid-1980s, studies of gifted girls could find no evidence of math anxiety (Weiner & Robinson, 1986). Sex-role expectations and attitudes are also in flux. Sometimes parental attitudes change in reaction to findings of psychological research: The highly publicized research of Benbow and Stanley (1983) has affected parental views of girls' math attitudes in a complex manner, confirming some parents' stereotypes and sending others to the defense of their daughters' abilities (Jacobs & Eccles, 1985). In studying gifted girls and women, we are observing a moving target, and our observations are changing our observed subjects.

Finally, value conflicts about women's roles now pervade society, education, and research. The education and guidance of gifted girls take place within the context of a society that is deeply conflicted in its attitudes toward women's roles. Although the majority of women in the United States now work outside the home, the deep ambivalence about women's rising aspirations is reflected in the many cautionary stories in the media about the dangers of "Superwomen," persistent criticisms and concerns about effects of nonmaternal child care, and the extraordinary interest in biologically based gender differences in abilities (Faludi, 1991).

Value conflicts and ambiguities about women's roles are also evident within psychology and education. Although most researchers on women's achievement use societally recognized measures of achievement such as educational attainment and occupational status, a number have questioned the practice of measuring women's achievement using male-oriented measures of achievement (Callahan, 1987; Eccles, 1985). Gilligan's (1982) proposal that women experience a different process of moral development than men has led to a broad interpretation of her theory to fit many observed gender differences. The separate spheres argument—that is, that men and women are basically different, inhabit different realities, and must be considered and judged within their own spheres rather than in comparison with one another—is one that reemerges in every generation, immediately following on the heels of the equity argument—that is, that women and men are more alike than they are different and should be treated equally in all respects (Tavris, 1992).

Despite rapid changes in women's status in some areas of the economy and changes in particular aspects of the psychology of women, the fact of continued differential socialization of girls and boys can hardly be denied. A few hours spent watching Saturday morning cartoons will bring home the striking differences in society's images of boys and girls. In children's toy commercials, boys continue to be depicted as action-oriented problem solvers playing with noisy, active toys in outdoor settings, whereas girls are quiet, pretty nurturers playing almost exclusively with passive toys that require grooming and dressing, almost invariably in the girls' bedrooms. In the cartoons themselves, male characters outnumber female characters, and boys are capable and adventurous while girls are helpful observers. As Sadker and Sadker's (1994) work shows, girls continue to receive less attention than boys throughout their education. They are called on less often in class, given fewer opportunities for leadership, and given less support for their goals. In our counseling laboratory, we have observed that young gifted women are deeply concerned about their role expectations and often confused and unclear about their goals. Nevertheless, many of our clients feel a need to hide their confusion by claiming impressive-sounding career goals such as business management, when in fact they have little interest in the actual goal or knowledge of how to pursue it. Young gifted women today seem to feel pressure to be highly achieving and work-oriented, but they have not learned the deeper lesson of the women's movement: that work, as well as relationships, is a source of meaning in women's lives.

Perhaps the best approach to take in a subject area fraught with value conflicts is simply to explain one's own biases and move on. My assumption is that gifted women are happiest when they are challenging the limits of their intellectual potential. In addition, I assume that the best type of achievement for both men and women is the attainment of one's own dreams and goals. Despite the advice of advocates who desire different standards for measuring the achievements of men and women, I will explore traditional measures of achievement of gifted females such as educational degrees and occupational prestige, not because they are the only measures of accomplishment but because they are markers of less measurable qualities of lifestyle, such as autonomy and opportunities for challenge. The use of these measures does not mean that gifted females can only be studied in comparison with gifted males. I assume here that gifted females are interesting in themselves.

Reports of gender differences in achievement test scores, educational degrees, occupational prestige, and attainment of eminence tell us little about individual gifted girls, but much about our society. Our knowledge of these differences, however, provides clues to potential societal restrictions on the freedom of an individual gifted girl to enjoy as many options as she deserves. These restrictions—whether lack of expectations of success, inadequate course taking, or absence of mentoring—can be remedied. The next sections review what is known about gifted girls and gifted female adolescents, followed by suggestions for education and guidance.

Gifted Girls: Trends and Problems

Giftedness is evident in girls at an earlier age than boys because gifted girls are more likely to show developmental advancement (Silverman, 1986). High-IQ girls tend to be taller, stronger, and healthier than girls of average IQ (Terman & Oden, 1935). Nevertheless, gifted girls may feel less physically competent than gifted boys or boys in general (Chan, 1988).

In the moderately gifted range, defined by Kerr and Colangelo (1988) as approximately the 95th percentile on IQ and achievement tests, gifted girls are as healthy mentally as they are physically. Studies comparing gifted girls with gifted boys and with average girls and boys consistently show gifted girls to have excellent social adjustment. Whether measured in terms of "social knowledge" (Terman & Oden, 1935), perceived self-competence (Chan, 1988), or absence of behavioral impairments on behavior rating scales (Ludwig & Cullinan, 1984), gifted girls are remarkably free from childhood adjustment disorders. At the very highest levels of ability, gifted girls may experience more adjustment problems. Terman and Oden (1935) and Hollingworth (1926) noted, fairly predictably, that the highest IQ children in general suffered more adjustment problems, probably as a result of their profoundly deviant intellectual abilities. Interestingly, eminent women, in retrospective accounts of their lives, remember feeling either "different" or "special" as children; whether the consequences were negative or positive, eminent women seemed well aware as girls of their deviancy from the norm (Kerr, 1985, 1994).

Gifted girls are more similar to gifted boys than to average girls in their interests, attitudes, and aspirations. Gifted girls apparently enjoy a wide variety of play activities, including many of those activities traditionally associated with boys: outdoor activities, adventurous play, sports, and problem-solving activities. They also frequently maintain feminine interests as well, such as playing with dolls and reading girls' magazines (Silverman, 1986; Terman & Oden, 1935). Eminent women remember girlhoods full of exploration, adventure, and voracious reading. As girls, eminent women also spent an unusually large amount of time in solitary activities (Kerr, 1985, 1994).

Although sex-role-stereotyped career interests are well established by second grade in the general population of girls and boys, gifted girls may have career interests more similar to those of gifted boys (Silverman, 1986; Terman & Oden, 1935). Young gifted girls have high aspirations and vivid career fantasies: They dream of being paleontologists, astronauts, and ambassadors (Kerr, 1985). Throughout childhood, gifted girls outperform gifted boys in classroom achievement, maintaining higher grades in all subjects. Gifted girls also outperform gifted boys on achievement tests throughout elementary school (Gallagher, 1985).

Adolescence brings changes in gifted girls' aspirations, expectations, attitudes, and achievement. The changes that occur for gifted girls today are more subtle than those that occurred fifty, twenty, or even ten years ago. Nevertheless, the direction of change is still the same overall, and it is one of *declining* involvement with former achievement goals. The changes are most evident in academic achievement test scores, course taking, and other academically related behaviors.

Gender Differences in Achievement and Aptitude Tests

Sadker and Sadker (1994) make a strong case for the existence of serious sex bias in the construction and item content of the major college admissions tests. Items concerning sports, wages, machinery, and other experiences much more commonly involving males than females seem to discriminate against girls, even those with excellent reading or math skills. It may be, then, that sex bias must always be taken into account when discussing variables affecting gifted girls' performance on achievement tests.

On American College Testing (ACT) exams taken during the senior year of high school, 61 percent of students scoring above the 95th percentile on the composite score are male; 72 percent of students scoring in the 99th percentile on the composite score are male (Kerr & Colangelo, 1988). With regard to the four subtests, males outperform females at the highest levels on the ACT mathematics, natural sciences, and social studies subtests. Only on the English subtest do females outperform males. Three times as many males earn perfect math scores, 5 times as many males earn perfect natural sciences scores, and 2.5 times as many males get perfect social studies scores (Colangelo & Kerr, 1990).

The lower scores for females on the ACT seem to be strongly related to course taking. Laing, Engen, and Maxey (1987) provided convincing evidence that much of the variance in ACT scores is accounted for by curriculum. Gifted adolescent females apparently not only take fewer and less challenging math and science courses than gifted males, but also take fewer and less challenging social studies courses.

More puzzling, however, are Benbow and Stanley's (1983) findings of extreme sex differences favoring boys at the highest levels of mathematical reasoning among gifted seventh graders. Benbow and Stanley's group was made up of seventh graders who scored at or above the mean for high school seniors on the Scholastic Aptitude Test, mathematical section (SAT-M). Their research is worth examining in some detail because it has been a source of controversy.

Note that the finding of gender differences in mathematical achievement test scores is nothing new; across many cultures, gender differences appear in mathematical measures by about tenth grade (Maccoby & Jacklin, 1974). These differences have been linked in the past to math course taking. Gender differences in math scores generally begin at the point at which girls stop taking math courses.

The Benbow and Stanley results are considered important, first, because the seventh graders in their study had had similar course experiences, and second, because the makers of the SAT-M consider it a test of mathematical reasoning ability rather than a test of mathematical achievement. Therefore, course taking alone could not account for the large differences in proportions of boys and girls scoring extremely high. There is a possibility that some native reasoning ability above and beyond mathematical operations is brought into play on this test, and that consequently gifted boys were found to be superior in this sort of reasoning. Also, critics of this study (Eccles, 1985; Kavrell & Peterson, 1984) have pointed out that the participants were a nonrepresentative sample of gifted girls and boys; they were all seventh graders whose school officials had publicized the Talent Search Program that sponsored the testing and whose parents had arranged for their testing on the SAT college entrance exams. It is possible, according to this argument, that some of the most highly mathematically gifted girls did not participate in the talent search. Studies have shown that gifted girls are less likely to enroll in advanced math classes (Benbow & Stanley, 1982), less likely to enter a gifted/talented program voluntarily (George & Denham, 1976), less likely to participate in accelerated math courses (Fox & Cohn, 1980), and less likely to be interested in science and engineering careers even when they are capable of them (Benbow & Stanley, 1984). Sex differences in achievement on the SAT also may be tied to speed of performance rather than actual competence in mathematics (Dreyden & Gallagher, 1989). Whenever tests are speeded and competitive, girls are less likely to achieve at their true level of ability (Silverman, 1993). Clearly, factors other than native ability can discourage even very brilliant girls from participating in the talent search in the first place.

Expectations of success and belief in the value of the task (Eccles, 1985), instrumental and expressive behavior (Hollinger & Fleming, 1988), and "exploratory" behaviors (Steinkamp, 1984) all have been linked to bright girls' achievement. All these are socialized perceptions, attitudes, and ways of approaching problems.

Studies that have explored the relationship of chromosomal patterns (Bock & Kolakowski, 1973) and pubertal hormones (Petersen, 1979) to math ability have produced mixed results. The first line of research has been pretty well disconfirmed; no differences have been found that could be linked to the X chromosome (Boles, 1980). The only study to show an indirect relationship between hormones and math achievement simply compared math scores and body types. Boys with more "feminine" physical characteristics and girls with more "masculine" physical characteristics were found to have higher math scores (Petersen, 1976). This finding would not support *masculine* superiority in math achievement so much as "androgynous" superiority.

Even if these studies did provide evidence of some biological basis for sex differences in mathematical reasoning, what difference should it make to teachers, parents, and gifted girls themselves? First, Hyde (1981) showed that sex differences, whatever their basis, account for less than 4 percent of the variance in math achievement. Most of the variability in achievement scores is within genders, rather than between genders. It is likely that differences in math ability are the result mainly of factors within our control, such as the shaping of expectations and confidence, rather than factors out of our control, such as gender. Therefore, the presence of biological differences could hardly be used as an excuse for discouraging gifted girls from mathematical pursuit, when the effect, if it exists at all, is so small.

Second, even the most august and rigorous math-related jobs in the world—for example, theoretical mathematician, astrophysicist, cosmologist—do not necessarily require the most extraordinary mathematical reasoning powers in the land. The vast majority of mathematically gifted girls, certainly all those who qualify by the talent search criteria, have the intellectual capacity for any math-related position existing today if to their intellectual ability they add the training, confidence, expectations, attitudes, and personality characteristics needed to explore the concept of number or the beginnings of the universe.

Career Aspirations

Changes seem to be occurring across society in gifted adolescent girls' career aspirations. Whereas highly gifted girls such as the top 1 percent of National Merit scholars usually maintained high career aspirations in adolescence (Kaufmann, 1981), until recently moderately gifted girls (those scoring in the upper 5 percent on IQ and achievement tests) tended to have declining career aspirations during adolescence (Fox, 1976; Kerr, 1983, 1985). More recently, however, gifted adolescent girls have been naming college majors and career goals that are frequently nontraditional for women (Kerr & Colangelo, 1988). Among 12,330 girls scoring in the 95th percentile and above on the ACT, about the same proportion of girls as boys chose majors in premedicine, prelaw, and mathematics. Health professions (17.9 percent), social science (14.0 percent), and business (13.0 percent) were the most popular majors of this group. Sharp disparities continued in only one traditionally male career—engineering, where the proportions were 30.5 percent males to 7.9 percent females choosing that major. When gifted adolescent girls were asked to name their career goals, they seemed to aim high. Dolny (1985) observed the same trend in his study of Toronto gifted students' aspirations. However, a recent study (Kelly & Hall, 1994) contradicts this trend, at least among eighth-grade gifted students. Kelly and Hall found that gifted girls, like average girls, had lower aspirations than their male counterparts.

Adjustment and Self-Esteem

There is strong evidence that the majority of moderately gifted girls, like gifted boys, have normal personalities during adolescence (Janos & Robinson, 1985; Lessinger & Martinson, 1961; Terman & Oden, 1935). That is, on personality inventories, girls and boys identified as gifted are usually similar or superior to average students on psychological characteristics associated with good mental health and adjustment. However, gifted adolescent girls may experience loss of self-esteem, social anxiety, and decreases in self-confidence. The American Association of University Women's 1992 study of girls and self-esteem showed a dramatic plunge in self-esteem for girls between the ages of 11 and 17. It seemed to repeat the findings of Groth's studies of gifted girls and women twenty years earlier. Groth's (1969) cross-sectional study had shown an abrupt psychological shift at age 14 from wishes and needs related to achievement and self-esteem to wishes related to love and belonging. Her study showed that gifted younger girls tended to dream about successes in school activities and accomplishments but that older gifted girls dreamed of popularity and intimate friendships. Kelly and Colangelo (1984) found that whereas gifted boys were superior to average boys in academic and social self-concepts, gifted girls were not similarly higher than average girls.

In Kerr, Colangelo, and Gaeth's (1988) study of adolescents' attitudes toward their own giftedness, gifted girls were evidently quite concerned about the impact of their giftedness on the attitudes of others. Although most of them believed that there were some social advantages to being gifted, females saw more disadvantages to being gifted than their male peers did. There was a deep ambivalence about the label *gifted* as well as concern about negative images others might hold of that label.

Perhaps the most significant work in the area of the adjustment of gifted adolescent girls has been done by Constance Hollinger and Elyse Fleming (Fleming & Hollinger, 1979; Hollinger, 1983, 1985; Hollinger & Fleming, 1984, 1988). Beginning with over 100 gifted girls identified on the basis of U.S. Office of Education guidelines, Hollinger and Fleming created a career development program aimed at overcoming barriers to gifted girls' achievement. Participants in the program have been followed closely since 1979, and frequent assessments have been made of their self-perceptions, self-esteem, and aspirations.

Of particular interest to Hollinger and Fleming has been the development of social self-esteem, which they believe is central to the realization of potential in gifted girls. Social self-esteem is made up of *instrumentality,* or the belief that one has the ability to act effectively and to make decisions independently, and *expressiveness,* a sense of responsiveness and caring, with instrumentality making the stronger contribution to high self-esteem (Hollinger, 1983, 1985). Social self-esteem seems to protect gifted girls from fears of social rejection that may accompany high achievement and serves to build the self-confidence needed to follow through on high goals. Self-confidence may be a better predictor of adult achievement than high grades or high aspirations (Eccles, 1985).

Hollinger and Fleming (1988) found that from sophomore year of high school through three and a half years after graduation, self-perceptions of instrumentality were predictive of occupational confidence and life satisfaction. Expressiveness, on the other hand, though not predictive of occupational confidence or life satisfaction, did predict social self-esteem in combination with instrumentality. The results of their research so far seem to show that gifted girls need to be encouraged to develop not only those instrumental characteristics associated with masculinity but also the expressive characteristics associated with femininity if they are to be highly achieving as well as socially confident. Gifted girls need to understand that they do not need to reject the nurturing, caring side of themselves in order to be bold and achieving. More will be said about Hollinger and Fleming's social self-esteem model later.

Good social adjustment in adolescence is not a prerequisite for eminence. Kaufmann (1981), in her study of the extraordinarily talented young women who had been named Presidential Scholars, found that they had received little recognition for their accomplishments in high school and were often perceived as loners. Eminent women often had unhappy, difficult adolescences (Kerr, 1985, 1994). For some, social rejection and the status of the "outsider" paradoxically lent them the freedom to develop independent opinions and free-ranging intellects. Therefore, in guiding gifted girls, it seems best to nourish the growth of self-esteem but to deemphasize the pursuit of popularity.

Identification

An early start may be critical to gifted girls' receiving an appropriate education. As mentioned earlier, gifted girls are more likely to show developmental advancement than gifted boys and are likely to be ready for kindergarten earlier than gifted boys (Silverman, 1986, 1993). Gifted girls do very well as early admittants to kindergarten (Callahan, 1979). Identification of giftedness becomes a problem only when schools require "proof" of giftedness. Although intelligence tests such as the Stanford-Binet, the Wechsler Intelligence Scale for Children—Revised (WISC-R), and the Kaufman Assessment Battery for Children (K-ABC; Kaufman & Kaufman, 1983) have been used with very young children, they often are not reliable measures of giftedness before ages 9 or 10 for children in general. Developmental scales are usually more effective at identifying deficits than advances in development. Nevertheless, a good intelligence test, administered carefully by a competent psychologist, will pick up the extraordinary verbal skills that are often the earliest signs of giftedness in girls (Silverman, 1986). Whenever possible, however, bright 4- and 5-year-old girls who simply show signs of school readiness—advanced vocabulary, precocious reading, math skills, and an eagerness for school social activities—should be given the benefit of the doubt and admitted early (Silverman, 1993). An early start helps ensure that gifted girls will be challenged, even when no other gifted programming is available. Where schools are locked into an age-in-grade format, early admission to kindergarten may be the only window of opportunity available to gifted girls.

In selecting tests for admission into a gifted education program, test bias must be considered (Kitano & Kirby, 1985). Tests that emphasize content that is more familiar to boys than to girls, such as word problems about mechanical toys or sports, may be biased against girls. Achievement tests with a heavier weighting of math and science items than language-related items will select more boys, particularly in the upper grades. Intelligence tests that deemphasize verbal skills and emphasize performance, that is, spatial-visual activities, also may be biased against girls, who receive much less practice than boys at puzzles and assembly.

Several approaches to identifying gifted girls for particular educational interventions have been found to be effective in predicting performance. One method is the use of different cutoff scores for admission to advanced course work in specific areas. It is difficult to prove that particular tests are sex-biased. Nevertheless, for some tests it is fairly easy to show that different aptitude scores for girls and boys actually predict the same levels of success in areas such as math and science. For example, a girl scoring 490 on the SAT-M in seventh grade may perform similarly in accelerated mathematics to a boy in seventh grade scoring 530. Therefore, in those subject areas in which gifted boys have generally received higher scores than gifted girls, it is possible that girls receiving scores slightly lower than boys may be able to perform at equivalent levels in the classroom.

A second method for identifying gifted girls is a multidimensional approach (Fleming & Hollinger, 1979). Gifted girls may possess a wide variety of skills and characteristics that contribute as much to their academic performance as aptitude for particular tasks—for example, leadership skills and creativity. A multidimensional approach will help ensure that girls with potential for high performance are identified above and beyond those who score well on objective tests of intellectual aptitude. The multidimensional approach is most useful in selecting gifted girls for broad-based programs of enrichment or other increased academic challenges. It is also useful for targeting girls who might benefit from specialized career education, guidance, and mentoring.

Finally, although tests and assessment devices are useful in predicting academic performance, few objective measures have been shown to be predictive of adult accomplishment of gifted women. Neither high IQ (Terman & Oden, 1947), high achievement test scores (Kaufmann, 1981), nor high grade point averages (Kerr, 1985) have been found to be associated with women's achievement. Torrance, Bruch, and Morse (1973) found that the Torrance tests of verbal creativity were more predictive of accomplishment in women than any measures of intellectual aptitude. Therefore, any measure of the intellectual aptitude of gifted girls must be used for short-term prediction and with a clear understanding of the many powerful nonacademic factors operating in determining the progress of a gifted girl toward the achievement of her potential. Sadker and Sadker (1994) remind us that biased achievement test scores can have a strong negative effect on girls' self-esteem. They add, "the SAT's send an even more devastating message to minority girls," because there is a gap between minority and white scores, as well as a gap between boys' and girls' scores. Identifying procedures should enhance self-esteem, not destroy it (p. 140).

Increasing Equity in the Classroom

Potential sources of bias need to be removed from the program of study as well as the identification procedures. Ample evidence exists of inequitable instruction in the classroom (Sadker & Sadker, 1985, 1994). Boys receive more attention from teachers than girls throughout their education. Boys are called on more often in class than girls. They are more frequently rewarded for calling out answers, whereas girls are more frequently reprimanded for the same response. Boys also receive more informative responses from teachers; Sadker and Sadker found that girls receive more bland, "accepting" responses from teachers, whereas boys receive more praise and criticism. Boys receive more instructional attention; they get detailed instructions on the correct approach to tasks. By contrast, girls frequently are simply given the right answers. These differential teacher responses do not seem to be the result of deliberate discrimination on the part of teachers; even staunchly feminist teachers exhibit similar patterns. Differential instruction seems to be both a response to different behaviors of boys and girls and a reflection of underlying socialized attitudes that are mostly unconscious.

Similar studies have not been done specifically with gifted children or in the context of a gifted education program. Nevertheless, there are some indicators that gifted girls suffer from differential treatment. In a study of attitudes toward gifted students, Solano (1977) found that when teacher attitudes were negative toward gifted students in general, they were more negative toward gifted girls. One study found that female teachers may be more discouraging toward gifted girls' aspirations than male teachers (Cooley, Chauvin, & Karnes, 1984). Fox (1976) found evidence that gifted girls were discouraged from taking advanced math courses, entering gifted education, and participating in summer opportunities for gifted students.

Although the causes of teachers' differential treatment of girls and boys may run deep, the remedy may not be difficult or complex. Sadker and Sadker (1984) found that most teachers wanted to teach in a nonsexist manner and were anxious to learn how. Even brief training workshops were effective in improving equitable behavior. Teachers can learn to call on girls as often as they call on boys; to give girls informative responses, praising and criticizing in detail; to reward girls' assertiveness in the classroom; and to resist "overhelping" girls by giving them answers or solving problems for them. Sadker and Sadker (1994) provide excellent examples of teachers on "the edge of change" who teach themselves to look at girls and maintain focus on them as they speak; who ask their classes to help them to be fair in responses; and who teach girls to demand their share of attention.

Another perspective on equity in classroom instruction is given by Dweck and Licht (1980), who showed that girls learn to attribute the causes of their successes and failures differently than boys. Possibly because of bland teacher responses and overhelping, girls learn to attribute their successes to luck and effort and their failures to lack of ability. This may lead them to avoid course work that they believe requires considerable effort and for which they believe they lack the ability (Eccles, 1985). Therefore, girls need to be taught to have confidence in their abilities and to believe that their efforts are effective. This may translate into teacher behaviors that encourage effort ("I know you can do this" or "I want you to try to solve the problem on your own").

Gifted girls must be given specific information about their superior abilities very early (Kerr, 1994). They should be helped to understand their intellectual strengths and to see how their abilities can help them in their classwork. Gifted girls need to perceive their giftedness not as a mysterious force out of their control but, rather, as a set of potentials that, when combined with effort, can lead to extraordinary accomplishment.

Changing teacher behavior is only one aspect of removing bias from the education of gifted girls. Boy-centered textbooks, literature, and activities may discourage bright girls from pursuing interests even in those areas in which they excel and which they enjoy. This can be particularly a problem in science and math classes, where experimenters, teachers, and the subjects of study are rarely female or feminine. However, language arts and social studies materials are also sometimes biased against females, and these should be checked for the balance of presentation. Do illustrative pictures have an equal number of males and females? Are female authors represented? Are the roles of women in history and current events represented?

Gifted girls' tendency to be able to read popular adult literature while still very young may occasionally have negative effects; popular novels and magazines are often much more sexist than school materials or age-appropriate materials. Restriction of the amount or type of reading engaged in by gifted girls is almost always a bad idea. However, teachers and librarians should discuss recreational reading materials with bright girls, and should point out stereotypes of women and girls in popular literature. "Inoculating" bright girls against negative portrayals of women with biographies of eminent women and stories about strong, active, courageous girls may be the best approach to combating sexism in print (Kerr, 1994).

What about Single-Sex Schooling?

One hope for "girl-friendly" education may lie in single-sex schooling. Proportionately more women scholars and leaders graduate from single-sex colleges (Kerr, 1985). Fox (1976) was able to maintain girls' interests and aspirations in math in an all-girl, female-led accelerated math class. A review of single-sex schooling (Hollinger, 1993) suggests, overall, more advantages to girls in all-girls schools than in coed schools.

Enhancing Achievement-Oriented Behaviors

Many theories and models have been proposed to explain women's achievement—or lack of achievement. Research-based models of achievement that have been applied to bright girls and women include Eccles's (1985) model of achievement; Hollinger and Fleming's (1988) social self-esteem theory; and Steinkamp's (1984) motivational theory. Each of these contains within it practical implications for educating and guiding gifted girls. In addition, case studies of eminent individuals can help in understanding guidance needs of gifted girls.

Achievement-Related Choices

Jacqueline Eccles's (1985) model of achievement-related choices assumes that many variables contribute to gifted girls' achievement and that these variables are related to one another in complex ways. Two of the most important components of achievement-related choices are *expectation for success* and *subjective task value.* That is, differential socialization of females can affect both their expectations for success in sex-role-stereotyped academic plans or career goals and their perceptions of how important or valuable particular academic and career goals might be. It is not clear if gifted girls lack confidence in their abilities. Moderately gifted girls (Terman & Oden, 1935; Kerr, 1985) seem to have less confidence in their intellectual abilities than highly gifted, particularly mathematically gifted, girls (Benbow & Stanley, 1982). Hollinger (1983) found a strong relationship between gifted girls' confidence in their math abilities and their plans to pursue math-related careers. Gifted girls also may value achievement goals differently. Like average girls, they may be more "people-oriented" than boys and may have different perceptions of sex-role-stereotyped occupations than boys do (Fox & Denham, 1974).

Therefore, it may be very helpful for gifted girls to increase both their confidence in their ability to achieve academic career goals and the degree to which they value these goals. Specific information about relative abilities can help increase the confidence of gifted girls in their goals: "You are probably able to read better than 9 out of 10 children your age" or "Your math skills are as good as those of kids who grow up to be mathematicians and scientists." Teachers should avoid vague or bland confidence-giving statements; they should back up their encouragement with solid facts.

Increasing the task value may be a matter of helping gifted girls to understand the consequences of academic decisions. For example, few gifted girls are aware of the absolute importance of mathematics to their future goals. Frequently, gifted girls drop out of math and science courses for superficial reasons, without realizing that most college majors leading to high-level careers and professions require four years of high school preparation in math and science (Kerr, 1985). Teachers need to be careful not to collaborate in gifted girls' plans to take less challenging courses in order to keep up their grade point average; instead, they need to emphasize the value of taking the most comprehensive and rigorous curriculum available.

Social Self-Esteem

According to Hollinger and Fleming (1988), social self-esteem, as noted earlier, is related to achievement and life satisfaction and is the product of two self-perceptions: instrumentality and expressiveness. *Instrumentality,* which is central to achievement, is an attitude and a set of self-perceptions related to the ability to act effectively, to make things happen, to have an impact. Women with high instrumentality are decisive, active, and risk-taking. *Expressiveness* is the self-perception of being caring, communicative, and affiliative. Women who are high in expressibility are interpersonally adept and sensitive while also possessing high levels of self-awareness and self-understanding. Expressiveness seems to protect girls from the social rejection that sometimes accompanies high intellectual ability in girls.

It is possible that instrumentality could be increased through leadership opportunities, development of decision-making skills, and many experiences of success in challenging activities. Even when they are very young, bright girls need to be given the opportunity to lead other girls and boys. They can lead task groups, captain sports teams, and teach skills they possess to others. Many curriculum units on decision making exist; the actual techniques used to teach decision making are probably less important than communicating to girls that their decisions have weight.

Throughout their education, gifted girls need to be encouraged to take risks. This means taking the most challenging course work available, engaging in play activities that are physically challenging and occasionally competitive, and learning to speak out and defend their opinions in groups. To encourage instrumentality in bright girls, teachers may need to reverse the common practice of rewarding compliant behavior and withdrawing rewards for, or even punishing, noisy and nonconforming behavior. Teachers might experiment with rewarding boisterousness and idiosyncrasies in gifted girls with humorous, approving responses.

Expressiveness is more likely to be gifted girls' strong suit. Nevertheless, it needs to be acknowledged and reinforced. Social skills need to be labeled as such and praised. Friendship skills and considerateness can be reinforced by opportunities to help other children and through cooperative problem solving.

Exploratory Behavior

Marjorie Steinkamp (1984) proposed a theory of motivational style which states that certain *exploratory* childhood behaviors set the stage for adult achievement in science. Exploratory behaviors flourish in an environment free of evaluation, responsibility, and externally imposed challenge. Exploratory behaviors take place in situations of uncertainty and ambiguity. According to Steinkamp, there is evidence that girls are socialized in our society to have a *compliant* rather than an exploratory motivational style. Compliant behaviors depend on external reward, need external feedback, take place only in the context of society, and function best under external locus of control.

The clear implication of Steinkamp's theory is that gifted girls need help in learning self-directed behaviors. They need to learn to work alone, to enjoy ambiguity and uncertainty, and to work without external reward or approval. This, again, may mean reversing the normal socialization processes. Instead of drawing girls who are playing by themselves into a group, teachers should consider leaving them alone. When a girl turns in a project that clearly required exploration of difficult, ambiguous, or uncertain issues, she needs praise and encouragement. In many ways, science experiments and activities provide these latter kinds of experiences. Creative play and schoolwork also seem important. However, Steinkamp warns that it is easy to transform an independent exploratory behavior into a compliant one simply by giving too much help, information, and feedback. It takes sensitive observation and careful reward to discover and encourage exploratory behavior. Finally, there is evidence that encouraging young women to be exploratory in science may be too little, too late. Interventions to enhance exploratory and decrease compliant behaviors may need to begin very early in the gifted girl's development.

Eminence and the Gifted Girl

Two studies of eminent individuals have important implications for gifted girls. Bloom's (1985) study of talent development in such individuals as concert pianists, Olympic athletes, and sculptors showed that a crucial step in the attainment of eminence was the development of an identity. Eminent individuals usually had the opportunity early in adolescence to identify themselves and be identified by others as "the class artist" or "the school athlete." Teachers may be able to help gifted girls toward the achievement of their potential by assisting them in their identity development. "You're the math whiz around here!" and "Lisa, you certainly are a scientist!" are the kinds of statements that can aid the identity development of girls who show strong inclinations toward the enjoyment of those fields.

Eminent women have been shown to demonstrate a great many of the qualities and behaviors that have been discussed here (Kerr, 1985, 1994). As children, they spent a great deal of time alone, during which they engaged in a great many exploratory behaviors: reading, trying out new skills, and seeking new ideas. If they were not rewarded for these behaviors, at least they were not punished. They felt "different" or "special" as children, depending on their self-concept, and this sense of uniqueness may have made nonconformity possible. In adulthood, they maintained the ability to remain separate from the crowd. In fact, eminent women were frequently perceived as having "thorns"—a dry wit or even a caustic, argumentative style. They demonstrated instrumentality in that they took responsibility for themselves, for their tasks, and for accomplishing their life goals. In addition, most eminent women created loving partnerships with another, often finding their love relationship through their work. Later, many of them competently integrated a mothering role into their other roles. This seems to be a case of integrating expressiveness and instrumentality, as Hollinger and Fleming (1988) advised.

The educational methods suggested by the experiences of eminent women include early educational experience, learning at a challenging pace, individualized instruction, and mentoring. It may be that these educational strategies interact with one another to enhance achievement-related behaviors. For example, the presence of a supportive mentor may help increase a gifted girl's confidence in her ability to meet the challenge of fast-paced learning.

The single most important commonality in the lives of eminent women seems to be that they "fell in love with an idea." Falling in love with an idea means committing oneself to a deeply held value, a theory, or an attitude (Torrance, 1979). It is the discovery of a calling or a vocation. People who have fallen in love with an idea have a deep sense of purpose. Falling in love with an idea seems to protect many women from succumbing to sexism, discrimination, and other pressures to conform to traditional women's roles (Kerr, 1985). Teachers can help gifted young women in the process of falling love with an idea by encouraging enthusiasm for particular ideas with related readings and opportunities to explore beyond the treatment in the classroom. As is the case with encouraging the growth of identity, it is important to discover specific talents and "passions" that are unique to each gifted girl. Generalized praise and encouragement may not be as useful as specific comments and observations: "Marie, when you play the violin, I can really see your love for the instrument and your passion for interpreting Bach," or "Your writing lately seems to me to be showing that you are finding your voice as a writer. I can always identify your work by its vivid descriptions and sharp humor."

Sometimes gifted girls and young women may need permission to fall in love with an idea, and sometimes they need help recognizing that they already are in love with an idea. A value-based career counseling intervention developed at the University of Iowa's Counseling Laboratory for Talent Development serves both of these purposes (Kerr, 1988). The value-based counseling approach includes group future planning; personality, interest, and values assessment; and intensive individual counseling. Participants are encouraged to imagine in detail their "perfect" future day; to examine roles and relationships; to understand how their interests, needs, and values make them unique; and to understand the importance of choosing a career based on their most deeply held values. Participants in the workshop have been found to increase their sense of identity and their development of purpose as measured by inventories of student development. In a two-day version of the workshop developed for talented at-risk girls, girls increase their self-esteem and self-efficacy as a result of the program (Kerr & Robinson, 1994).

Conclusions

Much has been learned since Lewis Terman and Melita Oden first described the gifted girl, but much remains to be learned. Specific educational and guidance programs for gifted girls are few and far between, and many programs lack the information they need to provide optimal conditions or to evaluate what they have accomplished. The International Symposium on Girls, Women, and Giftedness, held in May 1987, brought together for the first time teachers of gifted girls, researchers, and eminent women to discuss all facets of the gifted female (Ellis & Willinsky, 1991). Since that conference, the interest in gifted girls has accelerated, with both research and practice innovations increasing every year.

REFERENCES

American Association of University Women. (1992). *How schools shortchange girls: The AAUW Report.* Washington, DC: Author.

Benbow, C. P., & Stanley, J. C. (1982). Consequences in high school and college of sex differences in mathematical reasoning ability: A longitudinal perspective. *American Educational Research Journal, 19,* 598–622.

Benbow, C. P., & Stanley, J. C. (1983). Sex differences in mathematical reasoning ability: More facts. *Science, 222,* 1029–1031.

Benbow, C. P., & Stanley, J. C. (1984). Gender and the science major: A study of mathematically precocious youth. In M. W. Steinkamp & M. L. Maehr (Eds.), *Women in Science* (pp. 165–196). Greenwich, CT: JAI.

Bloom, B. S. (1985). *Developing talent in young people.* New York: Ballantine.

Bock, R. D., & Kolakowski, D. (1973). Further evidence of sex-linked major-gene influence in spatial visualizing ability. *American Journal of Human Genetics, 25,* 1–14.

Boles, D. B. (1980). Linkage of spatial ability: A critical review. *Child Development, 21,* 626–635.

Callahan, C. M. (1979). The gifted and talented woman. In A. H. Passow (Ed.), *The gifted and talented: Their education and development.* (The 78th yearbook of the National Society for the Study of Education, pp. 401–423). Chicago: University of Chicago Press.

Callahan, C. (1987, May). *Gender and the gifted: A roadmap for reflecting, questioning, and understanding.* Paper presented at the International Symposium on Girls, Women, and Giftedness, Lethbridge, Alberta, Canada.

Chan, L. K. S. (1988). The perceived competence of intellectually talented students. *Gifted Child Quarterly, 32,* 310–315.

Colangelo, N., & Kerr, B. A. (1990). Extreme academic talent: Profiles of perfect scorers. *Journal of Educational Psychology, 82,* 404–410.

Cooley, D., Chauvin, J., & Karnes, F. A. (1984). Gifted females: A comparison of attitudes by male and female teachers. *Roeper Review, 6,* 164–170.

Dolny, C. (1985). University of Toronto Schools' gifted students' career and family plans. *Roeper Review, 7,* 160–162.

Dreyden, J. I., & Gallagher, S. A. (1989). The effects of time and direction: Changes on the SAT performance of academically talented adolescents. *Journal for the Education of the Gifted, 12,* 187–204.

Dweck, C. S., & Licht, B. G. (1980). Learned helplessness and intellectual achievement. In J. Garber & M. E. P. Seligman (Eds.), *Human helplessness: Theory and applications* (pp. 197–221). New York: Academic Press.

Eccles, J. S. (1985). Why doesn't Jane run? Sex differences in educational and occupational patterns. In F. D. Horowitz & M. O'Brien (Eds.), *The gifted and talented: Developmental perspectives* (pp. 253–295). Washington, DC: American Psychological Association.

Ellis, J. L., & Willinsky, J. M. (1991). *Proceedings of the international symposium on girls, women, and giftedness.* Lethbridge, Alberta, Canada: University of Lethbridge.

Faludi, S. (1991). *Backlash: The undeclared war against American women.* New York: Crown.

Fleming, E., & Hollinger, C. (1979). *Project choice: Creating her options in career education.* (ERIC Reproduction Service No. E0185321).

Fox, L. H. (1976, August). *Changing behaviors and attitudes of gifted girls.* Paper presented at the American Psychological Association, Washington, D.C.

Fox, L. H., Benbow, C. P., & Perkins, S. (1983). An accelerated mathematics program for girls: A longitudinal evaluation. In C. P. Benbow & J. C. Stanley (Eds.), *Academic precocity* (pp. 113–138). Baltimore: Johns Hopkins University Press.

Fox, L. H., & Cohn, S. J. (1980). Sex differences in development of mathematically precocious talent. In L. H. Fox, L. Brady, & D. Tobin (Eds.), *Women and the mathematical mystique* (pp. 94–111). Baltimore: Johns Hopkins University Press.

Fox, L. H., & Denham, S. A. (1974). Values and career interests of mathematically and scientifically precocious youth. In J. C. Stanley, D. P. Keating, & L. H. Fox (Eds.), *Mathematical talent: Discovery, description, development* (pp. 140–175). Baltimore: Johns Hopkins University Press.

Gallagher, J. J. (1985). *Teaching the gifted child.* Boston: Allyn and Bacon.

Gardner, H. (1983). *Frames of mind: The theory of multiple intelligences.* New York: Basic Books.

George, W. C., & Denham, S. A. (1976). Curriculum experimentation for the mathematically talented. In D. P. Keating (Ed.), *Intellectual talent: Research and development* (pp. 103–108). Baltimore: Johns Hopkins University Press.

Gilligan, C. (1982). *In a different voice: Psychological theory and women's development.* Cambridge, MA: Harvard University Press.

Groth, N. J. (1969). *Vocational development for gifted girls.* (ERIC Document Reproduction Service No. ED931747).

Hollinger, C. L. (1983). Counseling the gifted and talented female adolescent: The relationship between social self-esteem and traits of instrumentality and expressiveness. *Gifted Child Quarterly, 27,* 157–161.

Hollinger, C. L. (1985). The stability of self-perceptions of instrumental and expressive traits and social self-esteem among gifted and talented female adolescents. *Journal for the Education of the Gifted, 8,* 107–126.

Hollinger, C. L., & Fleming, E. S. (1984). Internal barriers to the realization of potential: Correlates and interrelationships among gifted and talented female adolescents. *Journal of Youth and Adolescence, 14,* 389–399.

Hollinger, C. L., & Fleming, E. S. (1988). Gifted and talented young women: Antecedents and correlates of life satisfaction. *Gifted Child Quarterly, 32,* 254–259.

Hollinger, D. (Ed.) (1993). *Single-sex schooling: Perspectives from practice and research.* Washington, DC: Office of Educational Research and Improvement, Department of Education.

Hollingworth, L. S. (1926). *Gifted children: Their nature and nurture.* New York: Macmillan.

Hyde, J. S. (1981). How large are cognitive gender differences? A meta-analysis. *American Psychologist, 36,* 892–901.

Jacobs, J. E., & Eccles, J. S. (1985, March). Gender differences in math ability: The impact of media reports on parents. *Educational Researcher, 14,* 20–25.

Janos, P. M., & Robinson, N. M. (1985). Psychosocial development in intellectually gifted children. In F. D. Horowitz & M. O'Brien (Eds.), *The gifted and talented: Developmental perspectives* (pp. 149–195). Washington, DC: American Psychological Association.

Kaufman, A. S., & Kaufman, N. L. (1983). *K-ABC: Kaufman assessment battery for children.* Circle Pines, MN: American Guidance Service.

Kaufman, F. (1981). The 1964–1968 Presidential Scholars: A follow-up study. *Exceptional Children, 48,* 2.

Kavrell, S. M., & Petersen, A. C. (1984). Patterns of achievement in early adolescence. In M. W. Steinkamp & M. L. Maehr (Eds.), *Women in science* (pp. 1–36). Greenwich, CT: JAI.

Kelly, K., & Colangelo, N. (1984). Academic and social self-concepts of gifted, general, and special students. *Exceptional Children, 50,* 551–553.

Kelly, K., & Hall, A. (1994). Effects of academic achievement and gender on occupational aspirations and career interests. In N. Colangelo, S. Assouline, & D. L. Ambroson, *Talent development* (pp. 447–453). Dayton, OH: Ohio Psychology Press.

Kerr, B. A. (1983). Raising aspirations of gifted girls. *Vocational Guidance Quarterly, 32,* 37–44.

Kerr, B. A. (1985). *Smart girls, gifted women.* Columbus: Ohio Psychology Press.

Kerr, B. A. (1988). Career counseling for gifted girls and women. *Journal of Career Development, 14,* 259–268.

Kerr, B. A. (1994). *Smart girls two: A new psychology of girls, women, and giftedness.* Dayton: Ohio Psychology Press.

Kerr, B. A., & Colangelo, N. (1988). The college plans of academically talented students. *Journal of Counseling and Development, 67,* 42–49.

Kerr, B. A., Colangelo, N., & Gaeth, J. (1988). Gifted adolescents' attitudes toward their giftedness. *Gifted Child Quarterly, 32,* 245–248.

Kerr, B. A., & Robinson, S. (1994). *Talented at-risk girls: Encouragement and training for sophomores.* Symposium at American Psychological Association, Los Angeles.

Kitano, M. K., & Kirby, D. F. (1985). *Gifted education: A comprehensive view.* Boston: Little, Brown.

Laing, J., Engen, H., & Maxey, J. (1987). *The relationship of high school coursework to corresponding ACT assessment scores.* Iowa City, IA: American College Testing Program.

Lessinger, L., & Martinson, R. (1961). The use of the California Psychological Inventory with gifted pupils. *Personnel and Guidance Journal, 39,* 572–575.

Ludwig, G., & Cullinan, D. (1984). Behavior problems of gifted and nongifted elementary school girls and boys. *Gifted Child Quarterly, 28,* 37–40.

Maccoby, E. E., & Jacklin, C. N. (1974). *The psychology of sex differences.* Stanford, CA: Stanford University Press.

Meara, N. M., & Day, J. D. (1993). Perspectives on achieving via interpersonal competition between college men and college women. *Sex Roles, 28,* 91–102.

Petersen, A. C. (1976). Physical androgyny and cognitive functioning in adolescence. *Developmental Psychology, 12,* 524–533.

Petersen, A. C. (1979). *Hormones and cognitive functioning: Developmental issues.* New York: Academic.

Sadker, D., & Sadker, M. (1984, March). *Year II, Final Report, promoting effectiveness in classroom instruction.* Washington, DC: NIE Contract 400-80-0033.

Sadker, D., & Sadker, M. (1985, April). *Interventions that promote equity and effectiveness in student-teacher interaction.* Paper presented at the annual meeting of the American Educational Research Association, Chicago.

Sadker, M., & Sadker, D. (1994). *Failing at fairness: How America's schools cheat girls.* New York: Scribners & Sons.

Silverman, L. K. (1986). What happens in the gifted girl? In C. J. Maker (Ed.), *Critical issues in gifted education: Defensible programs for the gifted* (pp. 43–89). Rockville, MD: Aspen.

Silverman, L. K. (1993). *Counseling the gifted and talented.* Denver, CO: Love.

Solano, C. H. (1977). Teacher and pupil stereotypes of gifted boys and girls. *Talents and Gifts, 19,* 4.

Steinkamp, M. W. (1984). Motivational style as a mediator of adult achievement in science. In M. W. Steinkamp & M. L. Maehr (Eds.), *Advances in motivation and achievement: Women in science* (pp. 281–317). New York: JAI Press.

Sternberg, R. J. (1986). A triarchic theory of giftedness. In R. J. Sternberg & J. E. Davidson (Eds.), *Conceptions of giftedness* (pp. 223–243). New York: Cambridge University Press.

Tavris, C. (1992). *The mismeasure of women: Why women are not the better sex, the inferior sex, or the opposite sex.* New York: Simon & Schuster.

Terman, L. M., & Oden, M. H. (1935). *Genetic studies of genius: Vol. 3. The promise of youth.* Stanford, CA: Stanford University Press.

Terman, L. M., & Oden, M. H. (1947). *Genetic studies of genius: Vol. 4. The gifted-child grows up.* Stanford, CA: University Press.

Torrance, E. P. (1979). *The search for satori and creativity.* Great Neck, NY: Creative Synergetic.

Torrance, E. P., Bruch, C. B., & Morse, J. A. (1973). Improving prediction of the adult creative achievement of gifted girls using autobiographical information. *Gifted Child Quarterly, 17,* 91–95.

Tressemer, D. (1977). *Fear of success.* New York: Plenum Press.

U.S. Commissioner of Education. (1972). *Education of gifted and talented.* Washington, DC: U.S. Office of Education.

Weiner, N. C., & Robinson, S. E. (1986). Cognitive ability, personality and gender differences in math achievement of gifted adolescents. *Gifted Child Quarterly, 30,* 83–87.

39

Gifted Minority Students: Reframing Approaches to Their Identification and Education

MARY M. FRASIER, *Torrance Center for Creative Studies, University of Georgia*

There is no logical reason to expect that the number of minority students in gifted programs would not be proportional to their representation in the general population. However, the disparity between their participation in gifted programs, when compared to majority students, continues despite increased knowledge about the different effects that cultural backgrounds, environments, and socioeconomic status may have on the expression of gifted behaviors and despite the improvements that have been made in the assessment measures and procedures used to identify gifted potential. Gallagher and Coleman (1992), for example, report that at least 34 states now advocate the use of multiple criteria. The use of multiple criteria is a positive move away from relying on a single test score to identify students who will be eligible for gifted program services. This move also is compatible with recommendations by Gardner (1983, 1993), Renzulli (1978, 1988), and Sternberg (1981, 1982, 1988), who provide compelling evidence that giftedness is multidimensional and requires the use of multiple measures for identification.

Along with the recommendation to consider multiple criteria for identification, Gallagher and Coleman (1992) also note that 38 states now include specific instructions to address the special identification needs of culturally diverse populations, economically disadvantaged students, and disabled students in their regulations governing eligibility for gifted program participation. Ostensibly, recommendations like these should have had a significant and positive effect on addressing the underrepresentation of certain groups in programs for the gifted. Despite good intentions and recommendations, however, problems in identifying gifted minority students continue to challenge educators.

That the identification of minority students is still a challenge is noted by the edict in the Jacob K. Javits Gifted and Talented Education Act of 1988 to give highest priority "to the identification of gifted and talented students who may not be identified through traditional assessment methods (including economically disadvantaged individuals, individuals of limited English proficiency, and individuals with handicaps) and to education programs designed to include gifted and talented students from such groups" (p. 238).

The goal of finding effective ways to address the underrepresentation of minority and disadvantaged students in gifted programs was included in an earlier report on the education of gifted and talented children (Marland, 1972). In addition, the gifted literature is replete with discussions documenting problems in identifying minority students and recommendations to address these problems through differentiated assessment and instructional procedures.

One reason for this continuing challenge may be that the problems that negatively affect the identification and education of minority students essentially have not changed. These problems not only are long standing but, for at least the last 40 years, have almost consistently focused on issues related to (1) differences in test performance among racial, cultural, or ethnic groups; and (2) the effects of cultural, economic, and language differences or deprivations on the ability of minority students to achieve at levels associated with giftedness.

Whether or not these issues are the true source of identification and education problems, framing solutions around them has not served us well in our attempts to address the underrepresentation of minorities in gifted programs. For the most part, solutions developed around these types of problems have directed attention to deficiencies or weaknesses in the academic performance of minority students and to various ethnic or cultural differences as the primary cause for their low representation in gifted programs. A new perspective on the problems is needed if we are ever to address problems effectively in their identification and education.

Wiggins (1989) contends that "When an educational problem persists despite the well-intentioned efforts of many people to solve it, it's a safe bet that the problem hasn't been properly framed" (p. 703). For example, rarely has consideration been given to the more difficult challenge of examining the concept of giftedness from a multigroup perspective (Frasier, Garcia, & Passow, 1994). In fact, a major criticism by many minority scholars and educators has been that the concept of giftedness is solely defined from the perspective of one group, white middle class Americans. This single perspective does not sufficiently address the concept of giftedness in minority groups (Ford & Harris, 1990; Kirschenbaum, 1989; Machado, 1987; Patton, 1992; Tonemah, 1987).

Should the problems in identifying gifted minority students be reframed? What are the relevant issues that should be considered if the problems in identifying gifted minority students are reframed? What unique insights into assessment, programming, and curricula planning might be achieved if the problems in identifying and educating gifted minority students are reframed? The purpose of this chapter is to examine these issues by exploring them from a multigroup perspective and to present findings from research and practice that suggest more effective ways of addressing giftedness in minority groups.

The following sections present a definition of minority students; problems that have affected their identification and education; reasons for reframing problems associated with the identification and education of gifted minority students; one promising practice for facilitating a view of giftedness from a multigroup perspective; and finally a summary of the issues that were discussed and some suggestions for research and practice.

Who Are Minority Students?

Who are minorities? There is no clear-cut answer to this question, for the concept of *minority* has been defined in numerous ways. For example, minorities have been defined as "a population subgroup possessing social or religious interests that differ from those of the larger group" (Chaplin, 1985, p. 284). These differences subject minorities to various forms of segregation and unfavorable treatment that may be legal, quasi-legal, or purely social.

Minorities also have been defined by their economic, ritualistic, and political roles in a society and by the responses they have made to varying types of subjugation (Ogbu, 1978, 1994). Ogbu divides minorities into three groups: (1) autonomous minorities (people who are minorities primarily in a numerical sense); (2) immigrant or voluntary minorities (people who have moved more or less voluntarily to a society because they desire greater economic well-being, better overall opportunities, and/or greater political freedom); and (3) castelike or involuntary minorities (people who were originally brought into a society against their will, as in slavery, conquest, colonization, or forced labor). Children who are members of castelike minority groups, according to Ogbu (1994), typically "experience greater and more persistent difficulties with school learning" (p. 363).

Passow's (1982) description of disadvantaged students provides yet another perspective on minorities. He succinctly addresses the intermingling and interchanging of concepts related to the definition of *minority* when he observed that "The population pools in which the disadvantaged are generally found are the poor, racial, and ethnic minorities" (p. 20). While Passow cautions that the terms *minority* and *disadvantaged* should not be used synonymously, he also observes that population pools referred to as minorities are typically made up of African Americans, Latinos, and

Native Americans. This pool also includes Native Hawaiians and Asian American groups.

In summary, definitions of minorities, and by extension minority students, sometimes refer to ethnic group membership, or to political or economic status, or to values and beliefs that are different from those of a majority group. Other labels that have been used interchangeably to refer to minority students and their education have included *culturally different, culturally deprived, educationally deprived, economically disadvantaged, culturally disadvantaged,* and *at risk.* Concurrent with the use of these labels have been various views held about the educational potential of minority students as related to their diverse cultural, linguistic, and economic backgrounds. These views have revealed themselves in extensive discussions related to the concept of quality education, equality of educational opportunity, and the various social and political ideologies that characterize current discussions of school reform (Howe, 1994; Passow, 1982).

No matter how *minority* is defined, there is always the attendant risk of making unwarranted generalizations about minority individuals or groups, omitting a group that some feel should be included, or including a group that some feel should be excluded.

Changing demographics in this country are beginning to make the concept of *minority,* as it has been popularly used, passé. For example, many members of nonwhite groups currently refer to themselves as "people of color." The growth of multiculturalism and other movements that embrace, enhance, and celebrate the diversity between and within cultural and ethnic groups in the United States are also beginning to consider definitions that designate some groups as "minority" and others as "majority" as useless and nonproductive.

For purposes of this discussion, the primary reference groups will be African Americans, Native Americans, and Latinos. Students in these groups, often irrespective of their economic and achievement levels, have dominated discussions when problems in identifying minority gifted students are considered. They are also the students who most often have been the topic of research studies on the school performance of minority students.

Problems Affecting the Identification and Education of Gifted Minority Students

Problems affecting the identification of minority students have been enumerated in countless reports and need not be repeated here. A brief review of these problems as they affect the identification of gifted minority students has been included for background purposes. Frasier (1991a, 1993a) divided these problems into four categories: (a) access, (b) assessment, (c) accommodation, and (d) attitudes. Issues related to these problem categories are summarized in this section.

Access

Several factors are believed to limit the *access* of minority students for gifted program consideration. They include: (1) the generally low academic expectations that educators hold for culturally and linguistically diverse students (Clasen, 1994; Dusek & Joseph, 1983; Jones, 1988; McCarty, Lynch, Wallace, & Benally, 1991); (2) low rates of referral of their children for gifted program consideration by minority parents (Colangelo, 1985; Scott, Perou, Urbano, Hogan, & Gold, 1992; Wood & Achey, 1990); (3) the inability of educators to recognize gifted behaviors when exhibited by minority students (Bermúdez & Rakow, 1990; Bernal, 1980; Dabney, 1988; Leung, 1981); and (4) the minimal regard given to the influence of culture and environment on the manifestation of gifts and talent in different racial and ethnic groups and the effects of this on teacher referrals (Ford & Harris, 1990; Hale-Benson, 1982; Montgomery, 1989; Zappia, 1989).

Assessment

By far, the most frequently discussed reason for the limited participation of minority students in gifted programs is related to assessment measures and their use in identification. Especially criticized is the use of teacher nominations and tests as the ultimate way to determine a child's gifted potential. Ford and Harris (1990) attribute problems in assessment to an "over-reliance upon standardized tests, the reification of intelligence and IQ, and the use of unidimensional instruments to assess intelligence, a multi-dimensional construct" (p. 28). While Reynolds and Kaiser (1990) note that there is little or no evidence to substantiate claims of bias in most well-constructed tests of intelligence, a number of researchers and writers suggest otherwise. For example, Bernal (1980), Hilliard (1991), and Tonemah (1987) are among those who contend that testing instruments and practices developed in the Euro-American tradition are invalid measures for minority students. Borland (1986) attributes minority assessment problems to the pervasive bias found in American society. Hilliard (1991) affirms Borland's observation when he notes that mean score differences on standardized tests between majority and minority students more nearly reflect racial discrimination than low intelligence.

Accommodation

Persisting problems in the identification and education of gifted minority students also have been attributed to program designs and curricula that do not adequately address differences in their cultural and linguistic experiences. Efforts to ameliorate problems perceived to be created by these differences are reflected in the many remedial and compensatory strategies developed to prepare minority students better to "fit" into the form, structure, and functions of the dominant society. It has been observed that these accommodations are made without giving due consideration to the need of minority students to develop abilities valued by more than one culture, and to the need to help them acquire skills that allow them to move between and within at least two cultures, and to develop their sense of self-identity (Maker & Schiever, 1989).

Attitudes

The most pervasive reasons for problems in identifying gifted minority students are related to attitudes about gifted potential in these groups. Even if all of the access, assessment, and accommodation problems outlined above were solved, far more difficult problems related to attitudes about identifying gifted students need to be faced. In a study of state policies for identifying nontraditional students, Gallagher and Coleman (1992) described these problems: (1) concern that substantial increases in numbers of identified gifted children would *not* be accompanied by increases in resources for services, and (2) fears that programs will have to answer to parents of children *not* from special populations who demand that their children be included as well.

Maker (1983) alluded to similar inhibiting factors when she noted that efforts to address the identification of gifted culturally diverse students brought up counterobservations about the use of different tests and the possibility that the quality of gifted programs would diminish. These attitudes and concerns tend to be perpetuated by beliefs that minority group students are incapable of engaging in, or are uninterested in, intellectual endeavors.

How the gifted are described may provide one clue to the persistence of these less-than-positive attitudes about the possibility of gifted performers in minority groups. For example, one way of defining giftedness focuses upon individuals with outstanding ability and potential; another way emphasizes demonstrated productivity and creativity (Gallagher, 1994a). With the first definition, gifted children are viewed as those students who are performing tasks at much earlier ages and at more advanced paces than their chronological peers. Besides high IQ scores, other descriptions of gifted children include reading before they enter school, reading two grade levels or more above their current grade, or having mastered advanced mathematical concepts and tasks well before their peers. Gifted children are also described as having supportive families who encourage them in intellectual pursuits through the provision of assistance, resources, and experiences.

The second definition refers to children who demonstrate productivity and creativity in an area of human performance judged to be valuable for self or for society. Examples of areas deemed to be acceptable for recognizing gifted performance include those outlined by Renzulli (1988, p. 74): mathematics, philosophy, religion, life sciences, visual arts, social sciences, language arts, physical sciences, law, music, and movement arts.

Minority students are not typically thought of as gifted in either of these two ways. More often the focus is on developing and implementing programs and curricula to assist minority students in "catching up" with their peers. Numerous reports confirm that they do not, for example, perform as well as Anglos on formal tests (García & Pearson, 1994; National Center for Education Statistics, 1988; Natriello, McDill, & Pallas, 1990).

Further, the families of minority students have not been viewed as being supportive of intellectual development, either because they lack the skills, the interest, or access to necessary resources (Boykin & Toms, 1985; Harrison, 1985; Jenkins, 1989; Perrine, 1989). As a result the "deficit-deficiency" explanatory paradigm has encouraged insensitive and ineffective institutional responses to the ability of minority families to nurture academic achievement in their children (Jenkins, 1989). Weaknesses of minority families are highlighted, with little or no focus on their strengths.

Summary

The purpose of this section was to present a brief review of problems in identifying gifted minority students that have been articulated over the years. Effective solutions to them, however, will not be found in their reiteration nor in debates about whether or not they are the real problems. Effective solutions may ultimately depend on: (1) whether we choose to change our views about giftedness in minority groups and (2) how we use these new views to develop policies and procedures that better address giftedness in diverse groups.

Reasons for Reframing Problems in Identifying Gifted Minority Students

The goal of this section is to explore insights into the problems of identifying gifted minority students from two perspectives. The first perspective examines assessment issues as they relate to (1) barriers to reframing a concept that are based in tradition, (2) the utility of the IQ in an educational assessment program, (3) the merits of a contextual rather than a psychometric paradigm for educational assessment in a pluralistic culture, and (4) the relevance of cultural differences. The second perspective samples concerns related to a unidimensional view of giftedness.

Assessment-Related Reasons

The legacy of existing practices. Shore, Cornell, Robinson, and Ward (1991) observed that while entire models of identification and programming have been formulated around the idea of multiple talent or intelligence, there remains a great attachment to IQ as the defining quality of giftedness. Amid all the rhetoric about changing criteria for gifted program participation, core values and beliefs guiding identification practices remain focused on a student's ability to function at a high intellectual level based on their performance on intelligence tests, achievement tests, and teacher recommendations. It is true that other criteria have been added in attempts to address the multiple dimensions of giftedness as well as to accommodate children for whom the detection of their gifted abilities do not fit the traditional formula for identification. However, these assessment criteria are often viewed as alternatives, not valuable additives to the identification procedure. As Barbour (1992) noted, while recent definitions of giftedness have included other areas of importance, the capacity for cognitive activity has remained central to the definition and identification of giftedness. Paraphrasing an observation by Goodlad (1994), the goal still appears to be smoothing out the dissonance of other cultural beliefs, religions, and languages even as our schools become inhabited by students from increasingly diverse backgrounds.

Other comments by Goodlad relative to how schools can improve provide us with an opportunity to reflect on the need to reframe the problems in identifying gifted minority students. For example, he describes current restructuring efforts as being designed to improve the schools we have, not invent new ones to more adequately serve the needs of a growing diverse student body. A great deal of our thinking about schools and what goes on in them simply assumes the traditional definition. Goodlad further notes that modifications in traditional approaches to education, especially in our current society, require us to understand three things: (1) Change takes a long time, (2) change is not likely to occur if it depends heavily for success on the support of persons attached to the current setting, and (3) a fundamental change demands a new beginning, not adaptation to what exists.

Much of what has gone on in attempts to address the underrepresentation of minority students in gifted programs may be characterized as adaptations to what exists. As a result we are still wrestling with problems of identification. Goodlad's observations support a need for the field of gifted education to establish a vision of gifted education where the talents in diverse populations are core, not ancillary, to a reconceptualization of the concept of giftedness from a multigroup perspective.

Changing views about IQ testing to assess student potential. As noted earlier, most debates concerned with identifying gifted minority students center on testing issues. More specifically, the concerns relate to the proper use of IQ testing in the identification process, the use of alternative identification procedures, and the best ways to address cultural and social differences. A widely reported and well-supported finding from several studies, according to Shore et al. (1991), is that the major impediment to the identification of giftedness in culturally and socially different populations is the overwhelming dependence on test criteria based on middle-class reading skills in the majority language. Yet the IQ remains "the most universally advocated and used criterion for the identification of giftedness" (Shore et al., 1991, p. 53).

Newmann and Archbald (1992) suggest that a major limitation of standardized norm-referenced achievement tests is that they only report a student's overall score in relation to other students' scores. They tell us very little about a student's particular level of mastery on a specific task. Success is defined simply as scoring in the higher percentiles of the tested population. Newmann and Archbald advise that when "making evaluative judgments about individuals . . . we often need more than one indicator of quality. Any single indicator such as a percentile rank . . . limits the amount of information conveyed. . . ." (p. 80). A variety of performances over time are necessary to make quality assessments of students.

Pellegrino (1988) concurs. He noted that while mental tests of intelligence provide global indications of a person's performance relative to others, they are short on relating valuable information about a person's current cognitive capabilities. Our historical orientation to use tests as a means of classifying, predicting, and selecting, he contends, provides little information that is of diagnostic and prescriptive value.

In his call for a new measurement paradigm, Raven (1992) also argued that conventional tests fail to evaluate activities which lead people to observe, to think, to find better ways of thinking about things, or to communicate effectively. He proposed that adequate measures of competence should jointly measure the cognitive, affective, and motivational components of an activity, and concluded that it is meaningless to attempt to assess a person's abilities apart from their valued goals. A complete review of his Model of Competence is beyond the scope of this chapter. A few points from Raven's discussion of this model are presented here because of their relevance to reframing the problems involved in identifying and educating gifted minority students:

1. The need to describe the situation or context in which individuals find themselves

must be an integral part of the assessment process (p. 91).

2. It is the total number of competencies individuals display in many situations over a long period of time in order to reach their valued goals that we need to assess, not their level of ability in relation to any of them. An overall index of a person's "ability" or "motivation" is virtually meaningless (p. 92).
3. . . . a description of the types of behavior that people value and the competencies they display in the course of trying to reach them provides much more useful information than a single total score (p. 96).
4. The same qualities may look different in different contexts—indeed, copper looks and behaves very differently when it is combined with oxygen instead of sulphur. But it does not cease to be copper (p. 98).

A concluding observation from Raven's discussion of his Model of Competence emphasizes the need for teachers to study and be very familiar with their students' interests and talents. In addition, teachers must create situations where these talents can be expressed. Otherwise any statements made about, or ratings made of, high-level competencies will be meaningless.

The need for a new assessment paradigm. Berlak (1992) argues for the replacement of the traditional psychometric paradigm with one that he calls a *contextual* paradigm. Meanings of the psychometric versus contextual paradigms, as presented by Berlak, are presented here to illustrate their relevance to the identification of gifted minority students. The assumption that there is *universality of meaning* in assessment measures underlies the psychometric paradigm, according to Berlak. This assumption means that a consensus can be established about what standardized tests claim to measure. This meaning is believed to transcend social context and history and has essentially the same meaning for all individuals everywhere. In contrast, he asserts that a contextual paradigm accepts a plurality of meanings and would take into consideration the different histories, divergent interests, and concerns of individuals and groups. A system of educational assessment would consider a plurality of perspectives and differences in values and beliefs as givens and would treat these differences as assets, not obstructions to be overcome.

The use of standardized tests to rank students is a crucial component in the psychometric paradigm. Berlak contends that while this use of tests produces relative rankings of students, they provide little substantive information about what students know and are capable of doing, or where they may need help. Thus, students can be ranked or classified as belonging to a category, for example, high, average, or low achievers, but little more is promised that is useful to teachers for making programmatic or individual decisions. Those who are being assessed have little or no control over this method of evaluating their capacities or achievements. In contrast, a contextual paradigm allows input into the instrumentation and methodology followed in evaluating students. That is, rather than proceeding from a unidimensional view of giftedness, a contextual paradigm would encourage as well as seek input from the community of which a minority student is a member.

The relevance of cultural differences. Discussions of identifying and educating minority students virtually always indicate that cultural differences are an important factor to consider. The purpose of this section is not to debate the importance of cultural differences, but to consider two points of view regarding these differences and their relevance to the reframing of problems in identifying gifted minority students.

Ogbu's (1978, 1994) division of minorities into three subgroups was discussed earlier. Ogbu argues that the focus on educational strategies for minorities should be based on differences between these subgroups. For example, he contends that differences in the school performance of voluntary and involuntary minorities may be attributed to primary and secondary cultural differences. Primary cultural differences existed before two groups came in contact, while secondary cultural differences arose after contact with another group and in response to the contact situation. Both voluntary and involuntary minority group children may experience initial problems in interpersonal and intergroup relations and in academic work because they (1) may begin school with different cultural assumptions about the world and human relations, (2) may come to school lacking certain concepts believed to be necessary for academic achievement, and (3) may speak English poorly or be non-English-speaking. However, the primary cultural differences of voluntary minorities do not develop in opposition to another culture or as a strategy to protect their group's identity, sense of security, and self-worth. Learning the majority culture and language is not seen as threatening; learning the ways of the new culture is viewed as an immediate barrier to be conquered in order to reach long-range achievement goals. The cultural beliefs, values, and practices of a voluntary minority group are maintained according to their wishes.

Secondary cultural differences, however, develop as coping mechanisms by an involuntary minority group, usually under oppressive conditions imposed by the other culture. As a result, their cultural and language differences are maintained as markers of their identity in the face of perceived hostilities, not as barriers to be overcome. Schooling may be viewed as a strategy by their oppressors to displace their social identity, sense of security, and self worth. Ogbu (1994) contends that style, not content, separates secondary and primary cultural differences and may be at the heart of cultural difference problems associated with children learning in school. These stylistic differences may relate to communication style, styles of thought, and differences in learning style.

As a result of secondary cultural differences, Ogbu believes that involuntary minority children come to school with a cultural and language frame of reference that is not only different but is probably oppositional to that of the mainstream and of the school. Children who are members of involuntary minority groups are more often the topic of discussions related to their underrepresentation in gifted programs. It is Ogbu's belief that understanding their cultural differences is very important to the design of assessment and instructional strategies to address the needs of involuntary minority children. In addition, he suggests that involuntary minority adults should understand the impact of their differences on academic achievement and work proactively with their children to help them develop strategies that enhance the development of their talents.

The multicultural point of view (Banks, 1993a, 1993b) emphasizes educational equality for students from diverse racial, ethnic, and social-class groups. That is, "all students—regardless of their gender and social class and their ethnic, racial, or cultural characteristics—should have an equal opportunity to learn in school" (p. 3). Multiculturalists are concerned with the content and form of education that would permit each group to be recognized and respected for what its diversity contributes to the development of a healthy, viable society.

Rather than emphasizing cultural or other differences as the reason for academic success or failure, the emphasis is on using differences as the impetus for changing the structure of schools and the educational environment so that all children can experience opportunities for optimal achievement. Unlike Ogbu (1978, 1994), Banks (1993b) does not believe that membership in a group determines behavior even though this membership may make certain types of behavior more probable. Banks contends that the more we know about a student's level of identification with a particular group and the extent to which socialization has taken place within that group, the better equipped we are to predict, explain, and understand the student's behavior in a classroom.

The multicultural view emphasizes the need to focus on within-group heterogeneity rather than homogeneity. This is a familiar observation by persons who have suggested that a major problem in identifying gifted minority students is the tendency to indiscriminately characterize all members with the attributes associated with its least well performing members (Banks, 1993a; Kitano & Kirby, 1986;

Tonemah, 1987). As a result, group stereotypes (often negative) are perpetuated, regardless of individual behaviors to the contrary.

The multiculturalist's position, as well as the opinions regarding involuntary minorities offered by Ogbu, provide support for a multigroup perspective of giftedness that would take into account legitimate differences. Neither of these positions suggest making allowances for minority students, such as lowering admission requirements to gifted programs or setting quotas, features that do not enjoy strong support from minority scholars or minority parents. Instead, these positions clearly suggest the need to understand that differences in cultural experiences, values, and beliefs have important implications for designing appropriate assessment and instructional programs to address the ever-growing diversity in our school populations. Standards of excellence are not to be ignored because of these differences, but definitions of those standards must not favor one group over another, whether the group is distinguished by culture, gender, language, or economics.

Minority Concerns with a Unidimensional View of Giftedness

A unidimensional view of giftedness continues to be reflected in practices designed to assist minority students in either (1) meeting traditional eligibility requirements for gifted program participation or (2) meeting program requirements based on broadened conceptions of giftedness. For example, the short-term goal of a demonstration project implemented by Borland and Wright (1994) was to identify economically disadvantaged students who have potential for high-level academic performance and to provide them with intervention services that would help them develop their potential. A long-term goal was placement in classes for traditionally identified gifted students. This view does not invalidate earlier measures of giftedness. Rather, Gallagher (1994b) describes this view as an attempt to extend the traditional concept of giftedness "to meet more adequately the cultural diversity of today's American society" (p. 96).

Many concerns have been voiced by minority scholars and researchers regarding the limitations of this one-dimensional view of giftedness. Zappia (1989) contends that the problem of underrepresentation of minorities actually stems from our schools, our attitudes, and our values. She asserted that the problem is much greater than merely the choice of appropriate instruments and that the solution is complex. For example, because our society is culturally diverse, we must (1) use cultural indicators of giftedness, (2) find applicable alternatives to standardized tests, and (3) prepare teachers to recognize the creative behaviors of Hispanic and other minority students. Finally, she feels that bias should not be an issue limited to tests. The entire decision-making process must be examined for instances of bias. That is, attention must be given to the bias throughout the assessment process as well as the instructional planning.

Montgomery's (1989) concerns are with who sets standards for judging Native American giftedness. She asked "Why must educators identify American Indian students who are in the 'top' categories of performance, skills, or abilities?" (p. 80) Further, she wished to know who will benefit from a system that promotes gifted American Indian children. Her questions are not asked impertinently. Rather, she is concerned that individuals in the American Indian community be included in the process of determining the special talents of its children.

Grant (1989) raised concerns about the tendency to view Black students and other students of color as a special population needing special considerations. He contended that these students are in need of understanding and equal consideration in the identification and educational process. Given *equal* consideration, questions of *special* considerations might become moot.

Grant's views are echoed by other minority researchers and scholars. For example, Tonemah (1987) called for a moratorium on the use of terms like *minority* and *disadvantaged* when describing gifted Native American students. Ruiz (1989) called for a halt to treating "Hispanic students along with their associated antecedents—language and culture, families, neighborhoods, and academic training—in the framework of a problem orientation" (p. 64).

Bernal (1980) expressed it best when he stated his strong opposition to any effort to "doctor" traditional measurement techniques for minority students by adding points, selecting particular subtest batteries in the belief that they best reflect the abilities of minority children, or establishing any kind of quotas as a basis for minority students to participate in gifted programs. He argued that such recommendations further stigmatized minority students while still failing to recognize the gifted among them. Bernal urged, instead, that educators give greater attention to developing a core definition of giftedness. By doing so, he contends, there would be less reason to be bound by the cognitive preferences of the dominant ethnic group and greater reason to seek a valid and operationally useful identification and selection process for all children.

A Promising Practice for Viewing Giftedness from a Multigroup Perspective

Resolutions to ensure that students from traditionally underserved populations are not overlooked when assessing for gifted program services almost always include a recommendation to use multiple criteria for identification (Foster, Gallagher, & Coleman, 1993; Shore, et al., 1991). Almost all authors in a volume edited by Maker and Schiever (1989) recommended using "multiple assessment procedures, including objective and subjective data from a variety of sources" (p. 295) to address identification concerns of minority students. In addition, it is recommended that these multiple assessment procedures be culturally and linguistically appropriate.

The use of matrices, where points are assigned for tests scores that fall into preset intervals, has been criticized as being statistically and logically flawed (Feldhusen, Baska, & Womble, 1981; Treffinger, 1991). Problematic, according to Treffinger, is the practice of reducing complex profiles of diagnostic data to oversimplified categories or point totals, then creating arbitrary cutoff points for inclusion or exclusion in gifted programs.

Yet, evidence from many sources continues to affirm the utility of using more than one criterion when deciding a child's need for specific educational services (Hoy & Gregg, 1994; Newmann & Archbald, 1992; Shaklee, 1992; Shore et al., 1991). In addition, there is growing evidence that students admitted to gifted programs by multiple criteria equal the performance of students chosen by traditional means (Baldwin, 1994; Frasier, 1993b; O'Tuel, 1994; Shore et al., 1991).

An assessment procedure based on a multigroup perspective would attend to the concept of giftedness in ways that adequately accommodate the perspectives of different groups. According to Berlak (1992), such an assessment would consider plurality of perspectives and differences in values and beliefs as givens, and treat these differences as assets, not obstructions to be overcome. The following describes an educational assessment model that was designed to facilitate the identification of gifted potential in minority and economically disadvantaged student groups from a multigroup perspective. In addition, this model suggests a way to reframe the problem orientation in identifying gifted minority students to one that emphasizes their talents.

The Frasier Talent Assessment Profile (F-TAP)

The F-TAP model (Frasier, 1991b, 1994) is an assessment system that facilitates the collection and display of data from multiple test and nontest sources so that teams of educators have this information easily available to make recommendations about a student's need for gifted program services. It is based on the general notion that the gifted are a very heterogeneous group and that the methods and procedures used to identify and educate them must respond to that heterogeneity. The emphasis is on using tests and other measures that are reliable and valid for the abilities being assessed and are appropriate for the population with which they are being used.

Core attributes associated with the giftedness construct provide the foundation for the F-TAP model. The goal is to provide an effective way to recognize and develop gifted potential in diverse groups without unduly focusing on the preferences of one group over another. That is, rather than focusing (as has previously been done) on finding ways to assist minority and disadvantaged students to fit into the traditional paradigm of giftedness, the goal is to develop a procedure that assesses their gifted potential from a multigroup perspective.

Rationale. The concept of giftedness as a psychological construct provides the rationale for the construction of this model. A construct is a set of hypothesized traits, abilities, or characteristics abstracted from a variety of behaviors presumed to have educational or psychological meaning (Sax, 1980). Giftedness is thus a psychological construct. It is not a directly observable trait of an individual. Therefore, accurate inferences about giftedness depend very much on the choices of characteristics and behaviors that are observed and appraised in relation to this psychological construct.

Researchers have contended that lack of clarity about this construct has impeded optimal developments of methods and procedures to identify gifted potential in general (Hoge, 1988, 1989; Hoge & Cudmore, 1986) and specific methods to identify gifted minority students (Bernal, 1980; Culross, 1989). While formal definitions of the giftedness construct incorporate a broad range of cognitive, motivation, and personality characteristics, many methods to identify students for gifted programs continue to rely on IQ test performance as the primary indicator of a need for services (Hoge, 1989; Passow & Rudnitski, 1993). This view of a high IQ score as the necessary ingredient to determine giftedness perpetuates views that different behavioral manifestations of gifted potential by minority and disadvantaged students are still not sufficient. For example, Gallagher (1994b) observed that despite the improvements in the performance of students identified through many of the Javits Grant Demonstration Projects (Ross, 1994), there remain reservations "that many of the students might still not reach eligibility standards for the traditional gifted program" (p. 95).

For reasons such as these, the author's investigation was undertaken to develop a multigroup view of giftedness that transcended the barriers of identifying gifted minority students, especially when a single standard was used. Core attributes of giftedness were examined as a basis for resolving these barriers.

Core attributes of the giftedness construct. Core attributes of giftedness were identified from two sources: (1) a content analysis of checklists specifically designed to identify gifted minority students, and (2) an extensive search of the gifted literature to discover the typical traits, aptitudes, and behaviors exhibited by students identified as gifted (Frasier, Hunsaker, Frank, Finley, & Lee, 1994). Independent analyses were performed to identify the underlying concepts found in the lists of traits, aptitudes, and behaviors. Results of these analyses were pooled, discussed, and reanalyzed until a consensus was reached regarding ten core attributes that seemed to summarize findings from this literature and the checklists' descriptions of gifted children, regardless of background and environment. The *Dictionary of Psychological Terms* (Chaplin, 1985) was consulted for concise definitions of the following ten core attributes associated with the giftedness construct:

- Motivation (forces that initiate, direct, and sustain individual or group behavior in order to satisfy a need or attain a goal)
- Interests (activities, avocations, objects, etc., that have special worth or significance and are given special attention)
- Communication (transmission and reception of signals or meanings through a system of symbols—codes, gestures, language, numbers, etc.)
- Problem Solving (process of determining a correct sequence of alternatives leading to a desired goal or to successful completion or performance of a task)

- Memory (exceptional ability to retain and retrieve information)
- Inquiry (method or process of seeking knowledge, understanding, or information)
- Insight (sudden discovery of the correct solution following incorrect attempts based primarily on trial and error)
- Reasoning (highly conscious, directed, controlled, active, intentional, forward-looking, goal-oriented thought)
- Imagination/Creativity (processes of forming mental images of objects, qualities, situations, or relationships that are not immediately apparent to the senses. Problem solving through nontraditional patterns of thinking)
- Humor (ability to synthesize key ideas or problems in complex situations in a humorous way; exceptional sense of timing in words and gestures)

Methods and procedures developed for referrals, identification, and educational program planning were built around these core attributes.

Components of the F-TAP Model

Two major components of the F-TAP model are: (1) the Panning for Gold (PFG) observation form; and (2) the F-TAP, which consists of three sections—a sheet for recording demographic data on the student and professional recommendations, a profile format for displaying identification information (divided into three sections), and an Educational Services Plan sheet, which includes a place to record information that has significance for educational planning.

Panning for Gold (PFG) observation form. This is a four-page observation form on which teachers record evidence about a student's display of core attributes associated with the giftedness construct. The core attributes identified earlier are used as the basis for these observations. The last sheet of the PFG form, called the selection sheet, provides instructions to the nominator to note their recommendations for further assessments of the student(s) observed.

The F-TAP profile. In section 1 (the cover page) of the model, space is provided to record demographic information on a student and for a summary statement regarding recommendations for gifted program services. The assessment profile is contained in section 2 (the inner three pages). Two sets of scales are provided to allow for the interpretation of subjective and objective data that can be represented with numbers. These data are never summed to arrive at a total or composite score; the interpretation scales are aligned so that relevant comparisons can be made between the two types of performance results. A qualitative assessment section, section 3, is for recording performance data on a student that cannot be represented with numbers.

Educational Services Plan. The *Educational Services Plan* sheet facilitates the connection of information from assessment with instructional decisions. Four areas are included for this planning: (1) programming, (2) curricula, (3) counseling, and (4) evaluation. An Additional Information sheet is placed next to the Educational Services Plan sheet to provide a place to record certain status information about a student that is relevant to instructional planning. The sheet might include information about a student's learning style or environmental conditions that may impact on his or her performance.

Two observations concerned with assessment equity provide the rationale for separating *status* information from *functional* information. Gordon (1993) asserts that status characteristics, such as class, ethnicity, and gender, are not as important for assessment, but do have important implications for pedagogy. However, functional characteristics, such as cognitive style, culture, identity, language, source of motivation, and temperament, have important implications for both pedagogy and assessment. Hilliard (1994) concurs when he commented that information about a student's race, socioeconomic status, and gender are meaningful in education only from a political perspective. There is no defensible professional reason to have information about a person's race when making teaching and learning decisions.

Several studies have evaluated the effectiveness of this model (Cowan & Gollmar, 1994; Frasier et al., 1994; Hunsaker et al., 1994; Hunsaker, Frasier, Frank, Finley, & Klekotka, 1994; Schmeichel, 1993). Overall, the model has been judged effective as a way to (1) prepare teachers to observe the abilities of minority and economically disadvantaged students from a proficiency perspective, and (2) facilitate the collection and use of information from multiple sources when making decisions for gifted programs and services. In general, students identified using this procedure equaled the performance of students identified by more traditional methods. The most prevalent finding was that teachers were enabled to take a more holistic view of students and were able to view them from a more positive stance. The greatest barrier to be overcome is reducing the perception that an inordinate amount of time is needed to complete a comprehensive evaluation. There are also barriers that still need to be addressed in terms of state and local policies that are not designed to use results from a multiple criteria assessment as the basis for determining gifted program eligibility.

Summary

The format of F-TAP allows for the recording and interpreting of assessment information from multiple sources, for making decisions regarding the need for program services based on the information presented, and for planning comprehensive educational services. It allows for the optimal involvement of a number of individuals who are familiar with a child's functioning in various contexts, at home and at school. It provides a sound way to use information from objective and subjective sources when making professional recommendations for services. Most important for this discussion, the F-TAP facilitates the reframing of the problems in identifying gifted minority students by placing the emphasis on what a student can do that suggests a need for gifted program services. Finally, it addresses concerns that minority students are too frequently viewed from a problem-oriented perspective, and allows a way for these students to be given equal consideration for educational services that are appropriate for their talent development.

Conclusions

The purpose of this chapter was to explore issues from research and practice that offer insights into reframing problems associated with identifying gifted minority students. Several issues were discussed. One was concerned with the persistence of a problem orientation when addressing the underrepresentation of minority students in gifted programs. It was concluded that solutions developed around a problem orientation have hindered progress in effectively resolving identification and education issues.

Some issues were concerned with changes that needed to be made in the traditional assessment process. It is contended that minority students do not fare well in the assessment process because cultural indicators of giftedness that are unique to them are not a central part of the unidimensional view of giftedness that prevails in American society (Bernal, 1980; Ford & Harris, 1990; Hilliard, 1991; Ruiz, 1989; Tonemah, 1987; Zappia, 1989).

Other issues were concerned with the impact of using a unidimensional view of giftedness to define gifted potential in diverse groups: Who sets standards? How do we integrate cultural indicators of giftedness into an assessment system? What are applicable alternatives to standardized tests? Also, while terms like *disadvantaged* may be very important in describing conditions of children that may impact their education, such terms are misleading when they are used to designate groups of people.

Other assessment issues were less concerned with test bias against minority students and more concerned with the limitations of a single test score as the central measure of student ability. This concern with test score limitations extends to all students, regardless of their culture, gender, language, or economic status. One argument is that reliance on a test score for identifying gifted students provides little substantive information on which to base instructional interventions. In this regard, Raven (1992) specifically urges educators to refocus assessment activities to better emphasize the current goals of education—evaluating activities that lead people to observe, to think, to find better ways of thinking about things, and to communicate effectively. He also reminds us that while the expressed qualities of a competent individual may look different in different contexts, the essences of the qualities that symbolize competence are the same.

Berlak's (1992) argument for a new assessment paradigm is echoed in the writings of several gifted educators (Gardner, 1993; Renzulli, 1988; Treffinger, 1991). However, Berlak feels that an adequate system of educational assessment would consider a plurality of perspectives and differences in values and beliefs as givens. Differences would become assets, not obstructions to be overcome.

Based on the discussion in this chapter, the following suggestions may be important in formulating more adequate research on and practice with minority gifted students:

1. Hypotheses and practices developed to investigate giftedness in minority groups should establish the "why" of gifted education from the minority group's perspective.

For example, traditional reasons for identifying gifted students focus on their differentiated instructional needs and the benefits that accrue to our future as a society if their talents are fully developed. Traditional reasons for identifying gifted minority students tend to focus on improving their representation in gifted programs and on halting the loss of talent in their groups. Tonemah (1987) argued that the need to identify American Indian students must first be determined. The reasons for this need should be based on the collaborative values that parents, the tribal community, and the schools place on identifying students as gifted. Several writers suggest that identifying gifted students in different minority groups empowers these students to take charge of their own destiny and that of their group within the context of the larger society (Grant, 1989; Hilliard, 1991, 1994; Zappia, 1989). The importance of establishing these reasons at the outset is that they force the researcher or practitioner to consider giftedness from a multigroup perspective.

2. Practical activities and research designs that focus on gifted minority students should address differences according to the achievement-oriented and socialization strategies that are actually used within the group. Research and practice should not be based solely on status-type characteristics and strategies like income level, parent education, family configurations, and facility in the English language as the primary way to describe students. Clark (1983) contends that essential information about the character of a family is missed when "Social scientists and educators . . . use the surface characteristics of family composition and status to explain outcomes in children's school behavior" (p. 3). Others contend that within-group differences may be attributed to such things as degree of acculturation or assimilation or length of residence in the United States.

It is also important to factor into research and practice an understanding of where students are in their ethnic identity. Both Banks (1993b) and Cross (1991) have developed identity development stages that are important in understanding minority student's school performance.

A Closing Thought

One of the most important decisions we make as educators has to do with our recommendations regarding children's assignments to certain levels and types of services. It should always be the goal that these decisions are based on the best information that can be generated from research and practice, and are based on the best and most comprehensive information that can be gathered about children.

REFERENCES

Baldwin, A. Y. (1994). The seven plus story: Developing hidden talent among students in socioeconomically disadvantaged environments. *Gifted Child Quarterly, 38,* 80–84.

Banks, J. A. (1993a). Multicultural education: Historical development, dimensions, and practice. In L. Darling-Hammond (Ed.), *Review of research in education* (pp. 3–49). Washington, DC: American Educational Research Association.

Banks, J. A. (1993b). Multicultural education: Characteristics and goals. In J. A. Banks & C. A. Banks (Eds.), *Multicultural education: Issues and perspectives* (pp. 3–28). Boston: Allyn and Bacon.

Barbour, N. B. (1992). Early childhood gifted education: A collaborative perspective. *Journal for the Education of the Gifted, 15*(2), 145–162.

Berlak, H. (1992). The need for a new science of assessment. In H. Berlak, F. M. Newmann, E. Adams, D. A. Archbald, T. Burgess, J. Raven, & T. A. Romberg (Eds.), *Toward a new science of educational testing and assessment* (pp. 1–23). Albany: State University of New York Press.

Bermúdez, A. B., & Rakow, S. J. (1990). Analyzing teachers' perceptions of identification procedures for gifted and talented Hispanic limited English proficient students at-risk. *Journal of Educational Issues of Language Minority Students, 7,* 21–33.

Bernal, E. M. (1980). *Methods of identifying gifted minority students* (ERIC Report 72 ed.). Princeton, NJ: Educational Testing Service.

Borland, J. H. (1986). IQ tests: "Throwing out the bathwater, saving the baby." *Roeper Review, 8,* 163–167.

Borland, J. H., & Wright, L. (1994). Identifying young, potentially gifted economically disadvantaged students. *Gifted Child Quarterly, 38,* 164–171.

Boykin, A. D., & Toms, F. D. (1985). Black child socialization. In H. P. McAdoo & J. L. McAdoo (Eds.), *Black children: Social, educational, and parental environments* (pp. 33–51). Newbury, CA: Sage.

Chaplin, J. P. (1985). *Dictionary of psychology* (2nd ed.). New York: Laurel.

Clark, R. (1983). *Family life and school achievement: Why poor Black children succeed and fail.* Chicago: University of Chicago Press.

Clasen, D. R. (1994). Project STREAM: Support, training and resources for educating able minorities. In C. M. Callahan, C. A. Tomlinson, & P. M. Pizzat (Eds.), *Contexts for promise: Noteworthy practices and innovations in the identification of gifted students* (pp. 1–21). Charlottesville, VA: University of Virginia, Curry School of Education.

Colangelo, N. (1985). Counseling needs of culturally diverse gifted students. *Roeper Review, 8,* 33–35.

Cowan, R. S., & Gollmar, S. M. (1994). *Breaking traditional barriers: A new paradigm for gifted programs* (Interim Report No. 1). Lawrenceville, GA: Gwinnett County Public Schools.

Cross, W. E., Jr. (1991). *Shades of black: Diversity in African-American identity.* Philadelphia: Temple University Press.

Culross, R. (1989). Measurement issues in the screening and selection of the gifted. *Roeper Review, 12,* 76–78.

Dabney, M. G. (1988). An alternative model for identification of potentially gifted students: A case study. In R. L. Jones (Ed.), *Psychoeducational assessment of minority group children: A casebook* (pp. 273–304). Berkeley, CA: Cobb & Henry.

Dusek, J. B., & Joseph, G. (1983). The bases of teacher expectancies: A meta-analysis. *Journal of Educational Psychology, 75,* 327–346.

Feldhusen, J. F., Baska, L. K., & Womble, S. R. (1981). Using standard scores to synthesize data in identifying the gifted. *Journal for the Education of the Gifted, 4,* 177–185.

Ford, D. Y., & Harris, J. J. (1990). On discovering the hidden treasure of gifted and talented African-American children. *Roeper Review, 13,* 27–32.

Foster, A. H., Gallagher, J., & Coleman, M. R. (1993). *Suggested state guidelines for the education of gifted and talented children: Subsection 2—Non-discrimination policy* (Interim Report). Gifted Education Policy Studies Program at the University of North Carolina at Chapel Hill.

Frasier, M. M. (1991a). Eliminating four barriers to the identification of gifted minority students. In E. L. Hiatt (Ed.), *Update on gifted education: Identifying and serving diverse populations* (pp. 2–10). Austin: Texas Education Agency.

Frasier, M. M. (1991b). *Instruction manual: Using the Frasier Talent Assessment Profile (F-TAP).* Athens: The University of Georgia.

Frasier, M. M. (1993a). Eliminating the four persisting barriers to identify gifted minority students. *Gifted International, 7*(2), 60–65.

Frasier, M. M. (1993b). *Applying multiple criteria in the identification of gifted students in Georgia: Pilot project and performance study* (Report No. 1). Athens: University of Georgia, National Research Center on the Gifted and Talented.

Frasier, M. M. (1994). *A manual for implementing the Frasier Talent Assessment Profile (F-TAP): A multiple criteria model for the identification and education of gifted students.* Athens: Georgia Southern Press.

Frasier, M. M., Garcia, J. H., & Passow, A. H. (1994) *A review of assessment issues in gifted education and their implications for identifying gifted minority students.* State of the Art Paper, Athens: University of Georgia, National Research Center on the Gifted and Talented.

Frasier, M. M., Hunsaker, S. L., Frank, E., Finley, V., & Lee, J. (1994). *An exploratory study of the effectiveness of the Staff Development Model (SDM) and the Research-Based Assessment Plan (RAP) in improving the identification of gifted economically disadvantaged students.* Technical Report, Athens: University of Georgia.

Gallagher, J. J. (1994a). Current and historical thinking on education for gifted and talented students. In P. O'Connell-Ross (Ed.), *National excellence: A case for developing America's talent, An anthology of readings* (pp. 83–107). Washington, DC: U.S. Department of Education, Office of Educational Research and Improvement.

Gallagher, J. J. (1994b). A retrospective view: The Javits program. *Gifted Child Quarterly, 38,* 95–96.

Gallagher, J., & Coleman, M. R. (1992). *State policies on the identification of gifted students from special populations: Three states in profile* (Final Report). Gifted Education Policy Studies Program at the University of North Carolina, Chapel Hill.

García, G. E., & Pearson, P. D. (1994). Assessment and diversity. In L. Darling-Hammond (Ed.), *Review of research in education* (pp. 337–391). Washington, DC: American Educational Research Association.

Gardner, H. (1983). *Frames of mind: The theory of multiple intelligences.* New York: Basic Books.

Gardner, H. (1993). *Multiple intelligences: The theory in practice.* New York: Basic Books.

Goodlad, J. (1994). Why our schools don't get much better—and how they might. *Journal for the Education of the Gifted, 17*(4), 421–439.

Gordon, E. W. (1993). Human diversity, equity, and educational assessment. *CRESST Assessment Conference,* University of California at Los Angeles.

Grant, C. A. (1989). Black students and education: Points for consideration. In C. J. Maker & S. W. Schiever (Eds.), *Critical issues in gifted education: Defensible programs for cultural and ethnic minorities* (pp. 275–284). Austin, TX: Pro-Ed.

Hale-Benson, J. (1982). *Black children: Their roots, culture, and learning styles* (rev. ed.) Baltimore: Johns Hopkins University Press.

Harrison, A. O. (1985). The black family's socializing environment: Self-esteem and ethnic attitude among black children. In H. P. McAdoo & J. L. McAdoo (Eds.), *Black children: Social, educational, and parental environments* (pp. 174–193). Newbury Park, CA: Sage.

Hilliard, A. G. (1991). The ideology of intelligence and IQ magic in education. In A. G. Hilliard (Ed.), *Testing African American students: Special re-issue of the Negro Educational Review* (pp. 136–145). Morristown, NJ: Aaron Press.

Hilliard, A. G. (1994). How diversity matters. *Kappa Delta Pi Record, 30*(3), 114.

Hoge, R. D. (1988). Issues in the definition and measurement of the giftedness construct. *Educational Researcher, 17*(7), 12–16, 22.

Hoge, R. D. (1989). An examination of the giftedness construct. *Canadian Journal of Education, 14*(1), 6–17.

Hoge, R. D., & Cudmore, L. (1986). The use of teacher-judgment measures in the identification of gifted pupils. *Teacher and Teacher Education, 2*(2), 181–196.

Hoy, C., & Gregg, N. (1994). *Assessment: The special educator's role.* Pacific Grove, CA: Brooks/Cole.

Howe, K. R. (1994). Standards, assessment, and equality of educational opportunity. *Educational Researcher, 23*(8), 27–32.

Hunsaker, S. L., Frasier, M. M., Finley, V., Frank, E., Martin, D., Garcia, J., & King, L. (1994). *A report on the National Field Test of the Staff Development (SDM) and the Research-Based Assessment Plan (RAP)* (Report No. 1). Athens: University of Georgia, National Research Center on the Gifted and Talented.

Hunsaker, S. L., Frasier, M. M., Frank, E., Finley, V., & Klekotka, P. (1994). *Program performance of economically disadvantaged students placed in gifted programs through the research-based assessment plan: Technical report of the pilot project in its second year* (Technical Report No. 1). Athens: University of Georgia, National Research Center on the Gifted and Talented.

Jenkins, L. E. (1989). The black family and academic achievement. In G. L. Berry & J. K. Asamen (Eds.), *Black students: Psychosocial issues and academic achievement* (pp. 138–152). Newbury Park, CA: Corwin Press.

Jacob K. Javits Gifted and Talented Students Education Act (1988). P.L. 100–297, Title IV, Part B, Sec. 110l.

Jones, R. L. (Ed.). (1988). *Psychoeducational assessment of minority group children: A casebook.* Berkeley, CA: Cobb & Henry.

Kirschenbaum, R. J. (1989). Identification of the gifted and talented American Indian student. In C. J. Maker & S. W. Schiever (Eds.), *Critical issues in gifted education: Defensible programs for cultural and ethnic minorities* (pp. 91–101). Austin, TX: ProEd.

Kitano, M. K., & Kirby, D. F. (1986). *Gifted education: A comprehensive view.* Boston: Little, Brown.

Leung, E. K. (1981). The identification and social problem of the gifted bilingual-bicultural children. In The *Council for Exceptional Children*

Conference on the Exceptional Bilingual Child (pp. 1–24). New Orleans, Louisiana.

Machado, M. (1987). Gifted Hispanics underidentified in classrooms. *Hispanic Link Weekly, 5*(7), 1.

Maker, C. J. (1983). Quality education for gifted minority students. *Journal for the Education of the Gifted, 6*(3), 140–153.

Maker, C. J. (1989). Programs for gifted minority students: A synthesis of perspectives. In C. J. Maker & S. W. Schiever (Eds.), *Critical issues in gifted education: Defensible programs for cultural and ethnic minorities* (pp. 293–309). Austin, TX: Pro-Ed.

Maker, C. J., & Schiever, S. W. (Eds.). (1989). *Critical issues in gifted education: Defensible programs for cultural and ethnic minorities.* Austin, TX: Pro-Ed.

Marland, S. P., Jr. (1972). *Education of the gifted and talented* (Report to the Congress of the United States by the U. S. Commissioner of Education). Washington, DC: U.S. Government Printing Office.

McCarty, T. L., Lynch, R. H., Wallace, S., & Benally, A. (1991). Classroom inquiry and Navajo learning styles: A call for reassessment. *Anthropology & Education Quarterly, 22,* 42–59.

Montgomery, D. (1989). Identification of giftedness among American Indian people. In C. J. Maker & S. W. Schiever (Eds.), *Critical issues in gifted education: Defensible programs for cultural and ethnic minorities* (pp. 79-90). Austin, TX: Pro-Ed.

National Center for Education Statistics. (1988). *Education indicators.* Washington, DC: U.S. Department of Education, Office of Educational Research and Improvement.

Natriello, G., McDill, E. L., & Pallas, A. M. (1990). *Schooling disadvantaged children: Racing against catastrophe.* New York: Teachers College Press.

Newmann, F. M., & Archbald, D. A. (1992). The nature of authentic assessment. In H. Berlak, F. M. Newmann, E. Adams, D. A. Archbald, T. Burgess, J. Raven, & T. A. Romberg (Eds.), *Toward a new science of educational testing and assessment* (pp. 71–83). Albany: State University of New York Press.

Ogbu, J. U. (1978). *Minority education and caste: The American system in cross-cultural perspective.* New York: Academic Press.

Ogbu, J. U. (1994). Understanding cultural diversity and learning. *Journal for the Education of the Gifted, 17*(4), 355–383.

O'Tuel, F. S. (1994). APOGEE: Equity in the identification of gifted and talented students. *Gifted Child Quarterly, 38,* 75–79.

Passow, A. H. (1982). The gifted disadvantaged: Some reflections. In *Fifth National Conference on Disadvantaged Gifted/Talented* (pp. 19–27). Ventura, CA: Ventura County Superintendent of Schools Office.

Passow, A. H., & Rudnitski, R. A. (1993). *State policies regarding education of the gifted as reflected in legislation and regulation* (Collaborative Research Study No. CRS93302). University of Connecticut, Storrs, CT.

Patton, J. (1992). Assessment and identification of African-American learners with gifts and talents. *Exceptional Children, 59*(2), 150–159.

Pellegrino, J. W. (1988). Intelligence: The interaction of culture and cognitive processes. In R. J. Sternberg & D. K. Detterman (Eds.), *What is intelligence? Contemporary viewpoints on its nature and definition* (pp. 113–116). Norwood, NJ: Ablex.

Perrine, J. (1989). Situational identification of gifted Hispanic students. In C. J. Maker & S. W. Schiever (Eds.), *Critical issues in gifted education: Defensible programs for cultural and ethnic minorities* (pp. 5–18). Austin, TX: Pro-Ed.

Raven, J. (1992). A model of competence, motivation, and behavior, and a paradigm for assessment. In H. Berlak, F. M. Newmann, E. Adams, D. A. Archbald, T. Burgess, J. Raven, & T. A. Romberg (Eds.), *Toward a new science of educational testing and assessment* (pp. 85–116). Albany, NY: State University of New York Press.

Renzulli, J. S. (1978). "What makes giftedness?" Reexamining a definition. *Phi Delta Kappan, 60,* 180–184, 261.

Renzulli, J. S. (1988). The three-ring conception of giftedness: A developmental model for creative productivity. In R. J. Sternberg & J. E. Davidson (Eds.), *Conceptions of giftedness* (pp. 53–92). New York: Cambridge University Press.

Reynolds, C. R., & Kaiser, S. M. (1990). Bias in assessment of aptitude. In C. R. Reynolds & R. W. Kamphaus (Eds.), *Handbook of psychological and educational assessment of children: Intelligence and achievement* (pp. 611–653). New York: Guilford Press.

Ross, P. O. (1994). Introduction to descriptions of Javits grant projects. *Gifted Child Quarterly, 38,* 64.

Ruiz, R. (1989). Considerations in the education of gifted Hispanic students. In C. J. Maker & S. W. Schiever (Eds.), *Critical issues in gifted education: Defensible programs for cultural and ethnic minorities* (pp. 60–65). Austin, TX: Pro-Ed.

Sax, G. (1980). *Principles of educational and psychological measurement and evaluation* (2nd ed.). Belmont, CA: Wadsworth.

Schmeichel, J. (1994). *Comparing F-TAP to tradi-*

tional identification in terms of student progress (Evaluation Report No. 1). Kalamazoo, MI: Kalamazoo Public Schools.

Scott, M. S., Perou, R., Urbano, R., Hogan, A., & Gold, S. (1992). The identification of giftedness: A comparison of white, Hispanic, and black families. *Gifted Child Quarterly, 36,* 131–139.

Shaklee, B. D. (1992). Identification of young gifted students. *Journal for the Education of the Gifted, 15*(2), 134–144.

Shore, B. M., Cornell, D. G., Robinson, A., & Ward, V. S. (1991). *Recommended practices in gifted education: A critical analysis.* New York: Teachers College Press.

Sternberg, R. J. (1981). A componential theory of intellectual giftedness. *Gifted Child Quarterly, 25,* 86–93.

Sternberg, R. J. (1982). Lies we live by: Misapplication of tests in identifying the gifted. *Gifted Child Quarterly, 26,* 157–161.

Sternberg, R. J. (1988). A triarchic theory of intellectual giftedness. In R. J. Sternberg & J. E. Davidson (Eds.), *Conceptions of giftedness* (pp. 223–243). New York: Cambridge University Press.

Tonemah, S. (1987). Assessing American Indian gifted and talented students' abilities. *Journal for the Education of the Gifted, 10,* 181–194.

Treffinger, D. J. (1991). Future goals and directions. In N. Colangelo & G. A. Davis (Eds.), *Handbook of gifted education* (pp. 441–449). Boston: Allyn and Bacon.

Wiggins, G. (1989). A true test: Toward more authentic and equitable assessment. *Phi Delta Kappan, 70,* 703–713.

Wood, S. B., & Achey, V. H. (1990). Successful identification of gifted racial/ethnic group students without changing classification requirements. *Roeper Review, 13,* 21–26.

Zappia, I. A. (1989). Identification of gifted Hispanic students: A multidimensional view. In C. J. Maker & S. W. Schiever (Eds.), *Critical issues in gifted education: Defensible programs for cultural and ethnic minorities* (pp. 19–26). Austin, TX: Pro-Ed.

40

Providing Services to Children with Gifts and Disabilities: A Critical Need

LAWRENCE J. JOHNSON, *Arlitt Child and Family Research and Development Center, University of Cincinnati*
MERLE B. KARNES, *University of Illinois*
VICTORIA W. CARR, *University of Cincinnati*

History tells us that persons with both gifts and disabilities, given the opportunity to develop their potentials, can make a significant impact on society. Consider, for example, the contributions of Ludwig van Beethoven, Franklin D. Roosevelt, Helen Keller, Vincent van Gogh, Albert Einstein, and Thomas Edison. Unfortunately, attention to the gifts of persons with disabilities has been sorely neglected in society today. In fact, many stakeholders interested in identifying and nurturing the talents of individuals with gifts and disabilities have encountered considerable resistance among educators and representatives of funding agencies. All too often we hear such remarks as, "Yes, there have been and are gifted among the disabled, but why should we be concerned about these individuals; if they are truly gifted, their giftedness will emerge." We have no idea of the number of individuals with disabilities who have gifts that are never maximized because we fail to recognize, support, and nourish their potential.

Data regarding the number of gifted individuals with disabilities are sketchy, at best. Whitmore (1981) estimated that the number of gifted disabled might be as high as 540,000. Mauser (1980) found that 2.3 percent of the children with learning disabilities he tested in Illinois were gifted. Whitmore and Maker (1985) claimed that there were no accurate statistics on the incidence of giftedness among individuals with disabilities, but estimated conservatively that at least 2 percent of children with disabilities are intellectually gifted. Additionally, as Humphrey (1990) noted, up to 70 percent of *typical* children with gifts are overlooked when screened for programs by group-administered tests. One can only imagine the number of children with disabilities and special gifts who do not qualify for services by this identification procedure, which is too often the only one used for identification. If we believe that there are as many young people with disabilities who are gifted as in any other segment of the population, then we are vastly underserving these individuals.

Failure to identify and nurture giftedness among the disabled is unfair to them and to society. Our educational system assumes that all individuals must be given an opportunity to maximize their potential. Moreover, failing to actualize one's potential creates a breeding ground for frustration and poor mental health. Finally, as a society, we need all the gifts that can be made available. Failure to identify and serve children with gifts and disabilities is an indictment against our society and a problem we should not tolerate. As Whitmore and Maker (1985) aptly stated:

> It is obvious that appropriate educational programming for these children could release a very significant amount of creative productivity of great value to society and would also reduce the possibility of economic dependence in adult years, as is often the case when suitable employment cannot be obtained.

Gallagher (1988) discussed the leadership role the federal government should take in gifted education. He named children with gifts and disabilities as one target group that should receive top priority. However, in reviewing the literature to determine the status of education of children with gifts and disabilities, we are struck by how little has been or is being done for these individuals. Very little research has been conducted on the effectiveness of interventions with this population of children.

The purpose of this chapter is twofold: first, to emphasize that there are unserved or underserved children with gifts and disabilities, and, second, to foster a commitment to address this unmet need. To achieve these purposes, this chapter is divided into the following sections: (1) a historical overview of what has been done for individuals with gifts and disabilities, (2) barriers that have hindered identification and programming for these children, (3) provision of services for children with gifts and disabilities, and (4) implications of research and experience for educating children with gifts and disabilities.

Historical Overview

In the 1950s, for a short time following the launching of the Soviet Union's Sputnik, we became more interested in children with gifts. During this period special emphasis was placed on challenging the gifted, particularly in math and science. Mass screening to identify giftedness made use of achievement tests, teacher referrals, and, most often, intelligence test scores. Special programs were developed, many of which included segregated classes for the gifted.

In the 1960s concern shifted to culturally disadvantaged and minority children. The Head Start program was initiated in the summer of 1965 as a summer program and shortly thereafter was expanded to a full-year program. In the mid-1970s Head Start was mandated to serve children with disabilities. Although Head Start had a significant impact, its focus has never been on giftedness, and especially not on children with disabilities and gifts.

In 1971 Congress requested that the Commissioner of Education, Sydney P. Marland, Jr., determine the status of gifted education. The Marland report (1972) revealed that fewer than 4 percent of all gifted children were receiving special programming. Children with gifts and disabilities received virtually no attention at all.

The first book devoted entirely to young persons with gifts and disabilities, entitled *Providing Programs for the Gifted Handicapped,* was written by Maker (1977). This book includes descriptions of the work by Sanford and Karnes, who in 1975 received funds from the Bureau of Education for the Handicapped[1] for the development and demonstration of models for educating young children who were disabled and gifted. Sanford used a conceptual model derived from Bloom's taxonomy (Bloom, Englehart, Furst, Hill, & Krathwohl, 1956), and Karnes used a model derived from Guilford's (1967) structure of the intellect. Both programs were successful in identifying and providing services for children with both disabilities and gifts.

Of all subcategories of gifted disabled, children with gifts and learning disabilities have received the most attention. Books about gifted children with learning disabilities include *Learning Disabled Gifted Children* (Fox, Brady, & Fabin, 1983), *Teaching the Gifted/Learning Disabled Child* (Daniels, 1983), and *Helping Learning-Disabled Gifted Children Learn through Compensatory Active Play* (Humphrey, 1990). These books deal in depth with such important issues as characteristics, identification, programming, the role of the counselor, and compensatory experiences.

Whitmore and Maker published *Intellectual Giftedness in Disabled Persons* in 1985. These authors cited Mary Meeker, Merle Karnes, and Anne Sanford as the first educators to concentrate on this population. The book is a valuable resource, with case studies of individuals who are gifted and hearing-impaired, visually impaired, physically challenged, and/or learning-disabled. The needs of these children are delineated, along with identification procedures and discussions of the interactions between giftedness and their spe-

---

[1] Now the Office of Special Education Programs (OSEP).

cial needs. The authors emphasize that each child with gifts and disabilities is unique. Their guidelines for identifying and educating gifted children with disabilities are cited in sections of other books, such as *Guiding the Social and Emotional Development of Gifted Youth* (Delisle, 1992).

The Association for the Gifted, a division of the Council for Exceptional Children, established a national committee of educators of the gifted disabled. Subsequent to their meetings in 1976 and 1977, the Educational Resource Information Center (ERIC) created a category of *gifted handicapped,* but numbers of citations continue to be low.

The mainstreaming movement was brought about by Public Law 94-142, the 1977 Education for All Handicapped Children Act. Amended in 1990 and renamed the Individuals with Disabilities Education Act, Public Law 101-476, it still requires that children with disabilities have the right to a free, appropriate education in the least restrictive environment. The damaging effects of labeling and segregating children with disabilities had become a grave concern of professionals as well as parents (Hobbs, 1975). The orientation is away from a deficit model, emphasizing the disability, to a model that emphasizes the strengths of children with challenging conditions. The emphasis on what the child *can* do should increase the number of children with disabilities who are referred for gifted services.

Today, many states not only are broadening their definitions of giftedness to include exceptional abilities in areas other than general intellectual abilities and generic talents, they are searching for the gifted disabled as well. For example, the Kentucky Administrative Regulation for Programs for the Gifted in 1994 mandated that school personnel must take into consideration disabling conditions that may mask a child's true abilities.

Barriers Hindering Identification and Programming

Although regulations can provide the foundation for serving children with diverse abilities and disabilities, barriers to identification and programming for these children still remain. These barriers include the following: (1) inappropriate identification procedures that are receptive to the masking impact of disabilities; (2) stereotypic attitudes about what children with special gifts are like; (3) lack of information on the nature and impact of developmental delays associated with disabilities; (4) inadequate training of professionals; (5) lack of program models, research, and dissemination strategies; (6) lack of supportive technology; (7) lack of appropriate career counseling; and (8) inadequate funding. Each of these barriers will be described.

Inappropriate Identification Procedures

One barrier to identification of many gifted children with disabilities is the expectation that these children will demonstrate the same characteristics of giftedness as children without disabilities who are identified as gifted. It should be recognized that disabilities may obscure or suppress their gifts.

Instruments used in the identification of nondisabled gifted children may be inappropriate for use with children who are gifted with disabilities. It is the *use* of these instruments that is the important consideration. Adaptations must be made for some children with disabilities. For example, when identifying the gifted among children with disabilities, these children must be compared with each other, not with children without disabilities.

The procedure of identifying the gifts of children with disabilities on a one-time basis is faulty. Some children with disabilities have not had the opportunity to fully develop their potential. If they are given the opportunity, marked progress may occur. Adults must constantly watch for emerging gifts; identification of gifts must be an ongoing process.

Stereotypic Attitudes

Whitmore and Maker (1985) pointed out that expectations of typical children with special gifts may impede the identification of special gifts in children with disabilities. For example, gifted children may be expected to "look bright," but some physically challenged children who are very bright may look dull. This perception can even lead to an assumption of mental retardation. The child with hearing impairments whose language is absent or difficult to understand also may be labeled "mentally disabled" because, stereotypically, we expect a gifted child to have advanced language skills.

Additionally, some children with disabilities are not physically able to investigate their environments in the same way or to the same extent as typical children. Some classroom environments, especially early childhood settings, are geared to facilitate and expand on a child's tendency to explore. In these environments, children who actively explore gain a richer experience that is more likely to nurture and develop talents. For children with disabilities, these environments create an uneven playing field, which narrows their opportunities and further inhibits their gifts and talents (Johnson & Carr, in press). As Whitmore and Maker (1985) explain, "The most important needs that can be met by both educators and families are high expectations for success and an environment that facilitates achievement" (p. 59). Expectations must be within the capabilities of the child, of course. If a teacher or parent expects very little from a child, the child will produce very little. On the other hand, showing confidence in the child's ability to produce and supporting his or her efforts will bring positive results.

Lack of Information on the Nature and Impact of Developmental Delays

Gaps in information regarding the nature and impact of developmental delays associated with disabilities are a serious barrier to identifying the gifted among children with disabilities. It is risky to make a hasty diagnosis of a child when he or she is lagging behind in certain facets of development. For example, a child with a motor delay who has artistic gifts and talents will be delayed in presenting these talents because of the masking impact of the motor delay. In many instances the gifts of a child with a disability may be slow to appear, but with encouragement, support, and individually appropriate programming, they will emerge.

A source of hope for overcoming this barrier comes from activities that have resulted from the passage of Public Law 101-476, the Individuals with Disabilities Education Act (IDEA). This law mandates services to children with disabilities down to age 3 and provides incentives for states to provide services at birth. IDEA safeguards decisions about children with disabilities. For example, it requires a multidisciplinary team, including the parents, that shares information essential for diagnosis, educational placement, and programming. When this information is sparse, decisions regarding the child's potential and program needs may be inaccurate and result in inappropriate programming. For example, Lind (1993) and Webb and Latimer (1993) cited examples of gifted children who were referred for medical evaluations for suspected attention deficit disorders because the intensity of these children often confuses teachers and parents who misinterpret signs of giftedness. Thorough information gathering and collaborative decision making helps ensure appropriate programming and realization of a child's potential.

Inadequate Training of Professionals

Related to these three barriers, many persons working in the field are poorly equipped to identify and educate children with gifts and disabilities. Special educators trained to teach children with disabilities may have little knowledge about characteristics of gifted children or how to program for them. Their main orientation is to identify deficits. On the other hand, professionals in gifted education have little knowledge about disabilities or the effects of disabilities on learning. Finally, most mainstream educators have had little or no formal training that addresses either disabilities or giftedness.

Collaboration among all stakeholders, including parents and university faculty, will ultimately broaden our understanding of children with special needs. Collaborative efforts at various levels, such as student–adult, educators–administrators, and educators–service/resource providers, will provide a more accurate perspective on student needs and facilitate the development of individually appropriate programs (Pugach & Johnson, 1995; VanTassel-Baska, 1992). Through collaboration, the boundaries that now separate these groups will become less distinct, allowing us to combine expertise and resources to better address the needs of children with gifts and disabilities.

We must take serious steps to help professionals become better able to address the needs of children with gifts and disabilities. Inservice training is one way. Such training also aids communication among members of a child's multidisciplinary team. Preservice training is another avenue. Special educators should be required to take course work in gifted education; professionals in the gifted area should take course work addressing disability issues; and regular educators need to be familiar with both fields so that they can effectively accommodate the needs of children with disabilities and special gifts in inclusionary settings.

Lack of Program Models, Research, and Dissemination Strategies

Relatively few program models have been developed and tested. Likewise, we have a dearth of research findings to endorse or refute the interventions that have been developed and disseminated. When there are no models or research to guide practice, educators must rely on "gut feelings" and common sense. As Maker, Redden, Tonelson, and Howell (1978) noted, with few exceptions most research has been conducted with adults who are gifted and disabled, leaving a void of information regarding young children. Although they made this observation almost two decades ago, little has changed and many critical questions remain unanswered.

Not only is there a dearth of information to guide those attempting to provide services, but methods of disseminating information are lacking. The standard practice includes journals, texts, and conferences. These have been criticized as inefficient and not receptive to the needs and resources of service providers. Information published in written form may be three years old by the time it is published, which makes it potentially outdated. Although information presented at conferences tends to be more current, the number of teachers who are able to attend these conferences is extremely small.

As a field, we have been disseminating information in the same ways for decades. Clearly, it is time to use current and new forms of technology to develop innovative and timely ways to disseminate information. The best practices in working with individuals with gifts and disabilities should be more readily available to those who need the information most—the professionals working directly with these children and their parents.

Lack of Supportive Technology

Lack of funds for the needed equipment and materials for instruction is another barrier. To meet the special needs of the gifted disabled, a budget must be earmarked for the purchase of equipment and curricular resources. Whitmore and Maker (1985) wrote that "adaptive use of computers perhaps is the most promising single aid to improving instruction of disabled children" (p. 23). Today, the use of assistive technology, particularly as communication aids, enhances the lives of many individuals with disabilities.

Technology also is being used to assess children within the classroom environment and to develop individual education plans for children with special needs. The October–November 1994 special issue of *Exceptional Children* addressed technology-based assessment by reporting efforts to improve the quality of theories, methods, and technological innovations (Greenwood, 1994). Clearly there are opportunities for greater use of technology-based assessment and instruction in gifted education that will revolutionalize practice. Before this potential can be actualized, however, we must expand the availability of high-quality instrument software and provide adequate training to use such technology (Greenwood, Carta, Kamps, Terry, & Delquadri, 1994).

Lack of Appropriate Career Counseling

Historical cases of individuals with gifts and disabilities indicate that school systems did very little to promote the development of these children's abilities or to provide them with the kind of counseling they needed (Whitmore & Maker, 1985). Karnes (1984b) stated that if children with gifts and disabilities did develop their gifts or talents, "it was almost in spite of the educational program, not because of it" (p. 18). Customarily, individuals with disabilities were counseled into vocational training rather than advanced education and professional careers.

Instead of limiting the horizons of gifted children with disabilities, counselors and teachers should help them acquire the knowledge and skills they need to actualize their full potentials. These children need to develop realistic, healthy self-concepts and self-esteem; become as independent as possible; and have well-rounded lives that include hobbies, interests, and participation in activities. They need opportunities to explore different careers, to know their strengths and special abilities, and to match career goals with interests and capabilities. Hishinuma (1993) outlined a program for counseling youngsters with gifts and disabilities that emphasized individual and group counseling. Unfortunately, as a general rule, teachers and counselors are ill prepared to provide career counseling for children with disabilities and gifts.

Inadequate Funding

Perhaps the most serious barrier and the most difficult to solve is the inadequate funding of education. Schools are being asked to do more and more with less and less. Our educational system is increasingly serving children from diverse backgrounds, with family structures, cultures, languages, customs, interests, and socioeconomic levels that differentiate them from the majority. The level of preparation for these children and their families varies greatly, posing ever increasing challenges for the system. Further compounding this problem, most teachers are not representative of the ethnic and racial groups or the socioeconomic groups of the children they serve (Johnson & Pugach, in press). In a milieu of diminishing resources, administrators are forced to make hard choices on what to emphasize or ignore. In such an environment, it is easy for an administrator to ignore gifted education in the belief that children with special gifts will succeed despite the system's shortcomings.

We must recognize the complex and critical problems facing our educational system and realize that simple "quick fix" solutions will not be sufficient. Education must be supported at a level at which it is possible to provide adequate staff, who have the instructional materials and equipment necessary to address the diverse needs of children. We cannot afford to nurture the potential of some children while ignoring others. The children we work with today are our future; and to continue an educational system that does not embrace the needs of diverse children and families is destined to restrict that future.

Providing Services to Children with Gifts and Disabilities

It is imperative that we develop services to nurture the potential of children with gifts who also happen to have a disability. Such children are a precious resource that we cannot afford to squander. Identification procedures must consist of multiple measures, including informal observation, to ensure that children with disabilities are recognized and provided with a differentiated curriculum that maximizes learning opportunities. In order to provide needed services, teachers must expand their knowledge of how children's abilities and disabilities affect learning (Hegeman, 1981). They must become proficient in disability-related instruction and technology, adaptive curricular strategies, communication, and collaborative teaming. Without positive teacher attitudes and highly developed skills, it is unlikely that children with disabilities will receive any special services designed to nurture their gifts. Service provision must also include counseling to assist the student with disabilities in the development of a positive and realistic self-concept. The low self-esteem that often develops around the disability is combined with the often low and unrealistic expectations by others (Maker, 1977). We must recognize the potential for creative productivity to reverse the cycle of underachievement in children with gifts who are exhibiting delinquent behaviors or have learning disabilities (Baum, Renzulli, & Hebert, 1994).

Successful approaches are ones that accentuate a student's strengths and individual interests, as opposed to those that focus on remediating deficits (Baum, et al., 1994; Karnes & Johnson, 1986, 1987a, 1987b, 1987c). Educators can attend to children's strengths by providing opportunities for the development of creative gifts in children within a supportive classroom environment.

Unfortunately, as we noted earlier, there are few models that provide guidance for those wishing to develop programs for students with gifts and disabilities. We will look at some models in the following sections.

Retrieval and Acceleration of Promising Young Handicapped Talented

The earlier we identify potential gifts in children with disabilities and provide them with programming to nurture their abilities, the greater will be their chances for fully actualizing their potential. With this belief as a foundation, in 1974 Merle Karnes at the University of Illinois responded to a call from the Bureau of Education for the Handicapped for proposals to develop and demonstrate a viable model for identifying and programming for preschoolers with gifts and disabilities. Her model, entitled Retrieval and Acceleration of Promising Young Handicapped Talented (RAPYHT), has been replicated in over 20 states.

The RAPYHT project was originally developed to train teachers and parents to identify and program for gifted and talented preschoolers with mild to moderate disabilities (Karnes, 1978, 1979, 1984a, 1984b; Karnes & Bertschi, 1978; Karnes & Johnson, 1986, 1987b; Karnes, Shwedel, & Lewis, 1983a, 1983b; Karnes, Shwedel, & Linnemeyer, 1982). Experience and research with the model reinforced the belief that it is effective. The RAPYHT model has seven components: (1) general programming, (2) talent identification, (3) talent programming, (4) parent involvement, (5) interagency collaboration, (6) transitional procedures, and (7) evaluation. These components ensure individually appropriate programming.

General programming. This component is based on the assumption that giftedness is not a trait that will emerge irrespective of the environment. A deliberate effort must be made to provide children with disabilities with a program that encourages gifts and talents because of the difficulty with which these traits emerge in these children.

General programming in the RAPYHT model uses materials based on Guilford's (1967) structure-of-intellect model and includes activities to develop convergent, divergent, and evaluative thinking skills. General programming allows children to demonstrate their abilities more fully and encourages strengths or gifts to emerge by stimulating creativity, problem solving, and critical thinking. The activities in this curriculum have proved to be challenging and interesting to both children and teachers.

Talent identification. Children's talents and potential gifts are identified through the use of a Parent Checklist and a Teacher Checklist in the RAPYHT model. Both instruments focus on a child's performance in six areas of giftedness: intellectual, academic (separate subarea scales for reading, math, and science), creativity, leadership, visual and performing arts (art and music), and psychomotor abilities. Scores on the two checklists are summed and tabulated on a Talent Identification Summary. Teachers are encouraged to evaluate children separately, comparing children with disabilities with their peers with disabilities. Decisions regarding potential talent are made collaboratively by teams comprising parents, classroom teachers, and ancillary staff. It is anticipated that 10 to 20 percent of the children in a classroom will be identified as potentially gifted; a "wide net" approach is used to make sure that potentially gifted disabled children are not overlooked.

Talent programming. In-depth talent assessment, which is linked with programming, involves administering a curriculum-based assessment in each talent area. This assessment is based on observation and is conducted with those children identified as potentially gifted by the talent checklists. Results from this assessment are used to develop educational goals and to measure progress. There are many times during the day when children have opportunities to demonstrate their talents. If teachers are trained to observe children carefully and know the indicators of giftedness and talent, they will detect such traits. Teachers trained in the RAPYHT model become very adept at determining, with the help of the assessment instrument, the strengths a child has in a talent area and what should be done to assist the child.

Talent programming begins with an Individual Education Program (IEP) meeting. The multidisciplinary team determines ways to enhance the classroom environment to stimulate talent areas. This might include grouping children by strength (encouraging interaction between children with and without disabilities), enlisting the aid of a mentor, planning field trips, displaying artwork in the classroom, or procuring students' musical recordings. Advice in specific talent areas may be solicited from members of an interagency advisory committee. Talent programming typically begins in the second half of the year.

Parent involvement. Parents are encouraged to become involved in all components of the model. Parents participate in the talent identification process. Workshops are held to help parents acquire the knowledge and skills to promote the child's strengths at home. Booklets suggest activities for parents to enhance problem solving, creative thinking, and other types of higher level thinking. In each of the areas of giftedness, booklets are available to enhance a particular talent. Parents are also invited to become members of the interagency advisory committee and to volunteer in the classroom.

Interagency collaboration. Interagency collaboration is incorporated into the model in two ways. First, an interagency committee, including school staff, RAPYHT staff, and parents of children with and without disabilities, is created. Interagency committee members advise on programming for individual talent areas, adapting activities to meet children's needs, and identifying resources in the community. This group also helps identify consultants for the teachers and mentors for the children.

Transitional procedures. An important but often overlooked concern in gifted education arises when children move from one program to another. The RAPYHT model provides several ways to help the young child with gifts and disabilities to make a smooth transition from preschool to kindergarten. First, an attempt is made to identify the receiving teacher, who is then invited to visit the child in the preschool program. Also, a packet of information about the child is sent to the school that the child will attend. Finally, a meeting is scheduled in the fall among preschool personnel knowledgeable about the child, the principal of the elementary school, and the receiving teacher. The preschool teachers inform receiving teachers that they are available for consultative help if needed.

Evaluation. This includes both process and outcome evaluation. Parent and teacher feedback regarding the value of identifying and programming for each child's strengths is also collected. Over the years a great deal of research has been conducted on the model. The following is a brief summary of some of this research.

Karnes, Shwedel, and Lewis (1983b) evaluated the short-term impact of RAPYHT on 28 preschoolers with disabilities who were identified as having special gifts and talents. Children who had received RAPYHT programming made significant gains in their talent area, self-esteem, task persistence (motivation), and creativity.

In a second study, Karnes, Shwedel, and Lewis (1983a) investigated the long-term impact of RAPYHT programming. Of the 61 children who received RAPYHT programming between 1975 and 1981, 30 were located (a large number were from military families). Of these, 90 percent were in regular classrooms. Standardized achievement tests indicated that they scored at or above the 50th percentile in reading and math at each grade level. In addition, these children were rated by their teachers as above their classmates without disabilities on listening skills, self-assurance, memory, writing, independence, attention span, and willingness to try new activities.

The positive effects of the RAPYHT model on parents and teachers also were very encouraging (Karnes & Johnson, 1986). Parents were assisted in identifying children's strengths, developing a Talent Educational Plan, and participating in talent-based activities. Thus, parents developed skills and confidence in working positively with their children. Regarding teachers, as their perceptions of the children changed, their teaching efforts improved and they interacted with the children more positively. Lastly, the research indicated that if we want children to become more creative and think at higher levels, we must give them opportunities to do so and encourage and reinforce their efforts. Unfortunately, we often sell short children with disabilities by not having appropriately high expectations for them.

Bringing Out Head Start Talents (BOHST)

The RAPYHT approach also has been revised and used with children in Head Start programs. Although all children being served by Head Start programs can be described as "at risk," 10 percent of the population being served must have an identified disability. This variation of the model was entitled Bringing Out Head Start Talents (BOHST) and had components similar to the RAPYHT model. A field test of the BOHST project was conducted with 436 Head Start children, their parents, and their teachers in central Illinois (Karnes & Johnson, 1987a, 1987c). Data from this field test revealed that the model had a positive impact on teachers and all of the children—not just those identified as potentially gifted. The experimental children's creativity and problem-solving skills were significantly better than those of a comparison group. Interestingly, further analysis revealed that the group of children making the most significant gains were those who received general programming but were not identified as potentially gifted, a finding that indicated the importance of promoting creativity and problem-solving skills with all children.

Very Special Arts

Very Special Arts[2] is an international organization that provides opportunities in creative writing, dance, drama, music, and the visual arts for individuals with disabilities. Founded in 1974 by Jean Kennedy Smith, Very Special Arts seeks to promote worldwide awareness of the educational and cultural benefits of the arts and is designated by the United States Congress as the national coordinating agency for arts programming for people with disabilities.

Very Special Arts programs and training sessions are conducted in communities in all 50 states and the District of Columbia. The programs are implemented through a network of local, state, and national organizations. The international network extends to more than 55 countries around the globe. Very Special Arts demonstrates the value of the arts in the lives of all individuals and provides integrated learning opportunities for people with disabilities.

One of Very Special Arts' premiere programs is Start with the Arts, an instructional program that enables educators and parents to create meaningful learning experiences for young children. Designed to be implemented in inclusionary settings, Start with the Arts utilizes the arts in assisting young children with and without disabilities to explore topics commonly taught in early childhood programs. Start with the Arts encourages the use of creative play and provides educators with strategies and activities for integrating chil-

---

[2] John F. Kennedy Center for the Performing Arts, Washington, DC 20566.

dren with special needs into mainstreamed learning situations.

Conclusions and Implications of Research and Experience

The findings of research and experience indicate the following:

1. Contrary to widespread opinion, it is possible to identify indicators of above-average abilities and talents among children with disabilities.
2. Teachers can learn to identify potential gifts of children with disabilities more effectively if they have an instrument to guide them in observing children's behavior in natural settings.
3. Identifying and programming for children with gifts and disabilities are extremely important in terms of how these children perceive themselves.
4. Children with disabilities identified as potentially gifted, after being provided with a special program focusing on their strengths and fostering the development of higher level thinking and talents, are successful in inclusionary settings in the public schools.
5. Implementing a model that emphasizes the strengths or gifts and talents of children with disabilities promotes a more positive attitude among teachers toward these children.
6. In identifying gifts and talents among individuals with disabilities, the most appropriate procedure is to compare one child with disabilities with another in dimensions that are associated with giftedness or talent. To avoid overlooking those with potential, the top 10 to 20 percent of the population of individuals with disabilities should be viewed as potentially gifted.
7. Children identified as gifted disabled and provided an appropriate program at the preschool level retain these gifts and abilities over time.
8. Classroom teachers need to know more about disabilities and their impact on learning; therefore, teachers' preservice training should include required courses in special education of individuals with disabilities.
9. Special educators of persons with disabilities and specialists in the area of gifted and talented need to have a better understanding of each other's fields and must collaborate for the good of children.
10. Including children with disabilities and gifts in regular classroom settings is important and consistent with current philosophy. Segregating these children in special classes for individuals with disabilities is not conducive to their full development. They need good models, gifted persons with and without disabilities.
11. There is a scarcity of exemplary programming models for educating children with gifts and disabilities.
12. Funds should be made available to exemplary programs so they can provide technical assistance to sites interested in replicating their models.
13. More attention needs to be given to training counselors who understand giftedness and disabilities to better prepare them to collaborate with other educators and help children with many special needs develop a positive self-concept and choose and prepare for suitable careers.
14. Participation of parents in a program that promotes the gifts and talents children with disabilities has a positive effect on how parents perceive their child.
15. It is important that, in programming for children with gifts and disabilities, the IEP should be written for both the weaknesses and the strengths of the child.
16. An individualized program for children with gifts and disabilities fares best if there is a knowledgeable supervisor, coordinator, or administrator who advocates for these children and ensures that they are challenged. These children should be given opportunities to have a well-balanced, individually appropriate program and to pursue their interests.
17. Inservice training programs for personnel working with children with gifts and disabilities should include workshops focus-

ing on meeting the instructional needs of these children. Participants should include classroom teachers, teachers of children with disabilities, teachers of the gifted, supervisors and administrators, and ancillary personnel.

18. Children with disabilities and gifts should have continuity of programming, which means that there must be viable procedures for transitioning children from one level to another and for placing them in classes where teachers are cognizant of the special needs of this subgroup of children and know how to appropriately program for them. Parents must help ensure program continuity for their child.

19. Institutions of higher learning that are training teachers must include appropriate information in their programs and provide practicum experiences that will enable classroom teachers and teachers of children with special needs (disabilities and gifts) to individualize instruction for every student in their classrooms.

20. The federal government needs to provide leadership in the identification and programming for children with gifts and disabilities. Increased services for this group of children should be a top priority. When the federal government establishes a priority, states and local school systems usually are influenced to take more responsibility.

21. It is imperative that the fields of special education and gifted education work more closely together to better serve children with gifts and disabilities. This close collaboration should take place at the federal, state, and local levels.

We cannot continue to ignore our obligation to individuals with disabilities who are also potentially gifted. For the good of society and for the well-being of these individuals, we must put forth a greater effort to alleviate the problem of underserving such children. These children represent our future and we cannot afford to restrict that future by failing to provide an educational system that will enable these children to realize their full potential.

REFERENCES

Baum, S. M., Renzulli, J. S., & Hebert, T. P. (1994). Reversing underachievement: Stories of success. *Educational Leadership, 52*, 48–52.

Bloom, B., Englehart, M. Furst, E., Hill, W., & Krathwohl, D. (1956). *Taxonomy of educational objectives. Handbook I: Cognitive domain.* New York: McKay.

Daniels, P. (1983). *Teaching the gifted/learning disabled child.* Rockville, MD: Aspen.

Delisle, J. R. (1992). *Guiding the social and emotional development of gifted youth: A practical guide for educators and counselors.* White Plains, NY: Longman.

Fox, L., Brady, L., & Fabin, S. (1983). *Learning disabled gifted children.* Baltimore: University Park Press.

Gallagher, J. J. (1988). National agenda for educating gifted students: Statement of priorities. *Exceptional Children, 55*, 107–114.

Greenwood, C. R. (1994). Advances in technology-based assessment within special education, *Exceptional Children, 61*, 102–104.

Greenwood, C. R., Carta, J. J., Kamps, D., Terry, B., & Delquadri, J. (1994). Development and validation of standard classroom observation systems for school practitioners: Ecobehavioral assessment systems software (EBASS). *Exceptional Children, 61,* 197-209.

Guilford, J. (1967). *The nature of human intelligence.* New York: McGraw-Hill.

Hegeman, K. (1981). *A position paper on the education of gifted-handicapped children.* Paper presented to the Committee for the Gifted-Handicapped of the Association for the Gifted, Council for Exceptional Children, Reston, Virginia.

Hishinuma, E. S. (1993). Counseling the gifted/at risk and gifted/dyslexic. *Gifted Child Today, 16,* 30–33.

Hobbs, N. (1975). *The future of children: Categories, labels, and their consequences.* Report of the Project on Classification of Exceptional Children. San Francisco: Jossey-Bass.

Humphrey, J. H. (1990). *Helping learning-disabled gifted children learn through compensatory active play.* Springfield, IL: Charles C Thomas.

Johnson, L. J., & Carr, V. (1996). Curriculum in early childhood education: Moving toward inclusive specialization. In M. C. Pugach & C. Warger (Eds.), *What's worth knowing: How curriculum trends affect special education* (pp. 379–400). New York: Teachers College Press.

Johnson, L. J., & Pugach, M. C. (in press). The emerging third wave of collaboration: Expanding beyond individual problem solving to create educational system that embraces diversity. In W. Stainback & S. Stainback (Eds.), *Controversial issues confronting special education: Divergent perspectives* (2nd ed). Boston: Allyn and Bacon.

Karnes, M. B. (1978). *Identifying and programming for young gifted/talented handicapped children.* Presentation at the Council for Exceptional Children World Congress, Stirling, Scotland.

Karnes, M. B. (1979). Young handicapped children can be gifted and talented. *Journal for the Education of the Gifted, 2,* 157–172.

Karnes, M. B. (1984a). A demonstration/outreach model for young gifted/talented handicapped. *Roeper Review,* 7, 23–26.

Karnes, M. B. (1984b). Special children . . . special gifts. *Children Today, 13,* 18–23.

Karnes, M. B., & Bertschi, J. D. (1978). Identifying and educating gifted/talented nonhandicapped and handicapped preschoolers. *Teaching Exceptional Children, 10,* 114–119.

Karnes, M. B., & Johnson, L. J. (1986). Early identification and programming for young gifted/talented handicapped. *Topics in Early Childhood Special Education, 6,* 50–61.

Karnes, M. B., & Johnson, L. J. (1987a). Bringing Out Head Start Talents (BOHST). *Head Start Bulletin, 19,* 14.

Karnes, M. B., & Johnson, L. J. (1987b). Bringing Out Head Start Talent: Findings from the field. *Gifted Child Quarterly, 34,* 174-179.

Karnes, M. B., & Johnson, L. J. (1987c). An imperative: Programming for the young gifted/talented. *Journal for the Education of the Gifted, 10,* 195–214.

Karnes, M. B., Shwedel, A. M., & Lewis, G. F. (1983a). Long-term effects of early programming for the young gifted handicapped child. *Exceptional Children, 50,* 103–109.

Karnes, M. B., Shwedel, A. M., & Lewis, G. F. (1983b). Short-term effects of early programming for the young gifted handicapped child. *Journal for the Education of the Gifted, 6,* 266–278.

Karnes, M. B., Shwedel, A. M., & Linnemeyer, S. A. (1982). The young gifted/talented child: Programs at the University of Illinois. *Elementary School Journal, 82,* 195–213.

Lind, S. (1993). Are we mislabeling overexcitable children? *Understanding Our Gifted, 5/5a,* 8–10.

Maker, J. (1977). *Providing programs for the gifted handicapped.* Reston, VA: Council for Exceptional Children.

Maker, C. J., Redden, M. R., Tonelson, S., & Howell, R. M. (1978). *The self-perception of successful handicapped scientists.* Albuquerque: University of New Mexico, Department of Special Education.

Marland, S. P., Jr. (1972). *Education of the gifted and talented.* Report to the Congress of the United States by the U.S. Commissioner of Education. Washington, DC: U.S. Government Printing Office.

Mauser, A. (1980). LD in gifted children. *ACLD Newsbriefs, 130,* 2.

Programs for the Gifted and Talented, 704 Kentucky Administrative Regulation 3:385 (1994).

Pugach, M. C., & Johnson, L. J. (1995). *Collaborative practitioners, collaborative schools.* Denver, CO: Love.

VanTassel-Baska, J. (1992). *Planning effective curriculum for gifted learners.* Denver, Co: Love.

Webb, J., & Latimer, D. (1993). ADHD and children who are gifted. *Exceptional Children, 60,* 183–184.

Whitmore, J. (1981). Gifted children with handicapping conditions: A new frontier. *Exceptional Children, 48,* 106–114.

Whitmore, J. R., & Maker, C. J. (1985). *Intellectual giftedness in disabled persons.* Rockville, MD: Aspen.

41

International Perspective on Gifted Education

A. HARRY PASSOW, *Teachers College, Columbia University*

Education of gifted and exceptionally able children and youth has been a concern for most nations and cultures since Biblical days. Yet, until recently, there was a tendency on the part of Americans to think of gifted education as something "uniquely American." Some writers referred to such "classics" as Galton's (1869) *Hereditary Genius: An Inquiry into Its Laws and Consequences,* Lombroso's (1891) *Man of Genius,* and Stern's (1916) *Psychologische Begabungsforschung und Begabungsdiagnose (Psychological Giftedness Research and Identification of the Gifted).* However, except for a stray article here and there, American educators had little available to inform themselves of activities on behalf of the gifted and talented in other countries. Parkyn's (1948) *Children of High Intelligence: A New Zealand Study* was one of the few exceptions.

Thus, it was not until 1961 and 1962 with the publication of two *Year Books of Education* (Bereday & Lauwerys, 1961, 1962) that Americans and others, mainly British, got a first real look at education of the gifted from an international perspective. The two volumes contained 88 chapters by 87 contributors who discussed "what happens when attempts are made on a national scale to discover and to educate gifted children in all ranks of the population" in 26 nations (Bereday & Lauwerys, 1961, p. 1). Included were two chapters on increasing human resources in underdeveloped nations.

In the editors' introduction to the first volume, *Concepts of Excellence in Education,* Bereday and Lauwerys (1961) observed:

> All civilized societies have accepted as a duty the task of encouraging those with talent to cultivate their gifts and to pursue excellence. Such men and women would then promote the general welfare and demonstrate to the world the virtues of the group to which they belong. For the true worth of a city or a nation has always been thought to be connected with the number and the greatness of the creative geniuses, whether in the arts or the sciences, which it produces.
>
> These notions can be expressed in a form more directly related to the predominant concerns of modern nations, with their faith in progress and education, their democratic and egalitarian ideologies. We can say that cultural, social and economic advance depends upon educating all young people. Brains and talent are human resources which must not be wasted through failure to provide the right conditions for their development. *The attempt to embody this principle into educational policy raises complex and difficult problems.* (p. 1, emphasis added)

In introducing the second volume, *The Gifted Child,* Bereday and Lauwerys (1962) commented that they initially had thought they could provide a "review of the notions of talent throughout the world and the way in which these notions receive political, social, and cultural implementation in different school systems" in a single *Year Book,* but quickly saw that there was too much to be said and were forced to plan two volumes instead of one (p. xii). The reason, Bereday and Lauwerys (1961) pointed out:

> . . . we immediately encountered a major difficulty: There is no universal consensus as to what constitutes "giftedness," "talent," or "genius." In different cultural areas very different meanings are attached to such expressions as: "a very able man," "most promising," "very gifted," "very intelligent," "he has a great future before him." Of course, intelligence, beauty, gracefulness, strength, courage, and so on, are admired everywhere, but very unequally rewarded. The order of priorities, too, varies from place to place. Here, scientific skill is looked for rather than business

> acumen. There, intelligence and rationality are prized more highly than character or fighting prowess. (p. 1)

As for identification, Langeveld (1961) noted that each community and cultural group had its specific ways of selection and preparation for the different social functions and positions that existed. The institutionalization of modes of selection varied considerably and "may take place in the form of customs—derived from the gods or the ancestors—the 'best in national tradition,' common sense, etc.; or in the form of laws, institutions, castes, school systems, etc." (pp. 37–38).

The contributors from different countries indicated that, as diverse as opinions concerning the concepts of excellence, the institutional arrangements made to develop excellence and nurture talent potential were even more varied and controversial. For example, a Belgian author wrote that in 1921 a foundation called Fund for the Most Gifted provided bursaries on the basis of examination results at the end of the primary stage of education. This process was later modified to provide grants in the form of interest-free loans to university students. In 1951, prompted by a changing notion of equality, the foundation was renamed the National Fund for Studies. Reviewing the historical events that might "explain why Belgium is only moderately interested in the problem of the education of the very gifted," De Coster (1961) asserted:

> It can not be claimed that nothing has been done in Belgium for the gifted; far from it. But what has been done does not touch the schools. No attempt is made to detect the talented and the gifted from the very beginning of their primary school course, nor is there any provision of "special" education for them as there is for the physically handicapped or mentally retarded. (p. 238)

Radford (1961) described the Australian situation at that time as exhibiting "little expressed concern . . . about the best education for the gifted child" possibly because "most of the courses of study in secondary schools have in the past been written with the needs of the more able part of the student population in mind" (p. 227). He found no single definition of giftedness accepted by Australian educators nor did he think that there should be since:

> Most educators responsible for planning courses, organizing schools, and administering educational systems are aware of the literature on giftedness (and the educational development of gifted children), and know that any definition of "gifted" involves two things: (a) an arbitrary choice of what types of behavior will be included; (b) an equally arbitrary choice of dividing line between those regarded as gifted and those excluded whatever criteria are used. (p. 227)

Some other contributors, particularly the Western European authors, noted that while on the surface there was little attention specifically given to "the gifted," the structure of their national school systems was essentially geared to identifying and educating the most intellectually able—for example, the English grammar school, the French *lycée,* and the German *gymnasium.* Many national systems provided for ability grouping or streaming as a way of identifying able learners and channeling their education.

Creighton (1961) pointed out that "talent, in the Soviet view, is a human capability that finds its expression and development in a definite activity requiring that ability. Talent is specific, concrete, and reveals itself in activity; it therefore requires opportunity and special institutions and facilities for its development" (p. 317). Creighton described the networks of institutions throughout the Soviet Union—specialized schools and nonschool facilities (clubs, the Pioneers, cultural organizations, etc.)—that were available to develop talent potential.

World Council for Gifted and Talented Children

The First World Conference on Gifted Children, held in London in September 1975, expanded vistas for international perspectives on education of the gifted. It was at this conference that the World Council for Gifted and

Talented Children, Inc., was organized.[1] The conference was the brainchild of Henry Collis, at that time the director of the National Association for Gifted Children (NAGC) (United Kingdom) who practically singlehandedly promoted, organized, raised funds, solicited attendance, and moderated this first assemblage.

The first world conference drew over 500 participants from 50 countries, ranging from those that had governmental departments to those that were just beginning to think about the gifted. The conference proceedings titled *Gifted Children: Looking to Their Future* (Gibson & Chennells, 1976) includes 25 chapters dealing with all aspects of gifted education, plus another 25 in which individuals dealt with the topic: "What My Country Does for Gifted Children," providing a perspective and an overview of the common ground, the conflicts, the problems, and the possibilities created by a concern for developing talent potential in diverse societies and cultures.

At the final session, the chairperson of NAGC (UK), Felicity Ann Sieghart (1976), summed up the conference somewhat prophetically as follows:

> The end of one thing is often the beginning of another. I would like to think that now that we have found each other, that we have learned so much from each other, that we have made so many new friendships, we shall no longer feel quite so insular or perhaps isolated in our work for the gifted children of our own countries. I now feel convinced that this conference will mark the beginning of a series of world conferences, of world-wide trans-national professional and lay concern for gifted children, their problems, their future, and what we can do about them. (p. 376)

The World Council has never been a very large organization in terms of its membership numbers but it has unquestionably provided an international forum for stimulating research, exchanging information, sharing insights, and assisting individuals and groups from all over the world in fostering programs and services for gifted and talented. Its influence has far exceeded its membership numbers.

Since the 1975 conference when the World Council for Gifted and Talented Children, Inc., (WCGTC) was established as an organization, the council has sponsored a dozen biennial world conferences. These conferences have attracted as many as 1,700 participants from 55 nations. After each of the conferences, the publication of the proceedings has provided an even larger audience with international perspectives on research and theory, program, and practice.

Heller (1993) undertook a content analysis of the articles and papers included in the proceedings of the first nine World Conferences (1975–1991). Heller found that the articles could be classified under seven headings as follows: Educational or Instructional Processes and Programming, 35.0 percent; Personal Characteristics of Gifted/Talented, 25.0 percent; Development of Giftedness, 12.5 percent; Social Issues, 12.5 percent; Identification, 7.5 percent; Learning and Perception, 5.0 percent; and Physical/Mental Conditions, 2.5 percent. The bulk of studies (70 percent) involved educational psychology. Twenty percent of the papers were of a theoretical nature, and only 5.0 percent could be described as basic/experimental research; 20.0 percent were data-based/empirical studies; and 55.0 percent described programs and practices. Almost half of the papers (45.0 percent) dealt with gifted children in grades 4–8; 23.0 percent with students in grades 9–12; 13.0 percent with primary education; 3.0 percent with preschoolers; another 3.0 percent with higher education; and 13.0 percent with adult gifted. Whether Heller's content analysis of papers published in World Conference proceedings is congruent with ongoing international research and practice is, of course, difficult to determine. Nevertheless, the analysis describes what researchers and practitioners chose to share with other participants at these conferences.

Regional and National Organizations

By 1994 the World Council had cooperated in arranging for at least eight regional confer-

[1] The World Council for Gifted and Talented Children, Inc., is now headquartered at the Connie Belin and Jacqueline N. Blank International Center for Gifted Education and Talent Development. Nicholas Colangelo serves as Executive Administrator.

ences—three organized by the European Council for High Ability (ECHA); three by the Asia-Pacific Federation of the World Council; one by South African educators; and one by the Ibero-American Federation (Southern Hemisphere) of the World Council. These conferences were not strictly regional in that they usually attracted participants from many countries beyond the region. For example, the Second Asian Conference in Taipei, Taiwan, drew presenters and participants from a dozen nations outside the region. The regional conferences thus have served to provide forums for international perspectives that are not unlike those of the world conferences.

The First Southeast Asian Regional Conference on Giftedness, held in Manila in August 1990, attracted participants from the entire Asian region plus Canada, South Africa, and the United States. The proceedings included 31 papers arbitrarily grouped in three categories: The Broad Perspective (4 papers), An Interdisciplinary Approach to Developing Giftedness within the School System (14), and Society's Involvement in Developing the Gifted (13).

The proceedings of the Third European Conference of the European Council for High Ability (ECHA) included presentations on the following topics: Ability and Achievement (6 papers), Creativity and Innovation (7), Development of Gifted and Talent (6), Gender Issues (3), Special Groups (e.g., underachievers) (4), Identification and Psychological Measurement Problems (8), Gifted Education and Program Evaluation (5), Teachers of the Gifted (2), and Policy and Advocacy in Gifted Education (9) (Heller & Hany, 1992). In the United States, national associations such as NAGC and TAG and state groups have been in existence for four decades or more. They sponsor conferences, publish journals and newsletters, and actively engage in advocacy efforts. However, such organizations are a much more recent phenomena in most other nations around the world.

For example, Australia's First National Conference on the Education of Gifted and Talented Children took place in Melbourne in August 1983 under the auspices of the Special Projects Program of the Commonwealth Schools Commission. In Australia, programs and provisions for the gifted vary by state and territory—with some, as of 1983, even prohibiting such programs. Although there had been conferences sponsored by some of the seven state organizations, this was the first national conference. Some 500 teachers, parents, teacher educators, students, and administrators attended. In addition to the plenary session speakers, 82 presentations were made on every aspect of gifted education, indicating that the Australians were conducting studies and developing programs very much like those of their U.S. counterparts (Harkin, 1984).

Two years later, the Second National Conference was held, this time under the auspices of the newly formed Australian Association for the Education of the Gifted and Talented. The papers of 34 presenters included in the proceedings were grouped under the following topics: National and State Perspectives, including a perspective of provisions in New Zealand (6 papers), Identification and Selection Procedures (3), Gifted Children in the Regular School Classroom (8), Learning and Teaching About the Gifted: Inservice and Preservice Programs (4), Community-Supported Programs (4), Disadvantaged and Underachieving Gifted Students (3), Parental and Counseling Perspectives (3), and Research and Clinical (3).

In the opening paper, Braggett (1986a) provided a useful overview of education of the gifted in Australia by discussing four questions: (1) What are the difficulties faced by persons seeking to provide for the gifted? (2) What is the relevance of the policy statements issued at the system level? (3) What provisions are being made for gifted and talented children? (4) What are the trends emerging across Australia? Braggett observed that:

> The last decade has witnessed widespread change in Australian education. Each state and territory has now recognised the existence of gifted and talented children, either by a formulated policy or the creation of a special Task Force to provide for such children. Some states have developed system-wide provisions while others have handed over this responsibility to the regional office or to the local school. There is greater awareness of the need to cater to a wider range of abilities within the neighbourhood

school and important steps have been taken by many states to provide inservice education and greater consultancy services. (p. 27)

Braggett's observations and assessments were based on an intensive, comprehensive study he undertook for the Commonwealth Schools Commission in which he surveyed programs and activities in every Australian state and territory (Braggett, 1985). His report indicated that a dramatic change was occurring in Australia's efforts regarding the gifted since Radford's assessment in 1962. An accompanying publication consisted of a 676-item annotated bibliography grouped under more than 100 topics—clearly demonstrating that there was a rich body of literature concerning research, theory, policy, and practice in gifted education that was apparently not well known to Australians, let alone the international community (Braggett 1986b).

An International Perspective

The programs and proceedings from world, regional, national, and local conferences; the expanding number of books, journals, and newsletters; the exchanges of papers among researchers and policymakers; the interchange of consultants, teachers, and others across nations—have all resulted in a much fuller and different perspective on the education of gifted and talented around the world from that reported in Bereday and Lauwerys' two volumes, *Year Book of Education,* 1961 and 1962.

How different this perspective is can be seen in the publication of the *International Handbook of Research and Development of Giftedness and Talent* (Passow, Monks, & Heller, 1993). This 964-page handbook, with contributions by 80 individuals from 18 countries, contains thousands of references from nations around the world. Every chapter draws on research and literature from a number of countries, indicating that the chapter topic is of international concern. The eight chapters that provide examples of programs, policies, and issues regarding the ways nations identify and nurture giftedness reflect more similarities than differences. What is not clear with respect to gifted education, any more than it is with any other aspect of education and schooling, is how these commonalities are created.

It is difficult enough to describe education of the gifted and talented in the United States because of the diversity of conceptions, definitions, programs, provisions, policies, issues, and problems. To provide an international description is even more difficult, although there are both similarities and differences from country to country.

In countries all over the world, developed and less-developed, there is a concern for identifying talent potential and nurturing talented performance, whatever labels and terminology are applied to this population. The philosophical base and the underlying motivations for these concerns vary. In some instances, the motivation is one of developing specialized talents to meet societal needs; in others, the motivation stems from concerns for equality of educational opportunity and the full development of each individual for self-fulfillment as well as for meeting society's needs for brainpower and high-level performance.

Education of the gifted is inevitably tied to the availability of resources. In many countries there is considerable controversy as to whether limited resources should be spread as widely as possible or whether they should be husbanded for the most able. In some instances, the issue is as stark as deciding whether to broadly expand primary education or whether to use limited finances to enlarge secondary and tertiary education which serve smaller populations. In some developing countries, the "gifted" are those enrolled in secondary schools from which the few who go on to higher education are selected.

Despite a long history of programming for the gifted, such efforts are still debated as to whether they are elitist, undemocratic, and even necessary. Both proponents and opponents employ the arguments of egalitarianism and elitism to further or impede making appropriate provisions for the gifted. Variations of the perennial issue of equity vis-á-vis excellence (usually stated as equity *versus* excellence) are debated almost everywhere. Provisions for the exceptionally able are made under diverse political and economic systems, although the rhetoric used to support or attack programs differs. In fact, it has been observed "that, as in other fields, the more that is known, the more issues and controversies are fueled" (Passow, Monks, & Heller, 1993, p. 883).

In most countries, definitions, concepts, and constructs that guide research and practice are becoming much more diverse. While broader and more liberal definitions and conceptions of giftedness are being considered, as in the United States, *intellectual* and *academic giftedness* still dominate program and practice. A number of countries are adding *creativity* to their guiding concepts but, as in the United States, creativity has as many meanings as does intelligence. Most nations seem to focus initially on intellectual and academic development and only later move to the so-called nonacademic areas such as the graphic and performing arts.

It is generally recognized that many decisions regarding identification and education depend on one's definition or conception of giftedness. "Newer" concepts of giftedness—especially Sternberg's triarchic intelligence and Gardner's multiple intelligences—are finding their way into the literature and practice of many countries.

In the United States, the principle of using multiple sources of information in identifying the gifted has received widespread verbal acceptance, even though evidence of high intellectual aptitude is still central to most identification programs. While researchers in other nations explore or accept newer concepts of intelligence and giftedness, the basic identification procedures in most countries still involve assessment of intellectual or academic aptitude. This is true even in nations where psychological assessment is still at a relatively elementary stage. For example, since indigenously developed tests are often not available, a number of nations use adapted U.S. or British tests, recognizing the problems inherent in such adaptations. Few nations use as many different instruments and scales as can be found in the United States, where a national survey examined no fewer than 65 instruments purportedly measuring general intellectual ability, specific academic aptitude, creativity, leadership, and visual and/or performing arts aptitude for various age groups (Alvino, McDonnel, & Richert, 1981; see Chapter 7).

In the United States, the underrepresentation of minority, economically disadvantaged, and limited-English-proficient students in programs for the gifted has resulted in serious efforts to identify the gifted in those populations. Although the problem is comparable in many other developed nations, only a few, such as the Netherlands and Israel, have mounted enhanced searches.

The trend, emerging slowly in most countries, is one of designing and employing more authentic and complex assessments of talent potential. This trend is related to the exploration of broader concepts of intelligence and the inclusion of multiple talent areas.

The same broad array of programs and provisions for educating the gifted one finds in the United States is not yet replicated in most other countries. From the simplistic triad that was used to describe programs for the gifted three or four decades ago—*acceleration, enrichment in the regular classroom,* and *grouping*—there has been a proliferation of models and systems (Cox, Daniel, & Boston, 1985; Fox, 1979; Maker, 1982; Renzulli, 1986). There are exceptions, of course. For example, the Tannenbaum (1983) matrix model provided the framework for Singapore's curriculum for the gifted. Renzulli's (1977) Triad Model is being explored in several countries. Stanley's (1979) radical acceleration has been adopted by schools in China, Japan, and Germany.

Ability grouping and tracking have not been as contentious in most other countries as these practices have been in the United States. *Ability grouping, streaming, special classes,* and *special* or *selective schools* have a long history in many nations. Although selection practices, such as the 11+ process in England and Wales, have been modified or even curtailed in recent years, grouping tends to be less controversial in most countries than in the United States.

Most countries recognize the need for curricular and instructional differentiation for nurturing giftedness and talent potential. Although the same kind of national curriculum reform projects as one finds in the United

States are not as common in other nations, curriculum is of concern to most educators of the gifted. Differentiated curricula in mathematics and science and technology tend to be the focus in most nations. However, few countries seem to be developing special curricular materials for classes and programs for the gifted although, in many countries, the classroom teacher is expected to design differentiated experiences, often without appropriate training or support.

The theme of the Seventh World Conference, "Expanding Awareness of Creative Potentials" (Taylor, 1990), attracted a number of papers dealing with topics such as creativity; creativity in the arts; multiple talent development; student leaders, entrepreneurs, and inventors; futurists; technical-vocational gifted; computers and technology; and "whole person development." These papers described programs and studies in a variety of nations, suggesting broader curriculum interests than traditional academic subjects. In addition, there appears to be increased attention to the affective development of the gifted—to enhancing motivation and commitment, moral and ethical values, and metacognitive and thinking processes.

Formal, structured teacher education programs at the preservice or inservice levels such as those in the United States are not customary in most other countries. The United States is possibly the only country to have, in some states, special licensing or certification of teachers of the gifted. Specialized programs of education for teachers of the gifted are relatively rare.

In a number of countries—such as South Africa, Israel, New Zealand, and the United Kingdom—out-of-school, after-school, or extracurricular programs represent a significant component of provisions for the gifted. Such out-of-school provisions are often supplementary or complementary to in-school provisions. In some countries, greater use of community resources is seen as essential for developing talent potential. Museums, libraries, laboratories, art studios, and other agencies and institutions with educating potential appear to be increasingly utilized. Mentor programs which relate adult specialists and gifted students are becoming widespread as a means for extending the educational resources of gifted children.

Other aspects of nurturing the gifted—for example, guidance and counseling programs, parent involvement, and advocacy—also receive attention in countries around the world.

Finally, there has been a significant increase worldwide in research on giftedness and the gifted; in the aspects of talent potential and its development; in the evaluation of programs and practices; in the cross-national sharing of research; and even in the evolving interdependence of research and practice. Educating our most able children is indeed an international problem, an international challenge, and an international necessity.

Because education of the gifted does not occur in a vacuum but in a broad political, social, cultural, and economic context, policies and programs that affect educational policy and structure also impact on identifying and nurturing talent. Thus, to comprehend fully national efforts for the gifted requires some understanding of the context in which they exist. Such an understanding is usually limited in most international analyses, including this one, so that the viewpoints expressed are necessarily restricted to the interpretations of one observer.

REFERENCES

Alvino, J. J., McDonnel, R. C., & Richert, E. S. (1981). National survey of identification practices in gifted and talented education. *Exceptional Children, 48*, 124–132.

Bereday, G. Z. F., & Lauwerys, J. A. (1961). *Concepts of excellence in education. The year book of education 1961.* New York: Harcourt.

Bereday, G. Z. F., & Lauwerys, J. A. (1962). *The gifted child: The year book of education 1962.* New York: Harcourt.

Braggett, E. J. (1985). *Education of gifted and talented children: Australian provision.* Canberra: Commonwealth Schools Commission.

Braggett, E. J. (1986a). The education of gifted and talented children in Australia. In Imison, K., Endean, L., & Smith, D. (Eds.), *Gifted and talented children—A national concern* (pp. 13–28). Toowoomba, Queensland: Darling Downs Institute Press.

Braggett, E. J. (1986b). *Talented, gifted, creative: Australian writings.* Canberra: Commonwealth Schools Commission.

Cox, J., Daniel, N., & Boston, B. O. (1985). *Educating able learners: Programs and promising practices.* Austin: University of Texas Press.

Creighton, H. C. (1961). Facilities for the talented in the U.S.S.R.. In G. Z. F. Bereday & J. A. Lauwerys (Eds.), *Concepts of excellence in education: The year book of education 1961* (pp. 317–326). New York: Harcourt.

De Coster, S. (1961). The problem of intellectually talented children in Belgium. In G. Z. F. Bereday & J. A. Lauwerys (Eds.), *Concepts of excellence in education: The year book of education 1961* (pp. 236–240). New York: Harcourt.

Fox, L. H. (1979). Programs for the gifted and talented: An overview. In A. H. Passow (Ed.), *The gifted and the talented: Their education and development. 78th Yearbook,* Part I, National Society for the Study of Education (pp. 104–126). Chicago: University of Chicago Press.

Galton, F. (1869). *Hereditary genius: An inquiry into its laws and consequences.* London: Macmillan.

Gibson, J., & Chennells, P. (Eds.). (1976). *Gifted children: Looking to their future.* London: Latimer New Dimensions Ltd.

Harkin, D. J. (1984). *First national conference on the education of gifted and talented children conference papers.* Canberra, Australia Commonwealth Schools Commission.

Heller, K. A. (1993). Structural tendencies and issues of research on giftedness and talent. In K. A. Heller, F. J. Monks, & A. H. Passow (Eds.), *International handbook of research and development of giftedness and talent* (pp. 49–67). Oxford: Pergamon.

Heller, K. A., & Hany, E. A. (Eds.). (1992). *Competence and responsibility* (Vol. 2). Seattle, WA: Hogrefe & Huber.

Langeveld, M. J. (1961). The concept of excellence. In G. Z. F. Bereday & J. A. Lauwerys (Eds.), *Concepts of excellence in education: The year book of education 1961* (pp. 37–40). New York: Harcourt.

Lombroso, C. (1891). *The men of genius.* London: Robert Scott.

Maker, C. J. (1982). *Teaching models in education of the gifted.* Rockville, MD: Aspen Systems Corporation.

Passow, A. H., Monks, F. J., & Heller, K. A. (1993). Research and education of the gifted in the year 2000 and beyond. In K. A. Heller, F. J., Monks, & A. H. Passow (Eds.), *International handbook of research and development of giftedness and talent* (pp. 883–903). Oxford: Pergamon.

Parkyn, G. W. (1948). *Children of high intelligence: A New Zealand study.* Wellington, NZ: New Zealand Council for Educational Research.

Radford, J. J. (1961). Gifted education in Australia. In G. Z. F Bereday & J. A. Lauwerys (Eds.), *Concepts of excellence in education: The year book of education 1961* (pp. 41–46). New York: Harcourt.

Renzulli, J. S. (1977). *The enrichment triad model: A guide for developing defensible programs for the gifted.* Mansfield Center, CT: Creative Learning Press.

Renzulli, J. S. (Ed.). (1986). *Strategies and models for developing programs for the gifted and talented.* Mansfield Center, CT: Creative Learning Press.

Seighart, F. A. (1976). Closing comments. In J. Gibson & P. Chennells (Eds.), *Gifted children: Looking to their future* (pp. 375–377). London: Latimer New Dimensions Ltd.

Stanley, J. C. (1979). Identifying and nurturing the intellectually gifted. In W. C. George, S. J. Cohn, & J. C. Stanley (Eds.), *Educating the gifted: Acceleration and enrichment* (pp. 172–180). Baltimore: Johns Hopkins University Press.

Stern, W. (1916). *Psychologische begabungsforschung und Begabungsdiagnose (Psychological Giftedness Research and Identification of the Gifted).* Leipzig, Germany: Teubner.

Tannenbaum, A. J. (1983). *Gifted children: Psychological and educational perspectives.* New York: Macmillan.

Taylor, C. W. (Ed.). (1990). *Expanding awareness of creative potentials worldwide.* Salt Lake City, UT: Brain Talent–Powers Press.

42

Legal Issues in Gifted Education

FRANCES A. KARNES and RONALD G. MARQUARDT, *University of Southern Mississippi*

The most significant aspect of the legal framework in which gifted education operates is that, unlike the statutory legal protection provided the disabled student, there is no federal government mandate requiring school districts to provide special programs for gifted students. Consequently, gifted education proponents must look to state governments to establish the legal foundation to protect the interests of gifted students.

State governments take a variety of approaches in establishing the gifted education legal milieu. Approximately three-fifths of the states have passed a statutory mandate requiring special instruction for the gifted, with the balance of the states choosing the "permissive" route (Council of State Directors of Programs for the Gifted, 1994). The permissive statutory path simply means that school districts may, but are not legally required to, provide programs for the gifted. As explained later in this chapter, whether a state has a mandate in place is often a crucial factor in resolving legal disputes. The National Association for Gifted Children has issued a Position Paper on mandation, although not legally binding, which is shown on page 537. States also vary in the degree of state gifted education funding which, as will be seen later, often has legal consequences.

The reliance on the states for protection of gifted students makes monitoring legal developments in gifted education difficult. The number of states, the variety of legal procedural mazes operating in the states, and the fact that most states do not publish hearing officer and trial court decisions make the tracking of legal disputes burdensome.

In the past, researchers were relegated to state appellate court decisions, statutes, administrative regulations, and whatever bits and pieces could be garnered from state gifted education associations, professionals in the field, and parents. No systematic collection procedures existed to observe and record the resolutions to the variety of legal conflicts occurring in gifted education.

To help gifted education advocates in tracking legal issues, a Legal Issues Network (LIN) has been established at the University of Southern Mississippi.[1] All state gifted organizations have been invited to participate in LIN by establishing a committee to examine state laws and rules and regulations pertaining to gifted education. Created in 1994 to serve as a clearinghouse for information concerning legal issues, the Network publishes a newsletter describing legal developments in gifted education.

Procedures for Resolving Legal Issues

Methods for settling legal conflicts in gifted education range from informal discussions to state supreme court decisions. An axiom in this legal arena is that the best solution is to resolve the dispute at the lowest possible level. As the complainant proceeds up the ladder through negotiation, mediation, due process, administrative review, and the courts, costs and delays expand exponentially. If a matter reaches litigation, financial concerns take on great significance.

[1] Legal Issues Network, c/o Dr. Frances A. Karnes, Box 8207, University of Southern Mississippi, Hattiesburg, MS 39406-8207.

Position Paper:
Mandated Educational Opportunities for Gifted and Talented Students

The National Association for Gifted Children (NAGC) periodically issues policy statements that deal with issues, policies, and practices that have an impact on the education of gifted and talented students. Policy statements represent the official convictions of the organization.

All policy statements approved by the NAGC Board of Directors are consistent with the organization's belief that education in a democracy must respect the uniqueness of all individuals, the broad range of cultural diversity present in our society, and the similarities and differences in learning characteristics that can be found within any group of students. NAGC is fully committed to national goals that advocate both excellence and equity for all students, and we believe that the best way to achieve these goals is through differentiated educational opportunities, resources, and encouragement for all students.

The National Association for Gifted children supports mandating services to meet the unique needs of gifted and talented children.

Numerous studies, including the federal report *National Excellence: A Case for Developing America's Talent,* released in November 1993, have documented that needs of our nation's gifted and talented students are not being met. Programs for these students are currently often viewed as extracurricular and are available only on limited basis in some school systems, money permitting. The needs of gifted and talented students have been well documented by research and federal studies.

To educate all our children and allow America to compete in a global economy and all fields of human endeavor, the nation must provide an environment in which gifted and talented students, along with all of our children, can reach their full potential.

National Association for Gifted Children
1707 L Street, Suite 550
Washington, DC 20036

Negotiation

Within each school system there should be approved local, county, or parish board of education policies established for the purpose of resolving general educational issues. Such policies usually apply to concerns regarding gifted education. A general rule of thumb is to begin solving an issue at the source and proceed up the designated chain of command. For example, if the issue is in regard to assessment and eligibility criteria for admission to a program, then the place to begin would be with the person having responsibility for the testing. If there is disagreement over the program in which the gifted student was placed, the process of discussion would begin with the persons responsible for placement and/or programming. When an agreement cannot be reached at the point at which the issue began, then it is taken to the next level, which is usually the principal, the superintendent, and then the school board. In large school districts, there may be additional intermediate steps.

The person who is dissatisfied should gather the relevant documents: state laws pertaining to gifted education and related issues; state board of education rules and regulations; and local, county, or parish board rules and regulations. If there have been court cases and/or due process hearings, these should be reviewed if not privileged information. In addition to a thorough review of the above, accurate records of all meetings, phone calls, and other points of contact as to the time, place, persons present, discussion, and decisions made should be assembled. After each meeting, a letter should be sent to those involved with a summary and a written request for verification within a designated amount of time.

Additional guidelines for negotiation, as well as other steps in resolving an issue, are to be sure that facts are correct, not hearsay, and that records are kept of each action taken. Current state laws; state board of education policies and rules and regulations; and local, county, or parish board policies should provide the facts needed to understand the legal parameters.

Mediation

In the 12 states having *mediation* available to resolve issues in gifted education, this process may be used if negotiation has not produced the anticipated results through the board of education level (Karnes & Marquardt, 1991a). Mediation is a process by which disputes are resolved in an informal manner with a minimum of time, money, and emotional and psychological stress. Parents and educators may request to use the process through the state board of education or another state-designated agency. The mediation meeting can be scheduled within a short period of time and with a trained impartial mediator appointed.

The mediator should have training in mediation, good written and oral communication skills, and excellent interpersonal skills. The mediator, after hearing both sides of the issue, writes a mediation agreement with the assistance and the cooperation of both parties. The written document should be clearly worded with the specifics of what should be undertaken, who is responsible, the date at which it must be completed, and the name of the person who will monitor the process. Copies are given to both parties to sign and keep, and one is forwarded to the state agency given the responsibility for mediation.

Due Process

If mediation is not available or if an agreement cannot be reached through mediation, then in 28 states procedural *due process* may be employed (Coleman, Gallagher, & Foster, 1994). This is available under different provisions. In the states where the gifted are given the same rights as the disabled, due process is usually included within special education law and/or rules and regulations. There are a few other ways that states provide due process for the gifted. The most common are through general state due process procedures for all students, including the gifted; another means is through provisions specific to the gifted.

Commonalities and differences are apparent in reviewing procedural due process for the gifted. Written prior notice as to the date and time of the meeting, an electronic or written transcript of the meeting, having an open or closed meeting, having the student in question in attendance, having attorneys present, and expert witnesses on both sides to offer testimony are among the most common features. Differences occur in the level of the initial hearing, the jurisdiction, the selection and training of the hearing officers, and the route of appeal.

When a due process meeting has been completed, the hearing officer writes a report based on his or her interpretation of the evidence and within the parameters of local, state, and federal laws, rules and regulations, and policies. The hearing officer solely makes the decision regarding the dispute. Copies are forwarded to the appropriate parties, and to persons in the state agencies responsible for due process—usually the state superintendent of education. In the initial investigation of due process and the gifted, Karnes and Marquardt (1991a) discovered that over 100 hearings have been conducted.

Mediation and procedural due process differ in several ways. The latter is more costly in time and money, and it is more adversarial. Mediation offers the opportunity for both parties to write an agreement, while in due process the hearing officer writes the final document. The hearing officer makes the decision in which both parties must abide, unless an appeal is made.

The appeal process differs slightly from state to state. The most common is to appeal to the state superintendent of education, or to another person within the state department of education. Karnes and Marquardt (1991a) discuss the possible inherent conflict in such a structure and have provided a more equitable model. In addition, they present guidelines for states needing to establish and/or change procedural due process.

Courts

If the appeal to the state agency is not satisfactory, the parents or school officials may decide to take the matter to state or federal courts. Most educational matters are governed by state laws or rules and regulations and would be heard in the state courts. Federal courts are the appropriate forum in cases involving federal law and constitutional provisions. There are several points to keep in mind while making a decision to go to court. The complainant must know the current law(s), and understand that court cases are costly in time, money, and emotions. It may take years for the courts to make a ruling, and the attorneys' fees and court costs are very high. Persons having undertaken the court route described it as emotionally and psychologically draining whether the case is settled in their favor or not (Karnes & Marquardt, 1991b). Another rule of thumb is to hire an attorney with knowledge of educational law; the state bar association may have information on the topic. Before a commitment is made, be sure to know how the costs will be determined. Will there be a flat fee, an hourly rate, or a combination? There can be big differences.

Survey of Legal Issues

Certain legal issues consistently appear on the gifted education landscape. Space does not permit an analysis of every form of dispute, but the following are major conflicts which often arise between parents and school districts.

Early Admission to School

A recurring legal issue in gifted education is early admission to public school. Many states have statutes which specify that the child must reach a chronological age by a certain date, usually September 1, to enter the first year of school. School administrators are reluctant to ignore the age statute for fear of running afoul of state law and/or policy and procedures.

The best approach to overcoming the age barrier is to check the statute to see if it permits exceptions. Some states have written in the law circumstances that allow early admission. Some states, for example, allow a child transferring from another state who has been attending school to be admitted in the new state of residence. A few other states allow a child to be admitted early upon the showing that the child is mentally and physically ready to attend school.

Many states, however, rely heavily on requiring the child to be a designated age by September 1. Therefore, parents seeking early admission must find some way to circumvent the statute. The first step, of course, is to follow the designated maze through the school administration and school board procedures and, if necessary, to exhaust the administrative review process, including the state board of education. In most states, completion of this administrative gauntlet is a prerequisite for seeking judicial relief.

The model case in early admission is *Doe v. Petal Municipal School District* (1984). In this case, the parents had their 4-year-old daughter tested at a local college, and she was determined to be physically, emotionally, and mentally prepared to enter the first grade. In fact, the child was reading at the third-grade level. Standing as a barrier to the child's admission was the Mississippi school admission law that stated that a child must be 6 years old by September 1 for admission to the first grade (at that time, the state did not support public school kindergartens). After exhausting all administrative remedies, the father, a local attorney, took his plea to the county youth court.

Because the father had prepared his case well by obtaining the evidence that his daughter was ready to enter school, the county court judge issued an order to the school board to admit the child. The order provided the school district with the requisite legal protection it needed. Because in Mississippi, as in most states, youth court cases are handled secretly and the files are sealed, the child was protected from harmful publicity.

Provisions of Programs

Many parents resort to the courts in an attempt to force a school district to provide gifted education programs. Unless the state mandates that school districts provide gifted education opportunities, these suits brought by parents will for the most part be unsuccessful.

For example, if a district located in a nonmandated state chooses not to provide gifted education instruction, parental claims that their gifted children have been denied state or federal constitutional protections, such as due process of law or equal protection under the law, have been uniformly rejected by the courts. Gifted children are not a constitutionally protected class, nor have parents been successful in convincing courts to agree that state general education statutes or constitutional provisions dictate special instruction for gifted children. Instead, courts take the approach that these general education statutes mean that the child must be given the opportunity to attend school and that the educational experts will determine curriculum.

The best case embodying the above principles is the New York case, *Bennett v. New Rochelle School District* (1985). New Rochelle identified 109 gifted students for its newly established gifted education program. Unfortunately, the district only had funds to support 37 students, so a lottery drawing was used to select students for the program. A parent whose gifted daughter was not a lottery winner sued the district claiming that the school district's actions violated state statutory and constitutional law and the equal protection clause of the federal Constitution. The New York educational statute read that districts "should develop programs to insure that children reach their full academic potential." Bennett also claimed that the lottery process violated the Equal Protection Clauses of the New York and United States Constitutions.

These claims were rejected by the New York trial and appellate courts. The appellate court held that the word *should* in the statute provided the district discretion as to curriculum offerings. New York does not mandate that gifted education be provided to identified that gifted children, and the use of the word *should*, rather than *shall*, left room for the district to have flexibility in serving the educational needs of the gifted. Bennett lost on the equal protection claims as well. The court indicated that lotteries had been used in other educational matters in the past and the New York Department of Education had given prior approval to the district's gifted program and procedures.

The court seemingly did not wish to substitute its will for the expertise of professional educators. Karnes and Marquardt (1991a) tracked several cases in which parents have attempted to use ambiguous statutes or constitutional clauses—and all were unsuccessful in the courts. From a legal standpoint, it is much better for a specific state mandate to be passed by the state legislature *requiring* districts to serve the needs of its gifted students.

Racial Balance in Gifted Programs

Another problem is the maintenance of a proper racial balance in gifted programs. At the outset of many current programs, there was a tendency to use only IQ scores to select students for admission to gifted programs. These tests provided administrators a convenient and quantitative method to justify admission. Placing too great an emphasis on the standard intelligence test, however, frequently resulted in overlooking gifted minority students (*Vaughns v. Board of Education,* 1985; *Montgomery v. Starkville Municipal School District,* 1977).

Consequently, racial imbalance in gifted programs often became one issue among many raised by plaintiffs in district-wide desegregation suits. In attempts to correct this imbalance, court desegregation orders have forced school districts to develop a variety of procedures for identifying gifted children. Normally, districts involved in desegregation suits are required to adopt such admission criteria as teacher, parent, and self nominations, grades, and a variety of standardized and nonstandardized assessments. To be certain that their districts make a good-faith effort to avoid future discrimination, many administrators offer staff development for teachers to aid them in identifying gifted minority children. An advisory committee representing the constituent groups is helpful in making certain that minorities have input into the district's gifted program.

In matters of racial balance, concerned parents have another avenue of resolution besides the traditional approaches of negotiation, mediation, due process, and litigation. Because racial discrimination violates federal laws, parents can file a complaint that a gifted program is being run in a discriminatory manner with the U.S. Department of Education's Office for Civil Rights (OCR). OCR protects persons from discrimination based on race, sex, disability, or age. It investigates complaints and, if discrimination is discovered to exist, will insist that the school district modify its procedures to comply with federal law. Failure to comply may result in the withholding of federal funds from the district. A study of OCR letters of findings covering the years 1985 to 1990 found 46 complaints dealing with gifted education programs (Karnes & Marquardt, 1993). In almost every instance, the school district, after some negotiation, was able to convince OCR that it was operating a nondiscriminatory program and received a "school district is in compliance" determination. The OCR process provides federally protected gifted students and their proponents another avenue to solve disputes and escape the burden of going to court.

Carnegie Units

The awarding of Carnegie units for successfully completed high school courses for graduation varies from state to state. Some states allow seventh- and eighth-grade students to enroll in courses usually designated for those in grades 9 through 12, but will not award them Carnegie units toward graduation. These courses are taught by teachers certified to teach the high school–level academic content, require the same textbook, and apply the same standards in grading. Three families described their plights in working with local and state school districts and boards; there were positive outcomes in two of the situations (Karnes & Marquardt, 1991b). With 22 states empowered to grant Carnegie units to students upon the successful completion of advanced courses prior to admission to high school, and with an additional 8 states allowing the local districts to make the decision, the issue of awarding Carnegie units for high school courses taken before the ninth grade will remain in the forefront.

Transfer of Students

When a gifted student's academic, intellectual, or talent needs are not being met by a public elementary or secondary school, one possible option is to transfer the student to another district offering the needed advanced program. Several parents have undertaken this unusual step to resolve the lack of adequate instruction. A family in Mississippi had been denied a transfer, previously promised, after seeking legal counsel and going to court (Karnes & Marquardt, 1991b). They were so determined to receive an appropriate education for their elementary gifted daughter that they decided to sell their home in the county district and purchase another in a local district offering a gifted program. They stated that they would repeat the process, if they had to, in order to have her educational needs met.

A family in Illinois was given a transfer through annexing the family farm to the property of the adjacent school district (*Davis v. Regional Board of School Trustees*, 1987). After the school board denied the petition for transfer of the family home, the trial court granted the request of the parents and the appellate court upheld the decision of the trial court. The children were then afforded an appropriate education according to their abilities.

The state of Iowa allows all children due process hearings to determine the appropriateness of instruction, and parents of the gifted have employed this provision to seek instructional remedies. In two hearings, districts were ordered to provide tuition for the students to transfer to another district; in three others, the districts were given the choice of adjusting instruction or paying the cost of transferring the students. In only one situation was the family denied the transfer for their gifted child (Karnes & Marquardt, 1991a).

Appropriate Instruction

Once a gifted program is started, tension frequently arises between the school district and the parents as to the appropriateness of the instruction provided the gifted student. In states using the special education model, an Individualized Education Plan (IEP) is written for each child after consultation with teachers, counselors, parents, and the student. The plan, tailored for each child, would include a range of possibilities, for example, grade acceleration, advanced study in a particular academic area, off-campus instruction, or resource programs.

Resource programs allow districts to set aside a particular time each week when gifted students meet in a classroom and receive specialized instruction. These programs are economically efficient, allowing the district to serve a large number of gifted students. To some parents, however, these programs lack the degree of individualized instruction they believe their child should receive.

The resource program approach was the legal issue in what remains today the seminal case in gifted education, the Pennsylvania case, *Centennial School District v. Commonwealth Department of Education* (1988). Centennial used the resource approach to serve its gifted students, reserving 90 minutes each week to provide specialized instruction for students selected for the gifted program. Pennsylvania law placed gifted and disabled children under the *exceptional children* rubric, and the resource program allowed the district to meet the state mandate that gifted students be identified and given appropriate instruction.

A student in the Centennial School District was identified as intellectually gifted and having outstanding abilities in reading and mathematics. Believing he was not receiving appropriate instruction in the resource program in these two subject areas, his parents requested that the district provide him with instruction to serve his special talents in the regular classroom. The school district refused, fearful that if the district was forced to develop individualized instruction for him, other students would demand specialized instruction to serve their special aptitudes. The resource program, the district claimed, was the only economically feasible approach to fulfilling the state mandate to serve gifted children

Under Pennsylvania law his family had a right to request a due process hearing, and the impartial hearing officer ruled in favor of the student. Centennial appealed the decision to the state Department of Education, but they agreed with the hearing officer's ruling. The district then appealed its case in the Commonwealth Court of Pennsylvania, but lost again. Undaunted, the district appealed to the Pennsylvania Supreme Court.

The decision is one that supports gifted education, but is tempered by economic reality (Marquardt & Karnes, 1989). Correctly interpreting the (exceptional children) statutory mandate to require an IEP for each student, the supreme court stated that appropriate education for the gifted meant that the student's educational experience had to be tailored to the needs of the student. A resource program, the court concluded, lacked the individualized instruction required under state law.

The second thrust of the decision held that this individualized instruction need not "maximize" each gifted child's abilities. The school district was required to provide an individualized, appropriate curriculum to its gifted children, but did not have to allocate additional resources to do so. Pennsylvania's school districts were required to serve the needs of gifted students through the curriculum and instructional staff the districts had in place. Compliance with the state's mandate did not mean each district had to become a "Harvard or a Princeton" to develop fully the abilities of its most academically gifted students. The case provides a judicial precedent that gifted education proponents can use to support the demand for individualized, appropriate education for gifted students, particularly in states statutorily mandating that districts provide gifted education.

Teacher Certification

Teacher certification in gifted education presents a legal dilemma for gifted education proponents. On one hand, certification furnishes legal security for gifted education teachers in times of personnel reductions and serves as a safeguard against the hiring of untrained teachers for gifted education positions. The downside is that gifted education advocates do not wish to see the lack of certified teachers become a stumbling block to initiating or continuing gifted programs.

In *Johnson v. Cassell* (1989), Robert Johnson applied for a gifted education position in the Hampshire County, West Virginia, school district. Johnson possessed a master's degree, certification in gifted education, and eleven years teaching experience in gifted education. The candidate hired had no graduate degree, no certification, and no gifted education experience. After exhausting his administrative remedies, Johnson sued the district in the local trial court, lost, and appealed to the West Virginia Court of Appeals.

The appeals court noted that West Virginia law provided school boards discretion in personnel decisions, but the refusal to hire Johnson carried that discretion too far. The court ruled that the board's action was arbitrary and capricious and awarded Johnson the position.

A 1990 Pennsylvania case illustrates how the legal outcome can differ when a state does not require certification for gifted teachers. In *Dallap v. Sharon City School District* (1990), Vicky Linger, a gifted education coordinator, was retained while several more senior teachers lost their positions. Linger had developed the curriculum for the gifted students and evidently had established contacts throughout the community to support the program. To remove Linger from the gifted position, the superintendent concluded, would be "educationally unsound." She did not have, nor did the coordinator's position require, gifted education certification.

Dallap and several other more senior teachers sued the district and, after seven years of litigation, prevailed. After the case had made its way up through the lower courts, the Pennsylvania Supreme Court ruled that Linger be replaced by a more senior teacher.

Pennsylvania law, the court concluded, required that seniority in a subject area be the key factor in personnel reductions. While recognizing that Linger had been with the program since its inception and that she had considerable knowledge and experience in gifted education, the court held that because her certification was in English, the retention decision should be based on seniority in that subject area. If she had had certification in gifted education, seniority in this class of teachers would have been the benchmark for the personnel determination.

A similar case, but with a more positive outcome for the gifted education teacher, occurred in the 1993 Pennsylvania case, *Dilley v. Slippery Rock Area School District.* As in *Dallap,* a declining enrollment forced the Slippery Rock School District to reduce personnel. Mr. Dilley, who had seniority over the gifted education specialist, Kathleen Nachtman, saw his position diminished from full-time to half-time. Using *Dallap* as a precedent, Dilley claimed that since he had seven years seniority more than Nachtman, he should be given the gifted education post. However, the Commonwealth court held that Dilley was stretching the seniority factor too far. The gifted education job description required computer training, and Dilley did not possess computer skills. But more important, the district had sought, and received, a program specialist certificate for Nachtman. Dilley, of course, had no such certificate, and this allowed the court to distinguish this case from the *Dallap* litigation. Therefore, despite having less seniority than Dilley, the trained, experienced gifted education professional was able to retain her position.

Transportation

Woodland Hills School District v. Commonwealth Department of Education (1986), another Pennsylvania case, presents a clear victory for advocates of public school busing of gifted students to instructional sites. Decided on statutory interpretation of Pennsylvania's busing statues, the judge recognized the problems that working parents face in arranging midday transportation for their children.

Pennsylvania statutorily mandates that an appropriate education be provided to exceptional children. Included under the rubric of *exceptional* are disabled and gifted students. Pennsylvania law also allows a child to attend a private school but receive special education services at a public school site. Private school disabled children were bused to a public school site for midday educational services, but private school gifted students did not receive public transportation.

The school district justified not busing the gifted children in that gifted education teachers traveled to public schools to present gifted instruction. Under the state's general busing statute, the district was only required to provide equal busing treatment to all students. By busing public and private disabled children to instructional sites and not busing either public or private gifted students, the district claimed it was abiding by the statute.

Unable to convince the district to change its policy, parents of gifted private school children filed a complaint with the Pennsylvania Department of Education. The Department of Education ruled against the district, citing a statute specific to special education. Because, gifted students fell into the special education category, private school gifted students would have to be bused to the public schools for instruction.

Woodland Hills disagreed and filed suit against the Pennsylvania Department of Education. The Commonwealth Court agreed with the Department of Education that gifted children fit under the special education statute, and using a recognized rule of statutory construction held that a specific statute should take priority over a general law. The specific statute, the court concluded, required Woodland Hills to provide transportation to the private school students. Given that many parents would have difficulty in leaving work to transport their children in the middle of the day, the court's decision had a practical aspect as well as an equal treatment component.

Tort Liability

Summer residence programs, field trips, and transportation to and from instructional sites present opportunities for accidents. Moreover, because gifted students are intellectually advanced, parents and school personnel often assume they are as physically and mentally mature as adults. Case law suggests this is not the circumstance, and that teachers, counselors, and program directors must take preventive steps to make certain accidents do not occur.

A brief survey of selected case law illustrates the need for vigilance in protecting gifted children. For example, as a reward for her good academic work, a third-grade child was given the privilege of bringing a television cart from storage to the classroom. As the child rolled the cart down the hall, the television toppled, killing the 7-year-old child (*Dieringer v. Plain Township,* 1985). In another tragedy, two children attending the governor's school in South Carolina drowned while on a field trip to the beach ("Missing Boy's Body," 1986).

Four children in a Washington, D.C., summer gifted program were severely burned when chemicals exploded while the children were making sparklers in a laboratory experiment (Sargent, 1985). One of the children, Stewart Ugelow, described his injuries and recovery in Jill Krementz's book *How It Feels to Fight for Your Life* (1989).

A child enrolled in a residential program had to be airlifted to have leg surgery when a lack of communication following an accident exacerbated the child's injury (*Martinez v. Western Carolina University* (1980). Gifted education professionals should read this case—it depicts how *not* to handle an accident situation in a residence program.

Fraud and Misrepresentation

Although the *O'Neill v. Marjorie Walters* (1985) court case on fraud and misrepresentation has not been settled, it brings this issue into the arena of gifted education. The owner of a private elementary school advertised that teachers were certified in gifted education, indicated that the program was based on individualized instruction, and stated the curriculum was appropriate for gifted students. Several sets of parents disagreed and took the proprietor to court. The application of this type of situation to gifted education in public elementary and secondary education is apparent. However, a few questions may help districts avoid the accusation of fraud and misrepresentation. Are gifted students in specialized programs in fact receiving differentiated instruction? In states where certification/endorsement in gifted education is required, do all teachers working in special programs meet the state requirements?

Parents, teachers, administrators, school boards, and other concerned citizens may want to examine written materials and public oral statements regarding programs and services in comparison to the reality of such. Some districts and states have attorneys review all officially written education documents before they are circulated.

Home Schooling

When parents are dissatisfied with the education of their bright child, they will seek appropriate alternatives, one of which is home schooling. There are a number of questions to be asked pertaining to the gifted and the provision for their education in a home setting. If the district provides transportation to gifted programs, should the parents expect the same for their child in a home education program? If the school has a gifted program, may the child attend during the time that the specialized education takes place? If the local or state budget provides for differentiated materials or equipment, is the home-schooled child entitled to a prorated share? Is the student entitled to any instructional assistance from the teacher of the gifted? Should the child be involved in field experiences or extracurricular activities designated for the gifted and sponsored by the district? Although home schooling has never been found to be the focus of a due process hearing or a court case involving a gifted child, the fact that an increasing number of parents are involved in home schooling may make it a future legal issue.

Summary and Conclusions

Several conclusions can be reached concerning the legal issues involved in gifted education. There is no doubt that the most expeditious way to solve a dispute is through negotiation, mediation, or a due process hearing. In other words: Exhaust all the informal and quasi-formal means to resolving a dispute before seeking relief from the expensive, often frustrating, and cumbersome world of lawyers and courts.

But sometimes you just have to go court. Unless you can raise an issue handled in the federal courts such as disability, race, age, or gender discrimination, the case will be heard in the state court system. Reliance on state courts means that it is extremely important that the states have clearly written legislation and administrative regulations in place to guide the courts. As previously stated, judges are reluctant to incorporate protection for gifted students from general educational statutes and vague constitutional provisions.

The reliance on state courts to resolve legal issues means the court decisions rendered in a state are binding precedents in that state, but are not controlling in other states. Therefore, it is difficult to establish a national body of case law that can be described as being "what the law is in gifted education."

Nevertheless, some general legal conclusions can be extrapolated from existing case and statutory law. States should have early admission statutes in place that allow for the administrative processing of exceptions to a chronological age requirement. When states begin gifted programs, they should be certain that funds exist to serve all students identified as gifted; having a group of students identified as gifted and only serving a select group of them is an invitation to lawsuits. School personnel should develop an individualized educational plan for each child, keeping in mind the resources they have within the district to aid the student. When an appropriate education is not provided at the local level in public schools, parents may seek the option of school transfer.

Teacher certification in gifted education does protect the integrity of gifted education. Even courts that are most deferential to allowing educators and school boards control over hiring and firing decisions can understand that a certificated teacher possesses competency over a teacher having no training in gifted education.

Court decisions also reveal there are certain matters in which gifted education professionals must remain constantly vigilant in order to keep themselves and their programs out of court. Gifted educators assume a standard of care to their students, and this duty encompasses an obligation to foresee dangerous situations and to obtain competent medical care in a proper fashion when accidents occur. The same vigilance is necessary to prevent gifted programs from becoming limited to the cultural and racial majority in a school district. Districts must incorporate disparate procedures to identify the gifted from all segments of the community.

Regarding home schooling, questions pertaining to attending school only during the time of the gifted program, being given transportation, and prorating the teacher unit and instructional supplies are only a few yet to be answered.

Another issue that has not been resolved is the awarding of Carnegie units for advanced courses completed prior to admission to high school. States not allowing this practice should examine the manner in which this issue has been decided in other states. If younger students have completed advanced courses with the same content and under a certified teacher, it would appear unfair not to award credit to be applied toward high school graduation.

Extreme caution must be taken by local and state educational agencies and boards, as well as public, private, and parochial schools, in describing all aspects of their gifted education programs in printed form. Promulgated policies and procedures must be based in reality. The issue of fraud and misrepresentation may be the Achilles heel of gifted education.

REFERENCES

Coleman, M. R., Gallagher, J., & Foster, A. (1994). *Updated report on state policies related to the identification of gifted students.* Chapel Hill, NC: Gifted Education Policy Studies Program.

Council of State Directors of Programs for the Gifted. (1994). *The 1994 state of the states gifted and talented education report* (p. 4). Austin, TX: Author.

Karnes, F. A., & Marquardt, R. G. (1991a). *Mediation, due process and court cases.* Dayton: Ohio Psychology Press.

Karnes, F. A., & Marquardt, R. G. (Eds.). (1991b). *Parents' stories of hope.* Dayton: Ohio Psychology Press.

Karnes, F. A., & Marquardt, R. G. (1993). Pathways to solutions. *Gifted Child Today 16,* 38–44.

Krementz, J. (1989). *How it feels to fight for your life.* Boston: Little, Brown.

Marquardt, R. G., & Karnes, F. A. (1989). The courts and gifted education. *West's Education Law Reporter, 50,* 9–14.

Missing boy's body is found. (1986, June 30). *The Evening Post*, p. A-1.

Sargent, E. D. (1985, August 13). Science lab blast injures 4 D.C. pupils. *The Washington Post*, pp. A-1, A-8.

COURT CASES

Bennett v. New Rochelle School District, 497 N. Y. S. 2d 72 (App. Div. 1985).

Centennial School District v. Commonwealth Department of Education, 517 Pa. 540, 539 A. 2d 785 (1988).

Dallap v. Sharon City School District, 105 Pa. Commonwealth, 346, 524 A. 2d 546 (1987); 524 Pa. 260, 571 A. 2d 368 (1990).

Davis v. Regional Board of School Trustees, 507 N. E. 2d 1350 (Ill. App. 1987).

Dieringer v. Plain Township (Unreported 1985 Ohio Trial Court case).

Dilley v. Slippery Rock Area School District, 155 Pa. Commonwealth 357, 625 A. 2d 153 (1993).

Doe v. Petal Municipal School District, Forrest County, Miss. (Unreported Opinion) (1984)

Johnson v. Cassell, 387 S. E. 2d 553 (W. Va. 1989)

Martinez v. Western Carolina University, 49 N. C. App. 234, 271 S. E. 2d 91 (1980).

Montgomery v. Starkville Municipal Separate School District, 665 F. Supp. 487 (N. D. Miss. 1977)

O'Neill v. Marjorie Walters School for Gifted Children, 466 So. 2d 1295 (La. 1985).

Vaughns v. Board of Education of Prince George County, 758 F. 2d 983 (4th Cir. 1985).

Woodland Hills School v. Commonwealth Department of Education, 101 Pa. Commonwealth 506, 516 A. 2d 875 (1986).

43

Educating Teachers for Work with Talented Youth

JOHN F. FELDHUSEN, *Purdue University*

Teachers need special skills and understanding if they are to facilitate the personal, social, and academic development of talented youth. Some teachers undoubtedly can acquire those skills and understanding through their own practical experiences working with talented youth in the classroom. However, the daily demands of serving youth with a wide variety of ability and achievement levels and a diversity of interests, learning styles, and motivations, as well as the American tendency to focus on low-achieving or "problem" students, make it less likely that teachers will take time to study the special needs and characteristics of highly talented youth and determine how best to facilitate their learning. To be sure, teachers who work with highly talented youth in honors, accelerated, seminar, college track, or Advanced Placement classes have good opportunities to focus on and learn about the nature and needs of youth in those special classes without the distraction of slow or unmotivated students. However, most teachers, regardless of their teaching experience or situation, can and will profit from special training in the nature and educational nurturing of highly talented youth.

Research on teachers and the processes of teaching gifted and talented youth has been focused in three directions. One is to try to determine the *characteristics* of good or successful teachers of the gifted and talented as perceived by students or experts in gifted education. Another focus is on the *competencies* or specific skills needed to be a good teacher of gifted and talented youth. Finally, sometimes the focus has been on the process itself, assessing the *performance* of successful teachers of the gifted. All three approaches afford insights that can be useful in designing inservice education and college courses for prospective teachers of the gifted.

Characteristics of the Teacher

A major study (Bishop, 1968) concluded that successful teachers of the gifted could be characterized as:

1. Highly intelligent
2. Having cultural and intellectual interests
3. Mature and experienced
4. Striving for high achievement
5. Able to see things from students' points of view
6. Well organized, orderly, and systematic
7. Open to student opinions
8. Enthusiastic, stimulating, and imaginative

Maker (1975) reviewed the literature up to that time on characteristics of good or successful teachers of the gifted and concluded that the following were significant traits:

1. Ability to relate well to the gifted
2. Flexibility or openness to change
3. High intelligence
4. Imaginative
5. Respectful of individual talents
6. Accepts responsibility for individual children
7. Sees need to develop students' self-concepts

Hultgren and Seeley (1982) also reviewed the body of research then available on characteristics of effective teachers of gifted and talented youth and summarized their results as follows:

1. Mature, experienced, self-confident

2. Highly intelligent
3. Intellectual interests
4. Achievement oriented
5. Favorable attitudes toward gifted
6. Systematic and orderly
7. Stimulating, imaginative
8. Good sense of humor
9. Facilitates learning; does not direct
10. Hard working
11. Broad general knowledge and expertise
12. Recognizes individual differences

Whitlock and DuCette (1989) carried out a study of characteristics of ideal teachers of the gifted, but they departed from the survey technique and used intensive, in-depth interviews with ten excellent and ten average teachers of the gifted. They found that the excellent teachers were characterized by their enthusiasm, self-confidence, achievement motivation, general commitment to serve the gifted, ability to apply theory in teaching, and capacity to muster support for the gifted program.

These studies of the ideal teacher of the gifted seem to list virtues that should characterize all teachers or all leaders. They also indicate stable, long-range traits that may be useful in selecting teachers but of little value as guides in developing teacher education programs. As guides to selection, we can conclude that characteristics that match those often found in talented youth would be desirable in the teacher. These include:

1. Highly intelligent
2. Has cultural and intellectual interests
3. Strives for excellence or high achievement
4. Enthusiastic about talent
5. Relates well to talented people
6. Has broad general knowledge

Competencies of the Teacher

Far more productive for teacher preparation in gifted education would be clear delineation of the competencies, skills, and knowledge needed to work well with talented youth. Fortunately, one major line of research in gifted and talented education has pursued this approach.

Seeley (1979) reported the results of a survey to identify the competencies of teachers of the gifted and later followed with a larger national survey reported by Hultgren and Seeley (1982). In the latter study, 628 university personnel and school-based practitioners were the respondents. The top-ranked competencies were the following:

1. Knowledge of the nature and needs of the gifted
2. Ability to develop methods and materials for use with gifted
3. Skill in teaching higher cognitive thinking abilities and questioning techniques
4. Skill in facilitating independent research
5. Skill in individualized teaching
6. Ability to identify gifted and talented students
7. Skill in work with culturally different talented youth
8. Skill in counseling gifted and talented youth

For the most part, university personnel and school-based practitioners agreed in their rankings of these competencies. These competencies describe modifiable behaviors of teachers that could become goals, objectives, or outcomes of teacher education programs for work with talented students. However, the research focused on competencies to teach the gifted in general as though they were a homogeneous lot, and failed to recognize that the competencies needed by teachers to work with youth talented in mathematics or science might be very different from those needed to work with youth talented in art, music, literature, or computer science.

In recent research Nelson and Prindle (1992) surveyed teachers and administrators concerning basic competencies needed by teachers of the gifted, using the teacher competency survey instrument developed by Hultgren and Seeley (1982). The results yielded six basic competencies on which teachers and principals substantially agreed:

1. Promotion of thinking skills
2. Development of creative problem solving
3. Selection of appropriate methods and materials
4. Knowledge of affective needs
5. Facilitation of independent research
6. Awareness of the nature of gifted students

Nelson and Prindle also found that the teachers rated several other skills in working with the gifted significantly higher in importance than did administrators:

1. Group processes
2. Presentation of career education and professional options
3. Individual student counseling
4. Inservice for other teachers concerning philosophy and methods in gifted education

These results validate still further the findings of the Seeley and Hultgren research and point the way to appropriate teacher training.

Insights from Direct Observation of Teachers Working with Talented Youth

Both of the research approaches addressed so far, focusing on the characteristics and/or competencies of the teachers, depend on judgments of respondents who may or may not be experienced or familiar with actual classroom teaching of the gifted. Furthermore, the insights often derive from experience in general heterogeneous classrooms in which one or a few gifted and talented youth may be enrolled, not on experience with special classes for these students. However, several researchers have addressed the latter situation.

In a landmark study using direct observation of classroom teaching, Silverman (1982) observed "master" or experienced teachers and neophytes in training as they worked with gifted youth in the classroom, and concluded that there were large differences between them. The master teachers were able to (1) induce more and higher level thinking among students, (2) be less judgmental or critical, (3) get students to evaluate for themselves, (4) teach well while using presentations less, (5) ask more divergent questions, and (6) align themselves more closely with students as opposed to standing off formally as the teacher. Clearly, these insights into the processes of classroom interactions between teachers and students could be used to guide the development of teacher education programs, and they possess high validity. That is, they derive from the observation of real classrooms—real teachers dealing explicitly with real talented youth.

Starko and Schack (1989) carried out a comprehensive study with 57 teachers of the gifted, 85 regular classroom teachers, and 176 preservice teachers. One phase of the study asked the teachers to evaluate some specific teaching strategies in terms of their power to meet the needs of gifted and talented youth. The ideas of the 57 gifted teachers are of particular interest since they ostensibly derive from classroom experience. The strongest perceived needs according to these teachers were for:

1. Higher level thinking skills
2. Elimination of previously learned materials
3. Being grouped for instruction
4. Opportunities for independent study
5. Creativity training

While Starko and Schack found these needs rated high, they also found that teachers of the gifted often failed to use appropriate strategies to help students in these areas because the teachers did not feel confident or competent in using them.

Effects of Training in the Competencies

Research focusing on classroom interaction between teachers of the gifted and gifted students was carried out by Hansen and Feldhusen (1994). They studied the classroom competencies and performance of trained and untrained teachers of the gifted. The trained teachers had been taught many or most of the research-based competencies, skills, and knowledge in three or four graduate courses in gifted education. The first course was a general introduction to theory and current practice in gifted education. The second course focused on identification of talented youth, counseling, evaluation of programs, and assessment of student abilities and learning. The third course dealt with curriculum design and differentiation, teaching methods, and program development. The fourth course was an elective in one of the following areas: (1) individualized teaching of the gifted, (2) thinking skills, or (3) counseling the gifted. A total of 54 trained and 28 untrained teachers were observed in the classroom teaching gifted students, and were evaluated with the Purdue Teacher Observation Form (Feldhusen & Huffman, 1988). Their students completed the Classroom Activities Questionnaire (Steele, 1981).

The research revealed highly superior performance of trained teachers from both the observers' and the students' point of view. All of the differences were tested statistically and found highly significant. The major proficiencies or competencies shown by trained teachers far more than the untrained included:

1. Fast pacing of instruction
2. Emphasis on creativity and thinking skills
3. Teacher–student interactions
4. Appropriate motivational techniques
5. Student-directed activities
6. Use of media and models in teaching

Similarly, from the students' points of view the trained teachers used more higher level thinking activities and more discussion, emphasized student self-direction, lectured less, and motivated students with their enthusiasm. Thus, from both points of view training based on competencies identified in research translated into more effective teaching of talented students.

Story (1985) conducted an even more intensive observational study of teachers of the gifted who had had courses on teaching the gifted and were regarded as excellent teachers. She observed the teachers for 60 to 70 hours. She was guided in the observations by suggestions of leaders in gifted education concerning the competencies that should characterize good teachers of the gifted. She found that these teachers emphasize independent study and self-direction, use a multiplicity of resources in teaching, model "gifted" behavior, stress higher level thinking skills, and are flexible in classroom scheduling and activities.

Availability of Training in Gifted Education

If graduate training in gifted education can identify fundamental competencies that enable teachers to learn and use appropriate skills in teaching the gifted, it is appropriate to ask how widely available such training is. Parker and Karnes (1991) surveyed colleges and universities in the United States and Canada and found 127 institutions offering graduate degrees in gifted education. In addition, they found 25 "centers" emphasizing research, development, counseling, testing, youth programs, conferences, and library services, all focused on the gifted and gifted education as well as teacher training activities.

Approximately 25 states also offer an endorsement in teaching the gifted. The endorsement usually requires from 9 to 24 graduate credits and frequently requires a three-credit practicum. One result is that teachers have a strong inducement to seek the endorsement and upgrade their skills and professional credentials.

Inservice training for teachers of the gifted is most often offered on college and university campuses with classes offered late afternoons, evenings, weekends, and summers. However, with increasing popularity of distance education as a means of extending teacher training to more school personnel, off-campus training in gifted education has become more readily available. Hansen and Feldhusen (1990) described one such program in which up to 750 teachers enrolled during one academic year. The program offered the full range of courses for the fifteen-credit Indiana endorsement in gifted education.

Conclusions

Passow and Rudnitski (1993) carried out a major survey of state policies regarding education of the gifted. They found great variability in the ways different states acknowledge and require or fail to require educational services for the gifted, teacher training in gifted education, and teacher certification for teaching the gifted. They concluded that ". . . policies in all states would be improved were all teachers and other certified personnel required to have coursework dealing with the nature and nurture of the gifted and talented" (p. 56).

Twenty-nine "experts" in gifted education recently participated in a major national Delphi study of gifted education (Cramer, 1991). They concluded that all teachers should receive some basic education on the needs and characteristics of gifted and talented children. They also concluded that certification of teachers who work with groups of gifted children should be mandatory. Finally, they confirmed that gifted children require a differentiated curriculum and that teachers should be trained to develop and use such differentiated curriculum in their classrooms.

Although the instructional technology is available to prepare teachers for work with gifted students and many teachers are getting the training, it still is true that large numbers of gifted students receive no or very little differentiated or appropriate instruction to meet their needs. Instead, they are taught things they already know, taught at a very slow pace, and engaged in low-level thinking activities. Two recent large-scale studies (Archambault et al., 1993; Westberg, Archambault, Dobyns, & Slavin, 1993) surveyed 3,993 teachers throughout the United States and conducted structured observations in 46 classrooms. In the Westberg et al. study the observers were so dismayed by their observations that the report concludes as follows:

> All observers relayed personally to the researchers their dismay, discouragement, and in some cases, anger about the overall lack of differentiation in the instructional practices . . . provided to gifted and talented students. . . . (p. 143)

Equally disturbing are the results of the Archambault et al. survey study:

> It is clear . . . that teachers . . . make only minor modifications in the curriculum and instruction to meet the needs of gifted students. (p. 115)

The "know-how" and technology clearly exist to train teachers to work with gifted and talented students. To a limited extent our knowledge of the characteristics of good teachers of the gifted enables us to develop criteria and select teachers who will be able to meet the needs of gifted students in the classroom. Far more promising, however, is our understanding of the skills, competencies, and knowledge that teachers require in order to teach the gifted well. Armed with that information, we can design and conduct teacher education programs to prepare all teachers in the basics of working with the gifted and a cadre of highly trained and certified teachers to work with the gifted in special classes. Developments so far in teacher education show considerable success and bode well for the future of teacher preparation in gifted education and for the education of gifted and talented youth.

REFERENCES

Archambault, F. X., Westberg, K. L., Brown, S. W., Hallmark, B. W., Zhang, W., & Emmons, C. L. (1993). Classroom practices used with gifted third and fourth grade students. *Journal for the Education of the Gifted, 16*(2), 103–119.

Bishop, W. E. (1968). Successful teachers of the gifted. *Exceptional Children, 34,* 317–325.

Cramer, R. H. (1991). The education of gifted children in the United States: A Delphi study. *Gifted Child Quarterly, 35,* 84–91.

Feldhusen, J. F., & Huffman, L. E. (1988). Practicum experiences in an educational program for teachers of the gifted. *Journal for the Education of the Gifted, 12*(1), 34–45.

Hansen, J. B., & Feldhusen, J. F. (1990). Off campus training of teachers of the gifted: A program model. *Gifted International, 6*(1), 54–62.

Hansen, J. B., & Feldhusen, J. F. (1994). Comparison of trained and untrained teachers of gifted students. *Gifted Child Quarterly, 38,* 115–123.

Hultgren, H. W., & Seeley, K. R. (1982). *Training teachers of the gifted: A research monograph on teacher competencies.* Denver: University of Denver, School of Education.

Maker, C. J. (1975). *Training teachers for the gifted and talented.* Reston, VA: Council for Exceptional Children.

Nelson, K. C., & Prindle, N. (1992). Gifted teacher competencies: Ratings by rural principals and teachers compared. *Journal for the Education of the Gifted, 15*(4), 357–369.

Parker, J. P., & Karnes, F. A. (1991). Graduate degree programs and resource centers in gifted education: An update and analysis. *Gifted Child Quarterly, 35,* 43–48.

Passow, A. H., & Rudnitski, R. A. (1993). *State policies regarding education of the gifted as reflected in legislation and regulation.* Storrs, CT: National Research Center on the Gifted and Talented.

Seeley, K. R. (1979). Competencies for teachers of gifted and talented children. *Journal for the Education of the Gifted, 3,* 7–13.

Silverman, L. K. (1982). The gifted and talented. In E. L. Meyen (Ed.), *Exceptional children and youth* (pp. 184–190). Denver, CO: Love.

Starko, A. J., & Schack, G. D. (1989). Perceived need, teacher efficacy, and teacher strategies for the gifted and talented. *Gifted Child Quarterly, 33,* 118–122.

Steele, J. M. (1981). *The classroom activities questionnaire: Assessing instructional climate.* Mansfield, CT: Creative Learning Press.

Story, C. M. (1985). Facilitator of learning: A microethnographic study of the teacher of the gifted. *Gifted Child Quarterly, 29,* 155–159.

Westberg, K. L., Archambault, F. X., Dobyns, S. M., & Slavin, T. J. (1993). The classroom practices observation study. *Journal for the Education of the Gifted, 16*(2), 120–146.

Whitlock, M. S., & DuCette, J. P. (1989). Outstanding and average teachers of the gifted: A comparative study. *Gifted Child Quarterly, 33,* 15–21.

44

Federal Policy on Gifted and Talented Education

PATRICIA O'CONNELL ROSS, *Javits Program, U.S. Department of Education*

Over the past 40 years, sputtering attention has been paid to the education of gifted and talented students at the federal level. When there has been an interest in this student population, it has been embedded in the broader educational concerns of the nation. As a result, the arguments and rationales for special services for gifted and talented students have varied over time, depending on the larger sociopolitical issues of the day.

This chapter addresses federal policy on gifted and talented education over the past 40 years, and analyzes the current education reform debate and its impact on services for gifted and talented students.

A Brief History of Federal Involvement in Gifted and Talented Education

Before embarking on a discussion of federal involvement in gifted and talented education, it is important to acknowledge the conflicting beliefs in the United States about the role the federal government should take in education. The U.S. Constitution does not mention education as a federal responsibility, but it declares that all areas not mentioned explicitly in the Constitution are the responsibility of states and local communities. Unlike every other industrialized nation in the world, the United States has a limited federal involvement in education. Only about 6 or 7 percent of the budget for elementary and secondary education comes from federal taxes. Therefore, in education discussions at the federal level, there is intense disagreement about the extent to which the federal government ought to be providing direction and assistance to elementary and secondary education in the nation. This provides an important context within which to understand federal policy discussions concerning gifted and talented education.

The Sputnik Era

In the fall of 1957 the Soviet Union launched the first Sputnik satellite, simultaneously launching intense debate in this country about the quality of American education. Many voices claimed that the United States was losing the Cold War because of our inadequate educational system, in particular our "manpower" preparation in mathematics and science. It was believed that the most able students needed a more rigorous secondary education and broader access to higher educational opportunities. Many critics of the system decried progressive education's influence, as carried out by followers of John Dewey, and claimed that this approach focused more on the social development of students than on rigorous academic preparation. The U.S. public believed that the United States was in peril from outside forces if the education system was not improved.

As a result, Congress passed the National Defense Education Act of 1958, the first major federal legislation supporting education. Title V of this act provided assistance to states by providing funding for testing programs to identify able students, and for counseling and guidance to encourage students to develop their aptitudes and attend college, particularly in mathematics and science.

During this era, the rhetoric supporting programs for able students emerged from passionate concerns about our "race" with the Soviet Union and our ability to win the Cold War. Channeling able students into mathematics and science fields was the way to improve our relative standing with the Soviet

Union. The focus was on national need, not on self-fulfillment, and on the most able students, not the entire student body. With the success of the U.S. space program and the aversion of the Sputnik "crisis," support for able students waned.

The Rights of Special Children

The 1960s and 1970s can be characterized by the rise in demands for rights of individuals within U.S. institutions, particularly the disenfranchised. Massive support for poor, educationally disadvantaged students was initiated through Title I. In addition, a series of court cases found that children with handicaps were undereducated by U.S. schools. Court decisions led to a push for federal legislation to protect the rights of exceptional children in public schools. In early versions of the draft legislation for exceptional children, gifted and talented students were included as a category of exceptionality. At some point, language including gifted and talented students was removed from the draft legislation. Instead, Congress asked for a study on the status of gifted and talented education in the nation to:

> (A) determine the extent to which special educational assistance programs are necessary or useful to meet the needs of gifted and talented children, (B) show which existing Federal educational assistance programs are being used to meet the needs of gifted and talented children, (C) evaluate how existing Federal education assistance programs can be more effectively used to meet these needs, and (D) recommend which new programs, if any, are needed to meet these needs. (Public Law 91-230, Section 806)

The ensuing report to Congress, known as the Marland Report (U.S. Department of Health, Education and Welfare, 1972), was named after then Commissioner of Education Sydney Marland. It found that existing services for these students were all but nonexistent and went on to claim that

- There is an enormous individual and social cost when talent among the Nation's children and youth goes undiscovered and undeveloped. These students cannot ordinarily excel without assistance.
- Identification of the gifted is hampered not only by costs of appropriate testing—when these methods are known or adopted—but also by apathy and even hostility among teachers, administrators, guidance counselors and psychologists.
- Gifted and talented children are, in fact, deprived and can suffer psychological damage and permanent impairment of their abilities to function well which is equal to or greater than the similar deprivations suffered by any other population with special needs served by the Office of Education. (p. 3)

In response to this report, the 93rd Congress passed legislation that created an Office of Gifted and Talented in the U.S. Office of Education and provided modest funding ($2.5 million) to support research and development projects, as well as grants to state and local agencies.

In keeping with the rhetoric of the times that focused on student rights and equal opportunity, arguments for gifted and talented education centered on the need for helping students to develop their potential for their own well-being. The arguments also accused schools of creating an unfriendly environment for the brightest students, thus indicating that these students required special advocacy and programs in order for their needs to be met. These are many of the same arguments that were used for other special populations, including students who were economically disadvantaged, bilingual, migrant, and so on. The basic assumption at the time was that the regular education program was adequate to meet the needs of most children, but that there were special-needs students who required additional attention and support.

The federal program for gifted and talented students continued until passage of the Omnibus Budget Reconciliation Act of 1981. Caught in the recurring dispute over the appropriate federal role in education, the modest funds of the federal gifted and talented program were consolidated with 19 other programs into a block grant and sent out to states to spend at their own discretion.

Current Reform Initiatives and Federal Policy

In 1988 Congress reestablished a small federal program on gifted and talented education. The Jacob K. Javits Gifted and Talented Students Education Act of 1988 (P.L. 100-297) provides support for national demonstration grants, a national research and development center, and national leadership activities. The legislation specified that the program place special emphasis on economically disadvantaged students, limited-English-proficient students, and students with disabilities who are gifted and talented. It states that

> the Federal Government can best carry out the limited but essential role of stimulating research and development and personnel training, and providing a national focal point of information and technical assistance, that is necessary to ensure that our Nation's schools are able to meet the special educational needs of gifted and talented students, and thereby serve a profound national interest.

The Javits Gifted and Talented Education Program was created in the midst of the most intensive and sustained school reform movement in the history of the nation. Since the 1983 publication of *A Nation at Risk: The Imperative for Educational Reform* (U.S. Department of Education, 1983), there have been sustained efforts to improve U.S. education. The federal government has, in very modest ways, become involved in initiatives to improve American education for all children, rather than just for targeted populations, as was the emphasis in the past.

In 1989 President George Bush and the nation's governors met to develop a set of national education goals, providing for the first time a unified set of expectations for all of American education. The essential messages of these goals are that there should be higher standards for all children and that our education system should be the best in the world. Of particular interest for students with outstanding talents is Goal 3 of the National Education Goals, which states:

> By the year 2000, all students will leave grades 4, 8, and 12 having demonstrated competency over challenging subject matter including English, mathematics, science, foreign languages, civics and government, economics, arts, history, and geography, and every school in America will insure that all students learn to use their minds well, so that they may be prepared for responsible citizenship, further learning, and productive employment in our Nation's modern economy.
>
> (B) The objectives for this goal are that—
>
> **(i)** the academic performance of all students at the elementary and secondary level will increase significantly in every quartile, and the distribution of minority students in each quartile will more closely reflect the student population as a whole;
>
> **(ii)** the percentage of all students who demonstrate the ability to reason, solve problems, apply knowledge, and write and communicate effectively will increase substantially;

The underlying assumptions of this goal are that students at all levels of accomplishment, including the most talented, need to be performing at higher levels, and that more poor and minority students should be performing at higher levels. This is, in essence, the mission of the Javits program.

The National Education Goals presented a broad framework for national direction in education. In policy circles, the next debate centered on *how* to accomplish the massive task of improving all of education as envisioned in the National Education Goals. The concept of *systemic reform* emerged as the most powerful approach to achieving the National Education Goals. In essence, systemic reform holds that all elements of the educational enterprise need to be aligned to support higher levels of learning for all children. These elements include content standards, curriculum frameworks, professional development, assessments, and other policies related to education. As examples, teacher certification and licensure from the state should be aligned with teacher preparation programs that focus on the ability to teach high-level content in the core subject areas, and assessments of student knowledge ought to be aligned with challenging content standards. To facilitate reform at all levels of education, in 1994 the Clinton administration proposed and Congress passed Goals 2000: Educate America Act (U.S. Department of Education, 1994). The purpose of this act is to provide a framework for meeting the National Education Goals by:

> **(1)** promoting coherent, nationwide, systemic education reform;
> **(2)** improving the quality of learning and teaching in the classroom and in the workplace;
> **(3)** defining appropriate and coherent Federal, State, and local roles and responsibilities for education reform and lifelong learning; . . .
> **(6)** providing a framework for the reauthorization of all Federal education programs.

The overriding principles of Goals 2000 are that all children can learn in accordance with high, demanding standards and that to accomplish this challenging goal, education reform must take place at all levels of the system in a coherent and consistent way if a major overhaul of the educational enterprise is to take place. The legislation provides funds to states and local school districts to promote reform based on high standards. In this legislation, "all children" are defined as:

> students or children from a broad range of backgrounds and circumstances, including disadvantaged students and children, students or children with diverse racial, ethnic, and cultural backgrounds, American Indians, Alaska Natives, Native Hawaiians, students or children with disabilities, students or children with limited-English proficiency, school-age students or children who have dropped out of school, migratory students or children, *and academically talented students and children.* (emphasis added)

In addition, through the reauthorization in 1994 of the Elementary and Secondary Education Act there were substantial changes in the focus of K–12 education programs supported by the federal government. Public Law 103-382, the Improving America's Schools Act (IASA; U.S. Congress, 1994) contains the collection of elementary and secondary education programs supported by the federal government, and was reauthorized at about the same time that Goals 2000 was passed. Most of the programs in this legislation have been recast to incorporate the belief that *all* students can learn to higher academic standards, which represents a shift from a focus on reinforcement of basic skills for at-risk populations that was emphasized in previous legislation. Instead, IASA calls for acceleration and enrichment as strategies to improve the educational attainment of these students. Students in at-risk circumstances are expected to meet the same performance standards as other students. For example, Title I of this act, the program for economically disadvantaged students, states that:

> The purpose of this title is to enable schools to provide opportunities for children served to acquire the knowledge and skills contained in the challenging State content standards and to meet the challenging State performance standards developed for all children.
>
> **(1)** ensuring high standards for all children and aligning the efforts of States, local educational agencies, and schools to help children served under this title to reach such standards;
> **(2)** providing children an enriched and accelerated educational program, including, when appropriate, the use of the arts, through schoolwide programs or through additional services that increase the amount and quality of instructional time so that children served under this title receive at least the classroom instruction that other children receive;
> **(3)** promoting schoolwide reform and ensuring access of children (from the earliest grades) to effective instructional strategies and challenging academic content that includes intensive complex thinking and problem-solving experiences; . . .
> **(8)** improving accountability, as well as teaching and learning, by using State assessment systems designed to measure how well children served under this title are achieving challenging State student performance standards expected of all children.

Through this legislation, strategies that have typically been the hallmark of programs for gifted and talented students are now promoted for students most at risk of school failure. It suggests that all students should be taught using conceptually complex curriculum, and using problem solving, the arts, and acceleration and enrichment in order to create successful schools.

The Javits program (Title X, Part B) was reauthorized in IASA. Its original mission was expanded in order to align the program with the overall intent of IASA to set higher standards for all students and move away from isolated programs for special populations. The findings and purposes of the Javits act state:

> **(1)** all students can learn to high standards and must develop their talents and realize their potential if the United States is to prosper;
> **(2)** gifted and talented students are a national resource vital to the future of the Nation and its security and well-being;
> **(3)** too often schools fail to challenge students to do their best work, and students who are not challenged will not learn to challenging State content standards and challenging State student performance standards, fully develop their talents, and realize their potential;
> **(4)** the experience and knowledge gained in developing and implementing programs for gifted and talented students can and should be used as a basis to
> **(A)** develop a rich and challenging curriculum for all students; and
> **(B)** provide all students with important and challenging subject matter to study and encourage the habits of hard work.

The legislation continues to support research and development activities on gifted and talented education, but it also encourages the use of materials and teaching strategies developed by gifted and talented educators with all students.

National Excellence: A Case for Developing America's Talent

In an attempt to define the place of gifted and talented education within the context of educational reform, the U.S. Department of Education published in 1993 a national report on the status of gifted and talented education. *National Excellence: A Case for Developing America's Talent* offers a portrait of how the nation is presently serving gifted and talented students, and suggests the direction in which the nation should be heading to improve educational opportunities for these students. The report states:

> The United States is squandering one of its most precious resources—the gifts, talents, and high interests of many of its students. In a broad range of intellectual and artistic endeavors, these youngsters are not challenged to do their best work. This problem is especially severe among economically disadvantaged and minority students, who have access to fewer advanced educational opportunities and whose talents often go unnoticed. (p. 1)

To support this statement, the report goes on to provide evidence that

> Compared with top students in other industrialized countries, American students perform poorly on international tests, are offered a less rigorous curriculum, read fewer demanding books, do less homework, and enter the work force or postsecondardary education less well prepared. (p. 1)

The report claims that although effective programs for gifted and talented students exist around the country, most are limited in scope and substance, and most gifted and talented students spend most of their time in school in the regular classroom where few, if any, provisions are made for them.

To improve educational opportunities for talented students, the report makes the following recommendations:

- **Establish challenging curriculum standards.**
  As a part of the movement in education to establish standards for what students should know and be able to do in core subject areas, there should be assurance that standards are sufficiently high and flexible enough to accommodate the needs of gifted and talented students. Too often, standards are set at a minimal level rather than at a high level. To ensure that this happens, educators involved in gifted and talented education should be involved in developing the content standards.

- **Establish high-level learning opportunities.**
  To develop varied talents in students as recommended in the report, there should be a wide array of eduational options available to students. Even schools that provide services for gifted and talented students often use only one approach or accommodate only one kind of talent, and are not flexible in the approaches they use. It is essential to match each child's developing talent with appropriate experiences in order for the child to grow.

- **Ensure access to early childhood education.**
  There is a great disparity between the access that middle-class and poor children have to high-quality early childhood education. Poor children need to be offered rich and challenging educational opportunities in a preschool setting because these opportunities often are not available in their homes. In addition, it is essential to look for strengths in children from poor circumstances rather than focusing on their weaknesses, as is typically the case. These programs are essential if poor children are to be able to enter school fully prepared and able to match the accomplishments of more advantaged children.

- **Expand opportunities for disadvantaged and minority children.**
  It is essential to remove barriers to participation of poor and minority children in advanced learning opportunities and to support research and demonstration projects that are developing ways to work with diverse populations.

- **Encourage appropriate teacher training and technical assistance.**
  In order for change to take place, teachers must have skills and knowledge that give them tools to develop students' talents to the fullest. This is the key to implementation of changes in opportunites for students.

- **Match world performance.**
  The Report outlines results of international comparisons that show that even the brightest students in the United States are not as well prepared in mathematics and sciences as students in other countries. If the recommendations in the report are carried out, students in the United States should perform as well as students anywhere.

In the National Report, the U.S. Department of Education articulates the current beliefs regarding where gifted and talented education fits within the larger educational concerns of nation. It offers arguments based on national interest, as well as on the need to develop each individual in the nation to his or her full potential, especially students who do not currently have access to many advanced educational opportunities. These twin concerns are argued in the context of the need for all of education to be more substantial and rigorous.

To determine the impact of the National Report on policies and practices at the state and local levels, the Javits Program commissioned a study that was carried out by the Council of State Directors of Programs for the Gifted (CSDPG). A survey of states and selected local school districts was conducted to test the usefulness of producing national reports and to determine if this report had a positive effect on state policy and local school practice. Survey forms were completed by 36 states and Guam, and by local school district personnel in 8 states. In addition, 10 state directors were interviewed in depth, representing a sampling of states in different regions of the country.

Of the 36 states responding, more than 60 percent indicated that they had been able to influence change and garner support for gifted and talented education by using the National Report. Some resulting activities include placing a statewide emphasis on curriculum compacting, making presentations to state boards of education, using the report as a rationale for additional funding, broadening the definition of gifted, identifying more minority and low-socioeconomic-status students, increasing emphasis on professional development, increasing awareness of concern for accountability for results of services to gifted students, supporting mandates, and increasing local and regional networking.

The follow-up study also found that the states that were active in making change as a result of the publication of the National Report shared common features. These features included the timeliness of the National Report in relation to other efforts in the state, the level of commitment by state leadership to implementing recommendations of the report, and access to statewide networking of advocates and educators interested in gifted and talented education.

Conclusion

At the federal level, arguments to support gifted and talented education programs have changed over the years. During the Cold War, arguments for the national interest prevailed, citing the need to assert our dominance internationally. In the 1960s and 1970s, arguments supporting individual growth and developing full potential held sway. The current position takes a more holistic approach to improving services to students, with attention to gifted and talented students viewed as a part of a larger effort to raise expectations for all students.

REFERENCES

U.S. Congress. (1994). *Improving America's Schools Act of 1994* (Public Law 103–382). Washington, DC: Author.

U.S. Department of Education. (1983). *A nation at risk: The imperative for educational reform.* Washington, DC: Author.

U.S. Department of Education. (1993). *National excellence: A case for developing America's talent.* Washington, DC: Author.

U.S. Department of Education. (1994). *Goals 2000: A world class education for every child.* Washington, DC: Author.

U.S. Department of Health, Education, and Welfare. (1972). *Education of the gifted and talented.* Washington, DC: Author.

Name Index

Subject Index